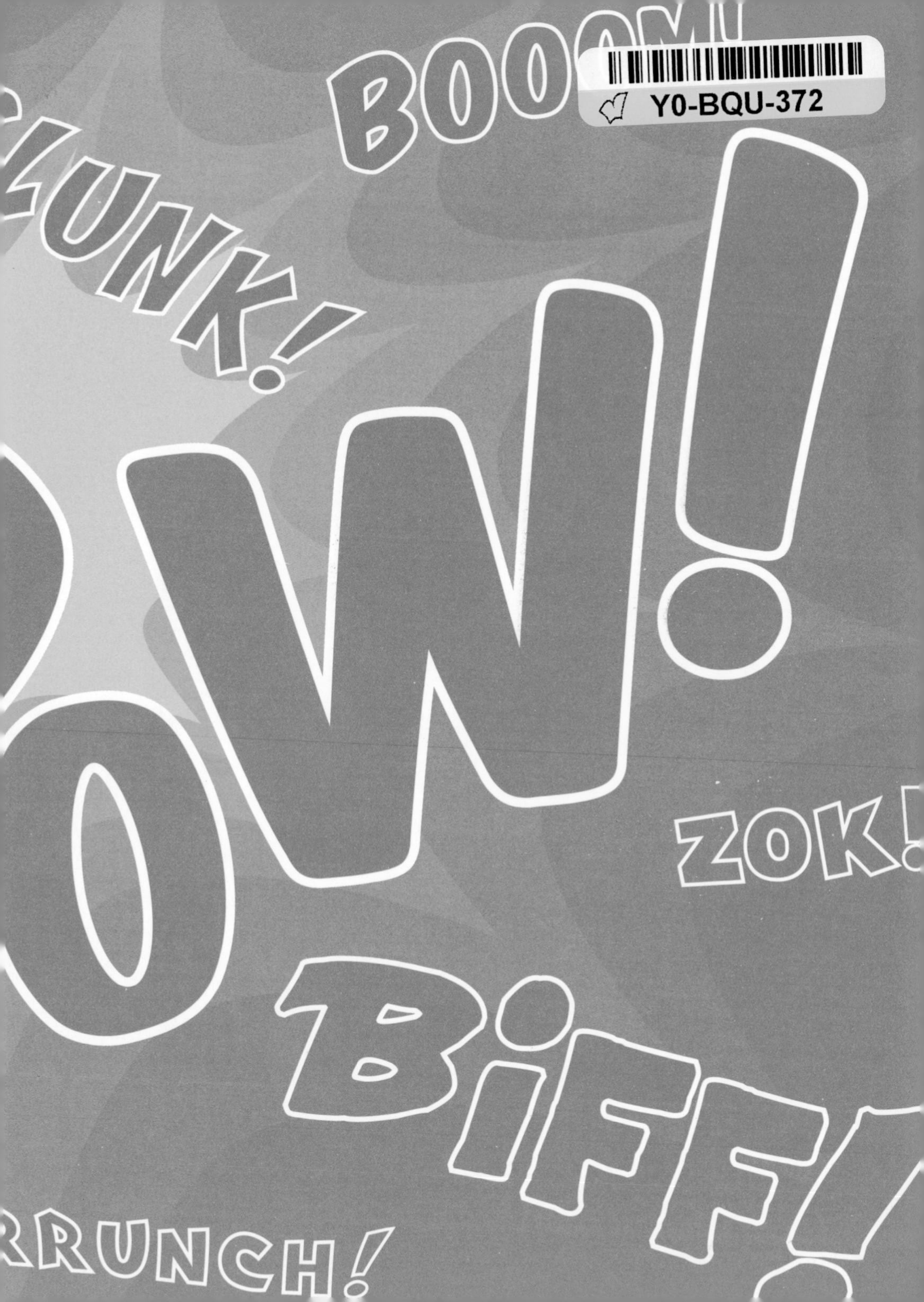
BOOO
LUNK!
OW!
ZOK!
BiFF
RRUNCH!

1001 COMICS
YOU MUST READ BEFORE YOU DIE

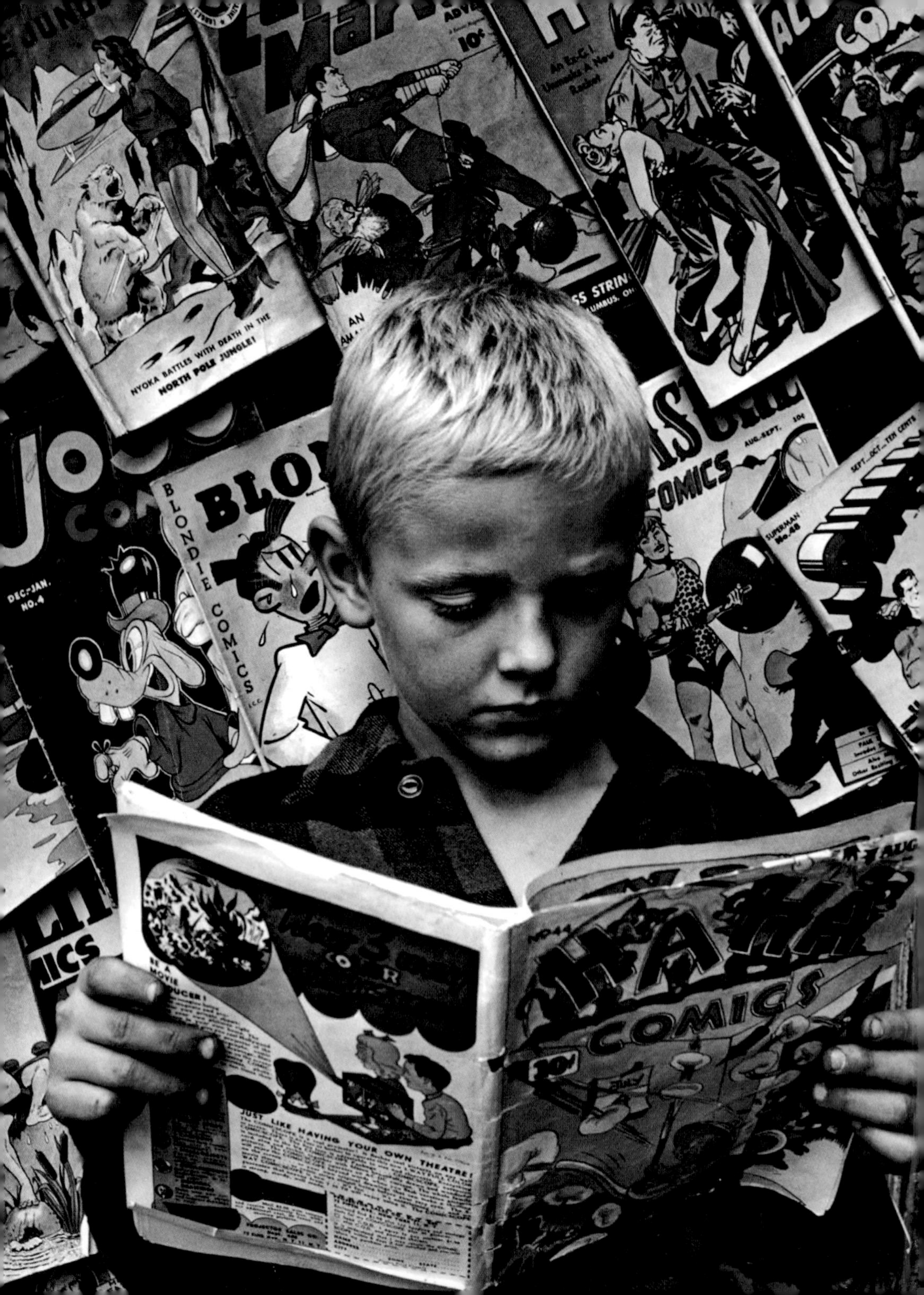
10¢
An Ex-G.I. Unmasks A New Racket
NYOKA BATTLES WITH DEATH IN THE
NORTH POLE JUNGLE!
BLONDIE COMICS
DEC-JAN.
NO.4
AUG.-SEPT.
10¢
COMICS
SEPT.-OCT.-TEN CENTS
SUPERMAN
No.48
BE A
MOVIE
PRODUCER!
JUST LIKE HAVING YOUR OWN THEATRE!
HA HA
COMICS
10¢

1001 COMICS
YOU MUST READ BEFORE YOU DIE

GENERAL EDITOR **PAUL GRAVETT**

FOREWORD BY **TERRY GILLIAM**

UNIVERSE

A Quintessence Book

First published in the United States of America in 2011 by
UNIVERSE PUBLISHING
A Division of Rizzoli International Publications, Inc.
300 Park Avenue South
New York, NY 10010
www.rizzoliusa.com

2011 2012 2013 2014 / 10 9 8 7 6 5 4 3 2 1

ISBN: 978-0-7893-2271-5

Library of Congress Control Number: 2011923857

QSS.GNOV

This book was designed and produced by
Quintessence Editions Ltd.
230 City Road
London EC1V 2TT
www.1001beforeyoudie.com

Project Editor	Simon Ward
Editors	Rob Cave, Becky Gee, Tamsin Oxford, Fiona Plowman, Frank Ritter
Designers	Alison Hau, Tom Howey, Rod Teasdale
Production Manager	Anna Pauletti
Editorial Director	Jane Laing
Publisher	Tristan de Lancey

Color reproduction by Chroma Graphics Pte Ltd., Singapore.
Printed in China by Toppan Leefung Printing Ltd.

Contents

Foreword

By Terry Gilliam

Ok , it's time for a confession. My first bit of porn was a comic book. Of course it wasn't the rich, detailed, uninspiring stuff that inundates the Internet today. No, we had to use our imagination. And it was Wally Wood who got mine going. I can't remember the exact issue of *MAD* that contained the *Adventures of Flesh Garden* with Wally's beautiful drawings of Flesh's incredibly sexy girlfriend, but my young, impressionable mind thought she was the hottest thing ever. Forget about the photos of the Venus de Milo in the section of Greek sculptures in the *Encyclopedia Britannica*. Wally Wood's pen and ink drawings stoked the sexual flames far more effectively. The timing was right. I had a need and Wally fed it.

With those guilty pleasures rampaging around my twelve-year-old mind and body (which was already dangling perilously far over the abyss of puberty), I knew that, for my own safety, my *MAD* comic had to be securely hidden. If my parents were to discover the sex-mad beast that was being spawned in their son's rapidly changing body, the results would have been catastrophic. I had to hide my precious comic in a secure place. But where? The garage! Several layers of building materials beneath my father's tool chest seemed like a safe hidey-hole. Wrong! Without any forewarning, it was decided that the garage needed a serious clean out and reorganization. My illicit comic was discovered and I, at long last, finally understood why God had made Man. To make belts. And belts were made for punishment. Whack! I was soundly whipped for having filth like that around the house. (Note: My parents were very nice, gentle people. This was at a time before child abuse had been invented.) Had I been touching myself? Whack! What other deviant acts had I been engaged in? Whack! These things were abhorrent to God and Jesus. Whack! Whatever pain I was feeling, my mother and father were hurting more, utterly disappointed to discover what an abomination their son had become.

These sordid events took place in the 1950s, during the days when the guardians of decency were fighting to ban the corrupting influence of comic books. Senate subcommittees had been formed. Protesters were in the streets. The good and the decent were up in arms to stop this evil that was destroying America's youth. Luckily, they failed.

But they were right. Comics were and are corrupting. And long may they remain so.

Comics were my escape route. Not that my life was unpleasant or difficult; in fact, I had a great childhood in the forested countryside of Minnesota and then, later, in the shining suburbs of Los Angeles. But those worlds were too pleasant, too limiting, too safe, and too reasonable. They didn't engage the darker corners of my imagination. A part of me felt imprisoned.

Comics were freedom. Depending on what was available at the corner shop, I could choose to live schizophrenically in a great throbbing metropolis as a bizarrely costumed, multiple-personalitied vigilante dealing brutally with major criminals, thwarting their evil designs wherever they blossomed. If I had some free time in the afternoon, I could head off to

Mars, no problem. Zapping from frame to frame with that red cape fluttering on my back, my own muscles soon understanding what it was like to fly. Every fiber of my body experienced that sensation. Admittedly, as I got older I realized I could fly only about three feet off the ground. But that was part of growing up. Actually, to be utterly honest, it wasn't until I was in my thirties that I was able to prove to myself, once and for all, that I was, in fact, unable to fly—not even a measly three feet off the ground. We can't be kids forever.

Long before the 1960s, and the onslaught of acid and other hallucinogens, there was *Little Nemo* to inhale. I learned to understand the infinite mutability of the "real world" while trying to deal with Windsor McCay's shape-shifting architecture. By the time I was old enough to inhale properly, Nemo's night journeys had rendered Buddhism and drugs unnecessary. Not only had comics saved me barrel loads of money and time, they had also provided me with a way to avoid real work and still make a living. All I needed was a piece of paper and a pen.

I learned to draw and write stories and jokes by copying the comics. For me, *MAD* was the most influential, not just for the sexy babes, but for the pastiches, the satires, the absurdities. These were forms and concepts that had altered the way I dealt with the world. Nothing was sacred. Pomposity must be punctured. Hypocrisy had to be exposed. Laughter was life-giving. Intelligence could be fun. Silliness was sublime. I copied Jack Davis's drawing style. I purloined Willy Elder's visual gags, and I worshipped Harvey Kurtzman. These guys became my heroes.

In college, I turned the arts and literature magazine into a humor magazine. Copies would be sent to Harvey in New York, and when I received an encouraging response from the great man himself, my academic studies were sacrificed to feed the interest this divine being had shown. Determined to make face-to-face contact with this Olympian, I made my way across America and, through a twist of fate that only occurs in comics, instantly became Harvey's right hand, the assistant editor of *HELP!* magazine. I was in heaven. My heroes and gods were my friends. And I was getting paid, working for $50 a week. That was $2 less than I would have made for not working. But, I had made the right choice. Or had I? The rest is history.

Let this be a warning. I was an innocent young man of potential who, through the dark influence of comics, set off on a long, painful, and degenerate path. I am still trying to come to terms with that error. If it hadn't been for comics and the corrupting impact they had on me I could have lived the dream. I could have been . . . a lumberjack!

London, United Kingdom

Introduction

By Paul Gravett

There can never be one history or one experience of comics. Each of us has a specific and personal relationship to these myriad stories depending on our circumstances, language, geography, and taste. Perhaps your parents indulged or encouraged your enjoyment of them as a child. Or perhaps your parents forbade you to read them at all, possibly making them even more illicitly desirable. Or maybe since you became a parent yourself, you have continued that veto for your own children. Perhaps you initially discovered comics characters via their small- and big-screen adaptations or as computer games, toys, cards, or other spin-off merchandising. Through the teenage years, many choose to put away childish things like comics, but a particular story can still surprisingly grab your attention and speak to you directly. Even in adulthood, it's never too late for that epiphany to make you rediscover—or discover for the first time—this deceptively simple yet complex and compelling storytelling vehicle.

It is precisely because of the individual nature of our relationship to comics that, as the general editor of *1001 Comics You Must Read Before You Die*, I drew on a wealth of perspectives from my team of sixty-seven experts in twenty-seven countries to compile this list. There have been other guides to comics before but most have their nationalist and linguistic biases, and none have been so determinedly international and exploratory as this one. I guarantee that you will not find all your favorites here, but I also guarantee that you will discover some brand-new favorites.

Inevitably, three of the greatest centers of comics creativity and production—the United States, Japan, and Europe, especially France—take pride of place here, but thanks to the global spread of contributors the most original, innovative, and distinctive comics from many other countries and cultures also appear. To make this book work in multiple language editions, the entries have been ordered by the year of first publication in the original language. As well as one of the few attempts at producing a true "world canon" of comics, this also results in an intriguing international chronology of how the medium has changed and continues to change.

To narrow this vast field, spannning years of daily newspaper strips to sagas hundreds, even thousands, of pages long, priority has been given to characters and concepts that originated first as comics over those derived from books, movies, or other sources. That said, you will still find Edgar

Key to symbols in the book

✎ Author
✎ Illustrator

Similiar reads/Also by
Titles in *bold italic* are featured in the book.

Burroughs's Tarzan, Disney's Donald Duck, and others here, alongside a few literary adaptations, too. Another concern was how far back in time this survey should go. Comics were not invented in a single, dazzling "eureka!" moment but have been metamorphosing for millennia. Arguably they can be traced back through prints, broadsides, children's books, illuminated manuscripts, scrolls, stained glass windows, and hieroglyphics to the earliest representational drawing on cave walls. We humans seem hot-wired to represent our world in symbols and icons, joining them up to give narrative meaning. *1001 Comics* could have focused on printed forms in the twentieth century, but I also wanted to highlight a few landmarks from the nineteenth century, led by the work of Genevan schoolteacher Rodolphe Töpffer, although there are many other antecedents and precursors. To explore these, I recommend Andy Konky Kru's burgeoning archive of early comics from 1783 to 1929 at http://konkykru.com/earlycomics.html.

An equally important decision was where to end this survey and it closes with some of the key works published in 2011. You may notice that almost the entire second half of the book is devoted to comics published since 1990. This reflects the recent and current extraordinary explosion of creativity in the medium worldwide, boosted, as I see it, by three huge shifts. First is the impact of women creators, who appeared on the scene as long ago as 1867 with Marie Duval in Britain, but on nothing like the scale and diversity witnessed in recent years. Second, the Internet has allowed cartoonists to express themselves online through web comics, cutting out the publishing, printing, distribution, and retail middlemen to reach a huge transnational readership with some outstanding results. Just as in the late nineteenth century, comics had anticipated many of the techniques and the public's acceptance of cinema so that comics then developed alongside film. A century later a similar fin de siècle interaction has emerged with the visual and verbal language of comics informing the Internet in its design and navigation, and again we have seen both media expanding in tandem.

Thirdly, and connected to this, is the gradual (re)blossoming of comics from almost everywhere imaginable. Comics occupy a peculiar place in world culture. Almost every other artistic form you can think of—music, literature, poetry, theater, dance, film, the visual arts—exist and even thrive in some form wherever you go. It seems only comics vary so much in their status, expression, and market from nation to nation, depending hugely on the country's politics, religion, literacy, economy, and exposure to outside influences. Communism, for instance, seems to have been very confused about comics. Mao's China heavily promoted palm-sized comics as a propaganda tool, whereas the Soviet Union deeply distrusted them as Western, capitalist juvenilia—and Russia largely still does. Each nation has its own attitude to the medium and its social, cultural, and political situation is not always conducive to generating a homegrown comics culture. Central and Eastern Europe, India, the Middle East, and Africa are awakening, albeit somewhat erratically. While Slovenia, especially through its state-supported magazine *Stripburger*, is an energetic ambassador for the region, neighbors such as Albania or Bulgaria seem almost inactive, so far. Egypt's first graphic novel was seized and its author and publisher fined, but the Arab Spring promises change.

These days a surprise hit can emerge from almost anywhere. Who could have predicted *Persepolis* by Iranian-born Marjane Satrapi or *Logicomix* from Greece and by a respected prose novelist? Globally and locally, there are passionate activists—festival organizers, independent publishers, academics, and new generations of writers, artists, and those all-important readers—who are contributing to building up a local scene and reaching out to a network around the world. Comics can cross language and culture barriers, enriching communication and understanding.

Many of the comics included in this book have originated in languages other than English, but rest assured that a substantial quantity have been translated or will be in the near future. The details of translated versions are always changing and I provide up-to-date information on my website (www.paulgravett.com) about what is available in English. This website is developing into a hub for articles, similar reads, creator profiles, and links, as well as sample covers and interior pages from many of the entries that we were unable to illustrate in this book.

Comics have become a greater part of my life than I could ever have expected. As an English boy, I grew up reading the short comic strips in my parents' newspapers: *Peanuts*, *Carol Day*, *Rip Kirby*, and *Focus on Fact* in the *Daily Mail*, and *Gun Law* and *Sporting Sam*'s worldless gags in the *Sunday*

Express. Progressing from *The Beano* and *The Dandy*, I started to get *Look and Learn*, which my parents bought me and my younger brother for its educational features. Little did they know that we always turned first to the two-page spread of the swords-and-spaceships comic *The Trigan Empire* with its stunning, full-color artwork by Don Lawrence.

In the shops, I soon spotted another weekly comic based on Gerry Anderson's futuristic puppet shows. Each week *TV21* was dated a full century in advance, as if beamed to readers from the future. Before videos, DVDs, or the Internet, with only three TV channels to choose from in Britain, watching *Thunderbirds* was an unmissable experience. Between episodes, a long week could be filled whenever you wanted by the comic versions painted in spectacular color by Frank Bellamy. Television also introduced me to Hergé's *Tintin* albums from the local library via the unpolished but thrilling Belvision animated cartoons. I discovered superheroes thanks to the colorful camp of *Batman* ("Same Bat-Time, Same Bat-Channel").

Comics changed as I changed. We grew up together. Just as my interest threatened to wane in one area, another vista would open up to me. On my first visit to a specialist comic shop, Dark They Were And Golden-Eyed in London's then-sleazy Soho, I bought my first fanzine. New collector pals and histories of the medium would lead me to the incredible achievements from the past. In 1977 I became captivated by both *2000AD* and *Heavy Metal*. I can never thank my French schoolteachers enough for enabling me to explore the "ninth art" of *bande dessinée*. I started a stall and mail-order service for self-published and small-press British comics, connecting to an array of youthful talent. I quit my dull nine-to-five existence in insurance for my first job in comics, managing the promotion of a new British adult comics magazine, *pssst!*. Since then, witnessing the rise of the graphic novel, comics journalism, graphic medicine, comics festivals, conferences, and exhibitions from Algeria to the Arctic Circle, and the long-overdue arrival of manga in translation, has been both amazing and inspiring.

How can anyone "give up" comics, when this medium is so varied and vibrant? Think of how much we can do with pictures. And how much we can do with words. Then imagine how much more we can do with them both. This is what comics, past, present, and future, can offer. For me, comics are for life. I hope some of these *1001 Comics* will become part of your life.

Index of Titles

#

A

B

C

N

O

P

Q

R

S

T

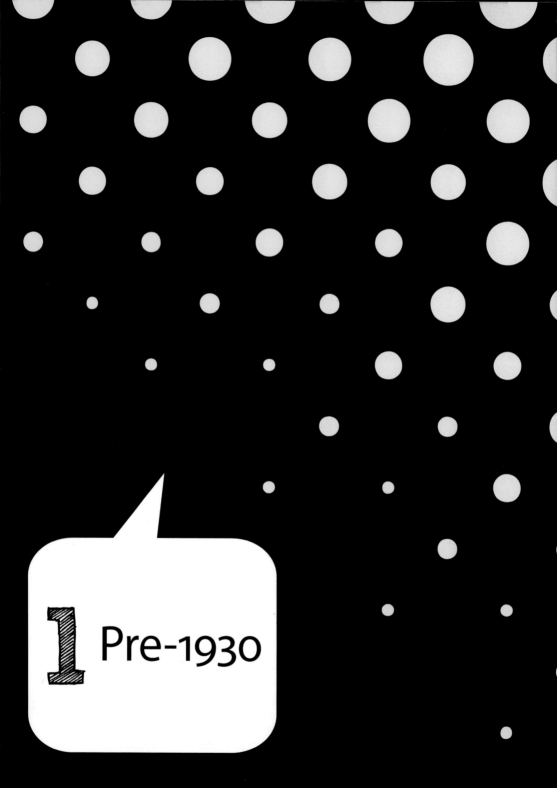

1 Pre-1930

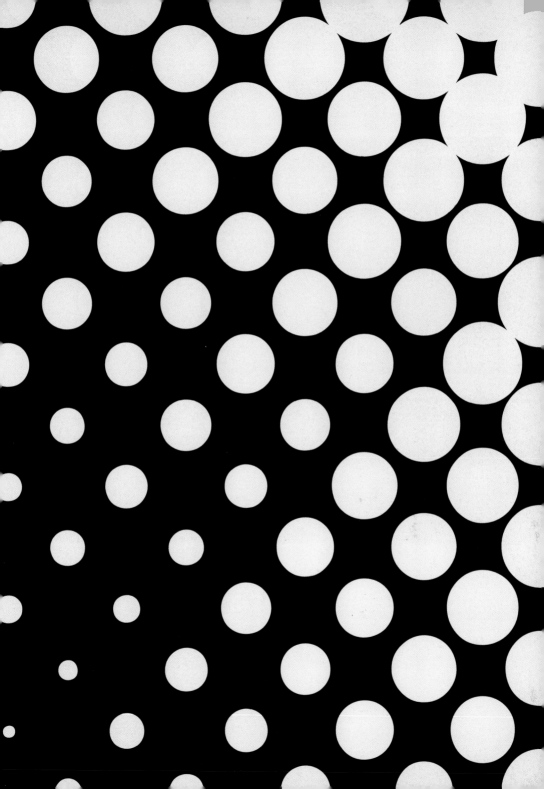

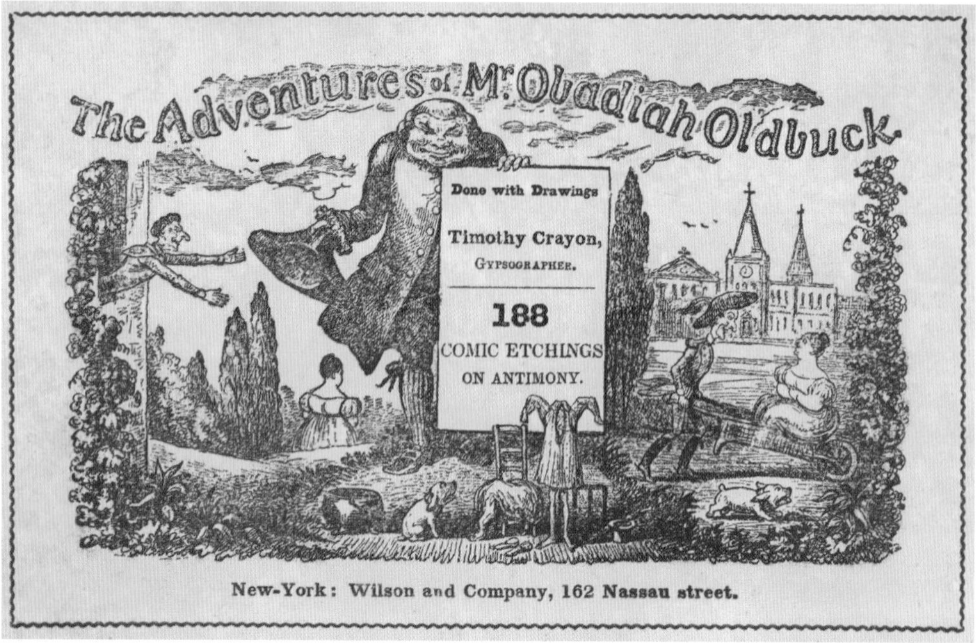
The Adventures of Mr. Obadiah Oldbuck.
Done with Drawings
Timothy Crayon,
Gypsographer.
188
COMIC ETCHINGS
ON ANTIMONY.
New-York: Wilson and Company, 162 Nassau street.

The Adventures of Mr. Obadiah Oldbuck 1837

Rodolphe Töpffer

Title in original language *Les Amours de Mr. Vieux Bois*
First published by Self-published (Switzerland)
Creator Swiss (1799–1846)
Genre Humor, Adventure

Rodolphe Töpffer, a French-speaking native of Geneva, Switzerland, was a schoolmaster prevented by eye disease from becoming a professional artist. He developed his own pictorial tales in the 1820s, and in 1827 he finished an early long story of the kind now called a comic—thirty pages filled with 158 panels of text and rough drawings, relating the mishaps of a funny man he named Mr. Vieux Bois (Mr. Ham-Handed). The strip resembled a chase movie, full of action and mishap. He didn't publish this first draft, but years later he redrew it into longer versions that he published himself as *histoires en estampes* (engraved stories), titled *Les Amours de Mr. Vieux Bois* (as 198 panels on eighty-eight pages in 1837; then, in an 1839 edition, as 221 panels on ninety-two pages). Whether or not he invented the comic, Töpffer established cutting, montage, and timing techniques as never before.

In an age of no copyright, his self-published *Mr. Vieux Bois* was soon pirated in France, and reworked into English-language editions as *The Adventures of Mr. Obadiah Oldbuck*—in 1841 (U.K.) with front art by Robert Cruikshank, then in 1842 (U.S.) as a forty-page issue of *Brother Jonathan Extra*. These predated authorized versions of his seventh album, *Mr. Cryptogame*—called *The Strange Adventures of Batchelor Butterfly*—in 1845 (U.K.), and in 1846 (U.S.). Töpffer's *The Adventures of Mr. Obadiah Oldbuck,* in the form of the 1842 *Brother Jonathan Extra*, can be seen as the first comic book in the United States, conceived in 1827. **HvO**

The front cover of the U.S. edition failed to credit Töpffer as author. ↑

Presto

The History of Holy Russia 1854

✐✐ Gustave Doré

Title in original language *Histoire Dramatique, Pittoresque et Caricaturale de la Sainte Russie*
First published by J. Bry Aîné (France)
Creator French (1832–83) **Genre** History

The History of Holy Russia is Doré's fourth and last comic book. After the Töpffer-modeled *Les Travaux d'Hercule*, his subsequent books would influence the layout of comics to come. *Holy Russia* was created at the peak of his career and displayed the full spectrum of his craft, but it was a risky endeavor and resulted in commercial failure. Sidestepping the labyrinthine details of Doré's professional career, *Holy Russia* was a project of a different nature. It was his first incursion into real history, and a most ambitious book, spanning more than a hundred illustrated pages with 500-plus images (each a singular woodblock), with text mostly written by him, including the small captions and the winding, if not frankly dull, narration. His drawings range from simple doodles to triumphs of line art, with great composition work at the start of the volume that deteriorated to rushed design solutions at the end.

His portrayal of the Russians is a mixture of mock historical research and gross caricature: for example, Russians were born from the union of polar bears and walruses, have always displayed a bellicose if not a bloodthirsty disposition, and are as much submissive as resentful, with crazed, capricious people for rulers.

The comic's scope of interest was curtailed further by its original price and its propagandistic tone. Still, its magnificent illustrations make it a wonder of graphic creativity: from the ink-stained page and a censoring vine leaf, to the "living" musical notes. All in all, it is one of the true original classics of comics. **PM**

⬆ *The History of Holy Russia* featured visual flourishes, such as the "living" musical notes.

Max and Moritz 1865

Wilhelm Busch

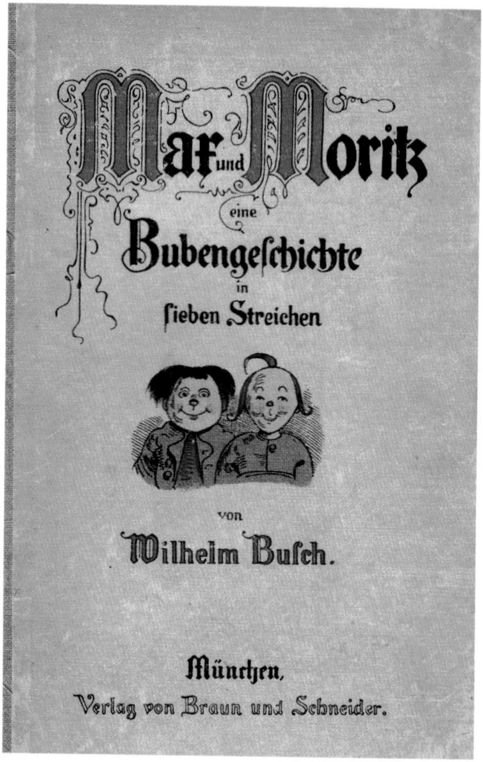
Max und Moritz
eine
Bubengeschichte
in
sieben Streichen
von
Wilhelm Busch.
München,
Verlag von Braun und Schneider.

First published by Self-published (Germany)
Creator German (1832–1908)
Genre Humor
Influence on *The Katzenjammer Kids*

Wilhelm Busch was famous in his own lifetime for his witty works and drawings. Today he is recognized as one of the pioneers of comics. Busch kept words and pictures spatially separate, and by doing so he introduced a narrative interdependence.

In the fifteen frames of his picture-story "The Virtuoso," Busch has a pianist introducing the reader to various musical styles, from the "Fuga del Diavolo" to the "Finale furioso." In the latter Busch portrays the wild movements of the pianist with the use of speed lines; he was the first picture-story artist to do so.

In Germany picture-stories were published in satirical magazines such as the *Fliegende Blätter* and *Münchner Bilderbogen*. The publishers of the *Münchner Bilderbogen* became rich through *Max and Moritz*, a classic of children's literature about two scallywags, but only paid Busch a pittance; he resigned as a result. His last page of pictures was aptly entitled "Die Hungerpille" (The Hunger Pill). Busch's satirical texts and picture-stories repeatedly ridicule the representatives of particular groups of society, especially the philistines with their self-satisfaction and dubious moral attitudes. Bourgeois bigotry and clerical sanctimony were also targets for his sharp pen.

Busch's *Max and Moritz* became a source of inspiration for *The Katzenjammer Kids*, a comic strip commissioned from Rudolph Dirks, a German living in America, for the U.S. newspaper magnate William Randolph Hearst. Highly successful, it became a blueprint for subsequent classic U.S. comic strips. **MS**

"Uncle, wild with fright, upspringeth / And the bedclothes from him flingeth."

Similar reads

Happy Hooligan Frederick Burr Opper
Mutt and Jeff Bud Fisher
The Katzenjammer Kids Rudolph Dirks
Yellow Kid Richard Outcalt

Ally Sloper 1867

✏✏ Charles Henry Ross and "Marie Duval"

First published by *Judy* (UK)
Creators Ross (British, 1835–97);
Emily Louisa Tessier (British, 1847–Unknown)
Genre Humor

Ally Sloper was arguably the first comics superstar due to his huge popularity in print and on stage. He was a Victorian antihero—a drunkard and ne'er-do-well, recognizable by his huge red nose swollen by alcohol, his shabby suit (often with a bottle poking out of the back pocket), crumpled hat, and patched-up umbrella. His genesis can be traced to 1867 in *Judy*, a rival publication to the British magazine *Punch*, though he had a false start in a penny dreadful some years earlier. Charles Ross was his creator, but his mannerisms owed much to Ross's wife, Emily Louisa Tessier (aka Marie Duval), who took up cartooning duties from 1869.

In 1873, a book was produced, priced one shilling, entitled *Ally Sloper: A Moral Lesson*, which collected the best strips from *Judy*. This was ostensibly Sloper's autobiography, and took in various of his scams, often undertaken in league with his Jewish pal, Iky Mo (such as overcharging punters at a magic lantern show, and pretending to be a blind beggar). Also included were his exploits as a war reporter in the Franco-Prussian War and his travels around the world. While Robert Cruikshank and Wilhelm Busch were obvious influences, art historian David Kunzle credits Duval with the use of techniques (distortions, unusual viewpoints) that only became standard in cartooning much later.

The book became the basis of stage acts (including some written by and starring Ross himself), and paved the way for Sloper getting his own weekly publication, *Ally Sloper's Half-Holiday* (1884). It is one of the genuinely amusing funny books of the early comics period. **RS**

Balthazar's Feast 1881

✏✏ "Caran d'Ache"

Title in original language *Un Festin de Balthazar*
First published by *La Vie militaire* journal (France)
Creator Emmanuel Poiré (French, 1858–1909)
Genre Humor

Emmanuel Poiré was born in Moscow, the son of a French officer of Napoleon. He moved to France in 1877, and after joining the French army he contributed satirical drawings to the army journal, *La Vie militaire*. Adopting the pseudonym "Caran d'Ache," which comes from *karandash*, the Russian word for pencil, Poiré first came to the public's notice with silhouette pen drawings of a famous Parisian nightclub, Le Chat Noir. He later provided black-and-white and color caricatures for publications such as *La Revue illustrée*, *La Vie Parisienne*, and *Le Figaro*.

Although d'Ache reveled in the challenge of the wordless story, he still felt words had an intrinsic role to play by virtue of their exclusion, and he enjoyed manipulating his images to overcome their absence. One short strip, *The Duelists and the Butterfly*, depicts two antagonists engaged in swordplay while another man captures a butterfly in a top hat. He approaches the duelists, puts the hat over one of their heads, and sees the other prodded harmlessly in the derriere.

D'Ache's pioneering status is best seen, however, in *Maestro* (1894). He proposed an ambitious series of wordless books to *Le Figaro* that, when completed, would comprise one of the world's earliest graphic novels. D'Ache was pleased that the story could be comprehended and enjoyed by anyone, regardless of their language. He was unable to finish the work, but its rediscovery and subsequent publication in 1999 by the Louvre Museum, Paris, has helped place d'Ache firmly in the pantheon of French cartoonists. **BS**

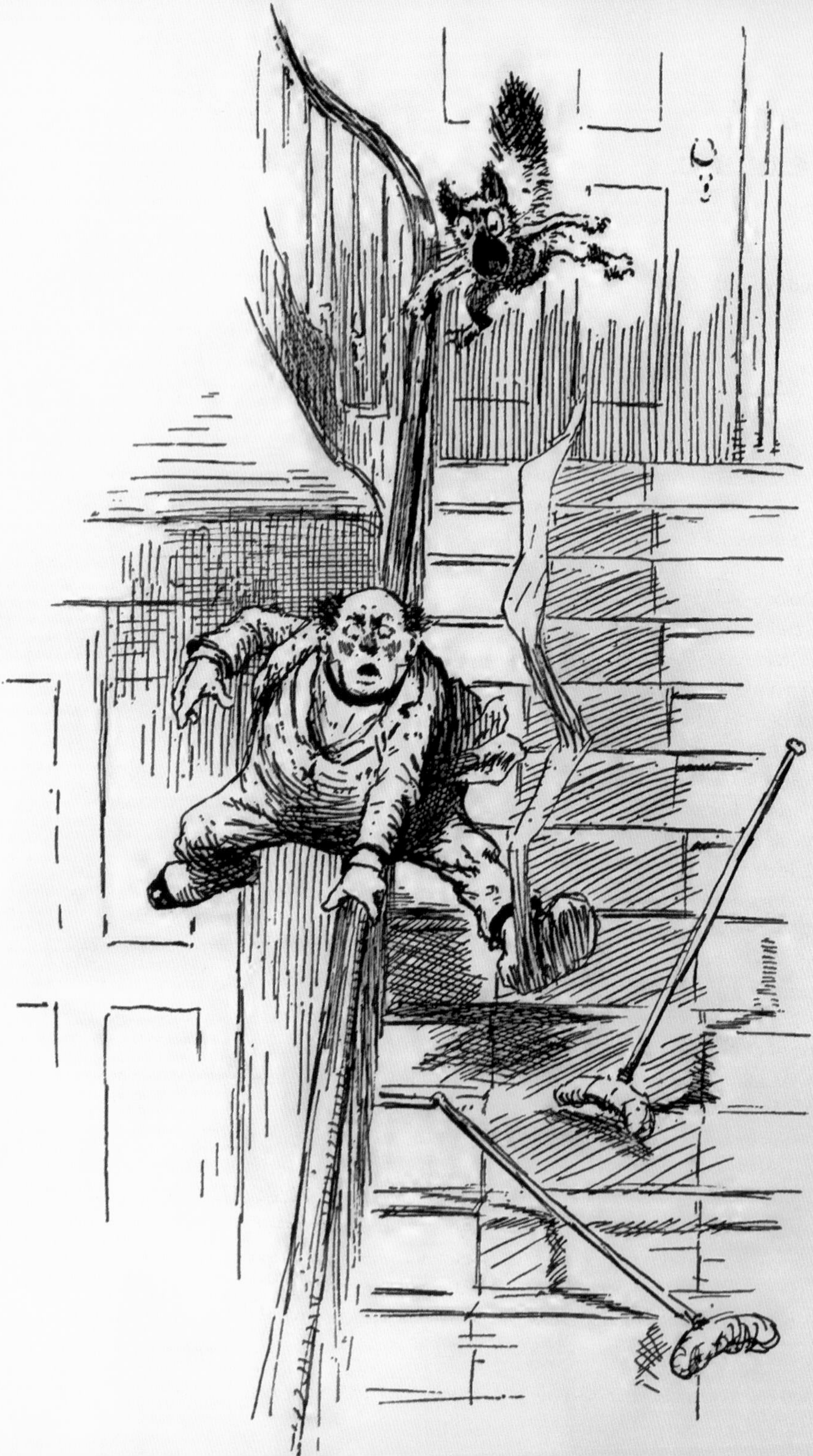

Stuff and Nonsense 1884

✐✐ Arthur Burdett Frost

First published by Charles Scribner's Sons (USA)
Creator American (1851–1928)
Genre Humor

A staff cartoonist for *Harper's Monthly* who was also renowned for his prints of the rural United States, Arthur Burdett Frost was a key figure in the golden age of U.S. illustration. His grotesque cartoons on everyday follies were a precursor to the daily newspaper comic strips, and his anthology *Stuff and Nonsense* highlights his pioneering work in time lapse and sequential imaging. It features both wordless and captioned stories, including his best known pieces—"A Fatal Mistake: A Tale of a Cat" (the zany tale of a cat who ingests poison) and "The Balloonists" (recounting the carnage left in the wake of two buffoons and their hot air balloon)—along with dozens of illustrated limericks. This harebrained and humorous medley highlights the brio of Frost's art, the incredible expressiveness of both his human and animal characters, and his remarkable ability to render brisk motion in single pen-and-ink images.

An illustrator of works by Lewis Carroll and Mark Twain, Frost received severe criticism in the twentieth century among figures of the Harlem Renaissance for his portrayal of black characters, especially in his illustrations for Joey Chandler Harris's *Uncle Remus* collections. Indeed, the original edition of *Stuff and Nonsense* features embarrassing Irish caricatures, which Frost himself removed from the 1888 edition.

Despite these criticisms, Frost's genuine technical mastery and artistic flourish can still be enjoyed by modern readers. The dynamism of his work is such that it anticipates not only later ballooned and paneled comic strips, but also animated motion pictures. **DN**

The Fenouillard Family 1889

✐✐ "Christophe"

Title in original language *La famille Fenouillard*
First published by *Le Petit Français Illustré* (France)
Creator Marie Louis Georges Colomb
(French, 1856–1945) **Genre** Satire, Adventure

Author, and later botanist, Georges Colomb didn't see it coming: the transformation of his illustrated serial into a near comic strip. From February to April 1889 his self-written, self-illustrated *A Day in the Country* (*Une partie de campagne*), ran for nine weeks as a serial in the weekly youth magazine *Le Journal de la Jeunesse*, published in Paris. For the first five weeks just one small drawing accompanied short, humorous text; the last four weeks brought two, three, even five pictures per episode. Colomb's story was about a fictitious Parisian family, *la famille Cornouillet*, a father and mother with two twinlike daughters, who started to explore their world. Colomb—who already had a good job as a teacher—wanted an amusing pen name; thinking of Christopher Columbus, he chose Christophe, signing himself calligraphically in the form of a whale.

Later in 1889 he expanded on the idea of his earlier Cornouillet family story, now a full-blown comic strip with all the text outside the frame. It ran under another title, *La famille Fenouillard*, and in another magazine, *Le Petit Français Illustré*, from August 31. Christophe drew fifty-three installments from 1889 to 1893, partly to amuse his young son, Pierre (b.1883). He changed the family home from Paris to a province, and sent them on a world tour as reluctant tourists—to the United States, East Asia, and across the Pacific. The parents were hosiers, papa always carrying his red umbrella and often losing his hat, with two daughters, Artémise and Cunégonde. Christophe was a brilliant observer, in image and in text. **HvO**

◀ A man hastily abandons his crutches to make way for the poisoned cat in *Stuff and Nonsense*.

The Yellow Kid 1894

Richard Felton Outcault

First published by *Truth* magazine (USA)
Creator American (1863–1928)
Genre Humor
Award Will Eisner Comic Book Hall of Fame (2008)

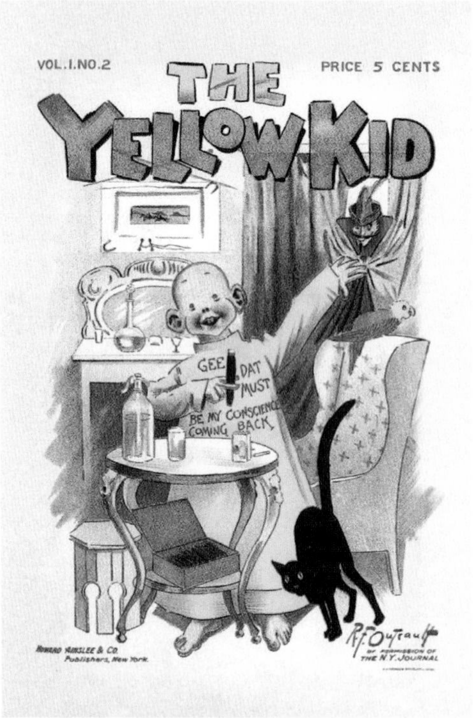
VOL.I.NO.2
THE YELLOW KID
PRICE 5 CENTS
GEE DAT MUST BE MY CONSCIENCE COMING BACK
R.F. Outcault
HOWARD AINSLEE & CO. Publishers, New York
BY PERMISSION OF THE N.Y. JOURNAL

"[Outcault] never had much schooling along the line of art, but it seemed to come to him."

***Lancaster Daily Eagle* obituary**

Richard Felton Outcault lived a distinguished life. He worked as a technical draftsman for Thomas Edison, became an editorial cartoonist whose talents sparked an early newspaper circulation war, and popularized an art form via his progressive use of the Yellow Kid.

A proto-bald headed Alfred E. Neuman (*MAD Magazine*'s iconic cover boy), the Yellow Kid first appeared in Outcault's *Hogan's Alley* panels, busy depictions of New York slum life. Starting as a background character, his distinctive appearance prompted comment, so Outcault increased his prominence, utilizing the kid's nightshirt as a billboard for the slogans with which he peppered his strips.

The great leap forward came with a strip published on October 25, 1896. "The Yellow Kid and his New Phonograph" comprised five sequential drawings where the text essential to each was contained *within* word balloons rather than being printed beneath. Outcault helped pioneer U.S. newspaper strips, and continued with the format, although not exclusively; he also numbered his panels to avoid reader confusion.

Astoundingly for such a seminal creation, the only book pulling together all Outcault's strips is Bill Blackbeard's long out-of-print 1995 publication *R. F. Outcault's The Yellow Kid: A Centennial Celebration of the Kid Who Started the Comics*. Blackbeard's collection of strips is archived online by Ohio State University.

Despite earning considerable sums of money via merchandising the character, Outcault was reportedly never keen on him. He resented the association between the slogans on the kid's yellow nightshirt and the disparaging term "yellow journalism," which refers to the inaccurate populist reporting of some papers. Outcault's new employers won a court decision over ownership, but realizing that he no longer controlled his creation, Outcault pursued other avenues of creativity. **FP**

The Katzenjammer Kids 1897

Rudolph Dirks

"Katzenjammer" is a German term with a dual meaning: it literally refers to cats howling outside, but is also a colloquial expression for a hangover. Both equally apply to the anarchic antics of Hans and Fritz, whose tricks on their mother and her boarder, the Captain, tried their patience and frequently earned retribution.

At the request of art editor Rudolph Block, Dirks created a strip based on *Max and Moritz*, Wilhelm Busch's illustrated morality tale, then largely unknown in the United States beyond the German immigrant population. His choice of phonetic, German-accented English highlighted the similarity.

There are legitimate claims for Dirks as the father of the comic strip. He popularized sequential narrative and word balloons, as well as several elements of visual shorthand, among them speed lines, beads of sweat, and the sawing of wood equated with snoring. Without his compelling storytelling, however, Dirks would be a footnote. His tricks and language were inventive, and his judgment sound. Moving the strip from New York to East Africa increased the possibilities for mayhem, although, in common with other strips of the times, what would now be considered offensive racial stereotypes began to feature.

Dirks requested a sabbatical in 1912. The most often repeated story claims he wanted to tour Europe, but contemporary cartoonists cite an inability to work with the tyrannical Block. The request was rejected, Dirks went anyway, and the paper had Harold Knerr continue the strip. It led to court, where Dirks was granted ownership of the characters, while the paper retained the name.

The very capable Knerr continued *The Katzenjammer Kids* in the *New York Journal*, while Dirks produced *The Captain and the Kids* for the *New York World*, until retiring to paint ten years before his death. **FP**

First published by *New York Journal* (USA)
Creator American (1877–1968)
Genre Humor
Adaptation Silent short film (1898)

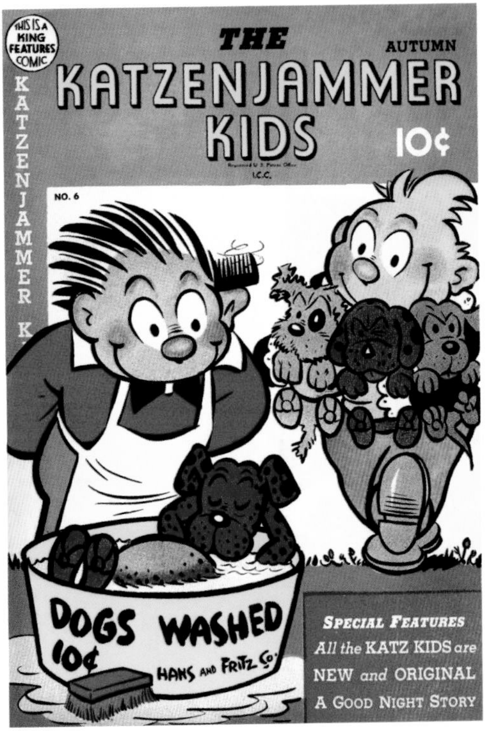
THIS IS A KING FEATURES COMIC
THE
AUTUMN
KATZENJAMMER KIDS
10¢
KATZENJAMMER K
NO. 6
DOGS WASHED 10¢
HANS AND FRITZ Co
SPECIAL FEATURES
All the KATZ KIDS are
NEW and ORIGINAL
A GOOD NIGHT STORY

"My friends! Let us drink to der health of Hanz und Fritz, dod gast dere little hides."

GOOD SHIP "SINKER" GOES DOWN WITH ALL HAND

Hans und Fritz, Alphonse et Gaston, Happy Hooligan an' Glo my Gus, All Swim Out—Drawn by Dirks, Opper, and "Bunny," assisted by G

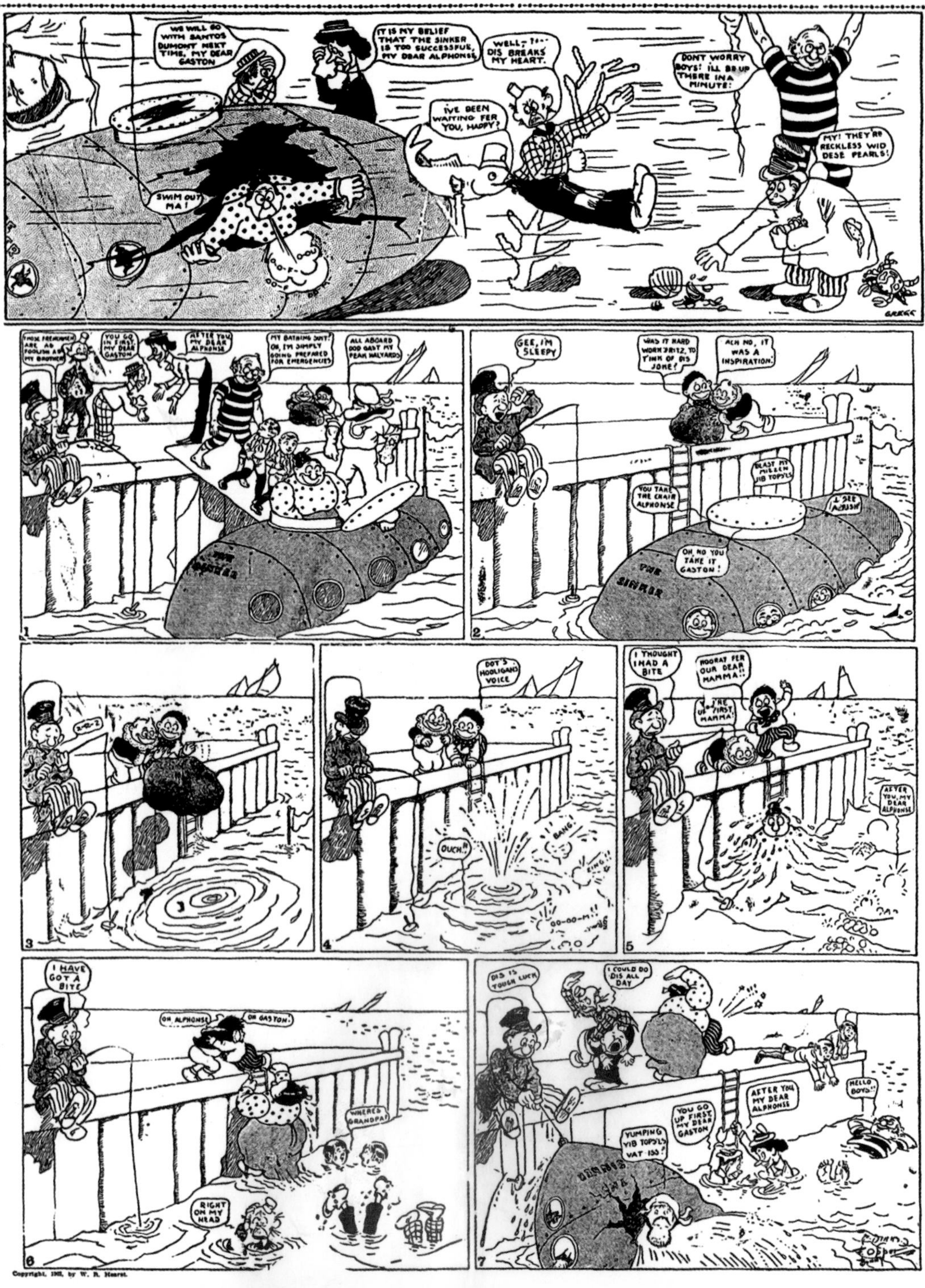
WE WILL GO WITH SANTOS DUMONT NEXT TIME, MY DEAR GASTON
IT IS MY BELIEF THAT THE SINKER IS TOO SUCCESSFUL, MY DEAR ALPHONSE
WELL-!!- DIS BREAKS MY HEART.
DONT WORRY BOYS! ILL BE UP THERE IN A MINUTE!
I'VE BEEN WAITING FER YOU, HAPPY?
MY! THEY'RE RECKLESS WID DESE PEARLS!
SWIM OUT MA!
O-O-F- O-OU
GREGG
YOU GO IN FIRST, MY DEAR GASTON
AFTER YOU MY DEAR ALPHONSE
MY BATHING SUIT? OH, I'M SIMPLY GOING PREPARED FOR EMERGENCIES
ALL ABOARD DOD GAST MY PEAK HALYARDS
GEE, I'M SLEEPY
WAS IT HARD WORK FRITZ, TO TINK OF DIS JOKE?
ACH NO, IT WAS A INSPIRATION.
BLAST MY MIZZEN JIB TOPS'LS
YOU TAKE THE CHAIR ALPHONSE
OH, NO YOU TAKE IT GASTON!
THE SINKER
Z-Z-Z
DOT'S HOOLIGAN'S VOICE
OUCH!!
BANG!
KING!!
OO-OO-M!!
I THOUGHT I HAD A BITE
HOORAY FER OUR DEAR MAMMA!!
AFTER YOU, MY DEAR ALPHONSE
I HAVE GOT A BITE
OH ALPHONSE!
OH GASTON!
WHERE'S GRANDPA?
RIGHT ON MY HEAD
DIS IS TOUGH LUCK
I COULD DO DIS ALL DAY
HELLO BOYS!!
AFTER YOU MY DEAR ALPHONSE
YOU GO UP FIRST MY DEAR GASTON
YUMPING YIB TOPS'LS VAT ISS?

Happy Hooligan 1900

✎ Frederick Burr Opper

First published by *New York Journal* (USA)
Creator American (1857–1937)
Genre Humor
Adaptation Short film (1900)

Reading early comic strips provides a vivid glimpse into the minds of comics fans of yesterday—few more so than *Happy Hooligan*, Frederick Burr Opper's long-running tale of a boho about town. Born in Madison, Ohio, just before the American Civil War, Opper was the son of Austrian immigrants. After moving to New York City while still a teenager, Opper studied briefly at the Cooper Union before apprenticing himself to Frank Beard, a star illustrator. Opper got his big chance when William Randolph Hearst offered him a position with the *New York Journal*.

Happy Hooligan, Opper's first *Journal* creation, tells the tale of a homeless Irishman and his hapless buddies. Published at a time when ethnic stereotypes were the accepted norm in the funny pages, the Hooligan's adventures around the world with his pals Montmorency and Gloomy Gus—whatever their implications about Irish immigrant intelligence—enjoyed enormous success, and made *Happy Hooligan* the first newspaper strip to make the transition to motion pictures.

Indeed, so popular was the Happy Hooligan in his day that, when the strip turned thirty, two U.S. presidents—Hoover and Coolidge—attended his "birthday party." Opper continued to draw *Happy Hooligan* until 1932, when the strain on his failing eyesight grew too great. After his death in 1937 the *New York Times* described him as the dean emeritus of American cartooning—a title well-earned after years of making the country laugh. **EL**

Buster Brown 1902

✎ Richard Felton Outcault

First published by *New York Herald* (USA)
Creator American (1863–1928)
Genre Humor
Adaptation TV (1951)

Richard Felton Outcault is best known as the creator of *Hogan's Alley*, the wildly popular depiction of slum life better known as *The Yellow Kid*. With *Buster Brown*, first published in 1902, Outcault proved he was more than a one-hit wonder. Designed for the upscale *New York Herald*, and influenced by the work of Charles Dana Gibson, Outcault drew Buster as a pretty boy with a pedigreed dog, flanked by an affluent New York family.

Buster's angelic looks did not deceive readers for long—he soon proved to be as much of a hellion as the Yellow Kid. Yet there was a crucial difference: each *Buster Brown* strip ended not in gleeful chaos but with Buster punished and penitent. Buster's resolutions to change and behave better filled the last panel of each strip—often drawing on the bibliophile Outcault's library of philosophy and world literature.

After three highly successful years, William Randolph Hearst came calling and Outcault left the *Herald* for Hearst's *New York Journal*. As lawsuits raged, competing *Buster Brown* strips appeared in both papers. Meanwhile, Outcault developed a Buster Brown merchandising empire, including reprint volumes, clothing, china, shoes, and more. Outcault quit the comic strip world a very rich man in 1921, but such was Buster's popularity that the strip continued in reprints until 1926.

Today, comic fans may have only foggy memories of little Buster Brown. But in a culture filled with cartoon bad boys—Bart Simpson and Dennis the Menace spring to mind—reading *Buster Brown* can feel a bit like finding the Rosetta Stone of childhood hijinks. **EL**

← Happy Hooligan is joined by other characters in a special episode.

The Upside Downs 1903

✎ Gustave Verbeek

Original title *The Upside Downs of Little Lady Lovekins and Old Man Muffaroo*
First published by *New York Herald* (USA)
Creator American (1867–1937) **Genre** Humor

A naturalized American of Dutch parentage, Gustave Verbeek was among the first newspaper cartoon strip creators, and died before comic books were five years old. Yet in the century since *The Upside Downs* first appeared his novel approach has never been matched. Verbeek's upside-down strips transcend mere gimmickry by virtue of the sheer planning required to create them, and his skill and imagination still impress.

An illustrator by trade, Verbeek embraced the new comic strips, creating a strip that flows in conventional fashion over the first six panels before requiring the page to be turned 180 degrees for the concluding six panels. *The Upside Downs of Little Lady Lovekins and Old Man Muffaroo*, to give the strip its full title, is a masterpiece of applied thought.

Verbeek's characters look eccentric. His design, however, assured that the billowing skirt of Lady Lovekins became Old Man Muffaroo's supernaturally large hat when the page was inverted, the ribbons waving from her hat transformed into his trousers, and her hair becoming his wild moustache. Their potato-shaped heads also served the reversal well.

As Verbeek grew more confident with the format, other details became more imaginative. A widely seen image has Muffaroo in the curved beak of a giant bird. When reversed, he is leaving an island by canoe as a large fish frolics beside him. A large tree-covered hill becomes a smoking fire, a genie becomes a bull, and a fire-breathing dragon a flaming city. One strip would be an achievement. Sixty-four is astonishing. **FP**

Dream of the Rarebit Fiend 1904

✎ "Silas"

First published by *New York Evening Telegram* (USA)
Creator Winsor McCay (American, *c*.1867–1934)
Genre Humor
Adaptation Short film (1906)

Winsor McCay (under the pen name Silas) called his comic strip *Dream of the Rarebit Fiend*, although his creation was more the stuff of nightmares: wild animals crush you in your bed; birds stuff straw and twigs into your mouth to build their nests; clumps of earth rain down on you as you look up from a coffin. Not quite the jolly entertainment the American public expected from the newspaper "funnies." McCay would open with a seemingly normal situation that gradually transforms to a shocking climax, before abruptly switching in the final panel to the dreamer startled awake. Every dreamer would then blame their bad night's sleep on a bedtime snack of Welsh rarebit—grated cheese mixed with beer or milk, poured onto toast and grilled.

McCay's strips often tapped into his own foibles, such as the dangers of automobiles, which he refused to drive. Diminutive men beset by domineering women reflect McCay, of slight build himself, and his larger, commanding wife Maude. McCay's younger brother suffered from mental illness and had been confined to an asylum. Fearing perhaps that madness might be hereditary, McCay reaffirms his sanity in every strip by illustrating that his traumatized sleepers are not insane but are simply victims of indigestion.

Comics scholar Ulrich Merkl has offered evidence that *Rarebit Fiend* imagery anticipated the creativity of others that followed. He highlights Luis Buñuel's surrealist film *L'Age d'Or* (1930), which featured iconic scenes such as a cow found in a woman's bed that had appeared years earlier in McCay's work. **PG**

"Silas" created a rarebit-fueled world of surreal nightmares. ➡

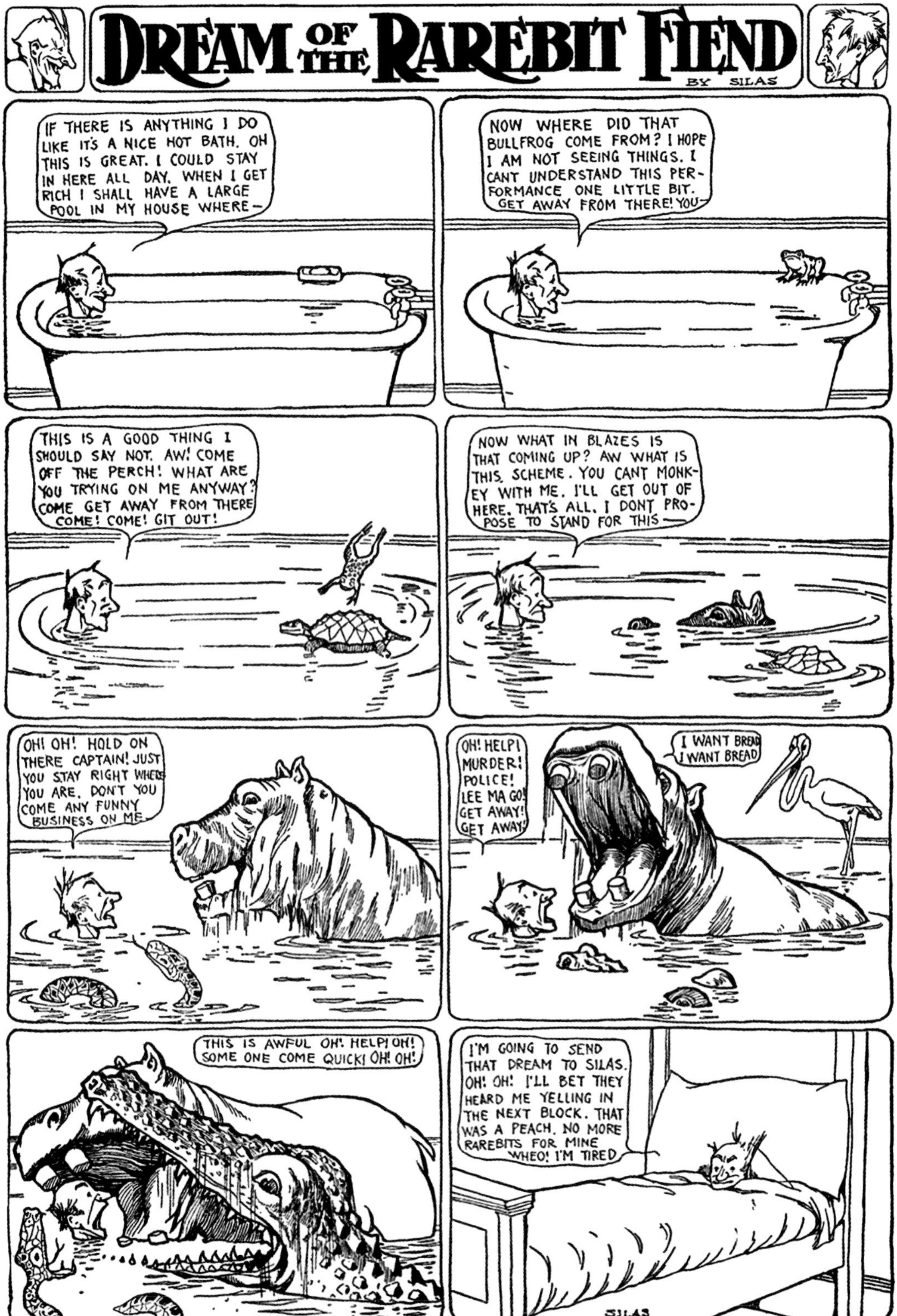
DREAM OF THE RAREBIT FIEND
BY SILAS
IF THERE IS ANYTHING I DO LIKE IT'S A NICE HOT BATH. OH THIS IS GREAT. I COULD STAY IN HERE ALL DAY. WHEN I GET RICH I SHALL HAVE A LARGE POOL IN MY HOUSE WHERE—
NOW WHERE DID THAT BULLFROG COME FROM? I HOPE I AM NOT SEEING THINGS. I CANT UNDERSTAND THIS PERFORMANCE ONE LITTLE BIT. GET AWAY FROM THERE! YOU—
THIS IS A GOOD THING I SHOULD SAY NOT. AW! COME OFF THE PERCH! WHAT ARE YOU TRYING ON ME ANYWAY? COME GET AWAY FROM THERE COME! COME! GIT OUT!
NOW WHAT IN BLAZES IS THAT COMING UP? AW WHAT IS THIS SCHEME. YOU CANT MONKEY WITH ME. I'LL GET OUT OF HERE. THAT'S ALL. I DONT PROPOSE TO STAND FOR THIS—
OH! OH! HOLD ON THERE CAPTAIN! JUST YOU STAY RIGHT WHERE YOU ARE. DON'T YOU COME ANY FUNNY BUSINESS ON ME.
OH! HELP! MURDER! POLICE! LEE MA GO! GET AWAY! GET AWAY!
I WANT BREAD I WANT BREAD
THIS IS AWFUL OH! HELP! OH! SOME ONE COME QUICK! OH! OH!
I'M GOING TO SEND THAT DREAM TO SILAS. OH! OH! I'LL BET THEY HEARD ME YELLING IN THE NEXT BLOCK. THAT WAS A PEACH. NO MORE RAREBITS FOR MINE WHEO! I'M TIRED
SILAS

Little Jimmy 1904

✐✐ James Swinnerton

First published by Hearst Corporation (USA)
Creator American (1875–1974)
Genre Humor
Adaptation Film: *Betty Boop and Little Jimmy* (1936)

There is a slim claim for James Swinnerton's *Three Bears* predating *The Yellow Kid* as the first U.S. newspaper strip, but it lacks illustration-to-illustration narrative. Swinnerton does earn his place, however, among the comic pioneers with his 1898 *Mr. Jack* strip.

The younger Swinnerton was a rambunctious man who had absconded from home aged fifteen, associated with boxers, and drank too much, in complete contrast to his innocent cartoon characters. Introduced as a single panel originally titled *Jimmy*, the protagonist was an easily distracted, naive young lad for whom the pleasures of exploration supplanted his daily tasks. This gradually evolved into Jimmy unknowingly creating constant mayhem around him.

Swinnerton's pages were not as packed as those of his contemporaries, making them easier to read today. It is astounding that he produced them at all, given a doctor's prognosis in 1906 of imminent death due to tuberculosis. Swinnerton relocated to Arizona where the cleaner air delayed his demise. "I forgot to die," he later claimed. The Arizona landscape profoundly affected his art as well. *Little Jimmy* strips were often set among the desert canyons and sunsets, and the additional color extended Swinnerston's painterly instincts.

During World War II Swinnerton temporarily ceased *Little Jimmy*, by then only a Sunday strip, to concentrate on the dramatic *Rocky Mason*. It was not well received, and *Little Jimmy* returned for another thirteen years, stopping only when increasingly shaky hands impaired Swinnerton's line work. **FP**

Little Nemo in Slumberland 1905

✐✐ Winsor McCay

First published by *New York Herald* (USA)
Creator American (c.1867–1934)
Genre Humor, Fantasy
Adaptation Musical (1908)

Winsor McCay was undoubtedly one of the most talented of the early comic strip pioneers and an individual who enormously expanded the parameters of the art form. McCay entered the newspaper world in 1897 and was soon drawing comic strips, but it was after moving to New York that he created his first important works—*Little Sammy Sneeze* and *Dream of the Rarebit Fiend*. In 1905 he created the first episode of *Little Nemo* for the *New York Herald*, and he would draw the feature off and on for the next twenty-one years.

Little Nemo appeared in the *Herald*'s Sunday comic section, and McCay reveled in the supplement's large pages and subtle color printing to produce a strip of great beauty. Typically, the story would start with the young Nemo asleep in bed; readers would follow him into his dreams, where he was often in the company of his friends Flip and the Imp, only for Nemo to fall out of bed in the last panel. The strip was less simplistic than that suggests, however; each week McCay's boundless imagination took Nemo and his readers into ever more surreal experiences. Nemo might find himself surrounded by ravenous lions, in a bed that sprouts legs, on the moon, or falling off the Earth itself.

McCay's creativity was too great to be constrained by one medium; he was also an editorial cartoonist, a showman, and a pioneer of animation. His 1914 feature, *Gertie the Dinosaur*, is widely regarded as the first important animated cartoon. He single-handedly went on to produce several more animated films, including one starring Little Nemo himself. **DAR**

The Kin-der-Kids 1906

Lyonel Feininger

First published by *Chicago Sunday Tribune* (USA)
Creator German-American (1871–1956)
Genre Humor
Award *The Comics Journal* Top 100 Comics

More than a hundred years after the publication of his classic *Kin-der-Kids* newspaper strip, the German-American painter Lyonel Feininger remains the best known artist to have turned his hand to comics. Following the 1907 cancellation of his second major strip, *Wee Willie Winkie's World*, Feininger retired from comics, becoming part of the *Der Blaue Reiter* (The Blue Rider) art group, and then teaching at the Bauhaus school for a number of years. The emphasis on form, line, and color found in his fine art is equally present in his comic strips, and Feininger was producing his own handcrafted Kin-der-Kids toys well into the 1950s.

In his introduction to *The Comic Strip Art of Lyonel Feininger*, historian Bill Blackbeard argues that *The Kin-der-Kids* was the first U.S. comic strip to feature any kind of continuity, with a group of young explorers setting off on an eventful voyage in the family bathtub, pursued by their skeletal adversary, Aunt Jim-Jam. In fact, narrative cohesion takes a backseat throughout the strip to the visual and verbal abstractions that typify works of early twentieth-century modernism.

The Kin-der-Kids appeared in the *Sunday Chicago Tribune* as a full-page, color visual treat and was the focal point of a campaign to attract educated, expatriate German readers who, it was thought, would favor high art European strips over the lowbrow, massively popular U.S. comics. Sadly, the readership proved indifferent to Feininger's esoteric, if undeniably gorgeous, flights of fancy. After less than thirty installments, *The Kin-der-Kids* was abruptly brought to an end mid story in 1906. **AL**

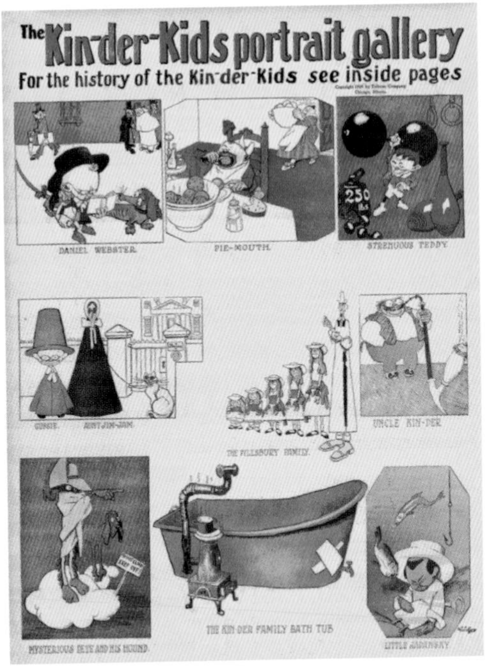
The Kin-der-Kids portrait gallery
For the history of the Kin-der-Kids see inside pages
DANIEL WEBSTER
PIE-MOUTH
STRENUOUS TEDDY
AUNTY JIM-JAM
UNCLE KIN-DER
THE KIN-DER FAMILY BATH TUB

"Feininger's visually poetic formal concerns collided comically with the fishwrap disposability of newsprint."

Art Spiegelman, comics author/artist

Similar reads
Krazy Kat George Herriman
Little Nemo Winsor McCay
Polly and Her Pals Cliff Sterrett
The Katzenjammer Kids Rudolph Dirks
Thimble Theatre E. C. Segar

Mutt and Jeff 1907

Bud Fisher

First published by *San Francisco Chronicle* (USA)
Creator American (1885–1954)
Genre Humor
Adaptation Animated series (1913)

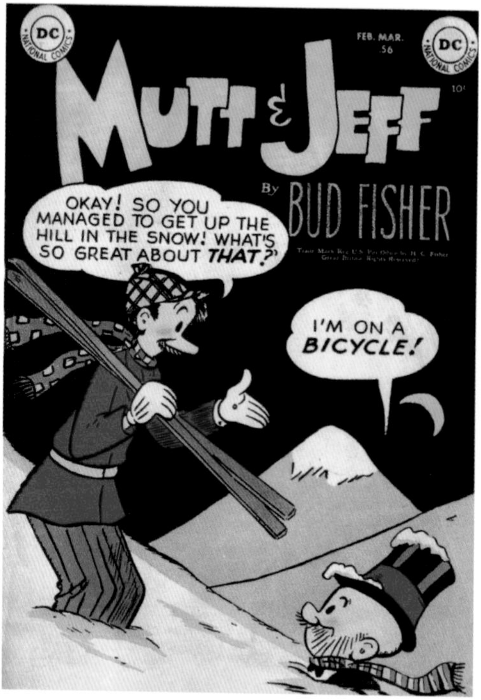

DC NATIONAL COMICS
FEB. MAR. 56
MUTT & JEFF
10¢
By BUD FISHER
OKAY! SO YOU MANAGED TO GET UP THE HILL IN THE SNOW! WHAT'S SO GREAT ABOUT THAT?
I'M ON A BICYCLE!

"People like Jeff because he is smaller, and almost every person in the world is for the little guy against the big one."
Bud Fisher

Before *Mutt and Jeff* there was, simply, Mutt, who starred in his own strip, *A. Mutt*, a daily cartoon about horse racing by an artist even more enterprising than he was prolific. More specifically, *A. Mutt* was a comic strip about betting on horse races. Mutt struggled financially to make ends meet, placing wagers on actual races that would occur shortly after the newspaper hit the stands. Mutt's successes (and more numerable failures) were tallied in each subsequent episode. Readers of the *San Francisco Chronicle*, the newspaper in which the strip first appeared, bet alongside Mutt on the races, which took place in the neighboring East Bay.

Fisher himself showed greater financial acumen than his character did (whose bets were based simply on which colorful-sounding horse names he fancied). Fisher managed to secure ownership of his work during an age when newspapers usually retained copyright over the creative work of their employees. According to one story, Fisher called in a correction to the production department just before the first episode of the strip went to bed, appending his own name to the copyright.

Eventually the comic made its way to syndication and made room for a good-hearted character by the name of Jeff. True to the popular vaudeville-style comedy of the day, slapstick ensued, and the bonding of short, stout Jeff and rail-thin Mutt was as much one of mutual antagonism (usually one-sided, with Jeff the butt of Mutt's pranks) as it was of camaraderie. The series was hugely influential on comic strips in the United States beyond establishing the early visual format—*Mutt and Jeff* lent a nickname to all future pairings of short/tall buddy duos. The comic strip also served as training ground for several assistants of Fisher, such as Maurice Sendak and *Krazy Kat*'s George Herriman. **MW**

Quadratino 1910

Antonio Rubino

In addition to being its graphic designer and illustrator, Antonio Rubino was the main artist of *Corriere dei piccoli*, a weekly Italian magazine published for children. Quadratino was a square-headed boy, and his visually surreal adventures were always based on the same scheme, following the classic six-panel model, with captions in rhymes.

Typically, in the first panel Quadratino escapes his family in search of exciting adventures, but something always goes wrong. In the middle of the story—somewhere in the gutters between the third and fourth panel—his head is struck and changed into a different geometrical shape. Finally, he goes back home and the last panel sees some helpful relative with mathematical expertise (Mom "geometry," Grandmother "mathematics," and Aunt "trigonometry") assist in restoring his perfectly square-shaped head. In one installment, he rolls down some stairs and his head becomes a sphere; in another he falls in the ocean and a shark bites off the "corners" of his square head.

While the intentions of magazine *Corriere dei piccoli* were clearly pedagogical—learning through entertainment—Rubino's work itself was motivated by a highly imaginative style, focusing on visual jokes and decorative elements that were inspired by artistic movements such as art nouveau, futurism, and the British retail designers, Liberty. Among dozens of his series for *Corriere dei piccoli*, this is the shortest—only seven episodes. However, it is possibly his most influential work, celebrated as one the most iconic comic strips in the publication's history. *Quadratino* is also probably the best conceptual homage to comics made by one of its artists—the square-headed character is an explicit metaphor for the actual panels of comic strips, and that makes *Quadratino* a series also about the visual development of comics. **MS**

Title in original language *Quadratino*
First published by *Corriere dei piccoli / Corriere della Sera* (Italy)
Creator Italian (1880–1964) **Genre** Humor, Children's

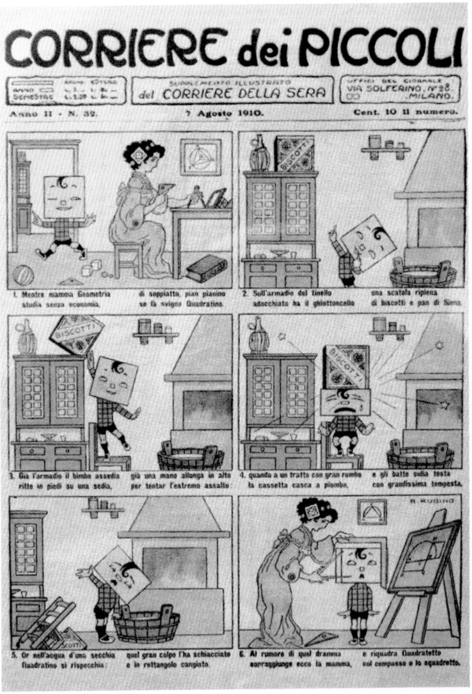
CORRIERE dei PICCOLI
SUPPLEMENTO ILLUSTRATO del CORRIERE DELLA SERA
VIA SOLFERINO, N° 28. MILANO.
Anno II - N. 32.
7 Agosto 1910.
Cent. 10 il numero.
BISCOTTI
1. Mentre mamma Geometria studia senza economia,
di soppiatto, pian pianino se la svigna Quadratino.
2. Sull'armadio del tinello adocchiato ha il ghiottoncello
una scatola ripiena di biscotti e pan di Siena.
3. Già l'armadio il bimbo assedia ritto in piedi su una sedia,
già una mano allunga in alto per tentar l'estremo assalto:
4. quando a un tratto con gran rombo la cassetta casca a piombo,
e gli batte sulla testa con grandissima tempesta,
A. RUBINO
5. Or nell'acqua d'una secchia Quadratino si rispecchia:
quel gran colpo l'ha schiacciato e in rettangolo cangiato.
6. Al rumore di quel dramma sopraggiunge ecco la mamma,
e riquadra Quadratetto col compasso e lo squadretto.

"[Rubino was] a key character in the transition from liberty to futurism."

Rossana Bossaglia, art historian

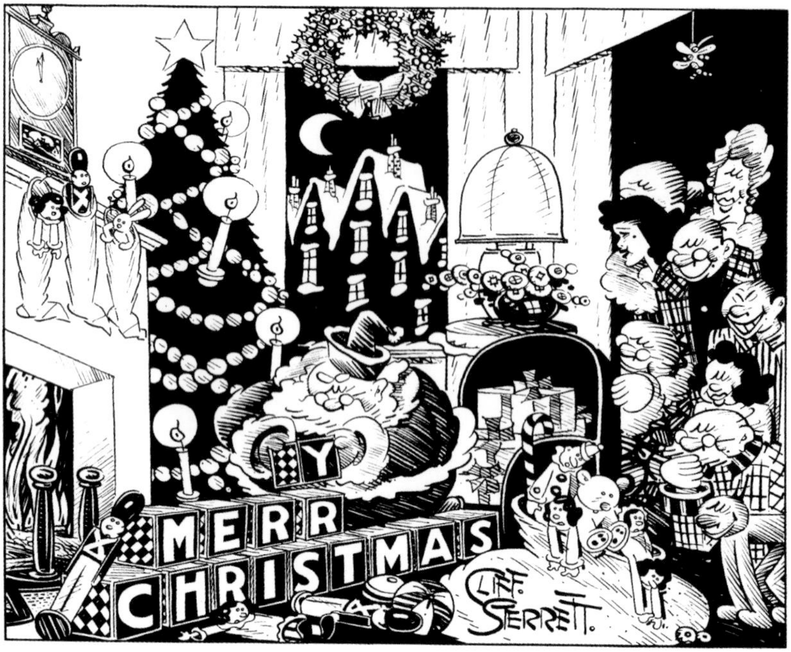
MERRY
CHRISTMAS
CLIFF STERRETT.

Polly and Her Pals 1912

Cliff Sterrett

First published by *New York Journal* (USA)
Creator American (1883–1964)
Genre Humor
Award Angoulême Prize for Inheritance (2006)

A hero to the cartooning cognoscenti, Cliff Sterrett, the creator of *Polly and Her Pals*, was born in Minnesota in 1883. He went to New York as an art student and then moved into newspaper illustration. Sterrett started his career as a strip cartoonist when he joined the *New York Telegram*, eventually drawing four strips simultaneously for that publication. In 1912, William Randolph Hearst, the great print mogul, saw Sterrett's *For This, We Have Daughters*, and asked the artist to create a story for his *New York Journal*. Hearst stipulated that a young woman should be the focus of the strip. Sterrett obliged with *Polly and Her Pals* (initially known as *Positive Polly*), a sweet-humored, slangy strip about the difficulties of living with a popular college student. Sterrett soon shifted his attention, however, from the eponymous young lady to her rambunctious family. Polly's crotchety "Paw" particularly captured Sterrett's imagination and dominated the strip for much of its forty-six year run.

Sterrett's strips are a joy to read, but contemporary cartoonists revere the strip for the artist's innovative style rather than its content. Sterrett shattered readers' expectations in the 1920s of how a house, flowers, or window should appear, creating landscapes in a bold, primary palette—including copious use of black—that pushed the boundaries of cartooning. Sterrett apparently mixed with abstract artists, which together with his love of Japanese prints undoubtedly influenced his work. Revisiting Polly's universe and the work of the remarkable Cliff Sterrett is highly recommended. **EL**

Polly and Her Pals is admired for its striking graphic art deco illustration. ↑

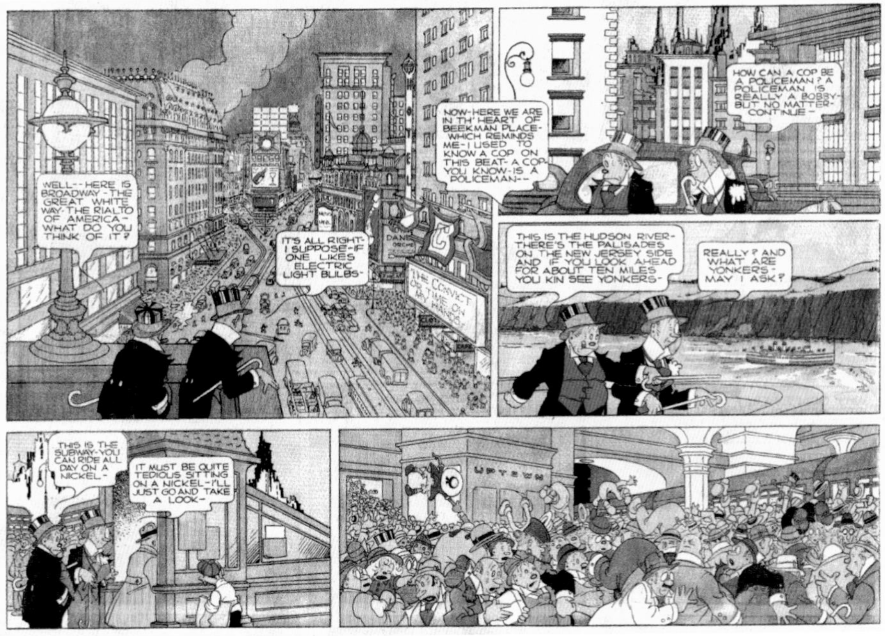
WELL--HERE IS BROADWAY-THE GREAT WHITE WAY-THE RIALTO OF AMERICA-WHAT DO YOU THINK OF IT?
IT'S ALL RIGHT-I SUPPOSE-IF ONE LIKES ELECTRIC LIGHT BULBS-
NOW-HERE WE ARE IN TH' HEART OF BEEKMAN PLACE-WHICH REMINDS ME-I USED TO KNOW A COP ON THIS BEAT-A COP-YOU KNOW-IS A POLICEMAN--
HOW CAN A COP BE A POLICEMAN? A POLICEMAN IS REALLY A BOBBY-BUT NO MATTER-CONTINUE-
THIS IS THE HUDSON RIVER-THERE'S THE PALISADES ON THE NEW JERSEY SIDE AND IF YOU LOOK AHEAD FOR ABOUT TEN MILES YOU KIN SEE YONKERS-
REALLY? AND WHAT ARE YONKERS-MAY I ASK?
THIS IS THE SUBWAY-YOU CAN RIDE ALL DAY ON A NICKEL-
IT MUST BE QUITE TEDIOUS SITTING ON A NICKEL-I'LL JUST GO AND TAKE A LOOK-
UPTOWN

Bringing Up Father 1913

George McManus / Emil "Zeke" Zekley

First published by King Features Syndicate (USA)
Creators McManus (American, 1884–1954); Zekley (American, 1915–2005) **Genre** Humor
Adaptation Film: *Father Gets into the Movies* (1916)

Bringing Up Father is often remembered as "Maggie and Jiggs," because the couple at its heart became such international stars. The strip appeared in 500 newspapers, in forty-six countries. Its basic scenario came from stage musical *The Rising Generation*, in which an Irish-American construction worker becomes rich. McManus once said that Jiggs's wealth, never explained in the strip, came from getting into the brickmaking business. His wife Maggie is determined that the family (including beautiful daughter Nora) will enter high society, attend the opera, and so on. Jiggs, though, would rather play poker and eat corned beef and cabbage with his old working-class pals. Out of these mismatched aspirations the strip spun decades of amusement. It also introduced a new level of domestic violence to the comics, unacceptable, perhaps, if Jiggs had been the perpetrator, but it was Maggie who regularly gave Jiggs black eyes and broken limbs.

McManus's art deco drawing style was influenced by Aubrey Beardsley and Japanese prints. With a simple line and a strong design sense, his color Sunday page was often spectacular; he was assisted by the excellent, uncredited, Zeke Zekley from 1935 onward. McManus's style strongly influenced the European *ligne claire* (clear line) school of Hergé's Tintin. *Bringing Up Father* mainly presented one-off vignettes, but there were continued stories, such as the family's tour of the United States in 1939–40, for which Zekley memorably drew detailed representations of several major cities. **GL**

↑ Jinks is shown New York during a tour he and Maggie make of the United States.

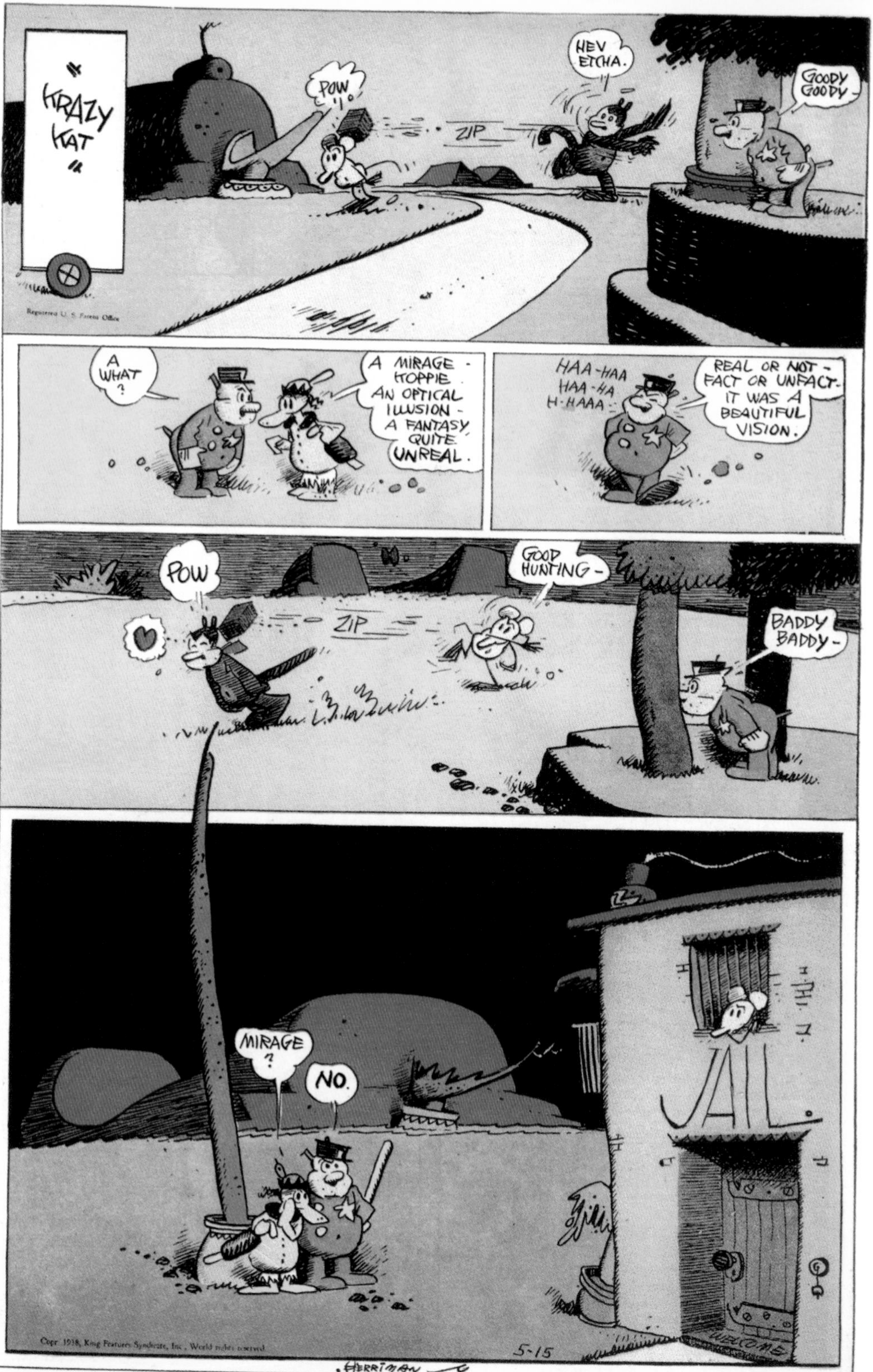
"KRAZY KAT"
Registered U. S. Patent Office
POW
ZIP
HEV ETCHA.
GOODY GOODY-
A WHAT ?
A MIRAGE - HOPPIE AN OPTICAL ILLUSION - A FANTASY QUITE UNREAL.
HAA-HAA HAA-HA H-HAAA
REAL OR NOT - FACT OR UNFACT - IT WAS A BEAUTIFUL VISION.
POW
ZIP
GOOD HUNTING-
BADDY BADDY-
MIRAGE ?
NO.
JAIL.
WELCOME
Copr. 1938, King Features Syndicate, Inc., World rights reserved.
5-15
HERRIMAN

Krazy Kat 1913

George Herriman

First published by King Features Syndicate (USA)
Creator American (1880–1944)
Genre Humor
Influence on *Wile E. Coyote* and *Road Runner*

On the face of it, this newspaper strip is about a mixed-up relationship between a mouse, a cat, and a dog. Krazy the cat (of ambiguous gender) is in love with the mouse, Ignatz. Ignatz despises Krazy and throws bricks at Krazy's head. Krazy, assuming this is a sign of Ignatz's love, looks forward to the bricks and cannot understand why Officer Pup keeps locking up Ignatz in prison whenever he catches him with a brick.

Krazy Kat's location, Cokonino County, evokes the great American landscapes of the Grand Canyon, Monument Valley, and New Mexico, yet it exists in a constantly shifting "reality" where all sorts of odd things can happen. While the narrative seems to relate to normal town life, the landscape serves as a reminder that civilization can be just a thin veneer.

There is a large supporting cast, including Kolin Kelly (a millionaire brick merchant), Gooseberry Sprig (The Duck Duke), Mme Kwakk-Wakk, Joe Stork ("purveyor of progeny to prince and proletariat"), and Gonzalo Gopher, all retaining something of their origins in their speech patterns. Among them, Krazy remains an innocent, unashamed of who he or she is, an independent commentator on the technological and social advances that come to Cokonino County.

Herriman's literary and visionary *Krazy Kat* is perhaps the *Citizen Kane* of comics. Although highly regarded by other comic strip artists and critics, it wasn't much loved by readers during its lifetime. In 1999 *The Comics Journal* voted it the best comic of the twentieth century, but it has been reprinted only sporadically. **NFI**

When a Feller Needs a Friend 1914

Clare Briggs

First published by *New York Tribune* (USA)
Creator American (1875–1930)
Genre Humor
Adaptation Musical (1919)

Clare Briggs belonged to a group of U.S. newspaper cartoonists who had what is known as "a fast line": Clare Victor Dwiggins, who drew *School Days*; Percy Crosby, who drew *Skippy*; Clifford McBride, who drew *Napoleon*; and George Herriman, who drew *Krazy Kat*. Their dynamic drawings were perfect for communicating movement, but they also conveyed the immediacy and speed of the new twentieth century.

On the contrary, however, as author Dennis Wepman put it: "Clare Briggs created a memorable panorama of middle-class, middle-brow, middle-America at the turn of the century." Rather than grand epics singing the progress of humankind or the brave new world of technological and scientific discoveries, Briggs dealt with the everyday foibles of the ordinary middle classes and evoked nostalgic memories of childhood in a Twainian, small-town America. Typical of Briggs's approach is the comic strip series *When a Feller Needs a Friend*. A "feller" needs a friend in various instances, but mostly when he fears ridicule. Briggs clearly shows his sympathies to be with the underdogs (and dogs). He celebrates the freedom and carelessness (in attire especially) of working-class urchins: he repeatedly shows middle-class boys in their Sunday suits looking at groups of Huck Finns and longing for adventure. Again and again, he shows stuffy boys being ridiculed.

Many of the titles of Briggs's comic strips, such as *When a Feller Needs a Friend* and *There's At Least One in Every Office*, were adopted as national catchprases. **DI**

← *Krazy Kat* takes place in a stylized version of western America.

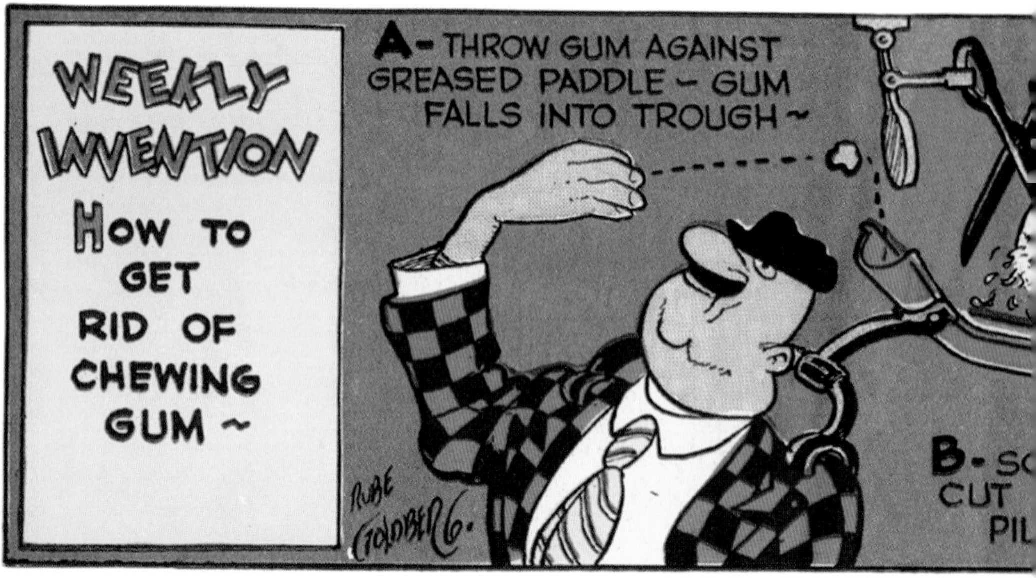
WEEKLY INVENTION
HOW TO GET RID OF CHEWING GUM ~
A - THROW GUM AGAINST GREASED PADDLE - GUM FALLS INTO TROUGH ~
RUBE GOLDBERG.
B - S
CUT
PIL

Rube Goldberg Inventions 1914

Rube Goldberg

First published by Hearst Corporation (USA)
Creator Reuben Lucius Goldberg (American, 1883–1970)
Genre Humor
Award Pulitzer Prize (1947)

Rube Goldberg was the middle of three sons with one sister. Cartoons were his calling, and at the University of California his campus magazine printed his very first. A 1904 graduate mining engineer, he quit his first job within months to become a newspaper cartoonist. After moving to New York in 1906, years of trying produced artful ideas, pictureplay, wordplay, and numerous fine cartoon series on sports and daily topics. His work often used text balloons and odd titles, like *Lunatics I Have Met* or *Foolish Questions* (of which the 1909 book cover had a talking head asking: "WHAT'S THIS—A BOOK?"), or "phony" titles such as *Telephonies* (about those who pretend to telephone), *Phoney Films*, or *Phoney Balonies*.

His longest running newspaper strip was *Boob McNutt* from 1915 to 1934, with simpleton Boob forever chasing love and disaster. (Goldberg himself married in 1916 and had two sons.) Around 1930 he grew tired, and later strip series were short-lived *(Bobo Baxter, Lala Palooza)* or downright misfires (political cartooning and the so-called realistic *Doc Wright*). The rest was self-promotion: chalktalks, Famous Artists courses, having the Reuben Award named after him, and so on.

His prime work was *The Inventions of Professor Lucifer G. Butts*. These cartoons pictured goofy devices meant to perform the simplest of tasks. In 1909, "Dwig" (Clare Victor Dwiggins) had done something similar in his *Schooldays* series, as did W. Heath Robinson in his series of "helpful solutions." Goldberg made it into U.S. dictionaries with "Rube Goldberg contraption." **HvO**

Chewing gum disposal the Rube Goldberg way. ↑

C- GUM ROLLS DOWN TROUGH, GATHERING FEATHERS AND FORMING FEATHER BALL-
D- FEATHER BALL ROLLS THROUGH TAR, BECOMING SMOOTH BLACK SPHERE- BOWLER HAPPENS BY, PICKS IT UP AND TAKES IT OFF TO BOWLING ALLEY!
7-16
The Register and Tribune Syndicate

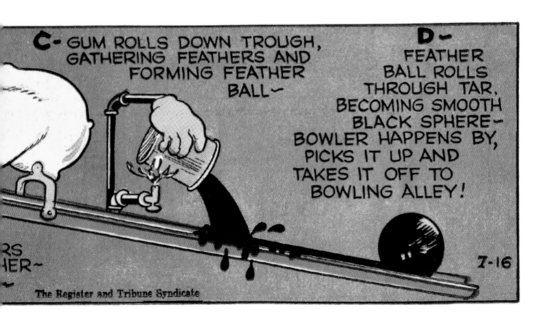

Punch Comic Strips 1916

H. M. Bateman

First published by *Punch* (UK)
Creator Henry Mayo Bateman (British, 1887–1970)
Genre Humor
Influence on Ralph Steadman

The great comic art natural Henry Mayo Bateman always wanted to draw, and his strong mother, Rose Mayo, even gave him her last name and sent some drawings to star illustrator Phil May for his advice.

Hounded by depression since youth, Bateman was saved early on by "going mad on paper." At barely twenty he decided to draw, not just people, but the moods people were in. In his strips he took to new levels every component of the 500 weekly gag strips of French trailblazer Caran d'Ache in *Le Figaro*—near-cinematic pages with frameless panels full of rule-breaking gaffers, perplexed bystanders, big heads, pop-out eyeballs, speed lines, and trembling bodies.

Bateman's *A Book of Drawings* (1921) alone had sixty-two strip pages. His forte was quasi-nonpolitical pictorial satire in pen, brush, ink, and color, in magazines such as *The Sketch* and *Punch*, along with highly paid advertising jobs, often full page with a single cryptic caption. Picturing British maids, judges, taxmen, press photographers, snobs, workers, modern art phonies, prohibition evaders, overpaid psychoanalysts, and other types, his magazine work was reprinted in hardcover. The title of his later highly successful series *The Man Who...* was originally conceived in 1909.

Wealthily retired from 1941, his latter days in the English southwest and in Malta were tainted with paranoia, especially about taxmen. He joked about it all in cartoons, caricatures, and strips, one to four pages long, some with word balloons. **HvO**

The Gumps 1917

✒ Sidney Smith

First published by *Chicago Tribune* (USA)
Creator American (1877–1935)
Genre Humor
Influence on *Sam 'n' Henry* radio show

Andy Gump looked like no cartoon character that had come before: a chinless opportunist with aspirations for a better life for his noisy, argumentative family: wife Minerva (Min), son Chester, and Uncle Bim. *The Gumps* was the brainchild of the *Chicago Tribune*'s editor and publisher Joseph Patterson. It premiered in 1917 and in three years went from the pages of the *Tribune* into newspapers across America. Patterson turned to one of the *Tribune*'s own cartoonists, Sidney Smith, to give his cartoon life. By the time Smith's contract came up for renewal in 1922, *The Gumps* was being read by twelve million people, and Smith negotiated the cartoon world's first million-dollar deal.

"I wasn't so much concerned about making them terribly funny, but I did want them to be true," said Smith. It was also one of the first, and certainly the most successful, "continuing story" strips, with plots left unfinished so that readers had to buy the next edition to find out what happened. Smith also used melodrama as no one had before. The 1921 introduction of the gold-digging Widow Zander and her intentions toward Andy's wealthy Uncle Bim represented the refining of stronger, suspenseful narratives. People on the street began asking for editions of the "Gump paper."

Smith continued *The Gumps* until his death in 1935, when the strip was given over to former sports cartoonist Gus Edson. But Edson was unable to emulate Smith's formula, and its popularity gradually waned until it was appearing in fewer than twenty papers, finally ending in 1959 after a run of forty-two years. **BS**

Mister Bonaventura 1917

✒ "Sto"

Title in original language *Signor Bonaventura*
First published by *Corriere dei piccoli* (Italy)
Creator Sergio Tofano (Italian, 1886–1973)
Genre Humor

For generations Mister Bonaventura was the one of the most famous characters of *Corriere dei piccoli* weekly, the main Italian comics magazine for children since 1908. Wearing a red tailcoat and a bowler hat, Bonaventura always begins his adventures as a penniless man and ends up a lucky millionaire. His initial misfortunes turn out to be blessings for other people (such as stumbling upon a thief), with the inevitable reward of a huge "one million" bank check. His microadventures were at this time a metaphor of average Italians and their everyday struggles with postwar austerity. The episodes followed the canonical *Corriere dei piccoli* model of six or eight panels, with captions in rhyming couplets using quaint language that was ironically divergent from the neatness of the drawings.

Sergio Tofano, perhaps best known as a comedy actor who worked with Vittorio De Sica and Luchino Visconti, was also a director, playwright, scene designer, and illustrator. He directed six theater adaptations of *Mister Bonaventura*, and one as a movie. Bonaventura himself became the first Italian multimedia character, used in advertising campaigns and as a sort of "licensing star" until the early years of television in the 1950s.

Tofano's drawing style is simple. His main influence is the abstract (and amused) side of futurist painting, especially that of Fortunato Depero (1892–1960), a painter, designer, and art director of early modern advertising campaigns. The result is a sort of *ligne claire* (clear line) blended with the energy of futurism and the fun and paradoxical vision of dada. **MS**

By locating a robber, Mister Bonaventura and his dog earn another bank check. ➡

CORRIERE dei PICCOLI

REGNO: ESTERO:
ANNO L. 19.- L. 32.-
SEMESTRE L. 10.- L. 17.-

SUPPLEMENTO ILLUSTRATO
del CORRIERE DELLA SERA
SI PUBBLICA OGNI SETTIMANA

UFFICI DEL GIORNALE:
VIA SOLFERINO, N° 28.
MILANO.

PER LE INSERZIONI RIVOLGERSI ALL'AMMINISTRAZIONE DEL « CORRIERE DELLA SERA » - VIA SOLFERINO, 28 - MILANO

Anno XXXI - N. 13 | 26 Marzo 1939-XVII | Centesimi 40 il numero

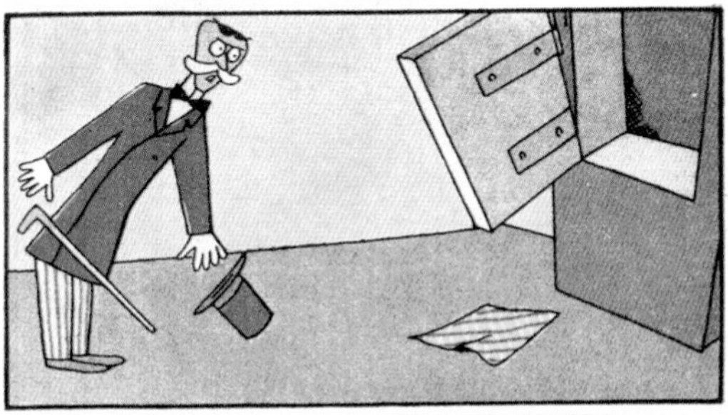

1. Qui comincia la sventura
del signor Bonaventura
e di un povero banchiere
cui vuotato hanno il forziere.

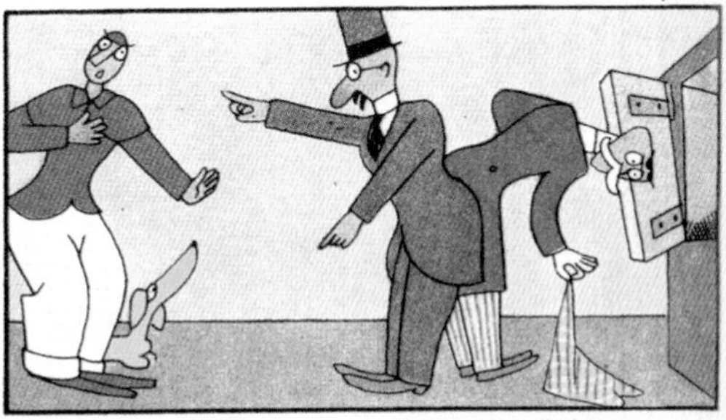

2. Un famoso poliziotto
viene, cerca sopra e sotto:
il colpevole, egli giura,
è il signor Bonaventura!

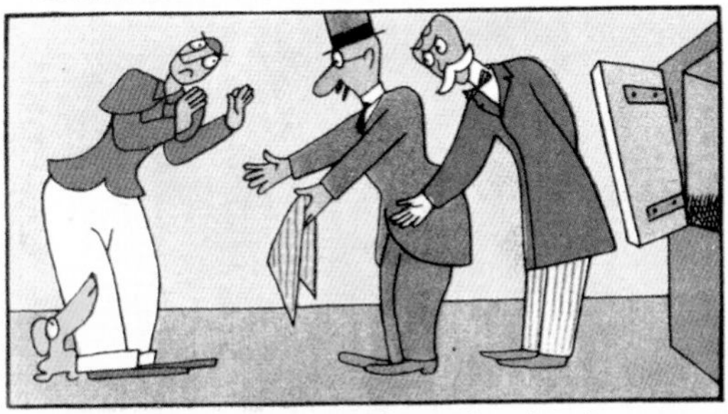

3. A conferma del sospetto
c'è per terra un fazzoletto
che smarrito certamente
ivi fu dal delinquente.

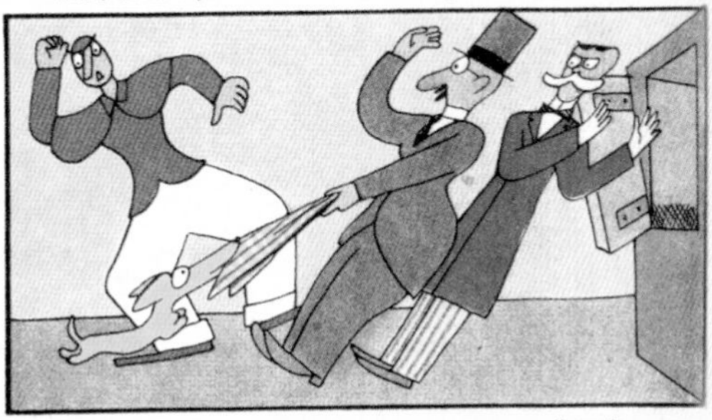

4. Ma di mano glielo strappa,
con un salto, il cane e scappa:
scappa come un disperato
con il corpo del reato.

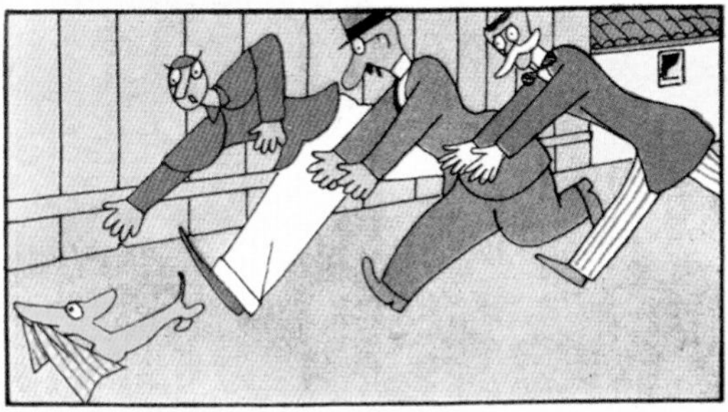

5. I tre restano perplessi,
poi si slanciano pur essi
dietro il cane, come il vento,
a un serrato inseguimento.

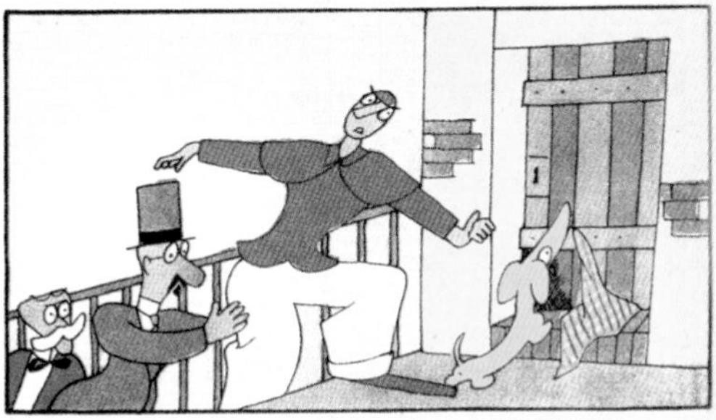

6. Ed il cane li conduce,
per viuzze senza luce,
ad un vecchio caseggiato
d'un quartiere malfamato.

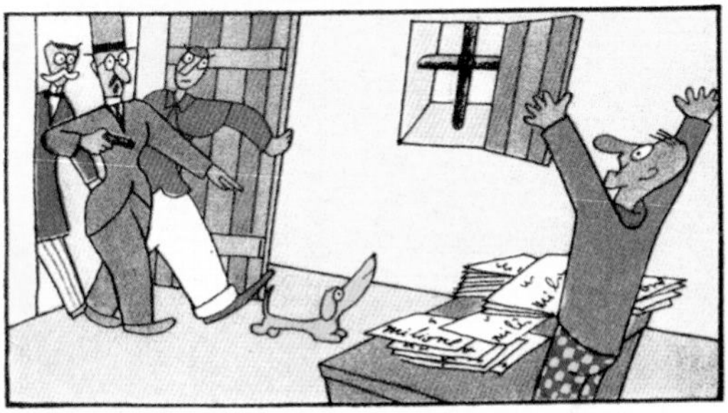

7. Penetrando dentro a un tratto
vi sorprendono sul fatto
il furfante che il forziere
ha vuotato del banchiere.

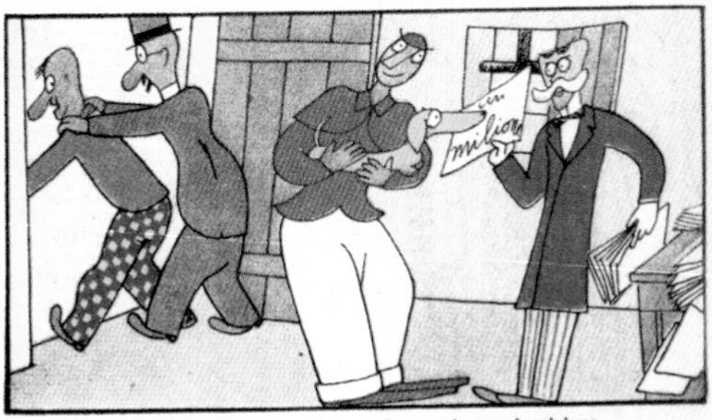

8. Riacquistato il capitale,
il banchiere liberale
fa una larga elargizione
al bassotto e al suo padrone.

Kathleen and the Great Secret

By Nell Brinkley

The American Weekly

Section of the San Francisco Examiner, Sunday, February 6, 1921

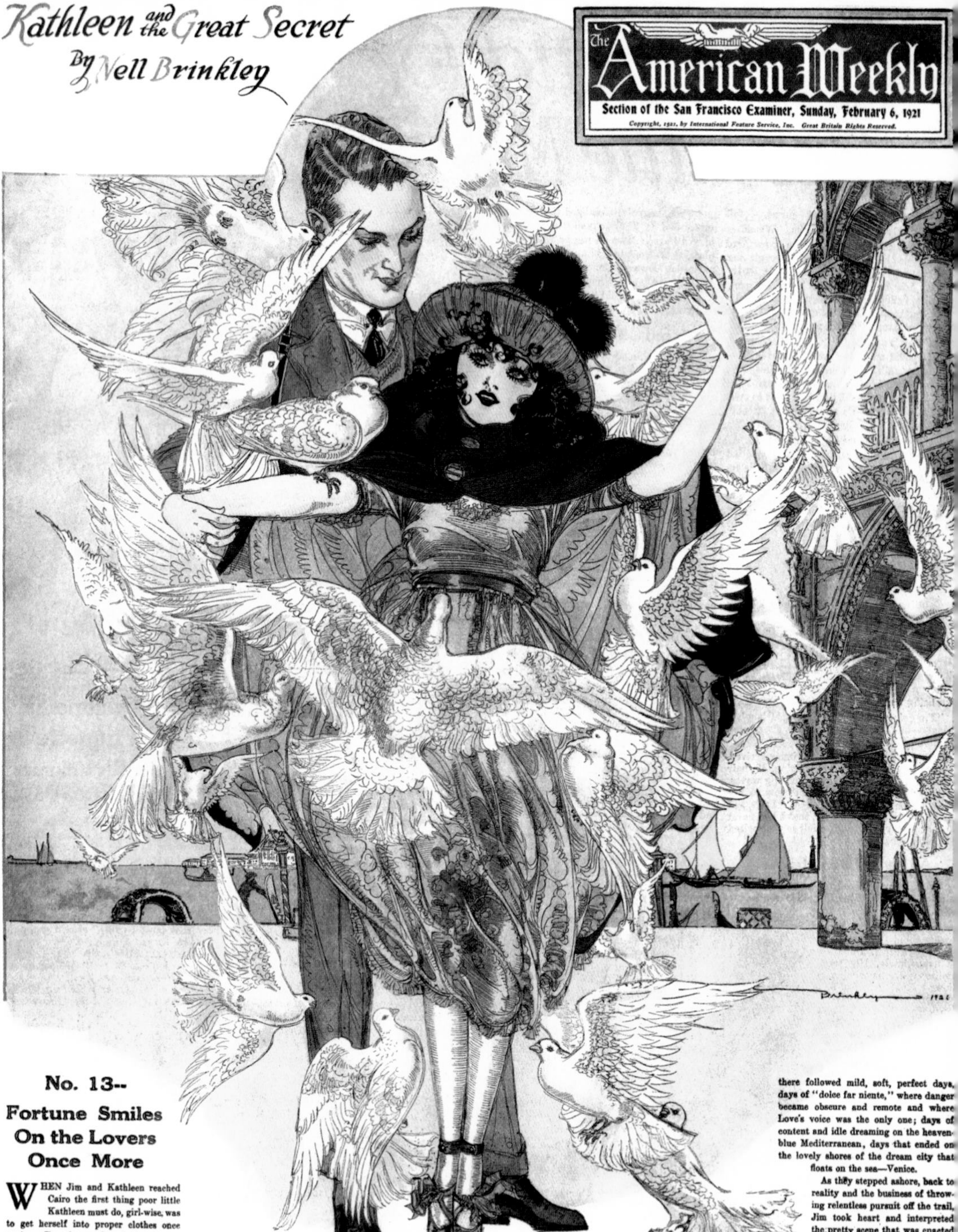

No. 13-- Fortune Smiles On the Lovers Once More

WHEN Jim and Kathleen reached Cairo the first thing poor little Kathleen must do, girl-wise, was to get herself into proper clothes once again. Jim also confessed that it was good to feel safe to eat and to sleep without nightmares and to shrug himself into the friendly feel of "civies."

Whlie they kissed and clung they whispered about the feel of Arab cloth, and the tinkle of tinsel-like silver stars and shuddered—and kissed again. Kathleen seemed more *Kathleen* and Jim more *Jim* in the clothes of the land and the time where their love began. Home, home-time—the clothes of home. How good!

In Cairo the two wayfarers, babes-in-the-woods, appealed to the American Consul, who procured passage for them to Venice on an Italian steamer. Meantime, like good hounds on a scent, the agents of the Power Trust, Stratton's concern, were searching for them—and warm on the trail.

For the two weary, lovers, however, there followed mild, soft, perfect days, days of "dolce far niente," where danger became obscure and remote and where Love's voice was the only one; days of content and idle dreaming on the heaven-blue Mediterranean, days that ended on the lovely shores of the dream city that floats on the sea—Venice.

As they stepped ashore, back to reality and the business of throwing relentless pursuit off the trail, Jim took heart and interpreted the pretty scene that was enacted there as a good omen for themselves and their love—for round Kathleen a rustling cloud of doves swirled in a snowy smother!

"Their wings are like the wings of Eros, son of Venus," said Jim to himself.

—*NELL BRINKLEY.*

(To Be Continued Next Sunday)

The Brinkley Girls 1918

✎✎ Nell Brinkley

First published by Hearst Corporation (USA)
Creator American (1886–1944)
Genre Romance
Influenced by *Ziegfeld Follies* (1908)

The creator of a universe of frilly flappers and wide-eyed romantic heroines, Nell Brinkley bestrode the world of early twentieth-century visual media. Comics historian Trina Robbins has finally edited and reprinted the illustrator's works in their original, luscious hues, and her collection, entitled *The Brinkley Girls*, is a reminder of why Brinkley's hold on her readers was so strong.

Brinkley arrived in New York City in 1906, having abandoned a career in political cartooning back home in Colorado. She acted as a kind of illustrator-at-large for the powerful Hearst newspapers, her nib veering from real-life murder trials to time-traveling make-believe. Readers immediately took to the "Brinkley Girl," with her masses of curls and twinkling smile, and eagerly bought the many products she adorned. From 1918 onward, they followed Brinkley's fluffy-haired heroines through such varied adventures as "Golden-Eyes and Her Hero, Bill," a World War I tale of a woman's incredible loyalty; the epic 1920s costume dramas "Kathleen and the Great Secret" and "Betty and Billy and Their Love Through the Ages"; and frothy flapper confections such as "Fortunes of Flossie" and "Dimple's Day Dreams." Robbins argues that Brinkley had a feminist side, and her inspiring "Heroines of Today" series from the late 1930s certainly supports that claim.

When Brinkley retired in 1937, the world she had created had been largely replaced by Hollywood melodrama and newspaper photographs. But her luxuriously detailed art still sparkles today, as Robbins's collection makes clear. **EL**

Gasoline Alley 1918

✎✎ Frank O. King

First published by *Chicago Tribune* (USA)
Creator American (1883–1969)
Genre Reality drama
Award National Cartoonists Society Humor Strip (1957)

Created by Frank O. King, *Gasoline Alley* presented a stolid, slice-of-life strip that intermittently moved into breathtaking unexpected action. The publisher wanted to exploit female readership by introducing a baby, but its protagonist Walt Wallet was a bachelor. A solution was found in having an abandoned baby left on his doorstep, whom he adopts and names Skeezix—slang for a motherless calf.

To help him with fatherhood he engages a nurse, Rachel, who is gradually introduced via an escalation of visual information. Film director Alfred Hitchcock used this technique in *The 39 Steps* in 1935, as did cartoonist Milton Caniff when he launched *Steve Canyon* in 1947. King's use of the part for the whole, however, had more sequential sophistication and gravitas. Frame by frame, the white-gloved nurse's features are obscured, first by a large, floppy hat, then by a kitchen cupboard, and finally under the wicker hood of a baby carriage. In the final frame, over two daily strips, Rachel is revealed as African-American. Within months, she was reduced to being a maid, and her features were reconfigured with stereotypically large lips. *Gasoline Alley* helped entrench this visual racial stereotype for years to come.

Despite its slow pace, the daily strip presents a captivating human drama. Its slowness provokes an impatient curiosity to see how it develops. The strip was pioneering in the way its characters naturally aged with it over time, most apparent with the foundling Skeezix. When King retired in 1959, he handed *Gasoline Alley* over to his assistant Dick Moores. **IR**

◄ Breathless prose heightened the allure of Nell Brinkley's elaborate visual confections.

The Bungle Family 1918

Harry J. Tuthill

First published by *New York Evening Mail* (USA)
Creator American (1886–1957)
Genre Humor
Influence on Art Spiegelman

Harry J. Tuthill was born in a Chicago tenement in 1886 and didn't sell his first drawing until he signed up as a cartoonist with the *St. Louis Star* in 1916. George and Josephine Bungle and their daughter Peggy debuted in *Home Sweet Home* (1918–24), based on Tuthill's own recollections of apartment life; it was retitled *The Bungle Family* in 1924. Considered one of the most underrated comics in U.S. history by Art Spiegelman (*Maus*), *The Bungle Family* inexplicably drifted into obscurity in the mid-twentieth century despite appearing in dozens of daily newspapers across America by the mid-1930s.

George and Josephine were typically middle class, their lives punctuated by regular altercations with neighbors, debt collectors, and, most spectacularly, each other. George vented the frustrations of a generation whose dreams were dashed by the Great Depression with dialogue that was appropriately real and coarse. Of all the "family strips" then in circulation, *The Bungle Family* provided the most realistic window into domestic American life.

Tuthill's ability to recognize the absurdities inherent in us all was born of a wayfaring early life that took him across much of the Midwest in a covered wagon. *The Bungle Family* was one of the earliest examples of "situation comedy" born of everyday experiences that, while often absurd, were always plausible. Though the early artwork was scratchy and the placement of its word balloons at times lacked grace, the situations were real, born of the true life experiences of a slyly sophisticated writer. **BS**

Passionate Journey 1919

Frans Masereel

Title in original language *Mon livre d'heures*
First published by Self-published (Switzerland)
Creator Belgian (1889–1972)
Genre Political fable

Belgian artist Frans Masereel was a pacifist, and in adopting engraving as a medium to spread his messages he was in good artistic company, from Jacques Callot to Francisco de Goya. His work, however, is more urgent than either Callot's or Goya's; as an artist who embraced realism, Masereel felt that his woodcuts needed to be simple and directly to the point. This sense of urgency was also provoked by the need to work quickly and solve technical problems. One such, identified by his biographer, Josef Herman, was "how to achieve maximum effect using poor quality paper, on which thin lines were simply lost."

Masereel produced expressionistic, black-and-white woodcuts for the pacifist newspaper *La Feuille* (*The Leaf*) in Geneva, where he lived from 1916 to 1922. Very aware of the suffering of the defenseless masses, he repeatedly attacked greed and the wealth won at the cost of millions of lives during World War I.

In 1918, as a consequence of his work for *La Feuille*, Masereel began to produce his wordless, graphic novels or his "novels in woodcuts," as artist Lynd Ward described them. Perhaps the most celebrated graphic novel was *Passionate Journey*. The fictional city he creates in it is as black as woodcut ink and the source of all evil: exploitation, alienation, poverty, sickness, despair, drunkenness. The novel's central character witnesses all this, but, as Herman expressed it, he is also, "Masereel's epitome of humanness [. . .]. His pathos is endearing: he is sometimes a rebel, sometimes a revolutionary [. . .], he is reaching towards life." **DI**

Frans Masereel created a threatening, expressionistic cityscape in woodcut. ➡

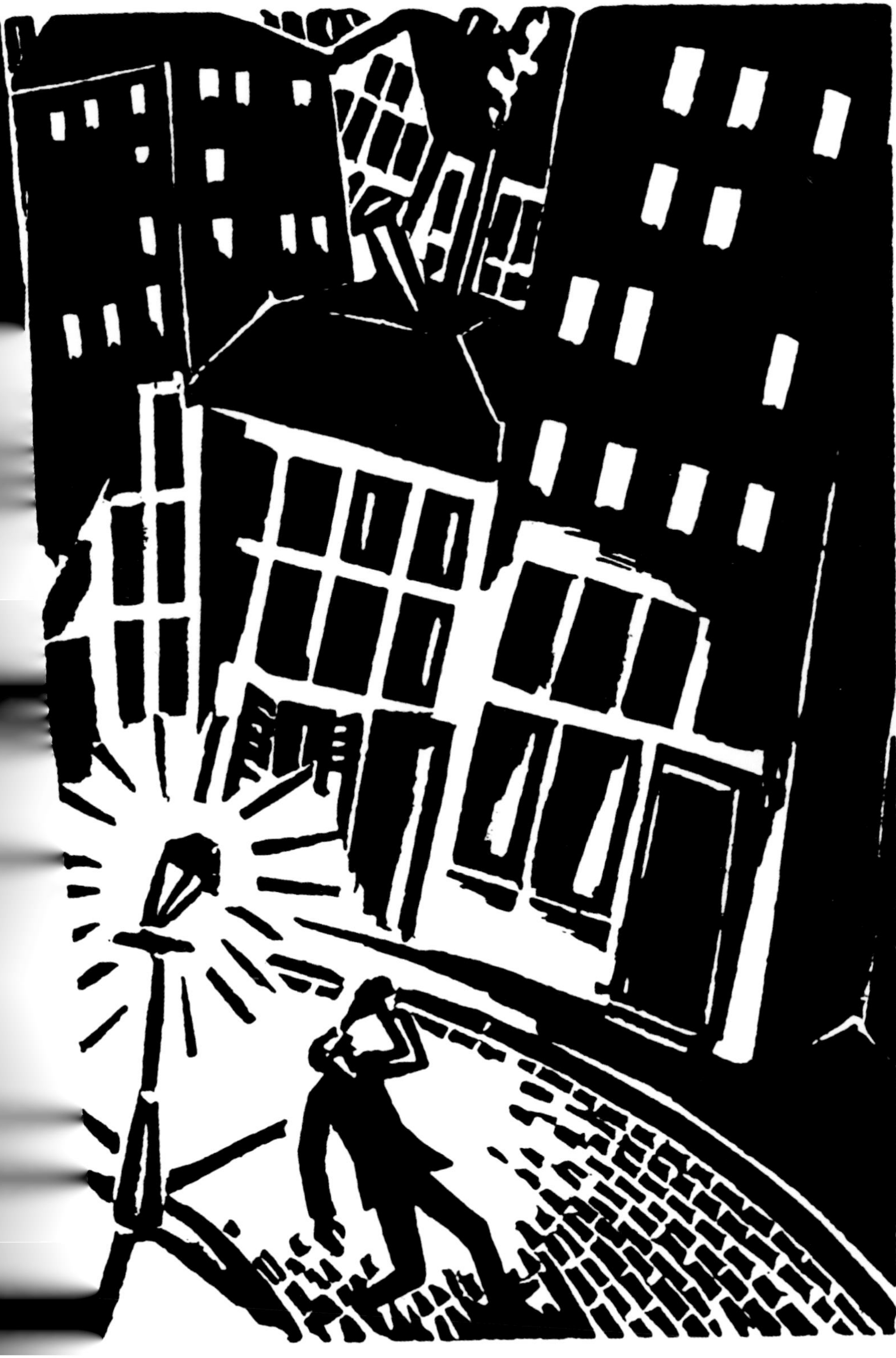

Barney Google and Snuffy Smith 1919

Billy DeBeck

First published by *Chicago Examiner* (USA)
Creator American (1890–1942)
Genre Humor
Adaptation Film: *Horsefeathers* (1928)

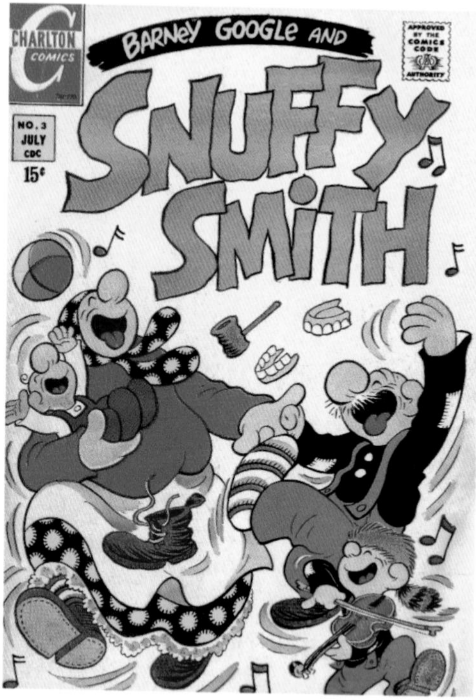
CHARLTON COMICS
BARNEY GOOGLE AND
SNUFFY SMITH
NO. 3 JULY CDC
15¢
APPROVED BY THE COMICS CODE AUTHORITY

Similar reads
Apple Mary Martha Orr
Danny Dingle Bernard Dibble
Mickey Finn Lank Leonard
The Bungle Family H. J. Tuthill
Tillie the Toiler Russ Westover

Barney Google was one of the most recognizable cartoon characters of the 1920s. His distinctive bulging eyes inspired a hit tune, and the strip several more. He starred in a series of short films in the late 1920s and subsequently an animated series. Barney's development was gradual. His first sighting, in *Married Life* in 1916, was as a tall, henpecked character named Aleck, who came to dominate the strip. DeBeck later reworked him under his familiar name in 1919 for *Take Barney Google, For Instance*, but it was two years before he assumed his familiar squat appearance.

The strip prioritized Billy DeBeck's love of sports and generally ran on the sports pages of newspapers, even during the long spells when DeBeck turned his hand to adventure and mystery stories. DeBeck's art style emphasized movement, and echoed both nineteenth-century editorial cartoonists and contemporary, fine-lined fashion illustrations. The strip was enormously influential in its day, and trickled down to underground cartoonists in the 1960s.

"I'm getting cold on this bird Zitz. How I do know he's on the up and up?"

Hillbilly Snuffy Smith, introduced in 1934, epitomized the hard times of the Great Depression. Despite the jokes made at his expense, he struck a chord with the public the way Barney had in the 1920s, and he soon shared equal billing with Barney.

DeBeck first saw his assistant Fred Lasswell's work on a church poster; he made him copy a Charles Dana Gibson illustration every day as training. When DeBeck died, Lasswell continued the strip until 2001. While his name still appears in the title, Barney Google is rarely seen, and John Rose is now responsible for the strip. **FP**

Pip, Squeak and Wilfred 1919

Bertram Lamb / Austin Payne

First published by *Daily Mirror* (UK)
Creators Lamb (British, 1889–1936); Payne (British, 1876–1956)
Genre Humor, Children's

The comic strip *Pip, Squeak and Wilfred* was so popular in the 1920s that it had its own fan club, the Wilfredian League of Gugnuncs (WLOG). This children's club was organized by London's *Daily Mirror* newspaper in 1927 to cater for devotees of the popular strip—about the simple, uncomplicated friendship of its three central characters—which had been running in the *Mirror* since 1919. WLOG's 100,000-plus members raised money for charity through rallies, parties, and an annual convention in London's Royal Albert Hall. The fans were themselves emblematic of the strip's wholesomeness and decency.

Further evidence of the strip's popularity lay in *Pip, Squeak and Wilfred* merchandise, including board games, greeting cards, annuals, a porcelain Wilfred released by Royal Doulton in 1927, and even a series of silent movies. This was clearly much more than just another comic strip—this was a phenomenon.

> *"I want three pies and three sausages please . . . thank you Auntie, we'll have some more if they're nice."*

Pip, Squeak and Wilfred was conceived by Bertram Lamb, who signed each strip "Uncle Dick." Squeak, a female penguin, was hatched on the African coast and made her way to London. Pip, a male terrier, was purchased from a home for lost dogs. Later in the series, Pip and Squeak take in Wilfred, a long-eared rabbit whom they discover chasing butterflies in a field of clover. Together, these three anthropomorphic characters—cared for by their human owner Uncle Dick and his maid Angeline—inhabit a surreal fairyland that is devoid of evil. This "Pollyanna" world was deliberately crafted for a postwar audience weary of death and the horrors of trench warfare. **BS**

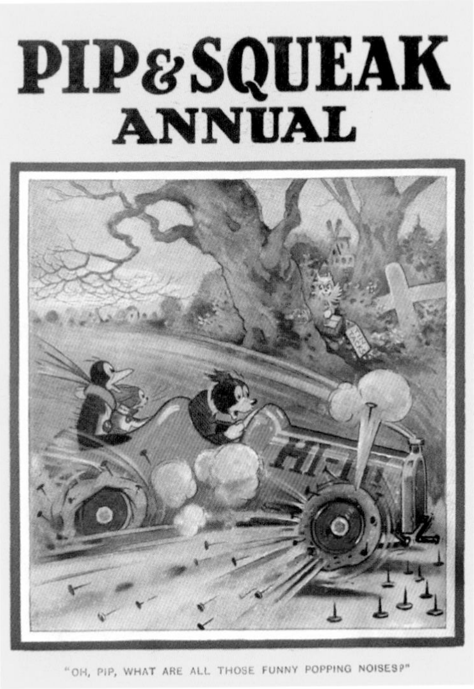
PIP & SQUEAK
ANNUAL
"OH, PIP, WHAT ARE ALL THOSE FUNNY POPPING NOISES?"

Similar reads

Bobby Bear *Daily Herald* newspaper
Eb 'n Flo Brian Segal
Rupert the Bear Mary Tourtel, Alfred Bestall
Teddy Tail Charles Folkard
Tiger Tim's Weekly Julius Stafford-Baker

Adamson's Adventures 1920

Oscar Jacobsson

Title in original language *Adamson*
First published by *Söndags-Nisse* (Sweden)
Creator Swedish (1889–1945)
Genre Humor

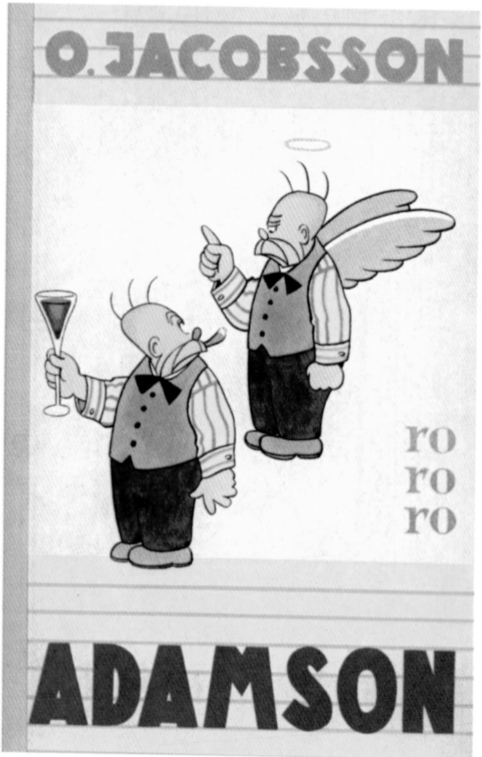
O. JACOBSSON
ro
ro
ro
ADAMSON

Similar reads
Bringing Up Father George McManus
Happy Hooligan Frederick Burr Opper
The Little King Otto Soglow

Adamson's Adventures was first published in 1920 in the Swedish humorous magazine *Söndags-Nisse*. The central character was a small, elderly gentleman who had only a few strands of hair on his head. Shown constantly smoking a big cigar and wearing a big hat, he had a solemn clownlike expression.

Being a wordless comic strip, Adamson's Adventures drew its humor from a variety of sources. For example, our expectations (and Adamson's) are confounded when he tries to retrieve a striped ball from the sea only to discover that the ball is the ample bottom of an irate swimmer in a striped swimsuit. Again, we laugh at his human feeble-mindedness when he berates his wife over their food bill, only to shower her with gratitude the moment his splendid dinner is on the table. The humor was universal, and the popularity of *Adamson's Adventures* grew outside Sweden in newspapers, magazines, and various collections published all over Europe, the United States, China, and Japan.

"Like the absence of speech, the absence of background gave it weight and importance."

Coulton Waugh, painter/cartoonist

Adamson's Adventures was a daily comic strip, usually presented in four black-and-white panels of equal size. The stories were quite simple, with the gag relying on physical action and facial expressions as there was no dialogue. Despite, or maybe because of this, the strip often took on a surprisingly philosophical air, with the little man struggling with everyday misadventures and not coming out on top. Often there was no real punch line in the last panel of the strip—more a sombre moment of contemplation, which made *Adamson's Adventures* stand out among its contemporaries. **FS**

Rupert the Bear 1920

Mary Tourtel, Alfred Bestall

Rupert the Bear was the fourth major comic strip to run in a British newspaper, and now having run for more than ninety years is by far the most significant. It was created in 1920 for the *Daily Express* and was aimed at attracting a young readership as part of a circulation war. Mary Tourtel was an accomplished illustrator who brought an elegant whimsy to Rupert and his anthropomorphic friends Bill Badger, Algy Pug, and Edward Trunk. Rupert's world was a gentle, quintessentially English idyll where animals lived like humans and magical adventures were always just around the corner.

Tourtel was a gifted artist, but the strip evolved into something more special after her retirement in 1935 when illustrator Alfred Bestall took over. Bestall shared Tourtel's economy of line, but he also displayed a genius for storytelling and an eye for landscape that British comic strips had not seen before. *Rupert the Bear* ran as a black-and-white daily strip in the *Express,* and yearly from 1936 hardcover annuals appeared. Here Bestall excelled with delicate watercolor covers and endpapers worthy of Arthur Rackham or Edmund Dulac.

"Bestall saw his role [as illustrator of Rupert the Bear*] as 'the most vitally important job in Fleet Street.'"*

Amanda Craig, author

Under Bestall the strip widened its horizons as the adventurous little bear traveled to fantasy worlds ruled by birds, savages, or pixies. The animals were joined by human characters, such as the Professor, his dwarf servant, and a Chinese girl, Tiger Lily. Indeed, the strip was a unique mixture of Asian iconography, bucolic village life, and an England that was forever stuck in the 1930s. Bestall retired in the 1980s, but Rupert remains a fixture in British culture. **DR**

First published by *Daily Express* (UK)
Creators Tourtel (British, 1874–1948); Bestall (British, 1892–1986)
Genre Children's, Funny animal

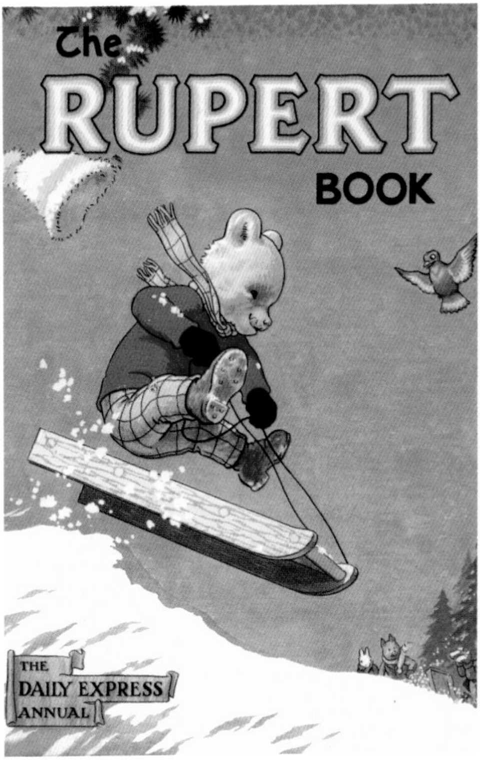

The
RUPERT
BOOK
THE
DAILY EXPRESS
ANNUAL

Similar reads
Oswald the Rabbit Walter Lantz
Owly Andy Runton
Teddy Tail Charles Folkard

Winnie Winkle 1920

✒️ Martin Branner

First published by *Chicago Tribune* (USA)
Creator American (1888–1970)
Genre Soap opera
Adaptation Film: *Winnie Winkle the Breadwinner* (1926)

A staple of the funny pages for seventy-six years, *Winnie Winkle* bridged the gap between a society where women did not work outside the home and the more emancipated world, providing the first depiction of a "working girl" in comics. Originally called *Winnie Winkle the Breadwinner*, creator Martin Branner launched the strip one month after U.S. women gained the right to vote in 1920.

A slim blonde who could have been the cousin of Cliff Sterrett's Polly, Winnie started out as a stenographer and explored various careers during the life of the strip. The difference between *Winnie Winkle* and later, better known "working girl" strips, such as *Brenda Starr*, is that Winnie's life was quiet. Much of the strip's drama revolved around Winnie's suitors and her family life, the latter dominated by her troublesome father and adopted brother, Perry. Although Winnie did not jump out of planes or join gangs like the adventuresome Brenda, she did have her moments, such as when she became a widowed mother during World War II, her experience mirroring that of many other women.

Widely translated, especially in the Netherlands (where brother Perry lived independently as "Sjors"), Winnie further entrenched herself in the collective subconscious when she became a muse of pop artist Roy Lichtenstein. After adventures in the Peace Corps and the fashion industry, Winnie retired for good in 1996. Sadly, there are no book collections currently available, but many original *Winnie Winkle* strips are held in the archives at Syracuse University, New York. **EL**

Pop 1921

✒️ John Millar Watt

First published by *Daily Sketch* (UK)
Creator British (1895–1975)
Genre Humor
Influence on *Blondie*

Pop was created for the *Daily Sketch* as a response to other popular newspaper strips, such as *Rupert the Bear*. The *Sketch* ran an advertisement calling for artists to submit new ideas, and the winner was John Millar Watt. Millar Watt was a surprising candidate in that he was already an established illustrator for *The Sphere* magazine and a graduate of the prestigious Slade School of Art. The feature he dreamed up, however, was more than worthy of his unexpected change of career.

The strip revolved around the rotund, blustering, put-upon Pop of the title, along with his wife, children, and best friend, the Colonel. Compared to both Falstaff and his U.S. comic character counterpart Jiggs from *Bringing Up Father*, Pop was forever despairing of his family and society at large. With his waistcoat, tails, and spats he was clearly a throwback to an earlier, more genteel era, and the strip's humor is often warm and poignant. Millar Watt drew the strip with great elegance and economy of line, although from time to time he also dazzled with his penmanship. He innovatively told the narrative through one continuous background, divided into four panels. He introduced silent panels to suggest a pause in time or a thoughtful reaction, and played around with pacing by delivering a punch line in panel three and a reaction in panel four. It remains a technique rarely seen today.

From 1929 the strip appeared in the *New York Sun*, where it ran for almost two decades. Millar Watt retired in 1949, although his replacement, Gordon Hogg, went on to draw *Pop* for another eleven years. **DAR**

Pop's success with readers inspired a series of annual collections, this one from 1925. ➡

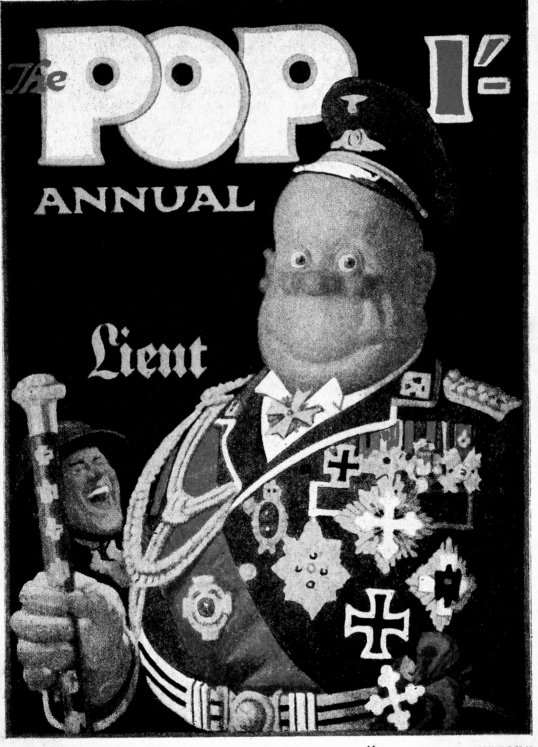

The POP ANNUAL

1/-

Lieut

80 PAGES OF CARTOONS REPRODUCED FROM "THE DAILY SKETCH"

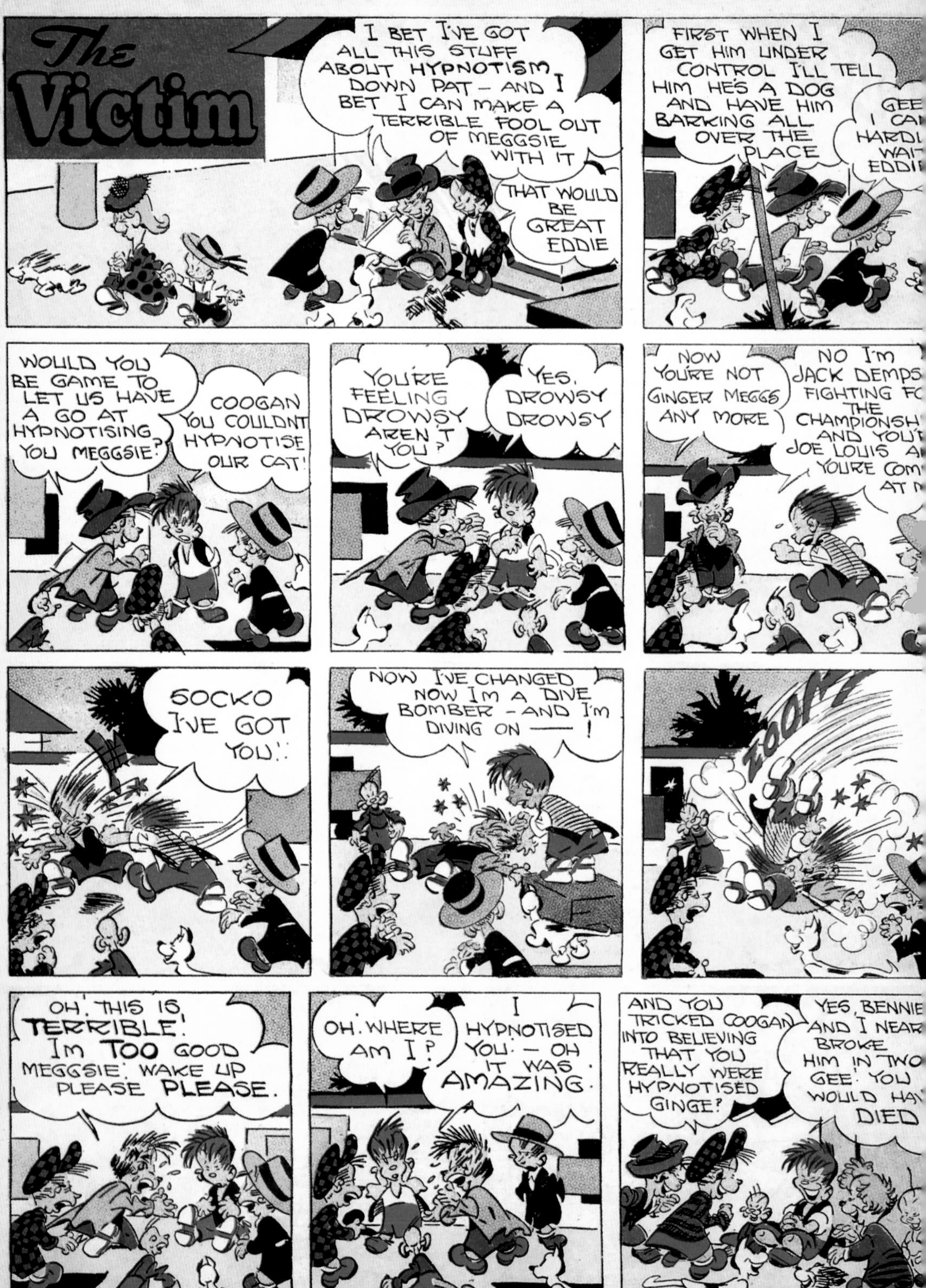
The Victim
I BET I'VE GOT ALL THIS STUFF ABOUT HYPNOTISM DOWN PAT – AND I BET I CAN MAKE A TERRIBLE FOOL OUT OF MEGGSIE WITH IT
THAT WOULD BE GREAT EDDIE
FIRST WHEN I GET HIM UNDER CONTROL I'LL TELL HIM HE'S A DOG AND HAVE HIM BARKING ALL OVER THE PLACE
GEE I CA HARDL WAI EDDI
WOULD YOU BE GAME TO LET US HAVE A GO AT HYPNOTISING YOU MEGGSIE?
COOGAN YOU COULDNT HYPNOTISE OUR CAT!
YOU'RE FEELING DROWSY AREN'T YOU?
YES. DROWSY DROWSY
NOW YOU'RE NOT GINGER MEGGS ANY MORE
NO I'M JACK DEMPS FIGHTING FO THE CHAMPIONSH AND YOU'R JOE LOUIS A YOU'RE COM AT M
SOCKO I'VE GOT YOU!!
NOW I'VE CHANGED NOW I'M A DIVE BOMBER – AND I'M DIVING ON —— !
ZOOM
OH! THIS IS TERRIBLE! I'M TOO GOOD MEGGSIE! WAKE UP PLEASE PLEASE.
OH! WHERE AM I?
I HYPNOTISED YOU! – OH IT WAS AMAZING.
AND YOU TRICKED COOGAN INTO BELIEVING THAT YOU REALLY WERE HYPNOTISED GINGE?
YES, BENNIE AND I NEAR BROKE HIM IN TWO GEE! YOU WOULD HA DIED

Ginger Meggs 1921

Jimmy Bancks

First published by *Sunday Sun* (Australia)
Creator Australian (1889–1952)
Genre Humor
Adaptation Film (1982)

In 1921 the editor of the *Sunday Sun*, Monty Grover, advertised for a comic strip about a group of boys who habitually get into trouble and are always being rescued by a girl. From among the contenders Grover selected a strip titled *Us Fellers* from an unknown illustrator named Jimmy Bancks. One of the boys in Bancks's strip was a red-haired troublemaker called Ginger Smith. Limits on color printing in the 1920s reduced the inks used in black line work to either red, yellow, and blue, meaning that the hero's signature red hair was born out of necessity rather than creativity.

By the third issue of *Us Fellers*, Bancks had quietly sent Grover's girl packing, maneuvered the renamed Ginger Meggs squarely into the strip's spotlight, and established his friends and family—father John, mother Sarah, brother Dudley, best friend Benny, girlfriend Minnie, his rival Eddie, and nemesis, Tiger Kelly.

The longest-running comic in Australian history, *Ginger Meggs* was one of the first Australian comic characters to exist in a recognizably Australian setting. Any Aussie boy ever born with red hair has been called Ginger at least once in his life. When Meggs moved from the *Sunday Sun* to the rival *Sunday Telegraph* in 1951, 80,000 readers moved with him.

When Bancks died in 1952 the strip continued under various artists and is now drawn by Melbourne cartoonist Jason Chatfield. "Creators come and go," Bancks once said, "but their characters live on." Prophetic words, indeed—Meggs's adventures can now be read today in more than thirty countries. **BS**

Minute Movies 1921

Ed Wheelan

First published by George Matthew Adams Service (USA)
Creator American (1888–1966)
Genre Satire

In 1918 a new groundbreaking strip satirizing the silent movie industry called *Midget Movies* debuted in the William Randolph Hearst newspaper *New York American*. Its creator was Ed Wheelan, who had begun poking fun at the silent screen and its stars in its pages months earlier despite not having a title. The strip quickly grew into its own week-long stories at a time when story continuity in comic strips was a rare and still emerging concept. After a dispute in 1920 Wheelan left the Hearst empire and took *Midget Movies* to the George Matthew Adams Service. The strip returned to papers in 1921 as the renamed *Minute Movies*.

Although *Minute Movies* took up the same amount of space as the other strips on the comics pages, it was separated into two tiers, which made each panel extremely small. Nevertheless, Wheelan used the space well, incorporating movielike close-ups of his elegantly attired leading man Dick Dare and leading lady Hazel Dearie, whose portrayal was so plausible that children would write in asking for autographs.

No genre was spared Wheelan's satire—Westerns, romance, drama, crime, even newsreels—there was no role or situation that debonair Dick or glamorous Hazel could not handle. Wheelan wrote, penciled, and inked the strip himself, and his fictional movie studio, created at a time of public interest in the burgeoning "dream factories" of Hollywood, grew with the industry. As talkies arrived his strips increasingly moved from parody to serious story lines which, ironically, led to its popularity diminishing and its eventual demise in 1935. **BS**

← Ginger Meggs is a red-haired boy with "a considerable talent for mischief."

Peter and Ping 1922

✎✎ "Storm P."

Title in original language *Peter og Ping*
First published by *Berlingske Tidende* (Denmark)
Creator Robert Storm Petersen (Danish, 1882–1949)
Genre Humor, Satire

It would not be entirely off the mark to describe Storm P. as the godfather of modern Danish humor. Over a five-decade long career, during which he produced tens of thousands of cartoons and became a household name, he defined the Danish sense of good-natured irony.

As Storm P.'s fame grew and his humor became more rounded, his work remained underpinned by his strong artistic commitment. His early career was characterized by his darkly humorous, strongly engaged satirical cartoons that integrated influences from his Scandinavian and German contemporaries, as well as from Norwegian painter Edvard Munch. As a strip cartoonist, however, he looked to the work of U.S. cartoonists Rudolph Dirks and Frederick Burr Opper.

Peter and Ping is Storm P.'s most famous comic strip. It appeared daily in the *Berlingske Tidende* (B.T.) newspaper, where it placed the author's trademark wit at the center of a four-panel grid. The strip narrated the experiences of everyman Peter Vimmelskaft in the city of Copenhagen, with a commentary provided by his sidekick, the dapper, talking penguin Ping. Some of the humor lies in the drawing of the characters themselves, with Peter and Ping dressed in identical suits and typically standing in identical poses with their hands in their pockets, discoursing with whoever should come along. The pair's puns, larks, quips, and japes were underpinned by a light, humorous take on the world that seeped inevitably into the Danish language and consciousness, establishing *Peter and Ping* as a much-loved national institution. **MWi**

Felix the Cat 1923

✎✎ Otto Messmer

First published by *Daily Sketch* (UK)
Creator American (1892–1983)
Genre Humor
Adaptation TV (1958)

Felix the Cat's history is one of success in early animation, merchandising, and television. He was the world's most popular cartoon character prior to the arrival of Mickey Mouse. With his vivacious personality, big grin, and expressive tail, Felix captivated viewers and later readers with his surreal, imaginative adventures.

There are disputes over his creation, however. It appears that U.S. animator Otto Messmer created him for the silent screen in 1919, although Australian producer Pat Sullivan—who owned the character and licensed him wholesale—ensured that his was the name linked with the animated feature. When Felix's strip debuted it was produced by Messmer but carried Sullivan's name; Messmer remained anonymous until three years after Sullivan's death in 1932.

Starting as a Sunday-only feature in 1923, Messmer produced gag-filled comic strip romps in between plotting and directing the continuing animation. His animation training ensured peerless storytelling, and his style evolved from scratchy to classic "bigfoot" cartooning (characters with oversized feet). The daily strip introduced in 1925 (with contributions from Jack Bogle) brought greater continuity, but both were infused with energetic whimsy. Cross-promotion later saw the animated films adapted for the newspaper strip. The Sunday strip was canceled in 1943, by which point Dell were reprinting Sunday pages as comics and commissioned Messmer to produce new *Felix* stories. Confident and endlessly varied, they are surreally creative, and Messmer's enjoyment is contagious. **FP**

Felix is instantly recognizable by his black-and-white colors and wide grin. ➡

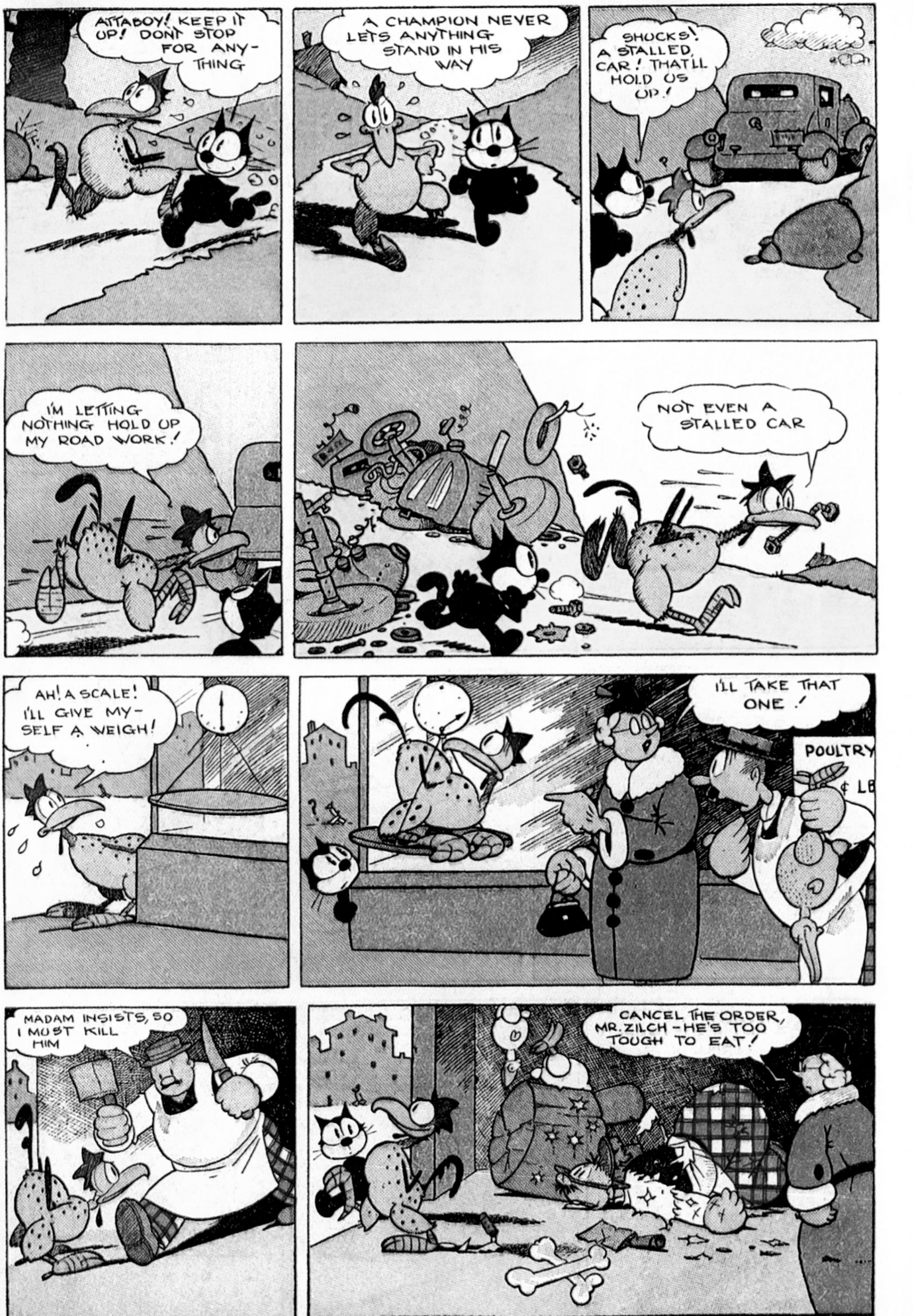

ATTABOY! KEEP IT UP! DON'T STOP FOR ANY-THING
A CHAMPION NEVER LETS ANYTHING STAND IN HIS WAY
SHUCKS! A STALLED CAR! THAT'LL HOLD US UP!
I'M LETTING NOTHING HOLD UP MY ROAD WORK!
NOT EVEN A STALLED CAR
AH! A SCALE! I'LL GIVE MY-SELF A WEIGH!
I'LL TAKE THAT ONE!
POULTRY
¢ LB
MADAM INSISTS, SO I MUST KILL HIM
CANCEL THE ORDER, MR. ZILCH - HE'S TOO TOUGH TO EAT!

Gédéon 1923

✏️ Benjamin Rabier

First published by Garnier / Hoëbeke (France)
Creator French (1864–1939)
Genre Humor, Funny animal
Adaptation TV (1979)

Benjamin Rabier, in over 150 books of personal drawings and writings, pictured the whole spectrum of human as well as animal action. From tiny things to turmoil in vast crowds and warlike scenes of mass destruction, he boosted the funny animal brand of comics like no one before. His animals walked and gestured like humans, were bottle-fed or clothed, cried, had dental pains, even smoked and laughed, and sometimes treated each other in very darned cruel ways.

Rabier had odd jobs in his youth, then in 1890, following four years in the army, he began a twenty-year career as an accountant. At the same time he did his pictorial storytelling, enjoying his work and fame in print. In 1907 he marketed himself and his comics in his self-published juvenile weekly *Histoire Comique*, with his photo proudly shown on its masthead. Only in 1910 did he drop his evening job and go full-time.

In reality he disliked animals, but by caricaturing them he made them his moneymakers. His loud "Benjamin Rabier" signature was inescapable, even on his most famous design: his early 1920s remake of a cheese trademark by the goofy name of *La vache qui rit*—the laughing cow. He did advertising work, animated cartoons, and, up to 1923, wrote and acted in vaudeville plays.

Gédéon is a youngish, long-necked yellow duck, partially clothed in coat, cap, or hat, who enjoys slyly smoking cigarettes. He can walk, swim, or fly—circling the world, delivering dirty tricks and moralistic messages, in sixteen full-color albums. **HvO**

Moon Mullins 1923

✏️ Frank Willard

First published by *Chicago Tribune* (USA)
Creator American (1893–1958)
Genre Humor
Adaptation Radio (1940)

Moon Mullins is an opportunistic young fellow who spends his days looking for a dame or a fast buck in bars or pool halls. A fast-talking rogue, his choices often led to a punch in the face or jail, but cartoonist Frank Willard ensured his universal appeal by keeping him good-natured and likeable. He surrounded Moon with other essentially good characters, including the popular Kayo, Moon's wise-beyond-his-years kid brother, who has a propensity for saying the wrong thing at the wrong time and getting him into trouble.

Over four daily panels Willard adroitly combined the soap opera elements of an ongoing cast with a solid gag at the end. The boarding-house setting marked the strip as one for a resolutely blue-collar readership; many small-town newspapers that ran only a single daily strip picked *Moon Mullins*. The young Willard shared some characteristics with Mullins, although the cartoonist's preferred location was the golf course. Assistant Ferd Johnson stockpiled replacement strips for deadlines that were threatened by Willard's many golf stints.

Moon Mullins was among the few newspaper strips in which no popular character joined the armed forces during World War II. Life in the vicinity of what had become the Plushbottom Boarding House continued as usual. Johnson began assisting on the feature two months after it started, and when illness later prevented Willard working he produced the strip on his own, ensuring a seamless transition when Willard died. *Moon Mullins* gradually became more gag-based as Johnson racked up a record sixty-eight years on the strip. **FP**

Lovable rogue Moon Mullins ensured the strip's long and popular run. ➡️

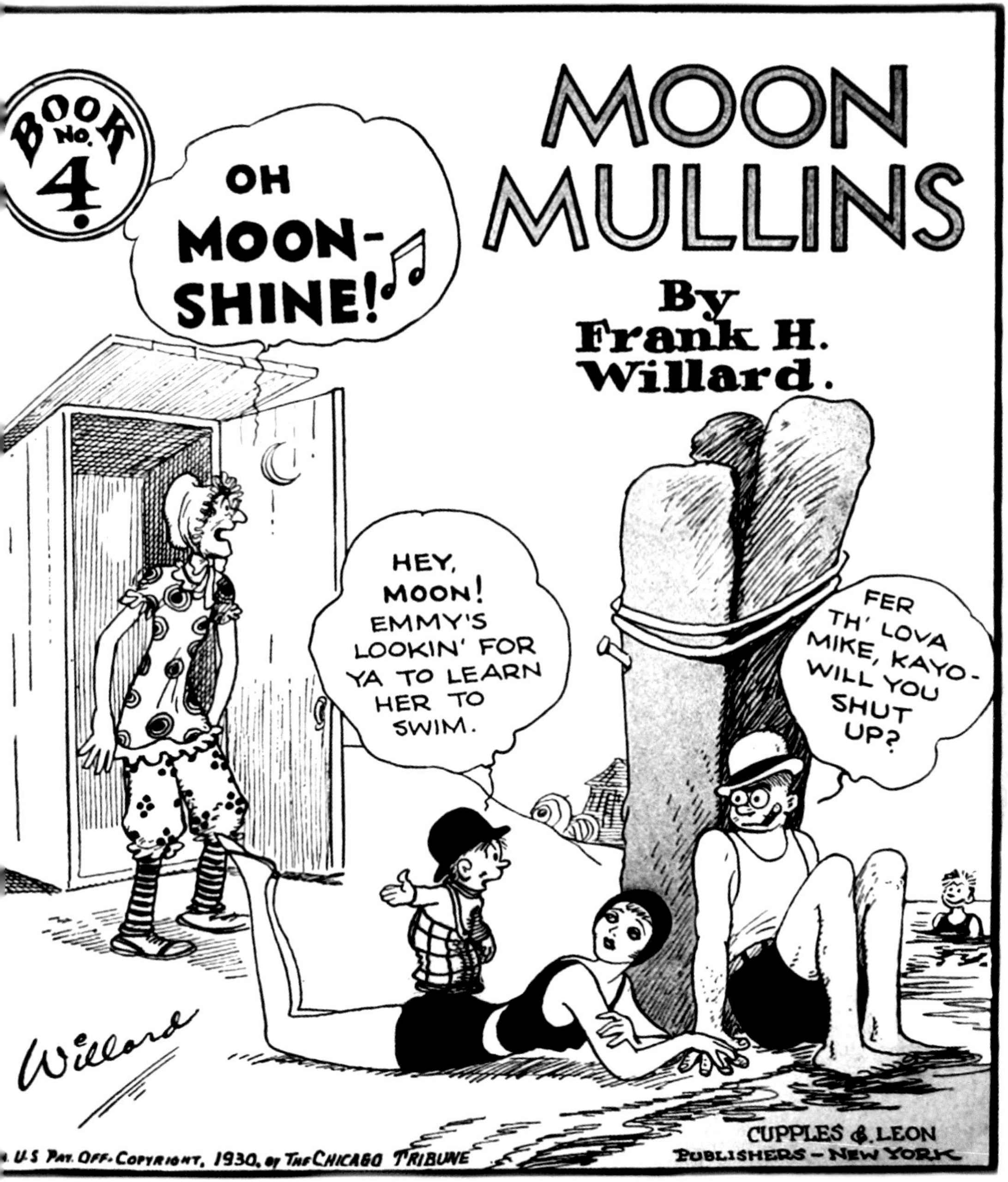
BOOK NO. 4
OH MOON-SHINE!
MOON MULLINS
By Frank H. Willard.
HEY, MOON! EMMY'S LOOKIN' FOR YA TO LEARN HER TO SWIM.
FER TH' LOVA MIKE, KAYO - WILL YOU SHUT UP?
Willard
U.S PAT. OFF. COPYRIGHT, 1930, BY THE CHICAGO TRIBUNE
CUPPLES & LEON PUBLISHERS - NEW YORK

Skippy 1923

✐✐ Percy Crosby

First published by Life Publishing Company (USA)
Creator American (1891–1964)
Genre Children's, Humor
Adaptation Film (1931)

Percy Crosby was not the first to produce a children's comic strip—other strips that appeared earlier in the history of the industry come more readily to mind: Richard Felton Outcault's *The Yellow Kid* and *Buster Brown*, Rudolph Dirks's *The Katzenjammer Kids*, not to mention *Little Jimmy* by James Swinnerton. These strips explored the antiauthority, irresponsible shenanigans of small kids. What was innovative about Percy Crosby's Skippy, however, was that he was also a loner and a young philosopher. As comics historian Bill Blackbeard

expressed it: "Skippy, hardly a kid in the usual sense, observed life through skeptical, jaundiced eyes. [His] view of the adult world was perceptive, ironic, and often bitter—reflecting Crosby's own philosophy and curmudgeonly cast of mind."

Skippy was drawn in a dynamic, sketchy line that appropriately conveyed the movement and the restlessness of young children. The influence of the series can clearly be seen in later comic strips, such as Bill Watterson's *Calvin and Hobbes* and Charles Schulz's popular *Peanuts* strip, which centered on another insecure loner, Charlie Brown.

In 1930 Crosby began a quixotic fight against the forces that, according to him, were destroying the United States. An extended story arc, "Skippy Versus the Mob: The Fight for Vesey Street and the American Soul," lasted for three months. The strip became increasingly political and preachy, and personal problems that would eventually lead Crosby to a mental institution did not help either. The strip was discontinued in 1945. **DI**

Skippy, known as the "All-American Boy," was based on his creator's childhood adventures. ⬆

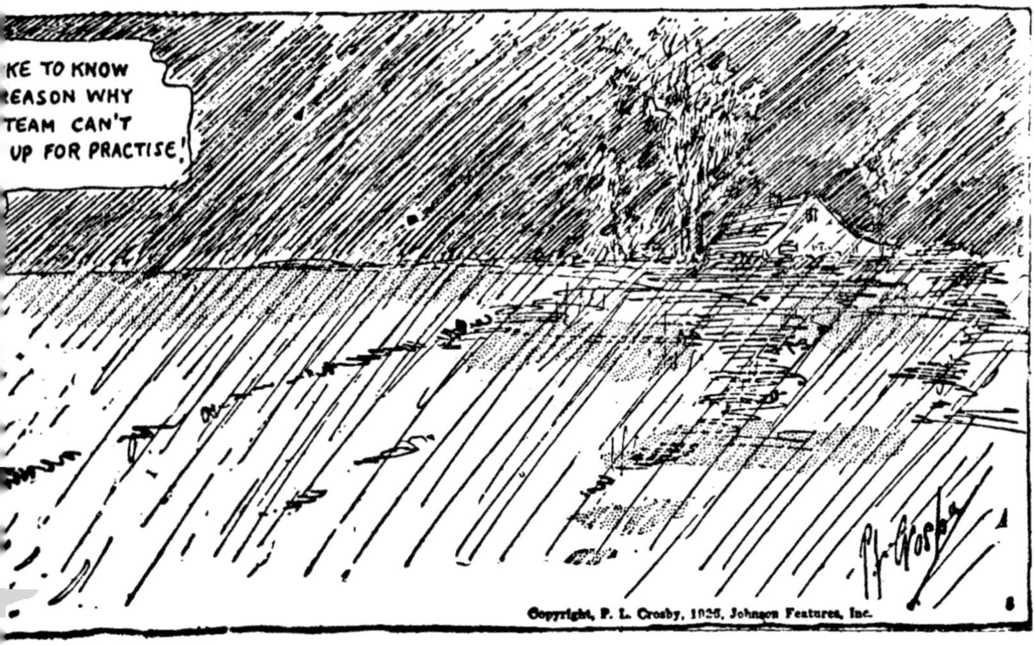
KE TO KNOW
REASON WHY
TEAM CAN'T
UP FOR PRACTISE!
Copyright, P. L. Crosby, 1926, Johnson Features, Inc.

Wash Tubbs 1924

Roy Crane

First published by Newspaper Enterprise Association (USA)
Creator American (1901–77)
Genre Adventure

Reading *Wash Tubbs* is like seeing the adventure comic strip evolve before your eyes: Roy Crane almost single-handedly created the visual language of the genre. The strip actually started life as a lighthearted, humorous feature about a jolly, round, bespectacled fellow named Washington Tubbs, who was intent on romance and fun. Within its first year, however, Crane had sent his hero out to sea in search of adventure.

There had been earlier newspaper strips that developed extended narratives, but Crane expanded elements such as close-ups, dramatic angles, evocative shadows, and sweeping vistas. He mixed a deceptively simple, cartoonlike delineation of his lead characters with increasingly accomplished backgrounds and more realistically drawn girls.

By 1928 the strip had firmly embraced action and adventure. This was underlined the following year by the introduction of Captain Easy, a rock-jawed soldier of fortune. With Easy on board, the pair roamed the world rubbing shoulders with pirates, sultans, con men, fallen aristocracy, and assorted ne'er do wells. Crane crafted every story with the lightest of touches, blending gripping action with warmth and humor.

A Sunday strip was launched in 1931 but was retitled *Captain Easy, Soldier of Fortune* two years later. The Sunday strip was Crane's high point as an artist, and both he and the public came to see Easy as the true star of the feature. In 1944 Crane left for rival syndicate King Features. *Wash Tubbs* was handed over to assistant Leslie Turner and ran in various hands until 1988. **DAR**

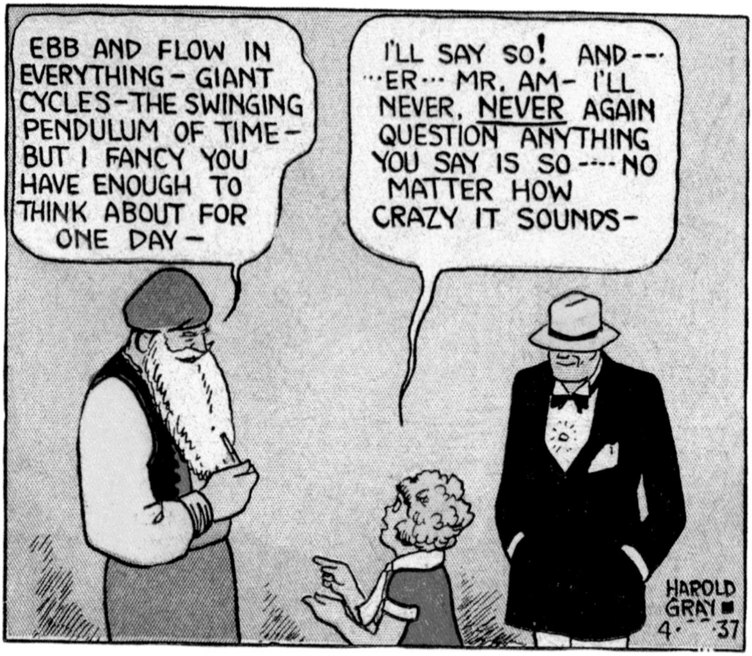
EBB AND FLOW IN EVERYTHING - GIANT CYCLES-THE SWINGING PENDULUM OF TIME- BUT I FANCY YOU HAVE ENOUGH TO THINK ABOUT FOR ONE DAY -
I'LL SAY SO! AND--- ...ER... MR. AM- I'LL NEVER, NEVER AGAIN QUESTION ANYTHING YOU SAY IS SO---- NO MATTER HOW CRAZY IT SOUNDS-
HAROLD GRAY
4-- 37

Little Orphan Annie 1924

Harold Gray

First published by *Chicago Tribune* (USA)
Creator American (1894–1968)
Genre Reality drama
Adaptation Film (1932)

If one wants to understand the United States, there is a large canon of literature on which to draw. Take, for example, Little Orphan Annie—an ageless troubadour of the human spirit who single-handedly tackles antisocial demons from the 1920s to World War II. Forever punching above her weight, the ten-year-old dishes out her own brand of justice. Like her creator, Harold Gray, Annie is a contradictory blend of the vigilante and the law-abiding. In the 1920s she uses trade union tactics to hound a shopkeeper who drove her out of town. In the mid-1930s, in an episode similar to Joseph Roth's *Rebellion* that chronicles the insidious rise of Nazism, a rabble-rousing demagogue exploits trade unionism to wreck the manufacture of a miraculous mineral that will bring earthly paradise to humanity, but his scheme backfires. "Daddy" Warbucks, an armaments millionaire and Annie's mostly absent guardian, loses his fortune but is uplifted by the indefatigable Annie. She sinks U-boats and forms the Junior Commandos (a group of children who collected scrap metal for the war effort).

Gray's conservatism and self-reliance policies alienated him from the Roosevelt administration, but with a readership of forty million in 1,000 newspapers, Annie was not openly opposed. The plucky Annie is protected by "Daddy" Warbucks's right-hand men—the sibilant Asp, the gargantuan, turbaned Punjab, and the magical Mr. Am who resembles Santa Claus. An enduring comic strip of great cultural relevance, *Little Orphan Annie* remains popular today. **IR**

Creator Gray made the red-haired Annie an orphan to give her the freedom to go where she pleased. ⬆

Destiny: A Novel in Pictures 1926

✎✎ Otto Nückel

Title in original language *Schicksal, Eine Geschichte in Bildern*
First published by Delphin Verlag (Germany)
Creator German (1888–1955) **Genre** Drama

Times were extremely difficult in Weimar Republic Germany between the world wars. Hyperinflation was rampant and unemployment massive. Otto Nückel's graphic novel *Schicksal, Eine Geschichte in Bildern* tells the tragic life story of a socially deprived woman during this period. In the wordless novel's very first image readers see an anonymous building situated in one of those nondescript places where the poor live in overcrowded conditions.

Nückel used leadcuts to illustrate. During World War I he had switched to lead because of the shortage of wood, but he liked the effect so much that he stuck with the technique. The leadcut allowed him to create gradations and the illusion of volume. The influence of silent cinema on his illustration work is obvious. The atmosphere and effect of the opening image, for example, is similar to that in German Expressionist films. Light and shadow contrast dramatically, particularly in candles and street lamps. The realism of Nückel's drawings is also reminiscent of the New Objectivity art movement that grew out of German Expressionism.

The story is melodramatic and has a sense of despair that confirms the story's deterministic title. The melodrama is toned down slightly in that readers almost never see the main character's face. She is the victim of deplorable social circumstances: poverty, her father's alcoholism, her mother's illness. Yet she is also the victim of her own poor personal choices—on one of these rare occasions her features are clearly seen. **DI**

⬆ Otto Nückel created an atmospheric shadowy world in *Destiny: A Novel in Pictures*.

Connie 1927

✐✐ Frank Godwin

First published by Ledger Syndicate (USA)
Creator American (1889–1959)
Genre Adventure, Science fiction
Collection *Famous Funnies* (1934–55)

Connie is one of the least known comic strips: it only circulated to regional newspapers during a run that ended more than sixty years ago. It has only been rescued from obscurity by comics historians.

Frank Godwin was a self-taught artist whose skills were honed from studying under U.S. artist James Montgomery Flagg. Godwin was seemingly at home in any medium and was much admired for his book and advertising work, as well as his black-and-white material. Two key elements characterized *Connie*: Godwin's fine-lined brushstroke art, and several surprising forays into new territory as Godwin's interests shifted. The early strips detailed standard dating problems, but as the Depression began to hit, Godwin had Connie Kurridge spend her days helping out among the dispossessed. At this stage the stories were very short, occasionally only twelve strips from start to finish.

Connie then pursued a newspaper career before learning to fly and adventuring around the world and involving herself in political affairs. Even this broader scope failed to satisfy Godwin for long, and he shifted emphasis once again. By 1939 Connie had become an astronaut and was jaunting about the universe meeting space pirates and aliens. Throughout Connie was a pioneering role model as a capable woman.

The science fiction run was scripted by Godwin's brother Harold. When the syndicate collapsed, taking *Connie* with it, Godwin developed *Rusty Riley*, the intricate art of which influenced the fantasy and science fiction artist Frank Frazetta. **FP**

Buck Rogers 1929

✐ Philip Nowlan ✐ Dick Calkins

First published by John F. Dille Co. (USA)
Creators Nowlan (American, 1888–1940);
Calkins (American, 1895–1962)
Genre Science fiction

The early daily *Buck Rogers* strips were adapted by Philip Nowlan from his 1928 novel, *Armageddon 2419 A.D.*, and drawn by the artist Dick Calkins. In 1929 it was renamed *Buck Rogers*. Set in the 1920s, Rogers is trapped in a collapsed mine, and a mysterious sleeping gas keeps him alive until he wakes 500 years in the future. People fly with the aid of rocket belts, robots abound, and gun-fighting derring-do is the order of the day. The plot concerns the invasion of the United States by a Mongolian race. Soon, however, Buck and girlfriend Wilma Deering are off to Mars and other planets.

Buck Rogers was the first science fiction comic strip serial. It was a massive success and lent its name to the language as shorthand for anything science fiction related. Reprints of *Buck Rogers* even helped to give birth to the new format of the comic book itself.

The Sunday strip, launched in 1930, was aimed at children. Although called *Buck Rogers*, it starred Wilma's younger brother Buddy. Signed by Calkins, the artwork was actually by the more talented Russell Keaton, who used the large color pages to great advantage. Keaton's *Buck Rogers* (1930–33) has a period charm comparable to Alfred Bestall's wonderful *Rupert the Bear*.

Later in the 1930s, Buck and Wilma entered the Sunday story line. Rick Yager took over the drawing, and the stories and artwork became darker. Yager stayed with the strip until the late 1950s, when Murphy Anderson and later George Tuska took it on. Revived in 1979 to tie in with the TV show, Buck enjoyed daily and Sunday art by artist Gray Morrow until 1982. **GL**

Buck Rogers was one of the first strips to present a continuous adventure story. ➡

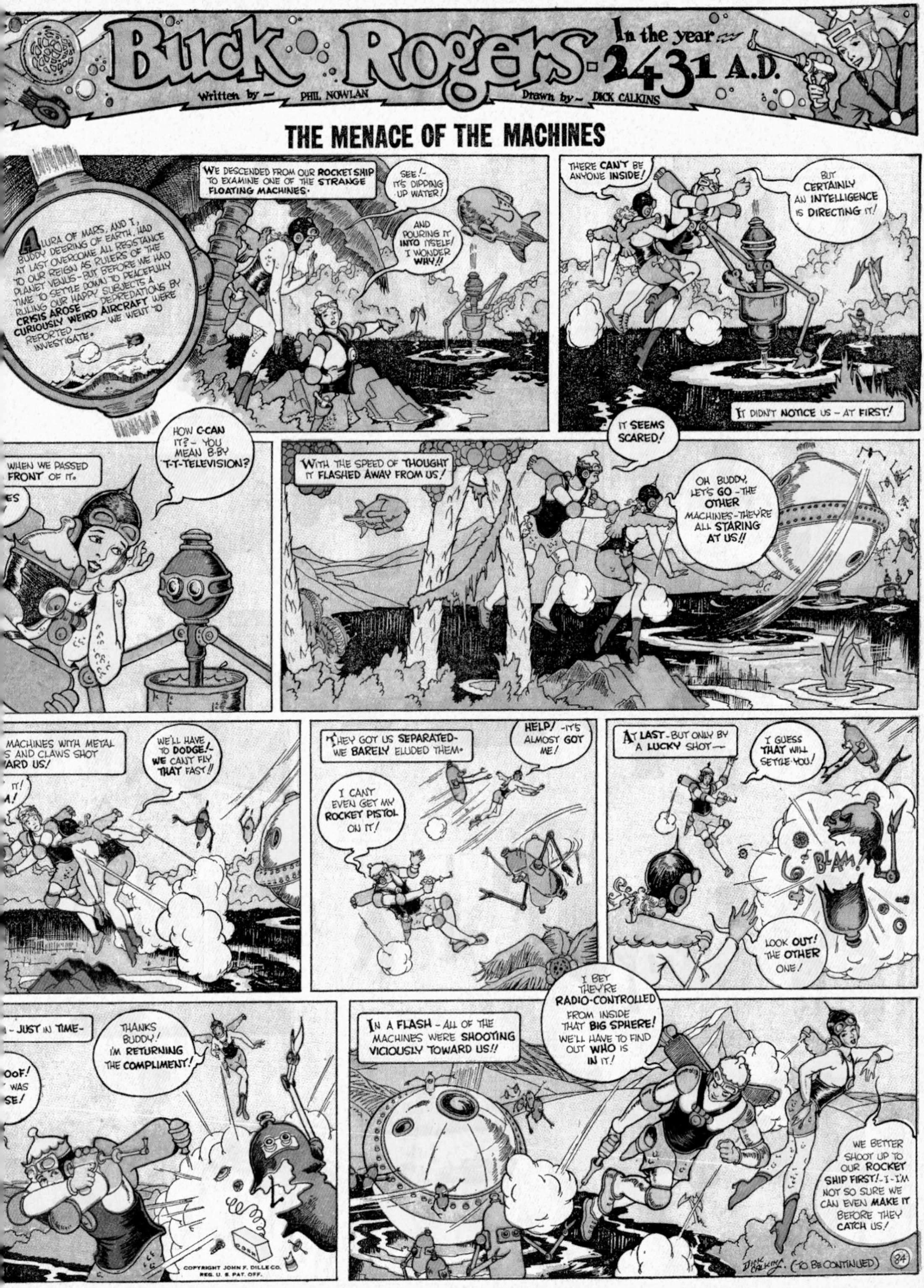
Buck Rogers - In the year 2431 A.D.
Written by — PHIL NOWLAN
Drawn by — DICK CALKINS
THE MENACE OF THE MACHINES
ALURA OF MARS, AND I, BUDDY DEERING OF EARTH, HAD AT LAST OVERCOME ALL RESISTANCE TO OUR REIGN AS RULERS OF THE PLANET VENUS - BUT BEFORE WE HAD TIME TO SETTLE DOWN TO PEACEFULLY RULING OUR HAPPY SUBJECTS A CRISIS AROSE — DEPREDATIONS BY CURIOUSLY WEIRD AIRCRAFT WERE REPORTED — WE WENT TO INVESTIGATE.
WE DESCENDED FROM OUR ROCKET SHIP TO EXAMINE ONE OF THE STRANGE FLOATING MACHINES.
SEE! - IT'S DIPPING UP WATER!
AND POURING IT INTO ITSELF! I WONDER WHY!!
THERE CAN'T BE ANYONE INSIDE!
BUT CERTAINLY AN INTELLIGENCE IS DIRECTING IT!
IT DIDN'T NOTICE US - AT FIRST!
WHEN WE PASSED FRONT OF IT.
ES
HOW C-CAN IT? - YOU MEAN B-BY T-T-TELEVISION?
WITH THE SPEED OF THOUGHT IT FLASHED AWAY FROM US!
IT SEEMS SCARED!
OH BUDDY, LET'S GO - THE OTHER MACHINES - THEY'RE ALL STARING AT US!!
MACHINES WITH METAL S AND CLAWS SHOT ARD US!
IT!
M!
WE'LL HAVE TO DODGE! - WE CAN'T FLY THAT FAST!!
THEY GOT US SEPARATED - WE BARELY ELUDED THEM.
HELP! - IT'S ALMOST GOT ME!
I CAN'T EVEN GET MY ROCKET PISTOL ON IT!
AT LAST - BUT ONLY BY A LUCKY SHOT —
I GUESS THAT WILL SETTLE YOU!
G'BLAM!
LOOK OUT! THE OTHER ONE!
- JUST IN TIME -
THANKS BUDDY! I'M RETURNING THE COMPLIMENT!
OOF!
WAS
SE!
COPYRIGHT JOHN F. DILLE CO. REG. U. S. PAT. OFF.
IN A FLASH - ALL OF THE MACHINES WERE SHOOTING VICIOUSLY TOWARD US!!
I BET THEY'RE RADIO-CONTROLLED FROM INSIDE THAT BIG SPHERE! WE'LL HAVE TO FIND OUT WHO IS IN IT!
WE BETTER SHOOT UP TO OUR ROCKET SHIP FIRST! - I - I'M NOT SO SURE WE CAN EVEN MAKE IT BEFORE THEY CATCH US!
DICK CALKINS
(TO BE CONTINUED)
84

Gods' Man 1929

Lynd Ward

First published by Jonathan Cape and Harrison Smith (USA)
Creator American (1805–1985)
Genre Drama

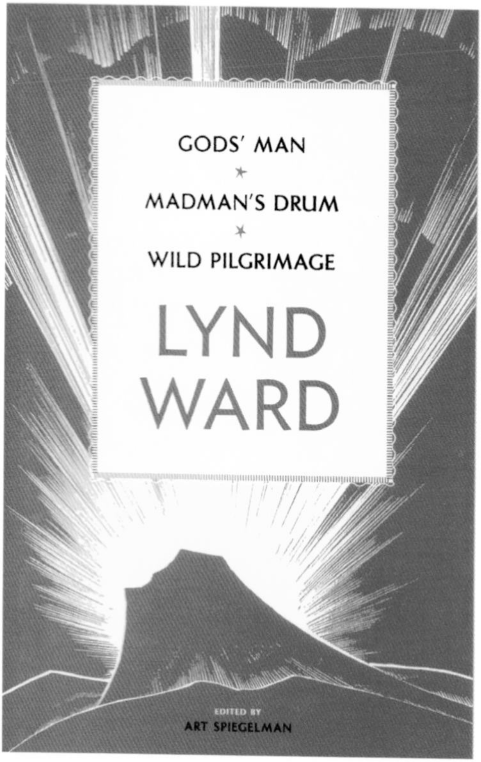
GODS' MAN
MADMAN'S DRUM
WILD PILGRIMAGE
LYND WARD
EDITED BY
ART SPIEGELMAN

Similar reads
Destiny: A Novel in Pictures Otto Nückel
Flood Eric Drooker
The Wild Party Art Spiegelman

Produced in a torrent of activity between the late 1920s and 1930s, this collection of Lynd Ward's six woodcut novels are a stunning example of artistic control over a notoriously taxing medium. The product of a rural, deeply religious Midwestern home, Ward grew up isolated from much of modern culture. Instead of learning storytelling from the funny pages, as did many of his illustrator peer group, Ward absorbed the classics, especially the Bible, significantly, an edition illustrated by Gustave Doré.

After studying art in New York and Leipzig, where he discovered the work of woodcut pioneers Frans Masereel and Otto Nückel, Ward produced *Gods' Man* in 1929. Hugely successful in its time, this stark, challenging work remains impressive today. Beginning when a young artist signs away his life in exchange for a mystical brush, Ward's tale takes readers on tour of the seedier side of the art world, while using an art deco and expressionist style.

"Ward's skill at miming expression and body language was impressive."
Art Spiegelman, author/artist

Ward followed *Gods' Man* with *Madman's Drum* (1930), a tale of the repercussions of the slave trade, and *Wild Pilgrimage* (1932), a representation of the proletarian struggle against the state. The woodcuts in his latter three novels—*Prelude to a Million Years* (1933), *Song Without Words* (1936), and *Vertigo* (1937)—express Ward's mounting anxiety over the status of world affairs while displaying an increasing level of technical achievement. Today, Ward's influence on cartoonists and storytelling remains strong, as the introduction by artist Art Spiegelman—a lifelong admirer of Ward's—emphatically confirms. **EL**

Popeye the Sailor 1929

Elzie Crisler Segar

First published by King Features Syndicate (USA)
Creator American (1894–1938)
Genre Adventure, Humor
Adaptation Film (1980)

Although more known by mass audiencies as an animated cartoon character rather than a comic strip one, *Popeye the Sailor*—or more accurately, *Thimble Theater*, the strip which carried his exploits (and which eventually was re-named after him)—is regarded virtually unquestionabily by most specialists worldwide as one of the masterworks of comics.

Thimble Theater orginally starred Olive Oyl and her brother Castor, and focused on their daily anecdotes. In 1929, the strip suffered a dramatic change as Castor, while looking for a sailor on Dice Island, meets Popeye for the first time. From then on, as the one-eyed, gruff seaman was integrated to the *Thimble Theater* cast of characters, the strip became a clever blend of satire and exotic adventure, with Olive Oyl becoming Popeye's eternal girlfriend. Segar added other emblematic characters, such as soft-spoken, hamburger-loving moocher J. Wellington Wimpy, Popeye's adopted "infink" Swee'Pea, the fabulous animal Eugene the Jeep, and the hairy, lovable monster Alice the Goon. A later addition was Popeye's long-lost father, Poopdeck Pappy.

"E. C. Segar was very good in his time . . . and he is even better in ours."

Mort Walker, artist

It's worth noting that Popeye's formidable strength was not actually derived from spinach, as his animated version would suggest, but from the magic Whiffle Bird, whom Popeye had to rub to become strong.

After Segar's death, the *Popeye* strip was continued successively by Bill Zaboly, Bud Sagendorf, Bobby London, and Hy Eisman. Popeye featured in countless licensed items, besides his long-running series of theatrical shorts made by the Fleischer Studio. **AMo**

POPEYE CARTOON BOOK

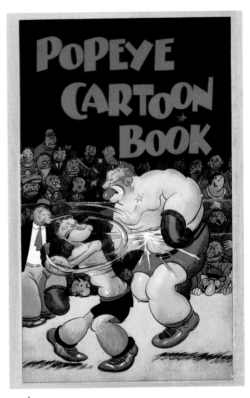

Similar reads

Sappo E. C. Segar
Smokey Stover Bill Holman
The Squirrel Cage Gene Ahern

2 1930–49

Blondie 1930

Chic Young

First published by King Features Syndicate (USA)
Creator American (1901–73)
Genre Humor
Award Billy DeBeck Award, Cartoonist of the Year (1948)

Blondie, one of the world's most read comics, is considered as the quintessential family strip. Interestingly, while King Features Syndicate's other successful family strip, *Bringing Up Father*, defined the rags-to-riches trajectory of its protagonists, *Blondie* shows the opposite: Dagwood Bumstead, the young member of a wealthy family, is disinherited when he marries working-class girl Blondie Boopadoop. The couple became an average American family, living in a suburban home, and have a son, Alexander, and a daughter, Cookie.

Unlike most strips, characters in *Blondie* grow up through the years: the Bumstead kids became young adults, and even Daisy, the pet dog, has five pups. Other supporting characters include Dagwood's dominant boss Mr. Julius Caesar Dithers, next-door neighbors Herb and Tootsie Woodley, and postman Mr. Beasley.

Most of the usual situations seen in *Blondie* remain virtually unchanged over the decades: Dagwood trying to get a raise from Mr. Dithers, Blondie trying to borrow some money from Dagwood (usually by luring him with a home-made pie) for a new hat, or Dagwood simply trying to take a nap or a bath without being disturbed by the kids, among a few others. Another of the strip's trademark characteristics was Dagwood's talent for creating gigantic sandwiches

Blondie also appears in comic books that combine reprints of the newspaper strip with fresh material. After Chic Young´s death, *Blondie* continues to appear, written by his son Dean and drawn by other artists. **AMo**

Quick and Flupke 1930

"Hergé"

Title in original language *Quick et Flupke*
First published by Les Éditions du Petit Vingtième (Belgium) **Creator** Georges Prosper Remi Remi (Belgian, 1907–83) **Genre** Humor

The Belgian comic artist Hergé, savvy and then only twenty-two years old, had just returned from the Christmas recess. At his desk in his employer's Brussels office he was meeting newspaper deadlines with spreads of his first *Tintin* serial. But when the newspaper weekly supplements were extended from eight to sixteen pages, and his editor asked for an extra strip, he created *Quick and Flupke*. He produced 315 strips of this series in ten years, mostly in the early 1930s, in the same children's weeklies as his *Tintin* strip, mainly as two-pagers, a total of 623 pages.

The bilingual artist Georges Remi, whose reversed initials sounded like "Hergé," was raised speaking Dutch and French. For sixteen years, until 1940, he published solely in French. With only a tiny audience, he dreamed of going into advertising. The *Quick and Flupke* strip was his seventh series, but only the third that he also wrote. It was a gag strip about two Brussels street kids, one always in a beret, the other with a scarf. They were modeled on the title duo in a well-known French film, *Les deux gosses* (1929), based on an 1880 children's classic from French writer Pierre Decourcelle.

Quick and Flupke, later better known from colored reprints, became a carefree playground for imaginative experiments involving all that Hergé knew about print and cinema. The characters' co-star was a local policeman, at first named Vertommen (Belgian Dutch or Flemish for "dammit"), and later just Agent No. 15. Of Hergé's nearly forty strips, his playful, almost naive *Quick and Flupke* is a particular joy to behold. **HvO**

HERGÉ

QUICK ET FLUPKE

GAMINS DE BRUXELLES

4me SÉRIE

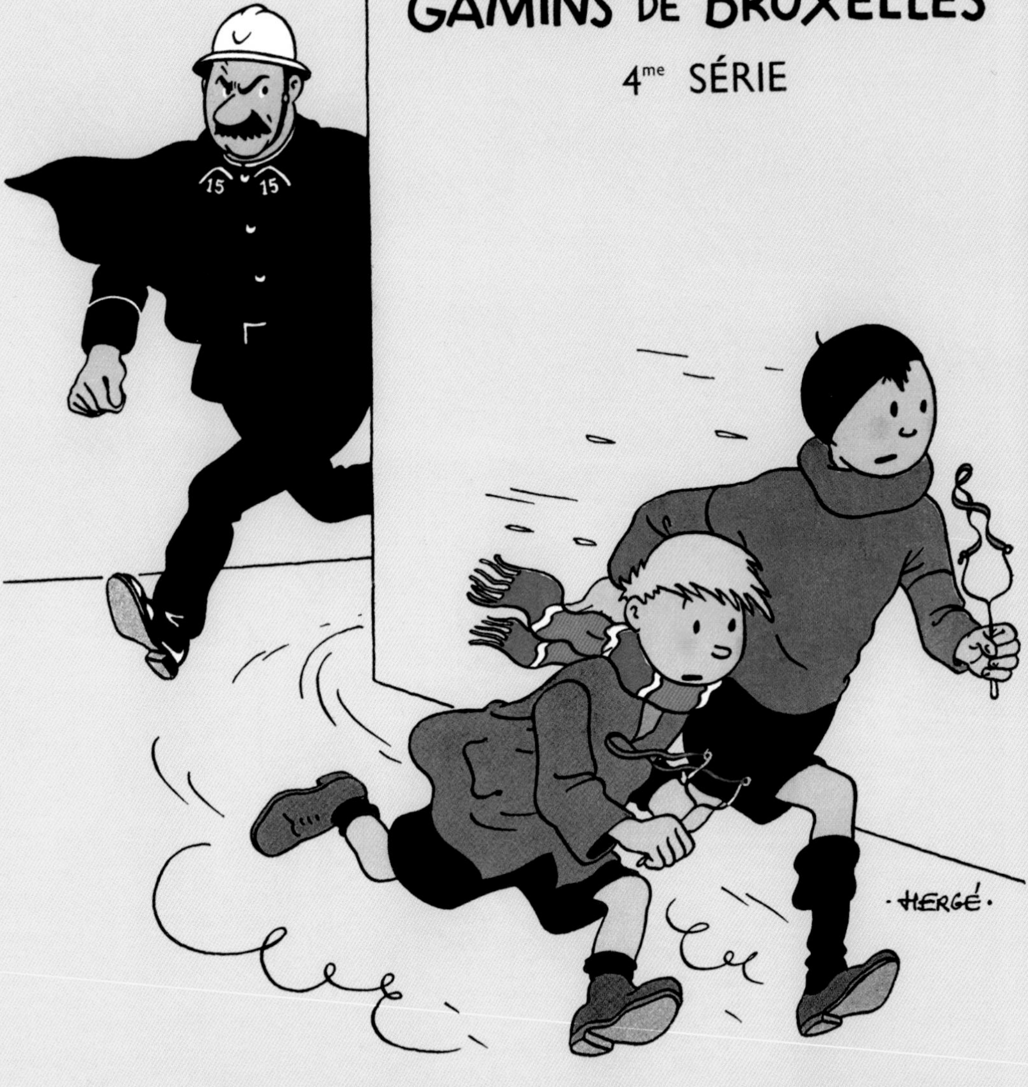
HERGÉ

CASTERMAN

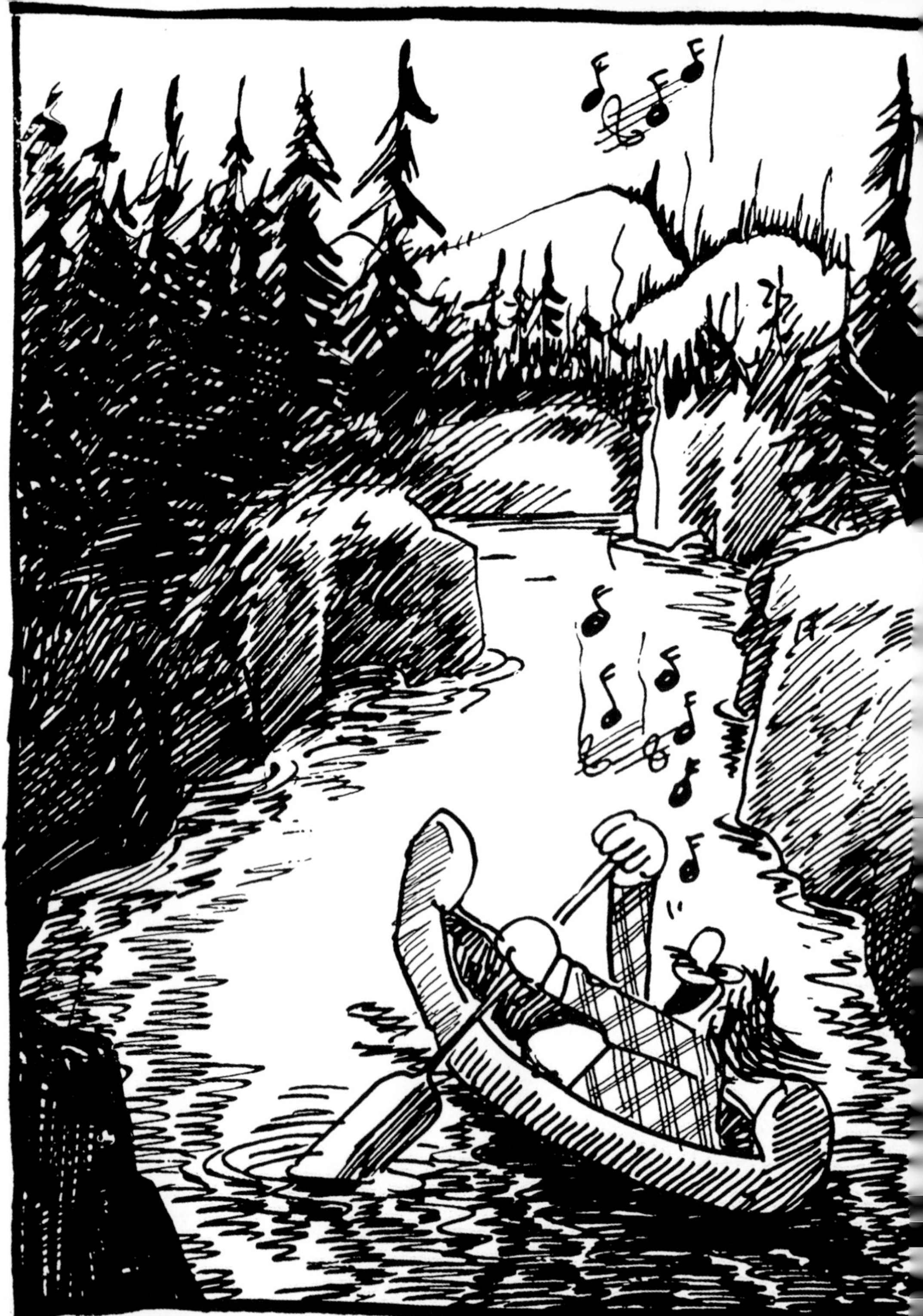

He Done Her Wrong 1930

✏️🖌️ Milt Gross

First published by Doubleday (USA)
Creator American (1895–1953)
Genre Humor
Award The "Milt Gross Fund" named in his honor

In the early 1930s it was somewhere between difficult and impossible to avoid the work of Milt Gross, particularly if you were Jewish. A friend of the great silent comic Charlie Chaplin, Gross was a prolific master of dialect humor, with books such as *Nize Baby* and his inspired *Hiawatta, Witt No Odder Poems*, written in his own peculiar amalgam of Yiddish and English, full of hilarious malapropisms. His strips became popular slapstick commentaries on contemporary Jewish culture and ethnicity. It is therefore somewhat surprising that his 256-page wordless comic, possibly the first American graphic novel, disappeared from public consciousness almost as fast as it was penned.

He Done Her Wrong parodies the staid action-romance adventures and melodramas of Hollywood. The girlfriend of a naive, muscular frontiersman (the hero) is stolen from him by a double-crossing baron who sabotages the frontiersman's business and flees with his money and his girl to New York. The hero travels to the city in pursuit of his true love, finds her, and, in a Keystone Kop moment, is hit on the head by a falling paint tin and a 2x4 timber. There are running gags too, including one spanning twenty-seven pages as Gross takes full advantage of the book's novel-like length.

Gross had a cinematic approach to storytelling. The book features close-ups when a detail needs emphasis, and multiple panels denoting speed when the narrative cranks up. The writer Stephan Becker was right when he described *He Done Her Wrong* as a "silent film transferred to paper." **BS**

Norakuro 1931

✏️🖌️ Tagawa Suiho

First published by Kodansha (Japan)
Creator Japanese (1899–1989)
Genre Humor
Adaptation Short films (1933)

Norakuro is the name of this comic's leading character, a stray black-and-white dog—*nora* (stray) and *kuro* (black). The original plot begins in 1931, with Norakuro joining the *mōkenrentai* (fierce dogs brigade). Norakuro's time in the army is full of slapstick comedy, and as the series progressed and gained more attention, so did Norakuro himself. He gradually gets promoted from private to sergeant, giving a new title to the series each time he moves up the ladder.

The outbreak of the Pacific War added fresh fuel to the children's craze for the series, and the dog became a national icon. In fact, he was used as a vehicle to accelerate support for the war. Only, in Norakuro's world, the enemy was an army of monkeys. This was a humorous take on the Japanese expression, "dog-monkey relationship," referring to two people who dislike each other. By the time Norakuro became the commanding officer of the brigade, the popularity of the series had reached a peak, with animated adaptations of the manga on the big screen. But following Japan's defeat in 1945, Norakuro was forced to leave the army for good. He returned, not as a soldier, but as an "ordinary" children's hero.

Norakuro's author, Suiho Tagawa, drew a picture of a tadpole at the end of all his titles as a symbol of his immaturity as an artist. The tadpole gradually grew limbs, but Tagawa never felt he could justify drawing a frog. When he announced his retirement in 1989 (the year he died), he gave his brothers his blessing to publish their version of Norakuro. **TS**

⬅️ *He Done Her Wrong* parodied the novels of Lynd Ward.

SANTA CLAUS!! UH YOU'LL HAFTA GIVE THE COUNTER-SIGN FER T'NITE. THEM'S ORDERS.
PEACE ON EARTH-GOOD WILL TOWARD MEN.
I'M SORRY--IT'S SWELL SANTA--BUT THAT AINT IT--I'LL HAFTA TAKE YOU TO THE GUARD-HOUSE. I HOPE YOU'LL UNDER-STAND.
IT REALLY SHOULD BE THE PASS-WORD JOE BUT NAZI THIRST FOR POWER HAS CHANGED IT.
THE COUNTERSIGN ISN'T CORRECT FOR TONIGHT'S ORDERS--BUT IT'LL BE ALL RIGHT---WE RECOGNIZE YOU---
THANK YOU CAPTAIN.
IN FACT I THINK WE'LL CHANGE THE COUNTERSIGN. YOURS IS MORE APPROPRIATE. DO YOU WANT ANY HELP DISTRIBUTING YOUR GIFTS SANTA?
YES, BUT MY GIFTS CANNOT BE CARRIED BY HAND---THEY ARE BY WORD OF MOUTH.
YES SANTA.
TELL THESE MEN WHAT THEY ARE PROTECTING. TELL THEM WHAT I HAVE SEEN AS I COVERED THE EARTH TONIGHT----
TELL THEM THAT THOSE OTHERS WHO WERE NOT ON GUARD---AND HAVE PAID IN SLAVERY---NOW PRAY THAT YOU WILL BE PROUD, STALWART--GUARDING THE MOST PRECIOUS OF ALL PROPERTIES--- FREEDOM---
HOLD IT--FIGHT FOR IT---I'VE SEEN WHAT HAPPENS TO THOSE WHO APPEASE THE ENEMY WITHIN AS WELL AS WITHOUT--THIS IS MY GIFT--I MUST GO NOW.
McNaught Syndicate, Inc.
I RIMEMBER HE SAID PEACE ON EARTH BUT NOT A DICTATER'S PEACE!! GOOD WILL TOWARD MEN--
GOOD NIGHT SANTA--AN' B'LIEVE ME WE WILL!
HAM FISHER

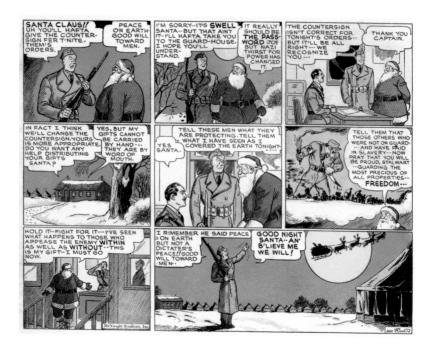

Joe Palooka 1931

"Ham" Fisher

First published by *The New York Daily Mirror* (USA)
Creator Hammond Edward Fisher (American, 1901–55)
Genre Sports, Adventure
Adaptation Film: *Palooka* (1934)

Syndicated in 2,000 newspapers to fifty million readers at its height, *Joe Palooka* was one of the most popular strips of the early twentieth century. The tale of a naive, blond heavyweight boxer answered the popular call for a "Great White Hope." There had been an embargo on boxing strips since 1908, when Jack Johnson became the first black heavyweight world champion. Later, Joe Louis asked *Joe Palooka*'s creator why his hero never fought a black opponent. Fisher replied that he could not draw Palooka beating up a black boxer, and Palooka could never lose. The average *Joe Palooka* story line is akin to Voltaire's *Candide*: the innocent lurching from adventure to adventure with his upstanding morals intact. A down-to-earth hero, Palooka often ends up dishing out well-meaning lifestyle homilies and even signed up for service in the U.S. Army in 1940. After fighting the war in style, Joe married his longtime love Ann Howe in 1949, making front-page news.

Fisher used many assistants in his work, but he devised the stories and drew all the faces. Animosity developed between Fisher and one assistant, Al Capp, whom Fisher accused of plagiarism in Capp's creation *Li'l Abner*. In retaliation, Capp parodied Fisher in his *Abner* strip. The more *Abner* became successful, the more Fisher's ire escalated. Public confrontations occurred, with the wittier Capp gaining the upper hand. In 1955, Fisher doctored Capp's artwork and claimed it was pornographic. Comparing the strips, the deception was transparent. Fisher was thrown out of the Cartoonists' Society and tragically killed himself not long after. **IR**

While serving in the U.S. Army, Joe Palooka wanted even Santa to follow military protocol. ↑

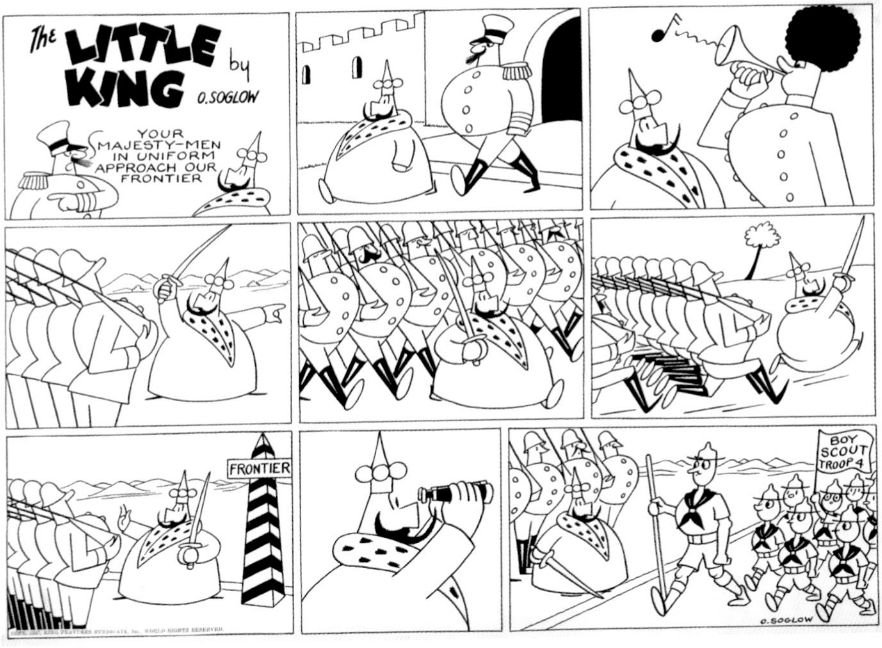
The LITTLE KING by O.SOGLOW
YOUR MAJESTY—MEN IN UNIFORM APPROACH OUR FRONTIER
FRONTIER
BOY SCOUT TROOP 4
O.SOGLOW

The Little King 1931

Otto Soglow

First published by *The New Yorker* (USA)
Creator American (1900–75)
Genre Humor
Award Reuben Award (1966)

After decades of telling their stories in expressive silence, by the 1930s motion pictures had embraced the world of sound and left the silent era behind. It is therefore ironic that while for comic books the early 1930s were also a time of experimentation, instead of adding words, some cartoonists began to reacquaint their readers with the virtues of "silent" wordless strips.

Pantomime comics experienced a resurgence, and one of the most interesting of the period focused on the daily rituals of an unnamed monarch, drawn by the Jewish-American cartoonist Otto Soglow. Soglow was annoyed by the "categorization" of society, our tendency to label people according to their gender, job, lineage, or ethnicity. So he created the almost wordless strip *The Little King*, concerning a mute monarch whose robes were as ill-fitting as he felt his title was. Desperate to escape a standard royal life, this small sovereign was constantly looking for excuses to be somewhere else; to slide down a banister, climb a tree, or play ping-pong.

Soglow crafted a world that was uncluttered, innocent, and filled with gentle, unhurried humor. He spent hours composing each panel, employing exaggerated curves in the chests of guards and courtiers to suggest they were full of "hot air," puffed up and self-important.

The Little King appeared in *The New Yorker* from 1931 to 1934, and, after being made an offer by publishing magnate William Randolph Hearst, thereafter as a newspaper strip in the Hearst press, as well as papers around the world through syndication. **BS**

↑ Otto Soglow often spent hours composing each panel, ensuring no line went to waste.

Tarzan 1931

✏️ "Hal" Foster and Burne Hogarth

First published by United Feature Syndicate (USA)
Creators Harold Rudolf Foster (American, 1892–1982); Hogarth (American, 1911–96)
Genre Action, Adventure

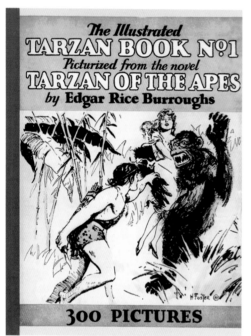

The Illustrated
TARZAN BOOK Nº1
Picturized from the novel
TARZAN OF THE APES
by Edgar Rice Burroughs

300 PICTURES

Similar reads

Akim Hansrudi Wäscher
Flash Gordon Alex Raymond
Nausicaä of the Valley of the Wind Hayao Miyazaki
Prince Valiant Hal Foster
Terry and the Pirates Milton Caniff

While the daily *Tarzan* newspaper strip (starting in 1929) adapted Edgar Rice Burroughs's novels, the full-color Sunday strips presented new stories from 1931, written by or approved by the Burroughs estate. When both Burroughs and the syndicate were unhappy with the first artist chosen after the first six months, Hal Foster took over the strip. When Foster left the strip in 1937 to launch *Prince Valiant* he was succeeded by the equally acclaimed Burne Hogarth.

Long considered one of the finest adventure strips ever, *Tarzan* combined epic story lines with beautiful illustration. Eschewing speech bubbles, the strip was presented as a narrative alongside the artwork. Foster's Tarzan fought alongside the French Foreign Legion against slavers, and met ancient Egyptians and Vikings in the hidden depths of Africa, while his artwork remained loosely inked, unusually impressionistic, and full of exotic grandeur. During his run, Hogarth kept the narrative and dialogue to a minimum, but followed Foster's lead in thrusting Tarzan from one deadly encounter to another. His artwork was earthier, more sharply inked, with every rippling muscle, fold of cloth, or landscape tightly defined.

Both cartoonists brought Tarzan into contact with hidden empires and dinosaurs, crooked prospectors, and beautiful princesses who longed for, but could never win, Tarzan's affections. Foster's two year sequence among the ancient Egyptians (Hogarth used some of the characters again later) and Hogarth's clash between the followers of the Sea and Fire gods are two of the best-regarded story arcs.

Tarzan himself captured the public imagination and around ninety Tarzan-themed movies have been made, in addition to television series and stage productions. He also appears in numerous computer games. The man in the animal-skin costume speaks to us all. **NFI**

Dick Tracy 1931

Chester Gould

Dick Tracy had no alias—you knew him by his squared-off chin and eagle nose. He lived in a city whose name was never made known to us. He was unstintingly honest, and a damn fine shot when honesty was not enough. He used gadgets because they helped catch the bad guy; ring cameras, two-way radio/wristwatches, and telephone wiretaps that appeared in the comics years before they were used in the real world. He even had a voice detector to help identify his villains, many of whom had the coolest names in comicdom: Flattop, Mumbles, Splitface, Itchy, Gargles, Pruneface, Tonsils, Cueball, and Breathless Mahoney.

The 1930s were unquestionably the strip's golden age, and the public's fascination with real life gangsters, such as John Dillinger and Bonnie and Clyde, saw detective strips abound in newspapers across America. Tracy's creator, Chester Gould, introduced a level of stylized, graphic violence not seen in comic books before, violence as a means to an end and that was used unambiguously by Tracy, who lived in an "eye for an eye" world. The strip's popularity reached a peak in the late 1950s but declined in the 1960s when the inventor of Tracy's two-way wrist watch, Diet Smith, designed the "Space Coupe," a craft that used Earth's magnetic forces to take Tracy to more overtly science fiction adventures on a colonized Moon.

A delightfully morbid, recurring motif throughout the strip was the ingeniously sadistic bevy of death traps devised for Tracy by his enemies, traps that were often accompanied by victorious, though predictably premature, "villain's speeches."

Tough-talking Dick Tracy has joined Raymond Chandler's Philip Marlowe in the pantheon of film noir characters that continue to influence popular culture today. The 1990 movie *Dick Tracy* starring Warren Beatty saw a successful revival of the character. **BS**

First published by *The Detroit Mirror* (USA)
Creator American (1900–85)
Genre Action, Adventure
Awards Reuben Award (1959 and 1977)

DICK TRACY
and DICK TRACY, JR.
AND HOW THEY CAPTURED "STOOGE" VILLER
CUPPLES & LEON Co. PUBLISHERS NEW YORK
CHESTER GOULD

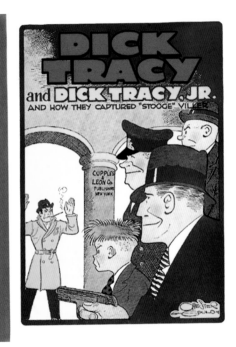

Similar reads

Batman Bob Kane
Detective Comics Malcolm Wheeler-Nicholson
Johnny Dynamite Ken Fitch and Pete Morosi
Rip Kirby Alex Raymond
The Green Hornet George Trendle and Fran Striker

The Four Immigrants Manga 1931

✎✎ Henry Kiyama

Title in original language *Manga yonin shosei*
First published by Yoshitaka Kiyama Studio (USA)
Creator Japanese (1885–1951)
Genre Reality drama

There's nothing particularly unusual about an American-based visual artist having found himself in unique circumstances for an extended period not merely thinking of but acting upon the idea of creating an autobiographical comic to document his experience. However, if that artist is visiting from Japan and the experiences date back to 1904—well, that is unusual, even groundbreaking.

Such is the case of Henry Kiyama, who was born Yoshitaka Kiyama in a small Japanese seaside village and took an Americanized forename when he and three buddies met up in San Francisco, each seeking their destiny on the alien shore: a businessman, an observer of democracy, a farmer, and Kiyama, an artist.

The fifty-two chapters of *Four Immigrants* were intended for serialization (one each week for a year), but that never transpired. Instead, Kiyama self-published the book, printing it back in his native country but registering the origin of publication as the corner of Sutter and Webster Streets: the heart of what remains of San Francisco's Japantown.

In chapter 20, a panel suddenly goes black. It is January 29, 1906: Kiyama had the luck to be in San Francisco for the infamous earthquake. His first instinct is to run for a bamboo grove, but of course there are no bamboo groves in the city. Later he witnesses influenza and the start of Prohibition. There is fun, too, but the tale of an Asian man in America at that time is a largely unpleasant one—when racism is not the issue, there are cultural misunderstandings aplenty. **MW**

Alley Oop 1932

✎✎ V. T. Hamlin

First published by Bonnet-Brown Syndicate (USA)
Creator American (1900–93)
Genre Humor
Adaptation Animated short film (1978)

Cartoonist V. T. Hamlin survived a variety of misfortunes in his life, including an arrow in the lip during childhood, poison gas in World War I, and being accidentally shot by his father on his way to producing *Alley Oop* in late 1932. The strip was originally set in the faux prehistoric land of Moo, where cavemen and dinosaurs coexisted. Caveman Alley was portrayed as resourceful yet boisterous and hot tempered with an equally hot-tempered but glamorous (and realistically drawn) girlfriend Ooola. He had adventures with his tame dinosaur Dinny and his pal Foozy, who spoke in rhyme. When not being harassed by dinosaurs they would antagonize the neighboring kingdom of Lem.

Hamlin's engaging scripts and underrated art, which betrayed a greater than passing interest in paleontology, served up a fast-paced and humorous adventure strip, but he eventually came to feel confined by its setting. At his wife's suggestion, in 1939 he had a twentieth-century time machine haul Alley from the past. From that point on, Alley was able to cause mayhem throughout time, even visiting the Moon. The novelty of a caveman pitching up in any era propelled *Alley Oop* to sustained success.

Cartoonist Dave Graue assisted Hamlin from 1950 and took over art duties in the 1960s when Hamlin's eyesight deteriorated. In 1971 he began writing as well, but it was a further two years before Graue was credited for his work. Now in production for over seventy-five years, *Alley Oop* is continued today by Jack and Carole Bender. **FP**

Alley Oop struggles with the experience of domesticating his dinosaur. ➡

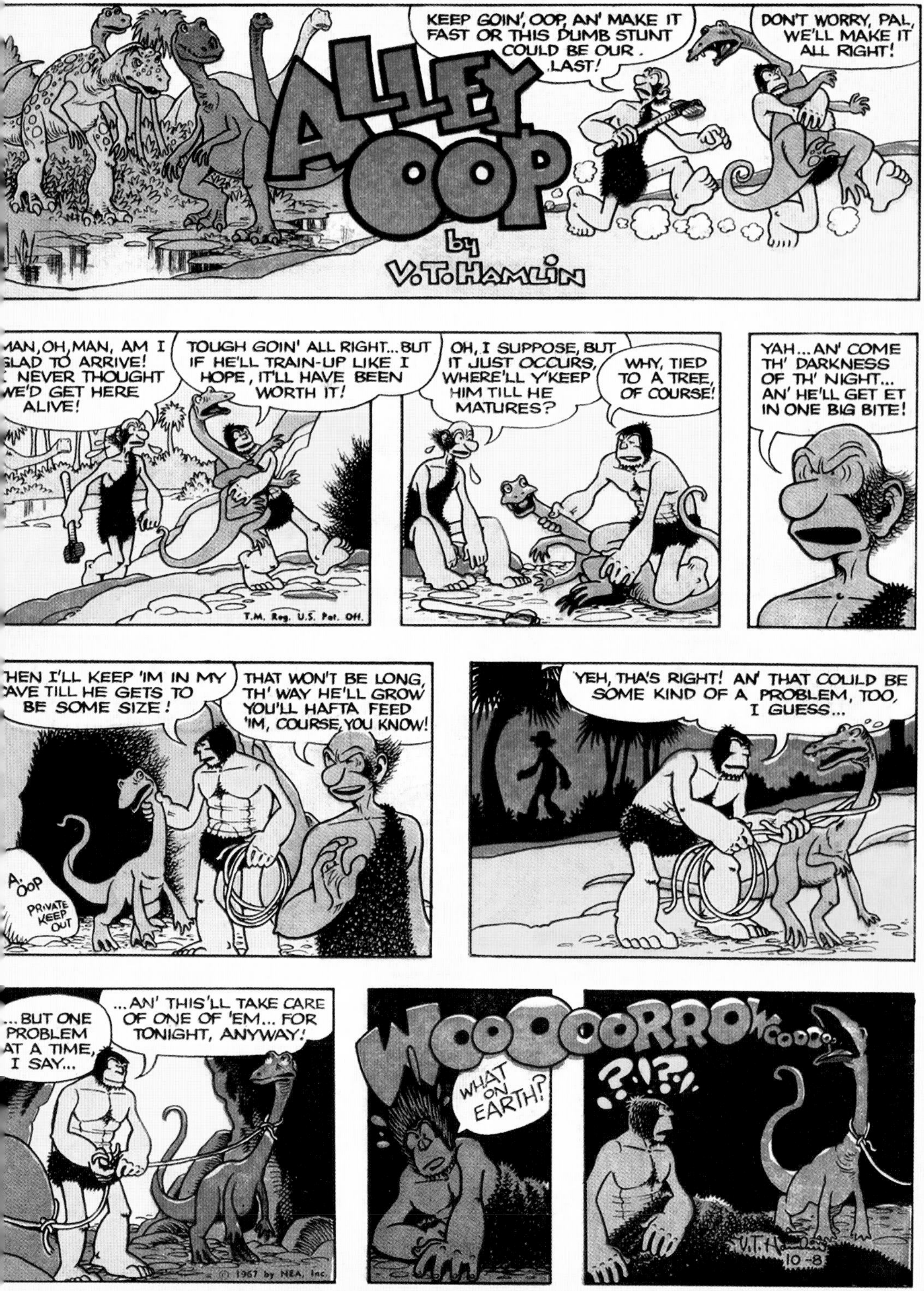

ALLEY OOP
by V.T. HAMLIN
KEEP GOIN', OOP, AN' MAKE IT FAST OR THIS DUMB STUNT COULD BE OUR LAST!
DON'T WORRY, PAL, WE'LL MAKE IT ALL RIGHT!
MAN, OH, MAN, AM I GLAD TO ARRIVE! NEVER THOUGHT WE'D GET HERE ALIVE!
TOUGH GOIN' ALL RIGHT... BUT IF HE'LL TRAIN-UP LIKE I HOPE, IT'LL HAVE BEEN WORTH IT!
T.M. Reg. U.S. Pat. Off.
OH, I SUPPOSE, BUT IT JUST OCCURS, WHERE'LL Y'KEEP HIM TILL HE MATURES?
WHY, TIED TO A TREE, OF COURSE!
YAH... AN' COME TH' DARKNESS OF TH' NIGHT... AN' HE'LL GET ET IN ONE BIG BITE!
HEN I'LL KEEP 'IM IN MY AVE TILL HE GETS TO BE SOME SIZE!
THAT WON'T BE LONG, TH' WAY HE'LL GROW YOU'LL HAFTA FEED 'IM, COURSE, YOU KNOW!
A. OOP PRIVATE KEEP OUT
YEH, THA'S RIGHT! AN' THAT COULD BE SOME KIND OF A PROBLEM, TOO, I GUESS...
...BUT ONE PROBLEM AT A TIME, I SAY...
...AN' THIS'LL TAKE CARE OF ONE OF 'EM... FOR TONIGHT, ANYWAY!
© 1967 by NEA, Inc.
WOOOOORROOWOOOO
WHAT ON EARTH?
?!?!
V.T. Hamlin 10-8

Jane 1932

✐✐ Norman Pett   ✐ "Don" Freeman

Jane at *War*

The original and
unexpurgated adventures
of the British secret weapon
of World War Two –
Jane of the DAILY MIRROR

HUBBARD

"Jane peeled (stripped off) a week ago. The British 36th Division immediately gained six miles and the British attacked in the Arakan. Maybe we Americans ought to have Jane, too."

American service newspaper, *Roundup*

Similar reads
Barbarella Jean-Claude Forest
Little Annie Fanny Harvey Kurtzman and Will Elder
Male Call Milton Caniff

First published by *The Daily Mirror* (UK)
Creators Pett (British, 1891–1960);
John Henry Gordon Freeman (British, 1903–72)
Genre Humor, Adventure

Jane and her dachshund, Fritz (full name: Count Fritz von Pumpernikel) were introduced in the first episode of *Jane's Journal—The Diary of a Bright Young Thing* in 1932. At first just a daily gag strip, Jane would often be shown dressing or bathing. In 1938, Don Freeman was hired as writer, and he developed *Jane* into a racy adventure strip that required Jane to do a great deal more undressing, whether she wanted to or not.

As World War II started, Jane became a chauffer, then secretary to a colonel. This allowed for misunderstandings with the colonel's wife and Jane's then boyfriend Basil, who was hoping Jane could wrangle him a commission. Further misunderstandings occurred when the colonel took Jane on M.I.6 business to secret locations where suspected spies lurked.

Jane took a turn in Naval Intelligence before returning to the colonel and meeting Georgie Porgie, with whom she would eventually sail off into the sunset in her final strip in 1959. Pett handed art duties on *Jane* to his assistant Michael Hubbard in 1948, while Freeman stayed on until 1953.

Pett based his drawings on actual life models, starting with his wife and then progressing to Chrystabel Leighton-Porter, who also portrayed Jane in the 1949 film, *The Adventures of Jane*. Though sketchy, Pett's artwork has an authenticity that adds to the eroticism of the strip. The height of Jane's popularity had to be during the war, when the it was read by seven million servicemen daily, according to the Canadian Armed Forces newspaper, *The Maple Leaf*, in 1945. **NFI**

Mickey Mouse 1933

✐✐ Floyd Gottfredson ✐ Ted Osborne

Original Title *Mickey Mouse the Mail Pilot*
First published by King Features Syndicate (USA)
Creators Gottfredson (American, 1905–86); Osborne
(American, *c.*1900–68) **Genre** Humor, Adventure

Originally written by Walt Disney, with art by Ub Iwerks and Win Smith, the *Mickey Mouse* daily comic strip was taken over in 1930, soon after its inception, by newcomer artist Floyd Gottfredson. At first reluctant to take on the assignment, Gottfredson ended up staying on the strip until 1975. Until the mid-1950s, when the strip became a gag-a-day affair at the syndicate's request, *Mickey Mouse* was an adventure strip, and a rollicking good one at that.

In his 1933 serial *Mail Pilot*, Mickey Mouse is still the plucky little daredevil from the early cartoons. After Minnie suggests he find a respectable job, Mickey decides to become a mail pilot. After weeks of training under mechanic Gloomy and instructor Captain Doberman, Mickey is sent on his first mission and attacked by a gigantic spider that's been making airplanes disappear. The spider and its web turn out to be catching devices for an air pirate dirigible where old Mickey Mouse enemies Pete and Shyster have set up their own air kingdom, complete with a farm and the city of Plunderville. Mickey leads an air raid on the pirate dirigible, rescuing a captured Captain Doberman and the snatched pilots and stopping the villains.

Modern readers might not recognize the Mickey Mouse they know in this story. Like all of his prewar adventures, this is a wonderfully entertaining, memorable story, full of action and gags. It was also the inspiration for the most infamous attack on American postwar complacency in the form of the 1970s counter-cultural underground comix *Air Pirates Funnies*. **J-PJ**

White Boy 1933

✐✐ Garrett Price

First published by Chicago Tribune-New York
News Syndicate (USA)
Creator American (1896–1979)
Genre Western

In the early days of the comic strip, before the understanding of what the medium could do became codified and restrictive, there was always the possibility of something eccentric and unique appearing. Garrett Price's *White Boy* was one of those special strips.

The series was commissioned by the Chicago Tribune New York News Syndicate, which wanted a Western feature that might appeal to a young audience, but what it got was charming and profound. Price was an accomplished illustrator of newspapers and magazines such as *The New Yorker*, and brought with him a gift for subtle realism and elegant minimalism. The "White Boy" of the title was a teenager who had been captured by the Sioux, and was in turn recaptured by another tribe in the days of the old West. Price had a deep understanding of the West, and in his seemingly simple tales of the boy and his relationship with the tribe, particularly the pretty young squaw Starlight, he showed a great knowledge and appreciation of the life and lore of the Native Americans, a sympathetic approach that was rare for the time.

Price's artwork on the strip is expressively bold, imaginative, and almost poetic, with a beautiful sense of color. Sadly, the syndicate failed to appreciate its brilliance, and in 1935 updated the series to a contemporary ranch setting, renaming it *Skull Valley*. With even Price himself regarding the venture as a failure, it was canceled in 1936. Subsequent generations have come to regard its earlier incarnation as one of the medium's true masterpieces. **DR**

Brick Bradford 1933

✎ William Ritt   *✎✎* Clarence Gray

First published by King Features Syndicate (USA)
Creators Ritt (American, 1902–72);
Gray (American, 1911–57)
Genre Science fiction

Brick Bradford was created in 1933 by journalist William Ritt. Inspired perhaps by the success of *Buck Rogers*, Ritt penned an engaging blend of science and mythology which, despite taking a long time to make the transition from small town newspapers to America's big cities, was intelligent, thoughtful, and slightly more scientifically plausible than *Buck Rogers*. Should Brick's spaceship venture too close to the Sun, for instance, he resorts to electrically chilled oxygen to see him through. There were subatomic worlds here too, worlds within worlds waiting to be explored.

Then there was Brick's "Time Top," a device shaped like a spinning top that enabled its occupants to travel through time. Making its debut in 1937 after being glimpsed briefly in a Sunday feature two years earlier, it appeared in the larger-format Sunday strip (though not the dailies) and was the first time machine to make regular appearances in a comic strip, predating a similar device in *Alley Oop* by four years. The Sunday strip went on to become the main vehicle for Bradford's daring space adventures.

By the end of the 1940s, Ritt had tired of his creation and handed authorship of the strip to his illustrator, Clarence Gray, who continued to write and draw it until ill health forced him to retire in 1952. A self-confessed "oddball artist," Gray drew on a flat desk and could produce half a dozen strips in under five hours. Paul Norris of *Jungle Jim* fame took over until the strip's demise on April 25, 1987, bringing down the curtain on five decades of adventures in time and space. **BS**

A Week of Kindness 1934

✎✎ Max Ernst

Title in original language *Une semaine de bonté*
First published by Éditions Jeanne Bucher (France)
Creator German (1891–1976)
Genre Drama

In 1933, German Dadaist and surrealist painter Max Ernst spent a vacation near Piacenza, Italy, and produced his collage work *A Week of Kindness* while staying there. It has seven chapters split across five booklets and was produced from old French pulp novels and Gustave Doré's illustrations for Milton's *Paradise Lost*. Ernst was fascinated by how old-fashioned these wood engravings seemed compared to the photo-mechanical reproduction processes that were beginning to replace them.

A Week of Kindness is subtitled "Les sept elements capitaux—Roman" (The Seven Deadly Elements—A Novel). Not a "collage collection" or "a cycle," but "a novel," as in "graphic novel." Surrealism questioned the very notion of the novel—noted surrealist André Breton considered it bourgeois and predictable. *A Week of Kindness* is not a written novel. It is a novel in pictures: Max Ernst wanted to subvert the term "novel" and shock the literati.

While *A Week of Kindness* might be difficult to read in a conventional manner—there is no definitive interpretation—each individual booklet at least has a recurring character for the reader to follow: Belfort's Lion, Oedipus, the rooster, and the falling woman. The themes Ernst touches on are also fairly evident: tyranny—Hitler rose to power the year that he created his book (booklet one), male sexual desire (booklet two), private vices in bourgeois households (booklet three), revolution (booklet five), and violence; lots and lots of violence. **DI**

Max Ernst made great use of existing illustrations while assembling *A Week of Kindness*. ➡

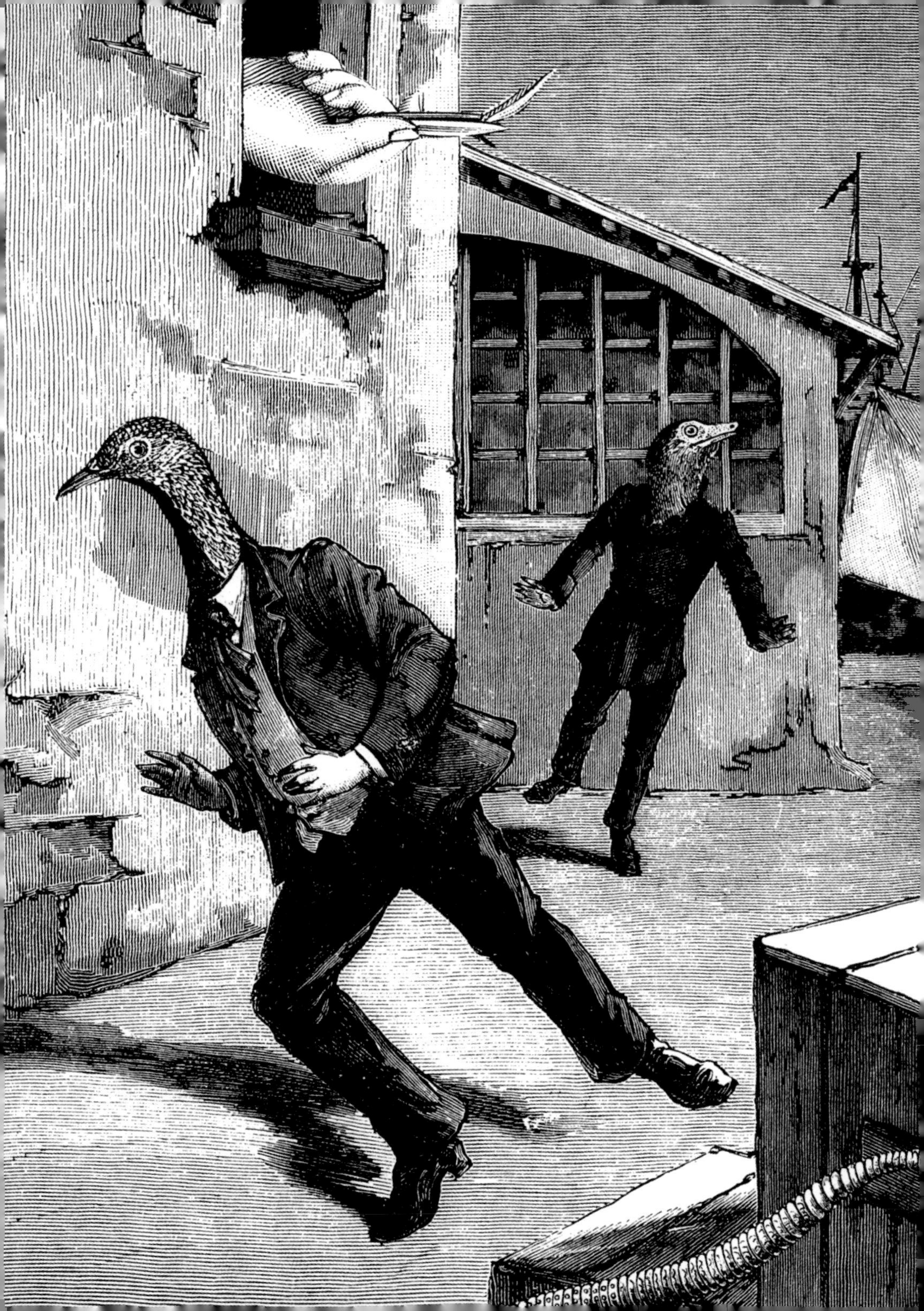

Terry and the Pirates 1934

Milton Caniff

No 18 OCT
TERRY
HOTSHOT
BURMA
TERRY
AND THE PIRATES
10¢
IN THIS ISSUE: MORE ALL-NEW HOTSHOT CHARLIE

"It wasn't just you who earned those wings . . . a ghostly echelon of good guys flew their hearts out in old kites to give you the know-how."

Colonel Corkin, *Terry and the Pirates*

Similar reads

Ballad of the Salt Sea Hugo Pratt
Male Call Milton Caniff
Scorchy Smith Noel Sickles

First published by Chicago Tribune-New York News Syndicate (USA)
Creator American (1907–88)
Genre Action, Adventure

Terry and the Pirates was the strip that made Milton Caniff famous. Charged with creating a story set in the Orient, the last romantic territory, Caniff enthralled readers with the adventures of Terry Lee, a bright young American lad who accompanies his older friend Pat Ryan to China in search of a gold mine.

Pat and Terry's right-handman, "Connie," is a Chinese caricature typical of the period, however the strip also had more progressive moments too: Terry's recurring love interest, April Kane, becomes a pilot in World War II. While the strips of the war years are less well regarded by some, their more patriotic bent won governmental praise and one (quoted in part, left) was even read out in the U.S. Congress.

Caniff left the strip in 1946 to create *Steve Canyon*, a strip he owned. George Wunder continued *Terry and the Pirates* until 1973, but his work was never as popular.

A big part of the appeal of Caniff's strips were his fascinating and beautifully rendered female characters, starting with the piratical Dragon Lady, the first of many mysterious villainesses. Later strong female characters included heiress Normandie Drake, Pat's true love who winds up married to a Nazi sympathizer, and Burma, a singer and con artist romantically involved with Terry.

Caniff used world events to provide a thrilling background for his characters' adventures, and after a few years of experimentation came into his own as a truly great adventure artist. His dramatic use of ink brought more life to a tiny black-and-white strip of squares than you'd think possible. **FJ**

Li'l Abner 1934

✐✐ Al Capp

First published by United Feature Syndicate (USA)
Creator Alfred Gerald Caplin (American, 1909–79)
Genre Humor, Adventure
Adaptation Film (1940 and 1959)

We were introduced to Li'l Abner as a six-foot-three, nineteen-year-old living in the hills with his Mammy and Pappy in Dogpatch, Kentucky. Seventeen-year-old Daisy Mae was clearly in love with him, but he considered her an "ornery no-account yaller-haired gal" and was generally repulsed by the thought of marriage.

His mother's sister, Beatrixe, Duchess of Bopshire, who has risen far from her hillbilly origins, invited Abner to New York to make a gentleman out of him. Before long, Abner found himself engaged to Mimi Van Pelt, the first of many brushes with matrimony.

Switching between Dogpatch and wherever Abner's next adventure took him, Capp built his strip on the humor to be found when mixing city and country manners and morals. Abner managed to avoid getting married until 1952, although he had many close shaves, especially on Sadie Hawkins Day, a day, invented by Capp in the strip in 1937, when women invite, or coerce, men to marry them. Other notable additions to *Li'l Abner* included a strip-within-a-strip *Fearless Fosdick*, a parody of Chester Gould's *Dick Tracy* in 1942, and the lovable and selfless creatures known as the Shmoos, created in 1948.

Abner's comedic adventures always enjoyed a good splash of danger, excitement, and romance, and as he introduced more fantasy elements Capp also played up the social and political satire, for instance with his version of Siberia, Lower Slobbovia. Mixing realism and caricature in his sharply inked artwork, Capp's characters are a delight. **NFI**

Betty Boop 1934

✐✐ Bud Counihan

First published by King Features Syndicate (USA)
Creator American (1894–1971)
Genre Humor
Adapted from Short films

Betty Boop debuted as a girlfriend to the dog-like Bimbo in "Dizzy Dishes," the sixth in the series of Talkartoon animated short features by Max Fleischer's Fleischer Studios in August 1930. Created to be a curvaceous cabaret singer, the character's decidedly canine appearance, with large teeth and dog-shaped ears, were a long way from the vampish Betty into which she soon evolved with pouting lips, curls, long eyelashes, short dresses, and flirtatious personality. Deemed too sexy by the Hays Production Code, a moral watchdog created in 1934 to "clean up" Hollywood's increasing "immorality," Betty's skirts were later lengthened and her overt sexuality was reined in. Effectively neutered, Betty was now a candidate for the comics pages of America's family-friendly newspapers.

In 1934, Fleischer Studios hired Bud Counihan, the creator of the 1920s strip *Little Napoleon*, to write and draw the new *Betty Boop* strip. Despite running for only twelve months as a daily, it continued until 1937 as a Sunday strip, which was for the most part single joke stories sprinkled with liberal doses of slapstick, Betty's adventures revolving round her younger brother Bubby and her own career as a budding actress. Sadly, the new strip was never destined to succeed with Betty, thanks to the Hays push for "decency," a sanitized version of the tempting siren she once was. Nevertheless Betty Boop has survived as one of the great sex symbols of animation and is still a role model for self-expression, a formidable achievement considering her all-too brief stay in the spotlight. **BS**

Father and Son 1934

✏️ "e.o.plauen"

Title in original language *Vater und Sohn*
First published by *Berliner Illustrierte Zeitung* (Germany)
Creator Erich Ohser (German, 1903–44)
Genre Humor

"Oh, who would not have gladly such a father?" **JS-Magazin**

Similar reads
Jimmy das Gummipferd Roland Kohlsaat
Nick Knatterton Manfred Schmidt

Father and Son is one of the most popular German comic strips, and has remained a classic with both young and old alike. It was on December 13, 1934 that the first comic strip of *Father and Son* was published in the *Berliner Illustrierte Zeitung*. Approximately 157 weekly episodes were published until December 1937, and, because of the comic's great popularity, they were reprinted each year in the form of an album.

Erich Ohser developed the silent comic strip under the pseudonym "e.o.plauen," which is made up of the initial letters of his first name and last name, followed by the town where he lived as a child. Ohser worked under a pseudonym because the National Socialists refused to admit him to the German journalists' and editors' union, effectively banning him from carrying out his profession. A political caricaturist for the Social Democratic Party newspaper *Vorwärts*, Ohser's ban came after he drew a cartoon of a man urinating in the snow to form the shape of a swastika.

The comic strip about the antiheroic pranks of the balding, plump father and his son soon became a resounding success. The lovable anarchic duo, with their childish jokes and penchant for making the authorities see red, was a pleasing alternative to the rigidity of everyday life under National Socialism. The simplified drawings and subtle humor did the rest.

Ohser's wordless sketches and discreet humor make the reader smile and laugh inwardly, but more importantly they stimulate reflection so that the drawings are not merely entertaining, but linger on in the reader's memory.

Ohser was arrested by the Gestapo in 1944 on the grounds of alleged defamation of Heinrich Himmler and Joseph Goebbels. Aware of the merciless sentencing of the People's Court, the artist took his own life in his cell on April 5, 1944, the day his trial was due to start. **MS**

Father and Son tackles daily life with gentle, slapstick humor. ➡

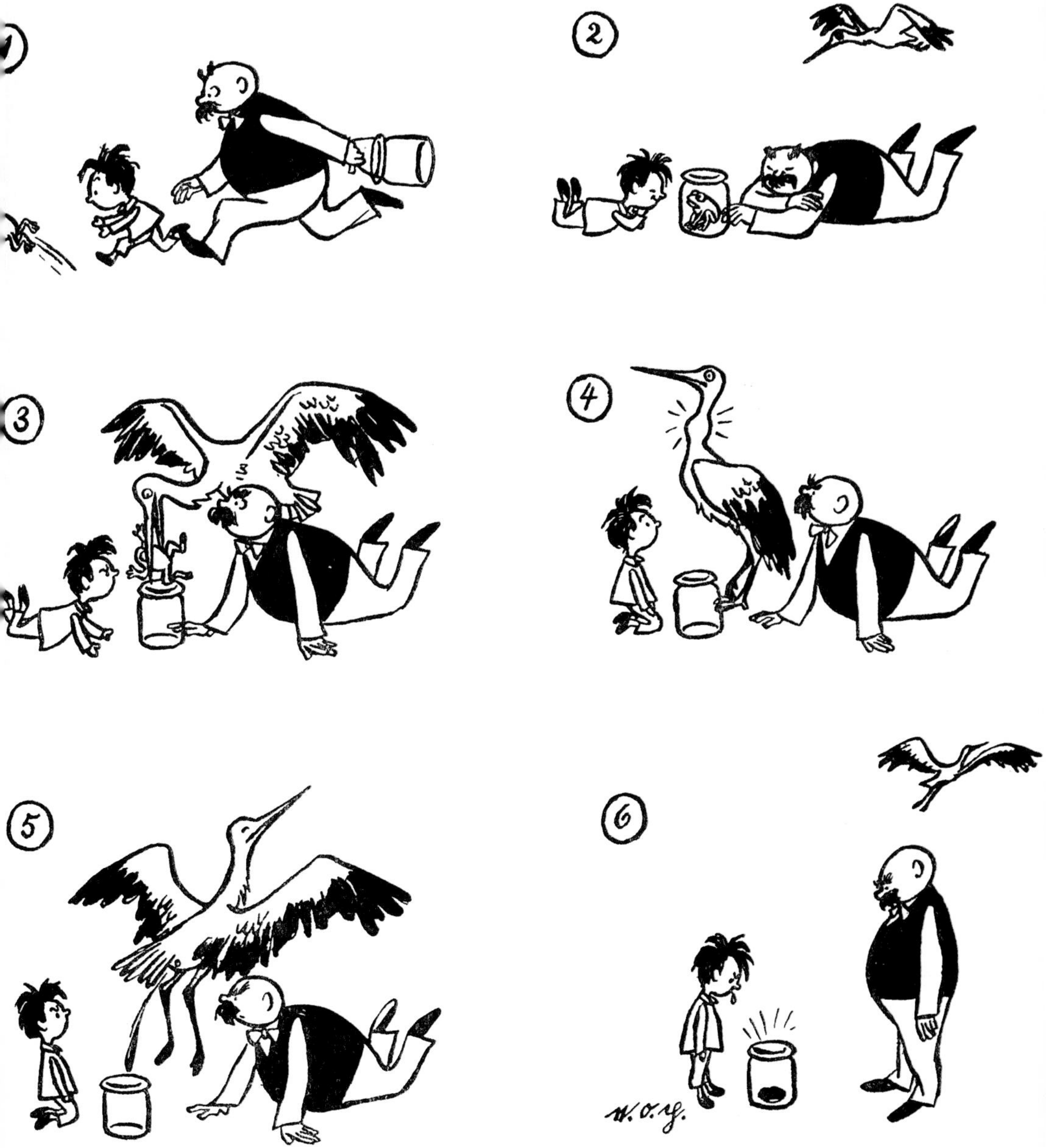
1
2
3
4
5
6

Mandrake the Magician 1934

Lee Falk Phil Davis

First published by *The New York Evening Journal* (USA)
Creators Falk (American, 1911–99);
Davis (American, 1906–64)
Genre Action, Adventure

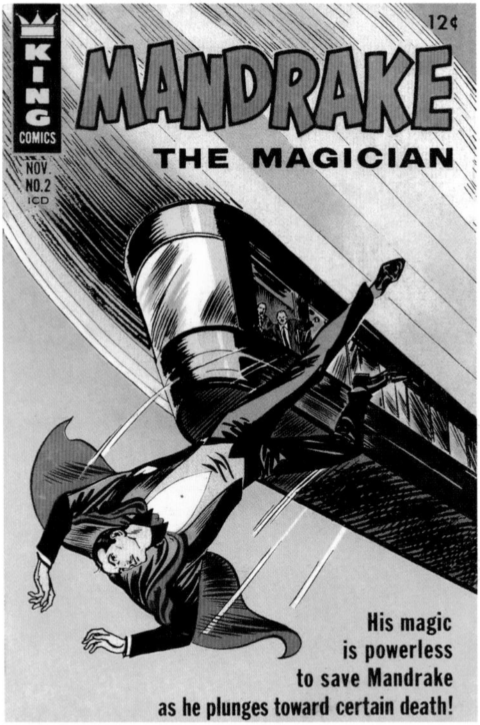
12¢
KING COMICS
MANDRAKE
THE MAGICIAN
NOV. NO.2
ICD
His magic is powerless to save Mandrake as he plunges toward certain death!

Similar reads
Dr Occult Jerry Siegel and Joe Shuster
Dr Strange Stan Lee and Steve Ditko
Merlin the Magician Don Zolnerowich
The Phantom Lee Falk

Lee Falk, the creator of *The Phantom*, was in his early twenties when he conceived the character of Mandrake, and when asked why the magician bore such a resemblance to its author, replied: "Of course he did. I was alone in a room with a mirror when I drew him."

Mandrake was based on Leon Mandrake, a Canadian magician who toured America in the 1920s. Falk drew the first two weeks' adventures, but his art was shaky and needed refining, so he enlisted the aid of illustrator Phil Davis. Davis took Falk's ill-proportioned figures and gave the strip a smooth, aesthetic rendering with realistic-looking characters. Together they created a forerunner of the comic book superhero, a master illusionist with supernatural powers and the ability to hypnotize his adversaries—and the only strip at the time that had a magician as its principal character.

"Mandrake gestures . . . the rifle seems to change into an umbrella!"

Mandrake's childhood was spent studying magic at Tibet's Collegium Magikos at the feet of his master Theron, who was, it would later be revealed, Mandrake's father. He settled in New York with Lothar, an African prince now serving as his valet and bodyguard, and Princess Narda, who became his fiancée and finally, in 1998, his wife.

In 1987, Mandrake appeared in Marvel's *Defenders of the Earth* comic, an adaptation of the 1986 animated TV series. This ambitious but doomed attempt to team him with The Phantom and Flash Gordon lasted just four issues. But Mandrake never needed to be part of a team to weave his magic. With his signature top hat, cape, walking cane, and wafer-thin moustache, he is both one of the most recognizable and dapper comic heroes of all time. **BS**

Secret Agent X-9 1934

Dashiell Hammett Alex Raymond

In the 1930s, Americans were seduced by the dark lure of gangsters and of the crime-busting law enforcement figures who fought them. In 1931, *The Chicago Tribune*'s *Dick Tracy* took the comic strip world by storm, and it wasn't long before publishing magnate, and the *Tribune*'s rival, William Randolph Hearst ordered up a tough, no-nonsense tough guy of his own—and he hired the best to give the strip life.

It is hard to think of a comic strip anywhere that began its run with a more enviable pedigree. Dashiell Hammett, the acclaimed mystery writer and author of *The Maltese Falcon*, would provide the words, and Alex Raymond, the creator and illustrator of a new strip called *Flash Gordon*, was hired to draw it. Sadly, however, it was a pairing that was never destined to prosper. Hammett left after just four stories and was replaced by Leslie Charteris, future author of *The Saint*. Raymond left in 1935 to focus on *Flash Gordon*.

"...the last time I saw you, you tried to hire a guy to kill me!"

Hammett seemed unclear if Agent X-9 was a spy, a detective, or a G-man. The character had no name, and it was deliberately vague on just which agency he worked for. It was a confused, muddled birth, and pity the poor reader. More writers and illustrators followed, notably Mel Graff, who provided art until the 1960s and gave Agent X-9 a personal life, various love interests, and a name: Phil Corrigan. Writer Archie Goodwin and illustrator Al Williamson brought fresh story lines and vivid visuals from 1967 to 1980, though despite Williamson's beautiful, atmospheric line drawings, a high water mark in American comics, the strip still failed to achieve massive popular success and the last issue appeared on February 10, 1996. **BS**

First published by King Features Syndicate (USA)
Creators Hammett (American, 1894–1961); Raymond (American, 1909–56)
Genre Crime, Action, Adventure

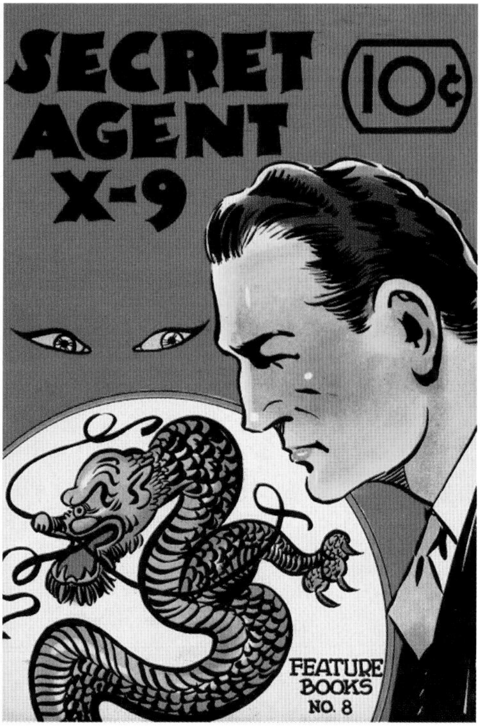
SECRET AGENT X-9
10¢
FEATURE BOOKS NO. 8

Similar reads

Dan Dunn Norman Marsh
Detective Comics Malcolm Wheeler-Nicholson
Dick Tracy Chester Gould
Red Barry Will Gould

Tank Tankoru 1934

Gajo Sakamoto

Title in original language *Tanku Tankuro*
First published by Yonen Club (Japan)
Creator Japanese (1895–1973)
Genre Fantasy

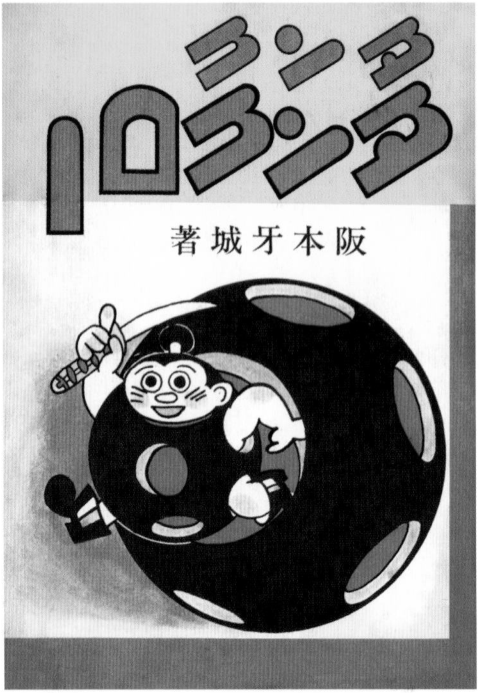
タンク・タンクロー
阪本牙城著

Similar reads
Boken Dankichi Keizo Shimada
Garagara Sensei Gajo Sakamoto
Kasei Tenken Taro Asahi and Noboru Oshiro
Marukaku-san Chyonsuke-san Shigewo Miyao
Norakuro Suiho Tagawa

Masaki Sakamoto's dream was to become a painter, but when his parents opposed this, he became a teacher. Undeterred, he studied painting in Tokyo, where he met Okamoto Ippei, a painter turned comic artist, at the first exhibition of the cartoonists' group Manga-kai; Ippei encouraged Sakamoto to take up comics himself. After a few years of creating a samurai serial in four-panel strips for newspapers, he broke out into longer, whole-page stories for Kodansha's monthly *Yonen Kurubu* (*Younger Children's Club*). Tank Tankoro is a large black iron ball with eight openings, like a bowling ball or tortoise shell, from which its human inhabitant can protrude his arms, legs, and head, and provide surprises to solve every emergency.

"To children, he must have looked like a chest full of toys."

Gajo Sakamoto

In "Man-Cannon Wind-Cannon," Tank is grabbed aloft by a magnet but escapes by popping out a pistol to shatter the chain, and wings and machine guns to become a plane. His persistent nemesis, Kuro-kabuto, eyes peering out of a shoulder-length helmet, retaliates with an egg-shaped cannonball full of troops and tanks shaped like elephants, whales, and tigers. Tank rescues his men by sprinkling water that freezes the tanks, but then the enemy's wind-cannon blows them all away, turning them into snowballs frozen onto a cliff.

Sakamoto enjoys breaking free from framed panels and unleashing spreads of crazy combat. Although tinged with the period's militarism, *Tank Tankoro* retains a charming surrealism and pioneered manga's robot obsession, influencing *Astro Boy*, *Doraemon*, and more. He also became the mascot for Sakamoto's hometown, Itukaichi, and NASA's reusable Space Flyer Unit. **PG**

Tank Tankoru, as a warplane, causes mayhem on the ground. ➡

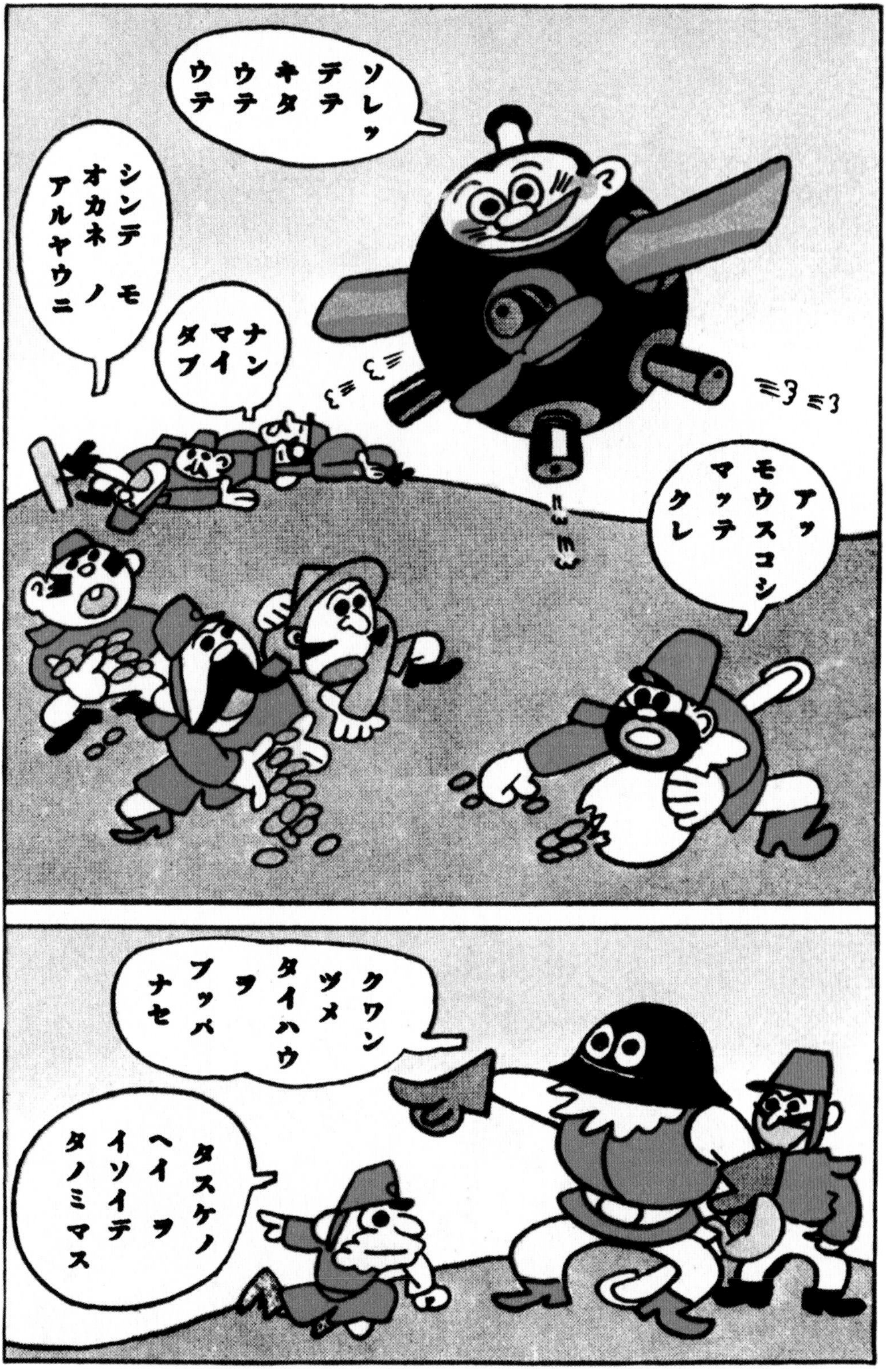
ソレッ デテ キタ ウテ ウテ
シンデ モ オカネ ノ アルヤウニ
ナン マイン ダブ
アッ モウスコシ マッテ クレ
クワン ツメ タイハウ ヲ ブッパ ナセ
タスケノ ヘイ ヲ イソイデ タノミマス

Flash Gordon 1934

Alex Raymond   Don Moore

First published by King Features Syndicate (USA)
Creators Raymond (American, 1909–56); Moore (American, 1905–86)
Genre Science fiction, Action, Adventure

Flash Gordon was not the only science fiction strip to follow the hugely successful *Buck Rogers*, but it was undoubtedly the best, and even outsold Buck's tales. Star American athlete Flash teams up with the lovely, gallant Dale Arden and scientific genius Dr. Zarkoff to travel to the planet Mongo, which threatens to destroy the Earth. Flash's struggles against its evil emperor Ming, while encountering the many exotic races populating Mongo's skies, forests, icy regions, and oceans, provided most of the action of Alex Raymond's fabulous run on the lush Sunday strips.

While Raymond soon employed Don Moore to write the strip, *Flash Gordon*'s main attraction was Raymond's artwork, and he is widely held to be the most imitated artist in American comics. With a full-color, full-size newspaper page on which to display his considerable illustration skills, Raymond started competently in 1934, then rapidly evolved his style. He reached amazing heights from 1938 to 1942, although for some modern readers his work lacks a flowing visual narrative. Raymond's last *Flash Gordon* was in 1944, when he enlisted in the U.S. Marines. In 1946 he returned to comics with a strip called *Rip Kirby*.

The early *Flash Gordon* pages had an additional topper strip drawn by Raymond, *Jungle Jim*, which was successful in its own right. *Flash Gordon* continued long after Raymond left, initially under Austin Briggs. Mac Raboy had a much-admired run as artist of the Sundays from 1948 to 1967, after which the strip seldom reached the the thrilling heights it once scaled. **GL**

MINGO IS A CITY OF FIESTA AND CARNIVAL, MADLY CHEERING "FLASH AND FREEDOM!" IN WILD JOY OVER THE END OF MING'S CRUEL REIGN.

Victory on Mongo is short-lived as Ming soon escapes! ➡

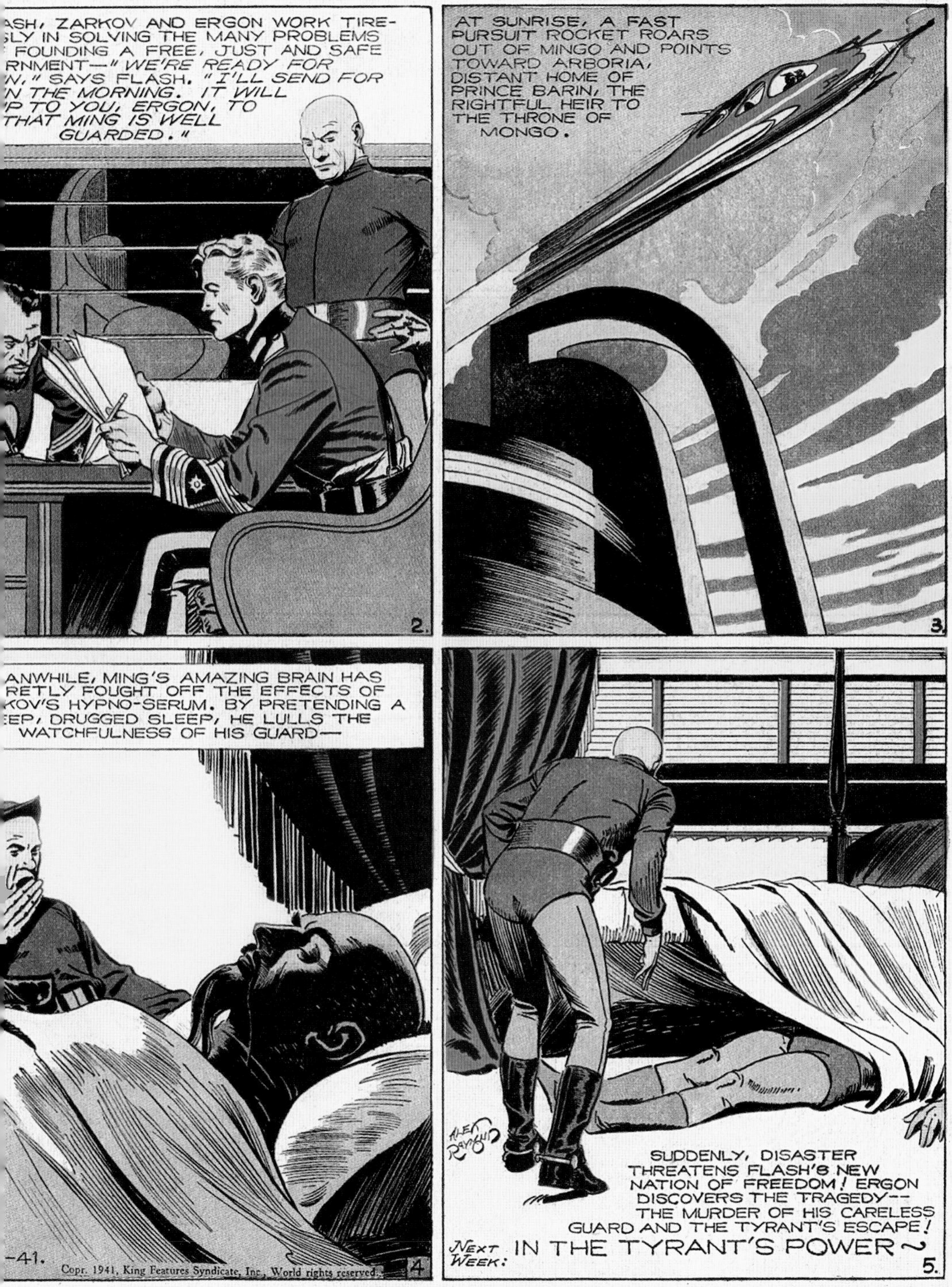
ASH, ZARKOV AND ERGON WORK TIRE-SLY IN SOLVING THE MANY PROBLEMS FOUNDING A FREE, JUST AND SAFE RNMENT—"WE'RE READY FOR N," SAYS FLASH. "I'LL SEND FOR N THE MORNING. IT WILL P TO YOU, ERGON, TO THAT MING IS WELL GUARDED."
2.
AT SUNRISE, A FAST PURSUIT ROCKET ROARS OUT OF MINGO AND POINTS TOWARD ARBORIA, DISTANT HOME OF PRINCE BARIN, THE RIGHTFUL HEIR TO THE THRONE OF MONGO.
3.
ANWHILE, MING'S AMAZING BRAIN HAS RETLY FOUGHT OFF THE EFFECTS OF KOV'S HYPNO-SERUM. BY PRETENDING A EEP, DRUGGED SLEEP, HE LULLS THE WATCHFULNESS OF HIS GUARD—
-41.
Copr. 1941, King Features Syndicate, Inc., World rights reserved.
4
ALEX RAYMOND
SUDDENLY, DISASTER THREATENS FLASH'S NEW NATION OF FREEDOM! ERGON DISCOVERS THE TRAGEDY-- THE MURDER OF HIS CARELESS GUARD AND THE TYRANT'S ESCAPE!
NEXT WEEK: IN THE TYRANT'S POWER ~
5.

Adventures of Tintin
The Blue Lotus 1934

"Hergé"

Title in original language *Le Lotus bleu*
First published by *Le Petit Vingtième* (Belgium)
Creator Georges Prosper Remi Remi (Belgian, 1907–83)
Genre Adventure

Having cut his teeth on strips such as *Quick and Flupke*, the Belgian bilingual artist Hergé created his first masterpiece in *The Blue Lotus*. For the first time, Hergé no longer simply relied on jokes, gags, and adventures to develop a story. *The Blue Lotus* is simultaneously dense, rich, human, and full of adventure, and for the first time the plot was explicitly inspired by a topical event—the Sino-Japanese conflict.

Lured to China by a mysterious Asian messenger who is hit by a dart of rajaijah, "the poison which makes you mad," Tintin arrives in Shanghai. The victim of several aggressive acts from the moment he sets foot in China, he makes contact with a secret Chinese society, the Sons of the Dragon, which is trying to disrupt the opium trade organized in China by a Japanese spy, Mitsuhirato, and whose drug-running nerve-center in Shanghai is an opium den called The Blue Lotus.

Having joined this noble cause, and determined to find the antidote for the terrible rajaijah, Tintin sets off in pursuit of Mitsuhirato and his drug-running thugs. On his travels Tintin often shows deep compassion for the suffering of the Chinese people. He witnesses sabotage operations led by the Japanese spy that result in part of China being invaded by Japanese troops. He is betrayed, imprisoned, tracked down, and in danger on numerous occasions, but the young reporter finally succeeds in foiling his enemies.

The Blue Lotus is the first true demonstration of Hergé's genius, energy, and inventiveness as an illustrator; his work remains unequaled today. **NF**

Patoruzú 1935

Dante Quinterno

Title in original language *Patoruzú*
First published by *Diario El Mundo* (Argentina)
Creator Argentinian (1909–2003)
Genre Humor, Adventure

Maradona, Gardel, Perón, and, of course, Patoruzú. The poker game of Argentinian chauvinists would never be complete without its poncho-wearing ace, the car-stealing and do-gooder aboriginal Patoruzú, created in 1928 by Dante Quinterno. From the comic strip's geometric, strong line, reminiscent of Chic Young of *Blondie*, to its definitive and iconic imagery (a mixture, in comedy as well as graphic style, of the Disney cartooning school and the facial gestures of Uderzó's characters), *Patoruzú* has become the most representative of Argentinian creations. Beginning as a second-string character in the daily strip *Las aventuras de Don Gil Contento*, Patoruzú was able to express the political and editorial complexities of Argentina.

Patoruzú's adventures and folkloric slang are tattooed into Argentina's day-to-day existence. At different times during the 1970s—the last decade of original *Patoruzú* stories—the historic World Cartoon Biennial and Argentina's bloodiest dictatorship both wanted the character as a emblem; sadly, the latter got it. That complexity is a part of the *Patoruzú* myth.

Quinterno's "perfect man among human imperfection" was an ideal, of Quinterno's skills and ambitions as well as of a comic era and its lifespan. *Patoruzú*, reprinted monthly in Argentina from the late 1970s, has become the last of the Mohicans, the last classic Argentinian comic where personalities are defined by physical features, where a screwball timing and use of space reigns, and where a sense of ingenuity is the best compass for a comic adventure. **JMD**

Zig and Puce in the 21st Century 1935

Alain Saint-Ogan

Title in original language *Zig et Puce au XXIème Siècle*
First published by *Dimanche Illustré* (France)
Creator French (1895–1974)
Genre Children's

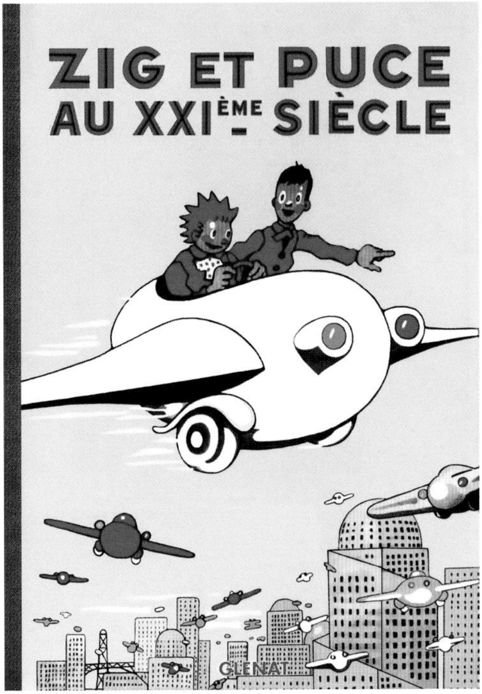
ZIG ET PUCE
AU XXIÈME SIÈCLE
GLÉNAT

Zig and Puce in the 21st Century is the ninth and best known of Alain Saint-Ogan's series, which traces the continually thwarted attempts of two young boys, often accompanied by a talking penguin named Alfred, to reach America and become millionaires. Making its first appearance in 1925 in the children's Sunday supplement *Le Dimanche Illustré*, the series quickly made its mark on French comics history, both in its huge success and as the first French series to regularly use speech bubbles.

Published in album format in 1935, *Zig and Puce in the 21st Century* is a rare early example of science fiction in French comics. The forty-six-page narrative recounts the story of the boys' accidental transportation into the future. Landing their hot-air balloon in the Paris of December 2000—a city with two Eiffel towers and a population that hovers above the ground on jetpacks—the young temporal tourists find themselves caught in a series of adventures, from incarceration in a mental institution to their accidental theft of a submarine, before finally being blasted into space in a rocket and discovering sentient life on Venus.

Aesthetically, with its dramatic, staccato changes in the young heros' fortunes, time periods, and locations, *Zig and Puce in the 21st Century* is a work of unwavering precision and linearity. Bearing muted influences of Art Deco and favoring clear lines and block shades, the album (and the series to which it belongs) is an early masterpiece of the Franco-Belgian aesthetic, one that would go on to inspire Hergé and the development of the classic *ligne claire* (clear line) form. **CMac**

"How is it possible that we've arrived in the year 2000?... If we were in the year 2000 we would be more than 80 years old and frankly, we don't look it!"

Similar reads
Blake and Mortimer: The Yellow "M" (*La marque jaune*) Edgar P. Jacobs
Zig and Puce on Venus Alain Saint-Ogan

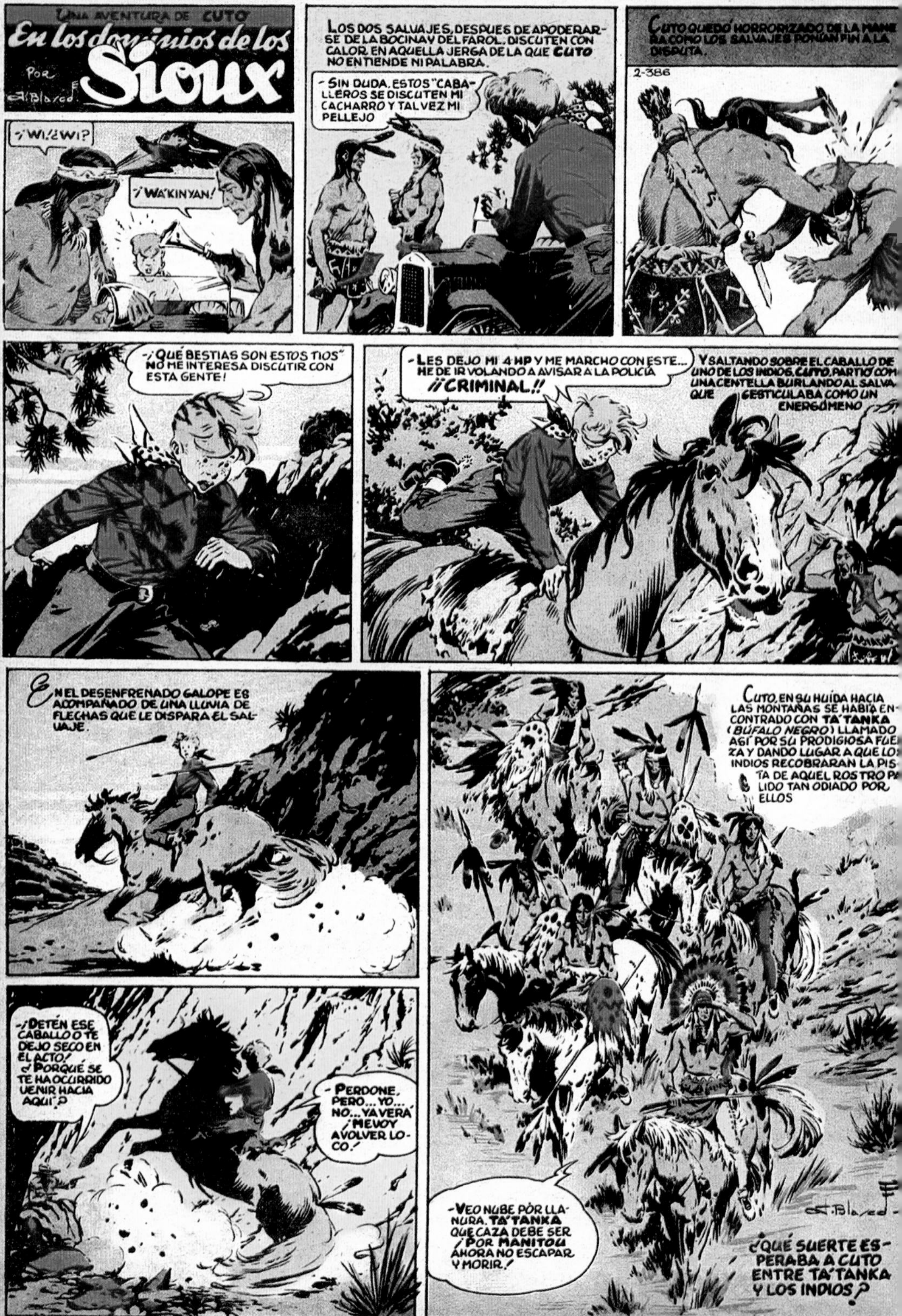

UNA AVENTURA DE CUTO
En los dominios de los Sioux
POR A. Blasco
¿WI, ¿WI?
¡WA'KINYAN!
LOS DOS SALVAJES, DESPUES DE APODERARSE DE LA BOCINA Y DEL FAROL, DISCUTEN CON CALOR EN AQUELLA JERGA DE LA QUE CUTO NO ENTIENDE NI PALABRA.
-SIN DUDA, ESTOS "CABALLEROS SE DISCUTEN MI CACHARRO Y TAL VEZ MI PELLEJO
CUTO QUEDÓ HORRORIZADO DE LA MANERA COMO LOS SALVAJES PONÍAN FIN A LA DISPUTA.
2-386
-¡QUÉ BESTIAS SON ESTOS TIOS" NO ME INTERESA DISCUTIR CON ESTA GENTE!
-LES DEJO MI 4 HP Y ME MARCHO CON ESTE... HE DE IR VOLANDO A AVISAR A LA POLICÍA ¡¡CRIMINAL!!
Y SALTANDO SOBRE EL CABALLO DE UNO DE LOS INDIOS, CUTO, PARTIÓ COMO UNA CENTELLA BURLANDO AL SALVAJE QUE GESTICULABA COMO UN ENERGÚMENO
EN EL DESENFRENADO GALOPE ES ACOMPAÑADO DE UNA LLUVIA DE FLECHAS QUE LE DISPARA EL SALVAJE.
-¡DETÉN ESE CABALLO O TE DEJO SECO EN EL ACTO! ¿PORQUÉ SE TE HA OCURRIDO VENIR HACIA AQUÍ?
-PERDONE, PERO... YO... NO... YA VERÁ ¡ME VOY A VOLVER LOCO!
CUTO, EN SU HUÍDA HACIA LAS MONTAÑAS SE HABÍA ENCONTRADO CON TA'TANKA (BÚFALO NEGRO) LLAMADO ASÍ POR SU PRODIGIOSA FUERZA Y DANDO LUGAR A QUE LOS INDIOS RECOBRARAN LA PISTA DE AQUEL ROSTRO PÁLIDO TAN ODIADO POR ELLOS
-VEO NUBE POR LLANURA, TA'TANKA QUE CAZA DEBE SER ¡POR MANITOU AHORA NO ESCAPAR Y MORIR!
A. Blasco
¿QUÉ SUERTE ESPERABA A CUTO ENTRE TA'TANKA Y LOS INDIOS?

Cuto 1935

✏️ Jesús Blasco

First published by *Boliche* (Spain)
Creator Spanish (1919–95)
Genre Adventure
Influence on TV: *The Mysterious Cities of Gold* (1982)

Cuto is an adventure strip created by the legendary Spanish comic creator Jesús Blasco. The title character, for whom Blasco adapted the physical features of his younger brother, Alejandro, first appeared in one-page gag strips in the comic *Boliche* as the leader of a gang of mischievous kids. While this first incarnation of Cuto was short-lived, Blasco reintroduced him in 1940, in the pages of the comic weekly *Chicos*, this time as an adventure hero, drawn in a realistic style.

Like Hergé's Tintin, Cuto was a teenage boy with no known relatives, freely living all kind of adventures around the world. Blasco couples a nearly perfect command of human-figure drawing with a mastery of action poses and a heart-throbbing narrative rhythm. *Cuto* became a popular success among the children of post–Civil War Spain, particularly during the most austere years of Franco's dictatorship. The series reached its peak between 1945 and 1947, when Cuto's two most famous stories were serialized in *Chicos*: "Tragedy in the East" (set in Tibet) and "In the Domains of the Sioux" (a Wild West story). The former, involving an evil Asian dictator, is a heartfelt statement on the horrors of war, and some have considered certain scenes as an allegory of the bombing of Guernica.

Later *Cuto* stories showed some decline, with the character finally leaving *Chicos* in 1951, although Blasco would revive him again sporadically in other periodicals (such as *Chito* in 1974). *Cuto* is today regarded almost unanimously by fans and scholars alike as among the higher masterworks in Spanish comics. **AMo**

Smokey Stover 1935

✏️ Bill Holman

First published by Chicago Tribune Syndicate (USA)
Creator American (1903–87)
Genre Humor
Adaptation TV animation: *Archie's TV Funnies* (1971)

Smokey Stover made its debut when gag-packed screwball humor was the fashion in the 1930s, yet it outlived the fashion by decades due to Bill Holman's continuing inventiveness.

Smokestack Stover was a fireman seemingly recruited from the Keystone Kops. A gangling, awkward youth, he drove to blazes in his two-wheeled "Foomobile," an impossible vehicle resembling a motorcycle sidecar, yet often seating two.

Ever-shifting visual surrealism was a hallmark of the strip. One week Chief Cash U. Nutt's desk would be stabilized by a large foot with a plant growing from the big toe, while the chief sat on a hand extended from beneath, while the next he'd be propped on a stool balanced by an outstretched hand on the floor.

In terms of its script, the strip depended on quick-witted fast-fired gags, inventive language, and plenty of puns. Holman loved his puns and packed his strips with them, verbal and visual, leading to an unusually dense read. The sheer level of intensity, though, was beyond even Holman on a daily basis, and for most of its run *Smokey Stover* appeared only on Sundays. The strip was dependent on his unique mind, and when he retired no one could succeed him.

Holman claimed the British humor magazine *Punch* as a key influence, but he hands us a legacy of his own: his mangled term for firefighters—"foofighters"—was adopted by pilots to describe U.F.O.s in the 1940s, from where it was adopted by the globally successful band of the same name in the 1990s. **FP**

← Cuto escapes a threatening situation—or does he?

Super Whiz Kids 1936

✐✐ Germán Butze

Title in original language *Los Supersabios*
First published by Publicaciones Herrerías (Mexico)
Creator Mexican (1912–74)
Genre Humor

Super Whiz Kids started as a comic strip in 1936, becoming a digest-sized, stand-alone, full-color, bi-weekly (and later weekly) comic book in 1953.

Germán Butze was deeply influenced by comic strips in the American Sunday papers. He developed an innocent and friendly cast of characters, where family dynamics, science, creativity, urban living, and social realism combined in a heartwarming, bittersweet tragicomedy. The series was unique because, rather than dealing with crime, adventure, sport, or the supernatural, it focused on three friends, Paco, Pepe, and Panza, and particularly on the life of Panza Piñón. As young scientists, Paco and Pepe have two main foes, the mad scientist "El Loco Solomillo" and Don Seve, Panza's grumpy grandfather.

Full of humor and lessons on the value of friendship, *Super Whiz Kids* told stories that offered tremendous insight into the social dynamics of urban, middle-class Mexico of the time, in which talented youngsters living with extended families had to contend with reactionary attitudes. Butze labored painstakingly on his pages, relied on extensive research for visual references, and aspired to literary craft and visual excellence. Although he tried to do the lettering himself, the issues contained pages with mechanical fonts on those occasions when Butze was unable to do them on time. Comparable to Gabriel Vargas's *Familia Burrón* (apart from that lack of consistency regarding the lettering, the complete original series represents one of the all-time best humorous comics for all audiences. **EPr**

The Broons 1936

✐ R. D. Low   ✐ Dudley D. Watkins

First published by D. C. Thomson (UK)
Creators Low (British, 1895–1980);
Watkins (British, 1907–69)
Genre Humor

The full-page comic strip *The Broons* (the Browns in English) made its debut in the Scottish newspaper *The Sunday Post* on March 8, 1936, and still appears there every week. Created by Robert Duncan Low and illustrated by the great English strip artist Dudley Dexter Watkins until his death in 1969, the Broons are a large, close-knit family of robust comic archetypes. There's Pa Broon, working man and put-upon patriarch; Ma Broon, the apron-wearing housewife; and their brood of eight children: muscular Joe, beanpole Hen (short for Henry), glamorous Maggie, Daphne the frump, Horace the swot, the identical boy twins, and the curly haired Bairn, a wise-beyond-her-years little girl who is particularly close to Grandpa Broon. The strip's dialogue, rendered in a unique regional patter, includes archaic expressions like "Jings!" and "Crivvens." R. D. Low had a broad Scottish accent, and he wrote just as he spoke.

The Broons live in tenement housing on Glebe Street, in a fictional city that appears to combine elements of Dundee (hometown of *Broons* publisher D. C. Thomson), Glasgow, and Edinburgh. They also spend time at their country cottage, called the "But An' Ben." Dudley Watkins's flair for depicting both rural and urban landscapes in a detailed, largely realistic style helped to anchor the semigrotesque cast of characters and their farcical escapades in something approaching the real world. Read nowadays, these same classic *Broons* strips offer a charming, nostalgic vision of the past, one where tradition and family comically collide with all the change and chaos of modernity. **AL**

The Phantom 1936

Lee Falk Ray Moore

First published by King Features Syndicate (USA)
Creators Falk (American, 1911–99); Moore (American, 1905–84)
Genre Adventure

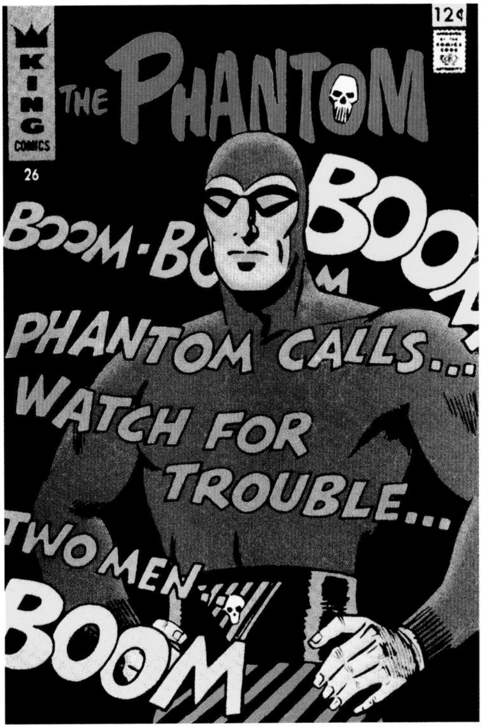
KING COMICS
12¢
THE PHANTOM
26
BOOM-BOOM
BOOM
PHANTOM CALLS...
WATCH FOR TROUBLE...
TWO MEN-
BOOM

The reputation of most newspaper strip creators rests on a single long-running feature, but Lee Falk created two, following *Mandrake the Magician* with *The Phantom*. Both have run continuously for seventy-five years.

Like Mandrake, The Phantom was a costumed adventurer, a forerunner to later comic book superheroes. His mythology included several novel concepts. Unknown to most, a dynasty of Phantoms was established in the sixteenth century by Christopher Walker, seemingly passing immortality and the title of "The Ghost Who Walks" down from father to son. The Phantom's calling cards were signet rings, one of which scars enemies with a skull imprint, while the other indicated those under his protection. He could also call on the services of a cadre of loyal warriors called the Jungle Patrol when required.

The character introduced in 1936 was the twenty first to assume the identity. Like his ancestors, Kit Walker operated from Skull Cave in Bengalla, a base that shifted its location from Asia to Africa in the 1960s.

Falk drew the first *Phantom* strips before employing a succession of artists, the most notable of whom was Sy Barry from 1962 to 1994. Falk, however, continued to write the strip until his death in 1999.

While undeniably popular in America, there are pockets of the world where the character's longevity and fanbase is astounding, particularly Scandinavia. Since Falk's death the Swedish publisher Egmont has recreated the American newspaper strip, often adapting stories from their licenced line of *Phantom* comics. **FP**

"Today, as always before, striking suddenly, mysteriously, the Phantom works alone."

Similar reads
Diabolik Various
Skull and Bones Ed Hannigan
The Panther Paul Wheelahan
The Question Steve Ditko
The Shadow Denny O'Neil and Mike Kaluta

Desperate Dan 1937

✎ Albert Barnes   ✎ Dudley D. Watkins

First published by D. C. Thomson (UK)
Creator Barnes (British, 1911–82);
Watkins (British, 1907–69)
Genre Humor

Desperate Dan, "the cowpoke from Cactusville," is the world's roughest, toughest cowboy. He's also one of the true iconic heroes of British comics, making his debut in the very first issue of the weekly comic *The Dandy*, dated December 4, 1937, and still appearing in the comic to this very day. To begin with he was an out-and-out villain, but the more familiar Dan quickly took over, still big and brash but now also brave, good-hearted, and utterly devoted to his Aunt Aggie.

At around the same time, the comic's overriding concentration on gigantism and impossible feats of strength as sources of humor also fell neatly into place. Typically we see Dan shaving off his stubble with the aid of a blowtorch, turning a lamppost into a flute, or riding a steamroller like a bicycle. His desire to help the weak and unfortunate is matched only by his appetite for Cow Pie, complete with horns sticking out of the crust.

The global popularity of the Western genre made the cowboy, epitomized by John Wayne, an obvious candidate for comic strip heroism, but Desperate Dan is a truly Scottish variation on a theme. Dan's hometown of Cactusville is equal parts Dundee and Texas, a neverneverland where it's not unusual to see a Native American chief sitting outside a High Street butcher's shop. English artist Dudley D. Watkins was an artist who somehow combined the detailed, realistic depiction of objects and locations with comically exaggerated faces and figures—and all in the same panel. It is this artful balance between the everyday and the fantastic that makes *Desperate Dan* such a charming read. **AL**

Prince Valiant 1937

✎✎ Hal Foster

First published by King Features Syndicate (USA)
Creator American (1892–1982)
Genre Adventure
Adaptation Film (1954)

To the unknowing, Hal Foster would seem at a career pinnacle in 1934. Aged thirty-six and acclaimed for his prodigious talent, he had been the artist of the Sunday newspaper strip *Tarzan* for three years. Foster was unhappy, though, with the quality of the scripts he illustrated, and felt his income was not commensurate with the prestige and circulation of the strip, from which author Edgar Rice Burroughs earned much more.

He resolved to create a feature from which he'd earn the bulk of the generated income. *Prince Valiant* would not appear until 1937, but he began it three years beforehand. An early decision was to give his new strip a historical setting at a time when the popularity of *Buck Rogers* and *Flash Gordon*'s futurism was peaking.

The enthused Foster stunned from the start, improved notably over the next five years, then settled in for decades of unsurpassed excellence. Valiant adventured across the Arthurian world, spreading nobility and common sense, while Foster's panoramic landscapes and meticulous depiction of pageantry, battle, and ordinary life was never skimped.

Collected editions reveal a formula to Foster's plots, but individual stories still read extremely well. Foster had introduced his distinctive text-beneath-illustration style in *Tarzan*, and an innovation for *Valiant* was letting his cast age over the course of the strip. By the time he handed over the art to John Cullen Murphy in 1972, former bachelor Val was married with four children. Foster continued writing *Prince Valiant* until 1980, his stories having thrilled for more than forty years. **FP**

Touches of irony enlivened Foster's script for *Prince Valiant*. ➡

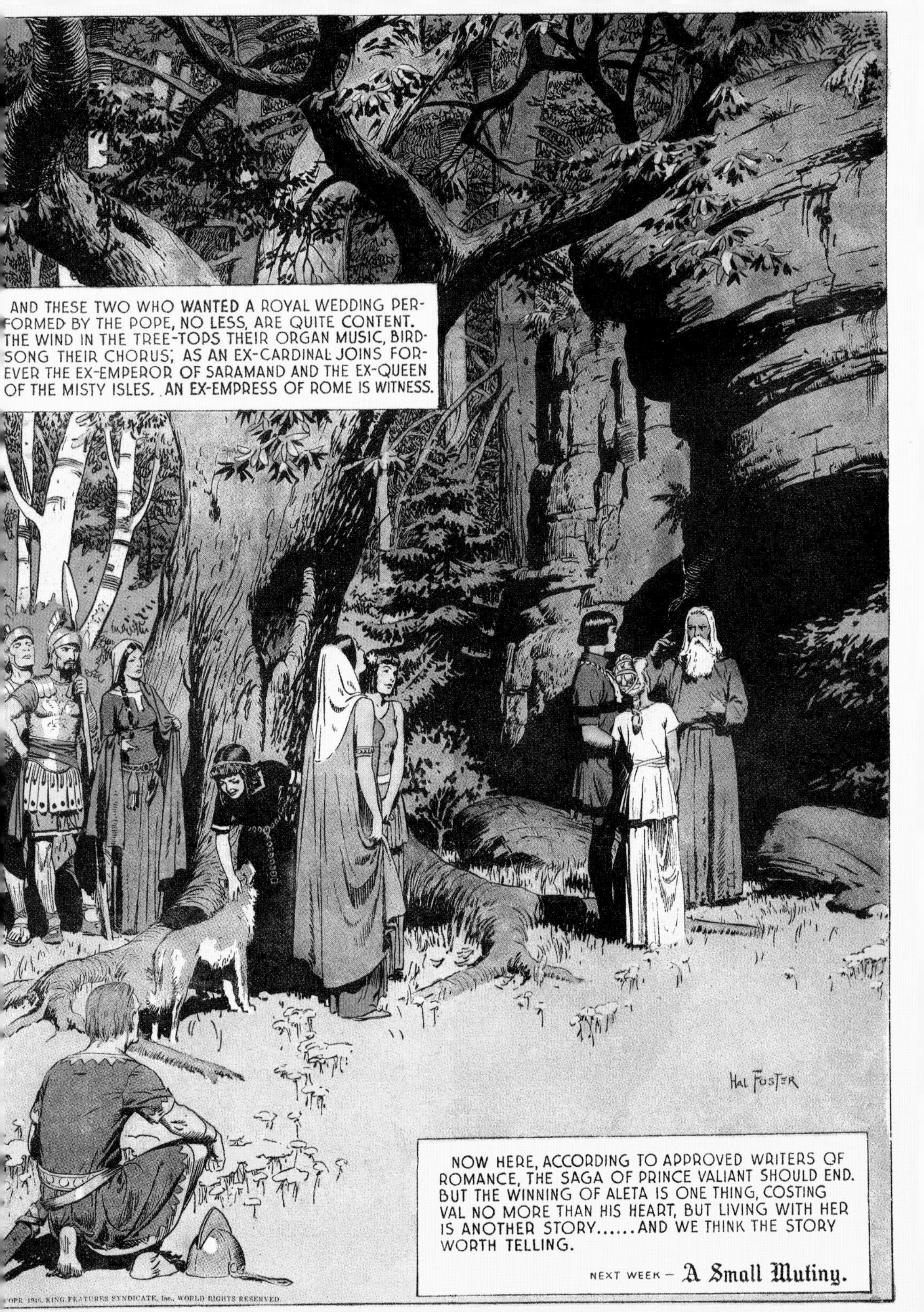
AND THESE TWO WHO WANTED A ROYAL WEDDING PERFORMED BY THE POPE, NO LESS, ARE QUITE CONTENT. THE WIND IN THE TREE-TOPS THEIR ORGAN MUSIC, BIRDSONG THEIR CHORUS; AS AN EX-CARDINAL JOINS FOREVER THE EX-EMPEROR OF SARAMAND AND THE EX-QUEEN OF THE MISTY ISLES. AN EX-EMPRESS OF ROME IS WITNESS.
HAL FOSTER
NOW HERE, ACCORDING TO APPROVED WRITERS OF ROMANCE, THE SAGA OF PRINCE VALIANT SHOULD END. BUT THE WINNING OF ALETA IS ONE THING, COSTING VAL NO MORE THAN HIS HEART, BUT LIVING WITH HER IS ANOTHER STORY...... AND WE THINK THE STORY WORTH TELLING.
NEXT WEEK — A Small Mutiny.
COPR. 1946, KING FEATURES SYNDICATE, Inc., WORLD RIGHTS RESERVED.

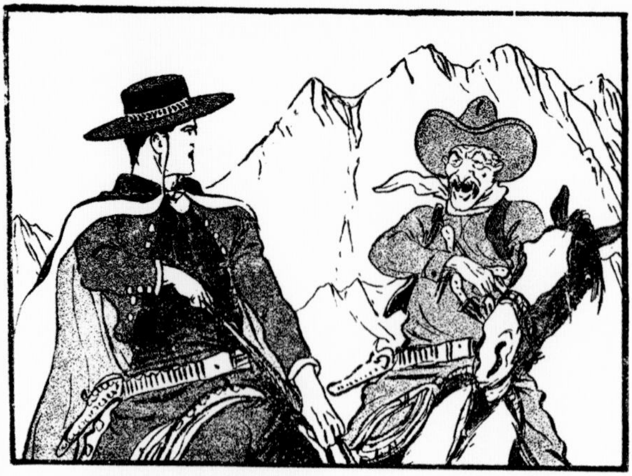

Odjednom je Crni Jahač naglo zaustavio konja i prodirno pogledao starca: »Bojiš li se smrti, Old Mickey?«

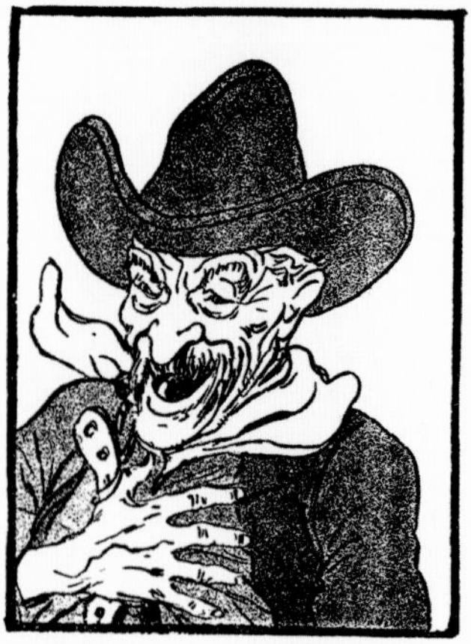

»Ja? Ha-ha-ha! Ja da se bojim smrti?!«

I TADA DV
JICA NAJ-
ODVAŽNIJI
LOVACA
DIVLJEG ZA
PADA STVO
RIŠE FAN-
TASTIČNU
ODLUKU

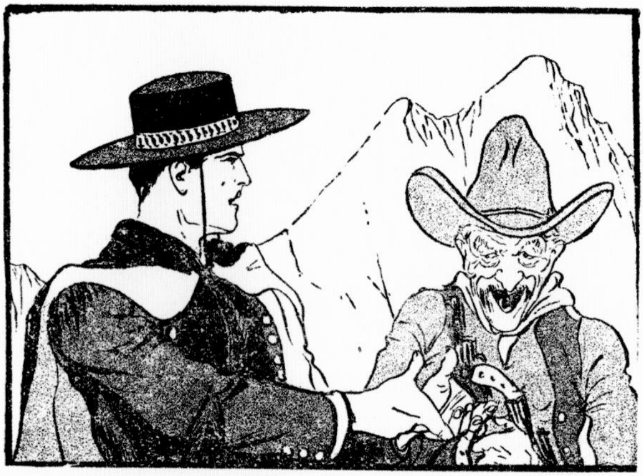

»Rekao si, da se ne bojiš smrti! Onda ćemo joj jašiti u susret! Podijeli to oružje, pa ćemo okrenuti konje...«

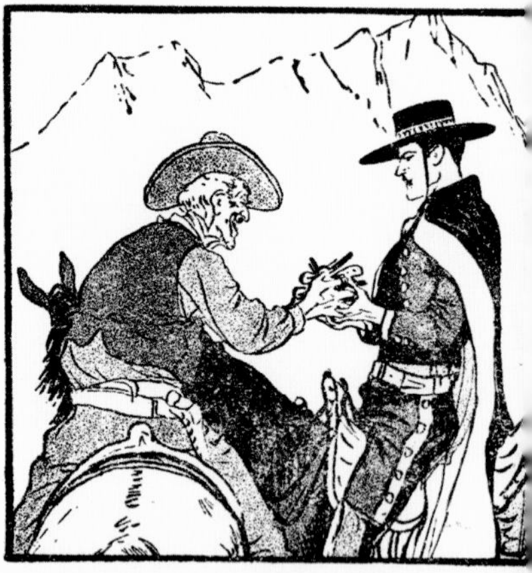

»Evo! Znam o čemu se radi... Vi misli
Dva protiv sviju... To će biti divota!«

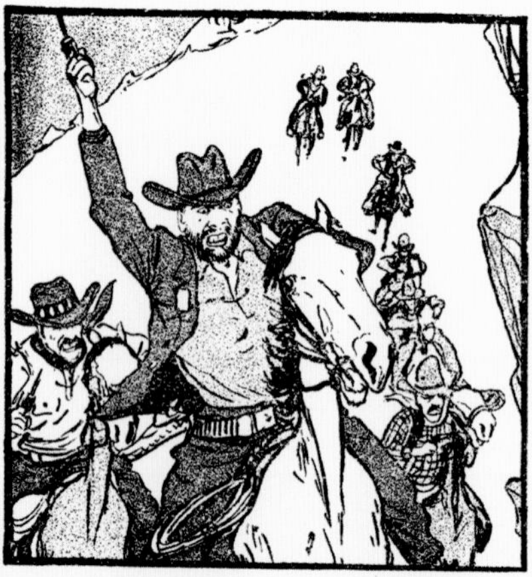

»Oprez ljudi! Pripremite oružje! Evo ih pred nama...«

PROSTOR
IZMEDJU
PROGO-
NJENIH I
PROGONI-
TELJA
NAGLO SE
SMANJIVAO

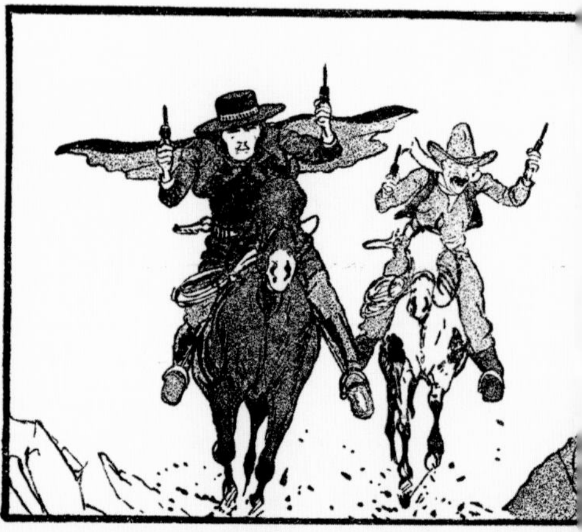

U paklenom tempu jurila su dva jahača
susret svojim progoniteljima...

The Old Tomcat 1937

✐✐ Andrija Maurović

Title in original language *Stari mačak*
First published by *Novosti* (Yugoslavia)
Creator Croatian (1901–81)
Genre Western

Andrija Maurović is probably the most distinguished artist from the comic culture of the former Yugoslavia. He serialized the first modern comics in the country in 1935 and continued to work on more than one hundred different comic series, plus numerous posters, book covers, illustrations, and oil paintings. His comics are recognizable for their cinematic scenes, their expressive use of contrasting areas of black and white, and their depiction of strong emotions on faces. His combination of visual and narrative elements is extraordinary and derives from him alone, without reference to his peers or artists before him. In particular, the comics he painted in oil, tempera, and ink between 1960 and 1962 testify to his unparalleled artistic ability.

Maurović's most popular comics were in the Western genre, and the most successful, if conventional, were his five episodes of *The Old Tomcat* series. Before World War II, the good guys in Wild West movies and comics were always good-looking and wore white hats. Many years ahead of his time, Maurović put into the leading role Old Tomcat, an old, silly, but charismatic gunslinger, poorly dressed, wrinkled, and toothless, and his friend Slow Death, a sickly poet with a parrot on his shoulder. The pair were ridiculed by vicious bandits, who were always rigorously punished for their crimes. The public adored Old Tomcat and Slow Death.

It has to be said that, outside the former Yugoslavia, the rest of the world needs to be introduced to Andrija Maurović and his masterpieces. His work deserves far wider appreciation and representation. **ZT**

The Burrón Family 1937

✐✐ Gabriel Vargas

Title in original language *La familia Burrón*
First published by Editorial Panamericana (México)
Creator Mexican (1915–2010)
Genre Humor

Gabriel Vargas's *The Burrón Family* is Mexico's most beloved and well known comic book. The full-color series predates by several decades Matt Groening's *The Simpsons* in achieving a merciless, yet funny and heartwarming cultural analysis of a society through an extreme focus on an individual family.

The series centers on Regino Burrón, a barber, and Borola Tacuche de Burrón, his wife, and their two teenage children, Regino and Macuca; also part of the clan is Foforito Cantarranas, who has been adopted by the family. The Burróns are a poor, working-class family struggling to make ends meet in an impoverished neighborhood of a large city. The comic strip focused firmly on working-class issues and sold 500,000 copies a week for decades. It offered comic relief and a clear reflection of the woes of life in the barrio, without the left-wing ideological weight of political cartoonist Rius or the macho escapism of the *Lucha Libre* series.

The illustration style of Gabriel Vargas, although carefully detailed and cartoony, was closer to its Latin American roots than to the European aesthetics of fellow Mexican cartoonist Germán Butze, creator of *Super Whiz Kids*. Vargas, who started as a newspaper editorial cartoonist, was awarded the Mexican National Journalism Prize in 1983 and the National Sciences and Arts Prize in 2003. After his death on May 25, 2010, the Mexican government descibed the strip as "an undeniable reference point for the nation's popular culture." *The Burrón Family* has been published in a series of hardcover collections by Editorial Porrúa. **EPr**

← The wily Old Tomcat pursues another adventure out West.

Nancy 1938

✐✐ Ernie Bushmiller

First published by United Feature Syndicate (USA)
Creator American (1905–82)
Genre Humor
Award National Cartoonists Society Award (1961)

Introduced in 1933, tomboy Nancy was originally a supporting character in *Fritzi Ritz*, a strip about a frivolous flapper created by Larry Whittington. Ernie Bushmiller inherited the strip in 1925 and made it his own, turning its former star into Nancy's "aunt." From 1938, Nancy took over, giving her name to the strip.

Bushmiller's spare style of drawing and storytelling went a long way to establishing *Nancy* as one of America's most iconic strip narratives, running in 880 newspapers by the 1970s. Early on, Bushmiller thought he could not draw in a representational manner and consequently pared down his drawing to the essentials, presenting readers with his own visual language in the form of a cartoon shorthand. Some have even compared these narratives to the unique codes of expression produced by self-taught artists or the mentally disturbed. Bushmiller's decision to employ a more realistic style for "aunt" Fritzi and other adults sat in stark contrast to the simplification of Nancy and Sluggo, her constant sidekick, and their environment. Both children were portrayed as being around seven or eight years old, but behaved like adults as they went about their daily adventures and fantasies. Much of the strip's humor was supported by a childlike approach to logic, making it both charming and widely accessible.

Like Mickey Mouse, Nancy has enjoyed an extended influential life both in the art world, featuring in works by Andy Warhol, Joe Brainard, and The Hairy Who, and in modern comics by such admirers as Bill Griffith and Mark Newgarden. **LC**

Red Ryder 1938

✐✐ Fred Harman

First published by Newspaper Enterprise Association (USA)
Creator American (1902–82)
Genre Western
Adaptation U.S. serial: *Adventures of Red Ryder* (1940)

Over twenty-six years starting in 1938, the popular Western comic strip *Red Ryder* was published in 750 newspapers, translated into ten different languages, and reached a U.S. readership of fourteen million. The series flourished on radio, in movies and serials, books, and rodeos. The Red Ryder BB Gun retains the longest continuous license for a merchandised toy. After Fred Harman retired from comics in 1963, he became a successful painter of Western scenes.

In the early 1930s creator Harman swapped ranch life for Hollywood, where he borrowed money and launched *Bronc Peeler*, a strip about a tough cowboy that the author syndicated himself. It floundered after three years, and Harman teamed up with business-savvy producer Stephen Slesinger to create *Red Ryder*. Harman's ranch near Pagosa Springs, Colorado, inspired his drawings depicting the adventures of a cowboy herding cattle and helping the law. The thickly drawn lines conjured up an enthralling vision of the West in the late nineteenth century.

Red Ryder works for his aunt, Duchess, a gutsy no-nonsense woman, who is nonetheless easy to trick. Red rescues her from various scrapes, helped by the ever alert Little Beaver, an Apache orphan adopted by Ryder. The astute Little Beaver interferes whenever a pretty girl comes Red's way, and is determined to keep him single. Red rides a magnificent, well-trained black steed called Thunder. The pacey stories—filled with excitement and drama but never implausible—often ended on excellent cliff-hangers. **IR**

The Sunday pages also featured Little Beaver in his own supporting topper strip. ➡

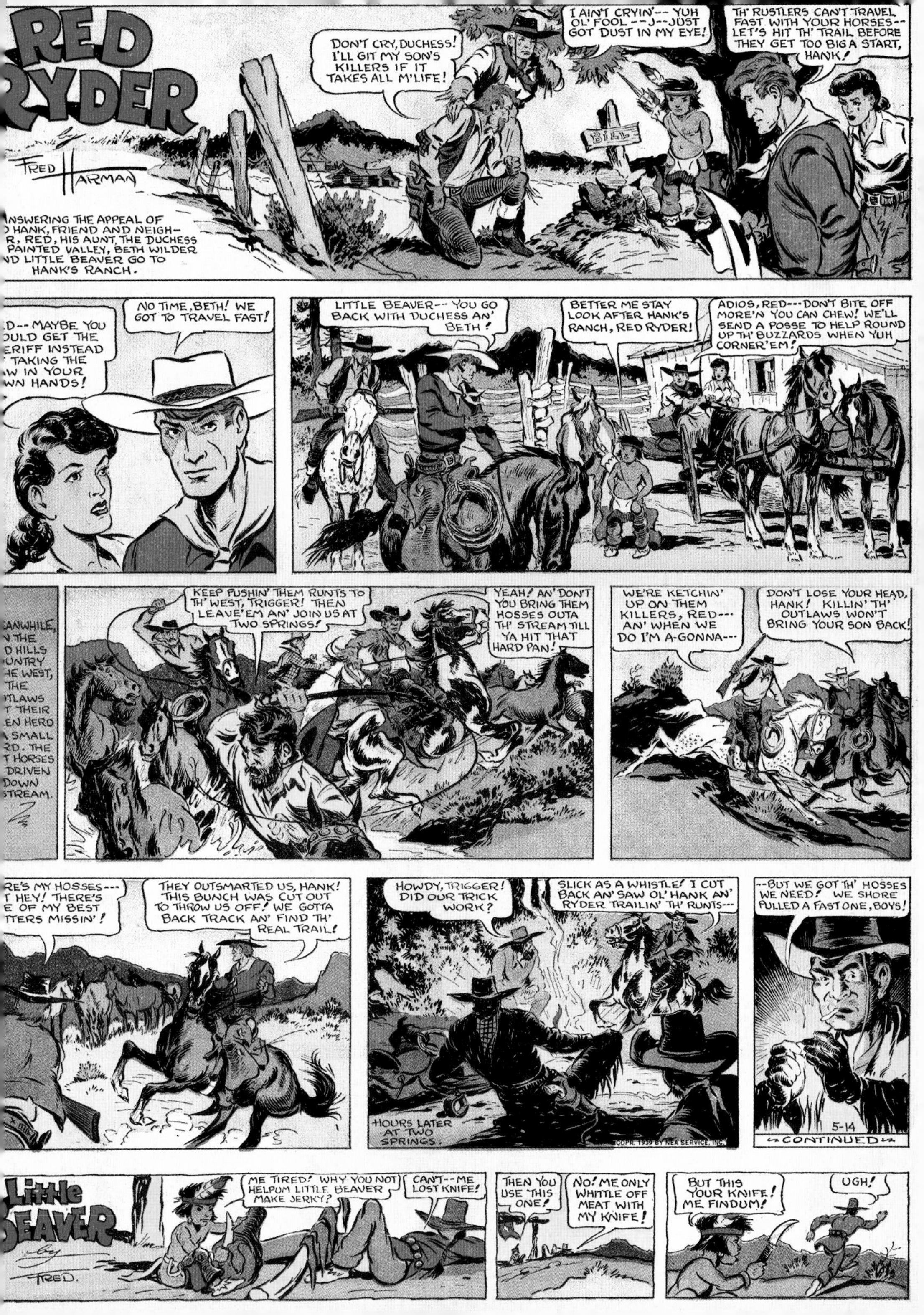

RED RYDER
by FRED HARMAN
NSWERING THE APPEAL OF D HANK, FRIEND AND NEIGH- R, RED, HIS AUNT, THE DUCHESS PAINTED VALLEY, BETH WILDER ND LITTLE BEAVER GO TO HANK'S RANCH.
DON'T CRY, DUCHESS! I'LL GIT MY SON'S KILLERS IF IT TAKES ALL M'LIFE!
I AIN'T CRYIN'-- YUH OL' FOOL --J--JUST GOT DUST IN MY EYE!
BILL
TH' RUSTLERS CAN'T TRAVEL FAST WITH YOUR HORSES-- LET'S HIT TH' TRAIL BEFORE THEY GET TOO BIG A START, HANK!
D-- MAYBE YOU OULD GET THE ERIFF INSTEAD TAKING THE W IN YOUR WN HANDS!
NO TIME, BETH! WE GOT TO TRAVEL FAST!
LITTLE BEAVER-- YOU GO BACK WITH DUCHESS AN' BETH!
BETTER ME STAY LOOK AFTER HANK'S RANCH, RED RYDER!
ADIOS, RED--- DON'T BITE OFF MORE'N YOU CAN CHEW! WE'LL SEND A POSSE TO HELP ROUND UP TH' BUZZARDS WHEN YUH CORNER'EM!
EANWHILE, N THE D HILLS OUNTRY THE WEST, THE UTLAWS T THEIR EN HERD SMALL RD. THE T HORSES DRIVEN DOWN STREAM.
KEEP PUSHIN' THEM RUNTS TO TH' WEST, TRIGGER! THEN LEAVE'EM AN' JOIN US AT TWO SPRINGS!
YEAH! AN' DON'T YOU BRING THEM HOSSES OUTA TH' STREAM TILL YA HIT THAT HARD PAN!
WE'RE KETCHIN' UP ON THEM KILLERS, RED--- AN' WHEN WE DO I'M A-GONNA---
DON'T LOSE YOUR HEAD, HANK! KILLIN' TH' OUTLAWS WON'T BRING YOUR SON BACK!
RE'S MY HOSSES--- T HEY! THERE'S E OF MY BEST TTERS MISSIN'!
THEY OUTSMARTED US, HANK! THIS BUNCH WAS CUT OUT TO THROW US OFF! WE GOTTA BACK TRACK AN' FIND TH' REAL TRAIL!
HOWDY, TRIGGER! DID OUR TRICK WORK?
SLICK AS A WHISTLE! I CUT BACK AN' SAW OL' HANK AN' RYDER TRAILIN' TH' RUNTS---
HOURS LATER AT TWO SPRINGS.
COPR. 1939 BY NEA SERVICE, INC.
--BUT WE GOT TH' HOSSES WE NEED! WE SHORE PULLED A FAST ONE, BOYS!
5-14
CONTINUED
Little BEAVER by FRED.
ME TIRED! WHY YOU NOT HELPUM LITTLE BEAVER MAKE JERKY?
CAN'T--ME LOST KNIFE!
THEN YOU USE THIS ONE!
NO! ME ONLY WHITTLE OFF MEAT WITH MY KNIFE!
BUT THIS YOUR KNIFE! ME FINDUM!
UGH!

Superman 1938

Jerry Siegel Joe Shuster

First published by DC Comics (USA)
Creators Siegel (American, 1914–96); Shuster (American, 1914–92)
Genre Superhero

No. 1
JUNE, 1938
ACTION COMICS
10¢

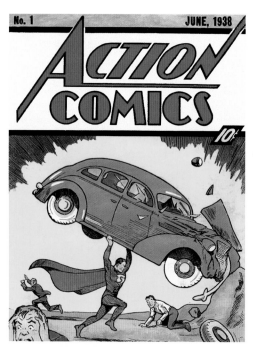

Similar reads
Superman: Kryptonite Darwyn Cooke and Tim Sale
Superman: Man of Steel John Byrne
Superman: Secret Origin Geoff Johns and Gary Frank
Superman: Whatever Happened to the Man of Tomorrow? Alan Moore and Curt Swan

A great shame regarding the earliest *Superman* stories (including his first appearances in *Action Comics*) is that the initial impact of the first true superhero (one with powers, a costume, and secret identity) can't be conceived by anyone familiar with its immense legacy.

Superman's debut was thrilling stuff in 1938. His composite elements have been endlessly discussed, but let's take Jerry Siegel and Joe Shuster at their word and accept Edgar Rice Burroughs's John Carter novels and the action films of Douglas Fairbanks as the primary influences. Shuster aspired to the lush art of Alex Raymond and Burne Hogarth, but he only managed a crude approximation of Roy Crane and Milton Caniff's cinematic style. Yet better artists who later tried to draw Superman as Shuster's eyesight deteriorated could not match the vigor he brought to his own creation.

"As the man of steel springs toward the window, the assassin fires a bullet into his own brain!"

For all his powers, over the years the *Superman* stories that linger longest are those eliciting an emotional response. From the earliest issues, Siegel's social conscience had Superman dealing with wife-beaters, rescuing trapped miners, and preventing a wrongful state execution, while supporting characters who questioned the ethics of munitions manufacture. *Superman* could easily be dismissed as a standard wish-fulfilling fantasy, but this stark assessment pales in comparison to all he has inspired.

In *Superman*'s first year Siegel and Shuster introduced Krypton, Lois Lane, and Jimmy Olsen. The following year they debuted Lex Luthor. That cast has seen *Superman* through decades of publication and spawned an icon that is still with us today. **FP**

Batman 1939

Bill Finger "Bob Kane"

The success of Superman, from his launch in *Action Comics*, kept publishers on the lookout for characters that fitted the new superhero formula. But what made Superman so special, so different, and a runaway hit? Bill Finger and Bob Kane's Batman inverted almost all of Superman and Clark Kent's characteristics—bar his heroism. Superman was an alien with superhuman abilities; Batman was human and relied on his mental and physical training. Superman fought openly and in broad daylight; Batman was a masked man, frequently operating at night. By presenting in almost every way the antithesis of Superman, Finger and Kane defined the limits of the superhero genre, and perhaps defined in Batman the most durable hero of all.

"It is the duty of every good citizen of Gotham City to report meeting a man from Mars in a public park."

Finger and Kane also devised a back story that took in Batman's unique origin and accounted for his thirst for revenge on criminals. Between 1939 and 1943 the pair set in motion themes that have been explored in superhero stories ever since; they also gave Batman a rogues' gallery of memorable villains, many of whom are exaggerations of one or more of the key characteristics of Batman himself.

Kane's cinematic artwork also introduced a new sensibility to the genre, a gothic sense of light and shadow. Kane understood the power of white space, and of bright yellow set against a field of black. Batman's costume exploited the dramatic possibilities of contrasting light and darkness, although the introduction of Robin in *Detective Comics* issue #38 (April 1940) moved the protagonists out of the shadows, adding more primary colors and witty dialogue. **RR**

First published by DC Comics (USA)
Creators Finger (American, 1914–74); Robert Kahn (American, 1915–98)
Genre Superhero

No. 27
64 PAGES OF ACTION!
MAY, 1939
Detective COMICS
10¢
STARTING THIS ISSUE: THE AMAZING AND UNIQUE ADVENTURES OF THE BATMAN!

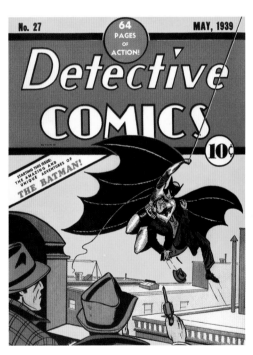

Similar reads
Green Arrow Mort Weisinger and George Papp
Green Lantern Bill Finger and Martin Nodell
Robin Bill Finger, Bob Kane, and Jerry Robinson
Superman Jerry Siegel and Joe Shuster
Wonder Woman William Moulton Marston

Mopsy 1939

Gladys Parker

First published by United Feature Syndicate (USA)
Creator American (1910–66)
Genre Humor
Influenced by *Dumb Dora* (1924–35)

BERKLEY BOOKS 336
MOPSY
BY GLADYS PARKER
BUT, BOSS, YOU TOLD ME NOT TO WEAR MY SWEATER IN THE OFFICE!
ANC
25c

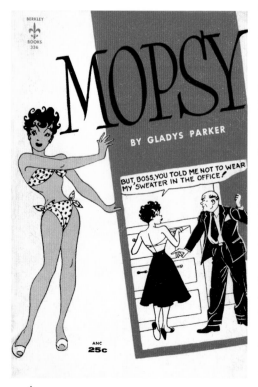

Similar reads

Boots and her Buddies Edgar Everett
Mazie the Model Larry Whittington
Tillie the Toiler Russ Westover
Winnie Winkle Martin Branner

When cartoonist Rube Goldberg happened to remark to Gladys Parker that her hair "looked like a mop," the latter cartoonist seized upon the name for her new comic strip about a savvy, single New York working girl. Similarities between the cartoonist and the character didn't end with the hair, however. Their facial resemblance was nothing short of uncanny. Parker also took to dressing in clothes worn by Mopsy, and even applied her own lipstick in an attempt to emulate the look she gave to her character's mouth. Writers always say that to be successful you need to write about what you know. Mopsy's remarkable three-decade-long run bears out this truism—although in the case of Mopsy, it was difficult to know where the life of the character ended and that of its creator began.

Mopsy debuted in 1939, on the eve of World War II. Initially she was a "flapper," a typically airy 1920s jazz-age girl, but soon she was contributing to the war effort, working in turn as a nurse and as a wartime factory worker. A *Mopsy* Sunday strip was added in 1945, but, in a reflection of the social norms of the era, Parker made the decision not to make Mopsy appear overly intelligent. It was her belief that making a woman obviously smarter than the men around her would be damaging to the strip's popularity.

Clothes and men were Mopsy's twin obsessions, and when it came to the opposite sex she proved herself manipulative, bold, and cheeky, characteristics that constantly led her to become embroiled in compromising—and entertaining—situations.

At its peak in the late 1940s, *Mopsy* was being published in more than 300 newspapers. A *Mopsy* paperback was published by Berkley Books in 1955, and there is no telling how long the popular series may have continued had it not been brought to an end with the retirement of its self-modeled creator in 1965. **BS**

Frankenstein 1940

Dick Briefer

Dick Briefer's *Frankenstein* certainly mellowed with the passing of the years. Debuting in 1940 in Prize Comics 7, Briefer's adaptation of Mary Shelley's character was found in early issues throwing tourists from the head of the Statue of Liberty, luring them to their grisly deaths on Coney Island, and squishing criminals with his bare hands. However, after returning home from fighting Nazis in World War II and settling in smalltown America, Frankenstein was given his own comic in 1945 and became a different monster. Once overwhelmed by anger at having been so hideously and needlessly formed, he now possessed a childlike innocence. He enjoyed smelling flowers, learned how to play baseball, and tried to be a good neighbor. Briefer even began to draw him with a distorted button nose. He had lighthearted adventures with Dracula, the Wolfman, and other nefarious creatures. He still killed people, of course, but only when aggravated, and his cruelty was never without cause.

From 1940 to 1949, and again from 1952 to 1954, Briefer worked alone on the strip without assistants, doing all the pencil work, lettering, writing, inking, and erasing himself. His strong brushwork, contrasting colors, and thoughtful compositions coexisted alongside balloons of often abundant text. Briefer returned to his original, darker portrayal of the monster in the 1952–54 period to satisfy a growing demand for comics depicting classic horror.

Frankenstein was canceled in 1954, falling victim to various anti-horror groups and the overly zealous Comics Code Authority, which was created to regulate what was deemed increasingly "inappropriate" material. Briefer, who created what many believed was the first continuing comic feature focusing on a horror character, then left the world of comic books and found work as a commercial advertising artist. **BS**

First published by Prize Comics (USA)
Creator American (1915–80)
Genre Horror, Humor
Influenced by Novel: *Frankenstein* (1818)

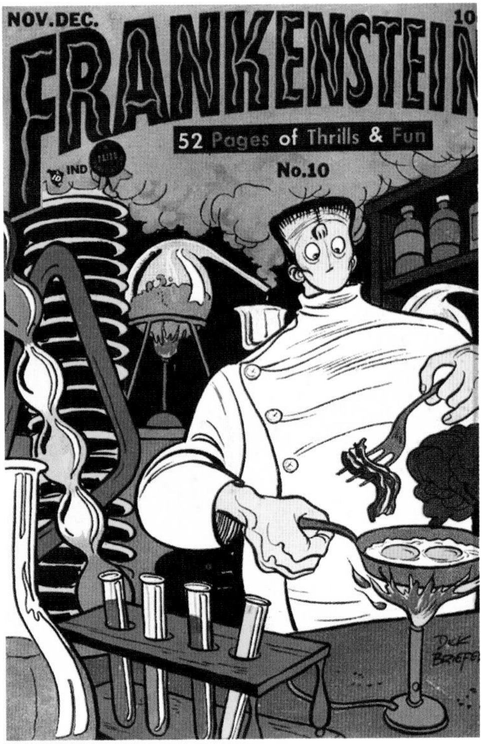
NOV.DEC.
10
FRANKENSTEIN
52 Pages of Thrills & Fun
No.10
DICK BRIEFER

Similar reads

Eerie Archie Goodwin
Tales from the Crypt William Gaines
The Haunt of Fear William Gaines
The Vault of Horror William Gaines

The Spirit 1940

✎ Will Eisner

First published by Quality Comics (USA)
Creator American (1917–2005)
Genre Superhero, Crime
Adaptation Film (2008)

As the 1930s came to an end comic book sales escalated. Extending stories in the comic book sections of Sunday newspapers seemed a natural progression. One of these, Will Eisner's *The Spirit,* first appeared early in 1940. Never a fan of superheroes, Eisner paid lip service to the genre by giving his creation, Denny Colt, an eye mask and an original story in which he is resurrected from the dead after being killed by his archenemy, Dr. Cobra. Otherwise, the character is basically a detective navigating the murky waters of the criminal underworld.

The Spirit was an immediate success, reaching its peak in presentation and storytelling after Eisner returned from service in World War II in 1944. One downside of the strip is the racial caricature of Denny's African-American sidekick, Ebony White. The depiction is unfortunate (although the character was treated well in the stories), but looking beyond this dated factor, *The Spirit* yields a bounty of treasure.

Stories such as "UFO" (September 28, 1947), which features an affectionate parody of Orson Welles as Awesome Bells, and "Meet P'Gell" (October 6, 1946), which introduced *The Spirit*'s femme fatale adversary, mix humor, drama, action, and pathos with consummate ease. Eisner's splash page compositions, often involving moody cityscapes, swooping perspective, or complex design elements, set the industry standard and are hugely influential. His cinematic storytelling brought new levels of sophistication to the medium. *The Spirit* ran for twelve years and is one of the most important series in comics history. **CH**

Brenda Starr, Reporter 1940

✎ Dale Messick

First published by Chicago Tribune Syndicate (USA)
Creator American (1906–2005)
Genre Adventure
Adaptation Film serial (1945)

In 1940, when world events shook civilization to its core, glamorous girl reporter Brenda Starr was on the spot with the scoop. As created by Dale (born Dahlia) Messick, Brenda combined the beauty of Hollywood star Rita Hayworth with the spritely look of the working "Brinkley Girls." Debuting a year before Miss Fury and even beating the arrival of the immortal Wonder Woman, the adventurous Brenda's influence soon extended beyond the panel borders, fueling the dreams of young women long before the feminist revolution.

Brenda Starr's path to fame was not an easy one. Taken on with trepidation by the Chicago Tribune Syndicate after several rejections, Messick's debut strip first appeared as a Sunday-only trial. It soon became clear, however, what a powerful cocktail of adventure, romance, and fashion could do in attracting audiences, both male and female. Over more than sixty globe-trotting years, Brenda enjoyed a thrilling series of adventures, jumping out of planes, cheating death on many occasions, and even sparking a love affair with an alluring man of mystery. The eye patch-wearing Basil St. John lingered in the strip until the final installment, together with friends Hank O'Hair and Twirl O'Curl who kept things lively when St. John was out of town.

Messick drew the strip until her retirement in 1970, when Ramona Fradon was the first in a series of female writers and illustrators who kept Brenda alive. On January 2, 2011 Brenda hung up her press card for good, although her character's tenacity still provides inspiration for women in comics everywhere. **EL**

Miss Fury 1941

"Tarpé"

First published by Bell Syndicate (USA)
Creator June Tarpé Mills (American, 1915–88)
Genre Superhero
Influenced by *The Cat Man*

Miss Fury has the distinction of being the first comic strip about a superheroine. She beat *Wonder Woman* to the punch by some six months when her strip was launched in June 1941. Bored socialite Marla Drake discovers that she has chosen the same fancy dress costume for a party as another woman. In disgust, she changes into a black, leopard-skin catsuit, an heirloom from her uncle. The costume turns out to have mysterious powers: once dressed in the costume Marla is immediately drawn into crimefighting. Marla is soon dubbed the Black Fury by the newspapers—the original name of the strip. The strip was renamed *Miss Fury* in September 1941.

Miss Fury is the creation of June Tarpé Mills, one of the few women to work as a writer or artist during the Golden Age of U.S. comics. Created as a Sunday funny, *Miss Fury* was popular and long-lived, and the series continued until 1952.

As the strip developed, it moved progressively away from the costumed superhero genre, and became more closely allied to adventure narratives such as *Terry and the Pirates*. Mills was influenced stylistically by Milton Caniff; her cinematic cutting, reverse angles, and long-shot/close-up combinations, as well as the interpolated silent panel sequences, show Mills's understanding of the medium's narrative. Mills also worked as a fashion illustrator, and Marla Drake—as well as her enemy and rival Erica von Kampf—possess wonderfully on-trend wardrobes for their period. Mills projected herself into the character of Marla Drake in many ways—even her cat Peri Purr was based on the author's own pet. **RR**

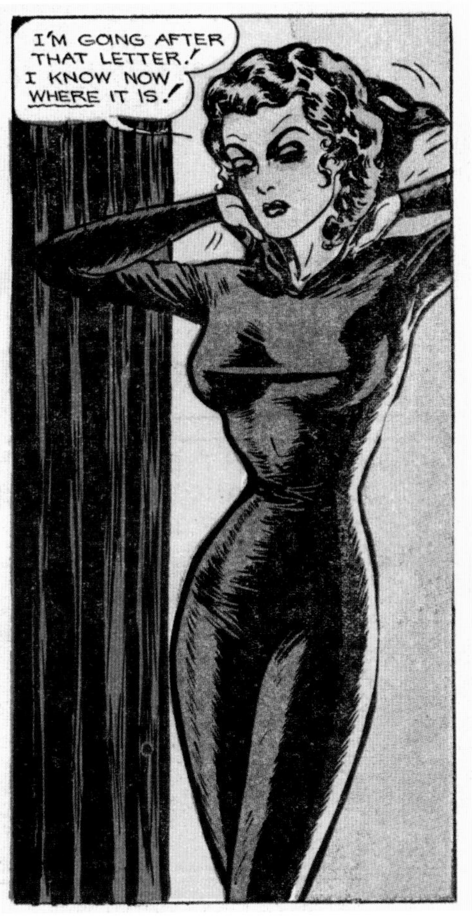
I'M GOING AFTER THAT LETTER! I KNOW NOW WHERE IT IS!

"At least no one else will be wearing the same thing! Good night, Francine!"

Plastic Man 1941

Jack Cole

First published by Quality Comics (USA)
Creator American (1914–58)
Genre Superhero, Crime
Adaptation TV series (1979)

POLICE
COMICS
SEPTEMBER No. 22
10¢
FEATURING
THE SPIRIT
DO YOU WANT TO LAUGH?...CRY?... AND SHUDDER??
READ JACK COLE'S TERRIFIC PLASTIC MAN STORY... "THE EYES HAVE IT!"
THE GREATEST TALE EVER TO APPEAR IN COMICS!

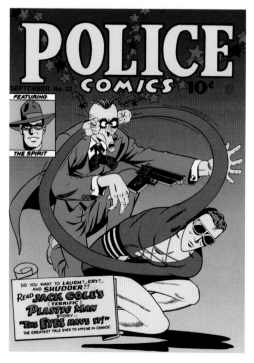

"Plastic Man goes oozing out of a keyhole, around a corner and up through piping that leads to a sink in the mad Nazi scientist's lab."

Thomas Pynchon, novelist

Having previously worked on *The Spirit* for Will Eisner, creator Jack Cole gave *Plastic Man* ("Plas") his debut in the first issue of *Police Comics* in 1941. Professional crook "Eel" O'Brien falls into a vat of chemicals during a factory break-in. He wakes up in a monastery, only to discover that his body has become infinitely malleable and ductile. These superpowers cause O'Brien to change his moral outlook, and he moves from a life of crime to become a crimefighter. In his enterprise, Plas is helped by the underworld contacts he acquired when operating on the wrong side of the law.

Although the influence of Eisner is evident, *Plastic Man* rapidly took on its own unique identity. Cole's world of madcap physical transformations neatly mirrors his topsy-turvy ethical landscape. As easily as a crook can become a crimefighter, Plas can transform himself into a parachute, a table, or a lampshade. *Plastic Man* is the first superhero who embraces the bizarre possibilities implicit in his superpower. The sly and surreal humor of the series was further stretched by the arrival of Plastic Man's sidekick Woozy Winks. Also an ex-crook, Woozy is "the man nature protects" and—at least in his early appearances—is able to walk unharmed through the most violent natural catastrophes.

Plastic Man survived beyond the Golden Age of comics, first being published in *Police Comics* and subsequently in his own comic book series. *Plastic Man* was canceled in November 1956, the same month that The Flash, now reborn, ushered in the next era of superheroes. There have been a number of subsequent attempts to revive the character, DC Comics having acquired the rights in 1956. Jack Cole's *Plastic Man* remains the most successful combination of humor and superhero fantasy ever created. It is a masterpiece, revered by Thomas Pynchon, Art Spiegelman, and many, many others. **RR**

Wonder Woman 1941

"Charles Moulton" Harry Peter

First published by All-American Publications (USA)
Creators William Moulton Marston (American, 1893–1947); Peter (American, 1880–1958)
Genre Superhero

Part of a generation of groundbreaking comic book superheroines, such as *Brenda Starr, Reporter* and *Miss Fury*, *Wonder Woman*'s popularity played a massive role in expanding women's place in comics. The character made her first appearance in *Sensation Comics*.

Her creator, the Harvard-trained psychologist Dr. William Moulton Marston, was convinced that men's warmongering tendencies were to blame for society's ills. Marston also claimed that comics—vilified by many—had a powerful part to play in shaping a better society. Combining these two convictions, Marston (under the pseudonym Charles Moulton) started to write the story of a young Amazon girl who is as beautiful as Aphrodite, as wise as Athena, and as strong as Hercules.

Wonder Woman's story begins when Captain Steve Trevor crash-lands on Paradise Island, the home of an Amazon civilization. Nursing him back to health, Diana, the daughter of the Amazon queen, falls in love with Trevor, the first man she has ever seen. She competes for the right to return him to his duties in the United States's armed forces. Arriving in the United States, she bribes a nurse called Diana Prince and assumes her identity. In a nod to *Superman*'s Clark Kent, Diana Prince wears glasses and soon becomes her own rival for Steve Trevor's love. Wonderful inventions such as the magic sphere, the Magic Lasso, and the indestructible bracelets that Wonder Woman uses to deflect bullets are all part of the appeal of this immortal character.

Created as a wartime heroine, *Wonder Woman* has experienced many incarnations over the decades and has appeared in many different media, notably television. Yet, no matter what transformations she undergoes, the superheroine remains true to Marston's original vision, a woman who can serve as a symbol of the bravery, nobility, and strength in all of us. **EL**

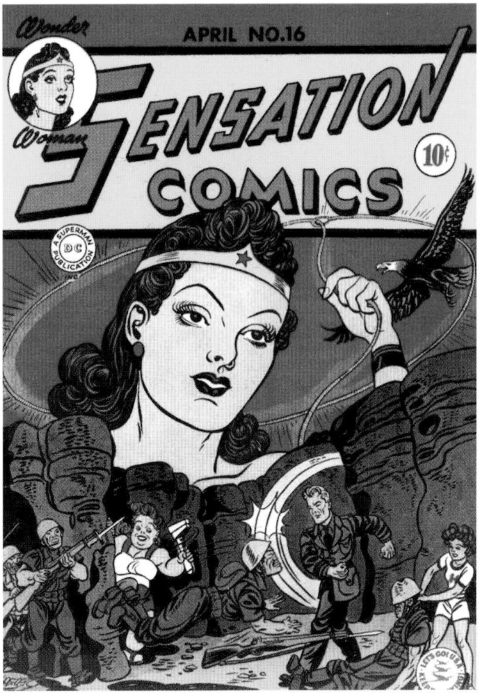
Wonder Woman
APRIL NO.16
SENSATION COMICS
10¢

"No woman can be the hero of a comic strip—but something compels me!"

Editor at *American Scholar*

Captain America 1941

Joe Simon Jack Kirby

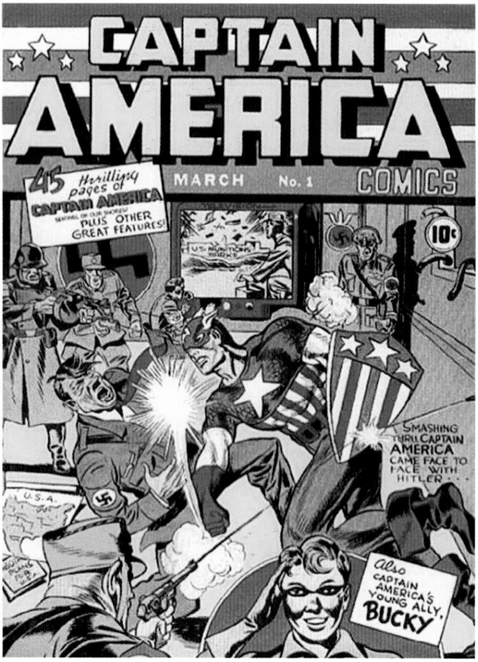
CAPTAIN AMERICA COMICS
45 thrilling pages of CAPTAIN AMERICA PLUS OTHER GREAT FEATURES!
MARCH
No. 1
10¢
SMASHING THRU CAPTAIN AMERICA CAME FACE TO FACE WITH HITLER . . .
also CAPTAIN AMERICA'S YOUNG ALLY, BUCKY

"We're in this war, Namor, and we're going to win it—but let's make sure we're still the 'good guys' when we do!"

Also illustrated by Jack Kirby
Fighting American
Mister Miracle
The Double Life of Private Strong
The Fantastic Four
The Incredible Hulk

First published by Timely/Marvel Comics (USA)
Creators Simon (American, b.1913); Kirby (American, 1917–94)
Genre Superhero

The newly formed team of Joe Simon and Jack Kirby scored their first major success at Timely (later Marvel) in 1940 with *Captain America*. The patriotic supersoldier, created by a government program to develop superior specimens to aid the war effort, was a year ahead of the United States joining the Allies after the attack on Pearl Harbor. A conscious political statement, it captured the rising patriotic mood of the time. With the added impact of the Captain slugging Adolf Hitler on the cover of the first issue, it sold half a million copies.

Kirby is regarded as one of the most important figures in comics, and here he displays an early flowering of skills that put him at the forefront of comics for four decades. His figures are sinewy and rubbery, they leap and contort effortlessly, and the quality of his drawing was far ahead of its peers. In issue #6 of *Captain America* Kirby introduced the double-page spread format, which became his trademark in the decades that followed.

With teen sidekick Bucky Barnes (continually thrown into the middle of danger despite having no special powers himself) Captain America met an array of memorable villains across the ten Simon and Kirby issues. The best remembered of which was super-Nazi nemesis the Red Skull (who was later revived along with Cap himself in the 1960s). His masked villainy is standard but the image of him is unforgettable.

Kirby was to collaborate with Simon on several other projects during his fifty-odd years in comics, including *Sandman*, *Sandy the Golden Boy*, *Newsboy Legion*, *Boy Commandos*, and *Manhunter*. **CH**

Tom Puss 1941

✎ Marten Toonder ✎ Piet Wijn and others

Title in original language *Tom Poes en Heer Bommel*
First published by *De Telegraaf* (Netherlands)
Creators Toonder (Dutch, 1912–2005); Wijn (Dutch, 1929–2010) **Genre** Humor

---

Dutch comics creator Marten Toonder was a born storyteller. He and his younger brother, Jan, obsessively talked each other to sleep as children with neverending tales of their own creation. They devoured the large, colorful English-language comics—worlds apart from Dutch comics—that their sea captain father sometimes brought home from his travels.

In 1933 Marten became house artist at magazine publisher Nederlandsche Rotogravure Mij (NRM), where he illustrated in a multitude of styles. The publications of his employers provided him with great inspiration, but he was underpaid and was never allowed to sign his own work. Although he was forbidden to have his work published elsewhere, he did so regardless. Influenced by Mary Tourtel's *Rupert Bear*, he created his own anthropomorphic bear, Thijs IJs.

Toonder finally broke free from NRM in 1940 and worked for himself. When Dutch newspaper *De Telegraaf* saw its supply of Disney's Mickey Mouse daily strips dwindle in 1941, they took on Toonder's *Tom Puss*. The inventive strip, about a clever white cat, blended musings, social criticism, and wordplay. The author created a sidekick for Tom Puss in the form of a clumsy but lovable brown bear in a checkered coat called Olivier B. Bumble (nicknamed "Ollie"), who became rich and lord of Castle Bommelstein. Toonder refused to credit the ghost artists he used but most of the artwork for *Tom Puss* was done by freelancers such as Piet Wijn. Several expressions used in Toonder's strips are now commonly used in the Dutch language. **HvO**

Gordo 1941

✎ Gustavo "Gus" Arriola

First published by United Features Syndicate (USA)
Creator Mexican-American (1917–2008)
Genre Humor **Award** National Cartoonists Society Humor Comic Strip Award (1957)

In the U.S. newspaper strips of the 1940s stereotypical portrayals of foreigners were commonplace: Italian men had moustaches; Australians lived in the bush; and Mexican men were lecherous, lazy scoundrels.

In 1941 Gustavo Arriola, a young Mexican-American animator in MGM's cartoon department, created *Gordo*, a Mexican bean farmer who was as prescribed, fond of chasing girls, taking siestas, and avoiding the call to manual labor whenever possible. When fellow Hispanics complained to Arriola that he was misrepresenting his own people, the artist decided it was time to bring some authenticity to the strip.

Gordo underwent a fundamental transformation in the mid-1950s when he was forced off the farm on which he had worked as a laborer. He purchased a bus that ran on alcohol, which he called "Halley's Comet," and became a tour operator, traveling across the United States. In the process he became an "accidental ambassador" for Mexico, with the bus used as a platform for introducing Mexican history and culture to readers across the United States. This highlighting of Mexican history and folk art gave the strip a powerful visual aesthetic not seen in U.S. comics pages at the time. "Gus can cartoon anything", declared *Peanuts*'s creator Charles Schulz.

With only brief respites for health reasons, Arriola continued to write and draw *Gordo* until its finale in March 1985, and in the process acquired a legion of fans from within the profession, many of whom recognized his Sunday color pages as stylistic triumphs. **BS**

Captain Marvel Jr. 1941

Ed Herron   Emmanuel "Mac" Raboy

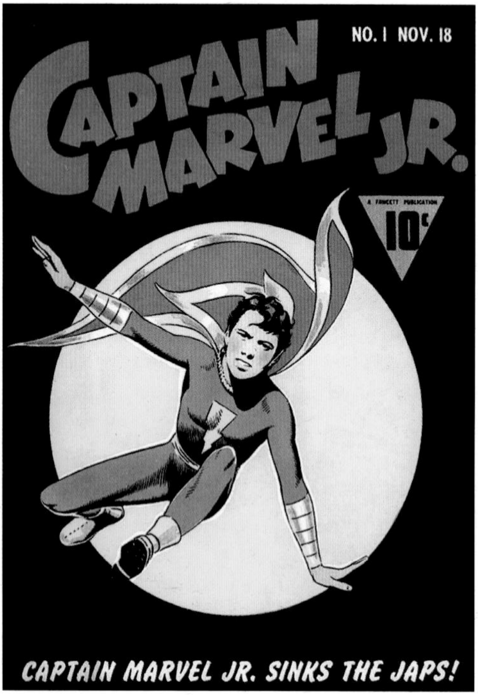
NO. 1 NOV. 18
CAPTAIN MARVEL JR.
A FAWCETT PUBLICATION
10¢
CAPTAIN MARVEL JR. SINKS THE JAPS!

"Do what's right for you as long as you don't hurt no one."

Elvis Presley

Similar reads
Batman
Captain Marvel
Justice League of America
Kingdom Come
Superman

First published by Fawcett Comics (USA)
Creators Herron (American, 1917–66); Raboy (American, 1914–67)
Genre Superhero

It is a little known fact that the most popular superhero of the war years was not Superman or Batman, it was in fact Captain Marvel. Such was the character's success that the decision was made to create a companion hero, but while young Billy Batson was transformed into the adult Captain Marvel, Freddie Freeman was about to become a super-powered boy, Captain Marvel Jr.

Freddie was an innocent bystander seriously injured during a titanic battle between Captain Marvel and Captain Nazi. To save the lad, Captain Marvel took him to the wizard Shazam, who transformed him into the blue suited Captain Marvel Junior, still a teenager but with extraordinary powers and an adult physique. The character was an instant hit, quickly starring in his own series in *Master Comics* and, within a year, also spinning off into a solo title. Both would run until 1953.

To become his super alterego Freeman only had to say the name "Captain Marvel," but chose to live a Dickensian existence as a crippled, orphaned newspaper vendor. As a hero he never acquired the villains gallery his mentor enjoyed; instead he had quirky, often fairy-tale-like adventures and boasted a fondness for Elvis Presley (his hairstyle and stance are known to have influenced Presley's act). The strip's great attraction was the early artwork of Mac Raboy, which combined an innate draftsmanship with a real sense of grace; his scenes of Captain Marvel Jr. flying were among the most elegant of the era. Raboy left in 1944 and, while no other artist quite matched his vision, the character retained an undeniably iconic appeal. **DR**

Archie 1941

✎✎ Joe Montana and John L. Goldwater

First published by MLJ Publications (USA)
Creator Montana (American, 1920–75);
Goldwater (American, 1916–99)
Genre Teen, Romance

Archie Andrews was introduced in issue #22 of superhero anthology *Pep*, along with best friend, Jughead Jones and Betty Cooper. Later rich debutante Veronica Lodge arrived, forming an eternal triangle. Although the dynamics of the relationship have changed over the years, essentially Betty loves Archie, who in turn loves Veronica. Immediately popular, Archie was launched in his own series in 1943.

The stories are set in the archetypal U.S. small town of Riverdale. Archie is meant to be a typical teenager, so he is girl-crazy and always in trouble with the school authorities. The rich supporting cast includes parents, notably Veronica's father, Hiram. Also appearing are Reggie Mantle, rival for Veronica's affections, and classmates Dilton (the egghead), Ethel (in unrequited love with Jughead), Moose (a dim-witted sportsman), and Midge (Moose's long-suffering girlfriend). African-American characters first appeared in the 1970s, while Indian, Mexican, and Japanese characters arrived later. In 2010, the first openly gay character appeared in Riverdale—Kevin Keller.

MLJ Comics founder John L. Goldwater is credited with creating the characters while their likenesses are the work of Bob Montana, whose artwork can be seen at its best in the *Archie* newspaper strip. Among the best *Archie* artists are Dan DeCarlo, George Frese, Harry Lucey, and Samm Schwartz. There have also been many different titles as Archie Comics experimented with oddball titles such as *Dilton's Strange Science* and *Jughead's Time Police*. **NFI**

Barnaby 1942

✎✎ "Crockett Johnson"

First published by PM (USA)
Creator David Johnson Leisk (American, 1906–75)
Genre Humor
Influence on *Flook*

Barnaby is a young boy who finds himself wishing for a fairy godmother after hearing a bedtime story from his mother. As he's wishing, a bright star appears outside his bedroom window and a winged man, Mr. O'Malley, flies through it. "Cushlamochree! Broke my magic wand!" he says, before explaining to Barnaby that he is his actual fairy godfather. O'Malley leaves before Barnaby's parents arrive to see what he's doing out of bed, but Barnaby is convinced it wasn't a dream when he finds the ashes from O'Malley's cigar (wand) on the carpet. Thereafter, Barnaby's parents think he has just dreamed up this fairy godfather and, despite Barnaby's attempts to have them all meet, there's always something that just prevents them doing so.

When Barnaby gets around to asking for a wish to be granted, O'Malley claims that his "fine Havana magic wand is a bit short to grant wishes with," but compensates by scrounging some of Barnaby's father's cigars as well as some food. Somehow O'Malley always manages to create trouble for Barnaby, whether it's blowing up his father's car after filling the inner tubes with gasoline ("I got too close with this fine Havana magic wand") or causing an ogre to come looking for a magic egg at Barnaby's house. The plots are driven by the entrepreneurial antics of O'Malley, who can suddenly become an international financier or a writer for a food column. Meanwhile, innocent Barnaby, sometimes with his friend Jane, finds himself rubbing shoulders with a talking dog, ghosts, witches, and other supernatural beings. **NFI**

Jingle Jangle Comics 1942

George Carlson

First published by Eastern Color (USA)
Creator American (1887–1962)
Genre Children's
Collection *Famous Funnies* (1942)

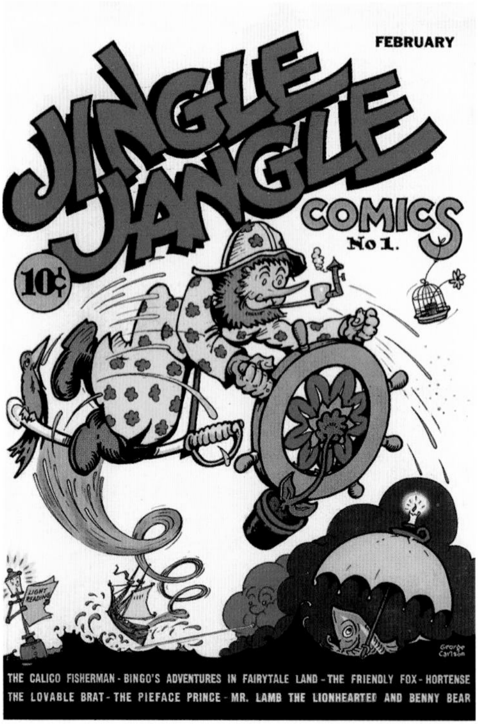
FEBRUARY
JINGLE JANGLE COMICS
No 1.
10¢
LIGHT READING
George Carlson
THE CALICO FISHERMAN - BINGO'S ADVENTURES IN FAIRYTALE LAND - THE FRIENDLY FOX - HORTENSE THE LOVABLE BRAT - THE PIEFACE PRINCE - MR. LAMB THE LIONHEARTED AND BENNY BEAR

"What he did was miraculous and happens only once in a particular art form."

Harlan Ellison, author

George Carlson's comics remain unique fifty years after his death. He composed his pages as an artist, not a storyteller, yet his storytelling is exemplary, honed by many years of drawing children's books. Carlson's figures are constantly in motion, bending this way and that, inhabiting a nonsensical, unstable world referencing nursery rhymes and surrounded by as many anthropomorphic variations on ordinary objects as you care to imagine. It was a world that captivated both children and adults with its strange charm.

Were these not patently comics aimed at younger children their most obvious successors would be the more chemically aided offerings of the 1960s underground cartoonists. An earlier touchstone would be *Krazy Kat*. Carlson brings George Herriman's jagged and off-kilter approach to his soft-edged subjects and shares his fondness for whimsical background detail.

Carlson produced the jacket illustration for *Gone with the Wind*'s first edition, but his only known comics prior to 1942 were for *Film Fun* over twenty years previously, those one page gag-strips providing a full movie. They were well drawn, with no hint of the flourishes to come. The same artistic eccentricity extends to Carlson's writing. His stories are fairy tales, immersed in verbal dexterity, alliteration, and the contortions of a unique mind.

The story titles alone soar: *The Double-Rich Banker and the Well-Watered Hat Tree*, *The Coffee-Eyed Hermit and the Unprisoned Princess*, and *The Sultan's High Class Plumber and the Very Little Leek*. Try translating those into French and Japanese.

A loving 400-word eulogy to Carlson in the *Bridgeport Telegram* after his death detailed a life of accomplishment. However, it sadly neglected to mention *Jingle Jangle Comics*, the only achievement for which he is remembered. **FP**

Powerhouse Pepper 1942

Basil Wolverton

Powerhouse Pepper, ostensibly a small and slow-witted boxer, is transported by his creator, Basil Wolverton, to many different locations from the Old West to a construction site, or the slopes of a ski resort, without any explanation. His occupation is secondary to his willingness to fight anyone who speaks out of turn or threatens the weak and innocent.

His fighting abilities are those of a superhero, including super strength and being impervious to bullets. Pepper might not exactly go looking for fights, but all roughnecks, criminals, and common or garden thugs are likely to find that annoying him can be hazardous to their health. Women rarely intrude on Pepper's world, except in an opening gag panel, but they are impossibly glamorous compared to the other characters Wolverton draws.

In the nonnarrative, six to eight page episodes Wolverton pitted his hero against a gallery of grotesques with large noses—be they crooked, beaked, or strangely doubled over—and wide mouths. Although a superhero, Pepper is of slight build, which makes bullies believe he is an easy target, but he always manages to take on the hulking brutes with an easy nonchalance.

Pepper appeared in *Joker Comics* as well as in five issues of his own title, with short runs in *Gay Comics* and *Tessie the Typist*. His regular appearances ended in 1948, but stories completed after that time appeared in various humor publications up until 1970.

Wolverton's artwork is clean, his figures exaggerated and sharply inked. Much of the humor of the strip lies in his use of language, which is rich with puns and alliteration. He fills the panels with sight gags and out of place signs (an arm reaches out of the sand next to a board saying "beach comber" for instance), and his irreverent and sometimes silly sense of humor gives this work a timeless appeal. **NFI**

First published by Timely/Marvel Comics (USA)
Creator American (1909–78)
Genre Superhero
Award Jack Kirby Hall of Fame (1991)

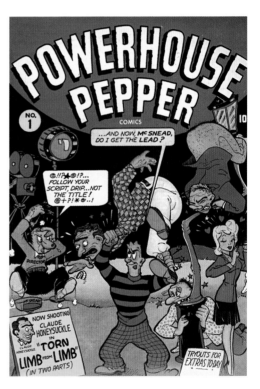

POWERHOUSE PEPPER
COMICS
NO. 1
10
...AND NOW, Mc SNEAD, DO I GET THE LEAD?
@.!!?★@!?... FOLLOW YOUR SCRIPT, DRIP...NOT THE TITLE! @+?!*@..!
DIRECTOR
NOW SHOOTING CLAUDE HONEYSUCKLE IN "TORN LIMB FROM LIMB" (IN TWO PARTS)
TRYOUTS FOR EXTRAS TO-DAY

"Powerhouse Pepper sailed through life in a sea of rhymes, rhythms, and alliterations."

Don Markstein, comics historian

Adventures of Tintin
The Secret of the Unicorn 1942
✐✎ "Hergé"

Title in original language *Le secret de la licorne*
First published by *Le Soir* (Belgium)
Creator Georges Prosper Remi Remi (Belgian, 1907–83)
Genre Adventure

For a number of reasons, *The Secret of the Unicorn* and *Red Rackham's Treasure* are notable landmarks in the history of *Tintin* and, therefore, by extension, in the history of comics. They form the first ever two-part Tintin adventure, giving Hergé greater space to explore moments of character and comedy alongside one of his typically fast-paced plots. Secondly, the participation of friend and fellow artist Edgar P. Jacobs pushed the artwork to even greater heights of verisimilitude, with objects, backgrounds, costume and décor all exactly researched and then rendered in Hergé's increasingly assured "clear line" style. Thirdly, *Red Rackham's Treasure* not only introduced Professor Tryphon Tournesol (Professor Cuthbert Calculus, in English), a delicious comic foil for the ever-exasperated Captain Haddock, but also confirmed the captain as the owner of Moulinsart (Marlinspike) Hall, a large country house that served as a key location in many subsequent *Tintin* adventures.

Unicorn is an urban mystery thriller, with Tintin and Captain Haddock acquiring three parchments that point to the location of some priceless treasure that once belonged to the pirate Red Rackham. Both volumes find Hergé trying out new storytelling devices, such as a long, intense flashback sequence that enters the narrative in a way that still feels strikingly modern. Produced under German occupation, at the time *Unicorn* and *Treasure* appeared to avoid "current affairs" but now it is not hard to see parallels between Red Rackham and any number of twentieth-century despots. **AL**

Adventures of Tintin
The Seven Crystal Balls 1943
✐✎ "Hergé"

Title in original language *Les 7 Boules de cristal* and *Le Temple du soleil* **First published by** *Le Soir* (Belgium)
Creator Georges Prosper Remi Remi (Belgian, 1907–83)
Genre Adventure

Back from the Andes where they have dug up the Inca mummy, Rascar Capac, all seven members of an archaeological expedition fall into a deep coma. Tintin, Haddock, and Calculus are present at the home of Bergamotte, the last of the seven archaeologists, when he also falls victim to this strange disease and Calculus is kidnapped.

Tintin and Haddock discover that their friend has been drugged and put on board a Peruvian cargo ship at La Rochelle so they immediately fly to South America. In Peru, they befriend little Zorrino, who acts as a guide, and set off in hot pursuit across the Amazon jungle and the mountains of the Andes.

This amazing voyage of the young reporter and his companions ends within the walls of the Temple of the Sun, a secret location from whence the descendant of the Inca kings still rules. Calculus, accused of sacrilege because he has innocently taken Rascar Capac's bracelet, is condemned, like the rest of group, to burn at the stake. Tintin's clever stunt to free them is one of the finest bravura moments of the series.

Hergé was inspired to create *The Seven Crystal Balls* and *Prisoners of the Sun* by the famous curse said to have plagued the archaeologists who discovered Tutankhamun's tomb in the 1920s. They are among the best of Tintin's adventures, with faultless storytelling and outstanding graphics vigorously glorifying adventure for adventure's sake. Almost seventy years after they first appeared, they can still be re-read with the same intense pleasure. **NF**

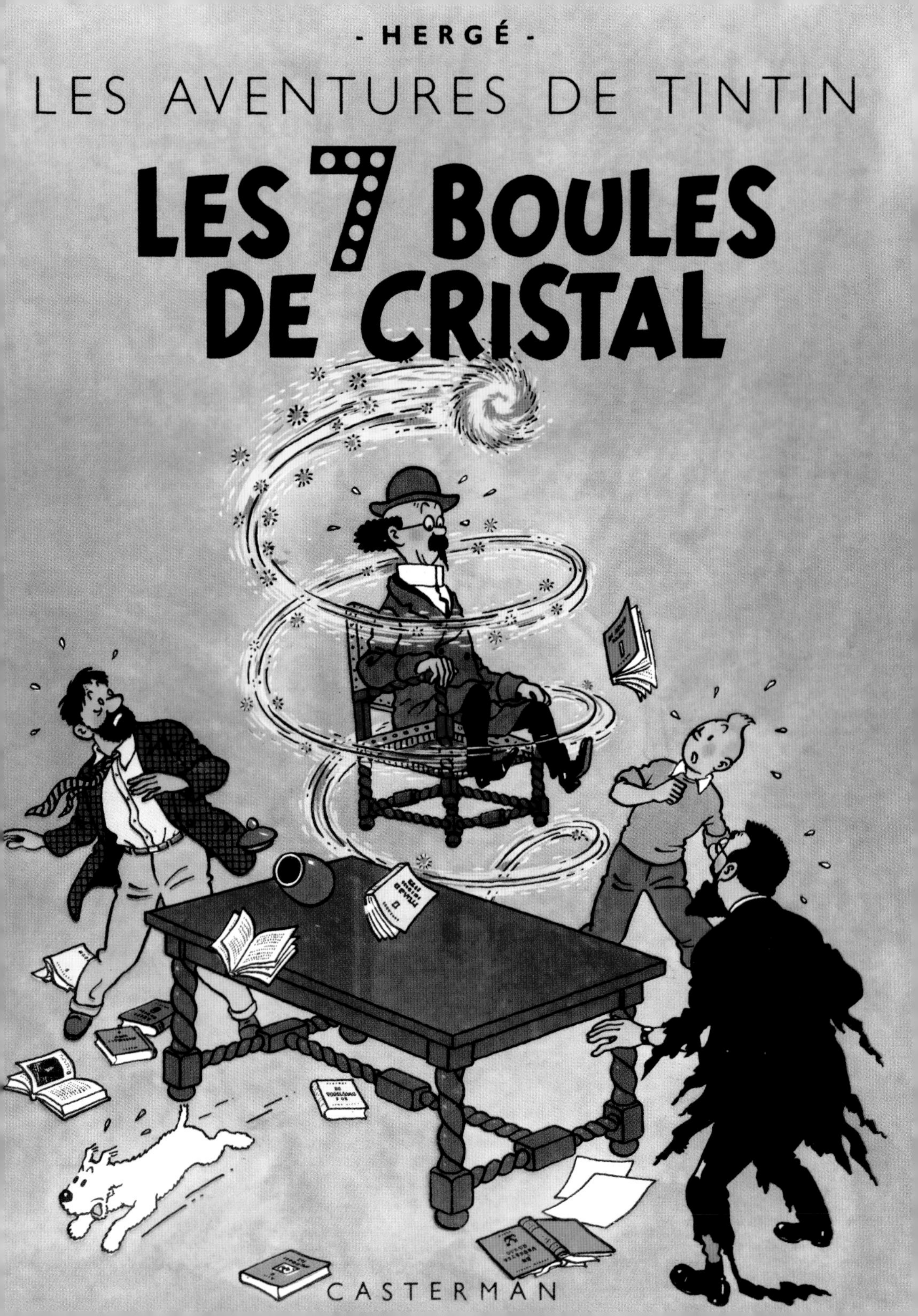
- HERGÉ -
LES AVENTURES DE TINTIN
LES 7 BOULES DE CRISTAL
CASTERMAN

Captain Marvel
The Monster Society of Evil 1943

Otto Binder · C. C. Beck

First published by Fawcett Comics (USA)
Creators Binder (American, 1911–74); Beck (American, 1910–89)
Genre Superhero

Around once every decade the Captain Marvel character is revived, although reworking him in the modern superhero idiom has achieved varying degrees of success. By contrast, the original Captain Marvel actively eschewed realism, as plucky, twelve-year-old newsboy Billy Batson became the world's mightiest mortal. Characterized by the deceptive simplicity of the artwork and an inherent innocence and humor, Otto Binder and C. C. Beck never forgot *Captain Marvel* was a vehicle for fantastic stories to entertain children. His fight against the Monster Society of Evil illustrates this perfectly.

Over several issues he butts heads with foes organized by the unseen villain Mr. Mind, who is later revealed as an alien worm. Years later Binder confessed that at the outset there was no fixed idea of the Mr. Mind character, but when the concept of "the World's Mightiest Mortal plagued by the World's Weakest Creature" occurred, it fitted elements neatly.

Captain Marvel was one of the most popular superheroes of the 1940s, but for all his success in dismantling Mr. Mind's schemes, the latter evaded capture. In an interesting reverse he would later feature in cliffhangers, about to be consumed by Nazi Hermann Goering or crushed on the sidewalk. This is not the first continued story in comics history, and it should be noted that a typical issue of *Captain Marvel* featured at least four stories. Yet the sheer ambition of continuing episodes that ran over two years resulted in success, and these comics are still worth reading today. **FP**

The Beast Is Dead! 1944

Victor Dancette · Edmond-François Calvo

Title in original language *La Bête est Morte!*
First published by Editions G.P. (France)
Creators Dancette (French, Unknown); Calvo (French, 1892–1958) **Genre** Drama

In the years preceding World War II, French children were used to anthropomorphic tales involving animals and nature, such as Yvonne Estienne's *The Story of a Beautiful Oak* (*La Belle Histoire d'un Chene*) about a giant oak tree (representing Vichy France) that protected the forest's flora and fauna (the French people) from an approaching storm (the German army). Comic books were banned when *The Beast Is Dead!* was first produced in 1944, appearing on French newsstands just three months after the German retreat from Paris.

Using animals as protagonists, writer Victor Dancette and illustrator Edmond-François Calvo portray Occupied France through the eyes of animals: Hitler and the German army are rabid wolves; Goering an overweight, preposterous-looking pig, and Goebbels a deformed weasel whose propaganda Dancette delights in mocking. The French people are rabbits and squirrels, the British are bulldogs, Mussolini a baying hyena, and the Americans herds of liberating bison. All the horrors and atrocities of war are laid bare, save for the Vichy government's collaboration with the Germans, which is ignored in favor of the French Resistance, including the depiction of General de Gaulle as a majestic white stork with a Cross of Lorraine around his neck.

Originally published in two volumes—*The Beast Is Unleashed* and *The Beast Is Devastated*—*The Beast Is Dead!*'s complex, bombastic, and voluminous prose might be difficult for contemporary children to digest and is perhaps a little dated, but Calvo's haunting illustrations are as remarkable as ever. **BS**

Calvo's rabbit nurse dispenses bedpans, cigarettes, and wine to the wounded. ➡

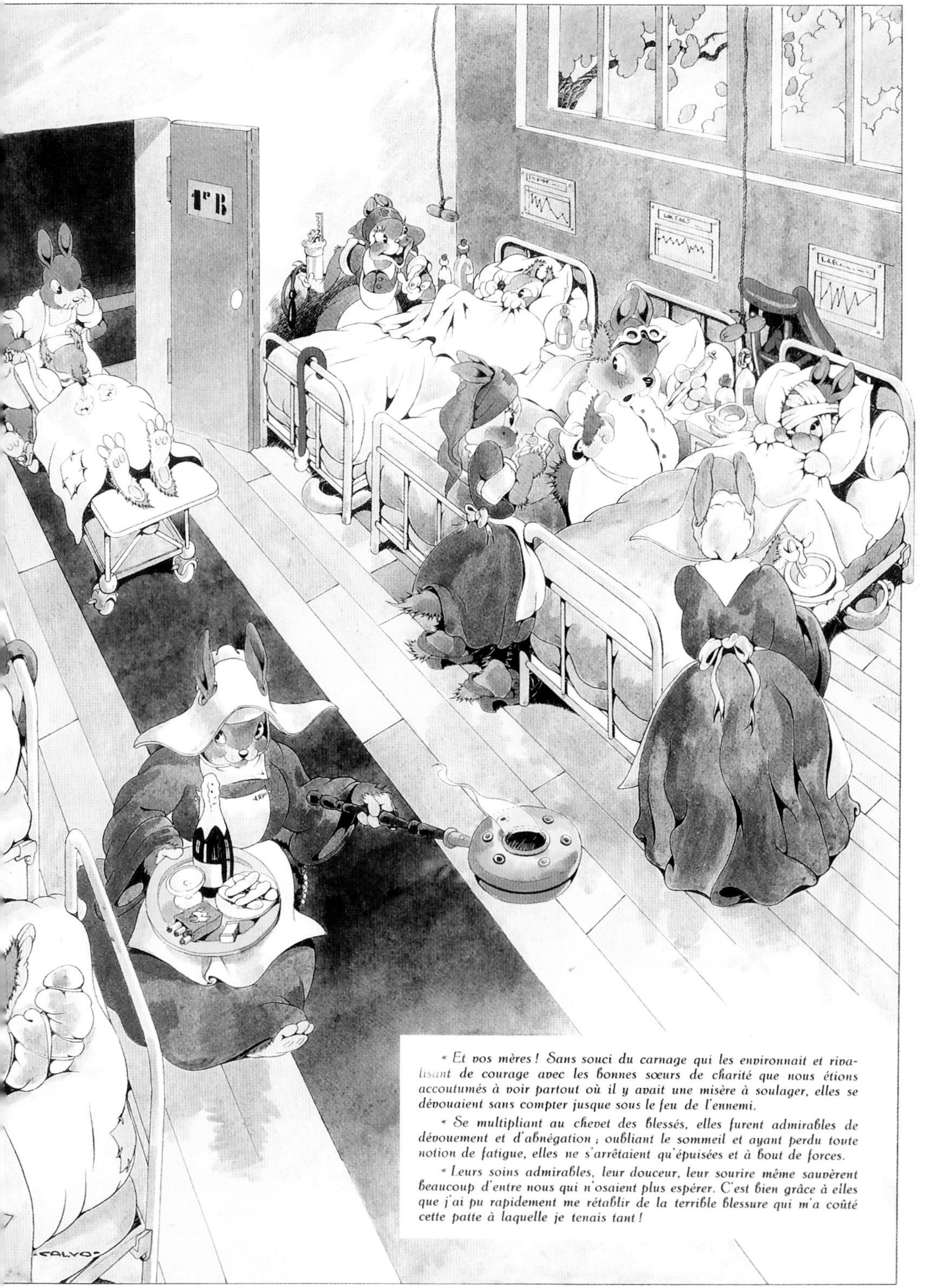
1r B
CALVO

« Et vos mères ! Sans souci du carnage qui les environnait et rivalisant de courage avec les bonnes sœurs de charité que nous étions accoutumés à voir partout où il y avait une misère à soulager, elles se dévouaient sans compter jusque sous le feu de l'ennemi.

« Se multipliant au chevet des blessés, elles furent admirables de dévouement et d'abnégation ; oubliant le sommeil et ayant perdu toute notion de fatigue, elles ne s'arrêtaient qu'épuisées et à bout de forces.

« Leurs soins admirables, leur douceur, leur sourire même sauvèrent beaucoup d'entre nous qui n'osaient plus espérer. C'est bien grâce à elles que j'ai pu rapidement me rétablir de la terrible blessure qui m'a coûté cette patte à laquelle je tenais tant !

The Ulises Family 1944

Joaquim Buigas Marino Benejam

Title in original language *La familia Ulises*
First published by *TBO* (Spain)
Creators Buigas (Spanish, 1886–1963); Benejam (Spanish, 1890–1975) **Genre** Satire

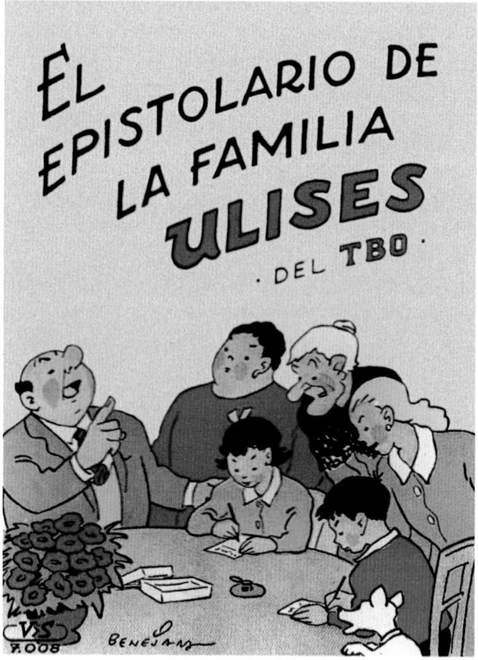
EL EPISTOLARIO DE LA FAMILIA ULISES
· DEL TBO ·
BENEJAM

Similar reads
Eustaquio Morcillón Marino Benejam
Melitón Pérez Marino Benejam
Pumby José Sanchís
Short Stories Josep Coll
Topolino Alfons Figueras

The Ulises Family is a humorous family strip published in the venerable Spanish comic weekly *TBO*—from whose title derives the word *tebeo*, used in Spain to designate any comic book—with scripts by Joaquim Buigas and art by Marino Benejam. Nearly always published as a one-pager on the magazine's back cover, *The Ulises Family* depicted the adventures and misadventures of a large middle-class family led by good-natured Don Ulises Higueruelo.

The rest of the Ulises clan included his dominant wife, Doña Sinforosa, posh elder daughter Lolín, who was perpetually in search of a boyfriend, mischievous younger children Policarpito and Merceditas, and their amiable grandmother Doña Filomena, an expert in medicinal plants. A lap dog, Treski, rounded up the family circle.

Deemed as a faithful reflection of the joys and griefs of the average Spanish family, *The Ulises Family* was set in an unidentified large city which undoubtedly could be Barcelona. Stories tend to depict the attempts of Don Ulises and his kin to climb socially by "keeping up with the Joneses," or simply trying to make a good impression when invited to an upper-class event, alongside other entertaining situations. However, mostly due to fate, such attempts usually ended in catastrophe, although not on a level with the violence of other Spanish humor comics such as *Mortadelo y Filemón*.

The apparently lighthearted, but often scathing, scripts were enhanced by Benejam's elegant and stylized artwork. After Buigas passed away in 1963, Carlos Bech took over the writing of this darkly satiric series. In 1969, due to vision problems, Benejam retired from drawing the strip and was replaced by José Maria Blanco until 1979. *The Ulises Family* has survived to this day through reprints. **AMo**

The Pioneers of Hope 1945

Roger Lécureux Raymond Poïvet

The International Assembly sends a spacecraft, *L'Espérance*, to a planet, Radias, that threatens the safety of Earth. On board is a crew of four men and two women, representing a large part of humanity: the Frenchman Robert (who was soon to be renamed Tangha), the American Maud, the Chinese Tsin-Lu, the Soviet Rodion, the Englishman Wright, and Tom, from Martinique. Confronted by the peoples and dangers encountered in space, this small cosmopolitan group is soon reduced to four.

Tangha and Maud take the role of a glamorous couple living out numerous adventures while at the same time trying to extend the field of human knowledge and spread the ideals advocated by Earth.

The period in which this comic was conceived (World War II had recently come to an end) naturally played an important part in the rather pacifist character of this series. The identity of the magazine for which *The Pioneers of Hope* was created (*Vaillant* was a magazine for the young and heir to the spirit of the Resistance) further strengthens this positioning. It is a work of science fiction, often humanist and enlightened, whose heroes fight not to conquer but for noble objectives such as knowledge and justice.

A realistic draftsman of great elegance, Raymond Poïvet succeeded in distancing himself from his most obvious source of inspiration, Alex Raymond, the American author of *Flash Gordon*. He developed his own style, which became a solid benchmark of Franco-Belgian strip cartoons thanks to the longevity of the series, which was published over a period of thirty years. A large number of Poïvet's drawings give the impression of being quick sketches, more like outlines than finalized works, with an unfinished character contributing to the unusual and very successful graphic effect of this very lovable series. **NF**

Title in original language *Les Pionniers de l'Espérance*
First published by *Vaillant* (France)
Creators Lécureux (French, 1925–99); Poïvet (French, 1910–99) **Genre** Science fiction

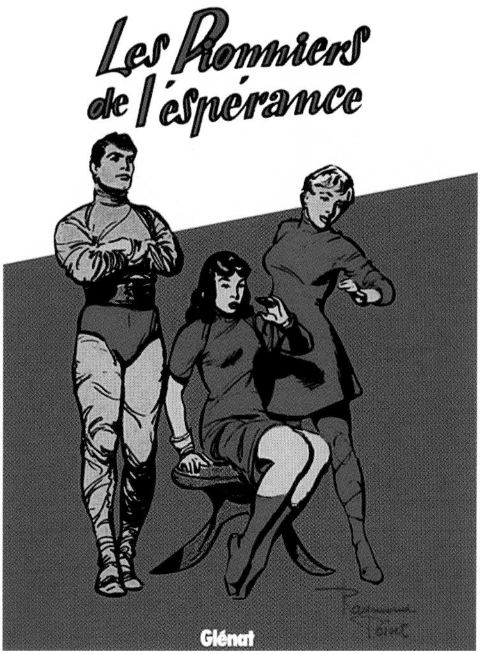
Les Pionniers de l'espérance
Glénat

Similar reads

Buck Rogers Philip Nowlan and Dick Calkins
Colonel X Marijac and Raymond Poïvet
Flash Gordon Don Moore and Alex Raymond
Nasdine Hodja Roger Lécureux and Pierre Le Guen
Tiriel Jean-Pierre Dionnet and Raymond Poïvet

The Fox and the Crow 1945

Cecil Beard   Jim Davis

First published by National Periodical Publications (USA)
Creators Beard (American, 1907–86);
Davis (American, 1915–96)
Genre Humor

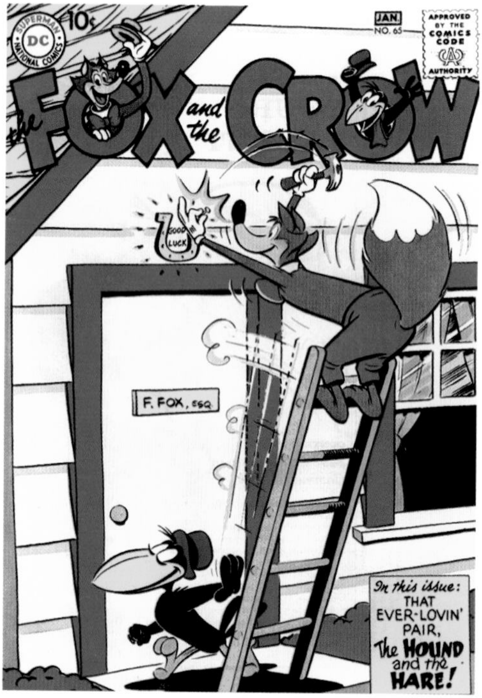
10¢
DC
SUPERMAN NATIONAL COMICS
JAN. NO. 65
APPROVED BY THE COMICS CODE AUTHORITY
the FOX and the CROW
GOOD LUCK
F. FOX, ESQ.
In this issue: THAT EVER-LOVIN' PAIR, The HOUND and the HARE!

Similar reads
Nutsy Squirrel Irving Dresler
Stanley and his Monster
Arnold Drake and J. Winslow Mortimer
The Dodo and the Frog Otto Feuer
The Three Mouseketeers Sheldon Mayer

The Fox and the Crow was originally a series of animated theatrical shorts produced by Columbia Pictures' Screen Gems studio. The first one, *The Fox and the Grapes*, directed by Frank Tashlin, set the pattern for the series, establishing a relationship between both characters not unlike Warner Bros.' *Road Runner and Coyote*.

The theatrical career of *The Fox and the Crow* was short-lived with just sixteen cartoons released between 1941 and 1950. The final three were made by innovative studio UPA after Screen Gems closed shop. However, *The Fox and the Crow* found new life in comic books and first appeared in issue #1 of *Real Screen Funnies*.

The stories depicted the attempts of cunning, Brooklyn-accented, cigar-smoking Crawford Crow to con selfish, petit bourgeois, and gullible Fauntleroy Fox. Fauntleroy Fox lived in a suburban house beside the tree that Crow called home. The latter would casually help himself to the Fox's properties, such as food and money, while using clever disguises and tricks to hide his thefts and machinations.

"We would be rolling on the floor in hysterics."

Cecil Beard

The series was first written by Hubie Karp and later by Cecil Beard (assisted by his wife, Alpine Harper) and usually drawn by Jim (James T.) Davis. Having worked in the animation field, Davis was able to apply frantic timing and slapstick humor to the comics, which made them look like storyboards. Other artists included Bob Wickersham, Owen Fitzgerald, and Kay Wright.

In addition to *Real Screen Funnies* (later renamed *TV Screen Cartoons* and canceled in 1961), *The Fox and the Crow* also appeared in *Comic Cavalcade* and in their own title from 1952, which lasted until 1968. **AMo**

Spike and Suzy 1945

"Willy" Vandersteen

Title in original language *Suske en Wiske* **First published by** *De Standaard* (Belgium) **Creator** Willebrord Jan Frans Maria Vandersteen (Belgian, 1913–90) **Genre** Humor, Adventure

Willy Vandersteen roamed the Antwerp docks and movie houses as a child. He was trained to join his father's business as a maker of ornaments, a dying trade after the 1920s, but he preferred the freshly printed juvenile magazines on the presses next to his father's workshop. By 1930, as a Dutch-speaking Boy Scout in Belgium, he copied Hergé's style and *Totor* strip. Even his Scouts' name, Sluwe Vos (sly fox), echoed Hergé's *Renard Curieux* (curious fox).

In 1936 he became a window-dresser. Under German occupation in World War II, when U.S. strips stopped in Belgium, he ventured into comics under the pen names Mik, Bobs, or Kaproen. After the war he wrote and drew eighty-one stories of his boy-girl duo, *Spike and Suzy* (*Suske en Wiske*). In the first, set in Eastern Europe's "Chocowakije," they were Rikki and Wiske; Tintin-lookalike Rikki was switched to Suske.

"A comic strip in a newspaper, the daily drop of publicity..."

Willy Vandersteen

Appearing in newspapers from 1945 to 1971, mostly with rhyming titles, these great comic adventures were full of echoes from foreign strips and films. Vandersteen teamed up his duo with Aunt Sidonie, strongman Jerom, and plumber detective Lambik (named after a type of Belgian beer). The book reprints were produced only in brown and blue.

Vandersteen's 1950s full-color stories in *Tintin/Kuifje* weekly were overtly in an Hergé style. Using lots of moralizing, and switching from lively Flemish to sterile Dutch or French, earned him a larger audience. With his studio he made many other strip series, comical as well as realistic, from *De Familie Snoek and 't Prinske* to *Bessy* and *De Rode Ridder*, and more. **HvO**

DE AVONTUREN VAN
SUSKE EN WISKE
DE KNOKKERSBURCHT
door
WILLY VANDERSTEEN
UITGEVERSMIJ. N.V. STANDAARD-BOEKHANDEL

Similar reads

Alley Oop V. T. Hamlin
Jean d'Armor Henry Le Monnier
Meester Mus Bob de Moor
The Adventures of Nero Marc Sleen
Wrill le Renard Albert Fromenteau

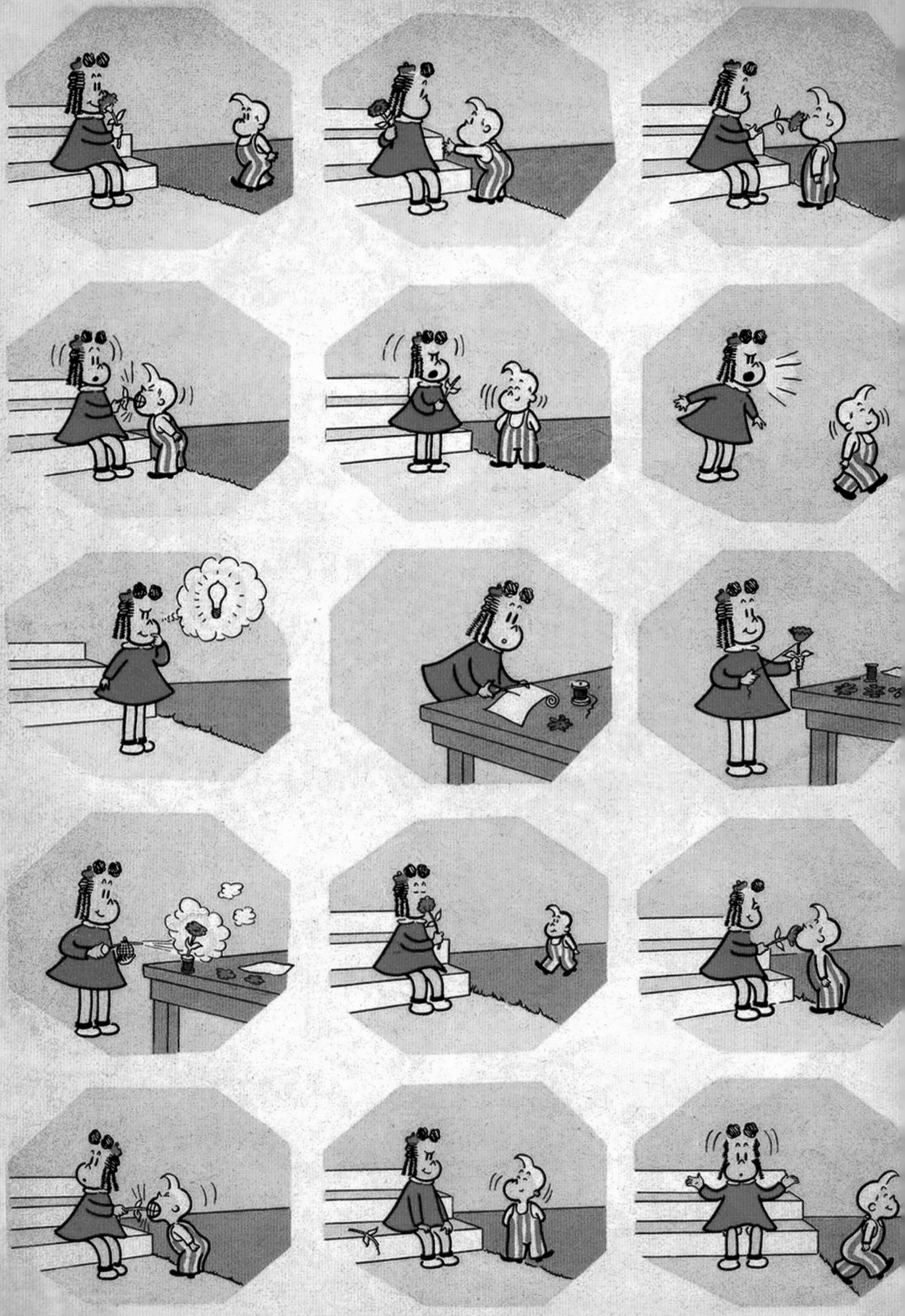

Little Lulu 1945

John Stanley ✏ *Irving Tripp* ✒

First published by Dell Comics (USA)
Creators Stanley (American, 1914–93)
Tripp (American, 1921–2009)
Genre Humor, Children's

The charming and amusing *Little Lulu* was originally created by "Marge" Henderson Buell as a single panel cartoon in 1935. When picked up for publication by Dell (with Henderson Buell exercising some editorial control), John Stanley introduced a whole neighborhood of characters for Lulu to interact with.

The Boys Club, whose members include Tubby, Iggy, Willy, and Eddie, have a straightforward rule: "No Girls Allowed." It is a rule that is broken if the boys really need Lulu's help, for example, but always on the understanding that Lulu's membership is temporary. Lulu might be young and occasionally naive, but she has a brain and takes no nonsense from anyone. Much of the humor arises from stories pitting female against male. The cast of girls usually features Lulu and Annie, Iggy's sister, and sometimes Gloria, Lulu's rival. Also appearing are the West Side Boys, a rougher, tougher group led by Spike.

Tubby, as his name suggests, is always looking to eat, preferably for free, but he also has a role as private investigator—the Spider—who is quick to blame Lulu's father for whatever trouble Lulu is in. A regular scenario featured Lulu telling a story to her bratty neighbor, Alvin, and Stanley concocted any number of reasons as to why Lulu should do so. These flights of fantasy had far more exposition than other comic strips.

Stanley drew the earliest stories himself, later writing and providing layouts for Irving Tripp. Robert Crumb, an avid reader in the 1940s, saw *Little Lulu* and *Donald Duck* as the best comics of the period. **NFI**

The Wonderful World of Sazae-san 1946

✏✒ *Machiko Hasegawa*

Title in original language *Sazae-san*
First published by *Fukunichi Shinbun* (Japan)
Creator Japanese (1926–92)
Genre Humor

The Wonderful World of Sazae-san can be regarded as the Japanese equivalent of *Blondie*. Created by Machiko Hasegawa, one of the very first woman cartoonists to achieve success in Japan, as a *yon-koma manga* (literally "four-panel manga"), it premiered on April 22, 1946, in the *Fukunichi Shinbun*, a newspaper from the author's hometown. It went nationwide in 1949 when it moved to Tokyo's *Asahi Shinbun*.

The cast of characters includes Sazae Isono, a lively housewife, Sazae's husband Masuo Fuguta; Sazae's brother Katsuo and sister Wakame; her parents, Namihei and Fune; Sazae's and Masuo's son, Tarao; and Tama, the family's pet cat. Over the years, the strip has mirrored the social changes undergone by Japanese society since the end of World War II. Its protagonists have aged at the same time: Sazae has evolved from a young twenty-four year old to a plump and kind old matron.

On February 24, 1974, the final *Sazae-san* strip was published, due to Hasegawa's retirement. Since then, it has been constantly reprinted in book form, making *Sazae-san* the most widespread Japanese manga ever. It has been adapted into radio shows, stage plays, live-action movies, and, since 1969, an animated TV series broadcast by Fuji TV. It is still in production to this day, making it the world's longest-running animated TV series of all time, with more than 3,000 episodes.

A dozen *Sazae-san* strip compilations have been published by Kodansha International in a bilingual English/Japanese edition known as *The Wonderful World of Sazae-san*. **AMo**

← Stanley's *Little Lulu* strips feature a cast of mischievous children.

Rip Kirby 1946

Alex Raymond

First published by King Features Syndicate (USA)
Creator American (1909–56)
Genre Action, Crime, Detective
Award Reuben Award (1949)

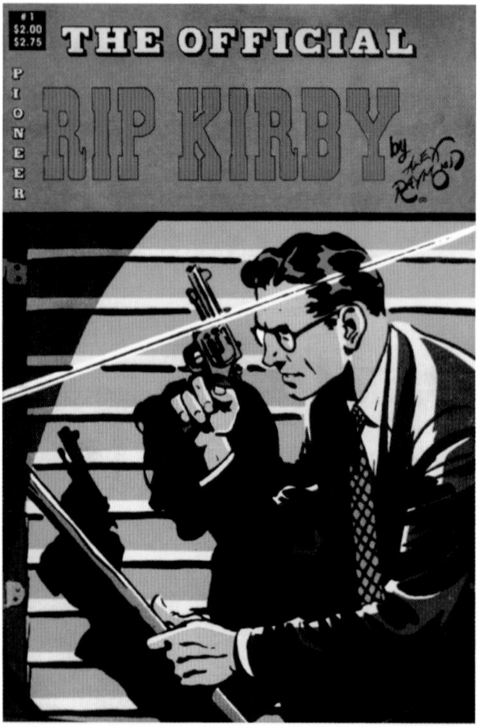

#1
$2.00
$2.75
THE OFFICIAL
PIONEER
RIP KIRBY
by Alex Raymond

Similar reads
Dick Tracy Chester Gould
Jim Hardy Dick Moores
Mickey Finn Lank Leonard
Secret Agent X-9 Dashiell Hammett and Alex Raymond

When Alex Raymond, the creator of *Flash Gordon*, returned to civilian life in 1946 after wartime service in the Marine Corps he did not resume work on his hit science fiction strip. Instead, he turned his attention to creating a new breed of private detective, *Rip Kirby*.

Rip Kirby's approach to solving crime broke ranks with the methods typically employed by other pulp detectives of the era. He punched less and thought more, and rather than a string of female suitors he had a single love interest—the pure and virtuous Honey Dorian. He was dapper, smoked a pipe, played the piano, and had Desmond, his balding butler and reformed safecracker, as his sidekick. But he was still a tough, no-nonsense ex-Marine.

"Rip wasn't the kind of private detective they were used to from pulp fiction."

Don Markstein, comics historian

Raymond approached the writing as if he were composing a novel. He had the dream of creating, in his words, "a very superior type feature" that had solid narratives without a hint of repetitiveness. Raymond had also developed into an exceptional portrait artist. His shadings, his use of grays and solid blacks, and the precision of his compositions were superb. His attention to detail was showcased in the rendering of everyday items such as clothing, curtains, and furnishings.

Fred Dickenson, a journalist who covered the hunt for criminal John Dillinger in the 1930s, took over the writing in 1952 and stayed with the strip for another thirty-four years. When Raymond was killed in a car crash in 1956 the illustrating duties were handed over to John Prentice who, during his own four-plus decades on the strip, made only subtle changes to the strip's nuanced and sophisticated look. **BS**

The Adventures of Sweet Gwendoline 1946

"John Willie"

Gwendoline is a blonde ingénue who is always getting into scrapes, which inevitably lead to her being tied up and gagged in intricate ways. And when she's not being kidnapped and restrained, she indulges in a little light bondage with her family and friends. Sir Dystic D'Arcy repeatedly carries Gwendoline off and Secret Agent U-69 rescues her, usually after giving her a whipping for getting captured in the first place.

You cannot underestimate how huge an influence the *Sweet Gwendoline* stories have had on erotic artists since John Willie published the first installments in the 1940s. He managed to balance an interest in the fetishistic trappings with a romping narrative, complete with daft cliff-hangers, and giving the kinky reader close-ups of rope techniques, gags, and heels while producing such a pretty product that those looking for more general titillation would not be put off.

> *"...it's difficult for [a model] to look miserable when working for me."*
>
> **John Willie**

Gwendoline's first eponymous outing has loose line and wash artwork, whereas later stories became more detailed and precise. They feature slender-waisted, well-endowed women who favor skintight trousers and skirts, skyscraper heels, and corsets. Willie's fetish world is decorously kinky, and all the bondage is done with a nod and a wink. In the spirit of silent movies, with the heroine tied to the rail track, the stories are lighthearted, with mustachio-twirling baddies, too-good-to-be-true heroes, and dark-eyed dominatrices—it was a giddy fantasy that indulged all the artist's particular fetishes.

Belier Press printed a previously unseen forty-page *Sweet Gwendoline* story called *The Golden Idol,* to accompany their reprints of the other five tales. **FJ**

First published by *Bizarre* (USA)
Creator John Alexander Scott Coutts (American, 1902–62)
Genre Erotic
Adaptation Film (1984)

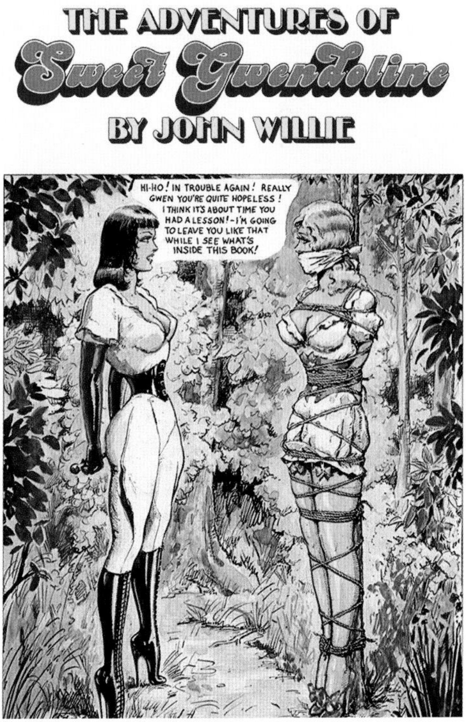
THE ADVENTURES OF
Sweet Gwendoline
BY JOHN WILLIE
HI-HO! IN TROUBLE AGAIN! REALLY GWEN YOU'RE QUITE HOPELESS! I THINK IT'S ABOUT TIME YOU HAD A LESSON! - I'M GOING TO LEAVE YOU LIKE THAT WHILE I SEE WHAT'S INSIDE THIS BOOK!

Similar reads

Bizarre Eric Kroll
Justine Guido Crepax
Sweeter Gwendoline Eric Stanton
The Story of O Guido Crepax

Citizen 13660 1946

✏️ Miné Okubo

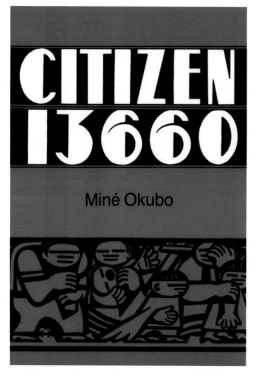

> *"We tagged our baggage with the family number, 13660, and pinned the personal tags on ourselves."*

Similar reads
American Born Chinese Gene Luen Yang
Barefoot Gen Keiji Nakazawa
Persepolis Marjane Satrapi
Safe Area Goražde Joe Sacco
The Four Immigrants Manga Henry Kiyama

First published by University of Washington Press (USA)
Creator Japanese-American (1912–2001)
Genre Autobiography
Award American Book Award (1984)

Miné Okubo, a talented artist who studied with Fernand Léger and collaborated with Diego Rivera, was traveling in Europe when World War II broke out. Returning home, she was shocked when Japanese bombers attacked Pearl Harbor. Even more shocking, however, was what followed: the mass internment of Japanese-Americans, Okubo included, regardless of their U.S. citizenship.

Citizen 13660 tells Okubo's story as she and her brother adapt to the indignities of life as second-class citizens. They are first taken to a racetrack outside San Francisco, where the shacks have been re-purposed so shoddily that workers have simply whitewashed over the hair of the horses that previously occupied the dwellings. The internees are then sent to Topaz, Utah, a place where the winds blow from all directions at once, and the arid desert surrounds them. Seething with frustration at their interrupted lives, the inmates stay as busy as they can—knitting, playing go, gardening.

The claustrophobia of the camp is almost palpable in Okubo's tightly packed narrative. Picturing herself in nearly every drawing, readers get the sense that as the camps suffocate her identity—the government has already stripped her of her family name—Okubo insists on an individual presence somewhere in the world, even if it is simply on a piece of paper. Some may wonder if this memoir is a comic book—each image is accompanied by a paragraph of text, with no thought bubbles or speech balloons. However, when words and pictures are used so powerfully to capture human experience, it seems petty to quibble over details. **EL**

Eric the Norseman 1946

✒ Hans G. Kresse

Title in original language *Eric de Noorman*
First published by 't Kasteel van Aemstel/De Tijd
(Netherlands) **Creator** Hans Georg Kresse (German-
Dutch, 1921–92) **Genre** Adventure, Fantasy

Hans G. Kresse grew up in Amsterdam, the son of a Dutch mother and a German father. The young Hans occupied himself by learning to draw through endless sketching and copying. In late 1938, at the age of sixteen, he published his first strip serial—an adaptation of E. R. Burroughs' *Tarzan of the Apes*—in scouting magazine *De Verkenner*. It was hand-lettered with captions in the pictures, and signed "H. G. Kresse."

He followed this with a cowboy strip, but then World War II broke out and with it came the German occupation. As a German national, Kresse served in Hitler's army in 1941–42, but against his will. He was later sent to a military asylum and declared unfit. Having learned animation techniques, he went to work for Marten Toonder in 1943. After the liberation of the Netherlands in 1945, he was imprisoned for his wartime work on an anti-Semitic film and a comic for a Nazi magazine, which he had only dared sign "H. Zwart."

In 1946 his epic *Eric the Norseman* started in daily black and white in the Flemish newspaper *Het Laatste Nieuws*. The strip featured splendid artwork, filmic lighting and framing, graphic violence, and tough Vikings. Sixty-six stories appeared in small comic books. He created many more strips and illustrations, many in color. Despite his success and pivotal role in Dutch comic history, personal happiness eluded Kresse. He became a Dutch national in 1953, married twice, and had children, but also divorced twice and suffered from an eye disease. In his 1970s *Indianenreeks* albums he championed the Native American Indian cause. **HvO**

Steve Canyon 1947

✒ Milton Caniff

First published by Field Enterprises (USA)
Creator American (1907–88)
Genre Drama
Award Reuben Award (1971)

In 1946 Milton Caniff was at the height of his powers, enjoying great success with *Terry and the Pirates*, but he was concerned that the strip was owned by its syndicate and not himself. Instead, he created a new feature for the fledgling Field Enterprises Syndicate, one that was to be wholly owned and controlled by him. This strip became the popular *Steve Canyon*.

Contractual commitments to *Terry and the Pirates* meant that Caniff was unable to put anything down on paper until barely a few weeks before the strip was supposed to start and, consequently, Field had to sell the strip unseen. Such was Caniffs's reputation that 125 papers took the feature on trust. Their confidence was well-founded, as the strip displayed verve and panache, with an added maturity in the writing. Steve Canyon was an air force veteran running Horizons Unlimited, an air haulage firm that took him across the globe in search of danger and adventure. Caniff devised him as a square-jawed, all-American hero with a girl in every port. He visited hot spots such as Burma, Africa, China, and the Persian Gulf and was pitted against a bevy of femme fatales, such as Copper Calhoun, Captain Shark, Madame Lynx, and Lady Nine.

Critics have noted imperialist attitudes in Caniff's work, and the strip took a more confrontational tone during the Korean War, when Canyon signed up for active service in Vietnam and the Middle East. The feature died with him in 1988 but it is fondly remembered as a masterfully crafted slice of adventure from one of the medium's most influential creators. **DR**

Murder, Morphine and Me! 1947

Jack Cole

First published by Magazine Village (USA)
Creator American (1918–58)
Genre Crime
Award Will Eisner Award Hall of Fame (1999)

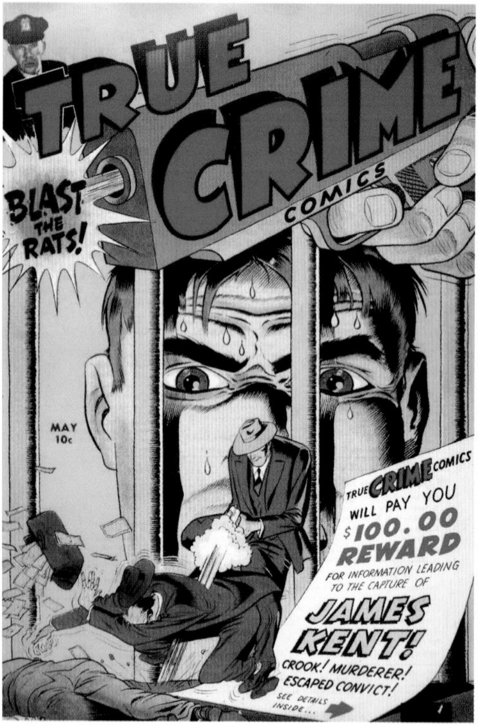
TRUE CRIME COMICS
BLAST THE RATS!
MAY 10¢
TRUE CRIME COMICS WILL PAY YOU $100.00 REWARD
FOR INFORMATION LEADING TO THE CAPTURE OF
JAMES KENT!
CROOK! MURDERER! ESCAPED CONVICT!
SEE DETAILS INSIDE...

Similar reads
Betsy and Me Jack Cole
Criminal Ed Brubaker and Sean Phillips
Hard-Boiled Defective Stories Charles Burns
King of the Flies Mezzo and Pirus

From his early success with the shape-shifting *Plastic Man* to his final offbeat family strip *Betsy and Me*, Jack Cole was a boundless innovator in the medium. When his attention turned to crime, he created this fourteen-page, 101-panel tour de force of histrionic anguish.

Tormented by her drug-induced nightmares, dope peddlar Mary Kennedy falls to pieces and breaks the fourth wall to confess her sordid history directly to the reader. She flashbacks to one evening in Los Angeles when a penniless addict breaks into her bedroom desperate for a shot of morphine. Callously she refuses him, but when he grabs her hair, she gives in, only to be terrorized by him pointing a syringe straight into her eyeball. Like the addict's wrecked body and Mary's panic,

"Who was the Big Boss of it all? You'll never guess, brother."

this panel quakes with emotion. It became notorious when American psychiatrist Dr Fredric Wertham extracted it out of context for the lurid picture section of his 1954 panic-inducing diatribe against comics, *Seduction of the Innocent*, as "a sample of the injury-to-the-eye motif." At this climax, Mary awakes screaming, from a dream, but also a trauma she cannot forget.

A flashback-within-a-flashback whisks readers next to Kansas City, where, lips aquiver, humble waitress Mary's thumping heart is stolen by tough guy Tony Petrillo, who leads her astray into a life of dope-dealing scams. Cole pulls out all the stops, distorting the shapes and lettering of his speech balloons to maximize emotion, emphasizing Tony's violent blows against Mary by making the entire panel teeter and vibrate. After one shocking twist reveals the "Big Boss" behind it all, Mary's shrill confessional wraps up with a warning about "the foolish folly of crime". **PG**

The Adventures of Nero and Co. 1947

"Marc Sleen"

Marc Neels, the son of a Flemish saloon keeper, took art lessons from the age of fourteen. In World War II he was forced into German military service, and, in late 1944 his first comic strip *De Avonturen van Neus* appeared. From 1945 he produced caricatures, cartoons, and courtroom drawings for the daily newspaper *De Standaard*, and had strips published elsewhere. In 1946, by reversing his last name, his pen name became "Marc Sleen."

Sleen loved the movies, especially the Hollywood musical *Hellzapoppin'* (1941), a film based on the popular Broadway show of 1938. Its sudden noises, devils in hell, sight gags, and madcap characters influenced him, setting him firmly in the direction of creating his own detective named Van Zwam.

"You have to laugh before you're happy [or] you may die without laughing."

This screwball hero was quickly outstripped by another character—a small, big-nosed, bald man who believed he was Nero, the mad Roman emperor, and assumed the ruler's name (along with laurel sprigs behind his ears). This Nero was to become his favorite antihero across 216 stories of *The Adventures of Nero and Co.* (which soon became the title of the series), together with a vast array of zany sidekicks, including Madam Pheip, a pipe-smoking battle-ax, Tuizentfloot, "the last pirate still alive," and Adhemar, Nero's eternally young, egghead son with just two long hairs sprouting from his head, just as his father had.

In 1989 Sleen held the world record for the most issues in a comic book series drawn by the same author. After 1992 fine artist Dirk Stallaert took over most of the drawing as his assistant. Together they decided to end the strip in 2002. After 1962 all Nero stories ended with dad's drinks and mama's waffles. **HvO**

Title in original language *De Avonturen van Nero en Co*
First published by De Nieuwe Gids (Belgium)
Creator Marcel Honoree Neels (Belgian, b.1922)
Genre Humor

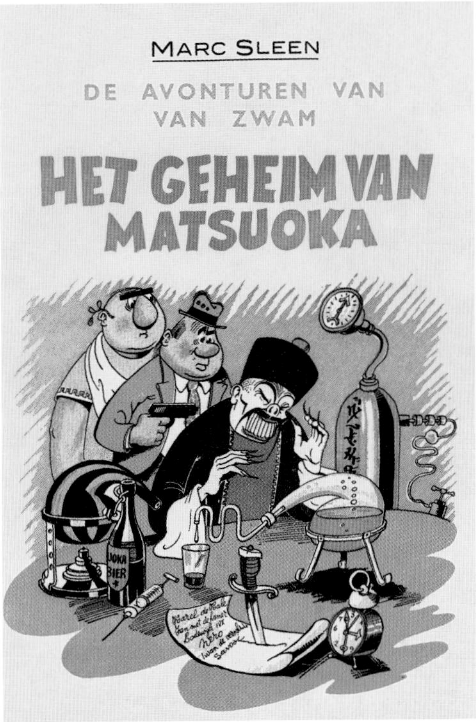
MARC SLEEN
DE AVONTUREN VAN
VAN ZWAM
HET GEHEIM VAN
MATSUOKA
JOKA
BIER

Similar reads

Lambiorix Willy Vandersteen
MAD Magazine Harvey Kurtzman
Nick Knatterton Manfred Schmidt
The Ghost of Sand Street Marc Sleen and Dirk Stallaert

Tarzan 1947

Gaylord Dubois Jesse Mace Marsh

First published by Dell Comics (USA)
Creators Dubois (American, 1899–1993); Marsh (American, 1907–66)
Genre Adventure

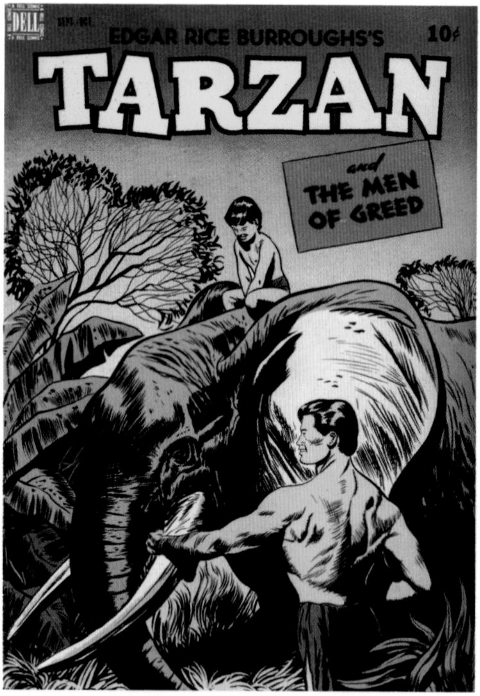
DELL
10¢
EDGAR RICE BURROUGHS'S
TARZAN
and
THE MEN OF GREED

"A Latino reading a comic book on the bus or at school, it was almost always a Tarzan book."

Gilbert Hernandez, creator *Love & Rockets*

Jesse Marsh's portrayal of Tarzan almost escapes the stigma of the white man lording it over the African continent. Other Tarzans in comics suffer from using the luscious African greenery as a mere backdrop to perpetrate the conceit of white supremacy.

Marsh's interpretation feels more acceptable, with fewer clichés and spurious observations, though never entirely so, for example the statement, "I smell white man blood," hardly bears analysis with modern eyes. Marsh's Tarzan slips into the indigenous flora and fauna as part of it, rather than coming from the masterly colonial race. Moral conflicts are seldom far from the surface. Villains are mostly white fortune hunters, rogue witch doctors, the occasional thwarted female, and some sorties into slavery.

Though well written by the prolific Gaylord Dubois, it is Marsh's chunky, earthbound graphics that propel the reader along a helter-skelter of adventure. The raging elements and the mischievous behavior of Tarzan's son, Boy, and his friend Dombie push the action along with vigor and alacrity. Flying between the trees from vine to vine, *Tarzan* (by Marsh) resembles the sense of weightless stone as conceived by Margritte.

It is unlikely that Tarzan's creator, Edgar Rice Burroughs, would have liked Marsh's version as much as Hal Foster's newspaper strip in 1929 with its excellent raw scratchiness, or Foster's successor in the late 1930s, Burne Hogarth, whose heroic muscularity earned him the label of the "Michelangelo of comics."

Launched in 1948, after appearing in the Dell *Four Color* series, the comic book *Tarzan* later returned to a glamorous, cinematic style thanks to Russ Manning. While the others aspired to the moving frame, Marsh's *Tarzan* represents the magnitude of the static frame and, with its absence of stereotyping, appeals across ethnic divisions. **IR**

Buck Danny 1947

Jean-Michel Charlier Victor Hubinon

First published by Spirou (France)
Creators Charlier (Belgian,1924–89); Hubinon (Belgian, 1924–79); Bergese (French, b.1941)
Genre Action, Adventure, War

The adventures of U.S. pilot Buck Danny are virtually unknown beyond the borders of the United States, which must seem odd to anyone familiar with the gung-ho Americanism of this Franco-Belgian comic.

With its flattering depiction of everyday life in the U.S. military, the fêting of its values, a preoccupation with its procedural minutiae, and an overwhelming, unabashed love of its aircraft, readers would be forgiven for thinking the strip was the product of a U.S. State Department propagandist.

The characters, all of whom have never aged, have flown World War II carrier-based dive-bombing Hellcats through to radar-evading Stealth bombers and, in the process have not only showcased the development of American aviation but also catalogued the flexing of the U.S.'s geopolitical muscles. From the Korean Peninsula to the shock of *Sputnik*, from the breakup of the Soviet Union to the Age of Terror, Buck Danny has seen it all.

The magic of *Buck Danny* has always been in its drawings. Despite early depictions of figures by illustrator Victor Hubinon appearing somewhat "rough," it was his portrayal of fighter aircraft, of dogfights and naval ships that showed off his rare gift for realism and a meticulous eye for detail.

Forty *Buck Danny* albums were produced from 1947 to 1979, followed by a four-year hiatus with the death of Hubinon before being picked up again in 1983 by Francis Bergese, a draftsman who continued its successful formula of historical fact and *Boy's Own*-style fiction.

Mission Apocalypse (1988) and *Mystery in the Antarctic* (2005) have been translated into English. *Buck Danny* survived the passing of two of its creators, itself a rare event in the world of Belgian comics, in which series tend to die along with their makers. **BS**

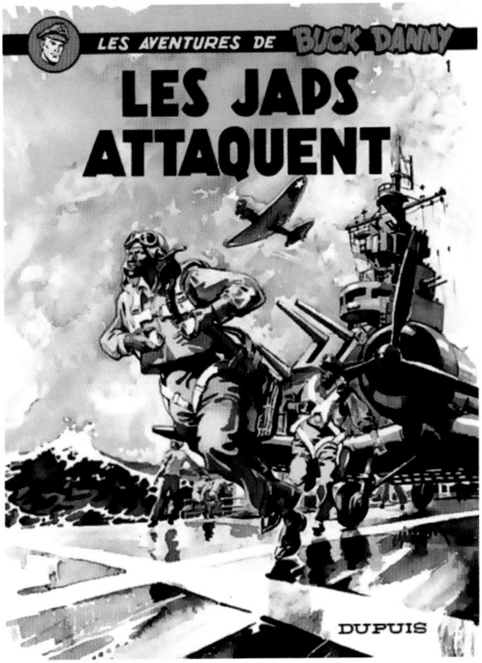
LES AVENTURES DE BUCK DANNY
1
LES JAPS ATTAQUENT
DUPUIS

"That rascal of a North Korean MIG fired a missile at me at point blank range!"

Alix 1948

Jacques Martin

Title in original language *Alix, La Tiare d'Oribal*
First published by *Le Journal de Tintin 9* (Belgium)
Creator French (1921–2010)
Genre Drama, Adventure

ALIX
JACQUES MARTIN
LA TIARE D'ORIBAL
casterman

Other *Alix* titles
Prince of the Nile (*Le prince du Nil*)
The Emperor of Chinarion (*L'empereur de Chine*)
The Ghost of Carthage (*Le spectre de Carthage*)
The Tower of Babel (*La tour de Babel*)
The Wild God (*Le dieu sauvage*)

Historical drama strips have long been among the most popular genres in Franco-Belgian comics, and Jacques Martin's *Alix* was one of the first and longest-lived. Martin was one of the great pioneers of French comics. After the war he combined his love of history and comic strips to create *Alix*. This super strip was to run in *Le Journal de Tintin* for more than thirty years.

Along with fellow artists Hergé and Edgar Jacobs, Martin was one of the creators of the *ligne claire* (clear line) school of art that was to define the look of French comics for decades to come.

The *Alix* series was set around fifty years before the birth of Christ in an era when a large part of the world was ruled by the Romans. Alix himself was born in occupied Gaul, the ancient name for France, and sold into slavery. Adopted by a Roman nobleman, the young Alix eventually joined up with the Roman cavalry and headed off with his young Egyptian friend Enak to experience a life of adventure.

Alix was one of a breed of fearless young comic strip heroes who, like the ever popular Tintin, seemed to encounter adventure and intrigue wherever they went. Martin delighted in illustrating for his readers the ancient world in all its glory—from Rome to Carthage, Sparta, and Alexandria, and from Egypt to China, Africa, and Persia. Ever the keen historian, Martin had his young hero Alix discover such legendary wonders of antiquity as the Tower of Babel and the Trojan horse, and these he invariably rendered with painstaking attention to detail and accuracy, adding immeasurably to the quality of the series. The strip was renowned for its historical accuracy.

The two volumes that made up the English translations of *Alix* were published by Ward Lock in the early 1970s. Sadly, however, the series remains relatively unknown outside of the French-speaking world. **DR**

Babe, Darling of the Hills 1948

Gordon "Boody" Rogers

Boody Rogers was christened Gordon, but his ball-kicking skills earned him a college nickname that stuck. He sold gag cartoons in the 1920s, and some of the earliest comics reprinted his newspaper strips, *The Funnies* in 1929 and *Deadwood Gulch* in 1931. By the time he was contributing to the earliest DC Comics in 1936, Gordon had become Boody, and it was under that name he produced his most memorable work in the 1940s, with superhero parody *Sparky Watts*, teenager *Dudley*, and *Babe*.

At first glance *Babe* (the subtitle *Darling of the Hills* was adopted in 1949) is an imitator of Al Clapp's *Li'l Abner* with the gender of the main protagonist changed for added teenage appeal. Although starting from a less than original premise, Rogers's unique mind shines through. Babe Boone is a hillbilly sporting sensation who derives her abilities from drinking the distilled bark of trees struck by lightning. She wrestles, boxes, and plays baseball for Mr. Teapot's Brookdale Blue Sox.

Rogers populated Babe's home of Possum Holler with a host of odd characters: Mister Guppy is a Merman who moves around land on crutches while avoiding Babe's father, who wants to fry his tail; hermit Mister Stalagmite lives on top of a mountain and converses in pictograms with a three-legged caveman hatched from a volcanic egg; and Mammy resembles a female Popeye. Meanwhile, Doctor Woeman develops a gender-switching potion, and there are also fetishistic centaurs.

The imagination and humor of the strip still engages, and if there is an influence on the strip beyond Al Capp, it can be seen in the work of Bill Holman, which is similarly offbeat and peppered with bizarre signs and wordplay. Rogers supplied eleven issues of *Babe* lunacy, assisted on some strips by 1950s bondage artist Eric Stanton, but ended his comics career in 1952 when he opened an art supply store in Arizona. **FP**

First published by Prize Comics (USA)
Creator American (1904–96)
Genre Humor, Teen
Collection *Boody: The Bizarre Comics of Boody Rogers* (2009)

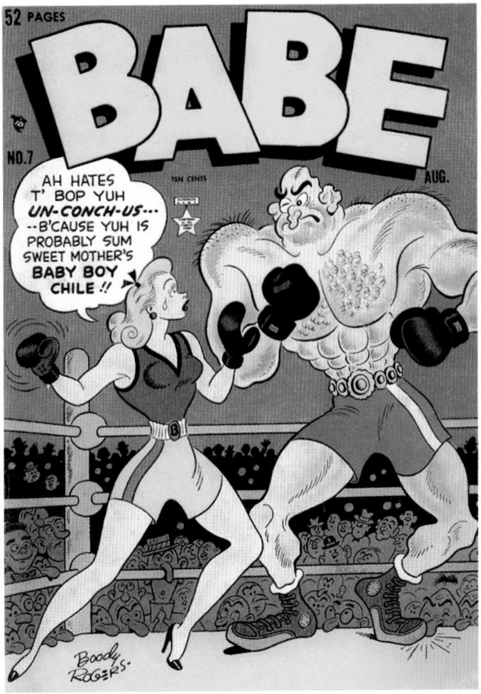
52 PAGES
BABE
NO.7
TEN CENTS
AUG.
AH HATES T' BOP YUH UN-CONCH-US··· --B'CAUSE YUH IS PROBABLY SUM SWEET MOTHER'S BABY BOY CHILE !!
Boody Rogers

Similar reads
Ace of Diamond Terajima Yuji
Football Family Robinson Tom Tully and Joe Colquhoun
Michel Vaillant Jean Graton
Ozark Ike Ray Gotto
Roy of the Rovers Stuart Green and Rob Davis

Pogo 1948

Walt Kelly

The
INCOMPLEAT
POGO
WALT KELLY

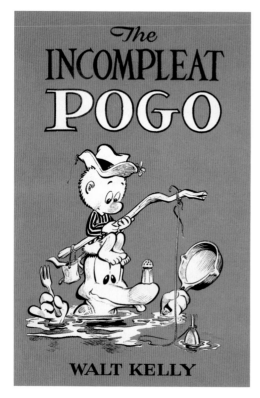

"You can do more with animals. They don't hurt as easily, and it's possible to make them more believable in an exaggerated pose."

Similar reads
Doonesbury G. B. Trudeau
Peanuts Schultz
Popeye E. C. Segar

First published by Simon & Schuster (USA)
Creator American (1913–73)
Genre Humor, Satire
Award Reuben Award (1951)

Former Disney animator and newspaper journalist Walt Kelly brought an astute political awareness to the comic strip when he began *Pogo*, his long-running political satire, in the 1940s. Set in Okeefenokee Swamp, and populated by a cast of anthropomorphic animals, the initial stories were more slapstick-centered than allegorical. Gradually, however, popular topics started to creep in, beginning when one of the characters, Dr. Howland Owl, an ill-informed, know-all, spouts off about atomic energy.

Kelly had already created Pogo the possum and Albert the alligator for Dell's *Animal Comics* in 1941, and he revived them when asked to draw political cartoons for the short-lived *New York Star* newspaper in 1948. When the newspaper dissolved, the strip was picked up by the Post-Hall Syndicate and ran continuously until 1975. It was produced by Kelly's wife Selby and son Stephen for the last two years after his death.

At the center of the strip is the double act of Pogo, a humble yet philosophical possum, and Albert, his dumb but loyal alligator friend. Pogo is self-effacing, Albert self-aggrandizing, Pogo quiet and retiring, Albert gung-ho and angry. Other characters include the superstitious turtle Churchy LaFemme, Porkypine, a grumpy and cynical porcupine, and Miz Mam'selle Hepzibah, a French skunk.

For contemporary readers ignorant of the period *Pogo* evokes, Kelly remains a great gag artist whose polished drawing, witty wordplay, and poetic language transcend the time and place of his material. **FJ**

Mickey's Inferno 1949

✎ Guido Martina ✎ Angelo Bioletto

Title in original language *L'Inferno di Topolino*
First published by Topolino/Mondadori (Italy)
Creators Martina (Italian, 1906–91); Bioletto (Italian, 1906–87) **Genre** Parody

Mickey's Inferno is the Italian version of the Disney parody-adaptation of Dante Alighieri's famous classic, *Inferno*. With Mickey Mouse (known as Topolino in Italian) as Dante and Goofy (Pippo) as Virgil, it was written in rhymes and reproduced the prosodic structure of the literary masterwork.

The story begins at the finish of a theatrical performance of Dante's *Divine Comedy*, costarring Mickey and Goofy. Envious of their success, Pete (Gambadilegno) hypnotizes his two eternal enemies. The two of them later go to the library so that they can learn more about Dante, and while grappling with a huge volume of the *Divine Comedy* quickly, fall asleep. They have a dream in which they find themselves inside the first part of Dante's *Inferno*, where Mickey-Dante meets Goofy-Virgil, thus beginning their long pilgrimage through a "dark and gloomy wood," unable to find their way to salvation.

The strip is true to Dante's depiction of Hell and to the original poem's division in cantos. However, Martina—a former teacher and one of the most prolific Disney comics writers—brings much more to the adaptation. He manages to rewrite Dante, using the same eleven-syllable rhymes, in a playful, surprising, and comical way. The result was a landmark publication that reached generations of Italian readers and helped legitimize the educational worth of comics. It also inaugurated the tradition of "Disney parodies," a long-lasting series of literary adaptations that helped reshape the Disney identity. **MS**

Condorito 1949

✎✎ Rene Rios

First published by Empresa Editora Zig-Zag (Chile)
Creator Chilean (b.1911)
Genre Humor

The most widely read comic in Latin America, *Condorito* is as recognizable to children and adults in Chile, Argentina, Brazil, and Venezuela as *Mickey Mouse* is to the average American. Created by Rene Rios, who first imagined his character while looking at a Chilean coat of arms featuring a deer and a condor either side of the crest, the strip follows the adventures of an anthropomorphic condor who lives in the fictional provincial Chilean town of Pelotilluhue. Condorito came to live among humans after he was thrown from his nest high in the Chilean Andes by his irate father. Condorito is lazy and wholly lacking in ambition, but nevertheless endears himself to readers with his innate goodness and irrepressible wit.

The strip's format is uncomplicated: each episode is a single gag, usually involving chauvinism and sexism reflective of macho Latin American cultural norms, but expressed in double entendres that are indiscernible to children. There is no continuity from one strip to the next, and most episodes end with the victim of some outrageous pun falling backward out of the panel, feet in the air, and landing with a classic "flop take." Condorito's signature statement—"I demand an explanation"—is part of the Chilean vernacular.

Created in response to Walt Disney's animated *Saludos Amigos*, which Rios felt misrepresented Latin American culture, *Condorito* went on to transcend borders to become the most successful, widely translated Spanish-language comic in history. It has an estimated eighty million-plus readers worldwide. **BS**

Young Hawk 1949

✎ Gaylord Dubois   ✎ Rex Maxon and Ray Bailey

First published by Dell Comics (USA)
Creators Dubois (American, 1899–1993); Maxon (American, 1892–1973); Bailey (American, 1913–75)
Genre Adventure, Western

Before European colonization, two Native American Indians, Young Hawk and Little Buck, travel on foot searching for their lost home. Although it is established later that the narrative occurs before the arrival of the eponymous horseman, this backup feature to *The Lone Ranger* starts with Young Hawk and his cousin Little Buck losing a medicine horse and getting lost chasing after it. Despite occasional anomalies, Native American Indian life with all its traditions was fastidiously researched and well drawn, initially with Rex Maxon's muscular, thick, wayward lines. Subsequently, artist Ray Bailey brought depth to the artwork, recalling a natural past with almost ethereal rendering. His light touch gave the strip a gentle authenticity.

A master of Westerns and adventure stories, author Gaylord Dubois wrote a staggering 3,000 comic books during his lifetime. In this series, the diversity of the Plains Indians and their social customs is well observed. Only one tribe knew how to make iron. Young Hawk shows how to make a sail for a canoe from half a tepee, and discovers how to carve a canoe from a single tree, instead of from easily splintered birch bark. From a wrecked Spanish galleon, Young Hawk and Little Buck learn about chain mail and ground meal. They meet coastal dwellers who row out to sea in vast wooden boats decorated with carvings to hunt a whale. Elsewhere on the coast, people fish using cattle on the beach to draw in nets. In later years, Dubois moved into areas of publishing more directly related to his faith, including scripted Christian comics. **BB**

Flook 1949

✎ Douglas Mount   ✎ "Trog"

First published by *Daily Mail* (UK)
Creators Mount (British, Unknown); Wally Fawkes (British-Canadian, b.1924)
Genre Satire **Influence on** *Private Eye* magazine

When Wally Fawkes was ten years old, his mother, Mabel, sensing her son's potential as an artist, gave him a fountain pen and a bottle of Indian ink. In the late 1930s he entered Sidcup Art College, just outside London, but could not afford to graduate despite having entered on a scholarship. In 1939, with Britain at war with Germany, the fifteen-year-old Fawkes found work at Woolwich Dockyards on the south bank of the River Thames, painting camouflage patterns onto factory roofs.

In 1942 Fawkes landed a job as a decorative illustrator for London's *Daily Mail* newspaper. It was not until 1948, however, while on a visit to the United States, that the newspaper's owner, Lord Rothermere, became acquainted with a U.S. comic strip called *Barnaby*, about a boy with an interfering fairy godfather. The proprietor asked Fawkes to illustrate a similarly themed strip, *Rufus*, initially written by Douglas Mount, in which the central character was a red-haired boy. When readers warmed to Flook, Rufus's quirky, odd-looking companion, *Rufus* was retitled *Rufus & Flook*, and eventually just *Flook*.

Fawkes's lighthearted strip evolved into a sophisticated political satire with the arrival of writer and jazz singer George Melly in 1956. Jazz musician Humphrey Lyttleton, comedian Barry Took, and film critic Barry Norman also contributed. Fawkes drew *Flook* for thirty-five years. The strip, increasingly critical of the Conservative government of Prime Minister Margaret Thatcher, was canceled in 1984 by the *Daily Mail*'s right-wing editors, but it lived on briefly in the pages of the *Daily Mirror* and its Sunday counterpart. **BS**

The small furry hero Flook rescues his friend and sidekick Rufus. ➡

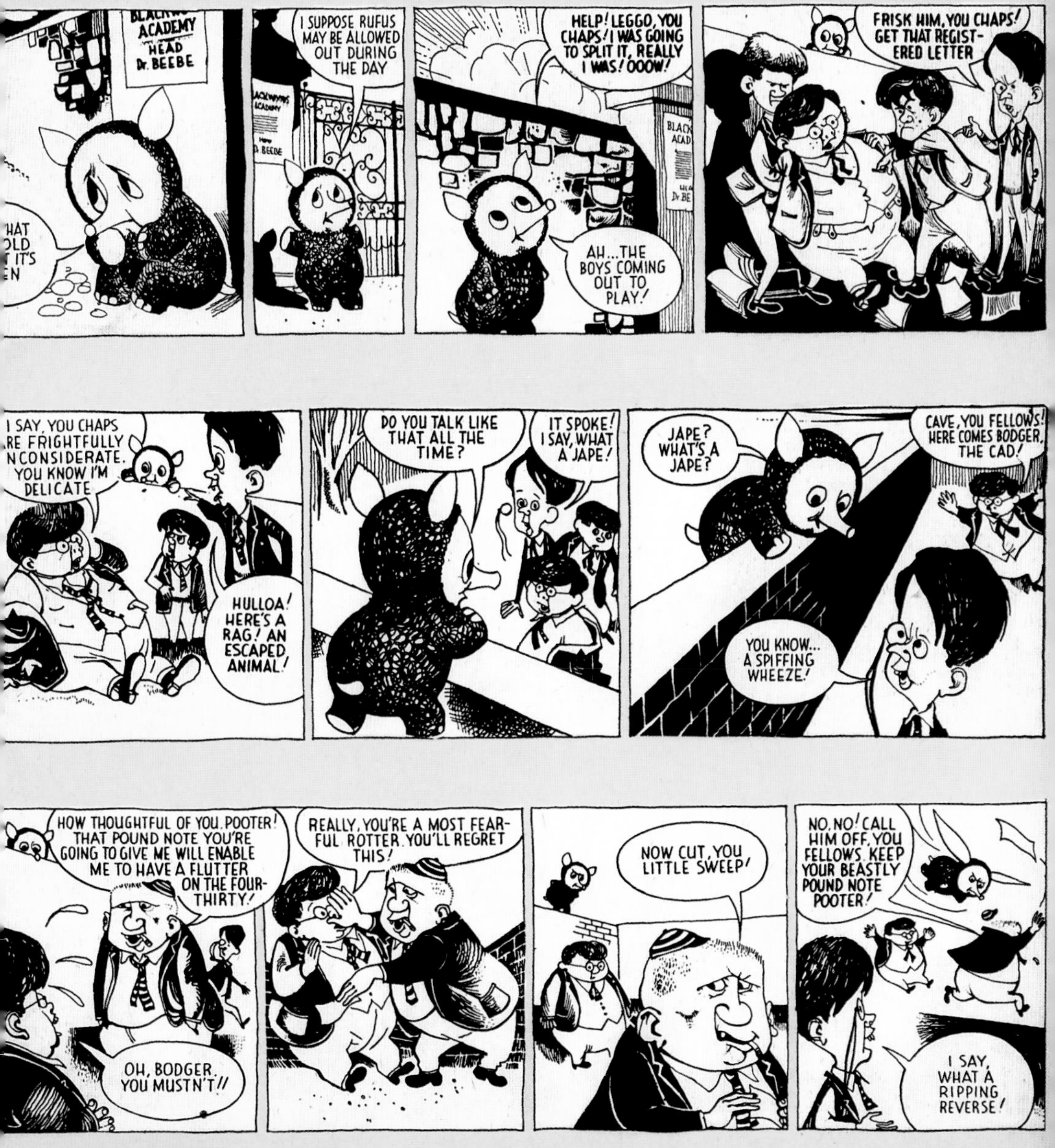
ACADEMY
HEAD Dr. BEEBE
I SUPPOSE RUFUS MAY BE ALLOWED OUT DURING THE DAY
HELP! LEGGO, YOU CHAPS! I WAS GOING TO SPLIT IT, REALLY I WAS! OOOW!
AH...THE BOYS COMING OUT TO PLAY!
FRISK HIM, YOU CHAPS! GET THAT REGIST-ERED LETTER
I SAY, YOU CHAPS RE FRIGHTFULLY NCONSIDERATE. YOU KNOW I'M DELICATE
HULLOA! HERE'S A RAG! AN ESCAPED ANIMAL!
DO YOU TALK LIKE THAT ALL THE TIME?
IT SPOKE! I SAY, WHAT A JAPE!
JAPE? WHAT'S A JAPE?
YOU KNOW... A SPIFFING WHEEZE!
CAVE, YOU FELLOWS! HERE COMES BODGER, THE CAD!
HOW THOUGHTFUL OF YOU, POOTER! THAT POUND NOTE YOU'RE GOING TO GIVE ME WILL ENABLE ME TO HAVE A FLUTTER ON THE FOUR-THIRTY!
OH, BODGER. YOU MUSTN'T!!
REALLY, YOU'RE A MOST FEAR-FUL ROTTER. YOU'LL REGRET THIS!
NOW CUT, YOU LITTLE SWEEP!
NO, NO! CALL HIM OFF, YOU FELLOWS. KEEP YOUR BEASTLY POUND NOTE POOTER!
I SAY, WHAT A RIPPING REVERSE!

White Indian 1949

"Frank Frazetta"

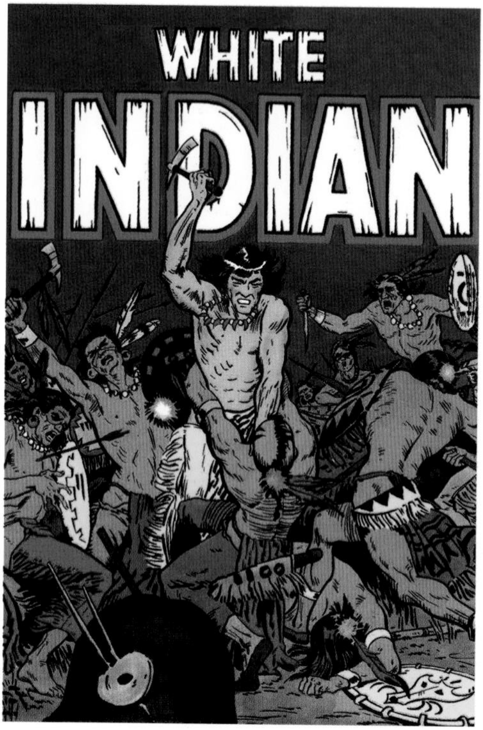
WHITE
INDIAN

"I think I'm a better line artist than painter . . . I was quite happy doing comics."

Frank Frazetta

Similar reads

Flash Gordon Alex Raymond, Austin Briggs, and others
Tarzan of the Apes Hal Foster
Terry and the Pirates Milton Caniff

Original title *Dan Brand and Tipi*
First published by Magazine Enterprises (USA)
Creator Alfonso Frazzetta (American, 1928–2010)
Genre Adventure, Fantasy

Young Alfonso Frazzetta, the eldest child of a jeweler with Sicilian-Italian roots in New York City, wanted to draw. He was a smart little Brooklyn kid with three sisters. Before he was seventeen he enjoyed eight years of lessons in a small local art school, was a churchgoer, and became a high-school dropout. In 1944 he proudly saw his artist's name Frank Frazetta in print in *Tally-Ho Comics*: eight funny pages of *Snowman . . . The "Something New" in Comics!* He created the strip with John Giunta, who greatly influenced him. Young Frazetta lived to fantasize, to see every cinema serial and film, and to find the most striking strips or illustrations.

Throughout the 1940s and 1950s he did many odd jobs: funny animal, swordfighter, cowboy, sci-fi (*Flash Gordon*), love, and horror comics. But his speedway hero Johnny Comet flopped in the newspapers. Inspired by Tarzan, Frazetta tried his hand at the white-man-in-the-jungle theme in his intense *White Indian* series (first titled *Dan Brand and Tipi*), and in 1952 with his stunning one-shot *Thun'da*. He then quit comic books (lousy pay, no say, no rights, loss of originals) to survive the 1950s by penciling Al Capp's *Li'l Abner* Sunday pages.

Later, having grown into a painter and a world-famous one-man fantasy art industry, supported by the business skills of his wife, Ellie, Frazetta set the rule: stylish eruptions of violence and sex, without gore. His men displayed strong backs and forearms, his women were bosomy with big buttocks. Always insisting that each job was done in less than a day, he lived his fantasy and kept it up until the end. **HvO**

Doug Wright's Family 1949

✐✐ Doug Wright

First published by *Montreal Standard* (Canada)
Creator British (1917–83)
Genre Humor
Influence on Chester Brown

Not widely known beyond the borders of Canada, Doug Wright is so beloved in the country where he lived his entire adult life that the national comic book awards are named in his honor. His newspaper strip *Nipper* (later changed to *Doug Wright's Family*) was launched in the *Montreal Standard* in 1949 and continued to run for more than three decades. During that time, Wright defined the Canadian suburban existence through the adventures of a tight-knit nuclear family.

As a visual stylist Wright had few peers. His lines were crisp, sharp, and filled with life. The spot colors that he employed provided a sharp focus for the reader's eye, and allowed him to eschew the kind of shading and cross-hatching that would have detracted from the slickness of his approach. More importantly, the strip was entirely wordless, the stories strung together by the expert use of images. The absence of text allows the strip to breathe, and allows Wright to devote precious space to the exact rendering of situational details that make the work feel alive.

The first decade of the strip focused on the adventures of Nipper, the young son of a quiet suburban couple. In the summer of 1960, a second son was born to the family, and all of the pieces of the puzzle came together. The peak of the strip's run occurred in the 1960s, when the relationship of parents to sons, and brother to brother, takes center stage. Wright's strip, although filled with a fair degree of the unvarnished realities of life, depicted an idyllic world of familial happiness, all without ever saying a word. **BB**

Lobey Dosser 1949

✐✐ Bud Neill

Original title *Sheriff Lobey Dosser of Calton Creek*
First published by *Evening Times* (UK)
Creator Scottish (1911–70)
Genre Humor, Western

As a port city, early twentieth-century Glasgow absorbed U.S. culture. To this day, the Glasgow Grand Ole Opry has a Confederate flag-folding ceremony to end the night. Early Western movies represented a glamorous world to people crammed into Scottish Victorian buildings, and they left a lasting mark on cartoonist Bud Neill.

Lobey Dosser is the sheriff of Calton Creek, a fusion of Glasgow and the Wild West, a genial law enforcer on his trusty, two-legged steed Elfie. Neill seemingly plotted story lines by the seat of his pants, producing shaggy-dog tales that he used as a vehicle for his strengths. The jokes, puns, and asides remain very funny today, all underpinned by Neill's good-natured worldview as he twisted the cliches picked up in his childhood. His cartooning is simple but imaginative. Lobey resembles an onion in a hat, while local villain Rank Bajin is a blob of solid black apart from his eyes and teeth. Bajin would often dominate the strip for days at a time.

Neill produced his work for a Glasgow audience, and Lobey's speech is a broad phonetic dialect, with plentiful parochial references to the likes of the Barras, Govan, Troon, and Millport. The unique character names (Rubber Lugs, Roona Boot, Breedan Mulk) possibly do not travel well. A "lobby dosser," for instance, was a Glaswegian term for a homeless person who slept in the accessible stairwells of tenement buildings.

Today, opposite Glasgow's Halt Bar, there stands a bronze statue of Lobey Dosser, Bajin, and Elfie, a testament to how highly they, and their creator, are still regarded in the city. **FP**

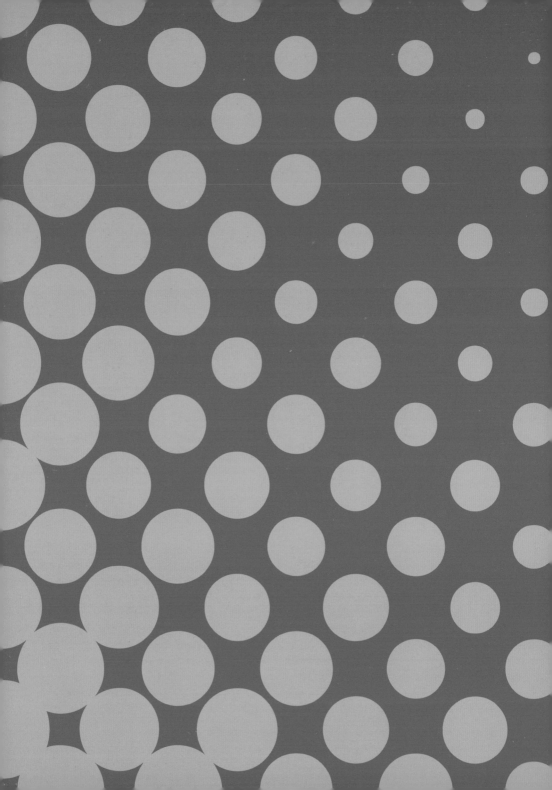

3 1950–69

Torchy in Heartbeat 1950

✎✎ Jackie Ormes

First published by *Pittsburgh Courier* (USA)
Creator American (1911–85)
Genre Teen **Notable mention** Founding member of the DuSable Museum of African-American History

Jackie Ormes should have been a name throughout the United States, but her comic strip, *Torchy in Heartbeat*, was limited to the black press. The strip featured in a number of Chicago-based newspapers from 1950 to 1956 with a circulation of 300,000. The first African American woman cartoonist, she was also a journalist, artist, socialite, and progressive political activist.

Torchy in Heartbeat was more socially aware than most comic strips, perhaps with the exception of *Little Orphan Annie*. Environmental pollution, prejudice, and corruption all fell under Ormes's microscope. Had her work been more widely distributed, it could have been a great force for progress. Nonetheless, her contribution to women's rights, equality, and leftist causes was considerable.

Torchy Brown's image as a strong, independent black woman contrasted with the usual stereotypical portrayal of black women at the time. While investigating a pollution scandal, Torchy—in her role as a nurse—has a pleasant encounter by the side of a lake with a white boy, until he realizes that she is from "over there" and he is therefore not supposed to talk to her.

The FBI compiled a 287-page file on Ormes with no mention of her being a cartoonist. The McCarthyites tried to get their hooks into her, but she did not waver. Ormes was an astute businesswoman who incorporated into the strip her designs for cut-out dresses (known as Torchy Togs), which paved the way in the late 1940s for the Patty-Jo dolls, a successful range of American black dolls that are now collector's items. **IR**

Mother Delilah 1950

✎✎ Jack Kirby (assisted by Joe Simon)

First published by Harvey Comics (USA)
Creators Kirby (American, 1917–94); Simon (American, b.1913)
Genre Western

Joe Simon and Jack Kirby brought the "kid gang" concept to comics in the early 1940s. In 1950, they produced some of their finest work by placing the idea in a Wild West setting and calling it *Boys' Ranch*. Clay Duncan, orphaned as a child and raised by Apache Indians, runs a ranch where similarly estranged children live under his care. *Boys' Ranch* was short-lived, sadly, but memorable. The story of "Mother Delilah" from the third issue, however, remains exceptional.

Delilah "Del" Barker, who runs the Last Chance saloon, takes Clay Duncan's rejection of a dinner invitation personally. She exacts revenge by becoming "mother" to Angel, a ranch boy with long blond hair. Angel yearns for a mother figure and responds positively to Del. When Clay warns her to back off, she responds by cutting off Angel's beloved golden locks. Angel feels humiliated—he is no longer a tough guy and unable to shoot straight. As his hair returns, so does his aim.

Kirby, who handled both script and art, showers the tale with overt references to the Old Testament story of Samson and Delilah. The overall style is a unique mixture. In having an elderly poet named Virgil Underwood comment upon events in verse, Kirby uses a "narrator as chorus" format. The artwork is raw and lively, but rises to more sophisticated levels where needed. Standout moments include the two silent panels depicting Angel's horrified reaction to his short hair and the redemptive power of the story's final tragic panel. It is easy to see why "Mother Delilah" was one of Kirby's personal favorites. **CH**

The character of Delilah was influenced by Marlene Dietrich's in *Destry Rides Again* (1939). ➡

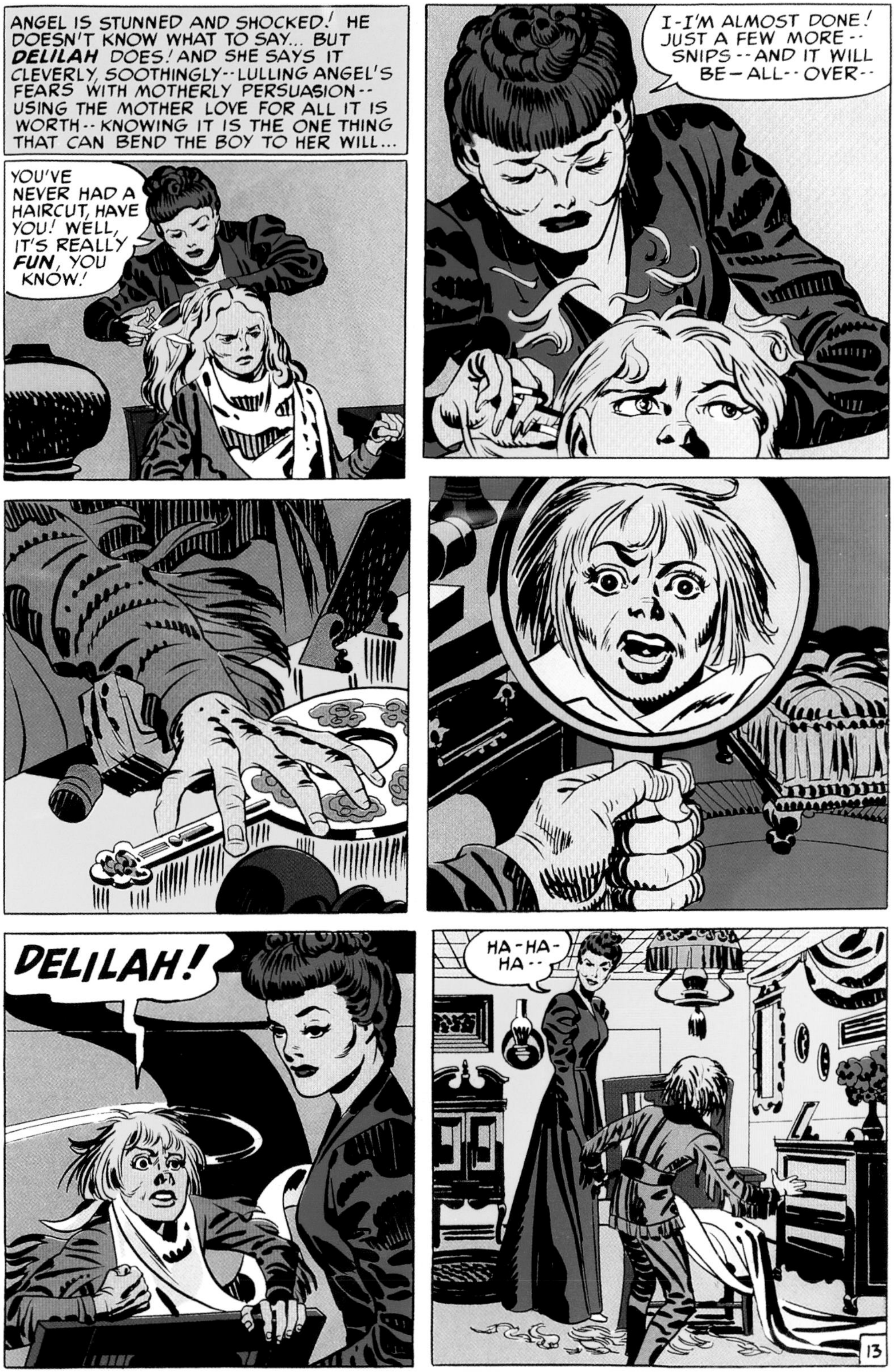
ANGEL IS STUNNED AND SHOCKED! HE DOESN'T KNOW WHAT TO SAY... BUT DELILAH DOES! AND SHE SAYS IT CLEVERLY, SOOTHINGLY-- LULLING ANGEL'S FEARS WITH MOTHERLY PERSUASION-- USING THE MOTHER LOVE FOR ALL IT IS WORTH-- KNOWING IT IS THE ONE THING THAT CAN BEND THE BOY TO HER WILL...
YOU'VE NEVER HAD A HAIRCUT, HAVE YOU! WELL, IT'S REALLY FUN, YOU KNOW!
I-I'M ALMOST DONE! JUST A FEW MORE-- SNIPS--AND IT WILL BE-ALL--OVER--
DELILAH!
HA-HA-HA--

Tales from the Crypt 1950

✎ Al Feldstein and William Gaines ✎ Al Feldstein and various

First published by EC Comics (USA)
Creators Feldstein (American, b.1925); Gaines (American, b.1922)
Genre Horror

TERROR
TALES FROM THE CRYPT
VOL 2
9.95
13.70
CANADA
FEATURING...
THE CRYPT-KEEPER
THE OLD WITCH
THE VAULT-KEEPER
DANGER
QUICKSAND
KEEP AWAY!
FELDSTEIN

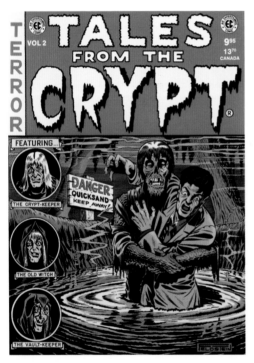

"Introducing a new trend in magazines . . . illustrated SuspenStories we dare you to read!"

Originally titled *The Crypt of Terror*, *Tales from the Crypt* was one of EC Comics's "new trend" all-horror titles that first hit newsstands in April 1950. Hosted by the original "Ghoulunatic," the Crypt-Keeper, the strip was accompanied by *The Vault of Horror* and *The Haunt of Fear*, hosted respectively by the Vault-Keeper and the Old Witch. All three bimonthly titles featured graphic horror stories, written by publisher William Gaines and editor Al Feldstein, and illustrated by a talented roster of artists including Feldstein himself, Johnny Craig, Jack Davis, Graham Ingels, Jack Kamen, and Wally Wood. All three titles came to a sudden end in 1954, when the industry introduced the Comics Code. EC's horror titles were named and admonished at the Senate Subcommittee on Juvenile Delinquency, and were singled out as offenders against innocence and good taste by Dr. Fredric Wertham, in his anticomics tract, *Seduction of the Innocent*.

EC's horror and crime comics paint a dark picture of the pursuit of the American Dream. Gaines and Feldstein crafted hundreds of six- and eight-page morality tales. One crime—usually committed in the pursuit of a fast buck—leads to another and before long the protagonists are caught in a horrific web of retribution. As the moral noose draws tight, Gaines and Feldstein employ coincidence or the supernatural as deus ex machina devices that appear unexpectedly to supply shock or twist endings—all gorily illustrated. The ironic hand of fate delivers justice where the punishment truly fits the crime.

EC can be blamed, in part, for the U.S. industry's twenty-year retreat into self-censorship. It is, however, perhaps preferable for a canon of comics as excellent as EC's to have existed with censorship rather than to have upheld a theoretical freedom of expression that nobody dared champion at the time. **RR**

The Girl Who Tempted Me 1950

Jack Kirby (assisted by Joe Simon)

Launching *Young Romance* in 1947, Joe Simon and Jack Kirby became pioneers of provocative, passionate tales of love in U.S. comic books. The genre became very successful very quickly, before the censoring Comics Code Authority in 1954 neutered it and the stories became mostly formulaic tearjerkers, and the weekday television soap operas seduced their readership.

In contrast, *The Girl Who Tempted Me* is a high-voltage Hollywood melodrama, largely Kirby's solo handiwork, with its fifteen pages narrated in the genre's usual first-person confessional style, although unusually this time not by a pining female but by a brawny male. Ethan, a self-proclaimed strong and righteous farmer, and his brother, Amos, meet Lola, an ex-carnival worker, upon her arrival from the big city. She soon sparks sibling rivalry between the brothers. Ethan is torn between his puritan denial of pleasure and Lola's "dark wisdom of sin shining brazenly in her eyes." He dramatizes his resistance to sultry Lola's allure into a battle for his soul. After tensions flare between the brothers, Ethan is sent off to visit "a fine girl" whom his mother wants him to wed.

Instead, Ethan rides off to confront Lola, his suppressed desires flaring up, mirrored by the mounting thunderstorm outside. As lightning strikes, Ethan's narrative captions all but vanish. Now is no time for thoughts, only the immediacy of actions and the fulfillment of passions. Finally, Ethan kisses Lola as the storm reaches an orgasmic crescendo, only to hurl her to the floor and curse her. Lola taunts him, "I'm life and I'm joy, Ethan—I'm yours." In the end, their love cannot be denied. Kirby's association with fantastical superheroics can, at times, overshadow his mastery of evocative body language, facial expression, and truly adult emotions laid bare on the pages of this, his finest romance comic. **PG**

First published by Prize Comics (USA)
Creators Kirby (American, 1917–94); Simon (American, b.1913)
Genre Romance

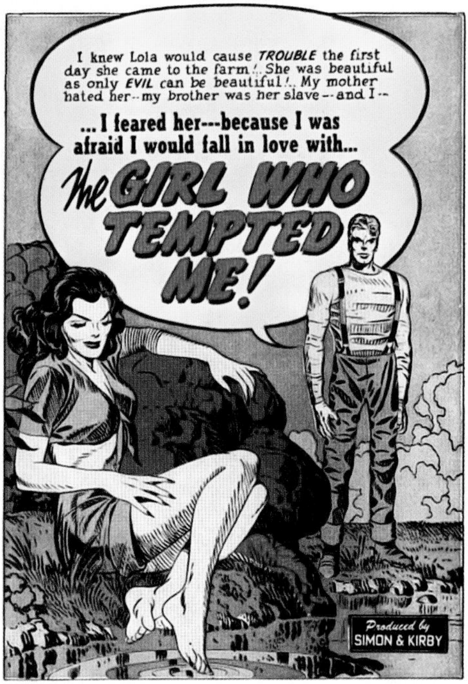
I knew Lola would cause TROUBLE the first day she came to the farm!.. She was beautiful as only EVIL can be beautiful!.. My mother hated her--my brother was her slave--and I--
...I feared her---because I was afraid I would fall in love with...
The GIRL WHO TEMPTED ME!
Produced by SIMON & KIRBY

"The horse had become a physical extension of my demon-driven brain! I was all animal now."

EAGLE-BRITAIN'S NATIONAL STRIP CARTOON WEEKLY

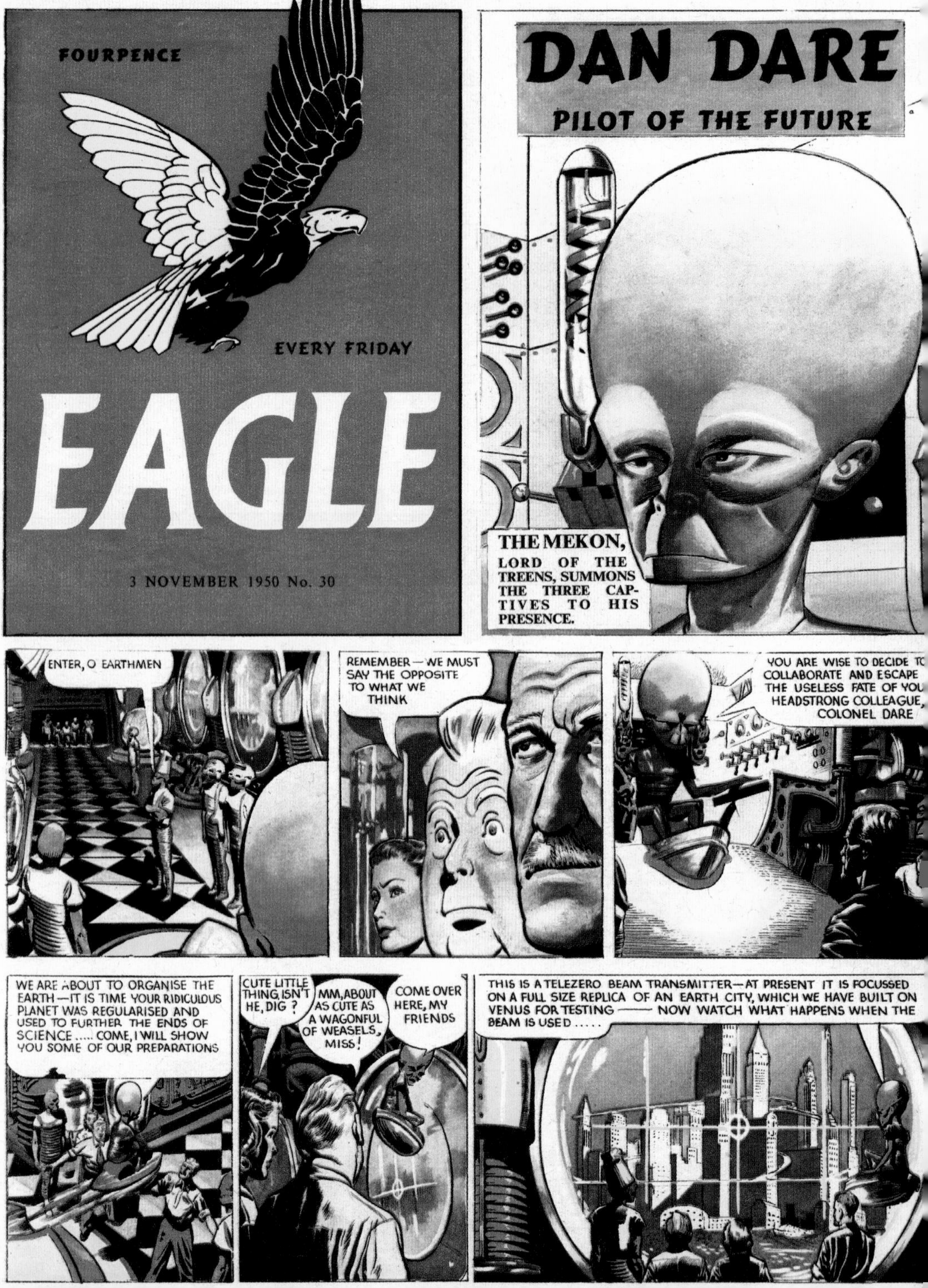

FOURPENCE
EVERY FRIDAY
EAGLE
3 NOVEMBER 1950 No. 30
DAN DARE
PILOT OF THE FUTURE
THE MEKON, LORD OF THE TREENS, SUMMONS THE THREE CAPTIVES TO HIS PRESENCE.
ENTER, O EARTHMEN
REMEMBER—WE MUST SAY THE OPPOSITE TO WHAT WE THINK
YOU ARE WISE TO DECIDE TO COLLABORATE AND ESCAPE THE USELESS FATE OF YOUR HEADSTRONG COLLEAGUE, COLONEL DARE
WE ARE ABOUT TO ORGANISE THE EARTH—IT IS TIME YOUR RIDICULOUS PLANET WAS REGULARISED AND USED TO FURTHER THE ENDS OF SCIENCE ..... COME, I WILL SHOW YOU SOME OF OUR PREPARATIONS
CUTE LITTLE THING, ISN'T HE, DIG ?
MM, ABOUT AS CUTE AS A WAGONFUL OF WEASELS, MISS!
COME OVER HERE, MY FRIENDS
THIS IS A TELEZERO BEAM TRANSMITTER—AT PRESENT IT IS FOCUSSED ON A FULL SIZE REPLICA OF AN EARTH CITY, WHICH WE HAVE BUILT ON VENUS FOR TESTING —— NOW WATCH WHAT HAPPENS WHEN THE BEAM IS USED .....

Dan Dare 1950

✎✎ Frank Hampson

Original title *Dan Dare: Pilot of the Future*
First published by Hulton Press (UK)
Creator British (1918–85)
Genre Science fiction, Adventure

Launched on April 14, 1950, as the flagship story for the new *Eagle* boys' weekly, *Dan Dare* was a revolutionary leap forward for British comics. It broke new ground with both its subject matter and the quality of its artwork. Frank Hampson's artwork is still breathtaking today. He combined a meticulous sense of form with a dynamic grasp of perspective. He worked with specially constructed, three-dimensional models, so that his spaceships would look convincingly solid.

Whether drawing a spaceport on Earth or a city on Venus, all are rendered with the same brightly colored, art deco–influenced forms. Hampson brought a visual unity to this depiction of the near future—the 1990s as seen from the 1950s. Clean-cut and heroic Dan Dare, comic sidekick Digby, patrician Sir Hubert Guest (chief of the British-dominated Space Fleet), and the brilliant Professor Jocelyn Peabody are some of the key characters whose adventures begin as interplanetary exploration and expand into interstellar voyages.

The *Eagle*'s policy was to encourage Christian values without explicitly preaching to its readers. The result is a solar system populated by races of varying moral and intellectual development—the isolationist Mercurians, the noble but decadent Therons, and the scientifically advanced but morally bankrupt Treens. Dan Dare meets every danger with a traditionally British stiff upper lip. *Dan Dare* was ably continued into the 1960s by Frank Bellamy, Keith Watson, and other artists. However, the post-1960s revivals of the character should not be confused (or compared) with the original. **RR**

King Aroo 1950

✎✎ Jack Kent

First published by McClure Syndicate (USA)
Creator American (1920–85)
Genre Humor
Award Chicago Graphics Award (Unknown)

King Aroo was a highly regarded comic strip in the 1950s that drew a wide audience across cultural boundaries, appealing to the same kind of readership as *Krazy Kat*. However, with the passage of time, the strip has slipped into obscurity outside of comic book devotees.

King Aroo rules the fictional kingdom of Myopia, along with his retainer Yupyop. They are the only humans regularly seen in Myopia, which is otherwise inhabited by intelligent animals: Mr. Pennipost is the kangaroo mailman and, if an expert is required, canine Professor Yorgle will inevitably offer his flawed services.

King Aroo remains an anomaly among the generally slick cartooning introduced in the 1950s. As a teenager, Jack Kent had corresponded with George Herriman, and while employed elsewhere refined his art until he started assisting on *Big Chief Wahoo*. Kent was talented, but as a self-taught artist his strips followed no disciplined formula. His rounded characters were created with loose brushstrokes, and his panels are sprinkled with whimsical background detail.

King Aroo revels in sophisticated wordplay and introduces philosophical topics, yet most precocious children would find it an enjoyable strip. When Kent's publishing syndicate collapsed in 1958, the *San Francisco Chronicle* commissioned the strip directly, but limited distribution eventually saw the end of *King Aroo*. When Kent selected strips for inclusion in *The Smithsonian Collection of Newspaper Comics,* he revealingly chose one that closes self-referentially with the message, "This is absurd, but is it art?" **FP**

◀ The *Dan Dare* series was renowned for its lavish artwork.

Nick Knatterton 1950

✎✎ Manfred Schmidt

First published by *Quick* magazine (Germany)
Creator German (1913–99)
Genre Parody
Adaptations TV (1977), Film (2002)

Nick Knatterton
AUFGEZEICHNET VON MANFRED SCHMIDT

Alle aufregenden Abenteuer des berühmten Meisterdetektivs

LAPPAN

"I conclude . . . these guys are not dangerous at the moment! I can see their trousers hanging on the washing line!"

Similar reads
Dick Tracy Chester Gould
Father and Son (Vater und Sohn) e.o.plauen
Jimmy the Rubber Horse (Jimmy das Gummipferd) Roland Kohlsaat
Tintin and Snowy (Tim und Struppi) Hergé

Nick Knatterton was conceived as a comic parody. Manfred Schmidt, the inventor of this quirky detective character, condemned the colorful, action-packed superhero comics emerging from the United States as the "most primitive of narrative forms."

Schmidt parodied the medium and, in particular, its superheroes, satirizing them in his own way. His check-suited, pipe-smoking heroes are inspired by Dick Tracy and Sherlock Holmes, and the character's name is a combination of Nick Carter and Nat Pinkerton, characters from two prewar detective story series.

Knatterton distinguishes himself not by the powerful muscular stature of a superhero but through his brilliant logical mind. His most common expression, "kombiniere," which, in context, meant "to deduce," became a catchphrase that entered everyday German speech. It was a favorite expression of the detective, especially in tricky situations.

Developing the "restless narrative" style of comics that has often been criticized in the past, Schmidt took the form a step further. His strips are filled with wild chaos, incorporating simultaneous courses of action, many small text blocks, and numerous speech bubbles, as well as a large number of arrows designed to be reading aids. The stories of Nick Knatterton are embellished with bizarre characters who are extremely overdrawn in their appearance, personality, and habits.

The mixture of slapstick action and tension has made *Nick Knatterton* popular worldwide. The first comic adventure of the master detective was published in the illustrated magazine *Quick* in 1950; just two years later, the first of the seven *Knatterton* volumes was published. Nick Knatterton lives on today as an advertising medium, a cartoon character, and a movie character, in spite of the relatively abrupt termination of the comic series in 1961. **MS**

Peanuts 1950

Charles M. Schulz

Peanuts debuted in seven newspapers in 1950 and, by the time creator Charles M. Schulz passed away in 2000, had appeared in 2,600 newspapers in seventy-five countries, and had been read by 355 million people in twenty-one different languages. It was one of the most popular comic strips of all time.

But what is the secret of the strip's success? If one end of the spectrum of comics characters is occupied by impossibly powerful beings such as Superman, at the opposite end are the zany and enchanting characters of *Peanuts*. A group of children and their animal friends, they live in a world controlled not only by unseen adults but by peers who are stronger and more confident than they are. The bittersweet humor of *Peanuts* lies in the characters' heroic attempts to make sense of the difficulties and failures that beset their lives, and in the daydreams and philosophical musings that help to make intolerable experiences more acceptable.

At the heart of the series are Charlie Brown, an anxious little boy for whom the baseball field is a challenge that mostly ends in humiliation, and Snoopy, his black-eared dog. Lying on the roof of his doghouse, Snoopy often shares his observations with Woodstock, a little yellow bird with whom only he can communicate. Around them are Linus and his verbose, fussbudget sister Lucy, Schroeder, Peppermint Patty, and others. The characters may only be simple drawings, but readers were quick to empathize with them.

Like the routine nature of childhood, the strip was repetitious: footballs were always jerked away, games were always lost, hopes constantly dashed. Schulz had a genius for writing the same thing over and over again, only the result was somehow different. For child readers, here was an adult who realized how they, too, wrestled with doubt and anxiety. As Schulz himself was fond of saying: "You can't create humor out of happiness." **BS**

First published by United Feature Syndicate (USA)
Creator American (1922–2000)
Genre Humor, Children's
Award Congressional Gold Medal (2000)

THE COMPLETE PEANUTS
The definitive Collection of Charles M. Schulz's comic strip masterpiece
INTRODUCTION BY GARRISON KEILLOR
DAILIES & SUNDAYS
1950 TO 1952
by SCHULZ

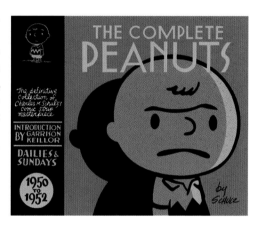

"[Schulz] brought . . . humor to taboo themes such as faith, intolerance, depression, loneliness, cruelty, and despair."

David Michaelis, biographer

Also by Charles Schulz

It's Only a Game
Li'l Folks
Peanuts 2000
You Can't Win Them All, Charlie Brown
Young Pillars

Blake and Mortimer
The Mystery of the Great Pyramid 1950

"Edgar P. Jacobs"

Title in original language *La Mystère de la Grande Pyramide* **First published by** *Le Journal de Tintin*/Editions du Lombard (Belgium) **Creator** Edgard Félix Pierre Jacobs (Belgian, 1904–87) **Genre** Adventure

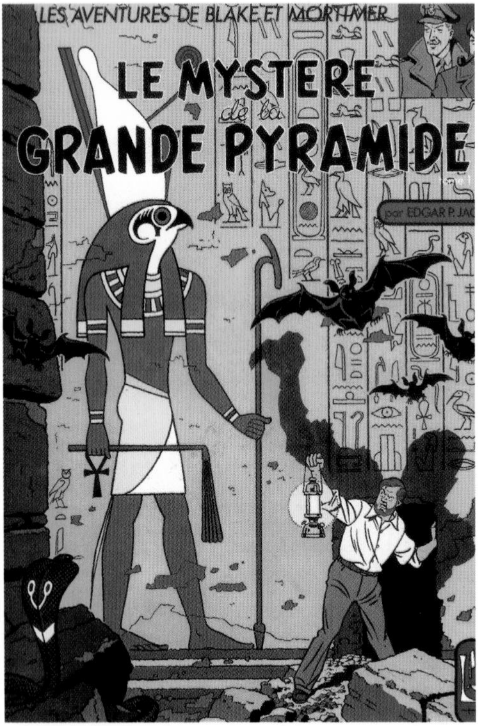
LES AVENTURES DE BLAKE ET MORTIMER
LE MYSTERE de la GRANDE PYRAMIDE

Similar reads

Baker Street Gary Reed and Guy Davis
By the Numbers (La vie de Victor Levallois) Laurent Rullier and "Stanislas"
Yoko Tsuno Roger Leloup

Edgar P. Jacobs must be the only comic creator who came to the art form after having spent fifteen years as an opera baritone. Heard throughout Belgium and France, he also designed sets for the productions in which he performed. He met Hergé while creating the set for a *Tintin* stage adaptation, and it is documented that elements of Captain Haddock's character were based on Jacobs's propensity for irascible invectiveness. Their friendship survived the rejection of a demand for equal credit on *Tintin* stories, for which Jacobs provided color and detailed backgrounds.

Jacobs then created his own feature for *Le journal de Tintin*, one way of ensuring that he finally got credit. Although *Blake and Mortimer* was serialized alongside *Tintin* and drawn in the same *ligne claire* style, Jacobs pitched his series to a more advanced audience. His English adventurers, Professor Philip Mortimer and M.I.5 agent Captain Francis Blake, are intellectual men—refined, knowledgeable, and cultured. Their interests encompass the past and embrace the future.

"If he wanted to shadow me, would he act in such a crazy manner?"

Jacobs never avoided explanation, judging that his audience appreciated background and technical information. He also believed that the story should dictate the page count, rather than the format. In *The Mystery of the Great Pyramid*, an old friend of Mortimer's is on the verge of a monumental archaeological breakthrough in Egypt, but strange events and an eccentric collector plague the research. Mortimer summons his investigative partner, but a shock awaits them both. This particular strip from the series lays the foundations for the pair's later cracking and unpredictable adventures. **FP**

Beetle Bailey 1950

Mort Walker

On September 4, 1950, what would later become the third most widely distributed comic strip of all time, *Beetle Bailey*, debuted almost unnoticed in a dozen newspapers. Six months later, the figure had grown to a paltry twenty-five, and there was talk of cancellation. Then the United States began sending troops to Korea, Beetle accidentally enlisted, and life for both Beetle and his creator changed forever.

Private Beetle Bailey is lazy and insubordinate, a constant thorn in the side of his superior officer, the short-tempered Sergeant 1st Class Orville P. Snorkel (Sarge). Real-life G.I.s, however, loved Beetle and would write to Mort Walker calling for Beetle's promotion and complaining that he had been a private for far too

"I've had it with you, Beetle! Come here!"

long. Walker's simple, graphic approach to drawing fit well with the reduced space comics were being given in newspapers in the early 1950s. As a gag writer Walker knew just what it took to make readers laugh. His characters, about twenty in all ("You can't have an army with two people in it"), changed in appearance over time—Beetle beefed up; Sarge became fatter.

And there was controversy, too. In the 1980s feminists railed against the sexist portrayal of a secretary, while others thought Walker ridiculed the U.S. war effort in Vietnam. Walker was well placed to write a strip highlighting the absurdities of army life. As an intelligence officer in World War II, he recalled how he was once given the task of making certain no one pilfered surplus watches and binoculars in Italy in 1945 so they could be run over by their own tanks. "Army humor writes itself," he once quipped. Walker's humor continues to entertain a loyal readership today. **BS**

First published by Dell Comics (USA)
Creator American (b.1923)
Genre Humor
Adaptation TV (1963)

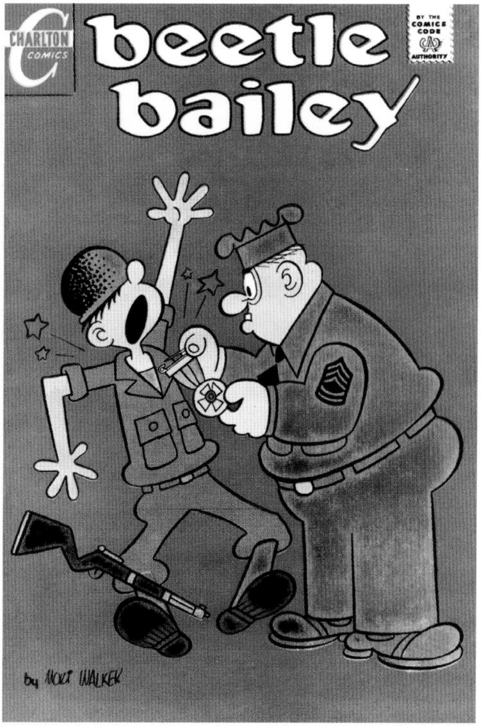
CHARLTON COMICS
beetle bailey
BY THE COMICS CODE AUTHORITY
by MORT WALKER

Also by Mort Walker

Boner's Ark
Hi and Lois
Sam & Silo
Sam's Strip

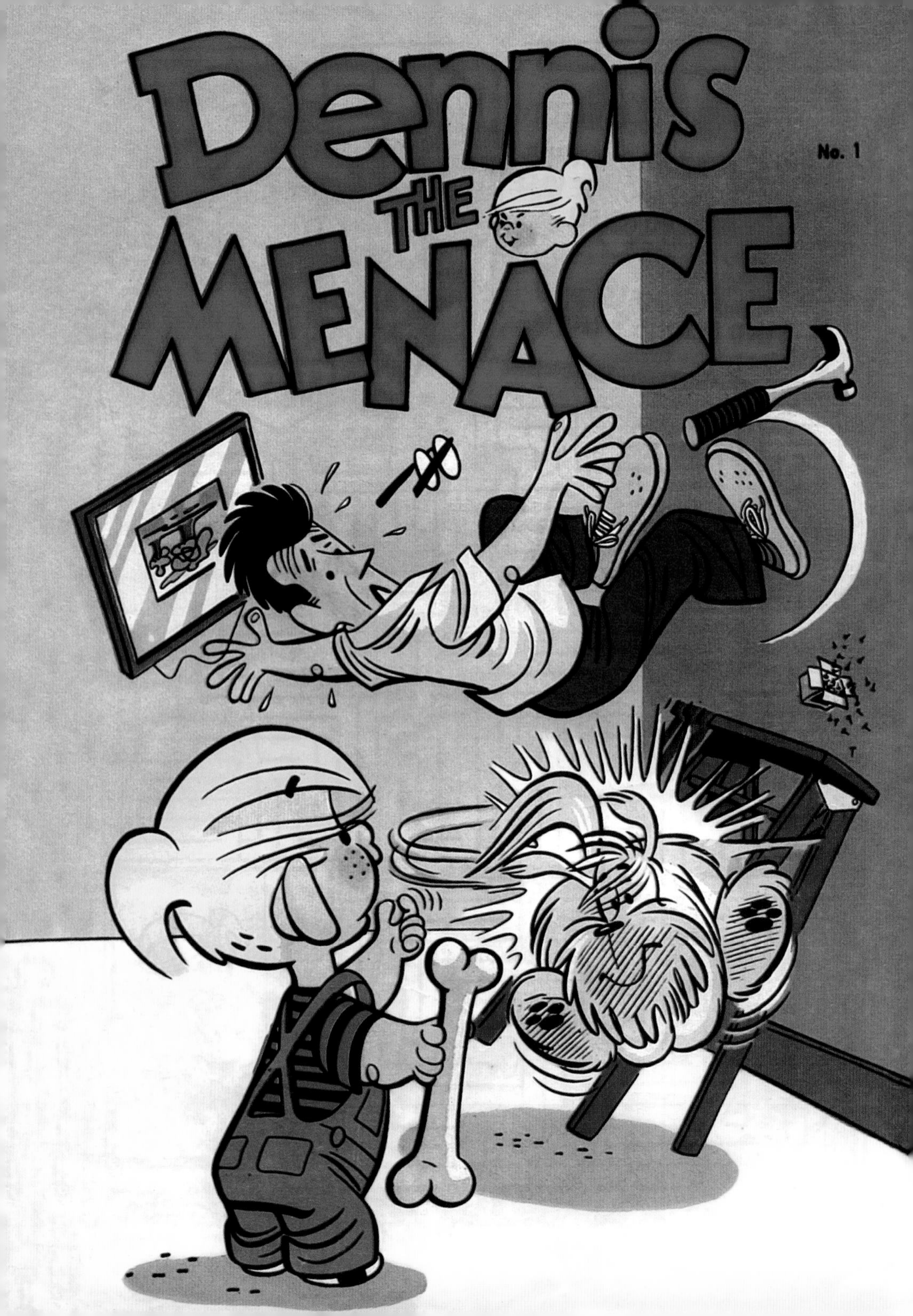
Dennis THE MENACE
No. 1

Dennis the Menace (USA) 1951

✏️ Hank Ketcham

First published by King Features Syndicate (USA)
Creator American (1920–2001)
Genre Humor, Children's
Award Reuben Award (1953)

First released on an unsuspecting U.S. public on March 12, 1951, Hank Ketcham's *Dennis the Menace* set the benchmark for misbehavior for the postwar, baby boom generation and their increasingly alarmed parents. A freelance cartoonist for the *Saturday Evening Post*, Ketcham was amazed by his own son's ability for causing chaos and before long had created one of the most enduring strips of the twentieth and twenty-first centuries.

Born in Seattle, Henry King Ketcham dropped out of college to work as an animator at Universal Studios and Disney. There he honed the fluid, bouncy line work and indelible character design that would be the strip's trademark. He enlisted in the U.S. Navy in 1942, drawing cartoons to promote war bonds. He and his family moved to Carmel, California after the war, where the real-life Dennis appeared in 1948. Sadly, Ketcham's wife, Alice, died in 1959. But none of this touched on the world of the cartoon, where Dennis is eternally five-and-a-half, and the worst thing that can happen is a ruined carpet.

Over the decades, Ketcham proved himself equally adept at both the single-panel gag cartoon and the multipanel Sunday strip, often drawing on a team of other writers and illustrators for inspiration. Success in other media soon followed, with a television series and a comic book (created with Al Wiseman and Ron Ferdinand, among others) both finding large audiences. Ketcham handed the strip over to his team for good in 1994, having trained those working with him to love drawing Dennis as much as he did. **EL**

Dennis the Menace (UK) 1951

✏️ Davey Law

First published by D. C. Thomson (UK)
Creator British (1908–71)
Genre Humor, Children's
Adaptation TV series (1996)

Appearing in print five days after his U.S. counterpart, the British *Dennis the Menace* is an altogether more truculent brute—a proactive troublemaker rather than a mischievous boy. The use of the same name was purely coincidental. The assignment to create a character to fit a name taken from the music hall song "Dennis the Menace from Venice" was given to Davey Law. Although early attempts failed to capture Dennis's wild nature, Law based the eventual look on a sketch provided by *The Beano* comic's Ian Chisholm. Dennis rapidly became the highlight of a comic then in decline, and in 1952 inspired cartoonist Leo Baxendale to contribute to *The Beano*; he noted the strip "pulsed with life. Somebody was carrying an intensity of creation into the drawing."

The vigorous art stemmed from Law's new freedom; he had been a staff artist shackled by a rigid house style for almost twenty years. With Dennis he had a surly, destructive child for whom mayhem was a way of life, and Law relished the change. Dennis was a force of devilment, frequently using the local joke shop's stock and relentlessly taunting "softy" Walter. He was the antithesis of the role models usually seen in comics.

Law labored over his pages and constructed his gags precisely. As his Dennis picked up other features in the 1950s, he became scratchier and sketchier, although not to the detriment of the strip. The current look was sealed in 1968 with the arrival of Gnasher, Dennis's anarchic dog. Mirroring Dennis in resembling nothing more than a mop-head on legs, Gnasher continues to revel in havoc with Dennis to this day. **FP**

Astro Boy 1951

Osamu Tezuka

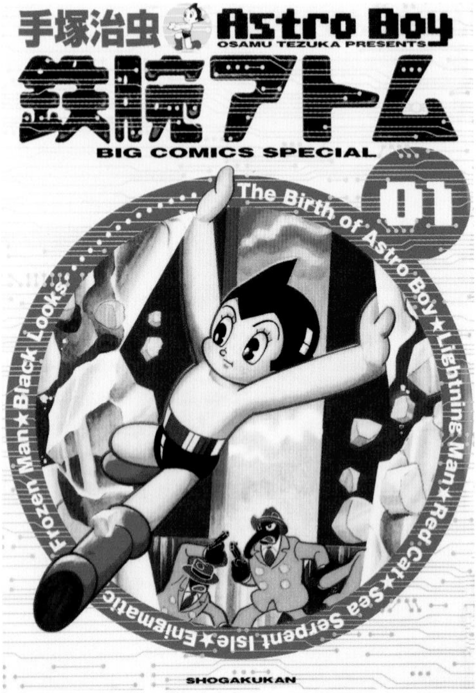
手塚治虫
Astro Boy
OSAMU TEZUKA PRESENTS
鉄腕アトム
BIG COMICS SPECIAL
01
The Birth of Astro Boy★Lightning Man★Red Cat★Sea Serpent Isle★Enigmatic
Frozen Man★Black Looks
SHOGAKUKAN

"This is it. This is what I was created for. This is my destiny."

Astro Boy

> **Also by Osama Tezuka**
> *Dororo*
> *Kimba the White Lion*
> *Metropolis*
> *Rainbow Parakeet*
> *The Three-Eyed One*

Title in original language *Tetsuwan Atomu*
First published by Kobunsha (Japan)
Creator Japanese (1928–89)
Genre Science fiction

Osamu Tezuka's *Astro Boy*, which launched in Japan in 1951, remains one of the most futuristic comics of all time. In fact, Tezuka's manga creation came long before Japan gained its reputation for its high-tech developments. The strip's timeless themes of hope, dreams, and justice have given Atomu the robot an iconic status in the world of Japanese science fiction.

The birth of Atom Boy in Tezuka's story is triggered by a tragedy in which Dr. Tenma, the director of the Ministry of Science, loses his only son named Tobio in an accident. Desperate, Dr. Tenma decides to revive Tobio as a robot, but when he realizes that Tobio is irreplaceable, he sells the robot to a circus. The robot later becomes known as Atomu. This type of narrative, where a protagonist is forced onto a road of hardship, is known in Japanese literature as *kishuryutan*. Atomu's dark history not only earns the sympathy of his audience, but also enhances his exuberance when he finally finds happiness and becomes a superhero. After being adopted by Professor Ochanomizu, Atomu used his powers and high-tech weaponry to fight villains for seventeen years, until the series ended in 1968.

Instead of the literal "Mighty Atom," *Tetsuwan Atomu* was renamed *Astro Boy* for the English-language market in 1963, when Tezuka developed his creation into an animated series in Japan and sold it to the American television channel NBC. Although a 2003 cartoon series in color was less successful, demand for Astro Boy has remained strong, prompting a 3-D film by director David Bowers in 2009. **TS**

The Cisco Kid 1951

✒ Rod Reed   ✒ Jose Luis Salinas

First published by Dell Comics (USA)
Creators Reed (American, Unknown);
Salinas (Argentinian, 1908–85)
Genre Western

Many countries have produced a truly great comics artist who stands out from everyone else: Alex Raymond in the United States, Frank Bellamy in Britain, Jesus Blasco in Spain, and Francisco V. Coching in the Philippines. In Argentina that accolade belongs to Jose Luis Salinas. By 1951 he had been working in his native comics industry for two decades, but it was with the creation of the U.S. strip *The Cisco Kid* that he found his greatest success.

The Cisco Kid character first appeared in a 1907 short story by O. Henry, "The Caballero's Way," although at this stage he was little more than a ruthless bandit. For later incarnations in films, radio, and television, he was reinvented as a dashing Mexican hero, and it was this version that persuaded King Features editor Sylvan Byck to bring the character to newspapers. Scripts were provided by Rod Reed, a comic book veteran and writer of the *Rusty Riley* strip, with art supplied by Salinas.

In the strip, the Cisco Kid was joined by his rotund sidekick Pancho, and the pair roamed around New Mexico and beyond looking for adventure, wrongs to be righted, and a hearty meal. Cisco himself was depicted as a handsome, snappy dresser complete with sombrero and embroidered shirt, who invariably found adoring girls wherever he went. Reed kept his scripts light in tone, but with enough action to satisfy the Western fans of the day. The strip was soon carried by more than 150 newspapers in the United States and abroad. Salinas excelled in depicting beautifully the dusty majesty of the Old West. **DAR**

Donald Duck and the Gilded Man 1952

✒✒ Carl Barks

First published by Dell Comics (USA)
Creator American (1901–2000)
Genre Humor
Collection *Walt Disney's Donald Duck Adventures* (1990)

Donald Duck is trying to earn enough money from stamp collecting to go to British Guiana to look for a rare one-cent magenta stamp. While searching the railroad station wastebaskets, he comes across his cousin, Gladstone Gander. Gladstone finds a stamp album belonging to a rich, absentminded collector named Philo T. Ellic, who gives him a reward, forgets about it, then gives one to Donald, too. The money enables Donald to fly to British Guiana with his nephews.

The ducks are not the only stamp collectors around, and the search proves difficult until an old man sends them on the trail of his postman father's mailbag, stolen by the legendary gilded man El Dorado. A veritable giant covered in gold, El Dorado is fascinated by all things silver, and the ducks use this to trick him and retrieve the missing mailbag.

On their return, the ducks find that the Guianan postal service intends to deliver a letter bearing the valuable one-cent stamp. It is sent to the United States, closely followed by Donald. To his dismay, the addressee has passed away, and Gladstone, being sole heir, gets the stamp. He quickly proceeds to sell it to Philo T. Ellic, who promptly loses it. When Donald finds the stamp and gives it back to him, he pockets a nice reward.

Even though Donald Duck was not his creation, it was Carl Barks who made him shine in the comic books in hundreds of stories, ranging from the epic to the comical. This one is a fine example of Barks at his storytelling best—a straightforward adventure tale with plenty of action and lots of gags. **J-PJ**

The Crushed Gardenia 1952

✎ Unknown   ✎ Alex Toth

First published by Standard Comics (USA)
Creators Toth (American, 1928–2006)
Genre Crime
Award Jack Kirby Hall of Fame (1990)

Dr. Paul Crane introduces *The Crushed Gardenia*, the story of Johnny Faber, a delinquent who eventually turns to murder. Crane tells the reform school warden that Johnny is a paranoid who needs help. This psychiatric appraisal is questionable even for its time—Johnny is really a sociopath with extreme narcissistic tendencies. The unknown writer brings standard melodrama to the story, but it would not make such an impression without the brilliance of Alex Toth's drawings.

Toth's work soared to its greatest heights in the 1960s and 1970s when he found the perfect mixture of expressionism and minimalistic, telling detail. He was a restless, driven man who, in later years, unable to satisfy his perfectionism, could not produce finished pages. His belief was that nothing should be wasted—every line should serve a careful purpose. Readers see this approach at an earlier stage of development in *The Crushed Gardenia*, which is already remarkable in its economy, drama, and strength of design and composition.

This average story is elevated to real greatness by the young Toth, who was already a master of the art form. Faber's face—contemptuous and without conscience—is rendered in a handful of loose strokes. The brooding Johnny on page five sits in darkness filled with the name of the girl who has rejected him—Ellie—his world overcome with the pain of his wounded ego. Toth makes extensive use of shadow and heavy black throughout, the abstractions always clear in intent and powerful, such as the chilling silhouette of Johnny holding his weapon on the final page. **CH**

The Indian 1952

✎✎ Francisco V. Coching

Title in original language *El Indio*
First published by Ace Publications, Inc. (Philippines)
Creator Filipino (1919–98) **Genre** Drama, Adventure
Notable mention Dean of Filipino Komiks Illustration

The Indian was serialized from 1952 to 1953 in five-page, biweekly installments within the standard Philippine anthology format containing four to eight continuing or complete stories. By 1952 Francisco V. Coching was the foremost Filipino comics creator, and his comic strips were so popular that film adaptations were being shot long before the stories were finished in print.

Unusual in the Filipino comics industry, Coching was one of the rare individuals who would write and draw their own stories. *The Indian* represented the culmination of Coching's artistic development and the ultimate example of his unique style as an illustrator. His brushwork was bold and frenetic; he sculpted figures that seemed to move even when they were standing still. Every major comic book artist from the Philippines, including Alex Niño, Alfredo Alcala, Nestor Redondo, Rudy Nebres, and Tony DeZuniga, cite Coching as a major influence on their work.

Coching himself never worked abroad, opting instead to create stories for his native readership. Set during the Spanish occupation of the Philippines toward the end of the nineteenth century, *The Indian* tells the story of Fernando, the son of a Filipino general and a Spanish noblewoman. Fernando goes to the Philippines in search of the truth about his father. Writing in an impeccable Tagalog language, Coching weaves an engrossing tale of love, honor, and quixotic values. *The Indian* was digitally restored by Komikero Publishing in 2004 and compiled in one volume that was published by the Vibal Foundation in 2009. **GA**

Francisco V. Coching strikingly rendered *The Indian* in black and white. ➡

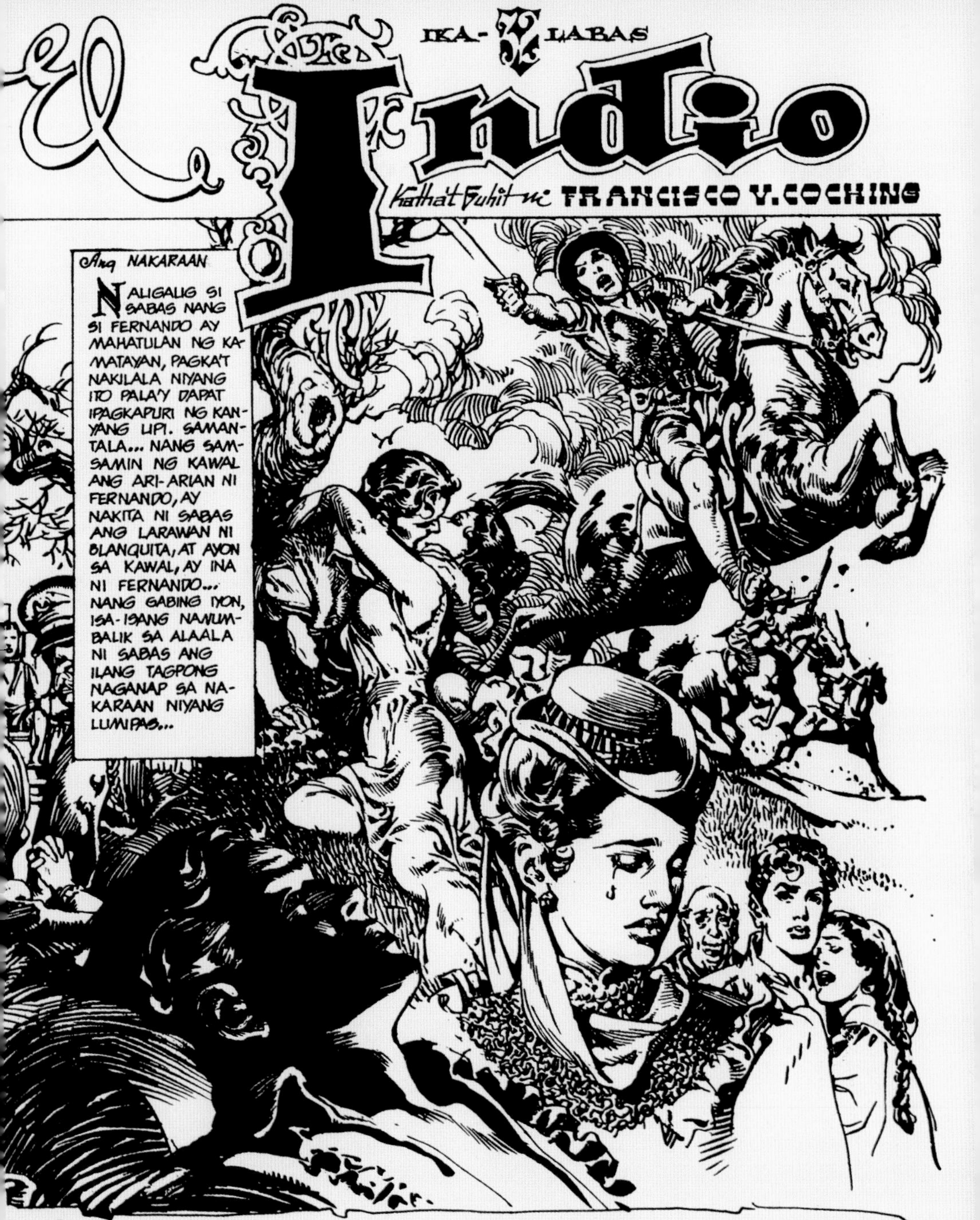
IKA- LABAS
El Indio
Kathat Guhit ni FRANCISCO V. COCHING
Ang NAKARAAN
NALIGALIG SI SABAS NANG SI FERNANDO AY MAHATULAN NG KAMATAYAN, PAGKA'T NAKILALA NIYANG ITO PALA'Y DAPAT IPAGKAPURI NG KANYANG LIPI. SAMANTALA... NANG SAMSAMIN NG KAWAL ANG ARI-ARIAN NI FERNANDO, AY NAKITA NI SABAS ANG LARAWAN NI BLANQUITA, AT AYON SA KAWAL, AY INA NI FERNANDO... NANG GABING IYON, ISA-ISANG NANUMBALIK SA ALAALA NI SABAS ANG ILANG TAGPONG NAGANAP SA NAKARAAN NIYANG LUMIPAS...

NOONG PANAHONG SIYA'Y NAPABANSAG BILANG ISANG DAKILANG TULISANG SI BARBARO... MULI NIYANG NAGUNITA ANG PUSPOS NG KATAMISANG PAG-UULAYAW NILA NI BLANQUITA... ANG LABIS NIYANG PAGKAHIBANG SA NAKALALANGONG ALINDOG NITO... NASUKAT DIN NIYA ANG KADAKILAAN NITO NANG SIYA'Y BIBITAYIN NA LAMANG AY NANIKLUHOD PA SA MAYKAPANGYARIHAN AT INIHANDOG ANG BUHAY BILANG TUBOS SA KANYANG KALAYAAN. AT HIGIT SA LAHAT... NANG MAKAMIT NI SABAS ANG KAPATAWARAN AY IPINAGPARAYA PA RIN NG BABAING ITO ANG KANYANG PAG-IBIG KAY TARCILA, NA DI NAMAN NAGLAON AT SUMAKABILANG BUHAY.

Donald Duck
A Christmas for Shacktown 1952

Carl Barks

First published by Dell Comics (USA)
Creator American (1901–2000)
Genre Humor
Award Disney Legends Award (1991)

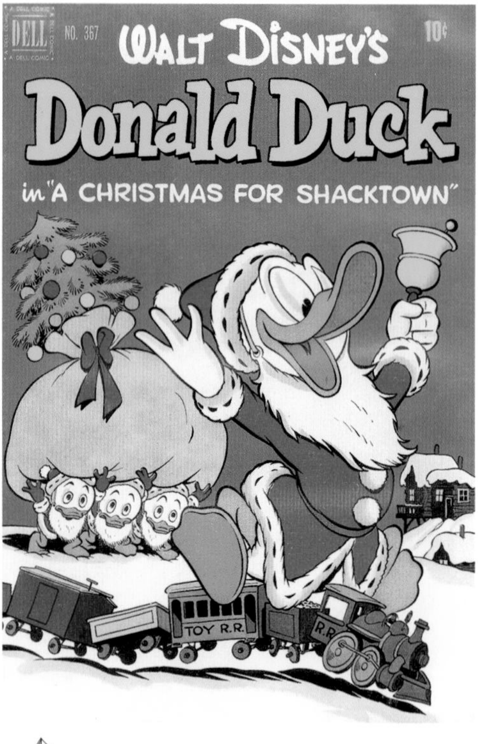
DELL
NO. 367
WALT DISNEY'S
10¢
Donald Duck
in "A CHRISTMAS FOR SHACKTOWN"
TOY R.R.
R.R.

Other *Donald Duck* stories
A Financial Fable
Houseboat Holiday
Omelet
Statuesque Spendthrifts

Not content with using nephews Huey, Dewey, and Louie and fiancée Daisy Duck as comic foils for Donald, Carl Barks also created lucky cousin Gladstone Gander, the maddeningly rich Uncle Scrooge, zany genius inventor Gyro Gearloose, bad-tempered neighbor Jones, and a host of other episodic figures to make life hell for his duck hero—who could be pretty unbearable himself. *A Christmas for Shacktown* starts out as a traditional holiday story, with Donald trying to help Daisy and the kids raise money for a Christmas party for poor children.

When asked for fifty dollars, Uncle Scrooge challenges Donald to raise half of it by himself before giving him the rest. After two failed attempts to con Scrooge into changing his mind, Donald enlists the help of his cousin Gladstone, who quickly finds the twenty-five dollars and an extra dime to boot. That extra dime, passed on to Scrooge, however, causes the rich duck's fortune to drop into a deep cavern, the bottom of which is so fragile that attempts to retrieve it might cause the cash to disappear forever in the underlying quicksand. In the end, Scrooge's fortune is saved by the very thing he disparaged as silly and useless—a toy train bought as a gift for the poor children of Shacktown.

"Mister, would you like to donate to a Christmas party for poor kids?"

This is a lively comedy with plenty of wry humor. Donald Duck's bumbling attempts at raising money, initially from passersby, then from his very rich but miserly relative ("World's richest duck—and darn well going to stay that way!"), climax with the hilarious catastrophe of a single dime breaking Scrooge's safe. The zany problem it causes (how to get the money back) makes for very entertaining reading. **J-PJ**

Uncle Scrooge
Only a Poor Old Man 1952

Carl Barks

Uncle Scrooge McDuck is Carl Barks's most enduring creation for the Disney universe. Donald Duck's impossibly rich uncle first appeared in 1947 and grew more and more popular over the years until he was given his own comic book title, starting with the *Four Color* anthology series in 1952.

This story is Scrooge's first solo outing. It begins with him taking a morning swim in his "money bin" while at the same time lecturing nephew Donald on the virtues of saving. Soon, however, Scrooge has to contend with the terrible Beagle Boys, who plan to rob him from the construction site they have set up next to his money bin. Scrooge manages to smuggle his money to the bottom of a nearby lake by using the Beagle Boys' own dump trucks. His relief is short-lived, though, because his hiding place is discovered and the Beagle Boys attempt various devious tricks to break the dam that holds the money lake. They eventually succeed, but Scrooge outsmarts them again and soon gets his fortune back.

"What's the use of having money if I can't have fun with it?"

In this beautifully drawn and superbly timed story, Barks starts to make the Scrooge character more rounded by giving him a past. The eccentric old coot turns out to have a long life of valuable experiences behind him that he draws on to keep outsmarting would-be looters. Having witnessed all the trouble his uncle has to go through just to keep his money, Donald thinks that Scrooge's billions are "a pain in the neck," but obviously Scrooge would rather have the money than peace of mind. And who can argue with a duck whose idea of fun is having a morning swim in a pool full of cash? **J-PJ**

First published by Dell Comics (USA)
Creator American (1901–2000)
Genre Humor
Award Shazam Award (1970)

DELL
NO. 386
WALT DISNEY'S
10¢
UNCLE $CROOGE
in "ONLY A POOR OLD MAN"
MONEY LAKE No. 1
PENNY WISE
DEPTH GAUGE 20 ft

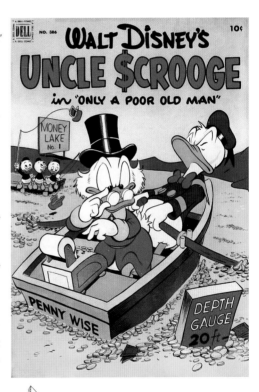

Other *Uncle Scrooge* stories

Back to the Klondike
Land Beneath the Ground!
The Lemming with the Locket
Tralla La

The Saint, the Man in the Silver Mask 1952

José G. Cruz José Trinidad Romero

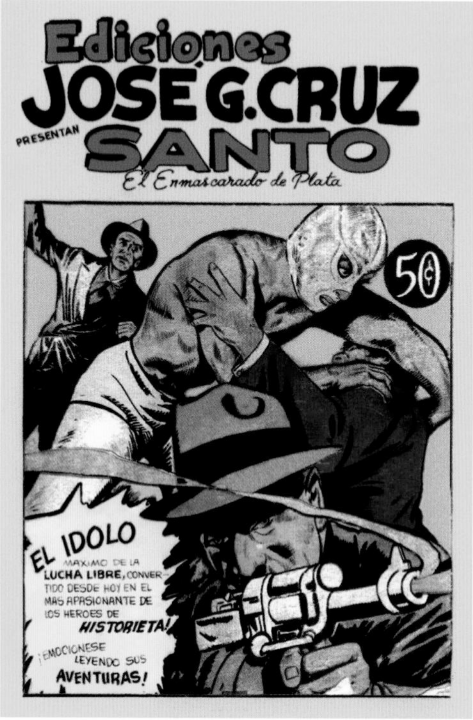
Ediciones
JOSE G. CRUZ
PRESENTAN
SANTO
El Enmascarado de Plata
50¢
EL IDOLO MAXIMO DE LA LUCHA LIBRE, CONVERTIDO DESDE HOY EN EL MAS APASIONANTE DE LOS HEROES DE HISTORIETA!
¡EMOCIONESE LEYENDO SUS AVENTURAS!

"[Guzmán] died of a heart attack. He was buried with his silver mask on."

Xavier Garza

Similar reads

Batman Bill Finger and Bob Kane
Canciones Inolvidables José G. Cruz
Dick Tracy Chester Gould
El Vampiro Tenebroso José G. Cruz
Sleepwalker (*Sonámbulo*) Rafael Navarro

Title in original language *El Santo, el enmascarado de plata* **First published by** Ediciones José G. Cruz (México) **Creators** Cruz (Mexican, 1917–89); Romero (Mexican, 1925–99) **Genre** Adventure, Fantasy

If there is a quintessential Mexican superhero, it has to be the *luchador* (wrestler). The real-life El Santo (Roberto Guzmán Huerta) is perhaps Mexico's most famous popular icon, after the Virgen de Guadalupe and José Guadalupe Posada's celebrated *Day of the Dead* graphics. By the time this series started in 1952, El Santo was already a celebrity, and José G. Cruz merged the fields of photography and comic books with the artistry of José Trinidad Romero. In spite of being technically a *fumetto*, or photo-comic, the publication advertised and defined itself as an *historieta*, or comic book.

Regular programming in Mexican television would not start until 1955, so the *The Saint, The Man in the Silver Mask* weekly photo-comic book was a product ahead of its time in visual and narrative terms. This first issue presented a masked vigilante defending the inhabitants of Santa Cruz against petty criminals. Fatally wounded, the hero asks his son to continue his struggle by wearing a silver *lucha libre* (free wrestling) mask to become El Santo. Possessing supernatural strength and athletic ability, El Santo's weakness was the removal of his mask. Romero's technique blended a noir photographic aesthetic that matched the half-tone style of other Mexican comics of the time.

El Santo was played by Roberto Guzmán himself, but often it was Horacio Robles, one of the magazine's editors, who would wear the mask for the photo shoots. *The Saint* remains an essential piece in the history of Mexican comics, and is one of the most sought after by collectors of comics and ephemera alike. **EPr**

MAD 1952

✐ Harvey Kurtzman   ✐ Harvey Kurtzman, Jack Davis, Bill Elder, and Wally Wood

First published by EC Comics (USA)
Creator American (1924–93)
Genre Humor
Adaptation Theater: *The MAD Show* (1966)

Long before it became a satirical magazine and a U.S. television sketch show, *MAD* was a comic book that dared to go where few other comic books had gone before. Although it only lasted for three years and twenty-three issues, *MAD*'s influence on those baby boomer artists who would later form the underground comix scene in the late 1960s was considerable.

Originally baptized *Mad Mag* by EC Comics publisher William M. Gaines, Harvey Kurtzman shortened the title to *MAD* and went to work hiring humorists as writers and artists with whom he could have a direct working relationship. The three artists whose work looms largest in the pages of *MAD* are Jack Davis, Wallace "Wally" Wood, and Bill Elder. Each possessed a unique style that made *MAD* stand out from its competitors. Wood had already been involved with EC's science fiction titles, while Davis had worked alongside Kurtzman on *Two-Fisted Tales* and *Frontline Combat*, but with *MAD* their collective creativity was fully unleashed, resulting in some of their most memorable work.

After a frustratingly slow start, *MAD* eventually took off with "Superduperman!," Wood and Kurtzman's scalpel-sharp lampooning of DC Comics's superhero Superman, that appeared as the lead story in issue #4 of *MAD*. Other revered comic book characters (Batman, Popeye, Prince Valiant, Flash Gordon, Little Orphan Annie, Plastic Man, Pogo), movie stars, television stars and shows, the national press, and magazine advertising would all later be given the same treatment as the crack team of *MAD* writers and artists went on the

attack. Even classic literature was fair game. Bill Elder's "Shermlock Shomes!" and "The Hound of the Basketballs!" (*MAD* issues #7 and #16) reduced Conan Doyle's master detective to a sleuthing klutz, while Davis's take on "Alice in Wonderland" (*MAD* issue #18) had Lewis Carroll's heroine meeting Bugs Bunny instead of a white rabbit.

Davis also supplied the art for "The Face Upon the Floor" (*MAD* issue #10), a retelling of H. Antoine D'Arcy's poem about an alcoholic artist who, after drawing a picture of his former lover Madeline on a barroom floor, drops dead at the sight of her beauty. This being *MAD*, however, Madeline's portrait was supplied by eccentric artist Basil Wolverton, who depicted her in the final frame as a bug-eyed, snaggle-toothed crone. Lena the Hyena, another of Wolverton's creations, featured on the cover of *MAD* issue #11 as "Beautiful Girl of the Month," a barbed parody of pictorial magazine *Life* that became one of *MAD*'s most iconic images. In his 1989 autobiographical strip "Ode to Harvey Kurtzman," Robert Crumb revealed, "The cover of *MAD* issue #11 changed the way I saw the world forever!"

MAD is seen as a precursor to the U.S. underground comix movement in its antiestablishment stance and ceaseless goading of corporate institutions. Bill Elder's "Mickey Rodent!" (*MAD* issue #19), for example, was an irreverent, four-fingered salute to the Disney corporation that predates Dan O'Neill and company's *Mickey Mouse Meets the Air Pirates* and Robert Armstrong's *Mickey Rat*. "Let's not forget," reminded Kurtzman in an interview with publisher Russ Cochran, "that Mickey is a huge, upright, talking mouse, bigger than a giant rat."

In 1955 Kurtzman revamped *MAD* into a magazine format before leaving EC that same year to write and edit the satirical magazines *Trump, Humbug,* and *Help!* It was *MAD*, however, that has proven to be Kurtzman's enduring triumph and masterpiece. **EP**

Frontline Combat 1952

Harvey Kurtzman   Harvey Kurtzman, Jack Davis, Bill Elder, John Severin, and Wally Wood

First published by EC Comics (USA) **Creators** Kurtzman (American, 1924–93); Davis (American, b.1924); Elder (American, 1921–2008); Severin (American, b.1921); Wood (American, 1927–81) **Genre** War

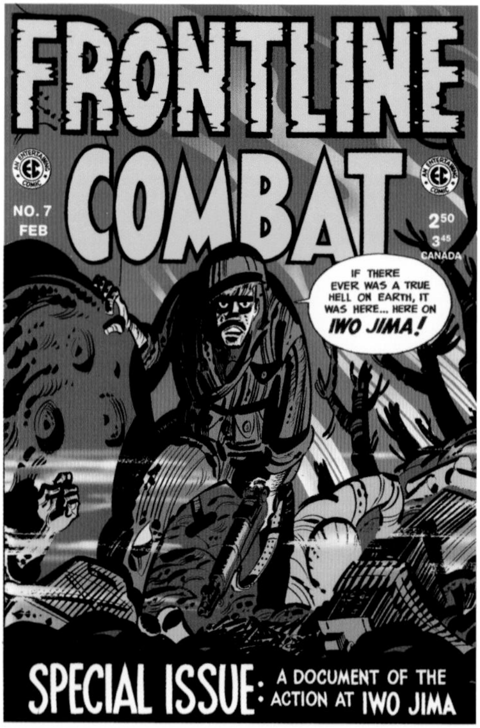
FRONTLINE COMBAT
NO. 7 FEB
2.50
3.45 CANADA
IF THERE EVER WAS A TRUE HELL ON EARTH, IT WAS HERE... HERE ON IWO JIMA!
SPECIAL ISSUE: A DOCUMENT OF THE ACTION AT IWO JIMA

Also by Harvey Kurtzman

Jungle Book

The Bedside MAD

The EC Archives: Frontline Combat with Jerry DeFuccio, Wally Wood, Jack Davis, and others

The first story in *Frontline Combat* #7, "Iwo Jima," introduces the island through the eyes of bomber pilots struggling to make it back to base after being hit by enemy flak. The plane is unable to get home, but there is a possibility of reaching the tiny volcanic island of Iwo Jima, which the U.S. Marines are still fighting for. The story takes this opportunity to introduce the geology of the island in some detail, as well as its geographic position at the extreme south of the chain of islands that straggle out southward from the Japanese mainland.

The second story, "The Landing," deals with the invasion of the island by the U.S. Marines, and is one of EC Comics's many war stories that turn on an ironic revelation about the perceived cowardice of one of the characters. "The Cave"—in typical EC style—switches the point of view around to the Japanese forces defending Iwo Jima, and again delivers an ironic comment on received ideas about heroism in different cultures. The final story, "Mopping Up," completes the circle. The Marines have made the island secure, and it is finally possible for the bomber featured in the first story to land safely. Two brothers are reunited—one from the bomber and one from the Marine Corps—but not before one of the protagonists has had his belief in the purpose of war tested to the very limit.

"Why am I here? Why? Why? What do I want with this crummy stinking volcano? Why are we dying for it?"

Under Harvey Kurtzman's enlightened editorship, EC's war comics portrayed the actions and emotions of men on both sides of the conflict with great realism. The stories deliver a powerful condemnation of warfare from a generation of writers and artists who had lived through the horrors of World War II. **RR**

Shock SuspenStories 1952

Al Feldstein and William Gaines   Al Feldstein, Jack Davis, Jack Kamen, and others

First published by EC Comics (USA)
Creators Feldstein (American, b.1925); Gaines (American, 1922–92); Davis (American, b.1924); Kamen (American,1920–2008) **Genre** Reality drama

Shock SuspenStories was launched by EC Comics to give readers a one-story taste of the kind of fare featured in its other titles. The first issue opens with "The Neat Job," a crime story illustrated by Jack Kamen. "Yellow," with artwork by Jack Davis, is typical of the stories featured in *Two-Fisted Tales* or *Frontline Combat*. "The Monsters" (artwork by Joe Orlando) is a fine example of the stories available in either *Weird Science* or *Weird Fantasy*, while the final story, "The Ring," (with artwork by Graham "Ghastly" Ingels) could have passed as one of the milder horror stories from *Tales from the Crypt*, *Vault of Horror*, or *Haunt of Fear*.

In issue #2, however, "The Patriots" appeared. Written, as usual, by Bill Gaines and Al Feldstein, with artwork by Jack Davis, it tells the fate of a blind veteran whose actions are misinterpreted by ultrapatriotic bystanders at a parade of troops arriving home from the Korean War. This was the first EC tale to put political and social commentary explicitly at the heart of the narrative. The story's topical theme of misplaced anti-Communist zeal typifies the liberal politics of *Shock SuspenStories*. Subsequent stories dealt with racism, anti-Semitism, and police corruption and brutality.

"Must pain be the only teacher? Can't we learn without pain? Can't we learn to love . . . instead of to hate?"

The cancellation of *Shock SuspenStories* in 1954, along with most of EC's comics, silenced a provocative and trenchant voice in U.S. comics that would not be seen again until the emergence of the underground movement in the 1960s. The influence of EC and *Shock SuspenStories* can be seen in the work of such diverse talents as Charles Burns, Robert Crumb, Jack Jackson, Spain Rodriguez, and many others. **RR**

IMPACT
NO.1
FEB.-MAR.
SHOCK
10¢
SUSPENSTORIES
JOLTING TALES OF
TENSION
IN THE
EC TRADITION!
FELDSTEIN

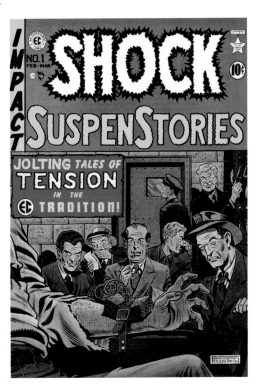

Also by Al Feldstein and William Gaines
Crime SuspenStories
Haunt of Fear
Tales from the Crypt
Vault of Horror

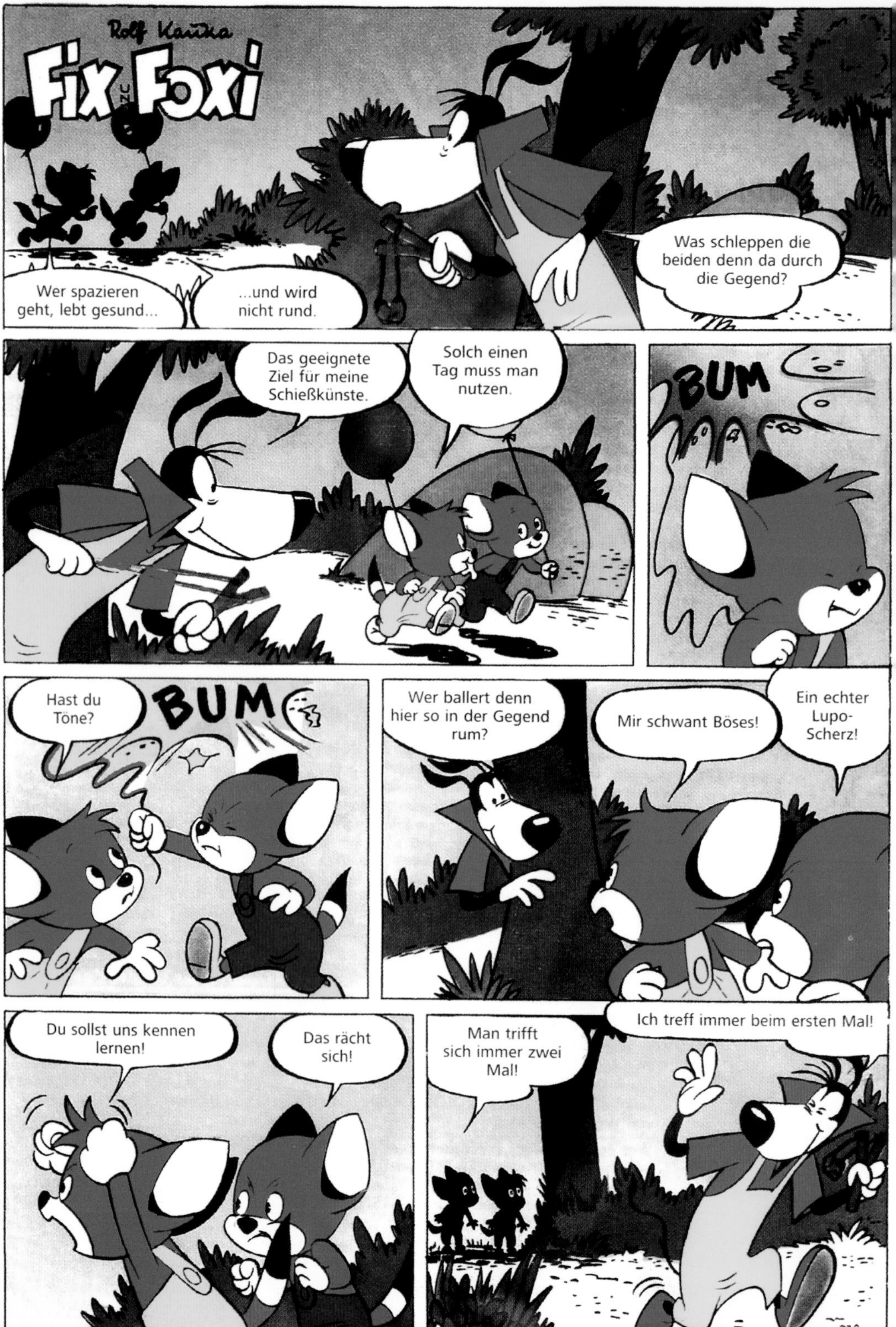

Rolf Kauka
Fix und Foxi
Wer spazieren geht, lebt gesund...
...und wird nicht rund.
Was schleppen die beiden denn da durch die Gegend?
Das geeignete Ziel für meine Schießkünste.
Solch einen Tag muss man nutzen.
BUM
Hast du Töne?
BUM
Wer ballert denn hier so in der Gegend rum?
Mir schwant Böses!
Ein echter Lupo-Scherz!
Du sollst uns kennen lernen!
Das rächt sich!
Man trifft sich immer zwei Mal!
Ich treff immer beim ersten Mal!

Fix and Foxi 1953

✑✑ Rolf Kauka

Title in original language *Fix und Foxi*
First published by Kauka Verlag (Germany)
Creator German (1917–2000)
Genre Children's

Fix and Foxi are not only the most famous German comic strip characters, their names are also behind the expression *fix und fertig*, or "exhausted," in German slang. The two young foxes, who are twin brothers, appeared as minor characters in Rolf Kauka's first published comics anthology series, *Till Eulenspiegel*. Kauka developed them in 1953 when he retold the traditional story of Reynard the Fox and Isegrim the Wolf. They became so popular that the series was renamed *Fix and Foxi*.

The two protagonists were examples with whom young readers could identify: broadminded, moral, educated, and socially committed. Fix, in yellow dungarees, is characterized as the more intelligent and pragmatic of the two; Foxi, dressed in blue, is a more cautious, thoughtful type. Their friend Lupo, a lovable cadger who wants to become a small-time criminal, provides all the chaos and excitement in the series. Lupo became the series' secret star and later had his own comic magazine, in which Kauka published the first translations of Franco-Belgian comics.

In 1951, after U.S. comic books made their appearance in Germany, Kauka founded a comics company, Kauka Verlag. There were still very few comics artists in the young Federal Republic of Germany, so he worked with graphic artists from Yugoslavia, Italy, and Spain. *Fix and Foxi* are children of postwar Germany. Although the series was inspired by U.S. comics, in particular the world of Carl Barks's *Donald Duck*, Kauka turned his back almost completely on humor and followed instead a purely educational approach. **MS**

Sgt. Kirk 1953

✑ Héctor Gérman Oesterheld   ✑ Hugo Pratt

Title in original language *El Sargento Kirk*
First published by Editorial Abril (Argentina)
Creators Oesterheld (Argentinian, 1919–77);
Pratt (Italian, 1927–55) **Genre** Western

In 1941, Italian publisher Cesare Civita arrived in Argentina after fleeing anti-Semitism in Europe. In Buenos Aires he established Editorial Abril, hiring Italian writers and artists, including Hugo Pratt (who arrived in the country in 1949). Pratt met Argentine comic book writer Héctor Gérman Oesterheld at Editorial Abril in 1951. A few months later they collaborated on *Sgt. Kirk* for *Misterix* magazine (although the story was also published in *Supermisterix*). In 1958 Oesterheld and Pratt revived the comic strip in Oesterheld's own publishing house—Editorial Frontera. *Sgt. Kirk* was also drawn by Jorge Moliterni, Horacio Porreca, and Gisela Dester, and, during the 1970s, by Gustavo Trigo (in the children's magazine *Billiken*).

Sgt. Kirk is a U.S. soldier who fought during the American Civil War and the Indian Wars. After taking part in a massacre in the latter, he questions his actions and decides to fight on the enemy's side. Kirk and a group of other characters—Maha (who belongs to the Chattooga people and is also Kirk's blood brother), Corto Lea (the inspiration for another Pratt creation *Corto Maltese*), a former outlaw, and Dr. Forbes (the "white shaman," as the American Indians call him)—live together on their ranch in Cañadón Perdido.

The series was superbly drawn by Hugo Pratt and incredibly well researched by both men. Oesterheld's humanism leads him to create a comic filled with antiheroes. Behind it all, however, is an antiracist message. As Sgt. Kirk puts it: "There are no palefaces or Indians . . . there are just men . . . just men." **DI**

← Primary colors dominate the artwork; Kauka stipulated that the foxes must be red.

Princess Knight 1953

Osamu Tezuka

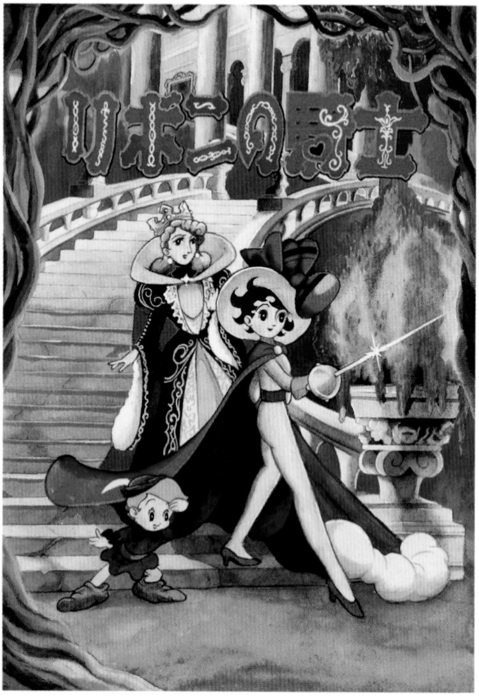
リボンの騎士

"Princess Knight is widely regarded as the progenitor of the modern girls' manga format."

Frederik L. Schodt, writer

Also by Osamu Tezuka

Fushigi na Merumo (Marvelous Melmo)
Metropolis
MW
W-3 (The Amazing Three)

Title in original language *Ribon no Kishi*
First published by Kodansha (Japan)
Creator Japanese (1928–89)
Genre Adventure

On *Princess Knight*, "god of manga" Osamu Tezuka employed the visual and storytelling innovations he had brought earlier to manga for boys. Set in the fictitious medieval kingdom of Silverland, Princess Sapphire is heir to the throne. But because she was born a girl—due to the mischief of the young cherub Tink (aka Choppy), who added a female heart to her male one—she cannot take her rightful place. The king raises and dresses her as a boy, keeping the secret from his people. The main villain is Duke Duralumon, who is suspicious of Sapphire's gender and will do anything to take the throne. Other menaces Sapphire has to face—together with sidekick Tink, who has descended to Earth to remove her extra heart—in order to defend her kingdom include Satan and his daughter Heckett.

Delightfully kitsch, *Princess Knight* shows, in addition to the omnipresent Disney imprint on most of Tezuka's works, influences such as European medieval-themed movies and, particularly, the *Takarazuka* all-female theater revue, which played an important role in the author's formative years. *Princess Knight* had a sequel in 1959, *Twin Knights*, starring Sapphire's son and daughter, as well as a remake of the original manga published in *Nakayoshi* and a science fiction–themed sequel published in *Shojo Friend* in 1967, drawn by Kitano Hideaki. That same year the comic was adapted into a fifty-two-episode animated television series, dubbed into English as *Choppy and the Princess*. A bilingual, English/Japanese version of the manga was published by Kodansha in 2001. **AMo**

The Heart of Juliet Jones 1953

✎ Elliot Caplin ✎ Stan Drake

First published by King Features Syndicate (USA)
Creators Caplin (American,1913–2000);
Drake (American, 1921–97)
Genre Soap opera

In 1953 Stan Drake was tiring of working in advertising and pondered a return to comics, which he had tried briefly prior to army service in World War II. He contacted King Features, who were developing a newspaper comic strip to compete with the popular soap opera strip *Mary Worth*, and was introduced to writer Elliot Caplin. Caplin was impressed with Drake's photo-realistic style, which he thought perfect for the concept—and the partnership for *The Heart of Juliet Jones* was born. It was an instant success. In the 1950s, soap operas, aimed at a romance-hungry female audience with newfound economic clout, saturated all forms of entertainment—from movies to radio to comics.

The strip chronicles the love lives of two dissimilar small-town sisters. Brunette Juliet is modest, mature, and successful. Her younger sister, buxom blond Eve, is flirty, flighty, and often in trouble. Their elderly widowed father, Pops, also plays a leading role as a succession of handsome, accomplished, and usually wealthy men fall for one (or sometimes both) of the sisters.

Caplin's storylines were praised for their quality, but it was Drake's artwork that gave the strip its lasting influence. His figure drawing captured naturalistic movement and expressive body language—achieved by using photographic reference. In this, he used the magazine and advertising illustration methods of the time. Perhaps Drake's greatest strength was his ability to draw accurate and varied expressions on his characters, from the most subtle to the most extreme emotions, his women still retaining their beauty. **TRL**

The Juggler of Our Lady 1953

✎✎ R. O. Blechman

First published by Henry Holt (USA)
Creator Oscar Robert Blechman (American, b. 1930)
Genre Drama
Adaptation Animation (1958)

Based on the 1882 story *Le jongleur de Notre Dame*, by Anatole France—itself based on a medieval legend—*The Juggler of Our Lady* was R. O. Blechman's first book. Some regard it as a picture-book rather than a comic, but most specialists consider it a pioneering example of the graphic novel—the borderless illustrations are presented in sequential form, with little or no text under each of them, and speech balloons are used. The work is in Blechman's trademark style: tiny characters drawn with a squiggly but expressive line, evolving on minimally developed but efficient backgrounds.

Wandering juggler Cantalbert joins a monastery to feel "part of a family" but is undervalued by the other monks because he lacks any particular talent apart from his ability to juggle. The tale is a variation on the theme that everybody is special in their own way, as Cantalbert's juggling earns him the blessing of the Virgin Mary. The medieval legend has Mary wiping Cantalbert's sweat after he falls exhausted from his efforts, and Blechman expresses this simply by showing a flower falling next to the fallen juggler.

The Juggler of Our Lady was adapted in 1958 as an animated short, made at the Terrytoons studio and directed by Al Kouzel and Gene Deitch; shot in CinemaScope and narrated by Boris Karloff, it was faithful to Blechman's designs. The entire book was reproduced to a minimal size and reprinted in Blechman's monograph, *Between the Lines* (1980), and a reissue of the original edition was published in 1997 with a foreword by Maurice Sendak. **AMo**

Jerry Spring 1954

"Jijé"

First published by Dupuis (Belgium)
Creator Joseph Gillain (Belgian, 1914–80)
Genre Western
Award Grand Prix Saint-Michel Belgium (1975)

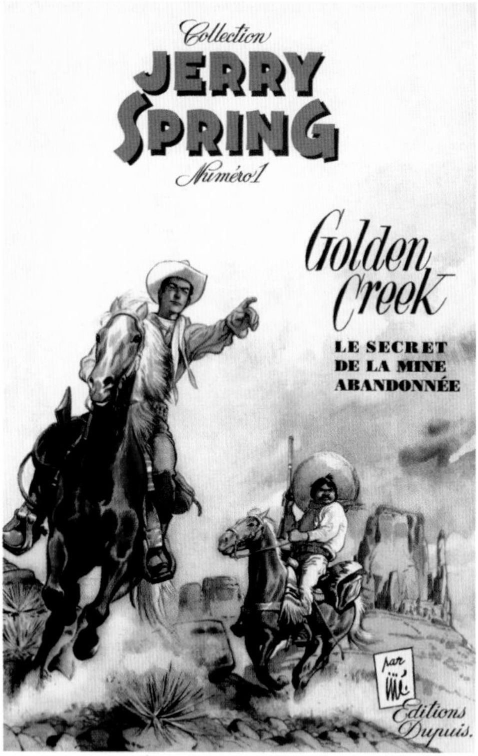

Collection
JERRY SPRING
Numéro 1
Golden Creek
LE SECRET DE LA MINE ABANDONNÉE
par Jijé
Editions Dupuis.

"I always preferred black and white."

Epitaph of Jijé (Joseph Gallain)

When he created *Jerry Spring*, Joseph Gillain (aka "Jijé") had been producing comic strips for Belgian publications for more than twenty years, particularly *Spirou*, to which he was an important contributor. In 1954, when his cowboy first appeared, his work rate was tremendous. In spite of his workload he started this new project because he had lived in the United States between 1948 and 1950 and wanted to reproduce the "awesome landscapes" he had seen there. Also, Editions Dupuis, publishers of *Spirou*, had not renewed the licence for *Red Ryder* (*Cavalier Rouge* in French), a long-running series by Fred Harman. There was room to welcome a new Western, more realistic than *Lucky Luke*, with which it shared the weekly's table of contents.

The shadowy gringo Jerry is accompanied by Pancho, a Mexican amigo, and, like in other Western comics (*The Cisco Kid*, for example), they struggle against the bad guys and defend the causes of oppressed peoples—American Indians, of course, but also African-Americans. This was so rare in the French publications of the time that it would permanently influence future generations of comic authors who wanted to tackle the genre. But it is also the graphic qualities of the series that fascinate. When he inked them, Jijé preserved the liveliness of the sketches. In his quest for spontaneity he preferred to work in black and white, and his many night scenes easily equaled the comic strips of the U.S. authors whom he had observed so well: Will Gould, Frank Godwin, Milton Caniff, and Noel Sickles.

Jerry Spring appeared in twenty-one albums up to 1979, and when Jijé called upon story line writers such as Maurice Rosy, René Goscinny, John Acquaviva, and Jacques Lob, it was more to acquire story threads from them than actual words. He usually rewrote the scenarios they delivered, thus preserving a narrative freedom as well as a graphic one. **CM**

Moomin 1954

✐ Tove Jansson

For those who delighted in the creative heights Tove Jansson reached with her *Moomin* children's books, her newspaper strips reveal how she further refined her narrative and artistic skills. In 1952, the Helsinki-born author jumped at a contract from the Associated Newspaper Syndicate in London to create, as they proposed, "an interesting strip cartoon, and not necessarily for children" that would use her upright, mouthless, hippolike clan "to satirize the so-called civilized way of life." Jansson's dream that the money from crafting "only six comic strips in a week" for the London *Evening News* would leave her free enough to pursue painting was soon dismissed in 1954 by the time-consuming challenges of devising *Moomin* serials in daily episodes of two to five panels.

A relative novice to the medium, she brought a sense of discovery to her comic strip, reveling in the playful possibilities of the form—vertically dividing pictures with trees, rope, or doors, for example. In contrast to the *Moomin* books published up until that time, she pared down the text for the comic strip to succinct yet expressive dialogue in balloons, while multiplying the pictures to animate as never before the foibles and charms of her eccentric cast, including the touchingly honest, romantic Moomin, the superbly feminine Snorkmaiden, the money-grabbing Sniff, and the lonely, ghostlike Groke.

Far from being a sideline, her strips—more than 800 in total over five years—are as fantastical and life-affirming as the original *Moomin* fables. Latterly, Tove assigned the writing to her brother, Lars, and then, in 1961, she assigned him the drawing also. Syndicated to forty countries, Jansson's strip gently celebrates the patience, accommodation, and understanding that were always at the heart of her complex, extended, alternative Moomintroll family. **PG**

Title in original language *Moomintroll*
First published by Schildts (Finland)
Creator Swedish-Finn (1914–2001)
Genre Fantasy, Children's

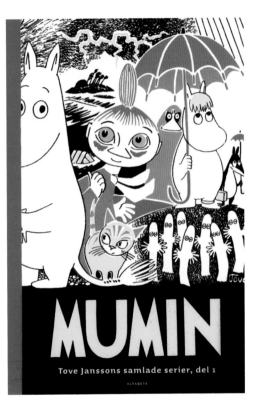

MUMIN

Tove Janssons samlade serier, del 1

ALFABETA

"I only want to live in peace and plant potatoes and dream!"

The Bash Street Kids 1954

✐✐ Leo Baxendale

First published by D. C. Thomson (UK)
Creator British (b.1930)
Genre Humor
Spin-offs *Pup Parade, Simply Smiffy, Singled Out*

From 1953 to 1954, over a six-month period, Leo Baxendale, a fan of *The Beano* as a child, introduced three strips to the comic that are still running more than fifty years later. Characters included Little Plum, who pastiched Native American culture, and Minnie the Minx, who reversed the gender of the already popular Dennis the Menace. The fame of *The Bash Street Kids* outstripped both.

Although Ronald Searle's three *St. Trinian's* books were popular then, the inspiration for Baxendale's anarchic school class originated with a Giles cartoon. *The Bash Street Kids* were initially presented in a series of gag-packed single illustrations, titled *When the Bell Rings*. These followed a British cartooning tradition dating back half a century to the comic series *Casey Court*.

At his peak Baxendale was astounding, melding the inventiveness of Heath Robinson with manic illustrations inspired by the efforts of his fellow *Beano* creators. He was offered three times his wage to take over the syndication of the *Little Sport* strip, but this failed to prise Baxendale from *The Beano*, although the offer of creating his own comic for Odhams lured him away in 1962. He had drawn 424 *Bash Street Kids* strips without a printed credit. In terms of talent and anonymous influence, he was a British Carl Barks.

In the 1980s Baxendale sued publishers D. C. Thomson over ownership and payment issues. The matter was resolved before trial. Neither party has spoken in public, but it is widely assumed that Baxendale was finally properly rewarded for the millions his characters have earned the company. **FP**

The Marsupilami Robbers 1954

✐✐ André Franquin

Title in original language *Les voleurs du Marsupilami*
First published by *Spirou and Fantasio* (Belgium)
Creator Belgian (1924–97)
Genre Humor

In *Spirou and the Heirs*, the comic book prior to *The Marsupilami Robbers*, Spirou and Fantasio went through various trials to secure Fantasio's inheritance from an uncle. The quest ended in the return of the most popular and inventive of André Franquin's creations in the Franco-Belgian *Spirou and Fantasio* series—the Marsupilami. This is a small, furry, yellow animal with black spots and a very long, strong tail. Known for its "Houba! Houba! Ha! Ha! Ha!" expressions, the Marsupilami is an animal prone to laughter and in possession of a great sense of humor, but it can become equally angry if harm comes to itself or its friends.

In this story, Spirou and Fantasio, grieved by the Marsupilami's apathy behind bars in the zoo, plot how to get the creature back to nature. Before they can act on their intentions, the Marsupilami is stolen for a circus act, and the two friends go through a number of trying events to get it back, with help from pet squirrel Spip and their eccentric friend, the Count of Champignac.

This *Spirou* comic book features the ideal mixture of adventure and humorous gags. Franquin's drawing style is sufficiently dynamic for the dramatic events, and his timing is close to perfect. He could draw anger so convincingly that readers would inadvertently duck for cover. Franquin also knew how to get the biggest payoff from night-shrouded pages, a solitary flashlight and an escapist monitor lizard. But the real star of the show is the Marsupilami, who is not only an incredibly ferocious and cute little beast but also a great friend and hilarious to experience at close quarters. **RPC**

LES VOLEURS DU MARSUPILAMI

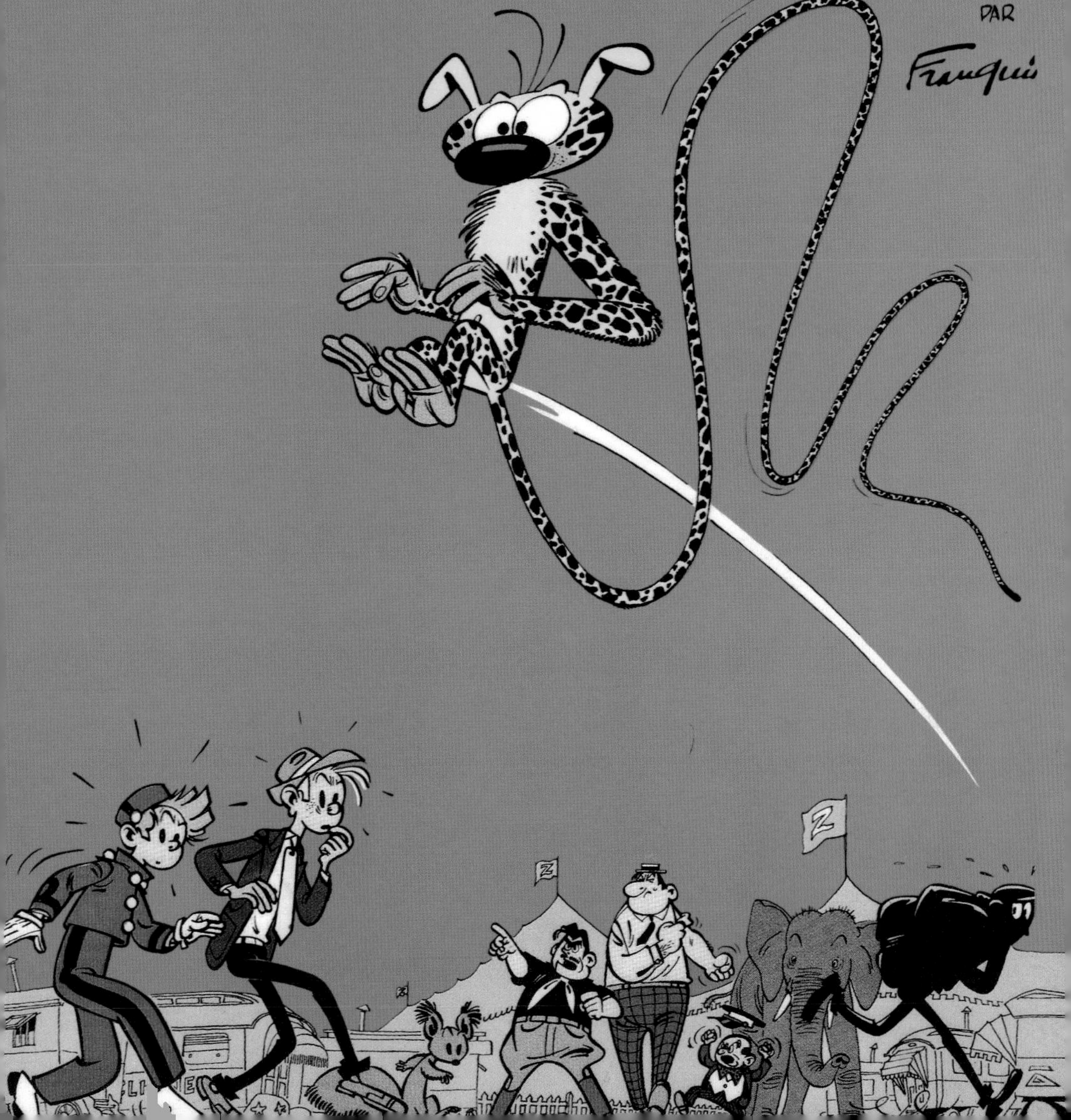
PAR
Franquin

Marvelman/Miracleman 1954

"Mick Anglo" and others

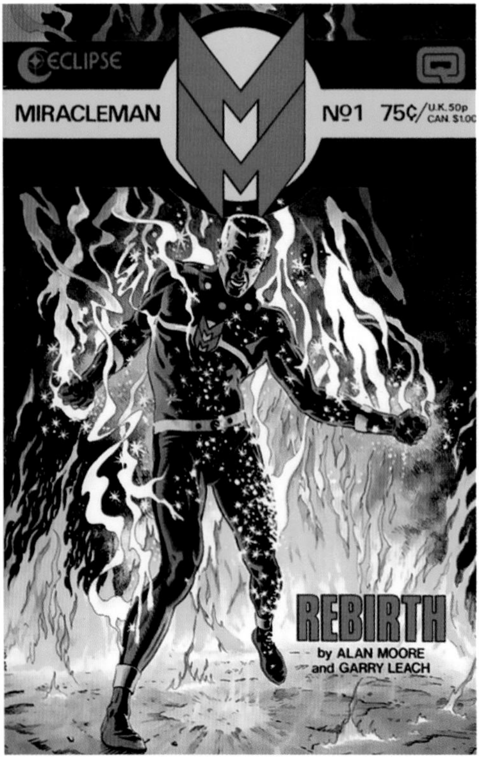
ECLIPSE
MIRACLEMAN
Nº1 75¢/U.K. 50p CAN. $1.00
REBIRTH
by ALAN MOORE
and GARRY LEACH

First published by L. Miller and Son (UK)
Creator Maurice Anglowitz (British, b.1916)
Genre Superhero
Award Eagle Award (1983)

When U.S. publisher Fawcett was forced to retire its best-selling superhero Captain Marvel because of a legal dispute over similarities to Superman, the British publisher of Captain Marvel's adventures, L. Miller and Son, needed to find a similar replacement hero. Miller hired Mick Anglo to come up with that replacement in 1954. Unlike the black-haired Captain Marvel, whose magic word was "Shazam!," Marvelman was a blond British lad named Mike Moran who shouted "Kimota!" to transform into the new but familiar superhero. Anglo produced *Marvelman* strips until 1963, but Marvelman's finest hour would be his revival in *Warrior* magazine by writer Alan Moore (aided by artists Garry Leach and Alan Davis) in 1982. Moore's reimagining focused on the realistic emotional impact of being a superhero on the adult Moran and his wife. To avoid further legal problems, *Marvelman* became *Miracleman* when the series was republished and continued in America.

Moore took the superhuman concept to its logical extreme in the third "book" in his trilogy, rendered evocatively by John Totleben, who captured both the wanton brutality of a truly unscrupulous supervillain destroying half of London and the "paradise" Miracleman imposes on humanity in its wake. Sadly, a further trilogy deconstructing Miracleman's utopia, penned by Neil Gaiman, was cut short once the comic's publisher went bankrupt. Ever since, *Marvelman/Miracleman* has been mired in legal disputes and kept out of print, but Moore's trilogy stands as one of the finest deconstructions of the superhero myth. **PG**

"This does sound silly in 1982, but in the fifties it made perfect sense. This is how I remember it, this is how it happened."

Also by Alan Moore
The Killing Joke with Brian Bolland
V for Vendetta with David Lloyd
Watchmen with Dave Gibbons

Rick Random 1954

✎ Harry Harrison and others ✎ Ron Turner

First published by Amalgamated Press (UK)
Creators Harrison (American, b.1925); Turner
(American, 1922–98)
Genre Science fiction

The success of Dan Dare spawned a small army of intrepid spacemen, and one of the best was Amalgamated Press's Rick Random, created by editor Ted Holmes. *Super Detective Library* was a British digest-sized comic which largely reprinted detective newspaper strips. To fit into the titles' concept, Rick Random was also a detective, working for the Interplanetary Bureau of Investigators.

The series was set in 2040, with the Earth and its surrounding planets united under the Interplanetary Council and space travel a norm. Random's cases were typically galactic in scale, involving far-off civilizations, space pirates, robots, time travel, and planets of sea and ice. From 1957, many of the scripts were handled by the U.S. science fiction writer Harry Harrison, but, typically for 1950s British comics, Rick himself was little more than a square-jawed cypher. The emphasis was on fast-paced action and awe-inspiring spectacle, and both were delivered with panache by artist Ron Turner.

Turner joined the series with its second installment, lending his fresh and inventive drawing to the strip for the next six years. He was a great science fiction fan and drew covers for numerous British pulps and paperbacks. His style was a mixture of luxuriously rendered art deco architecture and the surrealist abstractions of Joan Miró and Giorgio de Chirico that perfectly captured the hard-boiled noir action. Turner enjoyed a long career in comics but was never again quite so inventive. Fortunately his *Rick Random* strips have been reprinted repeatedly over the years. **DR**

Jeff Hawke 1954

✎✎ Sydney Jordan

First published by *Daily Express* (UK)
Creator British (b.1931)
Genre Drama
Collection *Overlord* (2008)

When Sydney Jordan approached Britain's *Daily Express* with a concept for a science fiction strip, the newspaper's editors suggested the cartoonist should give his hero the name Jeff Hawke and that he serve as a pilot in the mold of those in the Royal Air Force during World War II. Jordan agreed, and then duly sent his protagonist into space.

Wing Commander Hawke may have started out as simply an aircraft pilot, but he attracted alien life-forms at an alarming rate. The series was set in the then-future of the 1990s, when humankind could reach as far as Pluto and Britain had its own Space Agency. Hawke traveled even farther—20,000 light years farther, as a guest of the Galactic Federation—and that was when the strip really got interesting. In 1955 Jordan was joined by an old school friend, writer Willie Patterson, and the strip became noticeably wittier and more imaginative, bursting at the seams with bizarre alien life-forms. Among many memorable creations were the giant villain Chalcedon, the huge floating eyeball Tallid, and Kolvorok, who resembled a potato.

Jordan had started the strip as a gifted, if raw, artist but he steadily improved over the years. By 1969 he had matured into a great realist cartoonist, employing layers of mechanical tones to create an almost photographic effect in his art. Sadly, that year saw the departure of Patterson, and the strip was never quite the same after, although it continued until 1976. Despite its very British tone, the strip was syndicated widely across Europe and remains extremely popular in Italy. **DR**

Master Race 1954

✏ Al Feldstein ✏ Bernard Krigstein

First published by EC Comics (USA)
Creators Feldstein (American, b.1925);
Krigstein (American, 1919–90)
Genre Drama

Perhaps the shortest work in this book is this eight-page story originally published in the first issue of EC's abortive comic series *Impact*. Despite its brevity, "Master Race" is among the most celebrated of comics short stories, an intense elaboration of the potential of the form by one of its most assured graphic stylists.

Written and drawn at the height of the U.S. anticomic book movement in the spring of 1954, "Master Race" was unusual for its subject matter. Caught within a typical EC twist ending formula is a brief tale of the horrors of the Holocaust. Bernard Krigstein saw tremendous opportunities in this ordinary script, expanding it from six to eight pages to allow room for his visual experimentation. Permitted to let his creative energies run more freely for the first time, Krigstein crafted a masterpiece.

Each of the eight pages of "Master Race" is as carefully composed as any page in the history of comics. Krigstein uses panel shapes to structure the passage of time, stretching it and accelerating it so as to build dramatic tension. His images reference the paintings of modern masters, recalling the so-called "deviant art" that the Nazis had opposed so vehemently. Krigstein offered a serious work in the context of pulp publishing.

"Master Race" was not a success at the time it was published. It inspired few imitators, and EC closed down its comic book line shortly after it was published. Soon, Krigstein too would leave comic books for a career as a painter. His era was not prepared for the type of comics that he wanted to create. **BB**

Lance 1955

✏✏ Warren Tufts

First published by Warren Tufts Enterprises (USA)
Creator American (1925–82)
Genre Drama
Collection *Big Fun #5* (2007)

When Warren Tufts launched *Lance* in 1955 it was the first full-page color Sunday newspaper strip since *Prince Valiant* some twenty years earlier. Tufts had found fame at the beginning of the decade with his controversially adult-themed Western feature *Casey Ruggles*, but *Lance* was a more complete expression of his vision.

The titular character was one second lieutenant Lance St. Lorne of the U.S. 1st Dragoons, stationed on the Western Frontier of the 1830s, and the strip follows him as he explores the country from the high plains to the Rockies, from California to the Oregon trail. Tufts wanted to re-create an authentic vision of the West, and during the feature's six years Lance met up with such historical figures as Robert E. Lee, Henry Dodge, and Kit Carson. Inevitably, the strip included pitched battles with Indians, but dealt with them in a more mature, sympathetic manner that was far from the norm in its day.

Tufts was a gifted draftsman whose figure work rejoiced in a graceful realism, but more than anything else, the strip was a celebration of the visual splendor of the West, and it was Tufts's stunning landscapes that made it so memorable. For the carefully researched settings he would experiment with washes of color, occasionally dispensing with line work altogether, creating scenes of great beauty and power. Although the self-syndicated feature (and a daily strip added in 1957) was never the success it deserved to be in its homeland, it later gained a reputation among European fans as one of the great strips of the era. **DR**

Orpheus and Eurydice 1955

✒✒ Palle Nielsen

Title in original language *Orpheus og Eurydike første del*
First published by Hans Reitzels Forlag (Denmark)
Creator Danish (1920–2000)
Genre Fantasy

Palle Nielsen was one of the foremost Danish graphic artists of the postwar era. Highly prolific, his work encompassed many different print techniques as well as drawing. His preferred mode of expression was the graphic cycle, or series, which he—inspired by Frans Masereel and early woodcut novels—would often use in the service of a sequential narrative.

Orpheus and Eurydice is his best-known work. Totaling 118 linocuts, it spanned a large part of Nielsen's career, from the 1950s to the 1980s, crystallizing gradually the central concerns of his oeuvre. Loosely based on the classical myth, its succinctly captioned images tell the story of a man's journey in search of his lost love, abducted by the underworld.

The pawn of an oppressive society unraveling into chaos, Orpheus is essentially an automatonlike observer, walking in the ruins of culture, driven forward by his dawning sense of compassion. As in the myth, the end of part two posits a promise of transcendence, which is then snatched away at the beginning of the unfinished part three, where we find our protagonist back in the abyss. The narrative then becomes a crescendolike suite of thematically related images of escalating misrule, moving toward a resolution that—fittingly, perhaps—never happened.

A storyteller in the grand tradition, Nielsen's was an unflinching gaze into the self-negation of human civilization. His monumental architectural fantasies, reminiscent of Piranesi, embody simultaneously the beauty and menace of culture. **MWi**

PALLE NIELSEN

Orfeus og Eurydike

Første del

Orpheus and Eurydice

Part One

HANS REITZEL

"I feel I have to report on what I see, which is the complete hopelessness of our situation, but also that there is hope in the recognition of this situation."

Palle Nielsen

Also by Palle Nielsen

Narcissus
Passion
Scenario: Visions from the End of Time
Skammen
The Enchanted City

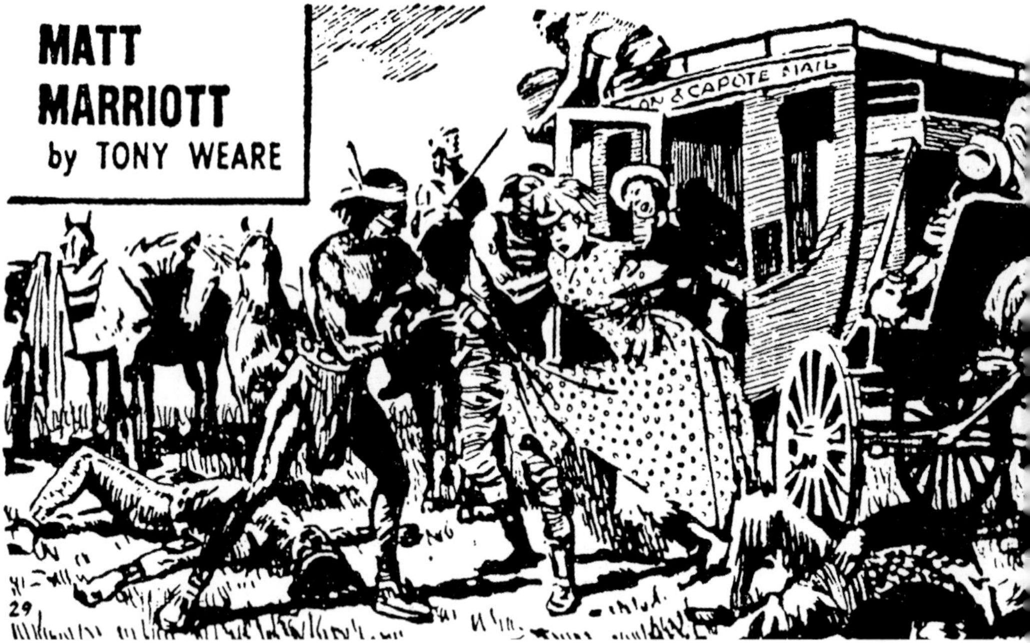
MATT MARRIOTT by TONY WEARE
& CAPOTE MAIL
29

Matt Marriott 1955

Reg Taylor and James Edgar Tony Weare

First published by Associated Newspapers (UK)
Creators Reginald Taylor (British, Unknown); Edgar (British, 1919–2004); Weare (British, 1912–94)
Genre Western

The most eye-catching thing about the *Matt Marriott* strip that featured in the British newspaper *Evening News* from 1955 until 1977 was not its Western setting, but its art. It is not initially easy to like Tony Weare's artwork. It lacks polish and glamour, yet such values are mere decorative qualities. Weare had a rougher approach best described by fellow artist David Lloyd: "His style on *Marriott* was that of a sketch artist—a portrayer of the instant. It was . . . naturalistic, raw, and unsophisticated—perfect for depicting the primitive quality of a realistic-looking Wild West." He also had a consummate control of hatching and cross-hatching techniques and a stunning ability to convey the time of day just by depicting light and shade. Lloyd admires Weare's sense of realism, too: "When we look at Tony's work it's as if we're just watching people going about their business through a lens that he has cleverly positioned for us, not viewing figures which are overtly posed for appropriate effect." He had a whole world of faces, human types, and body language inside his head. He could convey a facial expression with just a few brushstrokes, and his style matured during his run.

The strip was written originally by Reg Taylor, but James Edgar took over for most of its run, ensuring that the strip avoided simplistic goodies and baddies. The villains are violent, they rob and kill, but there is always a psychological reason behind their actions. Conversely, some so-called "good guys" behave very poorly. As Marriott put it: "When there's money involved most of the good guys become bad guys." **DI**

Tony Weare's chiaroscuro artwork on *Matt Marriott* gives his work a strong sense of realism. ↑

TRAGEDY ON THE PLAIN

Carol Day 1956

✒ Peter Meriton and others   ✒ David Wright

First published by Associated Newspapers (UK)
Creators Meriton (British, 1891–1961);
Wright (British, 1912–67)
Genre Romance, Drama

Carol Day is the story of a young upper-class English fashion model who also moves in the worlds of fine art and jazz music. Her adventures are in a soap opera style, often involving blackmail and other crimes, and a series of romances. Her strip, although not syndicated in the United States, was sold to more than twenty markets outside of Britain and remains greatly admired, especially by cartoonists.

David Wright was a pinup artist during World War II, then in the 1950s he drew a succession of "pretty girl" strips for weekly magazines. Peter Meriton wrote the strip initially, but the art was the real attraction. Wright's Charles Dana Gibson–esque brush and pen lines brought a hitherto unseen quality of artistry to the strip, while photo-reference helped create supporting characters with real individuality. The strip remains a pleasure to the eye—particularly its atmospheric scenes set at night or in fog—and is an enjoyable, if unchallenging, read. *Carol Day* is generally thought of as David Wright's work, and his writing collaborators are seldom remembered.

Although Wright had previously drawn nude or seminude pinups, Carol's stories were relatively tame, with no nudity involved. In attempting to reflect the changing postwar world, Wright was reportedly frustrated at how little his conservative readers would tolerate. When Carol discreetly consummated an affair with a married man (strictly between the panels), the *Daily Mail* received hundreds of letters in protest. Today we can appreciate the strip which, even in its time, was set in a vanishing world. **GL**

Black Blizzard 1956

Yoshihiro Tatsumi

Title in original language *Kuroi Fubuki*
First published by Hinomaru Bunko (Japan)
Creator Japanese (b.1935)
Genre Crime

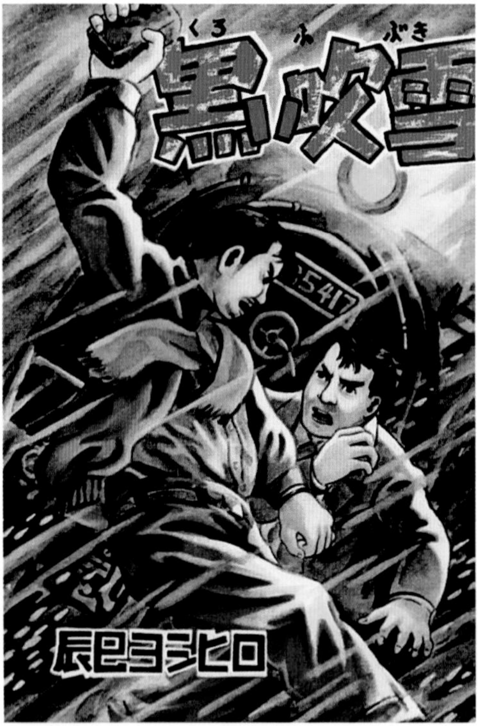
くろ ふ ぶき
黒吹雪
辰巳ヨシヒロ

Also by Yoshihiro Tatsumi
A Drifting Life
Abandon the Old in Tokyo
Good-Bye and Other Stories
The Push Man and Other Stories

A driven twenty-one-year-old talent with seventeen book-length manga already under his belt, Yoshihiro Tatsumi took just "one continuous streak of productivity" lasting twenty days to pour out this pacey noir thriller. Two men on the run, one a young pianist accused of murder, the other a hardened career criminal, find their fates entwined by the handcuffs locking them together. Taking refuge in an abandoned cabin, these polar opposites slowly form an uneasy alliance, and the pianist reveals how his love for a pretty young singer, forced to stay in the circus by her ringmaster father, drove him apparently to murder. Fleeing into the city, the pair resort to a macabre game of chance to decide who will cut off the other's hand and get away.

"The only way we're getting apart is if one of us loses his hand."

Inspired as much by Mickey Spillane as Alexandre Dumas, Tatsumi brings an appropriate rough dynamism to this convict drama, slashing panels with the diagonal lines of the biting snowstorm. If this same story had been told in a U.S. comic book such as *Crime Does Not Pay*, Charles Biro and his artists would have crammed it into a dozen dense pages at most. Remarkably, many manga authors in the 1950s could stretch such tales into full-length books, and Tatsumi makes full use of his 127 pages, heightening the urgency and tension by varying angles, slanting viewpoints, and letting sequences unfold visually, without dialogue. Tatsumi was in at the start of a boom in publishers catering for an older readership who visited some 30,000 pay manga libraries, not unlike video rental stores. He chronicled his youthful career crafting darker, more dramatic manga, which he renamed *gekiga* (graphic novel), in his 840-page autobiographical comic, *A Drifting Life*. **PG**

Tetsujin 28-go 1956

Mitsuteru Yokoyama

One of the most popular science fiction robot comics in 1960s Japan alongside Osamu Tezuka's *Astro Boy*, *Tetsujin 28-go* is the epitome of the genre that triggered the emergence of such titles as *Mazinger Z*, *Mobile Suit Gundam*, and *Neon Genesis Evangelion*.

A product of the Japanese military during World War II, the giant robot Tetsujin 28-go is the twenty-eighth model and most powerful of its kind. Taking inspiration from Frankenstein, Mitsuteru Yokoyama's robot is made entirely of solid iron, and its unbreakable gigantic body gleams with strength and power. The robot is remote controlled, meaning that it could go from hero to villain depending on who is "driving" it. Luckily, the remote control belongs to the well-dressed ten-year-old Shotaro Kaneda, whose signature style is a tie and jacket paired with shorts. Taken from his name, fans of young male characters are called *shotakon* (Shotaro complex). Manga creator Katsuhiro Otomo was so influenced by Shotaro that he named the central figure "Kaneda" in his own manga *Akira*.

"Good or evil, all is up to the remote-controller, Shotaro."

Set in postwar Japan, *Tetsujin 28-go* is a typical superhero story: a new villain emerges in every episode, and each adventure brings a newly advanced competitor for Tetsujin 28-go to fight. This simple but effective story has been adapted for a number of television series, the first of which aired in 1963 and reached the English-speaking market as *Gigantor*. Yokoyama, who passed away in 2004, was one of the most revered authors of postwar Japan, producing a number of hits in genres ranging from girls' comics to Chinese history. **TS**

First published by Kobunsha (Japan)
Creator Japanese (1934–2004)
Genre Science fiction
Adaptation Film: *Tetsujin 28* (2005)

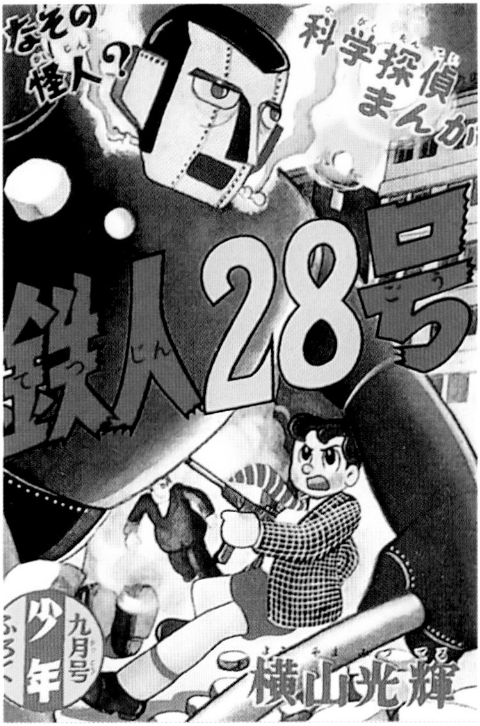
なぞの怪人?
科学探偵まんが
鉄人28号
少年 九月号 ふろく
横山光輝

Also by Mitsuteru Yokoyama

Akakage
Babel
Giant Robo
Princess Comet

Blake and Mortimer
The Yellow M 1956

"Edgar P. Jacobs"

LIMEHOUSE DOCK
EDGAR P. JACOBS
LA MARQUE JAUNE

"Mortimer, who has not missed a second of this incredible scene, almost cries out in amazement. . . "

Similar reads
King Ottokar's Sceptre (*Le Sceptre d'Ottokar*) Hergé
The Francis Blake Affair (*L'affaire Francis Blake*) Ted Benoît and Jean van Hamme
***The Mystery of the Great Pyramid* (*Le mystère de la grande pyramide*)** Edgar P. Jacobs

Title in original language *La marque jaune*
First published by Le Lombard (Belgium)
Creator Edgard Félix Pierre Jacobs (Belgian, 1904–87)
Genre Crime, Adventure

The Yellow M reprises the indispensable elements of any Edgar P. Jacobs adventure comic. The stiff-upper-lipped Eton-educated M.I.5 agent Blake and the more breezy but equally brilliant physics professor Mortimer come up against their implacable foe, the sinister Olrik, in a suspense-filled plot that evokes the cultural anxieties of the Cold War period: in this case kidnapping and brainwashing of members of the establishment.

Years of working in Hergé's studio made Jacobs a master of the clear line, but the flamboyance of his often symmetrical layouts and the grandiloquent narrative voiceovers give rise to a theatricality that contrasts with the less mannered ambience of the Tintin stories. The precision of the graphic line is deployed to convey the seductiveness of the social power wielded by his heroes. Blake's suaveness, Mortimer's panache and the taken-for-granted authority of the elites among whom they move are displayed against lovingly reproduced details of locations, such as a wood-paneled gentlemen's club, the British Museum reading room, and the Park Lane flat where Blake and Mortimer chastely and somewhat formally cohabit. However, the story takes them away from fashionable central London neighborhoods to the darkness and fog of the Limehouse docks, evoked by Jacobs with the sublime beauty of an expressionist film: shadowy industrial architecture looms, briefly illuminated by spotlights. Ultimately, order is restored and bromance underplayed: reunited with his friend after multiple ordeals, Mortimer's greeting is a laconic "Hello, Blake!" **AM**

Sennin Buraku 1956

✐ Ko Kojima

First published by Tokuma Shoten (Japan)
Creator Japanese (b.1928)
Genre Humor
Award Bungeishunju Manga Prize (1968)

The one-page manga series *Sennin Buraku* is the longest-running strip in Japan, published in the weekly *Asahi Geino* for more than fifty years. Its author, Ko Kojima, is renowned for his erotic comedy, with *Sennin Buraku* being his most popular creation.

Originally, Kojima used the fine tip of a Japanese *menso* paintbrush to create his signature ultrathin lines, because it allowed him to draw with the kind of delicacy impossible to achieve with a pen. In fact, Kojima's lines were so intricate that the technology during the 1950s and 1960s—when the comic gained its popularity—failed to print his illustrations clearly. The series' success certainly owes a lot to the artist's craftsmanship, spinning threads of fine lines that form beautiful slender, yet womanly, female figures.

Set in the Edo period, the stories takes place in Buraku, a small village on a sacred mountain inhabited by hermits with magical powers. The hermits spend their time drinking, singing, and using their powers to play tricks on normal people. Such tricks involve teasing beautiful women bathing in rivers, or disguising other hermits and humans to deceive such women. Openly erotic yet playful, Kojima's lively, lighthearted storytelling is part of the comic's charm.

Although it is a sex comedy, Kojima's female characters are not mere sex objects. Many of his stories are about empowered women who often get the better of lustful men. Kojima's work may be an expression of self-deprecating humor, but perhaps his weakness for female beauty speaks for many men. **TS**

Dreams and Somersaults 1956

✐ Maurice Henry

Title in original language *Rêves et culbutes*
First published by *Le Figaro* (France)
Creator French (1907–81)
Genre Humor

We are taught that the basic structure of narrative consists of a beginning, middle, and end. Maurice Henry followed this by reducing his comic strips down to three panels. Starting in 1956, the French newspaper *Le Figaro* published Henry's gag strip on a daily basis under the title *Rêves et culbutes* (*Dreams and Somersaults*). Like most of his single-panel cartoons, his strips do not require dialogue, harking back to turn-of-the-century French artists such as Caran d'Ache and Steinlen. The exploration of "silent" humor has a long Gallic tradition that is also evident in an enthusiasm for mime and in the films of Fernandel and Jacques Tati.

Before his cartooning career blossomed, Henry had been a member of the Paris surrealist group producing dreamlike drawings, poetry, and some surrealist objects. Black humor, a term coined by André Breton, is a touchstone to much of Henry's work, along with his reversal of logical order to impart a sense of the absurd. One strip has a pet shop owner showing a birdcage to a customer, who in turn indicates with hand gestures that he wants something bigger. A larger cage is produced and the customer departs happy. In the third and final drawing, we see the customer sitting in an armchair reading a newspaper. Behind him a cat sits in the birdcage while three birds are free to fly around the room. In 1979, the publisher Pierre Horay produced a book collection of 153 Henry strips titled *Gags*, laid out in a landscape format and bound, unusually, along its longest edge. Highly imaginative, Henry's work is quintessentially French. **LC**

Wulf the Briton 1956

Michael Butterworth Ronald Embleton

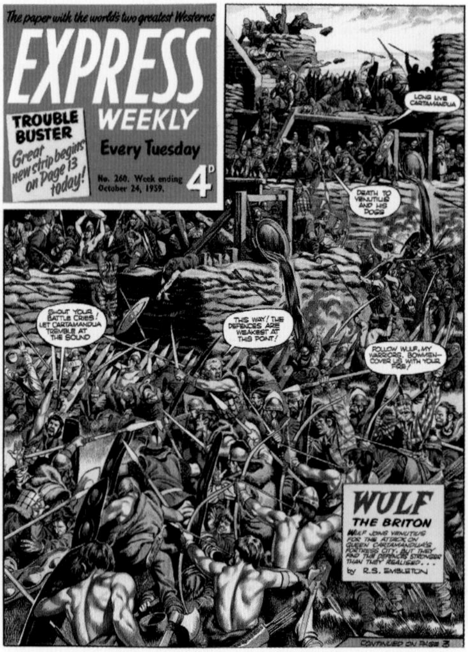
The paper with the world's two greatest Westerns
EXPRESS WEEKLY
TROUBLE BUSTER
Great new strip begins on Page 13 today!
Every Tuesday
No. 260. Week ending October 24, 1959.
4D
LONG LIVE CARTAMANDUA
DEATH TO VENUTIUS AND HIS DOGS
SHOUT YOUR BATTLE CRIES! LET CARTAMANDUA TREMBLE AT THE SOUND
THIS WAY! THE DEFENCES ARE WEAKEST AT THIS POINT!
FOLLOW WULF, MY WARRIORS. BOWMEN—COVER US WITH YOUR FIRE!
WULF THE BRITON
WULF JOINS VENUTIUS FOR THE ATTACK ON QUEEN CARTAMANDUA'S FORTRESS CITY. BUT THEY FIND THE DEFENCES STRONGER THAN THEY REALISED...
by R.S. EMBLETON
CONTINUED ON PAGE 3

"Remember, Greatorix. When we reach the village you must not eat or drink anything. . . If Turo and the villagers have done as I suggested, Baldur's in for a shock!"

Also by Ron Embleton

Biggles
Captain Scarlett
Colonel Pinto
The Wrath of the Gods

First published by *Express Weekly* (UK)
Creators Butterworth (British, Unknown); Embleton (British, 1930–88)
Genre Drama

The effect of *Eagle* on the 1950s British comics scene was electrifying. Rival publishers eyed its sales of a million copies per week with envy. Inevitably an avalanche of clones soon filled the stands; one of the most successful of these was *Express Weekly*. The comic was published by the mighty *Daily Express* newspaper group and boasted the same high-quality printing and color as its inspiration. The most fondly remembered of the title's strips was the longtime cover feature *Wulf the Briton*, written by the prolific Michael Butterworth.

Wulf was a slave living in Britain during the time of the Roman occupation who had to undergo seven trials before he could earn his freedom from his master Lucellus. Once freed, he joined up with fellow freedom fighters Greatorix and Basta in a valiant fight to drive the invaders from his homeland. The feature was drawn initially by Ruggero Giovannini, but from 1957 Ron Embleton, one of the greatest British comic artists, took over. Embleton's fully painted artwork was rich in keenly observed characterization and scrupulously researched historical detail, but it was in scenes of combat that he really excelled. Under Embleton, *Wulf* featured some of the most exciting scenes of battle ever seen in comics, with panoramic vistas of armies pitted against each other, sometimes filling an entire splash page.

From 1958 Embleton assumed the writing duties himself, and, if anything, both the strip and his art got even better. Sadly, in 1960 the clamor for war comics saw Embleton moved over to the aviation strip *Biggles*, and *Wulf* was canceled prematurely. **DAR**

Feiffer 1956

🖉🖉 Jules Feiffer

First published by *The Village Voice* (USA)
Creator American (b.1929)
Genre Humor
Award George Polk Award (1961)

The long-running, eponymous series that Jules Feiffer serialized in the New York alternative weekly the *Village Voice* from 1956 to1997 was urbane even by the most demanding definitions of the word. It was so rich with upper-middle-class Manhattanite navel-gazing, so questioning of cynical political authority, so agitated by societal ills, and so piercing in its depiction of sexual (and, closely related, romantic) maneuvering that it makes even the best films by Feiffer's contemporary, filmmaker Woody Allen, look like melodrama by comparison.

Feiffer has a unique visual poetry: individual characters appear side by side, balloonless spoken (and thought) text in multipanel strips that lack the standard subdivided boundaries. And despite the absence of word balloons or panel-separating grid lines, there is no temptation by the reader to misalign image and text, nor to mistake the whole thing as a hodgepodge.

The result is a comic that can look like a sketchbook entry tossed off in a café by an eavesdropping artist, yet the precision of Feiffer's storytelling, along with that storytelling's consistency over the course of four decades, is a testament to the consideration he brought to the effort. And it all only came to an end because of cost-cutting at the *Voice*, whose management seemingly forgot that Feiffer had won them a Pulitzer Prize in 1986. Feiffer mixed the longings of countless anonymous characters with those of repeat offenders, notably his depictions of U.S. maleness: the self-defeating Bernard and the comically macho Huey. **MW**

Wayang Purwa 1956

🖉🖉 Saleh Ardisoma

Title in original language *Wayang Purwa*
First published by Penerbit Melodi (Indonesia)
Creator Indonesian (Unknown)
Genre Fantasy

Descending from the Indonesian *wayang* (puppet theater) tradition, *wayang* is also the name given to a unique subgenre of comics that was particularly popular in Indonesia from 1955 through to the early 1980s. *Wayang* stories are typically adaptations of classic Indian mythology, mixed with some Islamic values and Javanese legends—the first *wayang* comic being *Mahabharata* from R. A. Kosasih.

Wayang Purwa is the masterpiece of this subgenre, a 545-page epic prequel to the Indonesian *Mahabharata* and *Ramayana*. It is a tale of the old gods in that universe, their origins, and their peculiar motives for their sometimes erratic or bizarre choices. Regrets, punishment, and the long-term consequences of worldly desires are the recurring themes throughout. And, as always in *wayang* stories, no character is purely good or evil.

The tale begins with the story of Manikmaya, third son of Sang Hyang Tunggal, who eventually inherited the throne of the universe. This episode also tells the origin story of Semar, who was the second brother, cursed to become ugly because of his ambition. In *wayang* mythology, Semar and his funny children are always regarded as the symbol of people's voice and wisdom. Saleh Ardisoma's art matured as the story progressed. His painterly sensibility was especially suited to evoking fantastic mythological landscapes and battles. His work eventually reached a wider audience in 1982, when the French publisher Trismégiste produced translations of *Manikmaya* in French and English. **HD**

The Completely MAD Don Martin 1956

Don Martin

First published by *MAD Magazine* (USA)
Creator American (1931–2000)
Genre Humor
Award Inductee into the Eisner Awards Hall of Fame (2004)

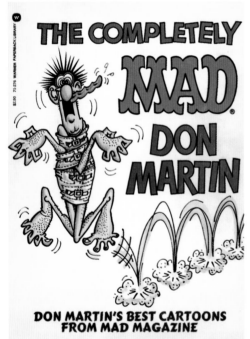

THE COMPLETELY
MAD
DON
MARTIN
DON MARTIN'S BEST CARTOONS
FROM MAD MAGAZINE

Similar reads
A MAD Look at Old Movies Dick DeBartolo and Jack Davis
Don Martin Bounces Back Don Martin
MAD's Snappy Answers to Stupid Questions Al Jaffee
The All New MAD Secret File on Spy Vs Spy Antonio Prohais
Viva MAD Sergio Aragones

Don Martin was the first major *MAD Magazine* cartoonist to be recruited by new editor Al Feldstein, following the departure of founder Harvey Kurtzman. Martin had previously only worked as a commercial illustrator, but the unhinged, slapstick energy of his work transitioned seamlessly to the comic page. Making his debut in issue #29 (September, 1956), Martin was an immediate hit with the readership, and as "MAD's Maddest Artist" he was awarded the rare accolade of a "department" all to himself.

Until 1988, when a dispute over royalties led Martin to join rival *Cracked* magazine, each issue of *MAD* tended to feature two or three short strips by Martin, not more than two pages long (longer stories, often featuring recurring characters such as Captain Klutz, or the duo Fester Bestertester and Karbunkle, were reserved for Martin's all-original *MAD* paperbacks). Martin's *MAD* strips always had anodyne titles—"In the Hospital," "One Day at the Beach," "Out West," and so on—and invariably concluded with a moment of painful injury, ridiculous coincidence, or professional incompetence. Martin's characters were drawn in the classic "bigfoot" tradition, although big noses, big ears, and big teeth were all just as prominent. Every gesture, movement, or facial expression in his comic strips were exaggerated to the point of delirium, augmented by equally over the top sound effects. Other writers, notably Don "Duck" Edwing, were sometimes responsible for the scripts on Martin's later work, but by then the "rules" of the artist's absurd universe were well established for others to follow. **AL**

"Martin was so damn visual, so visceral in his artwork, that even his unique 'sound effects' could evoke laughter."

Gary Larson

Uncle Scrooge

The Second-Richest Duck 1956

Carl Barks

First published by Dell Comics (USA)
Creator American (1901–2000)
Genre Humor
Award Inductee into the Eisner Awards Hall of Fame (1987)

Another prominent milestone in Carl Barks's run on *Uncle Scrooge*, "The Second-Richest Duck" introduced a new rival for the popular tycoon. While reading the newspaper, Scrooge is crestfallen to learn that another billionaire might now be the world's richest duck. Accompanied by Donald and his nephews, he leaves for South Africa, home of his rival. Flintheart Glomgold turns out to be very much like Scrooge, complete with his own giant money bin. After a night spent enumerating their various mines, farms, and possessions, the rivals conclude that the only way to decide who is richer is by unraveling the giant balls of strings both have been saving over the years to see which is longer. Thus begins a contest that takes the pair over miles and miles of African veldt, where rough terrain and the adversaries' respective dirty tricks greatly reduce the two balls. Eventually, Scrooge wins the contest by adding in the string he has been using to tie up his first dime.

"What makes the grumbling Scottish duck a symbol of pure Americana is that McDuck is a self-made man."

James Orbesen

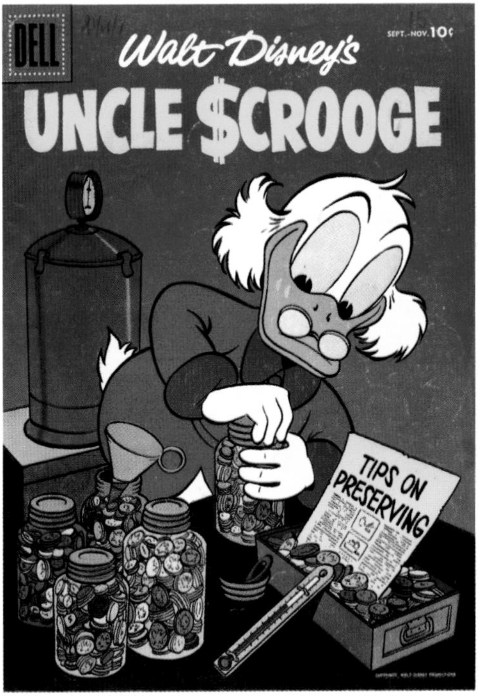
DELL
SEPT.-NOV. 10¢
Walt Disney's
UNCLE $CROOGE
TIPS ON PRESERVING

This tale stands out because it plays with Scrooge and Glomgold's particular personality quirks. They are so similar that they dislike each other at first sight. Their matching obsession is all the funnier because of the presence of Donald and his nephews as hapless observers. The way Barks structures the story is impeccable, starting with yet another attempt from Scrooge to demonstrate the virtues of saving to nephew Donald—who would rather spend his money on a soda—and escalating toward situations that are ludicrous yet logical. In the end Scrooge triumphs, but Donald would still rather have his soda. **J-PJ**

Other *Uncle Scrooge* stories

Land of the Pygmy Indians
The Midas Touch
The Phantom of Notre Duck
The Prize of Pizzaro
The Twenty-Four Carat Moon

Jiraiya the Ninja Boy 1956

Shigeru Sugiura

Title in original language *Shonen Jiraiya*
First published by Kobunsha (Japan)
Creator Japanese (1908–2002)
Genre Fantasy

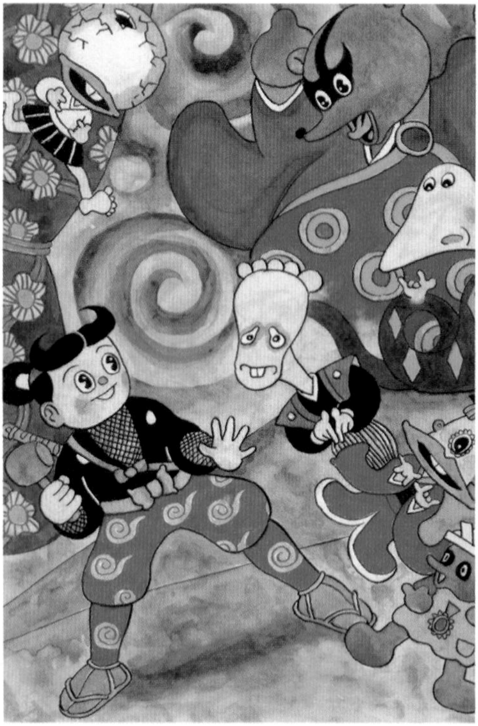

Similar reads

Mr. Xie's Night Walk (Kushii-kun no yoru no sanpo) Yuji Kamosawa
Mr. Robot (Misuta Robotto) Shigeru Sugiura
Little Z (Z-chan) Shingo Iguchi

Much of today's manga features movielike plot development and visual storytelling techniques that were developed by Osamu Tezuka, the groundbreaking "god of manga" in the 1950s and 1960s, but a contemporary of Tezuka, Shigeru Sugiura, pioneered a subversive parallel universe of idiosyncratic auteur manga.

Sugiura penned wackily absurdist stories filled with playful innocence. His unclassifiable, freewheeling fantasies and peculiar, painterly compositions were immensely popular with his initial audience—children—but they also earned him a cult following among adults with an avant-garde sensibility and inspired a generation of artists producing work for the magazine *Garo*. Sugiura was a close observer of popular culture, and his manga appropriated contemporary fads such as giant lizards, professional wrestling, science fiction films, and prewar U.S. comic books, mixing these disparate elements in tales loosely based on traditional Japanese folklore.

In 1956 Sugiura introduced Jiraiya the Ninja Boy, a shape-shifter traveling alternately by means of a giant toad, flying saucer, or rocket, sometimes accompanied by his friend the Star Princess. In one outlandish sequence, Jiraiya watches as a Popeye-like character emerges from a robot's head and battles a Superman clone—until interrupted by a giant warthog right out of an Albert Dürer woodcut! The narrative is deliberately archaic, the fights are hilarious, and the constant morphing of the characters is decidedly unsettling.

If Tezuka's round cartoonish "bigfoot" style can be compared to Disney, Sugiura's equally fluid art has a hard-edged surreality more akin to the work of the Fleischer brothers. In combining the winsome and the warped, Sugiura anticipates the adorable grotesqueries and parodic tone of Junko Mizuno by roughly forty years. **TL**

Sugar and Spike 1956

Sheldon Mayer

Cecil "Spike" Wilson, too young to talk to his parents, is delighted to find that he understands what his new neighbor, Sugar Plumm, has to say. Their parents cannot understand a word of the children's gibberish, but that does not stop the pair getting into a heap of adventures. Together they explore the world of grown-ups from their point of view, amazed that people squeeze themselves into telephones, for example, and discovering the uses of some grown-up words, such as "no." They often learn the hard way, however, that understanding each other will not help them when they do not know the rules. Being sent to sit on a stool in the corner is generally the worst they have to fear, although they are sometimes joined by Sugar's Uncle Charley, whose willingness to indulge them sometimes gets the better of him.

As the series continued, Sheldon Mayer began to expand the children's world, introducing more fantastical elements for the children to communicate with, such as a baby goblin, aliens, Herbert the aged lion (in his second childhood), and Eustace the mouse. Then there was the introduction of Bernie the Brain, whose appearance with one of his strange inventions precipitated all sorts of impossible hijinks. Unusually, Mayer encouraged reader participation, crediting his audience for ideas he used, particularly their costume ideas for his doll cut-outs as well as the coloring and "write your own comics" pages.

Convincingly portraying the thought processes of his young characters, Mayer's artwork has the feel of animation, but is not short on detail. Mayer's failing eyesight brought the monthly series to an end, but he created more stories for the European market on his recovery. DC Comics even published a further issue of *Sugar and Spike* in 1992 as part of their *Silver Age Classics* series. **NFI**

First published by DC Comics (USA)
Creator American (1917–91)
Genre Humor
Collection *Sugar and Spike Archives* Vol. 1 (2011)

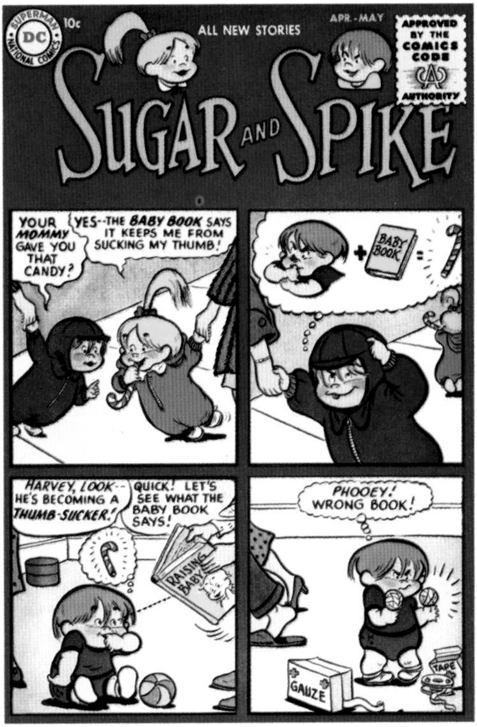
SUPERMAN DC NATIONAL COMICS
10¢
ALL NEW STORIES
APR.-MAY
APPROVED BY THE COMICS CODE AUTHORITY
SUGAR AND SPIKE
YOUR MOMMY GAVE YOU THAT CANDY?
YES--THE BABY BOOK SAYS IT KEEPS ME FROM SUCKING MY THUMB!
BABY BOOK
HARVEY, LOOK-- HE'S BECOMING A THUMB-SUCKER!
QUICK! LET'S SEE WHAT THE BABY BOOK SAYS!
RAISING BABY
PHOOEY! WRONG BOOK!
GAUZE
TAPE

Similar reads
Calvin and Hobbes Bill Watterson
Little Archie Bob Bolling
Little Lulu Marjorie Buell and John Stanley
The Kin-der-Kids Lyonel Feininger

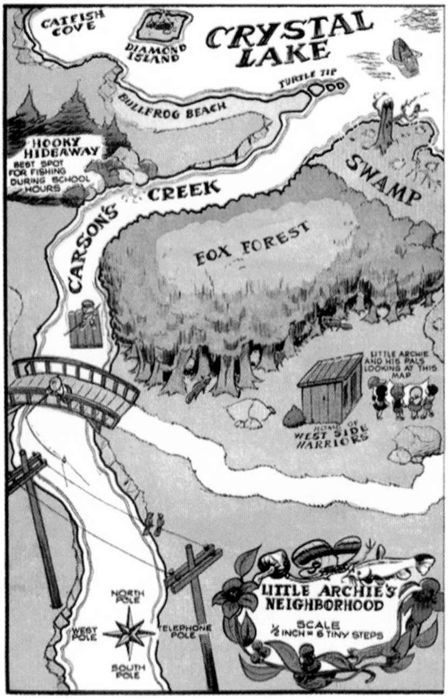
CATFISH COVE
DIAMOND ISLAND
CRYSTAL LAKE
TURTLE TIP
BULLFROG BEACH
HOOKY HIDEAWAY
BEST SPOT FOR FISHING DURING SCHOOL HOURS
CARSON'S CREEK
SWAMP
FOX FOREST
LITTLE ARCHIE AND HIS PALS LOOKING AT THIS MAP
HOME OF WEST SIDE WARRIORS
NORTH POLE
WEST POLE
SOUTH POLE
TELEPHONE POLE
LITTLE ARCHIE'S NEIGHBORHOOD
SCALE ½ INCH = 6 TINY STEPS
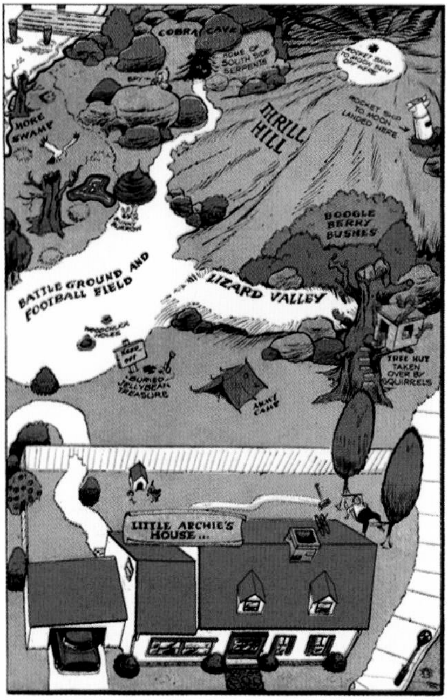
COBRA CAVE
HOME OF SOUTH SIDE SERPENTS
ROCKET SHIP TO MOON LANDED HERE
THRILL HILL
MORE SWAMP
BOOGLE BERRY BUSHES
BATTLE GROUND AND FOOTBALL FIELD
LIZARD VALLEY
TREE HUT TAKEN OVER BY SQUIRRELS
BURIED JELLYBEAN TREASURE
ARMY CAMP
LITTLE ARCHIE'S HOUSE...

This detailed map charts the world of Little Archie's childhood adventures. ↑

Little Archie 1956

✎✎ Bob Bolling

First published by Archie Comics (USA)
Creator American (b.1928)
Genre Humor
Adaptation TV animation: *Archie's TV Funnies* (1971)

Little Archie tells the stories of a younger Archie Andrews using characters established by the *Archie* strip and several new ones, including Ambrose, Evelyn Evernever, Fangs Fogerty, and Archie's dog, Spotty. When the children play, Archie is the leader of the "good" gang of boys, opposed by the Southside Serpents.

Archie's girlfriends, Betty and Veronica, take on a *Little Lulu* role, championing girls over boys and usually beating the boys at whatever they are doing. In one story, the boys are playing soldiers, but the girls want to play school. When the girls agree to be soldiers, the boys reluctantly agree to let them join in, but soon regret it when they find that being soldiers takes a lot of learning. These gender clashes are deftly plotted and a lot of fun. Betty and Veronica are not always the winners as Bob Bolling works hard to keep the punch line a surprise.

Bolling also took the opportunity to write "serious" adventure stories in which Little Archie, with either his parents or one of his friends, faces criminals or aliens or a monster. By contrast, Archie's recurring battles with Mad Doctor Doom are not to be taken seriously at all. The green doctor wants to rule the world, but Archie, his nemesis, is always there to foil his latest plot.

In a similar vein to Bolling's treatment of Betty (cute, willful, determined, and absolutely delightful no matter what she suffers) are his dramatic and moving stories about the girl from the wrong side of the tracks, Sue Stringly. Poor but cheerful, she gives readers a chance to learn something about nobility of character. **NFI**

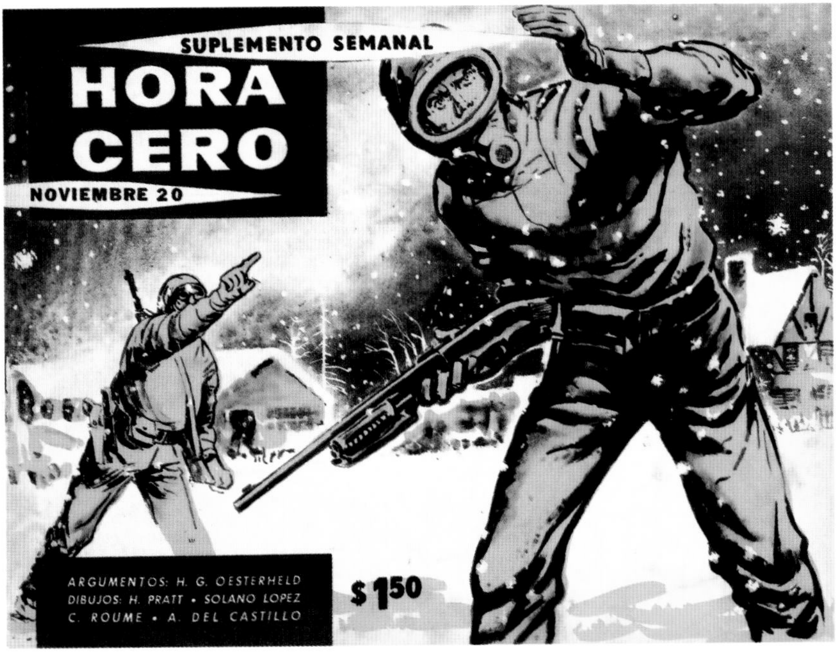
SUPLEMENTO SEMANAL
HORA CERO
NOVIEMBRE 20
ARGUMENTOS: H. G. OESTERHELD
DIBUJOS: H. PRATT • SOLANO LOPEZ
C. ROUME • A. DEL CASTILLO
$ 1.50

The Eternaut 1957

H. G. Oesterheld Francisco Solano Lopez

Title in original language *El Eternauta*
First published by Editorial Frontera (Argentina)
Creators Hectór Germán Oesterheld (Argentinian, 1919–77); Lopez (Argentinian, b.1928) **Genre** Science fiction

In 2010 history was made in Argentina with the approval by the Senate of September 4 as the country's *dia de la historieta*, or Comics Day. The date was chosen to commemorate the first publication of the cult series *The Eternaut* in *Hora Cero Suplemento Semanal*. *The Eternaut* tells the story of a group of characters caught inside a house in Buenos Aires by a deadly "snow" storm provoked by aliens called *los Ellos* (Them). The house belongs to one Juan Salvo, the series' protagonist, and the snowstorm marks the beginning of Earth's invasion by creatures sent by *los Ellos*. But if Juan was intended as the hero, Oesterheld's collectivistic views give the group's resistance acts priority over any individual's heroics. Intellectuals—Favalli and Lucas—collaborate with workers and men of action—Juan Salvo and Franco—to achieve important goals.

In the 1970s, Oesterheld joined an illegal leftist organization, the Montoneros. The military junta in control of Argentina arrested him in 1977 and is presumed to have murdered him and much of his family in early 1978. This has led some to see a political subtext in the first version of *The Eternaut*, but it was only with his remake of the tale in 1969 (drawn by Alberto Breccia) and its 1976 sequel *The Eternaut II* (drawn by Solano Lopez) that Oesterheld's politics became evident. In the 1969 version, the Western powers sell South America to the aliens, and in *The Eternaut II*, written while Oesterheld was in hiding, Salvo justifies sacrificing people in the fight against oppression. **DI**

↑ *Hora Cero* (*Zero Hour*), which first published *The Eternaut* in 1957.

VERY GOOD BANK, GIRLS! BUSINESS PRETTY GOOD?
ABOUT THE SAME!
HOW COME THERE WAS MORE IN THE BANK? HOW MUCH HAVE YOU BEEN CLIPPING?

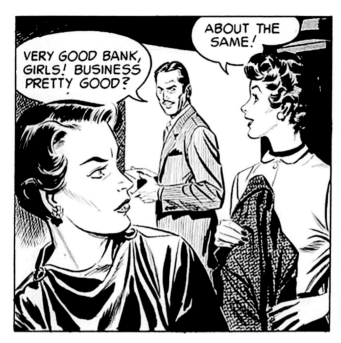

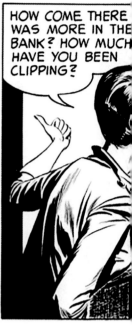

Andy Capp 1957

Reg Smythe

First published by *Daily Mirror* (UK)
Creator British (1917–98)
Genre Humor
Adaptation TV series (1988)

Reg Smythe had already experienced a fair amount of life before creating Andy Capp. He had joined the British Army after school, seen active service during World War II, and worked for the post office. Always a talented artist, Smythe (whose birth name lacked the "e") sold cartoons to supplement his income. Andy Capp's debut was a single panel in the style of many others he had sold, but Smythe was obviously taken with Andy, as his contributions for subsequent days all featured him and his wife Flo. The character sitting on a park bench with his flat cap pulled over his eyes and cigarette hanging from his mouth struck a chord. The characteristics that summed up Andy were in place from the start. He was work-shy but liked a smoke, a pint or three, a bet, and a game of darts, snooker, or football. If it meant neglecting his wife, he was not overly concerned. Flo, for her part, perennially stood by the door late at night, rolling pin in hand. Both provoked the other, and both gave as good as they got. Smythe claimed at one point that Andy and Flo were based on his parents.

It was September 1962 before Andy Capp became the familiar strip, reputedly to ease syndication in the United States. He may have been based solidly in Northern English working-class territory, but his archetype was global. At its peak, Smythe's well-constructed gags and elegant cartooning were syndicated to 1,700 papers spread over forty-eight countries. So prolific was Smythe that his work appeared for a year after his death. Since then, the strip has been continued by Roger Kettle and Roger Mahoney. **FP**

?—OH—I
T BEEN
ANY OF
© 1957 by The Chicago Tribune.
—LISTEN, YOU GOODY-GOODY. THEY FIGURE ON YOU CLIPPING! IF THERE'S ANY DIFFERENCE IN THE RECEIPTS, THEY'LL WONDER HOW COME, AND I'M NOT GOING TO LET THAT HAPPEN, SEE?!
LEONARD STARR 6-22

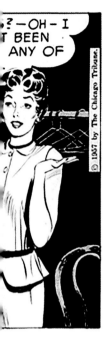

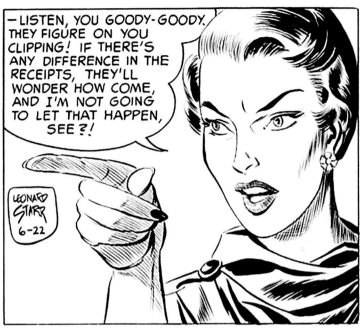

On Stage 1957

Leonard Starr

First published by Chicago Tribune-New York News Syndicate (USA)
Creator American (b.1925)
Genre Drama

Of the seven comic strip proposals Leonard Starr presented to the *Chicago Tribune* syndicate, *On Stage* was his least favorite. He felt that the life of an aspiring young actress on Broadway would have limited appeal and little scope for adventure. Happily, he was proven wrong, and from its first appearance on February 10, 1957, the strip turned out to be a huge success.

Starr came to the feature as an experienced comic book artist, but had also enjoyed great success as an advertising artist, and *On Stage* was drawn with the slickest Madison Avenue style and perfectionism. The feature epitomized the 1950s trend for realistically rendered soap opera strips, peopled with pipe-smoking Rock Hudsons and A-line wearing Grace Kellys. But Starr was not simply a great artist—over the life of the strip he proved himself to be a compelling storyteller, and it is the quality of the writing that propels the strip into the front ranks.

Readers first meet Mary Perkins as a gauche ingénue and follow her progress as her career takes her from the theater to television and films, encountering a fascinating menagerie of characters on the way. She meets her romantic lead, photographer Pete Fletcher, early on and, unusually, the pair are soon married, showing that Starr had more in mind than simply another romantic feature. Instead, he crafted stories of warmth and invention with an ever-evolving supporting cast of emotionally complex characters. Whether on Broadway, the French Riviera, or a Caribbean movie set, the strip was never less than compelling. **DR**

↑ Leonard Starr brought the skills he learned on Madison Avenue to his newspaper strip.

Gomer Goof 1957

André Franquin

Title in original language *Gaston*
First published by Dupuis (Belgium)
Creator Belgian (1924–97)
Genre Humor

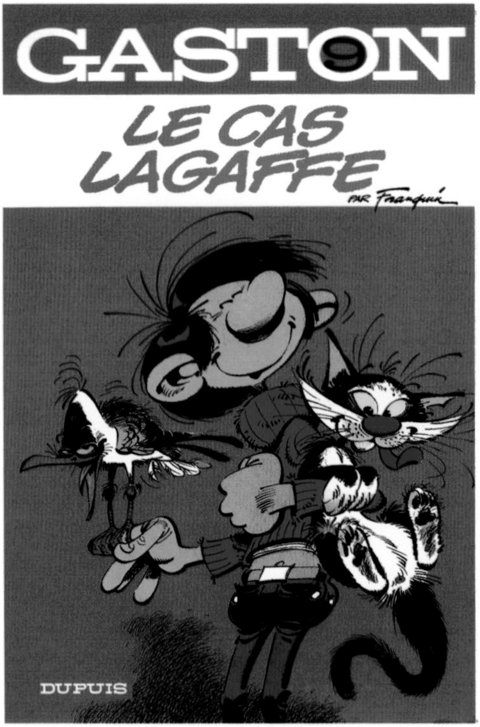
GASTON 9
LE CAS LAGAFFE
PAR Franquin
DUPUIS

Similar reads
Buddy Does Seattle Pete Bagge
Game Over Midam
Jonah Ken Reid
Kid Paddle Midam

One of the masterpieces of European humor comics, *Gaston* first appeared in the Belgian weekly comic anthology *Spirou* as a one-panel cartoon; it soon graduated to half-page (and later to full-page) strips. Although labeled as a *héros-sans-emploi* (hero without a job), Gaston Lagaffe is a young man who actually has work as an office boy at the *Spirou* headquarters. However, he spends most of his time there creating zany inventions, such as the Gaffophone (a giant harp whose sound can destroy an entire building), taking care of his pets, or simply dozing off. Usually these activities end in catastrophe, often making Gaston exclaim his catchphrase "M'enfin?!" (What the. . . ?!)

Gaston's long-suffering boss was originally Fantasio, taken from the *Spirou and Fantasio* series, which was also penned by André Franquin for publication in *Spirou*. Fantasio was later replaced by the short-tempered Léon Prunelle. Other characters include Gaston's naive girlfriend Jeanne, the harsh accountant Monsieur Boulier, the traffic cop Longtarin, and Monsieur De Mesmaeker, a wealthy businessman always trying to sign contracts with real-life comics publisher Jean Dupuis, but whose attempts to do so are always foiled by Gaston's gimmicks.

In the late 1960s, *Gaston* entered its creative peak, both in terms of artwork and gag development, and the protagonist became more of a nonconformist. However, from the mid-1970s, Franquin—suffering from depression and wanting to pursue other projects—gradually abandoned *Gaston*.

Gaston has been reprinted continuously in albums by Dupuis, and was adapted into an animated television series in 2010. The series is famous all over Europe but only a few *Gaston* gag pages have been translated into English. It appears as *Gomer Goof* in Fantagraphics's *Prime Cuts* and *Graphic Story Monthly*. **AMo**

Office boy Gaston snoozes within *Spirou*'s paper mountain. ➡

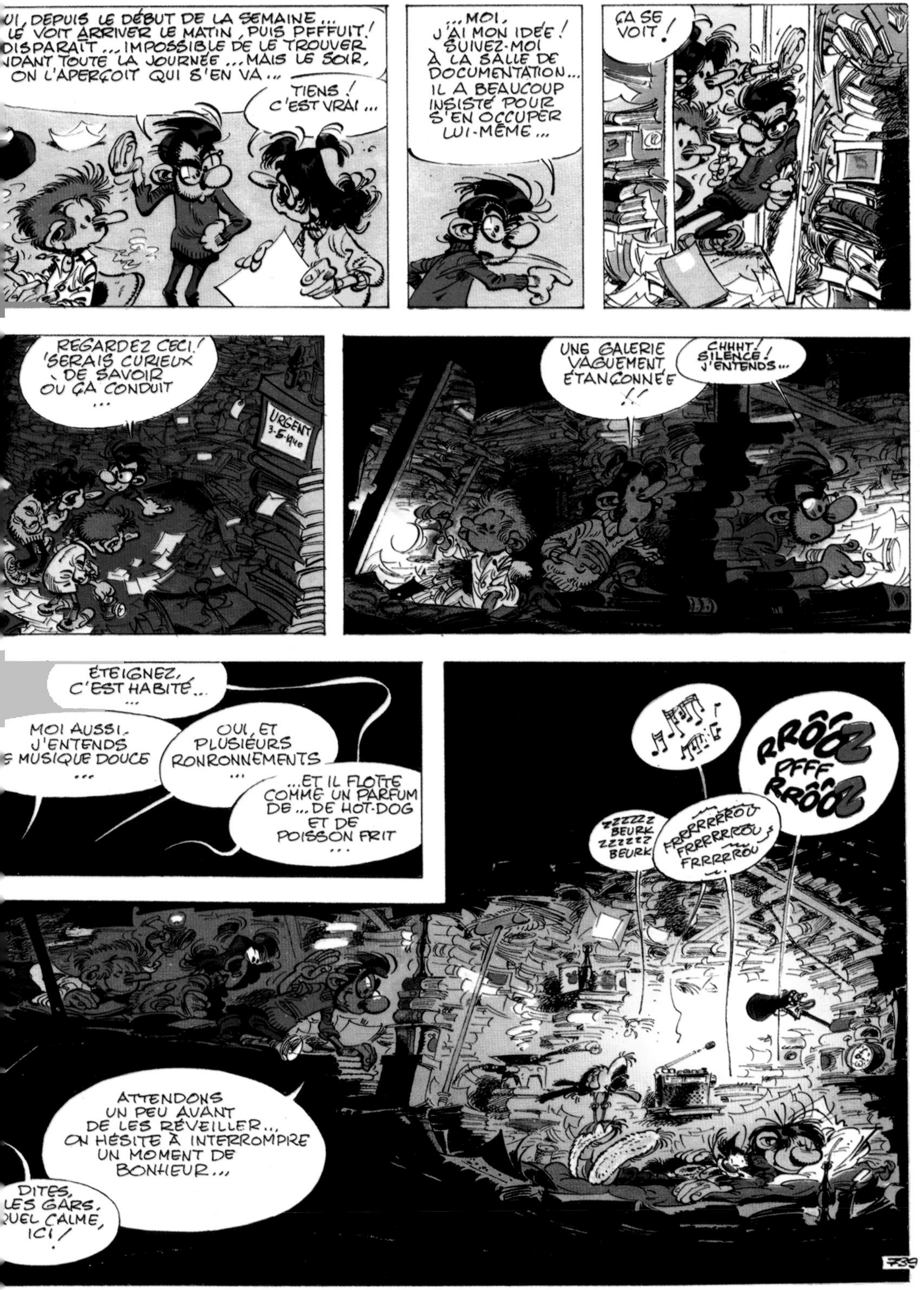
UI, DEPUIS LE DÉBUT DE LA SEMAINE... LE VOIT ARRIVER LE MATIN, PUIS PFFUIT! DISPARAÎT... IMPOSSIBLE DE LE TROUVER NDANT TOUTE LA JOURNÉE... MAIS LE SOIR, ON L'APERÇOIT QUI S'EN VA...
TIENS! C'EST VRAI...
...MOI, J'AI MON IDÉE! SUIVEZ-MOI À LA SALLE DE DOCUMENTATION... IL A BEAUCOUP INSISTÉ POUR S'EN OCCUPER LUI-MÊME...
ÇA SE VOIT!
REGARDEZ CECI! 'SERAIS CURIEUX DE SAVOIR OÙ ÇA CONDUIT...
URGENT 3-5-1940
UNE GALERIE VAGUEMENT ÉTANÇONNÉE!!
CHHHT! SILENCE! J'ENTENDS...
ÉTEIGNEZ, C'EST HABITÉ...
MOI AUSSI. J'ENTENDS E MUSIQUE DOUCE...
OUI, ET PLUSIEURS RONRONNEMENTS...
...ET IL FLOTTE COMME UN PARFUM DE... DE HOT-DOG ET DE POISSON FRIT...
RRÔÔÔZ PFFF RRÔÔÔZ
ZZZZZZ BEURK ZZZZZZ BEURK
FRRRRRRROU FRRRRRROU FRRRRROU
ATTENDONS UN PEU AVANT DE LES RÉVEILLER... ON HÉSITE À INTERROMPRE UN MOMENT DE BONHEUR...
DITES, LES GARS. QUEL CALME, ICI!
739

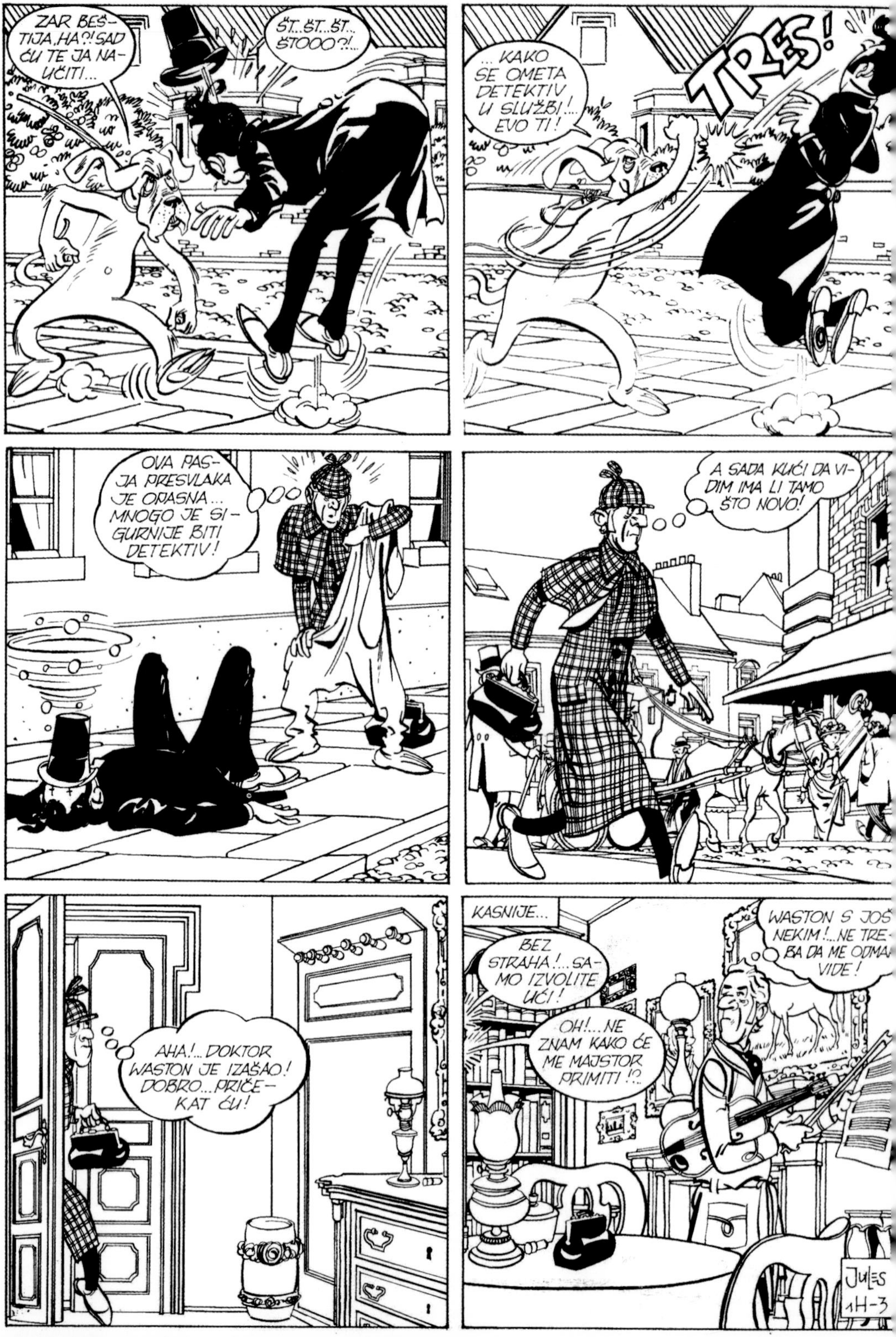
ZAR BEŠTIJA, HA?! SAD ĆU TE JA NAUČITI...
ŠT...ŠT...ŠT... ŠTOOO?!...
... KAKO SE OMETA DETEKTIV U SLUŽBI!... EVO TI!
TRES!
OVA PASJA PRESVLAKA JE OPASNA... MNOGO JE SIGURNIJE BITI DETEKTIV!
A SADA KUĆI DA VIDIM IMA LI TAMO ŠTO NOVO!
AHA!... DOKTOR WASTON JE IZAŠAO! DOBRO... PRIČEKAT ĆU!
KASNIJE...
BEZ STRAHA!... SAMO IZVOLITE UĆI!
OH!... NE ZNAM KAKO ĆE ME MAJSTOR PRIMITI!?
WASTON S JOŠ NEKIM!... NE TREBA DA ME ODMA VIDE!
JULES 1H-3

Herlock Sholmes 1957

✎ Zvonimir Furtinger ✎ Julio Radilović

First published by *Magazine Plavi Vjesnik* (Yugoslavia)
Creators Furtinger (Croatian, 1912–86);
Radilović (Croatian, b.1928)
Genre Humor

A major comic artist in the former Yugoslavia, Julio Radilović, or Jules, as he is better known, has had a long and prolific career as a comic artist producing numerous stories and illustrations. He is particularly known for the meticulous detail of his artwork and the precision with which he depicts clothes and weaponry of different historic periods, but Jules is also renowned for his storytelling abilities. Aside from his historical and adventure comics (*Past Centuries* and *Partisans*) and his fantasy comics (*Scouts' Adventures*, *Baca the Scout*, *Oliver*, and *The Knight Trueblood*, the last with the English writer Les Lilley), he is probably best loved for his amusing work on *Herlock Sholmes*.

Written by Zvonimir Furtinger, this parody of Sir Conan Doyle's famous detective is noted for its wit and humor. The stories are predominantly based on Sholmes's abilities as a master of disguise: he is able to disguise himself as anything imaginable, even if that thing is a tree and there is a dog nearby that needs to pee. One famous sequence has Sholmes disguised as a monkey while a monkey disguised as Sholmes is being congratulated by the detectives from Scotland Yard. The detectives do not notice "Sholmes" is acting like a monkey, despite his hanging from a light fixture.

Aside from comedy, the stories also have a very well-structured, classic detective narrative and are exciting adventures in their own right. There are nine books in the series, published locally and abroad, with cases involving dead people coming back to life and the discovery of Aladdin's lamp. **ZT**

Adam Strange 1958

✎ Gardner Fox ✎ Carmine Infantino

First published by DC Comics (USA)
Creators Fox (American, 1911–86);
Infantino (American, b.1925)
Genre Superhero

The late 1950s was a period of extraordinary creativity for DC Comics. In a burst of inspiration, its artists and writers dreamed up a pantheon of new strips to sustain it for the next five decades. Adam Strange, a sort of science fiction superhero, first appeared in *Showcase*, a title designed to preview potential new strips. After the usual three trial issues, he was deemed popular enough to spin off into his own series a year later in the pages of *Mystery in Space*.

The character was the brainchild of writer Gardner Fox and editor Julius Schwartz and was clearly influenced by Edgar Rice Burroughs's John Carter books. The series opens with archaeologist Adam Strange working on a site in Peru when all of a sudden he is struck by a ray (called a Zeta Beam) and transported to a faraway world called Rann, a technologically advanced world plagued by savage creatures. The ray was the creation of a scientist named Sardath, whose daughter Alanna frequently requires rescuing.

Two things helped elevate the comic book beyond the norm, and they were Gardner Fox's inventive scripts and Carmine Infantino's stylish artwork. Fox delighted in setting up perilous face-offs against a bizarre menagerie of alien menaces. Visually, the feature exuded a sleek modernity, with Infantino's infatuation with architect Frank Lloyd Wright evident in the futuristic cities of Rann. Infantino left the strip in 1964, and the feature died a year later, but while Adam Strange never enjoyed more than a cult following, the character has remained a part of the DC universe ever since. **DR**

◄ Herlock Sholmes keeps everyone on their toes with his awesome abilities of disguise.

The Smurfs
The Smurfs and the Magic Flute 1958

"Peyo"

Title in original language *La flûte à six schtroumpfs*
First published by Dupuis (Belgium)
Creator Pierre Culliford (Belgian, 1928–92)
Genre Adventure

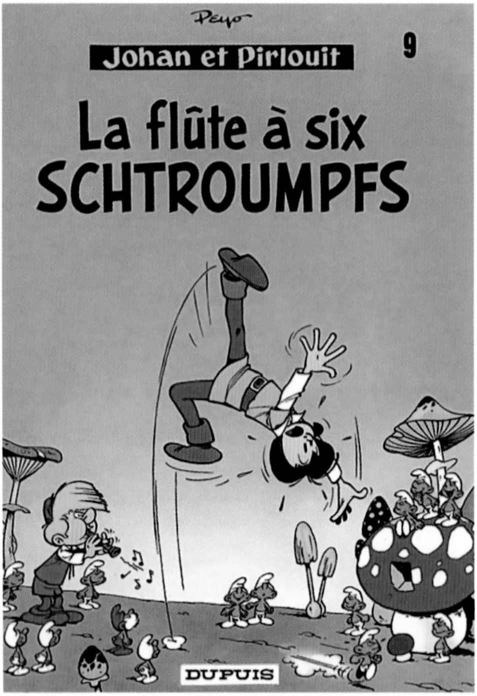
Peyo
Johan et Pirlouit
9
La flûte à six
SCHTROUMPFS
DUPUIS

Also by "Peyo"
The Cursed Country (Le pays maudit)
The Lord of Montresor (Le sire de Montrésor)
The Moonstone (La pierre de lune)
The Ring of Castellac (L'anneau des Castellac)
The Source of the Gods (La source des dieux)

This is the first story in which the Smurfs (or *Schtroumpfs*, as they are called in Belgium) appeared. Perhaps surprisingly, its stars were not intended to be the Smurfs at all but the young knight Johan and his funny little sidekick Peewit (Pirlouit in Belgium). Peewit is on a music-playing craze, but unfortunately for the inhabitants of the king's castle, he is not very good at it. Things go from bad to worse when he gets his hands on a peculiar flute that turns out to have magical powers: all who listen to it start dancing and, after a few minutes, faint.

A suspicious character by the name of Torchesac is interested in the flute, and, after ingratiating himself with Peewit, manages to steal it and use it to go on a looting spree. To try and stop him, Johan and Peewit seek the aid of their friend Homnibus the Enchanter, who magically sends them to the land of the original builders of the flute, little blue gnomes called the Smurfs. Johan and Peewit ask the Smurfs to make another magic flute to help them fight Torchesac. Meanwhile, Torchesac has allied himself with a local nobleman keen on conquering the neighboring counties. Johan and Peewit manage to intercept the plotters and, after a protracted magic flute duel, to defeat Torchesac for good.

"I've figured out how to get divine sounds from that instrument!!"

The story develops at a steady pace with plenty of humor along the way and is a finely crafted adventure tale from a creator at the peak of his powers. Peewit's puzzlement at the odd language spoken by the Smurfs and his attempts to speak it are very funny, but ultimately the Smurfs had the last laugh as they went on to have far greater success in their own strips. **J-PJ**

Gil Jordan
Murder at High Tide 1958

Maurice Tillieux

In Labron in the Morbihan, right in the middle of the "Pas du Malin" (Devil's Footstep), a road liable to flooding that links the mainland to the tower of the "Joyeux Chevalier" (Merry Knight), a car is found submerged in the water. There is no trace of the driver, who has probably been carried away by the rising tide, which can travel as fast as a horse. This initial scene, taking place beneath dark skies and in pouring rain, showcases Maurice Tillieux as first and foremost a creator of atmospheres. Influenced by the descriptions in detective novels, he liked to represent his characters with a certain realism, such as eating in a Paris café or wandering through disreputable backstreets on their way to sinister meetings. This was particularly bold at

"Now there's nothing left to do but wait for the low tide..."

a time when French censorship was extremely strict about publications intended for the young. As far as settings were concerned, Tillieux was especially fond of working-class districts of Paris and the mysterious atmosphere of Brittany. In this respect, *Murder at High Tide*, Gil Jordan's third adventure, is the perfect synthesis of his preferred settings.

Prepublished in *Spirou* at the end of 1958 (and published as an album in 1960), the investigation into the theft of antiques, led by the young detective Gil Jordan, takes the reader from France to London. In addition, the reader is regaled with numerous visual jokes and dialogue punctuated by plays on words.

Tilleux's clear line drawing style defines objects that have become status symbols. The cars are drawn in loving detail, including Jordan's Renault Dauphine, and especially the Facel Vega FV2, the inspiration for this wonderful, simple comic strip. **CM**

Title in original language *Gil Jourdan: La voiture immergée*
First published by *Spirou* magazine (France)
Creator Belgian (1921–78) **Genre** Adventure

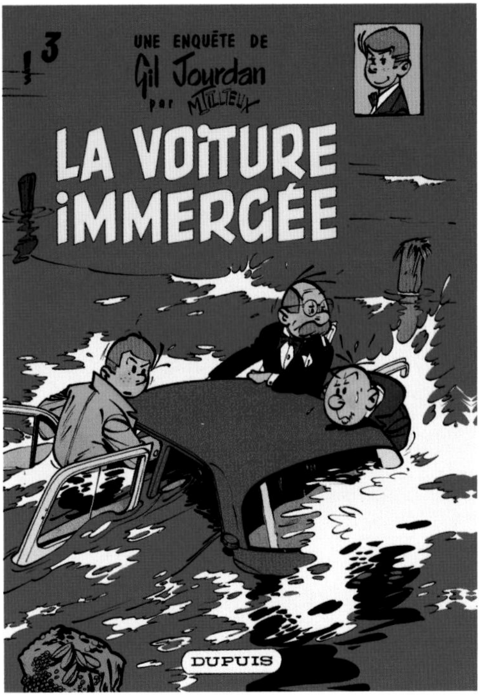
3
UNE ENQUÊTE DE
Gil Jourdan
par M. TILLIEUX
LA VOITURE IMMERGÉE
DUPUIS

Also by Maurice Tilleux
Libellule Escapes (Libellule s'évade)
The Pursuit (La poursuite)
The Red Monks (Les moines rouges)
The Three Stains (Les trois taches)
The Twilight Cargo (Les cargos du crépuscule)

Mort & Phil 1958

Francisco Ibáñez

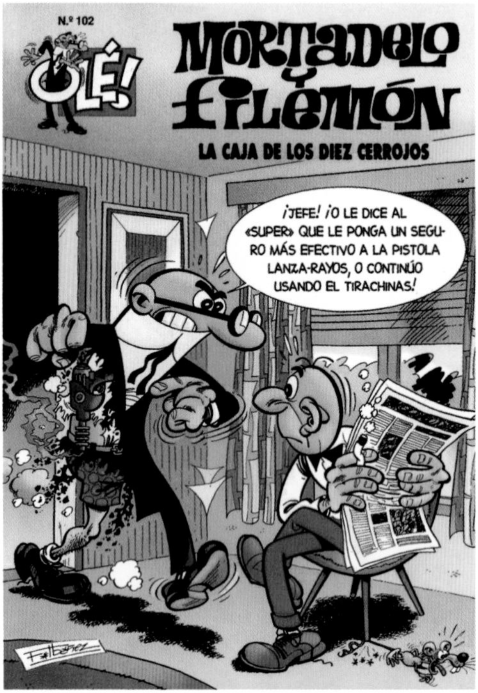
N.º 102
¡OLÉ!
MORTADELO Y FILEMÓN
LA CAJA DE LOS DIEZ CERROJOS
¡JEFE! ¡O LE DICE AL «SUPER» QUE LE PONGA UN SEGURO MÁS EFECTIVO A LA PISTOLA LANZA-RAYOS, O CONTINÚO USANDO EL TIRACHINAS!

"People who say that they [Mort and Phil] are kids' stuff are wrong. If I had to make a living on just what I would earn from the kids, I'd be cleaning windshields."

Francisco Ibáñez

Similar reads

Carpanta Josep Escobar
El Reporter Tribulete Cifré

Title in original language *Mortadelo y Filemón*
First published by *Pulgarcito*/Editorial Bruguera (Spain)
Creator Spanish (b.1936)
Genre Humor

To say that *Mort & Phil* is to the Spanish what *Asterix* is to the French or *Astro Boy* is to the Japanese would be enough to accurately define them as Spain's most popular comic characters ever, enjoyed by children and adults alike. Created by Francisco Ibáñez for the weekly comic *Pulgarcito* as one-page gags, the series stars a couple of bumbling sleuths: the bald, slim bespectacled Mort, a master of disguise, and the two-haired Phil. Heavily influenced by slapstick comedy, the series often relies on a relentless chain of quick-fire gags leading up to a chase scene climax.

In 1969 the two characters graduated to longer adventures, later compiled in album form, becoming secret agents at the service of the TIA, a spoof of the CIA. New supporting characters included the short-tempered TIA leader "El Super" and the failed inventor Professor Bacterio. The ever-growing success of the series encouraged publisher Bruguera to increase the quantity of the stories, even if it meant employing other artists, although these strips were never as popular as Ibáñez's tales. The series' original publisher went out of business in 1986, and since that time Ediciones B has continued to publish numerous new *Mort & Phil* tales from Ibáñez.

The pair have featured in countless licensed items as well as two animated cartoon series and three live-action movies. Their comic albums have been translated into several languages, but while their animated adventures have been dubbed into English, their strip adventures have not. **AMo**

Ompa-Pa the Redskin 1958

✒ René Goscinny and Albert Uderzo ✎ Albert Uderzo

Title in original language *Oumpah-Pah le peau-rouge*
First published by Le Lombard (Belgium)
Creators Goscinny (French, 1926–77);
Uderzo (French, b.1927) **Genre** Humor

Toward the end of 1951, René Goscinny was appointed head of the Paris office of the Belgian agency World's Press, and there he had a decisive encounter, with Albert Uderzo. Together they conceived Ompa-Pa, a young Indian living in contemporary America. The following year, Goscinny left for New York and took the Ompa-Pa project with him, convinced that U.S. publishers would be interested. However, it was not to be, and the six plates translated by his friend Harvey Kurtzman remained in a box.

It was not until May 1958 that Ompa-Pa made his official debut in the Belgian weekly magazine *Tintin*. Very little was left of the original story: the authors were no longer interested in the contrast between the modern world and traditional folklore. They decided to set the story in the eighteenth century, at a time when the colonization of the New World by various European kingdoms would make the stories much more exciting. In addition, they gave Ompa-Pa a blood brother, very different from him in both character and appearance. Thus, in only a dozen pages, the bravest warrior of the Shavashavah, Ompa-Pa, becomes best friends with Hubert de Flaky Pastry, a knight of the king of France, nicknamed Two-Scalp because of his removable wig.

Because of the lack of interest from Belgian readers, Goscinny and Uderzo decided to end the series and concentrate on other projects. But the five adventures published up to 1962 are hilarious and natural precursors to their other joint series: *Asterix*. **CM**

Sky Masters 1958

✒ Dick Wood and Dave Wood ✎ Jack Kirby

First published by George Matthew Adams Newspaper Service (USA) **Creators** Richard Wood (American, Unknown); David Wood (American, Unknown); Kirby (American, 1917–94) **Genre** Science fiction

As the 1950s drew on, U.S. public interest in the "Space Race" grew, and the George Matthew Adams Service sought to commission a space-themed newspaper strip to syndicate. Launching on September 8, 1958, *Sky Masters*, the adventures of the eponymous U.S. astronaut, was the result.

Sky works for the United States Space Force in a near-future world of space stations and gadgets. The technology may seem dated today, but it captured the readers' imaginations in the 1950s. After a few months the feature gained a full-page Sunday strip.

Visually, it was the perfect vehicle for Jack Kirby's developing interest in machinery and cosmic imagery. The artwork in the early strips was inked by Wally Wood (no relation to Dick and Dave) and tends to be the best remembered. Wood and Kirby's contrasting styles merge to create a beautiful whole that fully retains Kirby's dynamic layouts. The two admired each other enormously and enjoyed the collaboration. When Wally left, Kirby himself inked the strip for a while, trying to emulate Wood's atmospheric use of black and shadow. Dick Ayers later took over the inking duties. The final weeks of the strip in early 1961 were again inked by Kirby, this time in a much simpler style. Over time, Kirby also fell into doing much of the writing himself, making the strip his own.

Dated or not, the stories are simple and fun, and the visuals—especially during the first year or so—are among the very best of Kirby's work in the 1950s, offering a thrilling glimpse of things to come. **CH**

Jommeke 1958

✏️🖌 "Jef" Nys

First published by *Het Volk* newspaper (Belgium)
Creator Josef Nys (Belgian, 1927–2009)
Genre Humor
Award Gouden Adhemar (2005)

The national popularity of *Jommeke* requires being placed in perspective. Belgium has a population of ten million, only six million of whom are Flemish. *Jommeke* has sold 51 million books, and it is only the second best-selling Flemish comics series.

Jommeke is a plucky, upstanding lad whose adventures are shared with the similarly wholesome (but daft) Filiberke, distinguished by his black hair. Jommeke's parrot Flip is ever-present, and his parents seem largely unconcerned that his escapades often take him out of the country, never mind the neighborhood. He frequently foils the plans of the crooked butler Anatool, while other plots are prompted by Professor Gobelijn's latest inventions, such as a mirror coating enabling people to pass through any surface against which the mirror is placed.

"Jef" Nys took his cue from *Tintin*, working in a similar style with primary colors. He also had an impressive work ethic, crafting 250 *Jommeke* albums. During a typical week in the early 1960s he would produce twelve tiers of a *Jommeke* story for a daily newspaper, produce a weekly *Jommeke* cartoon, and draw another strip besides. These would often be biographies of prominent Catholic figures. He conceded the workload was excessive in the middle of the 1960s and concentrated exclusively on *Jommeke* from that point, hiring assistants, particularly Philippe Delzenne, from 1979. Since Nys's death, Delzenne and Gert Van Loock have continued his legacy, producing new *Jommeke* material under their own names. **FP**

Jonah 1958

✏ Walter Fearne 🖌 Ken Reid

First published by D. C. Thomson (UK)
Creators Fearne (British, 1933);
Reid (British, 1919–87)
Genre Humor

Ken Reid was one of the artists who revitalized *The Beano* in the 1950s and he got his big break with the creation of the newspaper strip *Fudge the Elf*, a feature that began in 1938 and continued until 1962, with a break during World War II while Reid was serving in the British Army. For the most part *Fudge* was a relentlessly innocent strip that only briefly touched on the more outlandish elements of Reid's artistic abilities. After working on a number of strips for *The Beano*, Reid partnered with writer Walter Fearne to create *Jonah*, a more suitable outlet for Reid's outré artistic instincts.

Jonah is a cursed sailor who has the unfortunate habit of sinking every ship he ever boards. Compelled to sail the seas, he overcomes his gormless nature to exhibit incredible ingenuity in contriving means of passage, as captains well aware of his reputation attempt to keep him ashore. As inventive as these scenarios become, the most memorable component of the strip is Reid's rendering of the title character. His Jonah is a true grotesque to make Basil Wolverton's heart swell with envy; a lumpy, pencil-thin sailor with ears pushed down by his cap, prominent buck teeth, and almost no chin.

Reid would usually receive a script requiring a dozen panels, and as more gags occurred to him he added more panels, often doubling the content on the page. After leaving *The Beano* in the 1960s, he created a series of memorable strips for other publishers, but it is a testament to his unique skills that *Jonah* lay dormant for thirty years after Reid's departure. **FP**

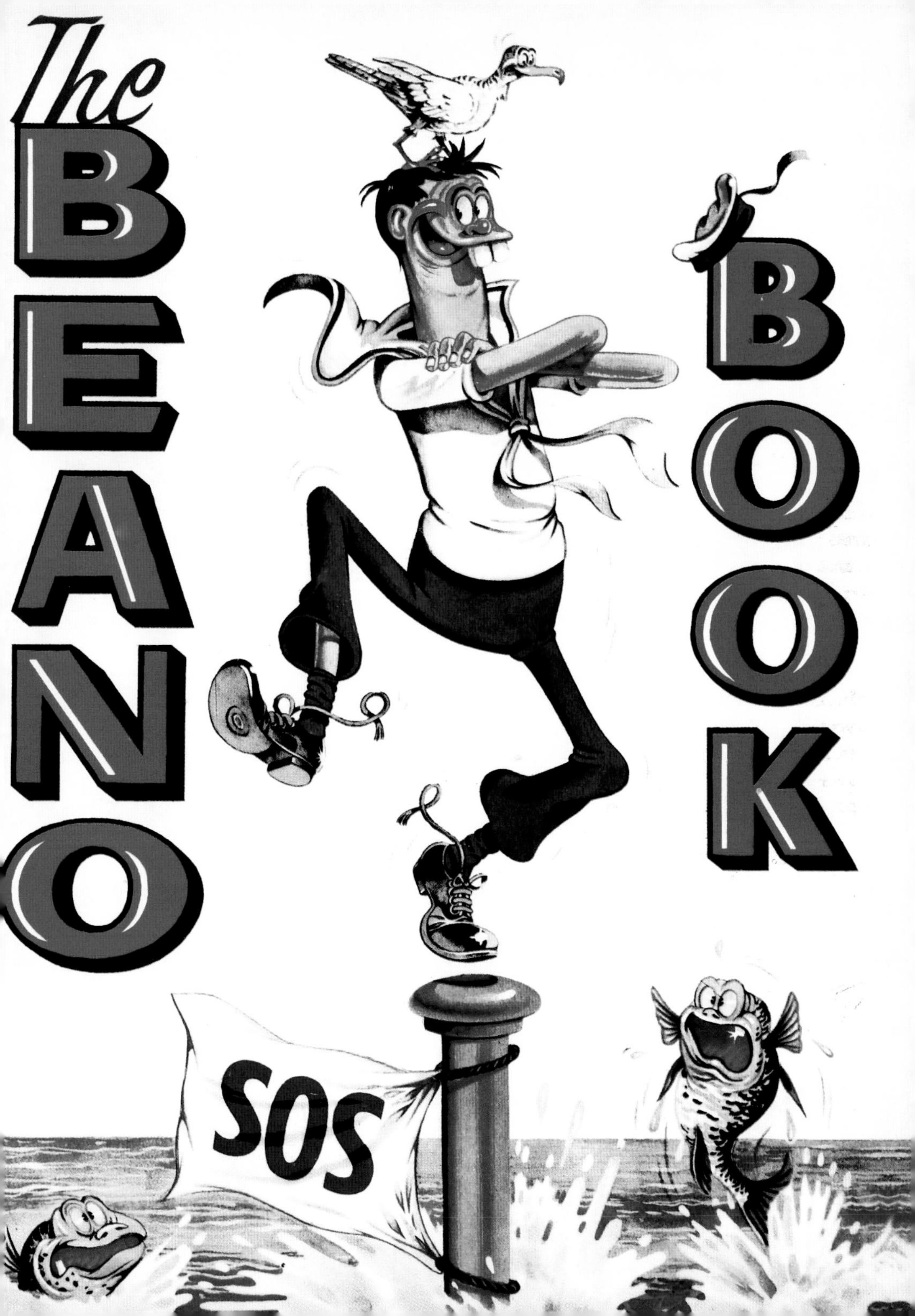
The
BEANO
BOOK
SOS

Speech bubbles within the comic:
here come the PERISHERS!
WHERE Y'GOIN' MARLON?
OVER TO THE OLE PIPE-YARD, MAISIE—WHERE WELLIN'TON LIVES!
'E'S BUILT 'IS TELEVISION S AN "E'S GOIN' GIVE A SHO
S249

The Perishers 1958

✏ Maurice Dodd   ✏ Dennis Collins

First published by The Mirror Group (UK)
Creators Dodd (British, 1922–2005)
Collins (British, d.1990)
Genre Humor

The Perishers is a strip about British kids (a "perisher" is British slang for anyone annoying) published in the *Daily Mirror* from 1958 to 2006. The strip was originally thought up by the newspaper's editor, Bill Herbert, as a British alternative to *Peanuts*, and this was certainly how it developed under the writing of Maurice Dodd.

The perishers of the title are a motley assortment of scruffy youngsters who go about their business in a world where adults are seldom seen or heard. The gang consists of Wellington, a young entrepreneur with a big cap and rubber boots who appears to live on his own in an abandoned station; his canine companion Old Boots, an Old English Sheepdog who thinks he is really an eighteenth-century lord under a spell; Maisie, a bossy obnoxious little girl who terrorizes her friends; Marlon, a boy who seems entirely devoid of brains; and Baby Grumplin', Maisie's little brother. Old Boots even has his own supporting cast with the inefficient, and improbably named, bloodhound B. H. (Calcutta) Failed, a pair of leftist insects with cockney accents, and Adolf Kilroy, a tortoise with a shell shaped like a German helmet.

A classic collection, *Omnibus No.3*, collects strips from the years 1964 to 1966, by which time the series had developed its own mythology, such as the rhubarb thrashing contest, Marlon's ketchup sandwiches with the one-inch ketchup filling, and Old Boot's annual peek into the crab pool at the beach, which regularly caused turmoil in the crab population as to the meaning of "the eyeballs in the sky." **J-PJ**

Prior to 1966, Wellington was shown living in a concrete pipe. ⬆

KER-UMBS, WELLIN'TON, YOU MUST BE PRETTY CLEVER!
OH! I DON'T KNOW...
ANY OTHER GENIUS COULD 'AVE DONE TH' SAME!
OH! THESE PERISHING KIDS!

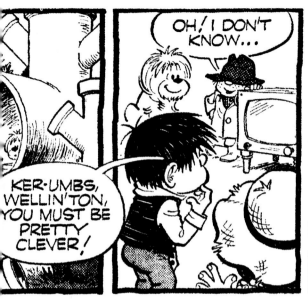

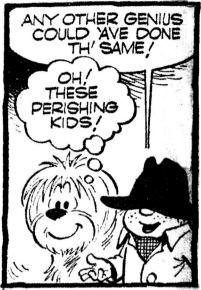

B.C. 1958

Johnny Hart

First published by *The New York Herald Tribune* (USA)
Creator American (1931–2007)
Genre Comedy
Award Reuben Award (1968)

In 2007 Johnny Hart passed away in a manner many illustrators would likely envy: sitting at his drawing board at his home in Nineveh, New York. Hart sold his first cartoon to *The Saturday Evening Post* in 1953. Five years later, after five rejections, *B.C.* debuted in *The New York Herald Tribune*. Hart based his cavemen and collection of various anthropomorphic animals on friends and colleagues. Wiley, the world's first bartender, was based on Hart's brother-in-law. Clumsy Carp was a near-sighted ichthyologist inspired by Hart's childhood friend Jack Caprio. And, of course, there was the naive B.C. himself, who likes to hang out with friends, discover the wheel, and harness fire.

The strip was simple enough: a joke a day in black and white with a color strip on Sundays. Background art was minimal, with boulders labeled "Patents" or "Shop Counter" to provide context for gags. As time went on, the modern world began to bleed subtlely into the strip, as did Hart's conservative religious views. His most controversial strip was in April 2001 when he depicted a lit Jewish menorah burning down to form a Christian cross, suggesting Christianity's ascendency over Judaism. As a result, the strip was pulled from some newspapers, including *The Los Angeles Times*.

In 1987, Hart, who was old enough to remember a time when contracts between cartoonists and publishers were more equitable, helped inspire the launch of Creators Syndicate, allowing cartoonists to own their characters and their names and, in Hart's words, "give the industry the dignity it deserves." **BS**

Jungle Book 1959

Harvey Kurtzman

First published by Ballantine Books (USA)
Creator American (1924–93)
Genre Humor
Award The Harvey Awards, named in his honor

Harvey Kurtzman's
JUNGLE BOOK

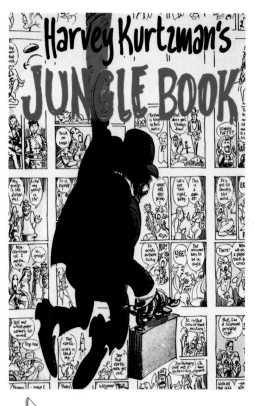

Similar reads
Dork Evan Dorkin
Goodman Beaver Harvey Kutzman and Will Elder
Slice of Life (Tranches de Vie) Gérard Lauzier

Justly revered as a brilliant artist as well as a legend of satire, it is surprising to consider how little of Harvey Kurtzman's full artwork actually saw print. For the final forty years of his life, the majority of his published art was rough layouts, buried beneath the pencils, inks, and paint of others. The 140 pages of *Jungle Book* form the largest collection of post-1952 Kurtzman art. It is magnificent: loose, expressive, and a textbook course in storytelling.

Jungle Book has an eccentric origin. Ballantine Books had successfully reprinted paperback collections of material from *MAD Magazine*, a title Kurtzman started and left over ownership issues. When it lost the rights, Ballantine approached Kurtzman to create new material. Having a point to prove, and at the time not editing a magazine, Kurtzman dipped his pen in ink and let his venom fly.

The question of abiding relevance is whether satire from 1959 stands up today. The answer is an unqualified "Yes." Kurtzman's sense of pacing, comic timing, and gag construction is so polished that it is not necessary to know that two of the four strips here originated as pastiches of popular television shows of the era (although a few specific minor elements may puzzle modern readers). It is a damning comment on the paucity of such shows that their clichés have been perpetually recycled since, rendering them instantly familiar here. A strip about the small-mindedness of rural America is also relevant today, in which a liking for books is suspicious enough to initiate a lynching. The strongest strip is titled "The Organization Man in the Gray Flannel Suit," in which Kurtzman really let rip, tackling the intellectual inadequacy of magazine publishing and drawing heavily on his own experiences in the field. Advertising dictating content is the only progression, a trend Kurtzman would have deplored. **FP**

RyePhie 1959

Sanho Kim

Although superhero is hardly the favorite genre in contemporary Korean *manhwa* (comics), one of the earliest popular hits in its history is a great superhero epic down to the bone. It has all the essential ingredients: a concealed identity, a secret hideout, super vehicles, a mask, and a cape.

In war-torn South Korea in the 1950s, reading *manhwa* was a favorite escape for the younger generation. Heroes fighting for justice could not be found in the real world, and every day was a fight for survival. The adventures of RhyPhie, the secret superhero who fights evil with the help of his trusty sidekick Ms. Swallow, provided some of the rare moments of justice on Earth in those troubled times. Unlike many of the other comics of that era, *RhyPhie* is not an overtly emotional story about a poor guy who rises from the ashes (to reflect the South Korea as it was immediately after the Korean War)—its setting is far more aspirational. It is the vision of a vastly advanced future where the superhero uses technology to fight against evil forces trying to take over the world. Flying in his vehicle faster than light, the hero involves himself in spectacular action with great power and courage. The fact that *RhyPhie* boasts superb art and great story structure also helps. The powerful artwork is an early mixture of Kirby-esque structure and manga drawing, resulting in a kind of illustration that is distinctively different. It turned out that this kind of well-made escapist fun gave more hope to its readers than the works reminding them of their real-life hardships.

After *RhyPhie* was published, Sanho Kim proved to have an adventurous spirit just like his character. He moved to the United States and even found employment in the U.S. comic industry, working at Charlton Comics as well as pioneering an enterprise for underwater tourism. **NK**

First published by Buonyi (South Korea)
Creator South Korean (b.1939)
Genre Superhero
Award Korean Order of Cultural Merit (2008)

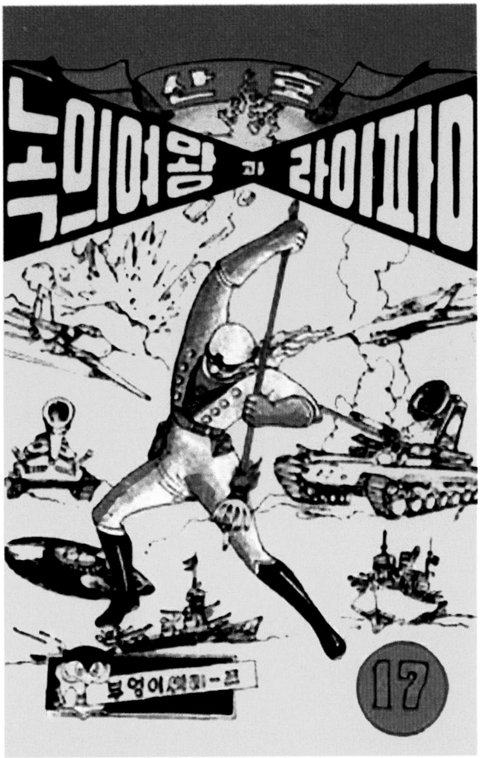

산호
녹의여왕 과 라이파이
17

Also by Sanho Kim

Cheyenne Kid
Dae Jyushin Cheguksa
Vampirella: Dragon Woman

GeGeGe no Kitaro 1959

Shigeru Mizuki

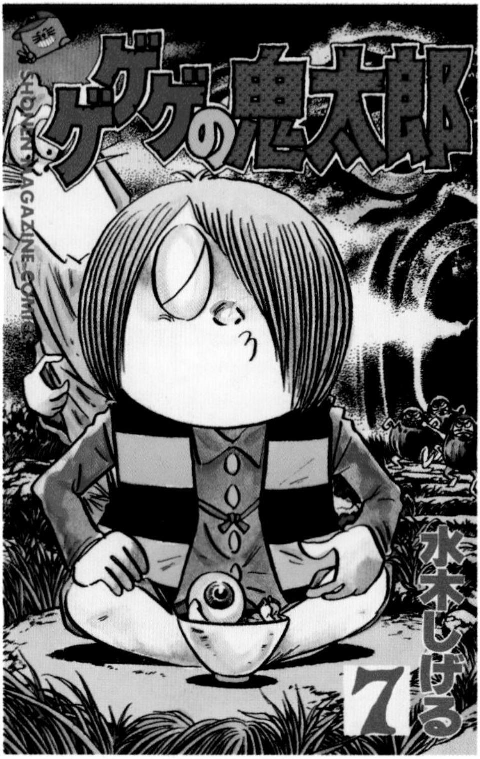
ゲゲゲの鬼太郎
水木しげる
7

"You're always real brave with Kitaro in those comics!"

from *The Great Yokai War* (*Yokai Daisenso*)

Also by Shigeru Mizuki
Akuma-kun
Hitler: A Biography
Yamato

Title in original language *GeGeGe no Kitaro*
First published by *Weekly Shonen Magazine* (Japan)
Creator Japanese (b.1922)
Genre Horror, Humor

When he created the series in the late 1950s for the Japanese network of lending libraries, Shigeru Mizuki gave it the title *Hakaba no Kitaro*, which literally means "Kitaro at the cemetery." It refers to the extraordinary ascendance of its leading character, whose first adventure tells the story of his fantastic genesis.

Born in the earth of a freshly dug grave, one-eyed and deformed, Kitaro is the progeny of a ghost and a living corpse. His mother died in childbirth, and his father, although his corpse has dissolved, survives as a speaking eye. Helped by his affinity with the world of the supernatural, Kitaro, the obvious ambassador, now travels between the world of the living and the world of the dead, defending the humans when the monsters become too threatening while reminding them to respect nature and its more obscure forces. Considering the original title a little too closely related to death, the publisher Kodansha changed it to *GeGeGe no Kitaro*. It was a historic success for Mizuki and his hero, who went on to become a manga superstar.

It is easy to see the attraction of Kitaro, the precursor of a mild gore school that subsequently became established in strip cartoons and the cinema. Incredibly modern in its conception, always subtle and funny in spite of its macabre theme, Kitaro succeeded in reconciling the Japanese with the world of the *yokai*, that pantheon of fantastic creatures (ghosts, spirits, monsters, zombies, and other chimeras) indissolubly linked to the collective animist imagination that is still alive in the archipelago. **NF**

Adventures of Tintin
Tintin in Tibet 1959

✐✐ "Hergé"

Title in original language *Les Aventures de Tintin: Tintin au Tibet* **First published by** Le Lombard (Belgium)
Creator Georges Prosper Remi Remi (Belgian, 1907–83)
Genre Adventure

While on holiday, Tintin learns that Chang, a Chinese friend due to visit him in Europe, was on board an aircraft that has just crashed in the Himalayas. Convinced against all the evidence that his friend has survived, the young reporter decides to go and look for him: he travels to the mountains of Tibet via Katmandu, flanked by the faithful Captain Haddock and his dog, Snowy.

Having arrived, the three members of the expedition set off to find the wreckage of the plane, but not without some difficulties. The superstitious porters are terrified by the invisible presence of the yeti, "the abominable snowman," which is thought to live in these desolate mountains. And the strange prints found in the snow seem to indicate that they are right.

The various clues found near the scene of the crash convince Tintin that his initial intuition was correct: Chang has survived the accident. But how can he find him? After numerous adventures, punctuated by further tracks of the elusive abominable snowman, and with the providential intervention and help of a friendly community of Tibetan lamas, Tintin, Haddock, and Snowy eventually find the young Chang, who only survived through the help of the dreaded yeti, which turns out to very kind and human.

Tintin in Tibet is the work of a mature author who had completely mastered the art of narrative and graphics. The final pages, in which the inconsolable yeti finds itself alone again and unable to resign itself to the departure of Chang and his rescuers, are among the most poignant of the whole *Tintin* saga. **NF**

Billy and Buddy 1959

✐✐ Jean Roba

Title in original language *Boule et Bill*
First published by Dupuis (Belgium)
Creator Belgian (1930–2006)
Genre Humor

Another of Belgium's legendary humor comics, *Billy and Buddy* could be labeled as a family strip, or more accurately as a boy-and-dog strip. It was created by cartoonist Jean Roba for the legendary magazine *Spirou*. First published as a one-shot *mini-récit* (a minicomic supplement), it quickly became a weekly one-page feature. Its humor involves comical situations between the two main characters: Boule, an ordinary red-haired kid, and his floppy-eared cocker spaniel Bill, and the various supporting characters, such as Boule's parents. One particular ongoing gag is the struggle Boule and his dad have getting Bill into a bath.

Roba's style fits ideally into that of the Marcinelle school (named after the Belgian town where *Spirou's* publisher Dupuis has its headquarters) of round, cartoony artwork with a dynamic, almost nervous line. This stands in great contrast to the Brussels school's *ligne claire* (clear line) style and its taste for farcical humor.

The *Billy and Buddy* strips have been reprinted in nearly thirty hardcover albums, while the characters have featured on many licensed items, starred in various advertising promotions, and have seen their adventures adapted into two animated television series (1975 and 2000). After Roba's death in 2006, the *Billy and Buddy* series has been continued by Laurent Veyron, who has worked to emulate faithfully Roba's style. First published in English during the 1960s in the British weekly *Valiant* as *It's a Dog's Life!*, the series' most recent English-language collections have been published by Cinebook. **AMo**

Blake and Mortimer
S.O.S. Meteors 1959

"Edgar P. Jacobs"

Title in original language *S.O.S. Météores*
First published by Le Lombard (Belgium)
Creator Edgard Félix Pierre Jacobs (Belgian, 1904–87)
Genre Science fiction

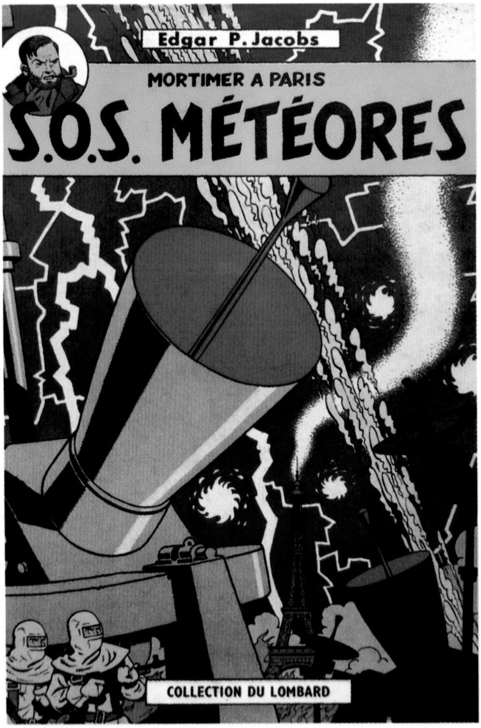

Edgar P. Jacobs
MORTIMER A PARIS
S.O.S. MÉTÉORES
COLLECTION DU LOMBARD

Similar reads

Lefranc: La Grande Menace Jacques Martin
***The Mystery of the Great Pyramid* (*Le mystère de la grande pyramide*)** Edgar P. Jacobs
The Time Trap (*Le Piège diabolique*) Edgar P. Jacobs

Another highly acclaimed entry in the *Blake and Mortimer* series, *S.O.S. Meteors* features a science fiction plot involving the control of the weather. On a mission from the British government to establish the cause of unusually bad weather in Europe, Professor Mortimer goes to visit his meteorologist friend Professor Labrousse in suburban Paris and unwittingly gets on the trail of the people responsible. Before he can get to the bottom of it he disappears, and it is up to his friend Captain Blake of M.I.5 to pick up the trail.

Blake is in Paris chasing a mysterious spy ring. He soon realizes that the ringleader is none other than arch-villain Olrik, working for the same unnamed foreign power that has been tampering with the climate. As he tries to warn the French commissioner, Blake is pursued by Olrik's gang throughout Paris. The story progresses through plenty of tricks and turns, leading to a vast underground base, straight out of a James Bond film, from where the requisite villainous scientist has been conducting his climate change experiments.

"One believed until now that . . . weather phenomena obey more or less precise and immutable laws."

S.O.S. Meteors is Edgar P. Jacobs at his finest. His clear line style and attention to detail are wonderfully appropriate when it comes to anchoring this fantastic science fiction tale of Cold War paranoia in everyday life. Just as that other Jacobs masterpiece, *The Yellow M*, always seemed to take place at night, *S.O.S. Meteors* is set in a succession of rainy, snowy, and overcast landscapes that mirror the political climate. Paris and its suburbs become a giant maze through which Blake and Mortimer are constantly on the move, trying to make sense of a quiet apocalypse. **J-PJ**

Fantomas: The Elegant Menace 1960

Guillermo Mendizábal and others   Rubén Lara y Romero and others

Title in original language *Fantomas, la amenaza elegante*
First published by Editorial Novaro (Mexico)
Creators Mendizábal (Mexican, Unknown); Romero (Mexican, Unknown) **Genre** Adventure

Fantomas, like most periodical Mexican comics published between the mid-1950s and the mid-1980s, is best understood as a corpus, a collective phenomenon of popular culture that once was more popular than radio, football, or television. Based on the 1911 character and situations created by Pierre Souvestre and Marcel Allain, the Mexican *Fantomas* weekly comic book series was originally written by Guillermo Mendizábal and illustrated with Rubén Lara Romero as its main artist, but many of the stories were published without authorial attribution.

The first and original series, published by Editorial Novaro, ran for two decades with incredible success. Fantomas, "the elegant menace," is a gentleman-thief-spy-detective-vigilante-bounty hunter of great wit and muscular physique, often dressed in top hat and tails and a skin-tight white mask. His background is European and of a high social class; he has no super powers but relies on sophisticated technological gadgets and attractive female assistants known by code names. His multireferential adventures take him around the globe facing both historical and fantastic foes. *Fantomas* remains a highlight of Mexican comics for its lengthy and complicated narrative arcs, where international political corruption, crime, and intrigue were set against a critique of capitalist exploitation and dictatiorial regimes.

"Fantomas came face to face with Hitler's Son . . . to rescue the Leader of the IV Reich's closest collaborator."

The series ceased publication in the early 1980s, leaving behind a collection of fascinating stories that help explain the cultural anxieties between Latin America and Europe during the 1970s. **EPr**

FANTOMAS
LA AMENAZA ELEGANTE
"6 SELLOS DE CORREO Y UNA DAMA EN PELIGRO"
$3.00

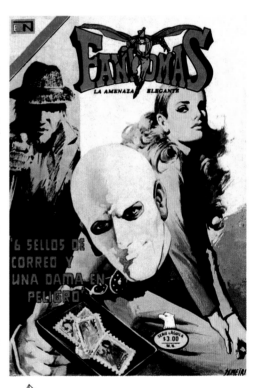

Similar reads
Batman Bob Kane
Kaliman Modesto Vazquez
Los Supermachos Rius
On Her Majesty's Secret Service Henry Gammidge

Fraser of Africa 1960

George Beardmore   Frank Bellamy

First published by Hulton Press (UK)
Creators Beardmore (British, 1908–79); Bellamy (British, 1917–76)
Genre Adventure

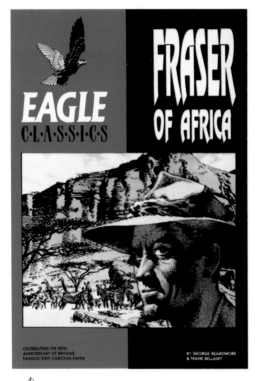

EAGLE
C·L·A·S·S·I·C·S
FRASER
OF AFRICA
CELEBRATING THE 40TH. ANNIVERSARY OF BRITAIN'S FAMOUS STRIP CARTOON PAPER
BY GEORGE BEARDMORE & FRANK BELLAMY

Similar reads
Black Panther in Jungle Action Don McGregor and others
Corto in Africa Hugo Pratt
Deogratias J. P. Stassen

Artist Frank Bellamy influenced just about every British comic artist that emerged in the late 1970s. He was self-taught, and his first comics work appeared in 1953. He produced numerous features for *Eagle* and its younger age group companion title *Swift* until 1965 before moving to *Thunderbirds* in *TV21*, then to the *Garth* newspaper strip in 1971. His science fiction work is excellent, but he is most highly regarded for his naturalism, which peaked on *Fraser of Africa*.

The distinctive palette that Bellamy used to convey the arid, scorched landscape in which the strip was set is immediately apparent. It was an effect that was decades ahead of its time. Subtle browns and yellows dominate, before Bellamy's illustrative skills catch the eye. Although appearing in *Eagle*, Bellamy approached the feature like a U.S. Sunday newspaper strip, producing a single page each week. Published in an era when Britain's colonial empire was diminishing, Bellamy imbued his realistically rendered cast with dignity, and his research was meticulous, avoiding the haphazard mixing of cultures or wildlife so typical of jungle stories in comics.

"I can't let them get away with it. Ona, you and I are gonna stop those poachers."

Biographical information about writer George Beardmore is less readily available. A regular contributor to *Eagle*, he maintained a career as a novelist into the 1970s. His three *Fraser* serials combined to a total of fifty-four pages, and their conservation agenda is surprising. They are well-plotted, in keeping with *Eagle*'s high editorial standards, but it is for Bellamy's work on the strip—which he cited as his personal favorite—that *Fraser of Africa* is remembered. **FP**

Fraser of Africa **charted the adventures of a white hunter in Kenya.** ➡

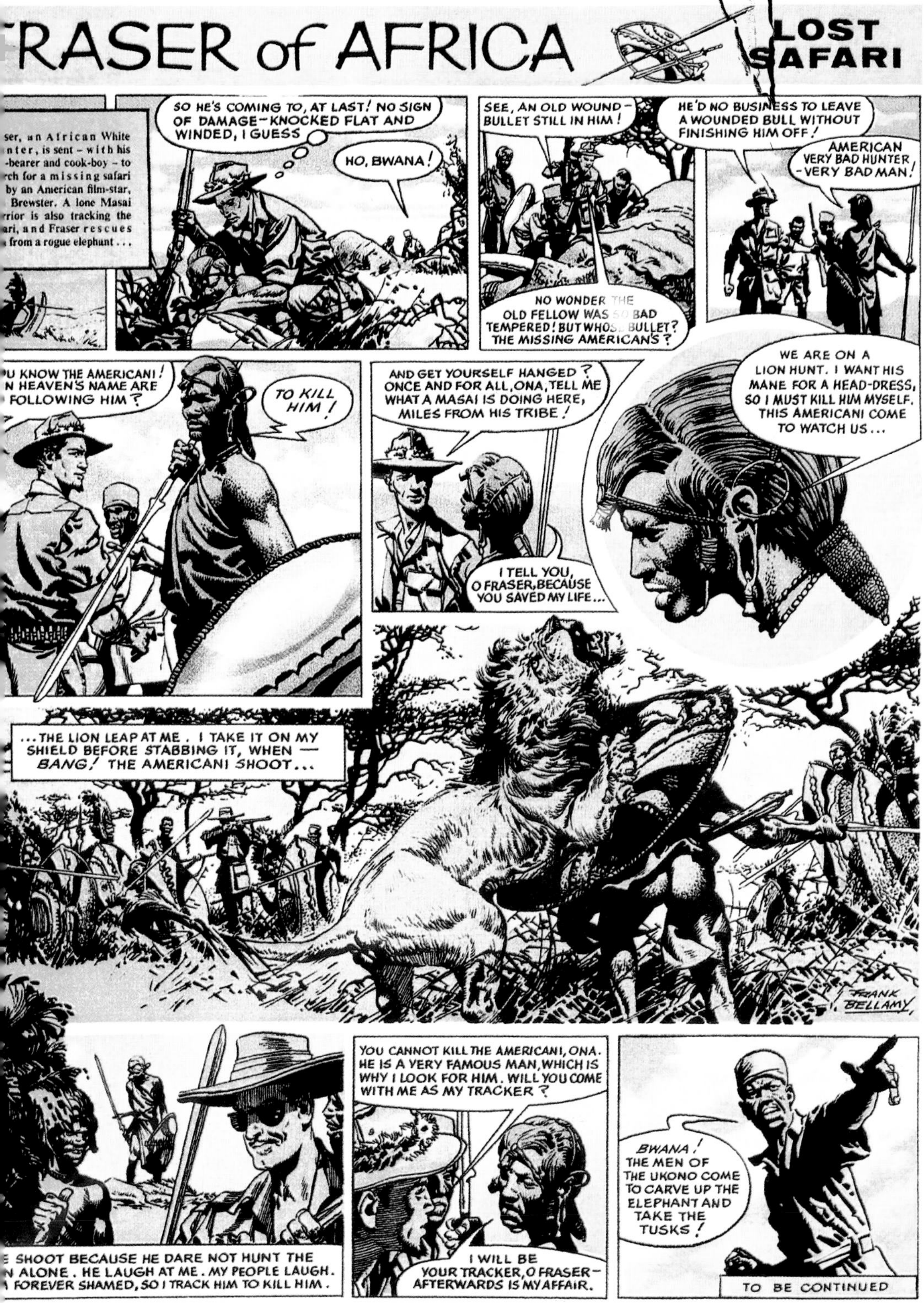
FRASER of AFRICA
LOST SAFARI
ser, an African White nter, is sent – with his -bearer and cook-boy – to rch for a missing safari by an American film-star, Brewster. A lone Masai rrior is also tracking the ari, and Fraser rescues from a rogue elephant . . .
SO HE'S COMING TO, AT LAST! NO SIGN OF DAMAGE – KNOCKED FLAT AND WINDED, I GUESS
HO, BWANA!
SEE, AN OLD WOUND – BULLET STILL IN HIM!
NO WONDER THE OLD FELLOW WAS SO BAD TEMPERED! BUT WHOSE BULLET? THE MISSING AMERICAN'S?
HE'D NO BUSINESS TO LEAVE A WOUNDED BULL WITHOUT FINISHING HIM OFF!
AMERICAN VERY BAD HUNTER – VERY BAD MAN!
U KNOW THE AMERICANI! N HEAVEN'S NAME ARE FOLLOWING HIM?
TO KILL HIM!
AND GET YOURSELF HANGED? ONCE AND FOR ALL, ONA, TELL ME WHAT A MASAI IS DOING HERE, MILES FROM HIS TRIBE!
I TELL YOU, O FRASER, BECAUSE YOU SAVED MY LIFE...
WE ARE ON A LION HUNT. I WANT HIS MANE FOR A HEAD-DRESS, SO I MUST KILL HIM MYSELF. THIS AMERICANI COME TO WATCH US...
...THE LION LEAP AT ME. I TAKE IT ON MY SHIELD BEFORE STABBING IT, WHEN — BANG! THE AMERICANI SHOOT...
FRANK BELLAMY
E SHOOT BECAUSE HE DARE NOT HUNT THE N ALONE. HE LAUGH AT ME. MY PEOPLE LAUGH. FOREVER SHAMED, SO I TRACK HIM TO KILL HIM.
YOU CANNOT KILL THE AMERICANI, ONA. HE IS A VERY FAMOUS MAN, WHICH IS WHY I LOOK FOR HIM. WILL YOU COME WITH ME AS MY TRACKER?
I WILL BE YOUR TRACKER, O FRASER – AFTERWARDS IS MY AFFAIR.
BWANA! THE MEN OF THE UKONO COME TO CARVE UP THE ELEPHANT AND TAKE THE TUSKS!
TO BE CONTINUED

The Fantastic Four 1961

Stan Lee Jack Kirby

First published by Marvel Comics (USA)
Creators Lee (American, b.1922);
Kirby (American, 1917–94)
Genre Superhero **Adaptation** TV series (1967)

IND.
APPROVED BY THE COMICS CODE AUTHORITY
THE Fantastic FOUR
1 NOV.
10¢
I--I CAN'T TURN INVISIBLE FAST ENOUGH!! HOW CAN WE STOP THIS CREATURE, TORCH?
JUST WAIT AND SEE, SISTER! THE FANTASTIC FOUR HAVE ONLY BEGUN TO FIGHT!
FEATURING: "THE THING!" "MR. FANTASTIC!" "HUMAN TORCH!" "INVISIBLE GIRL!" TOGETHER FOR THE FIRST TIME IN ONE MIGHTY MAGAZINE!
THE THREE OF YOU CAN'T DO IT ALONE! IT'S TIME FOR THE THING TO TAKE A HAND!
IT'LL TAKE MORE THAN ROPES TO KEEP MISTER FANTASTIC OUT OF ACTION!

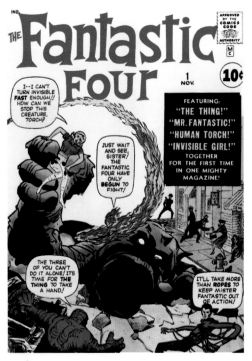

Similar reads
Challengers of the Unknown Jack Kirby
Justice League of America
Gardner Fox and Mike Sekowsky
The Avengers Stan Lee and Jack Kirby
The X-Men Stan Lee and Jack Kirby

In 1961 Atlas Comics was a small, struggling company. In a flash of inspiration, publisher Martin Goodman requested a superhero team book (echoing DC Comics's success with *Justice League of America*). It was assigned to editor/writer Stan Lee and plotter/artist Jack Kirby. "The Marvel Age of Comics" had dawned.

After a voyage in space and cosmic ray bombardment, scientist Reed Richards (Mr. Fantastic), his girlfriend Susan Storm (Invisible Girl), Sue's brother Johnny Storm (the Human Torch), and pilot Ben Grimm (the Thing) decide to use their newly acquired powers for the good of humanity as The Fantastic Four. For an amazing 102 issues, plus six new annual stories, Lee and Kirby chronicled their adventures monthly. From the start, they were different. Lee inserted more humor and soap opera than had been seen in superhero comics before. The bickering between the Human Torch and the Thing became a favorite theme among fans. The Thing, the only member permanently changed—into a huge, scaly monster—captured readers' imaginations. It always seemed possible his inner turmoil could turn into villainy.

Master villain Dr. Doom, Reed's former college mate, appeared in the fifth issue for the first of many stories. Doom was a twisted perfectionist who hid his scarred face behind a mask. His debut was the first "classic" of the run and remains a high point. As Kirby's imagination reached more grandiose peaks, the stories became increasingly fantastical. In a wonderful run of stories starting with issue #44, readers meet a hidden race of mutants named the Inhumans and see the coming of Galactus—a godlike alien who literally needs to eat planets to survive. The story, in issues #48 to #50, is widely regarded as the highlight of the run, and introduces the Silver Surfer as Galactus's herald, searching for planets for his master to consume. **CH**

The Fantastic Four do not hide their identities and enjoy the adulation of the public. ➡

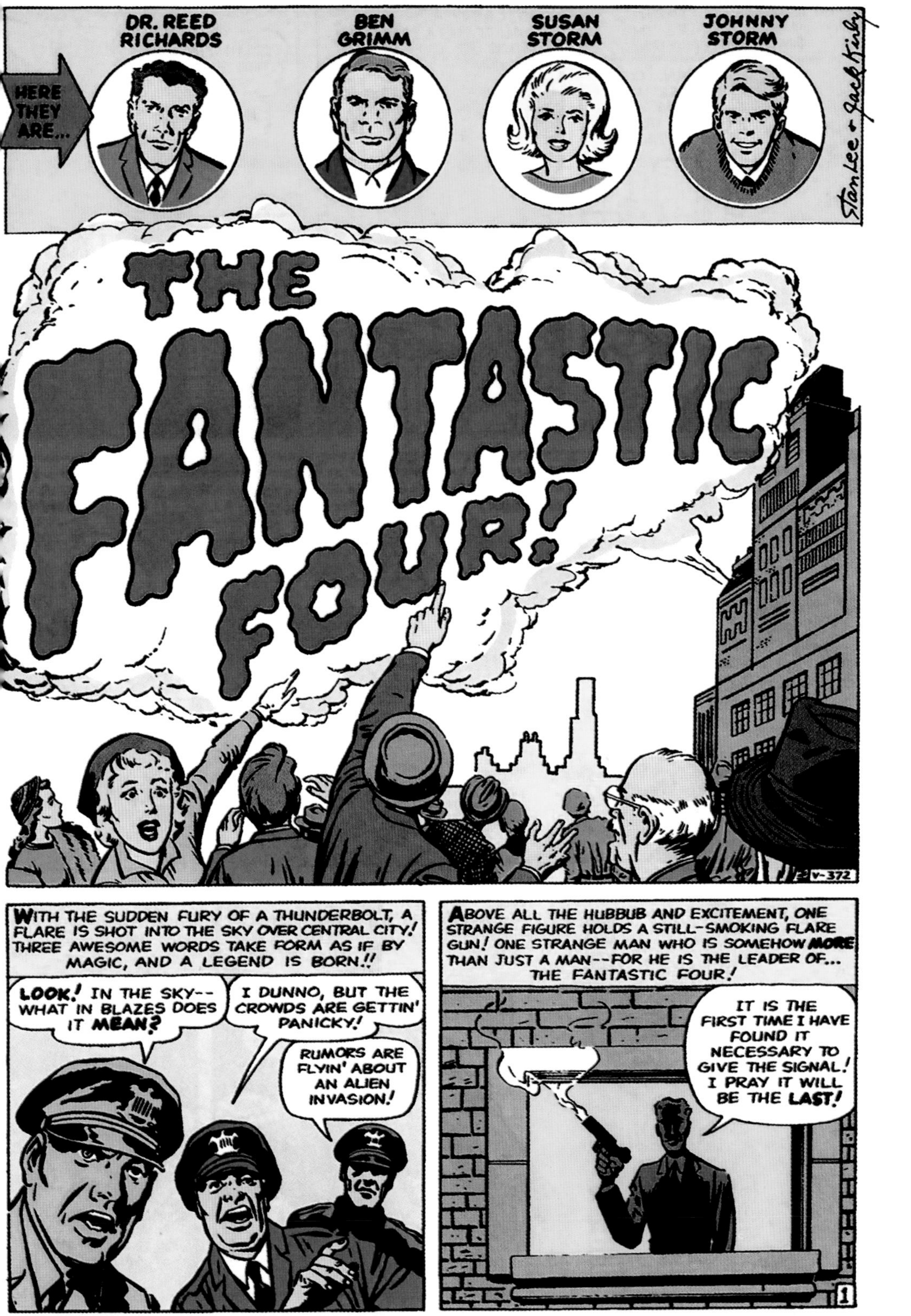

HERE THEY ARE...
DR. REED RICHARDS
BEN GRIMM
SUSAN STORM
JOHNNY STORM
Stan Lee + Jack Kirby
THE FANTASTIC FOUR!
V-372
WITH THE SUDDEN FURY OF A THUNDERBOLT, A FLARE IS SHOT INTO THE SKY OVER CENTRAL CITY! THREE AWESOME WORDS TAKE FORM AS IF BY MAGIC, AND A LEGEND IS BORN!!
LOOK! IN THE SKY-- WHAT IN BLAZES DOES IT MEAN?
I DUNNO, BUT THE CROWDS ARE GETTIN' PANICKY!
RUMORS ARE FLYIN' ABOUT AN ALIEN INVASION!
ABOVE ALL THE HUBBUB AND EXCITEMENT, ONE STRANGE FIGURE HOLDS A STILL-SMOKING FLARE GUN! ONE STRANGE MAN WHO IS SOMEHOW MORE THAN JUST A MAN--FOR HE IS THE LEADER OF... THE FANTASTIC FOUR!
IT IS THE FIRST TIME I HAVE FOUND IT NECESSARY TO GIVE THE SIGNAL! I PRAY IT WILL BE THE LAST!
1

The Death of Superman 1961

✐ Jerry Siegel ✐ Curt Swan

First published by DC Comics (USA)
Creators Siegel (American, 1914–96);
Swan (American, 1920–96)
Genre Superhero

Nowadays, death and resurrection are commonplace events in the superhero world. But in 1961, contemplating the mortality of superbeings—never mind that of Superman, the first and greatest superhero—was as unwholesome as the thought of shooting a president.

Still, one can understand why the idea of bumping off Superman appealed to writer Jerry Siegel. He had surrendered any claim to the character on his debut in 1938, then watched as Superman appeared not only in market-leading comic books but also in movies, newspaper strips, radio serials, and on a heap of merchandising that generated millions for publisher National (DC) comics. In 1961, Siegel was still grinding out Superman scripts with artist Curt Swan under the tyrannical hand of editor Mort Weisinger, who had controlled Superman's comic book universe since the mid-1950s.

In an effort to extend the narrative possibilities of the Superman formula, Weisinger hit on the idea of the "Imaginary Story," special tales that existed outside the standard rules and continuity of the comic. It was under this banner that "The Death of Superman" appeared, with the previously invincible superhero felled by his arch-nemesis Lex Luthor. The concluding section of this three-part strip opens with Superman laid to rest in a glass coffin, his demise mourned by a parade of humans and aliens. The intensity of feeling is understated but very real, so much so that in the final panel an editorial voice tells shell-shocked readers, "Well, let's not feel too badly! After all, this was only an imaginary story. . . . And the chances are a million to one that it will never happen!" **AL**

Spy vs. Spy 1961

✐✐ Antonio Prohías

First published by EC Comics (USA)
Creator Cuban (1921–98)
Genre Humor
Adaptation TV (1995)

Faced with the end of the free press in his native Cuba and tarred as a spy by Fidel Castro, cartoonist Antonio Prohías found himself out of a job. Instead of sticking around to see whether he would be jailed or simply censored, Prohías set out with his family for New York City. There he fell in with the crew behind *MAD Magazine*, the seminal humor magazine, and invented two immortal characters—the eternally warring, fedora-wearing saboteurs of *Spy vs. Spy*.

The concept behind *Spy vs. Spy* is simple—a spy clad in white tries to obliterate a spy clothed in black—and vice versa. They are identical in every respect—their long, pointed noses, their hats, their trenchcoats—but they are also sworn enemies. One of the most popular features in *MAD Magazine*, *Spy vs. Spy* appealed both for its encapsulation of the paranoia and pointlessness of the Cold War arms race, and for the sheer inventiveness of the destruction the spies inflict on one another.

Unusual in the United States, where wordless comics are relatively rare, *Spy vs. Spy's* silence adds to its elegant air of mystery. The mute format suited both the gags—leaving the focus on the ever more complicated booby-traps the spies use to blow each other up—and Prohías, who came to the United States speaking little English. Continued today by alternative cartoonist Peter Kuper (a founding editor of *World War 3 Illustrated*), readers can be sure that *MAD Magazine* has found an artist who understands the ironies underlying this classic strip—but who, just as importantly, can make readers laugh. **DI**

Spirou and Fantasio
Z is for Zorglub 1961

André Franquin

Title in original language *Z comme Zorglub*
First published by Dupuis (Belgium)
Creator Belgian (1924–97)
Genre Adventure

LES AVENTURES DE SPIROU ET FANTASIO 15
Z
COMME
ZORGLUB

In *Z is for Zorglub,* reporters Spirou and Fantasio become involved in a sequence of strange incidents masterminded by the mysterious scientist Zorglub. Intent on world domination, Zorglub uses the mind-controlling ray (Zorglwave) he has invented to build himself an army and set up a worldwide network of secret bases, using stolen technology. He wants Spirou and Fantasio's old friend, rival scientist Champignac, to work with him. Champignac, however, turns down his offer and Zorglub retaliates by kidnapping Fantasio. Champignac, having developed a protection against Zorglub's mind-control weapon, takes Spirou to Zorglub's headquarters, frees Fantasio, and drugs Zorglub into giving up his dreams of world domination.

Creator André Franquin continues the story in *The Shadow of Z.* When Spirou, Fantasio, and Champignac return home, they find a lone remaining member of Zorglub's army wreaking havoc. A few months later, Zorglub resurfaces, having reverted to his old ways. They trace him to his South American jungle base, and in the ensuing struggle Zorglub's mind is destroyed by his own experimental weapon.

At first glance, Spirou and Fantasio appear to take a back seat in their own adventures, yet it is their presence, and that of the vivid secondary characters, that anchors this duel of scientific geniuses to a human level and injects a great deal of humor. The fast-paced storyline warns against the possible misuses of modern science while poking fun at all authority figures, including that of bumbling would-be dictator Zorglub. **J-PJ**

"Do I have to tell you once again, Champignac, that only the universe offers the genie Zorglub a playing field big enough for him?"

Also by André Franquin
Pirates of Silence
Prisoner of the Buddha
The Moray's Keep
The Nest of the Marsupilamis
The Passenger of the Mésozoic

Bristow 1961

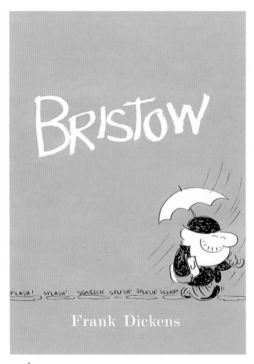

Frank Dickens

First published by *Evening Standard* (UK)
Creator British (b.1932)
Genre Humor
Adaptation Radio (1999)

BRISTOW
SPLASH! SPLASH' SQUELCH' SPLASH' SPLASH' SLURP
Frank Dickens

Similar reads
Albert Herbert Hawkins Frank Dickens
Andy Capp Reg Smythe
Augusta Angus McGill and Dominic Poelsma
The Gambols Dobs and Barry Appleby
The Perishers Maurice Dodd and Dennis Collins

Years before the television series *The Office* was even a glint in the eye of its creator Ricky Gervais, *Bristow* by Frank Dickens was making the workplace a great situation for comedy. Appearing every weekday in the London *Evening Standard* newspaper from 1962 to 2001 (and online at www.frankdickens.com ever since), the bowler-hatted Bristow is the epitome of the British postwar blue-collar worker. Eighteenth in line to become chief buyer in the monolithic Chester Perry organization, Bristow spends much of his working day doing anything but work. He is far too busy with other tasks: writing his magnum opus, *Living Death in the Buying Department*, playing table-top football with his colleague Jones, avoiding the wrath of his fearsome boss

"So I'll tell him I overslept. No! Why should I make excuses? I'm not afraid of him!"

Fudge, reminiscing about "the great tea trolley disaster," or planning his new career as a top brain surgeon.

According to Dickens, "My strip was originally conceived as an instruction on motor car maintenance," but by the time *Bristow* debuted in the *Aberdeen Press and Journal* on September 18, 1961, the basic, unequal struggle between the daydreaming protagonist and the crushing forces of conformity was already in place. The early strips are very crude, although Dickens's absurdist imagination and flair for punning dialogue are evident. By the strip's 1970s heyday, the artist had refined his ink line, settling into a pleasing visual shorthand of rounded faces and bodies occupying minimal interiors, ensuring that the strip's vast cast was instantly recognizable. All long-running comics have to be sustained by variations on a handful of scenarios. For more than fifty years, *Bristow* has done this better than most. **AL**

The Flash
Flash of Two Worlds 1961

✎ Gardner Fox ✎ Carmine Infantino and Joe Giella

In 1961, when this story was published, superheroes had been making a comeback at DC Comics for a few years. Updated versions of 1940s characters—a new The Flash and a new Green Lantern—had become the stars of their own comic books.

The Flash is the fastest man alive—not only does he run extremely fast, he can quite literally walk through walls by vibrating his own molecules. *Flash of Two Worlds* is based on the premise that this vibrating trick—performed by The Flash at a show he has been giving to local orphans—catapults him into another world much like his own. There, he meets the original Flash from the 1940s, whose adventures he had read as a boy and had been his inspiration for taking on The

"I can't tell you how excited I am to be going off on a case with my boyhood hero!"

Flash identity. It turns out that the two superheroes inhabit parallel worlds that "vibrate at different speeds." The modern-day Flash has turned up just in time to help his older namesake come out of retirement and stop three of his old adversaries—the Thinker, the Shade, and the Fiddler.

Flash of Two Worlds is a delightful example of the gentle lunacy that was prevalent during the superhero renaissance of the late 1950s. The characters' incredible powers are really magical, but have a pseudoscience veneer. During the story, The Flash surmises that when the original *Flash* writer Gardner Fox "was asleep, his mind was 'tuned in' on your vibratory Earth! That explains how he 'dreamed up' The Flash!" For preteen readers of the time, bringing together two generations of superheroes was both a novel and exciting concept. **J-PJ**

First published by DC Comics (USA)
Creators Fox (American, 1911–86); Infantino (American, b.1925); Giella (American, b.1928)
Genre Superhero

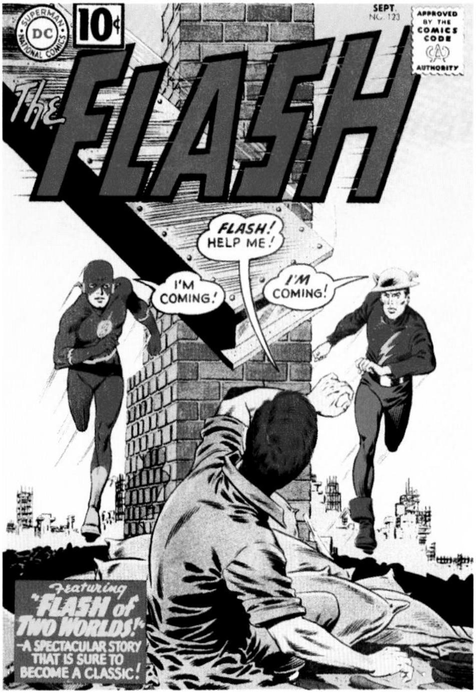
10¢
SEPT. NO. 123
APPROVED BY THE COMICS CODE AUTHORITY
THE FLASH
FLASH! HELP ME!
I'M COMING!
I'M COMING!
Featuring "FLASH of TWO WORLDS!" —A SPECTACULAR STORY THAT IS SURE TO BECOME A CLASSIC!

Similar reads

Fantastic Four Stan Lee and Jack Kirby
Justice League of America: Crisis on Earth-One! / Crisis on Earth-Two! Gardner Fox and Mike Sekowsky
The Flash: Vengeance of the Immortal Villain Gardner Fox and Carmine Infantino

Sa-lo-món 1961

Santiago "Chago" Armada

First published by Ediciones R. (Cuba)
Creator Cuban (1937–95)
Genre Humor
Influenced by Saul Steinberg

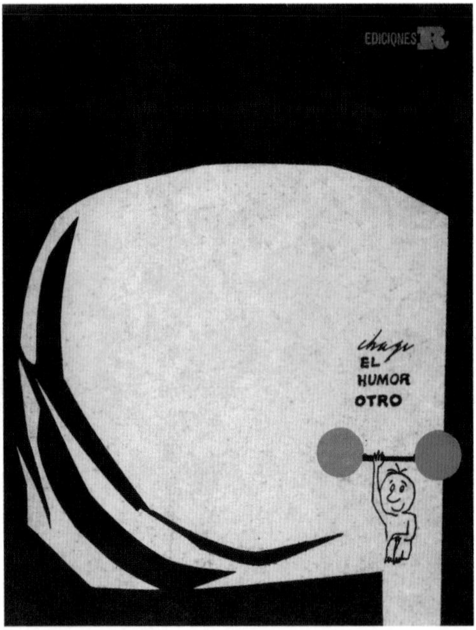
EDICIONES R
chago
EL
HUMOR
OTRO

Similar reads
Sabino Rafael Fornés
The Lonely Man (Hombre Solo) Antonio Mingote
The Lonely Ones William Steig
The Passport Saul Steinberg
Troya's Horse (El Caballo de Troya) René de la Nuez

Santiago "Chago" Armada was, according to Caridad Blanco de la Cruz, an "artist, humorist, cartoonist, sketcher, painter, designer, essayist, and poet." He was part of the Ejército Rebelde (Rebel Army) that fought Fulgencio Batista's dictatorship in Cuba.

In 1958 Chago Armada created his first comics characters: these were Julito 26 (he was named after Fidel Castro's liberation movement, M-26-7) and Juan Casquito. They appeared in the rebels' newspaper *El Cubano Libre* (*The Free Cuban*).

In 1960 cartoonist Rafael Fornés (creator of *Sabino*) founded the supplement *El Pitirre* (*The Kingbird*) of the newspaper *La Calle* (*The Street*), in which, influenced by Saul Steinberg, Armada began his conceptual (some would say, intellectual) humor. The process led a year later to his emblematic creation, *Sa-lo-món*, which was published in the newspaper *Revolución* (*Revolution*) from 1961 to 1963. Publication was ended (along with Fornés' *Sabino*) because Armada's philosophical, existential, and poetical work was quite different from the usual attack on North American imperialism, albeit at times humorous, then expected of Cuban cartoonists.

Sa-lo-món started as a very simple caricature and remained so until the end, but he gained a three-winged hat and, later, became a kind of blob from which a nib, a rifle, and a penis emerge. With *Sa-lo-món* Armada experimented with the form of comics, even to the extent of abstraction. He wanted to explore every aspect of the human condition (which, again according to Caridad Blanco, consists of "love, nothingness, existence, death, morals, ethics"). He also wanted to explore sex and eschatology: *la kaka* (the poo-poo).

Unfortunately, no *Sa-lo-món* compilation has yet appeared. Seventeen of the series' strips were published in *El Humor Otro* (*Another Kind of Humor*) in 1963 and thirty-three were published in *Signos* #21 in 1978. **DI**

With *Sa-lo-món*, Armada experimented with the form of comics. ➡

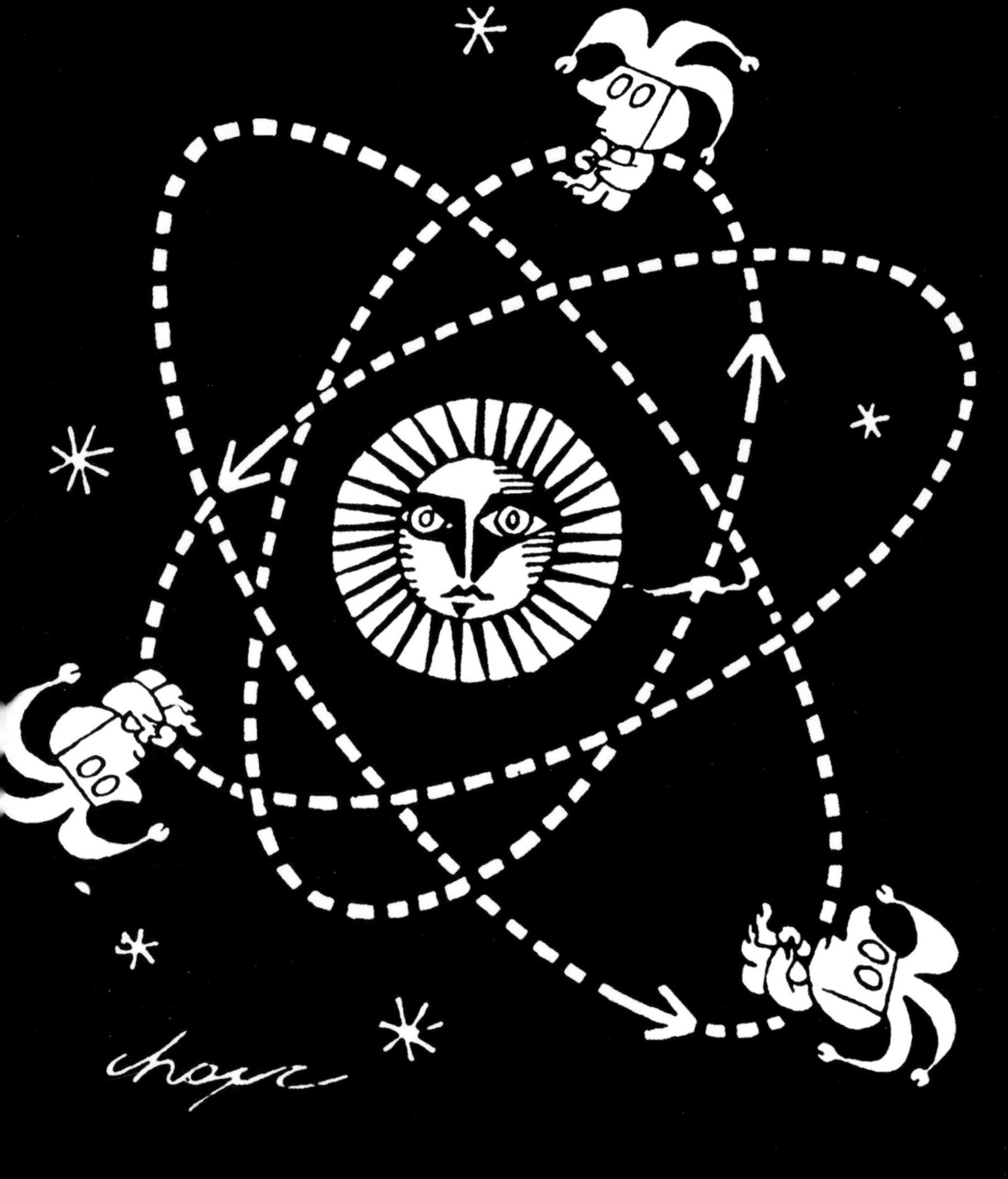

Sam's Strip 1961

✏ Mort Walker ✏ Jerry Dumas

First published by King Features Syndicate (USA)
Creators Walker (American, b.1923);
Dumas (American, b.1930)
Genre Humor

Many comics use self-referential jokes occasionally, but *Sam's Strip* is quite unique in the history of comics. A traditional comic strip, handled by one of the largest comics syndicates in the world, it was ahead of its time in that it was a metacomic. The main character, Sam, is himself a comic strip writer.

Sam's Strip was the brainchild of powerhouse comic strip creator Mort Walker, who was responsible for *Beetle Bailey, Hi and Lois, Boner's Ark,* and many others. When he was at his most productive, Walker worked on six strips simultaneously, and his studio was nicknamed "King Features West," since it supplied the King Features Syndicate with several of its most successful comic strips. Walker developed the idea for *Sam's Strip* together with his assistant Jerry Dumas, and they pitched it to King Features, who reluctantly added it to their list. Unfortunately, the humor proved too eclectic for a wide audience, and the experiment lasted only until 1963.

Sam is very much aware that he is a character in a comic strip. He talks directly to the reader, plays cards with characters from other strips, such as Dagwood and Snuffy Smith, harasses the cartoonist for poorly drawn images, and draws himself (badly). *Sam's Strip* was a comic strip for comics lovers, and clearly represented a breath of artistic freedom for Walker and Dumas, after having worked for some time on more traditional strips. Political comments about the contemporary period also feature prominently, making *Sam's Strip* a surefire hit for comics aficionados and history buffs alike. **FS**

Mort Cinder 1962

✏ H. G. Oesterheld ✏ Alberto Breccia

First published by Editorial Yago (Argentina)
Creators Hectór Germán Oesterheld (Argentinian, 1919–77); Breccia (Uruguayan, 1919–93)
Genre Fantasy

Life was difficult for Alberto Breccia and Hectór Germán Oesterheld during the early 1960s. The latter was facing the loss of his publishing company, Editorial Frontera, while the former's first wife was seriously ill. They both needed work and found it at *Misterix* magazine. Out of their collaboration there, *Mort Cinder* was born.

The concept for *Mort Cinder* (*morte* means "death" in Spanish) was simple: he is an immortal being who suffers many deaths only to be reborn each time. This gave Oesterheld sufficient latitude to place his character in many different ages and places in history, from Egypt to World War I. Usually the stories begin with the arrival of an artifact in the shop of Chelsea antiquarian Ezra Winston. The artifact then awakens memories in Cinder's mind, and these memories fuel his stories. *Mort Cinder* is the heir apparent to a couple of characters previously created by Oesterheld: time traveler Juan Salvo and space detective Sherlock Time. The series' stories are dark and pessimistic: they depict the horrors of war and the claustrophobic atmosphere of a prison. Mort himself originally started life as someone who was to be executed as a murderer.

Breccia drew the character of Ezra Winston as a much older version of himself, whereas Mort Cinder's face was based on the artist's assistant Horacio Lalia. With *Mort Cinder*, Breccia completely changed his style. He experimented with razor blades and other unorthodox instruments that he used to mark the drawing surface. His influence can be seen in the work of José Muñoz and Frank Miller, among others. **DI**

Breccia's chiaroscuro is expressionistic and masterfully executed. ➡

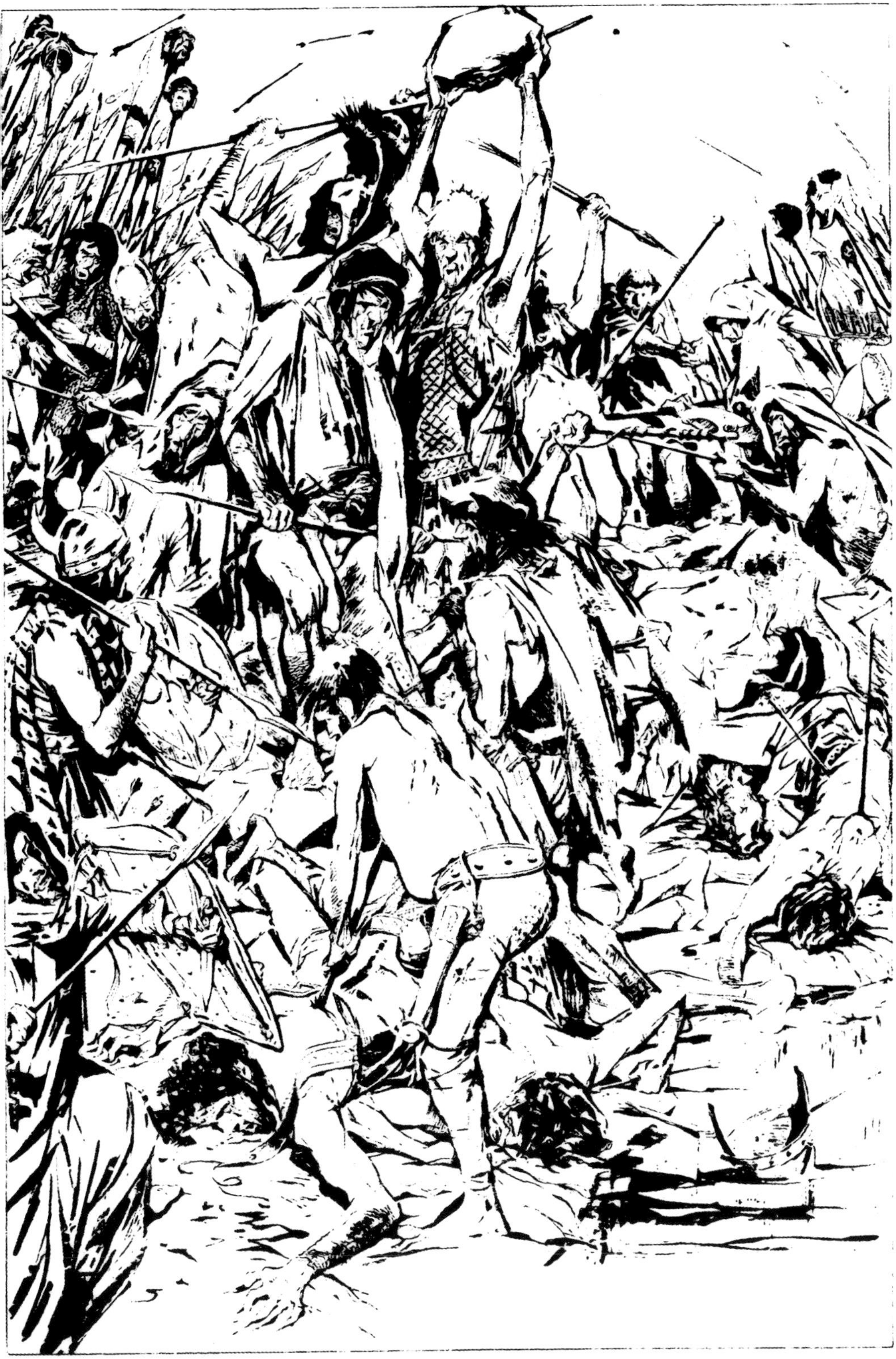

R. GOSCINNY **Astérix** A. UDERZO

Astérix gladiateur

Texte **René GOSCINNY**

Dessins **Albert UDERZO**

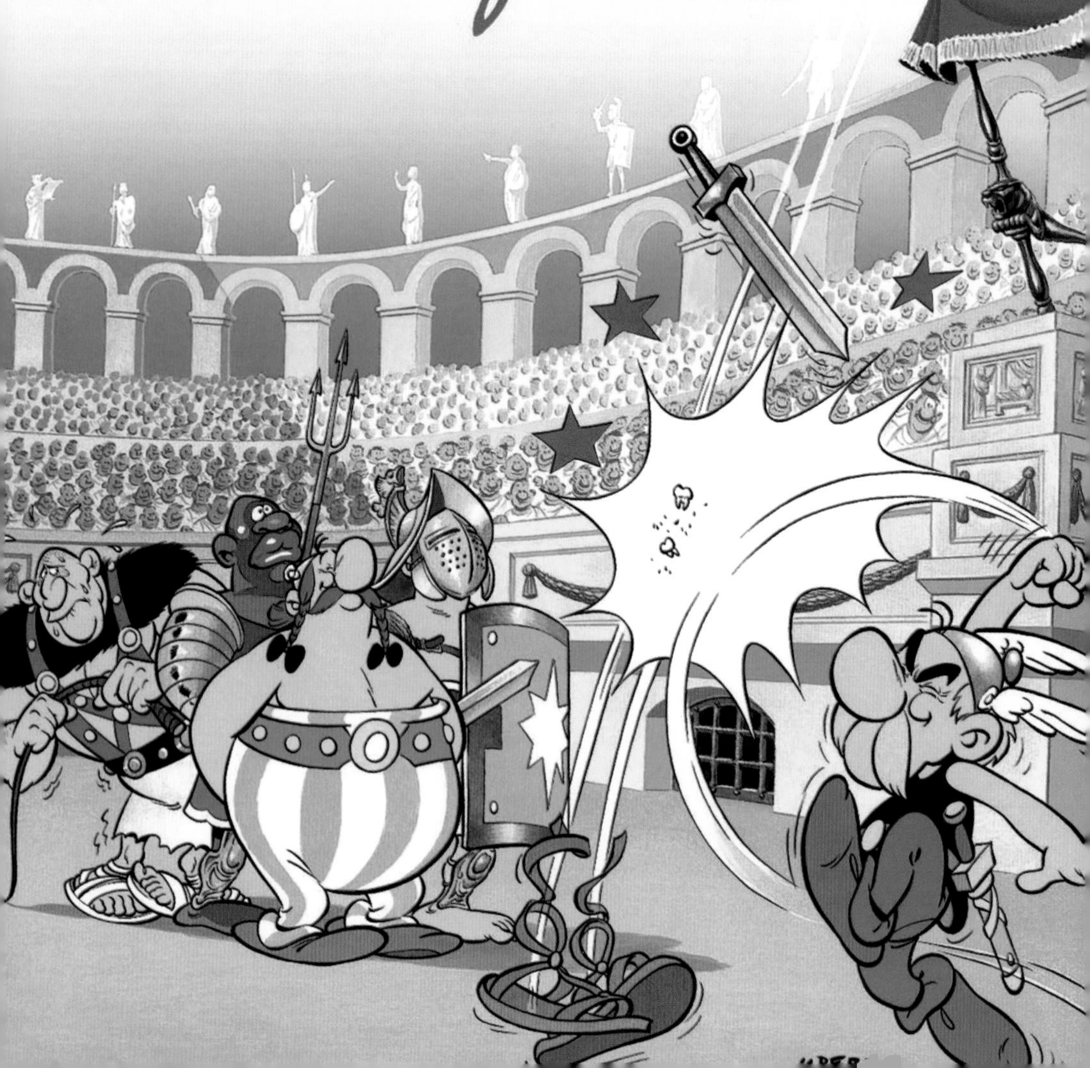

Asterix the Gladiator 1962

✐ René Goscinny ✐ Albert Uderzo

Title in original language *Asterix gladiateur*
Pre-published by *Pilote* (France, 1962) **First published by** Dargaud (France, 1964) **Creators** Goscinny (French, 1926–77); Uderzo (French, b.1927) **Genre** Humor

In 1949 the French passed a law banning the import of U.S. comic books, which had dominated the French market ever since GIs brought them to Europe in World War II. It was felt that the French comic industry needed an injection of patriotism, and in 1959 that injection came in the form of a diminutive, shrewd Gaul named Asterix. His sidekick is the tall, obese Obelix, whose unlimited strength is only matched by his appetite.

Asterix the Gladiator is the fourth volume in the perennially popular *Asterix* series. It is an "away" adventure, taking place not in France but in Rome. Asterix and Obelix sail on a Phoenician merchant ship from their rebel village on the Brittany coast to Rome. There they sign up as gladiators in order to infiltrate the catacombs and release their imprisoned village bard, Cacofonix, who is soon to be thrown to the lions.

Albert Uderzo's talent for taking historical settings and using them to make thinly veiled social commentary is seen when Asterix and Obelix visit a block of apartments that bear an uncomfortable resemblance to modern-day high-density living. The residents bicker and complain about the noise.

This volume includes the introduction of pirates, who appear in almost every subsequent book; the debut of Geriatrix, the oldest member of the village; and gladiator trainer Odius Asparagüs, based on a friend of the author's, who becomes the first "affectionate" caricature of the series. Obelix also begins to build his collection of Roman helmets and first utters the immortal phrase: "These Romans are crazy!" **BS**

Heros the Spartan 1962

✐ Tom Tully ✐ Frank Bellamy

First published by Hulton Press (UK)
Creators Tully (British, Unknown); Bellamy (British, 1917–76)
Genre Adventure

Heros the Spartan is notable for being the crowning early achievement of Frank Bellamy, a British comic book artist who became one of the chief architects of Gerry Anderson's science fiction creations, as depicted in *TV21*. *Heros* transplanted the *Eagle*'s moral values to the world of the first-century Roman Empire. Heros—a Greek orphan adopted by a Roman general—becomes a Roman soldier who lives by his own high ethical code. He worships the god Mithras—a mysterious religion that was widely practiced among Roman soldiers and was believed by some to resemble Christianity. Heros's strong morals frequently bring him into conflict with corrupt or decadent officials of the empire—as well as barbarians who threaten the *Pax Romana*.

Bellamy's artwork soars far above the requirements of Tully's relatively straightforward scripts, just as Bellamy's work also outshines the unsophisticated storylines of *TV21*. The double-page format, with panels running straight across the gutter, created its own rhythm, which suited the vigorous action and dynamically busy panels characteristic of Bellamy's art. His tendency to tell a story as a series of action-packed tableaux, punctuated by reflective moments framed in circular panel borders, also complemented the quietly moralizing tone of Heros, whose adventures function as a series of moral fables.

The sheer exuberance and fluidity of Bellamy's lines and painted colors, plus the inventiveness of his panel layouts, make one wish that he had produced more work for an adult readership. **RR**

The Steel Claw 1962

Kenneth Bulmer Jesús Blasco

First published by IPC Magazines (UK)
Creators Bulmer (British, 1921–2005); Blasco (Spanish, 1919–95)
Genre Science fiction

STEEL CLAW
#1 IN A FOUR PART MINI-SERIES
THE STEEL CLAW
QUALITY COMICS
NO1
DEC. 75¢
CAN. $1.10
Ten seconds ago
Lewis Randell was a man
...NOW HE'S A NIGHTMARE!
UNITED KINGDOM 60p

"The world will fear me now! They'll know I can do what I promise . . . and I'll make them pay!"

When the editors were first putting together the boys' adventure comic *Valiant,* they had thought that the blustering commando Captain Hercules Hurricane would be the star, but over the years The Steel Claw became the title's best-loved character. Interestingly, when he first appeared, The Claw's alter ego Louis Crandell/Lewis Randell was anything but lovable. In fact, he was a scheming, callous criminal.

Crandell is a young laboratory assistant with a steel right hand, the result of an accident, who turns invisible (except for his claw) when another experiment goes wrong and electrocutes him. Rather than dedicating himself to fighting crime, his first thought is to go out and rob a bank, and he embarks on a trail of destruction as he plots world domination. Author Kenneth Bulmer was primarily a science fiction novelist, and the strip clearly borrows from the story of H. G. Wells's *Invisible Man,* transported to contemporary Britain.

After the first serial Crandell was rehabilitated and became a more conventional hero, particularly after Bulmer was replaced by industry veteran Tom Tully in 1963. Tully wrote the series until its cancellation ten years later. His tenure saw The Claw tackle an increasingly outlandish gaggle of villains, such as Boulderman, Mr. No-Face, and The Vulture. What made the strip so readable, though, was the astonishing art of Jesús Blasco, whose photo-realistic style gave the strip a credibility its stories did not always deserve.

When Blasco left in the late 1960s, the strip deteriorated, although his return in 1971 coincided with its finest hour. The year-long "Lektrons" serial borrowed heavily from John Wyndham's *Midwich Cuckoos*, right down to the menacing children creating an air of rural horror. *The Steel Claw* was successful in translations across Europe, largely because of Blasco's artwork and his iconic image of the disembodied hand. **DAR**

Diabolik 1962

Angela and Luciana Giussani   Various

In the first issue of *Diabolik*, "The King of Terror" introduced one of the most famous and iconic antiheroes in Italian comics: a master thief dressed in an all-black costume who is interested in precious jewelry and huge amounts of money. His targets are mainly wealthy families, banks, or criminally enriched people. In every episode *Diabolik* devises clever techniques to scare his victims; he rarely uses firearms, preferring daggers, poison, and a variety of traps. Although a criminal, Diabolik has a strong ethical code: he is a modern, dark, ambiguous Robin Hood figure. He hates gangsters, drug dealers, extortionists, and torturers; he rarely kills, kidnaps, or blackmails, always taking into consideration honor, friendship, and gratitude. With the third episode of the series he had a talented partner in crime, his fiancée, the beautiful, blond Eva Kant. Eva's intelligence and independence made her a popular female role model, who featured in successful advertising campaigns.

Diabolik's amorality soon became, controversially, one of the reasons for his huge popularity. In fact the series helped establish a new subgenre of Italian comics—the *fumetti neri*—which focuses on antiheroes and villains. Some psychological and visual elements of *Diabolik* were inspired by the French crime novel series *Fantômas*. But the idea came to sisters Angela and Luciana Giussani as they observed the reading habits of Milan's commuters, who are heavy readers of crime fiction. *Diabolik* is well-known as the first comic book to use the digest "Italian pocketbook" format (4¾ x 6¾ in. / 12 x 17 cm).

A movie adaptation, *Danger: Diabolik*, directed by Italian horror master Mario Bava, is considered one of the best pop art films of the 1960s. Remembered for its costumes and set designs, it was heavily influenced by pop art, optical art, and psychedelia. **MS**

First published by Astorina (Italy)
Creators Angela Giussani (Italian, 1922–87); Luciana Giussani (Italian, 1928–2001)
Genre Crime

IL FUMETTO DEL BRIVIDO
DIABOLIK
IL RE DEL TERRORE
ROMANZO COMPLETO
LIRE 150

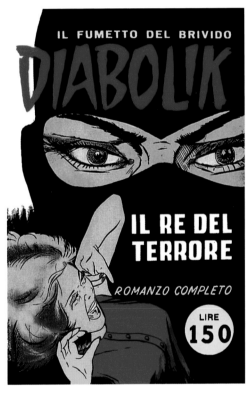

"You can feel a satisfaction not entirely peaceful (and therefore more exciting) in rooting for the bad guy."

Umberto Eco, literary critic and novelist

The Incredible Hulk 1962

Stan Lee and others   Jack Kirby, Steve Ditko, and others

First published by Marvel Comics (USA)
Creators Lee (American, b.1922);
Kirby (American, 1917–94)
Genre Superhero

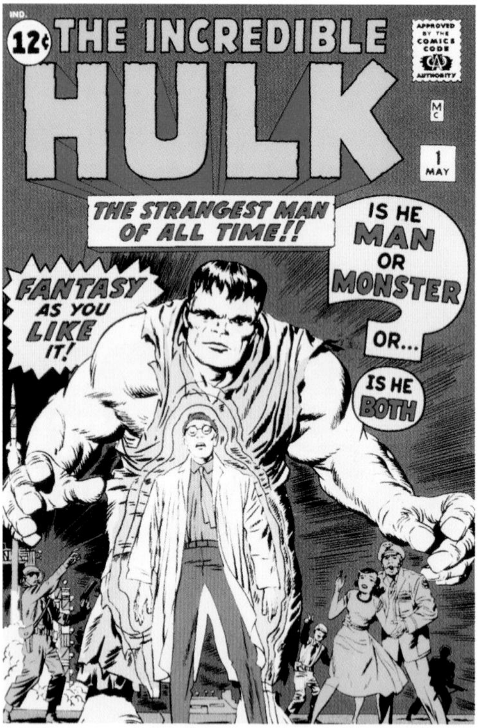

12¢
THE INCREDIBLE HULK
APPROVED BY THE COMICS CODE AUTHORITY
1 MAY
THE STRANGEST MAN OF ALL TIME!!
IS HE MAN OR MONSTER OR... IS HE BOTH
FANTASY AS YOU LIKE IT!

"The world hates the Hulk! They hunt me . . . hound me . . . try to destroy me! Why?"

Perhaps the most incredible thing about *The Incredible Hulk* is that this behemoth of the Marvel Comics universe was not an immediate success when he was launched in his own comic in 1962. Stan Lee and Jack Kirby were then at the top of their game, but the Hulk represented a daring departure even for Marvel's outstanding creative team. Here was a lead character in a superhero-oriented title that was completely devoid of the typical characteristics of a hero.

Bruce Banner, leading U.S. nuclear scientist, is testing his latest invention, the Gamma Bomb. Shortly before the bomb is due to explode, he becomes aware that a teenager (Rick Jones) has wandered into the test area. In saving Jones, Banner exposes himself to a massive dose of radiation from the bomb. Recovering in hospital, Banner experiences his first transformation into an immensely powerful, angry, and intellectually challenged monster: the Hulk. Subsequent issues recount Banner's attempts to prevent his transformations, General "Thunderbolt" Ross's relentless pursuit of the Hulk, and various crises when his strength and bravery become an unexpected force for good. Yet, surprisingly, after only five issues, the Hulk was relegated to being a backup character or antagonist in other character-led comic books.

These guest appearances cemented the Hulk's popularity with fans, and he subsequently returned in his own strip in 1968. He also gained a television series, turned temporarily gray, acquired a female counterpart (She-Hulk), and eventually starred in two movies of rather uneven quality. In 2002 the Hulk was given an outstanding reinvention in Mark Millar's *The Ultimates*.

The Hulk is a key character in the Marvel universe. As a symbol of subconscious rage released by a Faustian pact with nuclear technology, the Hulk is unsurpassed in contemporary narrative or mythology. **RR**

Thor 1962

✎ Stan Lee ✎ Jack Kirby

Dr. Donald Blake carries a walking stick that, when tapped on the ground, transforms him into the Norse god of thunder. It might not sound a promising idea, yet *Thor* became one of the finest comics of the 1960s. A devotee of mythology, Jack Kirby had used Norse gods in his earlier work, so it is not surprising that, as the Marvel Age of Comics snowballed, this would be among the deluge of concepts. "The Mighty Thor" debuted in 1962, in issue #83 of *Journey into Mystery*, immediately becoming the star feature. Kirby did not draw all the early stories, but he soon settled into a seven-year run from issue #101.

Other Asgardian characters, such as Thor's father, Odin, and evil half-brother Loki, were introduced early on but were seldom used effectively. The series often defaulted to standard superheroics. Then something happened. A series of backup stories from issue #97—*Tales of Asgard*—appeared. A mixture of Norse mythology, imaginative interpretation, and more fantastical aspects began to leak into the lead feature. Scripter Stan Lee also gave Thor and company a quasi-Shakespearean manner of speech—a much-debated approach that undoubtedly proved distinctive.

In issue #1 of the *Journey into Mystery* annual and continuing in issue #126, when it was retitled *Thor*, Greek mythology also featured with the appearance of Hercules. An outstanding run of books followed in issues #129 to #135, which introduced an alien race, the Rigellians, Ego the Living Planet (the cells of his surface become deadly humanoid marauders), and Kirby's unique take on Doctor Moreau, the High Evolutionary. After this astonishing outpouring of ideas, showing Kirby at his peak, the pace arguably slackened, but with many highlights, including an epic Ragnarok (*Death of the Gods*) story in issues #154 to #157 and an extended Galactus storyline in issues #160 to #169. **CH**

First published by Marvel Comics (USA)
Creators Lee (American, b.1922); Kirby (American, 1917–94)
Genre Superhero

IND.
12¢
JOURNEY INTO
MYSTERY
APPROVED BY THE COMICS CODE AUTHORITY
MC
83 AUG.
INTRODUCING... THE MIGHTY THOR!
THE MOST EXCITING SUPER-HERO OF ALL TIME!!
BEGIN THE SAGA OF THOR IN THIS ISSUE!

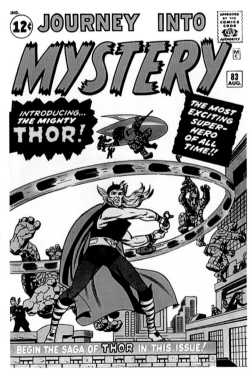

"In the name of omnipotent Odin—in the name of eternal Asgard. . . ."

Little Annie Fanny 1962

✏ Harvey Kurtzman ✏ Bill Elder

First published by Playboy Enterprises (USA)
Creators Kurtzman (American, b.1924);
Elder (American, b.1921)
Genre Adult humor, Parody

After the failure of the Hugh Hefner–published *Trump*, Harvey Kurtzman began working on this strip for Hefner's flagship magazine. *Little Annie Fanny*, a thinly veiled parody of Harold Gray's *Little Orphan Annie*, was a Candide-like figure—an exaggeratedly well-endowed blond, naive to the predatory sexual ways of men. The strip was originally conceived as a monthly feature, but Kurtzman was unable to maintain that level of productivity, and it appeared only occasionally in the magazine, skewering topical concerns ranging from Beatlemania and nudist resorts to Gay Liberation and the Ku Klux Klan.

The appeal of *Little Annie Fanny* resides in the convergence of *Playboy*'s adult satiric sensibility and the unusually high standard of the art. Taking advantage of the magazine's high-quality paper, Kurtzman enlisted Bill Elder to illustrate the strip in a fully painted style that set it apart from the poorly colored, flat illustrations dominating U.S. comic books at the time. Elder's carefully crafted panels provided the strip with a tremendous visual density, cramming in visual jokes almost to the breaking point and providing a manic sensory overload in every installment.

The golden age of the *Little Annie Fanny* strip coincided with the sexual revolution of the late 1960s and early 1970s, when Annie's adventures frequently involved her burgeoning feminist friend, Wanda Homefree. In retrospect, *Little Annie Fanny* reads as if it were from a time capsule as it satirically depicts the struggle between the sexes and the centrality of sex in shaping the American sensibility. **BB**

Barbarella 1962

✏✏ Jean-Claude Forest

First published by *V-Magazine* (France)
Creator French (1930–98)
Genre Science fiction
Adaptation Film (1968)

In a distant future, the young and very pretty Barbarella roams exotic planets and strange worlds where she has exciting adventures with all kinds of weird creatures: men, fantasy animals, extraterrestrials, robots, and so on. However, it was not because of their strangeness and their fantastic qualities that the saga of Barbarella left such a mark on its readers; it was more because of the personality of its heroine. Independent and free, she travels from planet to planet pursuing countless amorous encounters with charm and vitality, and looks for every opportunity to satisfy her desires.

Entirely dedicated to freedom, pleasure, and love, the episodic series conceived by Jean-Claude Forest made a radical break from the customs and practices that were prevalent at the time. French comics' first successful embodiment of an emancipated woman responsible for her choices, the character of Barbarella had all the traits necessary to become an icon, although her escapades in space and her suggestive outfits may, with the passage of time, seem restrained today.

Initially published in *V-Magazine*, Barbarella's adventures were collected and published in 1964 in an anthology. However, it was the cinema that put the character—the pioneering heroine of an adult episodic series, finally freed of its childish limitations—into the limelight. Adapted for the big screen by Roger Vadim in 1968, with Jane Fonda in the lead role, Forest's strip cartoon became one of the symbols of the turbulent 1960s, when many were keen to get rid of moral, social, and sexual constraints and conventions. **NF**

BARBARELLA

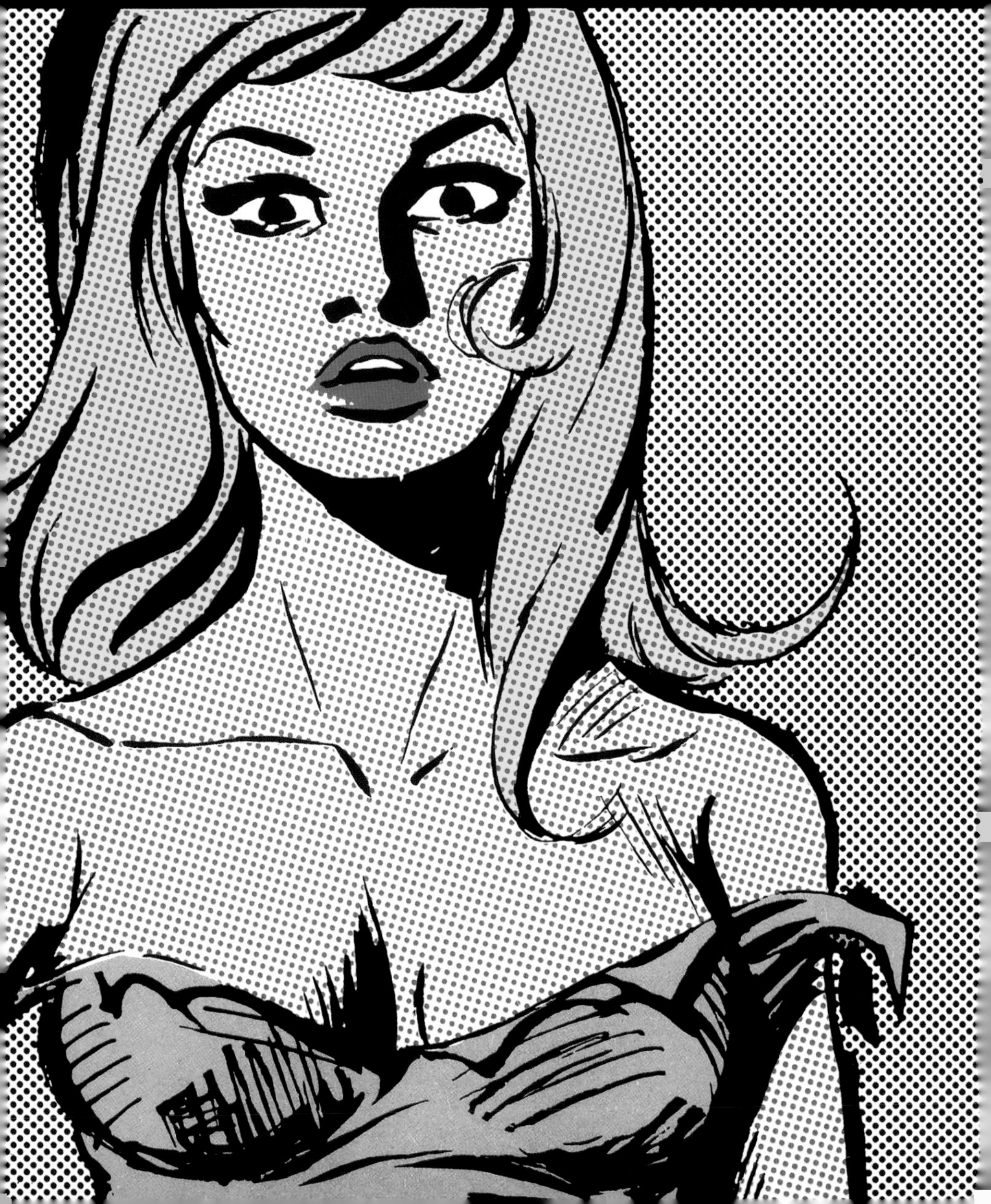

The Amazing Spider-Man 1963

Stan Lee   Steve Ditko

First published by Marvel Comics (USA)
Creators Lee (American, b.1922);
Ditko (American, b.1927)
Genre Superhero

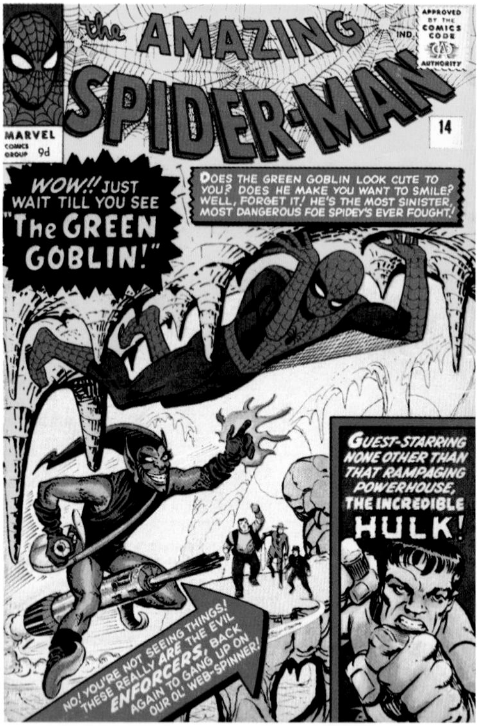
the AMAZING SPIDER-MAN
APPROVED BY THE COMICS CODE AUTHORITY
IND.
MARVEL COMICS GROUP 9d
14
WOW!! JUST WAIT TILL YOU SEE "The GREEN GOBLIN!"
DOES THE GREEN GOBLIN LOOK CUTE TO YOU? DOES HE MAKE YOU WANT TO SMILE? WELL, FORGET IT! HE'S THE MOST SINISTER, MOST DANGEROUS FOE SPIDEY'S EVER FOUGHT!
GUEST-STARRING NONE OTHER THAN THAT RAMPAGING POWERHOUSE, THE INCREDIBLE HULK!
NO! YOU'RE NOT SEEING THINGS! THESE REALLY ARE THE EVIL ENFORCERS, BACK AGAIN TO GANG UP ON OUR OL' WEB-SPINNER!

"Can they be right? Am I really some sort of crack-pot, wasting my time seeking fame and glory?"

Spider-Man first appeared in *Amazing Fantasy* issue #15—a title slated for immediate cancellation and therefore a suitable showcase for experiment. Stan Lee and Steve Ditko—both at their most inspired—created Marvel's first (and most successful) antihero. Bitten by a radioactive spider, Peter Parker's initial impulse is to use his newly acquired superpowers to make a fast buck. Only the death of Parker's Uncle Ben at the hands of a criminal whom Spider-Man allowed to go free steers him in the direction of fighting crime.

There had been earlier examples of antiheroes in superhero comics, such as Plastic Man, or, in a different sense, the Martian Manhunter. Yet Spider-Man's misadventures were chronicled by Lee and Ditko with a relentless emotional logic and a keen eye for the detail of the story's suburban setting. Everything is an uphill struggle for Parker: earning a living in order to support his widowed Aunt May, working his way through college, dealing with his irascible boss J. Jonah Jameson, or fighting an array of supervillains with a marked tendency to mirror Parker's misfit status. Dr. Octopus, the Green Goblin, the Lizard, the Sandman, Electro—no hero ever battled such a rogue's gallery of disturbed individuals.

Ditko's artwork for *The Amazing Spider-Man* is unique. His spiky lines and flattened perspectives look bizarre enough with *Dr. Strange*, but *Spider-Man* is a series grounded in suburban reality. Ditko makes teenage suburbia appear so exotic that the transformation of Peter Parker into Spider-Man never jars our sensibilities. *Spider-Man*'s subsequent evolution is far too intricate to detail here, but the three *Spider-Man* movies from 2002 to 2007 have wisely returned to the texture of the Lee–Ditko years. This fidelity to the character and his milieu puts the films among the most effective and successful superhero movies released to date. **RR**

The Avengers 1963

Stan Lee Jack Kirby

First published by Marvel Comics (USA)
Creators Lee (American, b.1922);
Kirby (American, 1917–94)
Genre Superhero

The Avengers began life as Marvel's response to DC Comics's success with the all-star superhero format of *Justice League of America*. Marvel's first superhero team—*The Fantastic Four*—featured characters specially created for the new title (albeit partly based on existing heroes), but *The Avengers* initially comprised characters who already had their own books: Iron Man, The Hulk, Thor, Ant Man, and The Wasp. In issue #4, Captain America himself was rediscovered, frozen in ice like Rip Van Winkle and oblivious to everything that had happened since 1944. The superhero genre was being revived, in all its golden age glory.

The rotating and evolving active membership of *The Avengers* quickly established a unique atmosphere for their stories. Not every Marvel superhero had what it takes to become an Avenger—even Spider-Man was turned down. But others, such as Hawkeye, Quicksilver, and the Scarlet Witch—with ambiguous or even villainous pasts—were admitted. The arrival of the Vision—an android—and his romance with, and eventual marriage to, the Scarlet Witch opened up powerful themes of diversity and tolerance. The theme of traditional masculinity under pressure was also explored through the troubled marriage of Yellowjacket (aka Ant Man) and the Wasp.

The team's semiofficial relationship with the U.S. government has also informed storylines. In the 1970s, the Avengers—with their collective ethic of heroic self-sacrifice—struggled to come to terms with the cynical attitude to political leaders that became widespread in the United States in the decade after the Vietnam war and Watergate. Writers such as Steve Englehart and Jim Shooter used *The Avengers* to reflect the political mood of the day. Mark Millar's *Ultimates* series continues to explore the intriguing question of a superhero team's relationship with government. **RR**

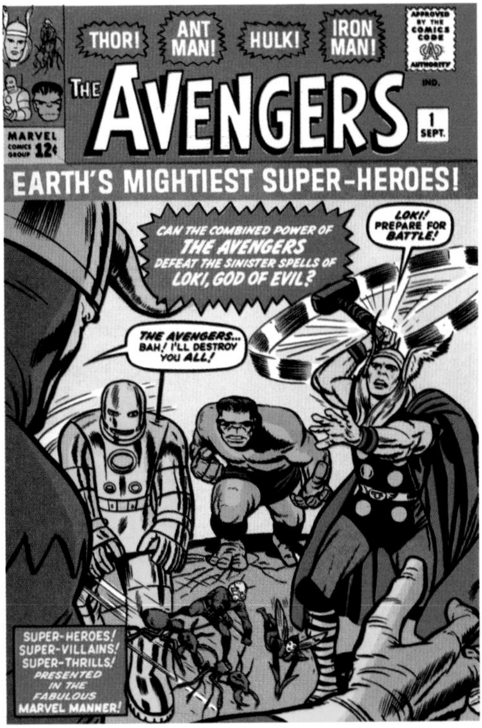
THOR!
ANT MAN!
HULK!
IRON MAN!
APPROVED BY THE COMICS CODE AUTHORITY
THE AVENGERS
MARVEL COMICS GROUP 12¢
IND.
1 SEPT.
EARTH'S MIGHTIEST SUPER-HEROES!
CAN THE COMBINED POWER OF THE AVENGERS DEFEAT THE SINISTER SPELLS OF LOKI, GOD OF EVIL?
LOKI!! PREPARE FOR BATTLE!
THE AVENGERS... BAH! I'LL DESTROY YOU ALL!
SUPER-HEROES! SUPER-VILLAINS! SUPER-THRILLS! PRESENTED IN THE FABULOUS MARVEL MANNER!

"Each of us has a different power! If we combined forces, we could be almost unbeatable!"

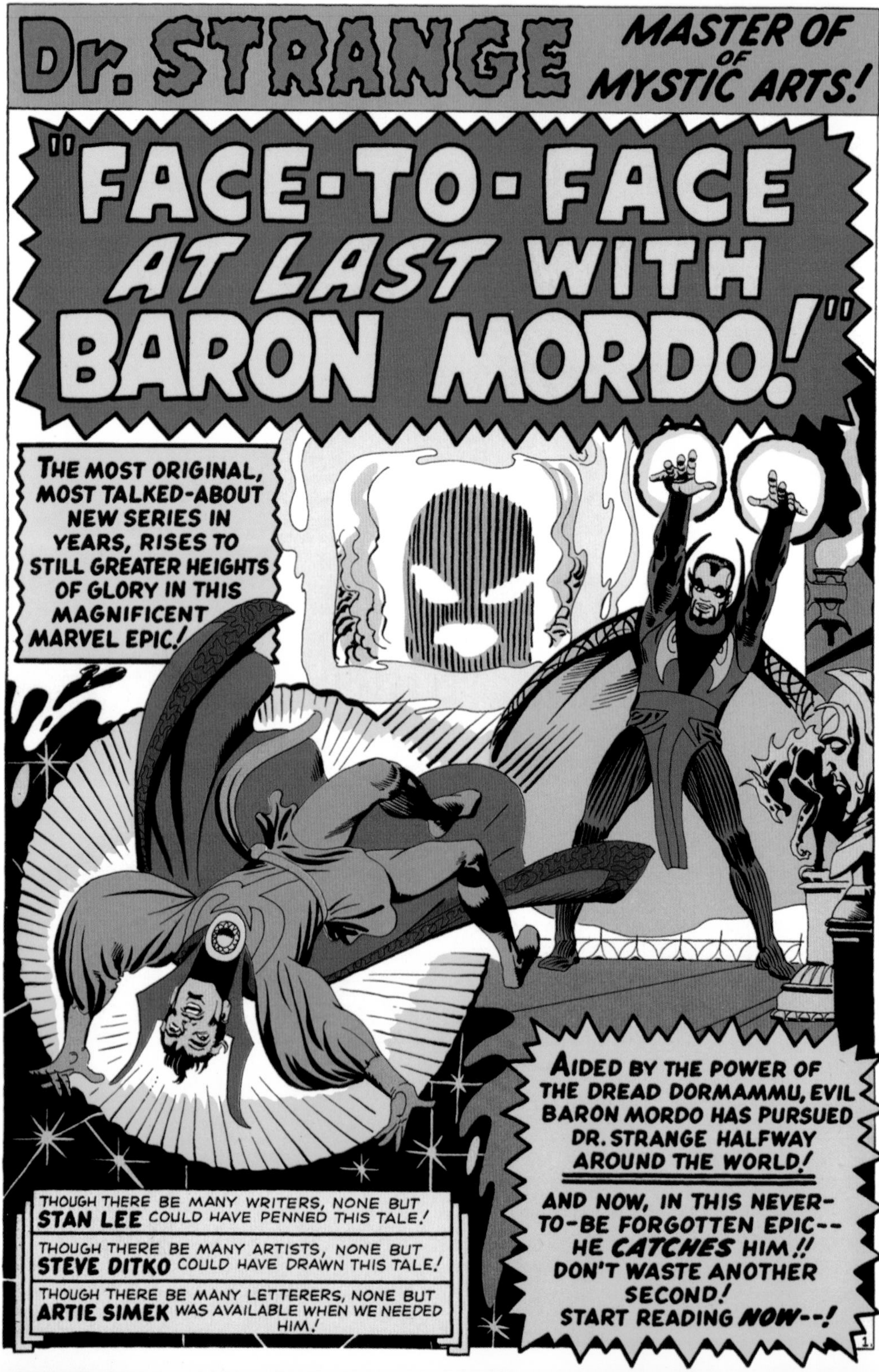
Dr. STRANGE MASTER OF MYSTIC ARTS!
"FACE-TO-FACE AT LAST WITH BARON MORDO!"
THE MOST ORIGINAL, MOST TALKED-ABOUT NEW SERIES IN YEARS, RISES TO STILL GREATER HEIGHTS OF GLORY IN THIS MAGNIFICENT MARVEL EPIC!
AIDED BY THE POWER OF THE DREAD DORMAMMU, EVIL BARON MORDO HAS PURSUED DR. STRANGE HALFWAY AROUND THE WORLD!
AND NOW, IN THIS NEVER-TO-BE FORGOTTEN EPIC-- HE CATCHES HIM!! DON'T WASTE ANOTHER SECOND! START READING NOW--!
THOUGH THERE BE MANY WRITERS, NONE BUT STAN LEE COULD HAVE PENNED THIS TALE!
THOUGH THERE BE MANY ARTISTS, NONE BUT STEVE DITKO COULD HAVE DRAWN THIS TALE!
THOUGH THERE BE MANY LETTERERS, NONE BUT ARTIE SIMEK WAS AVAILABLE WHEN WE NEEDED HIM!
1

Dr. Strange 1963

✎ Stan Lee   ✎ Steve Ditko

First published by Marvel Comics (USA)
Creators Lee (American, b.1922);
Ditko (American, b.1927)
Genre Superhero

On the heels of *Spider-Man*'s success, the team of Stan Lee and Steve Ditko turned their gaze toward the supernatural. Lee himself once said, "'Twas Steve's idea." Whatever the case, Dr. Strange (who made his debut in *Strange Tales* issue #110) was the perfect showcase for the wilder side of Ditko's visual imagination.

Stephen Strange is an arrogant surgeon who suffers an accident that ruins the tools of his trade—his hands. He treks to the Himalayas in search of a cure, encountering an elderly guru known as the Ancient One. Discovering the treachery of the Ancient One's pupil, Baron Mordo—who becomes a recurring foe in the series—Strange finds his inner hero and becomes a student of "the mystic arts."

Residing in his Sanctum Sanctorum in New York, Strange battles a procession of mystical opponents, his astral self often traveling to other planes of reality—giving Ditko the chance to draw many otherworldly, abstract, fabulously inventive landscapes. The visuals were beyond anything he had done before and created a hugely distinctive style template that has been much imitated. Lee reveled in the opportunity to compose numerous rhyming incantations, some of which are corny but give the strip a strong sense of identity.

Another regular foe was Dread Dormammu, a memorable figure whose head is a ball of flames. The second Dormammu epic (issues #130–146), featuring Eternity—an amazing Ditko visual of an entity representing the universe—ran for the rest of Ditko's tenure, and is the high point of a truly superb series. **CH**

Magnus: Robot Fighter 1963

✎✎ Russ Manning

First published by Gold Key Comics (USA)
Creator American (1929–81)
Genre Superhero
Award Comic Book Hall of Fame (2006)

Magnus: Robot Fighter was unusual in its attempt àt creating a coherent view of the future. The strip was set in the year 4000, in a world where robots control all aspects of society, including a subservient human race. Magnus has been raised from birth by a friendly robot named A1, and, after years of martial arts training, is able to crush metal with his bare hands.

In the first issue of his comic he defeats the despotic Pol-Rob (police robot) H8, freeing the population from years of oppression. In subsequent issues Magnus encounters a steady stream of fanciful, robotic human and alien foes, such as Mekman, the Robot Ghost, and Octo Rob. In developing his vision of the far future, writer and artist Russ Manning imagined a vast continent-spanning, vertiginous metropolis called North Am. The city was starkly divided into a wealthy, penthouse-dwelling elite—or cloud-cloddies—and the poor but cunning gophs, who subsist in its stygian lower levels. Interestingly, Magnus, and perhaps Manning, identify with the glamorous aristocracy, while the poverty-stricken gophs are depicted as irredeemably treacherous and ugly.

Visually the strip was seductively sleek, rendered with almost perfect brushstrokes. Rather eccentrically, Manning clothed Magnus in a pink, Romanesque, chain-mailed tunic, without any pants, and drew his girlfriend Leeja wearing a see-through dress. The comic ran for fourteen years, but Manning left after twenty-one issues to draw *Tarzan*. His interpretation of Magnus remains the definitive one. **DAR**

← The visuals for *Dr. Strange* had a surreal, psychedelic quality.

Modesty Blaise 1963

Peter O'Donnell / Jim Holdaway and others

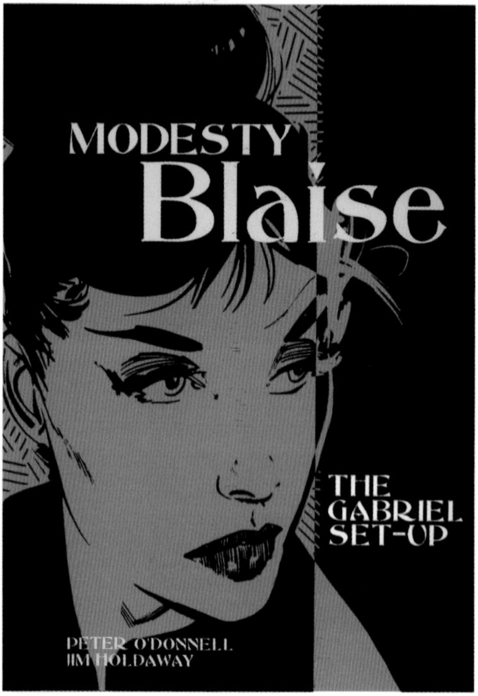
MODESTY
Blaise
THE GABRIEL SET-UP
PETER O'DONNELL
JIM HOLDAWAY

"Name's Modesty Blaise, out from England on a solo vacation, and she's keeping it solo. Rigorous tests have been made."

Similar reads
Garth Peter O'Donnell and Steve Dowling
Rip Kirby Alex Raymond
Romeo Brown Peter O'Donnell and Jim Holdaway
The Seekers Les Lilley and John M. Burns
Tug Transom Peter O'Donnell and Alfred Sindell

First published by Beaverbrook Newspapers (UK)
Creators O'Donnell (British, 1920–2010); Holdaway (British, 1927–70)
Genre Adventure

Modesty Blaise, at least in its first seven years when drawn by Jim Holdaway, is possibly the best ever daily adventure strip. Although she is sometimes referred to as a female James Bond, Modesty is not actually a spy. However, she often engages in freelance missions for Sir Gerald Tarrant of the British secret service.

In the first story, "La Machine," beautiful and wealthy former criminal Modesty Blaise and her cockney sidekick Willie Garvin are growing bored of their quiet lives. Inveigled into an assignment by Tarrant, they begin an exciting new life fighting (mainly) on the side of the law. Many stories refer to their shared past. Modesty's origins, which Peter O'Donnell based on a real refugee girl, are revealed in the short strip "In the Beginning."

Modesty and Willie possess their own strict moral code. Their relationship is based on total loyalty and an almost telepathic closeness of mind; they have no romantic or sexual longing for each other whatsoever. They are both fantastic characters with amazing mental and physical prowess, shown in their fighting and survival skills. The stories have intricate plots featuring plenty of gimmicks and taut cliff-hangers. Yet O'Donnell's writing is so skillful that readers always remain involved and convinced, and there are plenty of emotional moments, too.

Jim Holdaway excelled on *Modesty Blaise*: his photo-realism and mastery of the sketchy pen-and-ink line complemented the scripts brilliantly. Neville Colvin was his best successor, although Enrique Badia Romero drew more *Modesty* strips than any other artist. **GL**

Adventures of Tintin

The Castafiore Emerald 1963

✐✐ "Hergé"

Title in original language *Les Bijoux de la Castafiore*
First published by Casterman (Belgium)
Creator Georges Prosper Remi Remi (Belgian, 1907–83)
Genre Adventure

"The Castafiore Emerald" is Hergé's masterpiece, an astonishing work that deconstructs the codes of the adventure genre upon which the entire *Tintin* series had been based. In this album, the protagonists never leave home, and the crime under investigation—involving the loss (fantasized or real) of the diva's jewels—is a mere pretext for a series of red herrings. The real drama is provided by Captain Haddock's terror of Castafiore, a formidable female figure who is responsible, directly or indirectly, for a series of injuries and humiliations to the old sea dog.

Part of the work's importance lies in the amount of critical ink that it has generated, and the resulting acknowledgment of the medium itself as a worthy object of academic study. In 1970 the French philosopher Michel Serres described it as an exercise in the transformation of communication into noise, in keeping with Hergé's vision of modern media, as the propagation and circulation of misinformation is whipped up into a cacophony. Other theorists have focused on the psychological conflicts being enacted below the bland surface of everyday life at the Moulinsart château, which is depicted in Hergé's clear line style as a world without shadows.

A political reading can also be made: the album may be an attempt to dissipate the suspicion of racism that had clouded Hergé's reputation since his earlier works. Here he portrays a group of Romani as victims of racial prejudice, and as the origin of the only clear, pure, notes of music in the album. **AM**

Life? or Theater? 1963

✐✐ Charlotte Salomon

Title in original language *Leben? oder Theater?*
First published by Wanders Publishing (Netherlands)
Creator German (1917–43)
Genre Autobiography

Life? or Theater?—the title asks the question at the heart of this unique visual memoir by Charlotte Salomon, in which she draws her childhood in Berlin, her exile in France, and the discovery of her family's tragic secret. Salomon was born to a middle-class Jewish family in 1917 and attended Berlin Art Academy. With the rise of fascism, and the joint terrors of *Kristallnacht* and her father's arrest in 1938, Salomon was sent to her maternal grandparents in the South of France.

Arguably the first autobiographical comic, *Life? or Theater?* innovates as it straddles the genres of fine art, narrative, and music—so much so that Salomon coined the term *Dreifarben Singespiel*—"three-color songplay" to describe it. Created between 1941 and 1942 in a hotel in St. Jean Cap Ferrat, it is constructed from more than 700 pages of gouached pages and layers of tracing paper. Some pages have flowing texts; others have rich paintings of different sizes wrapped around each other like an intricate tapestry. Continuing monologues are presented through repeated drawings of protagonists, suggesting how a film could capture their speech.

The early pages are detailed and bright, whereas later ones seem hurried, urgent, and dulled in contrast. There is a sense that the artist knew she was running out of time. In 1943, married and pregnant, Salomon was sent to Auschwitz, where she died. *Life? or Theater?* is a memorial to the power of art and self-creation, to rise up amid the ruins of tragedy. Perhaps Salomon knew this when she gave the work to a friend before she was arrested: "Keep this safe. It is my whole life." **SL**

C Comics 1964

Various poets Joe Brainard

First published by Boke Press (USA)
Creator American (1942–94)
Genre Underground
Influenced by *The Nancy Book*

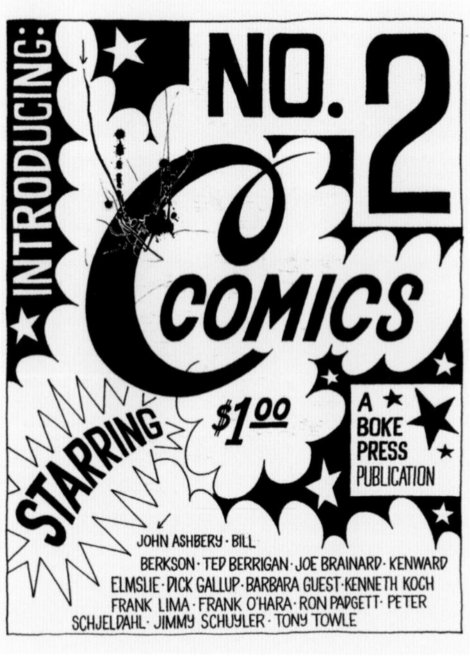
INTRODUCING:
NO. 2
C COMICS
STARRING
$1.00
A BOKE PRESS PUBLICATION
JOHN ASHBERY · BILL BERKSON · TED BERRIGAN · JOE BRAINARD · KENWARD ELMSLIE · DICK GALLUP · BARBARA GUEST · KENNETH KOCH FRANK LIMA · FRANK O'HARA · RON PADGETT · PETER SCHJELDAHL · JIMMY SCHUYLER · TONY TOWLE

Similar reads

Baffling Means Clark Coolidge and Philip Guston
How to Look... Ad Reinhardt
Joe Brainard: A Retrospective Constance M. Lewallen
So the Story Goes... Martin Fidler, Stephen Duncalf, Steve Wheatley, and Les Coleman

A leading light in the New York poetry community, Joe Brainard produced two issues of his collaborative *C Comics* in 1964 and 1965, offshoots of poet Ted Berrigan's *C Magazine*. Brainard chose to interfere with narrative continuity and introduce the element of chance by inviting poet friends to fit text into his existing sequences of drawings. This provided an opportunity for interpretation by the writer or often for a sense of disconnected randomness.

Described as a serious artist making nonserious art, Brainard's graphics show his interest in popular culture, with images of 1920s dancing couples, advertising symbols and logos, and references to gay magazines and comics characters—Ernie Bushmiller's Nancy being his favorite. He moved to New York in the late 1960s with poets Ted Berrigan, Dick Gallup, and Ron Padgett, all from Tulsa, Oklahoma. Brainard quickly became immersed in the poetry "scene," whose "mimeograph revolution" was driven by the poets themselves and reflected the spirit and politics of underground comix then emerging.

"C Comics is both an homage and a reinterpretation of the comic strip form."

Constance M. Lewallen, author and critic

All U.S. avant-garde poets of the day contributed to *C Comics*: Berrigan, Gallup, and Padgett, as well as John Ashbery, Bill Berkson, Kenward Elmslie, Barbara Guest, Kenneth Koch, Frank O'Hara, Peter Schjeldahl, and James Schuyler, among others. Disregarded by the poetry establishment of the period, this vanguard found more sympathy among painters, with Frank O'Hara acting as a go-between. Brainard continued his collaborations with poets until the 1980s. **LC**

C Comics was a unique collaboration between an artist and poets in the comic book medium.

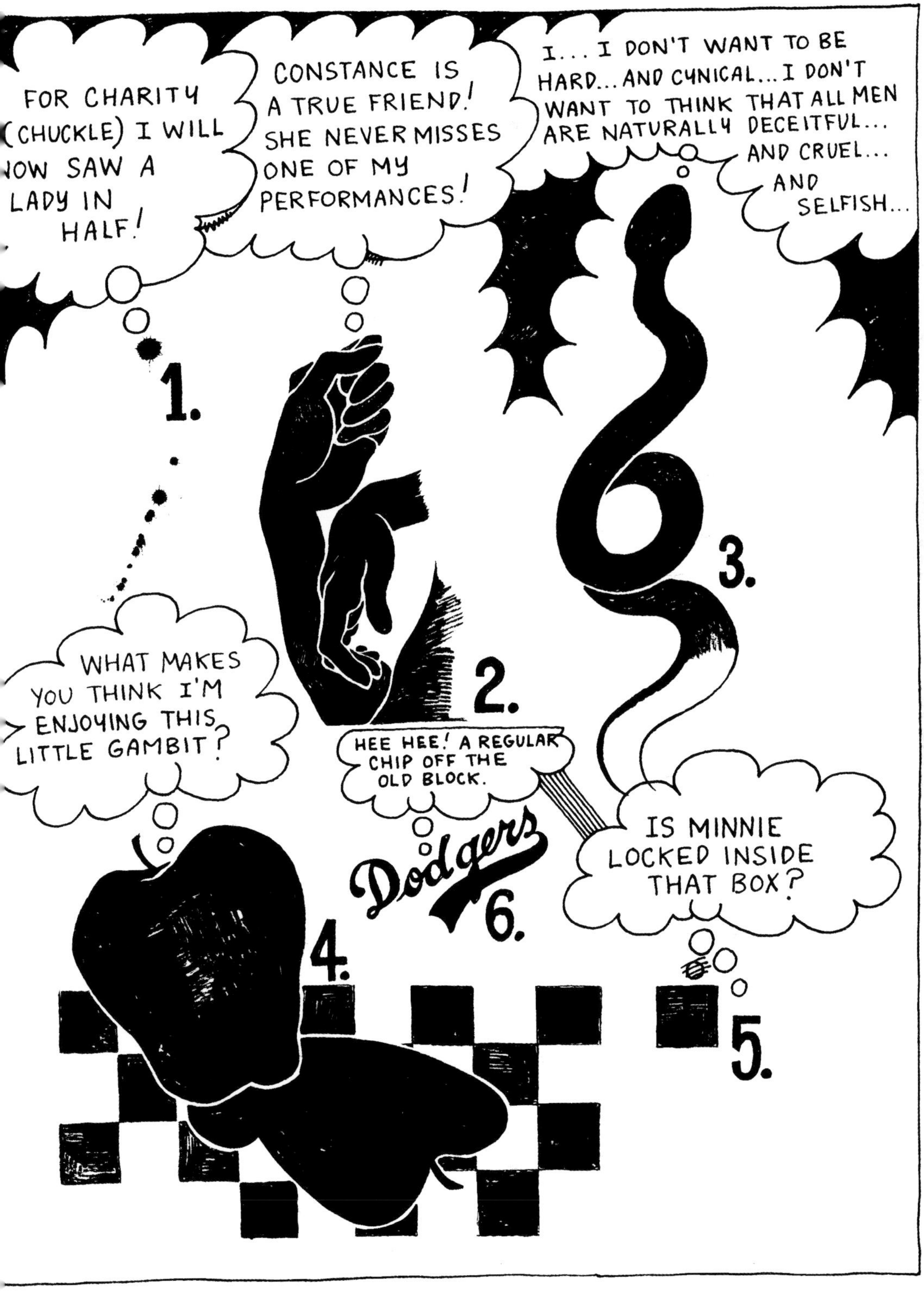
FOR CHARITY (CHUCKLE) I WILL NOW SAW A LADY IN HALF!
1.
CONSTANCE IS A TRUE FRIEND! SHE NEVER MISSES ONE OF MY PERFORMANCES!
2.
I... I DON'T WANT TO BE HARD... AND CYNICAL... I DON'T WANT TO THINK THAT ALL MEN ARE NATURALLY DECEITFUL... AND CRUEL... AND SELFISH...
3.
WHAT MAKES YOU THINK I'M ENJOYING THIS LITTLE GAMBIT?
4.
IS MINNIE LOCKED INSIDE THAT BOX?
5.
HEE HEE! A REGULAR CHIP OFF THE OLD BLOCK.
Dodgers
6.

Chaminou and the Khrompire 1964

✎✎ Raymond Macherot

Title in original language *Chaminou et le Khrompire*
First published by Dupuis (Belgium)
Creator Belgian (1924–92)
Genre Crime, Funny animal

Chaminou and the Khrompire takes place on the island of Zoolande, a civilization of anthropomorphic animals. Secret police agent Chaminou's vacation is interrupted by the news of a prison break by the dangerous throwback carnivore, the Khrompire. The Khrompire's escape has been engineered by state governor Crunchblott, a wolf, who wants to use him as a cover for his own animal-eating crimes. A chance meeting with an old friend, mouse prison guard Pépin, puts Chaminou on the trail, but he is soon kidnapped by Crunchblott and has a tough time foiling his plans.

This is both an adventure tale and a quirky satire. When the baddies want to make the Khrompire's appearance less conspicuous, a plastic surgeon turns him from a leopard into a very mouthwatering duck. Unfortunately for his flesh-eating cohorts, "only the shape has changed . . . It's still leopard flesh!" In an ironic twist on the consumer age, Crunchblott plots the kidnapping of a famous television personality, "merry Délysse pig," who advertises pasta, the only state-sanctioned food.

Raymond Macherot had already been successful with the *Chlorophylle* series about a country dormouse. But his new strip for Dupuis was very different and was met with incomprehension by the publisher: cynical and full of sophisticated humor, it centered on the power struggle within an animal society very like our own. Disappointed by the response, Macherot went on to create the *Sibylline* series about a strong-willed female mouse, which was much closer to *Chlorophylle*. **J-PJ**

The Wonderful World of Barry McKenzie 1964

✎ Barry Humphries ✎ Nicholas Garland

First published by *Private Eye* magazine (UK)
Creators Humphries (Australian, b.1934);
Garland (British, b.1935)
Genre Parody

Barry McKenzie was not supposed to be an Australian character; he was meant to be an Englishman—Alan Merryweather, in fact, from the north of England. It was Richard Ingrams, editor of the satirical London weekly magazine *Private Eye*, who thought McKenzie would work better as a culturally bereft Australian adrift in London. The character reflected all the caricatured portrayals of Australians.

Barry is an endearing, beer-guzzling lout—a "cultural terrorist," who urinates and copulates when and where he pleases. His creator, Barry Humphries, delighted in toying with the British perception of these Australian "colonials." The writing and imagery were unashamedly vulgar, with Humphries using euphemisms all but extinct even in Australia, such as "chunder," a little-used term among Sydney surfboarders meaning to vomit. Thankfully, British ignorance of Australian cultural norms allowed the publication of these and other scatological phrases. Despite being banned in Australia, *The Wonderful World of Barry McKenzie* was eagerly read in London by Australian ex-pats and travelers, as well as a growing core of English readers.

While Humphries wrote the dialogue—a blend of working-class chatter and schoolyard slang—political cartoonist Nicholas Garland supplied the inventive artwork. The brim of Barry's hat was borrowed from ANZACS Garland saw marching through Whitehall, and Barry's exaggerated chin was a homage to *The Dandy's* Desperate Dan. The strip was eventually canceled by *Private Eye* for its "tendency to go over the top." **BS**

Herbie 1964

"Shane O'Shea" Ogden Whitney

First published by American Comics Group (USA)
Creators Richard E. Hughes (American, 1909–74); Whitney (American, 1918–c.1970)
Genre Humor

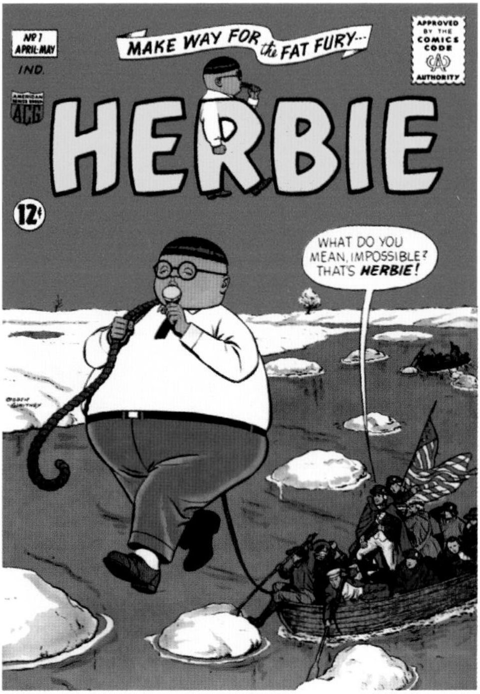

Nº 1 APRIL-MAY
IND.
MAKE WAY FOR the FAT FURY...
APPROVED BY THE COMICS CODE AUTHORITY
HERBIE
12¢
WHAT DO YOU MEAN, IMPOSSIBLE? THAT'S HERBIE!

The concept is this: an obese, lollipop-sucking kid with thick-lensed glasses can do anything, and the entirety of time and space is at his disposal. He speaks little, and in contracted fashion, yet animals and aliens can converse with him and accord him due respect. He is known to the famous and notorious, and the casually intoned threat of "Want me to bop you with this here lollipop?" usually ensures compliance. It is only Herbie Popnecker's parents who remain ignorant of their son's prowess. He made Cleopatra swoon, folk-danced for Soviet leader Khruschev, and spun dinosaurs by the tail, yet to his father Herbie is perennially "a fat little nothing."

This is an extraordinarily surreal strip of the type usually associated with a single creator, not a synthesis. When he launched this inspired lunacy in a 1958 issue of *Forbidden Worlds*, Richard E. Hughes had been almost single-handedly writing the output of American Comics Group for years, using assorted aliases to conceal the truth. It has even been suggested that "Hughes" itself was a further alias to distance him from anti-Semitism. Hughes benefited from the imposition of the Comics Code, transforming his writing into the imaginatively humorous to comply with its strictures, and *Herbie* exaggerated this whimsical style.

Ogden Whitney apparently based Herbie's look on his own boyhood form. His art is perfectly structured, with an uncommon flatness, as if his intention was to ensure every panel was bland and two-dimensional. This works in combination with the preposterous scripts for maximum humor. **FP**

"Lollipops. Have all flavors but hard to get cinnamon. Hard to get."

Similar reads
Arsenic Lullaby Doug Paszkiewicz
Brother Power the Geek Joe Simon
Flaming Carrot Bob Burden
Forbidden Worlds Richard E. Hughes and others
Les dents du recoin François Boucq

カムイ伝

1

夙谷の巻

赤目プロ
白土三平

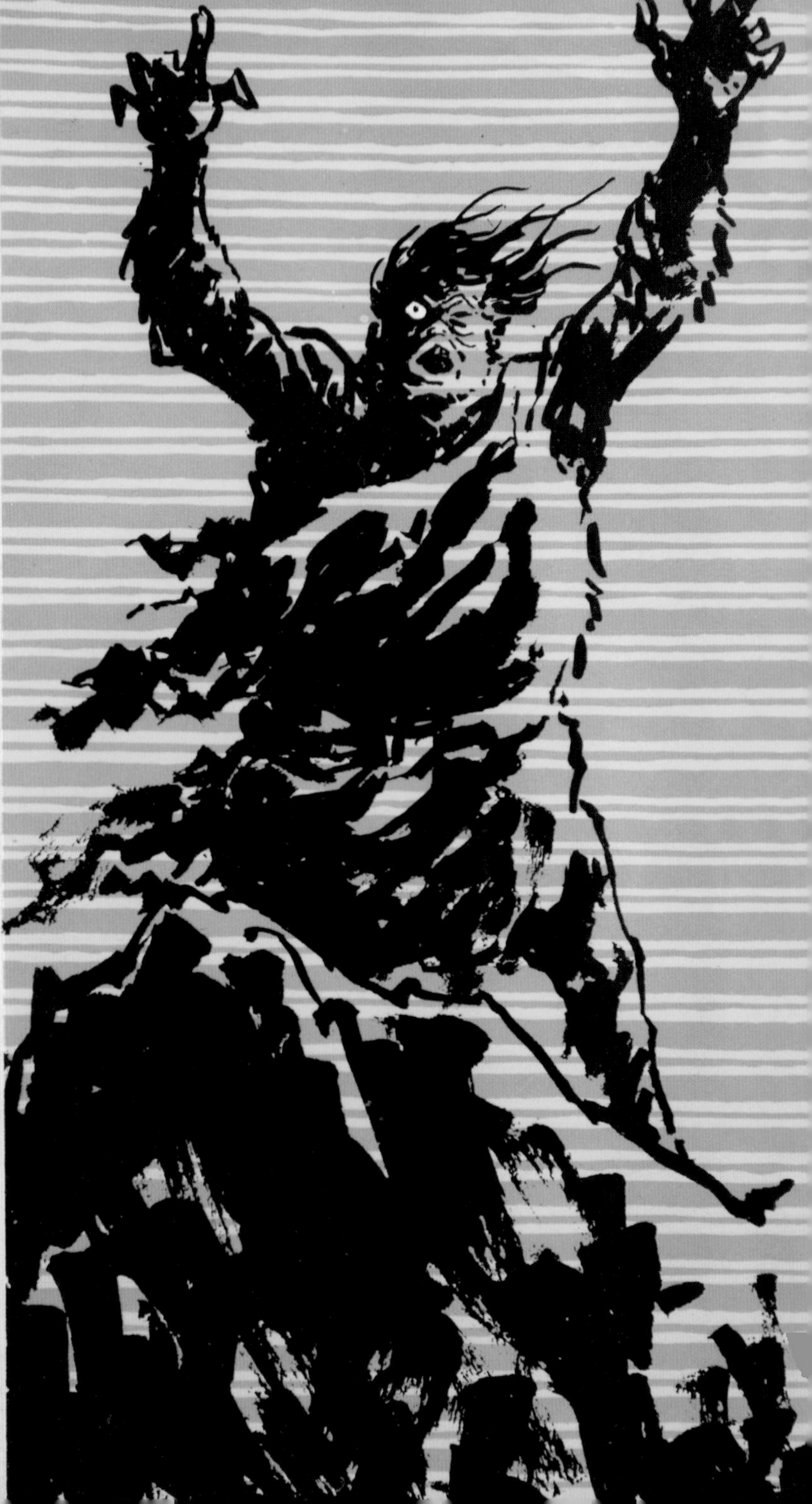

Legend of Kamui 1964

✏️🖊 "Sanpei Shirato"

Title in original language *Kamui-den*
First published by Seirindo (Japan)
Creator Noboru Okamoto (Japanese, b.1932)
Genre Adventure

During the 1930s, Sanpei Shirato was schooled at home by his father, a painter in the proletarian art movement, to save him from indoctrination by the official militaristic curriculum. Shirato began painting narrative cards for the postwar paper theater business, a natural training ground to switch to manga. After the success of *Ninja bugeicho: Kagemaru-den* (1959–62), he and publisher Katsuichi Nagai founded *Garo* magazine to serialize his next epic. Fortunately, Shirato could afford to work for free and pay his studio to help him produce around one hundred pages a month.

Legend of Kamui re-creates seventeenth-century feudal Japan by demonstrating the injustices meted out on the peasants, domestics, and pariahs by their corrupt rulers. Initially billing *Garo* as a "junior magazine," Shirato partly envisaged his well-researched serial, annotated with textual footnotes, as an antidote to textbooks that excluded these uncomfortable truths.

Kamui, an ancient word for "divinity," is the name given by an ogre to a pariah baby, who grows into a boy determined to elevate himself as a ninja. Adjusting his focus as he goes, Shirato devotes much of the first two chapters to another Kamui, a white wolf cub, originally intended as the human Kamui's companion. While continuing the stories of Kamui, man and wolf, Shirato increasingly highlights Shosuke, bright son of a peasant farmer and pariah mother, who teaches his communities to read, modernize, and protest peaceably. However, not even Shosuke can avert the incensed peasants' climactic, blood-soaked uprising. **PG**

The Complete Mafalda 1964

✏️🖊 "Quino"

Title in original language *Toda Mafalda*
First published by Primera Plana (Argentina)
Creator Joaquin Salvador Lavado (Argentinian, b.1932)
Genre Humor

Delightfully and irreverently cynical about the world she lives in, the young girl Mafalda is infused with righteous anger and childish wisdom. Like *Calvin and Hobbes*, this Argentinian strip delights in questioning accepted reality with touches of the surreal. Like *Peanuts*, it has characters and punch lines that live on well after the first reading. By rights, *The Complete Mafalda* should be as well-known to English speakers as both the aforementioned massively popular comic strips.

Mafalda is a six-year-old girl living in Buenos Aires during the 1960s; she loves the Beatles and wants a television, but she also worries about poverty, nuclear war, cultural imperialism, and the brain drain. The supporting characters include her overly sensitive best friend Felipe, the commercially minded Manolito, whose love of money tips into avarice, and petty bourgeois Susanita, who just longs to be a wife and mother. In their country of origin these funny, very human characters—whom readers come to know and love, quirks and all, from their hatred of soup to their patriotism—have become part of the national consciousness.

Despite the passing of the years and the fact that the original South American setting might initially seem culturally specific, this is a comic strip that is just as relevant—and more importantly just as funny—today outside its original milieu. Who could fail to love a young girl who looks at a soda siphon and sees a way to propel herself upward in her homemade space suit, and who wishes Fidel Castro would eulogize soup so that her country could feel justified in condemning it? **JSc**

King Smurf 1964

✎ "Peyo" and Yvan Delporte   ✎ "Peyo"

Title in original language *Le Schtroumpfissime*
First published by Dupuis (Belgium)
Creators Pierre Culliford (Belgian, 1928–92); Delporte
Belgian, 1928–2007) **Genre** Political fable

When Papa Smurf has to leave the village for a few days, the Smurfs find themselves leaderless. They decide to have an election, which is won by a Smurf who gets elected by promising the other Smurfs whatever they want. He dubs himself "King Smurf" and starts consolidating his power by setting up a private army and moving to a palace built by forced labor. A resistance movement soon emerges and takes to the woods. When the resistance launches an attack on the village, King Smurf is about to be defeated when Papa Smurf comes back from his trip and reconciles everyone.

King Smurf is part of the original series of comics created by "Peyo," which inspired the watered-down, animated television series. This story is the first long tale of the little blue gnomes cowritten with Yvan Delporte, then editor-in-chief of the weekly *Spirou* magazine in which it was originally serialized in 1964. The story benefits from Peyo's flawless storytelling and Delporte's great sense of humor, making it a tale that children can understand but that adults appreciate, too. It is also the earliest instance of the Smurfs displaying individual personalities. The interaction between Brainy Smurf, Jokey Smurf, Grouchy Smurf, and so on is hilarious.

Peyo and Delporte tell a very serious political fable in a lighthearted, funny manner. Rather like *Lord of the Flies*, the childlike Smurfs are left with no "grown up" authority and in a matter of days go from democracy to dictatorship and then to civil war. The rise and fall of the titular "hero" shows a brilliant analysis of the game of politics. **J-PJ**

Lost in Time 1964

✎ Jean-Claude Forest   ✎ Paul Gillon

Title in original language *Les Naufragés du temps*
First published by Chouchou (France)
Creators Forest (French, 1930–98); Gillon (French, 1926–2011) **Genre** Science fiction

Twenty years after the initial publication of *Lost in Time,* prolific strip cartoonist Jean-Claude Forest described the motivation behind his ambitious and highly successful project: "[I wanted to produce] a science fiction comic strip cartoon, a space opera, while respecting the conventions and constraints of a popular novel."

The premise is simple. At the end of the twentieth century, threatened with degeneration and perhaps even extinction by a disease known as the great plague, humanity sends two healthy creatures into space in order to preserve the species: a woman and a man, each in a state of hibernation in his or her own bubble. Awakened 1,000 years later by humans living in 2990, the man—Christopher Cavallieri—finds himself immersed in an interstellar society consisting of numerous forms of life plagued by various problems. Confronted with dangerous enemies, such as the Trasses—a race of invaders resembling rats—or the Tapir—a kind of super godfather of crime to match the vastness of the universe—he has countless arduous adventures as he tries to find Valerie, his twentieth-century companion, who has accidentally become lost.

Lost in Time owes much of its enduring success to the elegant graphic art of Paul Gillon, whose body of work is considered to be a major historic representative of realistic strip cartoons. The series displays great maturity—it is both action-packed and thought-provoking, and it can be enjoyed by children and adults alike—and also emanates a diffuse melancholy that gives it a particular charm. **NF**

Lost in Time lures its readers into disturbing imaginary worlds. ➡

...DU XXᵉ SIÈCLE. LE GRAND FLÉAU MENACE LA TERRE... L'HUMANITÉ EST EN DANGER. PLUS QUE LA MORT, ELLE CRAINT LA ...NÉRESCENCE. POUR SAUVEGARDER L'ESPÈCE, UN HOMME ET UNE FEMME SONT ENVOYÉS DANS LE COSMOS. LEURS CELLULES ...ALES SUIVRONT UNE ROUTE ELLIPTIQUE QUI LES CONDUIRA AUX CONFINS DU SYSTÈME SOLAIRE, PUIS LES RAMÈNERA VERS LA TERRE TOUS LES CENT VINGT-CINQ ANS.

PLONGÉS DANS UN SOMMEIL ARTIFICIEL ET PRÉSERVÉS DU VIEILLISSEMENT, ILS PEUVENT ESPÉRER SURVIVRE LONGTEMPS, JUSQU'AU JOUR, PEUT-ÊTRE, OÙ LE BERCEAU DE LA TERRE POURRA DE NOUVEAU PROTÉGER LEUR EXISTENCE ET CELLE DE LEURS ENFANTS...

MAIS LES HOMMES DE L'AVENIR SAURONT-ILS RECUEILLIR LES SURVIVANTS DU PASSÉ?

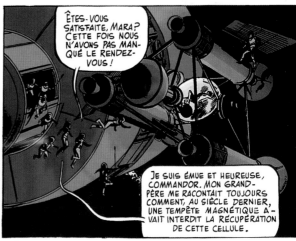

ÊTES-VOUS SATISFAITE, MARA? CETTE FOIS NOUS N'AVONS PAS MANQUÉ LE RENDEZ-VOUS!

JE SUIS ÉMUE ET HEUREUSE, COMMANDOR. MON GRAND-PÈRE ME RACONTAIT TOUJOURS COMMENT, AU SIÈCLE DERNIER, UNE TEMPÊTE MAGNÉTIQUE A-VAIT INTERDIT LA RÉCUPÉRATION DE CETTE CELLULE.

IL VIT! IL VIT! APRÈS TANT D'ANNÉES, C'EST INCROYABLE!

LES HOMMES DU XXᵉ SIÈCLE LUI ONT DONNÉ POUR MISSION DE SURVIVRE... DEPUIS MILLE ANS IL TIENT PAROLE... POURQUOI L'AVONS-NOUS RÉVEILLÉ?

Tiffany Jones 1964

✎ Pat Tourret ✎ Jenny Butterworth

First published by Associated Newspapers (UK)
Creators Tourett (British, b.1929);
Butterworth (British, Unknown)
Genre Adventure, Drama

If her first name evokes glamour and jewelry, her surname was surely chosen to sound as ordinary as possible. Tiffany Jones is every girl made good, 1960s style. She is the lass from the sticks who travels to London to make her fortune (accidentally) as a fashion model. Tiffany has been compared with Twiggy, but Twiggy arrived more than a year after Miss Jones. Women wanted Tiffany's lifestyle, whereas male readers simply wanted her. The formula was successful, and she appeared in more than one hundred newspapers.

Tiffany was launched with much fanfare as the first comic strip written and drawn by two women. Readers hoping for feminism in Jenny Butterworth's scripts may have realized from the first panel (Tiffany in her underwear) that it was unlikely. Pat Tourret's superb artwork, honed to an elegant polish in romance comics for teenage girls, lent itself well to lightweight stories of Swinging London.

However, there are more serious themes. When Tiffany's racing driver fiancé is killed on the track, she sinks into a convincingly portrayed depression. One of the best episodes takes her to Paris, where she falls for the glamourous lifestyle, falls in the River Seine, and falls in love with a struggling painter. In a neat reversal of the usual cliché, the artist leaves his bohemian life for a career in business, and Tiffany actually rejects him. There is a little bit of clean rock 'n 'roll in Tiffany Jones's 1960s London, but no dirty sex 'n' drugs. Realism it is not—fluff, perhaps, but gorgeously made fluff. Sink into it and enjoy. **GL**

The Wizard of Id 1964

✎✎ Johnny Hart and Brant Parker

First published by Creators Syndicate (USA)
Creators Hart (American, 1931–2007;
Parker (American, 1920–2007)
Genre Humor

A king of remarkably diminished stature rules tyrannically over a nominally medieval fiefdom, although historical accuracy is trumped by gag validity every time. He is petulant and cruel, particularly at any mention of his height, which is a frequent source of humor. The court wizard, after whom the strip is named, is featured no more frequently than the rest of what has expanded into a large, semiregular cast, many of whom can occupy the strip for days at a time. Wiz sometimes lives up to his billing, but often fails spectacularly—the chances of failure increasing exponentially depending on the vicinity of his wife.

The Wizard of Id exemplifies the maxim not to mess with success if the formula works. Three daily panels contain an introduction, set-up, and punch line. Listen carefully after reading and you can almost hear the rimshot, although the jokes rarely fail to raise a smile. Johnny Hart did not introduce sarcasm to newspaper strips, but his work emphasized it to a greater degree than previous strips. Hart was exceptional in his crediting of his assistants. While only his name is on the strip, he considered himself part of a writing team with Dick Boland, Jack Caprio, and Dick Cavelli. A friend of Hart's, Brant Parker was a Disney animator and regional political cartoonist who had never previously worked on strips. In the early days he also contributed to the ideas. Parker retired in 1997, and since then the strip has been drawn by his son Jeff, who had been assisting his father for ten years. The team Hart assembled continues to supply the gags. **FP**

Cybory 009 1964

Ishinomori Shotaro

First published by Akita Shoten (Japan)
Creator Japanese (1938–98)
Genre Science fiction
Adaptation TV (1968)

Joe Shimamura, the central character of this comic, is a troubled eighteen year old who escapes from a juvenile detention facility only to find his body transformed after being kidnapped by the evil Black Ghost Organization. Renamed Cyborg 009, all that remains of him is his brain trapped inside the body of a machine with the ability to move at extreme speed. His creator, Dr. Gilmore, also made eight other cyborgs: the genius and psychic baby Ivan (001); the flying Jet (002); Françoise (003), who has enhanced vision and hearing; Albert (004) whose body is entirely made of weapons; the Herculean Geronimo (005); the fire-breathing Chang Changku (006); Great Britain (007), who can transform into any object or creature; and Pyunma (008), who can survive under water without oxygen.

Black Ghost intended to use the cyborgs as soldiers, but Joe and his eight friends escape the organization with Dr. Gilmore. They struggle to overcome emotional hardships caused by who they are, but as battles against villainous enemies begin, the nine focus all their abilities on fighting for world peace. Enemies emerge, each inventing a more advanced cyborg in an attempt to destroy Dr. Gilmore's nine creations. But their individual powers, combined with their team tactics, firm friendship, and courage, always lead them to victory.

The comic has been adapted for film, television, radio, and theater. The characters have also been used as motifs for pinball machines at Japanese pachinko parlors, giving them an iconic status. Clearly a favorite with the author, Shotaro named his first son after Joe. **TS**

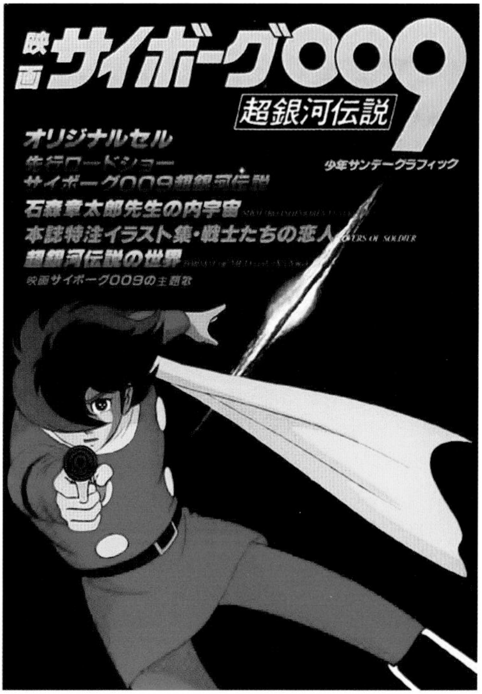
映画
サイボーグ009
超銀河伝説
オリジナルセル
少年サンデーグラフィック
石森章太郎先生の内宇宙
本誌特注イラスト集・戦士たちの恋人
超銀河伝説の世界

"They just wanted to develop more advanced high performance."

Also by Ishinomori Shotaro
Genma Taisen
Hotel
Kamen Rider
Ryujin-numa
Sabu to Ichi Torimono Hikae

The Trigan Empire 1965

✎ Mike Butterworth ✎ Don Lawrence

First published by Fleetway (UK)
Creators Butterworth (British, 1924–86);
Lawrence (British, 1928–2003)
Genre Science fiction

For anyone growing up in the 1960s and 1970s *Look and Learn* holds a special place in their affections. As an educational title it was the only comic that was allowed in schools, and on rainy lunchtimes the cupboards would be raided for back issues of the large, glossy magazine. However, the main attraction was not the educational articles. Instead, it was the two pages of *The Trigan Empire* comic strip in each issue that held the reader's attention so compellingly.

The strip, which began life in *Ranger* and moved over to *Look and Learn* in 1966, purported to chart the rise and fall of a suspiciously familiar empire on the faraway planet of Elektron. Governed by the Emperor Trigo, the Trigan Empire was clearly modeled on ancient Greece and Rome, with added aliens and monsters. Industry veteran Mike Butterworth gradually allowed the empire to evolve as Trigan City grew into a vast megalopolis and its horses were replaced by spaceships. In truth, however, the strip's real appeal was always Don Lawrences's grand, widescreen, painted artwork. Lawrence took delight in rendering Elektron's spectacular landscapes and bizarre creatures.

The strip ran until 1982 when the comic was canceled, but by then Lawrence was long gone. *The Trigan Empire* had become a sensation in the Netherlands, where the whole series was translated, although its creators never received any royalties. When Lawrence discovered this, he resigned on the spot and started working directly for the Dutch comic *Eppo* on *Storm*, the other highlight of his career. **DAR**

Asterix in Britain 1965

✎ René Goscinny ✎ Albert Uderzo

Title in original language *Asterix chez les Bretons*
Pre-published by *Pilote* (France, 1965) **First published by** Dargaud (France, 1966) **Creators** Goscinny (French, 1926–77); Uderzo (French, b.1927) **Genre** Humor

Anticlimax, who is Asterix's first cousin once removed, is an accomplished oarsman sent to France to enlist the aid of Getafix and his magic potion to help fight off the Romans laying siege to the village of Chief Mykingdomforanos. The village is the last pocket of unconquered British soil, the final stronghold of a nation given over to Rome by British soldiers who stubbornly refuse to fight on weekends and routinely cease hostilities to sit down to a glass of hot water and milk. Asterix and Obelix arrive in London with the potion but lose it in the River Thames. Once back in the village Asterix claims to be able to make the potion from some herbs he is carrying. Although it is only tea, it fortifies the village's defenders sufficiently to thwart the Roman assault. Tea then becomes the national drink.

Asterix in Britain is replete with more than its usual dose of stereotypical references—warm beer, mint sauce on lamb, and toast with marmalade to name a few. The book opened with a disclaimer, hoping that "the Gauls would have as good a sense of humor as the British."

The mistakes for which the series is renowned keep coming, including an argument between Asterix and Anticlimax as to which side of the road they should ride on, a premature argument as the Gauls did not ride on the right side of the road until the Napoleonic era some eighteen centuries later. There are also plenty of caricatures, such as Anticlimax's "V for Victory" sign when the Romans are defeated is a pointed reference to Winston Churchill. **BS**

R. GOSCINNY **Astérix** A. UDERZO

Astérix chez les Bretons

Texte René GOSCINNY

Dessins Albert UDERZO

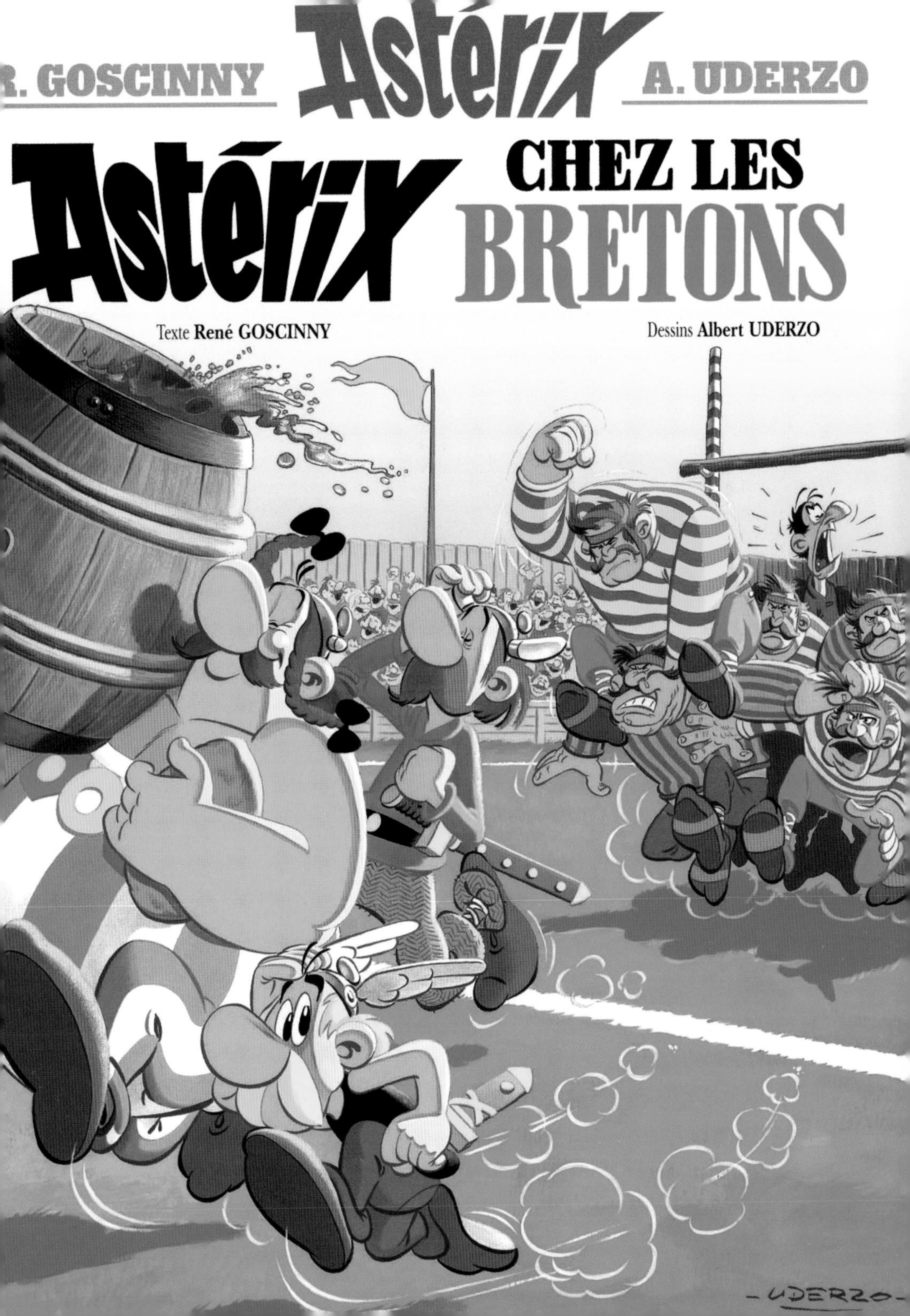
UDERZO

Ugh-Ugh Cocco Bill 1965

✎ Benito Jacovitti

First published by *Il Giorno* (Italy)
Creator Italian (1923–97)
Genre Western, Parody
Adaptation Animated series (2001/2004)

Cocco Bill is a cowboy, gunslinger, and a defender of the law—who likes chamomile tea. The series is a parody of the Western genre, full of stereotypical sheriffs, Indians, saloons, stagecoaches, and guns. "Full of" also describes Benito Jacovitti's unique style, for every panel is filled with elements—among them trademark salamis and fishbones—that make every episode a rich reading experience and a great collection of visual jokes.

In this story, Cocco Bill is resting in a village when it is attacked by a Sioux tribe led by Chief Crazy Horse. Cocco Bill helps the citizens but is imprisoned by the army. The Sioux want him for revenge, but he is also sought by the main villain, Bunz, a greedy businessman who has manipulated the Sioux to cause devastation, hoping to force impoverished farmers to sell up to him. Cocco Bill learns of Bunz's plan, bargains for a long time with the Sioux, Bunz, and Bunz's seven murderous brothers, and is fortunately released. Thankfully, he restores peace and brings the criminals to justice.

Jacovitti's inventive character building, and his surreal language of absurd neologisms and puns, made him a star for generations of young readers. One of the diverse successes of his long and somewhat controversial career (his parodic *Kama Sutra* had him dismissed by a Catholic publisher, and he defined his political position as "centrist extremist") was the 1950s and 1960s best-seller annual series *Diario Vitt*, based on children's school diaries. *Cocco Bill*, his most famous series, running from 1957 to 1998, is today continued by his former assistant, Luca Salvagno. **MS**

Monsieur Lambert 1965

✎ Jean-Jacques Sempé

First published by Éditions Denoël (France)
Creator French (b.1932)
Genre Reality drama
Influence on Anthea Bell

Although best known for his one-panel cartoons, Jean-Jacques Sempé has also created short, wordless comics and longer format narratives that use text and pictures to tell a story. *Monsieur Lambert* is the earliest example of the latter format, as well as Sempé's fourth published work, and his first original graphic novel.

The story takes place in the mid-1960s, in a small Parisian restaurant, Chez Picard, where local office workers come for lunch. Most are middle-aged men whose conversations revolve around either politics or football. Having lunch at Picard's under the motherly Lucienne's watchful eye is a daily ritual, and the unidentified narrator can tell the day of the week by what is on the menu. This reassuring routine is suddenly shattered when Mr. Lambert, the youngest habitué of a table of four football fans, starts arriving late for lunch. It turns out he has fallen in love. Lambert's friends follow the ups and downs of his relationship from afar, as football gets replaced—for a while—by romance in the conversations of his three remaining tablemates.

Sempé's first extended graphic narrative is an epic tale of the everyday. Important events that happen in the life of Monsieur Lambert are never shown. Only echoes filter into the well-ordered little universe of Chez Picard, always shown from the same angle, where Lambert's uncharacteristic lateness becomes a major event. The narrator's attempts at romanticizing the situation are constantly undermined by the down-to-earth dialogue, making the Parisian restaurant a stage where human foibles are gently mocked. **J-PJ**

Monsieur Lambert: a young man with young man's preoccupations. ➡

Peut-être le sujet de notre conversation n'intéresse-t-il pas tout le monde... peut-être...
eh oui...
ouais...

The Adventures of Phoebe Zeit-Geist 1965

✎ Michael O'Donoghue ✎ Frank Springer

First published by *Evergreen Review* (USA)
Creators O'Donoghue (American, 1940–94); Springer (American, 1929–2009)
Genre Humor

ADULT FANTASY ALBUM

PHOEBE ZEIT-GEIST
by MICHAEL O'DONOGHUE and FRANK SPRINGER

NO AMOUNT OF TAR PITS AND EX-NAZIS WILL EVER TARNISH THE NAME OF ZEIT-GEIST!

intro by FRANK THORNE

Similar reads
Barbarella Jean-Claude Forest
Little Annie Fanny Harvey Kurtzman and Will Elder
Long Sam Al Capp and Bob Lubbers
Sweet Gwendoline John Willie
Wonder Woman William Marston and Harry Peter

The time and the place: the United States in the mid-1960s. The magazine: the literary and modernistic bimonthly *Evergreen Review*. The strip: *The Adventures of Phoebe Zeit-Geist*, published in bimonthly installments from 1965 to 1967, three to eight pages at a time, mostly in black and white, plus loosely washed in secondary color, most often red, with superb lettering—all done on a shoestring budget and causing a sensation.

The heroine is Phoebe Zeit-Geist, an aristocratic expert in the martial arts and ballet. Drugged and abducted at the start, she is ordered out of her clothes, and, in most of the comic strip pages appears as the naked plaything of an endless chain of perverts—of the Nazi, blind Zen archer, necrophile, fungologist,

"Normally, I would disembowel this man with a few simple oriental combat maneuvers..."

Eskimo priest, gay gob, foot fetishist, marxist, tattoo artist, serial killer, counterspy, and lethal lesbian type.

A tour de force in form and content, *The Adventures of Phoebe Zeit-Geist* is one long sendup of the lady-in-distress theme. Its new, often surrealistic, adult settings give more of a theatrical than an erotic feel. The writer, boy wonder Michael O'Donoghue, loved playing the wacko in real life as well as in his pitch-black fiction. Frank Springer's philosophy was to draw better than anybody else and to get as many accounts as he could; both of which he did.

In 1970 O'Donoghue was cofounder of the trailblazing humor monthly *National Lampoon*. In its section of comic spoofs, he and Springer published more crazy strips, such as their 1971 *Tarzan of the Cows*. Springer also had a prolific ouput working with big authors and big publishers such as DC and Marvel. **HvO**

Gyatoruzu 1965

Shunji Sonoyama

Gyatoruzu, published between 1965 and 1975, is a gag comic, often told in six to eight pages, about a family of cave people and their struggle with nature, sex, and food. The father spends his time hunting and the mother provides him with a continuous stream of babies. The main character generally follows his primitive urges in any situation in which he might find himself. Whenever he sees a woman, he will try to have sex with her, and he kills and eats any giant woolly mammoth he encounters, the main source of food in this world. The next meal, competitor, or mate is often just beyond the horizon.

Shunji Sonoyama draws in a simple but very distinctive style, graphically very clear and playful. He produced many gorgeously drawn stories completely in color, in vibrant light red and gray watercolors. Relying as much on visual humor as on verbal jokes, Sonoyama plays around with the visual language of storytelling in comics and also finds numerous ways to exploit the graphic possibilities of the Japanese characters, known as the *kanji*. He often uses wild zooming effects to focus on the weird and funny details of life on the prehistoric plains. He evokes these landscapes with wide horizons and empty spaces, but can also fill the next page with mad action scenes or with rains and storms, the raw forces of nature.

"In . . . Shunji's view, primitive men were more human than modern people."

lambiek.net

The author used the strip for satirical comment on human nature and modern society. In the simple setting of his gags, he presents a human condition free from the pressures of the modern world and the oppression of the primitive human. **AE**

First published by Sunday Comics (Japan)
Creator Japanese (1935–93)
Genre Humor
Adaptation Animation (1974)

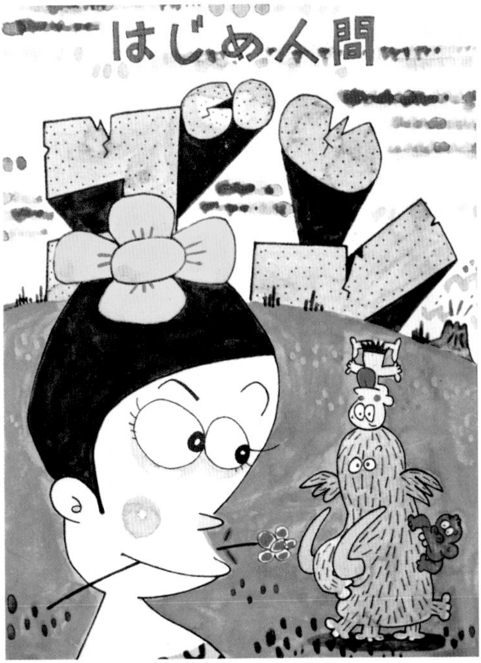
はじめ人間

Similar reads

Doraemon Fujiko Fujio
Ganbare Gonbe Shunji Sonoyama
Hajimeningen Gon Shunji Sonoyama
Kokkyo no Futari Shunji Sonoyama
Shonan Junai Gumi Tohru Fujisawa

Balthazar 1965

✐✐ Bob de Moor

First published by Lombard/Casterman (Belgium)
Creator Robert Frans Marie de Moor (Belgian, 1925–92)
Genre Humor
Influence on Johan de Moor

Bob de Moor, as a monolingual Fleming, at first spoke only Dutch. Raised in Antwerp, he was influenced by cowboy and swashbuckling movies, comics, and Disney cartoons. In World War II, when he was sixteen, a rather innocent anti-British cartoon of his was used in the pro-Nazi press. He did background drawing for Belgian animated cartoons, and at the war's end even had to work for the German occupier. Like other Belgian and Dutch artists (Vandersteen, Hergé, Jacobs, Toonder), whose work had served Nazi war propaganda, de Moor cheered the Allied soldiers at the 1944–45 liberation of Belgium, giving them self-made "souvenir of Belgium" postcards. In the same period, an exploding grenade ripped two fingers off his left hand.

After the war he made a wide variety of strips: comical, historical, nautical, futuristic. From 1951 onward, he was hired by Studios Hergé in Brussels. In the thirty-two years he worked there, he assisted with the last seven *Tintin* albums. Extra *Tintin* story remakes such as *The Black Island* proved time-wasting. However, at the studios he began to work on his own comics.

In 1965, with great joy, Bob de Moor created his own series, *Balthazar*, an original gag strip in humorous surreal settings, in the same free style he sometimes used to great effect to parody other strips. The *Balthazar* strips appeared irregularly in *Tintin/Kuifje* weekly and produced some lasting classics (such as his monument to the comic strip, or his deadline stress). Alas, the general reader did not warm to *Balthazar* fast enough and his editor pulled the plug. **HvO**

Valentina 1965

✐✐ Guido Crepax

First published by *Linus* magazine (Italy)
Creator Italian (1933–2003)
Genre Drama, Erotic
Adaptation TV (1989)

Valentina Rosselli is a beautiful young photographer and orphan, struggling in a world of men, and starting her career at a studio involved in advertising production. Valentina is twenty-three when she meets and falls in love with art critic Philip Rembrandt, a Dutch citizen living in the United States. He will be her partner in a long and erratic relationship that spans the series.

During her adventures, set in the very realistic context of lively Milan, she has personal and professional encounters through which Crepax explores her character from the mid-1960s to the 1990s. It is a social and internal journey where sex, desire, and psychoanalytical depth play a crucial role in shaping one of the strongest female characters ever, a symbol for a new generation of "true" contemporary women, increasingly independent and self-conscious.

The character design was inspired by early Hollywood diva Louise Brooks, but the most striking aspect, apart from the frequency of nude scenes, was Crepax's visual style, a peak in the 1960s European art-wise comics scene and still a model for authors such as Art Spiegelman and David B.

Influenced by masters of cinema, such as Sergei Eisenstein or Ingmar Bergman, and contemporary art, Crepax's layouts were sometimes as radical as abstract compositions, with single images decomposed in fragmented panels. In the first adventure, *La curva di Lesmo*, Valentina had just a cameo in the superherolike story of Phillip Rembrandt's alter ego Neutron, but such a magnetic appearance took her to icon status. **MS**

Valentina strips included sadomasochism and bisexuality. ➡

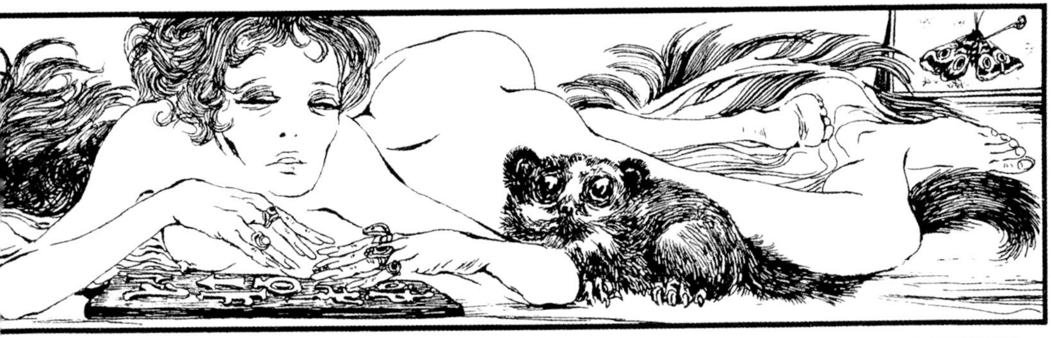

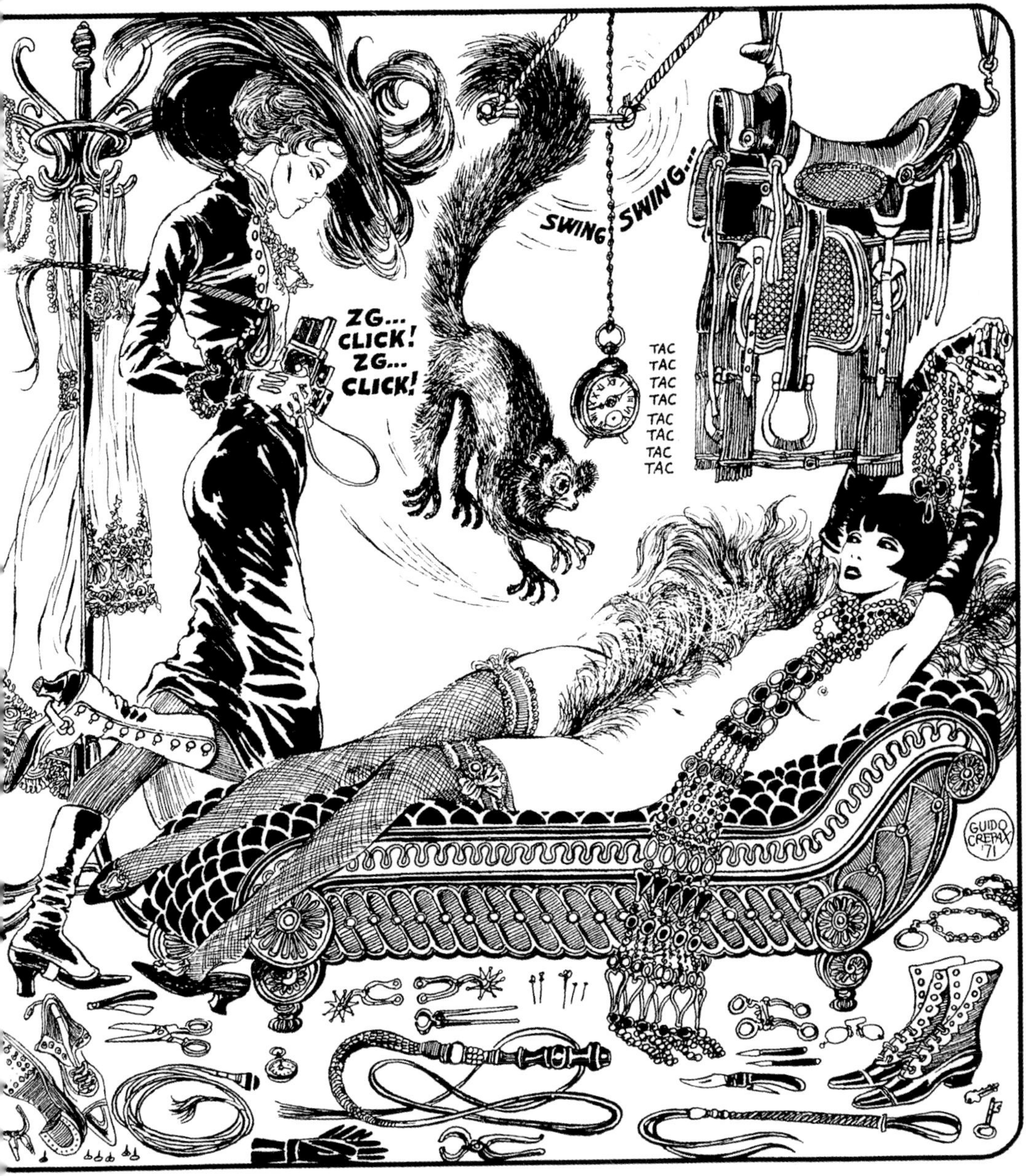
ZG... CLICK! ZG... CLICK!
SWING SWING...
TAC TAC TAC TAC TAC TAC TAC TAC
GUIDO CREPAX '71

The Masked Cucumber 1965

✏✏ Nikita Mandryka

Title in original language *Le Concombre Masqué*
First published by Vaillant (France)
Creator French (b.1940)
Genre Humor

MANDRYKA
Le concombre masqué
?
L'intégrale des Années Pilote
DARGAUD

Similar reads

Al Crane Alexis and Gérard Lauzier
Le Bandard fou Moebius
L'Écho des Savanes Nikita Mandryka
Les Miniscules Nikita Mandryka
Little Annie Fanny Harvey Kurtzman and Bill Elder

"Somewhere far, far away, in the middle of the desert of sweet follies . . . The Masked Cucumber, in his cactus-blockhouse, is slowly waking up. . . ." Thus, in a few words, Nikita Mandryka sets the scene at the beginning of one of his vegetable adventures. The setting is a crazy world created around his masked hero, a hero who would fascinate large numbers of French-speaking comic readers in the 1960s and 1970s.

Running counter to everything that could be considered "normal fiction" in a series of short stories, Mandryka develops a universe ruled by the absurd in which its recurring characters ponder the meaning of life. It is very obvious that the absence of apparent logic on the part of the cucumber and his

> *"It's destiny. . . . Some stick to it while others do not. Roles are distributed at the start, that's the power."*
>
> **Nikita Mandryka**

burlesque, almost surreal, adventures are the key to their inherent appeal. Following his imagination and using a narrative style that clearly does not exclude improvisation, Mandryka came to explore the dream world inhabited by his strange hero in silly stories and linguistic inventions. These reflected the free spirit and love of experimentation that personified the 1970s.

There is a deeper meaning, because *The Masked Cucumber* is also an expression of the author's interest in psychoanalysis, which he sometimes brings into the story. His love of rambling, and the incongruity of some of the situations, can be seen as an expression of the unconscious in comic strip cartoons, something that does not happen very often. Even today Mandryka's work is still unlike any other. Undoubtedly, a collective imagination at large. **NF**

Fritz the Cat 1965

R. Crumb

Ralph Bakshi's X-rated 1972 adaptation of *Fritz the Cat*, the early underground comic strip by R. Crumb, was such an outlandish event (a pornographic animated cartoon) that the sheer fact of its existence has risked obliterating the memory of the source material. Crumb axed the strip in 1972 after disagreements with the filmmakers. Crumb himself, in no way a fan of the movie, foresaw this effect. In a 1972 story called "Fritz the Cat: Superstar," he drew the hedonistic hero, high on success (among other things), being stabbed in the back, literally, by a female ostrich.

Women are usually the objects of Crumb's lascivious, if admiring, gaze, but here the ostrich, noticeably lanky like her creator, may well stand in for

"He started out based on a pet cat we had at home, and then he gradually evolved."

R. Crumb

the artist. Yet before Fritz was killed by a buxom ostrich and overshadowed by an animated doppelgänger, he was a randy, protohipster country boy whose fixation with sex led to all sorts of urban adventures: orgies, prostitutes, police evasion. Everyone is drawn as an animal, the police as pigs, naturally. True to Fritz's loose character, he was not serialized anywhere regularly and popped up in various publications, including *Help!*, *Cavalier*, and *The People's Comics*.

It may appear to modern readers that the mere presence of sex in a 1960s comic book gave it an X-rated reputation, but it is worth remembering that among the earliest Fritz stories is one in which he entices his younger sister to fornicate with him. The panels go into darkness, but all future Fritz sex would take place in the comic's equivalent of daylight. **MW**

First published by Sirk Productions (USA)
Creator American (b.1943)
Genre Underground
Adaptation Film: *The Nine Lives of Fritz the Cat* (1974)

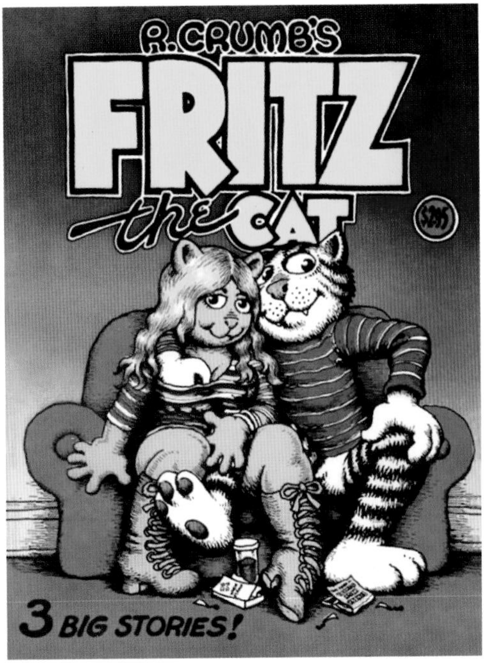
R. CRUMB'S
FRITZ the CAT
$2.95
3 BIG STORIES!

Also by R. Crumb
Complete Crumb: Mr Sixties
Mr. Natural
My Troubles with Women
R. Crumb Draws the Blues
The Book of Genesis

Enemy Ace 1965

Robert Kanigher Joe Kubert

First published by National Periodical Publications (USA)
Creators Kanigher (American, 1915–2002); Kubert (Polish, b.1926)
Genre War

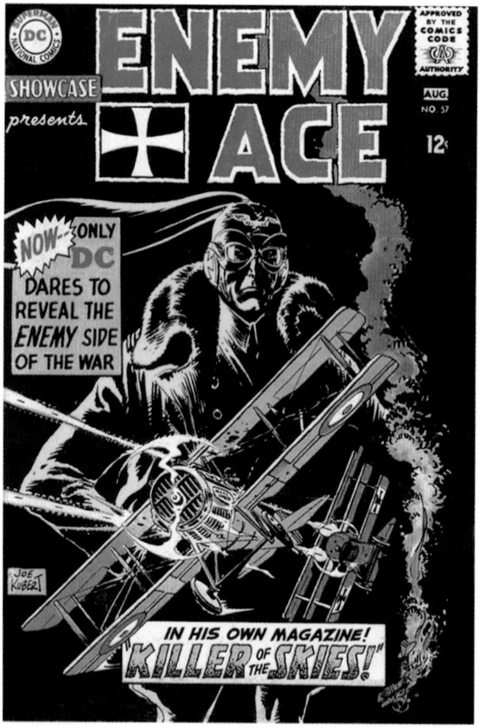
DC
SHOWCASE presents
ENEMY ACE
APPROVED BY THE COMICS CODE AUTHORITY
AUG. NO. 57
12¢
NOW--ONLY DC DARES TO REVEAL THE ENEMY SIDE OF THE WAR
JOE KUBERT
IN HIS OWN MAGAZINE!
"KILLER OF THE SKIES!"

Similar reads
Fax from Sarajevo Joe Kubert
Sgt. Rock Robert Kanigher and Joe Kubert
Viking Prince Robert Kanigher and Joe Kubert
Yossel Joe Kubert

"Human killing machine" Rittmeister Hans von Hammer is the Enemy Ace, a German fighter pilot flying an all-red Fokker triplane over the fields of France during World War I. Despite his prowess in the air—he downs his fifty-fourth aircraft during the first story—he suffers from loneliness. The awe of his fellow pilots sets him apart from them; his orderlies and female companions do not understand what it is to be a killer. His only friend is a black wolf that he visits in the forest.

In the third story readers learn more about von Hammer's fastidious code of honor when he unknowingly shoots down an English plane after the pilot has signaled that he has run out of ammunition. Accepting an invitation to a duel to avenge the pilot, von

"Do you know women call you the 'Angel of Death,' Rittmeister?"

Hammer takes to the air without ammunition himself in order to pay for his mistake. This is a crucial element of the stories that follow. The best of von Hammer's foes are gentlemen, as he is, fighting because they are at war, but refusing to be less than sportsmanlike about it. As the Hangman says while saving von Hammer's life after they collide over the English Channel, "We are eagles, von Hammer! If we are to die . . . it should be in the skies!"

In choosing to tell war stories from the enemy's point of view, creators Robert Kanigher and Joe Kubert went to great lengths to be authentic—from understanding the tactics of aerial warfare in World War I to researching the structure of the planes and the armaments of the period, to reading about the experiences of those who had actually fought in the war. All this added a credibility to the stories that made them highly effective and exciting. **NFI**

Kaliman, The Incredible Man 1965

Rafael Cutberto Navarro and Roberto Vásquez

Kalimán was originally a radio play series created by Rafael Navarro and Roberto Vázquez, aired for the first time in September 1963, in Mexico. The series, featuring a polyphonic stereo system known as "Illusound," had a loyal fanbase that equated the radio play with fantasy and adventure. Navarro and Vázquez had an astonishing success, breaking all records for Mexico and Latin America. The comic book series was a tie-in, originally adaptations of the radio storylines.

Little explanation is given regarding Kalimán's origin. He is presented as an Indian orphan adopted by Prince Abul Pasha from the valley of Kalimantan. His sidekick is Solín, an Egyptian boy, descended from pharaohs. Kalimán is blue-eyed and wears an all-white

"Fear not, Solin. I'll never let these monsters take you back to the village."

outfit with a jeweled "K" on his turban. The series' inside pages were mostly in black and white on half-tones on sepia pages (the covers were always in full color) and although some reprints and newer interpretations were made in full color, they were never as successful.

Kalimán's adventures were defined by a philosophy of peace set in a context of international adventures and continuous struggle with supernatural forces. Although not a superhero, Kalimán had some supernatural powers, such as control of mind over matter.

A true popular hero, Kalimán's dialogues have been passed on by generations of Mexicans as idiomatic expressions teaching the virtues of patience, self-discipline, study, and hard work. The series suffered from erratic editorial control and an inability to adapt to newer market conditions, and in spite of continous efforts to revamp it, the character is now officially a thing of the Mexican transmedia past. **EPr**

Title in original language *Kalimán, El Hombre Increible*
First published by Promotora K (Mexico)
Creators Navarro (Mexican, Unknown); Vázquez (Mexican, Unknown) **Genre** Adventure

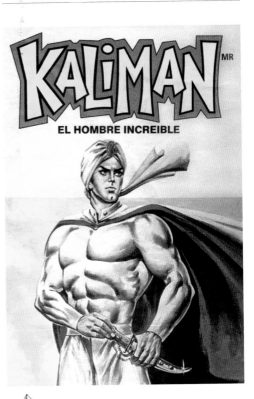

KALIMAN
MR
EL HOMBRE INCREIBLE

Similar reads

Doctor Strange Stan Lee and Steve Ditko
Fantomas Alfredo Cardona Peña and Rubén Lara Romero
Moon Knight Doug Moench and Bill Sienkiewicz

Blazing Combat 1965

Archie Goodwin Various

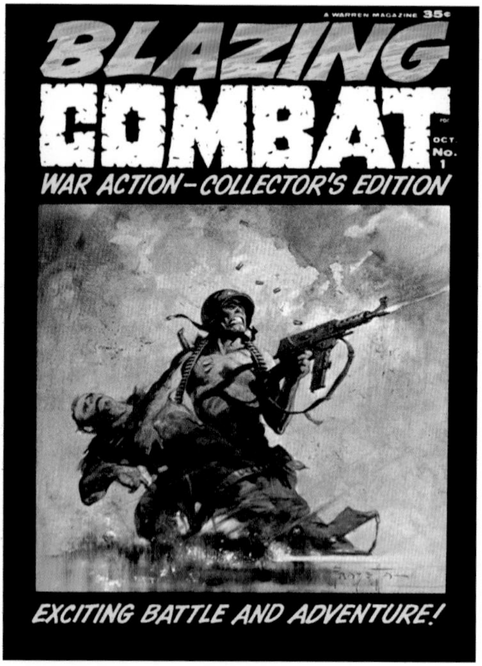
A WARREN MAGAZINE 35¢
BLAZING
COMBAT
OCT. No. 1
WAR ACTION – COLLECTOR'S EDITION
EXCITING BATTLE AND ADVENTURE!

"The [Blazing Combat] *stories were both gritty and realistic . . . showing the true horror of war."*

Steve Stiles, cartoonist and writer

Similar reads

A Sailor's Story Sam Glanzman
Charley's War Pat Mills and Joe Colquhoun
Frontline Combat Harvey Kurtzman and others
It Was the War of the Trenches Jacques Tardi
Two-Fisted Tales Harvey Kurtzman and others

First published by Warren Publishing (USA)
Creator American (1937–98)
Genre War
Award Eisner Award (1993)

In the early 1960s, publisher James Warren enjoyed some success with *Creepy* and *Eerie*—two horror comics that evaded the restrictions of the Comics Code thanks to their allegedly more adult, black-and-white magazine format. At this time Warren employed a number of creators who had worked for the notorious EC Comics in the 1950s, including Harvey Kurtzman, former editor of EC's groundbreaking war comics *Two-Fisted Tales* and *Frontline Combat*. With Kurtzman on hand as consultant, Warren launched his own war title, *Blazing Combat*, another anthology with powerful, full-color covers by Frank Frazetta and glorious monochrome interiors drawn by such greats as Reed Crandall, Gene Colan, George Evans, John Severin, and Wally Wood.

By his own admission, Warren—and his indispensable writer and editor Archie Goodwin—leaned toward the liberal side of life. Taking their cue from Kurtzman, many of the stories in *Blazing Combat* were broadly antiwar, often ending on an ironic twist that seemed to suggest war was always a messy, futile business, whatever the historical context.

Goodwin daringly wrote a number of scripts set in Vietnam at a time when the peace protest movement was just getting underway in the United States. Issue #2's "Landscape," drawn by Joe Orlando, was especially potent, ending as it did with the unthinking slaughter of an old Vietnamese man by U.S. troops. It led to *Blazing Combat* being denounced by the American Legion and banned from sale in U.S. military bases. Warren had no choice but to cancel the title after just four issues. **AL**

Leunig Strips 1965

✏️🖌️ Michael Leunig

First published by *Lot's Wife* (Monash University student newspaper)
Creator Australian (b.1945)
Genre Humor

Summarizing a life's work in a few paragraphs is never easy, and nowhere is it more of a challenge than with the life and work of artist and poet Michael Leunig. A state-declared "Australian living treasure" and author of more than twenty books, he has made claymation films and led protests on Australia's involvement in Iraq. His comic strips plumb deep, untapped, philosophical seams. They challenge our views on God, confront us with the darkness of depression, question our individual purpose, all the while using the guise of humor as a hook to drag us into often serious topics. Australians soon learned it was okay to trust Michael Leunig to do more than just make them laugh.

One week Leunig composes a piece about being ground down by tiredness, or how life allows us little time to be contemplative, or how when we cut ourselves off from nature we risk alienating ourselves from God. He describes his comic strips as therapeutic because, he says, they give readers time to pause. Leunig likes to imagine what people think and what they are afraid to say out loud. He worries that technology is becoming unfathomable, that television is corrosive, and that, as a species, human beings need far less stimulation than they are receiving. He laments that so many of us live reactively, instead of creatively.

It is impossible to get a handle on the world of Michael Leunig: his work cannot be reduced to a series of panels, or a "Best of" volume, or deduced from a phase or a period because there is too much there, and that is the genius of the man. **BS**

Star of the Giants 1966

✏️ Kajiwara Ikki 🖌️ Kawasaki Noboru

Title in original language *Kyojin no Hoshi*
First published by Kodansha (Japan)
Creators Kajiwara (Japanese, 1936–87); Kawasaki (Japanese, b.1941) **Genre** Drama

There is always opposition during times of great change. As postwar Japan moved into a happier and more contented era of lively cultural developments, manga writer Kajiwari Ikki expressed some resistance through the three themes of his creative world—"grit," "blood, sweat, and tears," and "passion." It was against this background that the sports manga *Star of the Giants* became a hit. While Kawasaki Noboru's dramatic illustrations received much acclaim, many could also predict the imminent arrival of the Kajiwara Ikki boom.

Ittetsu Hoshi, father of the central character Hyuma, used to be a gifted player in the baseball team the Giants. As an aspiring pitcher, Hyuma dreams of following in his father's footsteps. Although Ittetsu's career came to an end after being injured in the war, he is determined to make his son the star of the Giants. Under Ittetsu's Spartan methods, Hyuma's days of training are intensely harsh. Driven by overwhelming passion, however, Hyuma eventually makes it to the Giants team, where he is faced with a number of obstacles that will lead him to turn against his father.

Despite the story's serious tone and its significance in the history of Japanese sports comics, this vintage series has become the subject of numerous parodies in Japan. In particular, the scene where a raging Ittetsu turns over a table of dishes has become a classic joke. Although it happened only once during the five-year series, the concept has even been turned into an iPhone application. Taken seriously or not, *Star of the Giant's* survival across the decades is quite incredible. **TS**

Nick Fury, Agent of S.H.I.E.L.D 1966

Stan Lee, Roy Thomas, and Jim Steranko Jim Steranko and others

First published by Marvel Comics (USA)
Creators Lee (American, b.1922); Thomas (American, b.1940); Steranko (American, b.1938)
Genre Superhero

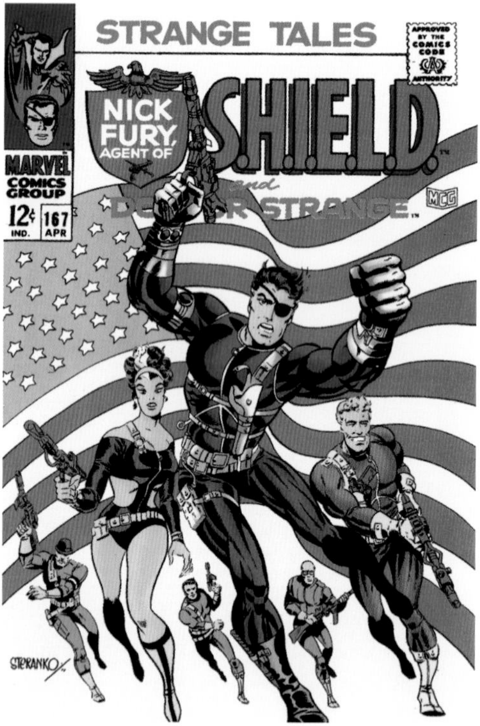
STRANGE TALES
APPROVED BY THE COMICS CODE AUTHORITY
NICK FURY, AGENT OF
S.H.I.E.L.D.
and
DOCTOR STRANGE
MCG
MARVEL COMICS GROUP
12¢ 167 IND. APR
STERANKO

Also by Jim Steranko
At the Stroke of Midnight
Captain America
Chandler: Ride Tide
X-Men

Seldom has an artist made such a deep and lasting impact from such a relatively small body of work as Jim Steranko with *Nick Fury, Agent of S.H.I.E.L.D.* First introduced in *Strange Tales* issue #135 (with artwork by Jack Kirby), Nick Fury was Marvel's Sergeant Fury from the war comic *Sgt. Fury and his Howling Commandos*—now updated as a James Bond–style superspy. The stories were imaginative, and Fury operated in an intriguing mezzanine world, a superhero without a costume or superpowers. With the arrival of Steranko, Fury began to evolve from a grizzled army veteran into a supersmooth ladykiller—while, in contrast, henchmen Dum Dum Dugan, Gabe Jones, and Jasper Sitwell remained relatively prosaic in their appearance.

In *Strange Tales* issue #159, Steranko introduced the outrageously glamorous and sexy Contessa Valentina Allegro de la Fontaine, Fury's partner in espionage and subsequently in the bedroom. Fury's relationship with the Contessa pushed the boundaries of what was then acceptable under the Comics Code. Cars, guns, aeroplanes—all the superspy accessories—were also in generous supply. One advantage that Fury (and Steranko) enjoyed over their television competition was the lack of budgetary restrictions on special effects. Encounters with the high-tech villains of Hydra, their ex-Nazi leader Baron Wolfgang von Strucker, and the Yellow Claw left an awe-inspiring trail of destruction in their wake.

Steranko's artwork and graphic design broke completely new ground. His covers, with their unified sense of graphic design, drew on elements taken from surrealism, pop art, and op art. Steranko's interiors—complete with dramatic splash pages, broken panels, abstract backgrounds, and collage effects have influenced every subsequent generation of artists in the comics medium. **RR**

Bat-Manga! 1966

Jiro Kuwata

Title in original language *Batman*
First published by Shonen Gahosha (Japan)
Creator Japanese (b.1935)
Genre Superhero

In the mid-1960s, when the camp *Batman* television show was due for syndication in Japan, a popular native creator of manga signed on to adapt the character for the local audience. The artist, Jiro Kuwata, was already famous for his hero *8 Man*.

Translation from one culture to another often entails a funhouse mirror effect, and that is certainly the case here. It is a remarkable thing to witness Batman, one of the biggest Western comics heroes, through the lens of what is arguably the planet's most comics-literate society, Japan. The result shows a Batman reminiscent of Bob Kane's original, but set upon by unfamiliar villains in surreal environs (all melting faces and eerie dream sequences) clearly rooted in the work of Osamu (*Astro Boy*) Tezuka, Kuwata's stated idol.

It is not that odd to see Batman, assisted by his sidekick Robin, fighting pterodactyls or facing down a villain named Death Man, but Japanese conventions make themselves felt. Some pages are drawn in color, others in black and white. Humorous commentary runs down the margins. Extensive wordless sequences effortlessly serve not only fights but also plot advancement. Then there is the habit of characters' faces changing depending on their emotions, often to an extreme that looks cartoonlike, not to mention the artist himself appearing in the comic and speaking directly to the readers.

That the manga, in 2008, became available in English owes much to Chip Kidd, a top U.S. book designer renowned for his Batman interest. Kidd's pursuit of the "holy grail," *Bat-Manga!*, as it was retitled, makes for an adventure unto itself, involving eBay fraud, missed opportunities, and corporate amnesia. When Kidd approached DC Comics for republication permission, no one at the company recalled it ever having existed. **MW**

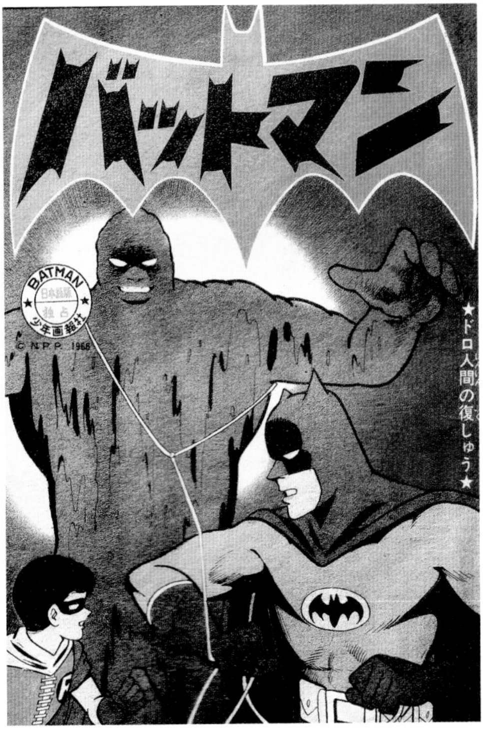
バットマン
BATMAN
独占
少年画報社
★ドロ人間の復しゅう★

Similar reads

Batman: Child of Dreams Kia Asamiya
MBQ Felipe Smith
Spider-Man: The Manga Ryoichi Ikegami
The Silver Surfer: Parable Stan Lee and Moebius

Lone Sloane
The Mystery of the Abyss 1966

Philippe Druillet

Title in original language *Le Mystère des Abimes*
First published by Eric Losfeld (France)
Creator French (b.1944)
Genre Science fiction

DRUILLET
LES 6 VOYAGES
DE LONE SLOANE
ALBIN MICHEL

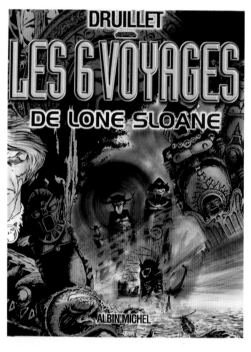

Other *Lone Sloane* stories
Chaos
Delerius
The Bridge over the Stars
The Isle of the Doom Wind
The Throne of the Black God

The term "space opera" was first coined in 1941 by Wilson Tucker, a U.S.-born science fiction and mystery writer, to describe melodramatic and romantic adventures set in outer space that were, in his opinion, "hacky, grinding, stinking." This jaundiced view persisted into the 1970s, when space opera was still being used as a tag for what was considered bad science fiction. Who knows how long the view would have held sway had artists such as Philippe Druillet not come along.

"The Mystery of the Abyss" was the first title to feature the Lone Sloane character. The cosmic adventurer, whose spaceship is damaged in the wake of the "great catastrophe," is captured by He Who Seeks, an abstract life-form that takes him into an alternate dimension

". . . an iron limb crashes into Sloane's painstakingly repaired rocket, destroying the work of . . . weeks."

where he is forced to wander, in a Silver Surfer–like way, galaxies that are not his own. With his companions, Kurt Kurtsteiner and Yearl the neo-Martian, he combats galactic warlords, demigods, and the evil Emperor Shaan. The allusion to opera was, of course, never about music but about scale. Philippe Druillet's artwork is panoramic, and his canvas the endless universe. Battles are epic, set against galaxies, nebulas, black holes, pulsars, and the sheer, infinite blackness of space.

In 1969 Druillet continued to develop *Lone Sloane* in *Pilote* magazine, and from 1974 in *Métal Hurlant*, the alternative magazine for graphic artists he cofounded with artist Jean Giraud. The latter saw him abandon panels in favor of full-page and double-spread drawings inspired by Hindu, gothic, and art nouveau architecture. The art was taken to new and spectacular heights by Druillet's use of computer-enhanced imagery. **BS**

Philippe Druillet's graphic art in *Lone Sloane* is spectacular and powerful. ➡

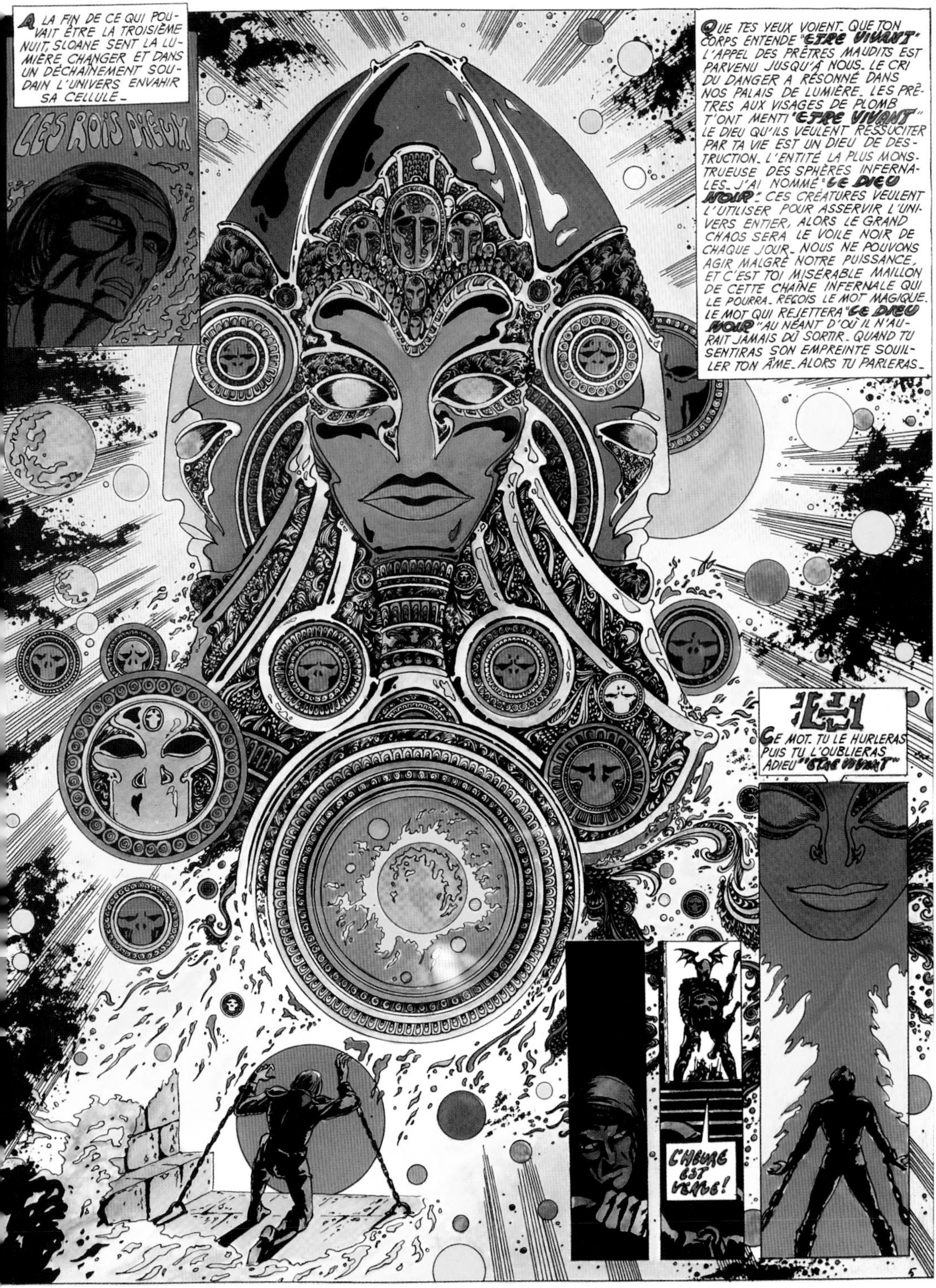
A LA FIN DE CE QUI POUVAIT ÊTRE LA TROISIÈME NUIT, SLOANE SENT LA LUMIÈRE CHANGER ET DANS UN DÉCHAINEMENT SOUDAIN L'UNIVERS ENVAHIR SA CELLULE–
LES ROIS DIEUX
QUE TES YEUX VOIENT. QUE TON CORPS ENTENDE "ÊTRE VIVANT" L'APPEL DES PRÊTRES MAUDITS EST PARVENU JUSQU'À NOUS. LE CRI DU DANGER A RÉSONNÉ DANS NOS PALAIS DE LUMIÈRE. LES PRÊTRES AUX VISAGES DE PLOMB T'ONT MENTI "ÊTRE VIVANT" LE DIEU QU'ILS VEULENT RESSUCITER PAR TA VIE EST UN DIEU DE DESTRUCTION. L'ENTITÉ LA PLUS MONSTRUEUSE DES SPHÈRES INFERNALES. J'AI NOMMÉ "LE DIEU NOIR". CES CRÉATURES VEULENT L'UTILISER POUR ASSERVIR L'UNIVERS ENTIER, ALORS LE GRAND CHAOS SERA LE VOILE NOIR DE CHAQUE JOUR. NOUS NE POUVONS AGIR MALGRÉ NOTRE PUISSANCE, ET C'EST TOI MISÉRABLE MAILLON DE CETTE CHAÎNE INFERNALE QUI LE POURRA. REÇOIS LE MOT MAGIQUE. LE MOT QUI REJETTERA "LE DIEU NOIR" AU NÉANT D'OÙ IL N'AURAIT JAMAIS DÛ SORTIR. QUAND TU SENTIRAS SON EMPREINTE SOUILLER TON ÂME. ALORS TU PARLERAS.
CE MOT. TU LE HURLERAS PUIS TU L'OUBLIERAS ADIEU
L'HEURE EST VENUE!

Creepy and Eerie 1966

Archie Goodwin Steve Ditko

First published by Warren Publishing (USA)
Creators Goodwin (American,1937–98); Ditko (American, b.1927)
Genre Horror, Fantasy

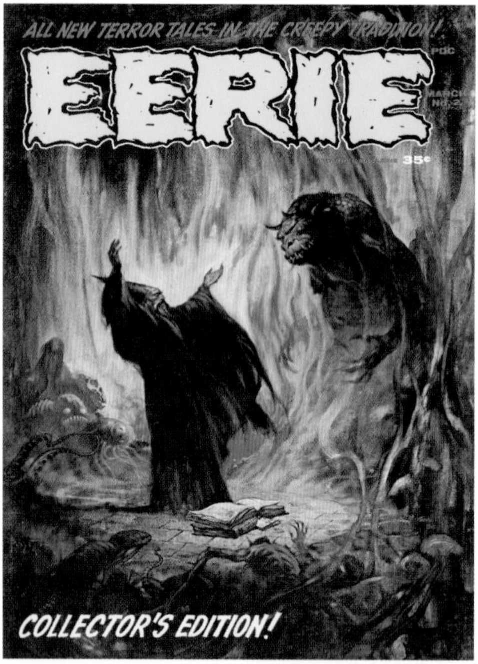
ALL NEW TERROR TALES IN THE CREEPY TRADITION!
EERIE
35¢
COLLECTOR'S EDITION!

Similar reads
House of Hammer Dez Skinn and others
Monsters Attack Mort Todd, Steve Ditko, and others
Spirit World Jack Kirby
Strange Avenging Tales Steve Ditko
Tomb of Dracula Marv Wolfman and Gene Colan

Steve Ditko's departure from Marvel in 1966 left fans wondering what he would do next. Charlton, where he worked on such characters as Blue Beetle and the Question, was familiar ground, but his appearance in Warren Publishing's black-and-white horror magazines was less expected. *Creepy* and *Eerie*, particularly during their early years, attracted a variety of notable artists, including Alex Toth, Gene Colan, Reed Crandall, Al Williamson, and many others. Ditko drew sixteen stories for Warren over the course of a year. All but one of the stories were scripted by Archie Goodwin and, without exception, display Ditko's artistic powers at their peak.

For most of these stories, Ditko used an ink-wash technique to depict textures and tonal gradations,

"You're a man of strange tastes, Mr. Danforth."

proving himself more than adept with this approach, using it to create moody atmospherics, magical landscapes (for example, "Second Chance," *Creepy* issue #13), and slavering monsters (as in "Blood of the Werewolf," *Creepy* issue #12). The arch-materialist Ditko, as always, proved himself a true master of depicting the supernatural in ways that challenged the reader.

Only three of the stories were not done in ink wash. "Collector's Edition" (*Creepy* issue #10), which tells of obsessive book collector Danforth's quest to secure a rare tome—the Marquis LeMode's *Dark Visions*—from oily dealer Murch, is worthy of special attention. It makes extensive use of fine pen, all textures and shadows rendered with meticulous line work, and stands out as one of the finest art jobs Ditko ever produced. The bottom-tier images on each page, showing a pair of hysterical eyes slowly closing, prefigure the story's conclusion visually, and are jaw-droppingly effective. **CH**

Being black and white, *Creepy* did not need the approval of the Comics Code Authority. ➡

SECOND CHANCE!

FOR A TIME AFTER HE DIED, EDWARD NUGENT DRIFTED IN A LIMBO WITHOUT DIMENSION, WITHOUT THOUGHT; LIKE A DREAMLESS SLUMBER... THEN, SENSATION WAKENED IN HIS FLOATING FORM AND HE FOUND HIMSELF DRAWN INTO A HALFWORLD OF HORROR, A SHIFTING, CHANGING NIGHTMARE THAT REACHED OUT AND ENGULFED HIM, AN AMOBEA UNIVERSE WRAPPING AROUND HIM, PULLING HIM TO ITS CORE...

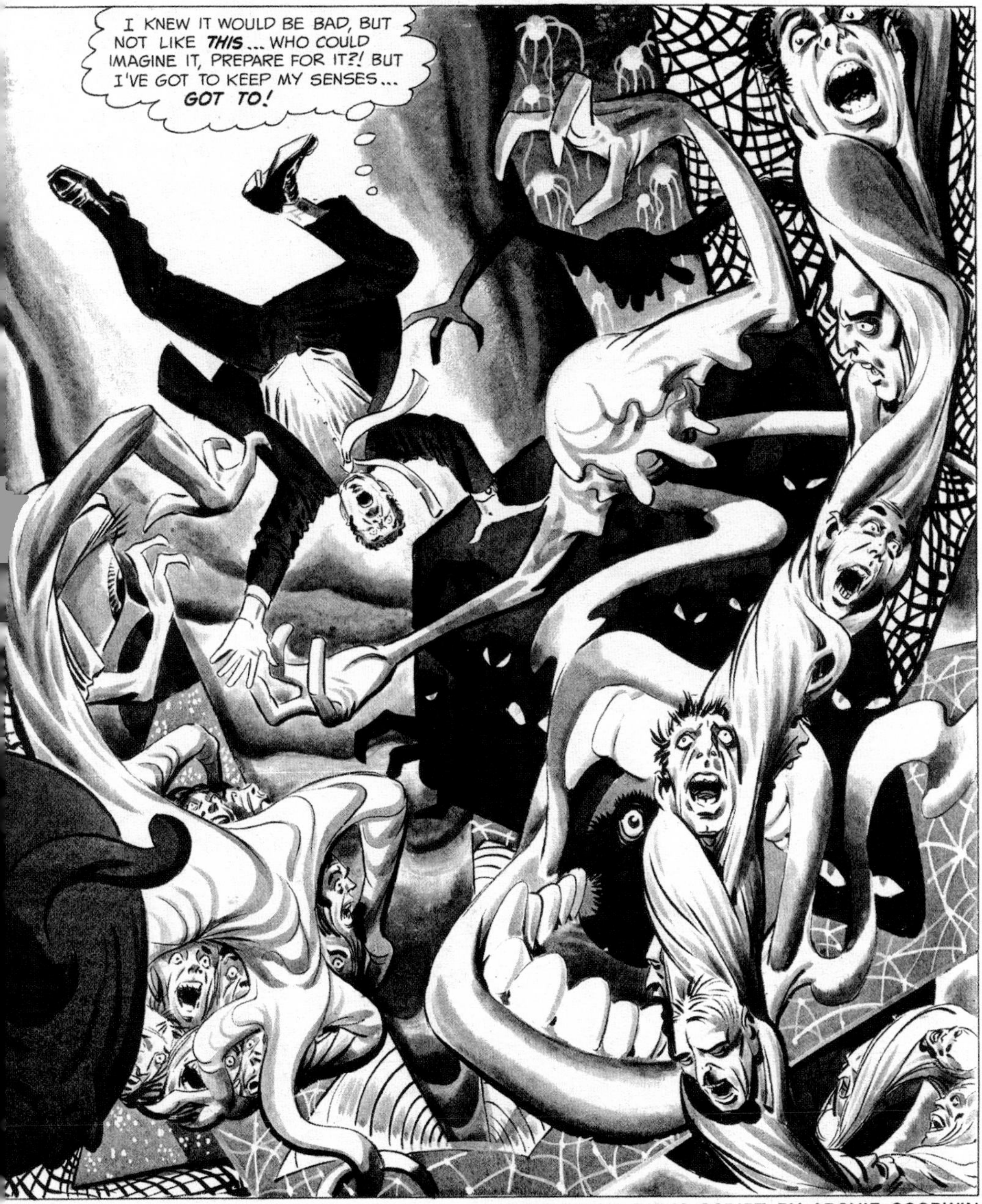
I KNEW IT WOULD BE BAD, BUT NOT LIKE THIS... WHO COULD IMAGINE IT, PREPARE FOR IT?! BUT I'VE GOT TO KEEP MY SENSES... GOT TO!

ART BY STEVE DITKO/SCRIPT BY ARCHIE GOODWIN

Cheech Wizard 1966

Vaughn Bodé

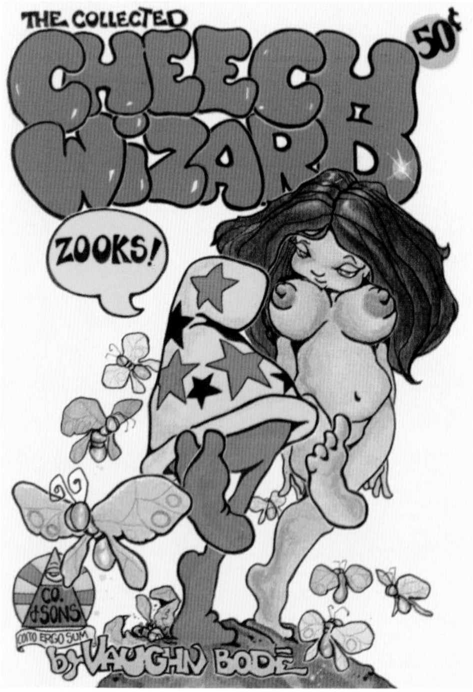
THE COLLECTED
CHEECH WIZARD
II
50¢
ZOOKS!
CO. & SONS
COGITO ERGO SUM
by VAUGHN BODĒ

"Cheech Wizard is the new Mickey Mouse of the 70s, but a far better head vehicle to communicate with."

Vaughn Bodé

Also by Vaughn Bodé

Das Kämpf

Deadbone Erotica

Purple Pictography With Bernie Wrightson

The Man

First published by *Syracuse Daily Orange* (USA)
Creator American (1941–75)
Genre Adult humor
Award Eisner Hall of Fame (2006)

Vaughn Bodé occupied an unusual place in the comics scene of the hippie era: although very much a part of the counterculture, most of his strips appeared in mainstream publications. His most famous creation, *Cheech Wizard,* appeared in *National Lampoon.* As a child, Bodé was a prodigious talent, who by 1960 had created more than 1,500 characters, his favorite of which was a mysterious being named Cheech Wizard, whose body was concealed by a large, star-covered hat.

While studying art at Syracuse University, he used his childhood creation in a strip for the student newspaper. As the counterculture took hold, Bodé embraced the underground scene, reviving *Cheech Wizard* for such titles as *The East Village Other*, *Gothic Blimp Works*, *Junkwaffel,* and *Last Gasp.* His big breakthrough came in 1972 when the strip started featuring in *National Lampoon* and reached a vast, hip audience. The strip was an unusual combination of hippie philosophizing, sex, and scatological humor set in a fantasy world populated by lizards and voluptuous girls. Bodé's art was colorful and attractive, and its apparent cuteness masked the often outrageous content of the stories.

In 1973 Bodé released his most personal work, *Schizophrenia*, which mixed typically scabrous *Cheech Wizard* strips with a brave autobiographical sequence about his life as a transvestite. He later performed scenes from *Schizophrenia* in a multimedia performance he called his Cartoon Concert. Tragically, he died a few days before his thirty-fourth birthday in an act of auto-asphyxiation that went horribly wrong. **DAR**

The Adventures of Jodelle 1966

✐✐ Guy Peellaert

Title in original language *Les Aventures de Jodelle*
First published by Eric Losfeld (France)
Creator Belgian (1934–2008)
Genre Adult humor

Jodelle is a spy and resident of Rome. Not the Rome we know, however, but a pseudofuturistic version of the ancient city complete with automobiles, nightclubs, television, neon, and caricatured celebrities straight out of the 1960s. Jodelle works for the despotic, guitar-playing Emperor Augustus, and when a plot by the Proconsuless to end his rule is uncovered, Jodelle and her associate Gallia are sent to uncover proof of her treasonous intent. They gain entry to her palace, but in the process Gallia is killed. With no time to mourn her loss, Jodelle escapes on a motorbike, clutching a diary that will prove the Proconsuless's guilt.

Notoriously sexy for its time, the lead character of *The Adventures of Jodelle* was modeled after French singer Sylvie Vartan and debuted in the satirical magazine *Hara-Kiri*. Along with Jean-Claude Forest's Barbarella and Michael O'Donoghue's Phoebe Zeit-Geist, the sexually liberated Jodelle represented a new breed of scantily clad heroines who battled as much to keep their clothes from falling off their voluptuous bodies and racing from one sexual encounter to the next as they did fighting bad guys. Of the three, however, *Jodelle* was the most aesthetic in terms of its art. Heavily influenced by the emerging pop art culture, Peellaert was at the vanguard of French erotic comics, and his flat, multicolored renderings perfectly illustrated *Jodelle*'s psychedelic, flower-powered, faux-Roman world. Peellaert followed *Jodelle* with *Pravda*, the adventures of a motorcycle-riding Amazon, before leaving comics to design album covers for The Rolling Stones and David Bowie. **BS**

The Genius Bakabon 1967

✐✐ Fujio Akatsuka

Title in original language *Tensai Bakabon*
First published by Kodansha (Japan)
Creator Japanese (1935–2008)
Genre Humor

Fujio Akatsuka's best-known gag comic, *The Genius Bakabon*, emerged thanks to the efforts of a persistent editor at *Weekly Shonen Magazine*, who, following countless rejections by the artist, finally convinced him to contribute to the publication. This was a bold gesture for both parties, because Akatsuka was already a favorite at the magazine's rival *Weekly Shonen Sunday* for his hit series *Osomatsu-kun*. Nevertheless, *The Genius Bakabon* became a huge success when it was released in 1967.

Initially, the comic focused on the daily life of a young, dopey boy, Bakabon (*baka* means "stupid"), but the leading role was eventually taken over by his wacky father—Bakabon's Papa. Bakabon's Papa was supposedly born a genius like his über-intelligent baby son Hajime, but the comic reveals that he lost his wit after it literally fell out of his mouth in an accident. Typically, an episode consists of an array of misadventures caused by the troublemaking father and mischievous Bakabon. Yet whatever the disaster, the day is always saved by the careless Bakabon's Papa's famous line, "That's alright!"

Akatsuka's approach to nonsense humor did not stop at the insane behavior of his leading character. Instead, the artist became increasingly experimental, for example, braving a dialogue-only episode with no illustrations, or drawing with his nondominant hand in another. He even tried to illustrate the characters in life-size, which meant he needed two full pages to draw a single head. These were the kind of jokes that only worked in print media, a priceless quality that took Japan's gag comic genre to a whole new level. **TS**

Deadman 1967

Arnold Drake · Neal Adams

First published by DC Comics (USA)
Creators Drake (American, 1924–2007); Adams (American, b.1941)
Genre Superhero

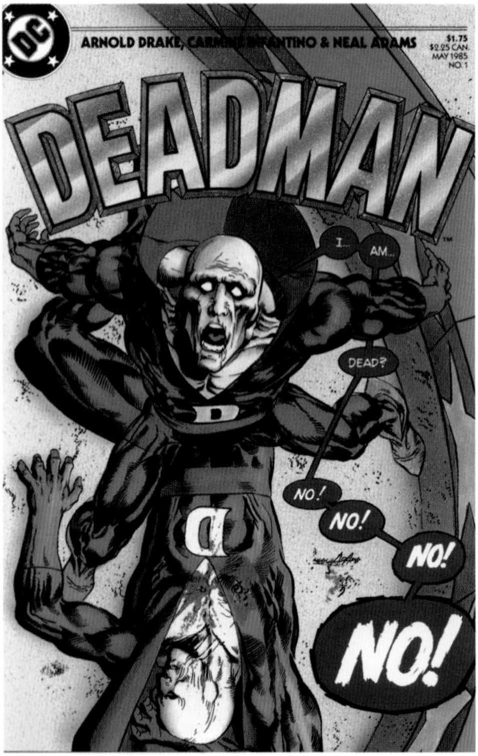
DC
ARNOLD DRAKE
NEAL ADAMS
$1.75
$2.25 CAN.
MAY 1985
NO. 1
DEADMAN
I... AM...
DEAD?
NO!
NO!
NO!
NO!

"This man who was just murdered is our hero! His story begins one minute later."

When writer Arnold Drake was assigned the creation of a continuing character for the comic anthology *Strange Adventures*, he drew on the late1960s fascination with Eastern mysticism and envisioned a ghostly hero.

Boston Brand, a circus trapeze artist who defies death nightly—cynically calling himself Deadman—is murdered by a gunman with a hook for a hand. The spirit of Deadman is granted the power to enter and control anyone's body by Rama Kushna, "the face of the universe." Taking a cue from the popular television show *The Fugitive*, whose protagonist searches for his wife's murderer, Drake had Deadman hunting his own killer, the mysterious Hook. Each story had an overarching quest from which Deadman was diverted to help someone in need. Writing with sophisticated, dramatic realism and infusing the hero with blunt, blue-collar emotionalism, Drake—and Jack Miller after him—wrote brutal, noirish crime scenarios about drug dealers, motorcycle gangs, evil circus performers, and smugglers of illegal immigrants.

Although Carmine Infantino drew the first story and designed the look of the character, including the cadaverous white mask, *Deadman*'s definitive interpretation came when artist Neal Adams joined the creative team with the second issue. Adams had cut his teeth on the newspaper strip *Ben Casey* and combined startling realism with wildly experimental page layouts. Adams could also make the fantastic credible. In one surreal story that he also scripted, Adams drew Deadman battling "misdirected wisps of imagination" to merge with—and save the life of—a character dying of a gunshot wound.

Despite fan acclaim, the series was canceled after twelve issues. Yet Deadman still became a perennial figure in the "DC Universe," and Adams one of the most influential U.S. comics artists of the 1970s. **TRL**

Tomorrow's Joe 1967

"Asao Takamori" Tetsuya Chiba

The brainchild of writer Asao Takamori and illustrator Tetsuya Chiba, *Tomorrow's Joe* was originally serialized in Japan between the late 1960s and the early 1970s, an era of resistance to authority among youth who opposed the nation's security treaty with the United States. When this boxing comic appeared in *Weekly Shonen Magazine* in 1968, it was those same young people who were attracted by Joe's rebellious character, his lower class background, and the setting of the plot, which was constantly synchronized with the time period in which they lived.

Evidence of the influence of the comic strip came in 1977 when hijackers of the Japanese Red Army were to boast in a statement that they "represented Tomorrow's Joe himself." However, the comic did not only appeal to extremists. By perfectly capturing the atmosphere of its time and digging deep into life as it was really lived in the slums, the comic gained a cult following all over Japan.

The story revolves around Joe, a troubled young man who is introduced to boxing while in a juvenile detention facility. His days of training are literally a roller-coaster ride of blood, sweat, and tears as he faces fierce competition in and out of the ring.

The appeal of Takamori's portrayal of Joe was that readers were able to witness his growth, not only as a boxer but as a rebellious teenager fighting his way to maturity. Readers became so attached to the comic that, following the dramatic and unexpected death of Joe's biggest rival, Rikishi, fans organized a funeral for the fictional character; seven hundred people came to participate in the extraordinary event.

Tomorrow's Joe was first developed into an animated series for television in 1970, followed by numerous adaptations such as video games, radio drama, and several films, including one in 2011. **TS**

Title in original language *Ashita no Joe*
First published by Kodansha (Japan)
Creators Asaki Takamori (Japanese, b.1936–87); Chiba (Japanese, b. 1939) **Genre** Drama

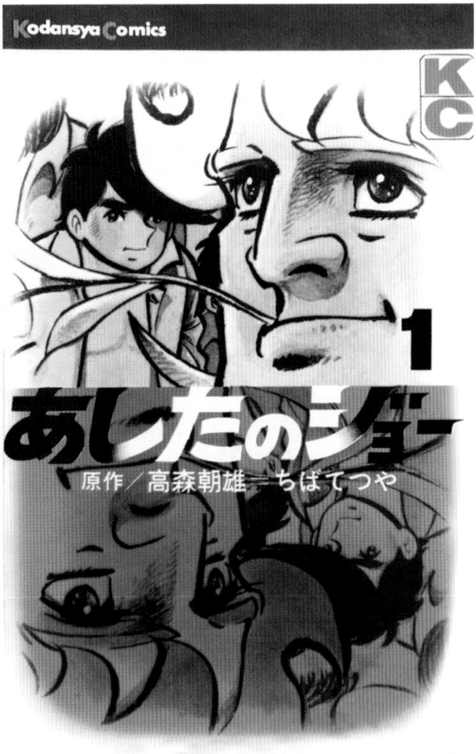
Kodansya Comics
KC
1
あしたのジョー
原作／高森朝雄　ちばてつや

"I've burned, I've burned out . . . all that is left is white."

Joe Yabuki

Mr. Natural 1967

R. Crumb

First published by *Yarrowstalks* (USA)
Creator American (b.1943)
Genre Humor, Underground
Award Harvey Special Award for Humor (1990)

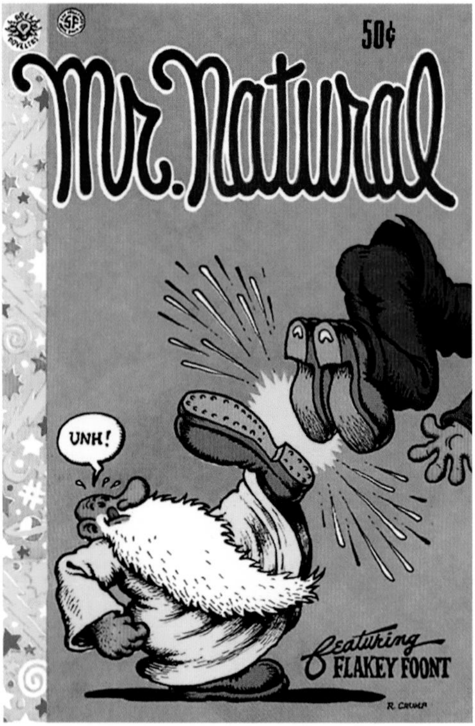
50¢
Mr. Natural
UNH!
featuring FLAKEY FOONT
R. CRUMB

"Come here, I'll let ya in on a secret! The whole universe is completely insane!"

The first star of underground comix, R. Crumb is still closely identified with the hippie era, but he was always something of an outsider. The fast-talking guru *Mr. Natural* starred in many of Crumb's early comics and was probably as close as his creator ever came to embracing the counterculture, although an undertone of distrustful cynicism is never far from the surface.

The year 1966 found Crumb at a crossroads, drawing greetings cards by day but also taking vast quantities of LSD. However, during that period he experienced an enormous outpouring of creativity that produced all the major characters that would fill his comics for the next ten years, foremost of which was Mr. Natural. After moving to San Francisco, Crumb quickly found success in *Yarrowstalks*, and then with his own comic, *Zap*. Over the next few years Mr. Natural starred in numerous publications, including *Hytone*, *Uneeda*, *The East Village Other,* and finally in 1970, his own title. Fred Natural himself was ostensibly the perfect hippie hero, a bushy-bearded shaman dispensing wisdom to his devoted followers. Indeed, in Mr. Natural's 719th meditation from issue #1 he meditates contentedly as a whole city springs up around him and then chants it out of existence again, all in the space of three pages.

However, Mr. Natural was always as much Groucho Marx as guru, and his refusal to ever give a straight answer was surely Crumb's way of telling his audience to trust nobody. By the mid-1970s his art had evolved into a finely cross-hatched level of detail and observation rarely seen in comics, although ruinous court cases and crippling tax bills had left him broke. To pay the bills he revived *Mr. Natural* for a weekly strip feature in the *Village Voice*, but there is a palpable sense of betrayal in the series. The once hippie icon was then beset by shallow young hipsters and jaded groupies. The 1960s as he had known them were definitely over. **DAR**

Corto Maltese
Ballad of the Salty Sea 1967

Hugo Pratt

Ballad of the Salty Sea was the first adventure story Hugo Pratt published featuring his celebrated comic character Corto Maltese, a mysterious Malta-born sailor who bums around the world during the 1910s and 1920s, regularly espousing heroic causes, often supporting the underdog, sometimes cynically promoting himself. Set against historically accurate backgrounds and mixing occult lore and philosophy into real events, with Maltese meeting a host of real-life figures, including international writers and politicians, Pratt's *Corto Maltese* stories are undoubtedly among the greatest adventure comics that have ever been created.

Maltese pops up at crucial times and places throughout history. This first adventure is set in the South Pacific islands just before World War I, in a veritable hotbed of rogues and thieves. The story begins when a Russian smuggler by the name of Rasputin rescues two teenagers, Cain and Pandora, much against his better judgment. The three of them later come across a tall, lean man tied to a raft, who has been left to die by pirates. This is how readers are introduced to the debonair and beguiling Maltese. Of course, there is every chance that he may well be a pirate himself.

The *Corto Maltese* series is endlessly fascinating. Books have been written about it, trying to get to the bottom of the character's appeal. Perhaps his unpredictable nature is the key to his magnetism, perhaps it is his misty past; the debate rages on.

Pratt's skillful art keeps readers on the edge of their seats. Dynamic and often audacious, the story is beautifully drawn. Pratt's panels never have one line too many, and the artist knows when to suggest something roughly and when to detail it, spotting blacks to dramatic effect. *Ballad of the Salty Sea* is a masterclass in how to tell a story clearly and succinctly, and yet with great panache. **FJ**

Title in original language *Una balata del mare salato*
First published by Self-published in *Sgt. Kirk* (Italy)
Creator Italian (1927–95)
Genre Adventure

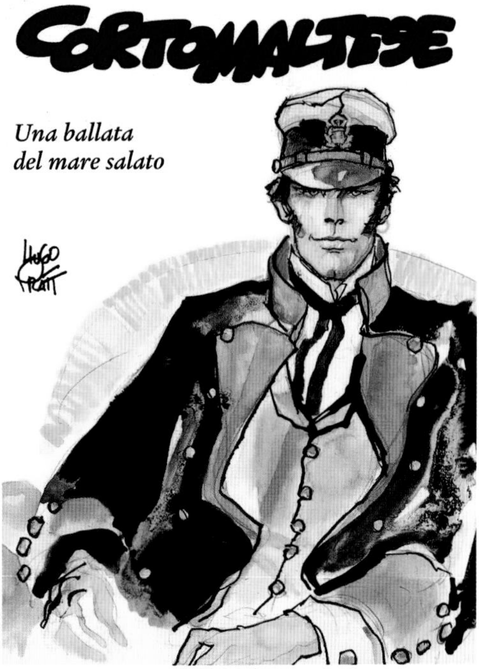
CORTO MALTESE
Una ballata
del mare salato
HUGO PRATT

GRUPPO EDITORIALE L'ESPRESSO

"I see, Mr. Pratt, that you're not afraid to dip a pen or brush in a bottle of ink and throw down a velvet-black line. . . ."

Will Gould

Lupin III 1967

✏️ "Monkey Punch"

Title in original language *Rupan Sansei*
First published by Futabasha (Japan)
Creator Kato Kazuhiko (Japanese, b.1937)
Genre Crime

The title of this comic refers to the name of its leading character, Lupin III, a notorious thief and the grandson of Arsène Lupin from the celebrated detective novels by French writer Maurice Leblanc. Kato Kazuhiko, more commonly known by his pen name of "Monkey Punch," leaves most things about Lupin to the readers' imaginations—details including his age, nationality, and education remain a mystery. Readers are told, however, that he has an I.Q. of more than 300, and that he has mastered his grandfather's teachings about theft and disguise as outlined in the "Robbery Bible." He has a weakness for beautiful women, and always warns his victims (and consequently his nemesis, Inspector Zenigata) before carrying out his robberies. Lupin's gang includes the voluptuous Fujiko Mine, gunman Daisuke Jigen, and Goemon Ishikawa XIII, the descendant of a Samurai swordsman.

The story lines and the artwork were innovatively Western when the comic first appeared, marking the beginning of a new era on the Japanese comic scene. *Lupin III* really took off when it was turned into an animated film. Blessed with excellent directors and matchless dubbers, it became a sensation. Many film productions followed, including *The Castle of Cagliostro* directed by Hayao Miyazaki in 1979. While the animated versions of *Lupin III* have retained the essence of the comic, they are less violent than the original. Surprisingly, Monkey Punch has not been involved with any of the animated films, although his reputation as the eminent creator of Japan's infamous icon stands firm. **TS**

Phoenix 1967

✏️ Osamu Tezuka

Title in original language *Hi no Tori*
First published by Various (Japan)
Creator Japanese (1928–89)
Genre Adventure

Osamu Tezuka completed twelve volumes of his manga series *Phoenix*, although the cycle remains unfinished due to Tezuka's death. Each of the books can be read independently, as they take place in different periods beginning with early civilization, then jumping backward and forward in time toward a convergence in the present. Although *Phoenix* was not published chronologically, the themes of evolution and reincarnation recur as characters from one volume and appear in new guises in others. The search for immortality, as embodied in the myth of the phoenix, is the starting point for each story.

The fifth volume, *Ho-o* (known as *Karma* in the English translation), is considered to be the best single volume. Set during the Nara period in eighth-century Japan, it depicts the lives of Gao, a bandit, and Akanemaru, a sculptor. Akanemaru was injured in his youth by Gao, who has since turned away from his evil past and also become a sculptor. When they both compete for the same commission, the truth about Gao's past threatens his life. The Phoenix and its promise of immortality drive the protagonists in different ways.

With the Phoenix as an impartial witness to the countless evolutions and destructions of life in its myriad forms, Tezuka addresses fundamental questions about existence. Each individual volume is complex, with its own set of richly drawn characters. The storytelling and artwork are consistently intelligent and moving as Tezuka sought innovative ways to tell his stories and help his readers feel them emotionally. **NFI**

COM こむ

月刊コミック・マガジン

創刊号

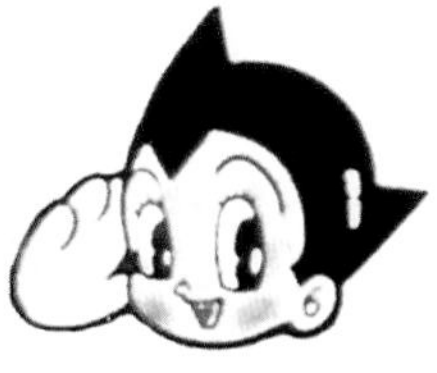

1967 1

んがエリートのためのまんが専門誌

塚治虫／火の鳥

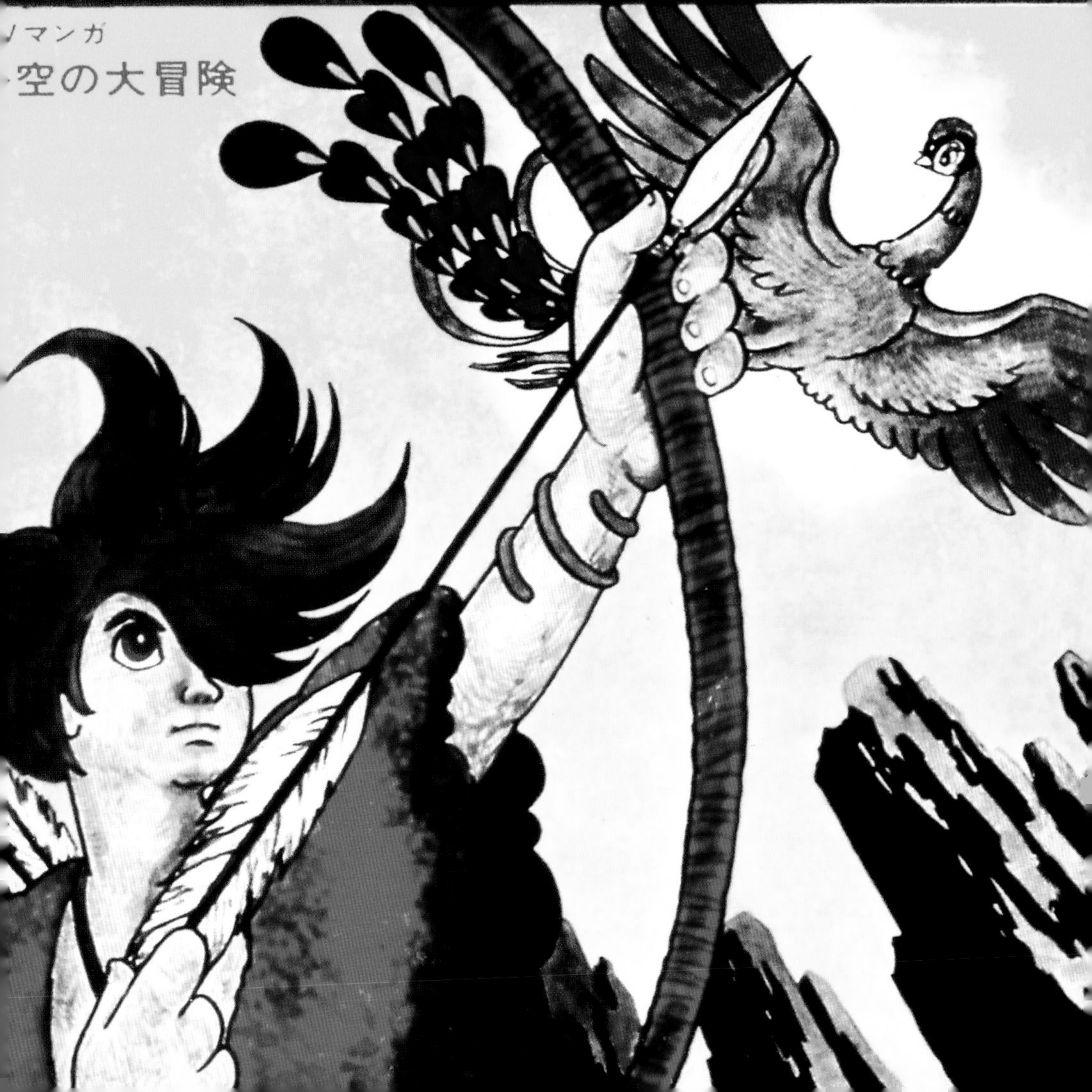
ノマンガ
空の大冒険

Wanderer 1967

✏️ Shinji Nagashima

Title in original language *Futen*
First published by Seirindo (Japan)
Creator Japanese (1938–2005)
Genre Humor

Amid the heightened tension of student activism in late 1960s to early 1970s Japan, many young people from all over the country migrated to Tokyo's Shinjuku district. Mostly aspiring artists, they rarely stayed at home, wandering around the streets as they engaged in conversation about film, art, and music. They found casual work, but only when they needed to. *Wanderer* revolves around the lives of such young people, with creator Shinji Nagashima as its main character.

Nagashima's depiction of the wanderer was based on his own itinerant lifestyle, although elements of the plot are fictional. In one memorable scene, Dan san (Nagashima's nickname) invites a girl whom he has just met to the Yamanote Hotel. Seemingly a portrayal of promiscuous youth, the comic soon reveals that the Yamanote Hotel is actually slang for the Yamanote line, a railway line that runs through Tokyo in a loop. Moments later, the couple are fast asleep, snoring loudly on a train. When they wake up, they decide to go for another one or two laps, and fall right back to sleep.

This was a period when the spirit of nihilism, rebellion, and the sexual revolution was reverberating throughout the world. Nagashima's masterpiece captured the nature of this generation and their sense of potential and freedom brilliantly. Renowned for constantly developing and experimenting with his illustrations, Nagashima uses a Picasso-like approach in *Wanderer*, and draws some of the faces and objects from multiple angles. **TS**

Terajima-cho 1968

✏️ Yu Takita

Title in original language *Terajima-cho Kidan*
First published by Kodansha (Japan)
Creator Japanese (b.1932)
Genre Biography

Terajima-cho was the name of prewar Tokyo's red light district. Its nickname was Akasen, or "red lines" (*aka* means "red," and *sen* means "line"), a reference to a tradition of using red pencil to mark such an area on a map. All districts with brothels were commonly known as Akasen, and they existed openly long after World War II. The author of this comic, Yu Takita, was raised in Terajima-cho, in a milieu of bars, prostitutes and their clients, and drunken men vomiting and urinating in the gutters. Takita vividly illustrates the district through his childhood eyes, watching visitors come and go.

In a memorable scene, Takita describes a seemingly helpful sign in an alleyway, saying "passageway this way." The so-called passageway is actually a blind alley, and the deceiving sign is a ploy to seduce potential customers. Growing up in this adults' world, surrounded by sultry women, Takita overheard adult conversations and witnessed Yakuza fights. Yet for him this was no tragic experience, simply normality for a young artist who did not know any different. The comic does no more than depict Takita's ordinary life, sketching his day-to-day observations with a nostalgic flavor, a hint of heart-warming humor, and no apparent plot.

Similar to *Terajima-cho kidan*, Takita's other famous work, *Dojo tsure zure banashi*, focuses on his everyday life while living in Kokubunji, Tokyo. In this piece, Takita uniquely places illustrations of objects such as a kettles and chocolates in the speech bubbles. Instead of using words, he cleverly expresses the characters' feelings through simple drawings. **TS**

The Fabulous Furry Freak Brothers 1968

Gilbert Shelton

First published by The Print Mint (USA)
Creator American (b.1940)
Genre Humor
Adaptation Film: *Grass Roots* (2011)

THE COLLECTED ADVENTURES OF
THE FABULOUS FURRY
FREAK
BROTHERS
LOVE IT OR
75¢
TOOT TOOT
DOPE
Gilbert Shelton

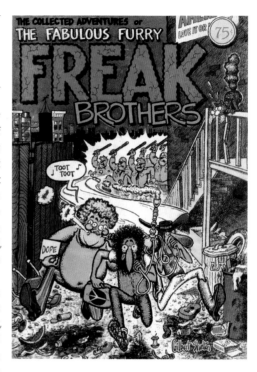

Created under the intoxicating influences of Harvey Kurtzman's *MAD Magazine* and the slapstick trios of the Marx Brothers and the Three Stooges, *The Fabulous Furry Freak Brothers*, by the Texan-born cartoonist Gilbert Shelton, first appeared in the early underground comic book *Feds and Heads*, published by The Print Mint in 1968. The three central characters—Fat Freddy (the slob), Phineas (the brains), and Freewheelin' Franklin (the cowboy)—are not actually biological brothers at all, but lowdown, hustling hippies who share an insatiable appetite for drugs, food, and beer.

The protracted business of acquiring and selling weed ("Oh no, Fat Freddy got burned again"), while frequently outwitting the hapless Norbert the Narc, forms the basis of many *Freak Brothers* strips, which tend to vary considerably in length and ambition. There are a number of very tightly plotted and executed one-page gag strips, and then there is the globe-trotting, three-issue-long "Idiots Abroad" story line, considered to be Shelton's finest. The strip also generated its own spin-off star in *Fat Freddy's Cat*, a flea-bitten beast that is about as far from cute as possible.

Harvey Kurtzman once described Shelton as "the true pro" of the underground, a compliment to Shelton's consistently high level of cartooning craft. There is nothing formulaic or by rote about his work on the *Freak Brothers*, and although it has come to epitomize a countercultural moment now long gone, the appeal of the stories is timeless and ageless, as worldwide sales of more than 40 million comics attest. **AL**

"Now, turn that bong over so it'll look like a sculpture and break out the rum so we'll seem natural!"

Similar reads

Dopin' Dan Ted Richards
Harold Hedd Rand Holmes
Philbert Desanex' Dreams Gilbert Shelton
The Fat Freddy's Cat Omnibus Gilbert Shelton
Wonder Wart-Hog Gilbert Shelton and Tony Bell

Asterix at the Olympic Games 1968

René Goscinny Albert Uderzo

Title in original language *Astérix aux Jeux Olympiques* **First published by** *Pilote*, collected by Dargaud (France) **Creators** Goscinny (French, 1926–77); Uderzo (French, b.1927) **Genre** Humor

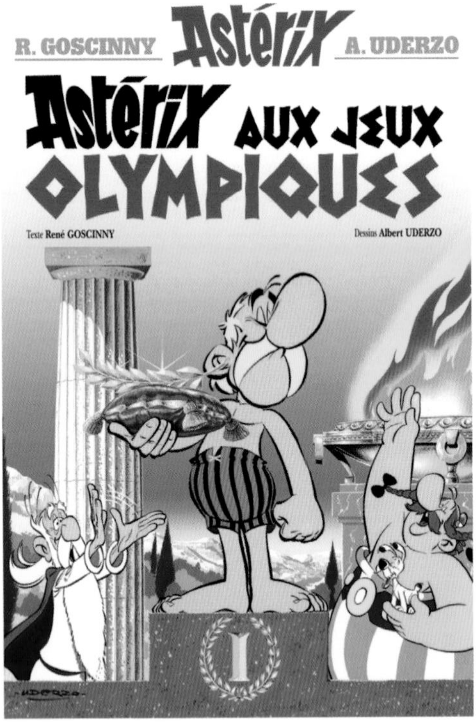
R. GOSCINNY
Astérix
A. UDERZO
Astérix aux Jeux Olympiques
Texte René GOSCINNY
Dessins Albert UDERZO

Other *Asterix* stories
Asterix in Britain
Asterix the Gaul
Asterix the Gladiator

Published in the same year as the Mexico City Olympics took place, *Asterix at the Olympic Games* sees our Gallic hero and his ever-present companion, Obelix, travel to Greece to compete in the games of 52 B.C. They do this after beating prideful Roman legionnaire Gluteus Maximus at running and then javelin throwing in the woods outside of their village, albeit unintentionally and with the aid of magic potion. Regrettably, when they arrive in Athens, our Gauls are told that their potion is considered an artificial stimulant and are forbidden from using it. The tale might be the first instance in sports of the banning of a performance-enhancing drug.

When the Greeks win every event, Asterix and a number of demoralized Roman athletes compete against each other in a hastily organized race designed to restore shattered Roman pride. The Romans win but only with the aid of a potion that gives them away by turning their tongues blue, so they are disqualified and Asterix is declared the winner.

"Athletes from Magnesia are on a milk diet, the team from Cos is on lettuce."

This, the twelfth volume in the *Asterix* series, sees everyone who lives Asterix's village make the journey to Athens, providing the reader with an opportunity to get to know several secondary characters a little better. Readers become privy to the age of one of the characters (Geriatrix is ninety-three), and we are left to ponder how he came to be married to the most beautiful woman in the village.

Despite René Goscinny's use of caricature and national and cultural observations there is nothing political about Asterix. For Goscinny and Albert Uderzo, all that mattered were the laughs. "Laughter," Uderzo once said, "was our daily life, our customs, our era." **BS**

Bat Lash 1968

Sergio Aragonés and Dennis O'Neil "Nick Cardy"

Forever sporting a flamboyant waistcoat and a flower in his hat, dandified gunfighter Bat Lash made his debut in 1968's *Showcase* issue #76 before graduating to his own short-lived seven-issue series. This atypical Western hero is, ostensibly, more interested in the finer things in life. However, a penchant for gambling and scams means that extricating himself from his latest self-inflicted predicament always takes precedence over his preferred pursuits of women, poetry, and the best recipe for pheasant in aspic.

Sergio Aragonés and Dennis O'Neil's scripts are liberally sprinkled with running gags and recurring themes, as the humorous elements of the strip dominate. The villains are often outlandish and over the top, giving artist Nick Cardy plenty of visual scope to fittingly flesh them out as memorable grotesques. Cardy's layouts are always inventive, and his art gracefully moves from slapstick to scenes of intense poignancy without ever seeming jarring or inappropriate. In later issues the series' tone changed significantly, providing a darker origin story for the character that focuses on his quest to avenge the events of his past. This dramatic shift in tone highlights the greatest strength of the book's writing: its ability to combine the pathos of Bat Lash's tragic backstory with its self-indulgently comedic approach to DC's Western line.

"I hate him. . . . He's the only man who made me feel like a woman!"

Bat Lash inverts the traditional role of the Western hero and adopts a sitcom sensibility to its subject matter, yet the creators never lose sight of the grim realities and harsher rules of its historical setting. *Bat Lash* is a comic that both embraces and shakes up the genre that spawned it, and is essential reading. **AO**

First published by DC Comics (USA)
Creators Aragonés (Spanish, b.1937); O'Neil (American, b.1939); Nicolas Viscardi (American, b.1920)
Genre Humor, Western

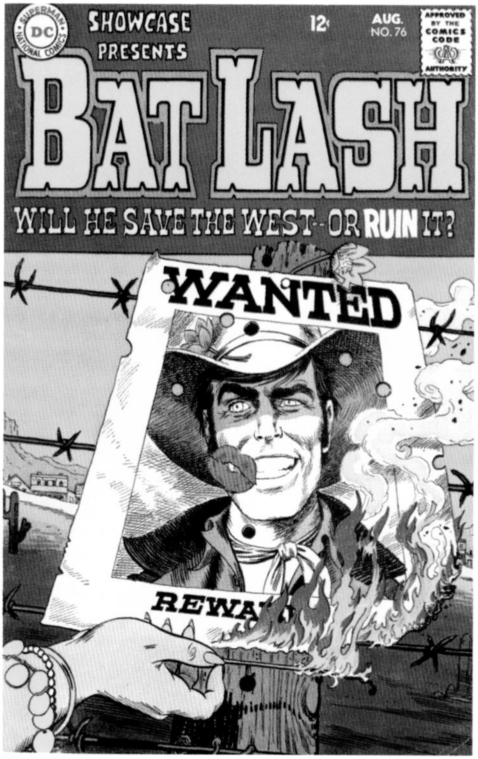
SUPERMAN DC NATIONAL COMICS
SHOWCASE PRESENTS
12¢
AUG. NO. 76
APPROVED BY THE COMICS CODE AUTHORITY
BAT LASH
WILL HE SAVE THE WEST—OR RUIN IT?
WANTED
REWA

Similar reads

Lucky Luke René Goscinny and Morris
Rick O'Shay Stan Lynde
Weird Western Tales John Albano and Neal Adams

Shameless School 1968

✏️✏️ "Go Nagai"

Title in original language *Harenchi Gakuen*
First published by Shueisha (Japan)
Creator Kiyoshi Nagai (Japanese, b.1945)
Genre Humor

Go Nagai may be known for his science fiction titles and their animated counterparts, such as *Mazinger Z* and *Devilman*, but originally he made his debut as a gag comic artist. Indeed, it was this early work in the genre that made him a household name.

As the title hints, the comic is set in a private elementary school for students who are utterly shameless, each eventful episode packed with Nagai's bizarre humor. The teachers featured in the story are particularly peculiar, such as the bearded Hige Godzilla sensei, who wears nothing but animal skin in the style of primitive man. The mildly sinister teachers' lives revolve almost solely around bullying the students. The immature, subversive gags are literally explosive, destroying the entire school by the end of every episode and always finding a way to strip off the girls' clothes. The so-called protagonist and central character, nicknamed Oyabun ("Boss"), is far from heroic, and the series heroine is one of his victims, Shuubei-chan.

When the comic featured a scene where Oyabun lifted Shuubei-chan's skirt, elementary school students from all over Japan copied the act. The nation's PTA was outraged, immediately labeling the comic a bad influence. After the incident, the act of skirt-lifting became something of a trademark of the comic, despite it happening only once in the entire series. Amusingly, the original idea did not belong to Nagai, but came from a television commercial for a gas station. *Shameless School*, published in *Weekly Shonen Jump*, was later developed into a series of films. **TS**

Iznogoud: The Caliph's Vacation 1968

✏️ René Goscinny ✏️ Jean Tabary

Title in original language *Les Vacances du Calife*
First published by Dargaud (France)
Creators Goscinny (French, 1926–77); Tabary (Swedish, b.1930) **Genre** Humor

To describe *Iznogoud* as a satirical comic strip set in Baghdad, although accurate, makes it sound a little more daring than it actually is. In truth, the Baghdad presented here exists outside of history and politics. It functions purely as an exotic backdrop and springboard for farce, one that allows writer René Goscinny to draw parallels with the fads and fancies of contemporary Western society. For example, the lead story in *The Caliph's Vacation*, the third *Iznogoud* album, takes aim at the overcrowded beaches, unfinished hotels, and desolate uniformity of the package holiday.

Goscinny, author of *Asterix* and *Lucky Luke*, began his collaboration with artist Jean Tabary in 1962, when they produced the strip *Les Aventures du Calife Haroun el Poussah* for the French comic magazine *Record*. This introduced the placid ruler of the title along with his scheming second-in-command, Grand Vizier Iznogoud, who quickly became the focus of the comic. Iznogoud, a great tragic-comic figure and thoroughly wicked man, is in the grip of one overriding obsession: to replace his boss as caliph. His elaborate schemes to bump off his superior inevitably end in failure and torment.

While *The Caliph's Vacation* may be the most varied and consistent *Iznogoud* album, each of the Goscinny-written volumes contains four ten-page-long stories that are minor masterpieces of bad punning and precisely orchestrated slapstick. The fine architecture of Goscinny's plots gave Tabary free rein to construct his own ornately detailed images of palaces and deserts, all drawn in a jagged, highly expressive pen style. **AL**

Zap Comix 1968

R. Crumb

First published by Apex Novelties (USA)
Creator American (b.1943)
Genre Underground
Award Will Eisner Comic Book Hall of Fame (1991)

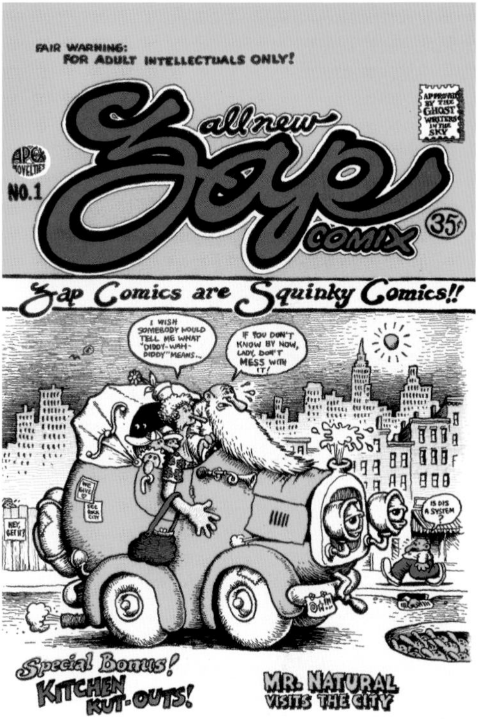

FAIR WARNING: FOR ADULT INTELLECTUALS ONLY!
APPROVED BY THE GHOST WRITERS IN THE SKY
NO.1
all new Zap COMIX
35¢
Zap Comics are Squinky Comics!!
I WISH SOMEBODY WOULD TELL ME WHAT "DIDDY-WAH-DIDDY" MEANS..
IF YOU DON'T KNOW BY NOW, LADY, DON'T MESS WITH IT!
IS DIS A SYSTEM ?
Special Bonus! KITCHEN KUT-OUTS!
MR. NATURAL VISITS THE CITY

Printed by *Beat* writer Charles Plymell and published by Don Donahue for his Apex Novelties imprint, the first issue of *Zap Comix* was the foundation for the entire underground comix movement. It also showcased Robert Crumb's drawing style and humor, opening it up to a wider, more hip audience. Although the majority of the early print run was sold on the streets of San Francisco by Crumb or his wife from a baby buggy, they would later be made available in retail outlets.

Zap #1 contains several of Crumb's best-known strips such as "Whiteman," a tale of white male America on the verge of a nervous breakdown, the much-bootlegged "Keep On Truckin'. . .," and "Mr. Natural Visits The City," a story that introduces Crumb's guru character Mr. Natural and his angst-ridden urban disciple, Flakey Foont, to the world. Other highlights are "Abstract Expressionist Ultra Super Modernistic Comics," a brain-tilting three-pager in which Crumb attempts to come to grips with modern art, an idea that would be explored more thoroughly in his 1973 sketchbook comic *Artistic Comics*, and the semiautobiographical "Definitely a Case of Derangement" where he questions his own sanity.

Somewhat confusingly, *Zap* #0 was published after the first issue, because the original publisher abducted the finished art. Crumb located photocopies of the pages, drew up a new cover, and handed the completed comic over to Donahue for publication. For successive issues of *Zap,* Crumb invited other artists to contribute, including S. Clay Wilson, Robert Williams, and Gilbert Shelton of *Freak Brothers*. **EP**

"'I want you should stop wasting your time reading these cheap comic books!': I bet this happened to you when you were a kid!"

Also by R. Crumb
Mr. Natural
My Troubles With Women

Rubric-a-brac 1968

Marcel Gotlib

Title in original language *La Rubrique-à-brac*
First published by *Pilote* (France)
Creator French (b.1934)
Genre Humor

GOTLIB
RUBRIQUE-À-BRAC
L'INTÉGRALE
DARGAUD

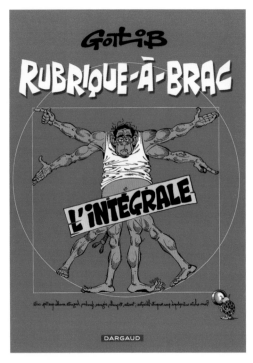

"To myself I am only a child playing on the beach, while vast oceans of truth lie undiscovered before me."

Isaac Newton

First appearing in the famous magazine *Pilote*, *Rubric-a-brac* (a portmanteau of *rubrique* and bric-a-brac) made its debut on January 11, 1968, in the form of a complete story on two plates. This format remained practically unchanged, apart from a few stories here and there with more pages, until the series came to an end in 1972. By then its author, Marcel Gotlib, had produced more than 400 pages of jokes and, in the eyes of several generations of unconditional, laughing readers, he had become a real idol.

When he started this series, Gotlib was already well known. He had been working for several years for *Pilote*, illustrating another series of humorous short stories, *Les Dingodossiers*, written by René Goscinny, the creator of *Asterix*. But Goscinny, snowed under with work (he was also the editor-in-chief of the magazine), decided to end the series while at the same time encouraging his illustrator to go it alone. The result was the birth of *Rubric-a-brac*: a very suitable name because the series—and this is its originality—does not have a particular subject, or rather, it covers them all.

Gotlib deals with any subject, from everyday life to historical events and animal chronicles or parodies, all in a hyper-expressive graphic style and with completely unrestrained humor. As time went by, some recurring characters began to stand out, introducing running gags into the series and implied references for its readers. For example, there is Isaac Newton developing his theory of universal gravitation after an apple fell on his head—and subsequently he is hit by just about any object, from a petanque ball to a whole rhinoceros—or the little ladybird who lives her life at the bottom of the pictures. For more than thirty years humorists in the world of strip cartoons, theater, and film have claimed to be influenced by Gotlib and his comic *Rubric-a-brac*, and he is still their mentor today. **NF**

Kake 1968

"Tom of Finland"

"Tom of Finland" (Touko Laaksonen) drew only gay men—in both meanings of the word. Almost single-handedly his artwork promoted a self-confident masculinity for gay men at a time when homosexuality was illegal and many were in the closet.

Drawing had become an outlet during his sheltered rural boyhood, and young Laaksonen devised his first strips at the age of eight. He moved to Helsinki in 1939 to study art and was soon experiencing his earliest sexual encounters with German soldiers, experiences that fostered his fetish for uniforms and boots. After the war, Laaksonen worked in advertising while developing his private homoerotic art, including his first multipanel story in 1946.

Inspired by pioneer gay U.S. illustrator George Quaintance, Laaksonen submitted work to the bodybuilding magazine *Physique Pictorial*, a rare outlet for postwar homosexual fantasies. Publisher Bob Mizer gave him his pen name in 1957—Tom of Finland—to highlight the exoticism of his new contributor. Tom's growing mastery of anatomy and subtle shading gave his muscular males, several based on Mizer's photographic models, an added potency, enacting visual stories told in five to fifteen panels, which Mizer sold for a costly U.S. $1.50 per page by mail order.

After trying a Finnish blond named Vicky, he changed to Mike, and then a Tarzan-style Jack, but in 1968 Tom hit on his leading man, Kake, a rugged, mustached, leather-clad rogue. Kake's wordless sexual escapades with soldiers, sailors, cops, cowboys, truckers, and construction workers would fill twenty-six booklets. For these comics, Tom simplified his toned illustration to a meticulous line but always lavished detail on his beloved leather and the ever-ready erections, exaggerated as in Japanese shunga or erotic prints to convey the participants' aroused self-perceptions. **PG**

First published by DFT (Denmark)
Creator Touko Laaksonen (Finnish, 1920–91)
Genre Erotic
Adaptation Film (1991)

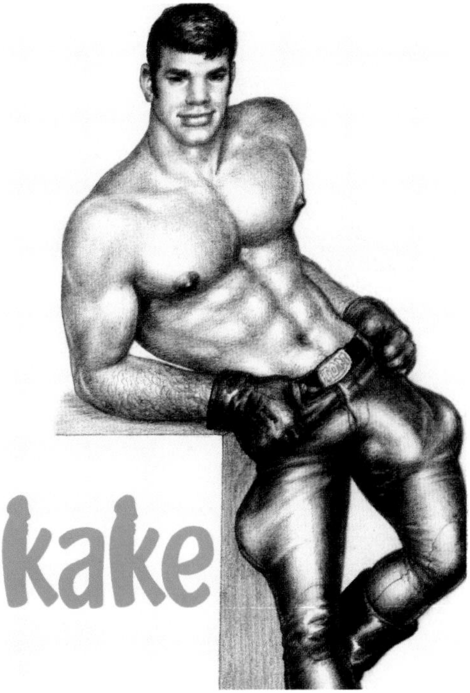
kake

"I work hard to make sure that the men I draw having sex are proud men having happy sex!"

"Tom of Finland"

Screw-Style 1968

Yoshiharu Tsuge

Title in original language *Nejishiki*
First published by Seirindo (Japanese)
Creator Japanese (b.1937)
Genre Autobiography

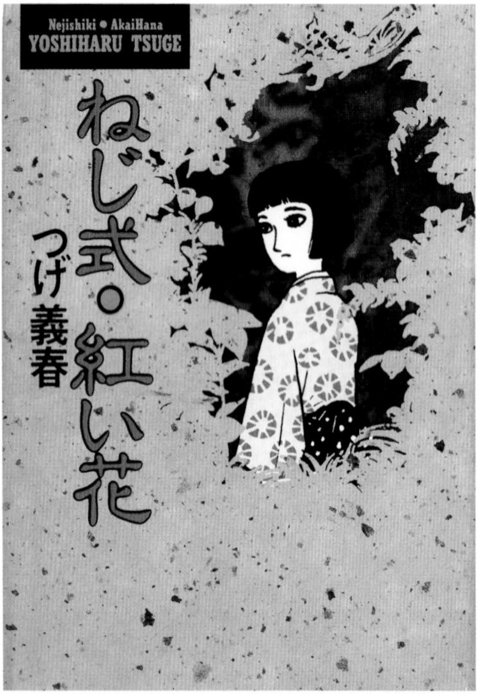
Nejishiki • AkaiHana
YOSHIHARU TSUGE
ねじ式・紅い花
つげ義春

Also by Yoshiharu Tsuge
Muno no Hito
Oba's Electroplate Factory
Red Flowers
The Sun's Joke
Yoshio no Seishun

Yoshiharu Tsuge is a cult figure in Japan. He is not known only for his comics because many of his stories were also adapted into films and television shows. He is known as an *ishoku kisai* (a "unique genius"). After a difficult childhood, Tsuge worked for the book rental library system. In an impoverished postwar Japan, these libraries offered cheap entertainment for adult readers in the form of bleak and realistic stories.

At this time the adult movement in Japanese comics was termed *gekiga* by Yoshihiro Tatsumi (*geki* means "drama," and *ga* means "image"). The genre was very influential in Tsuge's second period at the avant-garde magazine *Garo*. However, Tsuge suffered from chronic depression and once attempted suicide.

"The poetry Tsuge offers speaks eloquently of being alone in a changed world."

Bill Randall, writer and critic

Screw-Style was published in a special edition of *Garo* dedicated to Tsuge. It is the faithful transcription of one of the author's dreams. A man is stung on the arm by a jellyfish on a strange beach and sets off on a long search for a doctor. Losing blood, he develops a neurotic fear of dying from the wound. The search takes place in an illogical, hallucinatory world where people are evasive and unhelpful. Boarding a train (its driver wears a cat mask) to reach the next village, he is inexplicably returned to the one he has just left. A woman claiming to be a doctor becomes his lover and treats his arm by uniting the ends of his severed vein with a plumber's stopcock. To some, the boy's nightmarish experiences offer definite proof that comics can be an art beyond entertainment. *Screw-Style* was parodied, adapted to film, and even originated a video game. **DI**

"Compared to that, death is nothing . . . nothing at all." ➡

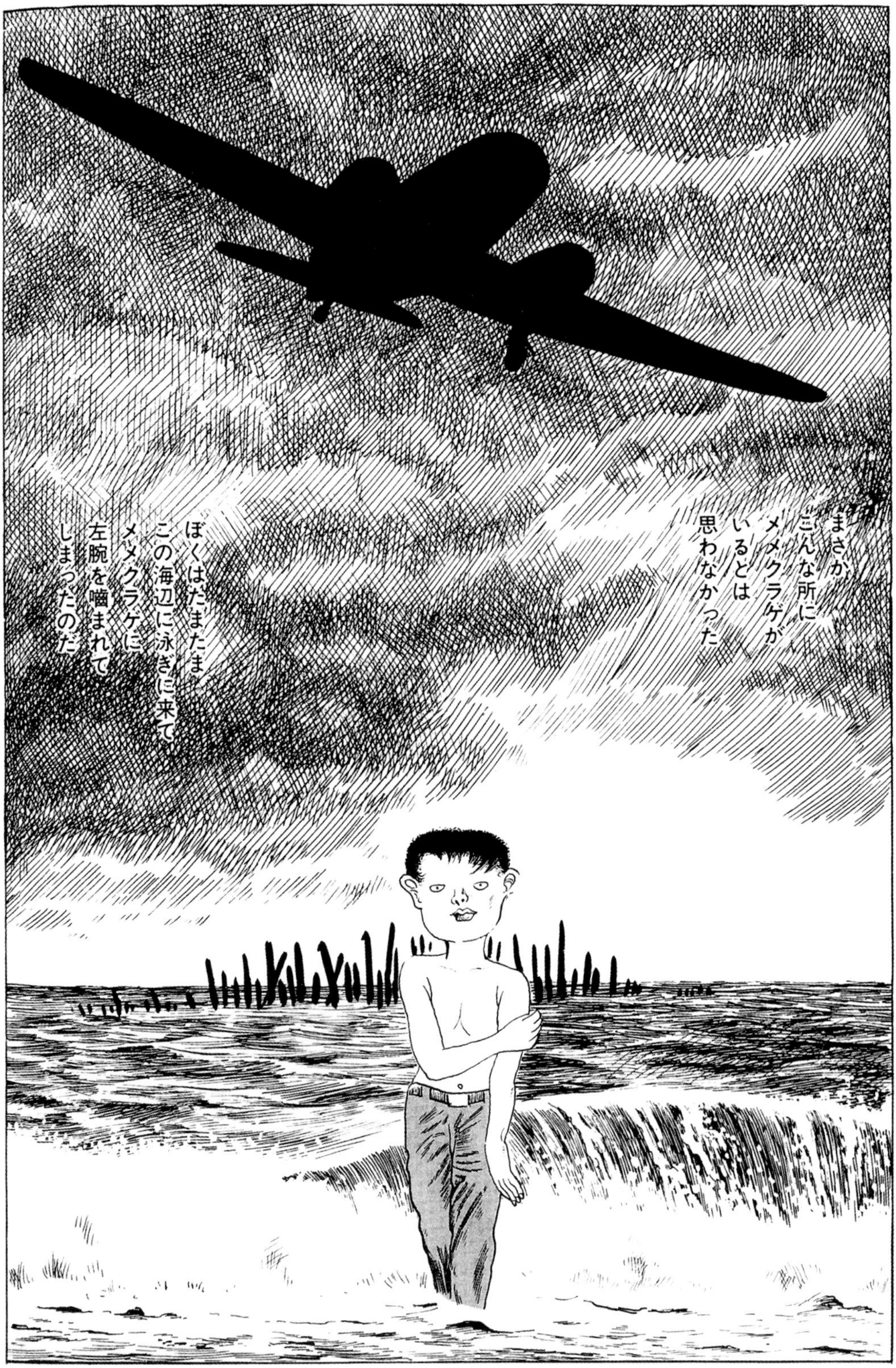
まさかこんな所にメメクラゲがいるとは思わなかった
ぼくはたまたまこの海辺に泳ぎに来てメメクラゲに左腕を噛まれてしまったのだ

The Silver Surfer 1968

Stan Lee John Buscema Jack Kirby

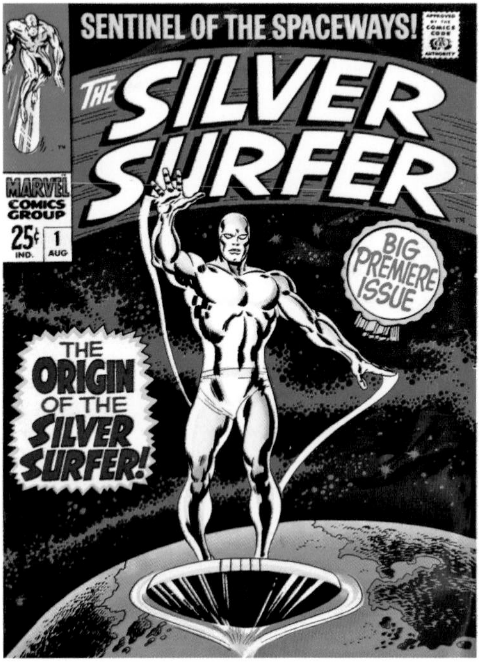
SENTINEL OF THE SPACEWAYS!
THE SILVER SURFER
MARVEL COMICS GROUP
25¢ 1 AUG IND.
BIG PREMIERE ISSUE
THE ORIGIN OF THE SILVER SURFER!

"You, who were the chosen of Galactus! You, who might have dwelled in the halls of the Gods! You have chosen instead the dunghills of Man!"

Also by Stan Lee and Jack Kirby
Fantastic Four
Silver Surfer
The Incredible Hulk
The X-Men

First published by Marvel Comics (USA)
Creators Lee (American, b.1922); Buscema (American, 1927–2002); Kirby (American, 1917–94)
Genre Superhero

The Silver Surfer entered the Marvel Universe in *Fantastic Four* issues #48 to #50 (1966), in a story line that also introduced Galactus, a devourer of worlds. Bearing a resemblance to the Hindu god Siva, Galactus is as indifferent to life as he is to suffering and death. The Silver Surfer, as Galactus's herald, seeks out worlds for his master to devour. In *Fantastic Four* issue #50, he rebels and throws in his lot with humanity. Galactus, as a punishment, imprisons him on Earth, forcing him to experience the planet that he has elected to save.

Relaunched with his own title in 1968, *The Silver Surfer* issues #1 to #18 tell the story of the Surfer's exile, his origin, and several attempts by his diabolical nemesis, Mephisto, to bend the Surfer toward evil. Lee, Buscema, and Kirby's distillation of Buddhism, Christianity, Hinduism, and other religions creates a richly ambivalent moral parable. The contrasting renditions of the Surfer add to the character's elusive mystique—liquid mercury in Buscema's sinuous rendition, muscular and charged with heroic angst. Later interpretations of the Surfer, by talents as diverse as Steve Englehart, Jim Starlin, and Moebius, have further enriched and developed this remarkable and unique character.

Although *The Silver Surfer* is situated firmly in the superhero genre, the theme and storylines are closely related to 1950s science fiction comics and literature. The millennial science fiction movies of the 1950s also anticipate the central theme of *The Silver Surfer*. The Surfer finally made his film debut in *Fantastic Four: Rise of the Silver Surfer* (2007). **RR**

Trashman 1968

"Spain"

First published by *East Village Other* (USA)
Creator Manuel Rodriguez (American, b.1940)
Genre Superhero
Collection *Zero Zero #2*

Trashman's publishing history is almost as hard to pin down as Harry Barnes himself, the underground guerilla fighter and the comic's eponymous hero. *Trashman* appeared from 1968 to 1969 in the *East Village Other*, from 1970 to 1976 in *Subvert Comics*, and subsequently in publications as diverse as *Screw*, *High Times*, *Weirdo*, and *Heavy Metal*. Equipped with his native intelligence, a powerful submachine gun, a staggeringly powerful motorbike, and paranormal abilities, Trashman leads the resistance against the shadowy tyranny that has covered the land.

Trashman's psychic superpowers include the ability to change his molecular structure and disguise himself as a piece of garbage—sometimes he is a banana skin, sometimes last week's copy of the *East Village Other*. *Trashman* retains its power to amuse and provoke chiefly because "Spain's" (Manuel Rodriguez) political concerns never succeed in swamping his narrative instincts. Spain is a romantic and libertarian Marxist, and *Trashman* consistently opposes tyranny and champions the cause of the underdog.

Spain's satirical tone is perfectly complemented by the nervy, heavily inked, and skewed perspectives of his artwork. The postnuclear society in which Trashman wages his guerilla war foreshadows the dystopias of *Judge Dredd* and *Mad Max*, but Spain's irony and lack of bombast make *Trashman* closer in spirit to the work of Howard Chaykin and the Hernandez Brothers. A gleeful combination of motorbikes, Marxism, and explicit sex is too entertaining ever to appear out of date. **RR**

The Stooped Ones 1968

"Rius"

Title in original language *Los Agachados*
First published by Editorial Meridiano and Editorial Posada (Mexico)
Creator Eduardo del Rio (Mexican, b.1934) **Genre** Humor

Eduardo del Rio, with the pen name "Rius," is one of Latin America's best-known political cartoonists, creator of the often imitated *For Beginners* series of books—a concept mixing iconographic research with comic strips and prose. An active Marxist editorial cartoonist, Rius created his first periodical comic book, *Los Supermachos*, in 1966. There he developed complex social, historical, and political themes with the goal of "raising the consciousness of the Mexican working classes," often including bibliographical references at the end for those who wanted to know more.

Rius left *Los Supermachos* in 1967 and created *Los Agachados*, whose first series ran successfully for nine years. *Los Agachados* was built on thorough research and a black-and-white cartoon style. In spite of the rural setting, *Los Agachados* had a middle-class urban readership. It is estimated that Rius addressed nearly 200 themes of all kinds in *Los Agachados*, all focused on a fierce critique of the Catholic Church and the corrupt elite.

The series' fictional universe was set in a typical Mexican town with recognizable stereotypes, the religious Catholic woman, the indigenous peasant, the mustachioed revolutionary, the liberal schoolteacher, the political party bureaucrat, and the corrupt police officer. It may be unfashionable nowadays to be so overtly ideological, but this series is still an essential piece in the history of liberal Mexican thinking, and an unparalled example of the once enormous power of comic books to promote political resistance. **EPr**

Philémon and the Shipwreck of the "A" 1968

✎✎ "Fred"

Title in original language Philémon et le naufragé du "A"
First published by Dargaud (France)
Creator Frédéric Aristidès (French, b.1931)
Genre Fantasy, Humor

Fred
Philémon
et le naufragé du "A"

"The greatest existential anguish is knowing where one is going, to be programmed. In my opinion, fantasy must be a part of life."

Everything begins when Philémon's father asks his son to collect water from the well because their pump has failed. In this well, which has not been used for many years, the young man discovers a bottle containing a message. A second message persuades him to dive into the well, watched by his talking donkey, Anatole. This is the start of a series of extraordinary events: Philémon is dragged to the bottom of the well where he comes across a gray shark, loses consciousness, and finds himself lying on a beach in a completely different reality. The new world around him has two suns, and not long after he awakes he meets a vegetable clock, a centaur called Vendredi (Friday), and Monsieur Barthélemy, a well sinker who has been shipwrecked on the island for forty years. It is from the old man himself, dressed as Robinson Crusoe, that Philémon learns he must find himself on the letter "A" of the Atlantic Ocean.

Frédéric Aristidès, known as "Fred," was a defector from the French magazine *Hara-Kiri*, which he left in 1965. The adventures of Philémon, conceived in the wake of this departure, were first offered to the Belgian weekly magazine *Spirou*, which rejected the project. They were then proposed to the French weekly *Pilote*, which accepted them immediately.

Two short stories were published before the first episode of the *Naufragé du "A"* (which appeared in 1968 and was later published as an album, in 1972). Fred is a storyteller, and it was during a family meal that he invented this story of letter islands in the Atlantic Ocean to amuse his son, Eric. His universe is very close to the fantasy genre so dear to Lewis Carroll, and while the script is very accessible in the first episode, this would not be the case in subsequent ones. The hero plays with the very codes of the medium, walking through walls and floors, challenging our perceptions just as Carroll did with his *Through the Looking-Glass*. **CM**

Rahan 1969

Roger Lécureux André Chéret and others

In 1969 a new weekly magazine made its appearance and became incredibly successful as the months went by: *Pif Gadget*. This was the new formula of *Vaillant*, a magazine launched after World War II and that was associated with the French Communist party. Readers discovered the imaginary adventures of a Cro-Magnon man, named Rahan, aka "the son of fierce times."

The basic idea was conceived by writer Roger Lécureux, who had wanted to explore this period of history. Several illustrators were approached, including Angelo Di Marco, but it was André Chéret who created the iconic identity of the character. Rahan has a statuesque, sculptural body and long blond hair. Bare-breasted, with an ivory cutlass hanging from his loincloth and a necklace of claws given to him by his father (each one of the claws representing a human quality), he travels through unknown lands and meets different people or obstacles that he must overcome.

The ideology of the scriptwriter was clear, but the anachronistic humanism of his hero was hailed with such great enthusiasm that a new magazine bearing the hero's name was launched in 1972. Because of the enormous amount of work involved, the publisher decided to entrust the illustration of some stories to the Italian artist Guido Zamperoni, without informing the official illustrator, and then to the Spanish artist Enrique Romero, too. Following the publisher's refusal to pay an advance on his royalties on the pretext that he was only an illustrator, Chéret instituted a number of legal proceedings which he won, the most important victory being the one that gave him the status of coauthor. The series continued with various publishers, and since 1999 it has been published by Editions Lécureux, run by Jean-François, the son of Roger Lécureux, who took over the writing after his father's death in 1999. **CM**

First published by Vaillant (France)
Creators Lécureux (French, 1925–99); Chéret (French, b.1937)
Genre Adventure

RAHAN
BIMESTRIEL
N°27
TOUT EN RECITS COMPLETS COULEURS
300 CFA - 5.00 FS 8F
LES MONSTRES DE LA PREHISTOIRE

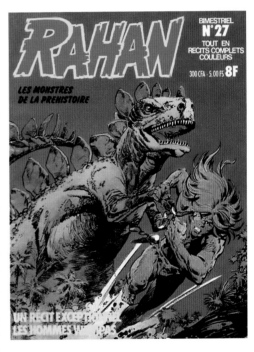

"As a child, I loved Rahan. And I agreed to come to France because I was going to meet him. . . ."

Marguerite Abouet, writer

Tex 1969

Gian Luigi Bonelli Aurelio Galleppini

First published by Cepim (Italy)
Creators Bonelli (Italian, 1908–2001); Galleppini (Italian, 1917–94)
Genre Western

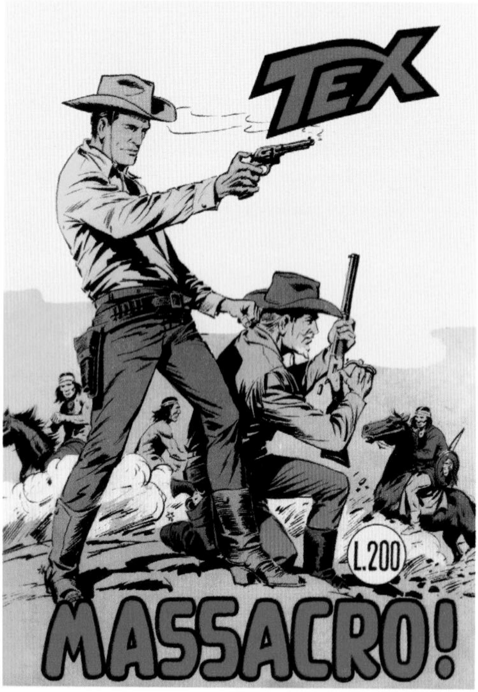
TEX
L.200
MASSACRO!

"Thinking of defeating Tex in terms of speed is like hoping to drain a lake using a sieve."

Giovanni Luigi Bonelli

Tex was created by writer Gian Luigi Bonelli and illustrator Aurelio Galleppini in 1948. After years as a comic strip minibook, it enjoyed renewed success in the 1960s as *Tex Willer*, in a bigger format and longer stories. *Tex* is the most famous title in the world of Italian comics, and is still a best seller, with more than 200,000 copies flying off the shelves every month.

Tex Willer the man is an Arizona ex-outlaw who turned ranger, an authentic tough guy with a strong sense of honor and justice. Tex kills only in self-defense and upholds the rights of others. Thanks to his marriage to a beautiful Navajo girl, Lilyth, he has also become a chief among Navajos—renamed Eagle of the Night—and a defender of Native American rights.

In one episode, "Attack at Fort Sumner," Tex and his closest friend, Kit Carson, follow a gang of arms smugglers across the plains, arrive in Goldena, and trap chief smuggler Fraser in the town. The criminal swears he will have his revenge and unleashes his bloodthirsty Apache accomplices upon the town's population. The rangers, helped by the cavalry, do not give in to this murderous rampage and soon save the town, but not without casualties. However, the worst fate is the one they reserve for Fraser. He is abandoned in the forest, wounded and surrounded by hungry wolves and the ghosts of the dead, with nothing but a solitary bullet in the barrel of his gun. The story, adapted from a previous short novel by Bonelli, is still remembered as the cruelest of the entire series, with a desperate, dark, and cynical ending. Another great adventure of the righteous sharpshooter is the compelling *Massacro!*

Inspired by Western movies such as John Ford's *Stagecoach*, *Tex* was a brilliant fusion of genres, where cowboys meet adventure, science fiction, horror, and comedy. As such, it anticipated the Spaghetti Western's radical reshaping of the Old West genre. **MS**

Alan Ford 1969

"Max Bunker" "Magnus"

"Magnus" (whose real name is Roberto Raviola) is an artist who established a new genre in Italian comics in the 1960s—*fumetti neri* (black comics). His bold, sharp, and characteristic shading provided a dark and mysterious appeal to his early comic works. He used this style to good effect over the years and delivered some truly intelligent and humorous stories, such as *Alan Ford*, as well as some with erotic storylines.

Magnus created *Alan Ford* with the writer "Max Bunker" (Luciano Secchi). The series is about an unlucky group of justice fighters with a sharp satirical twist. The *Alan Ford* comics were immensely successful in Italy and were introduced to Yugoslavian readers in the 1970s, in an excellent translation by Nenad Brixy, the scriptwriter, novelist, and editor from Croatia. The popularity of *Alan Ford* in Yugoslavia was extraordinary. Many generations of young people quoted the comics in everyday conversations. The reason for the success of these comics was the compassion that young Yugoslavians identified with the poor and good-looking Alan Ford. Despite the unfortunate circumstances of Alan and his friends, who had no money in their pockets and behaved modestly, they were somehow able to win their battles against extremely rich (but profoundly evil) criminals.

The comics included numerous witty conversations and interactions with colorful characters along the way, as well as astute observations on aspects of U.S. and Italian society. The primary characters of the *Alan Ford* series were The Number One (the supreme leader), Alan Ford (a naive young man), Minuette Macon (Alan's girlfriend), Bob Rock (a short and angry agent), Sir Oliver (a broke English nobleman), The Boss (Number One's right hand), and Jeremiah, the team hypochondriac. It is an eclectic cast with unique interactions that work remarkably well together. **ZT**

First published by Editoriale Corno, Max Bunker Productions (Italy)
Creators Roberto Raviola (Italian, 1939–96); Luciano Secchi (Italian, b.1939) **Genre** Humor

ALAN FORD
Presentazione di Carlo Della Corte
n. 1 L. 150 - mensile
IL GRUPPO TNT

"Better to live a hundred years as a millionaire than one week in poverty."

Doraemon 1969

"Fujiko Fujio"

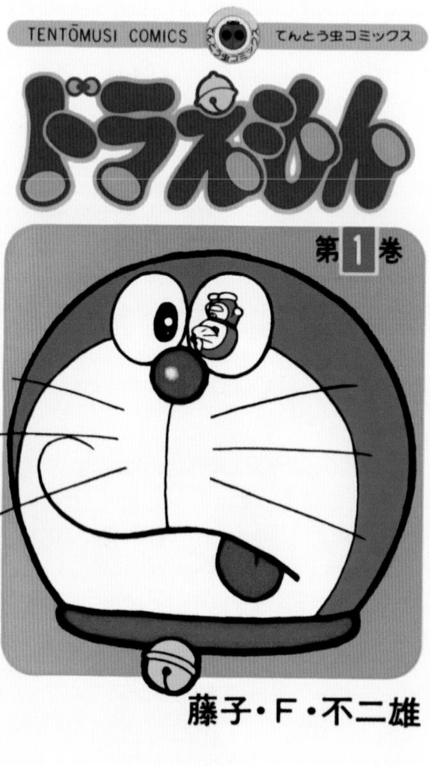
TENTŌMUSI COMICS
てんとう虫コミックス
ドラえもん
第1巻
藤子・F・不二雄

"*In the manga world,* Doraemon *. . . has been the equivalent of a home run with the bases loaded, repeated again and again.*"

Frederik Schodt, writer

First published by Shogakukan (Japan)
Creators Hiroshi Fujimoto (Japanese, 1933–96); Moto Abiko (Japanese, b.1934)
Genre Science fiction

Doraemon was originally published simultaneously in six different children's manga magazines by Shogakukan. The title character—whose name derives from Dorayaki, a popular pastry in Japan—is a robot cat from the twenty-second century. He suddenly appears one day in the top drawer of Nobita Nobi, a bespectacled, nerdish nine-year-old. Doraemon has been sent to the present by Nobita's descendants to stop him from becoming a failure as an adult.

Doraemon posseses a lot of gadgets, which he extracts from a pocket, similar to a kangaroo's pouch, that he has on his body. He uses these devices to help Nobita stay out of trouble, but because of fate, or Nobita's clumsiness, results are not always as expected. Supporting characters include Nobita's long-suffering mother, his gentle girlfriend Shizuki, big bully Takeshi, posh kid Tsuneo, and Doraemon´s sister, Dorami. The clean, round artwork and the simple but craftily told scripts, together with the appealing personalities of the main characters, have turned *Doraemon* into a manga classic. After Hiroshi Fujimoto and Moto Abiko ended their partnership in 1987, the former continued to produce *Doraemon* stories until he died in 1996.

A favorite among children, and a legendary icon in Japanese culture, *Doraemon* has featured in a long-running television anime series (the 1973 season failed, but new episodes were well received and total of more than 900 have been made to date), and in nearly thirty theatrical features. *Doraemon* has been published in several English/Japanese volumes by Shogakukan. **AMo**

King of Spades 1969

✐🖉 Luciano Bottaro

Title in original language *Re di picche*
First published by Alpe (Italy)
Creator Italian (1931–2006)
Genre Humor

Re di picche—King of Spades—is a special king, the king of the cards. He is also an aggressive and pitiless tyrant, always trying, but always failing, to expand his realm at the expense of the placid and lovable King of Hearts. Among his allies are Baron Catapulta, an avid counselor who sells him weapons at very high prices, and the Scannabue twins, who are terrible killers.

The series, loosely inspired by *Alice in Wonderland*, is a parody of military (and political) issues in which technologies and weapons are replaced by useless machines. Here, Luciano Bottaro's style goes in a more personal direction than in his previous works. Less rounded, more squared, its synthesis recalls Antonio Rubino: surreal, psychedelic, minimal in backgrounds, spectacular in color and decoration, and with the character design feel of a "paper toys" world. It is also a mix of Jacovitti, Carl Barks, and *ligne claire*, offering a "paper theater" experience of inventive drawings.

King of Spades was the first and most famous creation of Bierreci Studios, a group of authors, including Carlo Chendi and Giorgio Rebuffi, based in Rapallo, Italy. This and other Bottaro series of the 1950s and 1960s, such as *Pepito*, became best sellers in Italy, France, and Germany. Bottaro also gained renown in his career as one of the greatest Disney artists, especially for giving new life to characters such as Goofy, Hazel Witch, and Scrooge. He reinvented Rebo as a homage to one of the earliest Italian science fiction comics, created by movie master Cesare Zavattini and Italian Disney's first cartoon mastermind, Federico Pedrocchi. **MS**

Golgo 13 1969

✐🖉 Takao Saito

First published by Shogakukan (Japan)
Creator Japanese (b.1936)
Genre Crime
Award Shogakukan Manga Award (1975)

Meet the protagonist, Golgo 13. Name: Duke Togo. Date of birth: unknown. Age: unknown. Height: 182 centimeters. Weight: 80 kilograms. Blood type: A. Address: unknown. Nationality: unknown. The profile of Japan's most famous hit man, and the comic's central character, may not tell readers much, but the fact that the series has sold a total of more than 200 million copies and become one of the longest-running comics since its launch in 1969 says a lot more.

While Golgo 13 himself has not changed in the slightest, the world has transformed drastically throughout the decades of the comic's publication. The dissolution of the Soviet Union marked the end of the Cold War, then China, in the name of socialist market economy, became a capitalist country. Many readers assumed that the story's central theme of terrorism would go out of fashion and predicted that *Golgo 13* would lose its edge after the Cold War. Yet the world was faced with other problems, such as ethnic conflicts and limited wars, and *Golgo 13* was given plenty of reasons to stick around.

This comic has always been informative—from politics to economics, science, history, and even art— and Takao Saito's knowledge of current affairs is clear in the plot and overarching story lines. The *Golgo 13* series was serialized in Shogakukan's *Big Comic* magazine, and the title debuted in the United States in 1986 in graphic novel form (Leeds Publishing). In 2006 Viz Media released the first of thirteen volumes featuring a collection of selected stories. **TS**

Janus Stark 1969

Tom Tully Francisco Solano Lopez

First published by *Smash!* / Fleetway Publications (UK)
Creators Tully (British, Unknown);
Lopez (Argentinian, b.1928)
Genre Drama

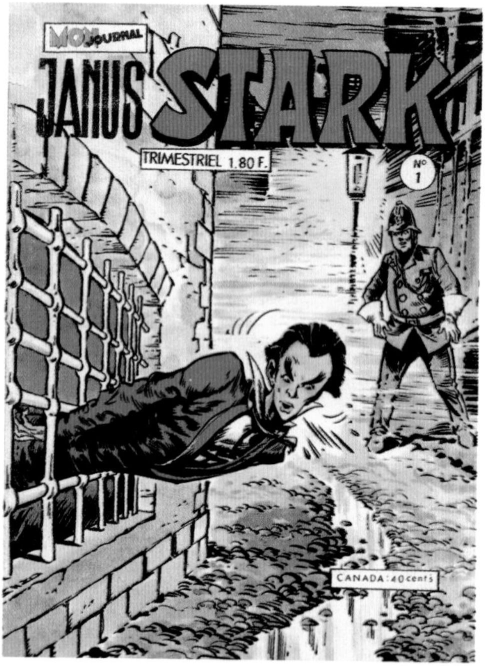

JANUS STARK
TRIMESTRIEL 1.80 F.
N° 1
CANADA: 40 cents

Also by Francisco Solano Lopez
Adam Eterno
Gigantus
Kelly's Eye
Kid Pharaoh
Raven on the Wing

One of the joys of British comics is the sheer variety of subjects they have tackled over the years, few stranger than *Janus Stark*. Fleetway editor Jack Le Grand was inspired by the great Houdini and dreamed up Janus Stark, a Victorian escapologist able to bend his body like rubber who roams the country solving crimes.

The strip was originally intended to run in the horror comic *Blackjack*, but when that title was abandoned it first found a berth in *Smash!* before transferring over to *Valiant*. In the strip readers first meet young orphan Janus as he escapes from the oppressive Hemlock Hall and encounters the Fagin-like Blind Largo. Under Largo's tutelage Janus becomes a master lock breaker and pickpocket, which helps him develop a music hall act as a great escapologist. However, his true power is the ability to stretch and contort his body into any shape, allowing him to squeeze through almost any opening.

"Behold, Janus Stark—master of illusion, son of the unknown!"

Principal writer Tom Tully sent Stark around the country and the world, and wherever he performed he would come up against wonderfully sinister villains such as Silvo the Dwarf or the Phantom Executioner. Artist Francisico Solano Lopez very much defined the look of British comics in this period, and with his studio he worked on as many as ten features at a time. *Janus Stark* typified his visual approach with its combination of dynamic, almost cartoonlike drawing and intensely rendered, dark brushwork. The strip ran until 1975. However, French translations from the publishers *Mon Journal* found such great success that when the British material ran out they simply commissioned new stories, which continued until 1986, more than twice the lifespan of the original series. **DAR**

Bogeyman Comics 1969

Rory Hayes

The innocent newcomer to the art of Rory Hayes will possibly be shocked by the childlike crudeness of his drawing style—a roughly scrawled set of panels loaded with a variety of strange characters, demons, and monsters, which, at first glance, look like the work of a maniac. Hayes's very personal and totally unique artwork was undoubtedly viewed at the time as an ugly horror show that bucked against the populist opinion of what the underground comix scene stood for.

His creepy lines seemed to belong more to the outsider art and art brut movements than the underground comix community, but the roots of his art were linked to the pre-Code 1950s horror comics. It was comic shop owner and publisher Gary Arlington

"Come to us, bear. We're going to eat you!"

who urged the budding comix creator to try producing a horror title of his own called *Bogeyman Comics*.

Edited by Arlington (who also supplied a short essay about EC horror comics titled "The Editor Reminisces"), Hayes scripted and illustrated five tales of "Horror in The Blood Vein" for *Bogeyman Comics*—three of which ("The Thing in the Room!", "Bits of Flesh," and "The Creatures in the Tunnel") feature Pooh Rass Bear, a variant on a teddy bear character that he and his brother Geoffrey had created during their formative years.

Elsewhere, "The Old Man" is narrated by the Bogeyman, a character on the scale of H. P. Lovecraft's cosmic horrors or Jack Kirby's planet-eating Galactus. Although much cruder, it still managed to instill a sense of unsettling psychedelic dread. *Bogeyman* ran for two more issues (with contributions from other artists included) but it is in issue #1 that Hayes's demented vision is at its most powerful. **EP**

First published by San Francisco Comic Book Co. (USA)
Creator American (1949–83)
Genre Underground
Influenced by *Tales from the Crypt*

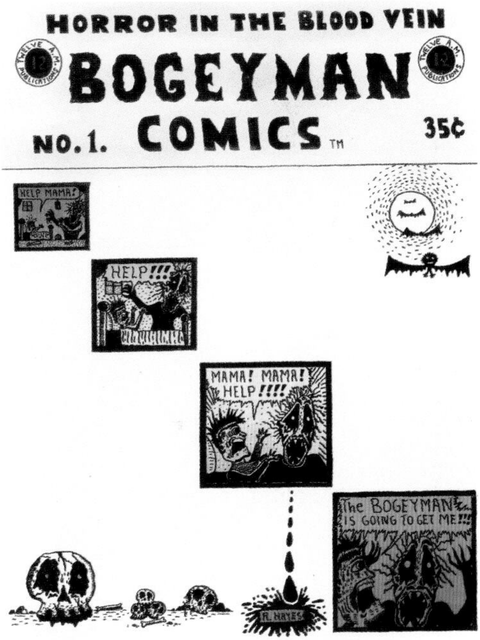
HORROR IN THE BLOOD VEIN
BOGEYMAN
NO. 1. COMICS TM
35¢
HELP MAMA!
HELP!!!
MAMA! MAMA! HELP!!!!
The BOGEYMAN IS GOING TO GET ME!!!
R. HAYES

Also by Rory Hayes
*C*nt Comix*
Insect Fear #2
Laugh in the Dark
Where Demented Wented: The Comics and Art of Rory Hayes

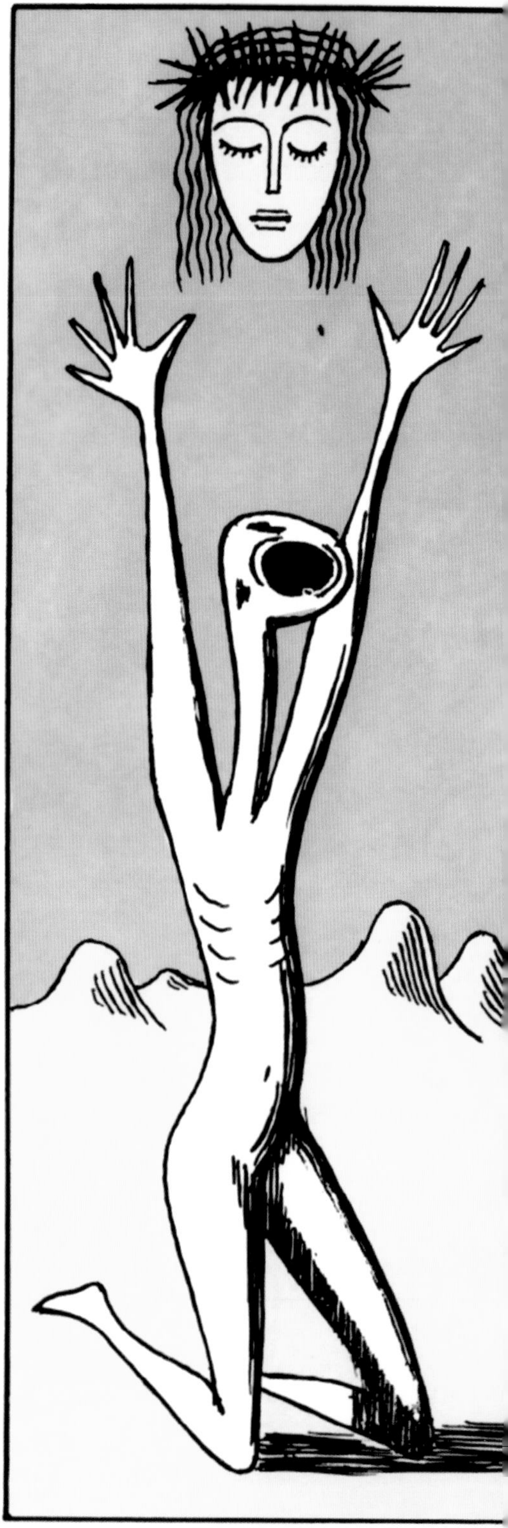
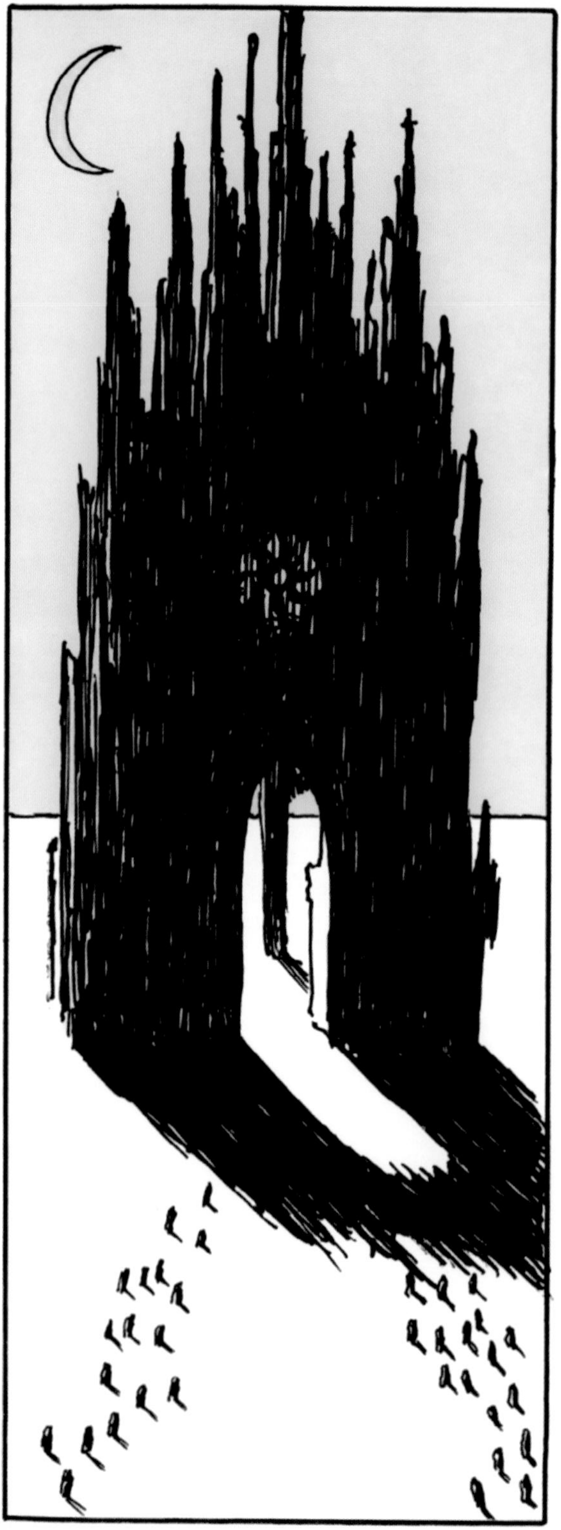

Poem Strip 1969

Dino Buzzati

First published by Mondadori (Italy)
Creator Italian (1906–72)
Genre Fantasy
Award Paese Sera Best Comics of the Year Award (1970)

The singer Orfi, a son of the noble Baltazano family, is the star of the Polypus nightclub. One night he sees his girlfriend, Eura, disappear, passing through a small door in the wall surrounding a mysterious mansion across the street. Eura dies, and Orfi starts a journey through the afterlife, which he can access thanks to his extraordinary musical abilities. He travels through a strange version of Milan where he meets many dead people and exists in a state of regret, without emotion or desire. To the keeper he sings stories about men, gods, and his lover, whom he finally meets and try to bring back to the world of the living.

The book is a reinvention of the myth of Orpheus and Eurydice, filtered by Dino Buzzati's interest in the fantastic, mysteries, and death. A reporter, editor, and critic for *Milanese Corriere della Sera* daily newspaper, Buzzati was not only one of the most famous Italian journalists, but also a highly appreciated and successful writer who practiced painting as his greatest pleasure.

Poem Strip was not his first comic art work (in 1945 he published *La famosa invasione degli orsi in Sicilia*), but it is his only graphic novel. Its general design was closer to a picture-book, with full-page images, long captions, and the large presence of nudes that was considered quite shocking for the time. The stylistic frame comes from surrealism, metaphysical painting (Giorgio de Chirico) and romantic expressionism, but the visuals are filled with contemporary references, from optical and pop art to Salvador Dalì, Hans Bellmer, Federico Fellini, and Wilhelm Busch. **MS**

Oh Wicked Wanda 1969

Frederic Mullally Ron Embleton

First published by *Penthouse* magazine (UK)
Creators Mullally (British, b.1918); Embleton (British,1930–88)
Genre Erotic

The heiress to a colossal fortune, Wicked Wanda first appeared in prose in the September 1969 issue of the adult magazine *Penthouse*, although she did not appear in comic book form until 1973. The brainchild of Frederic Mullally, *Oh Wicked Wanda* was drawn by illustrator Ron Embleton, veteran of the classic U.K. strips *Wulf the Briton*, *Captain Scarlet*, and the 1960s science fiction epic *The Trigan Empire*. *Oh Wicked Wanda* was a response to rival *Playboy*'s own piece of debauchery, *Little Annie Fanny*. Not to be outdone, *Oh Wicked Wanda*'s eight pages of painted panels overflowed with sex and scenes of bondage and domination.

A lust-filled dominatrix, Wanda finds a constant companion in Candyfloss, a blonde, bisexual teenager whom Wanda likes to call "Pusscake." She also has at her disposal her Puss International Force (P.I.F.), an army of obedient nymphettes led by General German Grrrr, whose name is a take on the feminist Germaine Greer. Males are mostly secondary considerations, possibly because *Penthouse*'s male readers had little interest in the addition of superfluous male characters. There are exceptions, such as the mad scientist and former Nazi J. Hoover Grud, a parody of the F.B.I.'s J. Edgar Hoover.

Over time, the overt sexuality of Wanda began to take a back seat to Mullally's political beliefs, and his increasing use of caricature depicting various celebrities included the multiple appearances of politicians such as Ted Kennedy and Richard Nixon. *Penthouse*'s founder and publisher, Bob Guccione, felt the strip had run its course by then and canceled it in 1979. **BS**

← "Whether I write or I paint, I pursue the same goal—telling stories." Buzatti

X-Men 1969

Roy Thomas · Neal Adams

First published by Marvel Comics (USA)
Creators Thomas (American, b.1940); Adams (American, b.1941)
Genre Science fiction

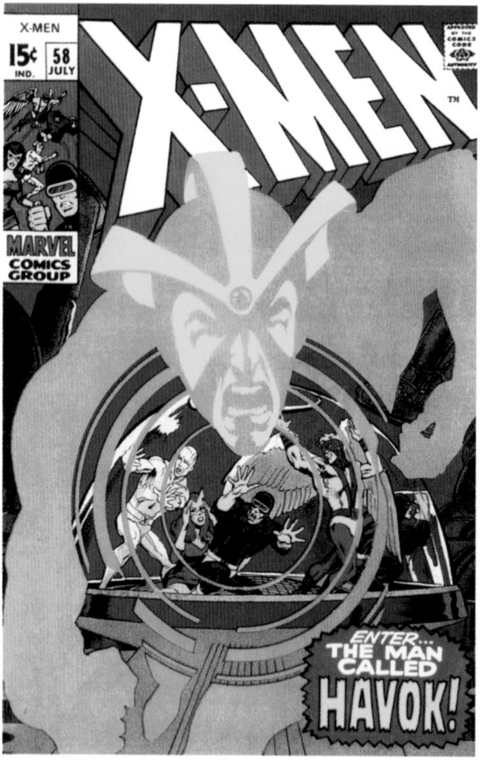
X-MEN
15¢
IND.
58
JULY
X-MEN
MARVEL COMICS GROUP
ENTER... THE MAN CALLED
HAVOK!

"My story isn't a pretty one, ladies and gentlemen, but it's true!! . . . Mutants are the greatest single danger facing mankind today."

Although Marvel's mutant superhero team was subsequently to become the company's most successful creation, the *X-Men*, during its first incarnation, was not a best-selling title. After a run of stories written by Stan Lee and penciled by Jack Kirby and Don Heck, the title slipped to reprint status before returning with a new lineup and creative team. Between the Lee years and the reprints came an interlude of nine issues written by Roy Thomas and penciled by Neal Adams. These issues—because of their inventive narrative and mold-breaking artwork—are some of the finest superhero comics of the period.

Thomas built on the theme of alienation, appropriate for a team of heroes "hated and feared by a world they are sworn to protect." Dramatic new villains appeared: Sauron (a *Lord of the Rings* reference) and the Living Monolith (an Egyptian god). Established menaces such as Magneto and the Sentinels were nuanced in a different way. The *X-Men* stories became more contemporary in their range of reference.

Adams's artwork is revolutionary. He is arguably the first artist working in the superhero genre to exploit fully the power of an image that explodes through its panel border. The reader seeks closure of a partially completed movement in the space outside the panel, creating a dynamic sense of action and tension. Jack Kirby and others anticipated this style, but Adams used the technique as an expressionist tool, heightening the reader's identification and involvement with the characters. This approach suits a comic that invites its readers to identify with superheroes who are continually pushed to the margins of society. Adams continued to develop his expressive style in subsequent work for DC Comics with Denny O'Neil, such as the *Green Lantern/Green Arrow* series and a long run on the many series of *Batman*. **RR**

Neal Adams's realistic artwork makes full use of color and space. ➡

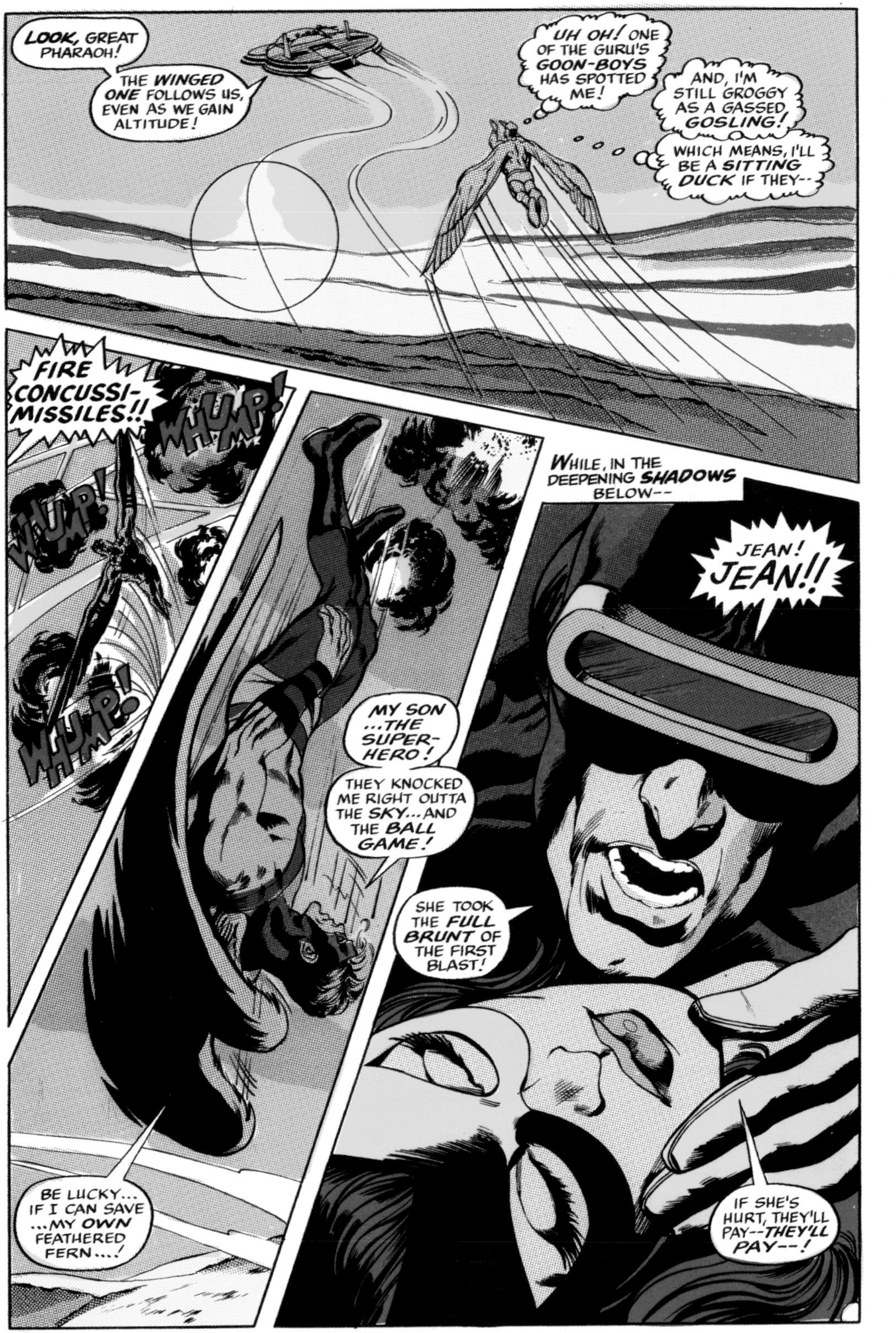

LOOK, GREAT PHARAOH!
THE WINGED ONE FOLLOWS US, EVEN AS WE GAIN ALTITUDE!
UH OH! ONE OF THE GURU'S GOON-BOYS HAS SPOTTED ME!
AND, I'M STILL GROGGY AS A GASSED GOSLING!
WHICH MEANS, I'LL BE A SITTING DUCK IF THEY--
FIRE CONCUSSI-MISSILES!!
WHUMP!
WHUMP!
WHUMP!
MY SON ...THE SUPER-HERO!
THEY KNOCKED ME RIGHT OUTTA THE SKY... AND THE BALL GAME!
BE LUCKY... IF I CAN SAVE ...MY OWN FEATHERED FERN...!
WHILE, IN THE DEEPENING SHADOWS BELOW--
JEAN! JEAN!!
SHE TOOK THE FULL BRUNT OF THE FIRST BLAST!
IF SHE'S HURT, THEY'LL PAY--THEY'LL PAY--!

4 1970–89

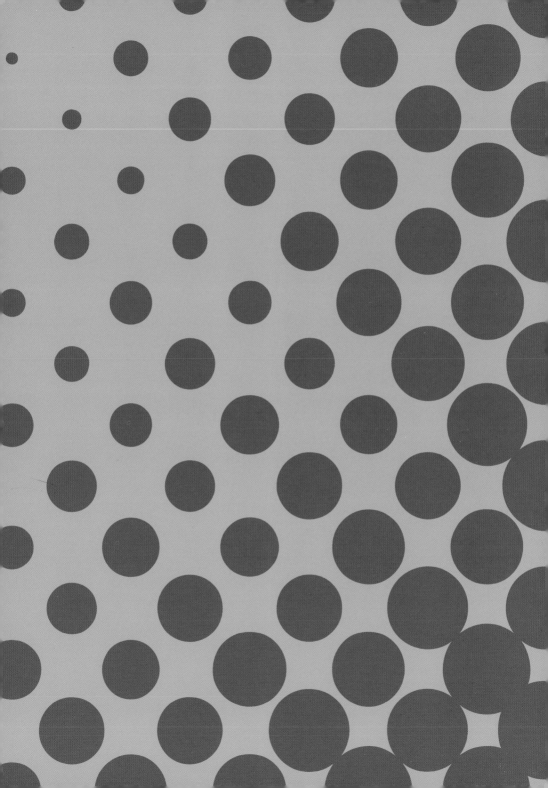

Monica's Gang 1970

Maurício de Sousa

Title in original language *Mônica e a Sua Turma*
First published by Editora Abril (Brazil)
Creator Brazilian (b.1930)
Genre Children's

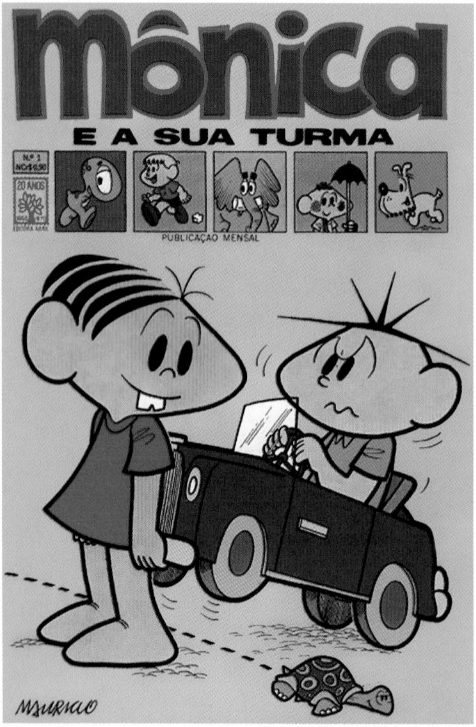

Mônica
E A SUA TURMA
PUBLICAÇÃO MENSAL
MAURICIO

Similar reads
Little Lulu John Stanley and Irving Tripp
Little Orphan Annie Harold Gray
Mafalda Quino
Nancy Ernie Bushmiller

Mônica is the biggest commercial success in Brazilian comics. There are six thick monthly comic books starring her gang, plus a number of thinner ones and special editions. Apparently aimed at children but reaching many older people as well, the comics star a toothy little girl in a red dress who rules her neighborhood. Mônica and her friends—Cebolinha, Cascão, and Magali—were created in the 1960s and graduated to their own comic books in the 1970s, starting in 1970 with Mônica. Since then they have changed very little visually, but the content has evolved.

Surrounding himself not only with tremendous artists (who draw within the established house style) but with teachers and educators, Maurício de Sousa has steadily broadened the reach of his characters. The same Mônica who sells diapers now also stars in giveaway comics about prevalent health issues.

"How weird Monica looks! / Yeah, weird as always."

In the first issue of *Mônica*, in a now classic situation, Cebolinha and the gang have a plan to depose Mônica as the "queen of the street," but they are simply not up to it. Mônica quickly establishes who is boss by punching them out with her blue rabbit, Sansão, who acts like a missile in her hands. Cebolinha, always the mastermind of such plans, gets hit first.

Innovation came in the "Mônica-teen" comics, a mangalike thick book in which Mônica and the gang have become teenagers. Also well worth reading are the special editions, *MSP 50* and *MSP+50*, published in 2009 and 2010. In these commemorative editions a number of younger creators pay homage to Mônica in their own styles, with creative results that are likely to broaden *Mônica*'s horizon further. **CB**

Ashura 1970

✏️ George Akiyama

Dubbed "the unstoppable king of Trauma Manga" by Takeo Udagawa in his book on underground manga, *Manga Zombie*, George Akiyama made quite a splash in August of 1970 with the publication of the first chapter of *Ashura* in *Shukan Shonen* magazine. Considered as a danger to public morals because of its unsettling depiction of dark human life, it was officially blacklisted in a number of prefectures in Japan.

Opening with nightmarish views of mountains of corpses, the story of *Ashura* begins with a young woman, pregnant and determined to survive, who is forced by hunger to resort to eating human flesh. Miraculously, she manages to give birth but, driven mad by lack of food, she throws her newborn boy in

> ## "The story got officially blacklisted as a danger to public morals." ComiPress

a campfire. He is saved from certain death only by a sudden thunderstorm, which douses the fire but at the same time drowns his poor mother. Burned and misshapen, young Ashura faces up to the harsh world he is born into with an amazing resiliency, leaving death and destruction in his wake.

Concerned with exploring the darkest recesses of the human soul, George Akiyama strikes at the core of the nuclear family in his tales, leaving children to survive on their own in a world where adults are either helpless or downright dangerous.

In *The Drifting Classroom*, published in 1975, Kazuo Umezu used a somewhat similar setting, but his story ended on a positive note, as reason prevailed over the monster dormant in all of us. Without a doubt, Akiyama's outlook is definitely bleaker. To him, we are all monsters, and it does not take much for the veneer of civilization to wear off. **XG**

First published by *Weekly Shonen Jump* (Japan)
Creator Japanese (b.1943)
Genre Drama
Adaptation Animation (proposed 2010)

ジョージ秋山
アシュラ 上

幻冬舎文庫

Also by George Akiyama
Derorinman
Horafuki Dondon
Kokuhaku
Zeni Geba

Yoko Tsuno 1970

✐✐ Roger Leloup

First published by Dupuis (Belgium)
Creator Belgian (b.1933)
Genre Science fiction, Adventure
Award Eurocon SF Award for Belgian comics (1972)

This series initially appeared in the Belgian comics magazine *Spirou* in 1970, with a first book following in 1972. More than forty years and twenty-four volumes later, *Yoko Tsuno* is still thriving under the artistic direction of its original creator, Roger Leloup.

The long-running strip follows the adventures of the eponymous Yoko, a young Japanese-born electronics engineer, and her two friends, Vic and Pol. Although several of the trio's escapades fall within the confines of classic sci-fi, the series is varied in both plot and setting. In addition to helping a race of alien refugees regain their home planet, and time-traveling to stop the destruction of Earth, Yoko and friends discover why a church organ in Germany causes all those who hear it to go mad, as well as track down a missing 1930s aeroplane filled with important documents.

Leloup, a one-time artistic collaborator of Hergé, uses the *ligne claire* (clear line) style throughout *Yoko Tsuno*, both in the series' stark lines and detailed backgrounds and in its unfailingly linear narrative. But nothing is traditional about his choice of principal character. Female, foreign, capable, and intelligent, Yoko is no dim-witted femme fatale stereotype. With a black belt in aïkido and impressive technological expertise, she is the brains *and* the brawn of this adventure series, with Vic and Pol firmly in the role of sidekicks. This intriguing mix of the traditional and the progressive, coupled with Leloup's innovative, technology-driven narratives, explain *Yoko Tsuno*'s long-running publication and its artist's high reputation. **CMac**

Ode to Kirihito 1970

✐✐ Osamu Tezuka

Title in original language *Kirihito Sanka*
First published by Shogakukan (Japan)
Creator Japanese (1928–89)
Genre Science ficiton

Dr. Kirihito Osanai is investigating a rare disease called monmow, found only in the isolated mountain of village Doggaddale. His superior, Dr. Tatsugaura, is convinced the disease is caused by a virus, but Osanai believes it is a degenerative and organic, and that the answer is to be found in the village itself. Having prepared a report to this effect for a medical conference, Osanai is easily persuaded by Tatsugaura that a month in the village will allow him to complete the diagnosis.

Once in the village, Osanai finds himself trapped by the villagers. To avoid being murdered, he marries Tazu, despite already having a fiancée at home. But soon Osanai succumbs to the disease, which will twist his body into a doglike shape before he dies. Discovering the origin of the disease, Osanai convinces the mayor to let him tell the authorities, but on the way he is kidnapped and taken abroad as a curiosity to amuse the rich. The remaining three-quarters of the story are concerned with his abuse at the hands of others and his attempts to find a cure and return home.

Tezuka's lifelong interest in medicine (he held a medical degree), which also inspired *Black Jack*, is to the fore here. He explores medical corruption, the role and fate of the outsider, and human transformation. *Ode to Kirihito* was, at the time, something of a departure for Tezuka, with its more experimental artwork and storytelling and very "adult" depiction of sex and violence. At more than 800 pages, it is a fast paced, tense read and, as always with Tezuka, a compelling examination of the human condition. **NFI**

COMコミックス増刊

きりひと讃歌

手塚治虫

上

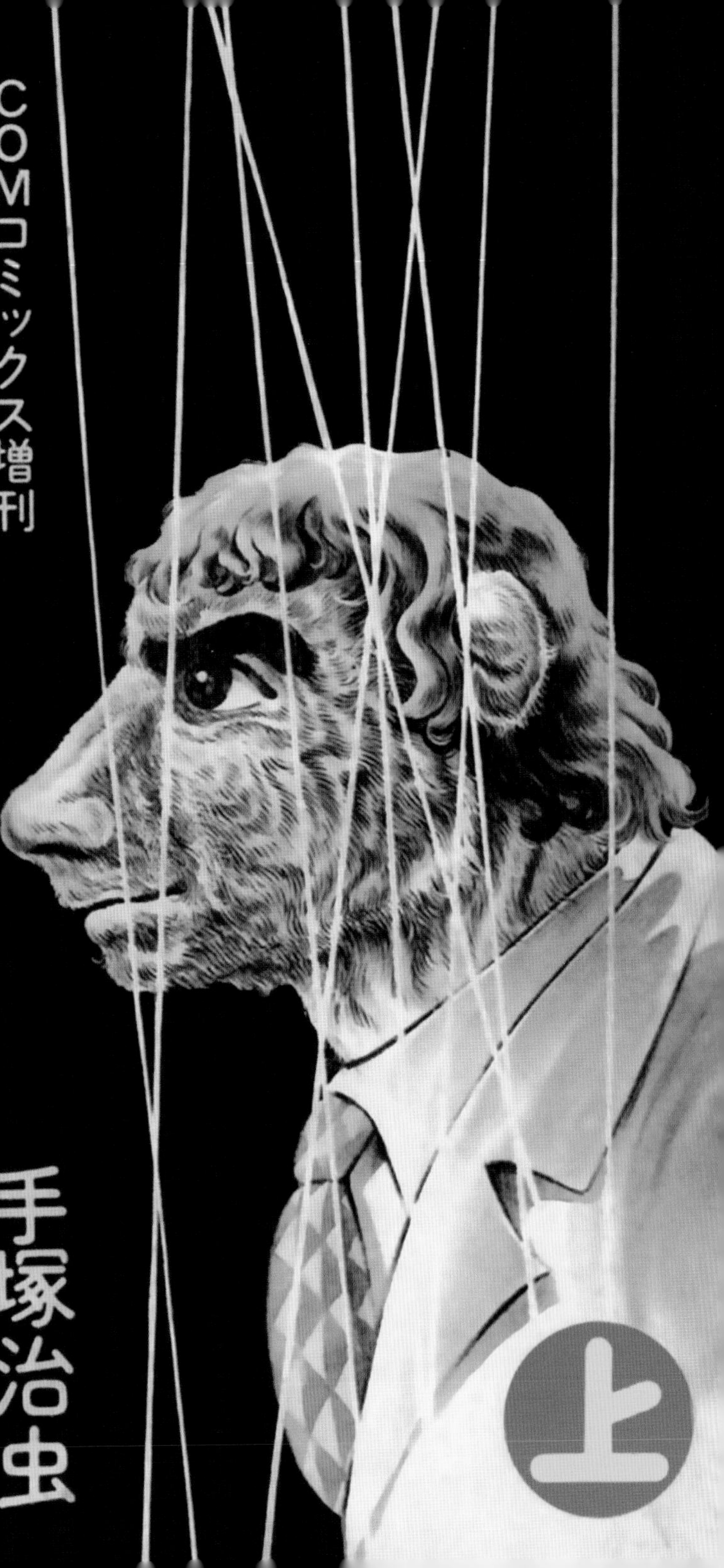

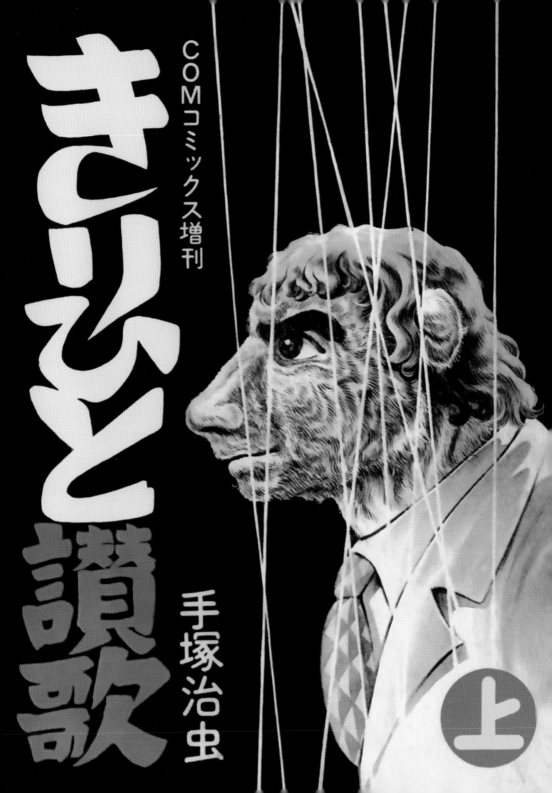

Lucky Luke
Tortillas for the Daltons 1970

René Goscinny Morris

Title in original language *Lucky Luke: Tortillas pour les Dalton* **First published by** Dupuis (Belgium) **Creators** Goscinny (French, 1926–77); Morris (Belgian, 1923–2001) **Genre** Humor

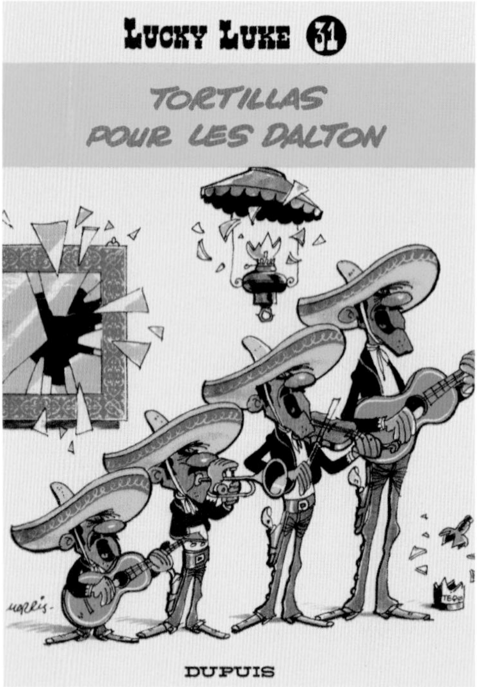
LUCKY LUKE 31
TORTILLAS
POUR LES DALTON
MORRIS
DUPUIS

Also by René Goscinny and Morris

Calamity Jane
Rails on the Prairie (*Des rails sur la Prairie*)
The Daltons Escape (*L'Évasion des Dalton*)
The Daltons Redeem Themselves (*Les Dalton se rachètent*)
The Rivals of Painful Gulch (*Les Rivaux de Painful Gulch*)

While traveling along the Rio Grande, the prison van transferring the Dalton gang to a new prison is hijacked and diverted to Mexico by the men of Emilio Espuelas, the most feared bandit in the country, in the hope of laying their hands on some treasure. When released, the Daltons propose that the gangs join forces; in exchange for being allowed to stay on Mexican soil, they will teach the Mexicans the techniques of U.S. organized crime—namely, how to rob a bank, a proven classic; until now the Mexican gangs have mainly raised money through kidnapping and ransom.

At the same time, Lucky Luke, flanked by his hilarious dog Rantanplan, has also crossed the Rio Grande. He has been asked by the U.S. government to chase the Daltons because the Mexican government has threatened diplomatic reprisals against America for having allowed the calamitous foursome into Mexico. Like the Daltons, Luke is faced by a strange environment and forced to get used to some puzzling things.

Lucky Luke, conceived in 1946, was a great success, and *Tortillas for the Daltons*, the thirty-first book of the series, was definitely one of the best. A prolific and always very imaginative writer, the brilliant René Goscinny used the same technique for his cowboy character and his Western universe as he did in another of his famous series, *Astérix*; he transposes his heroes into a foreign cultural context leading to numerous comic effects, both visual and linguistic.

As a result, we are regaled with jokes about siestas, tequila, chihuahuas, and mariachis, not to mention jokes related to the characters (the Daltons' stupidity and the amazing, enjoyably idiotic behavior of Rantanplan). Flowing, dynamic, and hyper-readable, Goscinny is at the peak of his form. Thrilling from beginning to end, *Tortillas for the Daltons* is also remarkable because of the graphic cleverness of Morris's illustrations. **NF**

Life in the Open Air 1970

Jean-Marc Reiser

Jean-Marc Reiser was an influential cartoonist whose work continues to polarize audiences decades after his premature death from bone cancer.

Reiser came to prominence in 1960 as one of the cartoonists responsible for *Hara-Kiri*, an influential establishment-baiting magazine with an editorial policy decreeing that nothing was sacred. Reiser's work is caustic, scatological, and often deliberately provocative, and his malicious nature, combined with a crude interpretative style of cartooning, put off many before they were able to appreciate the humanity of his work. Reiser berated political pomposity and railed against the system grinding down the ordinary man.

Life in the Open Air began in 1970 and continued in the monthly magazine *Charlie Mensuel* for the remainder of the decade. A series of wordless strips dealing with tribal life in Africa, the work has since attracted controversy for what are perceived as racist caricatures, although the tribespeople illustrated are no more grotesque and sketchy than Resier's usual figures. The humor in the strip was largely gag-oriented, but did stray into very dark areas. In a typically controversial strip, titled "The Famine," a plate is placed upside down on the ground in front of a group of starving people. At a signal, they lift the plate and consume the insects that have gathered beneath. But wildlife, Tarzan, and missionaries in particular are equally skewered as Reiser turns his attention to all aspects of life in Africa.

For all the outrage his work engendered, Reiser was appreciated by the comics community. In 1978 he became the fifth winner of the annual Grand Prize at the Angoulême Comic Festival. Reiser lived to see his work adapted as a movie, and at the time of his early death he had completed the film script for his comic strip *Vive les femmes!*; the film, starring Catherine Leprince, was released in 1984. **FP**

Title in original language *La Vie au grand air*
First published by *Charlie* magazine (France)
Creator French (1941–83)
Genre Humor

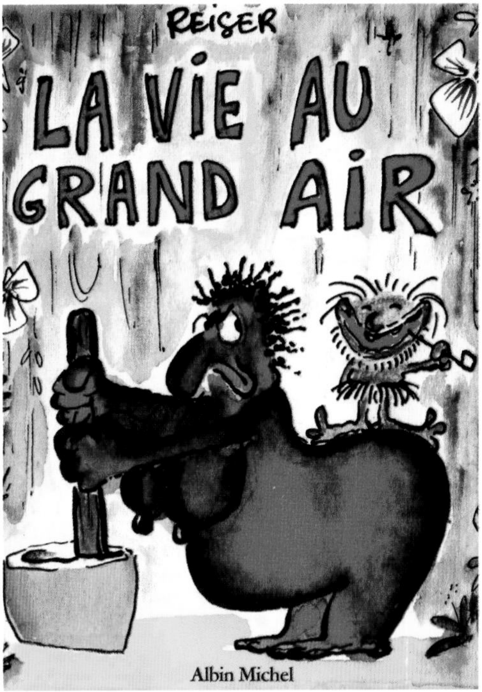
REISER
LA VIE AU GRAND AIR
Albin Michel

Also by Jean-Marc Reiser
Girlfriends (*Les Copines*)
Pervert (*Gros Dégueulasse*)
Pig Cartoons (*Dessins Cochons*)
The Oboulot Family on Holiday (*La Famille Oboulot en vacances*)

Jack Kirby's Fourth World/New Gods 1970

Jack Kirby

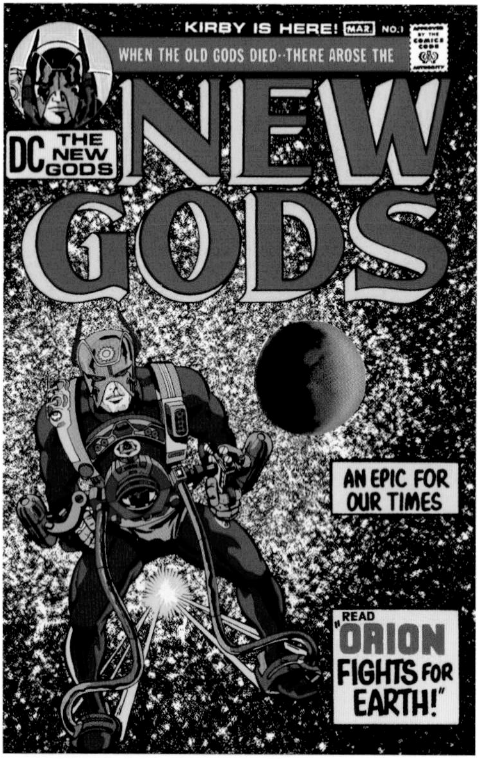
KIRBY IS HERE! MAR NO.1
WHEN THE OLD GODS DIED··THERE AROSE THE
DC THE NEW GODS
NEW GODS
AN EPIC FOR OUR TIMES
READ "ORION FIGHTS FOR EARTH!"

First published by DC Comics (USA)
Creator Jacob Kurtzberg (American, 1917–94)
Genre Superhero, Mythology
Award Shazam Special Achievement Award (1971)

Jack Kirby left Marvel for DC Comics in 1970, lured by the promise of greater creative control. The "Fourth World" was an idea he'd been developing since 1966; at the death of the Old Gods (Ragnarok), their world split into two sister planets, New Genesis and Apokolips. One is good, the other bad. Darkseid of Apokolips seizes control of his world, initiates hostilities with New Genesis, and seeks his ultimate goal, the Anti-Life Equation, which would give him control of all conscious life. The three titles—*New Gods*, *Forever People*, and *Mister Miracle*—focus on different sets of New Gods. The action is largely set on Earth, as Darkseid believes the Equation is within a human. Darkseid's son, Orion, raised on New Genesis, remains loyal to his adoptive world and stands against his father.

Often mentioned as pinnacles are *New Gods* #7 (a personal favorite of Kirby), which gives essential back-story on Darkseid's rise to power and how he and Hightfather of New Genesis exchanged sons in a pact to end their war (albeit temporarily); and *Mister Miracle* #9, which expands upon the history of Mister Miracle (Highfather's son) and how he finally escaped the hell of Apokolips. Both are superb, with the latter being one of Kirby's all-time best works.

It was not until 2007 that Kirby's vision of hardcover collections became a reality. *Fourth World* is a flawed masterpiece; most of it is genuinely great, and at its best it is almost transcendentally brilliant. It stands as one of the greatest and most ambitious projects mainstream comics has ever seen—read it immediately. **CH**

"I've read all the legends that were written before our time … I felt we had no legends of our own."

Jack Kirby

Also by Jack Kirby
Kamandi
The Demon

Zippy the Pinhead 1970

✏️✏️ Bill Griffith

First published by *The Berkeley Barb* (USA)
Creator American (b.1944)
Genre Underground humor
Influenced by Robert Crumb

If space is homogenous and time is isotropic, then what does that make Doris Day? If you enjoy pondering surreal quandaries such as this, then *Zippy the Pinhead* could be the comic strip you have always dreamed of.

Created by Bill Griffith, a New York native who originally planned to succeed Jackson Pollock, *Zippy* sprang forth from the California underground. But Griffith's unique approach to cartooning, merging high-caliber penwork with a refined and inventive use of language, soon found a wider audience, and King Features, the behemoth of American newspaper strips, picked up *Zippy* for syndication in 1986.

Early on, Griffith had the idea of creating a resonant environment for dadaist experiments by including characters representing both sides of human nature. Enter Zippy and his pal Griffy. Zippy, a microcephalic clown dressed in an enormous polka-dotted muu muu, is playful, fun-loving, and nonsensical. Griffy, uptight in a suit and tie, obsesses over life's details and the unhappiness they can bring. They have commented on everything from foreign policy to Garfield.

Zippy's message—that the surrealism of modern life can only be countered with more surrealism—has turned out to have had lasting appeal. Generations of slightly confused readers have enjoyed *Zippy* at the breakfast table or, as with many newspaper strips nowadays, online at the office. A person in a three-sided cubicle getting comics beamed into their brain through a screen—now that's a strange twist that even *Zippy* could not have foreseen. **EL**

Lone Wolf & Cub 1970

✏️ Kazuo Koike ✏️ Goseki Kojima

Title in original language *Kozure Okami*
First published by *Weekly Manga Action* (Japan)
Creators Koike (Japanese, b.1936); Kojima (Japanese, 1928–2000) **Genre** History

At the end of the seventeenth century in Edo (the former name of Tokyo), Ogami Itto, the *kaishakunin* (executioner) of the shogun, sees almost the whole of his family massacred by a powerful rival clan. His enemies want him to commit *seppuku* (suicide), but the executioner, rejecting the *bushido* (warrior's code of behavior), decides to stay alive and become a mercenary, offering himself and his warring skills to the highest bidder. He believes that choosing the cruel and bloody "assassin's path" is the only way to have a chance of one day avenging his family.

He changes his name to Kozure Okami (Lone Wolf) and now, as a *rônin*, or samurai without a master, he roams medieval Japan with his three-year-old son Daigoro as his only companion. Punctuated by numerous massacres, Lone Wolf's life is dominated by an unquenchable thirst for vengeance.

Told in several dozen albums, the epic story of *Lone Wolf & Cub* is undoubtedly a masterpiece. Few stories have managed to achieve such powerful universality. The image of a gloomy, taciturn man watching over a sleeping child in a simple wooden stroller with a pennant is not easily forgotten. The action is omnipresent, the fight scenes are consistently elegant, and the graphic treatment, which uses all the subtleties of black and white, is a masterpiece of classical realism. But *Lone Wolf & Cub* is also a true narrative gem: dense, complex, erudite, and detailed while also offering an unobstructed view of Japanese society in the Edo period. **NF**

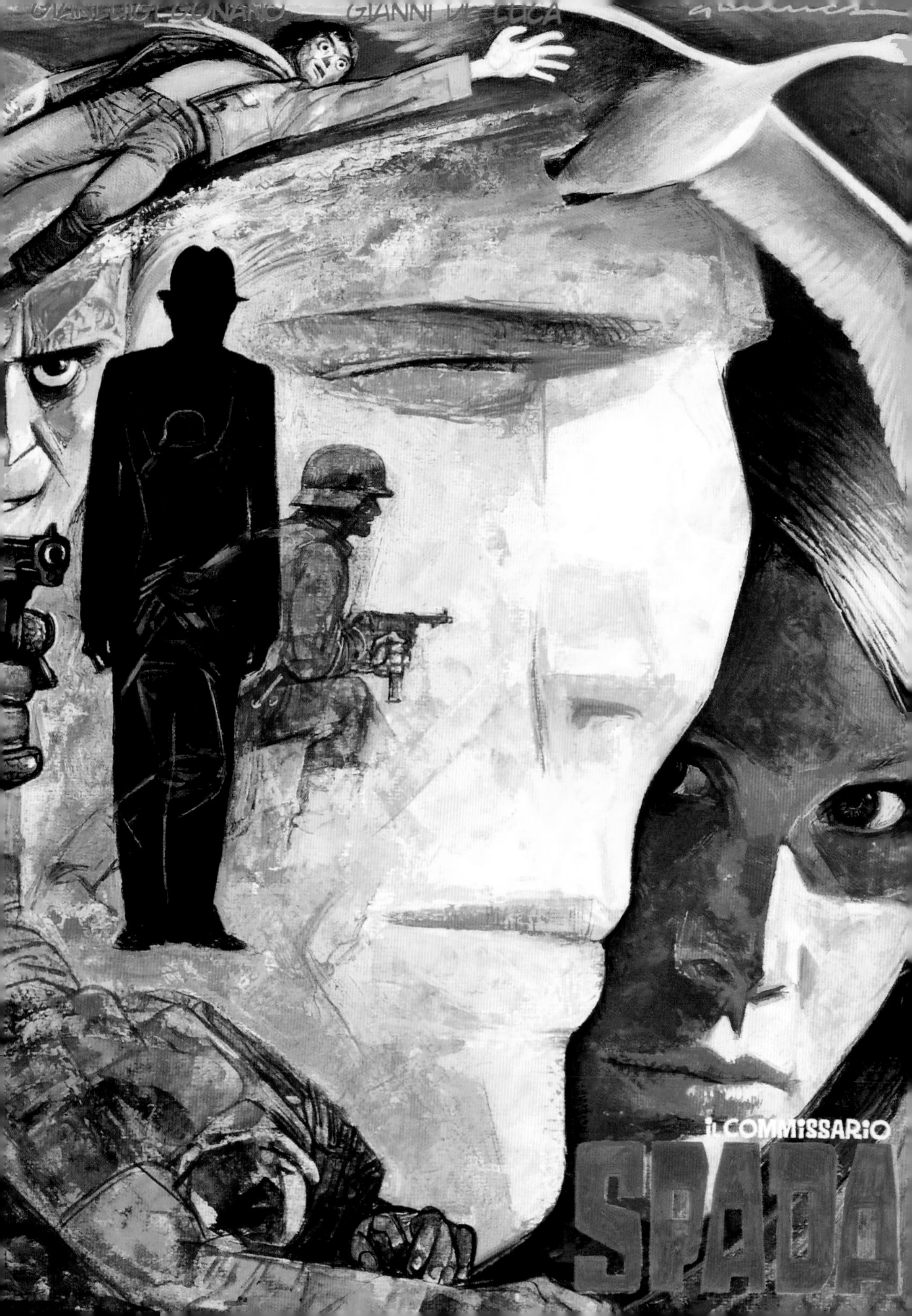
IL COMMISSARIO
SPADA

Commissioner Spada 1970

✐ Gianluigi Gonano ✐ Gianni De Luca

Title in original language *Il Commissario Spada*
First published by Edizioni Paoline (Italy)
Creators Gonano (Italian, b.1940); De Luca (Italian, 1927–91) **Genre** Crime

Intended as a classical crime series, this was one of the most disruptive and popular stories in Italian comics, both editorially and visually. Eugenio Spada is a criminal police detective who, over twelve years, deals with murders, thieves, criminal organizations, terrorists, and satanic sects. At the time of publication—the so-called "years of lead" dominated by spreading violence and the bullets fired by political terrorist groups—its portrayal of Italian society was unexpectedly realistic. The series appeared in the pages of children's weekly *Il Giornalino*—the oldest comics magazine in Italy, owned by a Catholic publisher—and soon it had a major impact on young readers, airing current and topical issues in a place traditionally used for light entertainment.

The strongest innovations came in visualization. Here, De Luca introduced some of his most radical experimentations in page layout. He stretched panels into every shape possible—diagonal, horizontal, round, zooming—expanding the knowing art of Chester Gould and Will Eisner in anticipation of Andreas, Sienkiewicz, and McKean. He used a sort of stereoscopical depiction of movement, putting characters on "background landscapes" without frames: the page became a "stage," and the action was drawn through a sequence of almost simultaneous micromovements of figures. Later, this work led him to his celebrated trilogy of Shakespeare adaptations, where every sequence is crafted in a landscape mode and readers are pushed to perceive a radical deconstruction of the page as a fictional, conventional space. **MS**

Miyoko Asagawa Kibun 1970

✐✐ Shin'ichi Abe

First published by Seirindo (Japan)
Creator Japanese (b.1950)
Genre Autobiography
Adaptation Animation (2009)

When considering Shin'ichi Abe's work, it is difficult to focus on a single volume. Most of his production has embraced the "watakushi manga" approach pioneered by Yoshiharu Tsuge with his seminal *Neji-shiki* (*Screw-style*), published in 1965. In watakushi manga—or I-comics, the manga version of the "shishôsetsu," or I-novel—authors use their feelings, dreams, and subjective experiences as story material.

In a sense, *Miyoko Asagawa Kibun* is a central piece of what constitutes a sprawling and yet largely hidden autobiographical project. It revolves around Miyoko, the love of Abe's life, and their early years in Asagawa. When first meeting her, Abe is overwhelmed by a feeling of "immediate nostalgia," wishing they had met earlier. This nostalgia pervades the book, which is a veiled exploration of his personal history, an autobiography in fragments, a collection of troubling moments and floating characters, of coded allusions and delicate references. There are few names, sometimes fewer words, because they are not always needed in the face of objects transformed by the intensity of the feelings attached to them, of sensuality remembered.

With his carefully etched line, Shin'ichi Abe carves out the most intimate moments in the relationship, revealing the hidden cracks with a frankness that can unsettle the reader, who is forced into the position of voyeur. And yet, the boldness of the art is only as strong as the restraint in the words, and in this apparent contradiction lies the complexity of a unique and thoroughly personal endeavor. **XG**

Green Lantern/Green Arrow 1970

Dennis O'Neil Neal Adams

First published by DC Comics (USA)
Creators O'Neil (American, b.1939); Adams (American, b.1941)
Genre Superhero

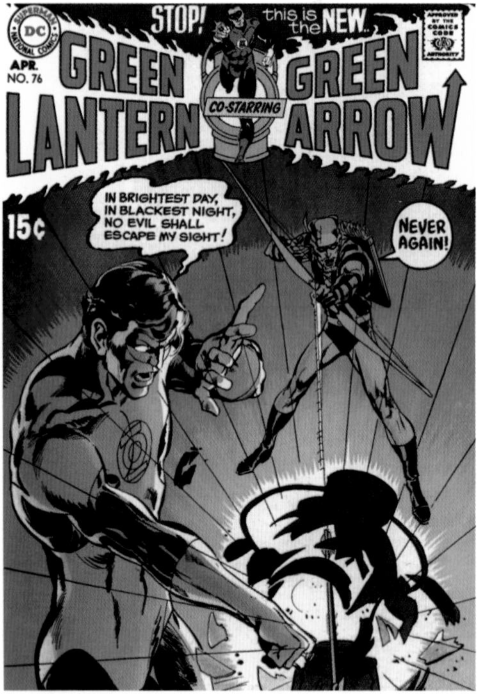
STOP! this is the NEW...
GREEN LANTERN
CO-STARRING
GREEN ARROW
APR. NO. 76
15¢
IN BRIGHTEST DAY, IN BLACKEST NIGHT, NO EVIL SHALL ESCAPE MY SIGHT!
NEVER AGAIN!

Similar reads
Amazing Spider-Man Stan Lee and Gil Kane
Batman Dennis O'Neil and Neal Adams
Iron Man: Demon in a Bottle David Michelinie and Bob Layton
Lois Lane Robert Kanigher and Werner Roth

When DC Comics decided to cancel *Green Lantern,* a series that first appeared in 1940, editor Julius Schwartz charged writer Dennis O'Neil and artist Neal Adams with a radical reboot: the hero and his new partner, Green Arrow, would explore real-life issues in what would be christened "social relevance" in comics.

In the seminal story "No Evil Shall Escape My Sight," Green Lantern rescues an obese man in a suit from a "punk" in a poor neighborhood. Expecting approval from bystanders, he is instead subjected to a barrage of garbage. Green Arrow informs him that the "victim" is a slumlord. The two then embark on a road trip to find the "real" America, with the traditionalist Lantern and iconoclast Arrow butting heads all the way. The stridently earnest narratives that follow deal with racism, pollution, cults, and drug addiction. In a controversial episode, Green Arrow's sidekick, Speedy, injects heroin, while another character dies of an overdose. Concurrent changes in the Comics Code, which for seventeen years had banned such depictions, allowed this issue to gain the seal of approval. Adams's Green Lantern was human, tortured, and self-doubting—the antithesis of the heroic icon of Gil Kane, the title's previous artist.

"Something is wrong! Something is killing us all! Some hideous moral cancer is rotting our very souls."

Insistence on social relevance was short-lived, however; after thirteen issues the series was cancelled. In hindsight the crusading seems heavy-handed and the mix with fantasy uneasy, but for two years these stories expanded the perceived potential of U.S. comics. And while the larger 1970s "relevance" fad faded, social commentary and more human characters were to endure in the superhero stories that followed. **TL**

Red Colored Elegy 1970

Seiichi Hayashi

Ichiro and Sashiko are two young artists working in the lower rungs of the animation business, living together in a hedonistic but listless manner and largely impervious to whatever is occurring on the "outside." They are kindred souls inimical to normal social expectations, lacking a clear idea of how to make a living or plan for their own future.

Although we witness their romance, we never fully participate in it. If ellipsis is the province of comics, *Red Colored Elegy* is at its core. Less about storytelling, or even character development, the book slowly generates an ambience, with each new sequence of images or calm splash pages building its nonverbal meaning. Emotions are conveyed less through the pair's facial expressions than by the dramatic theatricality and paused interaction of their bodies.

"What if you become a famous artist? I'll be known as your famous muse . . ."

Hayashi is searching for a fresh quality in his work, surpassing the themes and tones of gegika to create a form of adult manga that is relatively traditional where narrative is concerned. Considering the many references to drawing and comic making in this book, we can consider it to be at least partially autobiographical as it explores emotional nuances and the mixing of routine life, the oneiric, the perils of doubt, and the weight of the unspoken.

The art swings between minimalism and realism; some panels have white backgrounds, others are photo-perfect depictions of seascapes and temples. Visual metaphors and animationlike drawings create multiple layers of meaning and expression that convey the restless yet rich inner life of the characters. **PM**

Title in original language *Sekishoku Erejii*
First published by Shogakukan (Japan)
Creator Japanese (b.1945)
Genre Drama

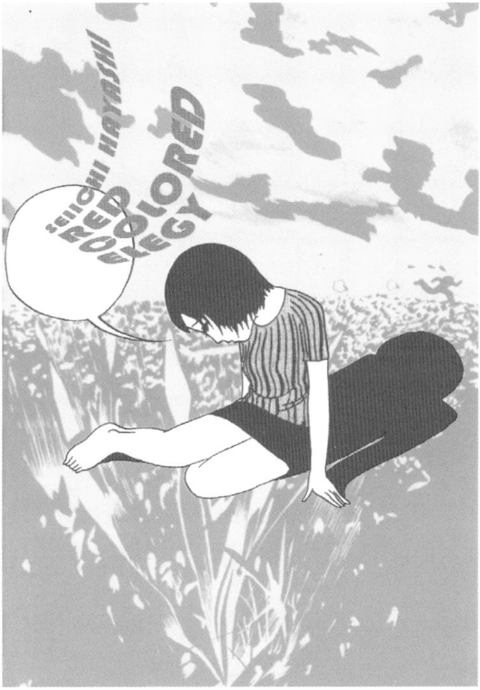
SEIICHI HAYASHI
RED COLORED ELEGY

Similar reads
A Nice Guy Shin'ichi Abe
A Single Match Oji Suzuki
Miyoko Asagawa Kibun Shin'ichi Abe
The Man Without Talent Yoshiharu Tsuge
Transparent Blue Oji Suzuki

Doonesbury 1970

✐✐ Garry Trudeau

First published by Universal Press Syndicate (USA)
Creator American (b.1948)
Genre Satire
Award Pulitzer Prize for Editorial Cartooning (1975)

An inadvertent chronicle of the public culture of the United States, for more than forty years *Doonesbury* has been the best proof that the U.S. comic strip need not cater to the lowest common denominator.

Garry Trudeau's comic strip has set the highest standard for U.S. satire. Despite often being sharp-edged in its commentary and willing to land harsh blows against its targets, *Doonesbury* is best characterized by its deeply felt compassion for the powerless, its complex depiction of moral issues, and its faith in the transformative power of human understanding. Throughout its long run, *Doonesbury* never lost its point of view, and never succumbed to the bitterness that defines too much of America's political discourse.

Having started as an intimate strip about college life, *Doonesbury* has, over time, developed an enormous, sprawling cast of characters—it reads more like an epic novel than a collection of topical gags. The way Trudeau's characters change—not simply age, but grow as people—has endeared them to generations of readers. Long after many of his political targets have faded from public memory, it is Trudeau's cast that readers remember most clearly.

Throughout its run, *Doonesbury* has not shied away from a single important cultural issue. Trudeau has chronicled wars (notably the second U.S. invasion of Iraq), the failings of eight presidents, and the gradual transformation of the U.S. family with an indefatigable sense of humor. *Doonesbury* is the landmark chronicle of the end of the twentieth century. **BB**

Bent 1971

✐✐ S. Clay Wilson

First published by The Print Mint (USA)
Creator American (b.1941)
Genre Underground
Influence on Robert Crumb

This early solo comic by S. Clay Wilson contains all the graphic elements that would make his work notorious. *Bent* is crammed with seedy and violent characters, all hell bent (no pun intended) on causing as much physical and sexual damage to each other as possible. The cover, awash with blood, knives, disembodied heads, murder, nudity, and sick surgery, is an indication that what lurks inside is not going to be pretty.

Wilson crams his pages with black-and-white detail, pushing the edge of the frame to its very limits with gore, semen, engorged penises, and severed limbs. His freak show of pirates, bikers, mad scientists, demons, drunkards, and freaks lurches out to pull readers into its world of sadism and madness. Roaming through *Bent* is the Checkered Demon (or "Checks" for short), a portly, short-horned demon wearing checked trousers, biker boots, and a leering grin who comes to the aid of a young girl abducted by female pirate captain Rosey Namrooth and her crew of lusty dykes. Elsewhere, Star-Eyed Stella finds herself ensnared by a biker gang, the Gypsy Bandits, in a surreal sexual tale that also involves a microscopic monk who mistakes her vagina for a cave and crawls inside. It is in the center spread of *Bent*, however, that Wilson really lets rip. The two-page illustration is called "Dwarf Snuffing Station #103" and is stuffed to the gunnels with scenes of dwarves being mutilated, murdered, and humiliated by a gang of crazed women.

Forty years on, Wilson's comics have lost none of their power to shock, amuse, and amaze. **EP**

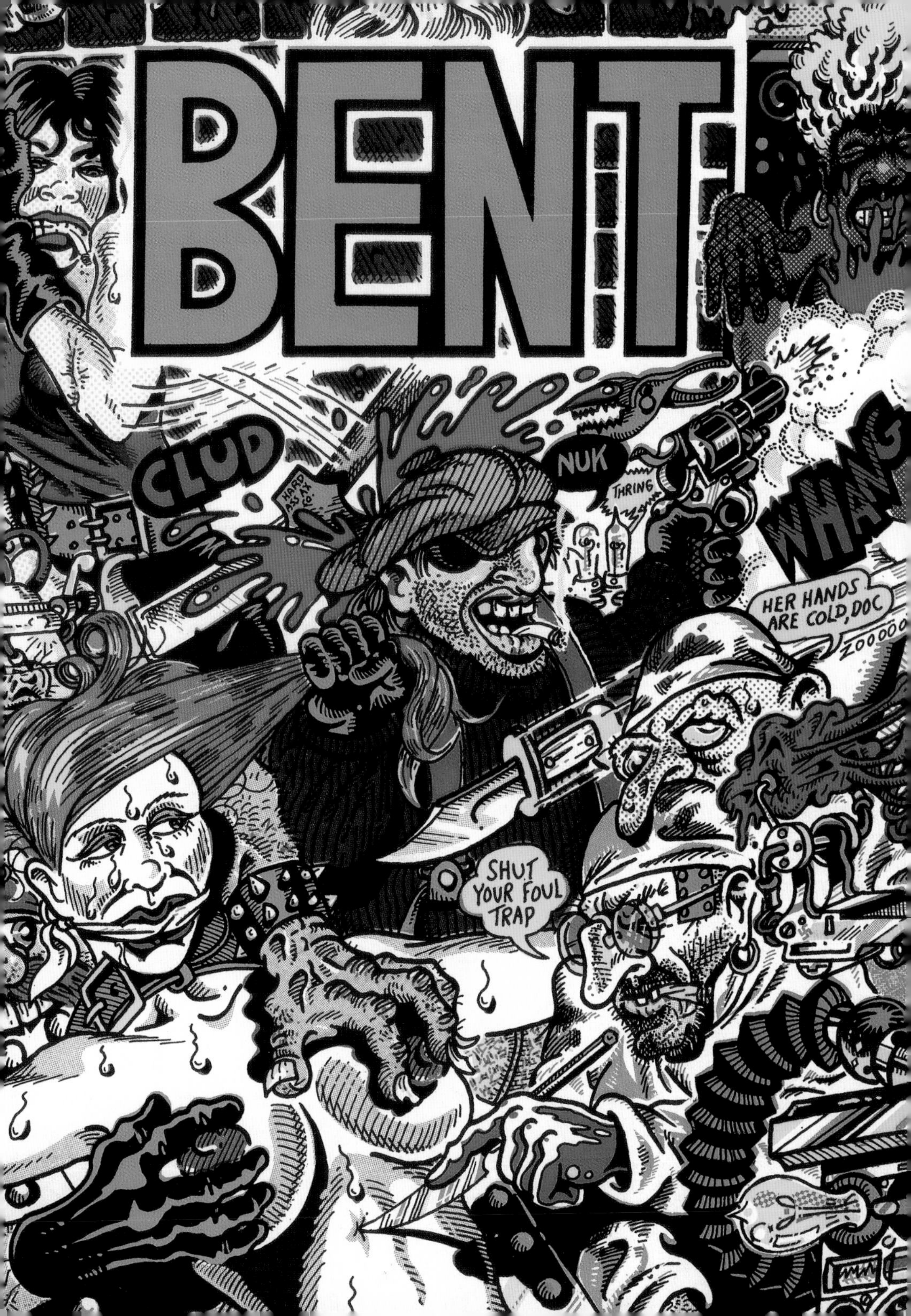
BENT
CLUD
NUK
THRING
HER HANDS ARE COLD, DOC
SHUT YOUR FOUL TRAP

Patty's World 1971

✎ Phillip Douglas ✎ Purita Campos

First published by IPC Magazines (UK)
Creators Douglas (British, Unknown);
Campos (Spanish, b.1937)
Genre Drama

Of the hundreds of girl strips published by IPC, *Patty's World* was both the longest running and the best. The feature, which first appeared in *Princess Tina*, was remarkable for its seemingly unremarkable concept: to chart the life, loves, and neuroses of an ordinary teenage girl. In a crowded marketplace dominated by stories about boarding schools, ballet, horses, or girls plagued by bizarre afflictions, the strip was a welcome dose of (often hilarious) reality.

Patty Lucas is a young girl living with her recently widowed mother and glamorous older sister. Her world revolves around school, friendships, and her unrequited love for the dashing Johnny Vowden. Within that framework, however, Phillip Douglas brilliantly dealt with such issues as jealousy (as Patty's mother marries again), miscarriages, unemployment, class, bereavement, and desire. He also had an acute ear for slang, and the strip resonated with the authentic voice of contemporary teenaged Britain. The strip's artist, Purita Campos, was attuned to the ever-changing world of fashion and had a vibrant, effervescent drawing style.

Patty's World ran for seventeen years in a succession of titles, including *Pink* and *Mates*, finally ending up in *Girl*, where it became the final strip ever published by IPC. In 2006, Glénat España launched a new series of graphic novels of Esther, the Spanish version of Patty. Esther is a middle-aged mother bringing up her own teenaged daughter named Patty, the product of a steamy one-night stand with Johnny. Thus, the cycle continues for another generation of readers. **DAR**

The Fosdyke Saga 1971

✎✎ Bill Tidy

First published by *Daily Mirror* (UK)
Creator British (b.1933)
Genre Drama
Adaptation Film (1977)

The year is 1902 and Josiah Fosdyke is unexpectedly rescued from poverty when he inherits Ben Ditchley's tripe empire at the expense of Ben's son Roger, the rightful but overlooked heir. Roger Ditchley, enraged at his disinheritance, becomes "the man with the world's biggest grievance" and spends the entirety of the strip's fourteen years gathering, one after the other, a coterie of inept accomplices to assist him in bringing about Fosdyke's early demise. The story is set in northwest England's gritty coal-mining hinterland.

The Fosdykes are a parody of English novelist John Galsworthy's Forsytes of *The Forsyte Saga*, an account of the rise and eventual fall of an upper-class British family. Born in Cheshire and raised in Liverpool, Bill Tidy was proud of his working-class roots and felt that northern working-class families should have their own slice of literary immortality, something that reflected their struggles and aspirations. "Their lives, thoughts, and dreams have been neglected for years," he once said. Unlike Napoleon and Snowball, the pigs of George Orwell's *Animal Farm* that show how power can corrupt, the Fosdyke family maintained their values.

The Fosdykes' misadventures spanned two world wars and beyond, and provided vivid depictions of the hardships encountered by the average Briton. The myriad of locations depicted, from the decks of the *Titanic* to the slopes of Mount Everest, provided its indomitable characters with a vast stage on which to showcase their determination to take the wonders of tripe to a waiting and grateful world. **BS**

Mickey Mouse Meets the Air Pirates Funnies 1971

Dan O'Neill, Bobby London, Gary Hallgren, and Ted Richards

First published by Hell Comics (USA)
Creators O'Neill (American, b.1942); London (American, b.1950); Hallgren (American, b.1945); Richards (American, b.1946) **Genre** Underground

The collective known as the Air Pirates produced two comics in 1971 that led to the Walt Disney Company issuing a lawsuit against them for breach of copyright. Disney was incensed by their depictions of famous characters such as Mickey Mouse, Donald Duck, Minnie Mouse, the Big Bad Wolf, and the Silly Symphonys bugs (retitled Sympathies) taking drugs and having sex. The case dragged on for several years, with Disney demanding over $2 million in damages and legal fees against chief Air Pirate Dan O'Neill. The case against O'Neill was finally dropped after he reluctantly agreed to stop infringing Disney's copyright.

In the two comics, the Air Pirates returned to the styles of past masters of the comic strip. Bobby London's *Dirty Duck* is a lovingly assembled remake of George Herriman's *Krazy Kat*, while Ted Richards' *Dopin' Dan* efficiently spoofs Mort Walker's long-running newspaper strip *Beetle Bailey* (with perhaps a trace of George Baker's *Sad Sack* thrown in for good measure). But it was Dan O'Neill who really got Disney's blood up, however, particularly in a scene where Mickey is performing the act of cunnilingus on an ecstatic Minnie Mouse.

With the full weight of Disney's empire against him, the unrepentant O'Neill drew and published the company's characters in a way that delighted his counterculture audience but infuriated his corporate enemies. One memorable cover for an issue of *Dan O'Neill's Comics and Stories*, a series he began in 1971, has one of the Three Little Pigs blowing out the brains of the Big Bad Wolf with a handgun. **EP**

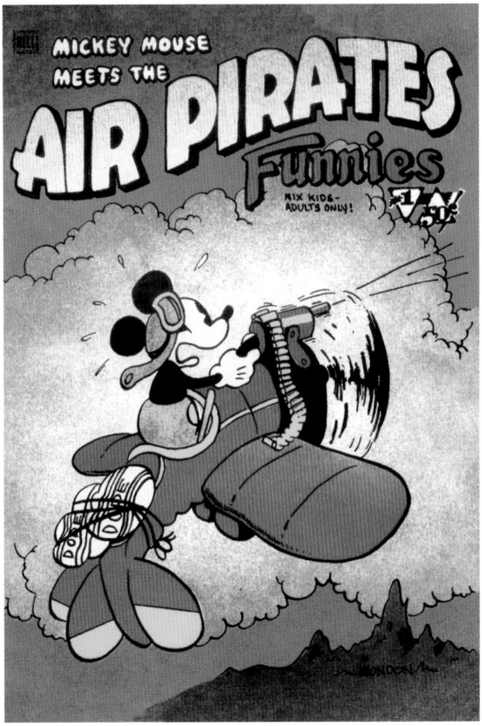
MICKEY MOUSE MEETS THE
AIR PIRATES
Funnies
NIX KIDS- ADULTS ONLY!

"The Air Pirates bring you A QUADRUPLE THREAT! and then some in clean, wholesome fun!"

Similar reads

Dan O'Neill's Comics and Stories
E.Z. Wolf
The Collective Unconscience of Odd Bodkins
The Dirty Duck Book
The Tortoise and the Hare

My Fears 1971

"Sió"

Title in original language *Mis Miedos*
First published by Buru Lan Ediciones (Spain)
Creator Enric Sió (Spanish, 1942–98)
Genre Horror

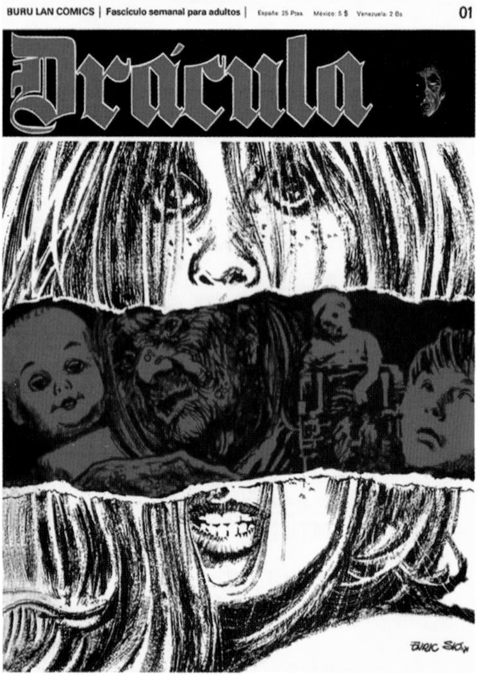
BURU LAN COMICS | Fascículo semanal para adultos |
01
Drácula
ENRIC SIÓ

Also by Sió
Aghardi
Lavinia 2016
Lord Shark
Mara
Nus and Sorang

Originally published in *Dracula* magazine, *My Fears* is a series of twelve short horror stories with no main character, each of them five pages long. Apart from the first story, "Eleonor," which is based on a tale by Juan Tebar, they were all written and drawn by Sió. Making full use of his considerable storytelling talent, Sió often devises revolutionary page layouts with a nearly photographic visual style comparable to that of other contemporaneous European innovative comic book artists, such as the Italian Guido Crepax.

Most of the stories deal with tormented young women who have larger-than-life problems with everyday objects or creatures: in "Krazy," a cat lover becomes the victim of her pet cat; in "Alicia," a young lady has troubles with her creaking floor; "Marian" presents a conflict between a grandmother and her granddaughter. Other episodes of *My Fears* worth noting include the aforementioned, dialogless "Eleonor," (where a vampire wants to bite a little girl, but she bites him first); "Eloise" (a man makes a pact with Death in order to be reunited with his late loved one); "Minins" (a young man—presumably the author himself—faces his childhood memories); and "Bittler Wraton" (a parody of *Battler Briton*, the popular British war comic strip which was briefly drawn by Sió in the early 1960s).

Dracula, the magazine in which these stories were published, was an anthology of adult horror and fantasy comic strips that also featured Esteban Maroto (with his sword-and-sorcery saga *Wolff*), Carlos Giménez, Josep Beá, and others. There was an English-language edition of *Dracula* published in the U.K. in 1972 by New English Library; additionally, material from issues one to six was compiled into a single volume in the U.S. by Warren. *My Fears* was never published separately in Spain in album form, although the French publisher Dargaud did so in 1980, under the title *Mes Peurs*. **AMo**

The Legion of Charlies 1971

Tom Veitch Greg Irons

The U.S. underground comics movement is widely regarded as having been primarily concerned with the issues of sex, drugs, and rock n' roll, but it was also on occasions intensely political. Poet and writer Tom Veitch was one of the most politically aware creators on the scene, and *The Legion Of Charlies* (published by Last Gasp in San Francisco) was the most visceral expression of his feelings of alienation and disgust

The story centers around the Vietnam veteran Lieutenant Kali, recently returned to the United States but still haunted by flashbacks of the atrocities he and his soldiers committed while on duty. Veitch links the Vietnam War to that other 1960s outrage, the killings by Charles Manson's "Family," by having Kali and a growing band of followers become possessed by Manson's demented spirit. In scenes of outrageous gore, the murderous group kills and consumes first Spiro T. Agnew and then other world leaders before being attacked in turn by a deranged President Nixon. The comic gleefully goes beyond the usual boundaries of good taste with scenes of unrelenting barbarity and cannibalism, while also somehow being hilariously funny.

The artwork of the comic was contributed by frequent Veitch collaborator Greg Irons, whose drawings in a detailed art nouveau–flavored style reveled in the excesses and frenetic pace of the script. Irons was one of the earliest artists to specialize in psychedelic posters, and after spending time in England working on the Beatles' movie *Yellow Submarine*, he embraced the underground scene with inspired gusto. Unfortunately, despite excellent work in titles such as *Heavy*, *Light*, *Grunt*, *Slow Death*, and *Skull*, he never became the star his talent deserved. Eventually he moved into the tattoo industry, where prospective clients increasingly sought him out until a tragic traffic accident ended his life at the age of thirty-seven. **DR**

First published by Last Gasp (USA)
Creators Veitch (American, Unknown); Irons (American, 1947–84)
Genre Drama

THE LEGION OF
CHARLIES
50¢
BIG C
LT. KALI
TITS
GORE

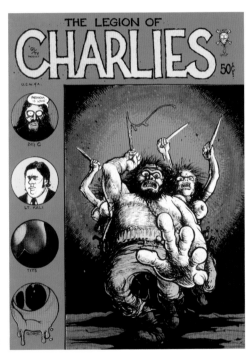

Also by Tom Veitch

Clash with Adam Kubert
My Name is Chaos with John Ridgway and Les Dorscheid
The Light and Darkness War with Cam Kennedy
The Nazz with Bryan Talbot

Achille Talon 1971

✏✏ "Greg"

Title in original language *L'indispensable Achille Talon*
First published by Dargaud (France)
Creator Michel Regnier (Belgian/French, 1931–99)
Genre Humor

Achille Talon is a fat, verbose, middle-aged Parisian bourgeois forever giving his opinion about everything and offering help in matters in which he is incompetent. The character was created by Greg in 1963 as a humorous filler for the weekly *Pilote* magazine, and one-page strips soon gave way to two-pagers. In the mid-1970s, Greg used the character in a more heroic role in longer adventure stories still peppered with plenty of satire about contemporary society. One of those stories, "Magnesia's Treasure," was published in English.

L'indispensable Achille Talon is a collection of two-pagers published in *Pilote* during the late 1960s, when the series was at its peak. Achille Talon is fighting with his eternal nemesis, next-door neighbor Lefuneste; trying to impress his snobbish girlfriend, Virgule de Guillemets; and annoying the short-tempered editor-in-chief of the weekly *Polite* magazine (a caricature of *Astérix* writer and *Pilote* editor René Goscinny).

Achille Talon is a well-meaning blunderer (in the Dutch version he is actually called Olivier Blunder) whose self-assurance spells his doom. When he tries out the "art of good manners" he just got from a book, he ends up in a fight with another good-manners fanatic who turns out to be the book's author. His two attempts at his editor's aptitude test are disasters: in the first case he's too bad, in the second, too good. And throughout, Achille Talon speaks to overflow, using a refined vocabulary that makes the strip both a paean to language and an indictment of its power to hide blatant incompetence behind a veil of words. **J-PJ**

Welcome to Alflolol 1971

✏ Pierre Christin ✏ Jean-Claude Mézières

Title in original language *Bienvenue sur Alflolol*
First published by Dargaud (France)
Creators Christin (French, b.1938); Mézières (French, b.1938) **Genre** Science fiction

Valérian and Laureline are two agents of a future Terran empire. First appearing in 1967 in the weekly *Pilote*, their series was originally straightforward space adventure but soon grew to incorporate a good dollop of satire and social commentary.

Welcome to Alflolol takes place on Technorog, a planet rich in all kinds of resources that have been exploited by the Terran empire for a couple of centuries. On an inspection journey, Valérian and Laureline meet a family of space-roving humanoid giants who turn out to be the original inhabitants of Technorog, which they call Alflolol. Extremely long-lived, Alflololians are very close to nature, and each has a special gift (healing, telepathy, telekinesis) that appears at puberty.

Their customs soon clash with the demands of the Terran empire, and things worsen when the remaining Alflololians turn up. Valérian tries to remain neutral and smooth things over between Earth and the Alflololians, while Laureline sides with the giants. The Earth government initially restricts the Alflololians to only a few zones, but when they cannot feed themselves they are asked to work in the Technorog factories. Well-meaning but totally impractical, the Alflololians make a mess of it, and finally they leave the planet in disgust and head back into space to find a new one.

Welcome to Alflolol is a biting indictment of the way Western civilization's obsession with progress has caused it to destroy nature and dispossess native people. It is also a very warm, funny, and fast-paced story, one of the best in the *Pilote* series. **J-PJ**

Lieutenant Blueberry
The Lost Dutchman's Mine 1971

✏ Jean-Michel Charlier 🖊 "Moebius"

Title in original language *La Mine de l'Allemand perdu*
First published by *Pilote* (France)
Creators Charlier (Belgian, 1924–89); Jean Giraud
(French, b. 1938) **Genre** Western

The story takes place in 1868 in a small town in Arizona, and Lieutenant Mike Blueberry, with old friend Jimmy McClure at his side, has been offered a temporary appointment as marshal. He overhears Luckner, a Dutch gold prospector with a dubious past, mention the existence of a fabulous mine somewhere in Apache territory, in the Hills of Superstition. The news spreads like wildfire, leading to numerous adventures and gunfights. Luckner flees, hotly pursued by Blueberry, McClure, and two bounty hunters.

The rest of the adventure takes place almost entirely on Apache land, in the sector of the "mesa of the dead horse," the alleged location of the gold mine. Luckner, whose absence of scruples becomes increasingly obvious, temporarily joins forces with one of the bounty hunters to locate the mine. Pursued by Blueberry and McClure, they all begin to realize that a menacing presence is silently following them. When it finally fires at them, pursuers and pursued discover to their great amazement that their invisible enemy is firing bullets made of pure gold.

Inspired by Western movies, the *Blueberry* saga, created in 1963 and consisting of about thirty volumes, has become a legend of the Franco-Belgian comic strip. The series is above all notable for the virtuoso graphic talent of Jean Giraud, aka Moebius. Two chapters bound together, "The Lost Dutchman's Mine" and "The Ghost with the Golden Bullets," mark a decisive turning point in the history of the series because of their visual sophistication and powerful narrative. **J-PJ**

FORT NAVAJO *une Aventure du* Lieutenant BLUEBERRY
LA MINE DE L'ALLEMAND PERDU
TEXTE DE CHARLIER
DESSINS DE GIRAUD
🌀 DARGAUD

"Lieutenant, this nugget is yours if you can get me a horse and let me leave quietly, okay?"

Also by Jean-Michel Charlier and Moebius
Ballad for a Coffin
Chihuahua Pearl
Fort Navajo
The Iron Horse
The Steel Fingers

The Man-Thing 1971

Steve Gerber and others John Buscema, Jim Mooney, Mike Ploog, and others

First published by Marvel Comics (USA)
Creators Gerber (American, 1947–2008); Buscema (American, 1927–2002); Mooney (American, 1919–2008); Ploog (American, b.1942) **Genre** Fantasy

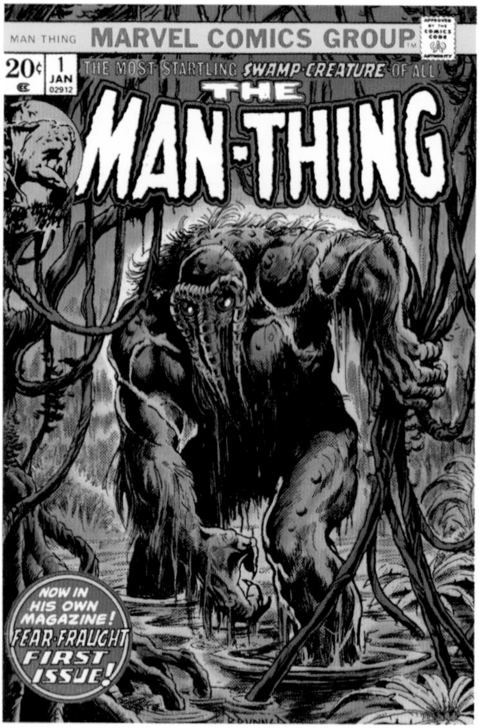
MAN THING
MARVEL COMICS GROUP
20¢
1 JAN
THE MOST STARTLING SWAMP-CREATURE OF ALL!
THE MAN-THING
NOW IN HIS OWN MAGAZINE! FEAR-FRAUGHT FIRST ISSUE!

Similar reads

Essential Defenders, Vol. 3 Steve Gerber, Gerry Conway, David Anthony Kraft, Ed Hannigan, and others; illustrated by Sal Buscema and Klaus Janson
Howard the Duck Steve Gerber with various artists

Originally conceived by Stan Lee and Roy Thomas, the Man-Thing was first introduced in *Savage Tales* #1 (1971). He was given his own feature in *Adventure into Fear* #11 (1972), and finally his own comic in December 1973, by which time Steve Gerber had emerged as the key writer for this most bizarre of Marvel's protagonists.

Biochemist Ted Sallis has devised a supersoldier serum of the kind that first created Captain America. Fleeing from terrorists intent on obtaining the formula, Sallis hides in Florida's Everglades swamps. He injects himself with the serum, but it combines with magical forces present in the Everglades to transform Sallis into a monster resembling a mobile chunk of mangrove swamp complete with the head of the Elephant Man. Sallis's identity is almost wholly obliterated. The Man-Thing is a creature driven by empathic emotions—nonmalevolent, but terrifying in appearance, and able to cause those who harbor fear to burn from his touch.

The allegory seems clear: the Man-Thing is a biochemical equivalent of the Hulk, a scientist transformed into a monster who takes revenge on behalf of natural forces that mankind has abused and misused. The Man-Thing's swamp is subsequently revealed to be the "Nexus of All Realities," which enables the creature to encounter inhabitants of many other worlds and dimensions: Dakimh the Enchanter, Wundarr (aka the Aquarian), and even Howard the Duck—as well as simultaneously defending his swamp against greedy real estate developers, vigilantes, and crooks.

Similarities exist between Marvel's Man-Thing and DC's Swamp Thing, whose original story was published after the Man-Thing's by some eighteen months. But the two monsters went their diverse ways, and Marvel never took legal action against their rival. A straight-to-video *Man-Thing* movie (2005) took some arguably unnecessary liberties with its source material. **RR**

Haxtur 1971

Victor de la Fuente

Haxtur, a parable on the miseries and ideals of mankind in a swords-and-sorcery setting, was the first personal work of renowned Spanish author Victor de la Fuente in the roles of both writer and artist.

First published in serialized form in the Spanish youth magazine *Trinca*, the story begins with its title hero, seemingly a Latin American guerrilla fighter, in the middle of a jungle. He seems to have survived a battle and is asking himself, "Why? Why do things happen? Why must death win over reason?" When he suddenly comes across a giant dragon, he kills it. This spontaneous act is followed by the appearance of four judges, symbolizing the Horsemen of the Apocalypse, who sentence Haxtur to wander through time and space for the crime of "having killed Father Time." During his quest for escape from his fate, Haxtur meets a variety of monsters, pretty girls in distress, evil robots, sorcerers, and werewolves. He eventually encounters a clone of himself and has to fight it; after this climax, the four judges appear again.

De la Fuente's script is enhanced by his elegant artwork, and in this he has acknowledged the influence of "Cisco Kid" (José Luis Salinas), among others, in his devising of innovative page layouts.

Haxtur actually caused de la Fuente some problems with Spanish governmental censorship—the comic was released in the waning days of General Franco's fascist dictatorship—but was hailed internationally as a comic masterwork of the 1970s. It was translated into several languages (appearing in English in 1979 in Warren Publishing's *Eerie* magazine), paving the way for other works by the same author in the heroic fantasy genre, such as *Mathai-dor* and *Haggarth*. *Haxtur* was reprinted in two albums by *Trinca*'s publisher, Doncel; much later, in 2008, the entire eighty-four-page saga was compiled into a single volume by Glénat. **AMo**

First published by *Trinca* magazine (Spain)
Creator Spanish (1927–2010)
Genre Fantasy
Influence on *The Wendigo* magazine's Haxtur Award

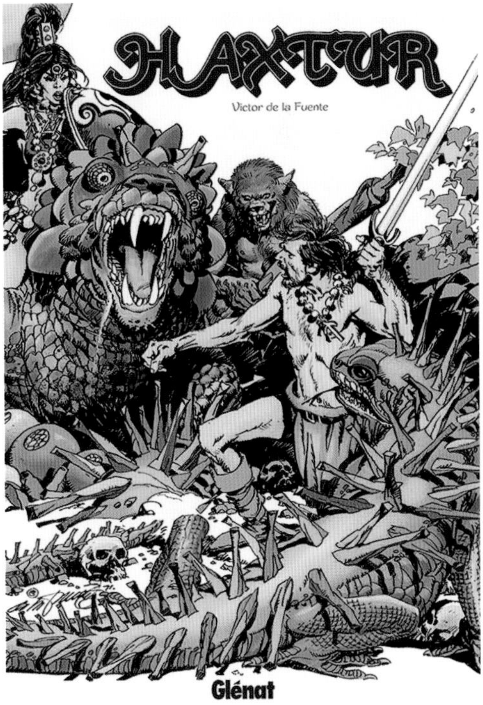
HAXTUR
Victor de la Fuente
Glénat

Similar reads

Conan the Barbarian Roy Thomas and Barry Windsor-Smith
Haggarth Victor de la Fuente
Mathai-Dor Victor de la Fuente

Binky Brown Meets the Holy Virgin Mary 1972

Justin Green

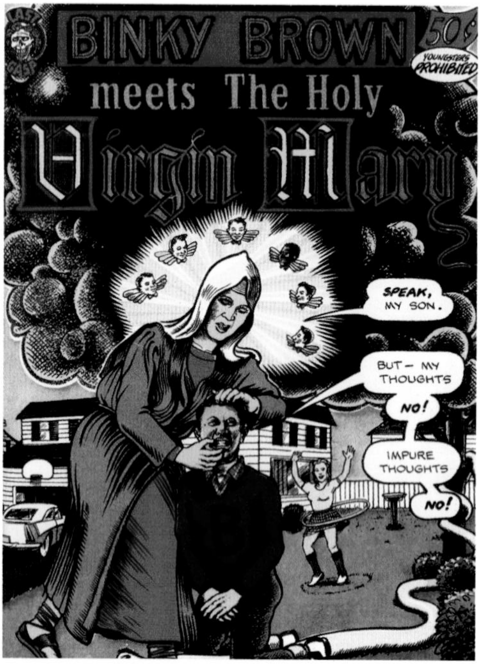
BINKY BROWN
meets The Holy
Virgin Mary
50¢
YOUNGSTERS PROHIBITED
SPEAK, MY SON.
BUT— MY THOUGHTS
NO!
IMPURE THOUGHTS
NO!

"A masterpiece of autobiographical revelation, a work that inspired me and helped me find my own voice."

Aline Kominsky-Crumb

Similar reads

Breakdowns Art Spiegelman

Dragon Slippers Roz Penfold

My New York Diary Julie Doucet

Need More Love Aline Kominsky Crumb

First published by Last Gasp (USA)
Creator American (b.1945)
Genre Autobiography
Influence on Art Spiegelman's *Maus*

Justin Green bracketed this seminal autobiographical comic within two very different moments of iconoclasm. The opening images show Binky Brown breaking his mother's statue of the Virgin Mary while playing with his stick and ball, an activity of Freudian significance. The event introduces us to the agonies of his struggle with sexuality, guilt, Catholicism—and obsessive-compulsive disorder: "Maybe I broke the Burjun Mary cause of the crack I stepped on yestiday."

Appearing in 1972, *Binky Brown* was one of the earliest autobiographical comics and a radical new development. Art Spiegelman articulated the debts that the genre owes to Green: "It now seems obvious that the form can achieve great intimacy, but before he [Green] came along, cartoonists were expected to keep a lid on the psyches and personal histories."

With this comic of conflicts, it hurts to laugh at Brown's sufferings and confusions as he flits between the fallible, fantastical, and phallocentric. He cycles and orgasms, endures torturous rays that emanate from his fingers and toes and transform them into penises, and delights in his 1958 Cadillac rubber fender guard.

Brown compounds his anxiety about the fate of his Jewish father with the rejections he receives from female schoolmates, even after he has prayed for them: "I'd like to kick you in the pants," says one ungrateful recipient of his attentions. Even the creator is ambivalent about the comic; in his written "Confession to my readers," Green (as Binky) warns: "It's probably a venal sin even to sell this comic to adults." **SL**

Buddha Kapilavastu 1972
✏️ Osamu Tezuka

First published by Ushio Shuppansha (Japan)
Creator Japanese (1928–89)
Genre History, Biography
Influenced by Biographies of Prince Siddhartha

Rather than produce a precise biography, Osamu Tezuka unfolds the life story of Prince Siddhartha and his quest for enlightenment as Buddha within a broader sweep of history, interweaving fact and fiction and expanding his peripheral characters. The prince himself only appears more than halfway through the first volume, "Kapilavastu," as a newborn baby.

Tezuka opens with a wordless episode, in which a starving wise man, who has collapsed in the snow, is discovered by a bear, a fox, and a rabbit who try to find him food. Returning with nothing, the rabbit sacrifices itself for him by jumping into the fire. In tears, the man sees the rabbit's spirit-form soar into the night sky. From this traditional Buddhist tale, Tezuka devises fine imagery to represent the connectedness of all life.

At the same time, Tezuka, as a showman eager to entertain, likes to insert humorous intrusions, almost as knowing winks to remind readers that, however realistic a comic strives to be, it is also a fabrication that only moves and speaks in our imaginations. His detailed, vivid settings, notably of beautiful trees and skies, contrast with his cartoonish humans and his cute and large-eyed animals. The style resembles the simplified figures dropped over lushly painted backgrounds in classic American animated films.

While Tezuka was not a Buddhist, he was morally concerned about our attitudes to life and nature, and not always optimistic. One of his strongest beliefs was in the communicative power of comics, amply proven throughout this enlightening *Buddha* cycle. **PG**

Trots and Bonnie 1972
✏️ Shary Flenniken

First published by *National Lampoon* (USA)
Creator American (b.1950)
Genre Humor
Influenced by *Little Orphan Annie*

Debuting in the "Decadence" issue of *National Lampoon* and running in that magazine for most of the next two decades, Shary Flenniken's *Trots and Bonnie* is one of the most unusual comic strips to have emerged from the tail end of the Underground comics movement. In chronicling the adventures of the teenaged Bonnie, her dog Trots, and her best friend Pepsi, Flenniken documented the rise of second-wave feminism with bitter irony and a mordant wit. Her faux-naive depiction of a highly sexualized teenage life put the strip at odds with moral puritans, and it has not been widely collected outside the pages of *Lampoon*.

Flenniken's art in *Trots and Bonnie* recalls the aesthetics of the comic strips of the early twentieth century, as do the frequently dated fashions of the strip's stars. Nonetheless, the topics addressed in the monthly strips were entirely contemporary. Bonnie, like *Playboy*'s Little Annie Fanny, was a sexual naif in a world gone crazy with lust. The comics were filled with risqué and bawdy humor that aggressively pushed the boundaries of good taste. In one, Bonnie and Pepsi earn money by appearing in child pornography; in another, they begin to produce their own pornography. Later, Bonnie is sexually harassed by her high school gym teacher.

Although the stories were envelope-pushing, the visuals were classical. The combination was rarely meant to titillate. Rather, *Trots and Bonnie* celebrated adolescent sexual precocity as a way of stripping back the hang-ups of the generation coming of age in the 1970s. The work is still ahead of its time. **BB**

Kamandi: The Last Boy on Earth 1972

Jack Kirby

First published by DC Comics (USA)
Creator Jacob Kurtzberg (American, 1917–94)
Genre Science fiction
Influenced by *Planet of the Apes*

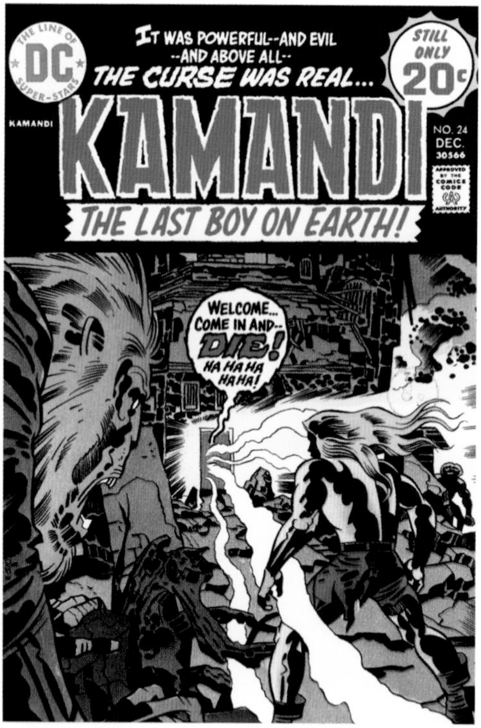
DC
IT WAS POWERFUL--AND EVIL
--AND ABOVE ALL--
THE CURSE WAS REAL...
STILL ONLY 20¢
KAMANDI
KAMANDI
NO. 24
DEC.
30566
THE LAST BOY ON EARTH!
WELCOME... COME IN AND-- DIE! HA HA HA HA HA!

Similar reads
Alarming Tales Jack Kirby
Deathlock Doug Moench and Rich Buckler
Planet of the Apes Gerry Conway, Doug Moench, and Mike Ploog

After DC Comics decided to cancel his series *The Fourth World*, the publisher asked Jack Kirby for new titles with specific themes. *Kamandi* was a request for a *Planet of the Apes*-type story in lieu of an officially licensed adaptation. Interestingly, Kirby had already done a postdisaster story, "The Last Enemy," in the first issue of *Alarming Tales*. Featuring sundry talking animals—not just apes—it appeared in 1957, six years before Pierre Boulle published his *Planet of the Apes* novel. Expanding on "The Last Enemy" proved highly effective.

Kamandi is a teenaged boy who emerges from an underground bunker on the death of his grandfather to discover an "After Disaster" world dominated by all manner of talking animals. Humans are reduced to the level of inarticulate beasts that are treated like cattle by the "superior" species. Nevertheless, he manages to befriend a number of atypical animals—including Dr. Canus, a dog scientist, and Prince Tuftan, a regal tiger—as well as discover some articulate humanoid mutants in the form of Ben Boxer, Steve, and Renzi. In addition to these allies are a semiarticulate girl, Flower, whom he befriends in *Kamandi* #6, shortly before her tragic death (an emotional highlight of the series), and her twin sister Spirit, introduced in *Kamandi* #12.

Kirby used this future world to mine all kinds of themes and concepts that interested him. Included among many notable stories is a homage to *King Kong* (*Kamandi* #7); a tale of mutation and germ warfare (issues #9 and #10); a *Westworld* riff in a 1920s gangster setting (issues #19 and #20); and the Charge of the Light Brigade enacted by dogs (issues #27 and #28), followed by a fascinating issue that deals with the Superman legend (*Kamandi* #29). As a nonstop adventure title, *Kamandi* is hard to beat in its boundless energy and inventiveness. The scripts are tight and the artwork is ablaze with dynamism and powerful design. **CH**

The Tomb of Dracula 1972

Marv Wolfman Gene Colan

When the dreaded Comics Code Authority restrictions were relaxed in the early 1970s, the companies under its jurisdiction began to test the new waters with mainstream horror titles. Artist Gene Colan secured the job of Marvel's *The Tomb of Dracula* by handing publisher Stan Lee a presentation drawing of his conception of Jack Palance as Dracula more than a year before the actor actually played the role on screen (in the 1973 Dan Curtis production).

The early issues of *Dracula* were a little unfocused due to the lack of a regular writer, but Marv Wolfman came on board with issue #7 and stayed with the title until its cancellation six years later. The team of Colan and Wolfman clicked almost instantly, and when Tom Palmer (one of the few inkers to do justice to Colan's pencil drawing) regularly took charge of the inking role, the book became a genuine classic.

For much of the series, the story involves the descendants of Jonathan Harker and Abraham Van Helsing, characters from Bram Stoker's novel, along with various other vampire hunters, in constant pursuit of the Prince of Darkness. *The Tomb of Dracula* issue #10 introduced vampiric vampire hunter Blade, who was later to star in his own Hollywood movies. Dracula's daughter, Lilith, was a regular guest star, and Dracula and his lover Domini had a son named Janus in issue #54 (a story far too complicated to detail here).

For Colan, *The Tomb of Dracula* was an opportunity to fully indulge his penchant for shadows and atmosphere, which often had been wasted on superhero and Western material. The comic remains one of the highlights of an impressive career that spanned more than sixty years. Virtually every page of the issues illustrated by Colan and Palmer is a winner, rich in mood, drama, and characters who ring true. A visual delight and a superb horror series. **CH**

First published by Marvel Comics (USA)
Creators Wolfman (American, b.1946); Eugene Colan (American, 1926–2011)
Genre Horror

TOMB OF DRACULA
MARVEL COMICS GROUP
20¢
1 APR 02143
DRACULA LIVES!
THE TOMB OF DRACULA
NIGHT OF THE VAMPIRE!

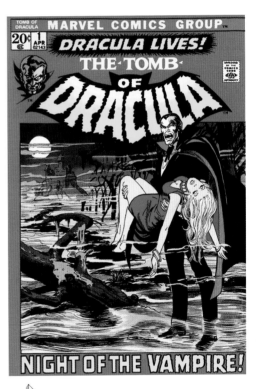

Also by Gene Colan

Detectives Inc.
Doctor Strange
Nathaniel Dusk
Night Force

Ayako 1972

✐✐ Osamu Tezuka

First published by *Big Comic* (Japan)
Creator Japanese (1928–89)
Genre Drama
Influenced by *Gekiga* (dramatic comics)

Released into civilian life in 1949 after several years in captivity after World War II, Jiro Tengé arrives back at the large rural estate owned by his family to find that the war has changed everything. The property is under threat of being divided up, and his clan is torn by tensions around four-year-old Ayako, the last-born of the family and seemingly the result of incest.

This deeply noxious atmosphere only worsens Jiro's own problems. Manipulated by U.S. secret services, he commits a politically motivated murder, which is soon followed by a second one intended to conceal his first crime. But there is one witness: little Ayako. In the best interests of the family, simultaneously confronted by the threat of difficult financial issues linked to the inheritance, the growing curiosity of the police, and the machinations of Jiro's shadowy employers, the Tengé clan makes a terrible decision: the girl will be locked up for life.

A portrait of a family sinking into degeneration over a period of thirty years, the *Ayako* trilogy fascinates not only because of the sophistication of the subject but also because of the emotional intensity and psychological depth of the characters, almost all of them highly immoral. At the same time, the very somber story gives insight into the political and economic situation in Japan in the immediate postwar years, including the agrarian consolidation forced on Japanese landowners by U.S. military authorities temporarily in charge of the country's administration. In *Ayako*, Osamu Tezuka created his masterpiece. **NF**

Mazinger Z 1972

✐✐ Go Nagai

Title in original language *Majingā Zetto*
First published by Shueisha (Japan)
Creator Japanese (b.1945)
Genre Action, Humor, Science fiction

Kouji Kabuto is a normal, everyday teenager living at home with his grandfather Juzo and little brother Shiro. One day an earthquake suddenly strikes and in the process opens up a secret passage. Kouji enters the passage and descends into a laboratory where he finds his injured grandfather and, to his astonishment, a giant mechanized robot. Kouji's grandfather is dying and with his final breath gives his grandson a frightening responsibility. Kouji must master the robot, named Mazinger Z, and use it against the evil Dr. Hell, the leader of an army of giant robots he discovered while on the mythical Greek island of Bardos. The young Kouji has no choice but to leave his childhood behind and take up his grandfather's fight himself.

Mazinger Z is a behemoth. Standing 60 feet (18 m) high and 20 tons in weight, it can run at 224 miles per hour (360 kph), fly at Mach 3, and possesses a formidable array of weaponry. Constructed from an impervious new alloy, Japanium (also called Super Alloy Z), and powered by Photonic Energy, it promises Dr. Hell one heck of a fight.

Later retitled *Great Mazinger* and *God Mazinger*, *Mazinger Z* was one of the first manga in the emergent mechanized super-robot "mecha" genre, and the first to place a human pilot inside a robotic giant—a development that other mangas would soon mimic. One of the great manga innovators, Go Nagai first imagined Mazinger Z while in a traffic jam, pondering just how good it would be if his car could transform itself, rise above the traffic, and take him home. **BS**

Amphigorey 1972

Edward Gorey

First published by Perigree (USA)
Creator American (1925–2000)
Genre Humor **Award** Horror Writers Association Lifetime Achievement Award (2000)

FIFTEEN
BOOKS
AMPHIGOREY
BY
EDWARD
GOREY

One of the major talents of illustrated books for half a century, Edward Gorey so completely defined his own visual style that "Goreyesque" has come to refer to a particularly dark form of gothic whimsy.

Gorey published more than four dozen short books during his lifetime, many with extremely small imprints that offered print runs to match. The four omnibus editions of his work collect most of these stories, with the first being the best. Originally published in 1972 and comprising work that was almost twenty years old at the time, *Amphigorey* opens with *The Unstrung Harp*, Gorey's first book and a tremendous example of his style. Gorey left the United States only once during his lifetime, but the struggles in *The Unstrung Harp* of Clavius Earbrass to write a novel so uncannily blended a feeling for upper-class Victorian England with a dreamlike sense of dread that many readers assumed him to be a British artist.

Other books in the collection explore the bizarre, the gloomy, and the mildly grotesque. Works in verse became his signature, and reading primers like *The Fatal Lozenge* and, most famously, *The Gashlycrumb Tinies* presage the fantastic gothic sensibilities of a filmmaker like Tim Burton. Gorey's drawings, which ranged from simple cartoons of colorful insects to intricately crosshatched portraits of depressive landowners, were superbly accomplished and could carry the story even in the absence of text, as in *The West Wing*. Few cartoonists were as consistent in their themes, and their pleasures, as Edward Gorey. **BB**

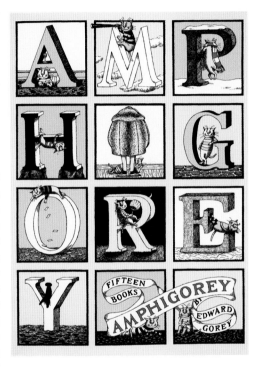

"Said a girl who upon her divan,
Was attacked by a virile young man,
'Such excess of passion,
Is quite out of fashion' / And she
fractured his wrist with her fan."

Also by Edward Gorey
The Abandoned Sock
The Epileptic Bicycle
The Fraught Settee

Delirius 1972

Jacques Lob   Philippe Druillet

First published by *Pilote* (France)
Creators Lob (French, 1932–90); Druillet (French, b.1944)
Genre Science fiction
Award European SF Award for Comics (1972)

LONE SLOANE
DELIRIUS
DRUILLET

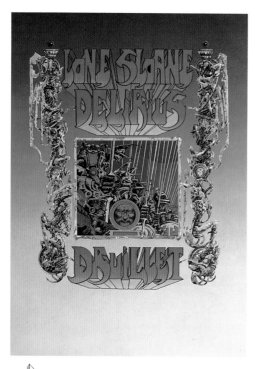

Also by Philippe Druillet
Chaos
Nosferatu
Salammbô
Vuzz
Yragaël with Michel Demuth

Philippe Druillet and his cult character Lone Sloane were already fairly well known when *Delirius* made its debut as a weekly comic in the magazine *Pilote*. The artist had created his hero in 1966 in his first book, *The Mystery of the Abyss*, and continued Lone Sloane's adventures in 1970 when he joined the team of *Pilote*.

But with *Delirius*, the saga of the red-eyed "neo-Earthling" takes on an extra dimension. The story, concocted by Jacques Lob, one of the most talented writers of French-language comic strips at the time, is at first glance rather traditional. A rebellious character on the run, pursued by the Imperator Shaan, Lone Sloane is recruited by the mysterious religious order, the Red Redemption. His assignment is to recover a fabulous treasure of accumulated taxes imposed by his employers on Delirius, a legendary planet of a hundred thousand pleasures. There are many traps and ambushes awaiting the hero, but Sloane manages to hijack the mission for his own benefit, sowing the seeds of chaos on the planet before he disappears.

"For years the great pirate Shonga has been planning his attack, and now the time has come!"

The portrait Druillet gives of this insane world is petrifying and extreme in every sense; it is somewhere between a cesspit and a dazzling vision. Passionately interested in science fiction and profoundly influenced by H. P. Lovecraft, the artist gives the impression of having personally explored another reality. His vision of a galactic universe, inhabited by thousands of life forms, is the stuff of dreams. With deconstructed pages, overwhelming panoramas, perspectives based on special effects, and epic imagery, Druillet, the creator of worlds, is himself a universe in his own right. **NF**

The Age of Cohabitation 1972

✐✐ Kazuo Kamimura

In Japan, as in much of the rest of the world, the end of World War II brought a new wave of births. The so-called *Dankai no sedai*, or baby-boomer generation, became the core of society in the late-1960s. During the immediate postwar period, values and attitudes in Japan underwent a tremendous change, influenced by factors such as Japan's military defeat, rapid economic growth, and student activism.

The Age of Cohabitation, which was first published as a serial comic in 1972, brilliantly captures life during this period through the story of a young couple. Former classmates in school, Kyoko, a typical Japanese office worker, and Jiro, an illustrator, decide to live together only three days after their first date. The idea of an

> "If love is beautiful, then the sin that a man and a woman commit must also be beautiful."

unmarried couple living under the same roof was outrageous at the time, but the naive pair—Jiro is just twenty-three years old and Kyoko even younger, at twenty-one—choose not to tie the knot. The purity of their love is beautiful yet fragile, and at times brutal—so brutal, in fact, that Kyoko begins to break down.

Kamimura's art is far from explicit in depicting the couple's sexual relationship, yet its elegance creates a sensual ambience like no other, inviting readers deep into their intoxicating, erotic world. His unique brushwork, reminiscent of paintings in the *Nihonga* style, is a rarity even among Japanese comic illustrators. The expression used for the title, *Dosei jidai* (literally meaning "a period of living together"), was invented by the artist himself, and received the Popular Word Award in Japan. In 1973, Kamimura's masterpiece was developed into a hugely successful film. **TS**

Title in original language *Dosei jidai*
First published by Bukkingu (Japan)
Creator Japanese (1940–86)
Genre Young adult, Drama

ACTION COMICS

同棲時代

上村一夫

Similar reads
He's Like a Devil (Akuma no youna aitsu)
Kazuo Kamimura
Lady Snowblood (Shurayukihime) Kazuo Koike
and Kazuo Kamimura
Shinanogawa Hideo Okazaki and Kazuo Kamimura

Zil Zelub 1972

✎✎ Guido Buzzelli

First published by *Charlie* magazine (France)
Creator Italian (1927–92)
Genre Grotesque
Award Yellow Kid Prize for Best Illustrator (1973)

In this story of a cello player undergoing an extremely weird hallucinatory adventure, Zil Zelub (an anagram of the author's name) wakes up to find he has lost control of his limbs. His legs, arms, and chest are physically detached from his body and have lives of their own (one arm, obsessed by sex, jumps on every beautiful woman it meets). To cure himself of his freakish condition, Zil tries a surgeon, a chiromancer, a psychoanalyst, and a politician—who cynically "sells" him to Choky, an unscrupulous businessman. Choky is responsible for the spread of a weird plague provoked by a mass of plastic hawks, a form of pollution caused by his chemical company. In a perverted society, Zil tries to regain control of his body and identity, but, defeated, he is unable to escape from his nightmare.

Formerly an illustrator, then author, of commercial comics, working on anything from sci-fi to war stories for Fratelli Spada in the 1950s and Fleetway in the '60s, Guido Buzzelli became a full-time auteur only in the '70s, following the critical success in France of his first graphic novel, *The Revolt of the Ugly* (1966), selected for *Charlie* magazine by an enthusiast George Wolinski.

Set in a society that is morally disillusioned, lacking any progressive vision for ending the class struggle, and drowning in filth created by the consumer culture, Buzzelli's more recent stories are skillfully drawn apologues on modern society; they are close to pataphysical theater pieces, Buñuel's cinema, and Goya's expressionist drawings. His work has earned him the sobriquet "the Michelangelo of Monsters." **MS**

Lady Snowblood 1972

✎ Kazuo Koike ✎ Kazuo Kamimura

Title in original language *Shurayuki-hime*
First published by Shueisha (Japan)
Creators Koike (Japanese, b.1936); Kamimura (Japanese, 1940–86) **Genre** Adventure

In this sweeping tale of a lonesome sword fighter slicing through a windswept Japan, Kazuo Koike presents the graceful assassin Yuki—whose name means "snow" in Japanese. Her peaceful-sounding name and natural beauty juxtapose with the cold and brutal violence she dispatches. Yuki is a sword for hire, following the call of the yen and leaving a trail of blood in her wake. Her code is not samurai but vengeance, and she is emotionally detached from her actions. As cold as her namesake, she has no qualms about forcing a coachman to rape his passenger, or about killing someone after promising not to do so.

Interspersed throughout the poetic violence are fascinating historical anecdotes that establish the time and place. Nineteenth-century Japan is rife with injustice: the Blood Tax Riot of 1873 is brought on by anger at conscription orders handed down by the government; women are kidnapped and forced into lives of prostitution. Descending like an avenging angel for the oppressed masses, Yuki destroys the Rokumeikan balls, ostensibly charity events for the Japanese ruling class but actually nights of scandalous debauchery.

This is an adult manga, and sex and violence are graphically illustrated throughout. The sexual violence is ugly and therefore sits uncomfortably with the somewhat gratuitous instances of Yuki stripped naked and fighting against villainous, slathering men. *Lady Snowblood* is a bleak story, and Koike's blood-splattered beauty in this beautiful and brutal epic influenced Quentin Tarantino's *Kill Bill*. **SW**

Lady Snowblood takes place in a world darkly rendered by Kazuo Kamimura's artwork. ➡

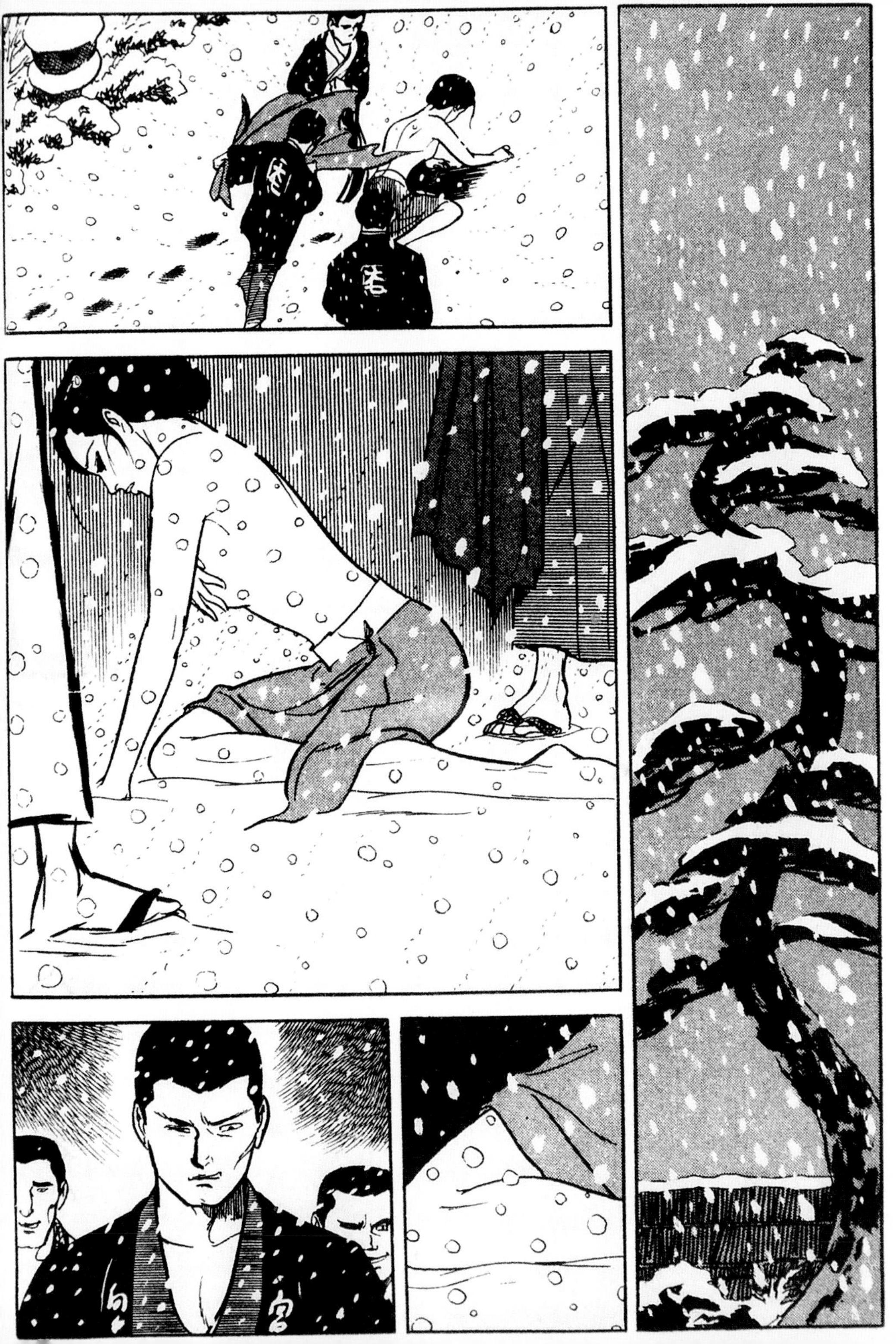

The Drifting Classroom 1972

✎✎ Kazuo Umezu

Title in original language *Hiyoryu Kyoshitsu*
First published by Shonen Sunday (Japan)
Creator Japanese (b.1936)
Genre Horror

On an ordinary day in the early 1960s, Yamato School, a primary school in Tokyo, suddenly disappears from the surface of the Earth, abruptly transported into the future with all its inhabitants—almost 900 pupils and their teachers. They find themselves on an extraordinarily inhospitable, completely uninhabited planet.

The story is told from the point of view of a brave young boy called Shô Takamatsu, who soon becomes the children's leader. Stimulated by the memory of his mother, with whom he sometimes manages to communicate telepathically, Shô organizes plans for their survival when faced with an incredible succession of terrifying dangers: attacks by monsters, diseases, volcanic eruptions, tsunami, and deadly confrontations between the children and their half-mad teachers.

Kazuo Umezu never explains the hyperhostile world to which he has transported his heroes, nor the reason for the sudden teleportation of the school. The point of *The Drifting Classroom* is its harsh representation of a human community reduced to its most primitive urges, plus its narrative boldness—explicit representation of the death of children was then a rarely transgressed taboo in manga. The readership of *The Drifting Classroom* extends far beyond the young age group for whom at first the story seems to have been intended. Even the graphic style, a kind of dusky, coal-black expressionism, is far from conventional manga. With this intense work Umezu redefined the aesthetic style of the horror story and set the standard for a genre that now flourishes in Japan. **NF**

Rose of Versailles 1972

✎✎ Riyoko Ikeda

Title in original language *Versailles no Bara*
First published by Shueisha (Japan)
Creator Japanese (b.1947)
Genre Teen

Rose of Versailles, Riyoko Ikeda's landmark work, made her a star of 1970s *shoujo* (girls' manga). Ikeda began the self-assured, windswept pages of this tale of prerevolutionary France when she was just a student, naming this epic tale for Marie Antoinette, the vivacious Austrian archduchess who became France's most infamous monarch.

In Ikeda's magnum opus, Marie shares the stage with Oscar de Jarjayes, a noblewoman who, in a bit of classic *shoujo* gender bending, dresses as a man and heads the Palace Guard. Unlike her royal employers, Oscar has her ear to the ground and realizes the precarious state of the monarchy, but she finds herself powerless to influence Marie, whose failings as queen are fueling the grumblings of revolution.

The arrival of a gorgeous Swedish count at Versailles further complicates matters for both women, but Ikeda also wants to depict life outside courtly circles. We follow Rosalie and Jeanne, two sisters born into poverty who—using very different methods—strive to propel themselves into the queen's orbit. But don't be fooled by the feathery, frilly artwork; *Rose of Versailles* perfectly balances the starry-eyed visual conventions of traditional manga with a plot rich in murder, manipulation, and royal malfeasance. Oscar in particular is a brilliant creation, admired by men and women alike but completely devoted to her duties. By the end of the story you'll regret that Marie didn't share Oscar's sense of duty, but you'll be elated by the intensity of the world that Ikeda has brought to vivid life. **EL**

Man from Utopia 1972

Rick Griffin

First published by San Francisco Comic Book Co. (USA)
Creator American (1944–91)
Genre Underground

This beautiful portfolio of drawings, strips, and panels from California artist Rick Griffin showcases both his accomplished draftsmanship and the personalized sense of spirituality that illuminates his work. Best known as a concert poster artist for groups such as The Jimi Hendrix Experience and the Grateful Dead (for whose 1969 album *Aoxomoxoa* he designed the cover), Griffin moved easily into underground comics.

Man from Utopia strayed from the regular comic-strip format without abandoning it altogether. Here, Griffin's spiritually motivated artwork and ideas appear around a series of cryptic panels and drawings. Griffin's conversion to Christianity in 1964 is strongly represented throughout with images of sacred hearts, the crucifixion, and the resurrection pulsating throughout. Also present are his now-familiar disembodied eye character (thought to be inspired by a near-fatal car accident that dislocated his eyeball) and his light bulb in the form of a dolphin's snout, both of which became recurring images.

In the center spread, an army of Roman centurion eyeballs is seen fighting against an opposing army of Nazi eyeballs; a black dolphin's head hovers between the two warring factions while a horned warhorse looms over a parapet. The title for the piece, presumably an antiwar statement, appears as a row of extracted teeth that gradually morph into helmets and finally a skull. It is this engrossing combination of mysticism and hallucinogenic surrealism that makes *Man from Utopia* unique in the world of comics. **EP**

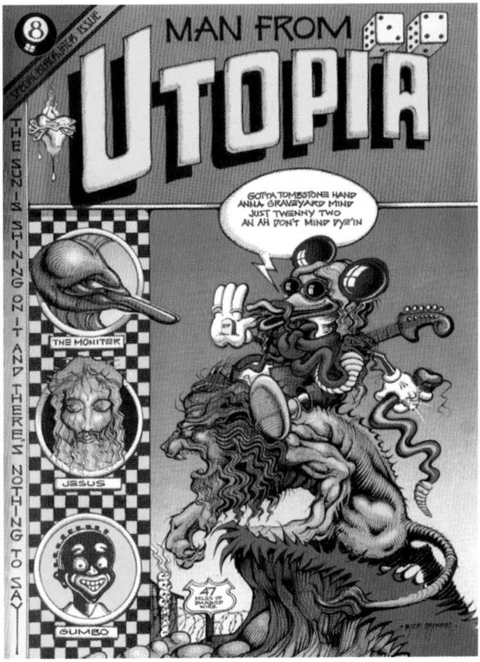
8
MAN FROM
UTOPIA
THE SUN-IS SHINING ON IT AND THERE'S NOTHING TO SAY
GOTTA TOMBSTONE HAND
ANNA GRAVEYARD MIND
JUST TWENNY TWO
AN AH DON'T MIND DYE'IN
THE MONITER
JESUS
GUMBO
47

"Meet me out on the hi'way, and bring me my runnin shoes, I'm on the road again, an' I ain't got time to lose!!!"

Also by Rick Griffin
All Stars #2 with various
The Gospel of John
Heart and Torch: Rick Griffin's Transcendence
Tales from the Tube with various
Zap Comix #3 with various

Devilman 1972

✏️ Go Nagai

Title in original language *Debiruman*
First published by Kodansha (Japan)
Creator Japanese (b.1945)
Genre Action, Horror

Go Nagai, dubbed the "possessed comic artist" by fans, launched *Devilman* as a serial comic in *Shukan Shonen* magazine. The central character, high-school student Akira Fudo, is told that the Earth is facing a terrible catastrophe. According to his old friend Ryo Asuka, the evil Demon Tribe that once ruled ancient Earth is about to come back to life after having been frozen for centuries, and the world needs an equally powerful hero to save it from invasion. Convinced by Ryo's words, Akira turns into Devilman, a demon with the heart of a human. But as Devilman's battles against the demons become more intense, his foes begin to possess humans. Fear drives humans to turn against each other and they begin to murder one another.

Devilman was initially based on the author's previous work, *Demon Lord Dante*, and was created with a TV animation tie-up already in mind. Although the two versions of *Devilman* started off with the same story, Nagai's plot started to deviate from the original concept as the two series progressed. Eventually the comic and the animated series followed two contradictory stories. The animation told a morality tale in the superhero genre, but when viewers picked up the comic version, they were shocked to find that not only did the plot differ completely but it included scenes of violent murders never seen in the animation.

Nevertheless, the classic *Devilman* comic would later become an inspiration for various new titles, including Nagai's own spin-offs *Violence Jack* and *Devilman Lady* and tribute comics by other authors. **TS**

Giraffes 1973

✏️ "Mordillo"

Title in original language *Giraffe di Mordillo*
First published by Editorial Nueva Senda (Argentina)
Creator Guillermo Mordillo (Argentinian, b.1932)
Genre Humor **Award** Phénix de l'Humour 1973

In the words of Marcel Marceau§§§, "the unexpected bursts out like a punch" from Mordillo's wordless humor. That a mime artist should define in words the work of an Argentinian cartoonist born in the 1930s—one who has become, according to Mordillo himself, "a citizen of the world"—is a paradox that defines Mordillo's take on the nonsense of our world. Be they full-page or sequential, Mordillo's comics express the idea of representing chaos by its opposite: total order—but a ridiculous order that exploits the one-dimensionality of the page as a source and not a limitation. Mordillo's gags are created through the betrayal of our sense of perspective: a giraffe appears to have the moon on its back, but when the animal walks, its neck crashes against the moon.

Giving order to the irrational with his use of wide shots and surgical distribution of color (the only white thing in his vignettes is the surface of the human characters), Mordillo demonstrates that every system of rules can be raw material for comedy. Mordillo lightheartedly destroys the world's physical limits by allowing cartoon logic and his strong sense of astonishment in solitude to undermine reason. His strong sense of space enables dadaist scene-placing, such as a soccer field inexplicably in the mountains.

Milan Kundera said that, "The true geniuses of humor aren't those who make us laugh more, but those who discover unknown areas in comedy." By that definition, and in many other inexplicable human ways, Mordillo is a genius. **JMD**

Mordillo finds irresistible comedy in the shape of a giraffe. ➡

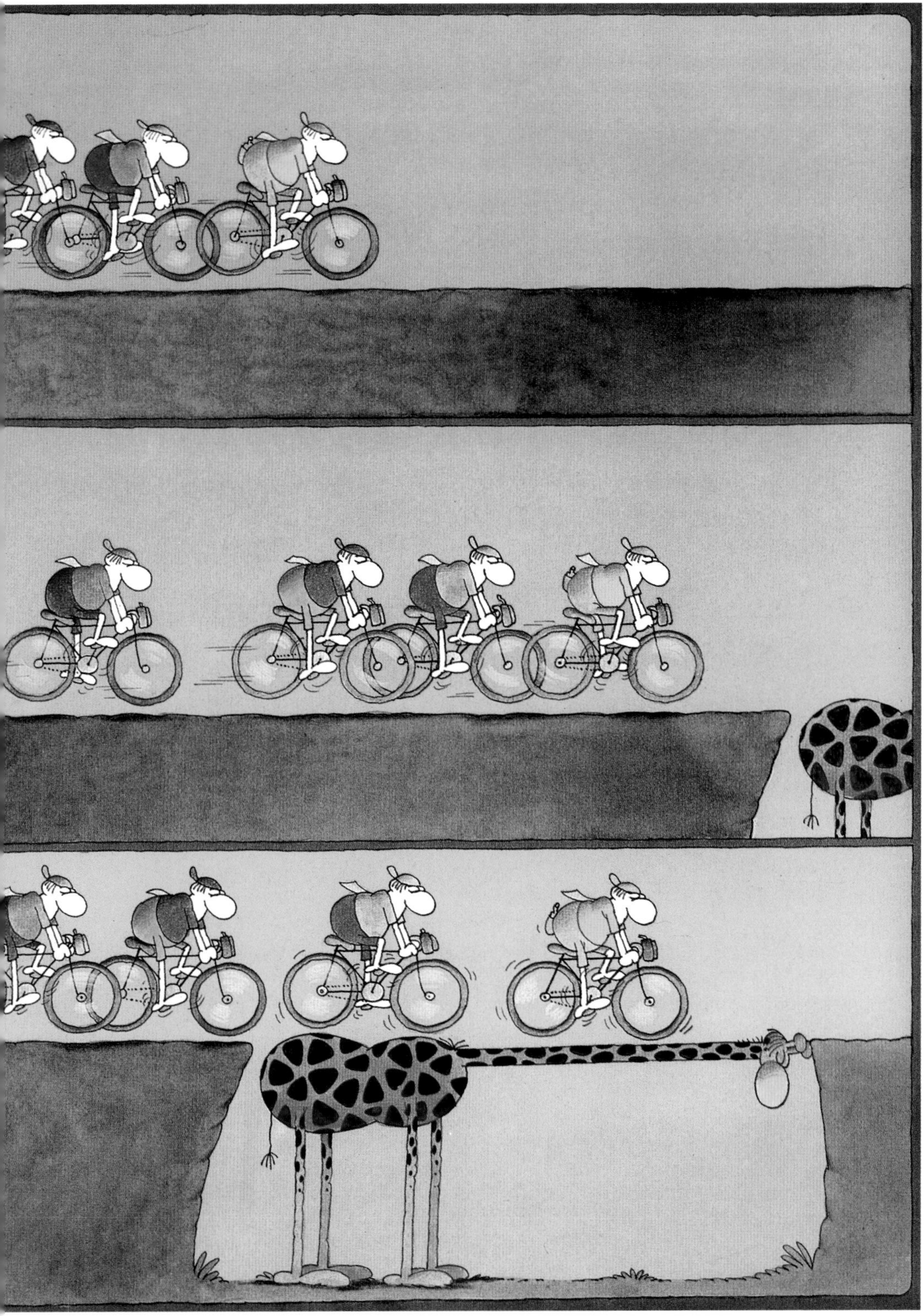

Barefoot Gen 1973

🖊 Keiji Nakazawa

Title in original language *Hadashi no Gen*
First published by Shueisha (Japan)
Creator Japanese (b.1939)
Genre Drama

Keiji Nakazawa and his mother were the only members of his family to survive the Hiroshima atomic bomb. When his mother died in 1966, he was told her ashes were too radioactive for him to keep. This final trauma led him to return to his childhood memories of the bombing in this semiautobiographical work.

Gen is a normal six-year-old boy living in Hiroshima in 1945, part of a loving family struggling to survive. While he and his brother innocently find ways to make the best of things, their father is ostracized for questioning the official line. Nevertheless, the war seems far away from Gen and his family until the day the bomb drops. In unsparing detail, Nakazawa shows us unimaginable horrors: men with their skin hanging off, a horse on fire stampeding through the flattened streets, Gen's family burning to death in front of him. The horror by no means ends with the bomb. The aftermath is no easier as Gen tries to look after his mother and her newborn baby in a dangerously irradiated world full of sickness and death.

It is clear that Nakazawa is haunted, not only by his memories of that fateful day and its aftermath, but by the whole mentality of Japanese society of the time—the kind of society that considered Koreans and Chinese as subhuman, and expected young men to undertake kamikaze missions because shame was a worse fate than death. *Barefoot Gen* is intended to educate children, and indeed should be read by them, but parents would do well to be cautious; there are few works of illustrated fiction that are more harrowing than this. **BD**

Sanpei the Fishing Fanatic 1973

🖊 Takao Yaguchi

Title in original language *Tsurikichi Sanpei*
First published by Kodansha (Japan)
Creator Japanese (b.1939)
Genre Fishing, Drama

No one could ever guess that the art of catching fish could be so influential before the arrival of *Sanpai the Fishing Fanatic*. But when the comic series hit its peak in late-1970s Japan, it caused a national phenomenon, with fishing stores opening all over the country and rivers overcrowding with aspiring fishermen. From traditional fishing to lure, fly, and netting, the comic introduced the audience to a plethora of fishing styles as Sanpei attempted to catch various "mystery" fishes.

The key to the comic's success was the fact that it was as informative as it was entertaining. Takao Yaguchi is a fishing enthusiast himself, and his expertise is evident in his detailed descriptions as well as the meticulously accurate illustrations of fish. Indeed, *Sanpai the Fishing Fanatic* became a delightful alternative to reading conventional fishing manuals.

Yaguchi, a latecomer in Japan's comic industry, made his debut at the age of thirty, in 1969. *Sanpai the Fishing Fanatic* was serialized only a few years later, between 1973 and 1983, in *Weekly Shonen Magazine*. The title won Kodansha's Children's Comics Award in 1974, and its animated series, broadcast for two years from 1980, was also a hit. The series then traveled abroad, launching in Korea, Taiwan, and Italy. Its twenty-first-century revival was also a success when Yaguchi released a new version of the series in 2001. This was followed by a film adaptation in 2009. *Sanpai the Fishing Fanatic* is a rare example of a comic where the passions of a young, unknown artist led to a fine piece of work destined to live on for decades. **TS**

Conan
Red Nails 1973

Roy Thomas Barry Windsor-Smith

First published by *Savage Tales* magazine (USA)
Creators Thomas (American, b.1940); Windsor-Smith (British, b.1949)
Genre Fantasy, Adventure

BACK BY POPULAR DEMAND!
SAVAGE TALES
FEATURING
CONAN
THE BARBARIAN
THE CITY THAT TIME FORGOT
KING KULL STRIKES!
BONUS: PHOTOS OF CONAN'S CREATOR! FACTS ABOUT CONAN'S CAREER! FANTASY IN THE CONAN TRADITION!

"Red Nails" was the last Conan the Barbarian adventure written by Texas pulp author Robert E. Howard before his suicide in June 1936. Howard admitted in a letter that it was "The bloodiest and most sexy, weird story I ever wrote," and this adaptation by Roy Thomas and Barry Windsor-Smith admirably captures much of the source text's morbid, sexually charged appeal.

By the time they came to produce "Red Nails," Thomas and Windsor-Smith had already crafted some twenty issues of *Conan the Barbarian* for Marvel Comics. After a slow start, *Conan* proved to be a big hit. In 1973, the black-and-white spin-off magazine *Savage Tales*, not subject to the restrictive demands of the Comic Book Code, provided the writer and artist with enough freedom to create this, their longest, most explicit, most intense collaboration. It finds Conan and his traveling companion Valeria reaching an isolated city-state populated by two dwindling, warring tribes. The two meet labyrinth-lurking beasts, occult ceremonies, hypnagogic visions, bisexual sorceresses, drug-laced plants, all in the stench of decadence and death.

In the space of five years, the British-born Windsor-Smith had grown from being a fairly crude Jack Kirby imitator into a more elegant and refined draftsman, one alive to the phallic, necrophiliac symbolism in the work of Aubrey Beardsley, or the Victorian Pre-Raphaelite painters. Thomas, at the time Marvel's leading writer and editor, was well skilled in the art of collaboration, and his script here is a concise and sympathetic distillation of Howard's singular, excessive vision. **AL**

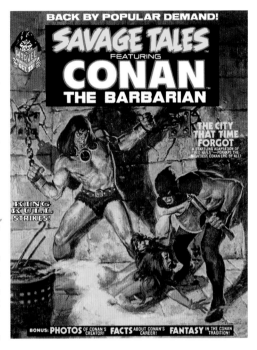

"On dusty rows of glass-covered shelves, countless human heads, perfectly preserved, stare at the intruders with emotionless eyes."

Similar reads
Blackmark Gil Kane and Archie Goodwin
Conan the Barbarian #24 ("The Song of Red Sonja") Roy Thomas and Barry Windsor-Smith
Elric #1–6 Roy Thomas, P. Craig Russell and Michael T. Gilbert

The Amazing Spider-Man
The Night Gwen Stacy Died 1973

Gerry Conway "Gil Kane" and John Romita

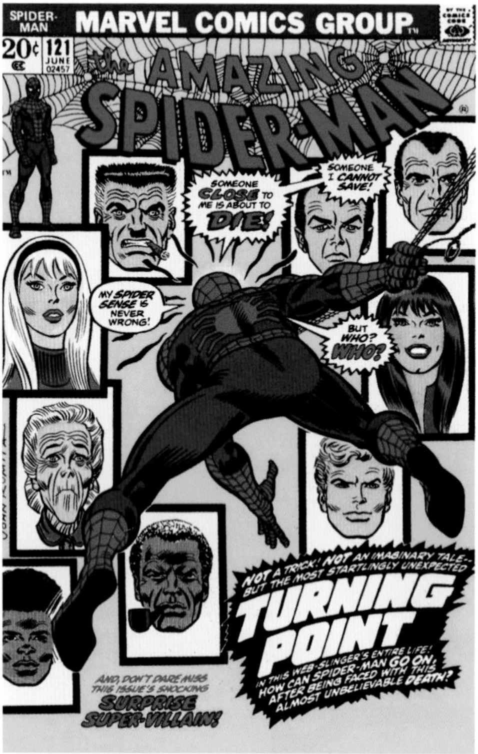
SPIDER-MAN
MARVEL COMICS GROUP
20¢ 121 JUNE 02457
the AMAZING SPIDER-MAN
SOMEONE CLOSE TO ME IS ABOUT TO DIE!
SOMEONE I CANNOT SAVE!
MY SPIDER SENSE IS NEVER WRONG!
BUT WHO? WHO?
NOT A TRICK! NOT AN IMAGINARY TALE-- BUT THE MOST STARTLINGLY UNEXPECTED
TURNING POINT
IN THIS WEB-SLINGER'S ENTIRE LIFE! HOW CAN SPIDER-MAN GO ON, AFTER BEING FACED WITH THIS ALMOST UNBELIEVABLE DEATH?
AND, DON'T DARE MISS THIS ISSUE'S SHOCKING SURPRISE SUPER-VILLAIN!

"You're the creep who's going to pay! You killed the woman I love, and for that, you're going to die!"

Similar reads

Amazing Spider-Man Stan Lee and Steve Ditko
The Death of Superman Dan Jurgens, Jerry Ordway, Louise Simonson, and Roger Stern; Jon Bogdanove, Tom Grummett, and Jackson Guice

First published by Marvel Comics (USA)
Creators Conway (American, b.1952); Eli Katz (Latvian-American, 1926–2000); Romita (Italian-American, b.1930)
Genre Superhero

The Amazing Spider-Man story "The Night Gwen Stacy Died" encapsulates the changes beginning to take place in the superhero genre in the early 1970s. During the Silver Age, it was a given that supporting cast members should not come to any permanent harm. The Thing's girlfriend Alicia might be captured and transformed into a monster, Thor's girlfriends might be abducted and held hostage, but it was against the unspoken rules for them to die. "The Night Gwen Stacy Died" broke all of those rules

The Green Goblin captures Peter Parker's girlfriend, Gwen Stacy, and holds her hostage atop New York's George Washington Bridge. Spider-Man arrives to rescue her, but Gwen is thrown off the bridge by the villain. Spider-Man believes he has rescued her, but in a brilliant use of the turning page, we learn that Gwen was already dead before Spider-Man scooped her up with a stream of his web-fluid. Gwen is dead, and there is nothing that Spider-Man can do about it. Defeating the Green Goblin (who also appears to die at the end of this story) cannot bring Gwen Stacy back to life.

Somewhat unusually for a character in a popular superhero comic, Gwen Stacy has stayed dead ever since (although she has reappeared from time to time in the form of a clone). Unlike the deaths of Dark Phoenix from the X-Men (1980) and Superman himself (1992), hers is not a temporary, reversible "comic book death," and its psychological effect on Spider-Man has been a key element in his evolving and maturing personality. **RR**

Gwen's death causes Spider-Man to learn a hard lesson. ➡

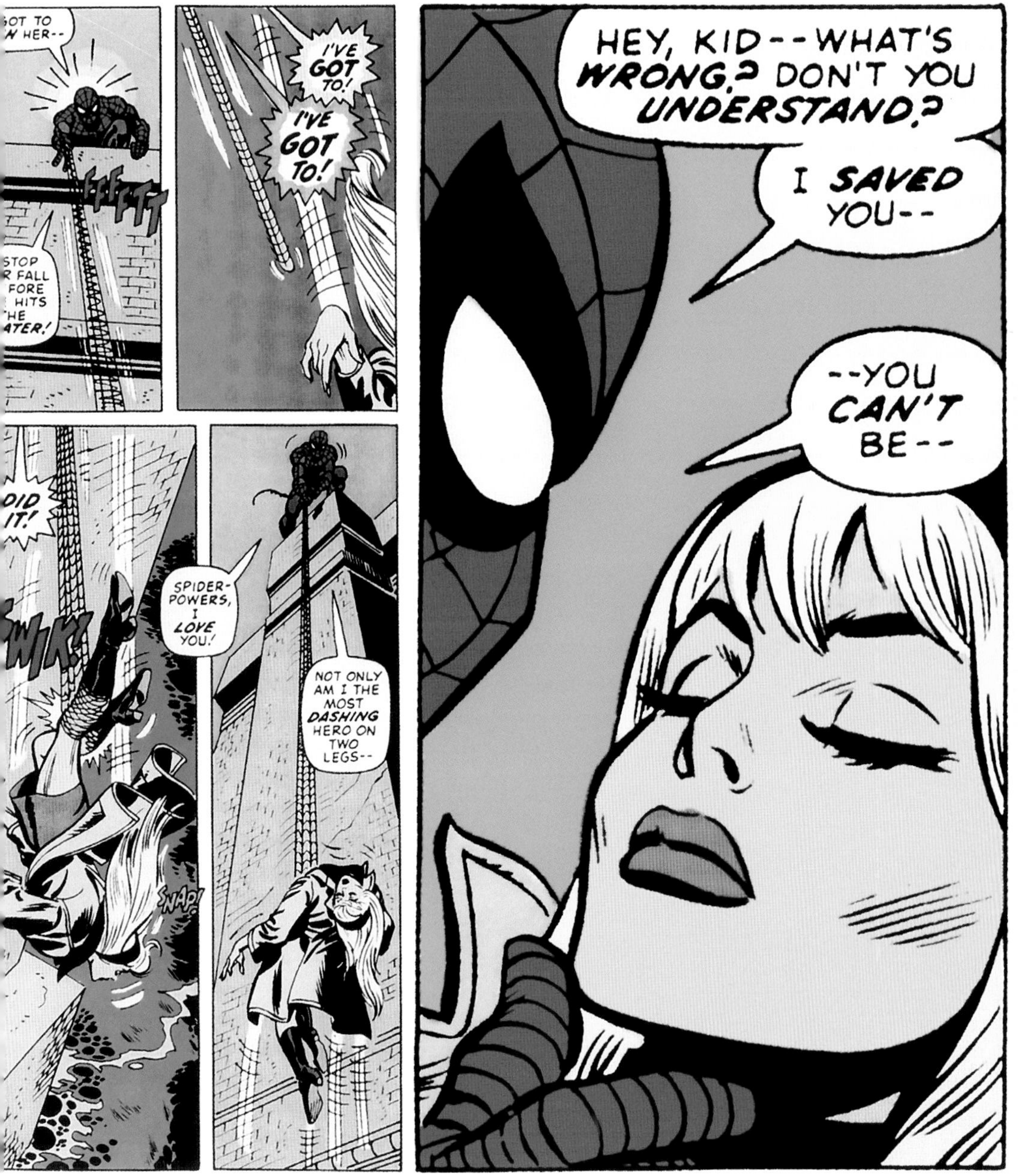
GOT TO
HER--
FFFTT
STOP
FALL
FORE
HITS
ATER!
I'VE GOT TO!
I'VE GOT TO!
DID IT!
WIK!
SNAP!
SPIDER-POWERS, I LOVE YOU!
NOT ONLY AM I THE MOST DASHING HERO ON TWO LEGS--
HEY, KID--WHAT'S WRONG? DON'T YOU UNDERSTAND?
I SAVED YOU--
--YOU CAN'T BE--

Asterix in Corsica 1973

✎ René Goscinny ✎ Albert Uderzo

R. GOSCINNY **Astérix** A. UDERZO

Astérix en CORSE

Texte René GOSCINNY   Dessins Albert UDERZO

"You don't like her, my sister? / But of course I like her . . . / So you like her, my sister!!! / Stop me or I am going to kill him, him and his imbeciles!"

Other *Asterix* stories

Asterix and the Goths (*Astérix et les Goths*)
Asterix in Belgium (*Astérix chez les Belges*)
Asterix in Britain (***Astérix chez les Bretons***)
Asterix in Spain (*Astérix en Hispanie*)
Asterix in Switzerland (*Astérix chez les Helvètes*)

Title in original language *Astérix en Corse*
First published by *Pilote*, collected by Dargaud (France)
Creators Goscinny (French, 1926–77); Uderzo (French, b.1927) **Genre** History, Humor

As in most Asterix adventures, the theme of *Asterix in Corsica* is relatively simple. The story is triggered by the Gauls fortuitously discovering a prisoner in the Roman camp of Totorum as they noisily celebrate victory over the Roman troops at the Battle of Gergovia. The prisoner, Boneywasawarriorwayayix, is a proud and easily offended Corsican (a pleonasm as we shall soon discover) who spontaneously describes his country as the "Romans' nightmare." This, of course, creates a bond. Curious to find out how the people in this faraway and unknown country treat their common enemy, Asterix and Obelix decide to accompany their new friend to Corsica. Their main mission there will be to prevent the local Roman governor returning to Rome with all the riches he has pillaged from the people—and at the same time to discover their picturesque and unexpected customs, a source of many surprises.

This was the last Asterix adventure to be published in *Pilote*, the magazine which followed the character from the very beginning, and as such it clearly confirms the talent and experience of the two creators. Uderzo's drawings, displaying a precision and energy rarely seen, are to be savored with relish. As to Goscinny's scenario, once again he plays with cultural references, delighting in bringing up the well-known (or supposedly so) peculiarities of the *Île de Beauté* (as Corsica is known) and its inhabitants: vendettas, chestnuts, siestas, diabolical cheeses, incomprehensible political intrigues, and naturally, the inhabitants' susceptibility. A little gem of humor and finesse, the story is a true delight. **NF**

Black Jack 1973

✒✒ Osamu Tezuka

Title in original language *Burakku Jakku*
First published by Akita Shoten (Japan)
Creator Japanese (1928–89)
Genre Drama

Osamu Tezuka completed medical school, but decided not to practice medicine. In part this was because of frustration at the Japanese medical system, and *Black Jack* is an idealized version of the doctor he might have been, albeit with the advantage of superhuman skills.

As a child, Black Jack was the victim of an explosion that scarred his body and paralyzed his limbs for many years. Now an unlicensed surgeon, he is often threatened by the authorities, but his reputation is such that anyone who can afford his services is willing to pay for them. That said, his fee is often outrageous, sometimes all that a patient has to give, and some clients are not at all happy about it. But this is in keeping with his attitude toward life—that it is priceless and always worth fighting for—and he expects his patients to feel the same way. Presenting an opposing viewpoint is Kiriko, a recurring character who performs euthanasia.

When not traveling, Black Jack lives with Pinoko, an eighteen-year-old female teratogenous cystoma that he removed from her twin sister and then placed in a plastic body. Pinoko calls herself Black Jack's wife and can be very jealous, but despite her physical age is an innocent, new to the world. Her mere existence always adds a poignancy to the stories in which she appears.

There are 242 *Black Jack* episodes, each of which usually run twenty pages. Tezuka fills each with drama as Black Jack challenges death and the evil that humans are capable of. Through it all readers feel real compassion for his patients, whether they are children or mobsters, deserving or undeserving, human or animal. **NFI**

Manhunter 1973

✒ Archie Goodwin ✒ Walt Simonson

First published by DC Comics (USA)
Creators Goodwin (American, 1937–88);
Simonson (American, b.1946)
Genre Superhero

Early Manhunter stories are framed as reports of John Kirk's (Manhunter) activities around the world as he is pursued by Interpol agent Christine St Clair. They begin with Manhunter's killing of a number of assassins who all look like him. Christine learns that Manhunter was saved from death and his body stored cryogenically until surgery was able to save him. That surgery also improved him, giving him enhanced healing abilities.

Manhunter's saviors belong to the Council, a group of the world's ten top minds who banded together near the end of World War II in hopes of saving the world. He learns the martial art of Ninjutsu from its last living master, Asano Nitobe, but rebels when he discovers that the Council has created an army of clones of him, each a trained assassin. Thereafter, the main thrust of the story has Manhunter gathering allies (including Christine and Asano) to aid him in bringing down the Council.

Archie Goodwin packed a great deal of story into each episode while still telling a ripping yarn that spanned the globe. Walt Simonson, on his breakthrough series, filled the pages with elegant detail, his design mixing larger and smaller panels as required to enhance the visual appeal of each page.

DC Comics originally published *Manhunter* as an eight-page backup story in *Detective Comics*. Goodwin and Simonson brought the story to a close in a final, feature-length episode guest-starring Batman. This very unusual occurrence was evidence of the good reputation enjoyed by the *Manhunter* series, which won six awards for both its writer and artist. **NFI**

Hägar the Horrible 1973

✒️ Dik Browne

First published by King Features Syndicate (USA)
Creator American (1917–89)
Genre Humor
Award Reuben Award (1973)

One reason that Dik Browne created *Hägar the Horrible* was that the strip he did with Mort Walker, *Hi and Lois*, was owned by the latter. He decided to create a character entirely owned by him, and from which his heirs might benefit. He credited the strip's name to his children, who liked to call him Hägar the Horrible.

Hägar is a more or less stereotypical Viking: fat, scruffy, a heavy eater and drinker, whose usual work is pillaging or invading neighboring countries with his tribe. His clan includes dominant wife Helga; well-mannered son Hamlet—more interested in books than in becoming a fierce Viking; and tomboyish daughter Honi; plus house pets Snert the dog and Kvack the duck. Other characters are Hägar's clumsy first mate, Lucky Eddie, and his village's medicine man, Dr. Zook.

Appearing in the 1970s, a decade that spawned few hit newspaper strips aside from *Doonesbury* and *Garfield*, *Hägar* became an instant success, eventually being syndicated in over 2,000 newspapers internationally. In addition to his daily strips and Sunday pages, now collected in dozens of paperbacks, Browne produced several *Hägar* longer stories that, published in book form, were aimed at the European market.

Hägar was made into an animated half-hour television special produced by Hanna-Barbera, and the character starred in a series of British commercials for Skol beer. Since Browne's death in 1989, the strip has been continued to this day by his son Chris, also a magazine cartoonist and creator of another strip called *Raising Duncan*. **AMo**

Didi Glitz 1973

✒️ Diane Noomin

First published by Self-published (USA)
Creator American (b.1947)
Genre Satire
Adaptation Musical (1981)

Didi Glitz, alter ego of comic artist Diane Noomin, is a single mother living in Brooklyn with her demanding, irritating daughter Crystal and her French poodle Pierre. Approaching forty, Didi espouses the values of a woman in 1960s middle-American suburbia. Her aspiration to live the American Dream leads to a vapid, lonely life and a series of disastrous relationships. Men are consistently portrayed as losers and creeps, while Didi's female friends are essentially gossips. On the rebound from two-timing Felix Kronsky, Didi has a fling with Eddie, a butcher who offers to show her "some really fresh meat." Eddie gets Didi pregnant, but as he is already married, he leaves her in the lurch.

Found in assorted underground anthologies and one solo comic, *Didi Glitz* is built around satirical obversation, unlike the autobiographical confessionals of Noomin's friend, Aline Kominsky (who encouraged Noomin to become a cartoonist in the first place, resulting in their joint comic *Twisted Sisters* in 1976). Didi briefly presents her own sharply ironic TV show, *Forty is Fabulous*, and runs a Rubberware (as opposed to Tupperware) party for her friends.

In a late story, "Didi Glitz in C'est Cheese," we see Noomin herself making a sculpture of Didi, whose drawn character exists within the clay. After arguing with her creator, Didi finally breaks free of her clay shell, commanding Noomin to "Look deep into my eyes! Follow the shining penpoint. . . ." Noomin replies, "Yes, master," a reminder of that cinematic moment when the dummy takes control of the ventriloquist. **LC**

Howard the Duck 1974

Steve Gerber Frank Brunner, Gene Colan, and others

First published by Marvel Comics (USA)
Creators Gerber (American, 1947–2008); Brunner (American, b.1949); Eugene Colan (American, 1926–2011)
Genre Satire

HOWARD THE DUCK
MARVEL COMICS GROUP
25¢ 1 JAN 02415
TRAPPED IN A WORLD HE NEVER MADE!
HOWARD THE DUCK
BECAUSE YOU DEMANDED IT-- THE FABULOUS FIRST ISSUE OF MARVEL'S MOST SENSATIONAL NEW SUPER-STAR!
AGAINST SWORD AND SORCERY, HOWARD STANDS SIDE-BY-SIDE WITH THE AMAZING SPIDER-MAN!

Howard the Duck appeared briefly in fantasy-horror series *The Man-Thing* as a throwaway character, but readers demanded more of the stogie-chomping, tough-talking duck, and he soon became the star of his own series. The perennial "stranger in a strange land," Howard is a fowl from another dimension transported to our world of "talking, hairless apes." He befriends shapely redhead Beverly Switzler and they decide to seek their fortunes; Howard a cynic, Bev the eternal optimist.

In his travels through America (which always seem to end up in Cleveland), Howard meets an assortment of weirdos and lunatics. He takes swiping beak-bites at superheroes (facing the Deadly Space Turnip); politics (he is a candidate in the 1976 presidential election); psychiatry (briefly placed in an insane asylum, he meets Winda, a girl whose parents believe she is demonically possessed because she "wike(s) to make funny faces and siwwy noises"); the media (mad scientist Dr. Bong has a bell on his head and has used unethical reporting to rise to power); and religious fanatics (such as the Kidney Lady, an old crone who thinks she is part of some world conspiracy against wholesomeness).

The series (an *Essential* book collects comics from 1975 to 1978) is a strange but compelling mixture of genre parody and social satire, with the titular hero expressing writer Steve Gerber's ideas. A hilarious, thought-provoking, and often touching romp through mid-1970s American society and popular culture, with inspired art by veteran artist Gene Colan, it also spawned a comic strip by the Gerber/Colan team. **J-PJ**

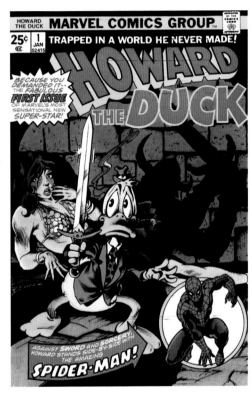

"You're a third party candidate and a duck! You expect to surmount those image problems alone?"

Similar reads
Bloom County Berke Breathed
Doonesbury Garry Trudeau
Giant-Size Man-Thing #4 Steve Gerber and various
Stewart the Rat Steve Gerber and Gene Colan

Bella at the Bar 1974

✎ Various ✎ John Armstrong

First published by IPC/Fleetway Publications (UK)
Creator Armstrong (British, b.1923)
Genre Teen
Influence on TV series: *Grange Hill* (1978)

Bella at the Bar ran from 1974 to 1984 in the teen comic *Tammy*, the title that shifted the focus of British girls' strips toward more realistic narratives that were antiauthoritarian, grittier, and darker. Nevertheless, there was humor in this story, albeit sometimes of a rather bleaker kind than previously. Created by Jenny McDade and John Armstrong, *Bella* featured a working-class orphan whose love of gymnastics helped her to battle through exploitation by her uncle and aunt and many other misfortunes, including blackmail, jealous rivals, and even imprisonment. Many writers worked on *Bella at the Bar* during the years it was published, notably Primrose Cumming (1915–2004).

The stories are typically about Bella's wit and resilience in the face of terrible odds. In featuring a contemporary "hard-done-by" working-class heroine who actively fights back and wins, uses slang, and wears casual clothing, *Bella at the Bar* was revolutionary. It also tapped into shifting cultural interests. Through both the British Amateur Gymnastics Association awards and the growth of televised contests, gymnastics was, in the 1970s in Britain, replacing ballet as a hugely popular and comparatively inexpensive activity for girls. The influence of televised gymnastics is very apparent, with an emphasis on showing Bella in action as a gymnast, her body often breaking the confines of the panel and exhibiting a great deal of energy and dynamism.

Bella's appearance was modeled on Armstrong's niece but was also influenced by gymnast Olga Korbut; both Olga and Bella wear their hair in bunches. **MG**

Jenifer 1974

✎✎ Bruce Jones and Bernie Wrightson

First published by Warren Publishing (USA)
Creators Jones (American, Unknown); Wrightson (American, b.1948)
Genre Horror

Artist Bernie Wrightson began illustrating the pages of Warren's horror magazines in the early 1970s. Although his art for a special edition of Mary Shelley's *Frankenstein* (*c.*1977–83) is generally considered his finest work, the story "Jenifer," scripted by Bruce Jones in *Creepy* #63 (1974), is among his best—a ten-page shocker that loses none of its power over time.

While on a hunting expedition, protagonist Jim discovers a girl about to be decapitated by a woodsman. He fires a shot to save her, and the dying man gasps the name "Jenifer." The girl is unable to speak, but worse, her face is a bug-eyed monstrosity atop a normal body. Yet, compelled by her gaze, Jim offers to adopt her rather than leave her at the mercy of the authorities. This puts a huge strain on his family, worsened when her violent tendencies show. Jim's wife and kids depart when his twisted relationship with Jenifer takes a sexual turn.

"Jenifer" was adapted by Dario Argento for the *Masters of Horror* TV series in 2005, which emphasized the sexual aspect—the man finds her irrationally seductive, not simply horrifying. In the original, Jim feels repulsed and little else—she compels him with her unspecified powers, or so it seems. Whatever angle you prefer, the array of haunting images—for instance, the moody overhead shot after Jenifer climbs into Jim's bed and he sobs, "Help me . . .," or his discovery of her feeding on the remains of a child in the basement—packs an enormous punch. A genuinely creepy story, matched by Wrightson's shadow-heavy atmospherics, it is a highlight of the Warren canon. **CH**

"Jenifer" offers an uncomfortable mix of violence and seduction. ➡

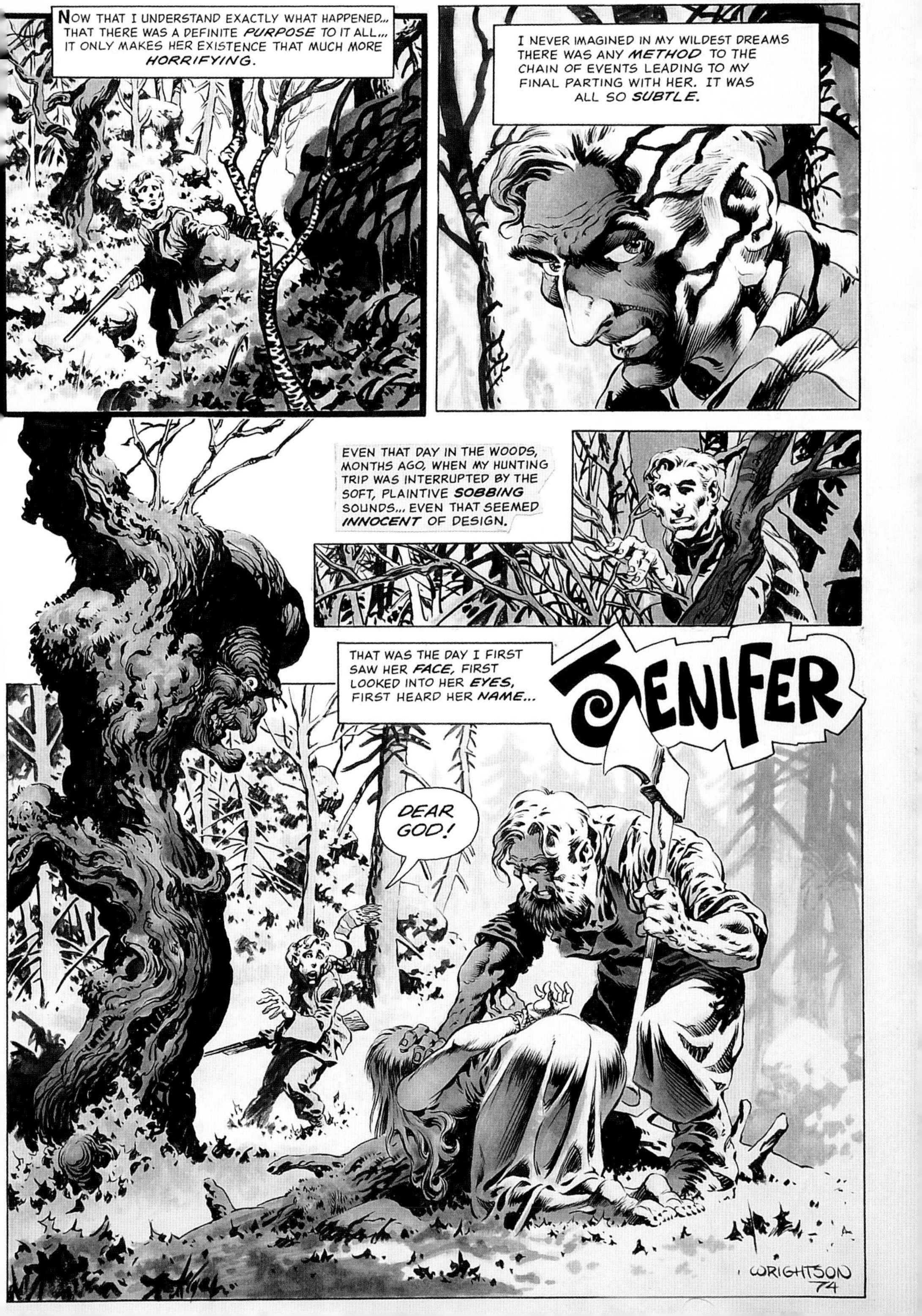
NOW THAT I UNDERSTAND EXACTLY WHAT HAPPENED... THAT THERE WAS A DEFINITE PURPOSE TO IT ALL... IT ONLY MAKES HER EXISTENCE THAT MUCH MORE HORRIFYING.
I NEVER IMAGINED IN MY WILDEST DREAMS THERE WAS ANY METHOD TO THE CHAIN OF EVENTS LEADING TO MY FINAL PARTING WITH HER. IT WAS ALL SO SUBTLE.
EVEN THAT DAY IN THE WOODS, MONTHS AGO, WHEN MY HUNTING TRIP WAS INTERRUPTED BY THE SOFT, PLAINTIVE SOBBING SOUNDS... EVEN THAT SEEMED INNOCENT OF DESIGN.
THAT WAS THE DAY I FIRST SAW HER FACE, FIRST LOOKED INTO HER EYES, FIRST HEARD HER NAME...
JENIFER
DEAR GOD!
WRIGHTSON 74

Thomas's Heart 1974

Moto Hagio

FLOWER COMICS

トーマの心臓 ②

萩尾望都

"For almost half a year, I have been thinking about my life, death… and one of my friends …"

Also by Moto Hagio

A Cruel God Reigns
A Drunken Dream and Other Stories
Hanshin
They Were Eleven

Title in original language *Toma no Shinzo*
First published by Shogakukan (Japan)
Creator Japanese (b.1949)
Genre Teen, Drama

Moto Hagio is considered the mother of modern *shoujo* manga. It is difficult to select one piece from her magnificent collection, but many readers would opt for *Thomas's Heart*, probably the first major manga dealing with *shonen-ai*, or female-oriented fiction focusing on male homosexual relationships.

One snowy day, a German boarding-school student, Thomas Werner, throws himself from the top of a bridge. He leaves a letter to Juli, with whom he was in love, but Juli had rejected him, believing himself unworthy of the love of Thomas or anyone like him. Only Juli's best friend, Oscar, understands Juli's feelings, while the other classmates see him as a cold and strong-minded intellectual. A couple of weeks after Thomas's death, a boy named Eric is transferred to the school. He looks very similar to Thomas, but his character is quite different. As the story unfolds, Juli is disturbed by Eric's open and straightforward behavior. Struggling with his feelings, Juli reacts in fear and anger. Hagio suggests that sometimes a "new breeze" that has the power to change can also be scary, even if it is love.

Hagio herself identified a question within this story, namely, how does a human recognize love for what it is? This is a simple but highly philosophical and religious issue of universal importance, and she expresses it brilliantly by borrowing the framework of *shonen-ai*. If you would like to know the answer to this question, you must read the story yourself. One thing: even though this story is not all tragedy, it is difficult to read it without crying your eyes out. **CK**

Alberto the Wolf 1974

✐✐ "Silver"

Title in original language *Lupo Alberto*
First published by *Corriere dei Ragazzi* (Italy)
Creator Guido Silvestri (Italian, b.1952)
Genre Humor

This famous Italian comic strip series is a comedy set on a farm starring a group of "funny animals" led by a wolf named Alberto. In the early days, the structure of the series was close to *Krazy Kat*'s oppositional dynamic. Alberto is in love with a chicken named Marta and tries to free her from the farm, but comes unstuck against the strict surveillance of a big, strong, bad dog named Mosé.

Over the years, the cast of McKenzie Farm has increased and become more complex. Alberto the Wolf is likened to a penniless but honest "average Italian man," idealist but sometimes fainthearted and immature as he systematically avoids Marta's wedding proposals.

The strip's main issues are family relations and friendships, with a special emphasis on the daily life and neuroses of couples. But in addition to the endless variations of humor gags and family situations, the strip deals with social commentary and satire. Examples include a much-debated story about gay rights (Alberto the Wolf decides to accompany his gay friend on a march), political terrorism, and the craze for TV and cell-phone technology.

Inspired by animation masters Chuck Jones and Tex Avery, as well as comic artists Jacovitti and Herrimann, Silver's drawing style recalls Walt Kelly's *Pogo*, with a more dynamic twist. Alberto the Wolf has become the most successful Italian character in the nonpublishing licensing market—clothes, gifts, back-to-school products, stationery—and he is highly sought after as a "spokewolf" for public service advertising campaigns, including those of the Ministry of Health. **MS**

The Arctic Marauder 1974

✐✐ Jacques Tardi

Title in original language *Le Démon des glaces*
First published by Dargaud (France)
Creator French (b.1946)
Genre Adventure

In the middle of the Arctic Ocean, the young Jerome Plumier, a medical student, is among the very few survivors of the mysterious 1889 shipwreck of the *Anjou*. Back in Paris, Plumier discovers that eight other ships have recently sunk in the same way, apparently after hitting an iceberg. The young man decides to join a scientific expedition that is leaving Brest to go and investigate these accidents.

Back in the Arctic, Plumier discovers that the shipwrecks were no accident. The ships were sunk by the underwater guns of an ingenious artificial iceberg, the "Arctic marauder," developed by two mad scientists, one of whom is Plumier's own uncle, Louis Ferdinand Chapoutier. The young man is persuaded to join his uncle in a plan to subject the world's largest cities to a bacteriological bombardment that will spread deadly diseases everywhere on the planet.

Jacques Tardi is fascinated by the imagery of the late-nineteenth century and is a master of illustration, inspired by Gustave Doré and Gus Bofa as much as by the masters of the classic strip cartoon. Adopting the playful approach of the serialized novel, he has a taste for larger-than-life characters and intrigues with constant developments. Tardi employs a devastating, omnipresent irony, and his great originality lies in a subtle balance between flaunted drollness and tacit despair. Strangely, he names one of his scientists Louis Ferdinand—the forenames of Céline, the great French nihilist writer, three of whose novels he was to illustrate with amazing brio fifteen years later. **NF**

Candy Candy 1975

✎ Yumiko Igarashi ✎ Kyoko Mizuki

First published by Nakayoshi (Japan)
Creators Igarashi (Japanese, b.1948);
Mizuki (Japanese, b.1949)
Genre Soap opera

One of Japan's most acclaimed *shojo* manga (manga aimed at young girls), *Candy Candy* tells the story of blonde, freckle-faced, tomboyish Candice White Ardley, alias Candy, an orphan who grew up in the orphanage Pony's Home, near Lake Michigan at the beginning of the twentieth century. She is adopted by a rich family whose children treat her badly, later finds a romantic interest who dies tragically in a horse accident, is then sent to an exclusive boarding school in London where she finds new friends and enemies—including a new love interest, the well-bred though anarchic Terrence Grandchester—and eventually returns to the United States, working as a nurse at the outbreak of World War I, among other adventures.

Using all the archetypical clichés of girls' manga—heroines with big eyes, handsome heroes, showers of flower petals—and the most effective elements of old-fashioned melodramas, Igarashi and Mizuki succeeded in creating what has been labeled a "soap opera for kids." Candy's strong personality and all the hardships she suffers along the way earned her a place in the hearts of millions of girls, and quite a few boys, too.

An animated adaptation, produced by Toei Doga in 1976, contributed to *Candy Candy*'s popularity outside Japan, particularly in Italy, where the original manga was published in color. This was even followed by new *Candy* stories drawn by Italian artists. Sadly, In recent years, a lawsuit between the authors regarding ownership of the character has prevented the manga from being reprinted. **AMo**

Paracuellos 1975

✎✎ Carlos Giménez

First published by Muchas Gracias (Spain)
Creator Spanish (b.1941)
Genre Autobiography
Award Angoulême (1981)

As well as being a great book, *Paracuellos* is a milestone in the history of contemporary comics. When it was first published in the mid-1970s, autobiographical comics were not common, and Carlos Giménez did much to expand the genre.

The story of *Paracuellos* is inspired directly by the author's life. In his early childhood, at the age of six, Carlos Giménez was placed in an Auxilio Social home, the state-run children's home of Franco's Spain. He spent eight years of his youth moving around such institutions—enough to accumulate a large stock of authentic memories and anecdotes to fill a comic.

Paracuellos is a series of simple short stories, varying in length from between two and twelve pages, that form the diary of a group of children in an orphanage, revealing the everyday events that make up their lives. The result could have been uplifting; instead it is horrendous. The enclosed space of the orphanage is depicted as a deeply neurotic place where perverse, corrupt, sadistic adults, steeped in Catholicism and the veneration of all things military, treat the children in their charge very poorly.

The only reprieve is the amusing relationships between the children themselves and their unfounded but deep-rooted hope of a better future, embodied by little Pablito (the alter ego of Giménez himself), who dreams of one day becoming a comics creator. While Giménez has produced many other comics during his career, this early pioneering work of autobiographical comics remains his most important achievement. **NF**

Polonius 1975

Philippe Picaret Jacques Tardi

First published by *Métal Hurlant* (France)
Creators Picaret (French, Unknown);
Tardi (French, b.1946)
Genre Science fiction

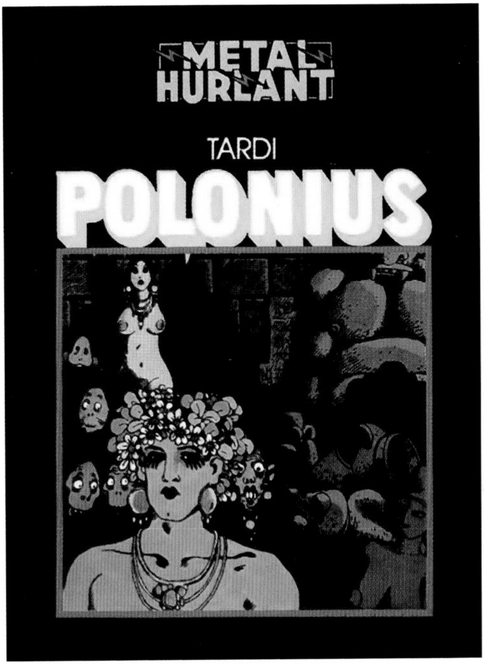
METAL HURLANT
TARDI
POLONIUS

Polonius is not what he appears to be. The name immediately makes one think of *Hamlet*, or a sword-and-sandal movie, and the story does contain certain historical attributes. However, the adventures of the titular character do not take place in the past, but in a distant future where humanity has regressed to more or less the same level as our ancient ancestors.

Like many other lonely people tired of an uncertain provincial life, Polonius has set off for the city of Ru in the hope of finding better living conditions. Captured and treated as a slave, he is noticed by Hegypios, one of the most powerful generals of the city, and swiftly becomes his protégé.

An idealist at heart, Polonius despairs at the corrupt, noxious atmosphere that dominates life in Ru. Together with Chimos, the last scholar in this depraved city, he organizes an expedition to the distant steppes with the aim of making discoveries that he hopes will rekindle the community's creative spirit, but his efforts are all in vain. In spite of the successful and productive results of his expedition, on his return he finds only desolation and death in the city. Despondent, Polonius watches in silence the final fall of Ru, decimated by a plague, haunted by carrion feeders, and littered with the grotesque idols created by the city's inhabitants, who have since renounced technology.

Tardi's fourth book, *Polonius* is a dark, tragic, and inconclusive rumination on the fate of humanity. The illustrator has not returned to science fiction since, but his later work retains the pessimism apparent here. **NF**

"Tardi has managed to create a nightmare through his illustrations, the kind of archaic nightmare which is as old as humanity and which is present in the unconscious of all of us."

Philippe Picaret

Also by Jacques Tardi
Déprime
Mouh Mouh
The Arctic Marauder (*Le démon des glaces*)

Alack Sinner 1975

✎ Carlos Sampayo ✎ José Muñoz

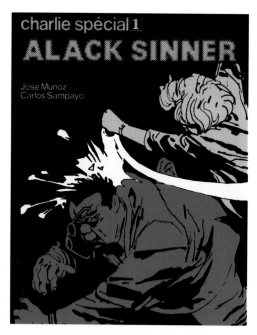

charlie spécial 1

ALACK SINNER

Jose Muñoz
Carlos Sampayo

> "The whole story of Alack Sinner and his daughter, for instance, is a transposition of what I experienced with my own daughter."

José Muñoz

Similar reads

5 Is the Perfect Number (5 è il Numero Perfetto) Igort
100 Bullets Brian Azerello and Eduardo Risso
One Trick Rip-off Paul Pope
Silverfish David Lapham
Stray Bullets David Lapham

First published by Linus (Italy)
Creators Sampayo (Argentinian, b.1943);
Muñoz (Argentinian, b.1942)
Genre Crime

In the best traditions of the crime novel, Alack Sinner is a former policeman who has become a private detective. His cases, often difficult and unrewarding, cause him to immerse himself in the murkiest neighborhoods and underworld areas of New York, in the beating heart of the great city, devourer of lives.

Although he does not shrink from violence when it is unavoidable, Alack is more a mediator than a warrior. Deeply disillusioned, he drags his disenchantment through the jazz-swathed nighttime streets. In the course of his wanderings, which involve more introspective melancholy than actual detective work, he meets a varied range of drop outs, social pariahs, and examples of human misery of every kind, often extreme or immoral in their own way, each declares that every night survived is a new victory over death.

While *Alack Sinner* is pure crime fiction, this is not a typical comic book adventure and pure action has a limited place. Numerous intense characters, even when they are comparatively minor, shine out for their depth and authenticity. From the first episode of the series, Sampayo's tales—sophisticated, dense, and taut—are remarkable for both their psychological depth and their marked political color. The masterly graphic interpretation of José Muñoz, a virtuoso of black-and-white art, results in a striking work. At the same time both expressionist and hyperrealist in its determination to stick to raw reality, the imagery of *Alack Sinner* has influenced generations of readers and artists alike. **NF**

Conquering Armies 1975

✏ Jean-Pierre Dionnet   ✏ Jean-Claude Gal

Title in original language *Les armées du conquérant*
First published in *Métal Hurlant* (France)
Creators Dionnet (French, b.1947); Gal (French, 1942–94)
Genre Science fiction

When inspired publisher Jean-Pierre Dionnet founded the legendary magazine *Métal Hurlant* in 1975 with his friends, graphic artists Jean Giraud (better known as Moebius for his science fiction work) and Philippe Druillet, it was to publish not only the authors he admired, but also to publish his own stories in the magazine. Trained in the early 1970s at *Pilote*, the publication that was home to many of the best French *bandes dessinées* of the period, Dionnet was a writer and was featured in the first issue of the magazine.

This work is immediately reminiscent of the science fiction popular at the time, particularly the epic fantasy of Robert Howard's tales of Conan the Barbarian or Michael Moorcock's Elric books. It consists of a series of short stories, from four to fifteen pages pages in length, set in a future or alternative world. Its theme is the conquests of a great military leader whose vast armies push forward ceaselessly.

Dionnet and his illustrator Jean-Claude Gal are fascinated by details: in parallel with the advance of the conqueror and his troops, the creators focus on the stories of lost or unlucky soldiers through tales of betrayal, failure, deception, and renunciation. Black, caustic humor is also evident in this landscape full of foul stenches and violent situations. Naturally it is Gal's imagery, constantly flirting with outrageousness and immoderation, that gives the work its weight. A highly gifted graphic artist with a great sense of realism, he went on to produce some fantastic work, but he was never as powerful as in this, his inaugural outing. **NF**

Footrot Flats 1975

✏✏ Murray Ball

First published in *The Evening Post* (New Zealand)
Creator New Zealander (b.1939)
Genre Humor
Adaptation Film: *Footrot Flats: The Dog's Tale* (1987)

Footrot Flats is a newspaper strip about a Border Collie sheepdog known simply as "the Dog," and his owner, farmer Wallace "Wal" Cadwallader Footrot. At school Wal's sporting prowess was poor, although he did prove adept at tractor reversing. Upon leaving school he purchased 400 acres of swamp in the center of New Zealand's North Island, which he called Footrot Flats. Wal doesn't have a serious love interest but he is quite sweet on Darlene Hobson, a hairdresser in the nearby town of Raupo. The ensemble cast of people and animals in the world of Wal and his dog includes Wal's niece Janice, local boy Rangi Jones, who likes to help Wal on the farm, Wal's neighbor Socrates, Aunt Delores, Aunt Dolly and her Welsh Corgi Prince Charles, Cecil the ram, and a cat called Horse.

Despite Ball's extensive depiction of animals, he does not resort to the anthropomorphism commonly found in similarly animal-studded comics. Here, The Dog is a dog, although his thoughts and character are expressed through thought bubbles. Overall, the characters altered little over the years with the exception of the Dog, who became slightly Snoopylike. Rangi, who grew from a child to a teenager, allowed Ball to show off his considerable illustrative skills in aging him almost imperceptibly year by year.

Footrot Flats has been collected in a series of books, adapted to the stage, and was even the basis of a film. The strip came to a close in 1994; Ball has suggested that the demise of his own dog and the state of New Zealand politics were the catalysts for its ending. **BS**

Frustration 1975
✐ Claire Brétecher

Title in original language *Les Frustrés*
First published by Brétecher (France)
Creator French (b.1940)
Genre Humor

The most well-known series by Claire Brétecher, the doyenne of French comics, *Frustration* first appeared in France's *Nouvel Observateur* magazine before becoming a series of five books published between 1975 and 1980. Over the span of hundreds of strips, *Frustration* combines a mix of socio-political satire and comedy that pokes fun at the problems of everyday life, and the key to its humor is Brétecher's witty deadpan dialogue.

The series follows a simple stylistic format throughout—each strip is made up of black-and-white frames containing almost no background detail, with very little movement and no change in perspective between frames. Armed only with simple drawings of mostly anonymous characters, however, Brétecher's sketches touch on a host of everyday issues.

Frustration was developed in the wake of the social upheaval in France that followed the turbulent protests of May 1968, the influence of which is clear throughout. A common target of Brétecher's satire is the fashionable pseudo-Marxist intellectualism of the post-1968 middle classes—particularly their habit of dramatically proclaiming the need for social change while refusing to get off the sofa. A feminist thread also runs through much of the series, too—although Brétecher herself does not describe her work as feminist—as female characters discuss abortion, divorce, and working motherhood. However, Brétecher's brilliance is cemented by her decison to highlight the comedy over the cause throughout, making *Frustration* an intelligent and truly funny read. **CMac**

Arzach 1975
✐ "Moebius"

First published in *Métal Hurlant* (France)
Creator Jean Giraud (French, b.1938)
Genre Science fiction
Influence on *Panzer Dragoon* video game (1995)

More than thirty-five years after its creation, *Arzach* surprises with its slimness. It consists of a handful of very short stories with no continuity between them, and fewer than forty pages altogether. Nevertheless it was with this restraint that Frenchman Jean Giraud, better known as Moebius, would forever change the way in which *bandes dessinées* are made and perceived.

In a vast and empty universe that is never explained, an austere, silent individual rides on the back of a large, white pterodactyl-like creature, taking part in strange adventures that involve danger and cruelty. For example, he attempts to rescue a beautiful woman from a tower, only to be given an unpleasant shock when he succeeds; in another sequence, he deliberately allows the woman's captor to fall to his death. Moebius decided to make a comic book that, without words, potentially could be universally understood. The stories apparently result from a dreamlike state of improvisation and radical experiment, similar to that practiced by surrealist writers in their automatic writing. Their meaning lies in the telling, although readers must try to work out the meaning for themselves.

Carried along by its extraordinary graphic quality and by its very strangeness, *Arzach* would soon achieve remarkable international publishing success. Comics creators, movie makers, painters, and graphic illustrators were enchanted and profoundly influenced by this U.F.O. of a comic, which had clearly arrived from the land of dreams. It was a literal demonstration of the power of the imagination through the medium of drawing. **NF**

Through the wordless *Arzach* strips Moebius has influenced numerous creators in the visual arts. ➡

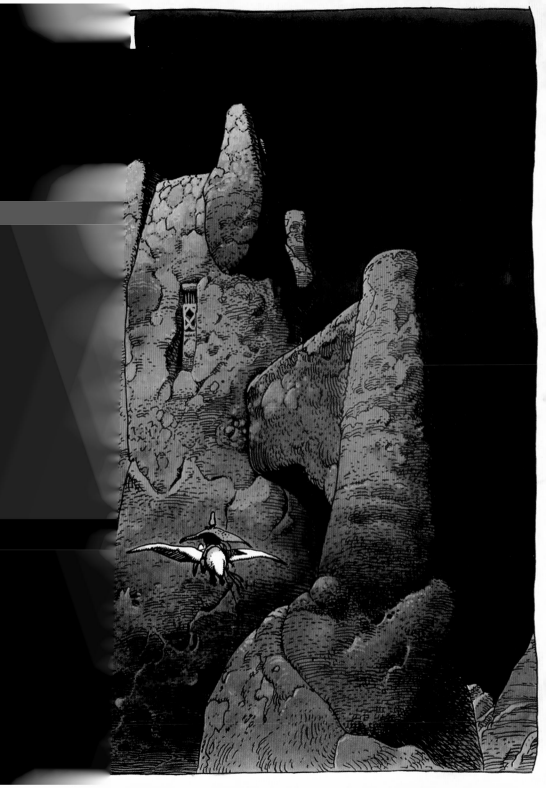

The Cage 1975

Martin Vaughn-James

THE CAGE
A Visual-Novel
MARTIN VAUGHN-JAMES

"Abandoned airfields, weed-covered bomb-sites, enigmatic bits of shell-casings, helmets, rusting away in woods and fields, that kind of thing."

Martin Vaughn-James on his influences

Similar reads

Arzach Moebius

Big Guy and Rusty the Boy Robot Frank Miller and Geoff Darrow

Soft City Axel Jensen and Hariton Pushwagner

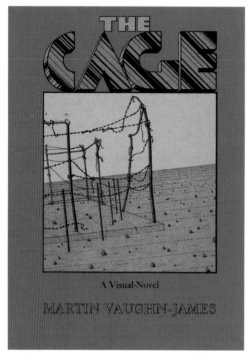

First published by The Coach House Press (Canada)
Creator British (1943–2009)
Genre Fantasy
Influenced by Alain Robbe-Grillet

Martin Vaughn-James was born in Britain, but he lived and worked in many parts of the world. It was in Canada during the 1970s that he started creating his visual novels. *Elephant*—a "boovie" (a portmanteau word mixing "book" and "movie")—was his first. The drawings were crude, Disneylike, and, in the artist's own words, comic book inspired. Surrealism and psychedelia can also be seen in the creator's work.

The essay, *Pour un nouveau roman,* by the French writer Alain Robbe-Grillet, was another crucial influence on Vaughn-James for *The Cage*. In his essay, Robbe-Grillet talked about the need for new literary forms for the new times of the 1960s. He rejected the nineteenth-century criteria (such as character development and psychology) used by bourgeois twentieth-century critics to judge contemporary novels.

The Cage's power is that it is a visual novel without human characters, but clothes and other objects depicted in it assume almost human form, taking the place of characters. In fact they're the ghosts of characters—to know more about them we just need to look at their rooms. Vaughn-James's has a desk and painting frames, the quarters of a comics artist. The destruction caused by time and men and a Deleuzian mixture of different times are other themes in this highly complex book. Vaughn-James linked his interest in debris to his memory of a post–World War II Britain. Time and war destroy everything in the end, everything that an artist tries to create in his or her room, in his or her cage, or in his or her ivory tower. **DI**

Warlock 1975

✎✎ Jim Starlin

First published by Marvel Comics (USA)
Creator American (b.1949)
Genre Science fiction
Influenced by Steve Ditko

Warlock stands at the peak of Jim Starlin's psychedelic and cosmic take on the "Marvel Universe." Picking up the mantle of the Silver Surfer (dropped from his own title in 1970), Warlock—along with Captain Marvel (whose adventures Jim Starlin also wrote and illustrated from 1973 to 1974), soon became the most philosophical and spiritually aware of Marvel's superheroes.

The 1970s were a period of relatively low editorial supervision at Marvel. It is said that creatives such as Starlin, Steve Gerber, and Steve Englehart delivered work directly to Marvel's production manager John Verpoorten for printing. (All this was to change with the arrival of Jim Shooter as editor-in-chief in 1978.) One result of this freedom was a lot of missed editorial deadlines, and a lot of filler or reprint issues. But this period also saw some of the most innovative work emerging from Marvel's marginal titles: *Howard the Duck*, *The Defenders*, *Morbius the Living Vampire*, *Captain Marvel*, and *Warlock*.

Jim Starlin's *Warlock* is a tormented figure. Accompanied by his satyrlike companion Pip, he battled his evil future self, the messianic Magus of the Universal Church of Truth and other menaces before the series was canceled in November 1976.

Starlin's artwork reached maturity during the course of his stint on *Warlock*. His ability to use a collage of individual panels as a means of dissecting action has roots in the work of earlier comic artists, such as Bernard Krigstein, but Starlin's use of this technique with eye-popping beauty is uniquely his own. **RR**

The Defenders 1975

✎ Steve Gerber ✎ "Sal" Buscema

First published by Marvel Comics (USA)
Creators Gerber (American, 1947–2008);
Silvio Buscema (American, b.1936)
Genre Superhero

Steve Gerber's run on *The Defenders* began with villains extracted from a 1950s reprint comic and a giant-size issue in which a model lost a limb to a car bomb. Two extended tales followed, tackling race hate groups and an invasion of Earth by alien lizards in the thirtieth century. Both were solid superhero stories with inventive quirks and unpredictable conclusions.

Gerber then stretched his imagination. A clown mask–wearing cult declared the entirety of New York to be bozos, a Soviet superhero arrived, Valkyrie investigated the past of her human persona and was jailed, and Dr. Strange developed a frat boy sense of humor. And that was not the half of it. Villains thrown into the mix included an elf with a gun; perennial losers Plantman, Porcupine, and Eel now empowered by a self-awareness course; a tentacled energy manipulating alien masquerading as both a golden god and an everyman; and the Headmen. Their leader boasted a gorilla's body from the neck down and was the most normal of the quartet. Even at Marvel in the 1970s, this was bizarre, experimental material.

With his artwork, Sal Buscema delivered quality superhero storytelling month after month for decades. There is never any need to puzzle over what is taking place on the pages, and these stories offer artistic differences with the smoother inking line of Vince Colletta and Jim Mooney contrasting Klaus Janson's brush style. Those who believe that Grant Morrison introduced surrealism to superhero comics need to acquire this thrilling seat of the pants series. **CM**

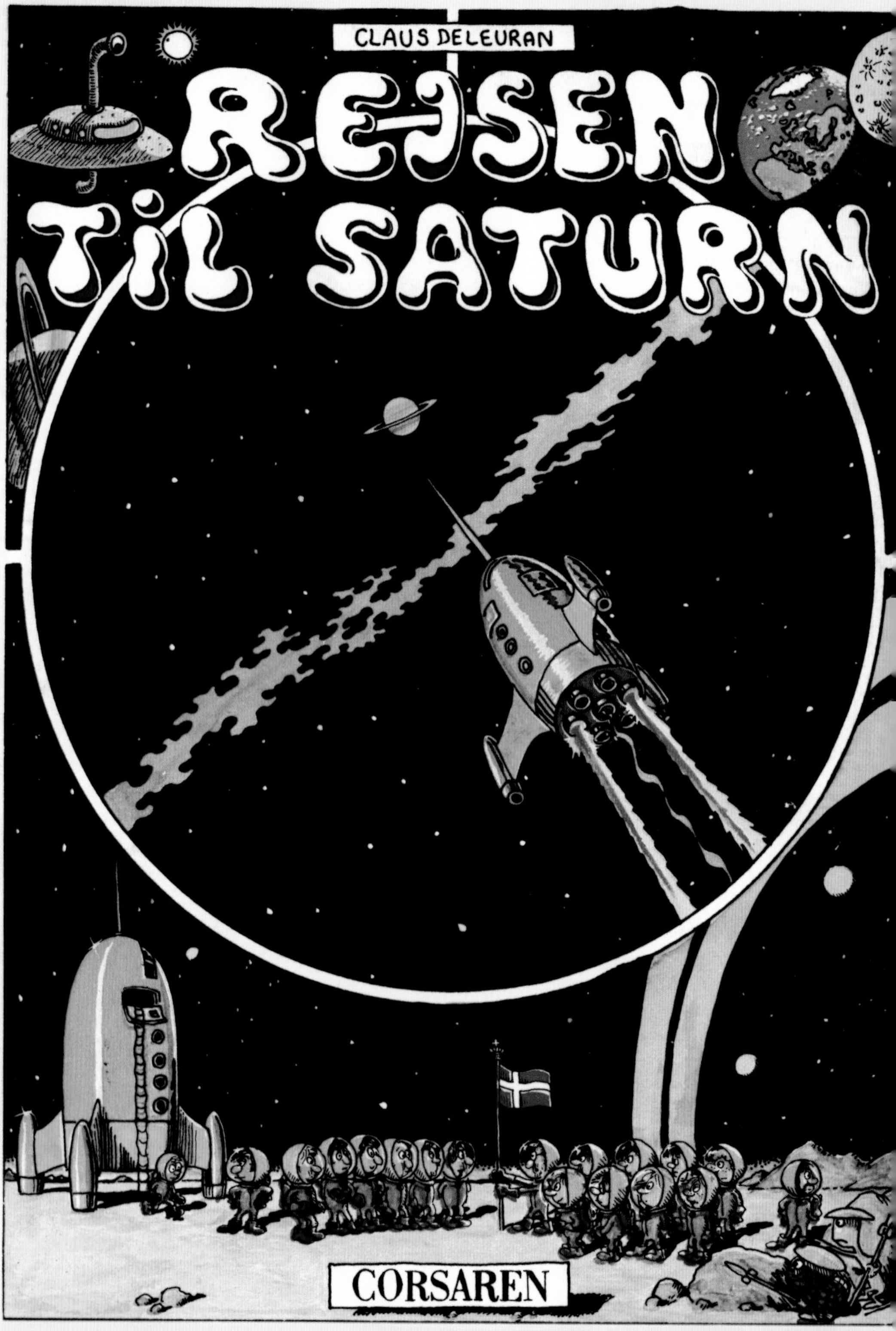
CLAUS DELEURAN
REJSEN TIL SATURN
CORSAREN

The Journey to Saturn 1976

✐✐ Claus Deleuran

Title in original language *Rejsen til Saturn*
First published by Corsaren (Denmark)
Creator Danish (1946–96)
Genre Humor, Satire, Science fiction

Drawn initially for leftist weekly *Wing Magazine*, *The Journey to Saturn* concerns a space mission undertaken by the Danish government to conquer the brave new territories of the sixth planet of the solar system. Although it is led by the macho captain Arne Skrydsbøl, the mission consists mainly of a bunch of hapless conscripts packing comics and bottles of beer.

Saturn's inhabitants, needless to say, are rather unimpressed by the might of the Danes, whose imperialist caper quickly founders. They end up being chased back to Earth by a UFO built of nougat ice cream, crammed with equally imperialist aliens bent on teaching the Earthlings a lesson. By that point, however, the journey has taken the travelers to where no man has gone before, from afternoon coffee on a planet at the far end of the galaxy to the pearly gates themselves, beyond which they have the dubious privilege of encountering a rather dysfunctional Holy Trinity. They also meet a rather perturbed slumbering space dragon who they cover with their weightless toilet waste.

The Journey to Saturn occupies a position at the heart of Danish comics; its broad anything-goes humor encapsulates the national spirit in its most generous aspect. As political and social satire, it easily transcended the left-wing dogma of its publication platform, offering a vibrant portrait of its time, but beyond that it is a witty and imaginative comics romp in the tradition of Carl Barks and Robert Crumb, wrought by a master of cartoon freestyle, equally at home with the comic, the realistic, the silly, and the fantastic. **MWi**

Wild Dogs 1976

✐✐ Alex Barbier

Title in original language *Lycaons*
First published by Éditions du Square (France)
Creator French (b.1950)
Genre Adult

When Alex Barbier burst upon the world of comics he caused as big a shock as the books of his inspiration William S. Burrough had to the world of literature two decades before. Barbier's first album, *Lycaons*, appeared in 1979 and collected the six chapters published in the French magazine *Charlie* between 1976 and 1978. Each chapter stands on its own, and readers can easily follow the characters' frequently blurred faces. A young, long-haired, male prostitute kicks off the series. He flees from a murder scene, is imprisoned, raped, then locked up. Later, the same character, called Pepito, becomes the object of the sexual desire of both women and men.

On the whole, the pages, divided in two, show bleak rooms, the interiors of American cars of the 1950s, parts of naked bodies, wild dogs, and disgustingly fat men. To compose these highly pictorial scenes, Barbier uses photographs with unusual framing, sometimes taken by himself. His technique of direct color was produced by mixing his inks more anarchically than other artists, sometimes as they were already spreading on the paper, conveying an impression of "blurred strokes," as the author once explained in an interview.

As far as the text is concerned, the language is extremely crude. There are no taboos. It mixes references to drugs, theft, paranoia, and sex into narratives that punctuate the images. An uncompromising artist, Barbier fell out of favor in the 1980s, only to be rediscovered in the 1990s by the Belgian publisher Fremok. In 2003, Fremok produced a new edition of *Lycaons*, which included some unseen early work. **CM**

Song of the Wind and Trees 1976

✏️ Keiko Takemiya

FLOWER COMICS

風と木の詩

② 竹宮恵子

"The first shojo manga to portray romantic and sexual relationships between boys."

Matt Thorn, manga historian

Similar reads
Banana Fish Akimi Yoshida
Emperor of the Land of Rising Sun (Hi Izuru Tokoro no Tenshi) Ryoko Yamagishi

Title in original language *Kaze to ki no uta*
First published by Shogakukan (Japan)
Creator Japanese (b.1950)
Genre Romance, Teen

Shuji Terayama, a famous Japanese poet, once said in the postscript for the first volume of this work, "from now on, *shojo* manga (manga for girls) will be categorized pre- and post-[*Song of the Wind and Trees*]." As this quote indicates, the 1970s was probably the most important era for girl's manga.

The story of *Song of the Wind and Trees* itself is set in late nineteenth-century France. Serge Battour is a fourteen-year-old boy who is transferred to a boarding school, where he meets the dauntingly beautiful Gilbert Cocteau. Rumor has it that Gilbert prostitutes himself to some powerful elder boys and teachers. Although his beauty is admired, most of the other students fear and despise him because of his "morally degenerate" behavior. However, Serge, who has been having a hard time himself because of his dark skin, tries to understand and save Gilbert. The more they get to know each other, the more they are attracted to each other.

Considering that this was created in the 1970s and was aimed at girls, the story is full of controversial topics: homosexuality, prostitution, rape, and incest. However, it is thoroughly and gracefully touching and never vulgar because of the creator's brilliant storytelling skill, as well as her beautiful, delicate, and detailed drawings. This is not only a sensual period drama but it also works as a metaphor for Japanese girls' anxiety and suppressed feelings toward their gender and sex. This is probably the biggest reason why this work is still considered one of the most pioneering pieces of girls' manga. **CK**

From Eroica with Love 1976

✎🎨 Yasuko Aoike

Title in original language *Eroica yori ai wo komete*
First published by Akita Shoten (Japan)
Creator Japanese (b.1948)
Genre Romance, Humor, Teen

First launched in 1976 during the Cold War, *From Eroica with Love* is set in a world of conflict. But in the world according to Yasuko Aoike, even the most serious political dilemma can be turned into a farcical tale.

The manga focuses on the adventures of a peculiar combination of characters. Dorian Red, Earl of Gloria, also known as Eroica, is the openly homosexual protagonist and the notorious leader of a British gang of art thieves. He often crosses paths (and flirts) with the homophobic conservative German Klaus Heinz von dem Eberbach, who serves in NATO. Eberbach's main adversary is Mischa the Bear Cub, a member of the Soviet Union's secret police, the KGB. The contrasting characters soon become entangled in this spy comedy, and although Eroica is the central character in the series, most readers would agree that Eberbach has almost completely stolen his limelight.

Aoike is one of the *24 nen gumi* (Year 24 Group), a group of female manga artists born around 1949 (the twenty-fourth year of Japan's Showa period) who are considered to have revolutionized girls' manga. As Aoike has done with this tale, such artists introduced innovative concepts to the girls' manga, including science fiction, fantasy, or homosexuality.

From Eroica with Love was originally published in Akita Shoten's *Princess* magazine until 2007, when it moved to *Princess Gold*. Its English-language version was first published in 2004. Aoike has also released a sister title, *Z*, which tells the story of Eroica through the eyes of one of Eberbach's beloved subordinates. **TS**

The Airtight Garage of Jerry Cornelius 1976

✎🎨 "Moebius"

Title in original language *Le Garage hermétique de Jerry Cornelius* **First published by** Les Humanoïdes Associés (France) **Creator** Jean Giraud (French, b.1938)
Genre Science fiction

Airtight Garage is a very interesting *bande dessinée* that appeared in very short episodes over a number of years in the late 1970s. It seems to have been developed section by section, with little sense of an overarching plot (or at times, it must be said, any direction at all). It is notable to science fiction fans for featuring Jerry Cornelius, a character created by Michael Moorcock, although he does not have as major a role as the strip's original name implies, and the character was later renamed Lewis Carnelian for the English version.

While many people may not read Moebius for his plotting, broadly speaking the story is a metaphysical tale with a fair amount of mysticism thrown in, set on a series of artificial worlds, one inside the next, like Russian dolls—its "hermetic" French title is carefully chosen because it refers both to an airtight seal and to the magical and religious teachings of various spiritualist touchstones, including Hermes Trismegistus and the Golden Dawn. Many of the worlds, or "levels," appear to have been created by Major Grubert, another recurring character in Moebius's own mythos.

Moebius explored the ideas of inner and outer space so beloved of the French Nouvelle Vague (New Wave) movement, and his artwork here is some of his best, possibly inspired by the lack of formal structure. Vast landscapes and mind-blowing spreads abound, with Moebius's trademark airiness and contrast between close details and white space. There is gorgeous figure work, and even if the story is a little nonsensical, this comic bears careful study for the artwork alone. **FJ**

MW 1976

Osamu Tezuka

Title in original language *Muu*
First published by Shogakukan (Japan)
Creator Japanese (1928–89)
Genre Political fable, Science fiction

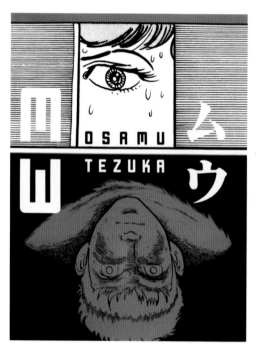

Also by Osamu Tezuka
A Story of Three Adolfs
Ayako
Black Jack
Ode to Kirihito
Phoenix

Catholic priest Father Garai and banker Michio Yuki are lovers. Fifteen years previously, they met as teenager and child on an island, far south of the Japanese mainland, that had a U.S. military base on it. A secret chemical weapon, code-named MW, leaked on the island, killing everyone except for Garai and Yuki. The U.S. and Japanese governments covered up the incident.

However, Yuki did not escape exposure to the gas unscathed, and grows up with no conscience, only a desire for revenge. He is a handsome, charismatic young man and a master of disguise in both male or female clothing. As a rising star in banking, he uses his position to reach the men he blames for the leak of the MW, casually killing their children along the way.

"He's lured me into an unholy union . . . he transforms himself into a woman and seeks my flesh."

Yuki is a smooth operator: he ingratiates people with his charm while plotting increasingly ruthless crimes. Garai is taken in by him, and although Yuki confesses his sins, Garai cannot bring himself to go to the police. He is drawn into deeper and deeper complicity in Yuki's crimes: "I despise him! It's just that my power to hate isn't strong enough." Not until Garai learns that Yuki plans to use the remaining MW for his own terrible ends does he find the will to act against his lover.

Tezuka contrasts charming evil with military and political corruption, while telling a twisted homosexual love story. Although Tezuka often reused his characters, partly in reference to the Buddhist ideas of reincarnation, Garai and Yuki are different—both wind up dying. Tezuka's artwork here is as inventive as always and the narrative is tense and serious. This is a dark and violent story with no easy answers. **NFl**

Bahadur
The Red Bricks House 1976

Aabid Surti and Jagjit Uppal Govind Brahmania

Title in original language *Bahadur: Lal Haveli Ka Rahasya* **First published by** Bennett Coleman (India) **Creators** Surti (Indian, b.1935); Uppal (Indian, b.1946); Brahmania (Indian, 1942–2009) **Genre** Adventure

Released in December 1976, months before a short-lived left-wing government trying to make India self-reliant kicked Coca-Cola out of the country in May 1977, *The Red Bricks House* was a similar attempt to "Indianize" comics. Bahadur, the comic's long-haired, iron-fisted vigilante, was created for Indrajal Comics to take on the imported U.S. syndicated comic characters introduced in 1964. Aabid Surti based Bahadur on an upright and resourceful 1970s Indian film hero and gave him the generic paraphernalia of his U.S. counterparts—a martial arts expert fiancée, a conscientious but underresourced police officer ally, and a trusty sidekick.

Illustrated with Govind Brahmania's rushed charcoal drawings daubed with garish colors, *The Red Bricks House*

"Bahadur's? You mean the son of the terror—Bhaiřav Singh, who was shot by the police chief?"

recounts Bahadur's transformation from a bandit's son impatient to avenge his father's killing by Vishal, a local police chief, into a thoughtful crime fighter who sets up the Citizen Security Force to mobilize villagers to defend themselves against the bandits terrorizing Jaygarh, a fictional hamlet in the real-life locale of the Chambal Valley in the central Indian state of Madhya Pradesh.

In 1979, after Surti's series ended its run, Jagjit Uppal was hired to resuscitate Bahadur. He swapped Bahadur's favored outfit of a saffron kurta for a skintight pink jersey, worn with cropped hair, and relocated him to Bombay, where his enemies were drug barons and arms smugglers. Together, the two authors brought to the project trite plots, bombastic dialogue, gauche sentimentalism, and the lurid machismo of popular Indian cinema, giving Bahadur a head start in gaining his cult status, which peaked in the 1980s. **HS**

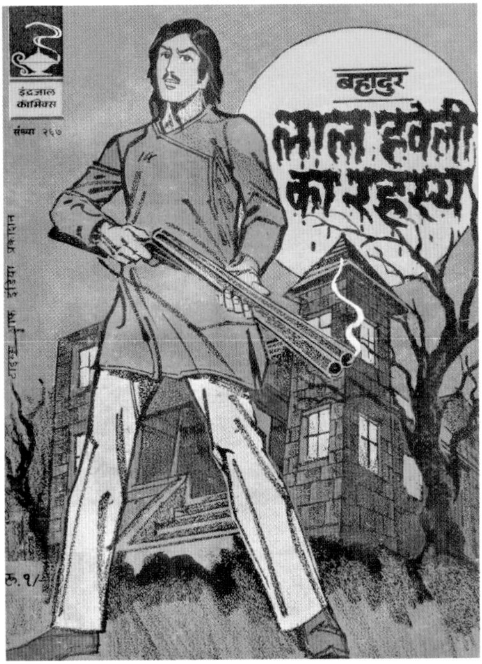
बहादुर
लाल हवेली का रहस्य

Similar reads

Dara, The Drug Barons Kamini Uppal and Pradeep Sathe
Detective Moochwala Ajit Ninan
Gardhab Das Neelabh and Jayanto Banerjee
Handa Bhonda Narayan Debnath
The Savage Oulaws Jagjit Uppal and Pramod Brahmania

working man's nightmare

STORY BY HARVEY PEKAR
ILLUSTRATED BY GERRY SHAMRAY

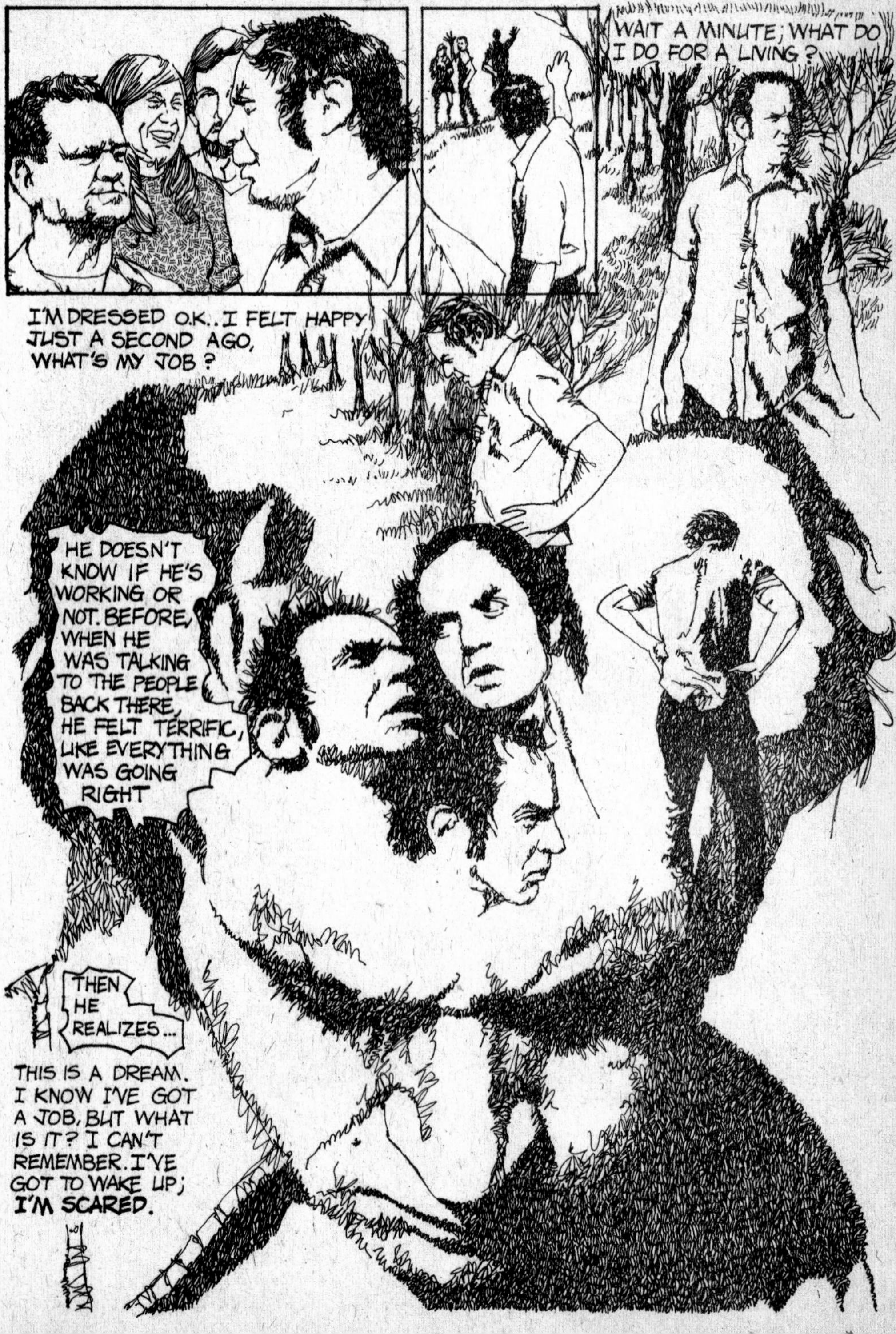
WAIT A MINUTE; WHAT DO I DO FOR A LIVING?
I'M DRESSED O.K.. I FELT HAPPY JUST A SECOND AGO, WHAT'S MY JOB?
HE DOESN'T KNOW IF HE'S WORKING OR NOT. BEFORE, WHEN HE WAS TALKING TO THE PEOPLE BACK THERE, HE FELT TERRIFIC, LIKE EVERYTHING WAS GOING RIGHT
THEN HE REALIZES...
THIS IS A DREAM. I KNOW I'VE GOT A JOB, BUT WHAT IS IT? I CAN'T REMEMBER. I'VE GOT TO WAKE UP; I'M SCARED.

American Splendor 1976

Harvey Pekar / R. Crumb and others

First published by Harvey Pekar (USA)
Creators Pekar (American, 1939–2010); Robert Crumb (American, b.1943)
Genre Reality drama

American Splendor is an autobiographical comic written by Harvey Pekar, the title of which is ironic. Unless he wins the lottery or lives through an unexpected thrilling adventure, there's nothing brilliant in the life of an everyman file clerk from Cleveland. Or is there? That's the point, really: it depends on where we look for brightness. Maybe there's more brilliance in simple everyday occurrences than in vacuous space operas.

In general, there are four kinds of stories in *American Splendor*: those in which there's no beginning, middle, and end (Pekar just cuts us a slice of everyday life, producing what we could call the "Harvey Pekar ending" in which there's no conclusion, the story just stops). There's also the stories in which Pekar pontificates on a particular subject, be that jazz or comics, exhibiting the pace of a stand-up comedian (silent panels before any given strip's "punch line" add gravitas or simply aid the comic timing). There are also stories about some person or other that Pekar knew, mainly in his work place, or heard about. Finally, there are stories in which the main interest is the transcription of an ethnic accent—as a jazz critic, Pekar was interested in the way people talk.

Pekar never attempted drawing properly himself. He created his scripts with rough grids and stick figures. A few great comics artists cocreated his stories: Robert Crumb (a fellow Clevelander who had a huge influence on Pekar's interest in the comics medium), stylist Frank Stack (who provided the art on *Our Cancer Year*, covering Pekar's brush with cancer), and the comics reporter Joe Sacco. **DI**

Sjef van Oekel 1976

Wim T. Schippers / Theo van den Boogaard

First published by Rijperman/Oberon (Netherlands)
Creators Schippers (Dutch, b.1942); van den Boogaard (Dutch, b.1948) **Genre** Adult humor, Alternative
Award Stripschapprijs (1989)

Theo van den Boogaard, one of eleven children in a Dutch Catholic family, was a comic strip virtuoso from his youth. Starting in the 1950s, he drew his own strips, inspired by Belgian comics creators Willy Vandersteen and André Franquin. While still in high school, his first self-made strip was published—a small comic book starring his comical detective hero Mark—and sold door to door by his father.

Van den Boogaard freely enjoyed the American *MAD Magazine* virtuosos, and, after moving to Amsterdam, drugs and his own gayness, too. In 1966, he began an impressive series of experimental cartoon strips and caricatures in a range of periodicals and styles. His work was regularly printed in a large format in the Dutch alternative press magazines *Hitweek* and *Aloha*, namely his *Striptease*, a *MAD*like satire, and his playfully erotic *Witje* strip series (featuring guest writers, such as Jan Donkers). In 1969, just as comix (X-rated U.S. comics) first reached the Netherlands, he created *Ans en Hans*, a comic strip that dealt with serious erotic and social issues.

In 1976, he teamed with writer Wim T. Schippers and they gave the looks of the Dutch actor Dolf Brouwers to the lead character in *Sjef van Oekel,* a strip full of taboo subjects published in the Dutch weekly *Nieuwe Revu*. Since then, van den Boogaard has adopted Hergé's pictorial approach with magnificent results—his finely detailed and colored artwork has become particularly "hot" in advertising and has appeared virtually everywhere in the Netherlands. **HvO**

← The art style of *American Splendor* varies with each of Pekar's different artistic collaborators.

Swan 1976

✐✐ Kyoko Ariyoshi

First published by Shueisha (Japan)
Creator Japanese (b.1950)
Genre Teen, Soap opera
Influenced by *Kitty and a Girl*

Ballet has been a popular theme for Japanese girls' manga ever since the genre was established. Typically, traditional ballet manga were set in small dance studios in Japan, and the plots usually consisted of fierce rivalries between ballerinas battling for the lead role. But in the 1970s, when real Japanese ballerinas began performing overseas, authors of ballet manga responded by moving their stories abroad as well.

One such manga, *Swan*, illustrates the life of Masumi, a country girl from Hokkaido, in Japan, who dreams of becoming a dancer. Thrown into the harsh and intense world of ballet, she endures both defeat and success, eventually flourishing globally, from Tokyo to London's Royal Academy of Dance, from the Bolshoi Ballet of Moscow to the New York City Ballet. Ariyoshi is evidently well versed in ballet, and the evidence is in her knowledge of ballet, techniques, competitions, and the lives of ballerinas backstage. Critics have praised her work for capturing the nature of the dance form.

Ariyoshi's distinguished artwork combines her G-nib pen's inks with dainty whites created using a fine tip brush, forming lines as delicate as the wings of a fairy. This distinctively original style is considered the author's signature. Ariyoshi's stunning illustrations are a feast for the eyes, with many fans regarding the work as an art book more than a comic.

Despite it being over three decades since *Swan* was first published, it remains in print today, along with its serialized sequel *Maia—Swan Act 2*, which chronicles the story of Masumi's daughter, Maia. **TS**

Mämmilä 1976

✐✐ Tarmo Koivisto

First published by Käyttökuva (Finland)
Creator Finnish (b.1948)
Genre Drama
Award Lempi Grand Prix (1991)

It's hard to find anything resembling Tarmo Koivisto's *Mämmilä* in the whole history of comics—or any art form either, for that matter. *Mämmilä* follows the contemporary history of the titular town over thirty years. As the series progressed, Koivisto painted an accurate picture of a small Finnish town developing from a relatively agrarian community to a participant in the global economy.

The model for *Mämmilä* is the town of Orivesi, an unremarkable place in the middle of Finland that happens to be Koivisto's birthplace. Instead of a small number of protagonists, the series has a cast of dozens of all ages and classes. They grow older in real time, some die, and a new generation is born.

Over the years *Mämmilä* covers a dizzying range of aspects of Finnish society—political, economic, sociological, and personal. In the beginning, many of the homes in the town lack electricity, and by the end its local entrepreneurs are doing business in the capital of the European Union. Readers see wooden houses change to cement buildings, politicians and business people scheming together behind the scenes, the arrival of the first African refugee, and so on. Koivisto draws in an economic, realist style, and his storytelling is inspired primarily by Carl Barks.

Mämmilä proved very popular, and the Finns recognized themselves within its pages—sometimes a bit too well. At least one reader attempted to sue Koivisto for violation of privacy, suggesting that events in the comic were taken directly from real life. **HR**

Mask of Glass 1976

Suzue Miuchi

Title in original language *Garasu no kamen*
First published by Hakusensha (Japan)
Creator Japanese (b.1951)
Genre Romance, Drama

Written by Suzue Miuchi, *Mask of Glass* is one of the world's longest running manga series. The core of the plot is the rivalry between two actresses—the main character, Maya Kitajima, and Ayumi Himekawa—who are battling for the lead role in a legendary play called *The Crimson Goddess*. What has kept readers captivated all these years is the extremity of the characters' passions for acting. When Maya is given the role of a doll, she fixes bamboo splints on to her entire body to give herself authentic movement, and in another scene Ayumi electrocutes herself to understand her character's emotions. The actresses' harsh and demanding preparation regime continues as they get tangled up in this fervent tale of complex relationships.

Equally intriguing is the turbulent history of the manga itself. First launched in 1976, it appeared in the biweekly *Bessatsu hana to yume* for more than twenty years, but in 1997 the series ceased serialization. It was then republished in collected editions starting from the beginning, but Miuchi changed the plot dramatically in these versions. In later volumes she redrew and rewrote her stories, completely ignoring the original plot. After its forty-first collected volume, Miuchi's rate of publication slowed considerably—the next volume was not released for another six years, with a further five-year wait for the next volume after that. Fortunately for impatient fans, the manga has now resumed serialization in *Bessatsu hana to yume*, and enough new material had appeared by 2010 for a further two collections to be published. **TS**

花とゆめ COMICS

ガラスの仮面

美内すずえ 1

Also by Suzue Miuchi

Amaterasu
Bara Monogatari
Dynamite Milkpie
Shirayuri no Kishi
Yokihi-den

Dark Thoughts 1977

✏️ André Franquin

Title in original language *Idées Noires*
First published in *Spirou* (Belgium)
Creator Belgian (1924–97)
Genre Adult humor

Widely hailed as a star genius of humor in the galaxy of Franco-Belgian comics, André Franquin took everyone by surprise in 1977 when his *Dark Thoughts* (*Idées Noires*) started appearing in *The Illustrated Trombone* (*Le Trombone Illustré*), a supplement to the children's magazine *Spirou*, and later in the adult monthly *Fluide Glacial*. Of course, it too was humorous, but whereas *Gaston Lagaffe*, today recognized as one of Franquin's unparalleled key works, conveyed a rather consensual, happy, schoolboy humor, these strips introduced a darker element: the humor of despair.

Indeed, the title says it all—as does its cover, which depicts Franquin as a paragon of depression. Perhaps this self-portrait is not far from the truth: almost everyone who knew Franquin mentions his dark view of life and his tendency toward chronic depression.

The inside pages are in keeping with the cover: a succession of one-page gags, quick and sharp, with the punch line usually based on the sudden, violent death of the involuntary hero. The graphic treatment of almost all the characters and situations in black on a white background enhances the power of the presentation. It should also be pointed out that the desire to indulge in hollow laughter is not the only driving force involved. Franquin took advantage of the opportunity to settle scores with groups of people he detested: hunters, the military, sports stars, and all institutions with binding rules. *Dark Thoughts* confirms an observation that so often turns out to be true: within most great comedy writers there lies a sleeping tragedian. **NF**

Maus 1977

✏️ Art Spiegelman

First published in *RAW* magazine (USA)
Creator American (b.1948)
Genre Biography
Award Pulitzer Prize (1992)

Art Spiegelman, the successful coeditor of U.S. comics anthology *RAW*, is the son of Holocaust survivor Vladek Spiegelman. Vladek is, in many ways, not a likable character: he is racist, exceptionally thrifty, and overwhelmingly difficult. His manner infuriates his son, creating a tense relationship between them. Yet when Spiegelman asks his father to tell his story of life during the war, an extraordinary tale of survival emerges. When placed in the context of the Holocaust, Vladek's frugal ways transform into exceptional resourcefulness.

Vladek is a privileged man at the start of the war. Drafted into the soon to be defeated Polish army, he is discharged in time to see the Holocaust begin in earnest: the creation of the ghettos, the executions, and "evacuations." With an extraordinary instinct for survival, Vladek goes underground with his wife, Anja, living from day to day on the streets of Sosnowiec. However, their luck does not last, and they are taken to Auschwitz.

In his artwork, Spiegelman portrays the Jews as mice and the Germans as cats, the Poles as pigs, and so on. It is a darkly effective approach, referencing both the anthropomorphic tradition of comics and the Nazi metaphor comparing Jews to a plague of rats. Spiegelman also bares his troubled soul for all to see, making the book not only about his father's incredible feats of survival, but also his own terrible guilt at surviving, a guilt that carries on through generations. *Maus* is possibly the finest, most extraordinary, and most powerful Holocaust memoir, and, as such, one of the most important comics ever published. **BD**

Spiegelman's anthropomorphic treatment of the Holocaust has won him awards and critical acclaim. ➡️

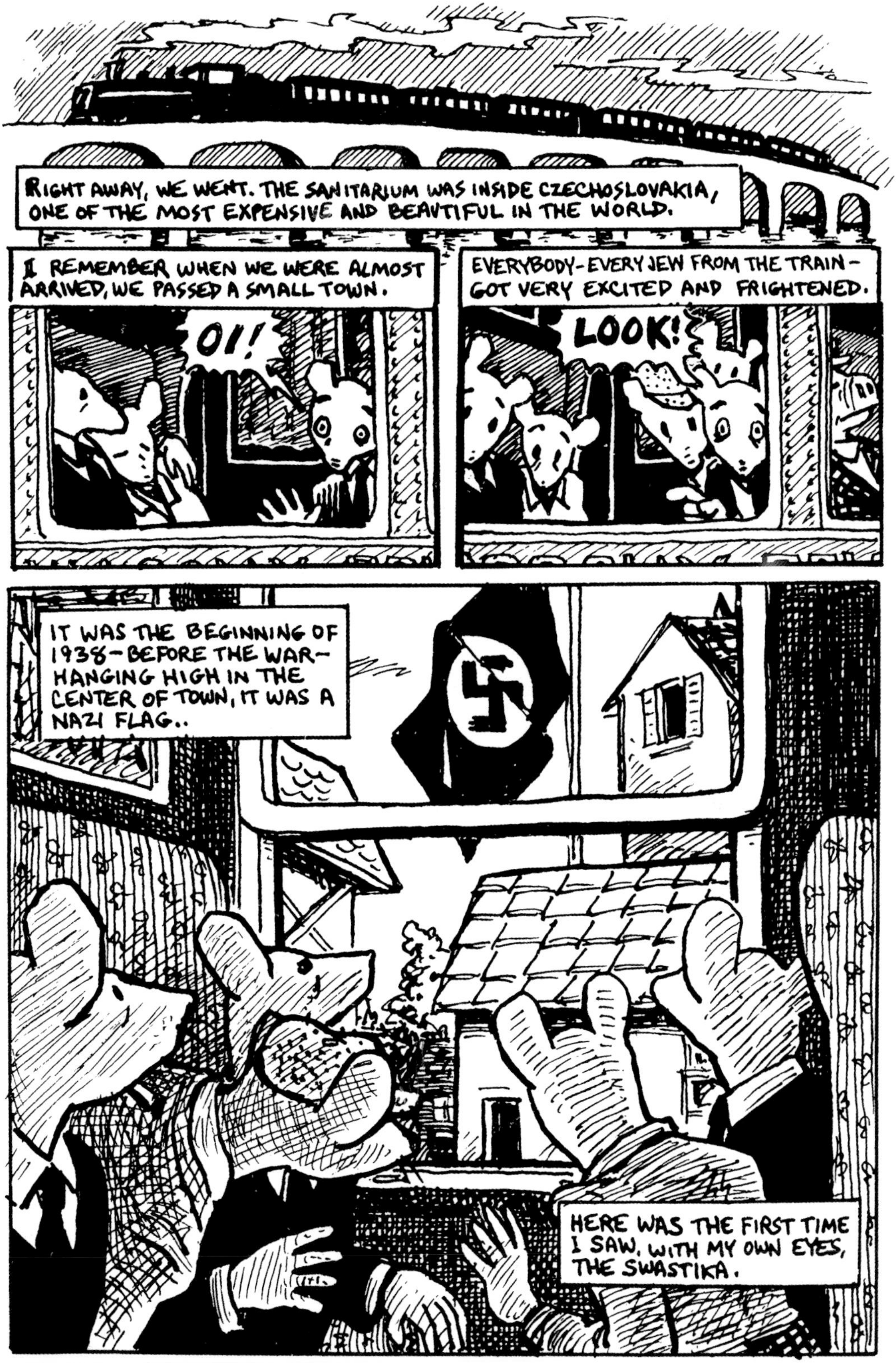
RIGHT AWAY, WE WENT. THE SANITARIUM WAS INSIDE CZECHOSLOVAKIA, ONE OF THE MOST EXPENSIVE AND BEAUTIFUL IN THE WORLD.
I REMEMBER WHEN WE WERE ALMOST ARRIVED, WE PASSED A SMALL TOWN.
OI!
EVERYBODY- EVERY JEW FROM THE TRAIN- GOT VERY EXCITED AND FRIGHTENED.
LOOK!
IT WAS THE BEGINNING OF 1938 - BEFORE THE WAR - HANGING HIGH IN THE CENTER OF TOWN, IT WAS A NAZI FLAG..
HERE WAS THE FIRST TIME I SAW, WITH MY OWN EYES, THE SWASTIKA.

Yakari and the Beavers 1977

"Job" "Derib"

Title in original language *Yakari chez les castors*
First published by *Spirou* (Belgium)
Creators André Jobin (Swiss, b.1927); Claude de Ribaupierre (Swiss, b.1944) **Genre** Children's

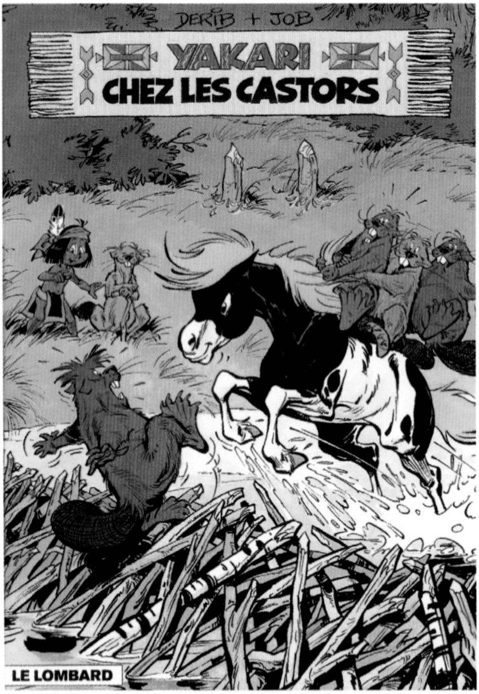
DERIB + JOB
YAKARI
CHEZ LES CASTORS
LE LOMBARD

Similar reads
Calvin and Hobbes Bill Watterson
Johan and Peewit (Johan et Pirlouit) Peyo
Owly Andy Runton
The Smurfs (Les Schtroumpfs) Peyo
Uncle Scrooge Carl Barks

A gentle series with no shocking conflicts deliberately aimed solely at younger children, the *Yakari* series is about a little Sioux boy who explores the countryside surrounding him in the days long before there was danger from white men or other tribes. What's more, Yakari has a special skill: the ability to communicate with animals.

A prodigiously talented artist in his teens, Derib moved to Belgium and landed a job working with Peyo on *The Smurfs*, later graduating to his own strips in *Spirou*. Job followed a career in journalism by founding *Le Crapaud à Lunettes*, a children's magazine, for which he hired Derib in 1967. Their first collaboration starred the comical owl Pythagore (Pythagorus), and their next introduced Yakari to the world.

Having discovered he can talk to animals after saving his pony in the first story, Yakari engages with another form of wildlife in each volume. He comes to understand how they live and to respect their environment. While animals act in almost human fashion around Yakari and communicate with him in turn, his friends lack such skills and cannot understand the animals at all. *Yakari and the Beavers* was the third of what is currently a thirty-five volume series of graphic albums. Job and Derib had already the established the format of Yakari's tales by this point, and it is as charming as the others. Yakari meets the beavers when he accidentally rides his pony through their dam. Having realized his mistake, he helps repair the damage and visits frequently thereafter, getting to know the beavers individually. This is also a volume where Yakari's friend Rainbow, becomes the first person to learn Yakari can speak to animals.

In the wake of its success, the series was adapted as animation in the 1980s, with a further, more acclaimed adaptation following in 2006. **FP**

Marie-Gabrielle of St. Eutrope 1977

Georges Pichard

Georges Pichard was one of a kind, an illustrator of extraordinary suppleness and variety whose early broad, comedy approach gradually evolved into an intricate and voluptuous style. His grasp of crosshatching makes Robert Crumb look clumsy, and his sense of page and panel design are exquisite, culminating in several works that are almost baroque in their complex balance and ornamentation. Unfortunately, his most eye-catching work generally features large-breasted, doe-eyed women being tortured in increasingly convoluted ways, usually by nuns. It can therefore be difficult for some people to reconcile an admiration for his immense artistic ability in the comic book form with his controversial subject matter.

Marie-Gabrielle of St. Eutrope is the pinnacle of his work, both in terms of art and sadism. It rolls the Sadeian picaresque format into a parody of a religious tale that tells you all the salacious details while pretending to offer moral instruction, and features several stories-within-stories that counterpoint each other.

Marie-Gabrielle takes her aged husband to a nunnery where dissolute women are sent to be purged of their wicked ways—which include "crimes" such as becoming pregnant out of wedlock or having feminist thoughts—to pick out a new servant from among the "saved." Along the way, she disapprovingly tells him the histories of several of the women being held there as they watch the extremely enthusiastic sisters punishing their charges. Of course, inevitably she winds up in the same place, having caused the death of her cuckolded husband, to be redeemed through pain herself.

Pichard creates a subtle context for all this debauchery through his command of facial expressions, and throughout there is a rich vein of humor, sometimes broad but often wry. *Marie-Gabrielle of St. Eutrope* works on so many more levels than just an erotic comic. **FJ**

First published by Glénat (France)
Creator French (1920–2003)
Genre Erotic
Influenced by Marquis de Sade

Marie-Gabrielle
Pichard

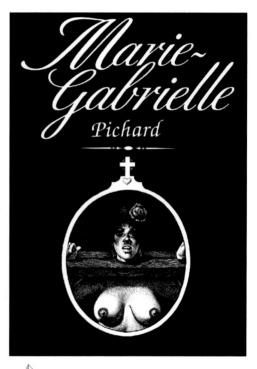

Also by Georges Pichard

Blanche Epiphanie
Caroline Choléra
Paulette
Submerman
Ténébrax

Den
Neverwhere 1977

Richard Corben

First published by *Heavy Metal* (USA)
Creator American (b.1940)
Genre Fantasy
Influenced by Film: *Neverwhere* (1968)

ARIEL BOOKS
27624/$7.95 ($8.75 in Canada)
NeverWhere
An Illustrated Epic Adventure Of Fantasy And Magic
RICHARD CORBEN
Foreword by FRITZ LEIBER

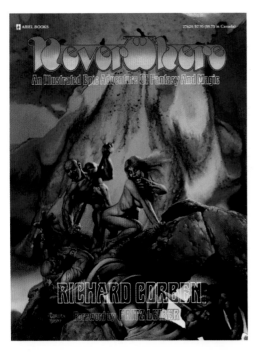

Similar reads
Arzach Moebius
Batman/Judge Dredd: Judgment on Gotham John Wagner, Alan Grant, and Simon Bisley
Conan: Red Nails Roy Thomas and Barry Windsor-Smith
Hellblazer: Hard Time Brian Azzarello and Richard Corben

Den comes to consciousness, naked, in a desert, barely aware of his own name, surviving on instinct. Having found shelter for the night, he discovers a lizard man drinking water but does not approach him. When an Indian girl, naked but for a noisy headdress, appears, Den decides to follow her. During a fight with the lizard man, who had also been following the girl, Den is knocked unconscious and remembers his name, David Ellis Norman, a man who built a gateway to another world.

After his uncle's disappearance, David had found instructions for the creation of a device that opened a hole into another universe. It was in stepping through in search of his uncle that David/Den found himself in the desert. Later, following a mysterious sorceress, Den intercedes to prevent a human sacrifice, and, after a desperate fight, finds himself in the company of a woman named Katherine Wells. Like Den, she comes from another time and place—London in 1892—and has been transformed in this new world.

The sorceress is using sacrifices to draw an ancient being to this strange world in an effort to try and control it. Rebels, led by Gel, who claims knowledge of Den from the past, oppose her and capture Den and Katherine, planning to kill them to prevent the sorceress from using them herself.

The strip is inspired by the works of Edgar Rice Burroughs (particularly his John Carter novels), the horror universe of H. P. Lovecraft (the being that the sorceress is summoning is called "Uhluhtc"), and pulp sword and sorcery tales. Although David is a scrawny young man, once through the portal Den is huge, heavily muscled, and very well endowed. Corben's artwork has an airbrushed realism, whether it's used for Den's muscles or the many weird and wonderful creatures that populate Neverwhere. Every page bursts with color, from the blue insects to the oily sky. **NFI**

Adèle Blanc-Sec
The Mad Scientist 1977

Jacques Tardi

A prolific young cartoonist, Jacques Tardi had already created the character of Adèle Blanc-Sec, a tough, impulsive, emancipated writer/adventuress, and penned her first two adventures before the more widely acclaimed third installment, *The Mad Scientist*, was published. The plot is set in Paris in January 1912, during the Belle Époque. In order to find material for the plots of her books, Adèle carries out investigations in the shadier parts of the city, coming into contact with a varied array of ruffians, crooks, and cranks of every kind.

Here, she crosses the path of a small community of scientists. The scientists have decided to bring to life a 300,000-year-old primitive man, *Pithecanthropus*, whose body has been miraculously preserved in the ice fields of Siberia. Against all expectations the experiment is successful, but it later goes out of control. One of the scientists takes possession of the creature and unveils his crazy plan: to make him the prototype of a new race of soldiers of the future, completely loyal to him. A series of chases through the spectacular setting of a snow-covered Paris at night follows, reaching its climax at the foot of Notre Dame cathedral.

The Mad Scientist includes most of the characteristics that form the appeal of Adèle Blanc-Sec's adventures: the endless twists and turns, the larger-than-life characters, an all-embracing sense of fantasy—not forgetting the irony and humor that are present throughout. The stamp of Adèle's character is also substantial and such an emphasis is common in comics today, but the choice of a woman to star in a series of adventures in the 1970s was a true innovation. The charm of the series also owes much to the enthusiasm of Tardi for the Paris of yesteryear, evident in much of his work. Under his brush, the city itself becomes a fully fledged character in the saga of Adèle Blanc-Sec. **NF**

Title in original language *Les Aventures extraordinaires d'Adèle Blanc-Sec: Le savant fou*
First published by Casterman (Belgium)
Creator French (b.1946) **Genre** Adventure

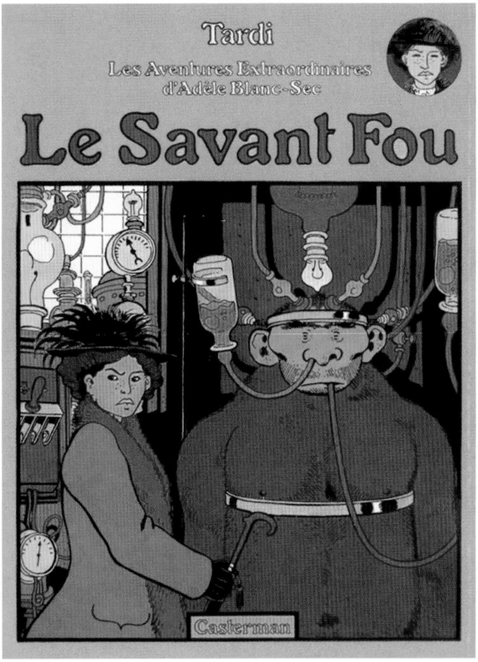
Tardi
Les Aventures Extraordinaires d'Adèle Blanc-Sec
Le Savant Fou
Casterman

Other Adèle Blanc-Sec adventures

Adèle and the Beast (*Adèle et la bête*)
Mummies on Parade (*Momies en folie*)
The Demon of the Eiffel Tower (*Le démon de la tour Eiffel*)
The Infernal Labyrinth (*Le labyrinthe infernal*)
The Secret of the Salamander (*Le secret de la salamandre*)

X-Men
The Phoenix Saga 1977

Chris Claremont John Byrne

First published by Marvel Comics (USA)
Creators Claremont (American, b.1950); Byrne (Canadian/American, b.1950)
Genre Superhero, Soap opera

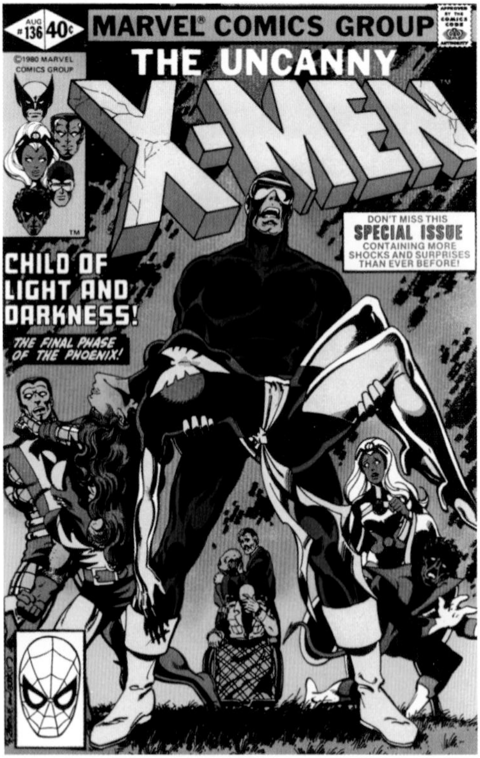

AUG #136 40¢
MARVEL® COMICS GROUP
©1980 MARVEL COMICS GROUP
THE UNCANNY
X-MEN
DON'T MISS THIS SPECIAL ISSUE CONTAINING MORE SHOCKS AND SURPRISES THAN EVER BEFORE!
CHILD OF LIGHT AND DARKNESS!
THE FINAL PHASE OF THE PHOENIX!

"Most of us were loners 'fore we became X-Men. The team's kinda given us the family we never had."

After Len Wein relaunched Marvel's team of mutant superheroes in 1975, Chris Claremont was tasked with writing their monthly adventures. After a brief run paired with artist Dave Cockrum, Claremont was joined by illustrator John Byrne in 1977. Their partnership on the title soon exemplified the depth of collaboration that is possible when two contrasting personalities explore their differences within a shared creative enterprise. The liberal Claremont and more conservative Byrne's conflicting attitudes are crystallized in the relationship between founder member and X-Men field leader Cyclops (Claremont), and the more cocksure, streetwise newcomer Wolverine (Byrne). Cyclops is the epitome of the team player, always using his powers responsibly and proportionately. Wolverine is the ultimate maverick, only operating reluctantly in the context of a team, and constantly challenging Cyclops's authority. Wolverine's loyalty is chiefly to his own ruthless but consistent code of honor. The remaining team members—Banshee, Colossus, Nightcrawler, and Storm—lend extra dimensions and subtler shades of meaning to this absorbing battle of wills.

The other surviving member of the original X-Men on the team (apart from their patriarch, Charles Xavier) was Jean Grey. Jean provides a natural focus for the rivalry between Cyclops and Wolverine, while simultaneously undergoing an extraordinary transformation herself into the ultrapowerful Phoenix, a potent being capable of great malevolence. This sinister metamorphosis poses an insoluble dilemma—what can be done with an individual in possession of world-destroying powers over which they do not have complete control? The Byrne/Claremont themes of group loyalty and individual self-knowledge are best expressed in their earlier stories, but their run is still a high-water mark in superhero storytelling. **RR**

Batman
Strange Apparitions 1977

✎ Steve Englehart and Len Wein ✎ Walt Simonson and Marshall Rogers

First published by DC Comics (USA)
Creators Englehart (American, b.1947); Wein (American, b.1948); Simonson (American, b.1946); Rogers (American, 1950–2007) **Genre** Superhero

With the first of the stories reprinted in this collection (which collects the *Batman* strips from *Detective Comics* #469–79 apart from issue #477), Englehart begins a series of subplots that received great acclaim from the comic's readers. Ostensibly facing the threat of Dr. Phosphorus, out to irradiate the whole of Gotham, Batman finds himself on the wrong side of the law when the City Council uses Commissioner Gordon's inactivity (due to injury) to make him persona non grata. The council's leader is Rupert Thorne, who's looking to eliminate Batman and increase his own influence in Gotham through his elevated position.

In the meantime, Bruce Wayne has met socialite Silver St. Cloud, who soon becomes his lover. When Bruce checks into a clinic to heal radiation burns he suffered while fighting Dr. Phosphorus, he is captured and unmasked by Professor Hugo Strange, who tries to sell Batman's identity to Batman's old foes. Thorne is also keen to learn Batman's identity and tortures Strange, but the Professor takes the secret to his grave.

That is ostensibly where the "apparitions" come in, as Strange's ghost appears in subsequent issues, helping Batman against the Joker and seeking revenge against Thorne. As for Silver, she too has unmasked Bruce as the Batman during his battle with Deadshot, but doesn't know what to do with the knowledge.

With stories that also involve Robin and the Penguin, Englehart covers much of what made Batman so popular. In many respects, this is the definitive Batman—a great detective, fighting on the edge of the law, but always with the interests of Gotham City in mind. While Simonson's work on the run suffers from some unsympathetic inks, the artwork by Rogers (inked by Terry Austin) ranks with the most iconic, with Batman a figure of the shadows, muscular yet lithe in action. **NFI**

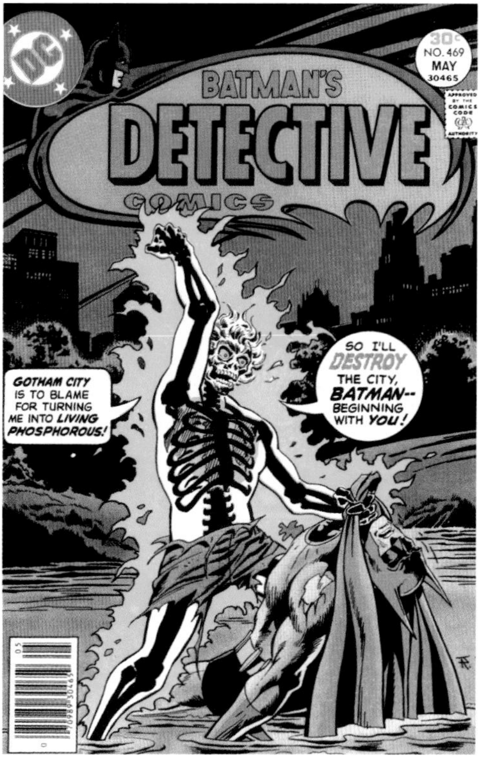
30¢
NO. 469
MAY
30465
BATMAN'S
DETECTIVE
COMICS
GOTHAM CITY IS TO BLAME FOR TURNING ME INTO LIVING PHOSPHOROUS!
SO I'LL DESTROY THE CITY, BATMAN-- BEGINNING WITH YOU!

"Just now I saw the Batman in action . . . I saw you—the man inside! The man I love!"

Reid Fleming: World's Toughest Milkman 1977

David E. Boswell

ACTION!
THRILLS!
ROMANCE
REID FLEMING
WORLD'S TOUGHEST MILKMAN
WANNA MAKE SOMETHING OF IT ?

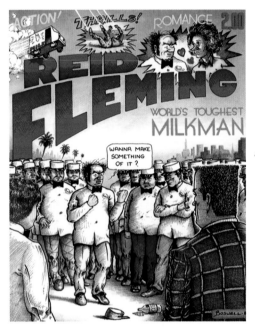

"I need rope! A hundred feet of rope, and make sure it's nylon! That milk is under pressure and could blow at any second!!"

Similar reads

Buddy Does Seattle Peter Bagge
Destroy Scott McCloud
Flaming Carrot Bob Burden
Milk and Cheese Evan Dorking
Naughty Bits Roberta Gregory

First published by David E. Boswell (Canada)
Creator Canadian (b.1953)
Genre Humor
Influenced by Josef von Sternberg

Reid Fleming is one of the great comic archetypes—an unimportant man who is perpetually angry, constantly confrontational and contrary, always wildly overreacting, "just because." When called a "skinhead" he chases down the culprits and blows up their car. The reader is left with a guilty admiration for this no-nonsense milkman's outrageously ballsy manner and way of behaving, yet his bravura rage ultimately gets him nowhere. The grandfather of countercultural slacker comic humor, Fleming's brief appearances are instantly memorable.

He bursts out of the page, a hard-drinking every(milk)man with a case of rye in the back of his truck. He behaves abysmally toward his employers and customers alike, threatening to urinate on their flowers if they don't pay their bills, and driving over their property with wild abandon. He is a man of simple pleasures: he wants to do his round as quickly as possible—assaulting anyone who makes fun of his uniform and getting one over on his hated supervisor Mr. Crabbe along the way, if he can—so that he can return home as soon as possible to watch television.

The jokes revolve around drunken milk float chases, his narcoleptic best friend's manhood, and his ultra square boss's attempts to get him fired, which always go awry. Boswell's work is immensely detailed, although later strips did loosen up a little, allowing for a greater sense of energy in the linework and some more frenetic action in the chase sequences. He reworks the same basic series of gags to great effect, always keeping one step ahead of his audience. **FJ**

Galaxy Express 999 1977

✐✐ "Leiji Matsumoto"

Title in original language *Ginga etsudo 999*
First published in *Shonen Gahosha* (Japan)
Creator Akira Matsumoto (Japanese, b.1938)
Genre Science fiction

Akira Matsumoto's science fiction space opera rarely appeals to mainstream audiences. Even his most successful mangas, such as *Otoko Oidon*, *Space Battleship Yamato*, and *Captain Harlock*, rarely appeal to non sci-fi fans. *Galaxy Express 999* is an exception, however, in attracting a far wider audience, and is considered the author's masterwork.

The story is based around a boy named Tetsuro Hoshino who joins the beautiful Maetel on a journey on the *Galaxy Express* through space. Tetsuro's destination at the end of the line is a faraway planet where he could potentially receive an immortal machine body for free. The pair travel to various planets, and Tetsuro gradually matures as new friends come and go.

Matsumoto's simple concept of an everyman character like Tetsuro going on an adventure with a beautiful woman is the ultimate fantasy of male readers. This, combined with the sudden sci-fi boom in 1970s Japan, made the comic a massive hit, consequently cementing Matsumoto's name in the genre. The comic was intended to be a fantasy set in space that also illustrated Tetsuro's coming of age in a *Bildungsroman*.

Inspired by Kenji Miyazawa's novel *Night on the Galactic Railroad* (*Ginga tetsudo no yoru*), the comic first appeared in *Weekly Shonen King* in 1977. While its animated series was also a hit, many fans were annoyed that it concluded the story before the original comic. Nevertheless, Matsumoto's masterpiece has since been developed into numerous spin-offs, guaranteeing that Tetsuro is in for a very long journey indeed. **TS**

The Beach Café 1977

✐✐ Régis Franc

Title in original language *Le Café de la plage*
First published in *Le Matin de Paris* (France)
Creator French (b.1948)
Genre Funny animal

Somewhere at the end of the world, with the infinity of the sea as the only horizon, the Beach Café provides for its handful of customers. In this world at the edge of the world, which is at the same time minimalist and full of detail, the cast are anthropomorphic animals. They deliver monologues, converse on all subjects—trivial or profound, funny or wicked, vain or surprisingly insightful—or just lie on the beach thinking.

The ensemble cast of characters, polished dialogue, and framing choices are evocative of the big screen, and within a few years of the strip's publication and massive success, its creator Régis Franc entered the world of film himself—both in front of and behind the camera—while continuing his work as a strip cartoonist.

Designed within the constraints of brevity as a daily newspaper strip, *Le Café de la plage* appeared in the center-left *Le Matin du Paris* between 1977 and 1980, and has neither a beginning nor an end. Instead it is a river, a stream, fed by digressions, flashbacks, and asides with numerous twists and turns.

Both in tone and in its form, the strip is an unusual creation that is very different from the rest of French comics culture. Paradoxically, this could be why it has had such a lasting impression on the medium. Subtly distanced, full of ironic references to literature and film, Franc's strip has attracted a wide audience thanks to the originality of its narrative while also maintaining an almost experimental nature. It is a genuine tour de force for *bandes dessinées*. **NF**

Lum 1978

✏️ Rumiko Takahashi

Title in original language *Urusei Yatsura*
First published by Shogakukan (Japan)
Creator Japanese (b.1957)
Genre Teen, Science fiction

Urusei Yatsura—the Japanese title actually translates roughly as "Those Obnoxious Aliens"—was the first major work of Rumiko Takahashi, the so-called "Princess of Manga." Its roots can be found in *Those Selfish Aliens* (*Katte na Yatsura*), a short story published in *Shonen Sunday* about Kei, a young paperboy kidnapped by a group of aliens.

Shortly afterward, Takahashi published the first chapter of *Urusei Yatsura* in the same magazine. The story begins as an alien race called the Oni invades Earth. Their leader declares, however, that they will halt the invasion if an Earthling defeats one of their race in a game of tag. The entrant for Earth is Ataru Moroboshi, a clumsy, lustful high school student; his opponent is Lum, the green-haired, tiger-striped bikini–wearing, sexy daughter of the alien chief. Ataru eventually wins the game and Earth is saved, but the price of his victory is high—Lum has fallen in love with him and plans to remain on Earth in an effort to win his heart. This leads to plenty of comical situations, resulting in one of the masterpieces of humor manga.

Urusei Yatsura ended its run in 1987 and was compiled into thirty-four volumes, paving the way for Takahashi's later successes. It was adapted into an animated series from 1981 to 1986, consisting of 195 episodes. Six full-length movies were produced, as well as a dozen OVAs (Original Video Animation, or animation specifically made for video). Viz Graphics published the series in English and renamed it *Lum* after the main character. **AMo**

Breakdowns 1978

✏️ Art Spiegelman

First published by Belier Press/Nostalgia Press (USA)
Creator American (b.1948)
Genre Alternative
Award Yellow Kid Award Best Foreign Author (1982)

If the only thing that Art Spiegelman had ever published was *Maus*, he could still be justifiably acclaimed as one of the most important cartoonists of all time. His 1978 collection, *Breakdowns*, gathered together a number of inspired short and experimental works in the comics form, testament to the cartoonist's aesthetic skill and astonishing intellectual curiosity.

Two of the most celebrated pieces included in the book relate to *Maus*, including the original three-page *Maus* strip published in *Funny Aminals*, and *Prisoner on the Hell Planet*, the autobiographical strip included in *Maus*. These strips, all created in 1972, suggest the scope of Spiegelman's artistic ambitions, as well as his experimentation with drawing styles. Other pieces expand the boundaries of the comics form through the playful manipulation of genre (*Ace Hole, Midget Detective*) or form (*Little Signs of Passion*).

Breakdowns also reveals Spiegelman's psychology more than any of his other works. The title refers equally to the process of arranging space on a comics page as to psychological crises. He finds, in the comics form, a near perfect way to express the anxieties that conflicted him. In this way *Breakdowns* can be seen as every bit as autobiographical as his more celebrated work.

The 2008 edition of *Breakdowns* contains material from the original book as well as a nineteen-page autobiographical introduction, *Portrait of the Artist as a Young %@&#!*. This mature piece demonstrates that, while Spiegelman's skills have evolved over the decades, his personal concerns have remained consistent. **BB**

Ranxerox 1978

Stefano Tamburini   Tanino Liberatore

First published by *Cannibale* magazine (Italy)
Creators Tamburini (Italian, b.1955);
Liberatore (Italian, b.1953)
Genre Science fiction

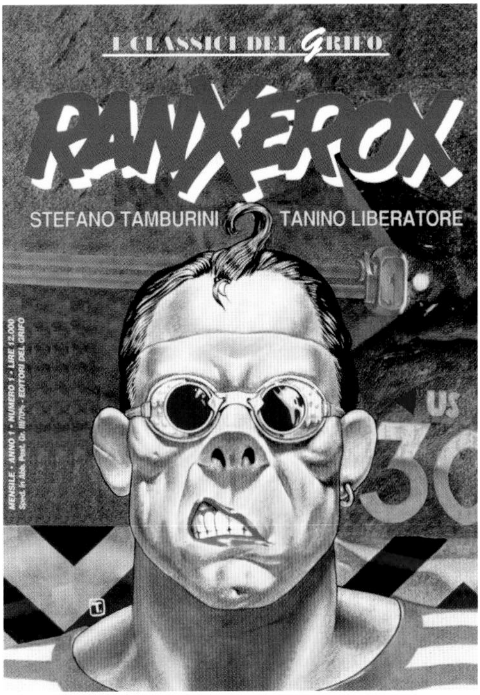

I CLASSICI DEL GRIFO
RANXEROX
STEFANO TAMBURINI
TANINO LIBERATORE

Ranxerox is a humanoid robot assembled by a university student by fitting together pieces of a Rank Xerox copier and other mechanical components. His stories are set in a violent and perverted megacity (loosely based on Rome) with almost Dantesque levels. Thanks to a loop in his circuits, the android falls in love with Lubna, a capricious Lolita of twelve who treats him mostly as her personal sex and drugs provider.

Their city adventures are absurdly violent; they deal with trisexual maniacs, the police, weird tycoons, and artists—when not taking drugs and meeting deviant friends, of course. Initially drawn by Stefano Tamburini, principal founder of magazines *Cannibale* and *Frigidaire*, and an activist in countercultural press initiatives such as *Stampa Alternativa*, and Andrea Pazienza, the series became a cult when Tanino Liberatore started delivering a new, hyperrealistic style on the pages of *Frigidaire* magazine. He redesigned Ranxerox as a nervous bodybuilder prone to sudden rages.

As a tragic parody of contemporary social struggles, with references to J. G. Ballard's visionary style and crude science fiction, *Ranxerox* is considered one of the leaders in Italian alternative comics. In 1980, the Italian subsidiary of Rank Xerox asked that the original name (*Rank Xerox*) be changed to avoid the brand's association with a character "whose adventures are a concentration of violence, obscenity, and foul language." The author's response was a panel where the character said, "So I'll have to break your asses," but he chose to change the name in the final version of *Ranxerox*. **MS**

"Ranxerox is a punk, futuristic Frankenstein monster, and with the underaged Lubna, they are a bizarre Beauty and the Beast."

Richard Corben, comic book creator

Similar reads

Aetheric Mechanics Warren Ellis and Gianluca Pagliarani
BrainBanx Elaine Lee and Jason Temujin Minor
Doktor Sleepless Warren Ellis and Ivan Rodriguez

The Star of Cottonland 1978

✐✐ Yumiko Oshima

Title in original language *Wata no Kuni Hoshi*
First published by Hakusensha (Japan)
Creator Japanese (b.1947)
Genre Fantasy, Romance

Yumiko Oshima debuted in 1968 with manga *Paula's Tears* (*Paùla no Namida*), which was serialized in *Margaret* magazine. A decade later, she launched *The Star of Cottonland* (*Wata no Kuni Hoshi*), which ran for nine years in *LaLa* magazine and, in 1979, it won the Kodansha Manga Award for girls' comics.

The plot opens with a forlorn, weak kitten, Chibi-neko, abandoned in a heavy rain, its white fur covered in mud. She is rescued by a young man named Tokio Suwano, who is studying to enter the law department of the local university. He takes Chibi-neko home, and the little kitten's new life with Tokio begins. Believing that she will one day grow into a human, Chibi-neko dreams of marrying Tokio. When Tokio meets the love of his life—a beautiful law student—the kitten is threatened and tries to grow up quickly. Throughout the story, Chibi-neko is drawn as a small girl with cat ears and a tail, although it is clear that the human characters only perceive her as a four-legged kitten.

Chibi-neko is further devastated to learn from Raphael, the leader of the cats in the neighborhood, that "a cat will always be a cat." Sympathetic, Raphael makes up a consolatory story about *The Star of Cottonland* (*Wata no Kuni Hoshi*), where a princess called Whitefield lives. He tells her that she must be Whitefield, but Chibi-neko is too young to realize that Raphael's storytelling is a signal of romance. While the story has a girls' comic sweetness, Oshima's careful dialogue expresses the characters' deep emotions while presenting the essence of human—and animal—nature with utter frankness. **TS**

HP and Giuseppe Bergman 1978

✐✐ Milo Manara

Title in original language *HP et Giuseppe Bergman*
First published by À Suivre (France)
Creator Italian (b.1945)
Genre Adventure

"Enough's enough!" is the exasperated cry that opens the first panel of *HP and Giuseppe Bergman,* a cry that encapsulates much of the spirit of the 1970s. In this story a production company with strange motives offers Giuseppe Bergman a chance to take part in a great adventure. In a bid to escape his mundane existence, Bergman decides to accept.

Bergman's destination is the great outdoors, where he is guided by a mysterious figure known only by the initials "HP." In time we learn that he is Hugo Pratt, the Italian comics master, whom Manara credits as an inspiration in his work. The meeting of the two men, and the subsequent start of the great adventure, prove sensational. Propelled into a remote region of the Upper Orinoco, Bergman meets dangerous animals and armed men, nearly drowns, and has other disturbing encounters. Also involved are drugs and sex (Milo Manara is masterly at drawing female bodies), without which no adventure is worthy of the name. Throughout the escapade, Bergman is conscious of the alternately irritated and amused gaze of HP, a father figure who is both helping Bergman and putting him under trial.

A vital work by an author in his prime, *HP and Giuseppe Bergman* is an adventure story that maintains a constant and subtle balance between the adventure itself and commentary upon it. It is a fascinating and enjoyably cynical reflection on the relationship between the real and the imaginary. Milo Manara, who later specialized in erotic works, never regained the tone and narrative sophistication of this book. **NF**

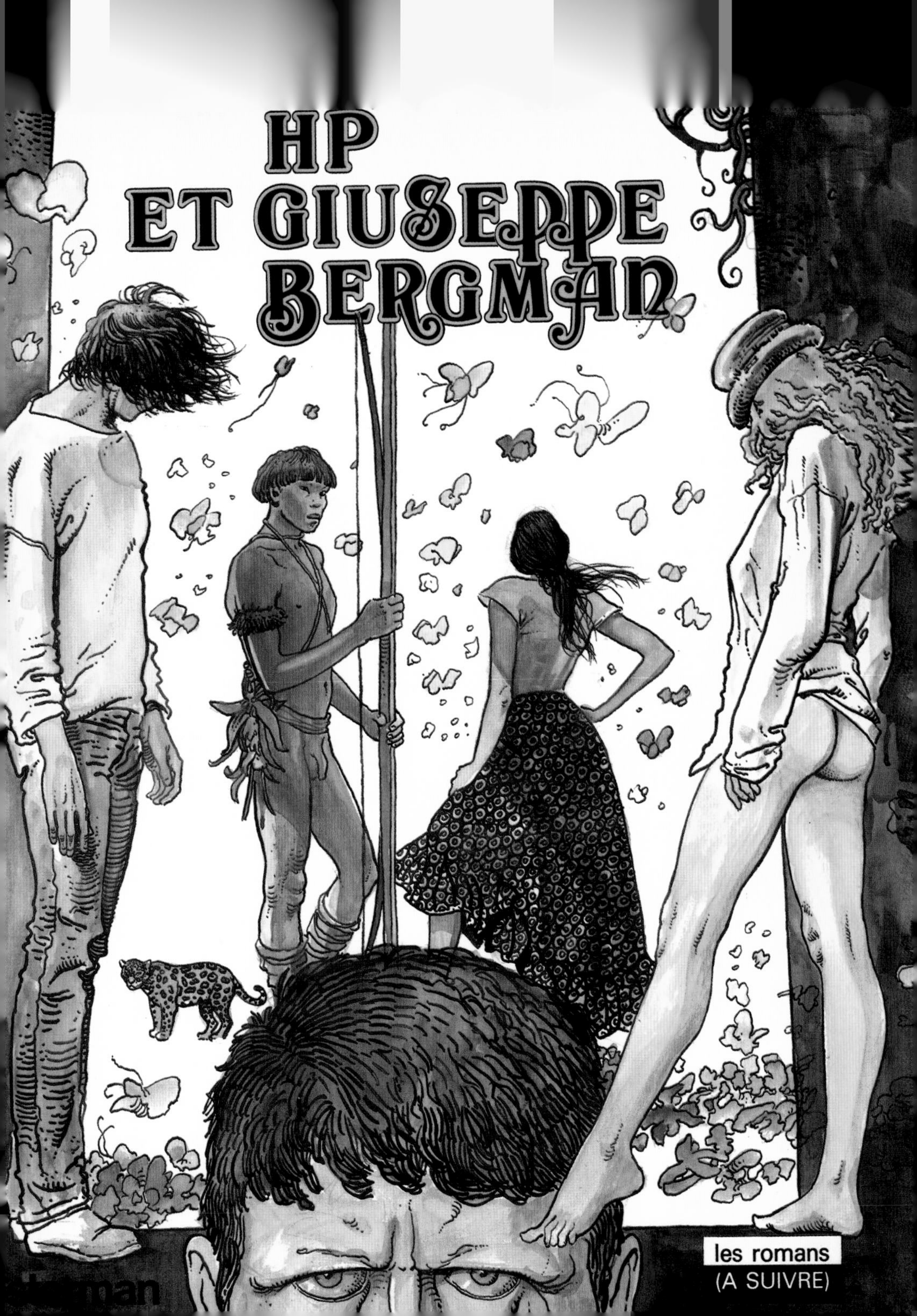
HP
ET GIUSEPPE
BERGMAN
les romans
(A SUIVRE)

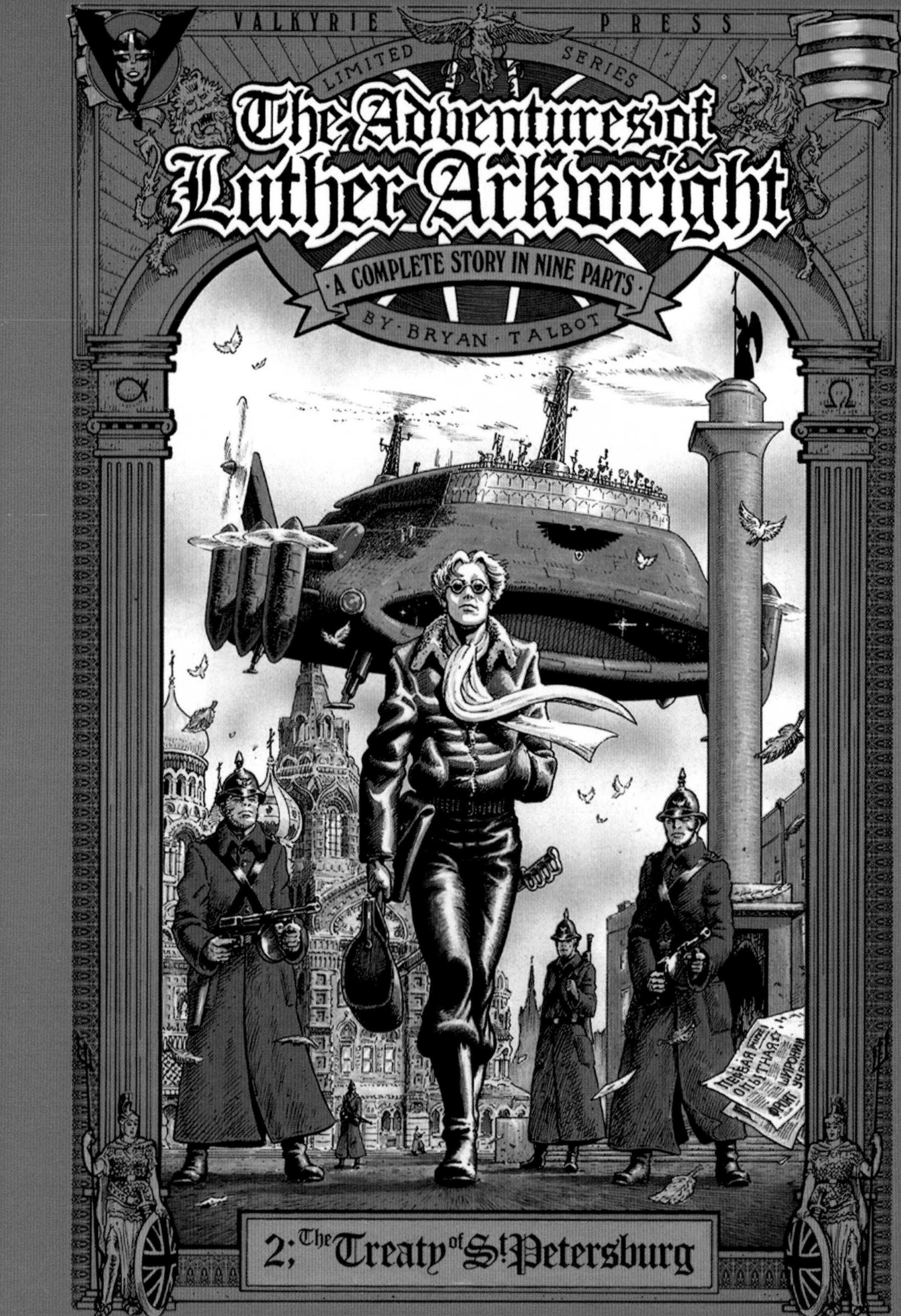
VALKYRIE PRESS
LIMITED SERIES
The Adventures of Luther Arkwright
A COMPLETE STORY IN NINE PARTS
BY BRYAN TALBOT
2; The Treaty of St Petersburg

The Adventures of Luther Arkwright 1978

Bryan Talbot

First published by Brainstorm Comics (UK)
Creator British (b.1952)
Genre Science fiction
Awards Four Eagle Awards (1988)

Luther Arkwright is utterly unique—the only man capable of crossing parallel dimensions and who has no dimensional counterpart. An agent of the idyllic central parallel 00.00.00, Arkwright is engaged in the cross-dimensional battle against the Disruptors—agents of chaos and destruction. Arkwright discovers an opportunity to draw out the Disruptors on parallel 00.72.87. In this world the puritanical rule of Cromwell and his descendents has been prolonged for hundreds of years by Disruptor agents, who took the Royalists's side and disrupted the balance of power in the British Empire. What follows is a tale of civil war, adventure, and derring-do, the story of a new messiah, and an excellent piece of science fiction.

Arguably Britain's first graphic novel, *The Adventures of Luther Arkwright* is a highly ambitious piece of work, meticulous in both style and substance. It shares many similarities with both *Doctor Who* and *Jerry Cornelius*, but comfortably holds its own against such comparisons. Highly experimental, it pushes the visual narrative of comics into new and relatively untried areas, including the use of subliminal hidden imagery, fragmented nonlinear narrative, and a highly elastic time perception.

Drawing on satirist William Hogarth and similar artists for inspiration, Talbot's beautifully rendered art feels historically familiar and very British. He effortlessly portrays epic events with grandeur and complexity, yet never drops the ball. *Luther Arkwright* is the cutting edge of comics; too complex and confusing for some, but if you stick with it, it will reward you. **BD**

Ken Parker
Ballad of Pat O'Shane 1978

Giancarlo Berardi *Ivo Milazzo*

Title in original language *Ken Parker: La Ballata di Pat O'Shane* **First published by** Edizioni Cepim (Italy)
Creators Berardi (Italian, b.1949); Milazzo (Italian, b.1947)
Genre Western

This is the most famous Italian Western comic since *Tex* and it boasts a cult status for its brilliant writing style and its vision beyond traditional stereotypes. Its main inspiration is *Jeremiah Johnson*, a movie directed by Sidney Pollack and starring Robert Redford, whose face was used as a model for Ken. Like Jeremiah, Parker is a trapper, and readers follow his adventures and travels across the American Frontier in the Old West. During the series Ken evolves profoundly and faces an array of existential and social issues, including racism, workers' rights, politics, and social exclusion.

Ken is more a victim of events than a hero, as he is forced to deal with situations bigger than he is, and is often defeated. He is rarely the leading character, with many victimized characters taking center stage: Eskimos, American Indians, and abused or cheated people. In this story, Ken is mistaken for a dangerous outlaw awaiting trial. Pat is an orphan seeking the criminal who murdered her family. She attends the trial and, fascinated by Ken's humanity, rescues him from prison by pretending to be his daughter. Too young for adult responsibilities, she is one of the best female characters created by Giancarlo Berardi, offering both a complex and realistic personality that enriches the story.

Combined with Ivo Milazzo's fine ink brushwork, Berardi offers a masterful example of his cinematic style of writing. There is a memorable "silent" sequence without captions or dialogue that is underlined only by some lyrics—like a movie soundtrack especially composed to create a mood. **MS**

Theories of Everything: Selected, Collected, Health-Inspected Cartoons 1978

Roz Chast

First published by *The New Yorker* (USA)
Creator American (b.1954)
Genre Humor
Award Honorary Doctorate of the Fine Arts (1988)

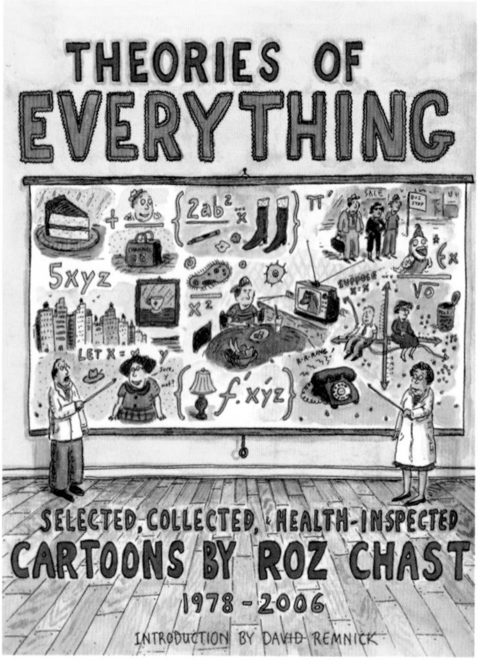
THEORIES OF
EVERYTHING
5xyz
SELECTED, COLLECTED, & HEALTH-INSPECTED
CARTOONS BY ROZ CHAST
1978 - 2006
INTRODUCTION BY DAVID REMNICK

A longtime contributor to *The New Yorker*, Roz Chast specializes in short, free-form gags that bridge the gap between the real and the surreal. Take, for example, Chast's "Bartlett's Unfamiliar Quotations," in which Plato advises us to never wear white after Labor Day, and Sigmund Freud suggests we get a subscription to "Schadenfreude Monthly" (unfortunately only available in Chast's world).

In many ways, Chast's strips echo Woody Allen's early stand-up comedy, in which neurosis is an end in itself. Her jokes feed upon self-absorption, her characters often so strenuously caught up in tiny details—the history of vanilla pudding, the biodegradability of their first novel—that they forget to live. A born and bred Brooklynite, Chast occasionally makes jokes that only native New Yorkers will understand, such as when she advocates the return of the "Miss Subway" pageant, albeit with some fundamental changes (the winners are not gorgeous young things but actual subway riders). But for the most part, her art simply expresses just how anxiety-inducing and vexing modern life can be.

"Outside of New York is so weird . . . you're in the middle of nowhere, but there's ALL THIS STUFF!"

Over Chast's career, her obsessions—mathematics, medicine, the suburbs, and processed foods—have waxed and waned. This was especially true during the Bush years, when her strips occasionally took a political turn. However, the stylistic trademarks of a Chast drawing—the angst-ridden faces, handwriting that comes as close to deadpan as it can, and her trademark watercolor tones—remain remarkably consistent. This collection will show you why Chast won her place as one of the brightest lights of American humor. **EL**

Similar reads
And the Pursuit of Happiness Maira Kalman
Lulu Eightball Emily Flake
Mondo Boxo: Cartoon Stories Roz Chast
The Complete Cartoons of The New Yorker Robert Mankoff

The Cartoon History of the Universe 1978

Larry Gonick

What's the unlikeliest combination to be found in a book? How about a title that could be considered a joke at first glance, a style of cartooning rooted solidly in 1960s underground comics, and a creator who graduated from Havard with a master's degree in mathematics? Larry Gonick's website welcomes you to the realm of the overeducated cartoonist, and it's a designation he backs up.

Having ascertained the title isn't a joke, consider the ambition—the history of the universe in cartoon form. In addition to delivering on the title, Gonick is a multitasking professor, slipping in lessons on philosophy, physics, mathematics, and plenty more besides. The project began as a series of comics, issued when paying work permitted the opportunity, then Doubleday took notice and commissioned volumes to sell in bookstores. Even then it took Gonick a further eighteen years to complete all five volumes.

"... [most accept] that the universe started with a bang, but no one can figure out how it's going to end!"

"Why start earlier than the birth of the universe?" asks Gonick, contemplating the original title. The final two are more commercially designated *The Cartoon History of the Modern World.* In terms of the universe humanity is a recent development, and the first volume picks up in the 1300s.

Gonick has a passion for his topics, but his style is anecdotal, punctuated by pomposity-pricking gags and endearing references to the creation of the strips. It's an adaptable format that has served him well, with spin-off projects galore. Although often somewhat looser in style, all are worth investigating for sugar-coated education or just plain entertainment. **FP**

First published by Rip Off Press (USA)
Creator American (b.1946)
Genre History
Award Inkpot Award for Excellence in Cartooning (1999)

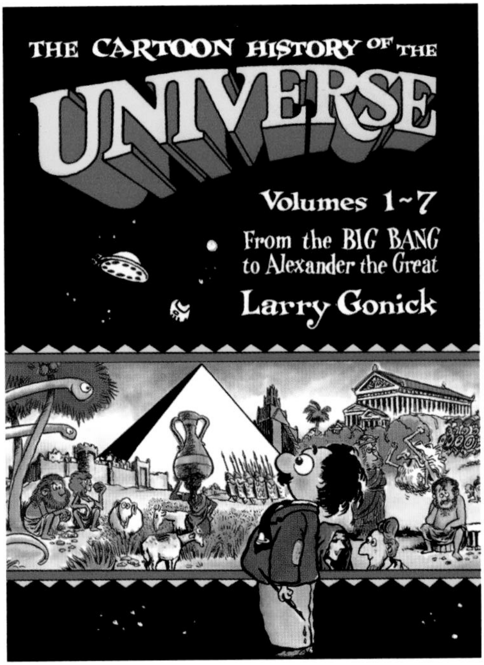
THE CARTOON HISTORY OF THE
UNIVERSE
Volumes 1~7
From the BIG BANG to Alexander the Great
Larry Gonick

Also by Larry Gonick
Kokopelli and Company
Kokopelli and Company: Attack of the Smart Pies
The Cartoon Guide to the Environment
The Cartoon Guide to Physics
The Cartoon Guide to Sex

Genius 1978

✐✐ John Glashan

First published by *Observer Magazine* (UK)
Creator John McGlashan (Scottish, 1927–99)
Genre Satire
Award Glen Grant Strip Cartoon Award (1981)

John McGlashan's Italian mother was from Lucca and his father was the Scottish painter, Archibald A. McGlashan. John attended Glasgow School of Art, but in the 1950s failed to make it as a London portrait painter. From 1959 on, shortening his last name to Glashan, he began publishing cartoons in the pocket-sized *Lilliput* magazine and elsewhere.

A uniquely personal style steadily emerged. Crazy cartoons peopled by bearded minimen drawn in black pen lines, who were dwarfed even more by vast architectural backgrounds and watercolor washes. Often comic strip–like, in page-long sequences, all frameless art and text, they were full of deeply philosophical thoughts by tiny men burdened with huge problems.

Not the least of his problems was that he was extremely well-trained in fine art but stayed forever bitter at his personal failure in it. In the 1950s comics were still being written off in *The Times Literary Supplement* as "a kind of literature not to be read, only looked at." But he wanted to be seen, to be read, to be paid. His wide-ranging comments on everything in the art, design, literature, and money establishments were often goofy and always razor sharp.

His masterpiece was *Genius*, a weekly strip cartoon about numbers, formulas for success, and making money. It starred wee inventor Anode Enzyme (IQ 12,794 and penniless), who was helping out Lord Doberman, the richest man in the world. Glashan's frameless strip drawings were often numbered. In the end he settled for landscape painting. **HvO**

Beau Peep 1978

✐ Roger Kettle ✐ Andrew Christine

First published by *The Daily Star* (UK)
Creators Kettle (Scottish, b.1951);
Christine(Scottish, b.1947)
Genre Humor

On the face of it, the brutal existence traditionally endured by the French Foreign Legion doesn't seem to be the ideal topic for a four-panel gag strip. Perhaps that setting indicates the level of original thinking that has kept the strip running for over thirty years. Nearly all the recurring characters were in place from the earliest days. Myopic Bert Peep joined the Legion to escape his formidable wife. His companions are the dim Dennis, the spontaneously violent Mad Pierre, incompetent chef Egon, Colonel Escargot, whose grip on sanity is tenuous, and Sergeant Bidet, within whom burns the near extinguished flame of efficiency. The generally incomprehensible Hamish turned up later as a means for Roger Kettle to satirize his hometown of Dundee.

The strip is a classic of setup and punch line, with recurring themes that never stray into repetition, a fine line few have trodden successfully for so long. Andrew Christine has claimed to be embarrassed by his early art, but the fundamentals slipped into place rapidly. Kettle had subscribed to *MAD Magazine* and was an avid *Peanuts* reader, but chanced on comics as a career. Applying for a journalist's position at Scottish publishers D. C. Thomson, he was asked to consider comics.

Christine also graduated from D. C. Thomson, and among his pre-Peep freelance assignments was Benny Hill's strip in *Look-In*. *Beau Peep* was launched along with *The Daily Star*, but Kettle recalls seventeen rejections beforehand. Collections are currently out of print, but strips are archived at www.beaupeep.com or available via auction. **FP**

The Rocketeer 1978

Dave Stevens

First published by Pacific Comics (USA)
Creator American (1955–2008)
Genre Superhero
Adaptation Film (1991)

Dave Stevens's entire penciling career, excluding cover illustrations, consists of fewer than 150 pages, with *The Rocketeer* making up 118 of those, which he completed over a seventeen-year period. His first professional employment was assisting Russ Manning in producing the Sunday *Tarzan* newspaper strip.

Stevens learned that drudgery, repetition, and long hours were staples of a regular career producing comics, and knew that wasn't for him. When *The Rocketeer*'s first publishers, surprised by the enthusiastic response to six pages in an anthology title, attempted to impose a schedule, it was destined never to work. Already employed in animation, Stevens couldn't maintain the schedule. *The Rocketeer* would outlive three publishers before completion, during which time Stevens earned a living doing film storyboards and illustrations.

Stevens set the adventure story in the 1930s, and the plot has stunt pilot Cliff Secord strapping on a prototype rocket pack to rescue a colleague at an air show. This attracts the attention of foreign spies, who want the rocket for themselves. Stevens researched period detail extensively, returned illustrative techniques to comics, and modeled his cast on real people. Secord's mechanic was comics and animation legend Doug Wildey, with whom Stevens was working in 1978. The 1950s glamour model Bettie Page was retrospectively paid for the appropriation of her likeness for Cliff's girlfriend. Stevens has a lot of fans for a man who claimed he rarely achieved the standards he set himself. **FP**

THE ROCKETEER
by
·DAVE STEVENS·
Introduction by
HARLAN ELLISON
all 5
ACTION
CHAPTERS

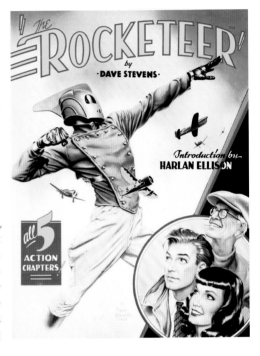

"I'm not averse to drawing superheroes, it's just at this point in time it's not as important to me as cheesecake."

Dave Stevens

Similar reads

Bettie Page Comics Jim Silke
Classic Star Wars Archie Goodwin and Al Williamson
Pin-Up Yann and Berthet
Somerset Holmes Bruce Jones and Brent Anderson
The Black Pearl Mark Hammill and Eric Johnson

Garfield 1978

✎ Jim Davis

First published by United Feature Syndicate (USA)
Creator American (b.1945)
Genre Humor
Award Best Humor Strip Cartoonist (1982)

Who could have guessed that the successor as top dog in the world of newspaper strips—taking the place of Charles M. Schulz's Snoopy—would turn out be a grumpy, lasagna-loving cat from Indiana?

Since 1978, when Jim Davis's *Garfield* first appeared in American newspapers, he has been building a fanbase that makes him the current world record holder as most widely syndicated comic strip. A misanthropic rebel, even by feline standards, Davis's kitty creation refuses to eat cat food, hates to do exercise of any kind, and treats his human and canine companions—hapless Jon and drooling Odie, respectively—with contempt. He may not sound like promising material for a cartoon strip, but Garfield, using a kind of dry humor that only a cat could pull off, managed to win the love of millions of global fans by just being himself, spawning a merchandising empire in the process. Perhaps Garfield is the kind of rule-breaker we would all love to be: curt with those who bore us, harsh to those we feel superior to, happy to eat anything warm, fresh, and delicious, and saying what we dare not.

With the future of the newspaper in doubt, the newspaper strip must also adapt, and Garfield has long been a pioneer in this regard, busting into film and television with gusto. While movies based on the franchise might not always be highly rated as artistic successes, they keep that fat orange cat in the center of the international collective consciousness—something newspapers increasingly struggle to do. This hilarious cat still has a few good lives left in him yet. **EL**

Garfield has the honor of being one of the most famous cartoon cats in history. ⬆

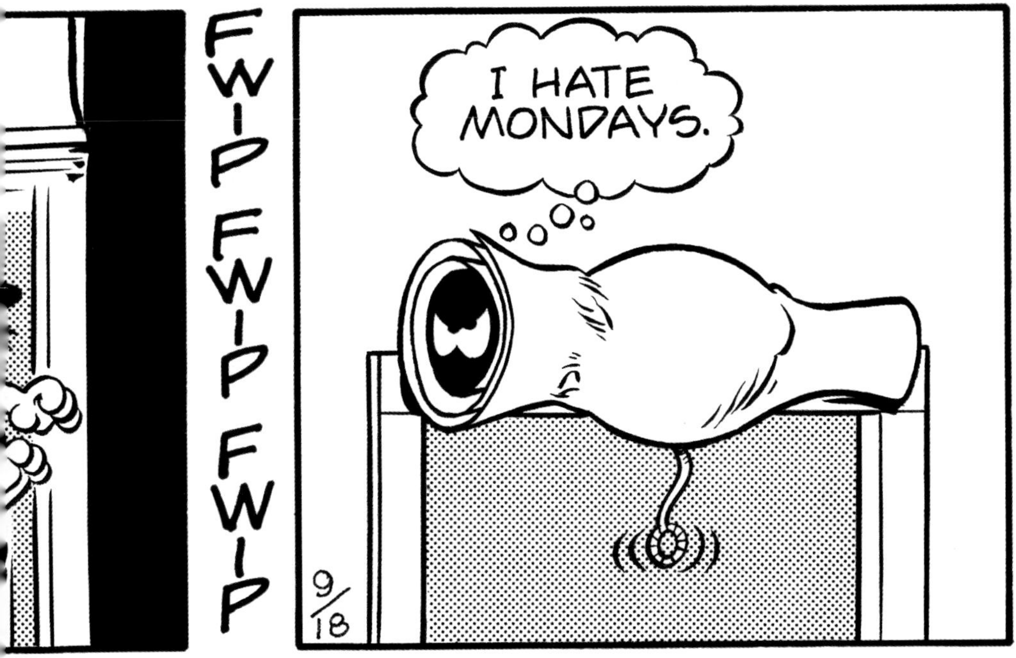
FWIP FWIP FWIP
I HATE MONDAYS.
9/18

Elfquest 1978

Richard Pini   Wendy Pini

First published by WaRP Graphics (USA)
Creators Richard Pini (American, b.1950); Wendy Pini (American, b.1951)
Genre Fantasy, Adventure

It may be cutesy, it may, over time and innumerable spin-offs and fan projects, have become sprawling and self-indulgent, but *Elfquest* is always good. When Wendy Pini and her astrophysicist husband Richard first created an idealized world of long-haired, huge-eyed elves riding on wolves and living in tune with nature, there was something of value in the idea.

At the center of the initial stories is a classic duo—Cutter, young and serious and not quite ready for the duties of being chief of the tribe, and Skywise, his wisecracking, older but more daring best friend. As humans start burning their forest home, they undertake a quest to search for their lost ancestors.

Pini's artwork is very clean-lined and attractive, her characters elegant, appealing, and childlike in their appearance. Initially the Pinis's storytelling ambitions were not so ambitious. The first fifteen or so black-and-white magazine issues develop plot rapidly as the questing elves find two versions of themselves—one that is a direct descendent of the legendary High Ones from whom all the elf people come, and the other barbaric. There are strong stand-alone stories and lots of work to individually characterize the many elves in Cutter's tribe, but soon it all changed.

Then things got complicated and, sadly, never as good. Although Wendy Pini continued to draw those *Elfquest* projects in which major events occur, she and her husband began writing for others. They handed over strands of the story to others, which currently spans over twenty-one centuries of Elf history. **FJ**

You Are There 1978

✎ Jean-Claude Forest ✎ Jacques Tardi

Title in original language *Ici Même*
First published by À Suivre (France)
Creators Forest (French, 1930–98); Tardi (French, b.1946)
Genre Adventure

With his bowler hat on his head, Arthur There spends his life running along the tops of the walls of Mornemont, a set of keys in his hand. In days gone by, his ancestors owned the whole of this vast area but a long succession of disputes between neighbors, as well as family arguments, resulted in the property being split up into numerous parcels of land, and he has been dispossessed of almost all his rights.

Only the walls and doors separating the parcels of land still belong to him, resulting in a strange situation: although driven off his land, Arthur There has complete control of all the comings and goings of those who have despoiled him. He even has—at the cost of a perpetual journey along the tops of the walls whenever someone rings for him—a right to open and close each of the entrances he controls. The money collected in this way serves to finance an endless trial, at the end of which he hopes one day to recover Mornemont. The plot thickens with the appearance of the compassionate, fierce little Julie, and the President of the Republic who, anticipating his next electoral defeat, hatches a complicated plot in which Mornemont is both the stake and the instrument.

Immersing oneself in reading *You Are There* is to discover a fascinating world and the prolific genius of Jean-Claude Forest, certainly one of the greatest storytellers of French comics in the 1960s and 1970s. Launched in 1978, this story, which was very innovative in terms of both content and format, has influenced a whole generation of writers. **NF**

A Contract with God 1978

✎✎ Will Eisner

Original title *A Contract with God, and Other Tenement Stories*
First published by Baronet Books (USA)
Creator American (1917–2005)
Genre Autobiography

It was the great comic book writer, artist, and innovator Will Eisner who helped popularize the term "graphic novel" by insisting his new work be treated as a novel and not as a comic. Eisner extended the comic book format to give substance and a sad nostalgia to his recollections of 1930s immigrant life and growing up in a Brooklyn tenement. His inspiration to create it came in the wake of his daughter's death, and through his grief Eisner brought the medium of the novel-length comic to a broader, more mature audience.

It consists of four interwoven short stories, all thematically linked, three of which occur in the same tenement building at 55 Dropsie Lane. The first story is the most personal and autobiographical: Frimme becomes angry at God when his daughter passes away because he did many good deeds and lived a virtuous life. In Frimme's estimation, God has reneged on their agreement. Life is hard here, and escaping the world of the tenements seems an impossible task. Eisner's towering urban backdrops conspire to keep them where they are, held fast within a fist made of bricks and mortar.

Frimme is transformed into an embittered, resentful man with an overwhelmingly sleazy appearance. The sense that he could not maintain his faith after his loss begs the question: was his contract born of faith or merely an attempt to safeguard himself from life's uncertainties? Groundbreaking for its time, Eisner's vignettes may seem somewhat naive now, but he still asks some very big questions. **BS**

Frimme berates God for the death of his daughter. ➜

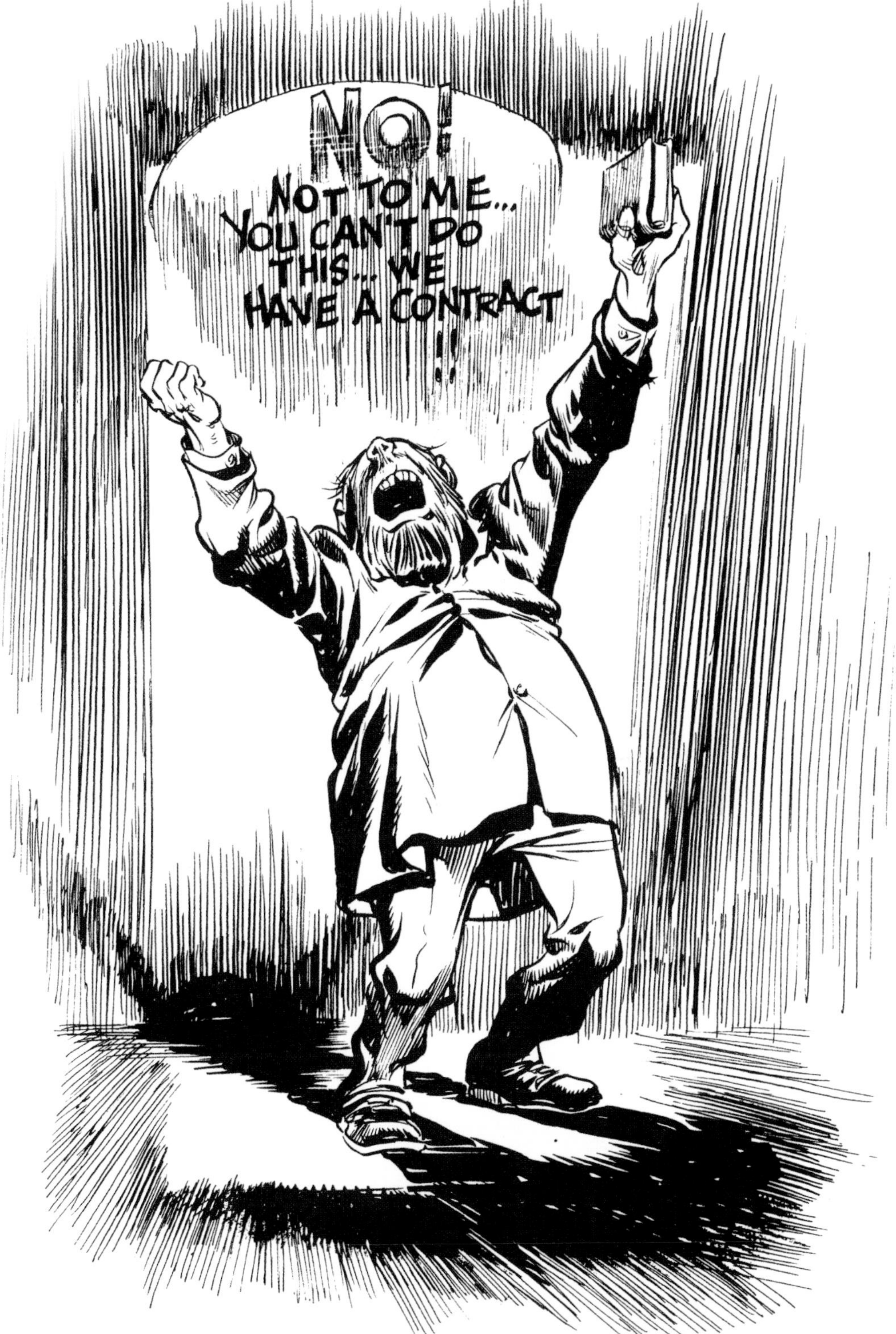
NO!
NOT TO ME... YOU CAN'T DO THIS... WE HAVE A CONTRACT!!

Omaha the Cat Dancer 1978

Kate Worley Reed Waller

No. 1
ADULTS ONLY
"OMAHA"
THE CAT DANCER
THE · FUNNY ANIMAL · NOVEL · by · REED WALLER

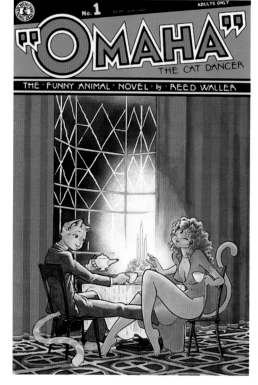

First published by Kitchen Sink (USA)
Creators Worley (American, 1958–2004); Waller (American, b.1949) **Genre** Erotic, Funny animal
Award Eisner Award Best Continuing Series (1989)

Omaha the Cat Dancer stands head and shoulders above the crop of liberal independent comics of the 1980s that celebrated sex. It's intrinsically about sex, rather than just featuring a lot of it, although it does that, too. Writer Kate Worley and artist Reed Waller, a couple when they began the book, created a sexy soap opera featuring anthropomorphic animals. In their magical, creative hands, even a chicken could be sexy.

Omaha the Cat Dancer is about a confident female cat named Susie Jensen, who, ironically, quits her male-dominated office job to become Omaha, a stripper. Her rich boyfriend Chuck fully supports the move, although his conservative father disapproves and will soon take steps to try and break them up. This is stripping as a feminist activity, and Omaha/Susie becomes involved in union politics and fighting antiporn protesters trying to shut down the club where she works. There are plenty of plot twists worthy of an American soap, and lots of animals getting it on, but the relationship between Omaha and Chuck is always central to the story.

Worley/Waller's view of the porn industry may be a bit starry-eyed—in a liberal society people ideally operate above board rather than be criminalized and ghettoized—but their understanding of relationships is mature and their wide cast of characters enables them to explore all sorts of emotions. The fur and feathers may put some people off, but they'd probably be put off by the liberal sexual agenda anyway. The sort of people who can get behind *Omaha's* politico-sexual agenda aren't going to be fazed by a tail or two. **FJ**

"A spunky, sexy, cleanly drawn, contemporary soap opera . . ."

Harlan Ellison, comic book creator

Similar reads

Diary of a Dominatrix Molly Kiely
Ironwood Bill Willingham
Lost Girls Alan Moore and Melinda Gebbie
Valentina Guido Crepax

Spirit of the Mountain Pastures 1978

✎✎ "F'murr"

Title in original language *Le Génie des Alpages*
First published by Dargaud (France)
Creator Richard Peyzaret (French, b.1946)
Genre Humor

They are called Côtelette, Particule, Gaelanne, Toussette, and Magouillette. They are the sheep spending the season in mountain pastures, guarded by an intellectual dog and his master, Athanase Percevalve, a lazy shepherd. They speak, as do all living things in those mountains, which are more fantastical than realistic. They live in groups but express sufficiently individual remarks to put an end to the commonly held prejudice that they do not have a personal opinion.

Behind them the scenery is amazing and constantly moving. In the fourth volume, *A Long Curly Silence* (*Un Grand silence frisé*), readers will see a lighthouse perched on a hilltop, an Indian on a funny flying tricycle, and the castle from the movie *The Lady with the Execrable Sock*, pushed by a stagehand. Two Swiss cuckoos throw themselves off the mountains that face each other to compete in a duel without apparent logic. The world of these stories from the Alps is close to nonsense.

Since its birth in January 1973 in the weekly magazine *Pilote*, a loyal public has been following the antics of this unusual herd. This pivotal volume sees the arrival of Athanase and marks a significant milestone in the series. The drawings of Richard Peyzaret, who signs his stories with the odd pseudonym F'Murr (or F'Murrr), become richer and more sophisticated over time.

The incoherence of the situations and the narratives barely conceal the social criticism that the author makes in his future works. *A Long Curly Silence* also includes three stories about Athanase's dream where he tames his flock. But this is only a dream. **CM**

Charley's War 1979

✎ Pat Mills ✎ John Colquhoun

First published by IPC Media (UK)
Creators Mills (British, b.1949);
Colquhoun (British, 1927–87)
Genre War

Charley's War was first printed in the weekly boys' comic *Battle Action* in 1979. The story follows underage Charley Bourne, who volunteers for the British Army in 1916 in the run-up to the catastrophic Battle of the Somme. Charley's initial enthusiasm is tempered by the grim realities of trench warfare as he copes with rats, flooding, poison gas, and daily bombardment by the Germans. The futility of conflict is vividly illustrated by the horrific loss of life, with the British Tommy as likely to succumb to the appalling leadership decisions of cowardly short-sighted officers as to enemy action.

The Great War is seen through the eyes of raw recruit Charley, and his harsh experiences are contrasted with his affectionate letters home. Pat Mills's reputation for meticulous historical research is present in each episode, while John Colquhoun's detailed art creates a hellish vision of life in the trenches, where death can come at any moment.

Mills later dropped the letters motif, which dragged the pace of the narratives, and following the end of the war, Charley and his friends were sent to fight in postrevolutionary Russia in 1919. Mills intended to end the story in 1933, with Charley broke and Hitler coming to power, but left the comic following a dispute. He was replaced by Scott Goodall, who took the story up to World War II and added a more conventional tone. However, the antiwar sentiments of these first episodes still stand up today. The original weekly stories have been collected and reprinted as part of an ongoing series from Titan Publishing. **TV**

Bernard Lermite 1979

Martin Veyron

First published by Editions du Fromage (French)
Creator French (b.1950)
Genre Humor, Adventure
Award Grand Prix du Festival de Angoulême (2002)

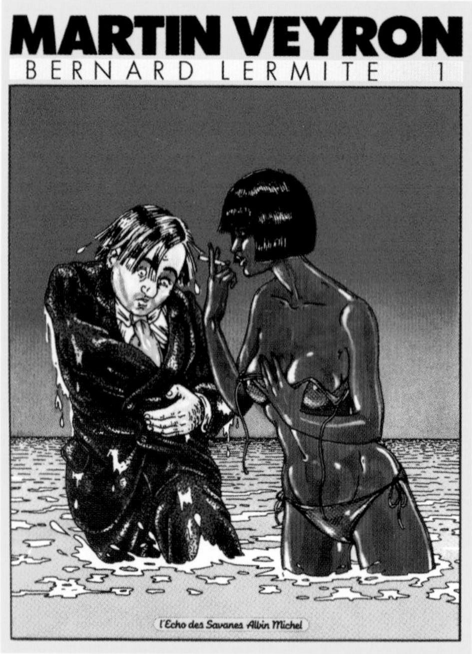
MARTIN VEYRON
BERNARD LERMITE 1
l'Echo des Savanes Albin Michel

Similar reads
Bienvenue à Boboland Charles Berberian and Philippe Dupuy
Cru bourgeois Martin Veyron
Donc, Jean Martin Veyron
Executive Woman Martin Veyron

The idle and permanently bemused young bourgeois Bernard Lermite first appeared in the journal *L'Echo des Savanes* in 1977, and then in album format starting in 1979. The first three albums are black and white, and the remaining four in color. The style has a slightly caricatural *ligne claire* realism, but the plots make no claim to credibility: the character is overtaken by chains of events considerably more improbable than those even in a *Tintin* adventure.

Like the adventurer with a quiff, Bernard Lermite finds himself on a desert island, but he has arrived there after being knocked off his bike by a hearse and subsequently embarking on a cruise with a not-so-grieving widow, who failed to foresee that her husband, who had gallantly faked his own suicide to facilitate his wife's dalliances with other men, would scupper the ship.

"Father Christmas doesn't deliver presents to all the children. / Just the good ones? / No, just the rich ones."

The appeal of the series lies in the offbeat and often cynical tone of the dialogue. The violent taboo-breaking of the 1960s has given way to inconsequential libertinage: sophisticated women are demanding in their sexual expectations of Bernard. This male fantasy is not without anxiety, though, prefiguring the terror of newly empowered professional women that looms large in Veyron's later albums.

In volume two, Bernard briefly regresses to infancy, and dreams of a line of breasts that turn into wolf heads with bared fangs. In volume four, the frenetic narrative is driven by a photograph of a dancer, an object of unquenchable desire. When the woman herself turns up in the plot, she is infinitely less alluring. **AM**

Bernard Lermite is characterized by humorous misadventures and lots of sex.

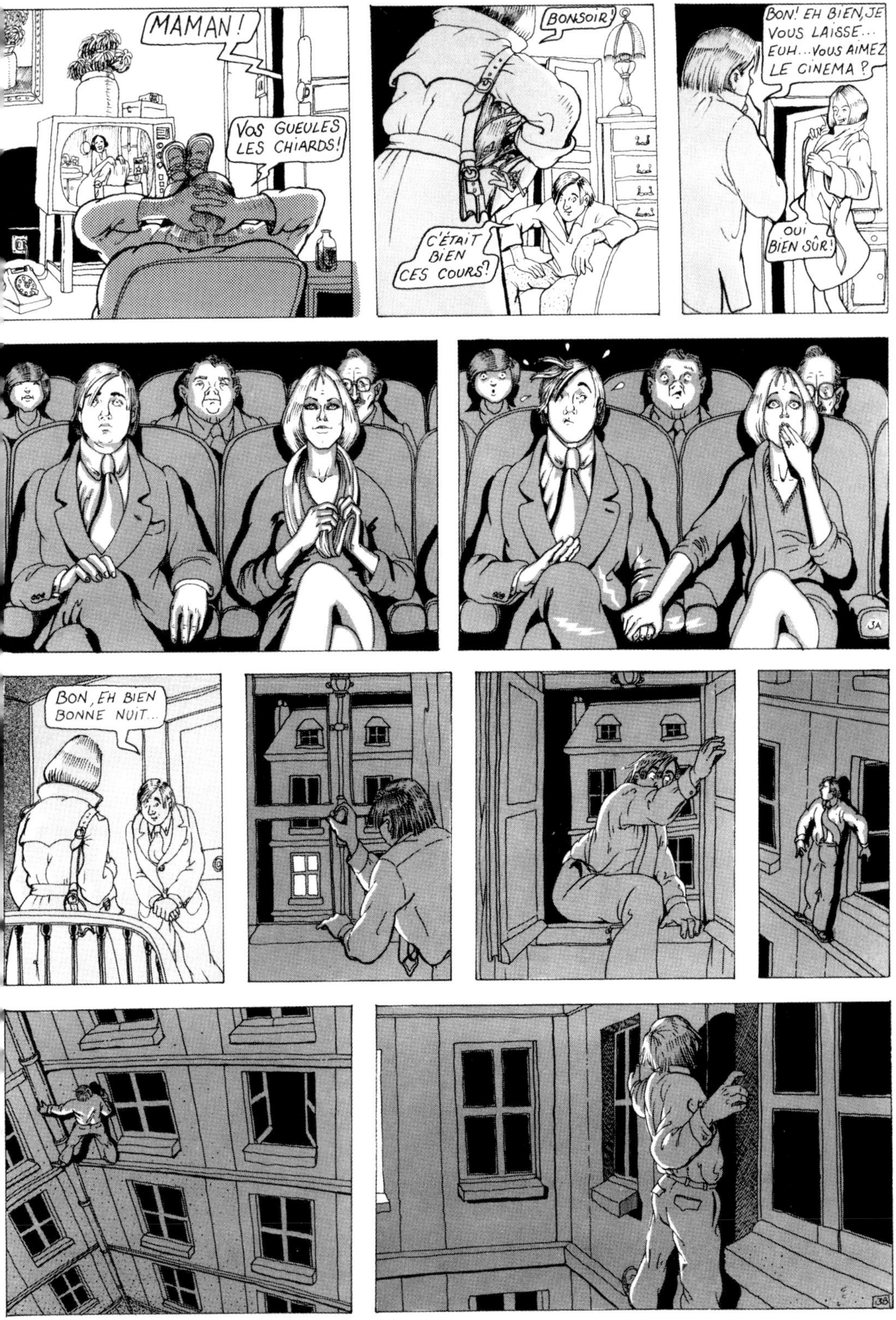
MAMAN!
VOS GUEULES LES CHIARDS!
BONSOIR!
C'ÉTAIT BIEN CES COURS?
BON! EH BIEN, JE VOUS LAISSE... EUH... VOUS AIMEZ LE CINEMA?
OUI BIEN SÛR!
3A
BON, EH BIEN BONNE NUIT...
3B

Viz 1979

✏️ Chris Donald, Simon Donald, and Graham Dury

First published by Self-published (UK)
Creators Chris Donald (English, b.1960); Simon Donald (English, b.1964); Dury (English, b.1962)
Genre Humor, Satire

Viz was a British humor publishing phenomenon in the 1980s and 1990s. In the early years it was quite outrageous, presenting thoughts and ideas that most people did not dare vocalize through the mouthpieces of characters such as "The Fat Slags" and "Sid the Sexist." It began life as a fanzine produced by brothers Chris and Simon Donald, and grew to become the third most popular magazine in the country, with sales of more than 1.2 million.

Viz comprises a mix of one-off and long-running characters, often with alliterative or explanatory titles such as "Roger Mellie, the Man On the Telly." Lampooning the traditional British boys' comic, there are also mock heroic tales, spoof ads, deliberately shoddy photo stories, take-offs of popular television shows, a fake letters page, and features full of surreal "facts."

Some of the strips featured in *Viz* are simply silly, many are topical and have a little more bite, while others, such as the Enid Blyton parody "Arse Farm," were simply surreal. As *Viz*'s popularity grew, several cartoonists joined the editorial board, including Graham Dury, Simon Thorp, and Davey Jones. Everyone is fair game for their satirical pens, but those that claim the moral high ground, such as newspaper columnists and members of the Royal Family, tend to get attacked with more bile than mere celebrities do.

Viz has developed over the years and frequently added timely characters, such as the hideously right-on "Modern Parents," the rave-obsessed "Wavy Davy Gravy," and leeching middle-class pupil "Student Grant." *Viz* can still get a smile but its glory years were the 1990s. **FJ**

Justine 1979

✏️ Guido Crepax

First published by Olympia Press (Italy)
Creator Italian (1933–2003)
Genre Erotic, Adventure
Influenced by *La Nouvelle Justine*

Guido Crepax was an astounding stylist whose free-form, often-psychedelic page layouts, spidery lines, and sense of patterning captured the spirit of the 1960s in his *Valentina* series. Clearly fascinated by the gothic and the erotic, he went on to adapt many classics (his version of *Dracula* is particularly good).

Justine is adapted from the picaresque novel by the Marquis de Sade about a young girl adrift in eighteenth-century France who is menaced and abused at every turn by seemingly virtuous people and outright libertines It brings together his two areas of interest perfectly. Crepax rarely simply adapts his chosen sources, and here he does a good job of capturing the philosophical spirit of the book without overcrowding it with dialogue. De Sade expanded his original twice, adding more philosophy to the sexual themes.

Crepax retains something of the Augustan structure of the writing in his script, and has a good ear for de Sade's black humor and sense of irony. He lavishes attention on all the kinky detail, embracing the frills and excesses of the period. One of Crepax's great strengths is capturing the visual style of an era in every aspect of his art, from the way panels are arranged down to the details of the period clothing.

Some of the page and panel designs in *Justine* are quite beautiful. All Crepax's heroines are elegant and elongated, and Justine is no exception, but Crepax gives her an air of innocence, clearly expressing the conflict and confusion she encounters when she begins to realize that virtue is never rewarded. **FJ**

Ada in the Jungle 1979

Francesco Tullio Altan

Title in original language *Ada Nella Jungla*
First published by Milano Libri (Italy)
Creator Italian (b.1942)
Genre Humor

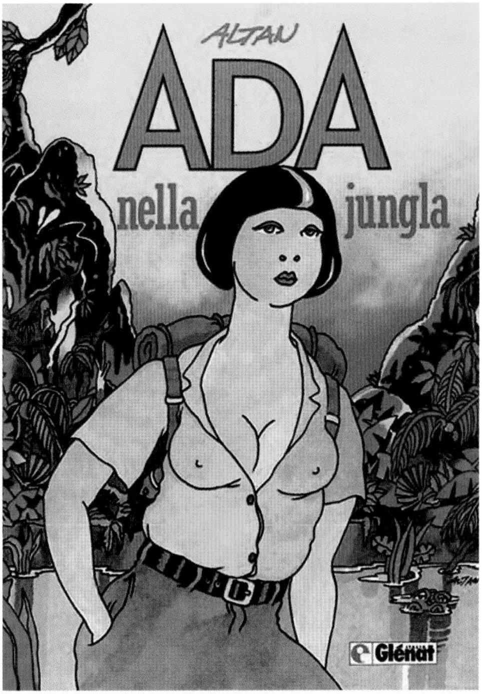
ALTAN
ADA
nella
jungla
Glénat

She is beautiful, luscious, intelligent, and mercenary—one could even add that her morals are confusingly elastic—but this was pretty much the case for everyone in the troubled year of 1939, when Europe and the rest of the world were about to topple into war. Summoned to the bedside of her dying Uncle Gordon, the glamorous Ada Frowz, who has been privately educated in a respectable young girls' boarding school, learns from the mouth of the dying man that the whole of his (considerable) fortune will be left to his son Percy, abandoned somewhere in Africa many years earlier. This seems to be a windfall for Ada, who clearly sees herself seducing Percy, and acquiring her uncle's legacy.

No sooner said than done, Ada sets sail for Africa, accompanied by Carmen, her Spanish maid. She does not yet know that she is dragging in her wake another of her cousins, Nancy, who is furious at seeing herself dispossessed and determined to murder Percy, so as to remain the sole inheritor. Evidently, this whole venture will bring no rest either to Ada or anyone else.

Every step in Ada's adventures is amusing and stimulating, filled with a malicious or sarcastic irony that the Italian artist has made the essence of his style. Beneath the panels he places a very effective system of sidebars which, in the same way as movie subtitles, add a counterpoint or a commentary to the action in progress. Combined with his very individual graphic style, it is apparent that, as an author, Altan is truly individual, in the best sense of the term. **NF**

"But are you not the Gowbo, the bearer of terrifying indigenous myths and taboos?"

Also by Francesco Tullio Altan
Cipputi
Colombo
Kiko
Pimpa
Trino

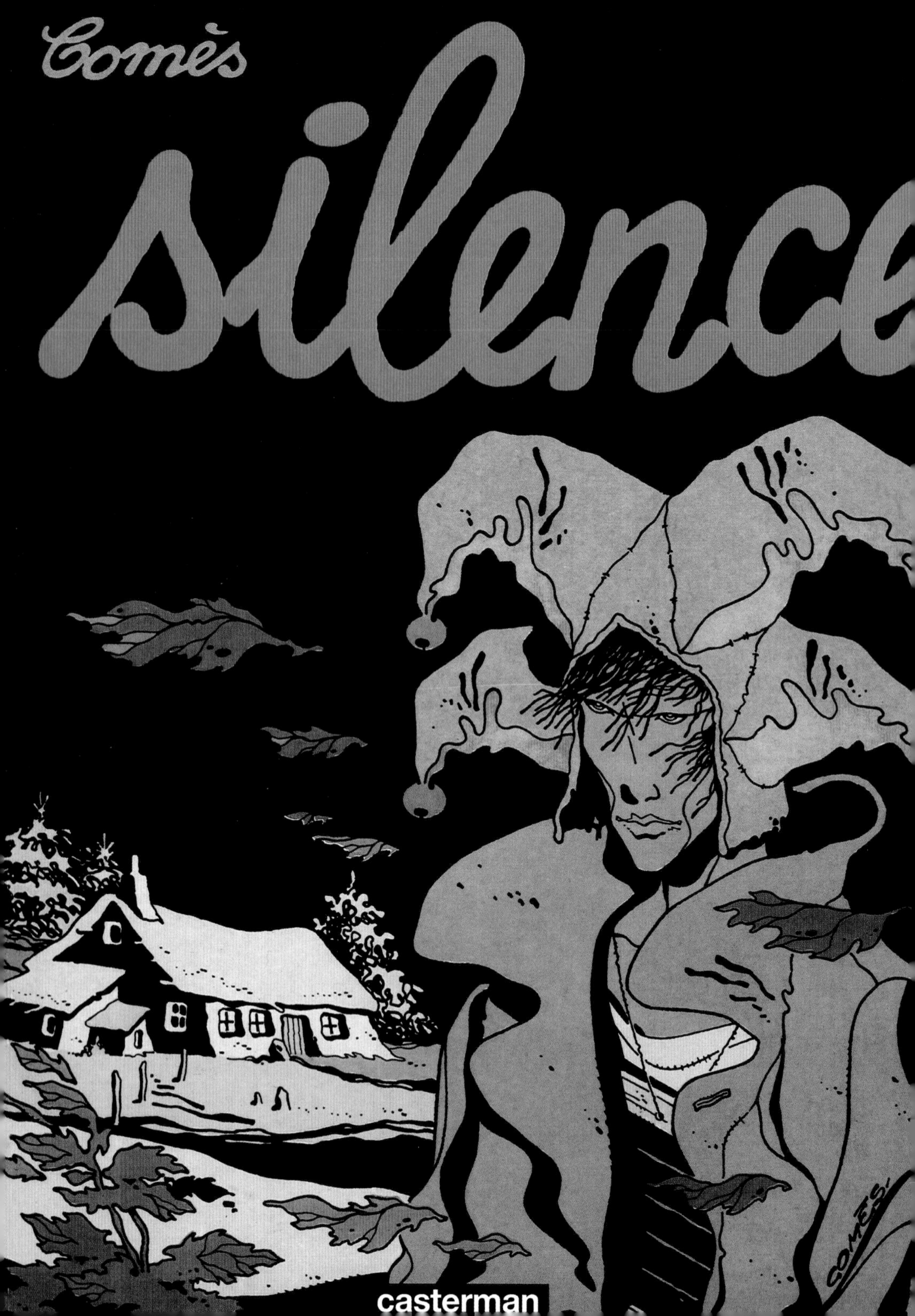
Comès
silence
COMÈS
casterman

Silence 1979

✎ Didier Comès

First published by À Suivre (France)
Creator Belgian (b.1942)
Genre War
Award Grand Prix Saint-Michel (1980)

The title of Didier Comès's album is also the name of the story's hero, an inoffensive simpleton. Silence is mute and he communicates with a slate on which he writes a few short sentences in a child's spelling. He is a farm laborer openly exploited by Abel Mauvy, a prosperous farmer whose vindictiveness toward the young man is difficult to understand.

It is only as the story develops and readers slowly discover the tragic origins of Silence that they realize the extent of the secrets that have been weighing on this corner of the Ardennes for many years. Secrets that Silence will, against all expectations, succeed in unraveling, with the help of a blind woman whom everyone treats like a leper, and Silence's only talent, an extraordinary empathy with nature and all living creatures that borders on telepathy. The story ends as tragically as it started, but ethics and justice are preserved while poetry and imagination, omnipresent in the world of Comès, play a major role.

Silence was first published in French-speaking Europe in the late 1970s, a decade marked by themes of regionalism and a return to nature in the wake of the hippie movement. This certainly played a part in its great success. After more than thirty years, the book is still a milestone in the development of Franco-Belgian comic strips, first and foremost because of its exceptional mastery, its originality, and its powerful narrative and graphic style. Comès is distinctive above all for his radiant black-and-white drawings that are produced with impressive virtuosity. **NF**

Tantrum 1979

✎ Jules Feiffer

First published by Alfred A. Knopf (USA)
Creator American (b.1929)
Genre Humor
Award Milton Caniff Lifetime Achievement Award (2004)

When a midlife crisis descends on Leo, an otherwise unremarkable husband and father, he literally wills himself into the body of a toddler. Although he retains all of his memories, intelligence, and awareness, Leo's new body allows him to regress into a state of pure id, begging women not for sex, but for the piggyback rides he so fondly recalls from his childhood.

Spurned by his inattentive family and tired of giving in to their needs, Leo hits the road, visiting, in turn, his parents, brother, and sisters. None are able to give him what he wants, so Leo pursues his own selfish ends with his brother's anorexic wife, and with the secretary with whom he has been having an affair. Not surprisingly, the hang-ups of these adults crimp Leo's self-loving style.

Tantrum was a breakthrough for Jules Feiffer, the longtime *Village Voice* cartoonist who, by the late 1970s, was equally well-known for his novels, plays, and screenplays. Working on a larger scale than his weekly strip, Feiffer produced *Tantrum* using one image per page. He turned out the images in a frantic, unpolished style as if they had been pulled from his pen in a hurry. They are vivid, stark, acute, and eminently entertaining. The art complements a sharp and polished dialogue that carries a story about life, midlife, and humanity with aplomb. What could be more appropriate for a book about a man who, after forty years, has given up giving and is ready to take, take, take. *Tantrum* is a mid-career masterpiece by one of the United States's preeminent cartooning talents. **BB**

Jeremiah 1979

✎✎ "Hermann"

First published by *Zach* (Germany)
Creator Hermann Huppen (Belgian, b.1938)
Genre Science fiction
Adaptation TV series (2002)

Hermann

JEREMIAH

L'INTÉGRALE / 1

Also by Hermann
Bernard Prince
Comanche
Hey, Nick! Are You Dreaming?
Sarajevo Tango
The Towers of Bois-Maury (Les Tours de Bois-Maury)

Toward the end of the twentieth century, racial tensions in the United States had caused the unthinkable—a nuclear conflict. In the ruins of America after the Bomb, devoid of any infrastructure or unifying authority, everything and everyone cannot be trusted. It is the survival of the fittest. A ravaged, declining world is prey to the antagonistic appetites of the human communities that have survived, and two lonely people will form an alliance to try and survive together.

"On the one hand, there is Jeremiah, part boy scout, part Tintin, and on the other Kurdy, a small but not unpleasant thug. Together, they represent Good and Evil. Actually they are one and the same person . . ." In this way the author of *Jeremiah*, Hermann Huppen, presents the two heroes of a series that was originally inspired by the postapocalyptic novel *Ravage* by French writer René Barjavel.

Thrown together on the roads of a country suddenly taken back several centuries, Jeremiah the idealist and Kurdy Malloy the amoral cynic write a sort of American ballad as endearing as it is chaotic: a new, original, violent version of the adventure of the American pioneers. Of course, it does not take much scratching beneath the surface of *Jeremiah* to detect the familiar surroundings and situations of the Western.

The author's history is closely linked to the Western genre since, before *Jeremiah*—the first of his series for which he also provided the story line—Hermann had produced the Western *Comanche* as a comic strip, which was also very popular, with a story line by the Belgian Michel Greg. Throughout its numerous episodes (nearly thirty), *Jeremiah* shows off the graphic power and the very physical dimension of Hermann's drawings, with the action taking precedence over everything else. It is an effective comic with a wide appeal, in the best sense of the word. **NF**

The Ranks of the Black Order 1979

Pierre Christin   Enki Bilal

Set in the 1970s, *Ranks of the Black Order* is a bittersweet meditation on comradeship and growing old. The story is about a left-wing group who fought against Franco in the Spanish Civil War reforming when an aged band of Fascists—the Ranks of the Black Order—start a campaign of terror.

When English journalist Pritchard sees reports of the massacre of an entire village he recognizes the perpetrators as members of the Ranks of the Black Order. However, his editor tells him that it is "ancient history, no one cares anymore." Pritchard calls up his former comrades, who are scattered across the globe, who have reached positions of influence in their fields, yet civilian life has failed to live up to their expectations. They answer the call not just because of idealism, but because once they thought they were changing the world for the better, and the reappearance of the Black Order gives them another chance to fulfill that dream.

By the end of the book their fears have been confirmed: neither they, nor the Black Order they have died to defeat, are really relevant or matter. Their sacrifices, now and back in the 1930s, are largely disregarded; the world doesn't care, and things stay the same no matter how much they change.

Writer Pierre Christin and artist Enki Bilal are incredibly adept at creating taut political thrillers, and this is no exception, even with such an aged cast. (Also penned by them, *The Hunting Party* is in a similar vein and equally excellent.) Bilal is superb at characterizing old people visually. His eye for build and stance conveys the weariness of old war horses making a final push, while his knack for detail and meticulous backgrounds bring to life the locations. *Ranks of the Black Order* is not afraid to ask big questions about age and altruism, or to serve up the unpalatable answers. A mature, thoughtful, and perfectly pitched story. **FJ**

Title in original language *Les Phalanges de L'ordre Noir*
First published by Casterman (France)
Creators Christin (France, b.1938); Bilal (Yugoslavian, b.1951)
Genre Adventure

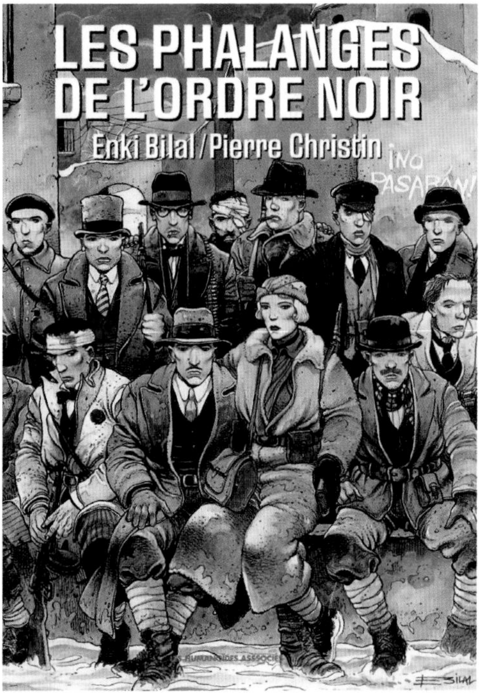
LES PHALANGES
DE L'ORDRE NOIR
Enki Bilal / Pierre Christin
¡NO PASARÁN!

Also by Christin and Bilal
Ship of Stone (*Le Vaisseau de Pierre*)
The City That Didn't Exist (*La Ville Qui n'Existait Pas*)
The Cruise of Lost Souls (*La Crosière des Oubliés*)
***The Hunting Party* (*Partie de Chasse*)**
Townscapes

The Bidochons 1979

Christian Binet

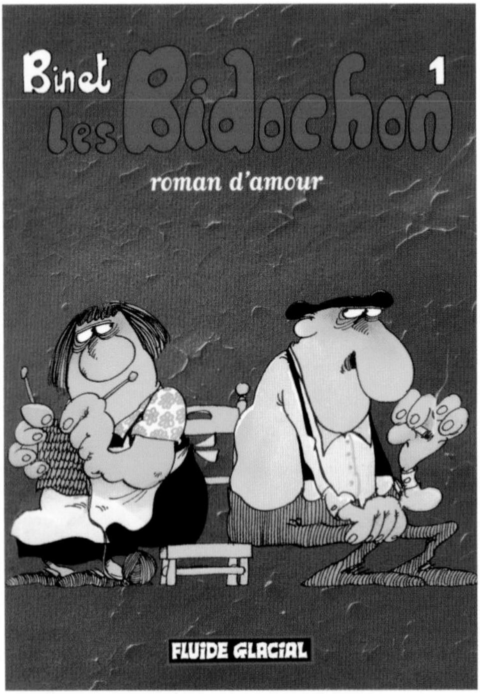
Binet
Les Bidochon
1
roman d'amour
FLUIDE GLACIAL

"I'm sorry I didn't recognise you. At the dating agency they said you were handsome, young, rich, and intelligent."

Also by Christian Binet
Contingencies (*Les Impondérables*)
Kador
Sir (*Monsieur le Ministre*)
The Infant Plague (*Poupon la Peste*)

Title in original language *Les Bidochon*
First published by Audie-Fluide Glacial (France)
Creator French (b.1947)
Genre Humor, Satire

Christian Binet's protagonists, Robert and Raymonde Bidochon, began their careers as supporting players in a saga, first published in *Fluide Glacial* in 1977, dedicated to their dog, the philosophical Kador, who intellectually outdistanced his owners by a considerable margin. The dim pair gained their own series two years later and achieved sufficient notoriety for their (non) exploits to be made into a play in 1989 and a film in 1996.

Binet sets an absurdist tone by omitting to draw elements of decor, indicating them instead with verbal labels and arrows, occasionally taunting his readers by evoking the magnificence of the invisible landscapes. The humor arises above all, however, out of the exuberant graphic line with which the artist renders the grotesque bodies—and bodily habits—of his middle-aged couple. The verve of the dialogue reaches sublime heights of scatology and crudeness in the mouths of the choleric Robert and the disgruntled Raymonde.

Yet the immense success of the series, sustained over three decades, is also attributable to its blistering social satire. Binet gleefully demolishes every aspect of the petit-bourgeois lifestyle to which the Bidochons aspire, from property ownership to cultivation of the body by means of beauty products. In the process, the consumerist rhetoric of status and advancement is deliriously misappropriated by the least glamorous couple ever to blunder through a comic book. Add in a few side-swipes at the imbecilic output of mainstream television and the insanity of French bureaucratic procedures and the result is pure genius. **AM**

Comanche Moon 1979

🖉🖉 "Jaxon"

First published by Last Gasp (USA)
Creator Jack Jackson (American, 1941–2006)
Genre History
Award Nominated for the Will Eisner Hall of Fame (2011)

Cynthia Ann Parker was the nine-year-old daughter of a white settler family from the Texas plains when she was kidnapped by the Comanches in 1836. Renamed Naduah, she was raised as one of their own, grew into adulthood, married a Comanche chief, and bore him three children. Along the way she refused all attempts by white traders to remove her from her new family.

Captured by Texas Rangers after a raid on her encampment in 1861, she was returned to her relatives but died brokenhearted in 1870. *Comanche Moon* details the rise of her eldest son, Quanah, as he led his nation in its struggle against white encroachment and his later years on an Oklahoma reservation working to reconcile whites and American Indians.

Jackson's book is an illustrated piece about a well-known and oft-told part of American history. What Jackson does here, however, is take the story and tell it in a way it has never been told before, visually. A self-taught historian working in a medium not noted for its dedication to historical accuracy, Jackson's depictions of buildings, weaponry, costumes, and even landscapes, owe their widely acknowledged authenticity to the hundreds of paintings and photographs he studied from the period.

Jackson's Old Satank was drawn from a photograph of the Kiowa chief Satank. His rendering of a buffalo hunt came from a 1919 painting by the great "cowboy artist" Charles Russell. The narrative of *Comanche Moon* encompasses almost a century of North American history, and is a genre all of its own. **BS**

Ardour 1979

🖉 Daniel Varenne 🖉 Alex Varenne

Title in original language *Ardeur*
First published by *Charlie* magazine (France)
Creators Daniel Varenne (French, b.1937); Alex Varenne (French, b.1939) **Genre** Political fable

In Europe at the end of the 1970s, the Cold War was still on everyone's minds, and the risk of a new worldwide conflict was seen as entirely plausible. It was in this particular historical context that the series *Ardeur* was born. From the generation that had reached adulthood when the Cold War was at its height, the brothers Varenne retraced the long journey of a French aviator flying across the ruins of a Europe devastated by World War III.

The countries of central Europe, for many centuries the favorite setting for the resolution of the continent's conflicts, was certainly at the epicenter of events: a witness of the nuclear horror, Ardeur, disfigured by serious burns, progresses toward the West, first to a Warsaw partially in ruins, where he has his face remade, and then to Berlin. Everywhere he is accompanied by the sinister ballet of the warriors of war—the militias, the corrupt, and profiteers—who have only one idea in their heads—to take advantage of the surrounding chaos, to use the survivors as tools, and to reconstruct a new world order.

It is an understatement to say that *Ardeur* is a dark tale. To give yet more power to this contemporary fable, the artist employs a very unusual graphic universe, all in light and shade, punctuated with great black surfaces. He is also one of the rare European artists, long before the Japanese comic strip set the example, to use screentones, a technique that contributes greatly to the singular atmosphere of *Ardeur*. This comic is an irreproachable artistic success. **NF**

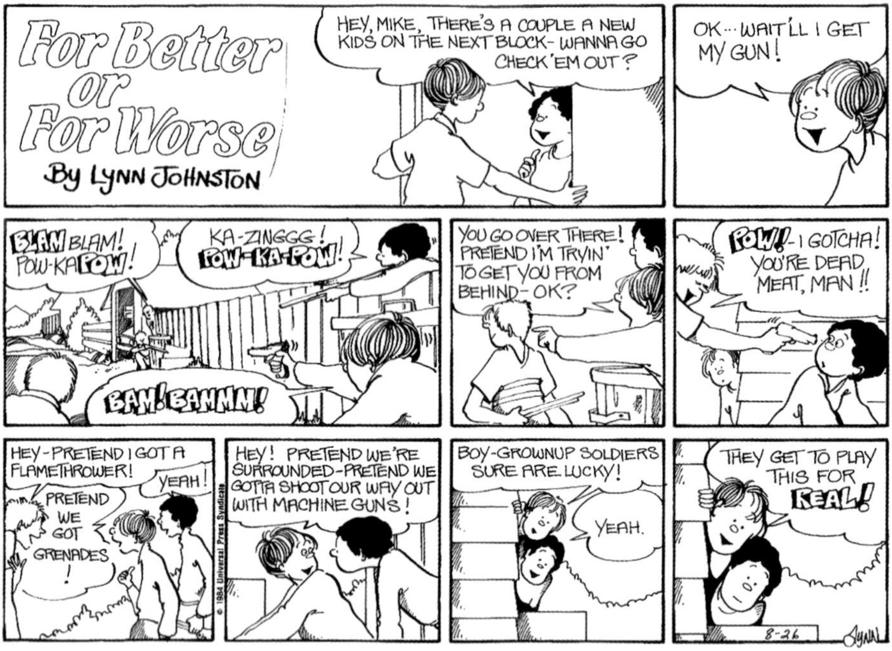
For Better or For Worse
By LYNN JOHNSTON
HEY, MIKE, THERE'S A COUPLE A NEW KIDS ON THE NEXT BLOCK- WANNA GO CHECK 'EM OUT?
OK... WAIT'LL I GET MY GUN!
BLAM BLAM! POW-KA POW!
KA-ZINGGG! POW-KA-POW!
BAM! BAMMM!
YOU GO OVER THERE! PRETEND I'M TRYIN' TO GET YOU FROM BEHIND- OK?
POW! - I GOTCHA! YOU'RE DEAD MEAT, MAN!!
HEY-PRETEND I GOT A FLAMETHROWER!
YEAH!
PRETEND WE GOT GRENADES!
© 1984 Universal Press Syndicate
HEY! PRETEND WE'RE SURROUNDED-PRETEND WE GOTTA SHOOT OUR WAY OUT WITH MACHINE GUNS!
BOY-GROWNUP SOLDIERS SURE ARE LUCKY!
YEAH.
THEY GET TO PLAY THIS FOR REAL!
8-26
LYNN

For Better or For Worse 1979

Lynn Johnston

First published by Universal Press Syndicate (USA)
Creator Canadian (b.1947)
Genre Humor
Award Reuben Award (1985)

Lynn Johnston always knew that one day she would be a cartoonist, but even she was flabbergasted when, in 1978, she mailed twenty examples of a strip based on her own family (husband Rod and two children) to Universal Press Syndicate and received in return an offer of a twenty-year contract.

She already had under her belt the hugely popular books *David, We're Pregnant*, *Hi Mum, Hi Dad*, and *Do They Ever Grow Up?* but it was the Johnston nee Patterson family of John, wife Elly, son Michael, daughter Elizabeth, and baby April that would change her life forever. Their escapades were, of course, largely whimsical, but there have also been controversies and loss. The family's Old English sheepdog, Farley, died. Grandparents have passed away.

There has been premarital sex. When Johnston created a gay character named Lawrence, she actually drew an alternate series just in case any newspapers chose not to run her gay-friendly panels. The Patterson family lived in the fictional Canadian town of Milborough, Ontario, and for most of their thirty-year lifespan in 2,000 newspapers across North America, and in eight languages throughout the world, have aged gracefully in real time, their obstacles, joys and aspirations captured in sharp focus by an astute, perceptive artist. In the wake of the strip's final episode in August 2008, Johnston embarked not on a new strip but on the same one—just reworked the way she says it "should have" been done. **BS**

Always fresh, funny, and astute, Johnstone's panel ran for thirty successful years. ↑

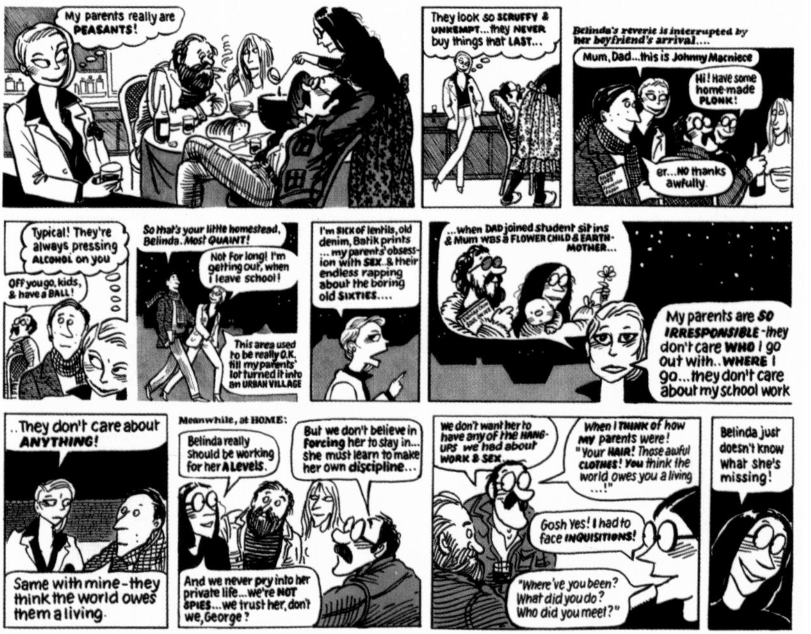
My parents really are PEASANTS!
They look so SCRUFFY & UNKEMPT...they NEVER buy things that LAST...
Belinda's reverie is interrupted by her boyfriend's arrival....
Mum, Dad...this is Johnny Macniece
Hi! Have some home-made PLONK!
er...NO thanks awfully.
Typical! They're always pressing ALCOHOL on you
Off you go, kids, & have a BALL!
So that's your little homestead, Belinda. Most QUAINT!
Not for long! I'm getting out, when I leave school!
This area used to be really O.K. till my parents' lot turned it into an URBAN VILLAGE
I'm SICK of lentils, old denim, Batik prints ... my parents' obsession with SEX..& their endless rapping about the boring old SIXTIES....
...when DAD joined student sit ins & Mum was a FLOWER CHILD & EARTH-MOTHER...
My parents are SO IRRESPONSIBLE - they don't care WHO I go out with.. WHERE I go...they don't care about my school work
..They don't care about ANYTHING!
Same with mine - they think the world owes them a living.
Meanwhile, at HOME:
Belinda really should be working for her A Levels.
But we don't believe in forcing her to stay in... she must learn to make her own discipline...
And we never pry into her private life...we're NOT SPIES...we trust her, don't we, George?
We don't want her to have any of the HANG-UPS we had about WORK & SEX...
When I THINK of how MY parents were! "Your HAIR! Those awful CLOTHES! You think the world owes you a living ...!"
Gosh Yes! I had to face INQUISITIONS!
"Where've you been? What did you do? Who did you meet?"
Belinda just doesn't know what she's missing!

Mrs. Weber's Diary 1979

Posy Simmonds

First published by *The Guardian* (UK)
Creator Rosemary Elizabeth Simmonds (British, b.1945)
Genre Humor, Satire
Awards Cartoonist of the Year (1980 and 1981)

Posy Simmonds, the middle child of five, came from a cheery dairy farmer's family west of London. At home, she was deeply into humor and satire in bound old *Punch* magazines, Victorian books, farm manuals, *Giles* annuals, 1950s American comics—and as a young girl started making little strips herself. Being ambidextrous, she could draw and paint with either hand. After boarding school in Caversham, she studied French civilization in the early 1960s in Paris, and then art and design in London, to become a professional illustrator in 1968. In May 1977 she was asked to do a strip for *The Guardian* newspaper. Her reply was a weekly series initially titled *The Silent Three*, after a secret society young Wendy and her classmates, Trish and Jo, founded.

While creating British characters at random, soon the focus was on the lives of prototype woolly liberals Wendy and George Weber and their family of six. In drawing them, she felt like she already knew them: Wendy a writer of children's books, and George a senior lecturer in liberal studies at a polytechnic. Over ten years, the strip grew into a minute reportage of everything British, new as well as old. It was full of sharply observed ways of speaking in the English language.

Her visual storytelling grew into her own collagelike blend of drawings, speech balloons, hand-lettered texts, and typesetting, in part handled by her graphic designer husband Richard Hollis. After two fine graphic novels, *Gemma Bovery* and *Tamara Drewe* (2005–06, also filmed), a third is now in the making. **HvO**

↑ The strip is a verbal and visual feast, an analysis of mores and morals.

Iron Man
Demon in a Bottle 1979

David Michelinie John Romita, Jr.

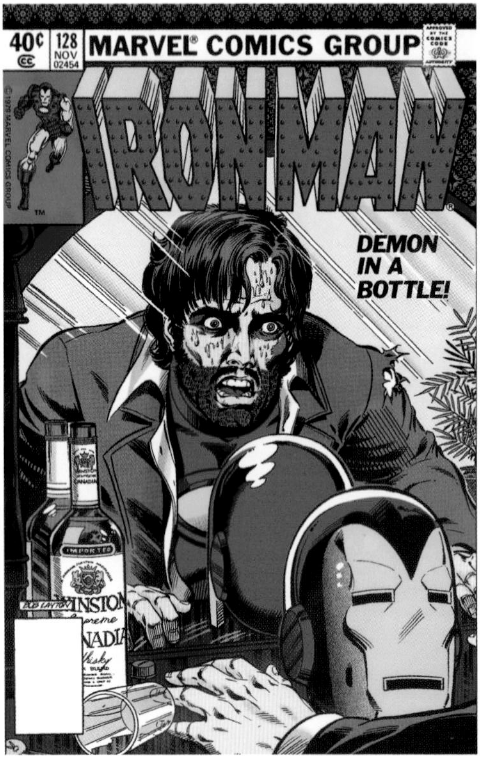
40¢
128
NOV
02454
MARVEL COMICS GROUP
IRON MAN
DEMON IN A BOTTLE!

"I saw that coming, but couldn't dodge it in time! Reflexes are off! I should never have had that fourth Martini . . . !"

Similar reads

Iron Man #103–7 Bill Mantlo, Keith Pollard, and George Tuska

The Amazing Spider-Man #96–98 Stan Lee and Gil Kane

First published by Marvel Comics (USA)
Creators Michelinie (American, b.1948); Romita, Jr. (American, b.1956)
Genre Superhero

Iron Man (and his alter ego Tony Stark) is Marvel's sybaritic superhero. But unlike playboy Bruce Wayne, Tony Stark has always pursued an ultra-pressurized career as inventor, scientist, and industrialist—a lynchpin in the U.S. military-industrial complex. Stark is an obsessive overachiever, creating extraordinary new weapon systems while simultaneously moonlighting as a costumed superhero.

He energetically pursues the celebrity lifestyle and an endless stream of glamorous young girls, and he has always enjoyed a drink or three. Stark's Dionysian appetite for life underscores his prowess in battle. But 1979's "Demon in a Bottle" story line undercut this version of the character and presented a very different and troubled Tony Stark to its readers.

The theme of alcoholism is developed slowly. In *Iron Man* #120, readers find Stark regretting his fourth Martini during a battle with the Sub Mariner. By issue #128, the original "Demon in a Bottle" story, we encounter an unshaven and hungover Tony Stark staring at his Iron Man mask like Hamlet contemplating Yorick's skull. Stark has clearly become an alcoholic.

This opening page is one of the most subtly disorienting images in mainstream superhero comics. Michelinie, Layton, and Marvel's editorial team deserve credit for slipping in this challenging and provocative story. The media paid little attention to the issue at the time, perhaps because this was a story about Iron Man. An alcoholism plot line with Superman or Batman might have made a bigger impact. **RR**

The Tokyo Drifter 1979

✐✐ Takashi Fukutani

Title in original language *Dokushin Apato Dokudami-so*
First published by Hobunsha (Japan)
Creator Japanese (1952–2000)
Genre Drama

In 1968, Japan became the world's second economy, and this postwar economic miracle continued for another two decades. At the height of the Bubble Economy in the 1980s, it was said that the land under the Imperial Palace in the center of Tokyo was worth more than the entire state of California. Japan was on top of the world, the poster child for success, and the land of plenty.

And yet, in the shadows of the skyscrapers of the business district of Shinjuku, the *shitamachi* lived on—the low city that was left behind by this march toward prosperity. For fifteen years, Takashi Fukutani told the story of these disenfranchised citizens, following Yoshio Hori, a young man who (like many others) had moved to the capital in the hope of a better life.

In a world of ordinary workers, corrupt cops, seedy bars, and transvestites, Hori struggles each month to make ends meet. Lazy, sex-obsessed, and not very bright, he is looking for love and lust in all the wrong places. His elaborate money-making schemes always fail (due to bad luck or sheer stupidity). Yet he helps one of his neighbors who has fallen on particularly hard times. Deep down, Hori is too nice for his own good.

The art is nothing flashy, a little dated but efficient, and particularly apt at rendering outrageous facial expressions. Sometimes repetitive and uneven in quality, Fukutani's stories are an ode to life and radiate a true tenderness for these people, who, even in the gloomiest situations, remain certain they will eventually know brighter days. **XG**

Kampung Boy 1979

✐✐ "Lat"

First published by Berita (Malaysia)
Creator Mohammad Nor Khalid (Malaysian, b.1951)
Genre Humor, Autobiography
Award Outstanding International Book (2007)

Kampung Boy is the childhood memoir of a boy, the small Malaysian village he grew up in, and the family and friends who raised him. Starting with his birth and continuing to his departure for middle school, Lat lovingly illustrates his father, the Meor brothers (his first friends and the ones who taught him to fish), his teachers, and his classmates.

Lat's career began at the age of thirteen when his comic strips were published in newspapers in neighboring Singapore. By the time he was seventeen he was earning an income from his comics. "The whole idea is to make people smile and feel like they are part of the whole thing," Lat said in an interview. True to his word, *Kampung Boy* is an invitation to readers to experience for themselves the town and customs that he grew up in and with: the strict classroom of his Koran teacher, Tuan Syed, fishing after school, a wedding at a neighboring village, and playing hide-and-seek.

His cartoon illustrations reflect a humorous sensibility and convey innocence and fun. Lat's rhythm and timing are expert, weaving together a series of events connected only by a location and its characters. His uncanny ability to fill the page, to illustrate both action and stillness, add to the humor and nostalgia of his autobiography. His upbringing was strict and Muslim, but not strict Muslim, and there is a complete, if not refreshing, absence of fundamentalism or disenfranchisement in the narrative. *Kampung Boy* is not merely a story of a simple time, but also of a simple place, yet none of it is simple-minded. **K-MC**

Modern Art 1980

🖊🖊 Joost Swarte

First published by Real Free Press Foundation (Netherlands)
Creator Jozef Willibrord Swarte (Dutch, b.1947)
Genre Satire
Award Stripschapprijs (1998)

Joost Swarte entered the art world in late 1970, when 60,000 copies of his six-page *The True Story of Mr. P.* were delivered door to door by the museum for modern art in the town of Eindhoven, also home to Dutch electronics giant Philips. It was a strip in "bigfoot" style in which he lampooned Philips's light bulb capitalism.

In the 1950s, Swarte often met relatives of his Belgian mother and fell in love with Vandersteen's *Suske en Wiske* comics in Flemish. When he quit his industrial design studies in 1970 he had already explored comix (X-rated U.S. comics) and the old comics masters. He excelled in angles, perspectives, lettering, and coloring. By the mid-1970s it all fell into place. While he neatly illustrated and designed books for the Amsterdam-based Real Free Press—for its series of classic U.S. strips (he even drew his own version of *Krazy Kat*)—he was asked by Bernard Holtrop, a Dutch expatriate cartoonist in Paris, to illustrate a hair-raising comic script starring Fred Fallo for the French monthly *Charlie*.

More French strips followed, some in true time-warp 1950s art deco settings, starring Jopo de Pojo, an odd young man with an enlarged black quiff and plus fours, a mix of *Tintin*, *Mickey Mouse*, and superhero aspects. A hardcover album of these stories, titled *Joost Swarte's Modern Art*, made this unique retro blend available in four different language editions in 1980.

For a 1977 booklet about comic strip authors working in the vein of Belgian grandmaster Hergé, he chose the title *De Klare Lijn*, the clear line, a label that proved to be unerasable. **HvO**

The Incal 1980

🖊 Alejandro Jodorowsky 🖊 "Moebius"

Title in original language *L'Incal (L'Integrale)*
First published by *Métal Hurlant* (France)
Creators Jodorowsky (Chilean, b.1929); Jean Giraud (French, b.1938) **Genre** Drama

The film director Alejandro Jodorowsky first met Jean "Moebius" Giraud in 1975 when the pair worked on an aborted *Dune* movie. Jodorowsky was so inspired by their collaboration that he devised a multipart epic comic book series that would showcase the artist's unbound imagination. By the time the first episode of *The Incal* appeared, Moebius had emerged as the most influential science fiction artist in the world, and this strip was to be his most expansive work.

The Incal itself is a sentient Chrystal that comes into the possession of a down-at-heel private investigator named John DiFool. The series was, essentially, a long chase scene as armies, races, creatures, and civilizations all competed to win it back. It is a story of bewildering complexity spread out over six parts (serialized in five volumes in France and three in the United States) and spawning numerous spin-off series.

Jodorowsky's hallucinatory script peopled the strip with a succession of bizarre creations, including a rat queen, the Meta-Baron, the Techno Pope, a concrete parrot, a wolf-headed freedom fighter, and, eventually, God. With such diverse inspirations as Mickey Spillane, Phillip K. Dick, and the Tarot, *The Incal* was effectively a metaphysical science fiction film noir on paper.

The series took almost ten years to complete, and Moebius was allowed to give full expression to his unique vision of the future. The world of *The Incal*, with its towering, overcrowded cities, alien lifeforms, and dreamlike dimensions was played out on a scale that only a visionary such as he could have achieved. **DAR**

The Incal was an ideal showcase for the talented Moebius. ➡

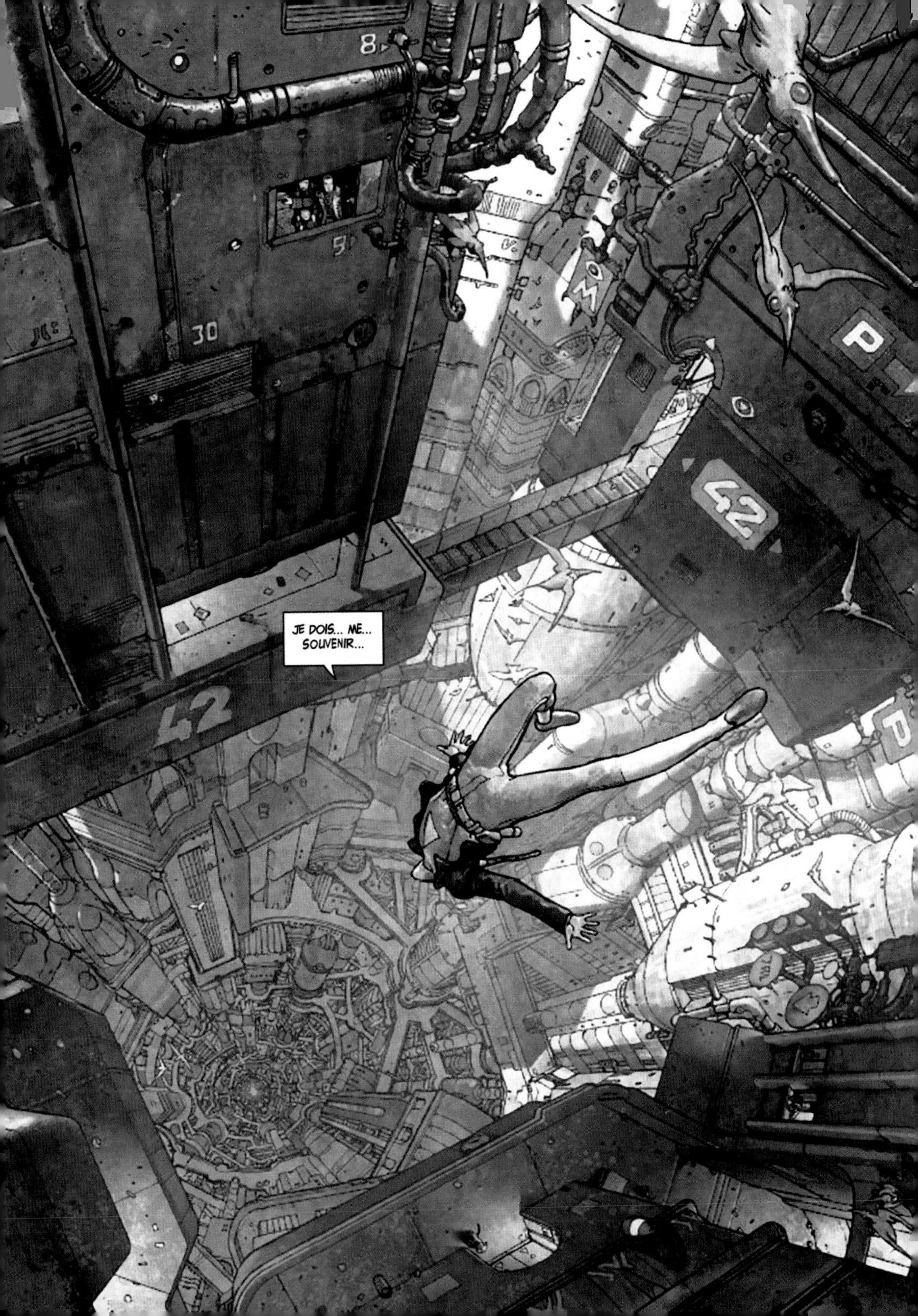
JE DOIS... ME... SOUVENIR...

Nemesis the Warlock 1980

✏ Pat Mills   ✏ Kevin O'Neill

First published by *2000 AD* (UK)
Creators Mills (British, b.1949); O'Neill (British, b.1953)
Genre Science fiction, Fantasy
Award Eagle Award for Best Graphic Novel (1983)

According to artist Kevin O'Neill, "I see *Nemesis the Warlock* as the start of my career proper." This great baroque fantasy strip, written by Pat Mills and originally serialized in the pages of the weekly British sci-fi comic *2000 AD*, gave O'Neill his first opportunity to pursue his flair for the grotesque and queasily repulsive.

Most of Mills and O'Neill's *Nemesis the Warlock* episodes are only four pages long, but every panel is teeming with angular, rigidly detailed drawings of deformed faces, semiorganic spaceships, gothic architecture, and gnarled alien landscapes. At the same time, both writer and artist are not afraid to indulge in a subversive strain of black comedy that sometimes nudges the strip closer to the humor work of earlier masters of sweaty, unapologetic ugliness, including Britain's Ken Reid, or America's Basil Wolverton.

The first few episodes of *Nemesis* quickly define the strip's dominant themes—intolerance, prejudice, fear of the "other," and the terrors of conformity. Readers meet the humans of the Termight Empire, determined to exterminate all other alien species and led by the semispectral necromancer Torquemada. Opposing them are Credo, the resistance movement headed by Nemesis, the cloven-hoofed "Lord of the Flies" who "Waits on the Edge of Your Dreams."

After chronicling the battle for some three years, O'Neill left to pursue other creative possibilities in 1983, infrequently returning to the character. While other talented artists have drawn installments of the *Nemesis* saga, O'Neill's singular version remains definitive. **AL**

The Nikopol Trilogy 1980

✏✏ Enki Bilal

Title in original language *La trilogie Nikopol*
First published by Dargaud (France)
Creator French (b.1951)
Genre Science fiction

Paris, 2023. Devastated by the legacy of two nuclear wars and under the thumb of a Fascist-inspired regime, the French capital is in a pitiful state. The tension rises when an enormous, pyramid-shaped extraterrestrial vehicle arrives above the astroport. The spaceship's inhabitants are the ancient Egyptian gods, who then engage in delicate negotiations with the authorities to obtain the huge quantities of fuel their spacecraft needs in order to leave. But France's ruthless dictator, J. F. Choublanc, stalls negotiations to take advantage of the situation in the light of imminent elections.

It is in this uncertain environment that one of the occupants of the pyramid, the falcon god Horus, who is in mortal conflict with his fellow deities, escapes into Paris. When a space capsule containing the body of a renegade soldier, Alcide Nikopol, who has been cryogenically preserved for thirty years, falls to Earth, Horus takes over his body in order to exact a revenge that has incalculable consequences.

Author Enki Bilal's powerful work was acclaimed when it appeared, becoming a major landmark in his career and the history of French-language comic books. He uses an impressive graphic vocabulary and has an outstandingly consistent imagination, largely inspired by the history of totalitarianism in Europe. *The Nikopol Trilogy*'s social commentary and its fine draftsmanship established Bilal as one of the major creators in the comic world universe. The story has been adapted into the video game *Nikopol: Secrets of the Immortals*, and the movie *Immortal (Immortel/Ad Vitam,* 2004). **NF**

Passengers of the Wind 1980

François Bourgeon

Title in original language *Les Passagers du Vent*
First published by Glénat (France)
Creator French (b.1945)
Genre History

F. Bourgeon
LES PASSAGERS DU VENT. 1.
La fille sous la dunette
Glénat

Set in the 1800s, François Bourgeon's historical epic follows the picaresque adventures of Isabeau de Marnaye, a rebellious young noblewoman whose hopes and ideals are at odds with her surroundings, very much a trait of Bourgeon's heroines. Seeking to escape her dreary aristocratic fate, she boards a French warship and saves one of the sailors, Hoel, who befriends her and soon becomes her lover.

Captured by the English, Hoel is rescued with the help of an English couple who are expecting a child out of wedlock, and they all flee to Africa on a slave ship. They witness firsthand the horrors of the "triangular" trade, where ships from Europe took manufactured goods to trade for slaves on the west coast of Africa, shipping them across to the Americas and exchanging them for sugar, coffee, and tobacco.

As well as being a great adventure tale, the *Passengers of the Wind* series is also a complex story of grown-up sexual relationships as the protagonists fall in and out of love, adding an extra dimension to what could have been a very lush and beautiful, but quite routine, adventure story. Bourgeon's artwork is extremely detailed and realistic—he's known as a painstaking researcher—and his artistic background in stained glassmaking informs the richness of his coloring with magnificent results. Bourgeon completed his original five-book cycle in 1984, producing the sequel, *The Bois-Caïman Granddaughter*, in 2009. Set in Louisiana during the American Civil War, it follows the adventures of Isa's descendent as she hunts for her ancestor. **FJ**

"If I did not do comics I would write, I might be able to make films or do theater, but I would create."

François Bourgeon

Also by François Bourgeon

The Bois-Caïman Granddaughter Parts 1 and 2 (La Petite Fille Bois-Caïman Livres 1 en 2)
The Curse of the Wood of Mists (Le Sortilège du Bois des Brumes)

Emperor of the Land of the Rising Sun 1980

Ryoko Yamagishi

Title in original language *Hi Izuru Tokoro no Tenshi*
First published by Hakusensha (Japan)
Creator Japanese (b.1947)
Genre History, Drama

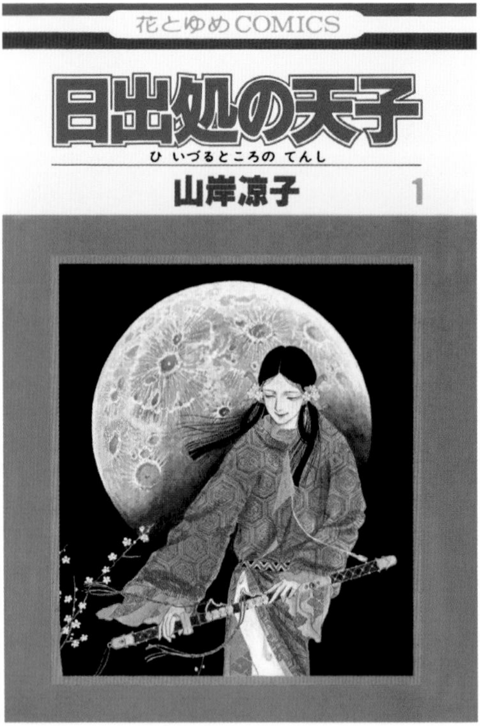
花とゆめCOMICS
日出処の天子
ひ いづるところの てんし
山岸凉子
1

Also by Ryoko Yamagashi
Arabesque
Banshee
Our White Room (Shiroi Heya no Futari)
Sphinx

Emperor of the Land of the Rising Sun tells the fictionalized story of Prince Shotoku, famous for his political work in sixth- to seventh-century Japan, and which largely contributed to the centralization of the nation's government. He is the second son of Emperor Yomei but, due to the law of primogeniture, he became a politician instead of succeeding to the throne.

The prince had many titles, but is referred to by his childhood name, Umayado no Oji, in the series. The comic illustrates ten years of his life, from his boyhood and through his youth. While basing the plot on historical figures and events, the author's imagination stretches beyond simple facts. She brings to life an original story with unique interpretations of historical events alongside additional supporting characters. Prince Shotoku is said to have been a very gifted man; according to legend, he was capable of listening to ten people at the same time. Ryoko Yamagishi's innovative interpretation of this legend assumes that the prince was psychic, and the author goes on to further explore the "what ifs" of history. Her artwork, on the other hand, attempts to depict the period as accurately as possible.

"If all my wishes are to come true, this arrow shall hit my target."

Despite her efforts, her most successful scenes are those with minimal background, emphasizing her fluent portrayals of traditionally taboo subjects such as homosexuality and incest. In fact, Yamagishi grasps all the classic themes of the *shojo* manga (girls' comic) genre, be it unrequited love, romantic rejection, or jealousy, with almost poetic ease. These were the key elements that attracted readers, leading the comic to win the Kodansha Comic Award in 1983. **TS**

Maison Ikkoku 1980

Rumiko Takahashi

Maison Ikkoku is one of several manga series that were produced at a great pace by artist and writer Rumiko Takahashi, and which originally appeared in the magazine *Big Comic Spirits*. With *Maison Ikkoku*, Takahashi wanted to get away from her fantasy comic book *Lum* (*Urusei Yatsura*), and deal with love in the real (albeit rather funny) world.

Although it might be assumed it was written for a female audience, the strip was actually aimed at men in their twenties and thirties. A bit like a Japanese version of Armistead Maupin's *Tales of the City*, *Maison Ikkoku* focused on the crazy lives of rooming house residents in 1980s Tokyo, and was based on Takahashi's own experiences. Central to the story is the long-running romance between Yusaku Godai, a poor student, and the house's manager, the sorrowful Kyoko, who has just lost her husband.

"I know you'll pass a mid-term someday! Just hang in there!"

Yusaku is a really nice guy, but the other tenants always take advantage of him, and he's easily misled. The rich, suave Shun Mitaka also has his eye on Kyoko, and, because of bad timing and misinformation, Yusaku and Kyoko spend much of the fifteen volumes of the series thinking the other isn't interested, is cheating, or has found someone else.

Takahashi's scripting is fast paced, and her dialogue often spot on, although the plotting is less realistic. It bears as much resemblance to the real world as a French farce, but it is quirkily funny. Her art is less sketchy than a lot of manga, with a polish and degree of prettiness that Western readers find very appealing. Comic distortion is used to point out the jokes and climaxes, which works very well among the more measured sequences. **FJ**

First published by Shogakukan (Japan)
Creator Japanese (b.1957)
Genre Romance
Adaptation TV anime series (1986–88)

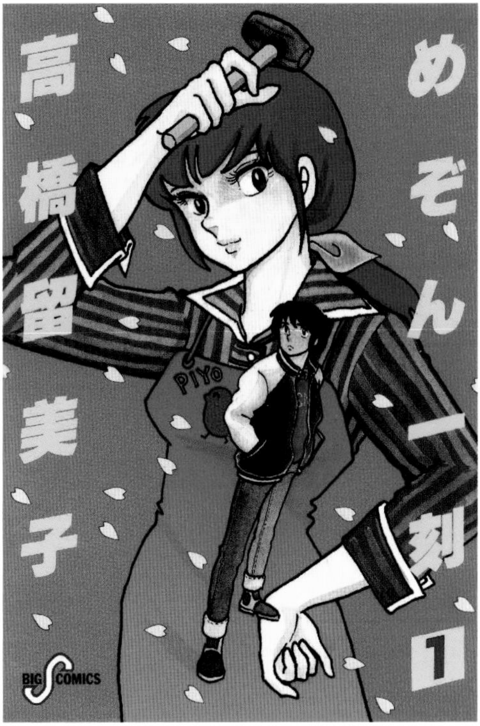
めぞん一刻
1
高橋留美子
PIYO
BIG COMICS

Also by Rumiko Takahashi

InuYasha, A Feudal Fairy Tale (*Sengoku Otogizoshi InuYasha*)
One Pound Gospel (*Ichi-Pondo no Fukuin*)
Ranma 1/2 (*1/2 Ranma Nibun-no-Ichi*)

Corto Maltese in Siberia 1980

Hugo Pratt

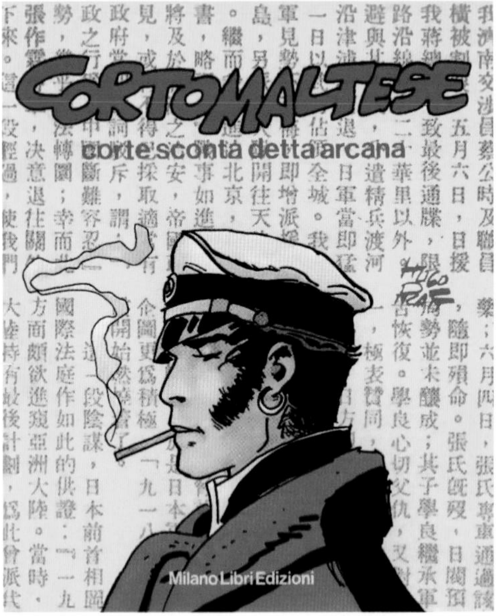
CORTO MALTESE
corte sconta detta arcana
Milano Libri Edizioni

Title in original language *Corte Sconta Detta Arcana*
First published by Linus (Italy)
Creator Italian (1927–95)
Genre Adventure

"You know, my mother was a gypsy of Gibraltar, a famous witch, and she knew her devils well. My father came from Wales. And was the nephew of an old sorcerer who lived in Tintagel where Merlin lived. . . ."

Also by Hugo Pratt
Corto Maltese: Ballad of the Salty Sea (*La Ballade de la Mer Salée*)
Jesuit Joe (*Jésuite Joe*)
Sergeant Kirk (*El Sargento Kirk*) with Héctor Oesterheld
The Scorpions of the Desert (*Les Scorpions du Desert*)

In Hong Kong, just as World War I ends, the sailor Corto Maltese is recruited by the secret society of the Red Lanterns. His assignment is to try and capture Admiral Kolchak's armored train on the border of Manchuria and Siberia. Kolchak was the leader of the White Russians who were fighting the Bolsheviks after they had seized power in Russia two years earlier.

After several very wild adventures on the Yellow Sea, then in Shanghai and on an aircraft, Corto Maltese eventually finds the famous train traveling on the Trans-Siberian railway. But he's not the only one in search of it. Thanks to its legendary load, Kolchak's train was bound to attract all sorts of people, all fighting to lay their hands on the Tsar's treasure, including Chinese warlords, allied troops, Manchu bandits, triads, and mercenaries.

With its great length (more than one hundred pages), *Corto Maltese in Siberia* is probably the most epic of the adventures of Hugo Pratt's hero. It is also the one with the greatest number of larger-than-life characters: the ferocious Ungern, directly inspired by a historical character of the period, who believes that he is a reincarnation of Gengis Khan; the striking duchess Marina Seminova, the archetype of the strong-willed women Pratt loves, and the mad Russian Rasputin, the malevolent alter ego whom Corto Maltese has to combat in most of his major adventures.

Graphically, Pratt is at his best here. Never has he been more flowing and dynamic than in this mature story, combining historical realism and a dreamlike quality that makes this a masterpiece. **NF**

Bloom County 1980

✐ Berkeley Breathed

First published by *The Washington Post* (USA)
Creator American (b.1957)
Genre Humor, Satire
Award Pulitzer Prize for Editorial Cartooning (1987)

When *Bloom County* first appeared in 1980 it took time for its creator to get the formula right. Characters came and went with some rapidity: "Major" Bloom, Mr. Limekiller, and Otis Oracle were just a few who were discarded. Even Opus, the endearing large-nosed penguin and herring addict was dropped in 1981, only to reappear in 1982.

When Berkeley Breathed did find the right mix—ten-year-old Milo Bloom the reporter, Steve Dallas the lawyer, and the wheelchair-bound, *Star Trek*–obsessed, war veteran Cutter John, among others—his irreverent small-town take on the nation's political and cultural bastions found its resonance. Breathed became inspired, at least in part, to create a strip that dealt with topical political issues in a humorous way because he felt that the comics page needed, as he succinctly put it, "a little kick in the ass."

It wasn't all plain sailing, with the cartoonist earning the ire of *Doonesbury's* Garry Trudeau for borrowing too heavily from his own firmly entrenched satire. The two strips ran side-by-side in the nation's papers for years after *Bloom County* took *Doonesbury's* place in *The Washington Post* and Trudeau moved his strip elsewhere. Breathed targeted everything from self-indulgent television evangelists to the government's antidrug policies, censorship, and apartheid. By the time this acerbic strip ended in August 1989 it was appearing worldwide in 1,200 newspapers. Not bad for someone who once spent his time doctoring photographs on the University of Texas's student newspaper. **BS**

Life in Hell 1980

✐ Matt Groening

First published by *Los Angeles Reader* (USA)
Creator American (b.1954)
Genre Humor
Award Reuben Award (2002)

When *Life in Hell* was first published in 1980 Matt Groening was employed as the paste-up artist and delivery driver for the paper in which it appeared. After being fired following staff changes, he transferred the strip to the rival free paper, *L.A. Weekly*, by which point his self-published collections had come to the attention of TV producer James L. Brooks, and subsequent talks with him led to *The Simpsons*.

In the early days *Life in Hell* was the exclusive province of Binky, created as a rabbit because Groening, honest about his limited cartooning skills, found him easy to draw. Binky was a set-upon everybunny, soon joined by a girlfriend, Sheba, and a son from a previous relationship, the one-eared Bongo. A human couple named Akbar and Jeff would occasionally hijack the feature to promote a succession of unconventional businesses like Tofu Hut, but would soon graduate to surreal conversations about their relationship.

Groening's strength as a cartoonist is his intelligent writing. He's adept at mining topics such as the enduring banality of everyday life, as well as regurgitating his own experiences for material. One memorable sequence (in "School is Hell") reworks Groening's fifth grade diary. Other recurring features are niche magazine suggestions and Bongo's single-panel denials in the face of overwhelming evidence. The strip was excellent for the first fifteen years, and has continued despite the success of *The Simpsons*, which inflated the circulation. Keeping to a promise he made in the 1980s, in 2007 the title changed to *Life Is Swell*. **FP**

Thorgal 1980

Jean Van Hamme   Grzegorz Rosiński

Title in original language *Thorgal: La Magicienne Trahie*
First published by Le Lombard (Belgium)
Creators Van Hamme (Belgian, b.1939); Rosiński (Polish, b.1941) **Genre** Fantasy

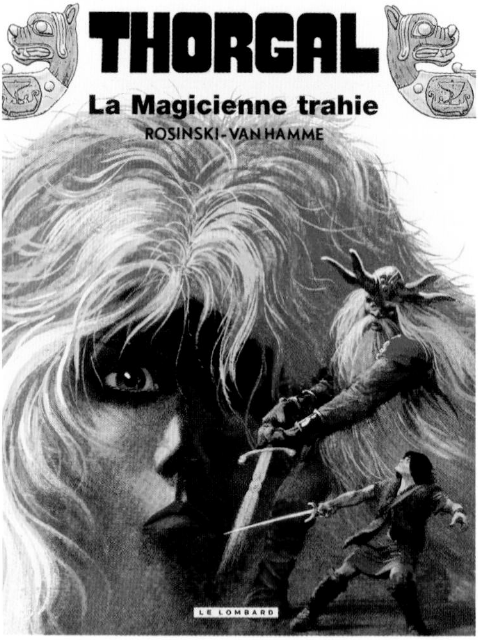
THORGAL
La Magicienne trahie
ROSINSKI-VAN HAMME
LE LOMBARD

Other *Thorgal* stories
Beyond the Land of Shadows (*Au-delà des Ombres*)
The Archers (*Les Archers*)
The Child of the Stars (*L'Enfant des Étoiles*)
The Eyes of Tanatloc (*Les Yeux de Tanatloc*)
The Island of Frozen Seas (*L'Ile des Mers Gelées*)

Thorgal is an exceptionally workmanlike series, in the best meaning of the word. It has been carefully crafted with a large cast of well-wrought characters who are introduced succinctly in exciting scenarios. Like a long-running television show, each episode is satisfying in its own right but moves the overall story along.

Jean Van Hamme knows how to pack plenty of action and character development into every page without being too wordy. Grzegorz Rosiński's art is a perfect match, clean and detailed, reminiscent of great adventure strips like *Prince Valiant*, but with a livelier line and less fondness for huge panoramas.

The series' appeal is very much that of genre fiction. There is a familiarity of structure, a revolving cast of well-loved characters, and the knowledge that, however much each story reveals, there will always be some new surprise lurking over the horizon.

The hero, Thorgal Aegirsson, is rescued as a baby by a clan of Vikings, and grows up to become an extraordinarily skilled archer, although some of his compatriots worry that he shows far too much tenderness to be a real Viking. It is eventually revealed that Thorgal is the child of advanced space travelers who came to Earth in search of alternative energy sources. Later volumes cover his childhood, and, as the series develops, he marries and his children go on to have their own adventures.

Thorgal would like to have a quiet life with his wife Aaricia, son Jolan, and daughter Louve. However, the gods have earmarked him for all sorts of missions. His children develop supernatural powers, Thorgal spends a period as a pirate captain after losing his memory, he is "married" to his great enemy Kriss of Valnor, and his entire family is enslaved and taken to Byzantium. Van Hamme uses all the opportunities that myth and history offer to fully develop this rollicking heroic fantasy. **FJ**

Crisp artwork and sharp dialogue bring Thorgal to life. ➡

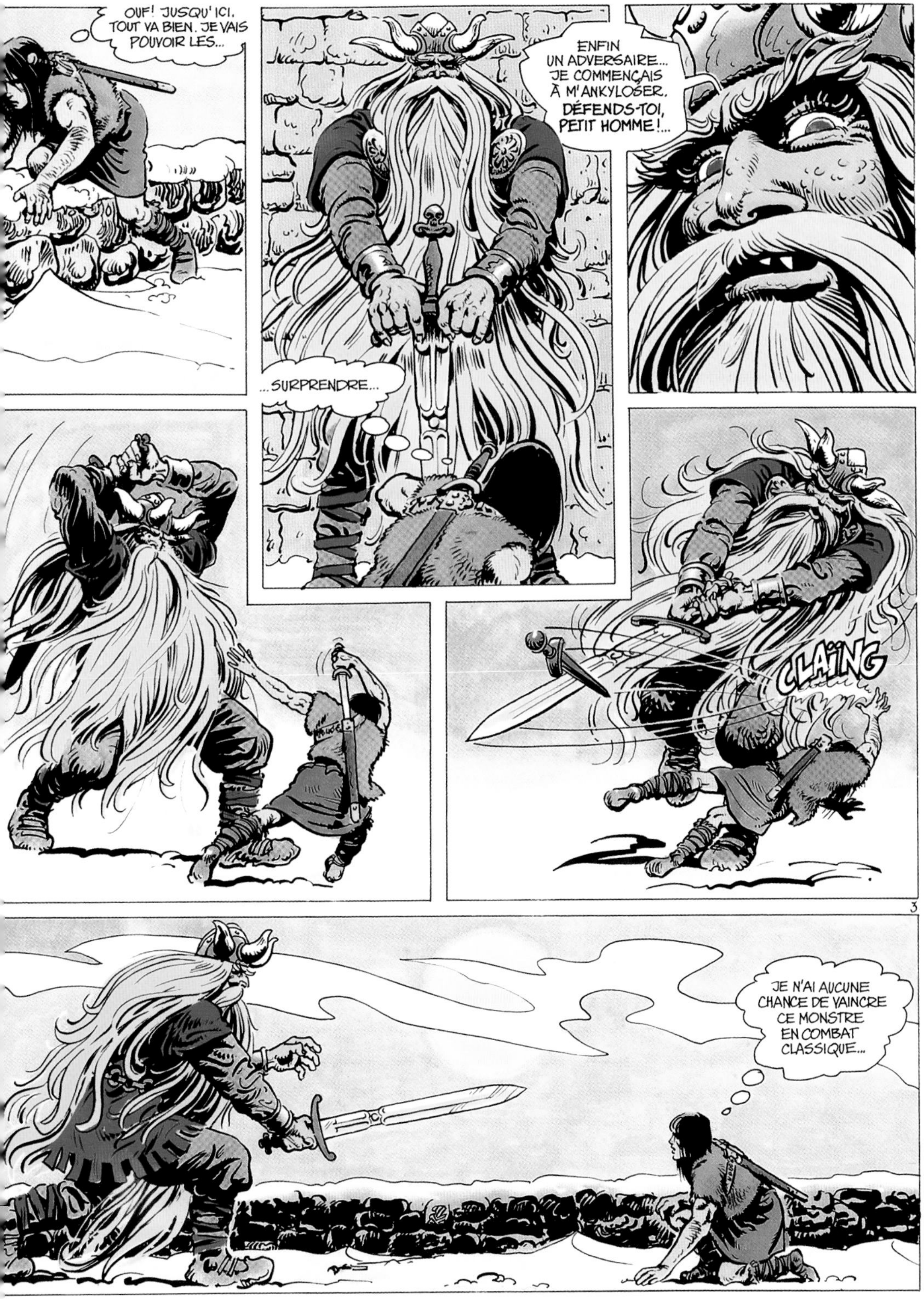
OUF! JUSQU'ICI, TOUT VA BIEN. JE VAIS POUVOIR LES...
...SURPRENDRE...
ENFIN UN ADVERSAIRE... JE COMMENÇAIS À M'ANKYLOSER. DÉFENDS-TOI, PETIT HOMME!...
CLAÏNG
JE N'AI AUCUNE CHANCE DE VAINCRE CE MONSTRE EN COMBAT CLASSIQUE...

Squeak the Mouse 1980

"Mattioli"

GLI ALBI DI BLUE
MATTIOLI
SERIE COLORE LIRE 8.000
SQUEAK THE MOUSE
THRILLS! LAUGHS! SEX! GORE!
SUGAR
PER ADULTI
V.M. 18 ANNI
Blue press

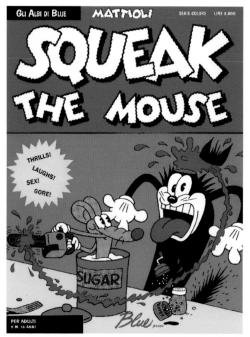

"Squeak the Mouse *can best be described as* Tom and Jerry *meets* Friday the 13th; *funny-animal splatterpunk.*"

***Frames Per Second* magazine**

Also by Mattioli

Friske the Frog
Joe Galaxy
M the Magician (M le Magicien)
Pinky
Superwest

First published by *Frigidaire* magazine (Italy)
Creator Massimo Mattioli (Italian, b.1943)
Genre Humor, Satire
Award Romics d'Oro (2009)

As a sort of X-rated version of *Tom and Jerry* and *Looney Tunes* animated cartoons, *Squeak the Mouse* tells of the cantankerous and violent relationship between a cat and a mouse constantly trying to kill each other in inventive ways. In every episode of this silent comic, the mouse is the bloodiest of the two, chasing the cat and often slaughtering his feline friends.

Contrasting with Mattioli's simple, childish character design, the situations depicted are strictly for adults: not the usual fare for mouse-and-cat interactions, but rather an anticonformist's mix of sexual encounters and brutal violence. The result is a satirical critique very close to *The Simpsons' Itchy & Scratchy Show*.

The most stunning ingredient of the work is its visual style, where Mattioli's inventive surrealism pushes characters toward odd solutions, and where the rhythm of the gags and actions is fast and syncopated.

After debuting in traditional weekly *Il Vittorioso* in 1965, Mattioli worked in London for magazines such as *Penthouse* and *Mayfair*, and created *M the Magician* for the French comics mag *Pif*. In 1973 he started his celebrated *Pinky*, an imaginative surreal gag series for the Catholic weekly *Il Giornalino*. After meeting with Stefano Tamburini—*Ranxerox* creator and comics mentor in the 1970s—he founded *Cannibale* in 1977 with Pazienza, Scòzzari, and Liberatore. It became the seminal Italian avant-garde comics magazine, where he started melding underground sensibilities and kids comics' stereotypes, rapidly becoming one of the main cult comics artists in Italy. **MS**

Domu 1980

✎✎ Katsuhiro Otomo

First published by Futabasha (Japan)
Creator Japanese (b.1954)
Genre Fantasy
Award Nihon SF Taisho Award (1983)

In the early 1980s, about two years before the launch of *Akira*, the unanimously admired masterpiece that kept the artist busy until the beginning of the next decade, Katsuhiro Otomo began working on a captivating story that was a combination of detective story, thriller, fantasy, and a disturbing chronicle of Japanese urbanity.

What is immediately striking about *Domu* is its sophisticated construction, a strikingly cinematographic and mature treatment of the subject matter, very impressive in a young author who had only entered the professional world of manga a few years earlier. The story starts on a large residential estate that looks ordinary, but isn't under the surface. It is the scene of a series of suspicious deaths: suicides and unexplained accidents, each incomprehensible and inexplicable.

The rhythm and tone of the narrative changes when two more victims are added to the list—a policeman investigating the murders and an adolescent living on the estate who cuts his throat with a box cutter in front of a witness. From then on, *Domu* changes dramatically. In the end, Otomo no longer cares about solving the mystery, and the identity of the guilty person is revealed relatively early on. The artist does not try to give a rational ending to his story, preferring to explore the dark abyss from which the characters of children emerge. This almost animist adventure, impressive in its graphic skills and imagination, pays tribute to the powers of the mind and marks a milestone in Otomo's creative development. In many respects it is a seminal work. **NF**

Anarcoma 1980

✎✎ "Nazario"

First published by La Cúpula (Spain)
Creator Nazario Luque Vera (Spanish, b.1944)
Genre Adult humor
Influenced by Tom of Finland

Anarcoma was published in a number of magazines such as *Rampa*, *El Víbora*, and various international titles from 1980, but this is the first book collection of her exploits. Named after its protagonist, Anarcoma, a transsexual prostitute-cum-detective operating in the seediest corners of Barcelona's Las Ramblas, the stories follow her adventures during which she encounters numerous crooks, frequent peril, fantastic traps, and easy fixes for a romp.

The portmanteau name "Anarcoma" comprises *anarco* (anarchist) and *carcoma* (woodworm) reflects the newfound sexual freedom and mirth that was shaking Catholic Spain after Franco's dictatorship. This included a laxer attitude towards sexuality and homosexuality in particular. In many respects author Nazario was a precursor of the countercultural movement—*la movida*" (the scene)—associated with Madrid, but in which other cities also played a crucial part.

The plot is dense with twists, parallel narratives, and cut-ins on every panel. It features a strange machine developed by Professor Onliyú, a real-life MacGuffin, although no one knows its purpose. Nazario's art is full of detail, texture, and rich color, and his characters are full bodied and imposing. Singer Marc Almond of Soft Cell even wrote a song about Anarcoma in 2007: "A stiletto scrapes the pavement / Leaving a red streak of paint / Breaks a sweat upon the sailors / To them she is a saint." She has been compared with Modesty Blaise, Lauren Bacall, and Humphrey Bogart—a combination leading to a funny, X-rated, hard-boiled saga. **PM**

Jack Survives 1980

✐✐ Jerry Moriarty

First published by Raw Books & Graphics (USA)
Creator American (b.1938)
Genre Autobiography
Notable mention Abstract expressionist solo artist

Jerry Moriarty's *Jack Survives* allowed him to identify and commune with the father he lost in 1953. Jerry got the sort of education that his father, Jack, never had and grew up to be a radical, largely solitary, artist and art teacher, a world away from his father's modest job, family life, and conservative values. It was only when Jerry reached forty, Jack's age when Jerry as a boy first remembered him, that he began to re-create everyday incidents in his father's life in comic form—a faulty TV set, shoe repairs, getting tangled in a dog's leash—and imagine how the "Jack" inside himself—what he calls "the better me"—might have reacted.

Layered in brushstrokes of black and white, and written with lyrical minimalism, his picture stories— part comics, part painting—were discovered in 1979 by Art Spiegelman, then a fellow instructor at New York's School of Visual Arts. He and Françoise Mouly premiered them in their seminal *RAW* magazine in 1980 and compiled many of them in 1984.

It was not until 2009's *The Complete Jack Survives* that every strip, drawing, and painting was meticulously remastered to expose their full tonal range and little seen under-drawing, alongside tender family photographs and commentary. He reflected, "My father has had time to become almost mythology to me, so Jack grows more poignant in my old age as I fuse myself with my dad." Jerry also survives today but, without Jack the comic character, whom he has replaced with another avatar named Sally. She represents his teenage experiences in large-scale painted sequences. **PG**

Touch 1981

✐✐ Mitsuru Adachi

First published by Shogakukan (Japan)
Creator Japanese (b.1951)
Genre Drama
Award Shogakukan Manga Award (1983)

Mitsuru Adachi's *Touch* was a breath of fresh air for the Japanese sports comics scene when it first appeared in *Weekly Shonen Sunday* in 1981. Although the theme of baseball was nothing new—an array of successful titles had already been established, such as *Kyojin no Hoshi*—it was the way in which Adachi executed the theme that made it refreshing. Unlike past titles, *Touch* wasn't about masculine, hot-blooded baseball-lovers. Instead, it was an emotional drama.

Initially the plot revolved around the eternal love triangle of twin brothers Tatsuya and Kazuya Uesugi and their childhood friend, Minami Asakura. While Tatsuya, the central character, is a slacker, Kazuya is a top player on his school baseball team and in love with Minami, the team's manager. As the awkward tension between the three becomes increasingly hard to ignore, the story takes an unexpected turn when Kazuya dies in a car accident. Kazuya's death prompts Tatsuya to join the school baseball team, deciding that he must keep his brother's promise to Minami to lead his team to the national high school championship. The fact that Tatsuya did this purely out of love for his brother and Minami, but never for baseball itself, was distinctly different to others of the same genre.

Perhaps the precise moment that made *Touch* a masterpiece was Kazuya's death. Adachi's prolonged depiction lasted weeks, the minimal dialogue and dramatic use of onomatopoeia taking readers on an intense and vivid journey through Tatsuya and Minami's heartbreaking devastation. **TS**

The Hunting Party 1981

Pierre Christin   Enki Bilal

Title in original language *Partie de chasse*
First published by Dargaud (France)
Creators Christin (French, b.1938); Bilal (French, b.1951)
Genre Drama

LEGENDES D'AUJOURD'HUI
PARTIE DE CHASSE
ENKI BILAL / PIERRE CHRISTIN
BILAL
DARGAUD

It is the beginning of the 1980s. A dozen influential leaders from Eastern Bloc countries and satellites of Soviet Russia meet somewhere in Poland to take part in a shooting party organized by their common friend and mentor, General Vasili Aleksandrovič Čevčenko. Remote from hostile ears, everyone can speak freely, with the exception of Čevčenko who is unable to make a sound after being struck with aphasia. Invited as an interpreter, a young French communist is present at this informal, very select meeting of top leaders.

What looks like a traditional gathering of old comrades-in-arms meeting for a bear-hunting party is far from innocent. How could it be when so many powerful men are brought together, men who have fought to survive in a totalitarian milieu? At this meeting of dinosaurs of the Soviet system, the young French idealist finally realizes (all too late) that his apparently fortuitous presence is no coincidence. He is there only as an instrument—in spite of himself and in bloody circumstances—of plans that he does not understand. Brutal, yes, but that is the way in the silent world of the state on the far side of the Iron Curtain when it teaches a lesson in "real socialism."

The Hunting Party is a caustic and cynical take on communism in Soviet countries, and it is also a bitter, cruel reflection on the seizing of power and the bloody measures taken to keep it. With Enki Bilal's masterly graphic interpretation adding an epic depth to Pierre Christin's script, *The Hunting Party* is one of the best illustrations of political analysis in strip cartoons. **NF**

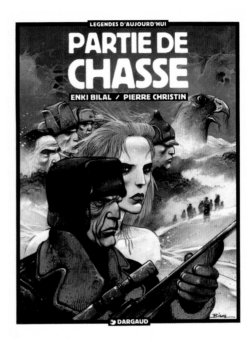

"I do not understand. Nothing was supposed to happen today."

Janos Molnar

Similar reads

The Ranks of the Black Order (Les Phalanges de l'Ordre Noir) Pierre Christin and Enki Bilal
The City That Didn't Exist (Le Ville qui n'existe pas) Pierre Christin and Enki Bilal
Valérian and Laureline Pierre Christin and J.-C. Mézières

Go, Bouzid, Go 1981

"Slim"

Title in original language *Zid ya Bouzid*
First published by SNED Editions (Algeria)
Creator Menouar Merabtène (Algerian, b.1945)
Genre Humor

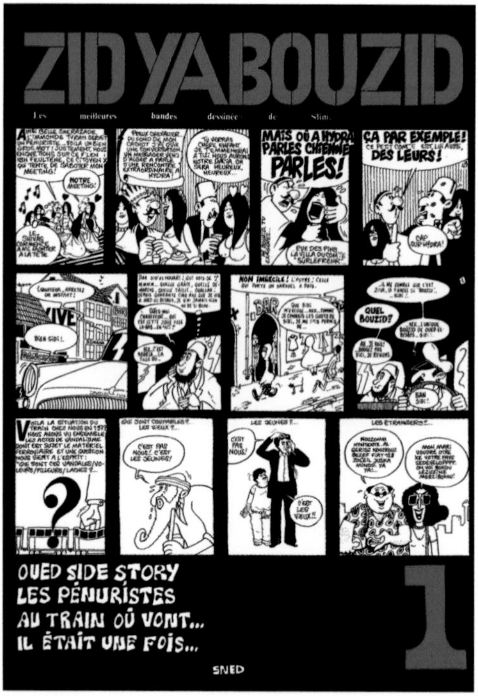
ZID YA BOUZID
Les meilleures bandes dessinée de Slim
OUED SIDE STORY
LES PÉNURISTES
AU TRAIN OÙ VONT...
IL ÉTAIT UNE FOIS...
SNED
1

Also by Slim
Go, Bouzid, Go 2 (Zid ya Bouzid 2)
Go, Bouzid, Go 3 (Zid ya Bouzid 3)
The Wonderful Bearded World (Le Monde Merveilleux des Barbus)
Walou on the Horizon (Walou à l'horizon)

In Algeria, an oil producing, secular, and Islamic country, the comic album *Go, Bouzid, Go* was published in 1981 for the first time by SNED editions. It was a huge public and critical success and it immediately went into all Algerian bookshops.

The comic strip encompasses the adventures of Bouzid El Bessebsi, a character who had appeared in national newspaper strips since 1969. Created by Slim, his characters Bouzid, his fiancée Zina, and his friend Mohand had represented the hopes and failings of the Algerian socialist dream. There are many reasons for Bouzid's appeal: he is a young North African folk hero, who with his fez, stick, and mustache, embodies all the virtues of the Maghreb fresh from colonial rule. His resourcefulness and outspokenness are matched only by his patriotism and idealism. In the early episodes Bouzid, in his fight against "speculators" and "enemies of the revolution," is definitely socialist. However, in the corner boxes with graffiti on walls, in the thoughts of the cat, another society is emerging: one that is not as rosy, not truly open, where the political police and state propaganda are masters.

"This cartoon is intended for all those who have never set foot in a train."

However, Bouzid, thanks to Slim's beautiful outline drawings, is a positive character: sassy and more lucid than some of the others, of course, but positive. There he remained until the late 1980s and the beginning of the civil war. After three albums (*Zid ya Bouzid 1*, *2*, and *3*) Slim began a second life. He had always been inspired by the French cartoonist Gotlib, so his next work was on the comic *Boite à Chique* that appeared in the weekly *Revolution Africaine*, and was a fierce and dry critique of society. **RA**

Zanardi 1981

Andrea Pazienza

This cycle of short stories looks at the daily lives of a group of seventeen- and eighteen-year-old high school students and bad boys: Zanardi, Colasanti, and Petrilli. In the first episode, in order to get compromising information from a teacher's house, Colasanti helps Zanardi blackmail a nerdy, homosexual schoolmate by sodomizing him while Zanardi takes pictures with a stolen camera.

Throughout the cycle Zanardi remains the leader; he is a tall, well-dressed boy who is cruel and detached, an impassive mastermind. Colasanti is handsome and fit, an occasional rent boy, and Zanardi's helping hand in his wrongdoings, but he also suffers from a lack of culture and cool. Petrilli is the group's most educated

"Patience [in Italian: pazienza] has its limits; Pazienza doesn't!"

member and an eternal loser, often humiliated by his two friends. In following episodes the teens will deal with drug dealing, rape, extortion, and vengeance.

The mood is that of a naturalistic view of teenage life and angst, and set in a recognizable Italian town. Teenage rebellion and disillusion are seen as tragic swings between desires and a deep existential void faced with violence and despair. The drawing and layouts reveal an incredible talent that merges painting and cartooning sensibilities from Renaissance art to Italian postmodernism, from Moebius to Carl Barks.

Andrea Pazienza's style is a blend of realism with a vital, expressive twist. As Zanardi is quite intense, Pazienza visually characterized him with a beaklike nose, conveying the image of a tall, young predator. Pazienza, known for his many satirical works and short stories, became increasingly popular and one of the most famous "comics auteur" icons in Italy. **MS**

First published by *Frigidaire* magazine (Italy)
Creator Italian (1956–88)
Genre Drama **Notable mention** Centro Fumetto Andrea Pazienza nonprofit organization

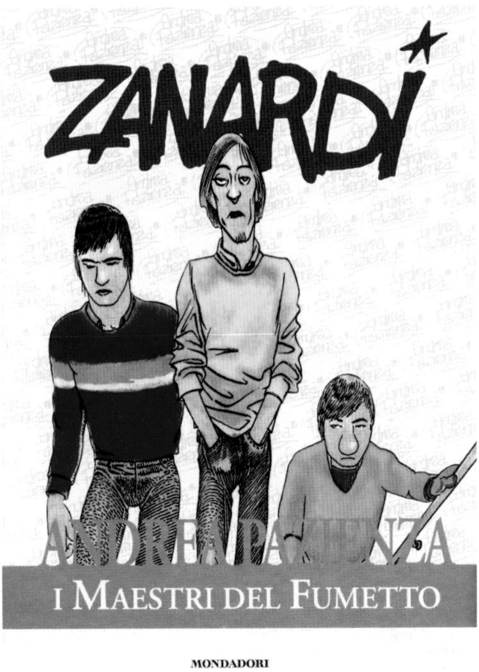
ZANARDI
ANDREA PAZIENZA
I MAESTRI DEL FUMETTO
MONDADORI

Also by Andrea Pazienza

Aficionados
The Extraordinary Adventures of Pentothal (*Le Straordinarie Avventure Pentothal*)
Why Goofy Looks Like a Pothead (*Perché Pippo Sembra uno Sballato*)

Necron 1981

Mirka Martini "Magnus"

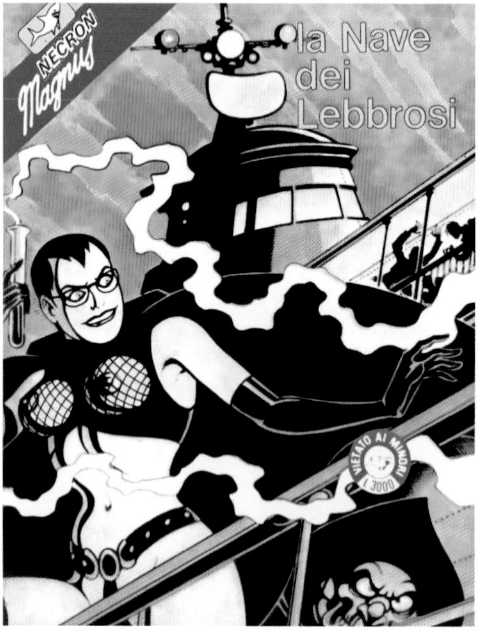

NECRON
Magnus
la Nave dei Lebbrosi
VIETATO AI MINORI
L. 3000

"Once I'm drunk, I won't mind so much being screwed by him! He's repulsive! His skin is warm and moist! Yuck! I prefer a cold corpse . . . I'll use you and then I'll kill you!"

Also by Magnus
110 Pills (*Le 110 Pillole*)
Alan Ford with Max Bunker
Kriminal with Max Bunker
Satanik with Max Bunker
Tex Willer with Claudio Nizzi

Title in original language *Necron*
First published by Edifumetto (Italy)
Creators Martini (Italian, 1942–99); Roberto Raviola (Italian, 1939–96) **Genre** Horror, Humor

Everything is in the title, or nearly so. An outstanding biologist working at the Institute of Histological Research in West Berlin (we are in the early 1980s, and the division of the world between the two opposing ideological blocs is still of topical interest), Doctor Frieda Boher is also a necrophiliac. Driven by lust, she recovers parts of various corpses stolen in the course of her work to make a living-dead slave of Herculean strength and inexhaustible vitality who would be entirely devoted to satisfying her perverted sexuality.

Alas, as a modern heir (although deeply depraved) of the famous Doctor Frankenstein, Frieda's creature deviates slightly from her original objective. Necron, the giant whom Frieda has brought to life, admittedly meets her sexual expectations, but he has two major and unforgivable defects: he is a cannibal and terribly sentimental, handicaps that will have to be dealt with, for the best and (especially) for the worst, in hilarious adventures full of violence, depravation, and excesses of every kind.

Conceived in Italy outside the boundaries of "decent" strip cartoons, *Necron* accepts its popular origins with an infectious enthusiasm. Running counter to all standards of decency, set between gore and grotesque hypersexuality, Magnus's creation can be described as the perfect culmination of trash humor and bad taste. The parallel with *eroguro*, very present in Japanese mangas, is obvious—the same love of provocation, extreme theatricality, and discretely ironic examinations of human passions. **NF**

Captain Tsubasa 1981

✎✎ Yoichi Takahashi

Title in original language *Kyaputen Tsubasa*
First published by Shueisha (Japan)
Creator Japanese (b.1960)
Genre Children's

It took a fair amount of ambition for Shueisha to launch the soccer-themed *Captain Tsubasa* in Japan in 1981 when young boys' hearts were predominantly occupied by baseball, one of the nation's many cultural imports from America. But despite the ambitious timing of its release, Yoichi Takahashi's masterpiece was a success when it arrived in *Weekly Shonen Jump*.

Japan did not have a professional soccer league at the time, and the sport was virtually unheard of. Takahashi's surprisingly dynamic vision placed its focus on elementary school boy Tsubasa Oozora, who dreams of not only becoming the best soccer player in the world, but winning the FIFA World Cup for Japan. Readers instantly took to Tsubasa and his implausibly skillful, exaggerated soccer moves that often led his team to miraculous victory. Tsubasa's signature "Flying Drive Shoot," where the ball is shot into the goal with such force that it sweeps up the defending opponents along the way, became a sensation.

The comic's themes of friendship, teamwork, and rivalry was engaging, sparking a soccer craze among boys all over Japan. It was so influential that when the Japanese League finally opened in 1993, many gave the credit to Takahashi. In fact, some of today's eminent soccer players grew up reading *Captain Tsubasa*, including Japan's Keisuke Honda, who has admitted to stealing moves from Kojiro Hyuga, and Spain's Fernando Torres, who is a fan of Wakabayashi the goalkeeper. In an interview Torres once said that the comic should be "essential reading for all aspiring soccer players." **TS**

If... 1981

✎✎ Steve Bell

First published by *The Guardian* (UK)
Creator British (b.1951)
Genre Satire, Humor
Award Cartoonist of the Year (1993)

Satire has been alive and well in comic books ever since the caricaturist James Gillray highlighted the absurdities of eighteenth-century British high society in *Punch*. Steve Bell, a self-confessed leftist, is happy to continue the tradition. Prior to *If...* he'd already plunged himself into plenty of editorial hot water with *Maggie's Farm*, a biting, unrelenting weekly tirade against Margaret Thatcher's Tory government published in the magazines *Time Out* and *City Limits* that was condemned as obscene in the House of Lords, no less.

Named after Rudyard Kipling's 1895 poem of rules and maxims for everyday living, *If...* began its caustic, satirical run in Britain's *Guardian* newspaper in 1981 and was used by Bell to encourage readers to question everything political, from the superficiality of politicians' peeches to their entrenched bureaucracies, economic and social policies, and military campaigns from the Falkland Islands to Afghanistan.

If... became the nation's preeminent platform for political satire, and Bell's lampooning had few boundaries. Victims have included Henry Kissinger as a turkey with a thick German accent, Iran's Ayatollah Khomeini draped in blood-stained robes, and George W. Bush drawn to resemble a primate. At a Labor Party conference in the 1990s, Bell was the first to notice a psychotic "glint" in Tony Blair's eye—which became his Blair motif. When it comes to satire, Bell was never one for pulling his punches. "It's almost your duty to do it, if you can," he once said of his job which is, as he sees it, to deflate political egos. **BS**

Nova-2 1981

🖉🖉 Luis Garcia Mozos

First published by *Totem* (Spain); *Heavy Metal* (USA)
Creator Spanish (b.1946)
Genre Drama
Award Warren Award (1972)

During the 1970s, Luis Garcia Mozos earned a reputation as one of comics' great radicals. While he created exquisitely crafted strips for *Warren* magazine in the United States and *Pilote* in France, he was also drawing politically impassioned stories for a variety of far-left titles and partying with Salvador Dalí. Garcia began work on what was to become his masterpiece *Nova-2*, in 1980, but what began as a science fiction tale changed when he heard about the killing of John Lennon.

The story abruptly stopped at page nine, and the first half of the strip became a meditation on hope and despair as, in a new narrative, a depressed comic book artist buys a gun and tries (unsuccessfully) to kill himself. The second half of the story tracks his life from the moment of conception through a childhood spent during the Spanish Civil War, and finally, his fate at the hands of his psychoanalyst. Throughout there are references and quotes from the likes of Allen Ginsberg, Diego Velázquez, The Beatles, and Alex Raymond.

Visually it was a tour de force, mixing delicate pen work with sequences rendered in sumptuous graphite, making it one of the most realistically drawn comics ever seen. For Garcia, the strip represented his sadness at the passing of the 1960s counterculture and his increasing disillusionment with Marxism. Choosing to syndicate the strip himself, Garcia flew to New York, where it was serialized to great acclaim in *Heavy Metal* magazine. The second half of the story appeared in the Spanish title *Rambla*, after which Garcia abandoned comics for a career in fine art. **DAR**

Cowboy Henk 1981

🖉 "Kamagurka" 🖉 "Herr Seele"

First published by *De Morgen* newspaper (Belgium)
Creators Luc Zeebroek (Belgian, b.1956); Peter van Heirseele (Belgian, b.1959) **Genre** Humor
Award Guezenprijs (Kamagurka, 1985)

The barrel-chested Cowboy Henk sports an ostentatious yellow quiff (a nod to *Tintin*), an extensive wardrobe (though more often than not he prefers a white T-shirt and jeans), and a pair of the clumsiest, round-toed black shoes imaginable. His chiseled, jutting jaw can be compared with that of the British cowboy *Desperate Dan*. Henk leads a contrary life, one colored with the poetry of surrealism and the absurd.

Apart from a few secondary characters, such as a neighbor named Freddy, who Henk enjoys playing practical jokes on, the supporting cast remain nameless and rarely appear beyond a single strip. In the tradition of adsurdity, each adventure contains its own internal logic. The happy-go-lucky Henk behaves as if he is oblivious of his reader, for example, when he takes his trousers down to defecate into a bird's nest, but then he will sometimes wink as if sharing the joke. In one episode, Henk rescues a "drowning" fish from a river and gives it the kiss of life, only for it to actually die.

In another, he deliberately blinds himself with a knife because he is familiar with the part of town where he is walking. Smiling, he taps his way along the sidewalk using a blind person's white stick, which has appeared from nowhere. Yet by the following strip, despite the depiction of blood pouring from his eye sockets, everything is back to normal, his blindness only temporary. Kamagurka and Herr Seele adapted their strip for television and radio, and *Cowboy Henk* still appears in the Flemish weekly *Humo*. A huge sculpture of his head adorns his hometown of Kortrijk in Belgium. **LC**

Cowboy Henk delivers sharp, funny, and often surreal humor. ➡

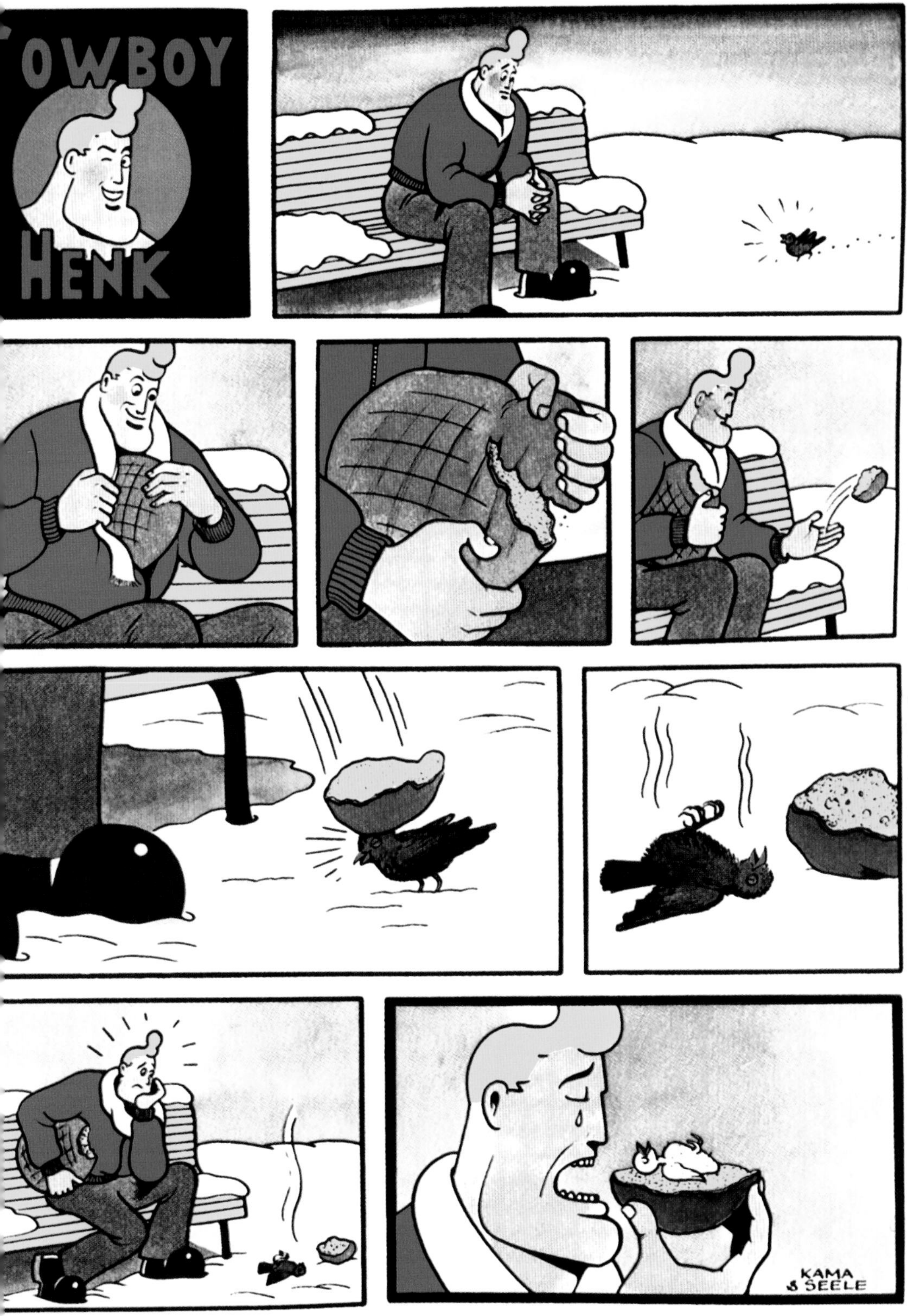
COWBOY HENK
KAMA
& SEELE

Akira 1982

Katsuhiro Otomo

First published by Kodansha (Japan)
Creator Japanese (b.1954)
Genre Science fiction
Award Kodansha General Manga Award (1984)

AKIRA
OTOMO KATSUHIRO
1
KODANSHA
SPECIAL PRICE
1000 yen

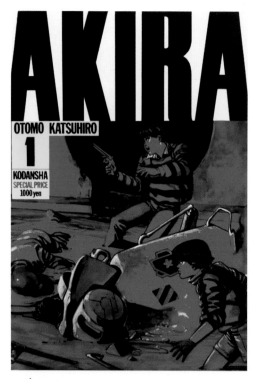

Similar reads
Battle Royale Koushun Takami and Masayuki Taguchi
Domu Katsuhiro Otomo
Dragon Head Minetaro Mochizuki
Nausicaä of the Valley of the Wind Hayao Miyazaki

Running to a whopping 2,182 pages, *Akira* is a dazzling, heady mix of youth rebellion, science fiction, romance, action, and fear of the apocalypse.

Kaneda is a fifteen-year-old rebel and leader of a biker gang who spend their after-school hours tearing up the highways of Neo Tokyo in the year 2030. His best friend and fellow biker, Tetsuo, is injured while swerving to avoid a withered-looking child on an abandoned section of road, after which he is taken away by the army. When Tetsuo returns, he has changed into an angrier, more violent young man with ever-growing psychic abilities. The ensuing clash between Kaneda and Tetsuo plays out against a backdrop of fierce political struggle between the government, army, and an underground resistance movement, all looking for the secret of Akira—a child who destroyed Tokyo thirty-eight years before, and may do so again.

Akira is a masterwork of action-fueled drama, and it contains some of the finest action sequences ever committed to page. Katsuhiro Otomo tells his story on a breathtaking scale, creating a sprawling, densely populated roller-coaster ride as the reader witnesses a city tearing itself apart, through coups d'état, epic battles, psychic dueling, the partial destruction of the moon, and the complete destruction of Neo Tokyo.

Otomo's black-and-white illustrations are highly detailed and more Western than a lot of other manga, using speed lines and dynamic camera angles to create a racing, highly cinematic narrative. *Akira* is a unique hybrid of Western and Japanese sensibilities, both in illustration style and substance, and has become a cultural phenomenon. Drawing inspiration from films such as *The Wild One* and *Bonnie and Clyde*, it is perhaps fitting that *Akira* is the book that opened the door to manga in the West. It also spawned video games and a 1988 animated film directed by Otomo. **BD**

Otomo's superb draftsmanship captures life in Neo Tokyo. ➡

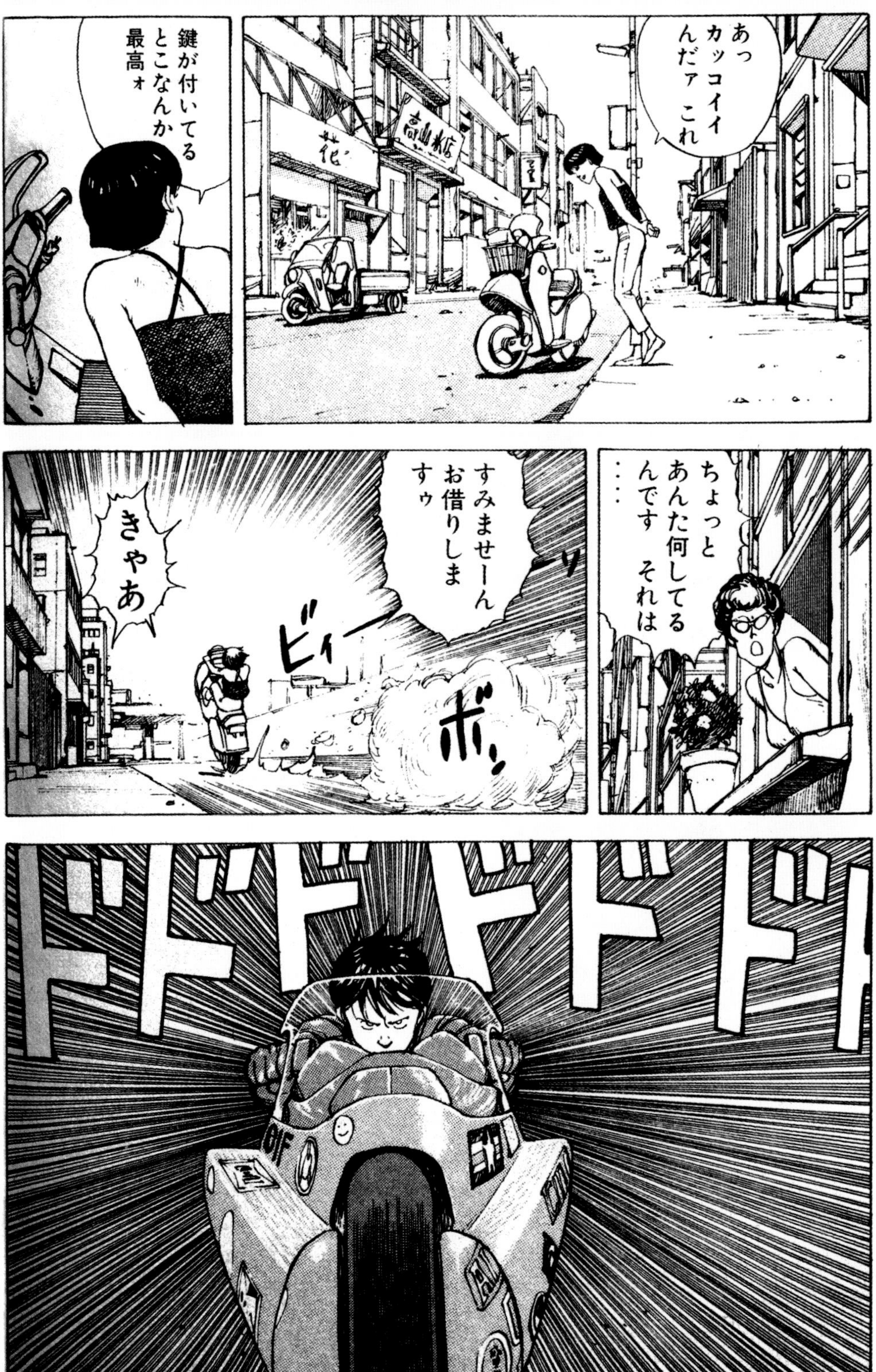
あっ カッコイイんだァ これ
鍵が付いてるとこなんか最高ォ
ちょっとあんた何してるんです それは・・・・
すみませーんお借りしますゥ
きゃあ
ビィーッ
ボッ
ドドドドド

Biff 1982

✎ Mick Kidd   ✎ Chris Garratt

First published by Pavement Press (UK)
Creators Kidd (British, b.1944); Garratt (British, b.1944)
Genre Humor, Parody
Influenced by *Eagle* comic

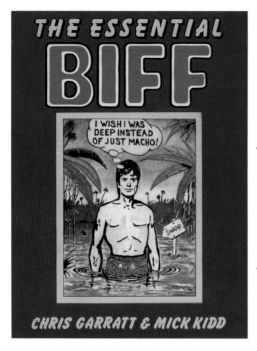

THE ESSENTIAL

BIFF

I WISH I WAS DEEP INSTEAD OF JUST MACHO!

SWAMP

CHRIS GARRATT & MICK KIDD

Similar reads
Ars Brevis Mick Kidd and Chris Garratt
Best of Biff Mick Kidd and Chris Garratt
File Under Biff Mick Kidd and Chris Garratt
The Bart Dickon Omnibus Borin Van Loon
The Caterer Steve Aylett

This tragicomic rooted in irony is created by Mick Kidd and Chris Garratt, hailed by British cartoonist Steve Bell as "two mad old farts from Leicestershire, locked in a long-distance comedy partnership since childhood." They started self-publishing *Biff* in a series of single-panel cartoons as postcards and as *Biff Quarterly* before evolving them into multipanel comic strips that appeared weekly in the *Guardian* newspaper for twenty years starting in 1985, eventually in color. The duo's apparently arbitrary use of the title *Biff*, taken from *Biffo the Bear* in the British children's comic *The Beano*, is a knowing decision by the creators. Biff is a character referred to only once in these strips. The nonrecurring characters live out their lives in a semiotic

> *"One moment I'm buzzing with joie de vivre, the next I'm slumped on the couch hitting the remote and the fatty snacks."*

and theoretical fog. They constantly try to impress, or verbally outmaneuver, their friends and colleagues. The "chattering classes" declare their seduction by language but fail to see their own ineptitude and stupidity.

The visuals look like they have been cannibalized from comics of the 1950s and 1960s, and are similar to the style of situationist comics that appeared in the French underground press at the time. The dialogue draws on theories of existentialism and postmodernism. Media moguls, college lecturers, artists, poets, writers, critics, advertising gurus, homespun philosophers, and rat-race escapees disappear in a smokescreen of words, while dilettante dabblers attempt to deal with the so-called cultural issues of the day. *Biff* strips continue to appear in British periodicals such as *History Today*, *fRoots*, and *Prospect*. **LC**

The Bluecoats

Black Face 1982

Raoul Cauvin "Lambil"

In 1969 Raoul Cauvin and Louis Salvérius published a series in the Belgian magazine *Spirou* about a group of friends in the American garrison of Fort Bow. After Salvérius's death in 1972, Willy Lambotte, known as "Lambil," took over as illustrator. The short stories then developed into long adventures, eventually adopting the forty-eight-page format of the series *The Bluecoats* (*Les Tuniques Bleues*).

The series takes place during the American Civil War. It features two Yankee soldiers, Sergeant Cornelius M. Chesterfield and Corporal Blutch. They are complete opposites: the former fights solely for the sake of glory, honor, and his country, and the latter not at all, however, they are united by an unshakable friendship. All of the stories draw on wartime historical events to create a compelling and exciting mix of fiction and fact.

"At West Point we were taught to use artillery fire to pave the way for a cavalry charge! / Well, here it's the opposite! [We charge] the cavalry!"

Although Blutch and Chesterfield's adventures are always farcical, they deal with serious questions, such as the slavery and racism that triggered the war. *Black Face* (in volume twenty, published in *Spirou* in 1982, then as an album the year after) follows the steps of a rebel so named because of his skin color. For one African-American leader who travels around the plantations, the Yankee abolitionists are far from the perfect liberators. In his eyes the Yankees are no better than the Confederates, since they ask him to polish the officers' shoes, dig latrines, and bury the corpses. This stupid war is not his and he ran away from it. What does he recommend to his brothers? To rise up against the oppressor and grab their freedom with both hands. **CM**

First published by Dupuis (Belgium)
Creators Cauvin (Belgian, b.1938); Willy Lambotte (Belgian, b.1936)
Genre Western, Humor

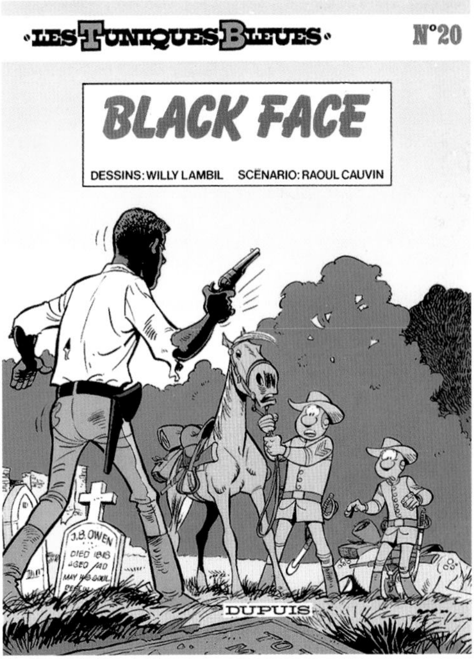

LES TUNIQUES BLEUES
N°20
BLACK FACE
DESSINS: WILLY LAMBIL SCÉNARIO: RAOUL CAUVIN
J.B. OWEN
DUPUIS

Other *Bluecoats* stories

Arabesque
Baby Blue
Bull Run
Drummer Boy
Miss Walker

It Was the War of the Trenches 1982

Jacques Tardi

Title in original language *C'était la guerre des tranchées*
First published by Casterman (Belgium)
Creator French (b.1946)
Genre War

1914
C'ÉTAIT
1918
LA GUERRE
DES TRANCHÉES
TARDI
casterman

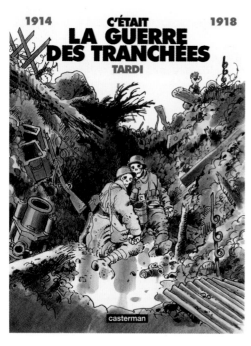

Similar reads

Adieu Brindavoine Jacques Tardi
Le trou d'obus (*The Shell Hole*) Jacques Tardi
Maus Art Spiegelman
Putain de guerre! (*Fucking War!*) Jacques Tardi
Up Front Bill Mauldin

By way of an incident or a character, World War I had been mentioned in all of Jacques Tardi's books prior to *It Was the War of the Trenches*. Even his famous cynical heroine, Adèle Blanc-Sec, is affected by it, albeit peripherally. But here the artist—himself the son of a soldier—takes a further, and decisive, step. He no longer looks at the war as an observer but immerses himself in its daily routines and horrors.

Many historians have debated the origins of World War I, but Tardi is more concerned with how the soldiers from all sides managed to live, fight, and survive in the trench environment. He ponders how it is possible to endure so much suffering, privation, madness, fear, and exposure to death to such a degree and for so long.

"And you, Englishman, you were sent as an ally and a neighbor, but I'm sure you're regretting it now."

There are no simple answers to such questions. In an effort to try and capture the unfathomable and the unutterable, Tardi records the everyday life of ordinary soldiers. He moves from one character to another when one dies—and many do—in an effort to keep as close as possible to the reality of the frontline soldiers. He shows the mud, the decomposing corpses, the human remains, the rats, the screams of the dying, the penetrating cold, the agonies that last all night, the first terrifying tanks, and the clouds of mustard gas.

With total bluntness and absolute accuracy, the artist avoids nothing: he describes the reality, piling detail upon painful detail. Apart from *Putain de guerre!* (*Fucking War!*), the 2008 work in which Tardi returned in detail to the war, graphic novels have never dealt with the subject with such intensity. As Art Spiegelman said in a rare endorsement, "It is one Hell of a book." **NF**

Tardi depicts soldiers' disillusionment with the war. ➡

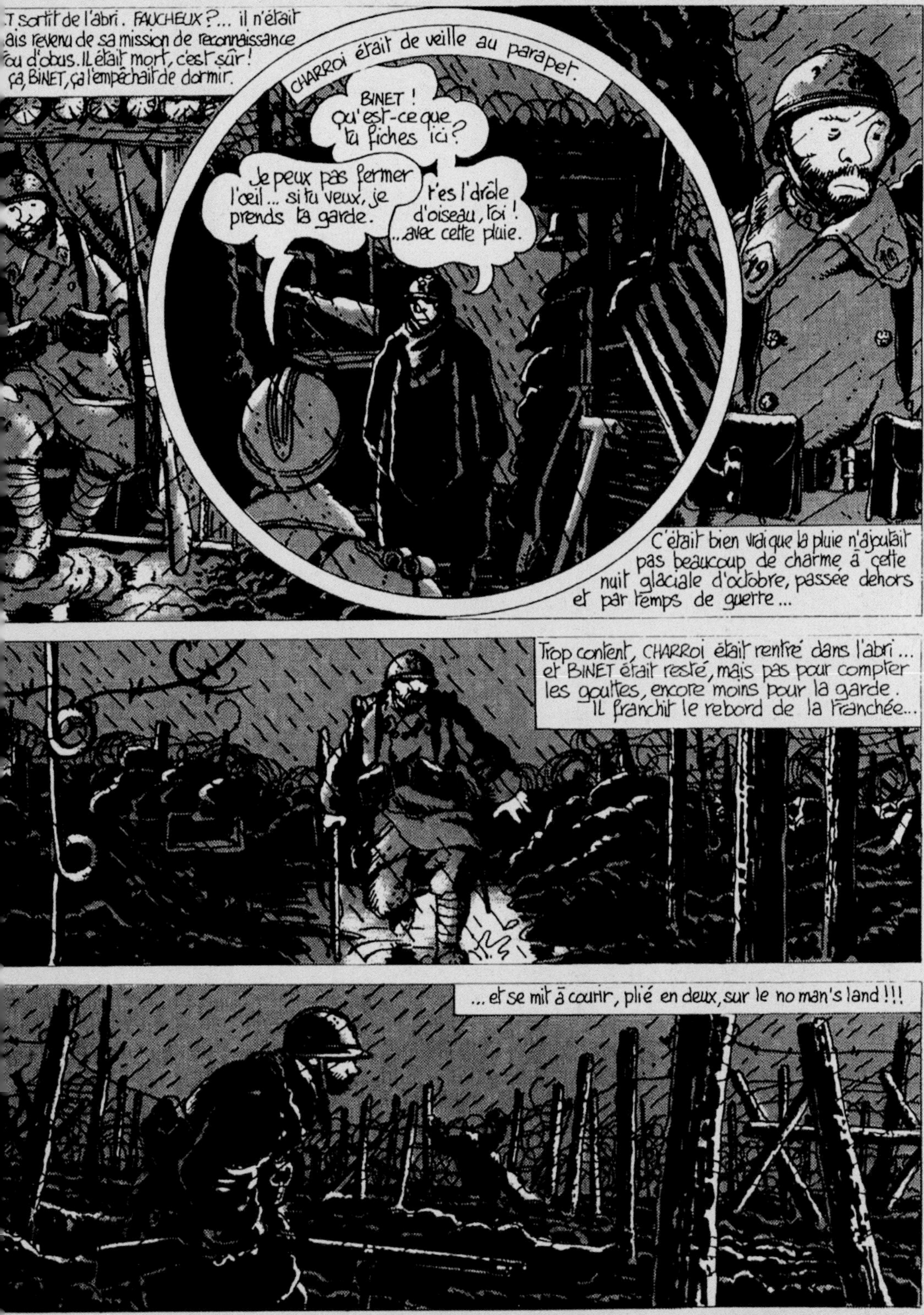
T sortit de l'abri. FAUCHEUX ?... il n'était
ais revenu de sa mission de reconnaissance
ou d'obus. IL était mort, c'est sûr !
ça, BINET, ça l'empêchait de dormir.
CHARROI était de veille au parapet.
BINET ! Qu'est-ce que tu fiches ici ?
Je peux pas fermer l'oeil... si tu veux, je prends ta garde.
T'es l'drôle d'oiseau, toi ! ...avec cette pluie.
C'était bien vrai que la pluie n'ajoutait pas beaucoup de charme à cette nuit glaciale d'octobre, passée dehors et par temps de guerre...
Trop content, CHARROI était rentré dans l'abri... et BINET était resté, mais pas pour compter les gouttes, encore moins pour la garde. Il franchit le rebord de la tranchée...
...et se mit à courir, plié en deux, sur le no man's land !!!

Groo the Wanderer 1982

✎✎ Sergio Aragonés and Mark Evanier

First published by Eclipse Comics (USA)
Creators Aragonés (Spanish, b.1937); Evanier (American, b.1952)
Genre Humor **Award** Reuben Award (1996)

SERGIO ARAGONÉS'
GROO
THE WANDERER
PC
"For the NEW Era in Comics"
$1.00 US
$1.25 Canada

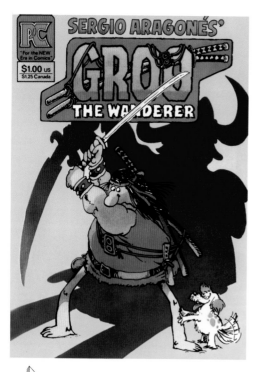

Other *Groo* stories

Groo and Rufferto
Groo Hell on Earth
Groo Mightier than the Sword
The Death of Groo
The Life of Groo

Groo the Wanderer is a master swordsman, quite possibly the best in his world. He is also, unfortunately for many people, of rather low intelligence, so much so that he is likely to forget whom he is fighting for and destroy his allies as well as his enemies. He would do well to heed his faithful and long-suffering companion, Rufferto—if only dogs could talk. Crossing Groo's path on numerous occasions (unless they can help it) are the Sage and the Minstrel, his archenemy Taranto (having served in the army with Groo in the past, he now only wants to kill him), and the witches Arba and Dakarba. Groo himself wants to spend more time with the beautiful warrior woman Chakall, but she usually manages to stay well away. Groo wanders from city to city, driven by the need to eat and fight. If he were not such an accomplished swordsman he would be driven out of everywhere he visits, given his propensity to cause chaos, whether it be physical, economical, or emotional.

"You will be sorry! Groo will return! People are always sorry when Groo returns!"

Mark Evanier

The *Groo* series is written and drawn by Sergio Aragonés, with scripting assistance from Mark Evanier, and lettering and coloring by Stan Sakai and Tom Luth. Aragonés is a superb cartoonist, and his panels are packed with story, character, and humor. The series contains many running jokes, from his hatred of being called a mendicant (although he does not know what it means), to his inability to be on board a ship without causing it to sink. Evanier jests that every *Groo* issue is the same, yet Aragonés's ability to tell the same jokes with a different inflection means they stay funny. **NFI**

Torpedo 1936 1982

Enrique Sánchez Abulí Jordi Bernet

Torpedo 1936 was first published in the Spanish edition of *Creepy* magazine. It was created by writer Enrique Sánchez Abulí for the publisher and artistic agent Josep Toutain, and it was Toutain's decision to have it illustrated by comic book legend Alex Toth. After drawing the first two episodes, however, Toth abandoned the project. He was replaced by Jordi Bernet, and a flourishing partnership was born.

The tale is set in New York during the Great Depression. Antihero Luca Torelli has left his native Sicily after killing a mafia boss in a vendetta. Torelli becomes known as "Torpedo," a tough, unscrupulous hitman who is respected by his peers and feared by his enemies. His only partner is Rascal, a bumbling sidekick.

"I gave him the image of a certain eccentric elegance, in the end a bit ridiculous . . ."

Jordi Bernet

Torpedo 1936 has been called *The Godfather* of comics. Abulí's drastic, grotesque scripts, sprinkled with a heavy dose of cynical dialogue, violence, and sex, reveal crime-infested New York's darkest face. The city and the characters' outfits are depicted beautifully; Bernet's expressionistic artwork shows great attention to period detail and is influenced by comic maestros such as Frank Robbins, as well as Hollywood noir movies.

In 1999 a lawsuit regarding the series' rights put an end to the saga, which has been reprinted in fifteen albums. Torpedo himself went on to feature in his own comic magazines in Spain and Italy, and the story was adapted as a stage play. An animated TV series was planned, but only one half-hour pilot episode was made before the project was dropped. Plans for a live-action movie were also shelved. **AMo**

First published by Toutain (Spain)
Creators Abulí (Spanish, b.1945); Bernet (Spanish, b.1944)
Genre Crime, Humor
Award Angoulême: Best Foreign Comic (1986)

Sanchez Abulí
TORPEDO
1
1936
Alex Toth
Jordi Bernet
BERNET

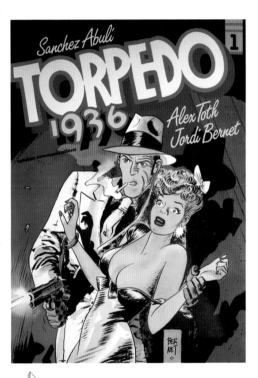

Also by Jordi Bernet
Betty by the Hour (*Clara de Noche*) with Carlos Trillo
Kraken with Antonio Segura
Retour with Enrique Sánchez Abulí
Sarvan (*Sarvane*) with Antonio Segura
Tex: L'uomo di Atlanta with Claudio Nizzi

Judge Dredd
The Apocalypse War 1982

John Wagner and Alan Grant   Carlos Ezquerra

First published by IPC Magazines (UK)
Creators Wagner (British, b.1949); Grant (British, b.1949); Ezquerra (Spanish, b.1947)
Genre Science fiction

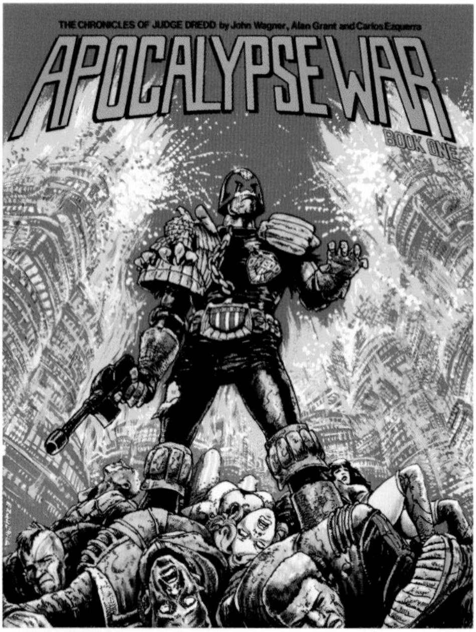
THE CHRONICLES OF JUDGE DREDD by John Wagner, Alan Grant and Carlos Ezquerra
APOCALYPSE WAR
BOOK ONE

"Surrender? Condemn my city to Sov-Block slavery? NEVER!"

Similar reads
Judge Dredd: The Pit John Wagner and various
The Last American John Wagner, Alan Grant, and Mike McMahon

By 1982 writers John Wagner and Alan Grant decided that Judge Dredd's home, Mega-City One, had grown too large. They decided to launch a war on their fictional city in an effort to reduce Dredd's vast world down to a more manageable size.

Prior to the events of the story—usually included in any reprint—Mega-City One is brought to its knees by Soviet Judge Orlok (in the story *Block Mania*) using a psychoactive agent in the water supply. Soviet rival East-Meg One launches a nuclear attack on Mega-City One, which destroys its laser defences and kills hundreds of millions of people, and the invasion begins. Outgunned, Dredd and his men have little choice other than to adopt hit-and-run guerrilla tactics to slow the Soviet advance, wherever and however they can, in what is called the Apocalypse War.

Wagner and Grant, clearly having enormous fun annihilating their own creation, craft a classic war story with a thrusting narrative in which large-scale and small-scale events are balanced with a skill few war stories ever match. This is Mega-City One's longest day, where the reader sees exactly what kind of mettle the Judges can boast. The story is also shockingly brutal and unafraid to show that in war it is the civilians that suffer the most. More than half of Mega-City One and all of East-Meg One are destroyed, leaving approximately 900 million people dead.

Carlos Ezquerra, *Dredd*'s visual creator, draws the strip with the confidence and flair that has made him a fan-favorite ever since. He is a man who knows how to draw war, and his gritty visuals give the rampant destruction a very bleak edge.

The events of "The Apocalypse War," a defining episode in *Judge Dredd*'s history, have impacted on the strip for more than twenty-five years and will continue to do so for as long as it sees print. **BD**

Soviet War Marshal Kazan launches the attack on Mega-City One. ➡

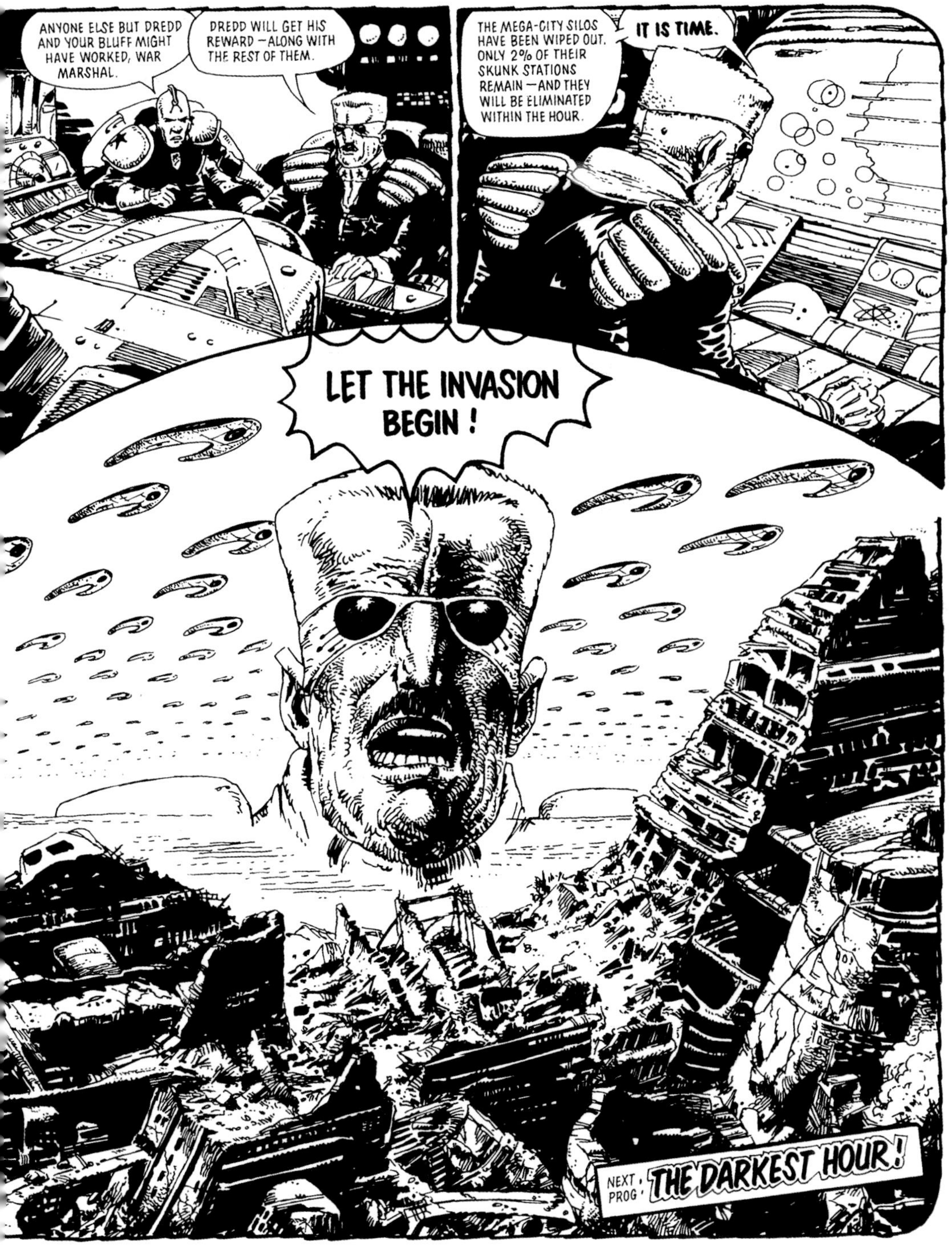
ANYONE ELSE BUT DREDD AND YOUR BLUFF MIGHT HAVE WORKED, WAR MARSHAL.
DREDD WILL GET HIS REWARD — ALONG WITH THE REST OF THEM.
THE MEGA-CITY SILOS HAVE BEEN WIPED OUT. ONLY 2% OF THEIR SKUNK STATIONS REMAIN — AND THEY WILL BE ELIMINATED WITHIN THE HOUR.
IT IS TIME.
LET THE INVASION BEGIN!
NEXT PROG: THE DARKEST HOUR!

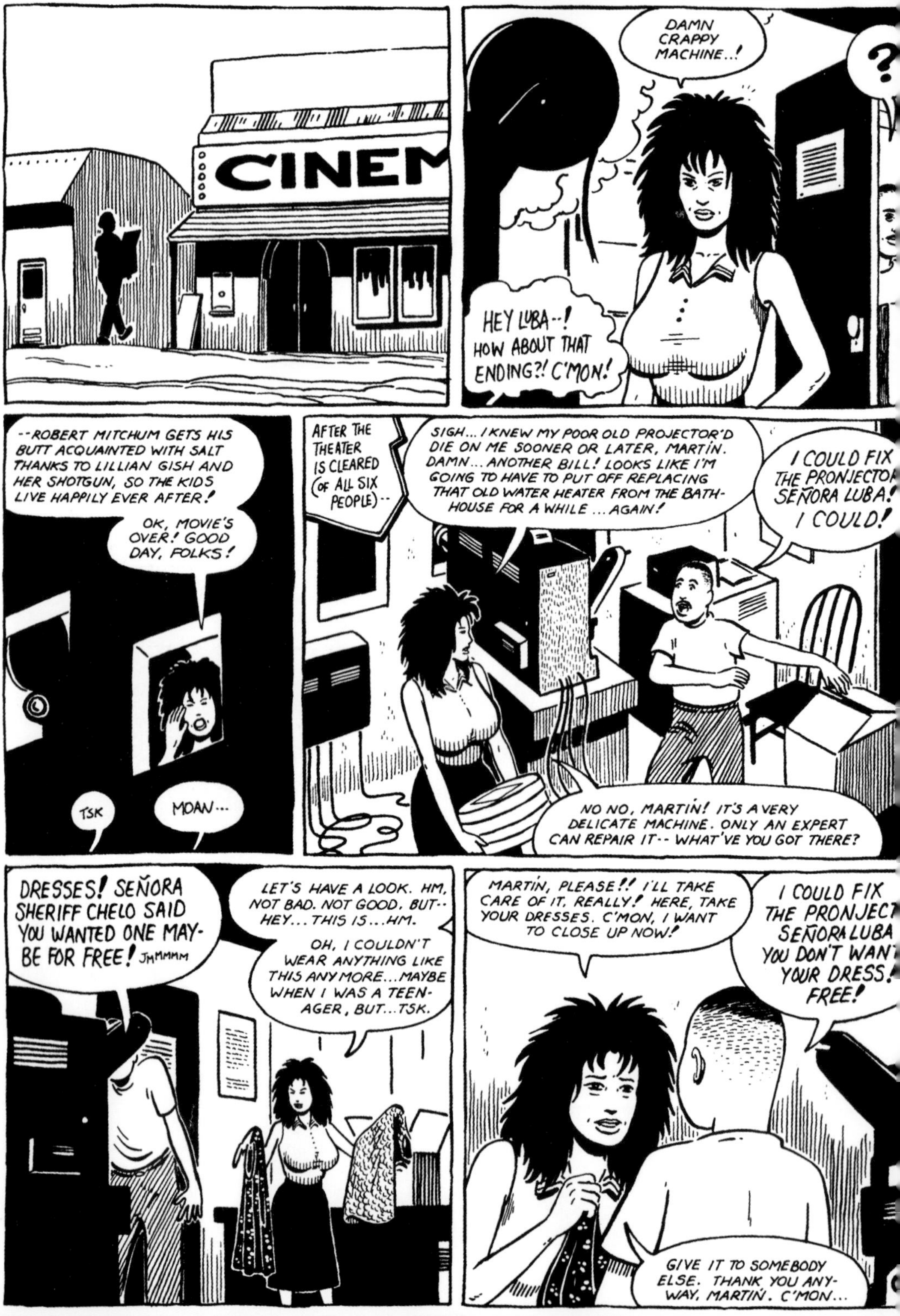
CINEM
DAMN CRAPPY MACHINE..!
?
HEY LUBA--! HOW ABOUT THAT ENDING?! C'MON!
--ROBERT MITCHUM GETS HIS BUTT ACQUAINTED WITH SALT THANKS TO LILLIAN GISH AND HER SHOTGUN, SO THE KIDS LIVE HAPPILY EVER AFTER!
OK, MOVIE'S OVER! GOOD DAY, FOLKS!
TSK
MOAN...
AFTER THE THEATER IS CLEARED (OF ALL SIX PEOPLE)--
SIGH... I KNEW MY POOR OLD PROJECTOR'D DIE ON ME SOONER OR LATER, MARTÍN. DAMN... ANOTHER BILL! LOOKS LIKE I'M GOING TO HAVE TO PUT OFF REPLACING THAT OLD WATER HEATER FROM THE BATH-HOUSE FOR A WHILE ... AGAIN!
I COULD FIX THE PRONJECTOR SEÑORA LUBA! I COULD!
NO NO, MARTÍN! IT'S A VERY DELICATE MACHINE. ONLY AN EXPERT CAN REPAIR IT-- WHAT'VE YOU GOT THERE?
DRESSES! SEÑORA SHERIFF CHELO SAID YOU WANTED ONE MAY-BE FOR FREE! JMMMM
LET'S HAVE A LOOK. HM, NOT BAD. NOT GOOD. BUT-- HEY... THIS IS...HM.
OH, I COULDN'T WEAR ANYTHING LIKE THIS ANYMORE...MAYBE WHEN I WAS A TEEN-AGER, BUT...TSK.
MARTÍN, PLEASE!! I'LL TAKE CARE OF IT, REALLY! HERE, TAKE YOUR DRESSES. C'MON, I WANT TO CLOSE UP NOW!
I COULD FIX THE PRONJECT SEÑORA LUBA YOU DON'T WANT YOUR DRESS FREE!
GIVE IT TO SOMEBODY ELSE. THANK YOU ANY-WAY, MARTÍN. C'MON...

Palomar 1982

✏️ Gilbert Hernández

First published by Fantagraphics Books (USA)
Creator American (b.1957)
Genre Drama
Award Kirby Award for Best Black-and-White Series (1986)

Love and Rockets was a comics masterwork published in pamphlet form from 1982 until 1996 created by three brothers: Gilbert, Jaime, and Mario Hernández. Such was its impact that in the world of alternative comics a fan is defined by one thing: who do they love more, Gilbert Hernández, or his brother Jaime?

"Los Bros Hernández" are of Mexican-American heritage. They grew up in southern California, where their mother immersed them from a young age in her favorite comics stories. When the brothers—still in their early twenties—were taken on by Fantagraphics Books, *Love and Rockets* soon became the place where they would seek some welcome relief from the mainstream of an art form that was obsessed by superheroes.

Gilbert "Beto" Hernández's ongoing *Palomar* story line exemplifies the brothers' approach to the medium. Named after the small Latin American town in which most of the action takes place, *Palomar* is best known for its central character, Luba, a strong woman of American Indian descent. Her enormous breasts and wild hair make her an object of desire for all of Paloma townsmen. A single mother, Luba works hard as the town's movie projectionist. Struggling to remain independent throughout these sexy, wistful stories, Luba only very occasionally entertains the idea of bringing a new man into her life.

Full of town politics, star-crossed romance, and even the occasional act of violence, the *Palomar* stories bring a wide, juicy line and a touch of Latin magical realism to the comic book world. **EL**

Nausicaä 1982

✏️ Hayao Miyazaki

Title in original language *Kaze no tani no Nausicaä*
First published by Tokuma Shoten (Japan)
Creator Japanese (b.1941)
Genre Science fiction, Fantasy

Nausicaä of the Valley of the Wind by Hayao Miyazaki was first published in 1982 in *Animage* magazine. Although the comic was not finished for twelve years, Miyazaki made an anime film of it in 1984 and founded Studio Ghibli on the back of its success.

The setting is a postapocalyptic world, a millennium after the war of the Seven Days of Fire. Much of the land is covered by poisonous forests infested by dangerous giant insects, and any understanding of how to use the aircraft and weapons that have survived the catastrophe has largely been lost. Nausicaä has been born into an essentially preindustrial, feudal world.

Nausicaä is the princess of a small, rural kingdom and has a deep compassion for all life. She is also a skillful pilot and fighter, and reluctantly gets drawn into a devastating war between two dominant empires. Helped by the unlikely alliances she forges through her humanity and courage, she tries to get all the nations to live in peace and harmony with the environment, but uncovers some disturbing secrets.

Miyazaki's sepia-inked art is precise, detailed, and delicate. He achieves an incredible dynamism and motion across the page. The rich array of characters, multiple themes, and densely interwoven plot ensure that the message, while worthy, is nuanced. Exploring conflict, politics, and religion, Miyazaki achieves a grand, epic sweep that is rarely seen in comics, and particularly in such a stunning action comic. Yet he also manages to keep the whole story accessible and relevant through the human qualities of his timeless heroine. **SB**

← A page from the story arc "Act of Contrition".

V for Vendetta 1982

Alan Moore   David Lloyd

$14.95 USA $19.95 CAN SUGGESTED FOR MATURE READERS
V FOR VENDETTA
ALAN MOORE
DAVID LLOYD
WITH STEVE WHITAKER AND SIOBHAN DODDS

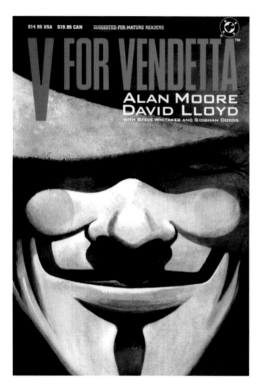

"Did you think to kill me? There's no flesh or blood within this cloak to kill. There's only an idea."

Similar reads

DMZ Brian Wood and Ricardo Burcielli
From Hell Alan Moore and Eddie Campbell
The League of Extraordinary Gentlemen Alan Moore and Kevin O'Neill

First published by Quality Communications (UK)
Creators Moore (British, b.1953); Lloyd (British, b.1950)
Genre Political fable
Adaptation Film (2006)

V for Vendetta centers on a battle of ideas. It explores the meaning of anarchy and the principle of taking sole responsibility for both one's own life and the world; fascism is also examined, with its rejection of personal responsibility and its wish to lose the self in a crowd.

Following a nuclear winter, England is ruled by the fascist party Norsefire. Sixteen-year-old Evey Hammond is rescued from rape and murder at the hands of the police, or "Fingermen," by a mysterious masked figure, a vaudevillian character in a Guy Fawkes costume known only as "V," whose first public act is to blow up Parliament. But such actions are just the beginning, and V embarks on a campaign of orchestrated chaos. At first V is an irresistibly romantic hero, but soon it is evident he is a hero with a very dark side. V has made himself a vessel of vendetta and has no identity of his own, describing himself simply as an idea. His vendetta is against the entire state, and his mission is to replace fascism with anarchy. Evey's presence at first seems incidental, but his rescuing her is no accident. Like everyone in this vicious cabaret, Evey has a part to play.

Densely written with a myriad of characters and featuring multiple intersecting plot lines, *V for Vendetta* is a treatise on the principles of anarchy. Illustrated by David Lloyd in a moody, noir style with deep blacks and, in the DC Comics edition, muted tones, the book has a very English, broken, real-world feel, a perfect backdrop for V's theatrical nature. The book has had considerable impact on the real world, with various protesters now being seen wearing Guy Fawkes masks. **BD**

Panorama of Hell 1982

✏✏ Hideshi Hino

Title in original language *Jigoku hen*
First published by Hibari Shobo (Japan)
Creator Japanese (b.1946)
Genre Horror

Addressing himself directly to the reader, an unknown painter explains that he creates "bloody hell paintings" in his blacked-out studio. He cuts himself and drinks hydrochloric acid in order to produce the vast amount of blood required to paint his canvases. He has just begun a huge painting called the *Panorama of Hell*.

The painter talks about his previous works, showing a guillotine that towers over his house, a river of blood alongside a railroad, a crematorium where headless corpses from the guillotine are burned, and a cemetery of executed prisoners dotted with animal heads on stakes. There are paintings of his family: his son, Krazy Boy, who steals pigs' eyeballs from the slaughterhouse; his artistic daughter, Krazy Girl; and his wife, who works serving zombies at a tavern. Additional paintings of his family establish a generational relationship with alcohol, violence, and blood.

Like the author, the painter was born in 1946 to a Japanese family living in Japanese-occupied Manchuria, in China. He travels to Japan with his then refugee family, and his mother goes mad during their journey. He grows up in a country where the people's psyche is affected by the bombing of Hiroshima. A childhood spent killing small creatures goes hand in hand with beatings by his parents, until he discovers that all his wishes are granted—from a house fire to train wrecks.

Blood, sweat, tears, and other bodily fluids flow freely through the pages of Hideshi Hino's grotesque story, and his characters are drawn realistically enough to retain their ability to shock. **NFI**

Starstruck 1982

✏ Elaine Lee ✏ Mike Kaluta

First published by Ilustración+Comix Internacional (Spain) **Creators** Lee (American, Unknown); Kaluta (American, b.1947)
Genre Science fiction

The 1980s was a time of experimentation in U.S. comics, but even amid that burst of creativity there was nothing as strange as *Starstruck*. The series began life in 1980 as an off-Broadway play cowritten by actress Elaine Lee, with costume designs by Mike Kaluta. The pair expanded the story into a comic for *Ilustración+Comix Internacional* and, later, *Heavy Metal*, which spawned a miniseries from Epic Comics/Marvel Comics in 1985.

The *Starstruck* comic series is a fiendishly complex space opera set in the far future with a wide cast of bizarre, mostly female characters. Lee told the endlessly expanding story through multiple narrators as well as various devices, including diaries, thoughts, memories, and explosive action. Prominent among the cast are adventurers Captain Galatia 9 and Brucilla the Muscle, the scheming Mary Medea, and numerous pleasure droids known as "Erotica Ann." Lee's writing is clever, sexy, profane, and outrageously funny, and she creates a sparkling cast of strong female characters. At the time Kaluta was rightly famed for his beautiful fantasy themed artwork, but here he proved himself to be a leading science fiction artist as well, creating an elegant art nouveau vision of the future. What the pair achieved in *Starstruck* is a perfectly realized universe of their own with a depth and complexity rarely seen in comics.

In 1990 an expanded version appeared from Dark Horse Comics. In 2010 IDW released the completed comic book series in color, plus an omnibus graphic novel including the spin-off adventures of the Galactic Girl Guides in 2011. **DR**

RAYMOND BRIGGS

When the Wind Blows

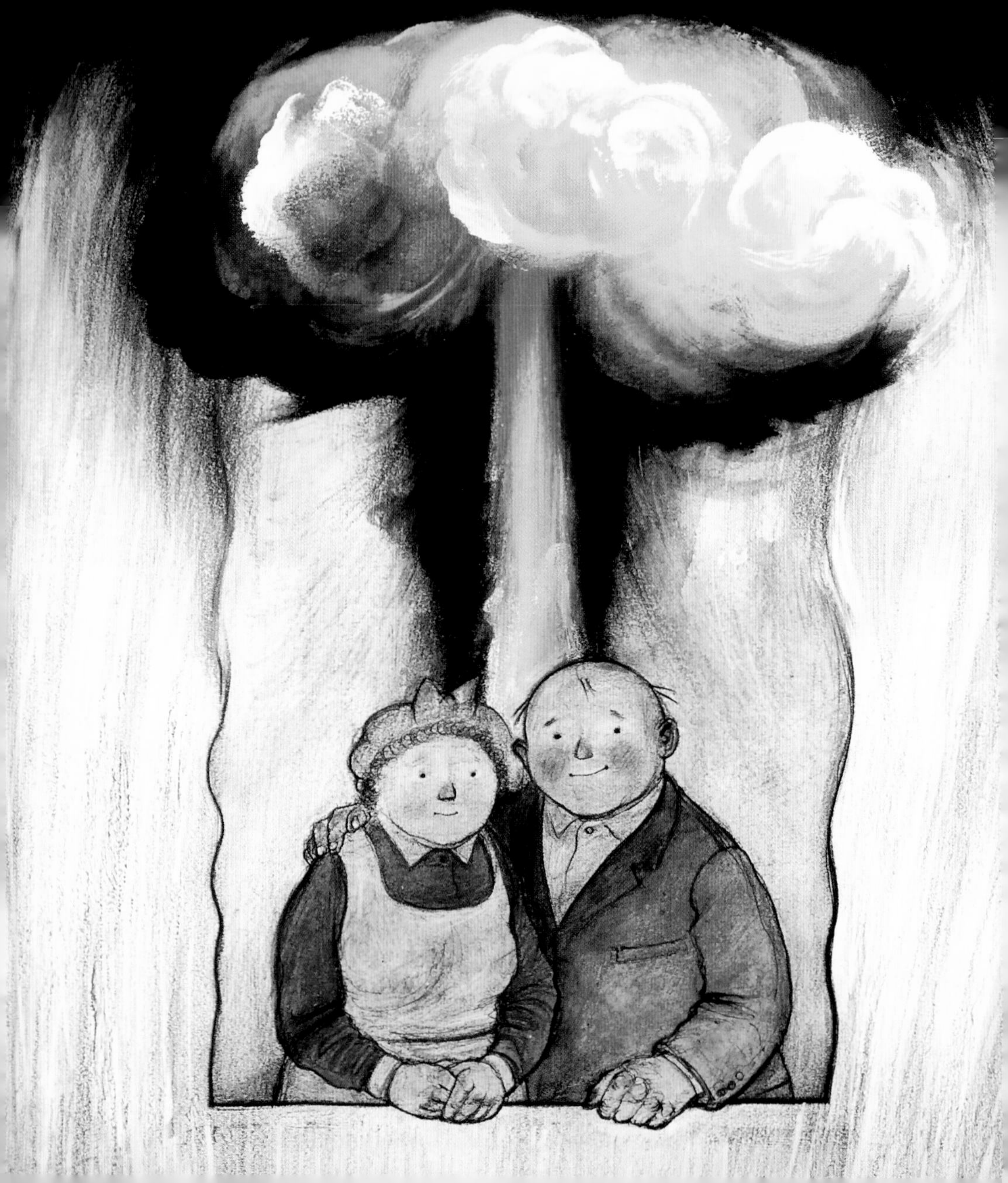

When the Wind Blows 1982

✐✐ Raymond Briggs

First published by Hamish Hamilton (UK)
Creator British (b.1934)
Genre Political fable
Adaptation Film (1986)

When the Wind Blows is a caustic and clinical dissection of the nuclear arms race that dominated the political and public arenas in the second half of the twentieth century. Raymond Briggs brings home the horror of a nuclear war by showing the effect on an ingenuous retired English couple, Jim and Hilda Bloggs. This gives the book a cozy, provincial feel, but Briggs's cold fury drips off every page—he is particularly contemptuous of the futile advice given by the government in the event of a nuclear war.

The first part of the book juxtaposes the Bloggs's everyday life with the vast machines of war. Sequences of bright, bucolic panels are interrupted by double-page splashes showing nuclear missiles, submarines, and bombers in dark, foreboding grays and blues. Jim cheerfully and scrupulously follows the official government guidelines, all the while showing the Blitz spirit that he believes will get them through.

The four pages depicting the inevitable nuclear explosion are extraordinary: a two-page splash, almost entirely white, followed by another that repeatedly shows the same panel of Jim and Hilda's makeshift shelter slowly becoming clearer and less visually distorted in the explosion's aftermath. After the bomb, the palette changes to the bleached colors of the encroaching nuclear winter, and dull purples, greens, and blues suggest radiation sickness. Jim and Hilda try to survive with dignity, never losing faith in the powers that be, while their lives are needlessly discarded by an indifferent military machine. **SB**

The Cabbie 1982

✐✐ "Martí"

Title in original language *Taxista*
First published by La Cúpula (Spain)
Creator Martí Riera y Ferrer (Spanish, b.1955)
Genre Crime

The Cabbie portrays a middle-aged, ultraconservative bachelor known by the alias of "Taxista Cuatroplazas" (Four-seater Cabbie) who works as a taxi driver-cum-sleuth. Driving his cab in an unidentified city that could be Barcelona, the protagonist is a lover of law and order whose urban adventures usually take him from the city center into the surrounding slums.

Known by his nom de plume, "Martí," author Martí Riera y Ferrer produces artwork that is influenced strongly by the style and layout of Chester Gould's *Dick Tracy*. Most pages conclude with a cliff-hanger ending, and the ugly, deformed faces of some of the characters in *The Cabbie* are a perfect match for the gallery of villains that Gould created for his detective strip. But Martí surpasses even Gould in terms of violence and atrocity. *The Cabbie* is an enlightening portrait of human miseries and flaws set in Spain in the early 1980s, during a time when social and economic problems grew after the death of General Francisco Franco.

Originally serialized in the monthly magazine *El Víbora*, *The Cabbie* was compiled into two books by its publisher, La Cúpula. In 2004 the *Cabbie* saga was reprinted in one volume by Glénat. Since the early 1990s, Martí has virtually abandoned comics.

The Cabbie was published in English by Catalan Communications in 1987 with a foreword by Art Spiegelman. It reappeared in 2007 in the one-shot *Calvario Hills* under the Fantagraphics imprint Ignatz, and Fantagraphics launched the first volume of a hardcover edition in 2011. **AMo**

Martin Mystère 1982

✎ Alfredo Castelli   ✎ Giancarlo Alessandrini

First published by Sergio Bonelli (Italy)
Creators Castelli (Italian, b.1947);
Alessandrini (Italian, b.1950)
Genre Adventure

Martin Mystère is a professor of archaeology and an adventurer. He is also a public figure who is involved in popular science journalism, inspired by writers such as Erich von Däniken. Based in New York, he spent much of his early life studying in Italy, where some of his adventures take place. Mystère is a mature man, accompanied by his girlfriend, and later wife, Diana Lombard, and a Neanderthal assistant named Java.

Mystère's adventures take him beyond archaeology. He investigates art, science, anthropology, science fiction, and parapsychology, retelling and fictionalizing cultural history. Some of the most memorable stories show Mystère delving into undisclosed relationships between inscrutable "Men in Black" agents and the Nazis' search for the Grail. A large subplot develops, centered on conspiracy theories and well-documented inquiries, that works toward an alternate history of civilization.

In the wake of adventures such as *Doc Savage*, this series was the first and leading one in the renovation of publisher Sergio Bonelli in the early 1980s. *Martin Mystère* was pivotal in launching a new era of modern genres that included horror in the form of *Dylan Dog*, and cyberpunk science fiction including *Nathan Never*, moving beyond traditional Western and post-Western series such as *Tex* and *Ken Parker*.

Creator Alfredo Castelli, a former editor of *Il Corriere dei Ragazzi*, is a passionate comics scholar, and many *Martin Mystère* episodes reference comic book history. In 2003 the series was adapted as an animated TV series targeted at a preadolescent audience. **MS**

Click! 1982

✎✎ "Milo"

Title in original language *Il gioco*
First published by Tattilo (Italy)
Creator Maurilo Manara (Italian, b.1945)
Genre Adult humor, Erotic

Among the most famous erotic comics ever produced, *Click!* tells the story of an attractive but passionless young woman named Claudia Cristiani who is married to a rich older man. She is abducted by a scientist who implants a remote-controlled device into her brain that causes her to become sexually insatiable whenever the remote control is activated. Throughout her adventures, Cristiani finds herself caught in embarrassing situations as a number of people get to control the evil machine that influences her, and which sometimes causes her to seek revenge against her cynical husband.

Click! was originally published in *Playmen*, an adult magazine from Tattilo Editrice. But the first installment of this short series became a best-seller only in 1984 in a book collection by Edizioni Nuova Frontiera, which inspired three sequels in 1991, 1994, and 2001.

After years working in mass-market erotic comics such as *Jolanda de Almaviva* and drawing satiric stories for *Telerompo* magazine, in *Click!* author Maurilio "Milo" Manara developed a more ironic method of dealing with middle-class hypocrisies and sexual desires. The beauty of Manara's women is legendary because of his ability to depict skinny, tall young girls in a torrid fashion. Their supermodel bodies are built from sexy details including luscious lips, perfect hair, and provocative gestures and poses.

Click! was the basis of the 1985 French film *Le déclic*, (*The Click*) starring Florence Guérin. In 1997, an English-language TV adaptation, entitled *Click*, was made into a series of seven ninety-minute episodes. **MS**

Pioneers of Human Adventure 1982

François Boucq

Title in original language *Les pionniers de l'aventure humaine* **First published by** Casterman (Belgium)
Creator French (b.1955)
Genre Humor, Fantasy

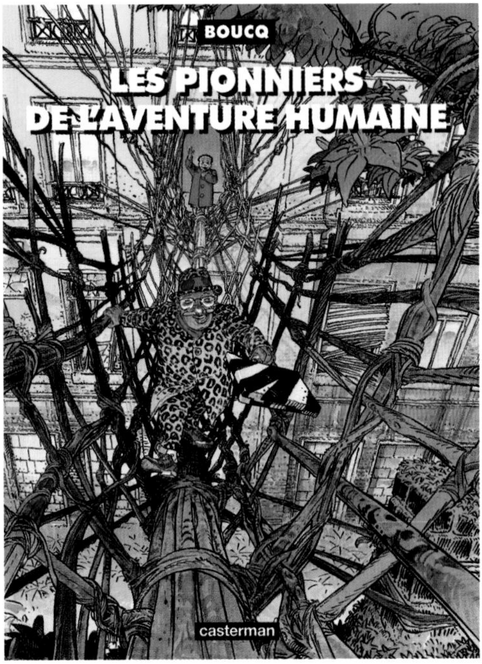
BOUCQ
LES PIONNIERS DE L'AVENTURE HUMAINE
casterman

An anthology of grotesque and satirical short stories, *Pioneers of Human Adventure* starts with a World War II Japanese commando brutally barging into a peaceful, present-day French apartment occupied by a mother and her four grown-up sons. It ends at the grandiose Niagara Falls with the ecstatic visit of a couple of lovers, who can already imagine themselves opening up a food kiosk to seal their passion.

Other stories feature a sculptor of cooked meats, who shares a painful confrontation with Leonardo da Vinci, and a gang of Neanderthals who escape by the skin of their teeth from a pterodactyl attack while in the company of Jérôme Moucherot, a heroic door-to-door insurance salesman clad in a leopard-skin suit.

The stories of *Pioneers of Human Adventure* have no common setting or recurring heroes, although the character of Moucherot, who appears in the story "Bengal Tiger," reappears in subsequent comics by author François Boucq. Nevertheless, all the stories share a powerful affinity for the surreal and absurd, which the author exploits with constant delight and an unusual inspiration that is very much his own.

Boucq is an extremely talented draftsman who feels at ease in all styles, and this is one of the reasons for his success. His realistic, energetic strokes can be excessive, but Boucq uses meticulous precision to make them a wonderfully comic element—especially when combined with anachronisms or outrageously incongruous situations, such as those where large African mammals play a major part. **NF**

"At dawn, only a structure remains. Impudent, as though the creatures who erected it wished to shout their being into the world's ear."

Also by François Boucq
Billy Budd, KGB (*Bouche du diable*) with Jerome Charyn
Bouncer with Alejandro Jodorowsky
Moon Face (*Face de lune*) with Alejandro Jodorowsky
The Magician's Wife (*La femme du magicien*) with Jerome Charyn

Pee Dog 1982

"The Shit Generation"

First published by Spooky Comics (USA)
Creators Gary Panter (American, b.1950); Jay Condom (American, Unknown)
Genre Adult humor

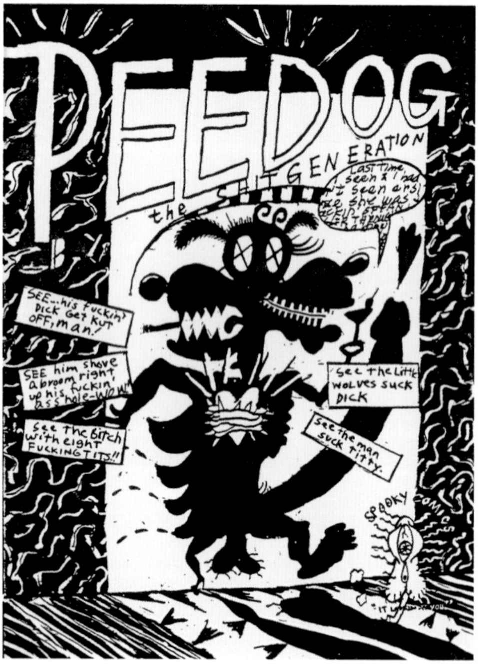

PEEDOG
the SHIT GENERATION
SEE..his fuckin' Dick Get KUT OFF, man!
SEE him shove a broom right up his fuckin ass's hole-WOW!
See the Bitch with eight FUCKING TITS!!
See the Little WOLVES SUCK DICK
See the man suck titty.
SPOOKY COMICS

Similar reads
Jimbo in Purgatory Gary Panter
Pee Dog vs. Poop Dog The Shit Generation
Pixie Meat Gary Panter, Tom Dehaven, and Charles Burns
The Asshole Gary Panter

Artist Gary Panter was involved in the Los Angeles punk scene during the 1970s when he produced drawings for *Slash* magazine and artwork for record album covers. Panter's grungy style developed when he joined forces with Jay "Condom" Cotton to become the collective called The Shit Generation. They embarked upon a series of projects that included a record album of their music and two issues of *Pee Dog*, a scatological, grotesque, often pornographic funny animal, underground comic that teeters on the edge of acid-blasted blasphemy. In short, a demented work of genius.

Panter said of *Pee Dog*: "We stayed up for a couple of nights drawing this sixteen-page comic together really fast and laughing really hard. It was really all about

"Behold the River of Pee. It is dirty because it accepts everything."

being infantile, stupid, dirty, and blasphemous. I think that for Jay and me it was also a spiritual thing."

To shield their true identities from any flak that *Pee Dog*'s publication and distribution might attract, they invented different personae. Panter went under the name of "Jocko 'Levant' Brainiac 5," and Condom chose "Eddie Nukes." Within these alteregos they developed a complex mythology: "It wasn't us. We imagined them as being a couple of nudists who were driving around the desert in an old Cadillac, dropping acid and selling or trading these old porno comics."

The result of this fantasy emerged in print as *Pee Dog II: The Captain's Final Log*. A handmade punk rock comic epic, it glues together elements of Leonardo da Vinci's painting *The Last Supper*, *Star Trek*'s Mr. Spock, and an anthropomorphic cartoon horse character named Quick Draw McGraw, who also served as the template for Panter's later work, *Jimbo in Purgatory*. **EP**

Locas 1982

Jaime Hernández

Locas is Jaime Hernández's ongoing contribution to *Love and Rockets*, an anthology that he created with his brothers Gilbert and Mario. Published in 1982, it defined the U.S. alternative comics movement of that decade.

Locas begins by incorporating a strong science fiction element, detailing the globetrotting adventures of rocket-ship mechanic Maggie Chascarrillo. The narrative then changes to focus on a fictional district of Los Angeles, Huerta (aka Hoppers), which is based on the Hernández brothers' hometown of Oxnard. The story relates the intersecting everyday lives of a diverse cast of characters from the California punk scene, low-rider gang culture, the pro-wrestling world, and the local Mexican-American community. But it is the intense

"... I was dancing and these geeks kept pinching my butt."

and vacillating romance between Chascarrillo and her best friend, Hopey Glass, that drives the story. *Locas* uses narrative time in a sophisticated way, interweaving self-contained vignettes and long, serialized stories, as well as flashback and fantasy, to relate the epic continuity of the characters' lives from childhood to middle age. This is combined with humor, magical realism, and astute social observation of the nuances of class, race, gender, and sexuality.

Jaime's bold black-and-white cartooning and spare economy of line draws on the gamut of the U.S. comics tradition, from the teen drama of Dan DeCarlo's *Archie* to the superheroic action of Jack Kirby by way of Charles M. Schulz's *Peanuts*. The rich layers and complex characterization of *Locas* make it unlike other alternative comics. Jaime spurns formal experimentation in favor of an accessible, story-driven visual clarity that captures the evolution of its unforgettable characters. **MG**

First published by Fantagraphics Books (USA)
Creator American (b.1959)
Genre Alternative
Influenced by Dan DeCarlo, Charles M. Schulz

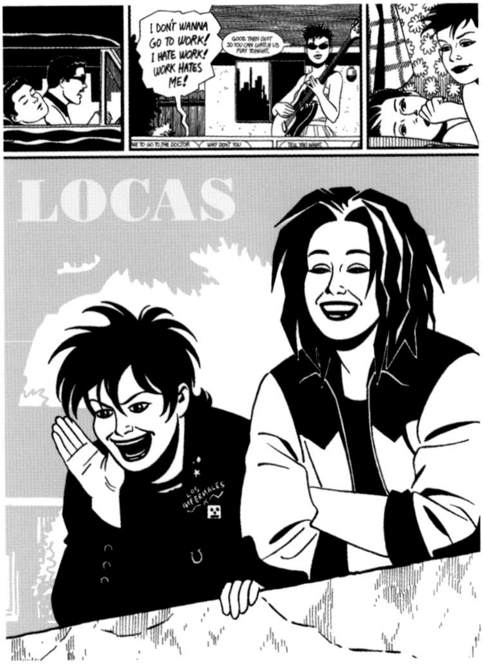
I DON'T WANNA GO TO WORK! I HATE WORK! WORK HATES ME!
LOCAS

Similar reads
Love and Rockets Jaime and Gilbert Hernández
Palomar Gilbert Hernández
Penny Century Jaime Hernández
Sloth Gilbert Hernández
Whoa Nellie! Jaime Hernández

Carmen Cru 1982

✐ Jean-Marc Lelong

First published by *Fluide Glacial*/Éditions Audie (France)
Creator French (1949–2004)
Genre Humor
Adaptation Play (1985)

An encounter with an elderly woman inspired Jean-Marc Lelong to create the character of Carmen Cru. She is tiny, immeasurably old, and incurably grouchy, with a cankerous face hidden permanently under a large rain hat. She spends her time ambling around town on her bicycle, ready to take advantage of the help her neighbors and passersby feel obliged to give her. She turns off the electricity supply to the building every time she leaves her apartment, and her long-suffering neighbors are charged with constantly carrying her bike up and downstairs while Cru reports them for harassment if they knock on her door to check on her. A world-weary character, unflinchingly distrustful of the human race in general, Lelong's elderly creation represents in her own laconic way a comically understandable picture of old age, while her bemused acquaintants provide a smartly satirical take on younger generations' reactions to it.

The strip first appeared in French magazine *Fluide Glacial* in 1982 before being published as a series of albums, and even became the basis for a play that toured France between 1985 and 1989. Each strip is produced in black and white with little background detail, the focus of the stories being very much on the figure of Cru and her curmudgeonly interactions with the people she encounters. Lelong's iconic artistic style renders Carmen Cru an unforgettably comic vision of glowering features, wrinkles, and oversized rainwear, but it is the disgruntled pensioner's dialogue that makes the series a classic comic. **CMac**

The Mercenary Baseball Team 1982

✐ Hyun-se Lee

Title in original language *Gongpoeui waeingudan*
First published by Koryoka (Korea)
Creator South Korean (b.1956)
Genre Drama

Only the winner can take the prize and everyone else will rot in hell. The desperate desire for success, even at the cost of everything else, was the overarching self-mocking sentiment in South Korea during the 1980s. The hit comics of that era went to extreme lengths to fulfill that sentiment. *The Mercenary Baseball Team* stars a band of losers. But, thanks to a hellish trainer, who trains them ridiculously hard, they return to the league to achieve record-winning streaks.

A group of well-managed elite players dominate the professional baseball league. For anyone cast out as an alcoholic, of lowly regarded ethnicity, or considered a second-rate loser, there is no way back in. This has all kinds of consequences; a player can become estranged from his family or lose his one and only love to a top player. But when one player meets a trainer who tells him to take revenge—putting him through training schedules that include getting beaten up everyday and climbing cliffs with bare hands—things take a turn for the better. In *The Mercenary Baseball Team* the desire to become a winner is so strong that a pitcher cuts off his own ring finger for a perfect knuckle ball. Such success is tempered by the ultimate price players pay for all they have sacrificed, including their own sanity. These factors make for a painful and mesmerizing story that is enhanced by edgy and powerful art.

The Mercenary Baseball Team is a landmark in Korean *manhwa* because of its mainstream popularity. It is one of the pioneering works that elevated comics to the status of serious adult fiction. **NK**

Roxanna and the Quest for the Time Bird 1982

Serge Le Tendre   Régis Loisel

Title in original language *La quête de l'oiseau du temps*
First published by Dargaud (France)
Creators Le Tendre (French, b.1946); Loisel (French, b.1951) **Genre** Fantasy

HISTOIRES FANTASTIQUES
LA QUÊTE DE L'OISEAU DU TEMPS
LA CONQUE DE RAMOR
LE TENDRE
LOISEL
DARGAUD

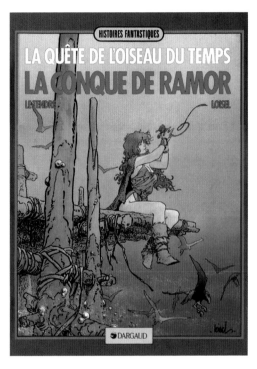

Régis Loisel and Serge Le Tendre's *Roxanna and the Quest for the Time Bird* fantasy series began in 1975 when it had a short outing in the ill-fated magazine *Imagine*. Both creators were very young, and when it reappeared seven years later in *Charlie Mensuel*, both had developed. By then Le Tendre had written for many genres; Loisel had refined his cute and puckish style with its buxom, tangle-haired heroines into one that would inspire a generation of fantasy storytellers.

Roxanna and the Quest for the Time Bird takes place in the fantasy world of Akbar, which is threatened by a vengeful god, Ramor. In an effort to thwart him, a powerful sorceress, Mara, sends her daughter, Pélisse (known as Roxanna in the English version), to persuade a former lover, Bragon, to embark on a quest to find the legendary Time Bird. What helps the story stand out from the crowd is the development of the individual characters: Mara and Bragon have to come to terms with the fact that they are aging and not what they once were, and there is a tinge of uncertainty and melancholy to the cycle. Le Tendre's plot developments also surprise his audience again and again.

However, it is the art that has drawn so many fans to the series. Loisel creates a detailed world that contains countless unfamiliar creatures, alien-looking hominids, giant birds, and spectacular, unfamiliar landscapes. His style is distinct with strong page compositions and visual characterizations. *Roxanna and the Quest for the Time Bird* is far from a typical fantasy quest story, with characters as rich and colorful as the scenery. **FJ**

"But enough! Time is pressing. You must make it quick. Mara awaits our return . . ."

Similar reads
Aquablue Thierry Cailleteau and Olivier Vatine
Elfquest Richard Pini and Wendy Pini
Thorgal Jean Van Hamme and Grzegorz Rosiński
Valérian and Laureline Pierre Christin and Jean-Claude Mézières

Fever in Urbicand 1983

Benoît Peeters   François Schuiten

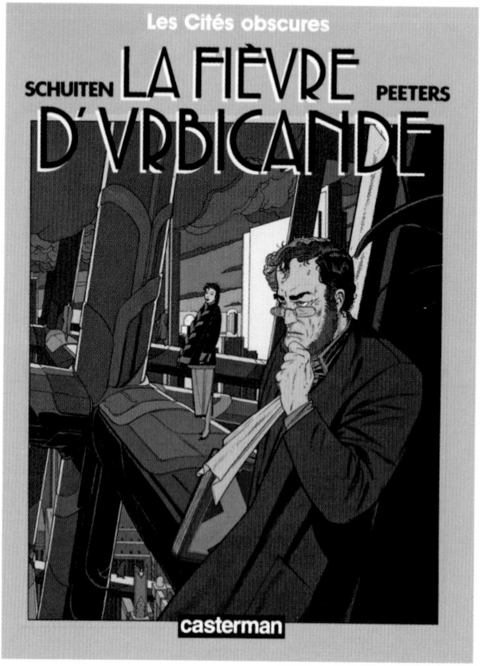
Les Cités obscures
SCHUITEN
LA FIÈVRE D'URBICANDE
PEETERS
casterman

"Though to the passive observer it doesn't seem anything very remarkable, it's a simple cubic structure totally empty . . ."

Also by Benoît Peeters and François Schuiten
Plagiat!
Souvenirs de l'éternel present
The Armillia Route (*La route d'Armillia*)
The Great Walls of Samaris (*Les murailles de Samaris*)
The Invisible Frontier (*La frontière invisible*)

Title in original language *La fièvre d'Urbicande*
First published by Casterman (Belgium)
Creators Peeters (French, b.1956); Schuiten (Belgian, b.1956) **Genre** Fantasy, Science fiction

Admired and respected for the visionary character of the architectural creations he has built all over the haughty city of Urbicand, the architect Eugen Robick is intrigued by a curious object he finds on a building site. The hollowed-out, cube-shaped structure has sharp ridges made of an unknown metal that no tool can cut or scratch. Even in Urbicand, famous throughout the Cities of the Fantastic for its wonders and revolutionary innovations, such an artifact is out of place. How to explain its nature and function—if indeed it has one?

Robick's astonishment turns into fascination when he realizes that the mysterious object is growing and expanding at the same time. Resolving the mystery of this strange structure becomes an all-consuming and futile obsession. Robick continues his search doggedly before despairing of ever solving the mystery, while the unexplained object grows inexorably, reaching gigantic proportions and becoming larger than the city itself.

Childhood friends, Benoît Peeters and François Schuiten started drawing imaginary cities in 1982 for *The Great Walls of Samaris* (*Les murailles de Samaris*). But it was *Fever in Urbicand* that laid the foundation for the series *Cities of the Fantastic* (*Les cités obscures*), a parallel world in which a network of dream cities with sometimes strangely familiar names appears to echo the cities of our world. *Fever in Urbicand* is an innovative creation from both a graphic and a narrative point of view. The comic won recognition when it first appeared, notably gaining the prize for the Best Album at the Angoulême Comics Festival in 1985. **NF**

Adolf: A Tale of the Twentieth Century 1983

✎✎ Osamu Tezuka

Title in original language *Adorufu ni tsugu*
First published by Bungeishunju (Japan)
Creator Japanese (1928–89)
Genre War

Set mostly in Germany and Japan during World War II, this is the first book in a five-part series. It tells the story of three men called Adolf: one historical, Adolf Hitler, and two fictional, Adolf Kamil and Adolf Kaufmann. Kamil is a Jew living in Kobe, Japan, and half-Japanese and half-German Kaufmann is his best friend.

Sohei Toge is a Japanese reporter sent to Berlin to cover the 1936 Olympic Games, where he discovers that his younger brother, Isao, has been murdered. When Sohei finds that the evidence of his brother's time in Germany has been erased, he is determined to investigate; he begins to search for a document that he believes his brother has sent back to Japan.

In Japan, Kaufmann's father is ordered to retrieve the document, which allegedly proves that Hitler has Jewish ancestors. Kaufmann continues his friendship with Kamil, refusing to give in to pressure from his school to disavow all Jews. However, after his father's death, Kaufmann discovers that he is being sent to Germany to join the Hitler Youth, despite his and his mother's protests. The story follows the growth of Kamil and Kaufmann as their lives are affected by Hitler and Sohei's hunt for his brother's killer.

Osamu Tezuka lived near Kobe in his youth, which gives the setting an added authenticity. He employs a realistic style in keeping with the heartbreaking subject matter. He uses few traditional manga exaggerations and portrays his characters—even Hitler—in a convincing fashion. His efforts won him the Kodansha Manga Award in 1986. **NFI**

Section Chief Kosaku Shima 1983

✎✎ Kenshi Hirokane

Title in original language *Kacho Kosaku Shima*
First published by Kodansha (Japan)
Creator Japanese (b.1947)
Genre Political fable

Manga is more a delivery apparatus than a storytelling norm, and there are wide varieties of manga. Yet it is still difficult for a Western audience to fully appreciate the cultural force that *Section Chief Kosaku Shima* is in Japan. A U.S. equivalent would be the character John Carter on the TV show *ER*.

But the differences are many, chief among them being that the title character of *Section Chief Kosaku Shima* is the center of the story, not part of an ensemble cast. The series has also run for a long time. It started in 1983 in the weekly magazine *Morning* (*Moningu*), and it is still published today. What the series have in common is intrinsically Japanese: even in the early twenty-first century, people might work for the same company and navigate the same bureaucracy for their entire career. The result is a story about decision-making, politics, and relationships, topics that are very familiar, at the outset, to manga's intended audience.

Kosaku Shima works as a salaryman at Hatsushiba Goyo, and the company is thought to be based on Matsushita, where its creator Kenshi Hirokane worked before he became a full-time artist. In time, however, Shima moves all the way up the ladder, and in 2008 becomes president of the company. The manga's title changed to reflect his elevation, and each story arc is named for Shima's current title.

Such is the impact of the series that *The Economist* covered Shima's promotion to the presidency, at which point more than thirty million bound volumes of the story had been sold. **MW**

Indian Summer 1983

Hugo Pratt "Milo"

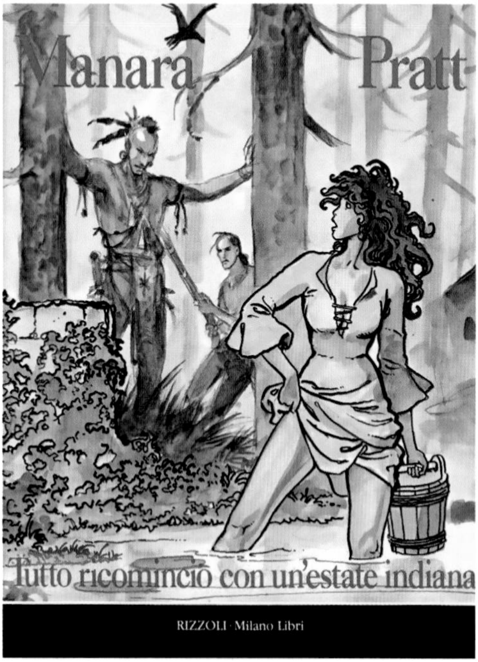
Manara Pratt
Tutto ricominciò con un'estate indiana
RIZZOLI · Milano Libri

"Stay still girl, in a little while you'll feel better . . . and give me a hand you two."

Abigail Lewis

Similar reads

El Gaucho Hugo Pratt with Milo Manara
Ernie Pike Héctor Oesterheld and Hugo Pratt
The Paper Man Milo Manara
Trip to Tulum Milo Manara and Federico Fellini
Wheeling Hugo Pratt

Title in original language *Tutto ricominciò con un'estate Indiana* **First published by** Milano Libri Editore (Italy) **Creators** Pratt (Italian, 1927–95); Maurilio Manara (Italian, b.1945) **Genre** Drama, Western

Indian Summer takes place in New England during the early seventeenth century. In this region of the New World, European settlers and indigenous peoples have learned to live together in a fragile armed peace. When two American Indians rape a young white woman, the delicate balance snaps. A settler, Abner Lewis, witnesses the attack and executes the rapists. Seeking revenge, the local American Indian tribes go to Lewis's farm, where the raped woman is being sheltered; they then proceed to New Canaan, a nearby fortified village inhabited by Puritans ruled with an iron hand by a sin-obsessed religious fanatic, the Reverend Pilgrim Black.

The action in *Indian Summer* portrays the fierceness of the fighting with exceptional spirit, and it also tells the story of the curse that affects the Lewis family collectively. All are ostracized because of the reputedly impure conduct of the mother, Abigail. As a sinner who has given birth to illegitimate children, she is a living affront to morality. One of her cheeks is disfigured by a branded letter "L"—for "Lilith"—inflicted with a hot iron.

Hugo Pratt is passionate about the frontier period in American history, when the native and colonial cultures often intermingled before the triumph of the European model. His story is a classic about the era. Pratt's friend, Maurilio "Milo" Manara, responds with a virtuoso graphic vocabulary that reflects the erotic dimension seen blossoming in his own solo albums. The rivalry between the two collaborators, both accomplished authors by the time they undertook this project, partly explains the success of the work. **NF**

Dykes to Watch Out For 1983

🖊🖊 Alison Bechdel

First published by *Woman News* (USA)
Creator American (b.1960)
Genre Adult humor
Influenced by Howard Cruse, Mary Wings, Jerry Mills

Before *The L Word*, there was *Dykes to Watch Out For*. But any fatuous attempt to link *Dykes to Watch Out For* with its more glamorous televisual cousin fails to honor Alison Bechdel's groundbreaking strip for its unique take on lesbian life in the United States. First published in small feminist and gay newspapers, the strip became a phenomenon, making comic book art out of a community the mainstream media still only reluctantly acknowledges. Spanning twenty-five years in the life of a small, close-knit gay community stranded somewhere in the U.S. heartland, *Dykes to Watch Out For* offers an anthropological view of women who keep one eye on their lovers, coworkers, and children—and the other firmly glued to cable news channel MSNBC.

Bechdel described it as half-Victorian serialized novel and half-op-ed piece. It is arguable that Presidents George W. Bush and Bill Clinton are as much characters in the drama as the lesbians of the title. From AIDS to gay marriage, transgender rights, the Iraq War, and the rise of the big-box retailer, readers get the women's take on every major issue to affect Queer America, all beautifully rendered with Bechdel's trademark squiggly crow quill. The characters neurotic Mo, cunning Sydney, hard-line Sparrow, and testy Clarice are smart, mouthy women; their articulate dissection of current events is a joy. But Bechdel's narrative does not stop with politics; there is romance after romance, marriage after marriage, and pregnancy after pregnancy as the women's lives evolve. The ladies may not fit usual stereotypes of lesbians, but their adventures keep readers hooked. **EL**

Fist of the Northstar 1983

🖊 "Buronson" 🖊 Tatsuo Hara

Title in original language *Hokuto no Ken*
First published by Shueisha (Japan)
Creators Sho Fumimura (Japanese, b.1947);
Hara (Japanese, 1961) **Genre** Science fiction

Fist of the Northstar is set in a world that has been destroyed by a nuclear war; the few survivors left are battling for control of what little uncontaminated food and water remains. Kenshiro is the inheritor of a deadly martial-arts style that enables him to use the human body's hidden meridian points to kill people from within, often with extremely gory results.

Kenshiro wanders the wasteland searching for his fiancée, who was taken from him by a rival martial artist, helping the weak but righteous to fight off the predations of the various tribes and clans that threaten them. The time span of *Fist of the Northstar* covers many years. As humanity regroups, a corrupt empire emerges that Kenshiro and his companions must fight. Then one of them is kidnapped by a band of warriors originating in a land where only great fighters survive. No matter how much order Kenshiro brings to a situation, he is always driven on to another that needs his violent form of attention.

The world Buronson (aka Sho Fumimura) creates in *Fist of the Northstar* is morally simplistic, although the series addresses its young male audience perfectly by emphasizing all the fighting styles and machismo. There is emotional conflict, too, when Kenshiro is pitted against family members and old fighting companions, but it is always within a martial arts context. Tetsuo Hara's art is functional rather than elegant, and his characters Westernized in style, with powerful, bulging muscles, which helps to make *Fist of the Northstar* accessible to a wide audience. **FJ**

American Flagg! 1983

Howard Chaykin

First published by First Comics (USA)
Creator American (b.1950)
Genre Science fiction, Satire
Influenced by Robert Fawcett, Al Parker

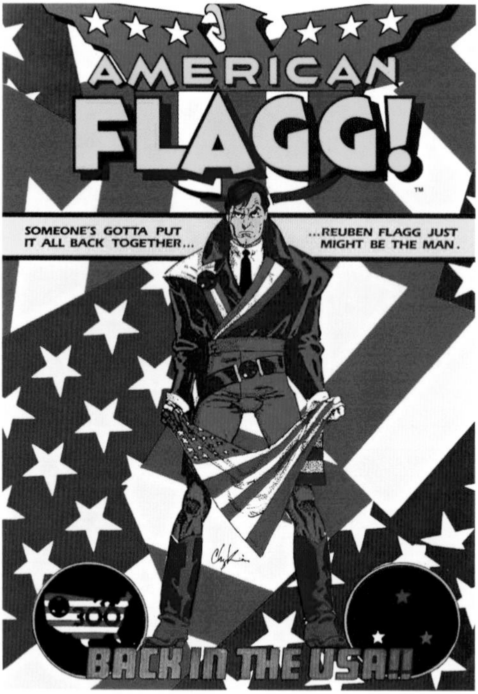
AMERICAN
FLAGG!
TM
SOMEONE'S GOTTA PUT IT ALL BACK TOGETHER...
...REUBEN FLAGG JUST MIGHT BE THE MAN.
BACK IN THE USA!!

Also by Howard Chaykin
American Flagg: Volume 1 (issues #1–7)
American Flagg: Volume 2 (issues #8–14)
Blackhawk, Book 1: "Blood and Iron"
City of Tomorrow
Howard Chaykin's Black Kiss

A mix of topical political satire and uncompromising artwork made Howard Chaykin's *American Flagg!* one of the most influential comics of the 1980s. In 2008, he remarked on how reality had come to resemble his predictions in *American Flagg!*: "Had I known it was going to get even worse than I predicted, I might as well have just shot myself then and split the difference."

Chaykin's hero, Reuben Flagg, operates in a future dystopia set in the year 2031. At this time, Western society is still attempting to recover from the disastrous events of 1996, known as the "Year of the Domino," which resulted in Africa annexing Europe and the U.S. government relocating to Mars, where life is marginally more secure than on Earth. The job of keeping anarchy at bay has been given to the Plex Corporation, and Chicago-based Flagg, a former porn star, is an agent for Plex—he is a Plexus Ranger. Flagg battles to reestablish law and order and eventually becomes President of the Independent Republic of Illinois, which secedes from the United States.

"American Flagg! . . . *stands out as Howard Chaykin's signature book.*"

Erik Larsen, Image Comics publisher

Chaykin wrote and illustrated *American Flagg!* for the first twenty-seven issues. Steven Grant and then J. M. DeMatteis replaced him, but sales of the comic declined. In 1988 First Comics persuaded Chaykin to return and wind up the story line. The result was twelve issues of *Amerikan* (sic) *Flagg!* where the action moved to Soviet Russia in the year 2032. Fans were unimpressed by Chaykin's return, and the actual extent of his creative contribution was also questioned. It is generally only the first twenty-seven issues of *American Flagg!* that are regarded as the real deal. **RR**

Theodore Death Head 1983

Pascal Doury

This Pascal Doury collection contains some of the most intense and disturbing drawing to be found in comics. The style is a heady mixture of outsider art and kitsch. Meticulously crafted scratchboard drawings, usually four to a spread, depict an anarchic world of psychotic individuals, more often than not with their genitals exposed and in a state of arousal.

It is Saturday night, and Theo drives over to his fiancée's home to pick her up and take her to the movies. En route, the driver of a shiny motor scooter, sporting a punk hairstyle and three arms, seduces Theo's sweetheart, and she jumps out of the car to ride pillion on the scooter. Having lost his girl, Theo drives on, witnesses a suicide, and returns home. He torments himself by looking through a small window in the adjoining wall to watch his neighbor engage in sex. Theo's neighbor has a shirt on, his trousers around his ankles, and two erect penises; his female companion is completely naked with the exception of high-heeled shoes and short stockings. She has two pairs of arms and hands of varying sizes, one holding a tube of cream, another applying it to her gaping vagina. Electric flashes and arm-movement lines add a frenzied excitement to the sexual violence that is about to take place. The subsequent spreads contain some of the most charged images known to comics, which suck the reader into a claustrophobic maelstrom.

"The 'violence' of an image happens in your head, it's not how you see it."

Bruno Richard, penciler

Doury's addiction to heroin lasted twelve years before it ended in 1991, and it is likely that this book was influenced by the experiences he encountered, or even initiated, while using the drug. **LC**

Title in original language *Théo tête de mort*
First published by Les Humanoïdes Associés (France)
Creator French (1956–2001)
Genre Adult humor

PASCAL DOURY
THÉO
TÊTE DE MORT
LES HUMANOIDES ASSOCIES

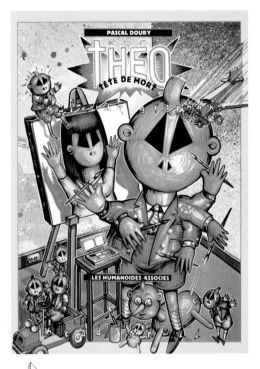

Similar reads

Elles Sont de Sortie Pascal Doury and Bruno Richard
Pornographie Catholique Pascal Doury
The Bogeyman Rory Hayes
The Checkered Demon S. Clay Wilson
The Mystery of Wolverine Woo-Bait Joe Coleman

Air Mail 1983

✎✎ Attilio Micheluzzi

First published by Bernardi (Italy)
Creator Italian (1930–90)
Genre Adventure
Influenced by Moebius, Hugo Pratt, Milton Caniff

Attilio Micheluzzi was an army brat who had a colorful past—including working as an architect for the Libyan royal family—before he became an illustrator in his forties. His early life informed his glamorous adventure stories such as *Petra Chèrie*, about a female pilot in World War I, and a lifelong interest in history enables him to depict a wide range of periods. He watched his father, a professional pilot, fly from an early age, and bringing the world of biplanes and dogfights to life is his great gift as an artist, as well as drawing in an authoritative and bold line. Many of his best works, including *Air Mail*, feature daring pilots.

Micheluzzi's work, both in art style and subject matter, is influenced by the great adventure artists such as Hugo Pratt and Milton Caniff. He often caricatures his villains and draws sketchy backgrounds, but his main characters are far more concrete, and he has an eye for pattern and detail not usually found in this style of art. His admiration for Moebius is seen in his ability to edit his line work, often leaving large areas of panels and pages blank or completely black. In *Air Mail* he uses a six-panel grid frequently, breaking out of this self-imposed order to great effect from time to time.

The story, which takes place in the United States during the early days of flying, features the adventures of an air-mail delivery pilot, Clarence "Babel" Man. He has to be reckless in order to do his job. Micheluzzi's writing is quite terse, and his characterization can be sketchy, but his scripts have the feeling of a Hollywood film, full of charismatic goons and wisecracking broads. **FJ**

Mister X 1983

✎ Dean Motter ✎ Gilbert and Jamie Hernández

First published by Vortex Comics (Canada)
Creators Motter (Canadian, Unknown); Gilbert Hernández (American, b.1957); Jaime Hernández (American, b.1959) **Genre** Science fiction

Only a professional illustrator-turned-writer would come up with a plot about a drugged architect trying to protect people from the psychological terrors of the city he designed.

Dean Motter's Mister X is an enigmatic figure that haunts his comics, just as the architecture he helped construct haunts the inhabitants of Radiant City. The city was intended to be constructed in a way that would alter its inhabitants' moods for the better. Thanks to cost cutting in the construction, its disconcerting vistas and strange angles instead unsettle and dehumanize people.

At times Mister X seems as much in the dark as the reader, dosing himself with drugs and trying to keep a lid on his emotions. He makes friends and enemies among those struggling to make sense of what is going on, including a depressed waitress named Mercedes, who tries to understand and protect him.

In the hands of the Hernández brothers, this pop art filtering of German expressionism is visually hugely stylish. The cityscapes dominate the action, and drawn in stark black and white with shadows that are not in the right place, the panels evoke disquiet. They set a style that subsequent artists, most notably Seth, adopted.

Mister X himself is very much a cipher onto which the reader can project. Motter's dialogue is suitably terse and intriguing, with much left unsaid and many plot twists that turn the premise of the story upside down. When Mister X's origin is revealed it only raises more questions in the reader. **FJ**

The Cat 1983

✎ Philippe Geluck

Title in original language *Le chat*
First published by Rossel (Belgium)
Creator Belgian (b.1954)
Genre Funny animal

The Cat appeared for the first time in a 1983 edition of *Temps Libres*, a supplement to the Belgian newspaper *Le Soir*. Philippe Geluck's straight-talking and witty cat has gone from strength to strength since then, and his weekly strips have been collected into more than twenty-six Casterman volumes.

An anthropomorphic creature, the Cat is human-sized (if rather corpulent), stands upright, wears a suit, and participates in everyday activities such as reading and driving. Each short strip is composed either of a brief succession of frames or a single large image. The Cat speaks to the reader, making a satirical commentary on modern life, with gags centered on humorous wordplay. Stylistically, each of Geluck's feline-focused strips is very simple, featuring almost no background detail and little movement or color. Geluck draws the Cat in a spartan style; his only features are two pointed ears and basic ovals for his eyes and a nose. The strip's humor and complexity comes from the Cat's dialogue, and comic content varies from ironical one-liners to self-reflexive jokes about his life as a fictional character.

As with other highly popular Franco-Belgian strips, *The Cat's* cultural presence surpasses its drawn image. It has spawned toys and calendars, become the focus of a touring exhibition, and even lent its name to a town square in Hotton, Belgium. With its consistently and unapologetically basic aesthetic, Geluck's creation is a testament to the endurance of intelligent comic writing and to the power of even the most simply structured of comics. **CM**

PHILIPPE GELUCK

LE CHAT

C'EST MOI...

C'EST LUI

casterman

"Time is money, I know. Time allows you to get money. But does money allow you to find time?"

Similar reads

Alert Fangataufa (Alerte sur Fangataufa) Philippe Geluck and Devig
Dilbert: Random Acts of Management Scott Adams
Mister O Lewis Trondheim
The Book of Bunny Suicides Andy Riley

Perramus: Escape from the Past 1984

✏ Juan Sasturain ✏ Alberto Breccia

First published by Bernardi (Italy)
Creators Sasturian (Argentinian, b.1945);
Breccia (Uruguayan, 1919–93)
Genre Political fable

"No mythic enterprise is going to save the shipwrecked from history, but the gesture of searching, and the voyage itself, justify our surrender and round up the unique sense. And I think this also applies to *Perramus*." With these words, Juan Sasturain, author of *Perramus*, defined the work that writer Osvaldo Soriano called "the first milestone work about the Argentine dictatorship."

In what became a serial work, Sasturain and illustrator Alberto Breccia pay tribute to comic book writer Héctor Germán Oesterheld, who had become one of Argentina's so-called "disappeared." If Oesterheld's *The Eternaut* (*El Eternauta*) presaged the dictatorial violence yet to come, then *Perramus* was the distorted memory of state-inflicted violence. It is a lively, Borgesian representation of Breccia's dogma: "The style is the concept, it is man."

While *The Eternaut* traffics the future, *Perramus* presents a ghost of the past. It recounts the efforts of a resistance group, the Volunteer Vanguard for Victory, when it attempts to overthrow the military government. Sasturain's anguished hero Perramus wants to forget his past, so much that he reinvents himself by taking the name he finds on the label of an overcoat. Breccia's Lovecraftian representation of the narrative uses an expressionistic gray scale as a way to define the hurt of a country ruled by marshal law.

Rabid and scarred, *Perramus* is an epic story without equal. It mixes both politics and adventure in what is a heartfelt search for Perramus's identity, and with that a search for his homeland. **JMD**

Dragon Ball 1984

✏✏ Akira Toriyama

First published by Shueisha (Japan)
Creator Japanese (b.1955)
Genre Action, Fantasy
Influenced by Osamu Tezuka, Walt Disney

When Akira Toriyama's *Dragon Ball* appeared in *Weekly Shonen Jump* in 1984, its adventurous plot captured a youthful audience instantly. The story follows the adventures of a young boy and girl, Son Goku and Bulma, when they set out on a journey to search for the seven legendary Dragon Balls used to summon the great wish-granting dragon Shenron. As their journey progresses they encounter numerous obstacles and antagonists that force Goku into conflict. Eventually his hidden physical strength and origin are revealed, causing the story to become more action oriented.

After countless battles, word of Goku's strength reverberates through the galaxies, which attracts the attention of increasingly strong aliens to challenge him. As the pressure piles on to protect the Earth and his loved ones, Goku undergoes inhumane physical training with the aid of the gods. Goku and his companions add a variety of techniques to their fighting styles as they stand together to face the evil that threatens them. Goku and his friends mature to become an increasingly tight-knit unit as they travel to other planets in order to save their people from extinction, gather comrades, fall in love, and die. Unexpected arrivals from the future warn them of possible devastation, and they attempt to save the universe from falling into despair and chaos at the hands of antagonists such as the Emperor Frieza, the lifeform Cell, and the monster Majin Buu.

Dragon Ball is a high-tempo, action-packed series considered to be one of the greatest comics of all time, and it has spawned films and video games. **TS**

Saga of the Swamp Thing 1984

✐ Alan Moore ✐ Stephen Bissette and John Totleben

First published by Vertigo/DC Comics (USA)
Creators Moore (British, b.1953); Bissette (American, b.1955); Totleben (American, b.1958)
Genre Science fiction

The first issue of *Saga of the Swamp Thing* was written by Martin Pasko and illustrated by Thomas Yeates. This revival went through various creators until 1984, when *Swamp Thing* cocreator and editor, Len Wein, solicited the British writer Alan Moore to take over scripting.

The trailblazing team of Moore, Stephen Bissette, and John Totleben reconceived the title radically as a genre-blurring mash-up of psychological terror, gothic romance, and science fiction adventure. The central character is transformed from a tragic hybrid into a plant god intrinsically connected to all vegetable life, using its powers to become as large as a mountain or as small as the flora in the human body. This gives a powerful agency to the natural world, which is usually disregarded by anthropocentric U.S. comics. Exceptions to that rule are Walt Kelly and Greg Irons, to whom the creators pay homage.

Drawing on literature and film, the series took the mainstream to a new level of sophistication. It explores philosophical, social, and sexual themes via the Swamp Thing's interactions with a host of well-conceived secondary characters, such as his human lover Abby and wheeler-dealer magician John Constantine. The artwork is remarkable for the dense intricacy of its lines, the subtle tonality of its coloring, and its ornate page layouts. *Saga of the Swamp Thing* is also important because of the radical way it advocates environmentalism. The series explores issues such as pollution, deforestation, and the threat of toxic waste, and so challenges an instrumentalist attitude toward nature. **MG**

FROM THE AWARD-WINNING WRITER OF WATCHMEN
ALAN MOORE

SAGA OF THE
SWAMP THING
BOOK ONE
STEPHEN BISSETTE   JOHN TOTLEBEN   VERTIGO

"Stories shape the world. They exist independently of people … The glaciers have their legends."

Similar reads
Hellblazer Jamie Delano and John Ridgway
The Sandman Neil Gaiman, Sam Kieth, and Mike Dringenberg
Swamp Thing Len Wein and Bernie Wrightson

The Magician's Wife 1984

Jérôme Charyn   François Boucq

Title in original language *La femme du magicien*
First published by Casterman (Belgium)
Creators Charyn (American, b.1937); Boucq (French, b.1955) **Genre** Drama, Fantasy

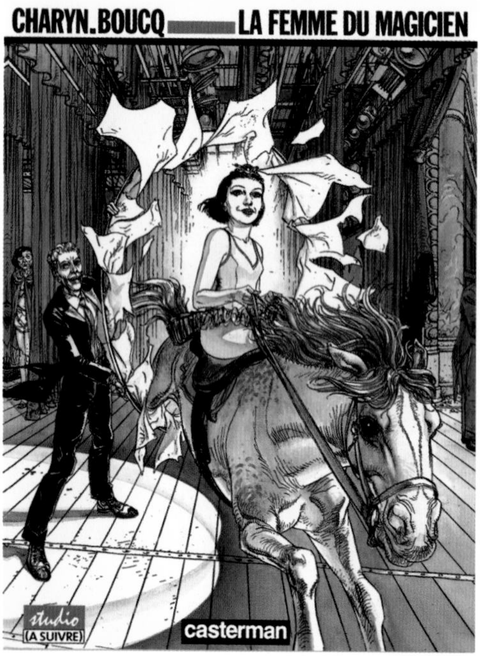
CHARYN.BOUCQ
LA FEMME DU MAGICIEN
studio (A SUIVRE)
casterman

Similar reads

Billy Budd, KGB (*Bouche du diable*) François Boucq and Jérôme Charyn
Bouncer François Boucq and Alejandro Jodorowsky
Pioneers of Human Adventure (***Les pionniers de l'aventure***) François Boucq

The lovely Rita knew the illusionist Edmond when she was a child. He was her mother's lover and amused himself by scaring Rita with strange tricks in the big house in Saratoga Springs where they lived. All three become star magicians and appear on stage all over the world, but things become even more surreal when Rita takes her mother's place and marries Edmond.

The strange relationship between Edmond and Rita encompasses attraction, repulsion, and magic. However, on the death of her mother, Rita decides to give up Edmond, as well as her magic act and the fame that goes with it. She goes to New York to lose herself in anonymity, becoming a waitress in a shabby hamburger joint. But it is there that her past resurfaces.

"No Edmond! I can't! I can't! I'm your wife, but . . . "

Haunted by memories and caught up by the dreamy, carnivalesque events of her childhood, she often becomes overwhelmed by the violence of the impulses that live within her. Rita comes to understand that there are unseen consequences to having ever become the wife of a magician.

French illustrator François Boucq was already established in the field of humor when he met the U.S. novelist Jérôme Charyn at the instigation of the French magazine *À Suivre*. Their ensuing collaboration proved to be exceptionally fruitful. *The Magician's Wife* combined Charyn's baroque imagination and Boucq's neorealist visual power. The strange love story, which takes place at the boundary between reality and the world of dreams, turned out to be one of the greatest successes in French-language comic strips of the 1980s. The duo went on to produce the excellent *Billy Budd, KGB* (*Bouche du diable*), first published in 1990. **NF**

The Two Guys on the Balcony 1984

✏️ Francis Masse

In a strange, drained Venice, two men exchange deep and sometimes rather outrageous thoughts on science and its latest advances. One of them is wearing a bowler hat and enjoys pontificating; the other wears a cap and plays the part of a guileless person whose astonished exclamations and naive questions continue to prompt further explanations from his companion. They discuss whatever seems strange and amazing.

The men's identities and the reasons why they are together on a balcony are unknown, but this seems unimportant, as readers are focused on the contemporary chemistry, physics, and biology under discussion. The men talk about weird attractors, paradoxical sleep, quantum mechanics, and continental

"... if you don't advance rather quickly, you know where the oars are ..."

drift. Their conversations move far beyond hard science to pseudophilosophy as topics range from giraffes, a gigantic bathroom, carnivorous flowers, and rutting cars to putting rhinoceroses out to dry.

The bizarre universe of Francis Masse's *The Two Guys on the Balcony* contains brilliance and nonsense, rigor and absurdity, erudition and madness, all in equal measure. Masse emerged as a personality in French comics in the 1970s but took a step back from the industry in the 1990s. Imaginative and radical, the illustrator has never compromised. This probably explains the fact that, although unanimously admired by his peers, he has not really enjoyed great popular success. To relish his black humor and fully appreciate his work, the reader needs to peruse the full dozen or so of his albums, which are clearly influenced by the great masters of illustration and painting. Today, as ever, they are still without equal within their genre. **NF**

Title in original language *Les deux du balcon*
First published by Casterman (Belgium)
Creator French (b.1948)
Genre Humor

MASSE ▬▬▬▬ LES DEUX DU BALCON

casterman

studio (A SUIVRE)

Also by Francis Masse
Lower Parts of the City (*Les dessous de la ville*)
Masse's Encyclopedia (*Encyclopédie de Masse*)
Memories of Land Overseas (*Mémoires d'outre-terre*)
Museum Tsunami (*Tsunami au musée*)
The Pond with the Pirates (*La mare aux pirates*)

The Towers of Bois-Maury
Babette 1984

"Hermann"

Title in original language *Les tours de Bois-Maury: Babette*
First published by Glénat (France)
Creator Hermann Huppen (Belgian, b.1938)
Genre Fantasy

HERMANN
LES TOURS DE
BOIS◇MAURY
TOME 1 - BABETTE
Glénat

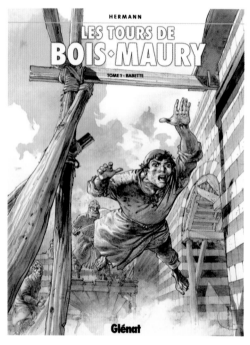

Similar reads
Bernard Prince Greg and Hermann
Comanche Greg and Hermann
Jeremiah Hermann
Hey, Nick! Are You Dreaming? (Nic) Morphée and Hermann

Hermann's *The Towers of Bois-Maury* is a great adventure story, but it veers away from straight action to focus more on characterization than any of his other works.

Sir Aymar de Bois-Maury is a nobleman wandering through medieval France, attempting to bring order to a world where war has made morality a costly luxury. The first volume in the series, *Babette*, finds De Bois-Maury staying with a fellow knight when another guest, Sir Geoffroy, is murdered. It transpires that Sir Geoffroy raped a local peasant girl, Babette, but her lover, Germain, is arrested for the killing. Tragically, the girl's own family beats her to death as she tries to aid her lover. De Bois-Maury is disgusted by the behavior of both nobles and peasants, and is unable to walk away without having found out the truth. His brisk and judgmental nature means he cannot resist attempting to force his ideals on those around him. Dispossessed of his own lands, he looks constantly for simple truths that will help him make sense of the world and which he can grasp onto—but he never finds them.

"It's merely that I learned different rules of chivalry from those that Sir Geoffroy embraces."

De Bois-Maury saves Babette's lover, but in a bitter epilogue Hermann shows the banished young man willing to sell his body and take up with thieves simply to survive. Hermann is interested in exploring the difficult ethical choices made by people in extremes, and his stories follow the fate of multiple characters.

Hermann's eye for period detail adds a richness to his visual storytelling, and his fine, somewhat sketchy, line gives his characters animation. No one is beautiful in the world Hermann creates, but all of his characters are distinct and individual. **FJ**

Rocco Vargas
Triton 1984

Daniel Torres

Some years after Rocco Vargas, the former pioneer of interplanetary exploration, ended his life of adventure to become known as "Armando Mistral," a successful science fiction writer and the owner of a fashionable music hall, Vargas's old friend and partner in crime, the engineer Covalsky, enters his life once more. Covalsky, wants Vargas, a former astronaut, to be part of his great project: dragging giant icebergs off the surface of Triton, a satellite of Neptune, to let them melt in Earth's atmosphere to put an end to a terrible drought that is affecting a large part of Earth.

Vargas refuses to help, but then Covalsky dies in a mysterious car accident. Vargas does not take long to realize that Covalsky's suspicious death is the work

"Think that your name makes you. Do you understand now why you must be the one to name yourself?"

of Colonel Mung, the diabolical head of the Saturnian secret service. By killing Covalsky and hence stopping his plan to end the drought, Mung hopes to ensure that Saturn retains the possibility of supplying water to drought-ridden Earth.

Prompted by Covalsky's daughter, Jill, who begs for his help, Vargas decides to become involved in the project. Vargas knew Jill as a child, and she has grown into an irresistible young woman. He heads for Triton on board his legendary spaceship, the *Estrella Lejana* (*Distant Star*).

In *Rocco Vargas: Triton,* creator Daniel Torres reinterprets classic imagery of science fiction comics by introducing humor, subtlety, and an elegant narrative. The result he achieves is an enjoyable pastiche of *Flash Gordon* revisited with the aesthetics of Raymond Loewy. **NF**

Title in original language *Roco Vargas: Tritón*
First published by Norma Editorial (Spain)
Creator Spanish (b.1958)
Genre Science fiction

Les aventures sidérales de Roco Vargas
TORRES
TRITON
UN AUTEUR
(A SUIVRE)
casterman

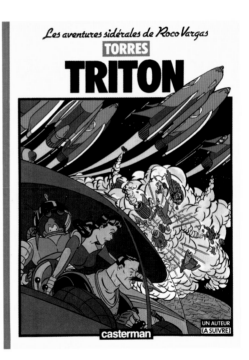

Similar reads
Flash Gordon Alex Raymond
Opium Daniel Torres
Ray Banana: Electric Lullaby (*Berceuse électrique*) Ted Benoît
Sabotage! (*Sabotaje*) Daniel Torres

Zot! 1984

Scott McCloud

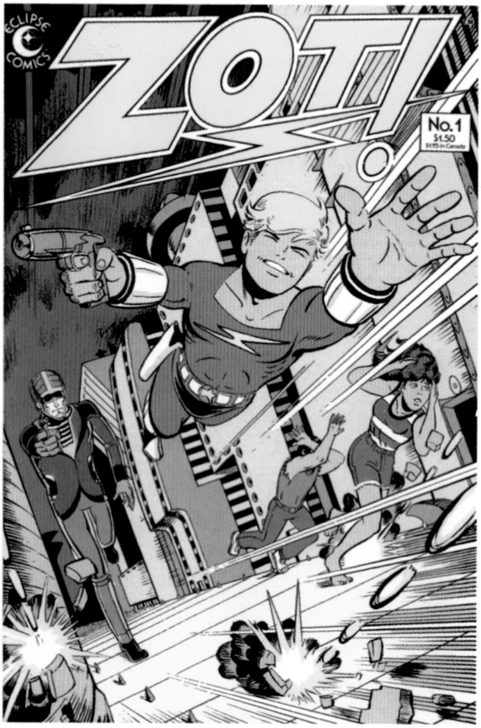
ECLIPSE COMICS
ZOT!
No. 1
$1.50

"Much of the storytelling drew heavily on my growing fascination with manga as well as alternative creators like the Hernández Brothers."

Scott McCloud

Similar reads

Astro Boy Osamu Tezuka
Mechanics Jaime Hernández

First published by Eclipse Comics (USA)
Creator American (b.1960)
Genre Superhero, Science fiction
Influenced by Philip Francis Nowlan, Colin Upton

Zachary T. Paleozogt, otherwise known as "Zot," comes from an alternate Earth in 1965. He behaves like a superhero, battling robots and hunting for a lost key to the Doorway at the Edge of the Universe. Jenny Weaver and her brother Butch find themselves on Zot's world facing the threats of the Church of De-Evolution, as well as super villains 9-Jack-9 and Dekko. The first three-quarters of the series presents exciting and inventive superhero adventures on both Zot's world and Earth.

In the final quarter, Zot is stranded on Earth, and although he still fights crime, the stories are about growing up in high school and the challenges faced by teenagers. In stories told from the point of view of different cast members, creator Scott McCloud explores their lives and contrasts them with Zot's utopian world. In the story "Normal," prompted by a homophobic attack on her brother, Pamela defiantly tells the whole school that she is a lesbian. Regular cast member Terry questions her own sexuality when she remembers how close she and Pamela used to be. Terry is in despair, but Zot promises that he and her friends will not desert her, leaving the question of whether or not she will have the courage to speak to Pamela. "Normal" was nominated for a Best Single Issue Harvey Award in 1991.

McCloud is best known for his theories about comics, but with *Zot!* he created a stylish, exciting, and upbeat comic that mixed superheroes with emotional drama. In spite of the science fiction trappings and fantastic premise, these are heartfelt stories that have much to say about the human condition. **NFI**

2001 Nights 1984

✐✐ Yukinobu Hoshino

Title in original language *Nisen'ichi ya monogatari*
First published by Futabasha (Japan)
Creator Japanese (b.1954)
Genre Science fiction

2001 Nights is a series of stories that postulate about the future and the possibility of space exploration and colonization. The stories span hundreds of years, and although each can be read individually, together they tell a much larger tale as discoveries, characters, and inventions are cross-referenced with each other.

In "Night 1: Earthglow," a group of world leaders discuss cooperation while looking down on Earth from space. "Night 2: Sea of Fertility" concerns a death while mining for minerals on the Moon and the discovery of a meteorite that holds fossilized fish, pointing to the possibility of other life in the universe. In "Night 4: Posterity," a spaceship is attached to the nucleus of a comet in order to use the comet's speed to reach a distant star in hundreds, rather than thousands, of years. Unfortunately, only frozen ova and spermatozoa and machines can survive the first part of the journey. In this moving tale, amid scientific explanations, Yukinobu Hoshino dramatizes the story of the parents left behind and the growth of their children in space.

Hoshino uses sharply inked photo-realism to depict scientific hardware with a somewhat looser figure work. *2001 Nights* can be wordy, but the explanation, dialogue, and silent passages work together to express something of the scale of the undertaking involved. Apart from obvious inspirations such as the film *2001: A Space Odyssey*, Hoshino references both Eastern and Western art and philosophy in an entertaining and thoughtful examination of what it might mean to leave Earth and face new worlds. **NFI**

Fires 1984

✐ "Jerry Kramsky" ✐ Lorenzo Mattotti

Title in original language *Fuochi*
First published by Milano Libri Editore (Italy)
Creators Fabrizio Ostani (Italian, b.1953);
Mattotti (Italian, b.1954) **Genre** Fantasy

A battleship, the *Anselm II*, casts anchor near Sainte Agathe, a deserted island in the southern hemisphere. Its mission is to explore the island and understand why strange happenings have occurred there recently .

A small detachment of officers land on the island. Among them is Lieutenant Absinthe, who is already perturbed by his dreams of flamboyant creatures that cannot be explained. Soon he develops empathy for the invisible creatures that inhabit the island. At first held back by his allegiance to his hierarchy, the officer soon becomes consumed and transfigured by the telluric force of his perceptions. Finally, he takes the side of the vibrant land, its exuberant natural forces, and its indomitable soul. But will his inner equilibrium, not to mention his humanity, survive the ordeal?

An animist fable in a magical setting, somewhere between shamanic trance and artistic creation, *Fires* is one of those rare comic strips that is immediately hailed as a masterpiece. Before this allegory of nature versus culture, few had envisaged using color to play a part in the narrative as a raw material pregnant with meaning. By opting, with amazing brio, for an intensely pictorial and chromatic comic strip, Lorenzo Mattotti and Fabrizio Ostani (aka "Jerry Kramsky") opened up the horizons of the medium. Mattotti sidesteps an explicit approach and rational chronology, and throughout the story, he favors a dreamlike dimension, and he makes his colors vibrate with an almost organic power. Breathtaking from beginning to end, *Fires* showed Mattotti had become a master of European comic art. **NF**

The Ballad of Halo Jones 1984

Alan Moore Ian Gibson

First published by IPC Magazines (UK)
Creators Moore (British, b.1953); Gibson (British, b.1946)
Genre Teen, Science fiction

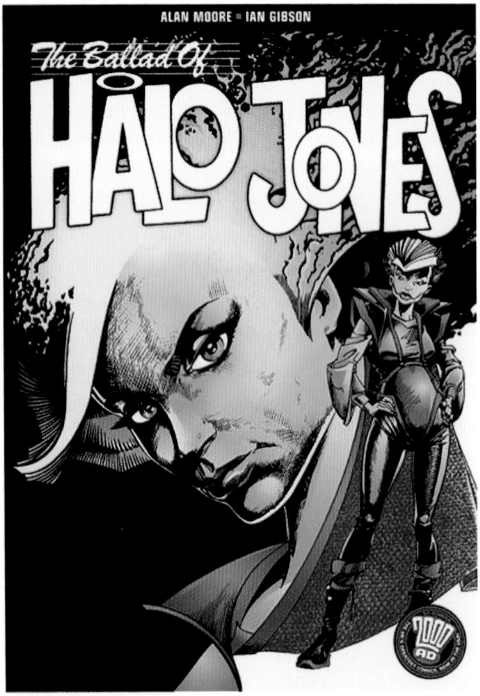
ALAN MOORE • IAN GIBSON
The Ballad Of
HALO JONES
2000 AD

Similar reads

Return of the Taxidermist John Wagner and Ian Gibson
The League of Extraordinary Gentlemen Alan Moore and Kevin O'Neill
The Spider Moon Kate Brown
V for Vendetta Alan Moore and David Lloyd

Halo Jones is an unusual character for a boys' science-fiction comic simply because she is a girl. Writer Alan Moore's decision to challenge convention and present a female lead character without any special abilities paid off handsomely and resulted in one of *2000AD*'s most fondly remembered characters.

Jones is a very average girl from the bottom of society in the fiftieth century. She lives in the Hoop, which is a floating, jobless ghetto with high crime and no prospects. Over the course of three books, Jones attempts to rise above the status given to her at birth, only to be continually beaten down by the world. The first book covers her life in the Hoop and her eventual escape, the second her new job as a stewardess on a year-long interstellar voyage, and the third her time spent in the military.

"Fresh air? Yeah, I think I remember breathing some of that once. It tasted of fish."

Like all good science fiction, Moore uses Jones's world to explore the problems of contemporary society. There are many extraordinary aspects to Jones's world, but they do not alleviate the staggering class inequality or the sense of futility and powerlessness felt by Jones and her friends. Her world feels utterly fantastic, yet unbearably mundane. The books showcase Moore's extraordinary imagination, particularly in his description of a battle raging on a planet so vast that its gravitational field slows down time. Ian Gibson's stylish and extravagant art is perfectly suited to the more feminine aspects of the story while running riot on its more fantastic elements and adding extraordinary levels of detail in every panel. This is a love letter to those at the bottom, whoever and wherever they are. **BD**

Odile and the Crocodiles 1984

Chantal Montellier

Title in original language *Odile et les crocodiles*
First published by Les Humanoïdes Associés (France)
Creator French (b.1947)
Genre Adventure, Political fable

Chantal Montellier's career began in the 1970s when she was one of a tiny number of female comic artists working in a male environment. This book sets out to counter the crude images of women that were then the norm in French comics, and, more generally, to combat misogynistic discourse. It uses some of the generic devices of the thriller, but in this feminist variant the heroine is not a victim but a perpetrator.

Actress Odile B goes on the offensive when a male judge acquits the three men who have raped her and she is accused of provoking them. She becomes an avenging vigilante. Armed with a paper knife, Odile dispatches various men, including a psychoanalyst, who

"My rapists were 'from a respectable family'... the judge expected me to be grateful that they'd deigned to rape me."

offers to cure her "hysteria" by reawakening her sexual desire. The title's "crocodiles" lurk in the spaces between chapters and frames, bursting into the fictional world at key moments. They represent the predatory, repressed unconscious of the society that Montellier portrays.

In Montellier's postpunk aesthetic, garish shades of green saturate elegant, realistic drawings, and texts, numbers, and arrows invade panels. In the dystopian world that she conjures up, public space has given way to sinister shopping malls. Some of the graphic elements emphasize the commodification of culture and sex, and the paranoia around security. But the walls of the city, and the book, serve as sites for resistance, with their anarchist symbols, anticapitalist graffiti, and quotations from Pier Paolo Pasolini. Scattered across the surface of pages are fragments of paper on which the words "Judith" and "Holofernes" can be read, giving a mythological resonance to Odile's exploits. **AM**

CHANTAL MONTELLIER
ODILE
ET LES CROCODILES
ACTES SUD - L'AN 2

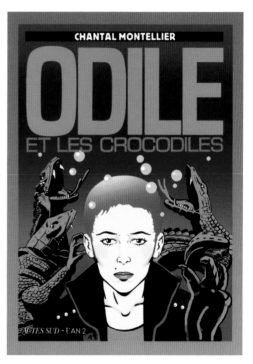

Also by Chantal Montellier

Chernobyl My Love (Tchernobyl mon amour)
Julie Bristol: Lying and Bleeding (Julie Bristol: Faux sanglant)
Social Fiction
The Damned of Nanterre (Les damnés de Nanterre)

XIII: The Day of the Black Sun 1984

Jean Van Hamme William Vance

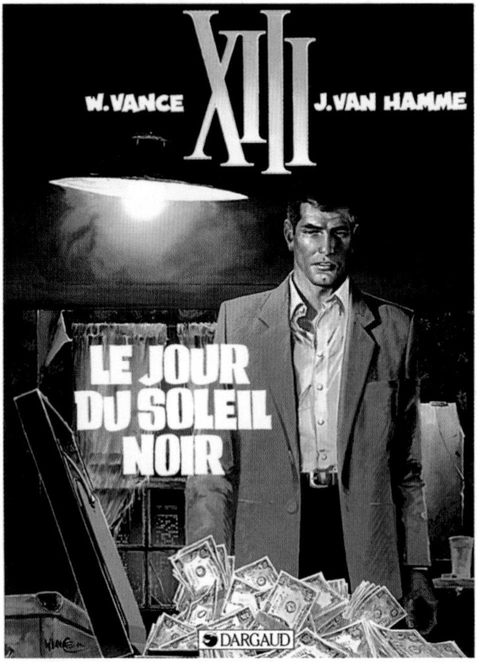
W. VANCE
XIII
J. VAN HAMME
LE JOUR DU SOLEIL NOIR
DARGAUD

"The doctor who took care of me was positive that my reflexes and instincts had remained intact . . . And my instincts tell me I am not an assassin."

Similar reads

Largo Winch Jean Van Hamme and Philippe Francq
Michael Logan Jean Van Hamme and André Beautemps
SOS Happiness (*SOS Bonheur*) Jean Van Hamme and Griffo
Thorgal Jean Van Hamme and Grzegorz Rosiński

Title in original language *XIII: Le jour du soleil noir*
First published by Dupuis (France)
Creators Van Hamme (Belgian, b.1939); Vance (Belgian, b.1935) **Genre** Adventure

The Roman numeral for thirteen, XIII, is tattooed on the lower neck of an unknown man who is found barely alive and washed up on the U.S. coast with a bullet through his head. He is rescued by an elderly fisherman and nursed back to health, but the bullet wound has erased his memory. An amnesiac stares back at a stranger's face in the mirror. He has no papers and no possessions on him. There are only two clues as to who he might be: a key sewn into his shirt collar, and the strange tattoo. When his life is threatened once more, he begins a desperate quest to rediscover his identity.

Inspired by Robert Ludlum's *The Bourne Identity*, Jean Van Hamme takes *XIII* in its own direction. The compelling characterization and complex plotting of this thriller gripped the Francophone public for more than twenty years through serialization in *Spirou* weekly and in nineteen albums. Caught in a game of escalating bluff and double-bluff, it becomes increasingly hard for XIII—and the reader—to know whom to trust. Tensions are heightened by the Kennedy-style assassination of a liberal U.S. president; the perpetrators can be traced to the corridors of power in Washington. Conspiracy and counterconspiracy, secrets of past lives and deaths, harrowing psychiatric treatment in a top-security prison, a Ku Klux Klan plot, and other elements intertwine with XIII's assorted aliases, but which of them, if any, is real?

Illustrator William Vance provides gritty realism and crisp clarity and composition. Several of his characters are thinly disguised portraits of celebrities, including Lee Marvin and Henry Kissinger. **PG**

Usagi Yojimbo 1984

🖉🖊 Stan Sakai

First published by Thoughts and Images (USA)
Creator Japanese-American (b.1953)
Genre Adventure **Award** Eisner Award for Talent
Deserving of Wider Recognition (1996)

Miyamoto Usagi, an anthropomorphic rabbit, is a *ronin* (masterless samurai). He goes on a warrior's journey that takes him through a Japanese landscape full of mystery, intrigue, and the occasional supernatural demon. For his plots, Stan Sakai draws on seventeenth-century Japanese culture, politics, and traditional folklore. He also sets his stories around specific Japanese crafts, such as pottery and kite making.

Sakai's main characters exist in a richly depicted world; Usagi meets people from all social classes and encounters good and bad in them all. Always willing to help those in need, he puts himself in danger because that is his fate as a *ronin*.

Many Usagi stories are completed in one or two issues, but Sakai has embarked on several longer tales. They include "Dragon Bellow Conspiracy," which features Usagi's potential romantic interest, Ame Tomoe, and her lord, Noriyuki; "Grasscutter," in which Tomoe searches for a legendary sword; and "Samurai," the story of Usagi's training under the old lion Katsuichi. Usagi encounters regular characters such as the bounty hunter Murakami Gennosuke; the Neko and Komori ninja clans; the enigmatic Jei, who claims to be a messenger of the gods; Usagi's son, Jotaro; and thief and entertainer Kitsune.

The stories are often humorous, with lighthearted tales separating the more dramatic episodes. There is a great deal of death in the series, but the brutality is undercut by Sakai's drawings of skulls over dying characters with comically grotesque expressions. **NFI**

The Collector 1984

🖉🖊 Sergio Toppi

Title in original language *Il Collezionista*
First published by L'Isola Trovata (Italy)
Creator Italian (b.1932)
Genre Fantasy

The Collector is the only recurring character in Sergio Toppi's work, and his adventures run to five volumes. A depraved aristocrat and dandy, he is a man whose life is entirely devoted to the quest for rare and mysterious objects. He travels through time and space to seek them, taking in the jungles of Borneo and the hills of Afghanistan. The Collector is a dangerous man who he will use any means necessary to secure the objects he seeks. But he is also a distinguished and elegant person; his passion is not motivated by economic interest but by an overwhelming desire to find the unique and become the ultimate collector.

The magic and spiritual atmosphere of Toppi's work is at its peak here. The series develops an animistic vision of the beauty of nature and the inherent truth that is expressed by well-crafted objects. After years of work in advertising for the renowned animation studio Pagot Film, Toppi debuted in the 1960s with *Il Corriere dei Piccoli* and rapidly started to amass a large body of historically inspired works for magazines such as *Linus* and *Sgt. Kirk*.

Toppi's visual style is one of the most idiosyncratic in the tradition of the European masters. He is admired by artists such as Frank Miller and David B., and devotedly followed by Walt Simonson. Toppi's line is characterized by a dense and hypnotic texture, full of details and arabesques. His layouts frequently comprise single splash-page images that push totemic figures into stunning close-up, capturing the reader's eye with their strange and mesmerizing poses. **MS**

Entresol 1985

✐✐ Tadeusz Baranowski

Title in original language *Antresolka profesorka Nerwosolka*
First published by MAW (Poland)
Creator Polish (b.1945) **Genre** Children's

Tekst & rysunki
Tadeusz Baranowski

Antresolka profesorka Nerwosolka

Młodzieżowa Agencja Wydawnicza

Also by Tadeusz Baranowski
Orient Men: Forever and For All (Forever na zawsze)
Where Does Soda Water Come From and Other Stories
 (Skąd się bierze woda sodowa i nie tylko)
Why the Nose of an Eskimo Lurks Inside a Whale
 (Na co dybie w wielorybie czubek nosa eskimosa)

Tadeusz Baranowski's *Entresol* was first published in album format in 1985. Aimed at young audiences, it contained two stories: one related to the exploration of outer space and the other to sea travel. However, this was no *Tintin*-esque comic strip for kids: it featured completely improbable plots, fantastic creatures, twisted protagonists, and eccentric wordplays, all drawn in a beautifully modern style, filled with audacious experimentation, surreal coloring, and expressionist shapes.

The plot of Entresol is nothing but a pretext for an exploration—not of outer space or the seven seas, but of the art form itself. Baranowski's work is sometimes, quite rightly, compared to Fred's *Philémon* series. It

"Get up on your feet, and help me lift this fallen comic strip."

originates from the same fascination with the comics medium and the understanding that it can become a worthy tool in the hands of an able artist. *Entresol*'s Profesor Nerwosolek and his maid Entomologia are among Baranowski's most popular comic book heroes. It is in this series that the author pushed the boundaries of the comics form, creating visual masterpieces that are full of humor and charm.

Tadeusz Baranowski published his first comic strips in the Polish magazine *Świat Młodych* in 1975, and quickly became one of the iconic creators during the twilight of Communist Poland. His humorous stories gradually became more surreal, offering a perfect escape from the often gray reality of crisis-ridden Poland in the 1980s.

Baranowski is virtually unknown outside of Poland, although he has published a number of short stories in the Belgian comic *Tintin* in 1984 and 1985. **MB**

Socker-Conny 1985

Joakim Pirinen

Socker-Conny was the most successful Swedish graphic novel of the1980s. Its publication in 1985 was a decisive moment in the development of the Swedish comics culture toward a more mature, adult-oriented medium, and it catapulted its creator to stardom.

Socker-Conny (which literally translates as "Sugar-Conny") tells the story of a clueless anarchic man. He is a child in an adult's body who has none of the inhibitions of a "normal" citizen. At the beginning of the story he attempts to steal some modeling clay from a toy store but gets caught and is fined. Although it is only a small sum of money, he cannot pay it. He tries different jobs to earn some money, but blunders all of them, destroying everything he comes in contact with and ending up owing everyone huge amounts of money. Pirinen's story is a brilliant satire of Swedish society in the yuppie era of the 1980s. It manages to be simultaneously realistic and surrealistic, leaping back and forth between the two styles effortlessly.

"With a good iron rod, you knock the world right off its feet!"

Socker-Conny was printed in black and white, which emphasizes Pirinen's beautiful, artistic inking and the seemingly inexhaustible crosshatching that fills each and every panel with endless details. Pirinen was also experimenting with layout and used new ways of arranging the panels on every page, which enhances the reading experience. The pages still feel modern and fresh today, more than twenty-five years later.

Pirinen has since created several other graphic novels, and written plays and short stories—all highly praised by the critics—and is rightfully revered as the grandfather of the alternative adult comics movement in Sweden. **FS**

First published by Galago (Sweden)
Creator Swedish (b.1961)
Genre Satire
Influence on Christina Alvner

SOCKER-CONNY
AV
JOAKIM PIRINEN

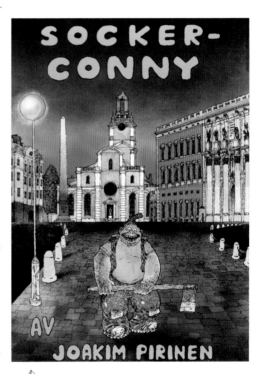

Similar reads

Bosnian Flat Dog Max Andersson and Lars Sjunnesson
Drafted for Life Joakim Pirinen
Epileptic **(*L'Ascension du haut-mal*)** David B.
Pixy Max Andersson
The Bear Family Joakim Pirinen

Wind of the Gods
Blood from the Moon 1985

Patrick Cothias Philippe Adamov

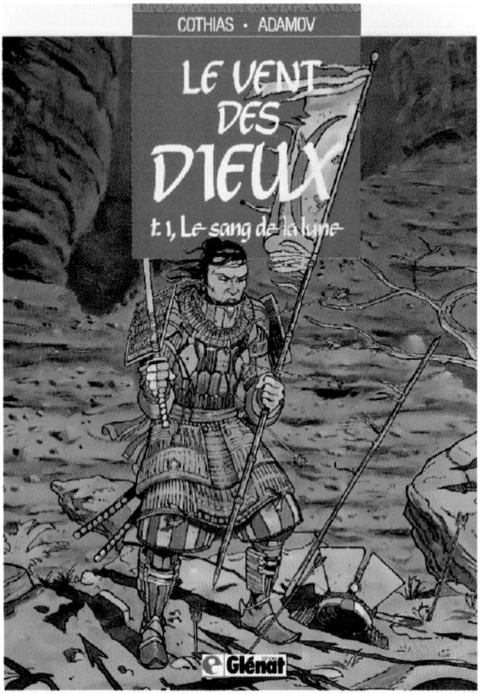
COTHIAS · ADAMOV
LE VENT DES DIEUX
t. 1, Le sang de la lune
Glénat

"It is really very flattering (and very enriching) to work with my collaborators . . ."

Patrick Cothias

Also by Philippe Adamov

Dayak
La malédiction de Zener with Jean-Christophe Grangé
Les eaux de Mortelune with Patrick Cothias
L'impératrice rouge with Jean Dufaux

Title in original language *Le vents des dieux: tome 1, Le sang de la lune* **First published by** Glénat (France) **Creators** Cothias (French, b.1956); Adamov (French, b.1948) **Genre** Adventure

This is a convoluted epic of court intrigue and samurai honor set in thirteenth-century Japan, a period when the Emperor's rule was shaky and various shogun were jockeying for power. The title *Wind of the Gods* refers to the wind that supposedly blows away human remains so that individuals can be reincarnated.

In the first volume readers are introduced to Qin Chen, a young warrior mistrusted by his overlord who is sent to subdue a group of rebels assisted by a carefully picked band of fellow samurai. Patrick Cothias's intention from the start was to create more than an action-packed story. Much of the first volume is taken up with conversations between the samurai on their long journey, during which they discuss their beliefs and ideals. They eventually betray Qin Chen, who is last seen tumbling to his death at the hands of the rebel forces. His lover, one of the shogun's concubines, outfaces her master during the repercussions from the rebel defeat. She warns Chen that he cannot defy the gods, and with this in mind the story ends as Chen sets out to discover his fate.

Despite the strength of Cothias's writing, this stands out as the artist's book. Illustrator Adamov draws the story in a delicate and detailed style. The milieu is rich and ornate, helped by the distinct outfits and hairstyles of the different samurai warriors. Although the artwork can sometimes feel a little stiff, there are occasional moments—Qin Chen's death metamorphosing into a bowl of goldfish, for example—that presage more exciting things to come in later volumes. **FJ**

Bell's Theorem 1985

✎✎ Matthias Schultheiss

Title in original language *Le Théorème de Bell*
First published by L'Echo des Savanes (France)
Creator German (b.1946)
Genre Adventure, Fantasy

Thirty-eight-year-old Shelby is in prison for life. To escape incarceration, the American detainee agrees to volunteer as a guinea pig in a medical experimentation program. After the early experiments prove to be very aggressive, he escapes prison but still has to learn how to cope with the strange and unpredictable effects of the unknown substances he has been given. Periodically seized by powerful hallucinations that seem to spring from another reality, Shelby moves to Labrador. There, alone in the heart of a vast wilderness, he comes upon the hideout, remains, and diary of Mark Amselstein, a physicist from Hamburg.

Hunted by mysterious pursuers who employ drastic measures, Shelby pretends to be Amselstein and manages to get on a flight to Germany. However, things are no more peaceful there: still plagued by inexplicable visions, Shalby gradually feels his identity being eroded, and he becomes confused by the insistent memory of Amselstein. In despair he plunges into the diary of the physicist, whose research revolved around Bell's theorem. A concept of quantum physics, Bell's theorem postulates that any part of the universe is in a hidden and immediate relationship with any other part.

Matthias Schultheiss constructs a fascinating story of hallucinatory flight, in which he develops his extreme characters and morbid, twilight moods. With an expressionist, graphic style and intense, saturated colors, he creates a bitter, violent realism that also has room for fantasy. It is a seductive, deeply personal, and instantly recognizable cocktail. **NF**

The Confessions of Julius Antoine 1985

✎ Serge Le Tendre ✎ Christian Rossi

Title in original language *Les errances de Julius Antoine*
First published by L'Echo des Savanes (France)
Creators Le Tendre (French, b.1946); Rossi (French, b.1954)
Genre Drama

When Serge Le Tendre and Christian Rossi initiated the *Julius Antoine* series in 1985, they were already experienced comics creators, and this is a mature, intelligent piece of work.

The eponymous character is a classic, bourgeois sophisticate, an architectural draftsman with a stylish lawyer girlfriend named Clemence and a smart convertible car. His life changes completely, however, when a chance encounter with old friends of his girlfriend leads to a growing obsession with their freespirited, teenage daughter, Lea. From there the story travels into darker territory when Antoine finds the girl's dead body and goes on the run from the police.

In its telling of a sordid, suburban murder, the story is reminiscent of the great French New Wave director Claude Chabrol. The story unfolds with a dreadful, cold logic and, like Antoine himself, readers are never quite sure of his innocence or guilt. Le Tendre's genius is to create a genuinely unlikable central character who could quite credibly be the killer. We first see Antoine as he sketches young girls in the street and his Lolita-like fixation is uncomfortably evident throughout. His obsession with Lea begins before he even meets her, and it is all too believable that his reckless fixation could lead to rape and murder. It is to Le Tendre's credit that readers still empathize with Antoine, even as he is hunted down by the police. Christian Rossi's art masterfully captures the mixture of carnality and despair that suffuses the story, and his evocation of the small French town is breathtaking. **DAR**

Mort Drucker's MAD Show-Stoppers 1985

Various   Mort Drucker

First published by EC Comics (USA)
Creator American (b.1929)
Genre Parody
Award Reuben (1987)

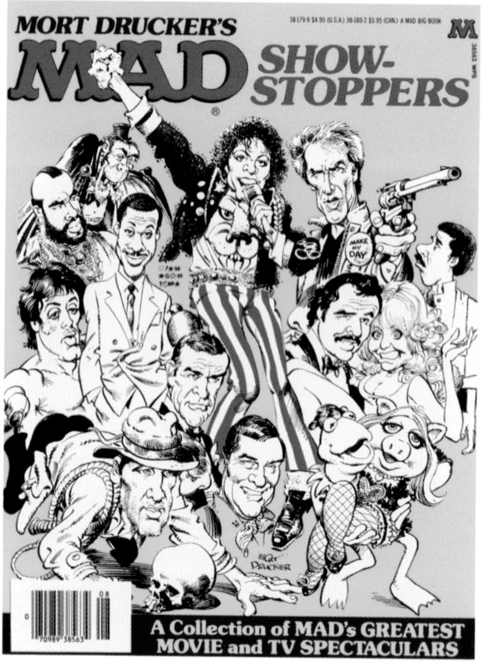
MORT DRUCKER'S
MAD
SHOW-STOPPERS
MAKE MY DAY
A Collection of MAD's GREATEST MOVIE and TV SPECTACULARS

Artist J. Scott Campbell remembers seeing Mort Drucker's drawings for the first time when he was eight years old. He was obsessed with a *MAD Magazine* cover featuring mascot Alfred E. Newman as Yoda from *Star Wars*. Inside was a parody sketch entitled "The Empire Strikes Out." Campbell loved the subject matter, but the rendering was a revelation: "I'd never seen an art style that so closely resembled real life while at the same time being so outrageously cartoony and funny looking." Drucker became a significant inspiration for Campbell.

Drucker's work experience uniquely prepared him for what would become his raison d'être—movie and TV show spoofs. Beginning at DC Comics, he honed his versatility correcting other artists' work, mastering myriad styles and tools. He next welcomed assignments in every DC comics genre, developing a vast visual vocabulary of place.

"He wouldn't just nail a likeness once, but many, many times over."

J. Scott Campbell, cartoonist

For freelance work, Drucker tapped diverse influences: for illustrations, he looked to the work of Robert Fawcett and Austin Briggs; for humor, Albert Dorne; for caricature, brilliant Britisher Ronald Searle and Al Hirschfeld, known for his stylized thespians. This amalgamation evolved into a distinctly personal style, and opened the door to *MAD Magazine* in 1956.

MAD Show-Stoppers collects spoofs from the 1960s and 1970s, two of Drucker's most fertile periods. Here one finds familiar faces: John Wayne in "True Fat," Marlon Brando in "The Oddfather," and Robert De Niro in "Raving Bully." Despite who's doing the writing—the scripts are undeniably clever—it is Drucker who breathes life into these lighthearted and never mean-spirited satires. **TRL**

Similar reads

Doonesbury Gary Trudeau
MAD about the 60s Various and Mort Drucker
MAD about the 70s Various and Mort Drucker
MAD about the 80s Various and Mort Drucker
Pogo Walt Kelly

Sambre 1985

"Balac" "Yslaire"

In 1985 Bernard Hislaire wanted to create an *histoire d'amour* that would emulate the passionate tragedies he had read as a youth. Under the pseudonym Yslaire, and with a script by Balac, he began *Sambre*, a darkly romantic fin de siècle tale of forbidden love.

The protagonists are Bernard Sambre, a young aristocrat at the time of the French Revolution in 1848, and Julie, a despised gypsy poacher with eyes the color of blood. With themes of sex, madness, jealousy, and the personal price of politics, Yslaire charts the destiny of a lineage cursed with "The War of the Eyes." In the opening scene, Bernard's father Hugo has committed suicide, convinced his dynasty is doomed. Bernard meets Julie, is rejected by his family, and follows her to Paris. There they are torn apart in the tumult of the revolution. The fifth and sixth volumes (of a planned twelve) continue the saga into the next generation, introducing Bernard and Julie's son, Bernard-Marie.

"Woe to him who loves a girl with eyes of fire, for he will cry a lifetime . . ."

Hugo Sambre

While intriguing and fairly literary, what sets *Sambre* apart from other European comics melodramas is the potent imagery: monochrome except for recurrent, dramatic splashes of crimson, focusing laserlike on details such as wine, blood, flags, fire, hair, lips, eyes. Red becomes, in effect, a character in the story, and Yslaire's emotionally charged yet tasteful eroticism sizzles.

After volume two, Yslaire became a writer as well as a comics artist. He also started digitally revising his work in "director's cut" editions and expanding the scope of the epic. In 2007 he began penning a multigenerational prequel—*The War of Sambre*—illustrated by various artists. **TRL**

First published by Glénat (France)
Creators Yannick le Pennetier (French, b.1954); Bernard Hislaire (Belgian, b.1957)
Genre Romance

YSLAIRE
BALAC
· SAMBRE ·
Plus ne m'est rien...
Glénat

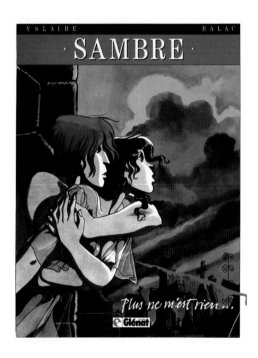

Similar reads

Memories of the Twentieth Heaven (*Mémoire du XXème ciel*) Yslaire
Sasmira Laurent Vicomte
The War of Sambre (*La guerre des Sambre*) Various and Yslaire

Comixtlán 1985

✐ Luis Fernando

First published by Editorial Resistencia (Mexico)
Creator Mexican (Unknown)
Genre Adult humor, Alternative
Influenced by Robert Crumb

Comixtlán perhaps best represents the feel and ethos of the alternative Mexican comics scene in the late twentieth century. The book compiles material originally published in newspapers and magazines between 1985 and the early 1990s, including strips from the most important alternative comics magazine in Mexico in the 1990s—*El Gallito Inglés* (*The English Cock*)—the country's closest equivalent to France's anthology title, *Métal Hurlant* (*Screaming Metal*).

Comixtlán is the work of the older, more mature Luis Fernando, who was a pioneer of graphic storytelling in his country. Fernando's black-and-white comics combine Mexican folkloric iconography and myths with a visual tradition that is deeply rooted in the U.S. and European experimental comics scenes. They range from the strictly poetic to political parodies and historical allegories.

Fernando strikingly blends poetic lyricism with a visual style that embodies a nonnationalistic sense of being Mexican. He constantly refers to the constructed nature of Mexico's historical discourses and articulates an imagery that remains critical of the impact of Catholicism and the monolithic Mexican state without becoming patronizing. His human and animal characters, like Edward Gorey's, are deceptively cute but reveal a darkness infused with the bloodiness of Catholic martyrdom. With its combination of modernity and enlightenment and tragicomic, barbaric violence and injustice, *Comixtlán* provides a graphic synthesis of what it is to be Mexican. **EPr**

The Useless Man 1985

✐ Yoshiharu Tsuge

Title in original language *Muno no Hito*
First published by Nihon Bungeisha (Japan)
Creator Japanese (b.1937)
Genre Autobiography

Yoshiharu Tsuge is renowned for using the methods of the "I-novel" genre (autobiography) to create his comics, or "I-comics." There are two styles in Japanese autobiography: one that deals with a public persona (*jiden*), and one that deals with private affairs (*watakuchi*). Tsuge's I-comics belong to the latter group. Writer Chokitsu Kurumatani has said of the confessional style: "I-novels question the root of one self's existence . . . this ominous and mysteriously unknown part that hides inside the grind of daily life." To dig deep within themselves, "I-novelists" do not present events as they really happened: they disguise the facts with fiction. Some readers of Yoshiharu Tsuge's *The Useless Man* failed to understand this distinction and searched on the banks of the River Tama for the author, selling ornamental stones like the graphic novel's main character, Sukezo Sukegawa. The comic strip is actually about a person who cannot make a decent living, who tries to make money within "the grind of daily life."

A deeper reading of Tsuge's story is about how to avoid depression and suffering, and face death. Tsuge believes in the Buddhist disappearance of the self: "What we name 'mu' means losing oneself, losing the self. And losing the self is losing one's anxieties, one's suffering." Tsuge's approach to one's mortality is "evaporation, to make oneself a point in the landscape." This explains why so many of his characters are seen with their backs turned to the readers inside a dense fog. They exist between the world of the dead and the world of the living. **DI**

The Survivor 1985

🖉🖉 Paul Gillon

Title in original language *La survivante*
First published by Albin Michel (France)
Creator French (1926–2011)
Genre Science fiction, Fantasy

By the time he started working on *The Survivor* series Paul Gillon was a veteran of the comics scene, with more than forty-five years of experience behind him. His extensive bibliography explains why the draftsmanship throughout the series is consistently superb—there are no page designs that do not work—but it also perhaps suggests why his mid-1980s tale of global decimation has a slightly old-fashioned air about it. Despite the fact that the heroine of the story spends a considerable amount of time bare-breasted, it remains the most decorous of sexy adventures.

In the first of four volumes, Aude, a young diver, emerges from a cave in which she has been trapped to find her companions turned to ash. She presumes there has been some sort of nuclear disaster and sets off for Paris to see if anyone else survived. Fortunately for her, as this is set in the near future, an army of robots are available to provide for her needs. Her chief problem is satisfying her sexual appetite, and soon she is getting it on with the automated help until a human astronaut turns up, making her favored mechanical partner jealous. In the following volumes, she has a child with him and makes contact with other survivors.

The Survivor's plot includes long introspective sequences that ponder the nature of existence. Gillon is very much a line artist, and in some printings of the story the coloring does him no favors. The art looks best in the collected *L'Echo des Savanes*/Albin Michel version, where the rather crude coloring anchors the line work and gives the unpleasant scenes more impact. **FJ**

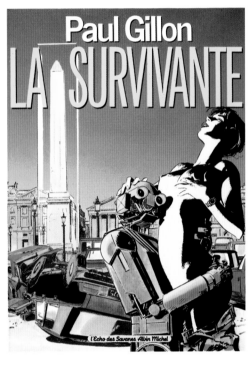

Paul Gillon
LA SURVIVANTE

l'Echo des Savanes Albin Michel

"The air's full of dust! What's that yellow light . . . ? Oh God! Don't' let it be what I think!"

Also recommended
La dernière des salles obscures with Denis Lapiére
Lost in Time (Les naufragés du temps) with Jean-Claude Forest
Nausicaä and the Valley of the Wind (Kaze no Tani no Naushika) Hayao Miyazaki

Druuna Morbus Gravis 1985

Paolo Eleuteri Serpieri

First published by Editions du Square, Dargaud (France)
Creator Italian (b.1944)
Genre Science fiction, Adult humor
Award Harvey (1995)

In a plague-ridden future where humans degenerate into hideous mutations, Druuna is a beautiful woman who discovers that Earth has long ago been poisoned, destroyed, and forgotten. The remnants of humanity are left floating aboard a spaceship called "The City." They live only to perpetuate the existence of Lewis, the ship's first commander, who has been merged with a computer (Delta) designed to keep him alive. Druuna searches for an antidote to the mutating plague known as "evil," but she finds herself trapped by mutants, monsters, and a mad scientist. During the series readers follow her journey—often in nightmarish dreams—in search of her lost lover, Shastar, and the forgotten world of humanity he had promised.

The focus of this postapocalyptic science fiction series is Druuna's sexual activity: she repeatedly fights men, monsters, and machines who oppose her and often force her to have sex. Inspired by French actress Valérie Kaprisky, Druuna's character is sadistically depicted as a nymphomaniac, always enjoying sex even when violence is involved.

Paolo Eleuteri Serpieri's skills are those of a former painter who clearly loves line drawing. His work shows the influence of Argentinian masters such as the early Alberto Breccia and Arturo Del Castillo, later mixed with Moebius and Caza. After debuting with classic Western comics, he moved to science fiction in the early 1980s, working for the magazine *Orient Express*. His work is notable for its perfectly crafted anatomies that enhance the sensual power of his drawings. **MS**

Calvin and Hobbes 1985

Bill Watterson

First published by United Press Syndicate (USA)
Creator American (b.1958)
Genre Humor
Collection *The Complete Calvin and Hobbes* (2005)

It is one of the simplest formulas for any comic strip, yet one of the most outstanding results, Bill Watterson's *Calvin and Hobbes* was the most beloved newspaper comic strip to emerge in the last quarter of the twentieth century. That it lasted for only eleven years undoubtedly contributes to its evergreen appeal.

Rereading *Calvin and Hobbes* today, one is immediately struck by the fact that the strip never had a growing period. It seemingly sprung from the artist's mind fully formed and proceeded to take its place in the pantheon of great U.S. comic strips. The relationship between the young Calvin and his stuffed toy tiger Hobbes was as fully fleshed out on day one as it would be when the strip ended, with thousands of memorable gags filling the days in between.

Watterson's drawing was immediately accessible and utterly charming. The manic energy required to bring the imagination of a young boy to life on the page is evident in virtually every line. Watterson could shift registers even within the limited confines of a daily strip, moving from cynical detachment to bewildered amazement in an instant. Nowhere was his visual range more evident than in the numerous Sunday page fantasies involving Calvin's alter ego, Spaceman Spiff, or a vast collection of killer dinosaurs.

Watterson's decision to retire from the strip at the height of his creative powers meant that his readers never had to suffer a period of decline. Watterson never gave anything other than his best, and *Calvin and Hobbes* will be read forever as a result. **BB**

Calvin and Hobbes get up to their usual lively antics. ➡

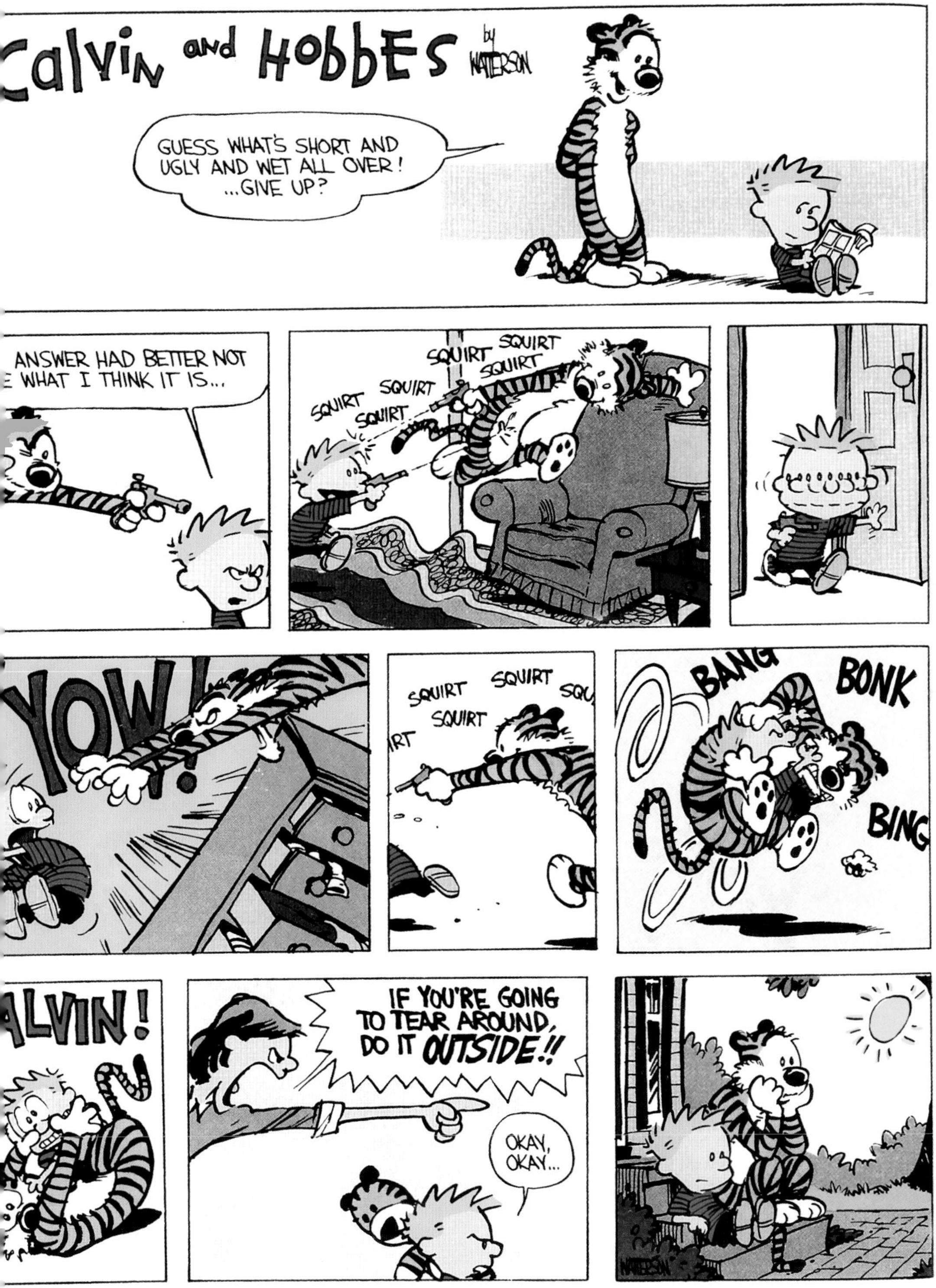
Calvin and HOBBES
by WATTERSON
GUESS WHAT'S SHORT AND UGLY AND WET ALL OVER! ...GIVE UP?
ANSWER HAD BETTER NOT
WHAT I THINK IT IS...
SQUIRT SQUIRT SQUIRT SQUIRT SQUIRT SQUIRT
YOW!
SQUIRT SQUIRT SQUIRT
BANG
BONK
BING
IF YOU'RE GOING TO TEAR AROUND, DO IT OUTSIDE!!
OKAY, OKAY...
WATTERSON

Banana Fish 1985

Akimi Yoshida

First published by Shogakukan (Japan)
Creator Japanese (b.1956)
Genre Drama, Adventure
Adaptation Radio (1996)

A rarity among comics for girls, *Banana Fish* is a hard-boiled action-drama. The main plot centers on the enigma surrounding an American soldier who went on an unexplained shooting spree against his fellow soliders during the Vietnam War in 1973. Since then the only words he has uttered are "banana fish." Fast-forward twelve years and the shooter's younger brother and leader of a street gang, Ash Lynx, is in New York investigating the incident with his best female friend, Eiji Okumura. Ash's rival, Frederick Arthur, is also on the case, and as the mystery unfolds, the three discover that a secret nuclear weapon development project is involved. The focus of the plot then shifts to the dark criminal underworld.

While such subjects were controversial for a typical Japanese girls' comic, readers of the *Bessatsu Shojo* comic were enthralled by the friendship between the handsome Ash and Eiji. The coldhearted Ash rarely shows a smile but opens up to Eiji, revealing his softer side and charming his female audience.

Akimi Yoshida tells her exciting story at a fast, heart-pounding pace but her artwork flawlessly captures the subtle changes in moods between scenes. The title of the comic strip comes from "A Perfect Day for Bananafish," a short story by American writer J. D. Salinger. Yoshida apparently based Ash on tennis player Stefan Edberg, Eiji on Japanese actor Hironobu Nomura, and Arthur on the musician Sting. The strip has also been developed into a radio drama as well as two theater productions in 2005 and 2009. **TS**

City Hunter 1985

Tsukasa Hojo

First published by *Weekly Shonen Jump* (Japan)
Creator Japanese (b.1959)
Genre Crime
Influence on *Angel Heart*

Ryo Saeba was just a child when the plane he was a passenger on crashed in the dense jungle of a Central American country that was being torn apart by a vicious civil war. The plane's only survivor, he was taken in by a rebel family and raised to be a freedom fighter. He eventually makes his way via the United States to Tokyo where he becomes a "sweeper"—someone who "cleanses" city streets and alleyways of crime. Morally ambiguous, with an ability to switch from hero to pervert within a single panel, Saeba can be protecting people from the vermin of Tokyo's underworld one minute and be a habitual womanizer and occasional assassin in the next. Despite his flaws, though, Saeba is in essence a heroic figure who drives through the streets of Tokyo in his trademark Mini Cooper, despatching criminals along the sights of his Colt Python .357 Magnum with unerring accuracy.

City Hunter does not spring from any personal angst from the mind of its creator. Tsukasa Hojo freely admits that the idea for the series just materialized in response to an everyday deadline. Nevertheless, his prowess as a draftsman and designer is highly apparent in the realism of its human figures, the accuracy of its firearms and ballistics, its detailed backgrounds, and the artist's ability to seamlessly blend humor with action. There is no doubting his dedication as an comic book artist: he spent around sixteen hours a day for six years creating the fluid lines that brought *City Hunter* to life, and in the process became one of Japan's most popular and celebrated cartoonists. **BS**

110 Pills 1985

"Magnus"

Title in original language *Le 110 pillole*
First published by *Totem* (Italy)
Creator Roberto Raviola (Italian, 1939–96)
Genre Erotic

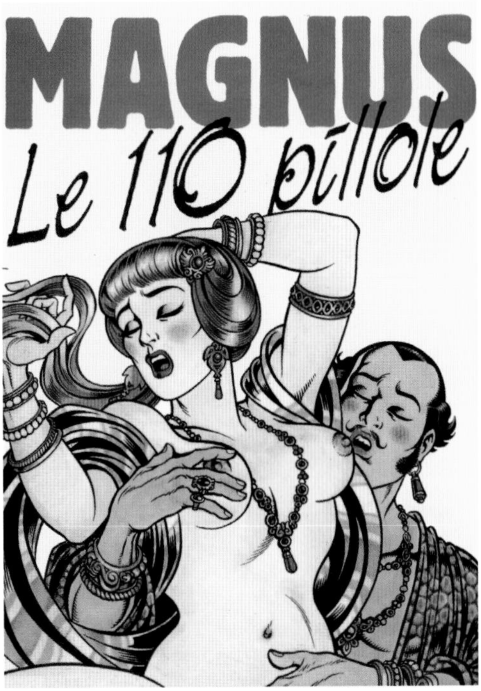
MAGNUS
Le 110 pillole

The story for *110 Pills* is based on a famous Chinese novel from the sixteenth century, *Chin P'ing Mei* (*The Plum in the Golden Vase*). It tells the story of Hsi-Men Ching, a wealthy and pleasure-loving pharmacist, and the six wives in his harem. An old monk gives the pharmacist 110 pills as a miraculous aphrodisiac, with the caveat to use it moderately. Instead, Hsi-Men abuses the pills and descends into a maelstrom of orgiastic sex and depravity. For a short time the lustful pharmacist attempts to regain the trust of his first wife, Madame Moon. However, he is soon drawn back to his addiction, straining himself mentally and physically before sinking into sickness and eventual death.

Roberto Raviola (under the pseudonym Magnus) is celebrated as one of the most prolific and eclectic writers in Italian comics. He has been the creator or cocreator of such popular series as crime comics *Kriminal* and *Satanik*, the historical *I Briganti*, the science fiction *Milady*, the satirical *Alan Ford*, and the socially and politically inspired spy story *The Unknown* (*Lo Sconosciuto*).

Together with *Le femmine incantate* and the pornographic *Necron*, *110 Pills* is among the masterworks of Magnus's erotic comics series. He depicts sex with anatomical explicitness, as well as skill and humor. The same diligence used in the graphic depiction of decor is employed to detail human bodies and sexual acts. His masterful use of dense crosshatching and figuration is inspired by nineteenth-century etching. **MS**

"He stuck Eros within the noir genre, as eighteenth-century libertines had not been able to do."

Antonio Faeti, critic

Similar reads
Casa Howard Roberto Baldazzini
Druuna Paolo Eleuteri Serpieri
Histoire d'O Guido Crepax
Il vizioso mondo di Keto Marco Nizzoli
Justine Guido Crepax

Watchmen 1986

Alan Moore Dave Gibbons and John Higgins

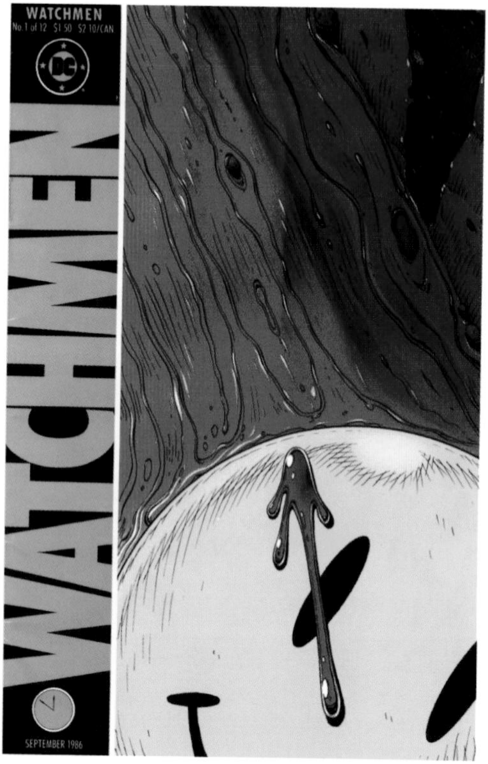
WATCHMEN
No. 1 of 12 $1.50 $2.10/CAN
WATCHMEN
SEPTEMBER 1986

"I don't believe in heroes . . . A hero is someone who has been set up on a pedestal above humanity."

Alan Moore

Also by Alan Moore

From Hell with Eddie Campbell

The League of Extraordinary Gentlemen with Kevin O'Neill

First published by DC Comics (USA)
Creators Moore (British, b.1953); Gibbons (British, b.1949); Higgins (British, b.1949)
Genre Superhero

It is difficult to separate *Watchmen* from the media hype surrounding its publication and its subsequent impact on the superhero genre. Originating as a stylishly designed twelve-issue series, it was rapidly repackaged as a graphic novel that has never been out of print. First approached by DC Comics for a new treatment of the superhero, Moore and Gibbons's proposal was deemed too radical. Instead, they created their own team loosely based on Golden and Silver Age archetypes. The result is widely seen as a postmodern deconstruction of the genre, in which the superhero is critiqued.

Gibbons's meticulous linework and strict, nine-panel grid layout, along with Higgins's use of flat color, present a world of clearly defined boundaries. The heroes themselves are spectacularly messy: morally ambivalent, ideologically suspect, psychologically disturbed, and socially and sexually inept. The plot nominally concerns an investigation into the murder of a costumed adventurer. More memorable is the interweaving of flashback character histories, symbolic repetitions, and literary allusions. For example, a Greek chorus of New Yorkers comments on escalating Cold War tensions, one of whom reads a pirate comic that acts as a metafictional parallel to unfolding events. Its incorporation through a range of juxtapositions and layerings marks but one example of the work's formal sophistication. While Moore laments the wave of dark, violent superhero revisionism that followed in its wake, it is this narrative complexity that is *Watchmen*'s legacy—a textbook of elaborate comics scripting. **MG**

BonoBono 1986

Mikio Igarashi

First published by Takeshobo (Japan)
Creator Japanese (b.1955)
Genre Humor, Funny animal
Award Kodansha Manga Award (1988)

Well-constructed comic strips can delve into profound themes without losing their humorous edge or lightheartedness, as *Peanuts* masterfully proved for several decades. Accessible, cute characters do represent aspects of society, and naive philosophical questions can provoke deeper thinking. *BonoBono* is on a par with the best in this arena.

The strip follows the everyday life of a young sea otter called BonoBono, his squirrel friend Shimaris-kun, his racoon friend and bully Araiguma-kun, along with other inhabitants of the forest. BonoBono, with his slow wit, cautious character, and infinite curiosity, continually asks seemingly silly but somehow profound philosophical questions either of his friends or himself. As neither his friends nor he can usually answer them, the questions are often left open. Surprisingly, this absence of direct answers encourages the reader to think about the questions themselves, which results in an almost Zenlike quality.

The strip is enhanced by its frequent use of visual repetition. The drawing style employs sparse lines but brilliantly captures the surroundings, and the same background is often repeated throughout the whole strip. As a result, it gives the sense of a long, uninterrupted shot. The slower pacing causes the reader to think at the tempo of the slow-witted protagonist. Although *BonoBono* achieved great acclaim with its animated TV series adaptation, this unique kind of reading experience works most effectively in the comic strip version. **NK**

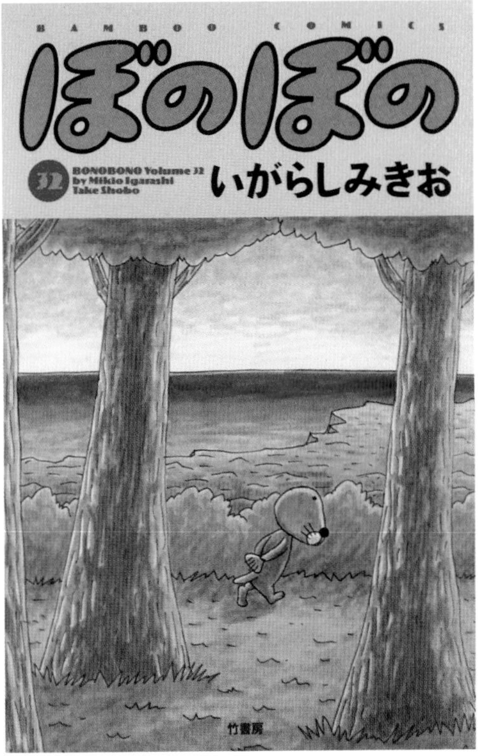
BAMBOO COMICS
ぼのぼの
32
BONOBONO Volume 32
by Mikio Igarashi
Take Shobo
いがらしみきお
竹書房

"BonoBono combines gag comic and philosophical questions, bringing up comparisons to Azumanga Daioh*"*

bonobono.co.tv

Also by Mikio Igarashi
Antaga warui
Nekuratopia
Ninpenmanmaru

Elektra Assassin 1986

Frank Miller Bill Sienkiewicz

First published by Epic Comics/Marvel Comics (USA)
Creators Miller (American, b.1957); Sienkiewicz (American, b.1958)
Genre Superhero

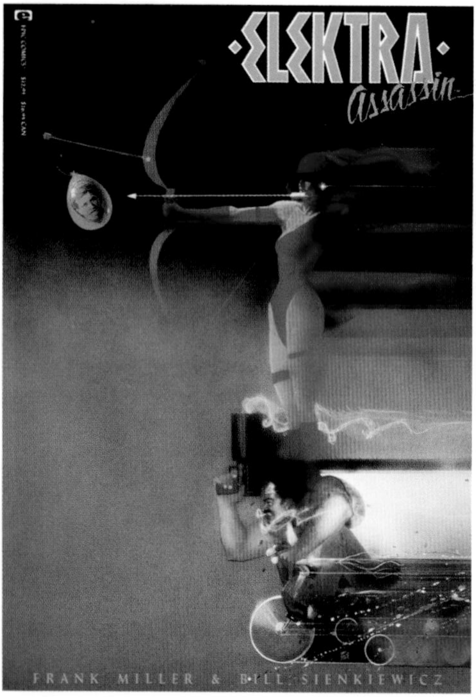
ELEKTRA
Assassin
FRANK MILLER & BILL SIENKIEWICZ

Also by Bill Sienkiewicz
Big Numbers with Alan Moore
Daredevil: Love and War with Frank Miller
Daredevil: The Man Without Fear with John Romita Jr.
The New Mutants with Chris Claremont
The Sandman: Endless Nights with Neil Gaman

Elektra: Assassin explodes off the page, a bewildering and bewitching bravura display from two of the hottest talents of its day—Frank Miller and Bill Sienkiewicz. Published starting in August 1986 as an eight-issue series, its dark and challenging content led it to be released under Marvel's Epic imprint.

Elektra, a ninja-trained assassin of Greek origin and ambiguous morals, was created by Miller during his first run on *Daredevil*. The series focuses on Elektra's attempt to prevent a shadowy supernatural foe known as the Beast from bringing about a nuclear holocaust. The Beast's most notable agent is Ken Wind, a JFK-esque presidential candidate, providing an opportunity for Miller to indulge his taste for political satire.

In essence this is hard-boiled, cyberpunk noir, with a dissolute SHIELD agent as protagonist and, in Elektra, the most fatale of femmes. The comic requires a certain sophistication from its readers. Miller's complex narrative suddenly switches to flashbacks, hallucinatory dream sequences, and overlapping stream-of-consciousness narration, with no warning except Sienkiewicz's gorgeous, jaw-dropping art undergoing corresponding changes in style. It is astonishing that Sienkiewicz manages to maintain what would have been elaborate for cover art throughout the whole book.

Elektra: Assassin is a truly collaborative work, and Miller and Sienkiewicz were clearly having the time of their lives. It is the cool and anarchic cousin to Alan Moore's *Watchmen*. While not as famous as its contemporaries, it is an ambitious, groundbreaking and influential work. Although initially challenging—especially the first two issues—the book quickly sweeps readers away with its frenetic momentum, and impresses with its perfect, mind-bending balance of narrative and art. **SB**

Nestor Burma
120, rue de la Gare 1986

Léo Malet Jacques Tardi

The end of 1941 is approaching when Nestor Burma, a prisoner of war in a German camp, hears the final words of a dying man. They consist of a mysterious address: 120, rue de la Gare. Liberated some time later, Burma hears the same address mentioned by one of his former colleagues on board a train waiting at a platform in Lyon when the man is promptly riddled with bullets in front of him. This is enough to reawaken Burma's investigative instincts—he was a private detective in Paris before the war. With only this incomplete address as a clue, and keen to avenge his dead colleague, he sets about solving this intriguing mystery in the difficult environment of a country still suffering in the aftermath of World War II.

The story of *120, rue de la Gare* is adapted from the classic French detective novel by Léo Malet. A compelling story, a genuine mystery, well-drawn characters, and a sufficiently complex hero (or antihero) to arouse the reader's empathy provide a solid grounding for the perfect thriller. In combination with the plot's intrigue, illustrator Jacques Tardi creates a distinctive visual atmosphere—reminiscent of the French cinema of the 1940s and 1950s he knows so well—and convincingly portrays the dark side of human passions.

Tardi knows exactly how to immerse his reader in the intimate details of a France still reeling and demoralized by years of German occupation, war, and endless shortages of everyday necessities. Ideologically close to the radical left (and thus in sympathy with the political views of Malet, a member of the anarchist movement as a youth), the illustrator chose to create images that highlight the collaboration of the French government of the period with the Nazi oppressors. Tardi also provided cover illustrations for the Fleuve Noir editions of Malet's novels from the 1980s. **NF**

Title in original language *120, rue de la Gare*
First published by À Suivre (France)
Creators Malet (French (1909–96); Tardi (French, b.1946)
Genre Crime

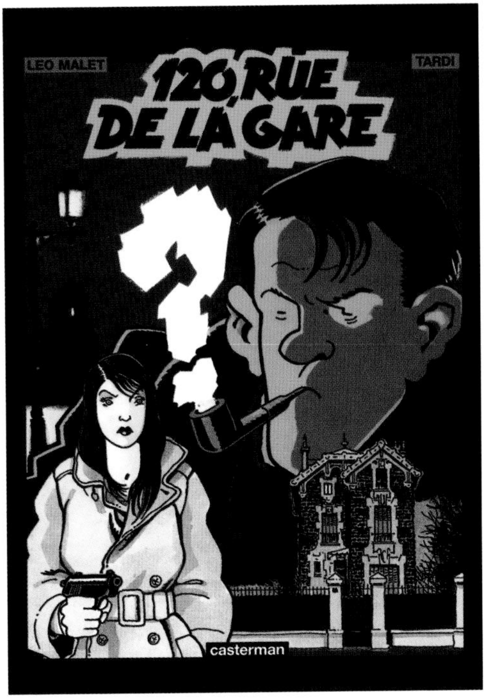
LÉO MALET
TARDI
120, RUE DE LA GARE
casterman

Also by Jacques Tardi
It Was the War of the Trenches (*C'était la guerre des tranchées*)
Polonius with Philippe Picaret
The Arctic Marauder (*Le Démon des glaces*)
You Are There (*Ici Même*) with Jean-Claude Forest

Dori Stories 1986

✎ Dori Seda

First published by Last Gasp (USA)
Creator American (1951–88)
Genre Autobiography
Influenced by *Weirdo*

Gap-toothed protopunk cartoonist Dori Seda first came to prominence in Robert Crumb's *Weirdo* magazine in the early 1980s. Her brief body of underground comic work, mostly autobiographical, is collected in *Dori Stories*, along with her *fumetti* (photo comics), paintings, and ceramics.

It is difficult to discuss Seda's work without becoming maudlin: she died young and alone for want of care, and this (along with one strip in which she seems to be advocating sex with her dog) is the thing people tend to remember about her rather than her extraordinary, zesty, self-deprecating talent.

Some of the work in *Dori Stories* is not the best quality, but after a few false starts she rapidly finds her own voice and visual style (which embraces detail and varied careful delineation with more frenzied inks) and tells readers about her life—the drugs and alcohol, the sexual hijinks, and her love for her crazy, underwear-sniffing dog. What shocks most about her stories—and they were designed to shock—is the offhand, almost breezy way she tackles her material. She may be telling you about terrible things, she may be whining about her life, but it is always underpinned by a sense of self-awareness and mordant humor. Seda knew how to pace a story and keep it interesting, something many later autobiographical artists failed to grasp. She presents a portrait of a woman you long to get to know better. You always wish for more, one more barroom confession, one more well-observed anecdote about sex, one more heroic reaction against the ordinariness of life. **FJ**

Concrete 1986

✎✎ Paul Chadwick

First published by Dark Horse Comics (USA)
Creator American (b.1957)
Genre Superhero
Award Eisner Award (2005)

In a refreshing twist on the superhero formula, when aliens take the brain of Ron Lithgow, a political speechwriter, and transplant it into their own concrete-sculptured behemoth, there is an agreeable absence of the requisite plethora of supervillains who suddenly appear to engage him in battle. Lithgow will, of course, have his battles—he is demonstrably different from all those around him—but his battles will be inner ones, of acceptance and how best to use his newfound strength to do good instead of just restrain evil. Lithgow, now known as Concrete, can at last champion the socially and economically disadvantaged.

The aliens responsible for Concrete's transformation are banished after the first issue. Concrete is then on his own, and no extraterrestrials will distract him, or us, from considering issues few superheroes ever had the time to bother with, such as: What can I do to make the world a better place? With the help of the CIA, Concrete exists under the guise of an experimental cyborg but naturally becomes alienated from the world he so desperately wants to help. What is surprising, however, are the moral positions he takes, such as aligning himself with a splinter group of hardcore ecowarriors.

Anomalies long ignored in comic books, such as the occasional yet obvious absence of male superhero genitalia, becomes a thorny issue here. Sex is Concrete's recurring Achilles heel. It is humbling to realize that for all his power, all is not well if you also happen to lack a penis. Despite his appearance, Concrete is one of us, after all. **BS**

Barney and the Blue Note 1986

Philippe Paringaux Jacques de Loustal

Title in original language *Barney et la note bleue*
First published by À Suivre (France)
Creators Paringaux (French, b.1944); Loustal (French, b.1956) **Genre** Drama

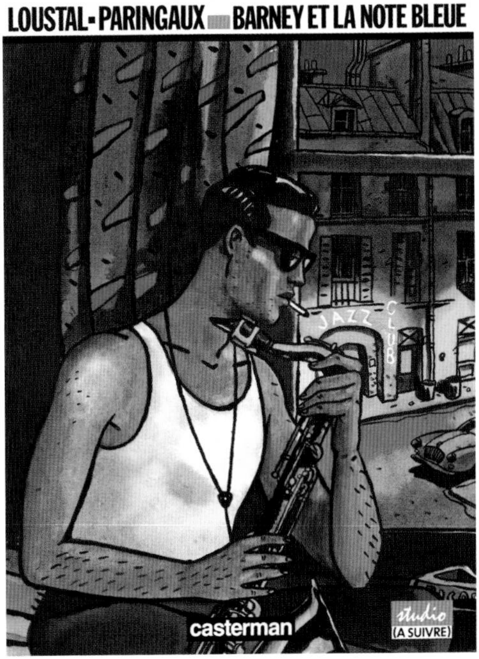

LOUSTAL-PARINGAUX BARNEY ET LA NOTE BLEUE
JAZZ CLUB
casterman
studio (A SUIVRE)

Illustrator Jacques de Loustal made his debut in the 1970s when he published a few drawings in the monthly magazine *Rock & Folk*, which at the time was the most influential music magazine in French-speaking Europe—a magazine whose editor-in-chief was Philippe Paringaux. It was therefore not surprising that when the two men collaborated, they chose to give one of their first major creations a title with a musical connotation: *Barney and the Blue Note*.

Loosely inspired by the life of saxophonist Barney Wilen, the book relates the meteoric career of a brilliant jazzman between the 1950s and 1960s. It shows the young prodigy's dreams and hopes of stardom, followed by his slow, irreversible fall from favor, characterized by a turbulent life and heroin abuse. "Barney was twenty years old," Paringaux wrote, "and his music was that of a man who had lived twenty lives."

Barney and the Blue Note is the familiar story of a jazz musician who struggles to develop his career beyond its early promise, but Loustal and his writer bring poignancy to the tale. Their album reflects the distinctive narrative technique developed by Loustal when he started working at the end of the 1970s: no speech bubbles or dialogue, but sequences of images backed by a cinematic voice-over narration. From chiaroscuro to images saturated with light, from slow tempos to howling choruses, from nostalgia to bitterness, here is a strip cartoon with a striking choreography—one of the most successful of its type in a decade that featured so many examples. **NF**

"Wilen had . . . a considerably accomplished technique and a real mastery of hard-bop forms."

www.loustal.nl

Also by Jacques de Loustal
A Romantic Young Man (*Un garçon romantique*)
Banana Tourist (*Touriste de bananes*)
Kid Congo
Hearts of Sand (*Coeurs de sable*) with Philippe Paringaux
Suns of Night (*Soleils de nuit*) with Philippe Paringaux

Cities of the Fantastic

The Tower 1986

Benoît Peeters François Schuiten

Title in original language *La Tour*
First published by À Suivre (France)
Creators Peeters (French, b.1956);
Schuiten (Belgian, b.1956) **Genre** Science fiction

Les Cités obscures
SCHUITEN
PEETERS
LA TOVR
casterman
les romans
(A SUIVRE)

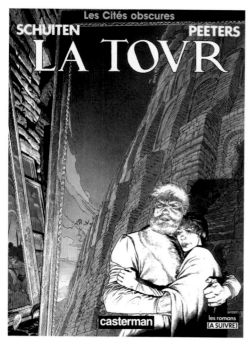

Also in the *Cities of the Fantastic* series
Brüsel
***Fever of Urbicand* (*La fièvre d'Urbicande*)**
The Leaning Child (*L'enfant penchée*)
The Road of Armilla (*La route d'Armilia*)
The Walls of Samaris (*Les murailles de Samaris*)

For thirty years Giovanni Battista has jealously guarded his sector of a city-state known as the Tower. He is a Keeper, one of the aristocracy of the workers of the Tower, a caste whose members maintain and repair the gigantic building. They have more or less devoted their lives to their task. These days, however, alone in the heart of the vast area for which he is responsible, Giovanni has lost faith in his life and his future. The inspector from whom he has been long expecting a visit has still not appeared, and there is no news from base, despite his numerous letters.

Time is short: never have there been so many cracks and collapses, and so much falling masonry.

"We are ignorant of the world of the [Cities of the Fantastic], *but that world is not ignorant of us."*

Even more worrying are the strange vibrations that are emanating from the bowels of the Tower. Breaking the Keepers' number one rule, Giovanni deserts his post to begin the long descent to the ground in the hope of referring to higher authority. His dangerous journey into the bowels of the Tower—a titanic construction that seems to have neither beginning nor end—proves to be an initiation. He discovers another reality where some answers are found, but at the cost of many new questions.

This is an epic exploration of a deteriorating construction, an odyssey full of illusions and false leads. Artist François Schuiten is visionary in his interpretation of the Tower, displaying impressive control and sophistication but still allowing for poetic interludes. *The Tower* is the most ambitious of the Peeters–Schuiten collaborations and conveys the radical otherness of the world of *Cities of the Fantastic* with great intensity. **NF**

Cromwell Stone 1986

"Andreas"

Cromwell Stone is just another passenger on the ship *Leviticus* when the theft of a mysterious key leads to mutiny, resulting in Stone and twelve other passengers being forced into a lifeboat and set adrift on the high seas. Against all odds, they find their way to land. Before going their separate ways, they make a pact to meet once every year thereafter. Each time they reunite, however, they learn that one of them has died.

Now, after ten years, the last three survivors are about to meet again; one of them, Jack Farley, has invited Stone to stay the night at his house before attending the reunion the following day. But as he arrives in the coastal town, Stone is overcome with anxiety and a sense of foreboding. Furthermore, he becomes convinced that he is being watched. For Stone the annual dwindling of the survivors' numbers smacks of more than just coincidence. Something sinister appears to be at work. His suspicions are aroused further when he arrives at Farley's house and a neighbor tells him that it is empty, and that no one has ever lived there matching Farley's description. Stone decides to rent the house for himself and attempts to resolve the mystery before he too loses his life.

"Ten years in a row the 20th of December has been a doomsday . . ."

Andreas crams vast amounts of detail into his carefully crafted, imaginary world, enclosing his panels within baroque-looking frames, filled not only with objects but also their shadows. Such a level of detail can overwhelm, but Andreas's technical brilliance manages to carry it off. *Cromwell Stone* provides readers with a high-caliber mix of art and mystery. Sequel volumes appeared in 1994 and 2004. **BS**

First published by Dark Horse Comics (USA)
Creator Andreas Martens (German, b.1951)
Genre Crime, Horror
Collection *Révélations Posthumes* (1980)

ANDREAS
Cromwell Stone
DELCOURT
COLLECTION
CONQUISTADOR

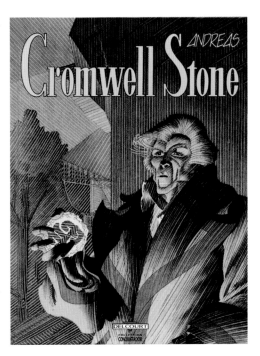

Also by Andreas Martens
Arq
Capricorne
Cyrrus
La Caverne du Souvenir (*The Cave of Memory*)
Rork

Freddy Lombard
The Comet of Carthage 1986

Yves Chaland and "Yann" Yves Chaland

Title in original language *La comète de Carthage*
First published by Les Humanoïdes Associés (France)
Creators Chaland (French, 1957–90); Yannick Le Pennetier (French, b.1954) **Genre** Adventure

CHALAND
Les aventures de Freddy Lombard
LA COMETE DE CARTHAGE
COLLECTION ELDORADO
LES HUMANOIDES ASSOCIES

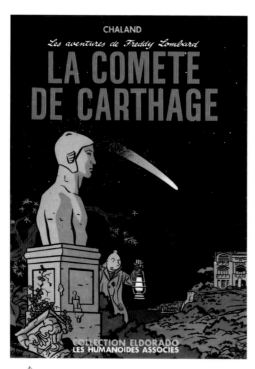

Also by Yves Chaland
Adolphus Claar
Bob Fish
Captivant
John Bravo
Le Jeune Albert

Yves Chaland was a master of the Franco-Belgian *ligne claire* (clear line) style, although he added his own twist—a much-imitated 1950s futuristic look with rounded forms and jazzy patterning. Chaland was instrumental in returning the *ligne claire* to popularity in the 1980s with his *Freddy Lombard* adventures.

The blond-quiffed and wedge-nosed Lombard, like Tintin and his forbears, travels around Europe during the uneasy Cold War period, getting into scrapes, accompanied by his two friends, Dina and Sweep. Unlike Tintin, he is something of a chancer, always sponging off his rich uncle. The strip has plenty of comic action and adult humor despite the often serious themes of Chaland and cowriter Yann's stories.

"Stop complaining! Others have been more desperate than we are now."

The Comet of Carthage is a delightful confection, and marks the point where Chaland gets the mix of thriller and comedy just right. His dialogue and plotting are often compared to the sharp romantic comedies of the 1930s, when women gave as good as they got. The story concerns a Phoenician princess who is the next intended victim of a homicidal painter.

As excitement builds, Chaland's art remains controlled, but manages to give a sense that it is bursting with energy. He avoids the static tableaux so typical of the *ligne claire* style by drawing on elements of children's humor comics, particularly Franquin. He breaks away from even outline inks and employs a bold brush style that is almost sensual. He isn't afraid of dense areas of black or heavy lines, and injects depth and movement into his panels, keeping the figures loose and expressive even when the backgrounds become detailed. **FJ**

Batman
The Dark Knight Returns 1986

Frank Miller

First published by DC Comics (USA)
Creator American (b.1957)
Genre Superhero
Award Kirby Best Graphic Album (1987)

Nobody, not even the Dark Knight, can live forever. It has been ten years since the last reported sighting of Batman, following the brutal murder of Robin at the hands of the Joker. With the exception of Superman (now working for the government), all other superheroes and crime-fighters have either been driven underground or voluntarily retired. Meanwhile, crime is worse than ever in Gotham City. On a dark and stormy night, overwhelmed by the atrocities listed on the news, Bruce Wayne can take it no longer, and returns as Batman to stamp his mark on the city once again. But with his reemergence come enemies old and new, including the Joker himself. Bruce Wayne is not a young man anymore: in his fifties, he lives in a world he no longer recognizes and is closer to Dirty Harry than the Caped Crusader of old. This is one final adventure he may not survive.

"This would be a good death . . . but not good enough."

Inspired by the tight storytelling of French *bande dessineé* albums, Miller crafts a dense and fractured narrative of a kind only really possible in the comics medium. Maintaining multiple simultaneous plot threads (sometimes set at different points in time), Miller carries Batman kicking and screaming into the 1980s world of nuclear threat, gang culture, moral decay, and political correctness. Miller has particular fun with the latter, using television vox-pops to satirize liberal commentators arguing against state-sponsored vigilantism, along with doctors who believe Batman to be a psychopath in his own right. That he may be, but more than anything Miller's Batman is a soldier of right and wrong who found himself too old to fight the war, but who would rather die in battle than in bed. **BD**

BATMAN
THE DARK KNIGHT RETURNS
BY
FRANK MILLER
WITH
KLAUS JANSON
AND
LYNN VARLEY
INTRODUCTION BY ALAN MOORE

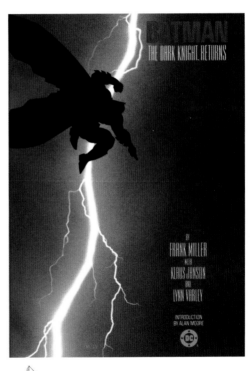

Also by Frank Miller
Batman: The Dark Knight Strikes Again
Batman: Year One
Daredevil: The Man Without Fear
Hard Boiled
Sin City

Batman
Year One 1986

Frank Miller / David Mazzucchelli

First published by DC Comics (USA)
Creators Miller (American, b.1957); Mazzucchelli (American, b.1960)
Genre Superhero

BY
FRANK MILLER
AND DAVID
MAZZUCCHELLI
YEAR ONE PART 1
BATMAN
404
75¢
THE HISTORY OF THE DC UNIVERSE is must reading
MAZZUCCHELLI

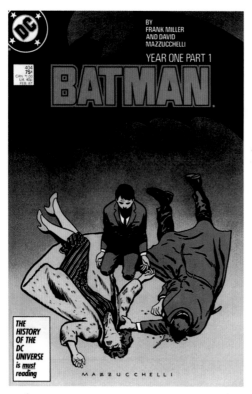

Similar reads
Asterios Polyp David Mazzucchelli
Batman: The Dark Knight Returns Frank Miller
Give Me Liberty Frank Miller and Dave Gibbons

Batman: Year One first appeared in 1986 as a four-part story spread over issues #404 to #407 of the *Batman* title. The story arc looks back to Batman's genesis in Gotham City, and re-imagines a number of events that have become deeply etched in the Batman mythology, such as Bruce Wayne's first donning of the Caped Crusader costume, Batman's first encounter with Lieutenant (not yet Commissioner) Gordon, and the origin of Catwoman. The plot centers on the start of the alliance between Batman and Gordon to deal with the deeply entrenched corruption in Gotham City that has spread to every aspect of civic life, including the police department. Nothing is easy or simple in this gritty story, which could be offered as "exhibit one" in any defense of the superhero genre against the charge of presenting the simplistic triumph of good over evil.

"Gotham City. Maybe it's all I deserve, now. Maybe it's just my time in Hell."

Frank Miller's vision of corrosive social decay appears to cut even deeper in this work than in his earlier graphic novel *Batman: The Dark Knight Returns*. The grim satire is perfectly complemented by David Mazzucchelli's moody and deliberately flat illustrative style, with occasional flourishes of chiaroscuro, color, and explosive action. The story deals with violence, but the narrative focuses more on the reactions of the characters to what they witness and perpetrate. *Batman: Year One* created a distinctly new twist on Batman, and added darker and realistic tones to the superhero narratives of the 1980s. *Batman: Year One* was developed as a screenplay but has never reached the screen. The story and its narrative style, however, are a major influence on Christopher Nolan's *Batman Begins* and its sequel *The Dark Knight*. **RR**

Daredevil
Born Again 1986

Frank Miller David Mazzucchelli

Daredevil: Born Again is the result of Frank Miller's return to the series in 1986. Miller had produced some of his earliest work for Marvel with *Daredevil*, and his stint as writer/artist on the title from 1981 to 1983 resulted in an impressive return to quality and popularity for a series that had spent much of the 1970s searching for consistency and direction. Miller's run introduced Elektra as a major new character, reinvented Bullseye as a major antagonist, and coopted the Kingpin (from Spider-Man) to become Daredevil's archenemy. In making these changes, Miller brought *Daredevil* back to his roots as a New York–based, film noir–inflected, crimefighting superhero—Marvel's closest equivalent to Batman. Batman may be a creature of the night, but

"And I—I have shown him that a man without hope is a man without fear."

Daredevil lives in darkness, having been blinded by an accident in his youth.

Daredevil: Born Again is the first of Miller's large-scale parables dealing with the dark side of the American Dream. The real protagonist of this story is not Daredevil, but his alter ego, attorney Matt Murdock. Miller and Mazzuchelli narrate the Kingpin's efforts to erase Daredevil's threat forever by destroying, but not killing, Murdock. The Kingpin's plot is part of his wider initiative to legitimize his criminal empire.

Mazzuchelli's artwork rises to the occasion. His depiction of Murdock's domestic life is shot through with a sense of imminent menace. The climactic action sequences are rendered from bewilderingly fractured perspectives that draw the reader deep inside the bone-crunching violence without ever yielding any complete understanding or narrative closure. The reader feels like a participant in the action rather than an observer. **RR**

First published by Marvel Comics (USA)
Creators Miller (American, b.1957); Mazzucchelli (American, b.1960)
Genre Superhero

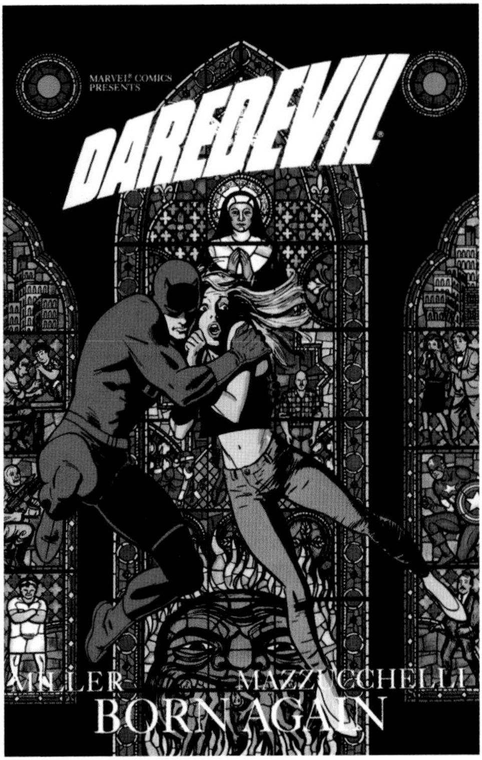
MARVEL COMICS PRESENTS
DAREDEVIL
MILLER MAZZUCCHELLI
BORN AGAIN

Similar reads

Batman: The Dark Knight Returns Frank Miller
Daredevil, Vol. 1 Frank Miller, Bill Mantlo, Marv Wolfman, and Roger McKenzie

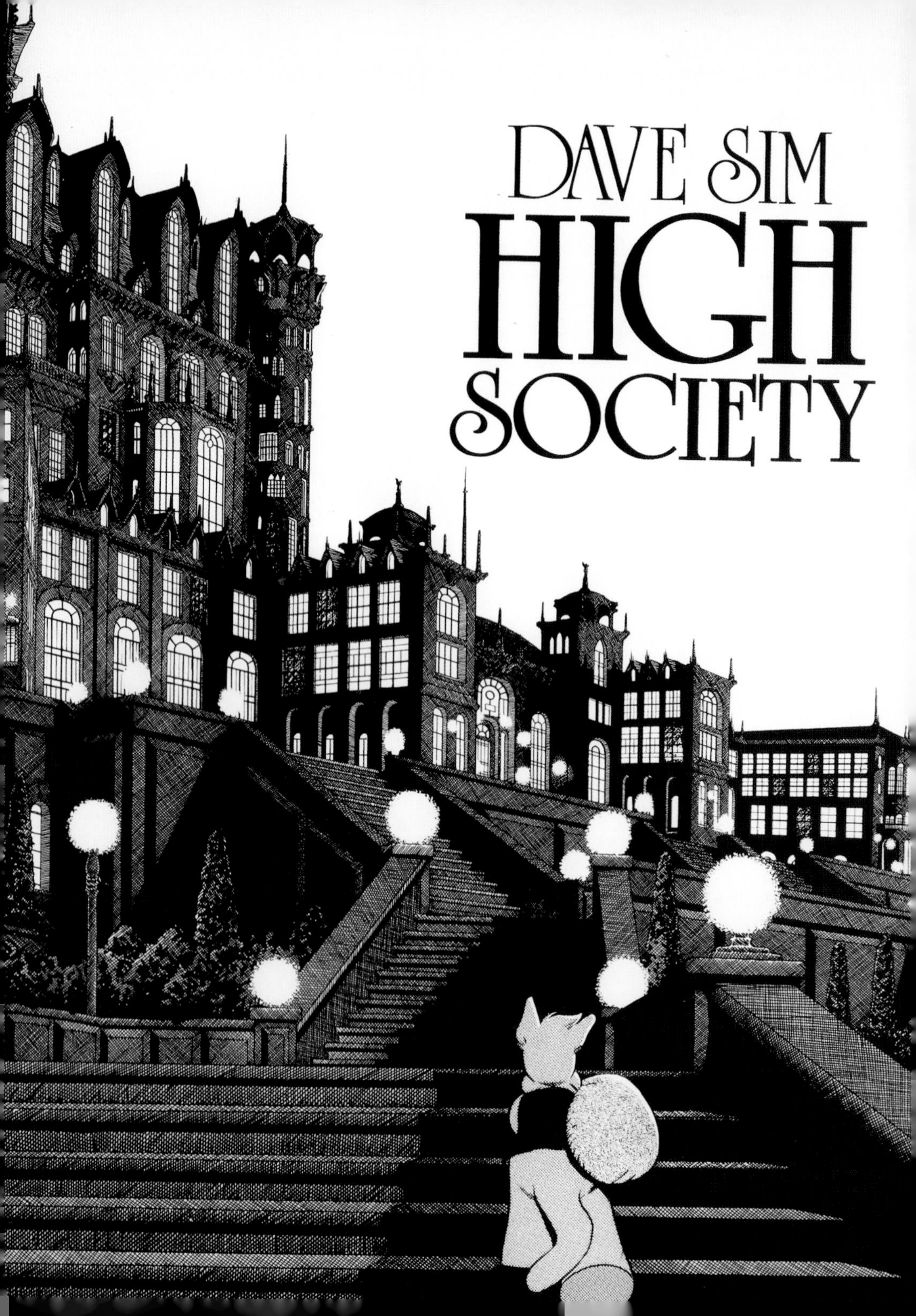
DAVE SIM
HIGH
SOCIETY

Cerebus
High Society 1986
✐✐ Dave Sim assisted by Gerhard

First published by Aardvark-Vanaheim (Canada)
Creators Sim (Canadian, b.1956);
Gerhard (Canadian, b.1959)
Genre Satire, Fantasy

What started out as one of the oddest experiments of the 1980s wound up as one of the most transformative comics of all time. Since 1977, Dave Sim had been serializing the adventures of Cerebus the Aardvark, a deft parody of Conan the Barbarian that was quickly running out of steam. With the twenty-sixth issue he dramatically changed the tone and direction of his work, thrusting his marauding antihero into the claustrophobic world of politics and high finance.

In the fictional city-state of Iest, Cerebus becomes a pawn in a highly fraught political game played against the diabolically clever Lord Julius. Aided by the manipulative Astoria, Cerebus struggles to negotiate a complex world that he does not fully understand. When the tense election is resolved, in hilarious fashion, by the vote of a single farmer in a snowy field, Cerebus finds himself Prime Minister. With his world literally turned on its head—Sim drew and printed the final pages of the book sideways—Cerebus is overwhelmed by his powerful position, enduring crisis after crisis before his government is toppled.

The image of politics Sim paints in the graphic novel is a dark one in which the primary characters are driven by vanity and greed. This is a lacerating view of human weakness, leavened by moments of humor that seem lifted from the best of the Marx Brothers's movies. Throughout, Sim experiments with new visual styles and storytelling formats, shedding his history as a simple parodist and emerging as a significant creative voice in his own right. **BB**

Five Star
Stories 1986
✐✐ Mamoru Nagano

First published by Kadokawa Shoten (Japan)
Creator Japanese (b.1960)
Genre Science fiction, Fantasy
Adaptation Anime film (1989)

If "epic" is defined in terms of a story that dramatically spans across time and space, nothing fits better in this category than *Five Star Stories*. A hybrid of Japanese mythology, medieval fantasy adventure, *Star Wars*, and Chinese warlord novels topped off by giant robots, *Five Star Stories* is an intergalactic epic that plays out across parallel universes over fifty-six million years.

In a future, distant galaxy where humans have settled and evolved, countries and planets are fighting each other for resources. Crucial combat assets are the giant robots called Mortar Headds, which can only be piloted by people with special physical capabilities, known as the Knights. They need the help of copilots—artificially made human computers known as Fatima. Within a predefined timeline of events, the story arcs freely take on the tales of interplanetary wars, the cruel fates of Knights and Fatimas, the lives of ordinary soldiers, and even dragons and princesses.

With great virtuosity, the author manages to mix many different genres into a comprehensive world. Wars are fought with infantry troops, space ships, giant robots, and magical dragons. Regardless of whether the characters are magicians, superbeings, or synthetic life forms, the happiness and tragedies are always very human. The drawing of the diverse Mortar Headds are stunningly beautiful and original, reflecting the varied cultures and eras in the story. Although notorious for its slow and only occasional new chapter releases in the Japanese magazine *Newtype*, *Five Star Stories* is well worth waiting for. **NK**

Dylan Dog 1986

✎ Tiziano Sclavi   ✎ Various

First published by Daim Press (Italy)
Creator Italian (b.1953)
Genre Horror
Awards Nominated for two Eagle Awards (2000, 2008)

This horror series was the best-selling monthly comic book in Italy for a decade, hitting its peak in 1993, when its circulation reached one million copies, and Dark Horse Comics published the English-language version.

The main character, Dylan, is a thirty-something ex–Scotland Yard policeman, now a private eye and self-titled as a "nightmare investigator." Although skeptical about paranormal activity, Dylan is frequently hired to deal with unexplained disappearances, mysterious serial killers, zombie appearances, and personality disorders. His investigations initially seek rational explanations before later turning to inexplicable solutions. Dark and romantic, Dylan has weird obsessive habits (he always wears the same shirt, jacket, jeans, and shoes) and hobbies (playing clarinet, building a galleon model), and tends to fall in love with his female clients. His best friend and assistant is a double of classic film comedian Groucho Marx, who speaks only in jokes. Throughout the entire saga, the special connections between Dylan and two ambiguous, immortal characters recur: deadly villain Xabaras and the ghastly Morgana, the latter initially his "ideal/dreamy girlfriend," but in reality his mother.

The impressive quality of the first one hundred episodes, which were mainly written in the wake of the new horror cinema in the 1980s by Tiziano Sclavi, is due to the disquieting atmosphere and suspense of his unsettling narratives. The text is tremendously elliptical and shows delirious David Lynch–like streams of associations, but the writing is always elegant. **MS**

Alex 1987

✎ Russell Taylor   ✎ Charles Peattie

First published by *London Daily News* (UK)
Creators Taylor (British, b.1960); Peattie (British, b.1958)
Genre Reality drama, Satire
Collection *The Full Alex Omnibus* (1998)

Alex is an investment banker whose adventures first appeared in the *London Daily News*. When the paper closed, the strip was picked up by the *Independent* but moved in 1992 to *The Daily Telegraph*—Britain's most right-wing paper, a strange home for a character whose right-wing attitudes are constantly being satirized.

Alex was twenty-five when the strip began in the late 1980s, and dating Penny and bantering with his colleague Clive. Alex is completely self-absorbed; he is obsessed with money and status. An early strip has him calling the telephone helpline for the Samaritans: "My name's Alex and I make forty thousand a year . . . Well, I've just had a car phone fitted in my new BMW," all because "I just thought you might like to hear some good news for a change."

Initial strips were straightforward jokes told over four panels, but these soon developed into the strip's most common format where the first three panels appear to be telling one story, while the fourth reveals that what appeared to be happening in the first three actually had a different context or reveals that the words spoken in the first three had another meaning. The characters age with the strip; Alex marries Penny and they have a son, Christopher. Alex faces unemployment and the trials of applying for a new job, but still survives in the banking world. Charles Peattie's art style veers toward caricature, but he fills the backgrounds with well-drawn details of people, vehicles, or places, whenever the occasion calls for them. **NFI**

JoJo's Bizarre Adventure 1987

Hirohiko Araki

First published by Shueisha (Japan)
Creator Japanese (b.1959)
Genre Fantasy, Adventure
Adaptation Anime movie (2007)

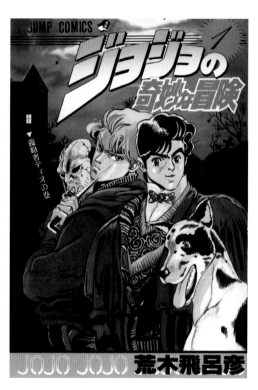

JUMP COMICS
1
ジョジョの奇妙な冒険
侵略者ディオの巻
JOJO JOJO
荒木飛呂彦

JoJo's Bizarre Adventure is a collection of loosely connected stand-alone stories featuring psychic battles that all have protagonists whose names can be abbreviated as JoJo. It was one of the pioneering mangas that popularized psychic battles between characters with different powers. These clashes resemble the game paper-rock-scissors where there is no absolute winner. By enhancing battles with elements of teamwork and intriguing puzzles, *JoJo's Bizarre Adventure* positioned itself as one of the most definitive *shonen* manga.

The first part in the series, *Phantom Blood,* takes place in Victorian England, when the long struggle between the Joestar lineage and the evil antagonist Dio Brando begins. In the next installment, *Battle Tendency*, the next generation of the Joestar family fight against ancient superbeings to save the world. In the third part, *Stardust Crusaders*, the series establishes the concept of Stand, a psychic power that is visualized as a strange humanoid and reflects the unique characteristic of its user. Some have the ability to stop time, while others have more complex powers, such as having the ability to read and manipulate an opponent's mind by opening comic book pages from his face. Some are downright silly; however, any Stand can potentially become lethal. Currently, the seventh offering, *Steel Ball Run*, is continuing the long tradition.

JoJo's Bizarre Adventure is influential in the manga world but also boasts a cult following for its excessively stylish poses, over-the-top dialogue, and rock music–inspired names of its characters and Stands. **NK**

"To know a man's Stand is to know his weakness! That is why Dio will beat you!"

Also by Hirohiko Araki
Autoto Man
Baoh
Deadman's Q
Gorgeous Irene
Magic Boy B.T.

Zenith 1987

Grant Morrison Steve Yeowell

First published by IPC Media (UK)
Creators Morrison (British, b.1960); Yeowell (British, b.1962)
Genre Superhero

FUNERAL IN BERLIN!
PROG 535 15 AUG 87
2000 AD
FEATURING JUDGE DREDD
28p
EARTH MONEY
IN ORBIT EVERY MONDAY
WW2 WAS JUST THE START OF...
ZENITH!

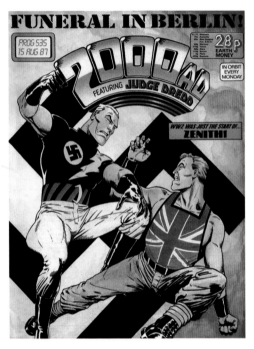

"I'm nineteen, I can fly, I can flatten ballbearings between my fingers and I'm practically invulnerable to damage. What can possibly go wrong?"

Shallow, materialistic, egotistical, self-centered, and generally unlikable, Zenith was a British superhero who reflected the Thatcherite zeitgeist of the 1980s.

Zenith is the only son of two members of a parents' generation of superheroes known as Cloud 9, who were created in a laboratory. That earlier generation, including Zenith's parents, had either mysteriously disappeared or lost their powers. Zenith himself has little interest in using his powers for good, preferring to use them to sell records. That is, until the return of an interdimensional being, Iok Sotot, on Earth to prepare the way for the return of the "many-angled ones."

Across four series of *Zenith*, Morrison explores the superhero mythology from a 1980s British pop-culture perspective. In the third series he introduces parallel universes that allow a multidimensional war across several worlds to take place between lost or forgotten British comic book characters from the 1960s and 1970s. Most memorably these include Robot Archie, now influenced by Acid House, and even a likable version of Zenith. Other characters include the Machiavellian Peter St. John, ex-Cloud 9 member and ex-hippie turned Conservative MP.

Morrison also highlights the culture gap between his and his parent's generation, heavily criticizing the passage from the permissive society of the 1960s to the monetarist society of the 1980s. But he also uses the series to explore his now trademark subjects of superheroes as myth, magic rituals, and multidimensional realities beyond our own.

Possibly Steve Yeowell's best-loved work, the illustration is colorless for the first three series, choosing to largely forgo outlines in favor of stark black-and-white shading. The result is a strongly noir-esque atmosphere that gives *Zenith* a dark, edgy tone that few superhero comic books ever achieve. **BD**

The Encyclopedia of Babies 1987

Daniel Goossens

A terrified silence has just descended on an air traffic control tower. The approaching Boeing is not answering calls and with good reason: its pilot is a baby who cannot yet talk. How to communicate with the cockpit so as to avoid a catastrophe? Commander Morton, who is head of the control tower, keeps his cool. He decides to contact the only professional who can solve this desperate situation—Professor Blair—a linguist who specializes in language learning and development. Having arrived at the tower while the ominous countdown is gradually ticking away and tension is rising fast, Blair decides to use the most reliable but also the most radical solution: to teach the baby the use of the subjunctive.

A very special kind of humor characterizes the universe of French comics creator Daniel Goossens. He is unique in the world of French-language comics for combining parody, absurdity, and nonsense together with numerous references and quotes from popular culture in all its forms, including literature, advertisements, films, soap operas, and TV programs. His writing often adopts a mock encyclopedic tone.

His atypical humor is frequently derived from the wild juxtaposition of universes or characters that have absolutely nothing to do with each other—such as here in "The Boeing Catastrophe" ("Le Boeing Catastrophe")—where he puts a baby sucking its thumb on a psychoanalyst's couch, or vast herds of babies are seen driven in the same way that cowboys drive cattle in Hollywood Westerns.

Goossens's surreal and sometimes disturbing graphic style is in keeping with the content of his narratives—surprising, personal, full of pop-culture references, and remarkably effective. His enthusiastic fans—and there are many of them—believe that Daniel Goossens is a genius. They could well be right. **NF**

Title in original language *L'Encyclopédie des bébés*
First published by *Fluide Glacial* (France)
Creator French (b.1954)
Genre Humor

GOOSSENS
L'ENCYCLOPÉDIE DES BÉBÉS
BOITE CRÂNIENNE
COIFFE JUVÉNILE
ORBITES OCULAIRES
DENTS DE LAIT (AMOVIBLES)
MUSCLES (SYSTÈME TRACTEUR ET RÉTRACTEUR)
MAXILLAIRE INFÉRIEUR
COUCHE (VUE EN COUPE)
FRONCES PROTECTRICES
MÉTA-TARSIENS
CHAUSSON DÉCORÉ AVEC DES BOMBARDIERS PARTANT EN MISSION ET DEUX BOULES
FLUIDE GLACIAL

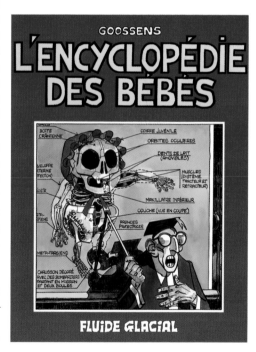

"This encyclopedia is addressed to non-babies, such as myself, so that I can better understand them, better love them, better classify them . . ."

Heinz 1987

✏️ René Windig and Eddie de Jong

First published by Gezellig en Leuk/Oog & Blik
(Netherlands)
Creators Windig (Dutch, b.1951); de Jong (Dutch, b.1950)
Genre Humor, Satire

In the late 1960s, five students in different classes at the highbrow Amsterdam high school, Barlaeus Gymnasium, created lowbrow strips that spoofed the classics. They were unsigned and drawn collectively, usually during class. The students sneaked relaylike in and out of classrooms and men's rooms to pass their art on to the next one. Speeding through corridors as if in a *Looney Tunes* cartoon, breaking all rules, they jokingly called themselves *De Vijf Slijmerds*—the five slimeballs.

Slimeballs René and Eddie, under their surnames Windig and De Jong, then began making comic strips professionally. Together they write, draw, ink, color, letter, and erase—forgetting who does exactly what. Satire and animalism define their work. In the mid-1970s they drew strips for the Dutch *Donald Duck* weekly. Their artwork was rated too crude by Disney but they hit back with a Disney parody in their self-published magazine *Gezellig en Leuk*. They also spoofed Mazure's 1940s detective strip *Dick Bos* in their hilarious *Dick Bosch*.

In 1987 they established themselves with a strip full of city street observations, sound effects, and movement starring Heinz, a big, fat cat. Often rude—vitriolic even—but with a heart of gold, Heinz walks and talks like a man in a world of goofs and idiots. Having featured previously in their *Rockin' Belly* strip, he was based on a real cat René once owned. Published as black-and-white daily newspaper gag strips with continuing themes, color has been added to thousands of *Heinz* dailies in annotated deluxe tomes. **HvO**

The Dutch strip *Heinz* focuses on the adventures of a grumpy tomcat. ↑

Maybe... Maybe Not 1987

✎✎ Ralf König

Title in original language *Der bewegte Mann*
First published by Rowohlt Verlag (Germany)
Creator German (b.1960)
Genre Humor

Ralf König's *Maybe... Maybe Not* was first published in 1987, not as a comic book as one would expect, but on the nonfiction list of a German publisher. It is a child of its time, a comic that was conceived in an eventful period for gender relations. At the end of the 1980s, self-help groups for men sprang up to encourage men to talk about their experiences and feelings.

König, a self-confessed homosexual, dwells with great pleasure on the helplessness of the so-called "stronger" sex. In his strip the women's movement meets the men's movement. Axel, a would-be macho man, is abandoned by Doro, the woman in his life. Deeply unhappy, he becomes friends with Walter, a homosexual who calls himself Waltraud. The devastated Axel is hitting rock bottom when Waltraud gives him shelter (and tries to seduce him several times in the process.) Axel is by no means averse to Waltraud's advances; he feels flattered and is attracted by the "female side" of gay men. Axel discovers a completely new side of himself, a "feminine" homosexual side that had been suppressed and which is wonderfully caricatured on the cover of the comic. He no longer has anything in common with his former macho self.

König could be described as the male version of French cartoonist Claire Bretécher. His observations on society are razor-sharp, and his characterization of his protagonists is spot on. With König everyone gets their just desserts, whether they be men or women, homosexual or heterosexual, macho or feminist. **MS**

Oriental Sketchbooks 1987

Jacques Ferrandez

Title in original language *Carnets d'Orient*
First published by Casterman (Belgium)
Creator French (b.1955)
Genre History, Drama

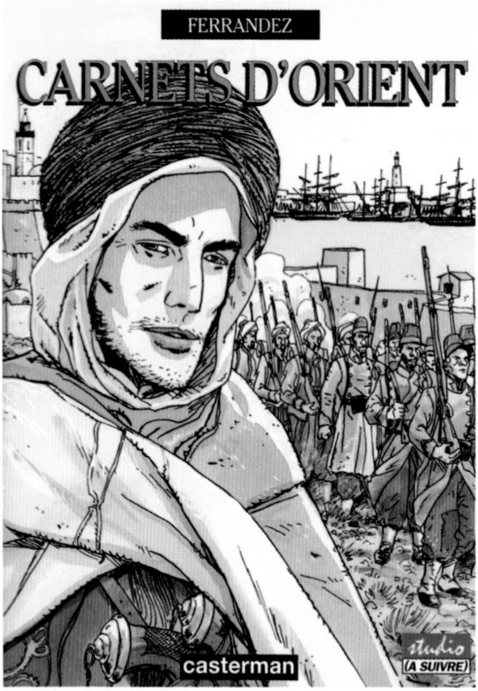
FERRANDEZ
CARNETS D'ORIENT
casterman
studio
(A SUIVRE)

Similar reads
Azrayen Lax and Giroud
Ce pays qui est le vôtre Kamel Khélif
D'Algérie Morvandiau
Petit Polio Farid Boudjellal
Walou à l'horizon Slim

Oriental Sketchbooks offers a remarkably complex view of France's colonial relationship with Algeria. The first series begins in 1836, six years after the French invasion, with the arrival in Algiers of fictional French painter Joseph Constant, and ends in 1954 on the eve of the insurrection. The second series is set during the war of independence, covering the period 1954 to 1960.

In the first volume, Jacques Ferrandez's detailed, watercolor and ink drawings are interspersed with pages from Constant's sketchbook. They include images of the beautiful Djemilah in a harem that are reminiscent of paintings by the French romantic artist Delacroix. Ferrandez sets a mythologized and eroticized version of Algeria alongside the more directly historical account that he offers through Constant's involvement with the real-life figure of Abd-el-Kader, leader of the resistance against the French.

"The Orient is a woman who entices us, then refuses. A woman who will always escape us."

In later volumes that portray the lives, both grueling and prosperous, of several generations of settlers, actual documents, newspapers, and pamphlets are reproduced. Here another potent mythology is exposed—that of the paternalist view of France as benefactor. In the fourth volume, *Le Centenaire*, the triumphalism of France's centenary celebrations of its rule over Algeria is contrasted with the deep disillusion of Broussard, a French army officer, now a hundred years old, who had truly believed that the colonial project was based on the extension of Republican ideals, not on ruthless exploitation. One senses that Ferrandez (who was born in Algeria) shares this doomed but seductive fantasy of what might have been. **AM**

Daily Delirium 1987

Miguelanxo Prado

Daily Delirium is a series of brief stories—each usually three to four pages long—with no main character. Within each episode, Miguelanxo Prado created a razor-sharp portrait of society in the late 1980s and early 1990s in which the absurdity and the reality of everyday situations rub shoulders. Topics include ever-changing technology, the deterioration of the environment, incompetent bureacuracy, the use and abuse of advertising, and sex. Sadistic old ladies, zealous government employees, overprotective mothers, henpecked husbands, and reckless drivers are among just some of the characters found in these tragicomedies. Some stories are based on actual events that happened to Prado or to his friends and relatives.

"Fuck Spielberg, his movie and all of these creatures . . . There's dinosaurs on everything."

Prado's other comics have focused on fantasy or slice-of-life stories, however, in *Daily Delirium* he demonstrates a skillful use of satire. The characteristic quality of his artwork also shines through: a masterful use of color and solid command of human figures are depicted in a clever blend of cartoony and realistic styles, coupled with richly detailed backgrounds and an innovative use of camera angles.

Originally published in the Spanish humor weekly *El Jueves*, the strip was subsequently reprinted in several albums. In 2003, Norma Editorial compiled all the material in a single volume, which was issued in English by ComicsLit. Some episodes were also published in the United States in *Heavy Metal* and in the United Kingdom in *X-Presso* (as *Unprobable Stories, Mostly*). Since 2010, some stories have also been available in a digital format for iPhone downloading. **AMo**

Title in original language *Quotidianía Delirante*
First published by *El Jueves* (Spain)
Creator Spanish (b.1958)
Genre Humor, Satire

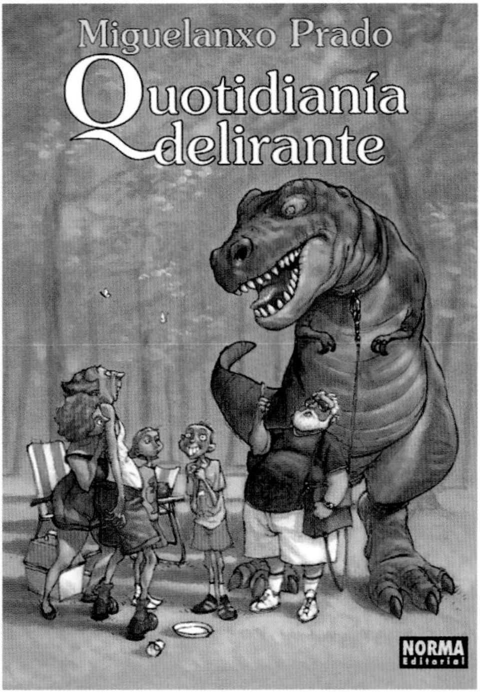
Miguelanxo Prado
Quotidianía delirante
NORMA Editorial

Also by Miguelanxo Prado
Chienne de vie
Demain les dauphins
Manuel Montano
Streak of Chalk (Trait de craie)
Stratos

Sensa Senso 1987

✐✐ Franco Matticchio

First published by *Linus* (Italy)
Creator Italian (b.1957)
Genre Humor
Award Treviso Comics Award (1994)

Gerald Jones is an eyepatch-wearing cat whose absurd and surreal adventures take place in a sort of *Alice in Wonderland*–like world. It is hard to know exactly on which side of the mirror he lives, however—fantasy or reality. His dreamy (and occasionally nightmarish) life seems to have no other purpose than to escape the real world.

In one episode that takes place at night, Jones's pillow comes to life and escapes the bedroom, seeking out his lover—a jute bag full of corn in a mill. Other surreal stories feature a rum-drinking snowman who tries to kill Jones; a girl whose hair turns into snakes; and a submarine that appears in Jones's bathtub.

Nothing is absolutely certain, and nothing much really happens in Franco Matticchio's fantastical world—a gentle, melancholic, sometimes dark place in which people and animals interact happily with inanimate objects. Most of his characters are searching for some meaning beyond the seemingly logical flat reality of the world. His witty and elegant line drawing style is reminiscent of Edward Gorey, Saul Steinberg, and Charles Addams.

Sensa Senso is a collection of the comic book stories by Matticchio that *Linus* published for many years, often featuring Gerald Jones. Mattichio is a talented illustrator and painter, as well as cartoonist, and the author of many picture books. In 1994 he also designed the animated opening credits for Roberto Benigni's movie *The Monster* (*Il Mostro*), which features a lonely bull terrier dog. **MS**

The Angriest Dog in the World 1987

✐✐ David Lynch

First published by *Los Angeles Reader* (USA)
Creator American (b.1946)
Genre Humor
Influence on *The Angriest Liberal in the World* (2003)

Movie director David Lynch created this comic strip for the alternative newspaper *L.A. Reader* where it ran from 1987 through to 1992. It was also published serially in the Dark Horse anthology *Cheval Noir*. It follows the "iteration" category devised by French comics theorist Thierry Groensteen in *The System of Comics* (1997). The strip always features the same four panels, depicting the backyard of a house where a dog lies growling. The first three panels show a scene during the day, while in the last panel it is dark with a glowing light appearing from inside the house. The introduction reads: "The dog who is so angry he cannot move. He cannot eat. He cannot sleep. He can just barely growl. Bound so tightly with tension and anger, he approaches the state of rigor mortis". The only differences in each strip are the speech balloons spoken by unseen characters in the house, which range from one-liners to dialogue. The last few strips published had their panels drawn as if they were burning, a fire that progressively consumed them until nothing was left. Lynch produced the cartoons during a period in which he was experiencing a lot of anger.

The jokes themselves are usually silly or even trite but this is typical of Lynch's humor, as seen in his films and in his cartoon series *Dumbland*. It is almost as if the main character is neither the dog nor the people speaking from inside the house, but rather the bleak world itself the strip portrays. Apart from the dog's bowls and leash, the backyard is lifeless: the tree seems to be stripped of all leaves and the ominous, polluting factory in the distance promises no respite. **PM**

Justice League International 1987

Keith Giffen and J. M. DeMatteis Kevin Maguire

First published by DC Comics (USA)
Creators Giffen (American, b. 1952); DeMatteis (American, b.1953); Maguire (American, b.1960)
Genre Superhero

When introduced in 1960, *Justice League of America* was an iconic title uniting DC's top superheroes. By 1987 superhero team-ups were commonplace, and the series was canceled. Diminished expectations greeted the announcement of a reboot. At a time when *Dark Knight* and *Watchmen* had struck a darker tone for superheroes, though, the renewed *Justice League* took the opposite route. It was deliberately bright, frothy, and funny.

Keith Giffen plotted the stories, but the dialogue was provided by J. M. DeMatteis. Known for dealing with weighty matters in the titles he wrote, DeMatteis defied expectation by providing sophisticated sitcom-sharp dialogue as a bunch of previously second-string characters bounced off each other. Memorable character standbys included a bump on the head transforming the odious Guy Gardner into a saintly reflection of himself, the satirizing of Batman's grim persona, the appearance of preposterous villains being greeted with laughter, and a world-weary Martian driven to Oreo cookie addiction by overseeing his inept colleagues.

Artist Kevin Maguire, unknown at the time, proved himself a master of expressions and posture. He defined the initial cast on the cover of his first issue in a much-homaged illustration. This would have all been window dressing without the strong plots. Giffen gave traditional fans the requisite dose of superhero action, foreshadowing, and guest stars whose insanity or inanity quotient ensured they fitted right in. Few followed their lead, but *Justice League International* remains highly readable—very, very funny. **FP**

$12.95 USA
$15.95 CAN
JUSTICE LEAGUE
A NEW BEGINNING
KEITH GIFFEN
J.M. DeMATTEIS
KEVIN MAGUIRE
AL GORDON
TERRY AUSTIN

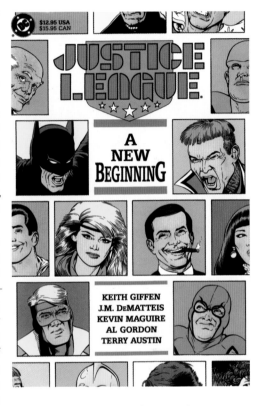

"My name's Guy Gardner . . . I'm declaring myself commander-in-chief of the spanking new Justice League. Any objections? I didn't think so."

Also by the same creators
Hero Squared
Planetary Brigade
The Defenders

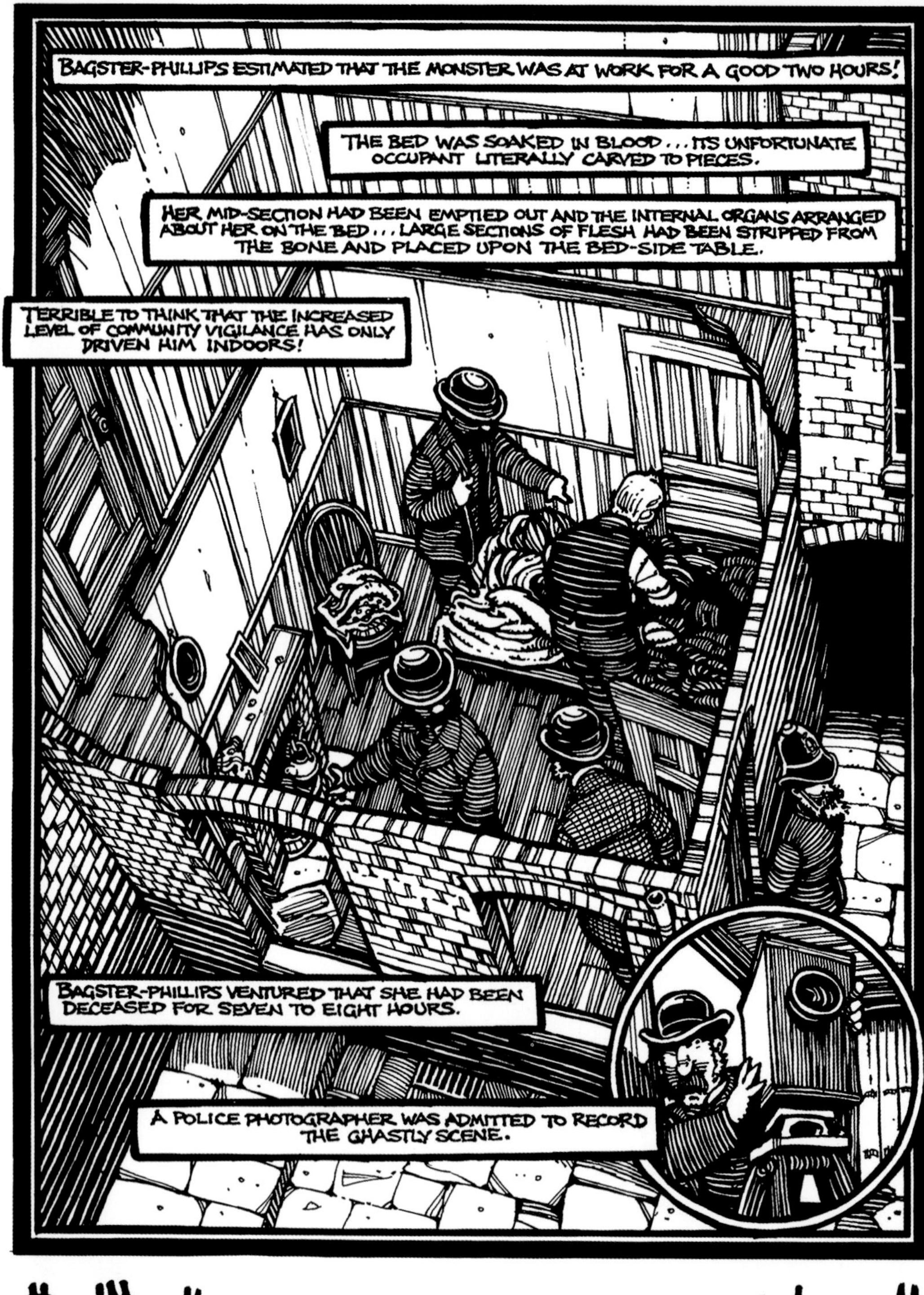
BAGSTER-PHILLIPS ESTIMATED THAT THE MONSTER WAS AT WORK FOR A GOOD TWO HOURS!
THE BED WAS SOAKED IN BLOOD... ITS UNFORTUNATE OCCUPANT LITERALLY CARVED TO PIECES.
HER MID-SECTION HAD BEEN EMPTIED OUT AND THE INTERNAL ORGANS ARRANGED ABOUT HER ON THE BED... LARGE SECTIONS OF FLESH HAD BEEN STRIPPED FROM THE BONE AND PLACED UPON THE BED-SIDE TABLE.
TERRIBLE TO THINK THAT THE INCREASED LEVEL OF COMMUNITY VIGILANCE HAS ONLY DRIVEN HIM INDOORS!
BAGSTER-PHILLIPS VENTURED THAT SHE HAD BEEN DECEASED FOR SEVEN TO EIGHT HOURS.
A POLICE PHOTOGRAPHER WAS ADMITTED TO RECORD THE GHASTLY SCENE.

A Treasury of Victorian Murder 1987

✏✏ Rick Geary

First published by NBM Publishing (USA)
Creator American (b.1946)
Genre Crime, History
Award National Cartoonist Society Award (1994)

Considering that he started out with straight-faced depictions of absurdities in *National Lampoon*, there is an element of the ridiculous in Rick Geary having carved a niche as comics' premier source for historical crime. He has also adapted Victorian novels, created a parallel series depicting twentieth-century murders, and produced serious biographies of J. Edgar Hoover and Leon Trotsky among others. Geary's interest in crime cases was stimulated in the 1970s when a former policeman and journalist friend displayed his extensive collection of articles and photographs. It was at the suggestion of NBM publisher Terry Nantier, however, that Geary's attention focused on three strange Victorian-era murders for the first volume.

The characteristic presentation of almost forensic detail arose as succeeding volumes dealt with a single event. Geary studies not only the crime itself, but all the motivating factors, continuing through to the fate of the perpetrators. Where the murders remain unsolved he presents all viable theories, but is careful not to intrude with his own suggestions. Geary's ornately detailed art offers that relatively rare instance in comics of a completely original and distinctive style. He is adept at visual juxtaposition, presenting ridiculous aspects of the cases in all sincerity, and despite his topic, Geary's depictions avoid any gratuitous indulgence. If there is any moral message to the series, it is that while murders are greater in number today, with a greater percentage solved, the motivations behind the crimes have remained consistent over the years. **FP**

Marshal Law 1987

✏ Pat Mills ✏ Kevin O'Neill

First published by Epic Comics (USA)
Creators Mills (British, b.1949); O'Neill (British, b.1953)
Genre Superhero, Parody
Collection *Fear and Loathing* (1990)

Marshal Law is set in an unspecified future in the U.S. urban conglomeration of San Futuro, created when an earthquake destroyed San Francisco. Genetic engineering has produced an army of superheroes with varying psychological problems—a side effect of their conversion. Marshal Law is the sole government-backed superhero hunter: when superheroes go rogue, he takes them down with maximum force and even greater pleasure.

When interviewed during the 1980s, Pat Mills was vociferous about how preposterous he considered the idea of superheroes. Given his antipathy for the genre, his customary deep research was painful, but paid off with utterly scabrous, and near libelous, parodies of DC Comics mainstays: the *Legion of Super-Heroes*, *Superman*, and simulacra of 1940s superheroes, resurrected in the belief that Nazis are still running loose on Earth. All were illustrated in equally appalling fashion by Kevin O'Neill, whose jagged, disturbing visuals are detailed and gag-packed, the latter drawing on the tradition of the anarchic and unsettling British children's comics he had grown up reading (Ken Reid was a particular influence). Indeed, it was O'Neill who prompted the series, designing the character and later providing the name as well.

The book's parody is not restricted to superheroes: Mills takes the opportunity to ridicule unthinking, flag-waving patriotism. However, the series would not work without a strong core. Strip away the parodic elements and each story works as an effective action thriller. **FP**

◄ Geary's text, rather than his art, provides the gory details of the murder.

Aquablue 1988

Thierry Cailleteau · Olivier Vatine and Ciro Tota

First published by Delcourt (France)
Creators Cailleteau (French, b.1959); Vatine (French, b.1959); Tota (Italian, b.1954)
Genre Adventure, Science fiction

AQUABLUE
THE BLUE PLANET
CAILLETEAU
VATINE
DARK HORSE COMICS

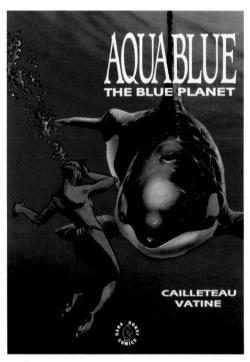

Similar reads
Incredible Science-Fiction Various
Meridian Barbara Kesel and Steve McNiven
Storm Martin Lodwijk and Don Lawrence
The Legend of Mother Sarah Katsuhiro Otomo and Takumi Nagayasu

A baby is the sole survivor of a tragedy in space. He is placed in an escape pod along with a robot to care for him. Eight years later, the child arrives on Aquablue, a planet where most of the surface is water, restricting humanoids to a few scattered archipelagos. The robot deactivates on contact with water and the child, named Nao, is raised to adulthood by the planet's natives.

What raises *Aquablue* above its science fiction predecessors is its subsequent plot strands. Nao's first contact with Earth occurs at eighteen when his identity as the heir to a multimillion dollar conglomerate is revealed. The business is run by his aunt, who views Aquablue as a substantial power source, not caring that her interference will leave it covered in ice.

"I'm unhappy when I see writers able to produce twelve albums a year. I envy them. I can't do it."

Thierry Cailleteau

Thereafter, Nao returns to Earth to present his inheritance claim, and a discovery is made that provides the Aquablue natives with technological parity to Earth's. In the best adventure tradition, just when everything looks bleakest, Nao comes up trumps.

Olivier Vatine met Thierry Cailleteau at art college in 1977. They created two series together prior to *Aquablue*, then drifted apart. Vatine's expressive characters and ability for depicting high-tech and less advanced societies equally convincingly had defined *Aquablue*. Purists wish he had completed the series, but Ciro Tota's work on the concluding chapter is equally effective.

Aquablue is a treatise about the way the Western world exploits nontechnological societies. Thankfully, this never overwhelms the well-constructed and fully realized vision of a future on display here. **FP**

In Search of Shirley 1988

"Cosey"

Two Vietnam veterans, Art and Ian, go on a journey to Italy to evade their responsibilities and escape the stifling tedium of 1980s small-town America, but an encounter with the elusive woman who had marked both their adolescences reopens old wounds and forces the pair to confront their own unrealized fantasies. The past invades the present in the form of memories of carefree moments from the long-gone hippie culture of the 1960s, past romantic ecstasy and loss, or nightmare visions of burning Vietnamese villages, sometimes with such intensity that the images give way to white. The style is realist, although an occasionally nonrealist use of color adds emotional force. However, objects and decor may not necessarily have immediate narrative

"... reading a comic is a very active kind of reading. Reading a comic is doing a lot of synthesis work."

Cosey

significance, but instead serve to evoke a mood. What is not said, or said obliquely, carries great weight here. There are many silent sequences in which the reader has to scan the page for narrative clues, leaving them to assemble the story from fragments. Cosey makes virtuoso use of inserts, zooming in on a detail (usually a face), presenting it simultaneously in close-up and as part of a wider narrative context: this has the effect of burrowing into the subjectivity of a character.

The end of the book is profoundly affecting. A series of images of objects evoke the everyday banality that now represents hard-won contentment for one of the two men. This, on the penultimate page, is where Cosey chooses to place the ending. The last page, a coda to the tale, is the most heart-wrenching depiction of renunciation in all of comic art. **AM**

Title in original language *Le Voyage en Italie*
First published by Dupuis (Belgium)
Creator Bernard Cosendai (Swiss, b.1950)
Genre Romance

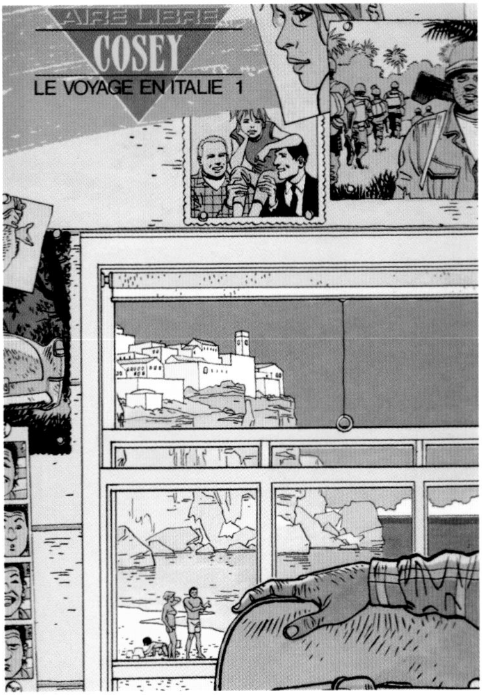
AIRE LIBRE
COSEY
LE VOYAGE EN ITALIE 1

Also by Cosey

In Search of Peter Pan (A la recherche de Peter Pan)
Orchidea
Saigon-Hanoi
Whoever Leads the Rivers to the Sea (Celui qui mène les fleuves à la mer)

The Spiral Cage 1988

Al Davison

AL DAVISON
The Spiral Cage
AN AUTOBIOGRAPHY

"Even a tarnished mirror will shine like a jewel if it is polished."

Buddhist text, quoted by the author

Similar reads

A Child's Life and Other Stories Phoebe Gloeckner
Epileptic (*L'Ascension du haut-mal*) David B.
Stitches: A Memoir David Small
The Minotaur's Tale Al Davison
Violent Cases Neil Gaiman and Dave McKean

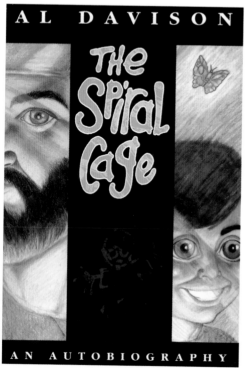

First published by Renegade Press (USA)
Creator British (b.1960)
Genre Autobiography
Influenced by Martin Luther King Jr.

In this utterly original personal account of a life with spina bifida, a life-threatening birth defect in which part of the spinal column is left exposed, Al Davison confronts many demons: the doctors who said he wasn't worth saving, the thugs who persecuted him, and even his own body. The story he tells of battling these foes in real life takes us into the mind of a Buddhist who needed to learn to fight to survive. Ranging wildly in style from the photo-realistic to the cartoony, the intensely detailed pen-and-ink images Davison conjures to evoke his early life vary from Blake-like visions to sequences reminiscent of animation. We follow, listen, and watch as the author fills his brain with Zen teachings, Gandhi's writings, Martin Luther King Jr.'s speeches, and the songs of Betty Boop, with the Invisible Man also thrown in. Again and again we see Davison's body—first in childhood, with his legs fused together, and then as an adult battling chronic fatigue syndrome. Perhaps when we see the adult nude figure of the author it's Davison's way of showing how far that tiny, paralyzed child has come, but these repeated images also challenge our notions of what a "correct" physique should be. There are moments of violence and despair—but there is also much of the miraculous events that surprise even Davison. *Spiral Cage* tells the story of someone becoming their own superhero, the person they need in order to be happy. It's also an inspiration to those who may themselves feel doomed by a "spiral cage"—their own DNA. What we do with what is only a building block is up to us. **EL**

A Hundred Tales 1988

✐✐ Hinako Sugiura

Title in original language *Hyaku Monogatari*
First published by Shinchosha
Creator Japanese (1947–2005)
Genre Fantasy

Set in the Edo period, a time spanning from 1600 to 1867 when Japan was isolated from the outside world, *One Hundred Tales* depicts a world where supernatural mysteries are believed to exist side-by-side with ordinary people, where the rational and fantastical collide.

Sugiura's work romantically depicts the normal lives of the people of the Edo period in an accessible fashion. Her story and the art are strongly supported by her rich knowledge of the Japan of the time, giving her manga both a solid foundation and a natural flow.

One Hundred Tales might remind you of dark nursery rhymes or fairy tales such as *Shockheaded Peter*, but it's full of classic Japanese horror stories, humor, and beautiful traditional motifs: *yokai* monsters, ghosts, spiders, racoons, rainy streets, and snowy fields—all unveiled in front of your eyes as you read.

Despite the meaning if its title, Sugiura's book actually contains ninety-nine episodes. This is because at a gathering to tell such scary stories, Japanese people traditionally sit in a circle with a hundred lit candles, taking turns to tell stories, extinguishing a candle after each tale is told. After the last candle is blown out, a real horror is believed to emerge: the author deliberately left this last story untold. Such gatherings are still popular today among Japanese people who enjoy a "chill" on a humid summer night, and as readers we are also able to taste a bit of this activity by reading Sugiura's work. *One Hundred Tales* will transport you back 200 years to a time in Japan when the border between reality and dark fantasy was very thin. **AT-L**

Jimbo in Paradise 1988

✐✐ Gary Panter

First published by *RAW* magazine (USA)
Creator American (b.1950)
Genre Science fiction
Influenced by Jack Kirby

One of the most influential cartoonists of his generation, Gary Panter is best known for his punk graphic sensibility that helped usher American comics out of an era focused on craft and into an age where comics became an expression of an individual artist's vision and ideas. More than almost any other cartoonist, Panter tied comics to the contemporary art world, and Jimbo was his avatar.

Jimbo is the spike-haired, kilt-wearing hero of Panter's postnuclear dystopia. Wandering the American wilderness and fighting mutants, robots, and aliens, Jimbo struggles to carve out a life amid a culture of deterioration, destruction, and decay. Light on plot but heavy on attitude, *Jimbo in Paradise* is a nightmarish vision of the end of the world seen through the broken kaleidoscope of American consumerism.

The appeal of Panter's work resides plainly in the visceral graphic power of his art. Changing visual styles from page to page, Panter's approach is rooted in a constant willingness to explore what comics have to offer as a communicative medium. The pages of *Jimbo in Paradise* shift from lovingly detailed character studies to images that seem to have been slashed out in a fury of ink. The final chapters, printed on green paper and with their homage to Picasso, are among the purest expressions of the comic book as art object.

Panter went on to chronicle Jimbo's adventures in Purgatory and Hell in order to complete a Dante-esque trilogy, but *Jimbo in Paradise* remains the standard by which his work is judged. **BB**

Tank Girl 1988

Alan Martin · Jamie Hewlett

DEADLINE
OCTOBER 1988
No1 £1.50
COMICS MEDIA MUSIC &
DEADLINE
DAVE ALLEN
JAH
wobble
DANNY
JOHN-JULES
HOUSE OF LOVE
BRIAN BOLLAND

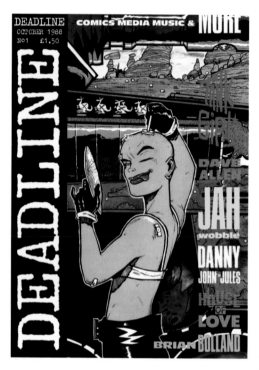

"Anyone here got a white handkerchief? Mine's got blood and snot all over it."

Similar reads
Dirty Plotte Julie Doucet
Dori Stories Dori Seda
My New York Diary Julie Doucet
Naughty Bits Roberta Gregory
The Pro Garth Ennis and Amanda Conner

First published by *Deadline* (UK)
Creators Martin (British, b.1966); Hewlett (British, b.1968)
Genre Adventure, Adult humor

Tank Girl began life as an ad for a fake comic strip hastily mocked up as filler for *Atomtan*, a fanzine created by Worthing College art students and roommates Alan Martin and Jamie Hewlett. Thanks to an invite to develop the strip in Brett Ewins, Steve Dillon, and Tom Astor's stylish independent comics and music magazine *Deadline*, it soon rose to cult status. Originally set in the Australian outback, Tank Girl's anarchic adventures featured a host of ninjas, mutants, time-traveling archaeologists, mafiosos, and bounty hunters, as well as memorable sidekicks Jet Girl, Sub Girl, and Camp Koala. Yet it was the central character herself, a beer-swilling, gun-toting, drug-taking, tank-revving, chain-smoking, kangaroo-shagging tour de force who was the undisputed star of the show, an icon that resonated with everyone from lesbian activists to "riot grrrl zinesters," while also being (mis)appropriated by fashion mags and Hollywood hacks.

Martin's narrative style is fragmented and spasmodic, paying tribute to William Burroughs and Jack Kerouac, and he often worked in obscure indie music lyrics and pop culture references. Even more striking was the artwork, which came into its own when the strip went full-color, channeling rave culture into a densely layered mixture of manic collage, psychedelic painting, and clean animation cel-style coloring.

Many *Tank Girl* books have been published since, but it remains hard to match the raucous irreverence, frenetic pace, and utter exuberance of the original *Deadline* strips. **MG**

Jamie Hewlett's anarchic illustrations defined Tank Girl's no-nonsense attitude. ➡

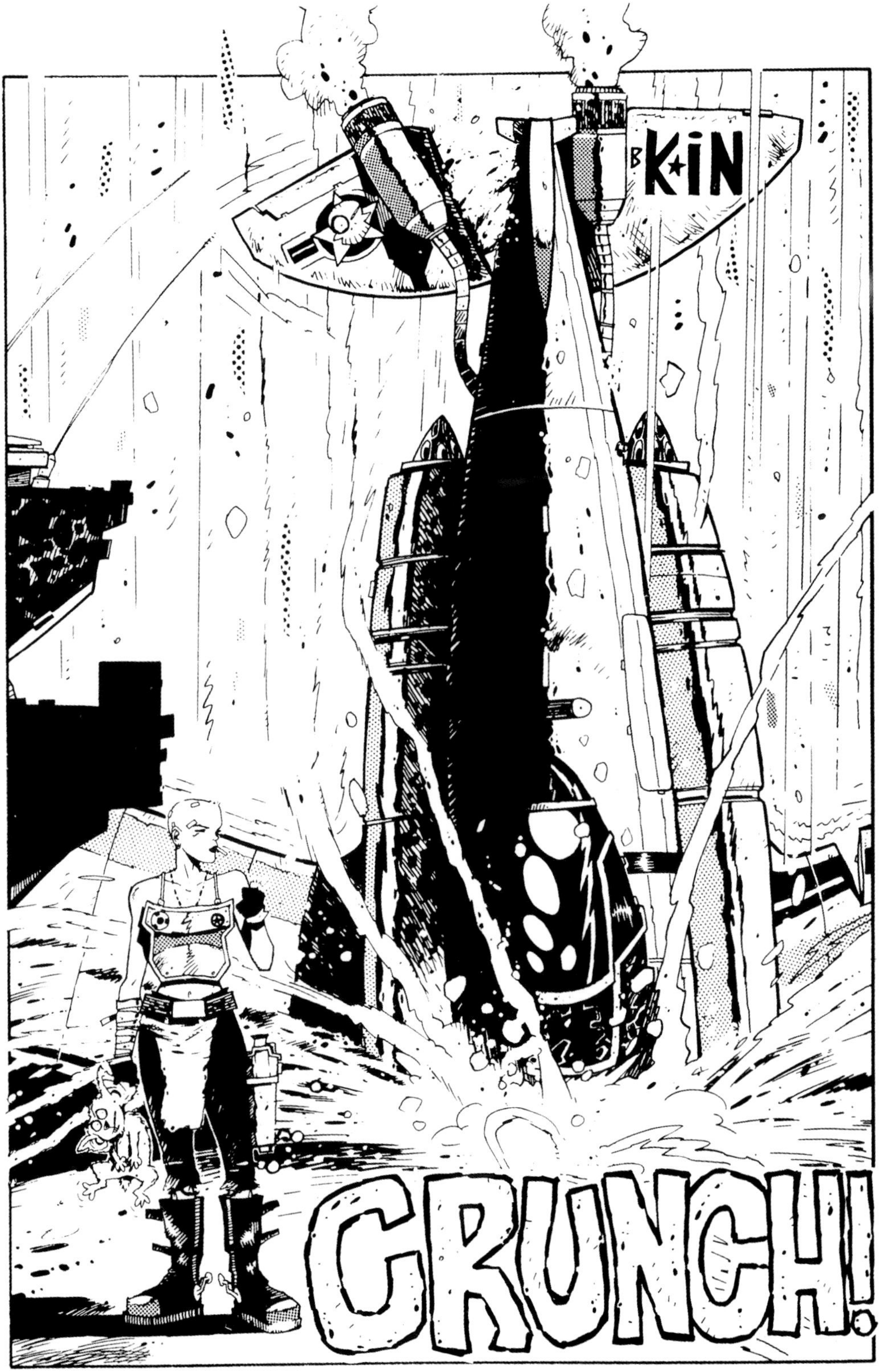
B K★IN
CRUNCH!

My Years of Youth 1988

🖊🖊 He Youzhi

Title in original language *Wo zi minjian lai*
First published by Les Amitiés franco-chinoises (France)
Creator Chinese (b.1922)
Genre Reality drama

"I was born in Shanghai in 1922, the only child of white-collar workers." The first sentence of *My Years of Youth* immediately sets the tone of this atypical book, a rare retrospective look by a fantastically talented Chinese cartoonist telling his own story.

My Years of Youth's Chinese title is *Wo zi minjian lai* ("I come from the people"), and one should point out here that this work is not really a comic strip in the sense that is normally understood today in the West. He Youzhi's book is produced as a *lianhuanhua*—a palm-sized picture book of sequential illustrations, a traditional Chinese form of comics.

This does not in any way diminish the impact and interest of the artist's work, which has been much admired and respected in his country for many years, even though it is almost unknown outside of China. With his direct, clear narrative, He Youzhi tells us about a China that no longer exists through anecdotes and scenes that are like miniature worlds.

The China of He Youzhi's childhood was rural, hard-working, happy, and often poor. Later on, as he enters adolescence and then adulthood, history intrudes with the Japanese occupation, the lack of job opportunities, and more poverty. Yet the illustrator never gives the impression of complaining. The tone is humble and sober, relying on elegant, precise drawings to convey his message. You only need to look at them to see why he is hailed as a master cartoonist. One must admire his whole approach and wish that every artist of the medium could achieve such brilliant simplicity. **NF**

Kings in Disguise 1988

🖊 Jim Vance 🖊 Dan Burr

First published by Kitchen Sink Press (USA)
Creators Vance (American, b.1953);
Burr (American, Unknown)
Genre Adventure, Political fable

Kings in Disguise is one of those little comic gems you always want to tell people about. Writer Jim Vance brings great humanity and understanding to his coming-of-age tale set in 1930s America, while artist Dan Burr's simple line work creates a classic, timeless story.

Freddie Bloch's family is falling apart. His father has disappeared and his older brother has been hurt stealing food. Freddie sets out from California for Detroit to find his missing father, not realizing the man doesn't want to be found. The romantic twelve-year-old is naive, and *Kings in Disguise* charts his growth and maturation, a journey that often comes in quick and painful bursts.

He falls in with a tubercular hobo named Sammy, who calls himself the King of Spain. Sammy teaches Freddie how to survive among the not-always-friendly traveling community and to get about by riding the rails while spinning him stories about the hobo way of life. Sammy's stories are like the Hollywood movies Freddie loves and speak to the romantic notion of life on the open road, free as a bird. But in reality, while some of the "free birds" help him on his way, others want to rob him or, frighteningly, make advances to him.

But the cruelest and most ruthless people Freddie encounters are those who still have something but don't want to share it with the rising tide of their poor and indigent countrymen. Particularly poignant is the story line about labor riots as Freddie witnesses firsthand how his once-proud homeland has become divided by fear and poverty. This is one of the few comic books that deserves to be called a novel. **FJ**

The Cowboy Wally Show 1988

Kyle Baker

First published by Dolphin Doubleday (USA)
Creator American (b.1965)
Genre Adult humor
Influenced by Hanna-Barbera cartoons

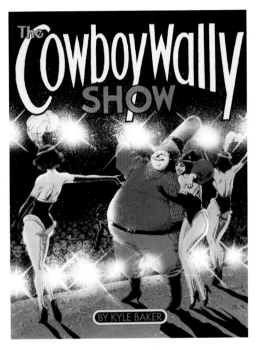

One of the funniest comics ever written, Kyle Baker's *The Cowboy Wally Show* is an outrageous send-up of an out-of-control celebrity culture. Cowboy Wally is symptomatic of everything that is wrong with American entertainment culture. He is a crass, vulgar, beer-swilling, belching, undereducated, simple-minded, and self-obsessed idiot who is inattentive to the needs of others. In short, he is the perfect comic foil for Baker's dark vision of America's culture of fame.

The Cowboy Wally Show opens as a documentary on the legend of this morbidly obese star. Beginning with his humble origins in Jeepersville, North Dakota, the book traces his rapid rise to glory, first as the host of a children's television program, then a game show host, a filmmaker, a soap opera actor, a newscaster, and finally a movie star. This fast-paced introduction is a showcase for Baker's gag-writing abilities, using deadpan humor and comic exaggeration to create a truly memorable buffoon of a lead character.

The rest of the book focuses on two long chapters following Cowboy Wally's career in the movies. "Sands of Blood" is an over-the-top parody of French Foreign Legion movies starring Wally's chronically depressed friend Lenny Walsh. The next section features Lenny and Wally in prison, vainly trying to produce a film version of Shakespeare's Hamlet from the confines of their cell without drawing the attention of the guards.

The Cowboy Wally Show was the breakthrough book in the long career of Kyle Baker, one of the most consistently funny of American cartoonists. **BB**

The Cowboy Wally Show
BY KYLE BAKER

"In one of the many rare interviews he has given, the legendary film star is as candid and witty as ever. With interviewer Oswald 'Glassy' Stairs, [he] traces his remarkable career . . . "

Also by Kyle Baker
Birth of a Nation: A Comic Novel
I Die at Midnight
King David
Why I Hate Saturn

Agrippine 1988

✐ Claire Bretécher

First published by Self-published (France)
Creator French (b.1940)
Genre Humor
Adaptation TV (2001)

Thirteen years after the first appearance of *Les Frustrés*, her celebrated strip satirizing the pretentious idealism of post-1968 French intellectuals, artist Claire Bretécher introduced the comic offspring of this generation in *Agrippine*. This strip, which would eventually be developed into a series of eight albums published over a period of twenty-one years and even inspire an animated television series, follows the grumblings of the eternally anguished teen Agrippine as she navigates adolescence, education, and a continually nagging feeling that life is both boring and pointless.

In classic Bretécher style, each *Agrippine* album presents a collection of short episodes, the majority just one page in length. Within each installment the panels are drawn simply, with little background detail or alteration of perspective. The focus is largely restricted to character dialogue. Within this simple recipe however, Bretécher's caricature of late-twentieth century adolescent dissatisfaction comes to life. Via pithy, intelligent, and superbly sarcastic dialogue, the mundanities of Agrippine's teenage existence are given a comic twist, from arguments with her parents to wondering what sex is like. The entirely comfortable but nonetheless "tortured" lives of Agrippine and her friends also allow the artist to revisit the existence of their bourgeois parents, whose attempts to retain the idealism of their earlier adulthood collapse under the realities of raising teenagers. Bretécher's witty dialogue and intelligent stories make *Agrippine* an original and funny addition to the French comics' scene. **CMac**

Here 1988

✐ Richard McGuire

First published by *RAW* magazine (USA)
Creator American (b.1957)
Genre Science fiction, Alternative
Influence on Chris Ware

Richard McGuire's *Here* first appeared in Art Spiegelman and Françoise Mouly's willfully avant-garde comics anthology *RAW*. Even in that urtext of experimental comics, *Here* stood out.

There are several experimental features in evidence within *Here*. First, each of the comic's thirty-six panels show the exact same location in space from the same perspective but depict different moments in time. What's more, sequential panels shift nonlinearly in time (with the year indicated in the top-left corner to guide the reader). Lastly, many panels have subpanels within them that work in the same fashion.

As if to ease the reader in, the first few panels proceed traditionally enough with the birth in 1957 of Billy, the strip's main character. The action then moves into subpanels as the main panel centers on both 1922 and 1971. After that all bets are off, with nonlinear jumps, multiple subpanels, and the timeframe shifting as far back as 500,957,406,073 B.C. Using Billy's life as something of a loose framing device, McGuire juxtaposes events across time for humor, pathos, and illumination. He demonstrates how a place can resonate with the echoes of past events.

McGuire really pushed comics into a bold, new direction and was a big influence on artists such as Chris Ware. It draws you into a world, glimpsed only through jumbled snapshots, that gives a sense of the place and its inhabitants far more efficiently than a straight narrative could. Ultimately, McGuire communicates the multiple implications of as simple a word as "here." **SB**

Hellblazer 1988

Jamie Delano and various John Ridgway and various

First published by DC Comics (USA)
Creators Delano (British, b.1956); Ridgway (British, b.1940)
Genre Horror, Political fable

With his trademark trenchcoat, biting wit, and ever-present cigarette, John Constantine debuted as a supporting character in Alan Moore's run on *Saga of the Swamp Thing* in 1985. An enigmatic master-manipulator, he cynically pulled the titular character's strings to stave off a number of paranormal threats. By 1988, the popularity of Constantine had grown to the extent that he was spun off into his own title, *Hellblazer*, wherein writer Jamie Delano revealed a more fallible and flawed chancer hiding behind the dapper facade of the controlling man of mystery.

Conceived as a British working-class warlock more likely to topple a demonic threat with a carefully constructed scam than the overt use of magic, Constantine is an amoral mystic detective just as likely to find himself in conflict with the forces of Heaven as he is those of Hell. Despite a track record for ruthlessly sacrificing friends for the greater good and an addictive, self-destructive personality, the character remains a sympathetic antihero; a cocky, occult everyman who the audience can both love and hate.

Hellblazer has retained a distinctively British flavor, due not just to the stewardship of a succession of mostly British writers including Warren Ellis, Garth Ennis, and Mike Carey, but also because it is steeped in British social and political commentary—all tinged with a requisite supernatural edge. The dark realism of artists like John Ridgway and Steve Dillon adds to the somber, gritty atmosphere—the true horror of Constantine's world is in its familiarity to the reader. **AO**

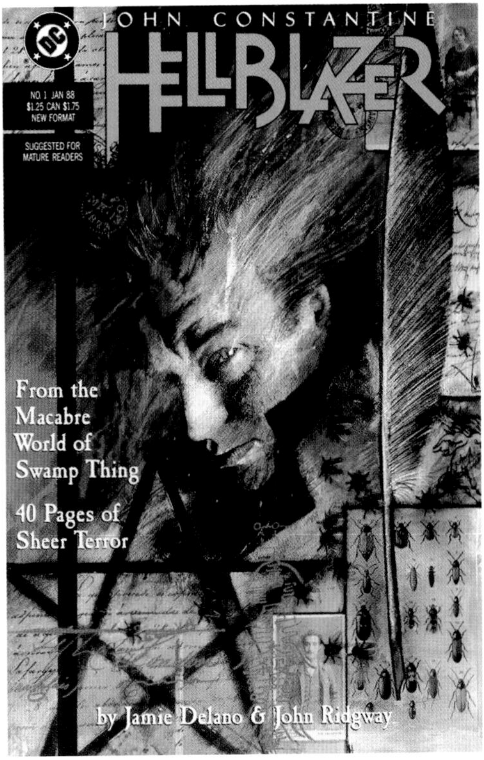
JOHN CONSTANTINE
HELLBLAZER
NO. 1 JAN 88 $1.25 CAN $1.75 NEW FORMAT
SUGGESTED FOR MATURE READERS
From the Macabre World of Swamp Thing
40 Pages of Sheer Terror
by Jamie Delano & John Ridgway

"Never look back's a good motto in our line of business. Too many bloody ghosts following."

Similar reads

Animal Man Dave Wood and Carmen Infantino
Saga of the Swamp Thing Alan Moore and Steve Bissette
The Books of Magic Neil Gaiman and various

Julius Knipl, Real Estate Photographer 1988

Ben Katchor

First published by *New York Press* (USA)
Creator American (b.1951)
Genre Adventure, Humor
Award Guggenheim Fellowship recipient (1995)

Ben Katchor explains how he created *Julius Knipl, Real Estate Photographer*: "I knew I wanted to do a strip about the city, and I knew of this profession: Real Estate Photographer. I didn't really know too much about what it meant except that people take utilitarian photographs of buildings for brokers to use for owners to show. I thought it a strange business, because it combines two professions that have all sorts of powerful connotations: real estate and photography, and yet it's kind of a pathetic profession; a man that goes around taking utilitarian photographs."

The Yiddish word *Knipl* (nest egg) refers to a small amount of money stashed away by Jewish housewives, while the character's first name brings to mind the Roman emperor—readers don't need to go far to see potentially funny dichotomies: the epic and the paltry, the comic and the tragic.

Katchor has a poetic, melancholic, and nostalgic view of the city. He is attentive to small details in human behavior. He's also attentive to the passage of time, to all that's ridiculously obsolete, a poet of all things ephemeral. His deceptively clumsy and crooked speech, paired with his balloons and apparently maladroit drawings, are part of an artisan-style effect that helps to group the strip among the antiquated objects it depicts. Katchor's washes and color combinations are superb, and three Julius Knipl books have been published so far: *Cheap Novelties, The Pleasures of Urban Decay*, *Julius Knipl, Real Estate Photographer,* and *The Beauty Supply District*—each a unique pleasure to read. **DI**

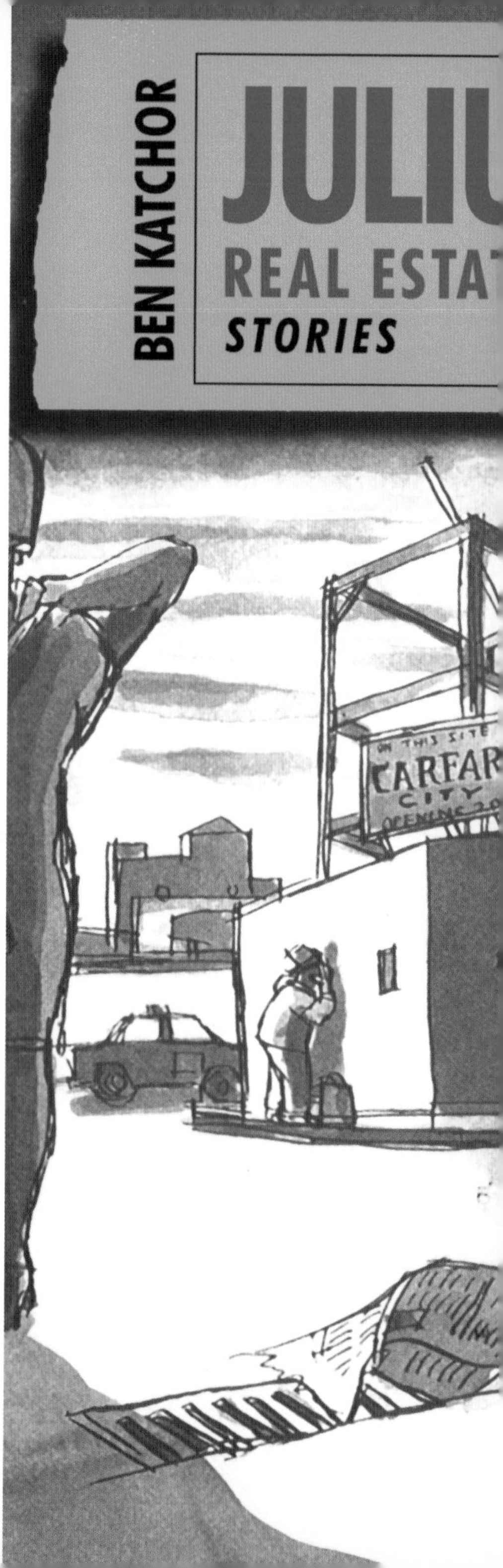
BEN KATCHOR
STORIES

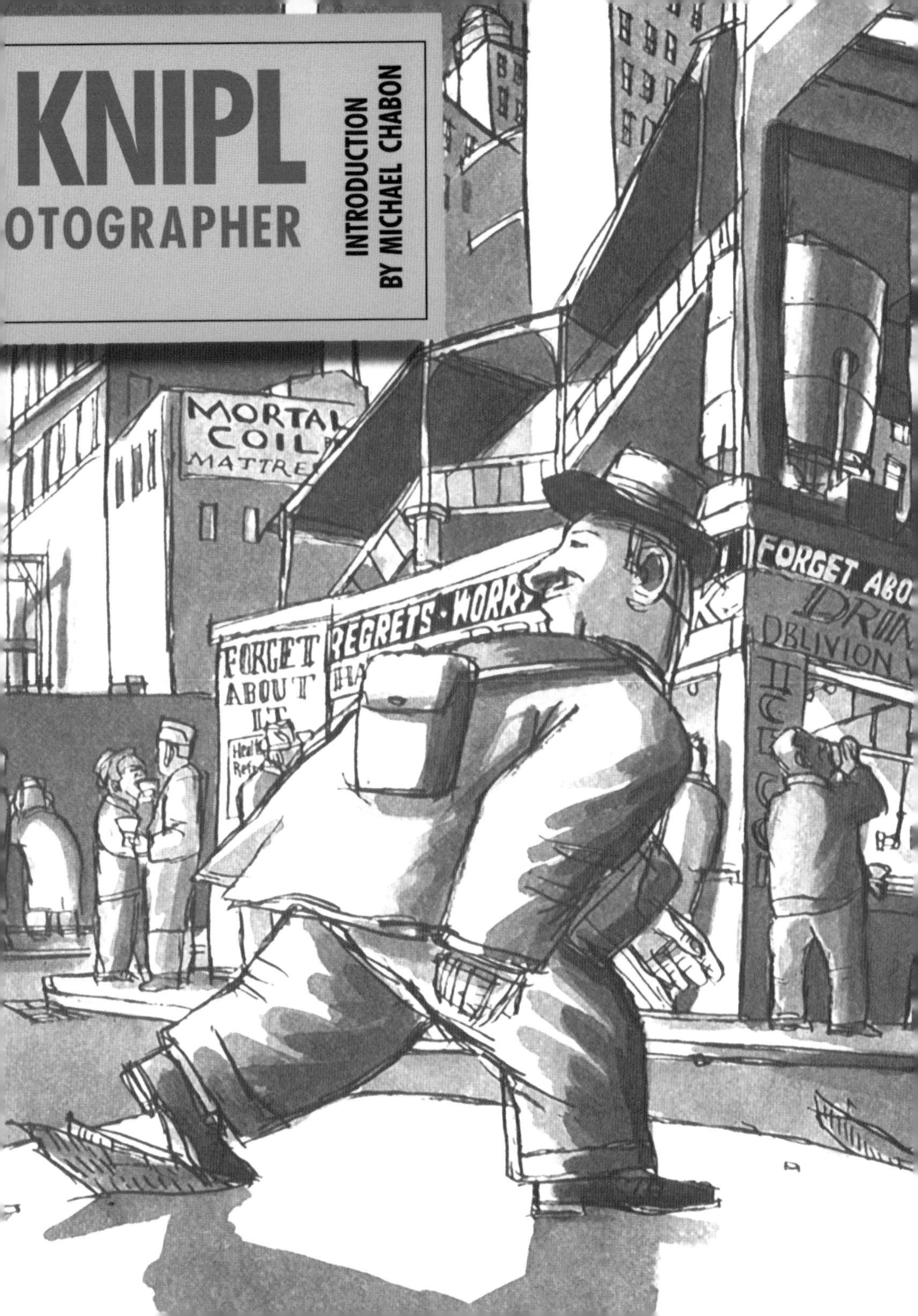
KNIPL
OTOGRAPHER
INTRODUCTION
BY MICHAEL CHABON
MORTAL
COIL
MATTRES
FORGET
ABOUT
IT
REGRETS · WORR
FORGET ABO
OBLIVION

Batman
The Killing Joke 1988

Alan Moore · Brian Bolland

First published by DC Comics (USA)
Creators Moore (British, b.1953); Bolland (British, b.1951)
Genre Superhero
Award Eisner Award for Best Graphic Album (1989)

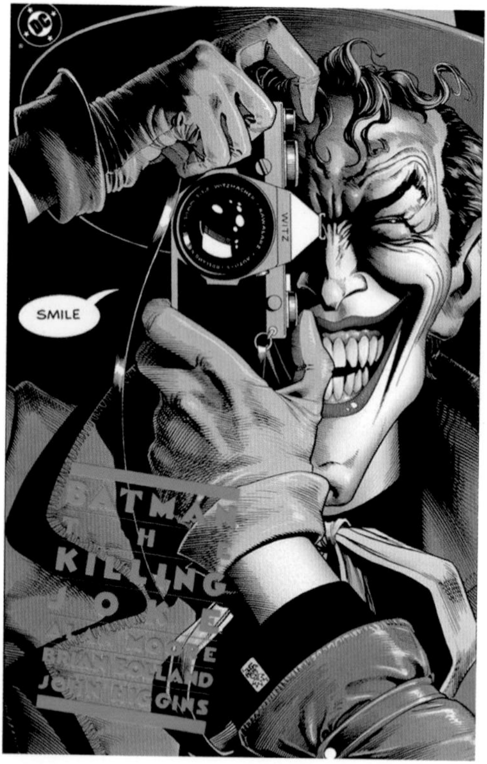

SMILE
BATMAN
THE
KILLING
JOKE
ALAN MOORE
BRIAN BOLLAND
JOHN HIGGINS

Similar reads

Batman: Arkham Asylum Grant Morrison and Dave McKean
Watchmen Alan Moore and Dave Gibbons

Alan Moore's psychological thriller serves the dual purpose of analysing the complex nature of one of comics' most enduring enmities and providing a possible origin story for the Joker. Batman is desperate to end the violent cycle of conflict between them, but the Joker is determined to taunt his nemesis with proof that even the sanest man is just a hair's breadth away from his own deep level of madness. To this end he imprisons the stalwart Commissioner Gordon in a derelict funfair and attempts to break him down mentally, the process having dramatic repercussions for his daughter and former Batgirl Barbara Gordon.

Batman: The Killing Joke was not without controversy on its original release. A pivotal early scene featuring the crippling of one character remains arguably the single most shocking moment in the long history of DC Comics's superhero universe, while the ending sits awkwardly with preceding events. *The Killing Joke* is a story that still has the power to significantly divide opinion among Batman aficionados. What is less contentious, however, is that Moore and Bolland's interpretation of the Joker—in turn vindictive and cruel, manic and childlike, contemplative and regretful—is little short of definitive.

There is also a rare opportunity on offer to experience Bolland at work on the sequential interior art of a superhero comic. Unsurprisingly, every intricate, detailed panel feels like a chapter in itself. Rereading the story is richly rewarded because his layouts are full of subtle nuance, telling expressions, and deeper symbolism that imbue the melancholy of Moore's tragic backstory for the Joker with profound sentiment. The true triumph of *The Killing Joke* is that, in a tale where the Joker is portrayed at his most vicious and unforgivable, he is also more human and sympathetic than he has ever been before. **AO**

The Sandman 1989

Neil Gaiman Sam Kieth and various

The Sandman, an anthropomorphic personification of dreams, is one of seven beings known as the Endless. Older than any god and bearing many names (although our titular character is mainly known as Morpheus), he is a regal, complex, and contradictory figure, capable of both terrible cruelty and great kindness.

Captured and held by occultists for seventy years in a botched attempt to capture Death (another being of the Endless), Morpheus eventually escapes to find his kingdom of dreams in ruins. He must restore order and rebuild his world, but he realizes that this time he must do more than that; his time in captivity has forced him to reassess his ways, and he finds himself wanting. He must change; but for a being as old as Morpheus, change is a difficult thing to accomplish.

Beginning as a DC horror comic with an interesting twist, *The Sandman* gradually evolved into an elaborate, highly intelligent fantasy series that incorporated a very wide range of myths, legends, and classic stories. Although the main story arcs are set in modern times, Morpheus is regularly relegated to bit-player roles in stories set across all of history. The reader sees the resplendent Baghdad of legend, runs with werewolves, and sits with a Roman emperor as he schemes. Neil Gaiman is in his element with the *Sandman* series, calling upon a lifetime of diverse reading and pouring it all into a complex, seventy-five-issue melting pot.

During its run, the *Sandman* strip gained a wide appeal, drawing in many readers who had never taken an interest in comics before. Unusually for a fantasy title, it achieved a demographic of readers that was fifty per cent female. It also attracted a World Fantasy Award. Ultimately, *The Sandman* is a story about stories, myths, and legends, hopes and fears, dreams and reality. But it is also about an immortal, dysfunctional family and the burdens its members carry. **BD**

First published by DC Comics (USA)
Creators Gaiman (British, b.1960); Kieth (American, b.1963)
Genre Fantasy

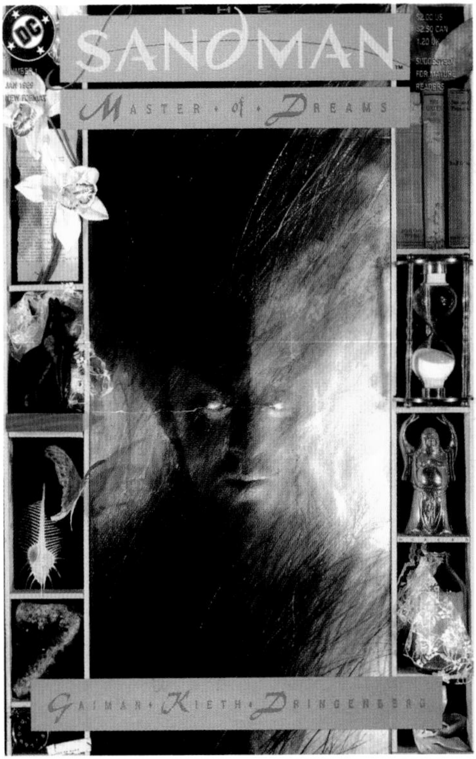
THE
SANDMAN
MASTER of DREAMS
GAIMAN KIETH DRINGENBERG

Similar reads

Signal to Noise Neil Gaiman and Dave McKean
Stardust Neil Gaiman and Charles Vess
The Books of Magic Neil Gaiman and Various

From Hell 1989

✎ Alan Moore ✎ Eddie Campbell

First published by *Taboo* (USA)
Creators Moore (British, b.1953);
Campbell (British-Australian, b.1955)
Genre Horror

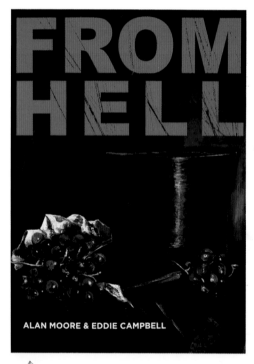

ALAN MOORE & EDDIE CAMPBELL

> **Similar Reads**
> *Berlin: City of Stones* Jason Lutes
> *Lost Girls* Alan Moore and Melinda Gebbie
> *The League of Extraordinary Gentlemen*
>   Alan Moore and Kevin O'Neill
> *The Plot* Will Eisner

As epic in scope as in ambition, *From Hell* is one of the defining works of the comics medium. Alan Moore and Eddie Campbell have crafted a fiction that includes almost every known fact about the Ripper Murders of 1888. Deliberately eschewing the "whodunit"in favor of a "whydunit" formula, Moore and Campbell reveal their Jack the Ripper—Sir William Withey Gull, royal physician and Freemason—early in the story.

The plot is largely based on a theory put forward by Stephen Knight in his book *Jack the Ripper: The Final Solution*, but this is just a starting point for a work of fiction that uses the Ripper murders to explore nineteenth-century London, Freemasonry, attitudes toward sex, gender, class, and the nature of magic.

"The one place where gods and monsters inarguably exist is within the human mind..."

Five prostitutes are blackmailing the artist Walter Sickert with the knowledge of an illegitimate royal baby. Sir William Gull is tasked to neutralize this threat. He sets about this work, but as he states, "Averting royal embarrassment is but the fraction of my work that is visible above the waterline." Gull is a misogynist who plans to use his murders and his occult knowledge as part of a work of magic designed to perpetuate the enslavement of women to the will of men.

The most important character in *From Hell* is London itself. The city is the true instigator of the Ripper crimes: a place of startling social inequality. In Campbell's hands it's a grimy, horrible place full of menace and degradation. What's more, *From Hell* is as much a damning indictment of modern society's attitudes to social and gender inequality as it is of those in the London of the past. **BD**

Ghost in the Shell 1989

Masamune Shirow

When it began, Masimune Shirow's manga appeared to be a straightforward science fiction adventure set in a future where a massive computer network runs the planet, but first impressions can be deceptive. The heroes are a team of covert operatives known as Public Security Section 9, created by a computer to combat techno-terrorism, particularly that of a shadowy figure known as the Puppeteer, the team's recurrent enemy.

The team are led by the hardheaded, no-nonsense Major Motoko Kusanagi, an android with a human brain. The team are both the ghosts within the massive computer system and ghost beings in artificial bodies; this is different from the literal translation of its Japanese title, *Kokaku Kidotai* (Mobile Armored Riot Police).

"The central cyber-brian barrier here is a complex maze of simulated experiences . . . "

After a few segments, Shirow's philosophical agenda started to creep to the fore as he immerses the reader more completely in his elaborate cyberpunk world, where androids keep cloned pets and possessing nonsynthetic versions of certain goods is a crime. Shirow increasingly has his characters begin to question their existences and the meaning of life. Kusanagi ultimately discovers the Puppeteer's secret and allows him to merge with her own consciousness, leading to further revelations. The creator effortlessly combines twisty, cyberpunk plotting with challenging philosophical conundrums.

Ghost in the Shell is not perfect, but it is unique. Shirow's characterization is quite sketchy, but he lavishes attention on technical details to create an amazing world that is never quite what it seems. A superb existentialist cyberpunk shoot-'em-up. **FJ**

Title in original language *Kokaku Kidotai*
First published by Kodansha (Japan)
Creators Japanese (b.1961)
Genre Science fiction

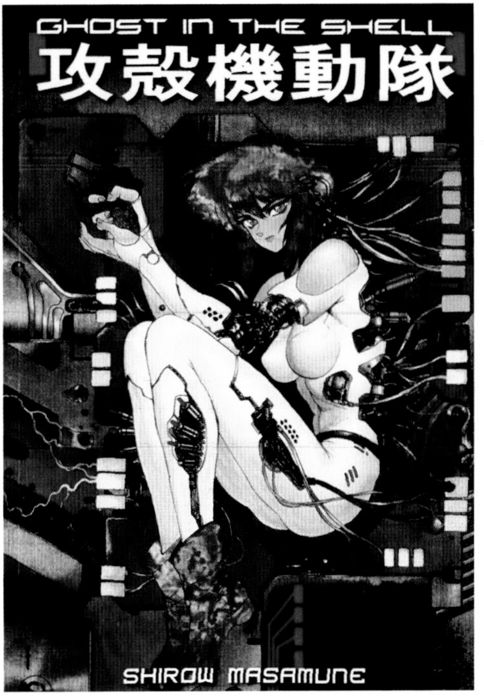
GHOST IN THE SHELL
攻殻機動隊
SHIROW MASAMUNE

Similar reads
Akira Katshiro Otomo
Appleseed Masamune Shirow
Hard Boiled Frank Miller and Geoff Darrow
Neon Genesis Evangelion Yoshiyuki Sadamoto
Ronin Frank Miller

Mark-of-the-Dog 1989

Silvio Cadelo

Title in original language *Voglia di cane*
First published by *Frigidaire* magazine (Italy)
Creators Italian (b.1948)
Genre Fantasy

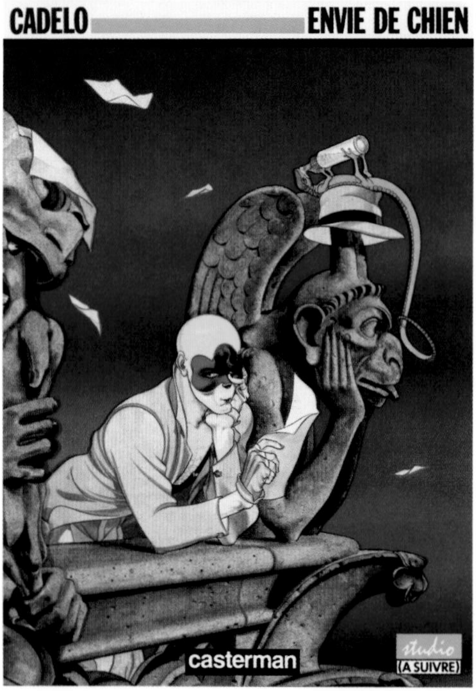
CADELO
ENVIE DE CHIEN
casterman
studio
(A SUIVRE)

Similar reads
Frank Jim Woodring
Going to Pieces François Schuiten
The Saga of Alandor (*La Saga d'Alandor*) Alexandro Jodorowsky and Silvio Cadelo
Two White Flies (*Deux mouches blanches*) Silvio Cadelo

When Silvio Cadelo joined *À Suivre*, the seminal Franco-Belgian comics magazine, he continued the adventures of *Mark-of-the-Dog*, a series he had begun two years earlier in the Italian comics magazine *Frigidaire*. Using ideas solicited from fans, he created four extravagantly surreal, grotesque stories about a melancholy masked killer loose on the streets of a futuristic Paris. The series was collected in its finished form in 1989.

The character is first seen hopping on one leg; not as an amputee, but as a monoped. He commits a murder and removes the victim's heart. He implants the heart in the body of his infant son to ensure he does not become a murderer. The son, who was conceived through hermaphroditic copulation, later rescues a lizard from a meat sandwich, and the lizard becomes his link to another world. And that's not the weird part.

"The unconscious, the imagination with its beauty and its monsters, are more real than reality."

Silvio Cadelo

The weird part is that you believe this is happening, that all of this is convincing, that the visuals create an internal logic for this mad, erotic, disturbing, and seductive world. The stories are not fragments of a dream; they add up to a consistent, coherent—albeit freakish—world, equally repulsive and lovely.

In 1994, Cadelo continued the saga of *Mark-of-the-Dog* in *Two White Flies* (*Deux mouches blanches*), which takes place in his father's world of origin and is—if it can be believed—even more bizarre. Beginning in 1995, at the initiative of Japanese publisher Kodansha, Cadelo further expanded the tale in a manga form as *The Children of Lutèce* (*Les enfants de Lutèce*). Sadly, these have yet to be translated into English. **TRL**

Heartthrobs 1989

Max Cabanes

It is the end of July 1956, and the nine-year-old protagonist of *Heartthrobs* is thinking of his recently deceased mother while throwing stones at a hen, which he ultimately kills. He's been sent away to stay with his aunt and uncle, and here he ponders the instinctive and passionate love he felt for his mother, trying to come to terms with her absence, but soon his attention is caught by a family moving in nearby, including a girl named Roberta, the catalyst for his prepubescent desires. Readers are offered a little window into the protagonist's psyche as he watches Roberta show her little sister a horse's genitalia. Each tale that follows catches the central character at a key stage in his development.

"Writing and drawing are tools of expression that are closely involved in my life."

Max Cabanes

Cabanes's extremely popular, semiautobiographical stories of growing up in the 1950s and 1960s beautifully delineate all the different stages of lust and longing, from the first realization of prepubescent arousal to the awkward teenage attempts to impress older girls with bad poetry. His memoir is bittersweet, capturing the time when the concept of the teenager was assaulting French provincial life, along with rock and roll.

Cabanes is a realistic artist who uses lush color to bring his beautiful women and gawky boys to life, but morphs into caricature at a moment's notice. Colors bleed and people's faces distort as the action become more intense, but throughout Cabanes displays a remarkable degree of observation and knowledge of body language, which really brings to life the emotions he's seeking to evoke. **FJ**

Title in original language *Colin-Maillard*
First published by Casterman (Belgium)
Creators French (b.1947)
Genre Romance

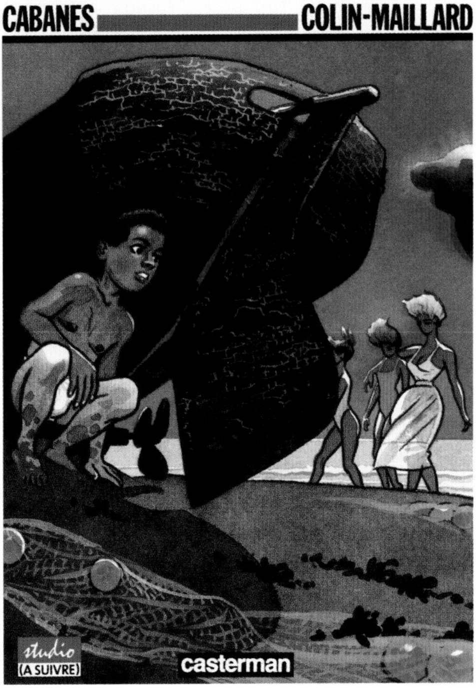

CABANES
COLIN-MAILLARD
studio (A SUIVRE)
casterman

Similar reads

A Taste of Chlorine (*Le Goût du chlore*) Bastien Vivès
Blankets Craig Thompson
Clumsy Jeffrey Brown
Likewise Ariel Schrag
Yukiko's Spinach (*L'Epinard de Yukiko*) Frédéric Boilet

Julien Boisvert
Neekibo 1989

✎ "Dieter" ✎ Michel Plessix

First published by Delcourt (France)
Creators Didier Teste (French, b.1958);
Plessix (French, b.1959)
Genre Adventure

French writer Dieter's first collaboration with artist Michel Plessix was *The Goddess with the Green Eyes* (*La Déesse aux jeux de jade*), a lighthearted Disney-esque adventure, in 1988. As Plessix's cartoony style became more realistic, the team began searching for new stories to tell. At the suggestion of their publisher the pair developed Julien Boisvert—a Tintin for grown-ups. The twenty-something civil servant was soon on globetrotting adventures with exotic locales, but these were also settings for self-discovery and character development—a journey both inward and outward.

The first volume of the four-part series, *Neekibo*, begins with Boisvert in Paris—spoiled, naive, and comfortable in his sheltered life. Reluctantly taking part in a humanitarian mission to Africa, he survives a plane crash and is rescued by an indigenous tribe. His predictable world is shattered by his exposure to a culture totally different from his own. He experiences his first love with a native woman, violence from racist mercenaries, and a rude awakening when he discovers the exploitive agenda of his own employers. Pretty heavy stuff for a Tintin-like figure!

The pacing of the stories is superb, and the psychological development of Boisvert is never forced. Plessix's lush watercolors over delicate pen-and-ink drawings create an utterly convincing sense of place. In later volumes, Boisvert marries, has a son, and confronts his father who abandoned him years earlier. Though not yet translated into English, Plessix's art remains a delight in these further albums. **TRL**

Sláine
The Horned God 1989

✎ Pat Mills ✎ Simon Bisley

First published by *2000 AD* (UK)
Creators Mills (British, b.1949); Bisley (British, b.1962)
Genre Fantasy
Influenced by Celtic myth

Sláine Mac Roth, a mighty warrior in the land of Tir Nan Og, has returned to be crowned king. Yet all is not well in the land of the young; the tribes of the Earth Goddess are threatened by the Formorians, a race of malevolent sea-demons, and the Drune Lords, a race of druids led by the evil Lord Weird Slough Feg. Sláine's best hope is to unite the tribes of the Earth Goddess by becoming the Horned God, the highest male deity in pagan lore, and husband of the Goddess herself. So begins Sláine's quest to find and unite the lost weapons of Atlantis, and in so doing claim the mantle of the Horned God. But herein lies danger; the tribes fear centralized power, as with it comes empire and dictatorship. Also, their deity cannot necessarily be trusted; as the Goddess herself says, "Sometimes I am your mother and hold you . . . Sometimes I am your sister and befriend you . . . Other times I am your lover who will stick one in your back."

Lavishly painted in full color by Simon Bisley, *The Horned God* was a groundbreaking comics work that significantly altered the form's landscape and inspired many artists working today. Drawing on his childhood exposure to Irish folk tales and Celtic myths, Mills weaves an intricate narrative that takes time in between battle scenes to explore the nature of Celtic society at the end of the last ice age and the relationship they had with a matriarchal god. It is not devoid of humor to go with its fantasy, either, particularly when it comes to flying boats or dragons. *The Horned God* feels very much like a genuine ancient myth. **BD**

Bisley's vertiginous artwork reinvents Britain's pagan past. ➡

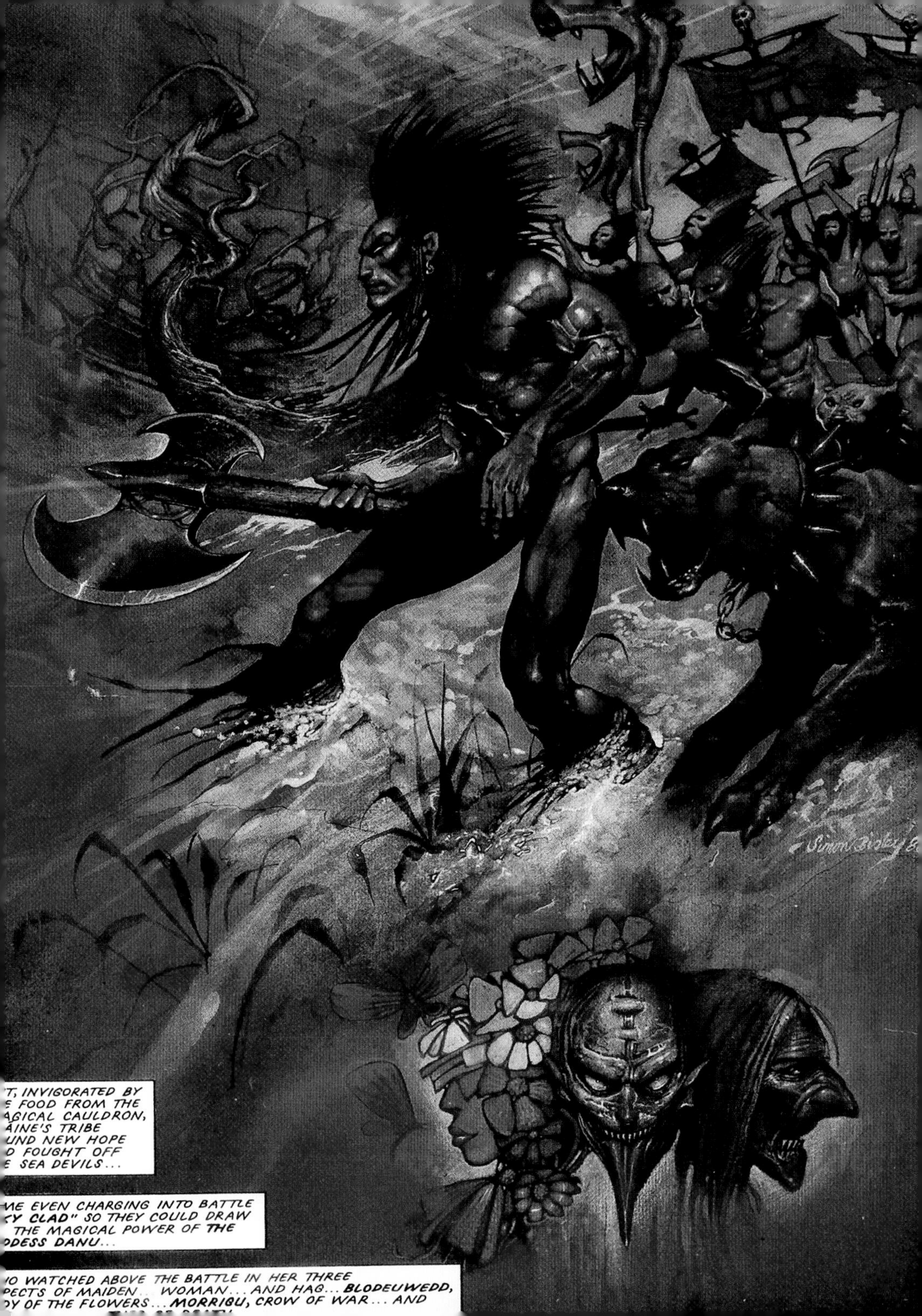
T, INVIGORATED BY
E FOOD FROM THE
AGICAL CAULDRON,
ÁINE'S TRIBE
UND NEW HOPE
D FOUGHT OFF
E SEA DEVILS...
ME EVEN CHARGING INTO BATTLE
KY CLAD" SO THEY COULD DRAW
THE MAGICAL POWER OF THE
DDESS DANU...
IO WATCHED ABOVE THE BATTLE IN HER THREE
PECTS OF MAIDEN... WOMAN... AND HAG... BLODEUWEDD,
DY OF THE FLOWERS... MORRIGU, CROW OF WAR... AND
Simon Bisley

Like a Velvet Glove Cast in Iron 1989

Daniel Clowes

First published by Fantagraphics Books (USA)
Creator American (b. 1961)
Genre Adult, Alternative
Influenced by *MAD Magazine*

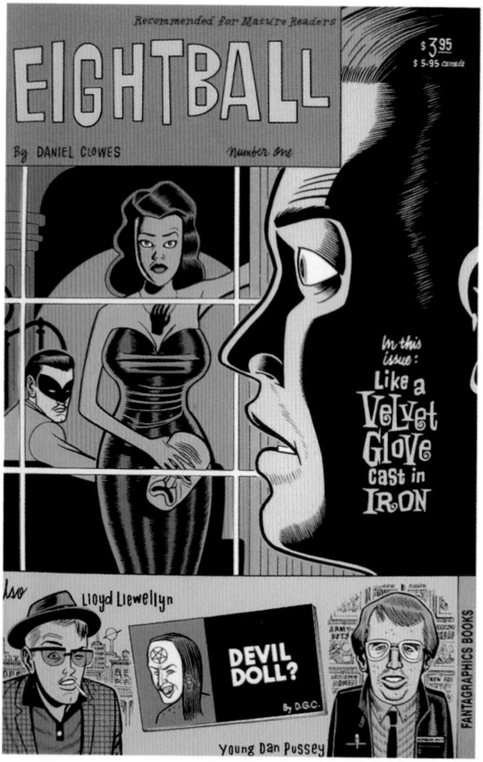
Recommended for Mature Readers
EIGHTBALL
$3.95
By DANIEL CLOWES
number one
In this issue: Like a Velvet Glove Cast in IRON
Lloyd Llewellyn
DEVIL DOLL?
By D.G.C.
Young Dan Pussey
FANTAGRAPHICS BOOKS

Similar reads
Black Hole Charles Burns
Ed the Happy Clown Chester Brown
Lloyd Llewellyn Daniel Clowes

Like a Velvet Glove Cast in Iron appeared in the first ten issues of Daniel Clowes's *Eightball*—one of the most important alternative comics of the 1990s. Compared with Clowes's previous work, *Lloyd Llewellyn*, *Like a Velvet Glove* introduced a dark and disturbing note that would come to characterize his style, although it is much more pronounced here than in his later, more realistic stories.

The comic opens with Clay Loudermilk—an unimpressive protagonist—visiting a pornographic cinema. He sees his estranged wife in one of the films and decides to find out more about its makers. Loudermilk is immediately drawn into a complex and surreal world of cults and conspiracies, psychopaths and freaks, fish-girls, and faceless dogs.

"This is incredible—I didn't know they made movies like this . . . these people are real sickos . . . "

The stylized, inky artwork and grotesque creepiness that pervades the book are somewhat similar to that employed by Charles Burns, but the weird, disjointed plot—with its dream sequences, flashbacks, and meta-textual narratives—and the dark and violent sexuality on display here are more reminiscent of the films of David Lynch and Luis Buñuel.

While there is much to surprise and amuse, *Like a Velvet Glove Cast in Iron* is very dark and very bleak. Clowes portrays a sinister and unintelligible world populated by a strange array of characters desperately trying to make sense of it all. The book is fascinating for its unique place in the work of one of comics most lauded creators, and is also an impressive, darkly surreal romp in its own right. *Like a Velvet Glove Cast in Iron* will take you to a disturbing place, but it may leave you, like Clay Loudermilk, feeling stranded and alone. **SB**

Batman
Arkham Asylum 1989

Grant Morrison Dave McKean

Batman: Arkham Asylum represents a culmination of the development of the superhero graphic novel. After the impact of *The Dark Knight Returns* and *Watchmen* in 1986, the book trade was hungry for new material of a similar quality. Comics publishers were keen to reinvent their flagship characters and market them to what was perceived as a more intellectually demanding audience. *Arkham Asylum* sits at the apex of this trend.

In the story Batman is forced to confront the possibility that, in his own way, he may be as deranged as the villains he has captured and sent upstate to the spooky confines of Arkham Asylum. But Morrison and McKean approach this relatively straightforward premise with blistering energy and intent, and—in the case of McKean's artwork—with a very real desire to upend the illustrational and narrative conventions of the superhero story and present an interplay of images that is closer to the formal language of fine art.

"The inmates seized control of the building early this morning. We don't know how it happened."

If the extraordinary result that is *Arkham Asylum* has shortcomings, then they lie in the almost too-complete success of McKean's artwork in sidestepping the conventions of narrative grammar. The entire book (and "album" feels like the only correct word) becomes a sequence of beautifully rendered tableaux to be savored for their technical invention more than to be read as narrative. But *Arkham Asylum* certainly succeeds as much as any graphic novel of its era in justifying its claims to be considered as art. And never has Batman, or his cast of villains here, including the Joker, Two-Face, Clayface, the Scarecrow, or Killer Croc, looked more frightening—or more seductive. **RR**

First published by DC Comics (USA)
Creators Morrison (British, b.1960); McKean (British, b.1963)
Genre Superhero

batman
aRKHAM aSYLUM
grant morrison
dave mckean

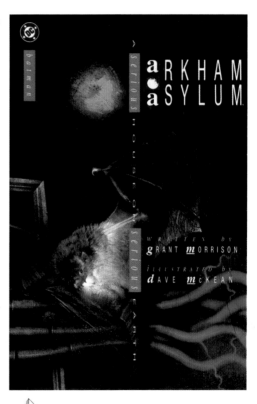

Similar reads
Animal Man Grant Morrison, Chas Truog, and Doug Hazlewood
Cages Dave McKean

Get a Life 1989

✏️ Charles Berberian and Philippe Dupuy

DUPUY ~ BERBERIAN

Monsieur Jean

Comme s'il en pleuvait

Les Humanoïdes Associés

"I wanted her to miss me, to feel miserable at the thought of me, alone in the night. I wanted her to find me and ask me to come back, so I could refuse."

Similar reads

Maybe Later Dupuy and Berberian
Mirror, Window Jessica Abel
Shortcomings Adrian Tomine

Title in original language *Monsieur Jean*
First published by Les Humanoïdes Associés (France)
Creators Berberian (French, b.1959); Dupuy (French, b.1960) **Genre** Romance

A four-handed drawing dynamo, the team of Philippe Dupuy and Charles Berberian are famous not just for the quality of their output but for the mysteries behind its production. They share all writing, penciling, and inking tasks, leading their readers to obsess endlessly over their working process: who did which drawing when? Since their first meeting in 1983, they have shared both a studio and a career, turning out innumerable elegant illustrations for a variety of clients. But their best-known creation is *Get a Life*, their long-running story of a young writer falling in and out of love.

First published in 1989 and collected in periodic volumes ever since, Monsieur Jean is, in so many ways, the quintessential Parisian. He goes to restaurants and parties with his close friends, the bossy Clément and charming Félix. He meets women, some of whom seem more alluring than others, and eventually, having found lasting romance, he decides to start a family. Influenced by great *ligne claire* (clear line) practitioners like Serge Clerc and Philippe Petit-Roulet, the series starts out with a clean, swooping line that becomes brushier and more vibrant as Jean's story progresses. Later installments are like visual jazz, especially when love leads Jean to New York City.

As part of a 1990s vanguard of introspective comics, Dupuy and Berberian played a crucial role in convincing French audiences that daily life was an important topic for cartooning. With the early years of this prize-winning series now available in English, *Get a Life* has found a new audience for his bittersweet ennui. **EL**

The Forever War 1989

🖊 Joe Haldeman 🖊 "Marvano"

First published by Dupuis (Belgium)
Creators Haldeman (American, b.1943);
Mark Van Oppen (Belgian, b.1953)
Genre Fantasy, Science fiction

As the United States continued a fruitless war in Vietnam, a war in which Joe Haldeman had fought, he wrote a bleak novel set in the future commenting on the dehumanizing effects of direct combat and how bureaucracy contrives to further life's complications. Highly acclaimed when published as a standard text novel, Haldeman adapted his own story for the graphic novel form as well.

William Mandella is conscripted, due to his high IQ and peak physical condition, to serve as part of a combat unit gathered to fight an alien race at that point unseen by any human. Traversing the great distances of space is feasible via black holes, but the toll for those using them is a diminished rate of aging in comparison to their friends and relatives at home. A reluctant soldier, Mandella's capacity for survival eventually floats him to high rank, and by then he is centuries old.

Marvano's thin-lined work here is astonishingly economical. His pages have a sparseness emphasizing isolation and the unknown, and a distancing effect necessary to the story. His handling of combat is subtle, and his people are created as individuals, even when used as cannon fodder. This is a Vietnam War allegory, but also a rumination on human nature. The vast timescales enable Haldeman to explore ideas of society, especially how population levels might be managed and how humanity might develop without sex.

This collaborative adaptation process appears to have been a satisfying experience for both parties—they've worked together several times since. **FP**

Berserk 1989

🖊🖊 Kentaro Miura

Title in original language *Beruseruku*
First published by Hakusensha (Japan)
Creators Japanese (b.1966)
Genre Adventure, Fantasy

First serialized in Hakusensha's *Young Animal* magazine, Kentaro Miura's tale of dark fantasy burst onto Japan's manga scene shortly after he received the young artist award at *Shonen Magazine*'s 34th Comic Awards.

Set in a historical era inspired by medieval Europe, the early stages of the plot are made up of fierce battles between Guts, the protagonist, and demon villains. These battles are mesmerizingly grotesque, and readers aren't given the slightest idea why Guts is facing demon hordes. Then, without any explanation, the story moves on to his reminiscences of his previous adventures with Griffith and Casca, fellow mercenaries in the "Band of the Hawk." This style, in which the story is told through a character's recollection, is not uncommon. But the fact that Miura allows the flashbacks to take over more than ten volumes of the series is truly extraordinary. During this period, the plot links the past, the present, and the future in a tangled chain of gripping events, slowly working toward the story's mysterious opening.

Kenshiro, the leading character in *Fist of the North Star*, is evidently the inspiration for Guts. Both wear their battle scars with pride, with Guts bearing "The Brand of Sacrifice" on his neck, and their respective tales each deal with themes of destruction and chaos. *Berserk* shares links with other manga series, too, particularly with the concept of naming its villains "God"—the enemies here are controlled by the evil God Hand, with Ryo Hanmura's sci-fi novel *Yoseiden* another possible key influence. For those who like their comics full of visceral action, *Berserk* is a very satisfying read. **RB**

5 1990−99

Paradise Town 1990

✐✐ Masahiro Nikaido

Title in original language *Gokuraku cho itchome*
First published by Asahi Sonorama (Japan)
Creator Japanese (b.1948)
Genre Humor

Love-hate relationships with more hate than love seem pretty universal as far as in-laws go. This type of relationship is all the more visible in a patriarchal culture with a strong sense of family and where the daughter-in-law is expected to care for the parents-in-law.

Paradise Town is a slapstick comedy about Noriko, who has been stuck with her old parent-in-law in the home for the elderly known as "paradise town." Noriko is tired of caring for her mother-in-law, who always stays in bed, bosses Noriko about, and hopes she will die soon. So Noriko decides to speed up matters by trying to kill her mother-in-law. Unfortunately for her, this is a comedy and the in-law outwits her every time. Even though she is lying in bed and coughing all the time, the mother-in-law can pull out great martial arts moves to protect herself and throw her daughter-in-law in the air. However, in the last panel of each short episode, everything returns to how it was originally, as if nothing has ever happened.

Paradise Town is filled with hilarity Bugs Bunny-style, which is accompanied by a subtle social commentary on tensions within a traditional family. Using simple drawing lines, each episode has the same structure of attack, defend, and return to normal, and moves in a fast staccato pace either in just four panels or one page at the longest. In the first half, the stories feature the mother-in-law, who happens to be a masterful martial artist, and the latter half deals with the father-in-law, who is simply supernatural. Push him over the cliff, he will fly home safely. **NK**

Give Me Liberty 1990

✐ Frank Miller   ✐ Dave Gibbons

First published by Dark Horse Comics (USA)
Creators Miller (American, b.1957);
Gibbons (English, b.1949)
Genre Science fiction

In a world forever besieged by conflict, the spirit of hope and freedom is embodied in a determined, willful, and brave African-American woman, who travels from the housing projects of Chicago into space and to the very center of existence. Through the epic renderings of Dave Gibbons, readers follow the story of Martha as she rises through the ranks of the PAX Peace Force, witnesses the extinction of the American Indian race, selflessly defends the dwindling Amazon rain forest, and allows herself to fall in love. Typically, Frank Miller's heroine is physically and mentally punished as she struggles toward her goal of liberty. Her loved ones die, she is incarcerated and hospitalized, and yet she continues to strive when all seems lost. With her close-cropped blond hair, heavy firepower, and earring bearing the logo of peace, Martha is a symbol of overcoming adversity as she battles her way out of poverty and tries to overcome a corrupt government.

The early issues are satirical and gleefully mock the media, warmongering, and the dominance of corporations such as Fat Boy Burgers that are depleting the Earth of its natural resources. Following *Give Me Liberty,* Miller and Gibbons continued their impassioned project, filling out Martha's inspiring life with several short stories, as well as *Martha Washington Saves the World* and 2009's *The Death of Martha Washington,* which are collected together in an epic 600-page edition. Miller and Gibbons have, for now, concluded their powerful and loving tribute to liberty, courage, and their indomitable female warrior. **SW**

Martha is brainwashed and renamed Margaret Snowden. ➡

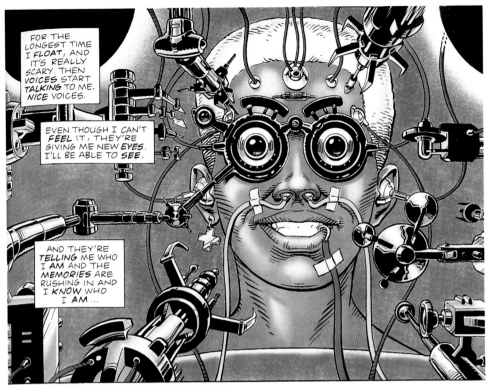

FOR THE LONGEST TIME I FLOAT, AND IT'S REALLY SCARY. THEN VOICES START TALKING TO ME. NICE VOICES.

EVEN THOUGH I CAN'T FEEL IT, THEY'RE GIVING ME NEW EYES. I'LL BE ABLE TO SEE.

AND THEY'RE TELLING ME WHO I AM AND THE MEMORIES ARE RUSHING IN AND I KNOW WHO I AM...

THE NEW PERSONALITY IS TAKING, SIR. SHE SEEMS TO WELCOME IT.

CONGRATULATIONS, SIR. I BELIEVE THIS IS A FIRST.

FIRST. ONLY USED ON ROBOTS BEFORE. COLLATE MILITARY SECRETS FROM WASHINGTON MEMORY. PREPARE SNOWDEN FOR DUTY.

Sanctuary 1990

✐ Sho Fumimura ✐ Ryoichi Ikegami

First published by Shogakukan (Japan)
Creators Yoshiyuki Okamura (Japanese, b.1947); Ikegami (Japanese, b.1936)
Genre Crime

Sanctuary is often accused of having a fascist agenda in its somewhat unlikely story of two refugees from Cambodia and their quest to politicize Japanese young people. However, it owes more to Ayn Rand's brand of libertarianism, in which the individual can make all the difference.

Having been caught up in Pol Pot's genocide, the two Japanese-born heroes seek shelter in their homeland but are horrified to find how apathetic and spineless the Japanese people have become. Asami, the more serious one, goes into politics, which is pretty much what you would expect for someone wanting to mend the political system. The other boy, the rather dashing Hojo, becomes a *yakuza*. The point is, of course, that the poles that lead to the top of their chosen professions are equally slippery, and both professions are violent, corrupt, and dangerous.

The joy of *Sanctuary* is watching as increasingly complex motivations and machinations are unveiled among the huge cast of characters. There is occasional explosive violence and extremely elegantly drawn sex, but most of the important sequences are talking heads, and the majority of the series is taken up with meetings, conversations, and arguments. Artist Ryoichi Ikegami has a way of making discussions seem very dynamic. His old men may be wrinkly, but, like Milo Manara, he could not draw an ugly young man or woman to save his life. He does a magnificent job of keeping readers gripped throughout Sho Fumimura's complex narrative twists and turns. **FJ**

Madman 1990

✐✐ Mike Allred ✐ Laura Allred

First published by Caliber Press (USA)
Creator American (Unknown)
Genre Superhero
Collection *Madman Gargantua* (2007)

Madman was Mike Allred's breakthrough title, a clever hipster superhero strip with its roots in the U.S. alternative tradition. Drawing on pop art, old science fiction serials, and his own weird sense of humor, Allred created a fantastic world of aliens, mad scientists, and beautiful girls. Initially drawn in black and white, the series went through various publishers and eventually became an alternative smash hit, rendered in dazzling color by star colorist Laura Allred.

Frank Einstein, the "Madman" of the title, is an accidental hero, a rough identity in a white costume that provides the stepping-off point for any number of strange stories. However, Allred's engaging art style and plotting took this anxious, amnesiac, reanimated hero and turned him into a very unique star. Motivated by love for his friends (a colorful supporting cast of romantic robots, mad scientists, and brightly colored aliens) and most of all for his girlfriend Joe, Frank is the kind of hero who inspires love. Over the years, different planets, mutant street beatniks, and attacking alien intelligences have vied with mundane concerns such as getting a job and staying focused, and each new challenge is viewed through the bright goggles of Frank's otherworldly innocence.

In a comic book world where superheroes were becoming darker and increasingly gritty, Allred's Frank stood out as a guy who was heading toward the light, seeking peace, trying to improve himself, and make the world a better place—expressed in blaring colors, expressive figurework, and quirky expressions. **JD**

Big Numbers 1990

Alan Moore   Bill Sienkiewicz

First published by *Mad Love* (UK)
Creators Moore (British, b.1953); Sienkiewicz (American, b.1958)
Genre Drama

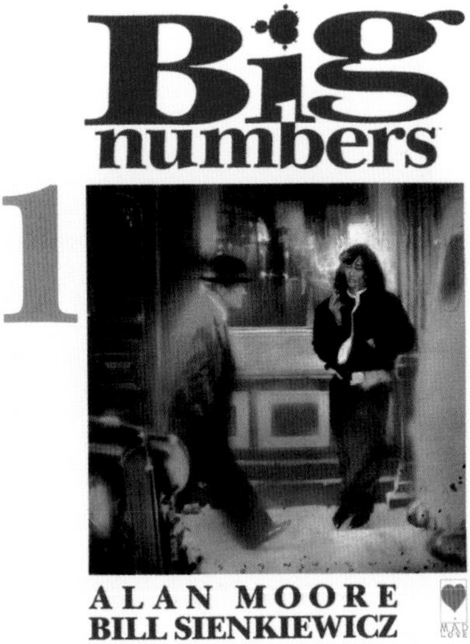
Big numbers
1
ALAN MOORE
BILL SIENKIEWICZ

Originally conceived as a 480-page graphic novel to be serialized in twelve chapters, *Big Numbers* united two of the most prominent comics creators of the 1980s for what promised to be a magnum opus. Alan Moore, at the time the most celebrated writer in comics, and Bill Sienkiewicz, coming off the career-defining success of *Elektra: Assassin,* combined forces to tell an unlikely story about fractal mathematics and U.S. investment in the British town of Hampton. Only two issues were published before Sienkiewicz opted out of the project, although a third, unfinished, chapter has circulated in samizdat form for many years.

The story revolves around writer Christine Gathercole returning to her family in Hampton after many years away. Here, she encounters a wide array of supporting characters, from tobacconists to patients and workers in a local psychiatric hospital. Looming over them all is the impending transformation of the town as a monumental new commercial building is slated for construction.

What was clear from the beginning was that each creator was pushing himself in new ways. Moore's story was intricately plotted, featuring dozens of characters whose lives would collide with each other over the course of the novel-length work. Sienkiewicz's art reached new heights, combining a strong sense of expressionism with photo-realist tendencies in luxurious gray tones and washes. This is the most important comic that never was, and the short fragment that remains is worth seeking out. **BB**

"Now, this sheet of paper's got length and width, but no thickness. So we say it's two dimensional, right? But a ball, on the other hand, that's got three dimensions. So, if we take our paper and we do this . . . "

Also by Bill Sienkiewicz
Elektra Assassin
Moby-Dick
Slow Dancer
Stray Toasters
The New Mutants

Peter Pan 1990

Régis Loisel

First published by Editions Vent d'Ouest (France)
Creator French (b.1951)
Genre Drama
Influence on *Lost Boys*

LOISEL
Peter Pan
Londres

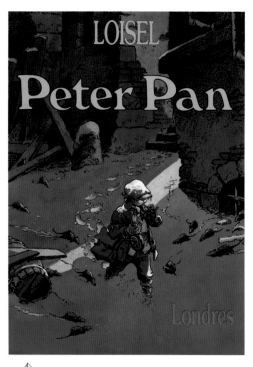

Similar reads
Father Christmas Raymond Briggs
Lost Girls Alan Moore and Melinda Gebbie
Peter Pank Max
The Lost Marc Andreyko and Galen Showman
Tintin: Breaking Free J. Daniels

Prior to this comic book series, Régis Loisel was best known for his fine art skills. It is no surprise then that his drawing is stunning, yet still improving throughout the series. When displaying how grim Victorian England could be, or positing that fantasy creations can be as appalling as humans, Loisel is dark and gruesome. However, he can illustrate happy and tender moments equally well. Never skimping on detail, Loisel's characters come alive and inhabit plausible locations.

As presented in J. M. Barrie's original novel, Peter Pan was a fully rounded and mischievous character. He ruled over the Lost Boys, ran wild in Neverland, and led a devil-may-care existence of perpetual youth, tormenting the other inhabitants of his island. Many writers have produced sequels to Barrie's work, but prequels are rare. "How did Peter develop?" is the questioned pondered by Loisel.

Over six albums he reveals his answer. Volume one ("London") has little of the cheer and light associated with Peter, because it is set in darkest Dickensian territory. Peter lives with an abusive alcoholic mother who dispatches her son at night to fetch her gin, unconcerned if he needs to sell himself in order to obtain it, and threatening to kill him should he return empty handed. Despite enduring an appalling existence, Peter still entertains a group of boys from the local orphanage.

Throughout the series, Loisel takes the randomly fused constituent parts of Barrie's world and provides logic and consistency. Where he is less likely to appeal to fans of the traditional story is by focusing on the darker elements, as if in response to decades of saccharine interpretations, and via the controversial introduction of a Victorian flavor previously unconnected to Peter Pan. **FP**

Road to America 1990

"Baru" and Jean-Marc Thévenet "Baru"

In the late 1950s, the young Saïd Boudiaf leaves Algeria, which is in the throes of terrorist attacks and civil war, for France, where he starts a brilliant boxing career. It seems that nothing can stop the new champion, who goes from victory to victory. Having become famous, Boudiaf is approached by representatives of the Algerian insurrection movement in Paris who ask him to pay the "revolutionary tax" demanded from all the "brothers" living in France. The boxer refuses. He is only interested in the sport, his career, and Sarah.

The insurgents put pressure on Boudiaf through Sarah, who is an active sympathizer with the Algerian independence movement, and the French authorities decide to exploit the champion's career by turning him into the symbol of an integrated Algeria. The obstinate boxer remains recalcitrant until the eve of the world championship. He is finally overcome by the events of October 17, 1961 in Paris, when the French police open fire on a peaceful protest by thousands of Algerians, killing dozens of people.

As in many of his books, Baru portrays a hero who comes from a humble background but is determined to do well in life. However, this human trajectory is only a structure that frames a much wider message, social and political in essence. Very familiar with the subject of immigration (Baru is himself the son of an Italian immigrant who spent his childhood and youth mixing with working-class North Africans, of whom there were many in France in the 1950s and 1960s), the artist asks the delicate question of allegiance with great subtlety. What is required for a person to feel that they belong to a social or cultural community? Can the heritage of one's own origins be ignored and given up? And can the personal equation of an individual take place outside of history? All these questions are still urgently topical. **NF**

Title in original language *Le Chemin de l'Amérique* **First published by** L'Echo des Savanes/Albin Michel (France) **Creators** Hervé Barulea (French, b.1947); Thévenet (French, b.1955) **Genre** Drama

BARU
JEAN-MARC THÉVENET · DANIEL LEDRAN
LE CHEMIN DE L'AMÉRIQUE
l'Echo des Savanes Albin Michel

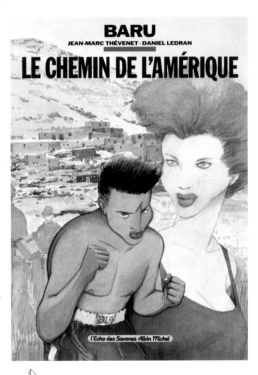

Also by Baru

Fais péter les basses, Bruno !
L'Autoroute du soleil
L'Enragé
Les Années Spoutnik
Quéquette Blues

Judge Dredd
America 1990

John Wagner Colin MacNeil

JOHN WAGNER
COLIN MACNEIL
JUDGE DREDD
IN
AMERICA
BOOKS

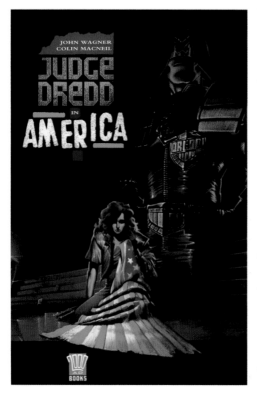

"Justice has a price. The price is freedom."

Similar reads

Judge Dredd: Total War John Wagner and Henry Flint
Savage: Taking Liberties Pat Mills and Charlie Adlard
The Last American John Wagner, Alan Grant, and Mike McMahon
V for Vendetta Alan Moore and David Lloyd

First published by Rebellion Developments (UK)
Creators Wagner (British, b.1949); MacNeil (British, b.1966)
Genre Science fiction

Written as an introduction into the world of *Judge Dredd* for new readers, "America" is one of the finest Dredd stories. Dredd himself barely features, relegated to the role of faceless figurehead of a brutal and uncaring police state. Instead, two would-be lovers take centerstage in a tragic tale of doomed romance.

A baby girl, born in Mega-City One to immigrants from the Puerto Rican Wastes, is named America in honor of the country that took them in. But this is not America anymore. As we follow her life through the eyes of her best friend and would-be lover Bennett Beeny, America Jara's beliefs in freedom and democracy set her on a collision course with the fascist dictatorship of the Judges. Beeny tries to live a good life within the system, but Jara becomes radicalized, eventually joining a prodemocracy terrorist group called "Total War." When Judge Dredd starts to investigate the group, Beeny must decide exactly where he stands.

John Wagner's *Judge Dredd* has always walked a thin line between dark satire and heroic adventure, yet here Wagner steps off the line altogether and makes Dredd a hate figure—a stark warning of what it is to live in a world where your life is not your own, where the police have absolute control. Fully painted by Colin MacNeil in neon hues, Mega-City One looks colorful but muted, as if the city itself is sick with fever.

There are thirty years' worth of *Judge Dredd* stories in existence, and many of them have been collected into books. For those who are looking for a place to start, there is no place better than here. **BD**

Baby Blues 1990

✐ Jerry Scott ✐ Rick Kirkman

First published by DC Comics (USA)
Creators Scott (American, b.1955); Kirkman (American, b.1953)
Genre Humor

With titles such as "Guess Who Didn't Take a Nap," "I Shouldn't Have to Scream More Than Once," and "Never a Dry Moment," it is not difficult to imagine the adult readers of this disturbingly true-to-life strip nodding their tired heads as they witness the latest parenting challenges Darryl and Wanda MacPherson face at the hands of their three children: Zoe, Hamish, and Wren.

Although humor abounds in the comic's panels, realism is never neglected in favor of slapstick and pratfalls. Wanda has breastfed all her children and has stayed at home with them at the expense of a career, choices that not only present a good role model but also, significantly, allow for more interplay between parent and child. When Wanda takes the children shopping, the supermarket announces that a cleanup is required in aisles one, two, three, four, five, "and most likely on aisle six." Darryl is asked to untangle several feet of dental floss and later is forced to ask Wanda to play catch with him because the children have better things to do. The pace of the strip is slower than real time by a ratio of about three to one, drawing out every tantrum, every meal time, and every diaper change—events that are funny enough, but a whole lot funnier if you happen to have kids.

Inspired by the birth of illustrator Rick Kirkman's second child, the creators of *Baby Blues* are mercifully quick to point out that none of the characters are based on any actual persons, although such anonymity can have a kicker: these adorable, mischievous children could be anyone's. They might even be yours. **BS**

The Last American 1990

✐ John Wagner and Alan Grant ✐ Mike McMahon

First published by Epic Comics (USA)
Creators Wagner (British, b.1949); Grant (British, b.1949); McMahon (British, b.1953)
Genre Science fiction

Set thirty years after nuclear Armageddon, *The Last American* charts the journey of Captain Ulysses S. Pilgrim through a postnuclear wasteland that was once the United States. Cryogenically frozen just before the war, his mission is to find survivors and restore law and order. As he travels the length and breadth of the country, accompanied by three army androids in a fruitless search for survivors, Pilgrim's sanity is pushed beyond breaking point as he comes to realize the truth: he may very well be the last man alive.

The Last American is a relentlessly pessimistic book, a cold and angry mirror to the logic of "mutually assured destruction," and it mixes the dark humor and insanity of Stanley Kubrick's *Dr. Strangelove or: How I Learned to Stop Worrying and Love the Bomb* (1964) with a macabre horror of a kind unique to the nuclear scenario. Mike McMahon's stylistic, almost cubist illustration at first seems at odds with the subject, but McMahon is a master of visual storytelling and uses his distinctive style to hammer home the surreal nature of nuclear war. Using muddy reds and dark grays (and apparently no ink brush), he effortlessly describes an alien landscape of human creation, hostile to all life. McMahon is often regarded as an illustrative genius, and *The Last American* may well be his greatest work.

Despite being written in the final year of the Cold War, *The Last American* is a strong reflection of the anxieties of that time, joining Mick Jackson's *Threads* and Raymond Briggs's *When the Wind Blows* as a stark warning to future generations. **BD**

Five Seasons: Autumn 1990

"Django" Igor Kordej

Title in original language *Les Cinq Saisons: Automne*
First published by Dargaud (France)
Creators Nenad Mikalački (Serbian, b.1978); Kordej (Croatian, b.1957) **Genre** Drama

HISTOIRES FANTASTIQUES
LES CINQ SAISONS
AUTOMNE
KORDEY
DJANGO
DARGAUD

Igor Kordej is a talented and highly prolific comics artist from Croatia. He started his career in the late 1970s as a member of New Panel, a group of artists who revitalized the local comics scene at the same time as Moebius, Philippe Druillet, and others from Les Humanoïdes Associés were changing the scene in France. Kordej's early works are fondly remembered by fans: *Metro*, *The Stranger*, *Stars*, *Vam* (based on the book by Vladimir Colin), *Have You Seen the Girls?* (based on the song by the Slovenian rock group Bulldozer), and others.

Five Seasons: Autumn is a unique and surprising graphic novel, magnificently drawn and painted by Kordej and written by Nenad Mikalački, alias "Django."

"The implementation of movie directing is an important characteristic of Kordej's comic narratives." **Svetozar Tomić, reviewer**

The story is complex, but the reader will not struggle to follow its many exciting layers, thanks to Kordej's ability to montage the pages and retain the clarity and dynamic of the story. The main character is Toulouse-Lautrec, the long-suffering French artist from the late nineteenth century, who has a bizarre connection with a long-suffering Japanese circus artist. Both are equally isolated, misunderstood, mocked, and physically disadvantaged. There is also a whole gallery of other characters, vividly brought to life by Django and Kordej, such as Toulouse-Lautrec's father, his servants, two students from Serbia and Croatia, and the local whores. These women sympathize to some extent with the diminutive artist, but this does not stop them from cheating him out of his money. This graphic novel remains one of the masterpieces of former Yugoslavian comics. **ZT**

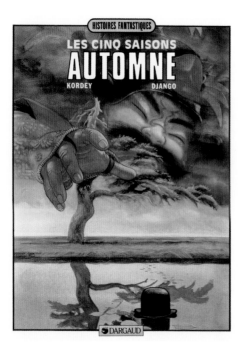

Also illustrated by Igor Kordej

New X-Men
Smoke
Tarzan: A Tale of Mugambi
Tarzan: Carson of Venus
The Secret History (*L'Histoire Secrète*)

Why I Hate Saturn 1990

Kyle Baker

Anne is a writer for *Daddy-O*, a magazine that is written for the type of hip New Yorker who would not be caught dead reading it. She spends much of her free time drinking and avoiding hard work. Her life makes sense until the day that her baby sister, Laura, arrives on her doorstep. Laura ushers chaos into Anne's life. She has been shot; she is being hunted by her ex-lover; and, by the way, she is the Queen of the Leather Astro-Girls of Saturn.

Tired of working on projects over which he had little control, Kyle Baker created this unusual work as a sort of comic book sitcom, a unique showcase for his razor-sharp wit. The dialogue is as pointed as anything you will find in films, zipping along as a series of barbed one-liners. However, *Why I Hate Saturn* is unusual among contemporary comics for its near total absence of word balloons. The dynamically rendered images sit atop dialogue in a way that harkens back to the earliest examples of the comics form, but the sensibility of the work is cutting-edge cool. The contrast between the antiquated form and the "of the moment" topicality lends the entire work a deeply ironic feeling that accentuates the alienated nature of the leads.

> *"I wrote* Why I Hate Saturn *at a time when comic books had stopped being fun for me."* **Kyle Baker**

Why I Hate Saturn is the story of a woman whose life is badly disrupted by forces beyond her control. As Anne spirals ever closer toward the chaos that surrounds her, the narrative itself takes on a gonzo tone. By the end, when rocket launchers are unleashed in the deserts of Arizona, readers may find themselves wondering just how they got here, but they will know that they have been on one hell of a ride. **BB**

First published by Piranha Press (USA)
Creator American (b.1965)
Genre Humor
Award Harvey Award (1991)

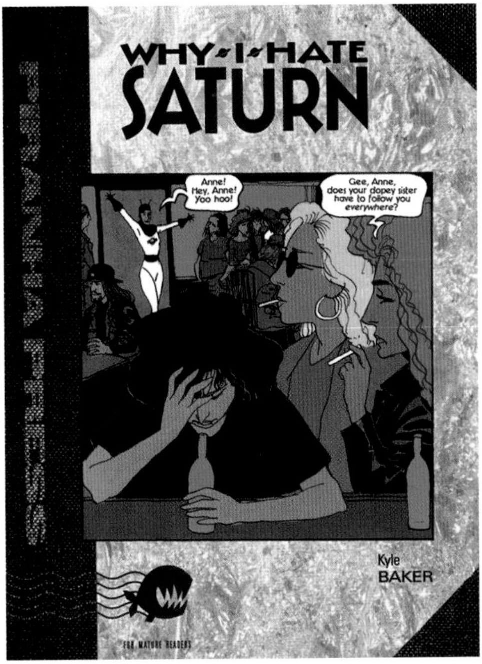
WHY I HATE SATURN
Anne! Hey, Anne! Yoo hoo!
Gee, Anne, does your dopey sister have to follow you everywhere?
Kyle BAKER

Also by Kyle Baker
Birth of a Nation: A Comic Novel
I Die at Midnight
The Cowboy Wally Show
Truth: Red, White and Black
You Are Here

Parasyte 1990

Hitoshi Iwaki

First published by Kodansha (Japan)
Creator Japanese (b.1960)
Genre Horror, Science fiction
Award Kodansha Manga Award (1993)

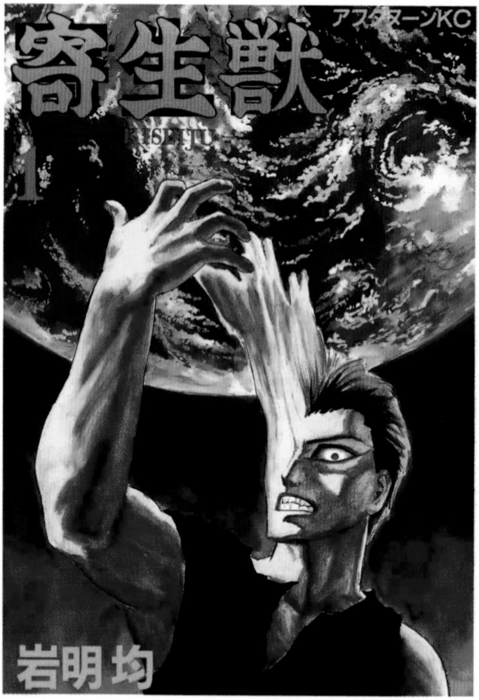
アフタヌーンKC
寄生獣
1
岩明均

Similar reads
Arms Ryoji Minagawa and Kyoichi Nanatsuki
Historie Hitoshi Iwaaki
Hone no Oto Hitoshi Iwaaki
Inugami Masaya Hokazono
Tanabata no Kuni Hitoshi Iwaaki

The term "parasite" commonly refers to a being that lives on another living being in order to get its nutrition, often harming its host in the process. In *Parasyte*, an unidentified, freely transforming species awakes on Earth and starts to possess humans. The creatures eat their host's brain and control the remaining body. Their biologically predefined command is simple and clear: eat the humans. For a small number of infected people, the new species did not manage to eat the brain. As a result, the protagonist, Shinichi, shares a body with the being that replaced his right hand, which calls itself Righty. Together they must find a way to survive the attacks of other infected humans and understand the meaning of their existence.

"Does a species not deserve to live if it is harmful to humans?"

Parasyte is overflowing with skeptical questions about humanity. It is not the new species but the humans who are the parasites . By being on top of the food chain, humans have destroyed nature in many ways. However, living beings still have the right to live, and the same applies to the newborn predator species. The distinctly barren artwork works well to carry out the inhuman looks of the infected people, and is all the more effective when depicting regular humans who are even more inhuman than the parasites. With dry dialogue and occasional narration, the author masterfully addresses many ironies of human existence, both in nature and in society.

Parasyte became an instant favorite with the critics and influenced a whole generation of dystopian science fiction thriller mangas with its bleak question on whether humanity is really worth surviving. **NK**

Largo Winch: The Heir & The W Group 1990

Jean Van Hamme Philippe Francq

The day-to-day running of a global conglomerate does not sound like the ideal topic for a comic. Backstabbing, political intrigue, and unfettered greed are, however, staples of many a classic drama, and *Largo Winch* began life as a series of novels written by Jean Van Hamme, based on his business school background.

A parallel career writing *bande dessinée* proved more lucrative, and *Largo Winch* fell by the wayside for a decade until Van Hamme began considering another title to complement his successful *Thorgal* and *XIII* series. When he began working on *Largo Winch*, artist Philippe Francq was relatively inexperienced, with fewer than five titles under his belt, but his accomplished storytelling and adaptability have defined Largo's world. Equally convincing at depicting boardroom conversations, rural

"The child of misery adopted by the richest businessman in the world."

scenes, and intimate moments, Francq's modified *ligne claire* style is easy on the eye and deceptively simple.

The Heir opens with the murder of ruthless businessman Nero Winch at the hands of an unidentified board member. The board discovers the company has been bequeathed to Nero's adopted son, Largo Wiczlav, a man Nerio had secretly groomed and who is currently languishing in a Turkish jail cell. A reluctant inheritor, Largo proves to be a natural at evading boardroom and real-life assassins, as Van Hamme and Francq turn out a page-turning thriller.

The template for the series was set with these initial volumes. In the first, a seemingly inescapable trap is sprung, leaving the adventurous Largo out on a limb before his skills pull him from the brink in the second. The stories are modified to excise all nudity for the more prudish English-speaking audience. **FP**

Title in original language *L'héritier & Le Groupe W*
First published by Dupuis (Belgium)
Creators Van Hamme (Belgian, b.1939); Francq (Belgian, b.1961) **Genre** Adventure

LARGO WINCH
PHILIPPE FRANCQ • JEAN VAN HAMME
L' HÉRITIER
REPERAGES
DUPUIS

Also by Jean Van Hamme
Corentin
Domino
S.O.S Bonheur
Thorgal
XIII

The Books of Magic 1990

Neil Gaiman John Bolton, Scott Hampton, Charles Vess, and Paul Johnson

First published by DC Comics (USA)
Creators Garman (British, b.1960); Bolton (British, b.1951); Hampton (American, b.1959); Vess (American, b.1951); Johnson (British, b.1958) **Genre** Fantasy

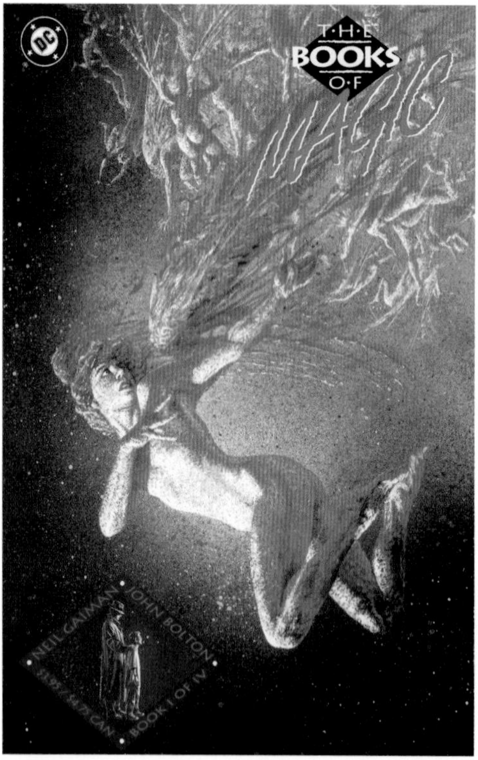
T·H·E
BOOKS
O·F
MAGIC
NEIL GAIMAN • JOHN BOLTON •
BOOK I OF IV

Also by Neil Gaiman
Black Orchid
Sandman
Violent Cases

Tim Hunter is an average bespectacled English boy, who actually has the potential to be the most powerful magician of his age. The whole magical world can feel his presence, but Hunter is as yet unaware of his importance. In an effort to steer his destiny, four magical figures from the DC Universe decide to give Hunter a tour of the magical realm so he can make a more informed choice and determine his own fate.

Divided into four distinct chapters (or books), Hunter is first shown the birth of the universe and is walked through a brief history of magic by the Phantom Stranger. He is then taken on a road trip of the magical side of the United States by occult conman John Constantine before being led by supernatural detective Doctor Occult to the realm of Faerie, and finally into the future with the sinister Mister E, to the end of time itself. Hunter learns many things, but above all he learns that magic is not free; everything has a price.

"In Faerie, there is only one time: Now. Twilight."

The Books of Magic is a very rich story, drawing as it does not only on the entire back catalog of magical characters from the DC Universe, but also on myriad myths and legends, closely following Joseph Campbell's *Hero's Journey* structure of storytelling. Each chapter is beautifully painted by a separate artist, each highly distinctive. John Bolton and Paul Johnson, who open and close the book, have a more chaotic style, ideal for witnessing the birth and death of the universe; the watercolor tones of Scott Hampton convey a more relaxed style for Hunter's U.S. road trip; and the serene illustrations of Charles Vess are perfect for the enchanted forests of Faerie. **BD**

Rogan Gosh 1990

Peter Milligan   Brendan McCarthy

Rogan Gosh first appeared in a colorful, trendy, and short-lived U.K. anthology *Revolver* in the early 1990s. Playfully named after a popular curry, this stylish and accessible experimental comic will appeal to those familiar with William Burroughs as well as to fans of the contortions of comic book continuity. It follows an elegant waiter in a cheap Indian restaurant and his surly, racist customer on a dizzying ride through bizarre, hallucinatory (and often hilarious) worlds, inspired by the vibrant excesses of cheap, mass-market comic books from India. Ambiguous, battling story lines race after a cast of colorful characters, headed by the eponymous Rogan Gosh, an Indian mystic superhero complete with sitar gun, holy cow, and extraordinary trainers.

"If I'm going to live an illusion I wish it to be my own illusion."

Peter Milligan's high-octane musings on life, death, and the nature of existence are explosively rendered by Brendan McCarthy as vivid, psychedelic gods, monsters, and weird, living environments. Dark intrusions of grimy reality expand the story with sudden shocks of emotional depth, but nothing interrupts the flow. Words and pictures swirl over each other in a seamlessly intense synthesis that seems more the work of one person than two. The story—short enough to read at a single sitting, yet crammed with enough fascinating detail to reward repeated readings—drifts associatively through a painterly and organic space where different cultures collide.

Revolver came at a point in time when color printing inside comics was as cheap and accurate as the covers, and McCarthy's artwork takes full advantage of this new freedom. In places, the color is so bright it leaps from the page. This masterpiece of the rave generation stays true to its roots: bright, brash, and entertaining. **JD**

First published by Fleetway (UK)
Creators Milligan (British, b.1962); McCarthy (British, b.1962)
Genre Alternative

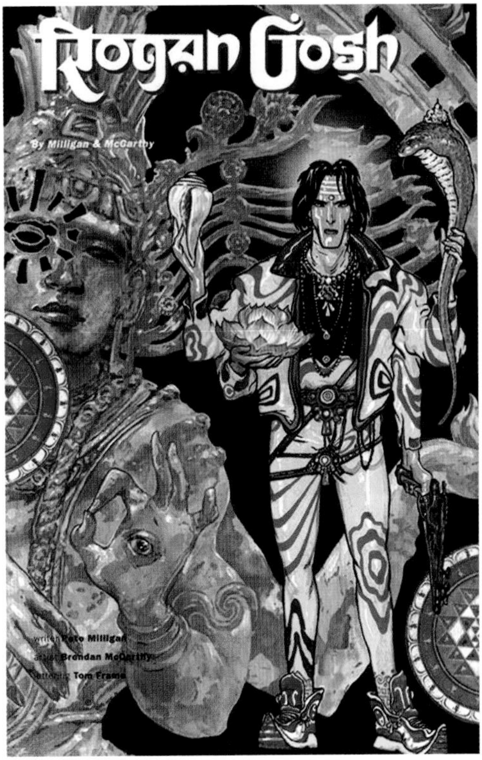
Rogan Gosh
By Milligan & McCarthy

Similar reads

Frank Jim Woodring
Really & Truly Grant Morrison and Rian Hughes
Vinanarama Grant Morrison and Philip Bond

Mauretania 1990

Chris Reynolds

First published by Penguin (UK)
Creator British (b.1960)
Genre Science fiction
Influenced by *Batman* (1940)

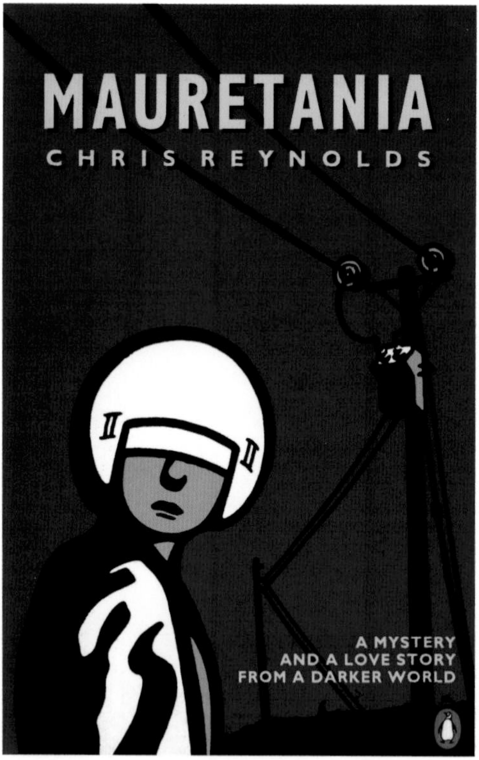
MAURETANIA
CHRIS REYNOLDS
A MYSTERY AND A LOVE STORY FROM A DARKER WORLD

Similar reads
Adventures from Mauretania Chris Reynolds
Silver Age Superman Ed Pinsent and Mark Robinson
The Dial and Other Stories Chris Reynolds

Susan finds herself unemployed when her company closes down. Unexpectedly, she is immediately hired by another firm, Reynal, but her new employer seems only interested in her old company. Susan finds out that Reynal is really a front for Rational Control, a "trendy new police force." Rational Control is interested in a young man called "Jimmy," whom they think is responsible for several other companies closing down.

Jimmy is a strange youngster who wears a helmet with the Roman numeral "II" written on the sides, and who seems compelled always to retrace his own steps. When Susan is sent to him under the pretense of seeking a job at his company, he tells her that he is indeed the cause of the closures, but that his actions are not arbitrary but involve "nodal points," which affect reality if certain things are done at the right time. Jimmy's office is raided by Rational Control in his absence, but then the local power plant mysteriously shuts down. Jimmy has ways to change the world.

"Chris Reynolds is preoccupied with notions of time and space allegory."

***Speakeasy* magazine**

Chris Reynolds has created a world gone strange, a quiet Earth almost devoid of people. The few who remain perpetuate everyday routines that seem devoid of meaning. Reynolds lets his story unfold at a slow and contemplative pace, never really explaining what is going on, merely hinting that certain causes have certain effects and leaving readers to ponder the mysteries of a universe suddenly grown immense.

At the end of the book, a couple of stories explain the relationship between Jimmy and Monitor, a character resembling him from the original, mostly self-published *Mauretania* comics. **J-PJ**

Frank 1990

Jim Woodring

Jim Woodring's *Frank* stories transport readers back to that place in childhood where anything can happen, where the things you read about in story books might or might not be real. Something about the shapes, the colors, and the choice of words combine to hypnotize a part of your adult brain and take you there.

Frank is Woodring's "everyanimal," a furry, four-legged thing with a mostly benign nature, wandering a phantasmagorical landscape full of random decorative objects and patterns. But Frank is not all nice and cuddly. He is subject to fits of panic and anger, which is not surprising because he has to protect himself and the other animals against the attacks of the Manhog and a creature called Whim.

"What we see is only a tiny fraction of what's to be had."

Jim Woodring

All the *Frank* stories are wordless, dreamlike adventures in which logic is suspended, and yet they all have a sense of inner cohesion. Woodring's style of drawing, with its soft and rounded forms and slightly fuzzy line, is reminiscent of early animation styles from the 1920s and 1930s, and shares that same sense of anarchic vision where one object can transform into another and seemingly harmless things turn out to be threats.

The stories feel right on an intuitive level. They speak to something inside readers and are equally revelatory and puzzling to both adults and children. Are they a representation of facets of human nature? Are they weird doodles the artist came up with late at night? Beautifully drawn and beautifully presented, every time you look at these stories you will draw a different conclusion. **FJ**

First published by Fantagraphics Books (USA)
Creator American (b.1952)
Genre Funny animal, Fantasy
Adaptation Short animated cartoons (2007)

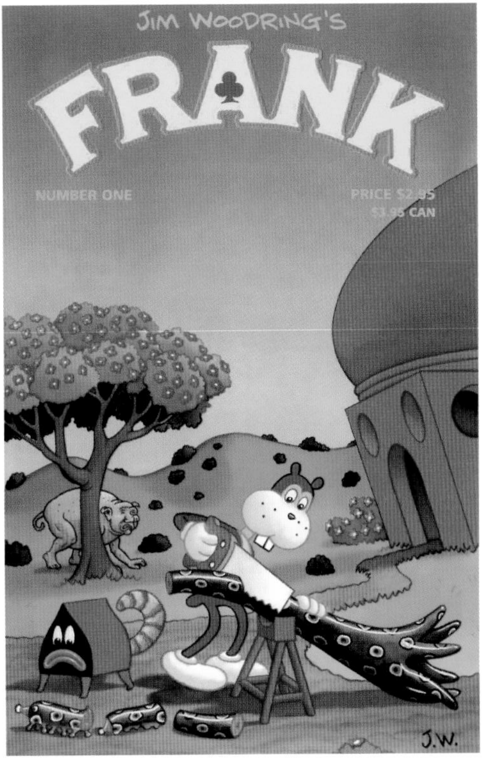
JIM WOODRING'S
FRANK
NUMBER ONE
PRICE $2.95
$3.95 CAN
J.W.

Similar reads
Jimbo in Purgatory Gary Panter
Krazy Kat George Herriman
Peter and the Wolf Miguelanxo Prado

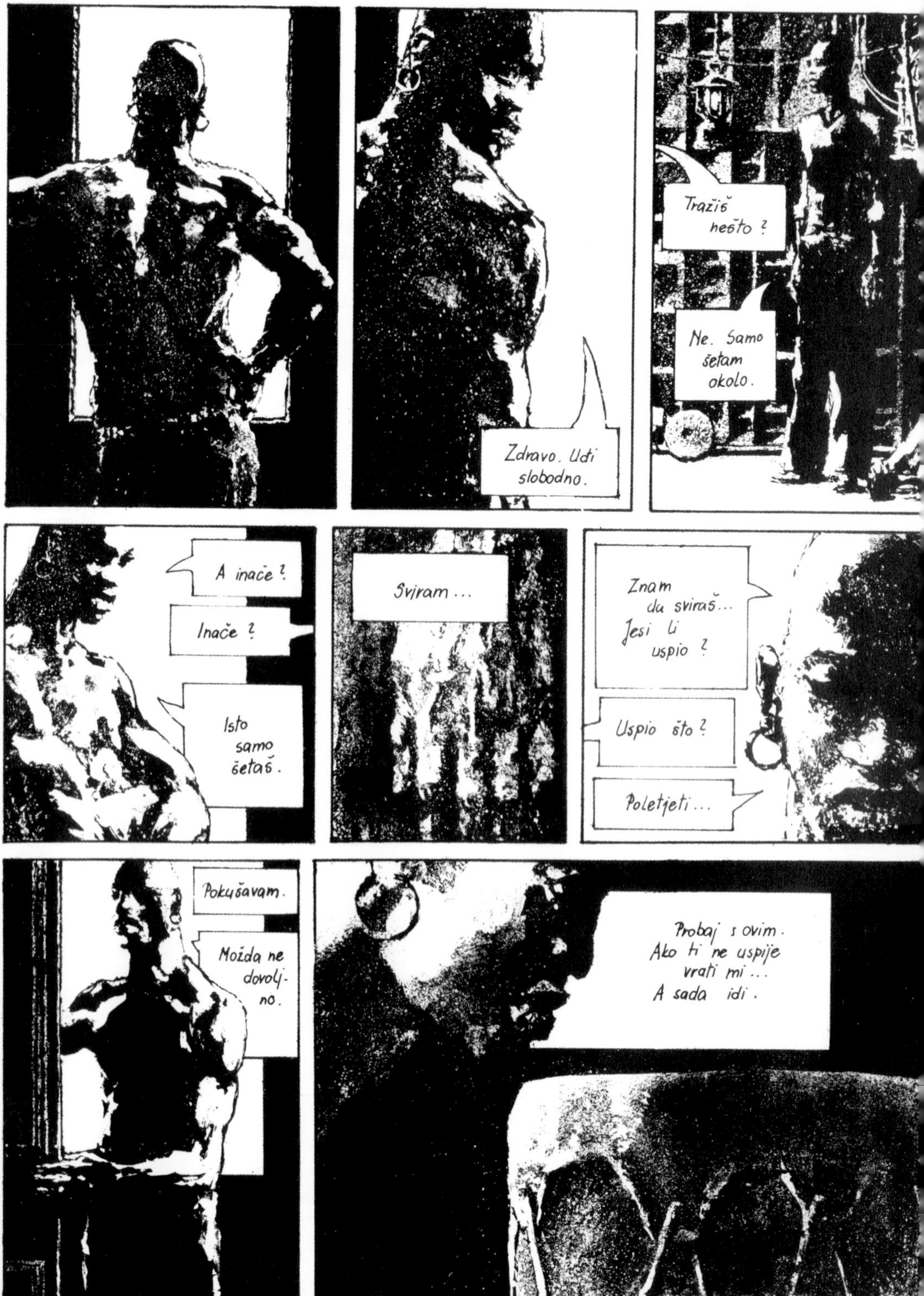
Zdravo. Uđi slobodno.
Tražiš nešto?
Ne. Samo šetam okolo.
A inače?
Inače?
Isto samo šetaš.
Sviram...
Znam da sviraš... Jesi li uspio?
Uspio što?
Poletjeti...
Pokušavam.
Možda ne dovolj-no.
Probaj s ovim. Ako ti ne uspije vrati mi... A sada idi.

Rhythm of the Heart 1990

✐✎ Danijel Žeželj

Title in original language *Ritam srca*
First published by Moria and Sky Comics (Croatia)
Creator Croatian (b.1966)
Genre Drama

Danijel Žeželj, who has both lived and published in Croatia and abroad, is a well-recognized artist. He acquired his domestic admirers in the late 1980s and later had fans around the world. His unsettling and unusual black-and-white panels, almost without words, are relatively static but reach inner meanings and feelings that stay with readers' memories forever. His unique approach to drawing and painting keeps him without real comparison in the contemporary Ninth Art.

Early in his career, Žeželj's work was very intellectual, almost hermetic, with more emphasis on metaphors than on storytelling. Later, and particularly in recent years, there is much more narrative in his graphic novels. His storytelling has improved, and his comic books that have always followed the "rhythm of the heart" are now following the "rhythm of the story," too.

Rhythm of the Heart is a good example of Žeželj's early work. His unique method, poetic and mythic at the same time, tells the sophisticated story of a black musician who is trying to express his dreams and memories through his music. This task is related to and compared with the effort of a young boy who is trying to draw pictures in the sand. These tasks will not bring success and happiness to either of the two characters.

This is a lyrical and intellectual graphic novel with metaphysical symbolism. It is developed by the use of a unique drawing style, panels carefully arranged on the page, and a flowing narrative, very slow in pace but filled with heady emotions. **ZT**

Even a Monkey Can Draw Manga 1990

✐ Kentaro Takekuma and Koji Aihara   ✎ Koji Aihara

Title in original language *Saru demo kakeru manga kyoushitsu* **First published by** Shogakukan (Japan)
Creators Takekuma (Japanese, b.1960);
Aihara (Japanese, b.1963) **Genre** Comedy

In order to truly enjoy this book, readers probably need to know some manga in advance and be able to handle a bit of nudity, sexual expression, and toilet humor. However, for adult lovers of manga, this is a painfully funny parody of other "How to Draw Manga" textbooks.

The story is about Kentaro Takekuma and Koji Aihara, the authors themselves, learning to draw manga chapter by chapter in their quest to become bestsellers. While sharing their recipes for success, with hilarious examples told in a slapstick jokey tone, they reveal a surprising number of bare truths, especially about the manga industry's formulae.

Their first important lesson is how to come up with a good pen name, because Japanese manga artists often adopt a distinctive pen-name that sometimes contains hidden meanings or wordplays. In the chapters, that follow, Takekuma and Aihara explain such basic techniques as drawing panel borders, facial expressions, and human figures, but in a unique, satirical way. They go on to describe the plot elements of hit manga from different genres, accompanied by their bizarre analyses. For example, they compare *shonen*, or boy's manga, to a shish kebab, the meatballs on a skewer representing one battle after another. "Everyday is a battle!" is the best way to make boy's manga. Their overengineered struggles with the creative process are brilliantly funny, and their how-to-draw steps expose a slew of manga taboos, derived from their critical view of the clichés in Japanese comics. **AT-L**

← Moody, oppressive artwork dominates Žeželj's haunting story.

Love That Bunch 1990

Aline Kominsky-Crumb

First published by Fantagraphics Books (USA)
Creator Aline Goldsmith (American, b.1948)
Genre Autobiography
Influenced by R. Crumb

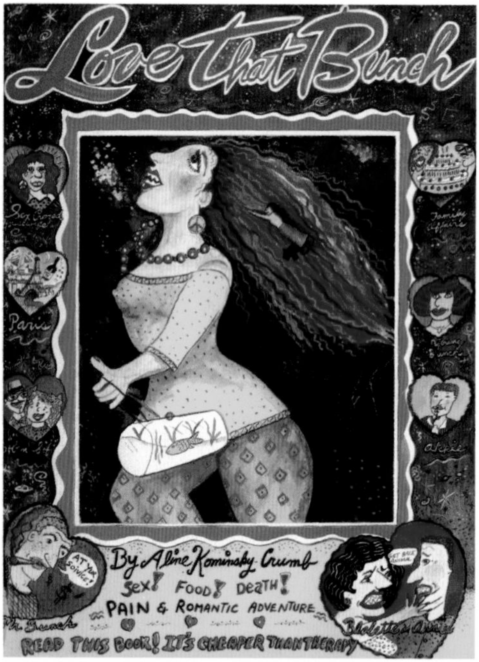
Love That Bunch
By Aline Kominsky Crumb
Sex! Food! Death!
PAIN & ROMANTIC ADVENTURE
READ THIS BOOK! IT'S CHEAPER THAN THERAPY

Similar reads
Make Me a Woman Vanessa Davis
Need More Love: A Graphic Memoir Aline Kominsky-Crumb
The Complete Dirty Laundry Comics Aline Kominsky-Crumb, R. Crumb, and Sophie Crumb
Twisted Sisters Diane Noomin (ed.)

Aline Kominsky-Crumb's wild stories starring the Bunch, her wayward and winsome alter ego, first appeared in girls-only anthologies such as *Wimmen's Comix* and *Twisted Sisters* in the 1970s and 1980s. Inspired by countercultural cartoonists such as Kominsky-Crumb's life partner, R. Crumb, Kominsky-Crumb and her contemporaries valued stories that spoke about women's real experiences—however shocking the results may have been.

Beginning before the birth of the Bunch, this autobiographical collection follows the eponymous heroine through her upbringing in a suburb gone mad with consumerism. Seeking fulfillment in sex, drugs, and rock 'n' roll (but primarily the former), the Bunch ends up in a series of outré situations: losing her virginity to a teenage rapist, cheating on her husband because she is sure he is going to cheat on her, and playing groupie tourist in New York City, among other escapades. However, the Bunch also has a gentler side. Readers can follow the teenaged Bunch during her internment in a militaristic summer camp, watch as she accompanies her now-widowed mother on her rounds as an advertising salesperson, and listen in as she drives her daughter around, all the while dreaming of a sadomasochistic encounter with a bank teller (nothing much changes in BunchWorld).

Kominsky-Crumb's ear for dialogue knows no equal, and the various characters—her mother Blabette, father Arnie, and the Noodle (her nickname for R. Crumb)—each clamor for the readers' attention, but none with more charm than the Bunch herself. Kominsky-Crumb's art may appear awkward and naive—and she may frequently complain about not being able to draw—but do not be fooled. Influences from the German expressionists to the cubists and beyond can be seen in her intensely detailed panels. **EL**

Quimby the Mouse 1990

✏️🖋️ Chris Ware

In his 1990 *Acme Novelty Datebook, Volume One*, Chris Ware described his project *Quimby the Mouse* as "a somber/subtle silent cartoon with the staccato medium of the comic strip." A few years after discovering the magazine *RAW*, he had decided to contribute in his own way to the revival of an art form to which he was already devoting most of his creative energy. His experimentation with the comic strip format enabled him to push back the boundaries of the comic strip beyond every convention of the genre. In his opinion, only by experimentation could he, as the illustrator/narrator, rediscover the purity of approach necessary to mold his art around content that was deeply important to him.

Ware's symbolic choice of a mouse (Quimby) and a cat's head (Sparky) is an intergenerational tribute to a long line of murine and feline characters, including Mickey Mouse, Krazy Kat, and Felix the Cat, not to mention the unforgettable Maus. The minimalist stories concerning Quimby are set in a quirky version of everyday life, full of nonsense, irony, malaise, and melancholy. The tales meander through all kinds of mental brooding, which can be irritating in its constant repetition but useful in ridding the reader of troubling sensations and emotions. Striking constants in these comic strips include the generally identical formatting of the frames, their small size, and their hallucinatory appearance. Beyond these extraordinary narrative expedients, the layout of the pages can almost appear to be an afterthought.

The endless stream of minuscule drawings closely reflects the inner world of childhood and memory. Allusions to an "idealized" house in the country lend an autobiographical character to *Quimby*. In the same way, the disturbing two-headed mouse evokes an inconsolable sense of loss of a loved one. **JS**

First published by Fantagraphics Books (USA)
Creator Franklin Christenson Ware (American, b.1967)
Genre Humor
Influenced by *Peanuts*

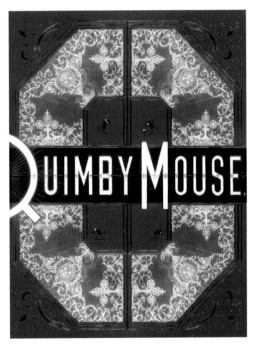

Also by Chris Ware
Is That All There Is? with Joost Swarte
Jimmy Corrigan, the Smartest Kid on Earth
Lonely Comics and Stories
Rusty Brown
The Acme Novelty Library: Building Stories

Battle Angel Alita
Rusty Angel 1990

Yukito Kishiro

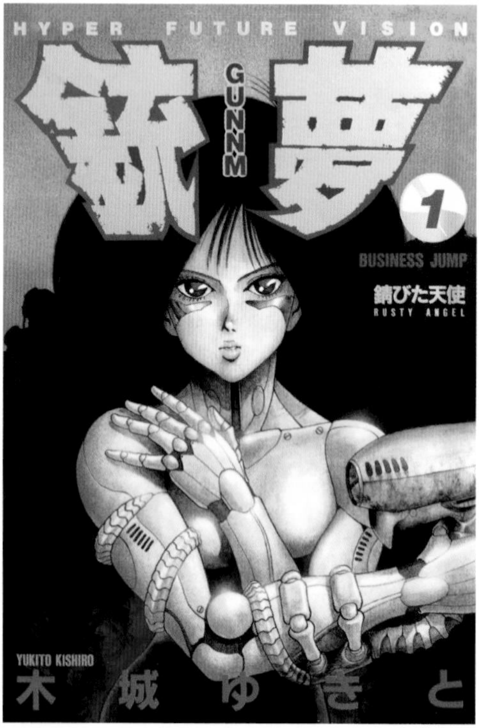
HYPER FUTURE VISION
銃夢
GUNNM
1
BUSINESS JUMP
錆びた天使
RUSTY ANGEL
YUKITO KISHIRO
木城ゆきと

"What are you calling 'scraps?' Can't you see, Gonzu? She's a genuine human being!"

Similar reads

Appleseed Masamune Shirow
Ashen Victor Yukito Kishiro
Berserk Kantaro Miura
Oblivion Joseph Kosinski
Tanpenshu Hiroki Endo

Title in original language *Gunnm*
First published by Shueisha (Japan)
Creator Japanese (b.1967)
Genre Science fiction

In a brutal and technologically dependent futuristic world, a cybernetics doctor named Daisuke Ido discovers the remnants of a cyborg in a scrap heap. He gives the cyborg a body, life, and a name: Alita. At first, Alita has no memory of her previous life, and Daisuke tries to mold her into a happy and carefree young girl. However, when the doctor is threatened, Alita's past and true calling as a hunter-warrior come to the surface.

Battle Angel Alita is a thoughtful and action-packed saga, and Yukito Kishiro balances the action sequences between graphic and gory violence (a brain-eating cyborg monster is a particularly vivid creation) and the angelic grace of Alita. She glides through maelstroms of mechanics, blood, and oil, and through panels filled with motion and disorienting angles. The art and story is fast, unpredictable, and alive with the threat of real danger, as seen when Alita is horrifically ripped apart.

The world is a gray, oppressive one where power belongs to the most technologically advanced. Despite this bleakness, there are flashes of tenderness and beauty, such as in Alita's love for her creator/father Daisuke and in her gentle features. The juxtaposition between the mechanical and the human is the central theme running throughout the artwork and the narrative. In pages filled with metal piping and machines, individuals appear in danger of being overwhelmed, making it all the more important that humankind—and what it means to be human—survives. Despite the science fiction trappings, this is a story of a girl growing up and trying to figure out her purpose. **SW**

Shade the Changing Man 1990

✎ Peter Milligan   ✎ Chris Bachalo

First published by DC Comics (USA)
Creators Milligan (British, b.1962);
Bachalo (American, b.1965)
Genre Drama

Peter Milligan is one of the most wildly inventive writers to work in mainstream comics, although his creativity comes with a caveat. Let him create his own series or reinvent an existing title and he is likely to be thought-provoking, entertaining, erudite, and witty. Shoehorn him into the rigid continuity of long-established characters and plot constraints and it is as if he has been put in a straitjacket.

Thankfully, *Shade the Changing Man* is a title that Milligan adapted from Steve Ditko's equally eccentric 1970s series. He discarded everything except the idea of an other-dimensional alien adjusting to Earth and a reality distorting accoutrement, here called the Madness vest. Chris Bachalo's excellent art confidently depicts Milligan's vivid imaginings. However, *Shade the Changing Man* is only consistently good from issue #33. The starting premise of Shade occupying the body of the man who murdered Kathy George's parents prompted an unlikely relationship, and his bond with the louche Lenny is fleshed out. From that point onward, Milligan produces a writhing and distinctly uncomfortable character study, with others thrown in to complicate matters.

There is an ending to the story in issue #50, after which Bachalo departs. However, Milligan was persuaded to continue writing, despite his initial reluctance. His scripts remain high quality and, at first, they are allocated to strong artists (Sean Phillips, Mark Buckingham). Despite a dispiriting finale, it is worth struggling through for the closure. **FP**

Crayon Shin-chan 1990

✎✎ Yoshito Usui

First published by Futabasha (Japan)
Creator Japanese (1958–2009)
Genre Comedy
Adaptation TV anime (1992)

Crayon Shin-chan is one of Japan's most popular comics of all time, alongside *Sazae-san*, *Chibi maruko-chan*, and *Doraemon*. The gag comic centers on the everyday lives of Shinnosuke (nicknamed Shin-chan) and his family, who live in a suburban neighborhood in Kasukabe near Tokyo. Shin-chan is a troublemaking five-year-old who drools over beautiful women and glamourous models, and embarrasses adults with his bizarre actions. Being an unpredictable character, however, he can suddenly act ten times his age, hilariously showing incredible calmness and maturity much to the surprise of the adults around him.

Shin-chan's signature "moves," such as revealing his naked bottom and flashing his private parts, are certainly blushworthy, and whether the comic is appropriate for children has been questioned. Indeed, *Crayon Shin-chan* was serialized originally in *Weekly Manga Action*, a magazine for adults that had previously published titles such as *Kozure Ookami*, *Dosei jidai*, and *Lupin III*. Nevertheless, when the comic hit the small screen as an animation series in 1992, it became overwhelmingly popular with children. Although Shin-chan's outrageous nature was toned down for television, the Japanese PTA once voted *Crayon Shin-chan* the least favorable comic for children to read. However, the undeniable truth is that whether it is a bad influence or not, it is exactly the kind of comic that appeals to children. After the sudden death of Yoshito Usui in 2009, the production of the comic was handed down to members of the author's team. **TS**

Bone 1991

Jeff Smith

First published by Cartoon Books (USA)
Creator American (b.1960)
Genre Fantasy, Comedy
Award Eisner Award (1993)

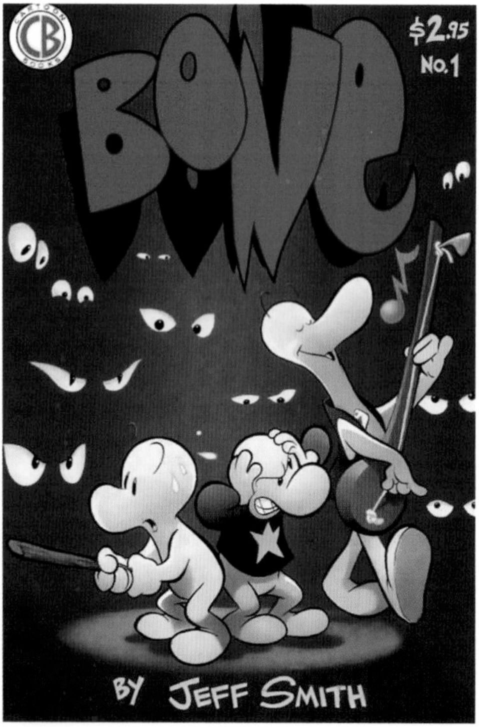

CARTOON BOOKS
CB
BONE
$2.95
No.1
BY JEFF SMITH

Similar reads
Bone Prequel Jeff Smith
Pogo Walt Kelly
RASL Jeff Smith
The Far Side Gary Larson

Jeff Smith began drawing characters for what one day would be called *Bone* when he was still in kindergarten. At the age of nine, he was captivated by Walt Kelly's *Pogo* comic strip, and his drawings soon reflected the *Pogo* style. By age ten, he was writing and drawing his own *Bone* adventures, which he called "Fone Bone—costarring Phoney Bone," and his first black-and-white, self-published issue appeared in 1991. Thirteen years and fifty-five sporadically produced issues later, Smith's epic adventures of goofy Smiley, idealistic Fone, and the greedy Phoney have won ten Eisner Awards and been lauded by *TIME* magazine's comic columnist Andrew Arnold as "the best all-ages graphic novel yet published."

"As sweeping as the Lord of the Rings."

***TIME* magazine**

Smiley, Fone, and Phoncible are cousins who live in the fictional town of Boneville, which the reader never sees. The first issue begins with them suddenly homeless after being run out of town. With nowhere to go, no water, and an unreliable map that "looks like it's been drawn by a five year old," they argue their way across an unforgiving desert, survive a swarm of locusts, and eventually enter a mysterious valley where they encounter ratlike creatures, a friendly farm girl named Thorn, talking possums, and the unseen, malevolent presence of the Lord of the Locusts. The Bones are now at the center of a climactic struggle between good and evil.

Their often comic escapades occur amid fantastical landscapes, and the vast array of creatures that call the valley home imbues *Bone* with a *Lord of the Rings*–type grandeur—with some liberal doses of humor. It is an undoubted triumph. **BS**

Gon 1991

Masashi Tanaka

In *Gon Eats and Sleeps*, the first Gon story published, a small, squat dinosaur of indeterminate type intimidates a grizzly bear by head-butting it, eating its hard-won catch of fish, and using it for a bed. All of this is depicted without dialogue, narration, or sound effects. In *Gon Goes Flying*, Gon is living in a nest with young golden eagles, sharing the fish their mother brings and protecting them from a predatory bobcat. In *Gon Glares*, set in Australia, Gon defends all sorts of animals, including koalas and kangaroos, from a dingo trying to feed her two cubs.

Each adventure features Gon in a different setting with different animal costars. There is no particular logic to this. Gon is as at home in Australia as he is living with penguins, facing piranha, or roaming the African savannah. Gon has adventures underwater (under a tortoise shell), underground (where there are lots of insects and a giant spider), in the desert, and climbing a snow-covered mountain.

> *"Manga should be without grammar."*
>
> **Masashi Tanaka**

Masashi Tanaka's artwork is heavily textured in black and white with a photo-realistic approach to the animals and their surroundings. Despite this accuracy in their depiction, Tanaka still manages to anthropomorphize each animal without destroying the illusion of realism. There are exaggerations of expression (in what might be called a typical manga style), but they are fully in context and serve the humor of the strip. In later stories Tanaka develops a looser inking style, which gives the work a more cartoony effect. *Gon* is witty and funny and leaves behind a sense of justice served, the cute and cuddly protected from the worst that nature has to throw at them. **NFI**

First published by Kodansha (Japan)
Creator Japanese (b.1962)
Genre Funny animal, Adventure
Influence on *Age of Reptiles*

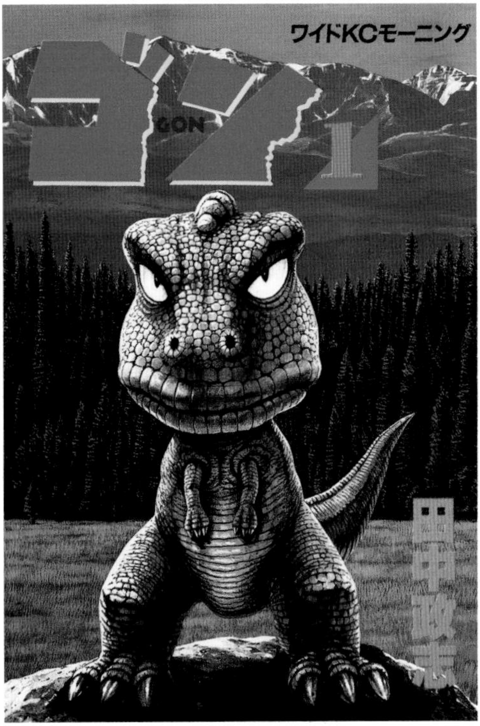
ワイドKCモーニング
GON

Similar reads

A.L.I.E.E.E.N Lewis Trondheim
Frank Jim Woodring
Louis Metaphrog (John Chalmers and Sandra Marrs)
Unidentified Prince Object U.P.O. Tanaka Masashi

Lost Girls 1991

Alan Moore Melinda Gebbie

First published by *Taboo* (USA)
Creators Moore (British, b.1953); Gebbie (American, Unknown)
Genre Erotic

LOST
ALAN MOORE
MELINDA GEBBIE
GIRLS

Similar reads
A Disease of Language Alan Moore and Eddie Campbell
From Hell Alan Moore and Eddie Campbell
Promethea Alan Moore and J. H. Williams III
Small Favors Colleen Coover
Watchmen Alan Moore and Dave Gibbons

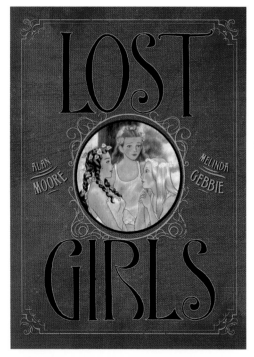

In a hotel in Austria, shortly before World War I, three women meet. They have one trait in common: each had something extraordinary happen to her on the onset of puberty. One is Alice, from *Alice in Wonderland*, now an aging lady still talking to the little girl she used to be, left forever young behind the looking glass. The second is Wendy, from *Peter Pan*, grown up and married to a dull businessman whose only interest is his job. The third is young Dorothy, fresh from Kansas and *The Wizard of Oz*. After a chance meeting, the three start telling each other their respective tales, which turn out to be quite different from the ones in the books. Here, the only magic is sex, with all its liberating, intoxicating, and sometimes threatening power.

"Pornographies are the enchanted parklands where the most secret of all our many selves can safely play."

The tales are interspersed by sexual escapades between the main characters, who slowly come to realize that their childhood experiences were positive and empowering. However, when the war breaks out, the hotel has to be evacuated, and the fragile erotic utopia is swept away by violence and death.

Lost Girls is a highly literary work, being a re-reading of children's fairy tales in the style of the classic erotica of the nineteenth and early twentieth centuries. It is also a collection of graphic pastiches of some of the genre's great illustrators of that period. Alan Moore and Melinda Gebbie extol the power of sex to make human beings more aware of who they are and what they want from life, without being naive about the possible dangers of giving in to one's unchecked desires. Nevertheless, they come out squarely on the side of making love, not war. **J-PJ**

I Never Liked You 1991

Chester Brown

It is common knowledge that many writers start their careers by writing about their past. Among many autobiographical cartoonists working in the early 1990s, a trio in Toronto gained some prominence: Seth, Joe Matt, and Chester Brown. The latter started producing autobiographical comics with the short story "Helder," published in his comic book *Yummy Fur*. Previously, he had written an absurdist horror series under the title "Ed the Happy Clown" and a highly unorthodox adaptation of the Bible. Chester Brown's autobiographical graphic novel *The Playboy* was serialized in *Yummy Fur*. *I Never Liked You*, also published in *Yummy Fur* before being collected as a graphic novel, is a sequel of sorts to *The Playboy*.

"The stuff people are reluctant to talk about is often the stuff that's most important, I think."

In *The Playboy* and *I Never Liked You*, Chester Brown tells the story of his childhood, focusing on himself as a teenager. The former book is about the shame that young Chester felt because he was obsessed with *Playboy* magazine. His strict religious education engendered this sense of guilt. *I Never Liked You* is a coming of age story that recounts Brown's inability to get on with girls, being bullied, and, most importantly, his relationship with his schizophrenic mother. It is also about repressing language (he was not allowed to swear because of his upbringing) and, consequently, repressing one's feelings (he never seemed to be able to put them into words). Brown portrays his young self in a hieratic, detached way. The glasses, without the eyes, help to convey his quasi-autism. Chester Brown cites his role model as Harold Gray, of *Little Orphan Annie* fame. **ID**

First published by Drawn & Quarterly (Canada)
Creator Canadian (b.1960)
Genre Autobiography
Award Harvey Award (1990)

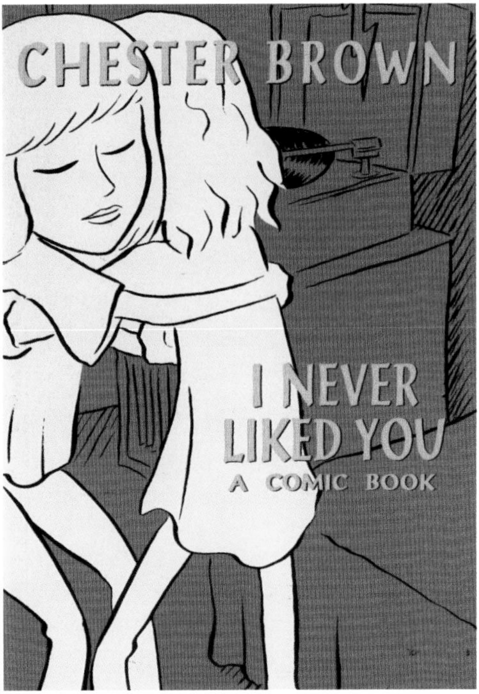
CHESTER BROWN
I NEVER LIKED YOU
A COMIC BOOK

Also by Chester Brown

Ed the Happy Clown
Louis Riel
Paying For It
The Little Man
The Playboy

The Walking Man 1991

✏️ Jiro Taniguchi

Title in original language *Aruko Hito*
First published by *Morning Party* (Japan)
Creator Japanese (b.1947)
Genre Reality drama

These are stories about almost nothing, of disarming simplicity and absolute clarity. In modern Japan at the very end of the twentieth century, a man wanders haphazardly on foot through the streets whenever he has the time—day and night—with no other reason than to enjoy each moment with all his senses and to savor the indescribable luxury of watching life go by. On the surface, nothing or very little happens. However, everything depends on one's point of view or state of mind. For this man, the rustling of the branches of a cherry tree, the sight of a starlit sky, the company of a young dog, or the feeling of water on his skin all become precious moments, experiences of life to cherish like special gifts.

When Jiro Taniguchi began writing *The Walking Man*, his humanist approach and receptiveness to themes linked to nature had already been seen in several of his earlier works, which included adventure stories such as *Blanco the Dog* or sport-inspired ones such as *K*. But never before had he abandoned himself to the peaceful, contemplative hedonism that pervades the stories of *The Walking Man*. In absolute contrast to the excesses and effects of action strip cartoons, with *The Walking Man* he invented the concept of a serene manga, more or less motionless.

Welcomed as a revelation by readers, the book was a turning point in the work of its artist. Since then Taniguchi has continued to work in an introspective vein, delving deeper into the intimate and the sensitive, but always with great propriety and tact. **NF**

Jonas Fink 1991

✏️ Vittorio Giardino

Title in original language *Jonas Fink: l'infanzia*
First published by *Il Grifo* (Italy)
Creator Italian (b.1946)
Genre History

Jonas is an introverted child of Jewish origins living in Prague. In October 1950, he witnesses the unjustified arrest of his father by the Communist police, during the antibourgeois purges set by the regime. He is then raised by his mother and has to cope with many forms of discrimination and economic problems that press upon him. In the first volume, Jonas leaves school and tries to find employment in menial jobs while still seeking the place where his father is imprisoned.

The story of a boy that must become a man all too soon is a sad and moving depiction of the gray atmosphere of the Stalin and Khrushchev era in Czechoslovakia, where its inhabitants try to live normal lives, only to be systematically interrupted by invasions of privacy by the secret service government. Inspired by a long correspondence with relatives resident in Eastern Europe during the Cold War era, Vittorio Giardino was moved to write this saga after the fall of the Berlin Wall in 1989. The project is intended as a trilogy, with the third part ending in the Prague spring of 1968. The book won the Angoulême Prize for Best Foreign Work in 1995 and a Harvey Award in 1999.

Giardino began his career in comics in his forties, starting in 1979 with private detective *Sam Pezzo*, a crime fiction inspired by Dashiel Hammett. He later created one of the best-known Italian graphic novels, *Hungarian Rhapsody*, starring the ex-secret agent Max Fridman. Giardino is one of the greatest heirs of the *ligne claire* tradition, and his passion for precision is evident in the brilliant crafting of architecture and detail. **MS**

To the Heart of the Storm 1991

Will Eisner

First published by Kitchen Sink Press (USA)
Creator American (1917–2005)
Genre Autobiography
Award Harvey Award (1992)

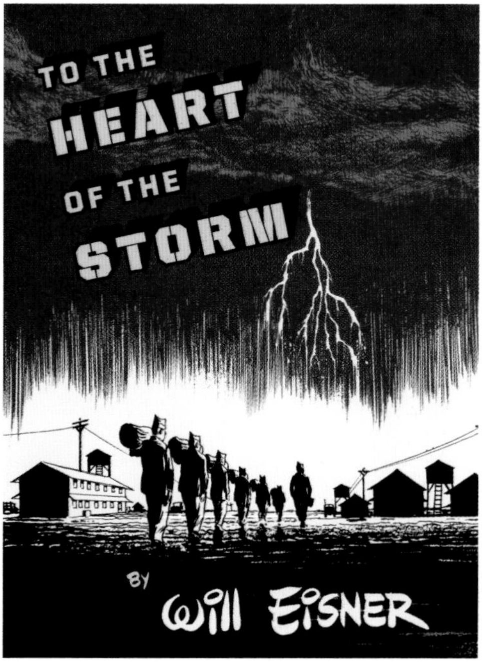
TO THE
HEART
OF THE
STORM
BY
Will Eisner

Although this book was originally planned as pure fiction, it takes the form of a "thinly disguised autobiography." It begins in 1942. Young Willie has been drafted shortly after the United States enters World War II, and he and other new recruits are on a train heading for boot camp. His mind wanders back to his earlier days during the long journey. The train's window becomes a kind of cinema screen onto which are projected his memories—a beautiful graphic touch, one of many. His own youthful experiences of anti-Semitism, which the looming specter of Hitler brings into focus, form the bulk of the narrative.

Back to 1928 and Willie's family have moved to a new home. The local Italian kids pick on Willie and his younger brother for being Jewish. His father advises him to fight stupidity with intelligence—which he soon does, to good effect. Skip ahead to 1930 and beyond, the family struggles during the Depression, the shadows of poverty and prejudice ever present. Toward the end, Willie meets his best friend from his adolescent days, Buck, and finds that Buck holds anti-Semitic views. Willie stands silently in the rain and readers share his wordless inner turmoil.

The convincing dialogue, theatrical staging, and adept use of shadow convey a wealth of reality and power through a cartoonish veneer. The feel of the various eras jumps off the page. Eisner was seventy-four when he wrote *To the Heart of the Storm* and continued to produce great work for more than a decade. His enduring craft was remarkable—and this is one of his best. **CH**

"It took me a year to produce. At the end it turned out to be a period of deep therapy."

Will Eisner

Similar reads

Jew Gangster Joe Kubert
Love and Rockets Gilbert Hernandez
Maus Art Spiegelman
Persepolis Marjane Satrapi
Street Code Jack Kirby

Weapon X 1991

Barry Windsor-Smith

First published by Marvel Comics (USA)
Creator British (b.1949)
Genre Superhero
Adaptation Film: *X-Men Origins: Wolverine* (2009)

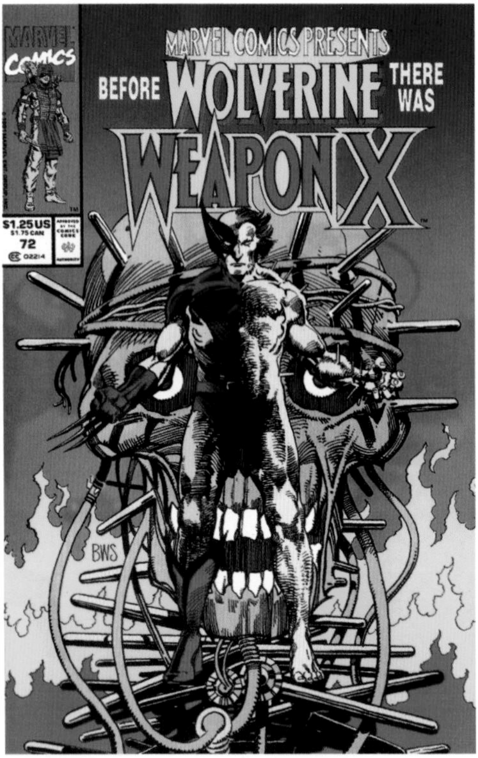
MARVEL COMICS
MARVEL COMICS PRESENTS
BEFORE WOLVERINE THERE WAS
WEAPON X
$1.25US
72
BWS

Similar reads
Deadpool Fabian Nicieza and Rob Liefeld
Old Man Logan Mark Millar and Steve McNiven
Punisher Max Garth Ennis and Steve Dillon

Wolverine first appeared in 1974 as a supporting character in an *Incredible Hulk* story line before beginning his career as an X-Man in 1975. He is one of comics' most morally ambiguous characters, constantly balancing his anger and bloodlust with heroic ambitions, and aside from Deadpool (with whom he shares some DNA), he is Marvel's most mysterious superhero. Throughout Wolverine's career, there have been hints about his past, and the amnesiac Canuck has desperately tried to piece together his troubled history. In 1991 Barry Windsor-Smith gave this fan-favorite character his definitive origin story.

Under medicinal lighting and with panels filled with vivid splashes of cold blues and blood reds and endless wires attached to our hero, *Weapon X* explains with businesslike formality the various stages that went into making Logan the ultimate killing machine. Windsor-Smith relies heavily on omnipresent captions that impart snippets of terrifying pronouncements, such as the relentless order to "Feed" in the fateful moment when Logan's skeleton is laced with adamantium.

There are trademark moments of violence, but for the most part a silent, unconscious, and traumatized Logan is subjected to extraordinary levels of clinical brutality: tied down to medical tables, experimented on, and brainwashed. Starring the mysterious Professor (a dark mirror reflection of the *X-Men*'s saintly Professor X), the narrative creates believable people out of all the characters and effectively shows both sides of the legendary Experiment X—that of the pioneering scientists and of the test subject. Before he becomes part of Experiment X, Logan is shown as a drunken dropout and a loser, and this origin tale makes the undeniable point that without the nightmarish procedures he underwent, Logan would never have become the hero that readers know today. **SW**

Windsor-Smith's captions reveal only fragments of critical conversation.

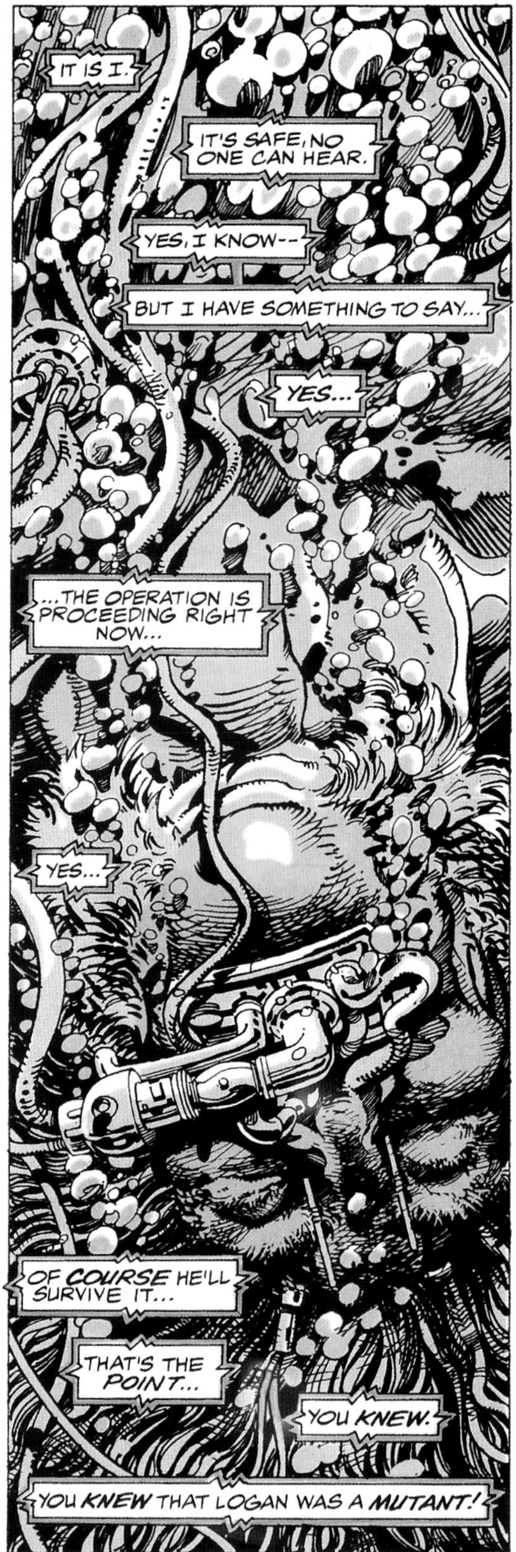
IT IS I.
IT'S SAFE, NO ONE CAN HEAR.
YES, I KNOW--
BUT I HAVE SOMETHING TO SAY...
YES...
...THE OPERATION IS PROCEEDING RIGHT NOW...
YES...
OF COURSE HE'LL SURVIVE IT...
THAT'S THE POINT...
YOU KNEW.
YOU KNEW THAT LOGAN WAS A MUTANT!
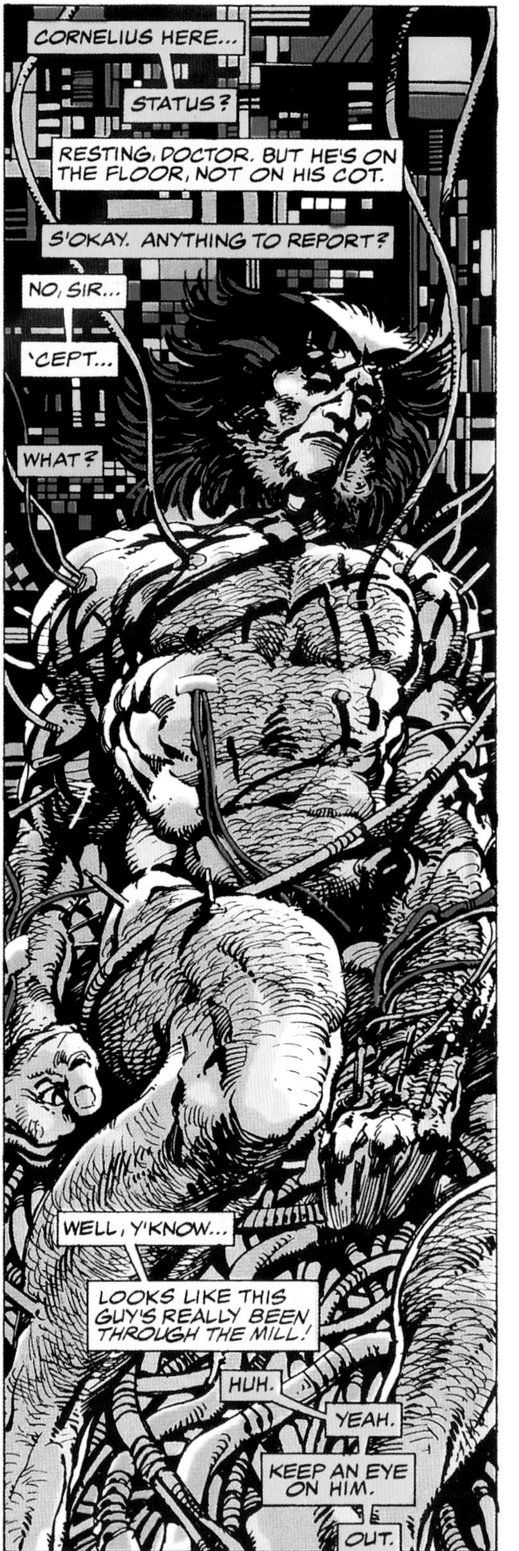
CORNELIUS HERE...
STATUS?
RESTING, DOCTOR. BUT HE'S ON THE FLOOR, NOT ON HIS COT.
S'OKAY. ANYTHING TO REPORT?
NO, SIR...
'CEPT...
WHAT?
WELL, Y'KNOW...
LOOKS LIKE THIS GUY'S REALLY BEEN THROUGH THE MILL!
HUH.
YEAH.
KEEP AN EYE ON HIM.
OUT.

Metropol 1991

Ted McKeever

TED McKEEVER'S
METROPŌL
METROPOL 1
VOLUME 1
$2.95
EPIC COMICS
HOTEL

"Don't these weaklings know that the time to step off their high 'n' mighty pedestal has come."

Similar reads

Battle Angel Alita Yukito Kishiro
Plastic Forks Ted McKeever
Transit Ted McKeever
V for Vendetta Alan Moore and David Lloyd

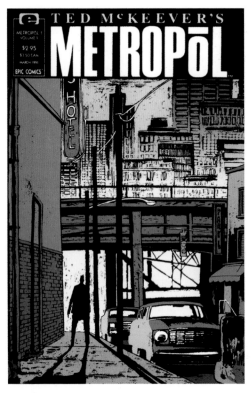

First published by Epic Comics (USA)
Creator American (Unknown)
Genre Science fiction, Adventure
Award Harvey Award (1992)

Ted McKeever's artwork is twitchy, unsettling, and full of little dots and lines and skuzzy stains and ugly black lumps, usually depicting the underbelly of society, the industrial heartlands of cities, and the hidden realms of tramps and outsiders. He has an eye for the darkly humorous, and developed from parodying superhero wannabes in *Eddy Current* to the epic *Metropol*.

Metropol is set in the same world as his previous comic, *Transit*, and concludes some of the story lines begun there. A crumbling city whose inhabitants have given up on it and themselves is the perfect place to start the end of the world. A plague that devastates the city also causes some of the dead to be reborn as angels or demons, who must then fight for control. A handful of angels tries to protect the remaining humans against an army of devils, to no avail. Much of the story is told through the eyes of a human caught up in metaphysical events he cannot understand, and flashbacks, visions, and dream fragments add to the somewhat perplexing nature of the narrative, which tends to progress in very short bursts, often of seemingly unconnected events. McKeever's vision of hell on Earth is somewhere between John Milton and Franz Kafka, so do not expect a happy ending.

McKeever kept tight control over *Metropol*, inking and coloring it himself in a muted palette that suggests urban decay and grubbiness, and employing much heavier blacks and harsher lines than previously. His art here looks extremely confident, blocky, and powerful, perfectly matched to the scope of his story. **FJ**

Madam and Eve 1992

✏️ Stephen Francis   ✏️✏️ Rico Schacherl

First published by *Weekly Mail* (South Africa)
Creators Francis (American, b.1972);
Schacherl (South African, b.1966)
Genre Humor

Madam and Eve's creators first collaborated on the satirical magazine *Laughing Stock*. Stephen Francis and Rico Schacherl describe their content as "domestic life and politics in New South Africa," which provides a very broad range for social satire. The strip is syndicated in thirteen publications, but primarily it is produced for a daily newspaper, thus permitting a rapid reaction to current events and a daily readership of four million. A sequence produced in 2010 as South Africa hosted the World Cup immediately responded to the home team's fixtures and results, and featured several gags about vuvuzelas, then being heard outside South Africa for the first time.

The Madam of the title is the feisty Gwen, now in late middle age and based on Francis's mother-in-law. Having lived in South Africa her entire life, while not racist, she is finding it difficult to come to terms with post-apartheid society. Eve is referred to as a "domestic maintenance assistant," for which she is paid very little, and also has an assortment of money-earning sidelines. Other regulars are Eve's eight-year-old cousin Thandi, and Gwen's grumpy mother, who subsists on gin and tonic and a constant diet of television.

It should be noted that Schacherl also contributes to the writing, which can be scathing at times. The depiction of Jacob Zuma coincides with how the rest of the world sees him, but Nelson Mandela, highly regarded outside South Africa, is portrayed here as venal and image-conscious. A television sitcom based on the strip debuted in 2000 and ran for three seasons. **FP**

NonNonBa 1992

✏️✏️ Shigeru Mizuki

First published by Shinchosha (Japan)
Creator Japanese (b.1922)
Genre Fantasy
Award Angoulême (2007)

NonNonBa is an old lady who lives in Sakai-minato, a small seaside community where little Shigeru also lives. Taken in by the child's family after her husband's death, NonNonBa comes to play an important part in Shigeru's life. She is an inexhaustible source of stories on the the *yokai*, fantastic creatures that inhabit the ancient Japanese animist world. As a result she becomes the "supernatural initiator" of Shigeru, who relishes these numerous stories, fairy tales, and legends, always on the cusp between dread and fascination.

With NonNonBa's stories, the *yokai* gradually play an increasingly important part in the life of the young Shigeru (whose prolific imagination does not need this additional stimulant), to the extent of soon overshadowing "real life." *NonNonBa* is the moving account of the interaction between the daily life of this small community and Shigeru's forays into the invisible worlds of his dreams, guided by a formidable cohort of monsters, ghosts, zombies, and other horrible creepy-crawlies. The old lady does not know it, but she has played a major part in awakening a love of fantasy tales in the man who years later would become one of the most famous pictorial storytellers in modern Japan.

NonNonBa is a gem of simplicity and freshness: an excellent example of what a family strip cartoon should be, with its sophisticated, intelligent treatment making it appealing to both children and adults. Throughout these 400 pages of pure graphic and narrative delight, Shigeru has taken great pleasure in reviving the enchantment of childhood with amazing sincerity. **NF**

Madwoman of the Sacred Heart 1992

✎ Alejandro Jodorowsky   ✎ "Moebius"

Title in original language *La folle du Sacré-Cœur*
First published by Les Humanoïdes Associés (France)
Creators Jodorowsky (Chilean, b.1929); Jean Giraud
(French, b.1938) **Genre** Drama

Alain Zacharias Mangelowsky, known as Mangel, is a well-respected Heidegger specialist at the Sorbonne University in Paris. Discussing philosophy and religion, dressed in violet, and with the following of a guru, his classes are like a stage for his preaching.

When his life crumbles before his eyes (a divorce, lack of respectability), he becomes involved with a group of religious freaks who believe they are enacting the return of the new Messiah. Mangel himself is the appointed progenitor. These characters are also involved with a Colombian drug cartel and acts of kidnapping, violence, and sexual magic. Many "miracles" happen around Mangel, but he always dismisses them as mere coincidences (or Jungian synchronicities) because he has no religious faith.

In many respects, the elements that make up this comic book are the same as those that Jodorowsky has expounded and examined time and again in his books, films, theater, and comics. Whereas his *Incal* saga connects these territories with the staples of space opera, *Madwoman of the Sacred Heart* brings them closer to home, questioning all the barriers that are constructed between philosophy and religion, reason and faith, sexuality, self-expression, politics, and the individual. Moebius's haunting art fluctuates between *ligne claire* and the more textured drawing of *Blueberry*, with a simple and classical approach to storytelling that leaves room for the narrative to thrive. The bright color palette also does much to express effectively the story's atmosphere. **PM**

Sof' Boy 1992

✎✎ Archer Prewitt

First published by Self-published (USA)
Creator American (b.1963)
Genre Alternative
Award Eisner Award (1997)

Archer Prewitt's *Sof' Boy* is no superhero, but his indestructible quality bears some affinity to a superpower and to Plastic Man's elasticity in particular. White and squidgy, Sof' Boy has the attributes of a molded, soft rubber toy. His form is simple and his features, dominated by a wide, expressive mouth, are minimal. He possesses the naive temperament of the eternal optimist and wants to be everybody's friend. He and his trusty companions, Herbie the cat and Pidgy the pigeon, are innocence personified. They live in a cardboard box on the crime-ridden streets of Chicago, and readers are confronted with the violent environment where Sof' Boy lives a charmed life.

In an early strip, after saying his customary "Good morning!" to Herbie, it takes only five panels before Sof' Boy is run over by a steamroller. In later episodes he is ripped to pieces by a crazed dog that shakes him as if he were a rag doll, his head is ripped off, he is shot, he is vomited on by an inebriated vagrant, and he has a lit firework stuffed into his mouth. In one dramatic strip, a wolflike dog barks at him from a window left ajar for ten hours. The final frame shows the dog foaming at the mouth and the windowsill dripping with saliva.

Sof' Boy always recovers from his misadventures with punks, prostitutes, down-and-outs, and rats. Amazingly, he and Herbie are always laughing, and when alone Sof' Boy is often surrounded by musical notes as if humming to himself. There is no question that *Sof' Boy* is a reflection of life in contemporary America. Whether it is a critique is less certain. **LC**

The invincible dough boy survives yet another mishap. ➡

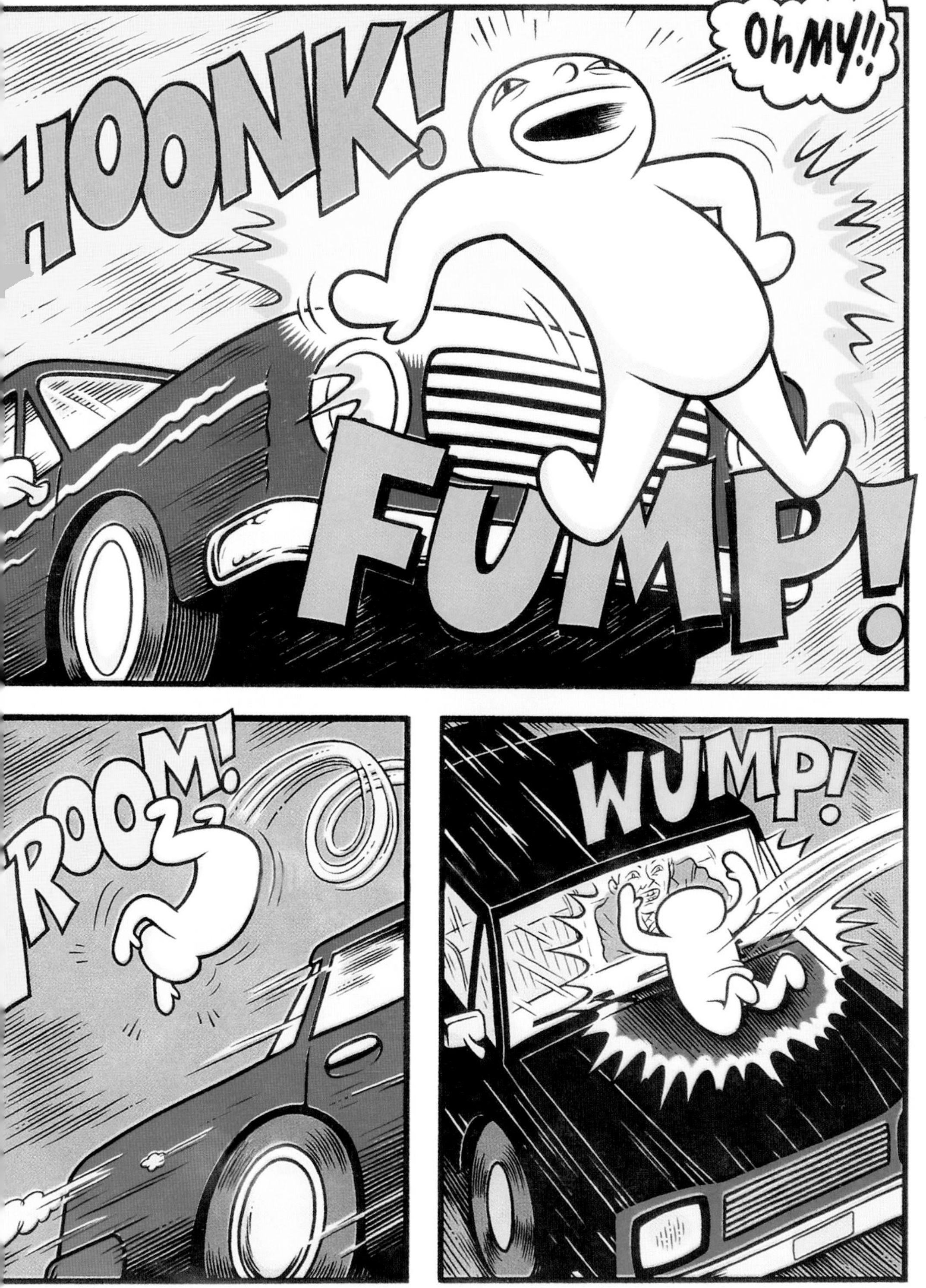
HOONK!
OhMY!!
FUMP!
ROOOM!
WUMP!

Button Man
The Killing Game 1992

John Wagner   Arthur Ranson

First published by Fleetway (UK)
Creators Wagner (British, b.1949); Ranson (British, b.1939)
Genre Crime
Award Eagle Award (2000)

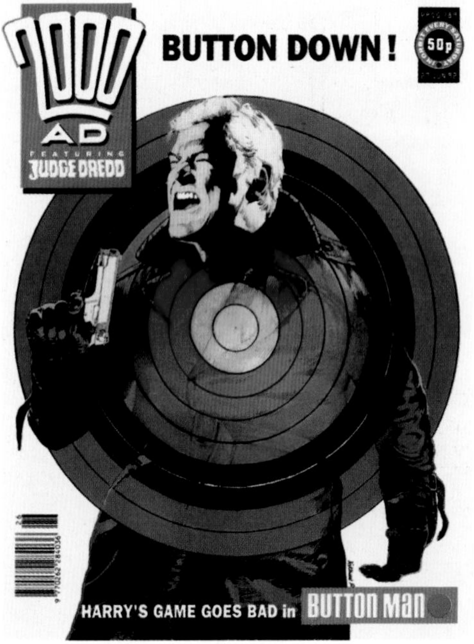
2000 AD
FEATURING
JUDGE DREDD
BUTTON DOWN!
50p
HARRY'S GAME GOES BAD in BUTTON MAN

Similar reads

A History of Violence John Wagner and Vince Locke
Button Man: The Confessions of Harry Exton John Wagner and Arthur Ranson
Colère Noire Philippe Marceé and Thierry Smolderen
Kickback David Lloyd

Button Man is the story of Harry Exton and his indoctrination into the secret world of "The Killing Game"—a modern version of gladiatorial combat, fought secretly on the streets of Britain between "Button Men" for the pleasure and profit of the superrich. Like the gladiators of old, it is a high-stakes game. Winning a match can mean a lot of money; losing can mean your life. Harry Exton, a former soldier and retired mercenary, is supremely good as a Button Man. When one of his defeated adversaries tells him "You can't quit—not in this game," Harry decides to find out for himself if that is true.

Written by *Judge Dredd* creator John Wagner, *Button Man* represents modern noir at its blackest.

"I left the key and a thousand in cash with Wiley. He'd been looking for a place to winter up anyway."

Wagner is a master at creating antiheroes, and Harry Exton is arguably his darkest creation. Exton is undeniably a psychopath, a man who kills not for freedom, love, or revenge, but for pleasure and profit. He is a professional killer in a world of killers, more ruthless and sadistic than the rest. Yet when his cold, detached, and self-centered logic is laid out through the first person narration, readers cannot help but root for him. Arthur Ranson's photo-realistic art lends a chilling realism to the book, reflecting Exton's own calm, measured, and unemotional sense of purpose. Yet the art style is able to lend a sense of cinematic drama and tension to the most sedate of scenes.

This is a quintessentially British, hard-boiled crime thriller that sits well with such classics of the genre as Graham Greene's *Brighton Rock* or Mike Hodges's *Get Carter*. It is, as one character says, "A cold fish." **BD**

Streak of Chalk 1992

Miguelanxo Prado

When Raul, on his yacht, approaches a little island in the middle of the ocean that is not charted on any known map, he is immediately struck by its strange appearance and unreal atmosphere. A long white jetty extends like a streak of chalk against the blue background of the sea; an uninhabited lighthouse is attacked by seagulls; a lone house is used as a grocery, a canteen, and who knows what else. Something certainly appears to be lurking beneath the surface.

Readers experience the sensation of being unable to distinguish between dream and reality as they discover, with narrator Raul, the geography of this highly unusual island. The characters who inhabit it are equally intriguing, such as Sara, the main occupant

"Here everything seems absurdly useless, without any justification beyond the simple fact of existing."

of the house; her son Dimas, dumb and violent; and in particular the withdrawn and uncommunicative Ana, who recently arrived on the island to wait for someone. Raul is irresistibly attracted to her, and in the space of a few days the pair form a clumsy and unfulfilled relationship, consisting only of evasion, avoidance, and sidesteps.

After a brutal, tragic sequence, the story ends for the couple with two diverging vanishing lines and on a final temporal pirouette that raises doubt as to the exact course of events. This mysterious sense of unknowing is, of course, where the strength of the story lies. Miguelanxo Prado's breathtaking art is also key to the fascination of *Streak of Chalk*. With this powerful work, the Spanish artist moved beyond the pleasant picturesqueness of his earlier creations to join the ranks of the masters. **NFI**

Title in original language *Trazo de tiza*
First published by *Cimoc* (Spain)
Creator Spanish (b.1958)
Genre Drama

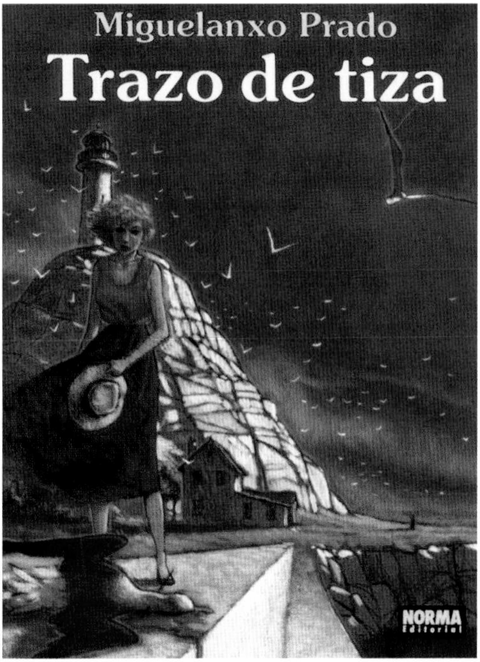
Miguelanxo Prado
Trazo de tiza
NORMA
Editorial

Also by Miguelanxo Prado
Daily Delerium
Manuel Montano
Papeles Dispersos
Segno di gesso
Tangents

My Troubles With Women 1992

✏️ Robert Crumb

First published by Last Gasp (USA)
Creator American (b.1943)
Genre Underground, Humor
Award Eisner Hall of Fame (1991)

My Trouble With Women consists of a series of short stories from the 1980s in which Robert Crumb explores and to some extent analyses his relationships with women and his *portmanteau* of fetishes. Such subject matter caused him a lot of trouble during his earlier career, when his directness about sex and the way he objectified women were often misunderstood and certainly proved thoroughly objectionable to large parts of the feminist counterculture.

Crumb's long-term partner, Aline Kominsky-Crumb, pops up with her views from time to time as he looks at what affected his sexuality in stories about his early sexual fumblings—such as "Footsey"—and how sex is played out in daily life. In the very funny "Dirty Laundry Comics" the Crumbs each draw themselves, a device they would later develop into a series of stories. The ageing Crumb worries about growing old and still being sex-mad, and how reading his work might affect his daughter. By contrast, in "If I Were King" he lets his imagination run riot in an orgy of dominating, firm-thighed, bubble-butted women in clumpy shoes.

Crumb is a fantastic draftsman, a great slapstick cartoonist, and master of a dozen different styles. He lays bare every crack and crevice of his soul, knowing full well that he will probably be castigated for his misogyny and called a racist, a Neanderthal, and who knows what else. It is almost as if he feels compelled to reveal all—from his desire to hurt women to his periods of impotence. His works are confessional comics at their best. **FJ**

Flood! A Novel in Pictures 1992

✏️ Eric Drooker

First published by Thunder's Mouth Press (USA)
Creator American (b.1958)
Genre Political fable
Award American Book Award (1994)

The message of Eric Drooker's highly acclaimed, wordless graphic novel is that modern man is insular and big cities alienate people. His central everyman character (which the book later hints may actually be the artist himself) bustles about an unnamed city full of dark and oppressive buildings, wandering into areas where prostitution and homelessness are rife. The rain pours down on whore and homeless and artist alike, and he is so focused that he does not see or care about the floodwaters rising around them all.

Drooker's natural calling is illustration, and it shows in his work. *Flood!* is frequently made up of sequential images, not panels in a comic strip, and to get the most out of them the reader needs to study each one carefully, which can interrupt the flow of "reading." Each image is powerful and individually beautiful, but it is hard to decide whether they constitute a graphic novel or a collection of interconnected pictures. The lack of words is certainly an approach that has reached beyond the insular world of comic book readers and found Drooker's work many fans in all walks of life.

Drooker uses a "woodcut" style that references a number of early twentieth century artists, particularly the Belgian painter and illustrator Frans Masereel. His worked-over lines and weighty blacks convey the pent-up intensity of his characters, and he cleverly uses occasional brightly colored symbols—from universal ones such as a red heart to logos lifted from corporate America—as visual shortcuts, adding to the book's universal appeal. **FJ**

Drooker's stark black-and-white style clearly shows an expressionist influence. ➡️

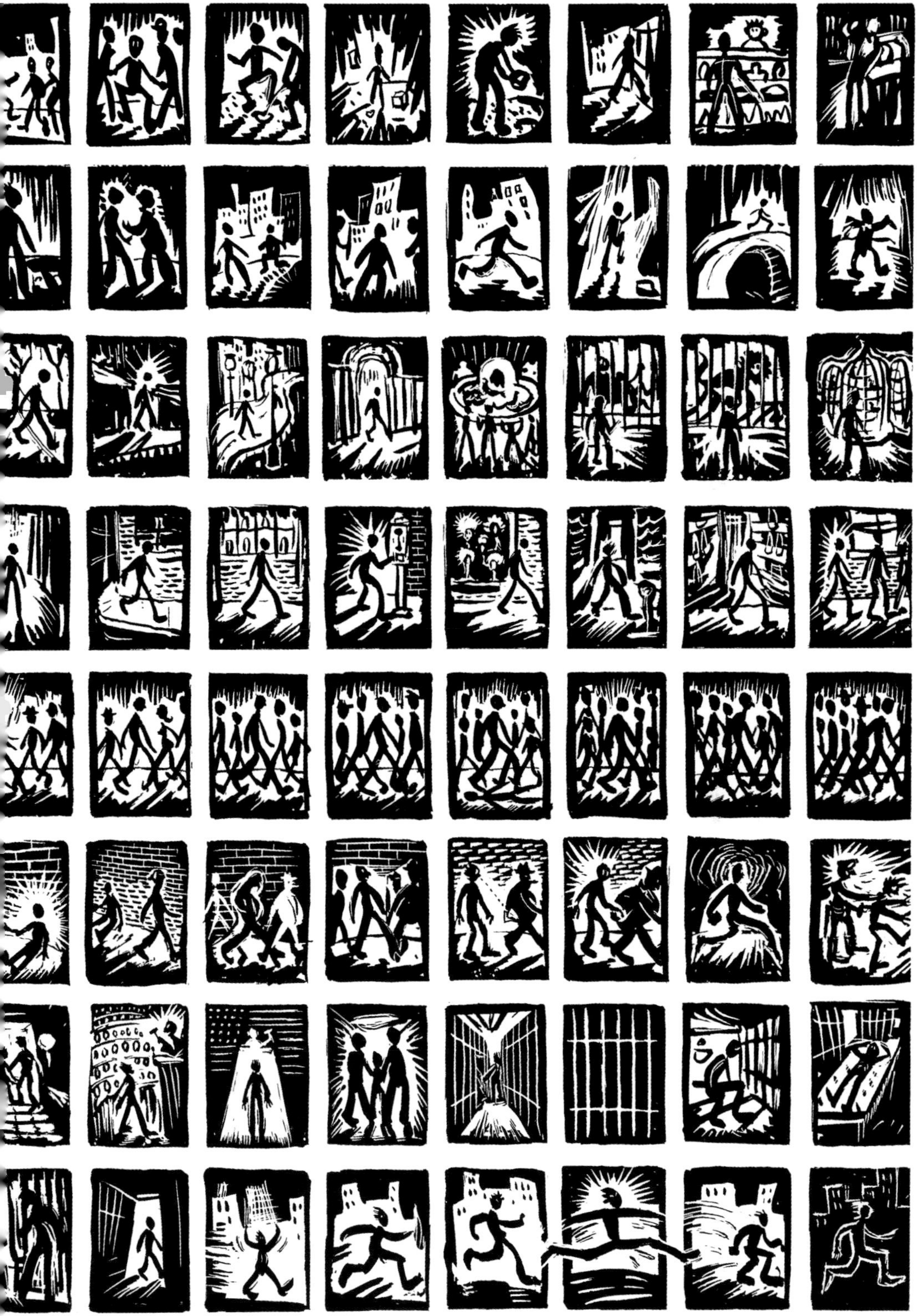

King 1992

Ho Che Anderson

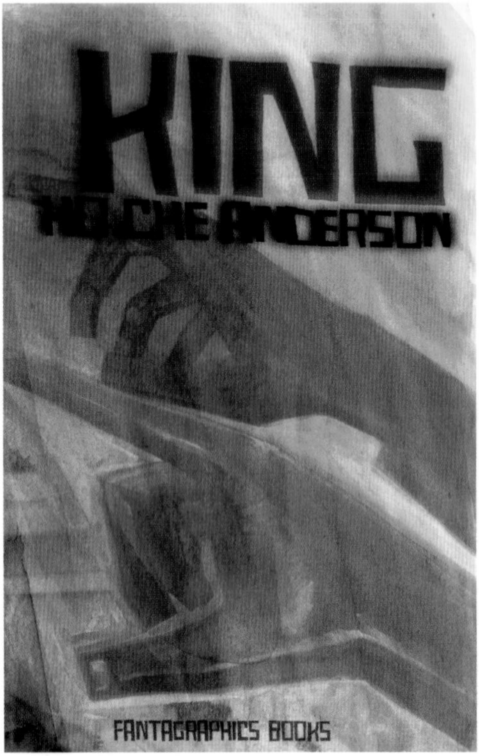
KING
HO CHE ANDERSON
FANTAGRAPHICS BOOKS

"Maybe he didn't always do the right thing—but he always tried."

Also by Ho Che Anderson
I Want to Be Your Dog
Sand & Fury
Scream Queen
Wise Son: The White Wolf
Young Hoods in Love

First published by Fantagraphics Books (USA)
Creator Canadian (b.1969)
Genre History, Biography
Award Harvey Award (1991)

At nineteen years of age Ho Che Anderson was a struggling artist, working odd jobs to help pay his bills and mailing out samples of his work in the hope that someone somewhere would eventually notice him. Someone did. An editor at Fantagraphics Books approached him and asked if he would develop a story based on the life of Martin Luther King, Jr., hero of the U.S. civil rights movement. It was, in the words of Anderson, a "profound and life-changing" experience.

King started as a ninety-page summation but grew to span three volumes and ten years of Anderson's life, and in the process became a milestone in the history of the biographical comic. Volume 1 (1992) began with watercolors but quickly reverted to black and white, as well as collages and mixed media as it focuses on the crusader's early life. Volume 2 (2002) includes King's 1963 "I have a dream" speech and saw Anderson begin to experiment with drawing his illustrations over old black-and-white photographs that echoed the abstract imagery of Frank Miller. Volume 3 (2003) was drawn in full color and culminates with King's assassination at the Lorraine Motel in Memphis, Tennessee, in 1968.

King is a stirring example of the graphic novel's unique ability to illuminate and educate. Archive material, multiple narratives, interviews, and documented quotes combine with Anderson's clever use of line drawings, splash pages, and approach to shading and shadows that occasionally make it difficult to discern skin color. *King* was released as a single volume by Fantagraphics in 2010. **BS**

Sailor Moon 1992

🖉🖉 Naoko Takeuchi

Title in original language *Bishojo Senshi Sera Mun*
First published by Kodansha (Japan)
Creator Japanese (b.1967)
Genre Superhero

Back in the 1990s something unbelievable happened—girls all over the world started to read comics. The reason for this was the publication of a manga called *Sailor Moon*, which was among the first wave of popularity for Japanese comics. There are many reasons for the enormous success of this series. At first glance it is nothing more than a superhero story for girls. Its main heroine, Usagi Tsukino, is an ordinary school girl, until the day she meets a talking cat called Luna. Usagi discovers that she is Sailor Moon, a reincarnation of Sailor Soldier, and thanks to a magical brooch, she is able to transform herself and fight the forces of evil. Soon other Sailors emerge and join forces to form a team fighting for "love and justice." The "love" part certainly helped to attract a female audience, even in countries with an undeveloped comics culture. The whole plot is a fusion of myths and beliefs from many parts of the globe. The Sailors' team is based on friendship and trust, and consists of unique yet archetypal characters to whom girls can relate.

The stylish artwork also helped to attract a female readership. The Sailors themselves are beautiful (which appeals to some male readers, too) and sport frilly dresses and unique haircuts. The composition is very dynamic, and in addition to the main layout there are side notes from Naoko Takeuchi to his fans, which helps readers to connect with the author. Sailor Moon has become very successful in wider merchandising terms, and the brand includes gadgets, animations, games, CDs, and even musicals. **RB**

Underworld 1992

🖉🖉 "Kaz"

First published by Fantagraphics Books (USA)
Creator Kazimieras G. Prapuolenis (American, b.1959)
Genre Adult humor
Collection *Ink Punk: Underworld Three* (1998)

Underworld started life as a self-syndicated strip appearing in several alternative weeklies, principally *The New York Press*, *Seattle Stranger*, and *Chicago Reader*. Kaz's beautiful-ugly subculture is peopled by a motley collection of cartoon reprobates, such as the "anti-Popeye" Sam Snuff, Creep Rat, Nuzzle, Ducky Duck, Petit Mort, and Smoking Cat. Murder and mayhem, disease, cruelty, and necrophilia are portrayed so poignantly that the only reaction is to laugh—out loud. Born of a "punk" aesthetic, these stories, with their bleak outlook on life, are among some of the funniest to emerge from the United States in recent years—if you like your humor black. The demented characters who inhabit these strips are locked into the world of comics history with their visual referencing of Disney, Segar, Chester Gould, Basil Wolverton, and others. The compactness of each wildly imagined story line is compelling. In one strip, Kaz confronts the dilemma facing the comic artist. A young aspirant arrives for his first lesson with the unshaven, cigar-smoking Mr. Snud. The kid is instructed to undertake a catalog of debauchery in his life. "Then, and only then, will you be qualified to draw Bumper the Delightful Bunny-Poo."

In 2001 *The New York Press* axed the strip on the grounds that it had a policy of not running any strips beyond ten years—*Underworld* was then in its eighth year. After Kaz's abrupt dismissal, other artists submitted proposals for his coveted place. Among them was Kaz himself, who sent in four panels, each containing a single word: "Kiss," "My," "Hairy," and "Ass." **LC**

Rock 'n' Roll Zoo Necronomicon 1992

"Savage Pencil"

First published by Music Comics (UK)
Creator Edwin Pouncey (British, b.1951)
Genre Underground
Influenced by Cal Schenkel

Savage Pencil's Rock 'n' Roll Necronomicon
And to any Disc Jockey who air plays a 'NECRONOMICON' Release comes a bonus opportunity of meeting the Elder God of your choice !!!
©'81 Savage Pencil
RADIO BIG JOBS

Also by Savage Pencil
Bad Thorts
Corpsemeat Comix
Dead Duck
Destroy All Monsters with Ken Hollings
Nyak-Nyak! with Andy Dog and Chris Long

In 1976 the year of the first Ramones album and the early Sex Pistols singles, the British rock 'n' roll music magazine *Sounds* began printing a bizarre strip by Edwin Pouncey under the pen name Savage Pencil. Titled *Rock 'n' Roll Zoo*, it looked like something a teenager might scrawl on loose leaf paper while sitting in algebra class and struggling valiantly to remain oblivious to the subject matter.

And that is a compliment. Capturing teen-hormone frenzy in all its stunted glory is no easy matter. Not that *Zoo* was concerned with teenagers, per se. Its focus was rock 'n' roll, then in its own awkward, teenlike phase between its 1960s flowering and its MTV-curated 1980s professionalization. Pencil drew

"It really didn't apply to me, it referred to my imaginary publishing company."
Edwin Pouncey

and wrote with a mix of sloppy affection and antic disgust about the egos and shenanigans of rock, with particular interest in brain-damaged bands and the drugged-out journalists who love them. His caricatures looked like bloated dust mites and undernourished wildlife, their faces either blank spheres or garbled mazes of internecine lines. Pencil's closest peers may be Gary Panter, who shares his shaky hand and abiding love for the psychedelic fringes of punk rock, and Pushead (aka Brian Schroeder), the artist who gave many punk/metal bands their graphic sensibilities.

In 1992, a year after *Sounds* closed, *Rock 'n' Roll Zoo* appeared in a book, *Savage Pencil's Rock 'n' Roll Necronomicon*. The comic continued in *Top*, published in England by Tower Records. Later, Pencil drew the *Trip or Squeek* strip in *The Wire*, a magazine dedicated to experimental music and sound. **MW**

Titeuf 1992

"Zep"

How do you assess a comic strip that has become a social phenomenon—when expressions used in a strip cartoon enter everyday language and are used by people without really knowing where they come from? This was the case in France with *Asterix*, and it is now also true of *Titeuf*. Originally published in issue #5 of *Sauve qui peut* (a Swiss fanzine published by AtoZ), the project was first offered to various French-speaking publishers who all rejected it until Jean-Claude Camano commissioned its author, Philippe Chappuis, alias Zep (a reference to Led Zeppelin), to produce a hardback album. With a print run of 4,000 copies, it was published by Glénat in 1993. Fifteen years later, the same publisher announced a print run of 1.8 million copies for the French edition of the twelfth album, clear proof of its amazing popularity.

"I suddenly felt there was something going on between Titeuf and me."

Zep

Titeuf is a young boy with a blond shock of hair. The author follows his daily adventures both at school and at home. His friends include Manu, Titeuf's timid best friend; Hugo, a fat boy in a red sweater; Vomito, who vomits for the slightest reason; and Jean-Claude who splutters because he has a dental brace. Titeuf spends most of his time with his friends wondering about sex and the grown-up world, interpreting everything he hears in hilarious ways. Believing he is in love with a girl named Nadia, his clumsy amorous techniques never lead to anything. The stories are usually presented in the format of one-page sketches, based on gags and comic situations. Adapted for television, the big screen, and video games, *Titeuf* has become a comics icon with thousands of marketing by-products. **CM**

First published by AtoZ (Switzerland)
Creator Philippe Chappuis (Swiss, b.1967)
Genre Humor
Award Sierre Comics Festival Prix du Public (1996)

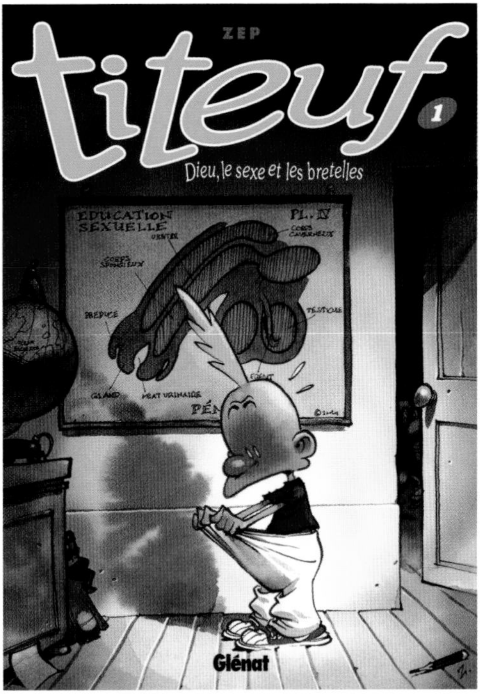
ZEP
titeuf
1
Dieu, le sexe et les bretelles
EDUCATION SEXUELLE
PL. IV
Glénat

Also by Zep
C'est pô juste
Dieu, le sexe et les bretelles
L'amour c'est pô propre
Nadia, se marie
Tchô, monde cruel

Palestine 1992

Joe Sacco

First published by Fantagraphics Books (USA)
Creator Maltese-American (b.1960)
Genre History
Award American Book Award (1996)

PALESTINE
MATURE READERS
$2.50; CANADA $2.95
FANTAGRAPHICS BOOKS

Similar reads
Footnotes in Gaza Joe Sacco
The Photographer Didier Lefèvre and Emmanuel Guibert

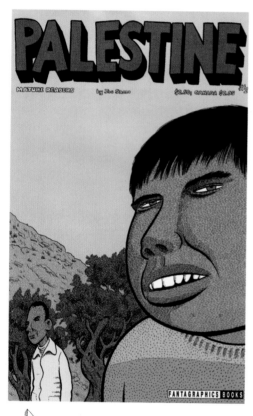

Joe Sacco defines himself as a cartoonist, although he graduated from the University of Oregon with a degree in journalism. After a few false starts as a journalist, he decided to try and make a living out of his hobby, cartooning. He joined *The Comics Journal* as a staff writer and began traveling. An interest in Middle Eastern politics took him to Israel and the occupied territories from 1991 to 1992. He explained his reasons for going: "I felt the American media had really misportrayed the situation, and I was really shocked by that. I grew up thinking of Palestinians as terrorists, and it took a lot of time, and reading the right things, to understand the power dynamic in the Middle East was not what I had thought it was." Using literary techniques (like the New Journalists of the 1960s and 1970s Tom Wolfe, Truman Capote, and Hunter S. Thompson), Sacco dramatized the stories of the people he interviewed, giving them a voice they might never otherwise have had. These were eventually published in a collection called *Palestine.*

"Well, we've heard it on the news, but CNN never made it seem this tough."

Frank Stack, cartoonist

The strip starts with the baroque, underground-inspired layouts of Sacco's early work. His caricatures are over the top, and the point of view is through a fish-eye lens. Over time this style was toned down. Thick lines in the foreground combine with thin lines in the background to help create aerial perspective and depth of field. Hatchings and crosshatchings mix with stipplings to give texture, if not much volume, to the drawings. Artistically, Sacco became more of a realist without giving up caricature. This evolution was inevitable because a visual journalist needs to faithfully describe places and events. **DI**

Sacco portrays the fearful paranoia that accompanies life in *Palestine.* ➡

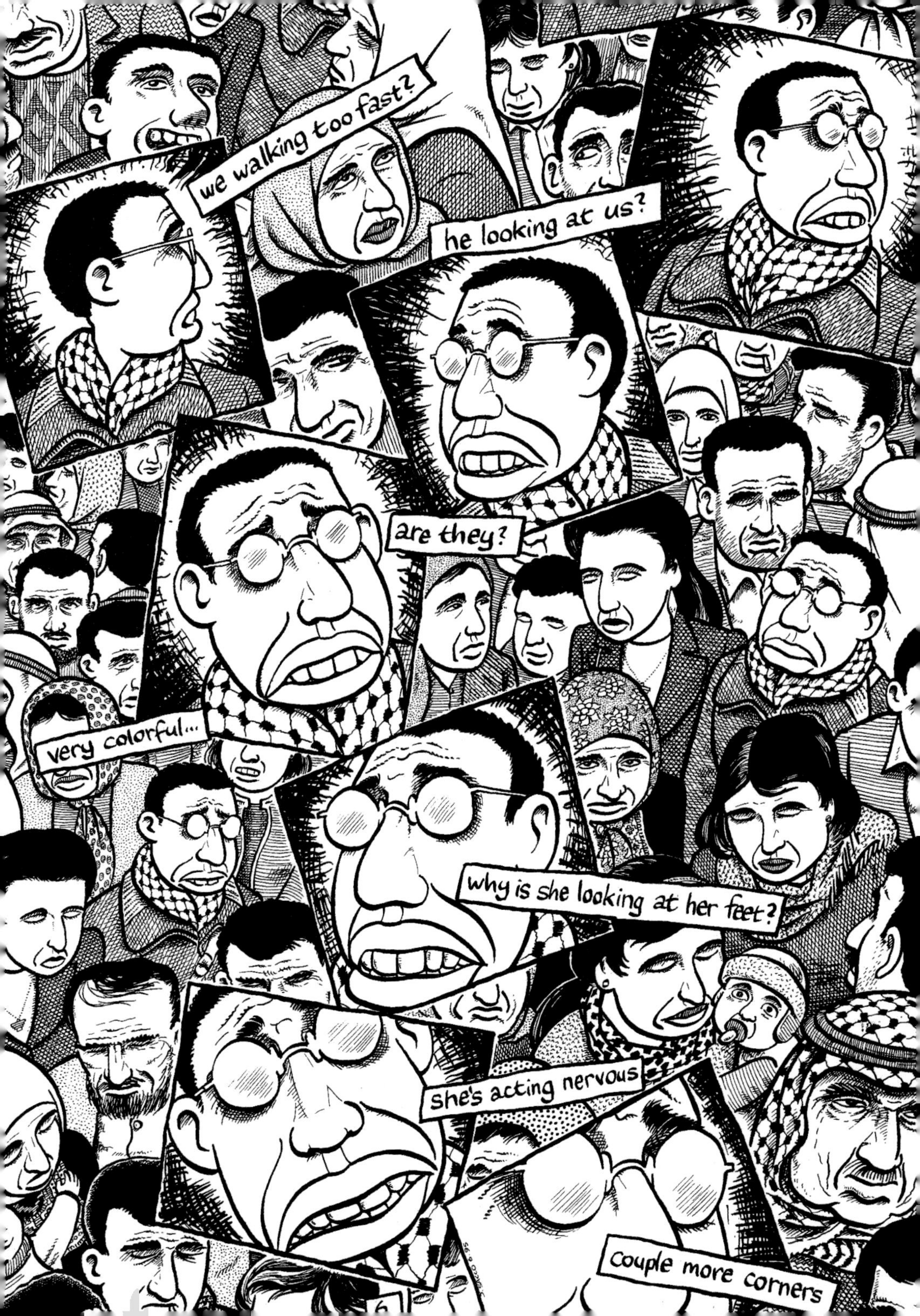
we walking too fast?
he looking at us?
are they?
very colorful...
why is she looking at her feet?
she's acting nervous
couple more corners

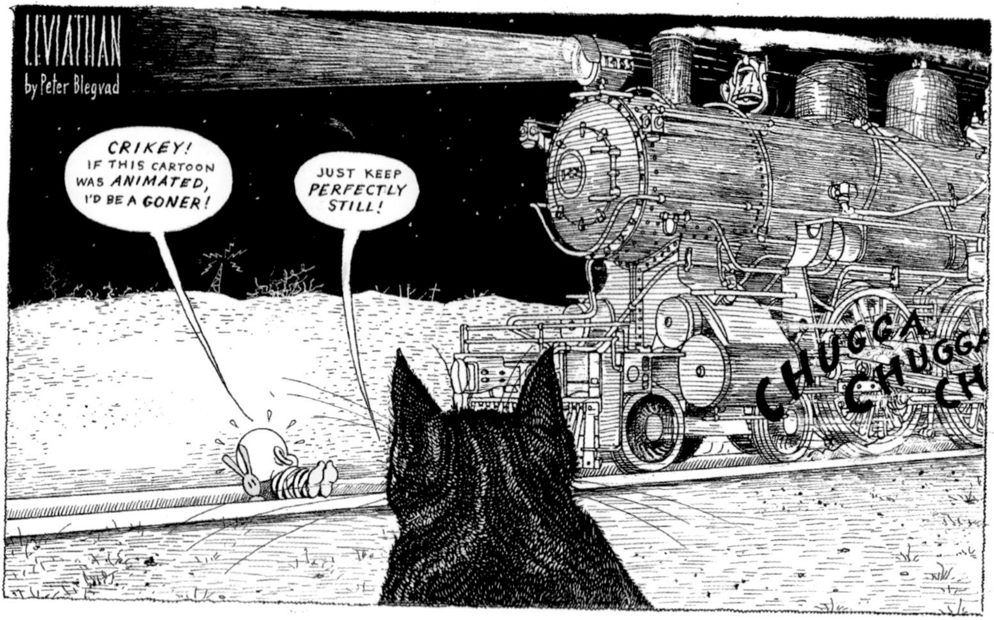
LEVIATHAN
by Peter Blegvad
CRIKEY! IF THIS CARTOON WAS ANIMATED, I'D BE A GONER!
JUST KEEP PERFECTLY STILL!
CHUGGA CHUGGA CH

Leviathan 1992

Peter Blegvad

First published by *The Independent* (UK)
Creator American-English (b.1951)
Genre Satire
Award Sony Award (2003)

The child of writer Lenore and illustrator Erik Blegvad, son Peter was smothered in ink and paper. He grew up as a flippant, rule-breaking individual in a relaxed, leftist milieu of freethinking and wordplay. An early Beatles fan, with no idea what to do, he had one foot in the United States and one in the U.K. He was obsessed with liquids—water, India ink, alcohol, milk—1960s psychedelia, and comix. He dreamed up his own verbal, poetical, visual, and musical brainchilds, even taping his sleeptalking to study drawing from memory.

He survived by painting and penciling backdrops for books based on the *Peanuts* TV specials. His personal artwork and stints as a musician (in Slapp Happy and solo) he saw as labors of love. In 1992 his art was finally noticed by the *Sunday Review*, a king-sized magazine of the *Independent* newspaper in London. His wondrously surreal cartoon strip *Leviathan*—starring Hand, Cat, Mama, Papa, Rebecca, and Levi, a faceless, almighty, highly talkative baby—ran weekly for seven years. In basic black and white with color accents, it was drawn using a quill pen and brush. (Going digital failed. Cat simply said: "I refuse to be drawn by a mouse!")

Throughout its 377 episodes, Blegvad revealed his views, loves, and interests in a flood of rhyme, picture rhyme, and crosshatching, together with references to dada, Duchamp, Yeats, and God. Some strips appeared in *The Book of Leviathan* (2001). Pondering low wages and high acclaim, Blegvad continues to work in music and teaching, and does "eartoons"—cartoons for the ear—for BBC Radio. **HvO**

Baby Levi faces yet another frightening end. ↑

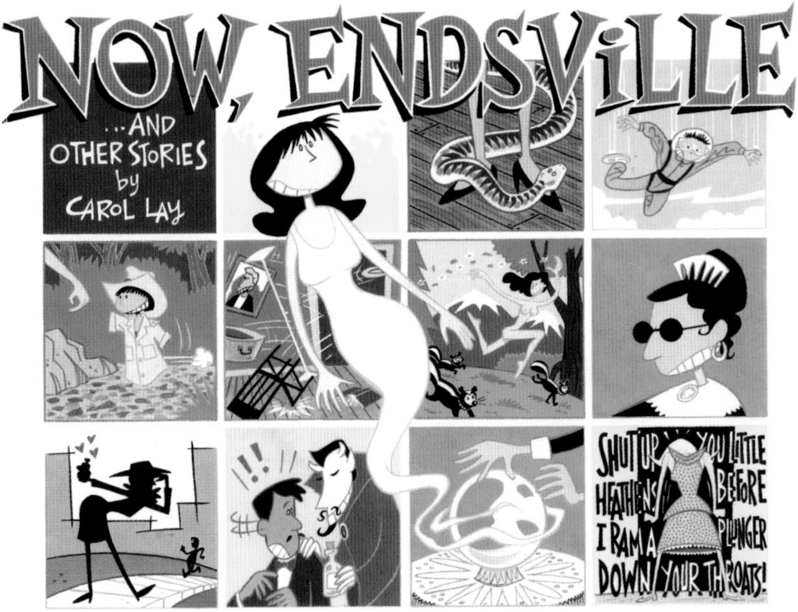
NOW, ENDSVILLE
...AND OTHER STORIES by CAROL LAY
SHUT UP YOU LITTLE HEATHENS BEFORE I RAM A PLUNGER DOWN YOUR THROATS!

Now, Endsville 1993

Carol Lay

First published by *The Village Voice* (USA)
Creator American (b.1952)
Genre Parody
Influence on Kim Deitch

While working on movie storyboards in 1987, Carol Lay was offered her own comic strip. Her lead *Good Girls* story featured Irene Van de Kamp, a woman raised by an African tribe with tribal scarring and lip plate, who returns to society as a disenchanted heiress. Drawn in the style of traditional romance comics, the parody gave an early insight into the skewed mind of its creator

Lay's talent flourished via limitation. Unable to combine an ongoing comic with higher paying illustration work, she conceived the whimsical and thought-provoking *Story Minute* strips—eight to twelve panels providing a complete yarn. Although hilarious, these are not gag strips where a replacement writer could turn out an approximation—they are totally fused to Lay's viewpoint. Confident with the format, Lay returned to longer narratives, including the title strip *Now, Endsville*. Jill will not settle for any dull guy and is prepared to wait for what she wants. Steve bungee-jumps into her life, and the story wanders down ever more unpredictable avenues. Another narrative concerns Madame Asgar, an eccentric, blind brewer of infallible potions, who is employed by an exploitative businessman to create wealth from the rain forest he has just bought.

Lay's cartooning is joyful and impeccable, characterized with deft strokes. The *Story Minute* collections are long out of print, but can be found archived at www.waylay.com, and the format continues in her current *WayLay* strip appearing in the online magazine *Salon*. **FP**

↑ *Now, Endsville* shows the unique quirky sensibility of its creator.

The Marat/Sade Journals 1993

Barron Storey

First published by Tundra Publishing (USA)
Creator American (b.1940)
Genre Biography, Alternative
Influence on Dave McKean

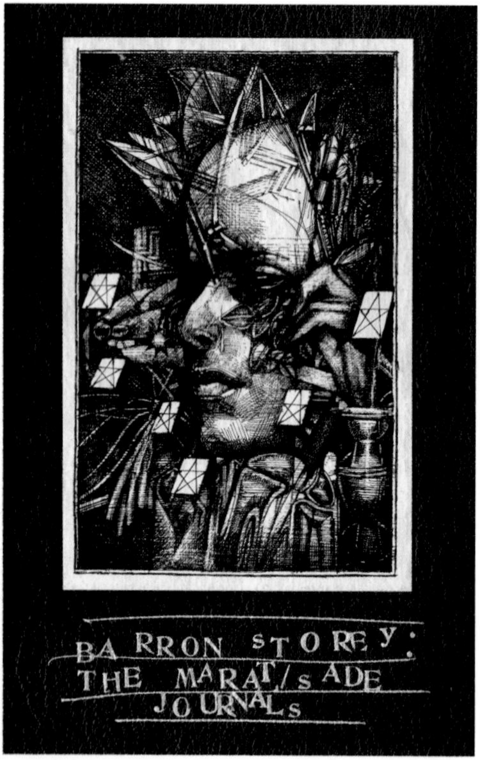
BARRON STOREY:
THE MARAT/SADE
JOURNALS

Similar reads
Hic Sunt Leones Frédéric Coché
Life? Or Theater? (Leben? Oder Theatre?) Charlotte Salomon

Although artist and teacher Barron Storey's comics output is small (this is his first foray), readers can recognize in them perfect examples of where the comic book, art book, and graphic diary come together. To label *The Marat/Sade Journals* "graphic novel" is perhaps too limiting. Describing it as an "adaptation" is also problematic. The title itself points to Peter Weiss's namesake play, *Marat/Sade*, which could be seen as its backbone, but Storey also throws in odds and ends from Shakespeare, Peter Shaffer, and a handful of films and songs. Furthermore, as the prologue discloses, the principal source for this comic book is basically "the personal journals of the aging artist." Many of the drawings have self-standing titles, and

"I adore her body but she doesn't realize that its beauty resides in its perfect appropriateness. . . ."

also poach numerous different sources. To a certain extent then, Storey's comic can also be regarded as autobiographical.

Storey has pushed the boundaries of comic books to unprecedented places. Arguably, it could be said that his influence has been felt mostly through the work of his friends and students—from Dave McKean to Bill Sienkiewicz, Kent Williams, and George Pratt—but also in younger generation artists, such as David Choe and David Mack, not to mention writers (try reading *Batman: Arkham Asylum* as a superhero variation of *The Marat/Sade Journals*). Using collage, photography, painting, text (of both the intelligible and the illegible kind), mixed media, and varying visual and graphic methodologies, Storey's art (and *Marat/Sade* in particular) displays a wide repertoire in which meaning is built, shattered, rebuilt, and put in a constant flux. **PM**

Kane 1993

Paul Grist

Kane is an absolute delight. It is a gripping, funny, sometimes surreal, hard-boiled police procedural comic drawn in a clear, clean style. Self-published since 1993 by Paul Grist, an artist who definitely knows when less is more, *Kane* is loosely centered on the eponymous detective hero and his sometimes mundane, sometimes spectacular cases. It is set in the fictional city of New Eden and combines some very English elements with a traditional U.S. format. Grist frequently pays homage to the U.S. television show *Hill Street Blues* with many in-jokes and references.

When introduced, Kane is at the center of an investigation into the shooting of his corrupt partner, which makes the other police, especially his rookie partner Page, suspicious of him. Rather than placating them, Kane throws himself into his work. Using a sole character in crisis as his window into New Eden's police department, Grist then begins to expand the book as an ensemble piece, gradually developing his multiple characters while slowly revealing what life in New Eden is really like. For long stretches of the narrative Kane barely appears, and Grist uses a variety of clever devices to indicate flashbacks and fantasies, sometimes changing narrator mid story.

"You use the gun to distance yourself from the target, instead of letting it bring you closer."

Grist has an arch sense of humor, and *Kane* is shot through with a mordant wit reminiscent of *Sin City*. His crisp artwork, with its sharp angles and deep shadows, is very absolute in contrast to his story lines, which make sudden cuts between events and time periods. The visual world of *Kane* may be black and white, but its moral world certainly is not. **FJ**

First published by Dancing Elephant Press (UK)
Creator British (b.1960)
Genre Crime
Influence on Jim Connolly

PAUL GRIST
KANE
1
DANCING ELEPHANT PRESS
£1.80

Similar reads

Gotham Central Greg Rucka, Ed Brubaker, and others
Jack Staff Paul Grist
Sin City Frank Miller

Leon the Stuff 1993

Sylvain Chomet Nicolas de Crécy

Title in original language *Léon la came*
First published by À Suivre (France)
Creators Chomet (French, b.1963); de Crécy (French, b.1966) **Genre** Satire

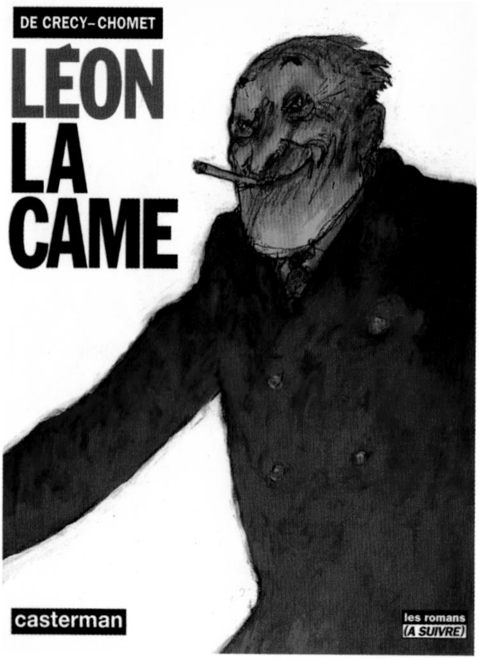
DE CRECY-CHOMET
LÉON LA CAME
casterman
les romans (A SUIVRE)

"De Crécy's loose, organic illustrations breathe life into his characters and give energy to his panel movement."

Library Journal

On the eve of his one hundredth birthday Léonce Houx-Wardiougue, the founder of a famous cosmetics company in the 1920s to which he gave his name, leaves a hospice where his family have deliberately left him and forgotten all about him. In fine form, the old man has decided to remind his beloved family of his existence. His family is worried and upset: how can they deal with the return of the old man whose clairvoyance, outspokenness, baffling behavior, and embarrassing past (he was a former trade unionist who took part in the 1930 uprising) have an absolutely devastating effect?

Naturally, the indestructible Léonce delights in spoiling the lives of his family and their marketing and advertising lackeys, with the important exception of his grandson Geraldo-Georges, a timid, self-effacing boy with whom, against all expectations, he forms a close and loving bond. Tremble, you wicked people, *Leon the Stuff* is in town and he is not happy: indignation and irritation at every turn, death to all idiots and long live the revolution!

When this ferocious fable concocted by Nicolas de Crécy and Sylvain Chomet was first published in France, it caused a sensation—and not surprisingly. The scenario is a brilliant device that is used to pulverize everything it attacks: human spinelessness, the bourgeoisie, and the deceptions of communications professionals. Only love—represented here by the meeting of the neurotic Geraldo-Georges and a young legless cripple—escapes unscathed in the end. The drawings are as astonishing as the story. Immediately noticed when his first book was published, de Crécy is exceptionally talented in graphic art techniques, which transfigure everything he touches. *Leon the Stuff* is irreverent and in a class of its own; it won the René Goscinny Prize in 1996. **NF**

The Blue Notebook 1993

André Juillard

The best known and most remarkable of the many stories by André Juillard is probably also, paradoxically, the least representative of all his work. An eminent specialist in historical comics, which he illustrated prolifically from when he started in the mid-1970s, Juilliard broke with his previous work when he started *The Blue Notebook* in the early 1990s. For this he chose a contemporary subject, free of any reference to history, and he worked entirely on his own, without a writer. The book earned him an avalanche of awards and is still one of his most brilliant achievements.

The apparently simple story is that of the classic love triangle. A young woman, Louise, is seen naked in her Paris apartment by Armand, from the elevated Metro nearby. Armand, a good talker, approaches the young woman and succeeds in seducing her. Louise, however, soon puts an end to what feels like an affair without a future, especially as she has just met Victor, a tormented character whose sensitivity touches her deeply. Their relationship is just about to blossom when Louise finds a blue notebook sent anonymously in her mailbox. This is Victor's private diary, the opening lines of which tell how once, in the elevated Metro, he glimpsed the naked body of Louise.

More complex and sophisticated than it at first appears, *The Blue Notebook* appeals through its unexpected narrative structure, which covers the same events several times from different perspectives. More so than in any of his other works, here Juillard is the ultimate artist of clarity. With relentless attention to detail and an absolute readability, his drawings enrich the pages with their warm, bright colors, bringing the story of *The Blue Notebook* vividly to life. The reader is united with Louise, and all those like her, and all the men who have one day fallen in love with the image of an unknown girl glimpsed in the big city. **NF**

Title in original language *Le Cahier bleu*
First published by À Suivre (France)
Creator French (b.1948)
Genre Drama, Romance

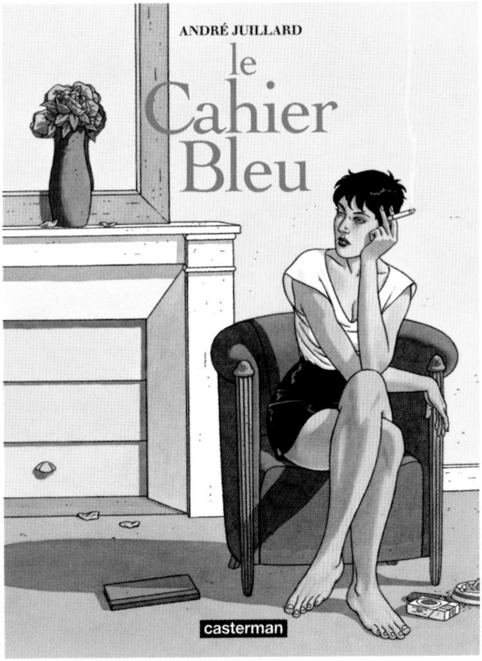
ANDRÉ JUILLARD
le Cahier Bleu
casterman

"We get a sense of the city and the loneliness that can come from romantic intrigue."

Christian Perring, critic

Strange Embrace 1993

David Hine

First published by Tundra Publishing (USA)
Creator British (b.1956)
Genre Supernatural
Influenced by David Lynch and Roman Polanski

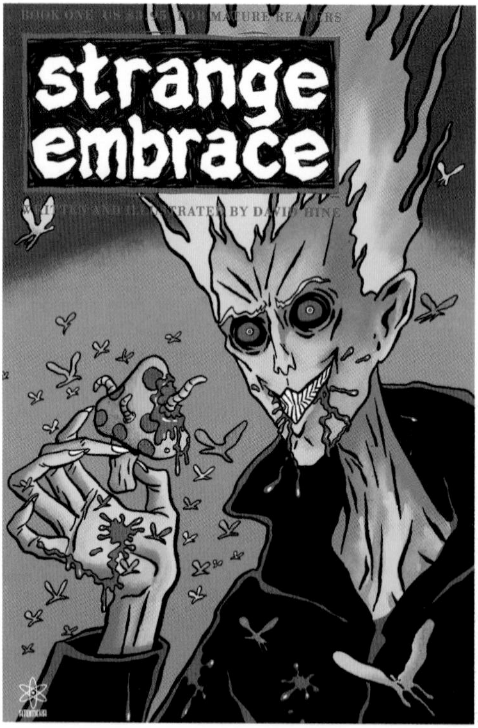
strange
embrace

Similar reads

A Treasury of Victorian Murder Rick Geary
From Hell Alan Moore and Eddie Campbell
Taboo edited by Stephen R. Bissette
Uzumaki Junji Ito

Strange Embrace is almost impossible to categorize neatly. It is an hallucinogenic ghost story, mixed with a critique of English sexual hypocrisy and misogyny, then crossed with the most gleefully sordid melodrama. Referring to fetishism, loneliness, and misplaced affection, it is told with black humor, compassion, and anger at the calculated cruelty of the old ruling class. There's nothing else quite like it in comics and it deserves to be much better known than it is.

A large part of the comic's story line is set in the Victorian era. Readers learn about the dark family secrets of masochistic recluse Anthony Corbeau, who may or may not be the central character of the tale. As if in homage to that greatest and most ambiguous of all Victorian ghost stories, Henry James's *The Turn of the Screw*, David Hine uses a variety of narrative techniques—letters, diaries, flashbacks—to unfold, slowly and very carefully, his tale of young innocence corrupted and made malevolent. James always paid close attention to the architecture of his plots, and Hine does likewise; by the end of the fourth and final issue of *Strange Embrace*, all the different strands of the story have been brought together and resolved in an extremely satisfying but quite unexpected manner.

"No one in their right mind leaps around in front of idols sticking nails in themselves."

Hine's jagged, deliberately ugly artwork is perhaps not quite as accomplished as his scripting, but it grows more adept as the series progresses, and is at all times perfectly in keeping with the story's surreal heart. African tribal art signifiers are used particularly effectively to extend the critique of imperial theft and despoilment that runs throughout the comic. **AL**

Casanova's Last Stand 1993

Hunt Emerson

In a "third-rate castle in Dux, Bavaria," an aging roué holds on to his precarious position as librarian by telling a lord of equal age ribald tales to stir his manhood. He himself is invigorated by telling the lord's stupid son about his amorous escapades, whether the lad wants to hear them or not. These are the depths to which Casanova, once the toast and scandal of Europe, has sunk, and he knows it. No one quite believes in the exploits he describes, so when a buxom female guest arrives at the castle, Casanova is determined to gain her affections—despite the fact that she clearly detests the farting, pox-ridden old man.

Hunt Emerson, Britain's greatest underground cartoonist—the description does not do justice to his

"... what better way to go than in the company of a lovely young woman ... with lovely young...."

profane comic genius—presents genuinely funny excerpts from the great libertine's life, counterpointing the high-flown prose of his memoirs with the visual reality of his situation, before embarking on the tale of the roué's "last stand." Throughout the story there are glimpses of Casanova as a sad and lonely little boy, abandoned by his mother, unable to make up for her lack of affection no matter how many women he beds, but this drifting, melancholy core is countered by brilliant sight gags.

Emerson's genius lies in editing his material deftly, giving readers just the right amount of saucy flashbacks and poignant moments before embarking on the comedic cavalcade of the main story. Few graphic novels can make readers guffaw and giggle and also bring a tear to the eye, but this is one of them—rich, witty, crude, and very moving by turn. **FJ**

First published by Knockabout Comics (UK)
Creator British (b.1952)
Genre Parody
Influenced by Casanova's memoirs

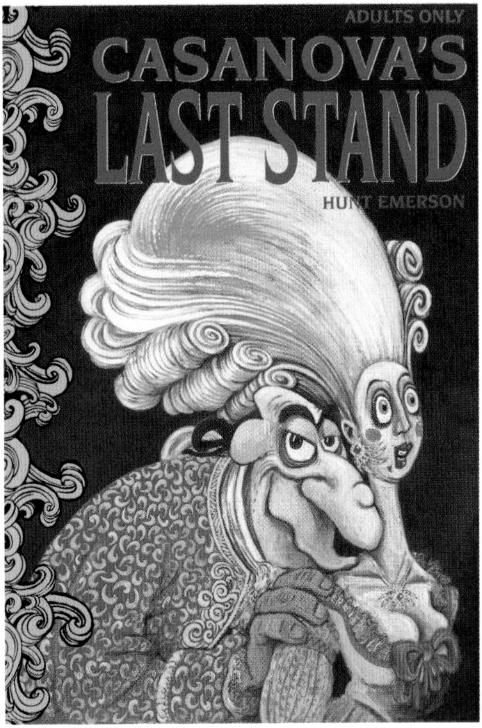
ADULTS ONLY
CASANOVA'S
LAST STAND
HUNT EMERSON

Also by Hunt Emerson

Lady Chatterley's Lover
Outrageous Tales from the Old Testament
The Rime of the Ancient Mariner
The Seven Deadly Sins

Enigma 1993

Peter Milligan Duncan Fegredo

First published by DC Comics/Vertigo (USA)
Creators Milligan (British, b.1962); Fegredo (British, b.1964)
Genre Superhero

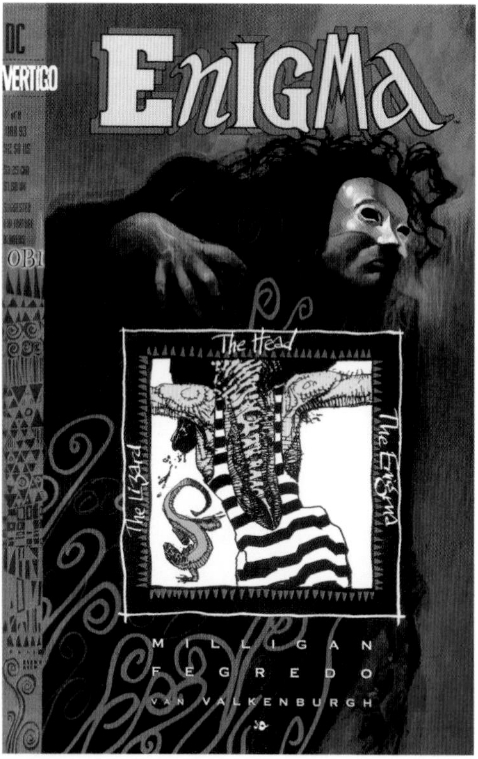
DC
VERTIGO
ENIGMA
The Head
The Lizard
The Enigma
MILLIGAN
FEGREDO
VAN VALKENBURGH

Also by Peter Milligan
Girl with Duncan Fegredo
Rogon Gosh
Shade, the Changing Man

Michael Smith is a twenty-five-year-old telephone repairman who lives a dull, lifeless existence until characters from the comic book he used to read as a child start coming to life. When the Enigma and the grotesque villains—the Head, the Truth, and Envelope Girl—from the short-lived comic he appeared in suddenly become real, Michael somehow senses that he is connected to his boyhood hero. An encounter with the brain-sucking Head leaves Michael near death, but he miraculously pulls through and leaves his former life and girlfriend behind to look for the creator of the old *Enigma* comic, Titus Bird. Michael offers his help to Titus, who is pursued by a cult who has sprung up believing he is some kind of messiah. Together, they

"I don't believe it. He's screwing one of my characters. / So report the son-of-a-bitch to the Writers' Guild."

discover a link between the strange events and an isolated farm in Arizona where a grisly murder took place twenty-five years earlier. They manage to find the Enigma and get the truth from him, but not before Michael has fallen in love with the superhero from his past. When the Enigma must leave what may be his final fight, Michael and Titus are with him.

Enigma is a strange story told by a narrator who remains unseen until the last page of the last chapter, where the reason for many weird occurrences is made clear. In the end, the central question of the book—did Michael cause the Enigma to come to life?—finds a very clever answer that sheds a new light on the whole story. Writer Peter Milligan sends his hero on a perilous journey of self-discovery, ably abetted by artist Duncan Fegredo's moody and quirky depiction of a twilight America. **J-PJ**

Ghost World 1993

Daniel Clowes

Meet Enid Coleslaw and her best friend Rebecca Doppelmeyer. Their story began when Daniel Clowes saw a piece of Chicago graffiti that shouted "Ghost World." The words encapsulated his feelings about the modern urban wasteland, where lives are only half lived and nothing seems permanent. Perhaps it takes an outsider to understand outsiders, but *Ghost World* offers several convincingly tender yet unpatronizing portraits of contemporary U.S. teenage girls.

It is no coincidence that Enid Coleslaw is an anagram of Clowes's name. Surviving high school hell brings two opposites together: confused, bespectacled, Jewish extrovert Enid, and her quiet, prettier blond foil Rebecca, united in their thrill-seeking and contempt for conformity. In a series of short, cumulative episodes, Clowes delves into their complex relationship and their confused relations with their mutual boyfriend, Josh. Their fierce, contradictory closeness is tested and broken after graduation by the pressures of home life, college, work, and desire, which both force them to grow up and grow apart.

"God, don't you just love it when you see two really ugly people in love like that?"

Clowes's slightly larger than life caricatures are constantly shrouded in an eerie greenish glow, as unnatural as artificial strip lighting or a flickering television, as they pass through a suburban wilderness of fake 1950s diners, cavernous supermarkets, and sterile apartments. Clowes cowrote the screenplay for the *Ghost World* movie with director Terry Zwigoff, but his original solo comic offers a much darker take on the self-destructive bewilderment of two girls' waning adolescence and looming adulthood. **PG**

First published by Fantagraphics Books (USA)
Creator American (b.1961)
Genre Teen
Adaptation Film (2001)

DANIEL CLOWES
GHOST WORLD

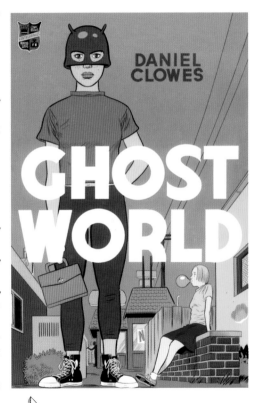

Also by Daniel Clowes
Art School Confidential
Ice Haven
The Death Ray

McConey 1993

✎▱ "Lewis Trondheim"

Title in original language *Lapinot*
First published by L'Association (France)
Creator Laurent Chabosy (French, b.1964)
Genre Humor

Lapinot (McConey in the English translation) is just about the least likely hero of a mainstream comics series imaginable. A quiet, retiring young rabbit living in present-day Paris, he is surrounded by a cadre of friends including the exuberant Richard, the intellectual Pierrot, the womanizing Titi, and Nadia, Lapinot's girlfriend. Over the course of ten volumes, Lapinot is embroiled in a series of misadventures featuring monsters, cowboys, and cursed stones, all of which impact variously on the absolutely mundane quality of his daily life.

The character debuted in Lewis Trondheim's 500-page epic *Lapinot et les carottes de Patagonie* (*The Spiffy Adventures of McConey*), a book with which the artist was attempting to teach himself how to draw. *Slaloms*, the first of the core series, was published in 1993 by L'Association as a black-and-white album. Two years later, the series moved to Dargaud, where the books were released as hardcover, full-color albums.

One of the most striking things about the *Lapinot* series is the way that it plays with time. Several of the volumes are set in the past, including *Blacktown* (a Western), *Walter* (a turn-of-the-century monster tale), and *Vacances de printemps* (set in Victorian England). In each of these books, the cast maintains their characterization and continuity, even while the world changes around them. The strength of *Lapinot* is Trondheim's remarkable sense of comic timing and his ability to gently mock genre conventions. His characters are knowing about popular culture and filter their experiences through it. **BB**

Sin City 1993

✎▱ Frank Miller

First published by Dark Horse Comics (USA)
Creator American (b.1958)
Genre Crime
Award Eisner Award (1997)

Returning to the crime arena that served him so well during his *Daredevil* run a decade earlier, Frank Miller constructed *Sin City*. It is a bleak place, perpetually steeped in darkness and rain, and seemingly entirely fused from the seediest quarters hosted by any large city. The lawless operate with impunity as the cowed, law-abiding turn a blind eye and accept their roles as prey and mute witnesses to atrocities.

Miller populated his creation with memorable characters: Marv the mug pushed that inch too far, Miho the pint-sized assassin, Hartigan the upright cop who cannot drop a case, and pole dancer Nancy who has a secret. Some are down on their luck, some are victims of events, some are what they are to survive, but all are fatally flawed. This is the cast of Damon Runyon's *Guys and Dolls* transported to Hell.

His art always on the dark side, Miller unleashed a symphony of black for *Sin City*. The only white on some pages is an obscured figure and the dashes representing the omnipresent rain. When Miller departs from this formula for a single, sparsely used spot color in volumes four and six, it increases the unsettling element.

Miller explored *Sin City* over seven volumes and several decades, deftly cross-referencing his cast. Leads from one series recur as background characters in another, and the same night in the same venue plays host to simultaneous events. *Sin City* relies heavily on the lone male hero archetype, but rarely has a film adaptation so closely resembled the source, and rarely has a source been so cinematically constructed. **FP**

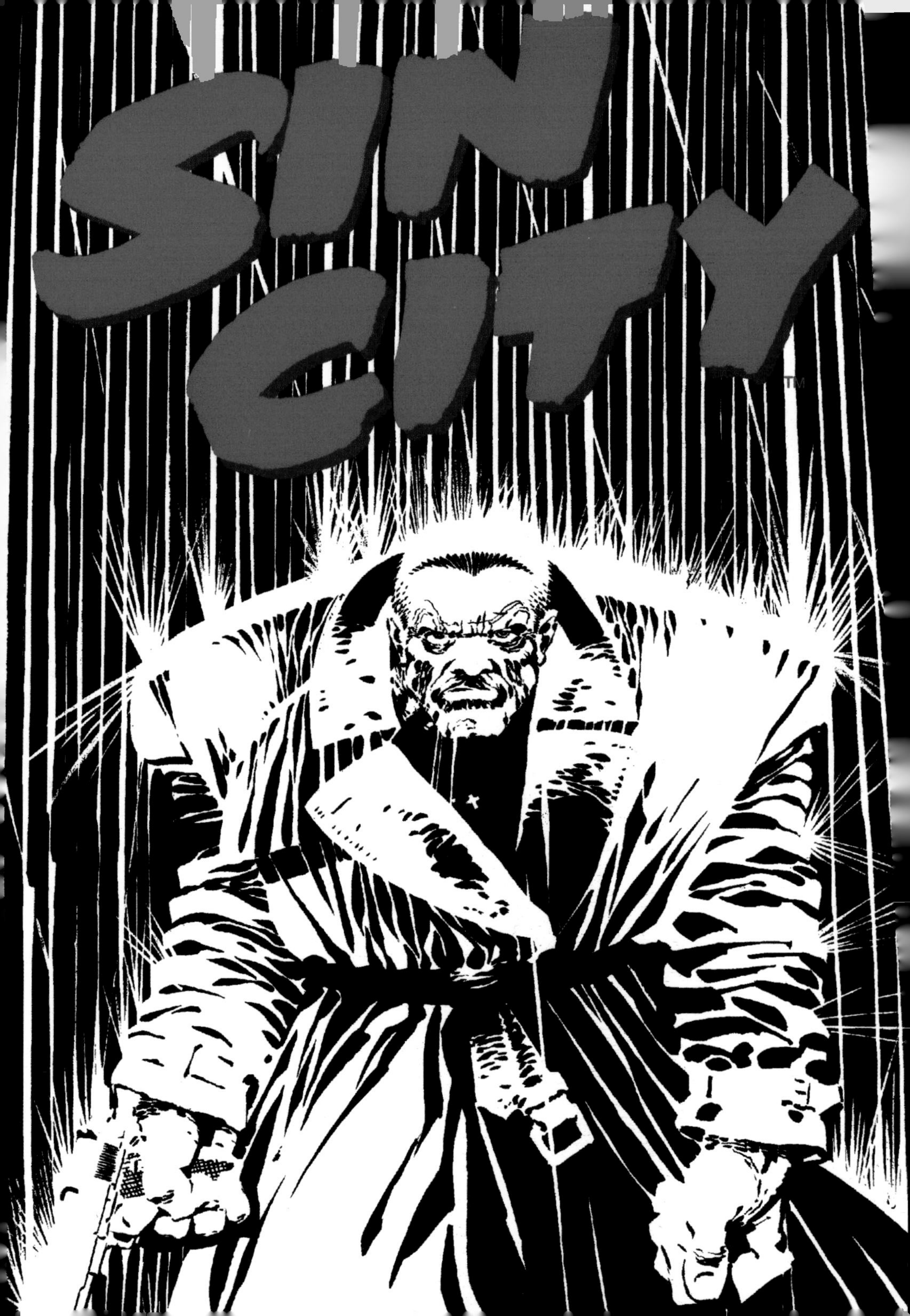
SIN CITY™

Understanding Comics 1993

Scott McCloud

First published by Tundra Publishing (USA)
Creator American (b.1960)
Genre Reference
Influence on *Logicomix*

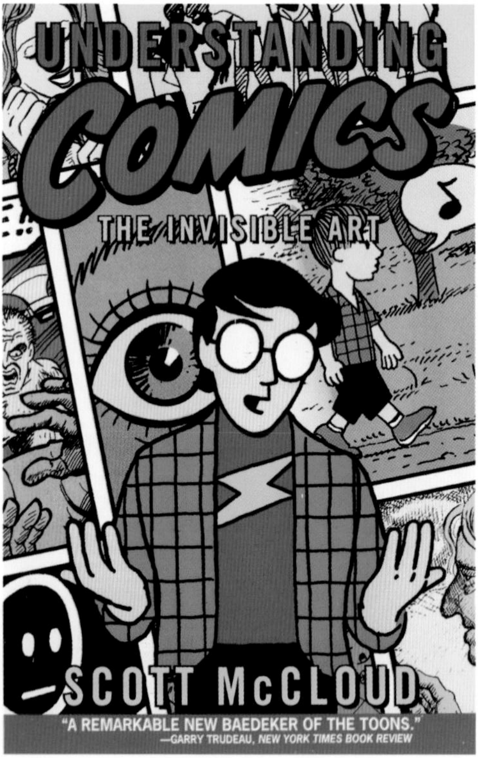
UNDERSTANDING
COMICS
THE INVISIBLE ART
SCOTT McCLOUD
"A REMARKABLE NEW BAEDEKER OF THE TOONS."
—GARRY TRUDEAU, NEW YORK TIMES BOOK REVIEW

Similar reads
Comics and Sequential Art Will Eisner
Making Comics Scott McCloud
Reinventing Comics Scott McCloud

What defines the comic as a medium? How is it different to any other artistic medium? How does it actually work? Building on the pioneering work of Will Eisner and others, Scott McCloud has created a graphic novel in which he lifts the lid on the medium itself and reveals that there is far more going on in a single page than you might previously have thought.

Beginning with an attempt to define what comics actually are (a harder task than one might think) and revealing some surprising historical uses of comics-style narrative—notably the Bayeux Tapestry and ancient Egyptian tomb paintings—McCloud goes on to deconstruct the actual vocabulary of comics. He explains the power of the simplified image and explores at length the strength of juxtaposition in telling a story, as well as the elasticity of time both within and between panels. Other topics include the use of quality of line to express emotion, the application of color, and even a broad definition of art itself.

"Today the possibilities for comics are—and always have been—endless."

Scott McCloud

Understanding Comics is an exhaustive but entertaining study of what makes the medium come to life. McCloud's narrative is complex and cerebral, but is also clearly laid out. This in itself is a triumph for he uses the techniques he describes to literally illustrate the point he is making.Consequently, many comics editors consider *Understanding Comics* required reading for anyone planning to make a living in the comics world. Indeed, many comics professionals working today regard it as having been invaluable in their careers. **BD**

Understanding Comics deconstructs the comics medium using its own techniques.

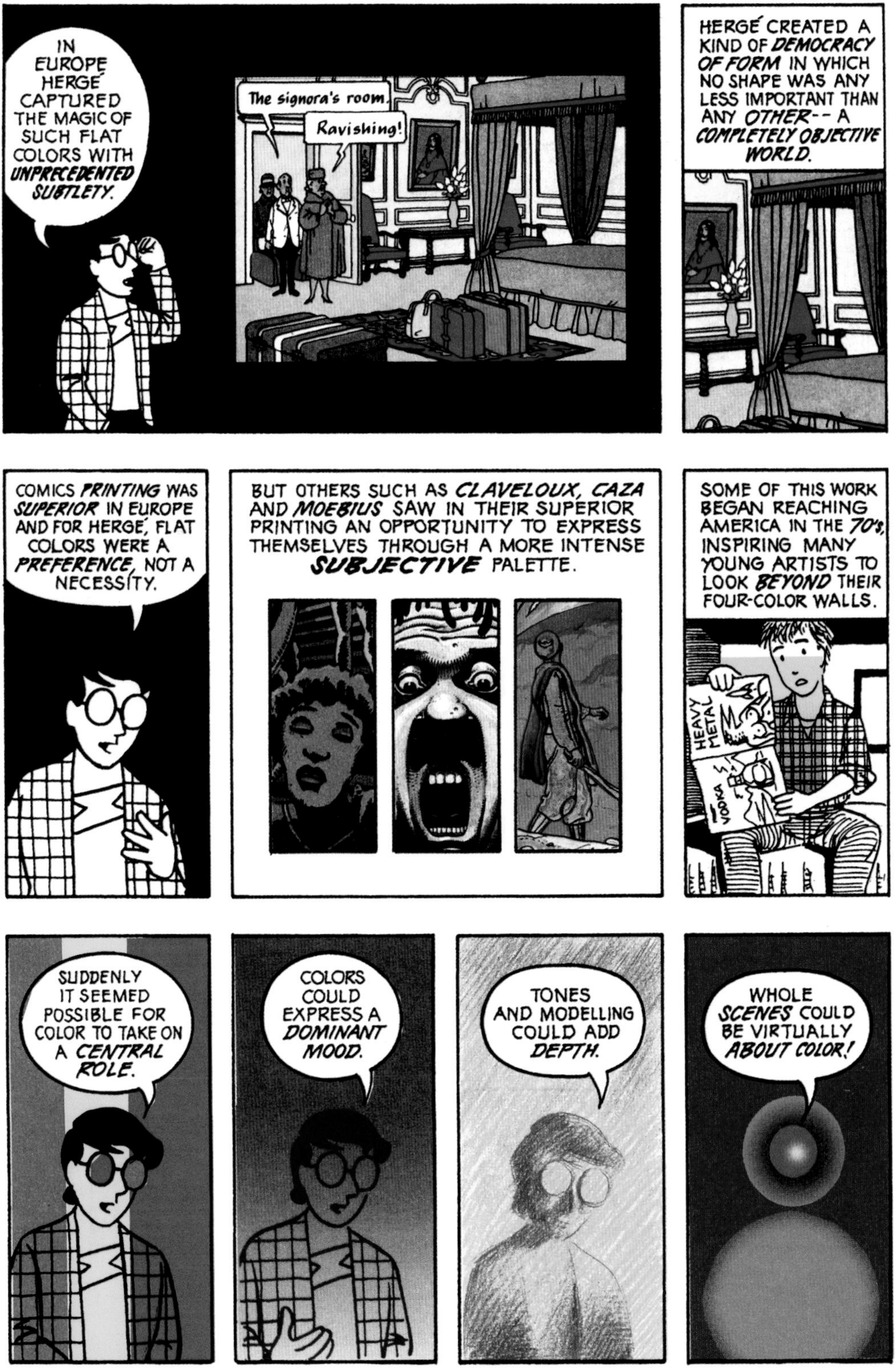
IN EUROPE HERGÉ CAPTURED THE MAGIC OF SUCH FLAT COLORS WITH *UNPRECEDENTED SUBTLETY.*
The signora's room.
Ravishing!
HERGÉ CREATED A KIND OF *DEMOCRACY OF FORM* IN WHICH NO SHAPE WAS ANY LESS IMPORTANT THAN ANY *OTHER*-- A *COMPLETELY OBJECTIVE WORLD.*
COMICS *PRINTING* WAS *SUPERIOR* IN EUROPE AND FOR HERGÉ, FLAT COLORS WERE A *PREFERENCE,* NOT A NECESSITY.
BUT OTHERS SUCH AS *CLAVELOUX, CAZA* AND *MOEBIUS* SAW IN THEIR SUPERIOR PRINTING AN OPPORTUNITY TO EXPRESS THEMSELVES THROUGH A MORE INTENSE *SUBJECTIVE* PALETTE.
SOME OF THIS WORK BEGAN REACHING AMERICA IN THE *70's,* INSPIRING MANY YOUNG ARTISTS TO LOOK *BEYOND* THEIR FOUR-COLOR WALLS.
HEAVY METAL
VODKA
SUDDENLY IT SEEMED POSSIBLE FOR COLOR TO TAKE ON A *CENTRAL ROLE.*
COLORS COULD EXPRESS A *DOMINANT MOOD.*
TONES AND MODELLING COULD ADD *DEPTH.*
WHOLE *SCENES* COULD BE VIRTUALLY *ABOUT COLOR!*

Ikkyu 1993

Hisashi Sakaguchi

Title in original language *Akkanbe Ikkyu*
First published by Kodansha (Japan)
Creator Japanese (1946–95)
Genre History, Biography

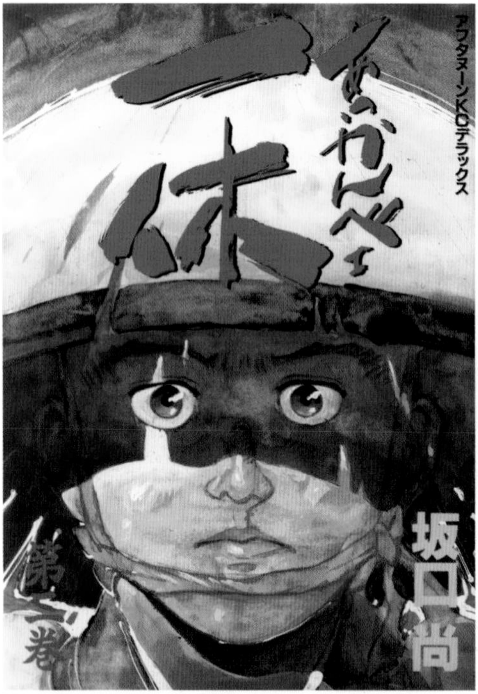
一休
アフタヌーンKCデラックス
坂口尚

Similar reads
Buddha Osamu Tezuka
Emperor of the Land of the Rising Sun Ryoko Yamagishi
King Ho Che Anderson
Onmyoji Reiko Okano
Vagabond Inoue Takehiko

Ikkyu is a 1,200-page fictionalized biography of a fifteenth-century Japanese Buddhist monk—one of the most significant and eccentric figures in Zen history. It is also the last work of Hisashi Sakaguchi, a "Zen master" of comics who died a few months after depicting the death of his hero on paper. Ikkyu was an enigmatic, mystical, and ribald character, renowned as both an ascetic and a libertine, iconoclastic and intolerant of hypocrisy. Sakaguchi's graphic novel follows Ikkyu's lifelong quest for enlightenment, from his childhood in a Kyoto monastery to his travels as a vagabond across Japan. Of great significance are Ikkyu's relationships with women, who always provide him with transcendent experiences. Although living in poverty and material self-denial, the monk saw no contradiction in partaking of the pleasures of the flesh.

In 1420 Ikkyu was meditating in a boat on Lake Biwa when the sound of a crow sparked his *satori*—sudden enlightenment. This incident is portrayed with eloquent simplicity by Sakaguchi in a series of panels depicting the fading light as the lonely monk is lost in memories and regrets. Out of the blackness comes the "caw" of a passing bird—stretched over two pages—startling Ikkyu into momentarily forgetting everything, even his sense of self. As the sun rises over the lake, the monk feels himself reborn, at one with his surroundings.

Sakaguchi's art is classic and straightforward, in dramatic high-contrast black and white, awash in historic—especially architectural—detail. At times it is cinematic—think Akira Kurosawa—at others poetic, taking on elements of traditional Japanese prints and Noh theater. Sakaguchi's narrative is quiet, reflective, and lyrical. Reading this contemplative work is akin to studying a *koan* (a riddle used in Zen Buddhism)—the meaning or answer lies within the reader. As Ikkyu says: "Only one *koan* matters . . . you!" **TRL**

Tokyo University Story 1993

Tatsuya Egawa

When Naoki Murakami sees Haruka Mizuno at a high school tennis meet, it is love at first sight. Tatsuya Egawa's *Tokyo University Story* follows their relationship from high school to college and beyond in a serialized soap opera that ran for eight years and eventually filled thirty-four volumes.

What begins as a simple love story becomes a convoluted tale of sex and obsession, with recurring diversions into extended daydreams and delusions—Egawa's favorite theme. Haruka is a kindhearted, cheerful, and caring girl; Murakami, however, is a somewhat psychopathic figure. He is passionate about Haruka, but his compulsions and numerous dalliances seem to doom their romance. Egawa's frequent and frank portrayal of "sweaty sex" in the course of the series saw him accused of being a pornographer—even in tolerant Japan. However, his blunt depiction of physical love also included pregnancy and explicit childbirth.

Egawa's stylized drawings are characterized by extreme facial expressions and startlingly cinematic storytelling techniques. When Murakami fails an entrance exam, Egawa shows his reaction to the news in a fourteen-page sequence. From a close-up of the posted exam results, a page-by-page backward pan reveals Murakami standing in front of the bulletin board, his shoulders slumped in depression. Egawa transitions to gradually more distorted wide-angle views and increasing darkness as the reader feels Murakami's pain. Other Egawa experiments and narrative devices include transparencies, cartoon avatars, graphs, diagrams, comics within comics, and impromptu "lectures."

Tokyo University Story was adapted into a live-action movie directed by Egawa in 2006. However, the original comic, in all its provocative messiness and flamboyant use of the medium, is his true masterpiece. **TRL**

Title in original language *Tokyo Daigaku monogatari*
First published by Shogakukan (Japan)
Creator Japanese (b.1961)
Genre Soap opera

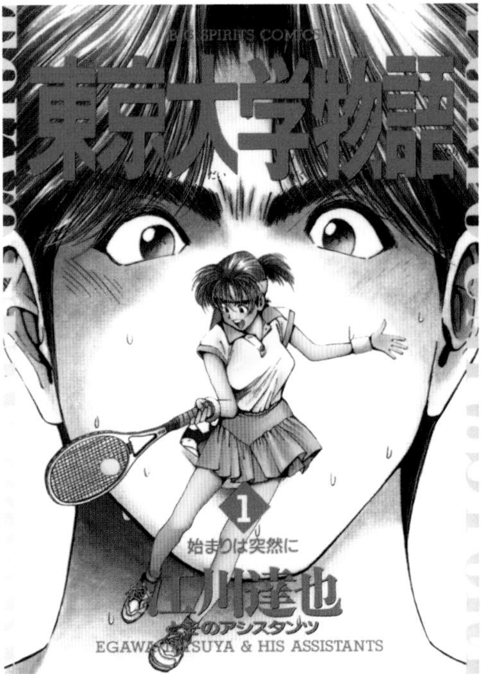

東京大学物語
1
始まりは突然に

Similar reads

Be Free! Tatsuya Egawa
Golden Boy Tatsuya Egawa
Great Teacher Onizuka Tohru Fujisawa
***Shameless School* (*Harenchi Gakuen*)** Go Nagai
The Last Man Tatsuya Egawa

Onmyoji 1993

Reiko Okano

First published by Hakusensha (Japan)
Creator Japanese (b.1960)
Genre History
Award Shogakukan Manga Award (1988)

陰陽師
岡野玲子
原作・夢枕獏

Similar reads
Calling Reiko Okano
Inana Reiko Okano
Petshop of Horrors Matsuri Akino
Youmi Henjou Yawa Reiko Okano

Combining Feng shui, Shinto, and Buddhism, feudal Japanese culture invented a way of understanding the flow of the world and even designated royal shamans to perform the task. *Onmyoji* is a fictional story about Seimei Abeno, the most legendary shaman of all. He is the spiritual protector of the capital, who prevents attacks from harmful demons and ghosts. He is also in charge of straightening out irregularities of nature, such as appeasing the skies to make it rain during a severe drought. Together with the good-willed Hiromasa, the only trusted friend of Seimei, who otherwise tends to distance himself from human society, they are a feudal Japanese Sherlock Holmes–Watson team who solve paranormal cases.

"Actually, I do not care at all what becomes of the capital of humans or that lord of ours."

The author, Reiko Okano—who is the daughter-in-law of "manga god" Tezuka Osamu—goes to considerable lengths to create a detailed and authentic feel of the era. Instead of resorting to flashy Chi blast fights, which are so common in manga, the spells used to restore the natural order of things are based on philosophy, religion, and even geometry. In one fascinating example, Seimei plays the ancient Chinese board game Go against an evil god, with the future of the capital at stake. Each part of the board corresponds to the actual layout of the spiritual barriers of the city itself. Also, poetry and music are noted among the prime strengths that can ward off evil forces. Backed by the superb artwork combining elements from ancient Japanese and Chinese folk art to visualize the supernatural creatures, *Onmyoji* is a gracefully unique work. **NK**

The Maxx 1993

✎ Sam Kieth   ✎ William Messner-Loebs

The main character of *The Maxx* series is a homeless man named Dave who lives in a cardboard box in an alley. His friend Julie Winters, who previously endured an assault and has trouble coping with life, is his self-appointed social worker. Both can enter a parallel world, the Outback, which is actually a manifestation of Julie's subconscious, where Julie is the Jungle Queen and Dave her protective spirit animal, a rabbit named the Maxx. Reality and the Outback intertwine, and the challenge for both Julie and Dave is to stay sane as they keep on shifting between their identities in the two worlds. For this they need the help of a teenager named Sarah, and her father, who was once the villain known as Mr. Gone.

"I kept wanting to ask 'How can rocks fly?' But in context it seems like a dweeby question."

This implausible set-up should not be as engaging as it is, but Sam Kieth manages to pull it off with the help of Messner-Loeb's well-written and believable dialogue, a long line of colorful and interesting characters, along with fast-paced action sequences and funny one-liners. Childhood traumas, imaginary animals, real-life crime, and distorted dreams are mixed together in amazingly beautiful, dynamic drawings. The bizarre mix of real and imagined worlds is made intelligible by means of a variety of different drawing styles, expressive colors, speech balloons, and experimental layouts. Kieth's pages look just as crazy and wild as his story.

The Maxx is over the top but it succeeds in telling a very moving story about the way that love can overcome all obstacles and get us through the most difficult times. It shows how loved ones can help conquer the darkness inside us. **RPC**

First published by Image Comics (USA)
Creators Kieth (American, b.1963); Messner-Loebs (American, b.1949)
Genre Superhero

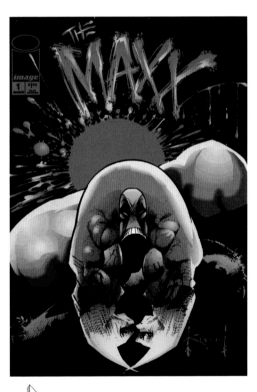

Similar reads
Four Women Sam Kieth
The Invisibles Grant Morrison and others
The Sandman Neil Gaiman and others
Zero Girl Sam Kieth

Space Dog 1993

Hendrik Dorgathen

First published by Rowohlt (Germany)
Creator German (b.1957)
Genre Science fiction
Award Max & Moritz Prize (1994)

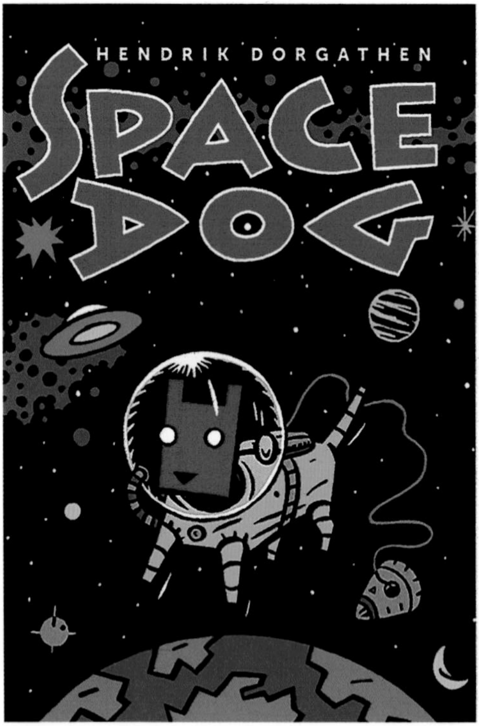
HENDRIK DORGATHEN
SPACE DOG

If one were to judge Hendrik Dorgathen's *Space Dog* according to the strict criteria of many comics experts, then it would probably not pass the test as a comic. This is because *Space Dog* is wordless, with none of the typical characteristics of a comic such as speech bubbles and words. The idea is not new: the Belgian painter, draftsman, and graphic artist Frans Masereel had experimented with a sequential narrative in pictures without words in *My Book of Hours*, published in 1919. Influenced by Masereel's angular woodcut pictures, Dorgathen's pioneering graphics incorporate the pixel art that was popular in the 1990s, spiced up with bright primary colors.

The eponymous protagonist is a little red dog who grows up in bucolic, idyllic surroundings but longs to see the big wide world. He travels to the city and finds himself in an animal shelter when he is thought to be a stray. There he is discovered by a NASA worker. The simple country dog is then transformed into the world-famous Space Dog, because in space there are extraterrestrial creatures who enable the dog to speak the language of humans. The whole world listens to Space Dog as he addresses the United Nations General Assembly, pleading for peace and criticizing the nuclear power lobby. Space Dog behaves like a human celebrity—he has affairs with starlets, tries his luck as a singer, and succumbs to alcohol. In reality he is searching for his lost love, a female dog he met briefly before he was taken to the animal shelter by the dog catchers.

Space Dog is a timeless story that is reminiscent of classics of the past, while still being highly contemporary in its graphic and narrative style. It bridges the gap between comic and illustration, and between art and animation, while skillfully combining all these forms. **MS**

Similar reads
Hundert Ansichten der Speicherstadt Martin tom Dieck
In Vitro Marc Caro
***Passionate Journey* (*Mein Stundenbuch*)** Frans Masereel
Slow Hendrik Dorgathen

Strangers in Paradise 1993

Terry Moore

Katchoo and Francine are two female friends who share an apartment. Francine has a boyfriend, Freddy, although she worries about his commitment to the relationship. Katchoo is actually in love with the apparently straight Francine, but turns to a man named David for the affection that Francine cannot give her. Initially played for laughs, with the humor springing from both Francine's ignorance of Katchoo's true feelings and her troubles with Freddy, the story takes a more serious turn when readers learn about Katchoo's past. She was once a lesbian call girl for Darcy Parker, who is David's elder sister. A dead senator and a lot of stolen money add up to a dangerous situation.

The series leaps backward and forward in time to show Francine married to Brad and with a five-year-old daughter, Ashley. Darcy is seen trying to blackmail Katchoo into a final job. More is revealed about Katchoo's motivations and her relationship to Darcy Parker's girls, while, in another time, Francine's mother reluctantly summons Katchoo to see Francine, who is depressed over her forthcoming marriage. The central plots that develop from all these narrative elements focus on whether Francine and Katchoo will ever recognize their love for each other and whether Katchoo can escape a police investigation into her past.

Creator Terry Moore writes in a naturalistic style, often using text pieces to tell more story or allow for longer dialogues. Artistically, the relatively simple lines are embellished with ornate inking, but the whole ensemble is visually pleasing. The reader may feel teased by the frequent interruptions and restarting of relationships, but Moore explores in-depth the lives and decisions of his characters. The complex web of relationships, together with a suspenseful thriller story, make for an engaging and entertaining read. **NFI**

First published by Antarctic Press (USA), but mostly self-published
Creator American (b.1954)
Genre Drama

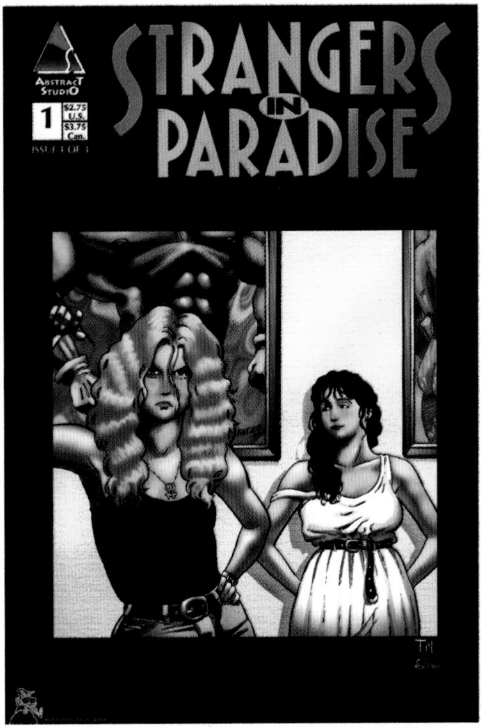
Abstract Studio
1
$2.75 U.S.
$3.75 Can.
Strangers in Paradise

Similar reads
Locas Jaime Hernandez
Omaha the Cat Dancer Kate Worley and Reed Waller
Tales from Sleaze Castle Terry Wiley
Tangents Miguelanxo Prado

The K Chronicles 1993

✑ Keith Knight

First published by *San Francisco Weekly* (USA)
Creator American (b.1966)
Genre Humor, Autobiography
Award Harvey Award (2007)

Keith Knight's strips are the comics equivalent of the observational comedian, in which he notes and comments on the annoyances of daily life. As such, he does not present the activities of a recurring cast of characters but draws his material from current events as they happen. One feature of *The K Chronicles* is the strand entitled "Life's Little Victories" (about fortuitous moments such as finding one has all the ingredients at home for a dish without having preplanned it), for which readers themselves have submitted topics.

An African-American whose work often reflects the specific experiences of African-Americans in his country, Knight covers an astonishingly broad canvas. Six pages of a collection, opened at random, deal with the disappearance of 1970s cover bands in San Francisco; the millennial U.S. presidential election; concerns about his mother clearing out the basement of the family home and discovering his nude drawings; stunt/dare reality television game show *Fear Factor*; annoying habits of former roommates; and his ignorance of foreign languages. Elements of Don Martin in the loose-limbed and expressive cartooning and the genial nature of the strips both contribute to Knight's success.

Knight's work is set in the real world and often addresses political, social, or racial issues .Controversies have been rare, but in 2008 a storm brewed when Knight relayed the true story of a couple who, when asked by a door-knocking pollster which candidate they would vote for, replied "the nigger." Uncompromising, yes, but it is Knight's humor that shines through. **FP**

Our Cancer Year 1994

✑ Harvey Pekar, Joyce Brabner, and Frank Stack

First published by New York Press (USA)
Creators Pekar (American, 1939–2010); Brabner (American, b.1952); Stack (American, b.1937)
Genre Biography

In 1987, professional whiner and old fart extraordinaire Harvey Pekar discovered he had cancer. A few years later he decided to depict his struggle with the disease for the reading public. This is a harrowing book that does not flinch from the horror of cancer. It is not a triumphant survivor's story, nor is it dramatized into a neat structure. Instead, it deals with all the minutiae of daily life lived in the shadow of the disease.

Cowritten with Joyce Brabner, Pekar's wife, *Our Cancer Year* presents a dual narrative. The story passes from one to the other, giving it pace and highlighting tense moments as well as tender and funny ones. Pekar, whose financial future was always precarious, simultaneously fights the disease while worrying about his ability to support his family and stop them being evicted from their apartment. There are no heroic confrontations, no brave speeches, just terrified people trying to muddle their way through.

Artistically, *Our Cancer Year* is a triumph. The story is illustrated by Frank Stack (better known as underground cartoonist Foolbert Sturgeon) a longtime friend who had contributed extensively to Pekar's *American Splendor*. Stack's style has always been sketchy, but here it seems to unravel in sympathy with Pekar's declining health; the pen-and-ink artwork looks like it was done straight to paper, without intermediate drafts, which gives a sense of urgency to events. Drawing parallels between his experience and the first Gulf War, which was occurring at the same time, Pekar's emotional account is a memorable exploration of a couple in crisis. **FJ**

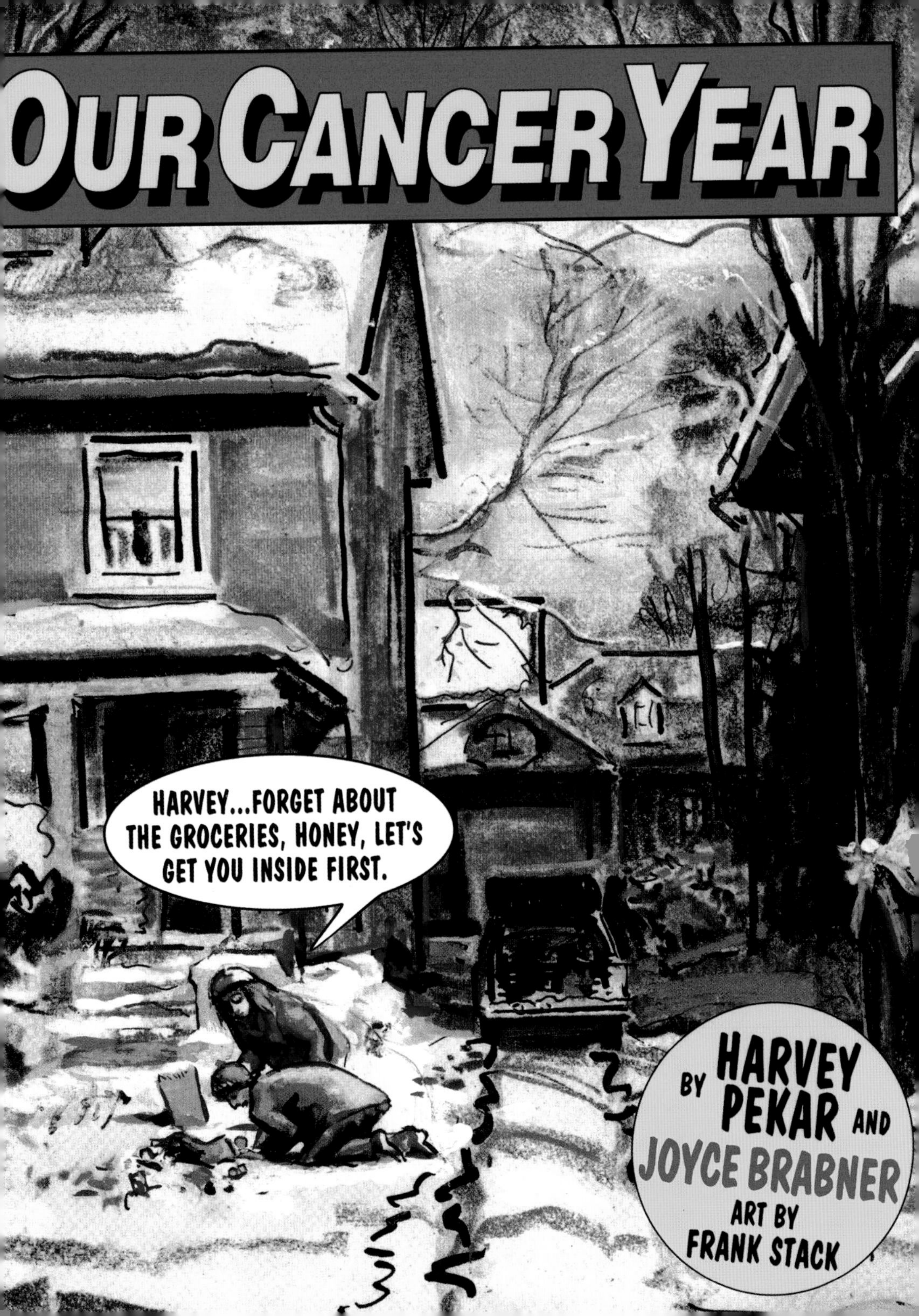
OUR CANCER YEAR
HARVEY...FORGET ABOUT THE GROCERIES, HONEY, LET'S GET YOU INSIDE FIRST.
BY HARVEY PEKAR AND JOYCE BRABNER
ART BY FRANK STACK

The Silence of Malka 1994

Jorge Zentner Rubén Pellejero

Title in original language *El Silencio de Malka*
First published by Glénat España (Spain)
Creators Zentner (Argentinian, b.1953); Pellejero (Spanish, b.1952) **Genre** Fantasy, Drama

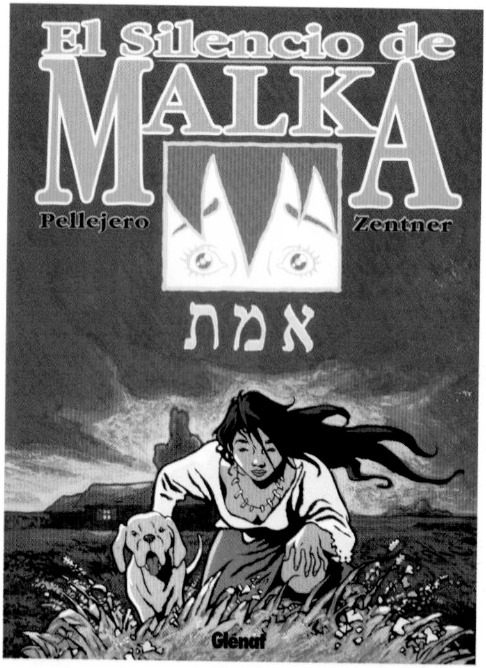
El Silencio de
MALKA
Pellejero
Zentner
אמת
Glénat

The Silence of Malka focuses on the Ukranian-Jewish families from the region of Bessarabia who, at the end of the nineteenth century, emigrated to Argentina in order to flee from the pogroms common in Russia at the time, and settling in the rural province of Entre Ríos, in the eastern part of that country (writer Jorge Zentner's grandparents were one such family). The title heroine, Malka, a perky red-haired little girl, acts as a link between the five chapters into which this eighty-two-page graphic novel is divided. Zentner adds to the historic background a fantastic element from Jewish folklore: the legend of the Golem. Malka's uncle Zelik, suffering from financial problems after having settled in Argentina, receives a calling from the prophet Elijah. He tells Zelik to create a Golem from mud and that it will become a real-life man. Things start to get complicated when Rosita, the granddaughter of Tomasa, the local folk healer, falls in love with the living Golem.

"This book was emotionally special. It was my family's history . . ." **Jorge Zentner**

The well-researched script by Zentner blends harmoniously with Rubén Pellejero's artwork, here a bit more stylized in comparison to his earlier work, and showcasing a clever use of color. This was Pellejero's first work in which he applied color directly onto the pages and page layouts. The latter are worth a special mention because some sequences are spectacular, such as Malka's dream before leaving Argentina and the Golem's desperate race in search of a country doctor. The final chapter, which features Malka as a young lady, offers a particularly faithful portrait of 1920s Buenos Aires. *The Silence of Malka* won the Alph-Art Award for Best Foreign Album at the Angoulême Festival, among other awards. **AM**

Also by Rubén Pellejero
A Bit of Blue Smoke (*Un Peu de Fumée Bleue*)
Âromm
Dieter Lumpen
Monsieur Griffaton
Taboo

Pirates of the Tietê and Other Barbarians 1994

Laerte Coutinho

Laerte Coutinho has enjoyed a long and successful career since the 1970s as one of Brazil's premier cartoonists. His popular daily strip, *Pirates of the Tietê,* first appeared in the 1980s. Under military rule in Brazil, cartoons generally featured humor spiked with considerable political satire. Many cartoonists did not survive the dawn of democracy in 1985—politics was all they knew how to lampoon.

Laerte's work, on the other hand, truly blossomed when the free press for which he fought came into existence. He is among the few Brazilian cartoonists whose work has steadily gained in depth and reputation, and who has taken his original daily strip to places it had never been before. He has consistently created wilder

"Father, help me! / Say ten Hail Mary's and then grab an urn of rum . . ."

characters and situations, and his acid wit still continues to fire shots everywhere like a gyrating machine gun.

Pirates of the Tietê and Other Barbarians is a collection of stories that were originally published in the magazine *Circus*. The comic strip centers on a group of iconoclastic, marauding pirates who loot and torture anyone they encounter on their travels—just for the fun of it. They are helped by their creator's ability to grasp the essentials of anything he chooses to portray.

Laerte's strip is still popular, even if the pirates themselves are long gone. They had their fun, even with werewolves, and were amusingly susceptible to good poetry. Laerte adapted the strip for a film version in 2003. The other stories in the collection demonstrate that Laerte never did just one thing, even back in the 1990s. These concise, sharp, award-winning stories, drawn with the ease of a master, never miss the opportunity to make readers laugh. **CB**

Title in original language *Piratas do Tietê e Outras Barbaridadesf*
First published by Circo Editorial (Brazil)
Creator Brazilian (b.1951) **Genre** Humor

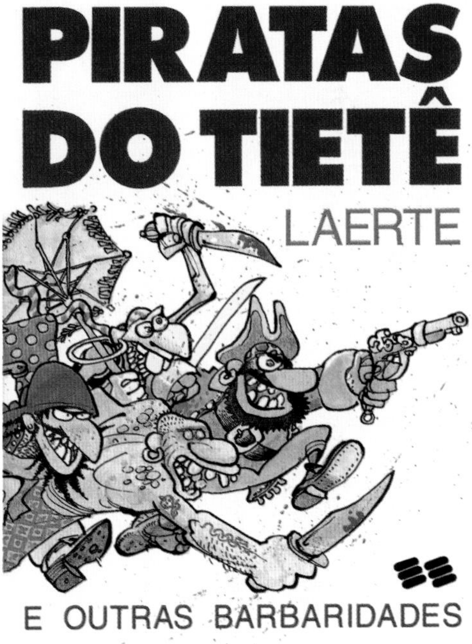
PIRATAS DO TIETÊ
LAERTE
E OUTRAS BARBARIDADES

Also by Laerte

Laertevisão
Muchacha
Sudden Stories (*Histórias Repentinas*)
The Three Amigos (*Los Tres Amigos*) with Angeli and Glauco Villas Boas

City of Glass 1994

Paul Auster and Paul Karasik David Mazzucchelli

First published by Avon Books (USA)
Creators Auster (American, b.1947); Karasik (American, b.1956); Mazzucchelli (American, b.1960)
Genre Crime, Adventure

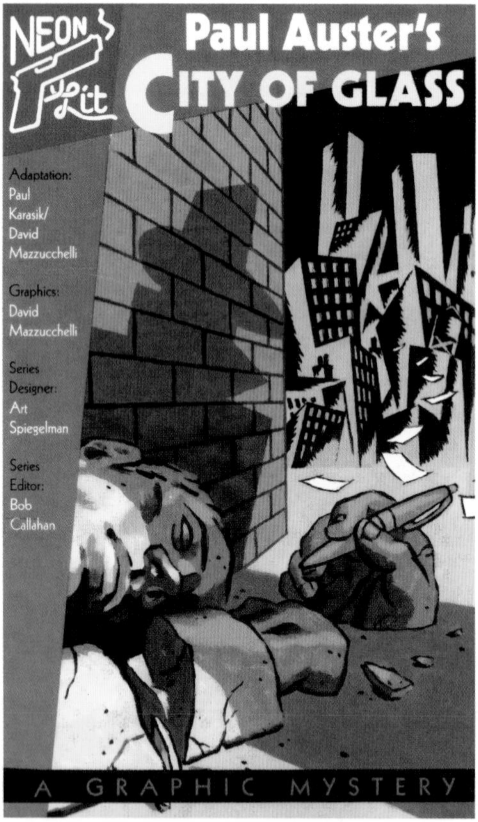
NEON Lit
Paul Auster's
CITY OF GLASS
Adaptation: Paul Karasik/ David Mazzucchelli
Graphics: David Mazzucchelli
Series Designer: Art Spiegelman
Series Editor: Bob Callahan
A GRAPHIC MYSTERY

"It was a wrong number that started it. . . ."

The question: why adapt one of the most celebrated novels of the 1980s as a comic book? The answer: to make it even better. This seems to have been the attitude adopted by Paul Karasik and David Mazzucchelli when they turned their attention to Paul Auster's widely lauded postmodern detective novel of the same name. They stood a very good chance of failing at the task, and this only serves to highlight the extent of their achievement and makes this tale even more inspirational.

Paul Auster's original novel, *The City of Glass*, tells the story of Quinn, a depressed writer of mystery novels who is drawn into a case involving the Stillman family when he accidentally takes a call meant for the private investigator, Paul Auster (a nod to the original author). This is not a traditional crime story, and as Quinn investigates the situation, he begins to lose himself in the process. The novel explores the psychological ramifications of loss, and Quinn ventures into himself as much as he explores the city where he lives.

For Karasik and Mazzucchelli, the problem of visually presenting a novel in which very little happens in terms of narrative excitement necessitated an entirely new way of approaching the comics page. Mazzucchelli's sparse art goes from the representational toward deep abstraction, literalizing the philosophical issues that structure the story. *City of Glass* is a profound work, and one that reflects both an astonishing familiarity with the source text and a thorough understanding of the way that comics operate.

City of Glass was one of a very small number of crime novels adapted for comics with the support of notables such as Art Speigelman, and it is, by far, one of the best. Indeed, it is fair to say that it is one of the most successful adaptations of a novel produced in the comics form. **BB**

The novel and the comic complement one another perfectly. ➡

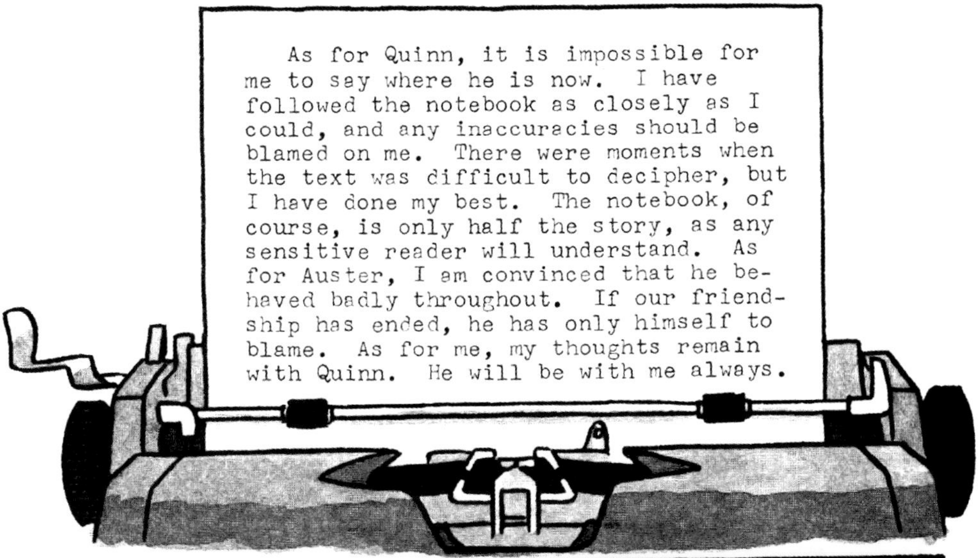
As for Quinn, it is impossible for me to say where he is now. I have followed the notebook as closely as I could, and any inaccuracies should be blamed on me. There were moments when the text was difficult to decipher, but I have done my best. The notebook, of course, is only half the story, as any sensitive reader will understand. As for Auster, I am convinced that he behaved badly throughout. If our friendship has ended, he has only himself to blame. As for me, my thoughts remain with Quinn. He will be with me always.

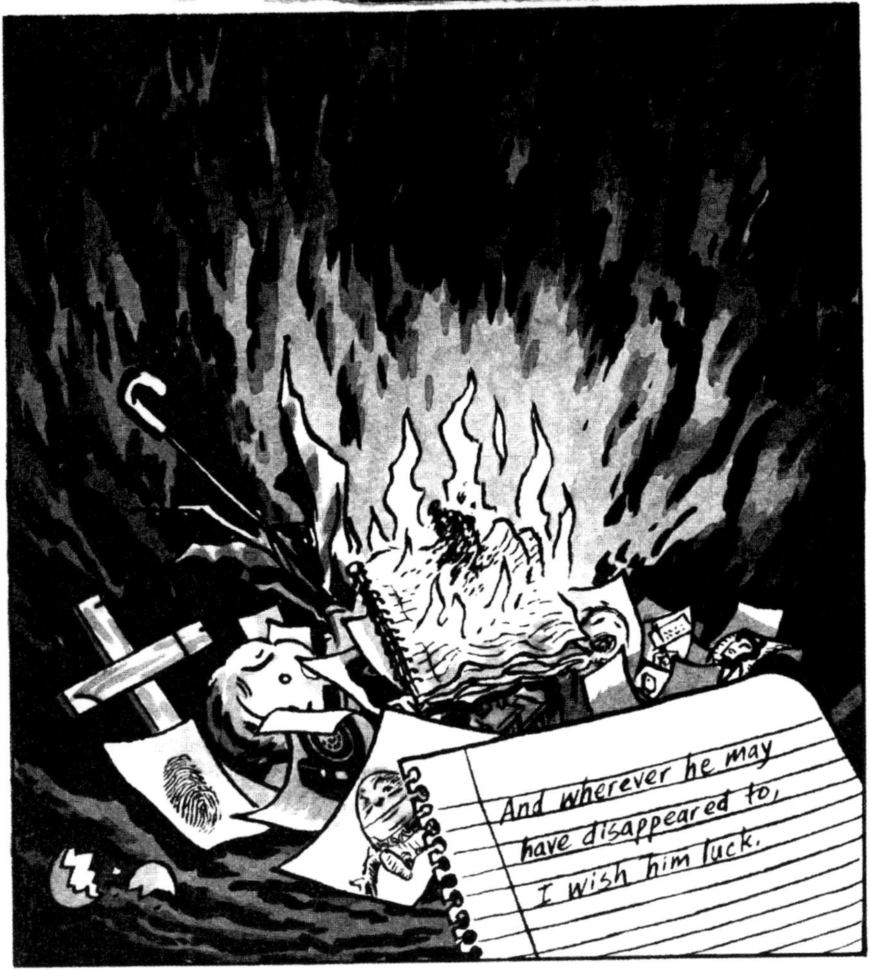
And wherever he may have disappeared to, I wish him luck.

The Highway of the Sun 1994

"Baru"

Title in original language *Taiyo Kosoku*
First published by Kodansha (Japan)
Creator Hervé Barulea (French, b.1947)
Genre Adventure, Drama

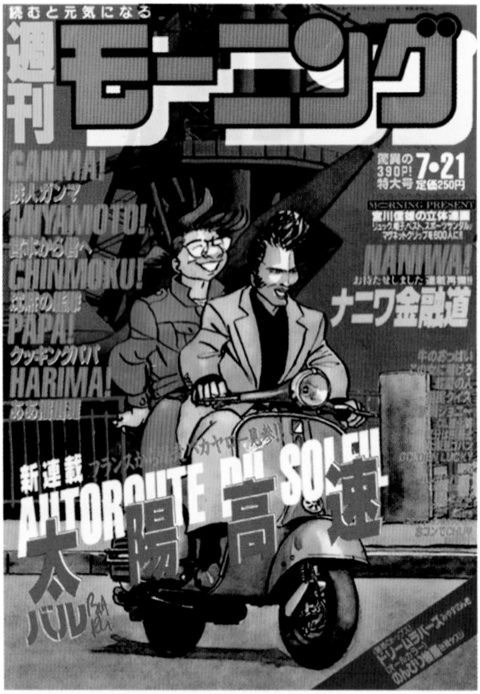

週刊モーニング
7•21
ナニワ金融道
AUTOROUTE DU SOLEIL
太陽高速

Also by Baru
Quéqette Blues
Road to America (*Le Chemin de L'Amérique*) with Jean-Marc Thévenet
The Communion of Mino (*La Communion du Mino*)
Vive la Classe

The publishing itinerary of *The Highway of the Sun* was very unusual. It was a Japanese publisher, Kodansha, that first commissioned this vast project (more than 400 plates) within the context of an experiment: to introduce European authors to the Japanese market through regular publication in *Morning*, one of Japan's weekly magazines for adults. This experiment enabled the French author Baru to conceive his project in a format that was very unusual at the time: the graphic novel. Soon published as a book by Casterman, *The Highway of the Sun* was so innovative and attractive that it was awarded the prize for the best album at the Festival of Angoulême in 1996.

It is remarkable not only because of its format and its length. If this French-style paper road movie remains a standard reference work, it is because it perfectly synthesizes the amazing originality of Baru's strip cartoons. It offers an unambiguous social and political commentary, a charming representation of working-class France, and an acute sense of movement and action.

The story follows the adventures of two characters—Karim and Alexander—brought together by fate. Karim, a good-looking, twenty-two-year-old North African charmer, has just been discovered in bed with the wife of the leader of a right-wing party. It is only the quick thinking of Alexander that allows him to escape from the husband's bodyguards who have orders to kill Karim. This results in a crazy pursuit that takes the fugitives right across France. During their mad escapade they encounter all kinds of fascinating, inspirational, and sometimes pathetic human beings. This exhilarating graphic novel delivers a magnificent display of narrative and graphic energy, while at the same time settling a few scores with some noxious, unpleasant, and unfortunate creatures. **NF**

Lanfeust of Troy
Ivory of the Magohamoth 1994

Christophe Arleston   Didier Tarquin

Ivory of the Magohamoth was the first of eight volumes in Christophe Arleston's *Lanfeust of Troy* series, published between 1994 and 2000. Largely unknown to Anglophone readers, this high fantasy series has spawned several sequels and spin-offs.

In the world of Troy, each and every human has a unique magical ability that they use in their everyday lives. The hero of the series, Lanfeust, can heat metal at will and uses this power to become an apprentice blacksmith. When a passing knight asks him to mend his sword Lanfeust is captivated by the weapon's handle. Carved from the ivory of a mythical beast and with the ability to develop incredible and all-encompassing powers, it is a truly powerful substance. Lanfeust embarks on a journey with the sage, Nicolede, and his two daughters, C'ian (who is bethrothed to Lanfeust) and Cixi (who constantly teases and torments Lanfeust), to the University of Magic to learn more about his powers. Inevitably they encounter dramas and obstacles as the quest takes them through Arleston's convincing world, full of incredible locales and beasts, all superbly penciled by Didier Tarquin.

If the essence of French literature lies amid the tension between classical high order and the freedom of *l'esprit Gaulois*, then Lanfeust defiantly positions itself toward the latter. Arleston takes the currency of high fantasy and trades it with the earthier coin of the traditional *fabliaux*, or traditional humorous verse tales. The books are soaked in wordplay, bawdy innuendo, scantily clad ladies, and lashings of scarlet violence (the deaths in the first volume alone are literally uncountable), but, like René Goscinny's best *Asterix* adventures, linguistic and subtextual playfulness is rife. Readers can only hope any official English translations will be handled by writers as dextrous as Anthea Bell and Derek Hockridge. **DN**

Title in original language *Lanfeust de Troy*
First published by Soleil Productions (France)
Creators Arleston (French, b.1963); Tarquin (French, b.1967) **Genre** Fantasy

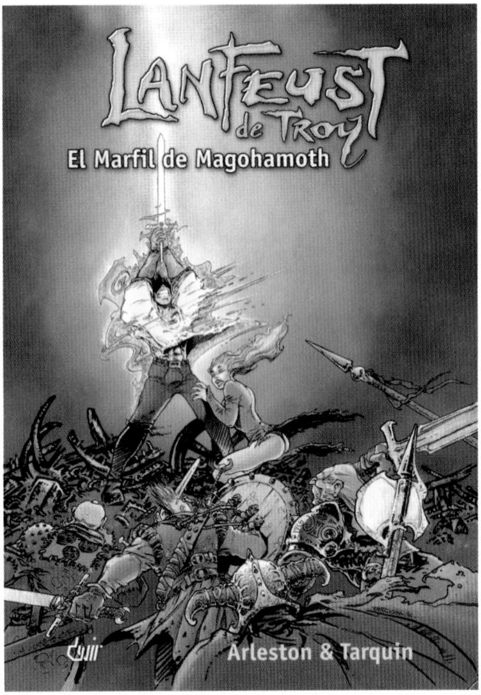
LANFEUST de TROY
El Marfil de Magohamoth
Arleston & Tarquin

Also in the *Troy* series
Conquerors of Troy (Les Conquérants de Troy)
Lanfeust Odyssey
Lanfeust of the Stars (Lanfeust des Étoiles)
Legends of Troy (Les Légendes de Troy)
Trolls of Troy (Trolls de Troy)

Marvels 1994

✎ Kurt Busiek   ✎ Alex Ross

First published by Marvel Comics (USA)
Creators Busiek (American, b.1960);
Ross (American, b.1970)
Genre Superhero

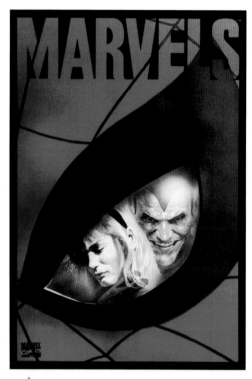

> **Similar reads**
> *Astro City* Kurt Busiek, Alex Ross, and Brent Anderson
> *Justice* Jim Krueger, Alex Ross, and Doug Braithwaite
> *Kingdom Come* Mark Waid and Alex Ross
> *The JLA/Avengers* Kurt Busiek and George Perez

Marvels is a graphic novel that retells the broad outlines of the history of the Marvel Universe as seen from the perspective of newspaper reporter Phil Sheldon. The story cleverly interweaves the development of the Marvel superheroes with major events of U.S. and world history from 1939 to the 1970s. Kurt Busiek and Alex Ross emphasize the strangeness, and even horror, of "Marvels" (superheroes) living in the same world as ordinary people.

The arrival of the Marvels means that the world can never be a cozy place again—much like the historical intervention of Nazism, the Holocaust, and the atom bomb. Artistically, *Marvels* is a tour de force by the visionary Ross, his painted panels bringing

"It is with considerable difficulty that I remember the original era of my being."
Human Torch

amazing vitality to the flames of the Human Torch, the sinister appearance of the mutant X-Men, and the first sighting of Galactus. The story line—in keeping with many of the more thoughtful superhero stories of the 1990s—focuses on the effect of the existence of superheroes on the mentality and mental well-being of the man or woman in the street.

By reinventing the Marvel universe from the point of view of the bystander, Busiek and Ross signaled a way forward for the superhero genre, which had become mired in the violent genre deconstructions that proliferated in the aftermath of *The Dark Knight Returns* and *Watchmen*. Viewing world history through the lens of the superhero has subsequently informed such successful works as Busiek's *Astro City*, Ross's *Kingdom Come*, Darwin Cooke's *The New Frontier,* and Mark Millar's *Ultimate Avengers*. **RR**

Yellow Negroes 1994

Yvan Alagbé

Title in original language *Nègres Jaunes*
First published by Amok Éditions (France)
Creator French (b.1971)
Genre Drama

Yvan Alagbé met Olivier Marboeuf in the early 1990s; both men were unhappy with commercial comics and shared a desire to express themselves more effectively in comics. Together they created Amok Éditions in 1992. Their editorial described their vision: "Deep childhood nostalgia condemns comics' efficiency vis-à-vis the real world and corners it on the periphery of contemporary stakes. Amok wants to be at the core of a creative confrontation with reality."

The anthology *The Headless Horse* (*Le Cheval sans tête*) was their flagship title, but they also published their own and other creators' books. Their priority was the immigrant postcolonial experience in France and the history of colonized peoples. The first version of

"I wanted to do something cool, less sensitive."

Yvan Alagbé

Yellow Negroes was published in *The Headless Horse*. It was considerably altered by Alagbé for the definitive album edition because his drawing style had evolved significantly since its initial publication. His new style made more use of negative spaces and was a lot more elegant and simple. It was, as he put it, more cool and detached, which he felt was important when dealing with such sensitive themes as racism and rootlessness.

Hugo Frey discovered a great visual device used by Alagbé in the book: black people's skin color is toned up or down according to white people's racism. They are defined by other people's gazes, not by what they are. *Yellow Negroes* tells the story of Mario, an ex-harki Argelian who sided with the French. He is a pitiful character, not accepted by white society but unable to be an African again either. **ID**

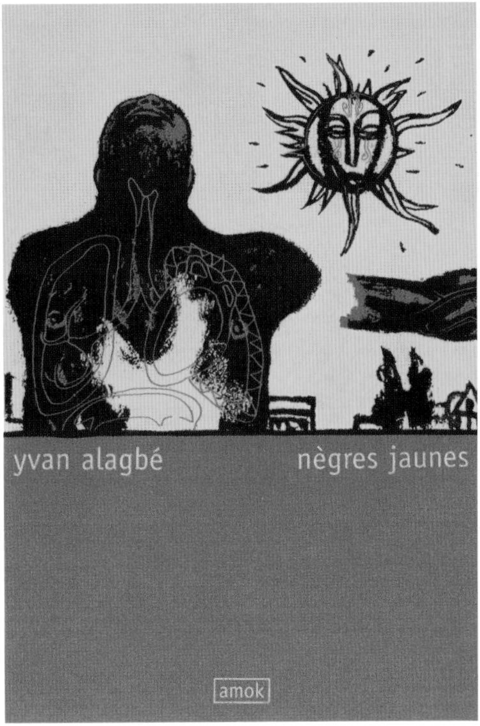
yvan alagbé
nègres jaunes
amok

Similar reads

A City on a Tuesday (*Une Ville un Mardi*) Olivier Marboeuf
Dyaa Yvan Alagbé
Les Exilées, Histoires Nabile Farès and Kamel Khélif
Qui a Connu le Feu Yvan Alagbé and Olivier Bramanti

The Tale of One Bad Rat 1994

Bryan Talbot

First published by Dark Horse Comics (USA)
Creator British (b.1952)
Genre Reality drama
Award Eisner Award (1996)

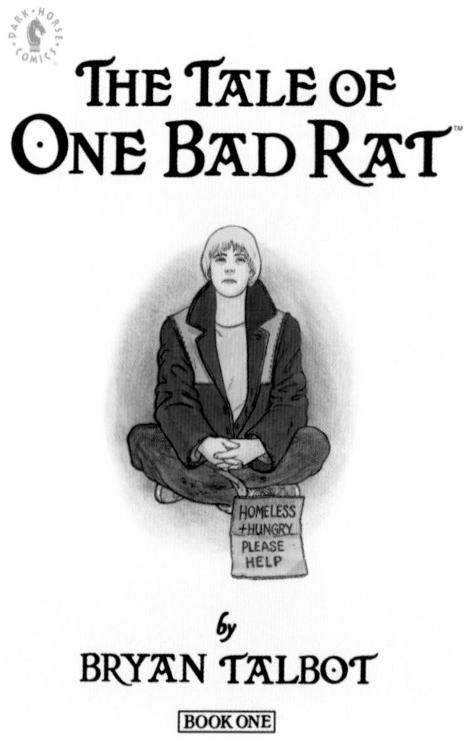
DARK HORSE COMICS
THE TALE OF ONE BAD RAT™
HOMELESS +HUNGRY PLEASE HELP
by
BRYAN TALBOT
BOOK ONE

Similar reads
Alice in Sunderland Bryan Talbot
Ctrl Alt Shift Unmasks Corruption Various
Psychiatric Tales Darryl Cunningham

The Tale of One Bad Rat is the sorrowful but ultimately uplifting story of Helen Potter, a young girl who runs away from her sexually abusive father and uncaring mother. Living rough on the streets with no self-esteem, harassed by strangers, and fantasizing about suicide, Helen finds herself embarking on a journey in the footsteps of her hero, Beatrix Potter. Traveling north from London to the tranquil beauty of the Lake District and accompanied by a huge imaginary rat, Helen eventually realizes that she must face her demons and gather the strength that she needs to come to terms with her abuse, as well as confront her abuser.

One of the true originals in the medium, *The Tale of One Bad Rat* is about overcoming the shadows of the past and functions as a self-help book as much as a powerful drama. Ever since publication, Bryan Talbot has received a constant stream of letters from abuse survivors for whom Helen has been an inspiration. You do not have to have been sexually abused to take something away from this book; victims of bullying, domestic violence, and many other forms of abuse will also find Helen's journey helpful.

"You were the most important person in my life. I idolized you. Then you started to molest me."

Sexual abuse is a brave subject to tackle in any medium, but Talbot approaches it with a calm, measured maturity that makes *The Tale of One Bad Rat* a landmark moment in comics. The clear and comfortable illustration style is deliberately designed to be accessible, even by those who would not normally read comics, and Helen's journey has been a gateway into the medium for many. *The Tale of One Bad Rat* is a transformative experience for all who read it. **BD**

Brooklyn Dreams 1994

J. M. DeMatteis Glenn Barr

First published by Paradox Press/DC Comics (USA)
Creators DeMatteis (American, b.1953); Barr (American, b.1958)
Genre Drama, Autobiography

J. M. DeMatteis likes to describe his mini-series *Brooklyn Dreams* as a "thinly disguised autobiographical account" of his senior year in high school. It is a personal journey in which he uses the fictional character of Carl Santini to find the answers to big questions: family, God, the need for love, and the inevitability of death. "I find fiction is a better doorway into the truth than memoir," he once said.

Santini spent his childhood living in the New York suburb of Brooklyn, and, as the narrator in *Brooklyn Dreams,* goes back into the memories of his old neighborhood, taking a fresh look at some of the pivotal moments during his senior year of high school and dissecting them from the perspective of adulthood.

"I'll weave you some lies about my life. With a little luck, they just might turn out to be true."

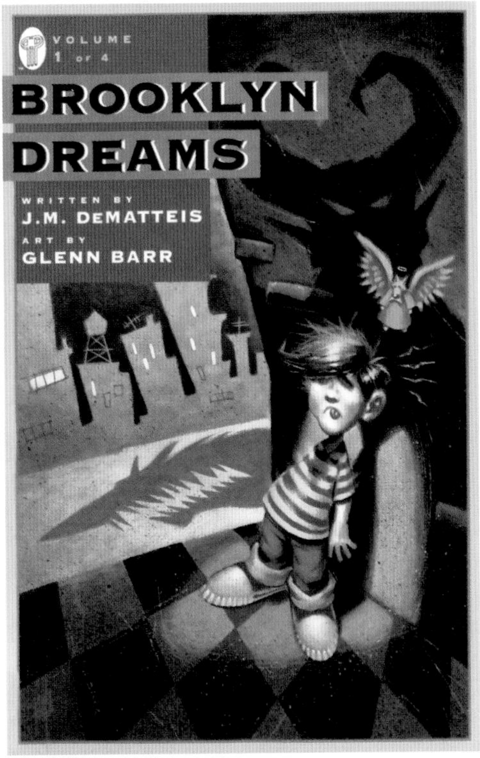
VOLUME 1 OF 4
BROOKLYN DREAMS
WRITTEN BY J.M. DEMATTEIS
ART BY GLENN BARR

Brooklyn Dreams was released in four ninety-six-page issues under the DC Comics imprint Paradox Press, a vehicle for more sophisticated, thought-provoking titles, featuring story lines outside the normal realm of DC's superhero-filled universe. The fact that Paradox ultimately failed to take off is no reflection on DeMatteis's hypnotic tale. It is illustrated in pencils, inks, and watercolors in a mangalike style by Glenn Barr.

DeMatteis's characters are so real and well defined that readers might question whether or not they are fictitious. The stray dog Santini meets is not really his guardian angel, but his many digressions, such as his description of his melodramatic Italian-Catholic father and nervous Jewish mother, overflow with grit and realism. The 1970s Brooklyn neighborhood he and Barr so vividly re-create delivers a tale where digressions are an integral part of a memorable journey. **BS**

Similar reads
A Contract with God Will Eisner
Road to Perdition Max Collins
Seekers into the Mystery J. M. DeMatteis

Buddy Does Seattle 1994

Peter Bagge

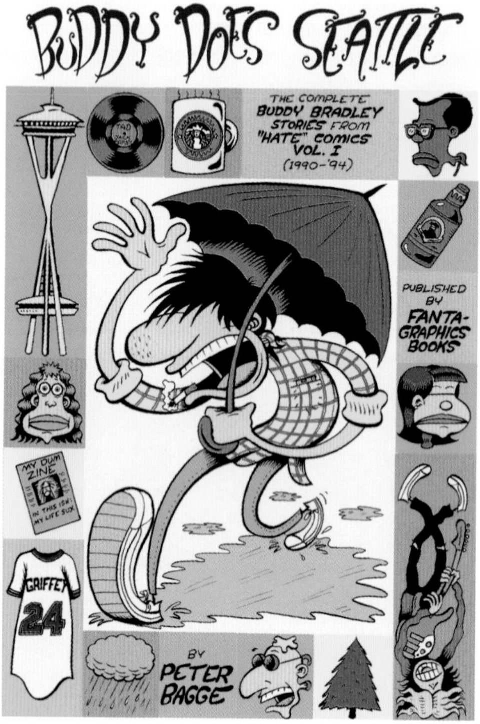
BUDDY DOES SEATTLE
THE COMPLETE BUDDY BRADLEY STORIES FROM "HATE" COMICS VOL. I (1990–'94)
PUBLISHED BY FANTAGRAPHICS BOOKS
MY DUM ZINE
IN THIS ISH: MY LIFE SUX
24
BY PETER BAGGE

"There's a very fine line between humor and tragedy—especially since I use the former to deal with the latter."

Also by Peter Bagge
Apocalypse Nerd
Fun with Buddy and Lisa
Hey Buddy!
The Bradleys

First published by Fantagraphics Books (USA)
Creator American (b.1957)
Genre Autobiography, Humor
Award Harvey Award (1991)

Buddy Does Seattle is a collection of several stories from Peter Bagge's *Hate* comic series. His whiny loser protagonist, Buddy Bradley, leaves home and the bosom of his not-so-loving family to strike out on his own. Heading for Seattle, he expects to enjoy life away from his bratty sister and square parents, but has not anticipated the joys of sharing a cruddy flat with a bunch of weirdos and losers. There is also the small matter of actually making a living.

Bagge's sharp eye dissects the slacker culture of the early 1990s with relish, using his wild and distorted style of drawing—one of the most expressive and distinctive around—to caricature the would-be cool people. Everything is exaggerated, from boggle-eyed, frothing-mouthed anger to apathy, where the characters look like they are about to become a puddle on the floor. Engaging though the extraordinary art is, it is Bagge's dialogue that shines.

Bagge contrives to make Buddy look well-balanced for much of the book, in spite of his interaction with a gaggle of unusual human beings. Buddy gives up in the end and goes home with his tail between his legs after a series of disastrous relationships with crazy women. Bagge's creation is full of gross physical humor as well as rapier-sharp commentary on youth culture. Bagge invests so much in his characters and their frustrations and insecurities that they seem ready to burst out of the page. Since 2009, Bagge has contributed a regular comic strip to *Discover Magazine* and he published his graphic novel *Second Lives* in 2010. **FJ**

Maakies 1994

✒️ Tony Millionaire

First published by *New York Press* (USA)
Creator American (b.1956)
Genre Humor
Adaptation Animated TV series (2007)

Rumor has it that Tony Millionaire created the first *Drinky Crow* strip, about "a little bird who drank booze and blew his brains out," on a paper napkin at his local bar. The bartender offered him free beer every time he did another drawing, and this encouraged him to develop the character until the *New York Press* spotted him and asked him to draw a regular strip. He incorporated *Drinky Crow* into the surreal world of *Maakies,* and a cartooning superstar was born.

Certainly Millionaire seemed to appear out of nowhere in the 1990s, a mature—some might say jaundiced—voice, with his cast of polished grotesques drawn in a disturbingly realistic style. Many of the *Maakies* strips feature only Uncle Gabby, a drunken monkey, and the equally alcoholic Drinky Crow engaged in badinage—or sometimes just throwing up a lot. Others introduce a wider cast and are set on what appears to be a pirate ship crewed by a series of bizarre and unsavory figures. Vomit, mordant humor, and suicide feature heavily throughout, and nothing ever goes well for the antiheroes.

Maakies is an anarchic strip, and Millionaire sometimes has members of his family draw them in childish scribbles, or invites guest cartoonists. The visual style references a hodgepodge of early illustrators— Millionaire appears to collage bits in from older strips— and is dense and unrelenting, with tiny panels running as a secondary strip alongside the main one. Equally unrelenting are the rather depressing themes, which manage both to tickle and disturb. **FJ**

Monster 1994

✒️ Naoki Urasawa

Title in original language *Monsuta*
First serialized in *Big Comic Original* (Japan)
Creator Japanese (b.1960)
Genre Crime

In 1986 Düsseldorf, a young and brilliant Japanese surgeon, Kenzo Tenma, saved the life of a young boy, Johann. The boy was a refugee and the survivor of a mysterious family massacre. However, the child disappeared as soon as the surgeon completed the operation, and Tenma's three colleagues were inexplicably murdered. Nine years later, Tenma, who is now senior consultant at a large hospital, comes across Johann again. The circumstances are bloody and the meeting brief, but it is long enough to realize that the young man is at the root of these tragic events.

This is when Detective Heinrich Runge arrives on the scene; he is methodical, determined, and obstinate, convinced that Tenma is the perpetrator of all the murders. Forced to flee, the doctor decides to track down Johann—his only hope of proving his innocence. This is the start of an incredible pursuit, punctuated by further murders and obscure messages, warning Tenma of the imminent arrival of Monster, something no one will be able to stop.

Published in serial form for seven years and then as a series of eighteen books, *Monster* is a major benchmark in the recent history of Japanese strip cartoons. Luxuriant and full of rich hues, this thriller is a brilliant narrative construction that has its roots in the darkest corners of Europe's recent history and the totalitarian fantasies that developed there. It contains numerous characters and themes, including eugenics, paranoia, conspiracy theories, manipulations, and perversions of science. **NF**

The Tragical Comedy or Comical Tragedy of Mr. Punch 1994

Neil Gaiman   Dave McKean

First published by Gollancz (UK)
Creators Gaiman (British, b.1960); McKean (British b.1963)
Genre Fantasy
Adaptation BBC radio play (2005)

the tragical Comedy
OR
Comical tragedy
OF
BY NEIL GAIMAN AND DAVE MCKEAN
MR. PUNCH
A VG GRAPHIC NOVEL

Similar reads
Arkham Asylum: A Serious House on a Serious Earth Grant Morrison and Dave McKean
Cages Grant Morrison and Dave McKean
Signal to Noise Neil Gaiman and Dave McKean
Violent Cases Neil Gaiman and Dave McKean

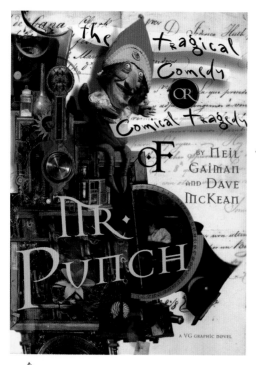

As the full title of Neil Gaiman and Dave McKean's graphic novel indicates, *Mr. Punch* is generically unclassifiable. On the surface the story follows the recollections of the narrator's visits to his grandparents by the sea and an encounter with a faintly sinister Punch and Judy man. Along with everyday experiences, such as fishing on the beach are introduced strange encounters with a mad grandfather, a hunchbacked great-uncle, a mermaid sideshow, and an unwanted pregnancy.

This is paralleled with the folk narrative of the Punch and Judy show about the archetypal trickster, Mr. Punch. It is one of a series of graphic collaborations between Gaiman and McKean from the late 1980s and early 1990s that resulted in some of the most genuinely innovative and intriguing work seen in the field of comics. Their first collaboration, *Violent Cases*, told the imperfectly recalled story of a young boy's memories of his father, an osteopath who once treated Al Capone. This established themes later taken up and developed in *Mr. Punch*. As with much of Gaiman's writing across different media, the story is concerned with memory and the unreliable nature of remembering the past. Unsurprisingly, there are characteristic gothic touches within the theme of buried family secrets.

"The greatest, oldest, wisest play there is: the comical tragedy, the tragical comedy, of Mr. Punch."

This is faultlessly married to the sometimes jarring and disorienting visuals from McKean, whose style owes more to graphic design and avant-garde art than conventional comics (see, for example, his outstanding *Sandman* covers). *Mr. Punch* offers the perfect synergy of author and illustrator, and for many readers it is Gaiman and McKean's best work. **TV**

Distorted photographs and drawings deliver a surreal collage of Mr. Punch's world. ➡

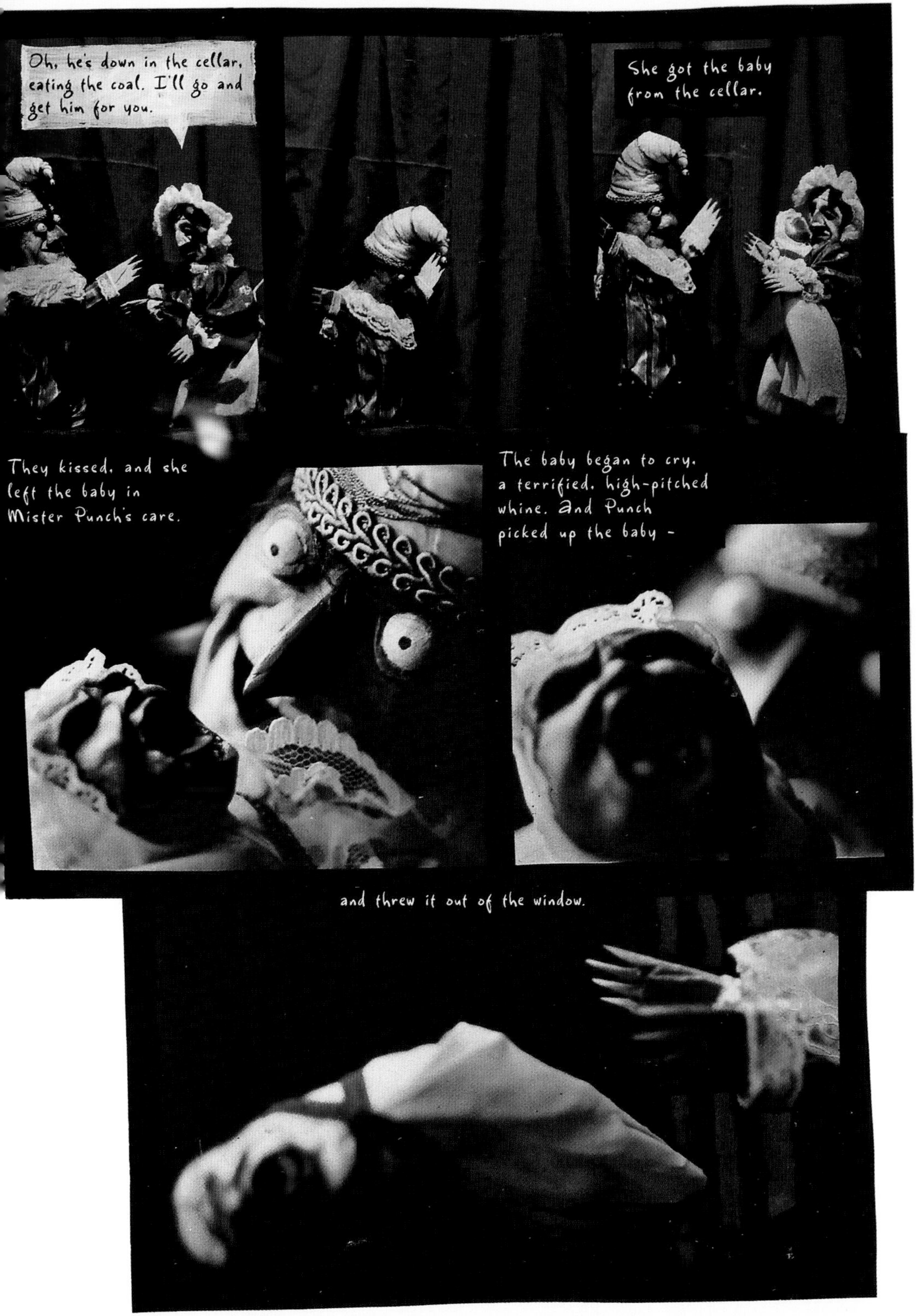
Oh, he's down in the cellar, eating the coal. I'll go and get him for you.
She got the baby from the cellar.
They kissed, and she left the baby in Mister Punch's care.
The baby began to cry, a terrified, high-pitched whine. And Punch picked up the baby -
and threw it out of the window.

The Life and Times of Scrooge McDuck 1994

Don Rosa

First published by Gladstone Publishing (USA)
Creator American (b.1951)
Genre Humor
Award Eisner Award (1995)

Walt Disney's
The Life and Times of
$crooge McDuck
Companion
by
DON ROSA

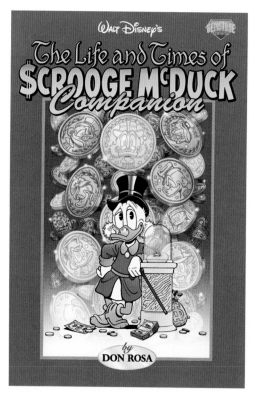

"The main reason I accepted the assignment was just for the fun of it."

Don Rosa

With *Duck Tales* a successful television cartoon in the early 1990s, Disney needed a chronological history for Uncle Scrooge McDuck. Carl Barks had conceived the character in 1947, but he had created his material before continuity became commonplace in comics. For more than twenty years, elements of Scrooge's past were dropped in, often merely as asides, as and when they suited the story that Barks was working on at the time, and these were rarely referred to again.

In lesser hands, cataloguing Scrooge's life might have been a dry exercise, but Don Rosa was already widely considered the spiritual heir to Barks. His stories were well researched, inventive, and entertaining, and his art expressive and gag-packed. Rosa began by classifying the Barks *Scrooge* stories as canonical and ignoring those by lesser talents, then wove a twelve-part epic around the random details.

Throughout the series, Scrooge progresses from a young duck earning his first dime in Glasgow into the miserly sourpuss that Donald Duck meets decades later. The telling spans the world, incorporating initial encounters with the Beagle Boys, the Gearloose Family, and Flintheart Glomgold, and defines the McDuck family tree as Rosa revisits Scrooge highlights, weaving his own tales around them. Rosa often incorporated historical speculation in his stories, and the success of *Life and Times* resulted in even more stories from Scrooge's past, where he went on to meet other significant and well-known figures. These stories formed a collection known as *The Life and Times of Scrooge McDuck Companion.*

While never matching Barks's prodigious output, Rosa produced a significant body of work before retiring in 2007. He cited a combination of declining eyesight and constant frustrations with his publisher, including poor rates and lack of royalties for stories selling millions of copies globally. **FP**

Starman 1994

James Robinson Tony Harris

DC Comics's superhero universe is built on the concept of legacy, on the idea of heroic dynasties proudly passing down the champion's mantle to the next generation. *Starman*'s Jack Knight represents a deliberate subversion of that tradition. Son of the Golden Age Starman and the epitome of the reluctant hero, Jack is more interested in acquiring memorabilia for his junk shop than he is in his father's heroic past. Only when his brother David is murdered as part of a revenge plot against the Knight family does Jack resignedly agree to take on the name, if not the costume, of Starman.

Unlike the neverending narratives of traditional superhero comics, *Starman* was published over seven years as a finite series with a defined beginning, middle, and end. This allowed James Robinson to foreshadow future events months—sometimes even years—in advance. It also gave his greater, overarching story line a tautly plotted, complex feel and made the series into a superb narrative.

The philosophy that continuity enriches rather than encumbers a story line is on show throughout the series, with Robinson fashioning compelling and accessible stories from the most obscure minutiae of DC history. Opal City, the comic's setting, becomes a memorable supporting character in its own right, with a beautiful art deco design by original artist Tony Harris, and a rich, exploitable back story.

Beyond the obvious superheroics, *Starman*'s mix of themes is as eclectic as the contents of Jack's junk shop. It is about ephemera, pop culture, and the thrill of finding that one rare collectible—about obligation, families, and the sacrifices we make for them. However, most of all, it is about one man, initially so disdainful of the superhero world, discovering his own innate heroism, a sense of responsibility, and an understanding of the importance of the Starman lineage. **AO**

First published by DC Comics (USA)
Creators Robinson (British, b.1963); Harris (American, b.1969)
Genre Superhero

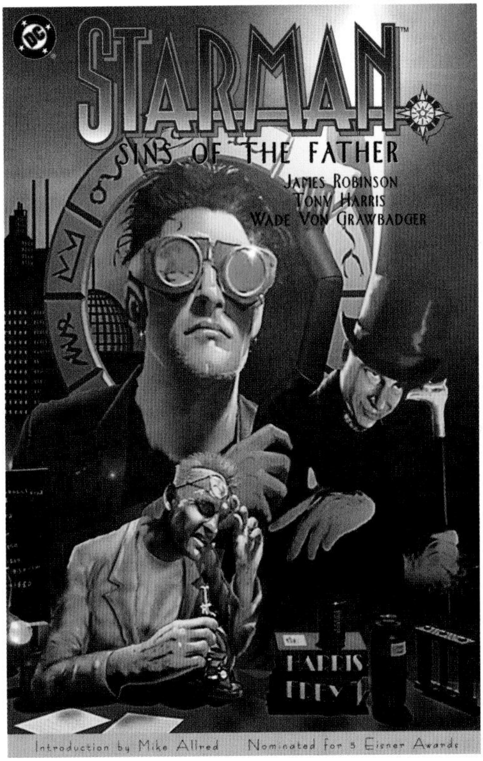
STARMAN
SINS OF THE FATHER
JAMES ROBINSON
TONY HARRIS
WADE VON GRAWBADGER
Introduction by Mike Allred   Nominated for 5 Eisner Awards

"I am not a hero. In no way. And even more . . . most definitely . . . I am not Starman."

The River of Stories 1994

✐✐ Orijit Sen

First published by Kalpavriksha (India)
Creator Indian (b.1962)
Genre Reality drama
Influenced by The Narmada Valley crisis

THE RIVER OF STORIES

A Graphic Novel by
Orijit Sen

KALPAVRIKSH, 1994

"These damned tribals always choose the most inaccessible places for their settlement."

India's first graphic novel, Orijit Sen's *The River of Stories*, has remained a hallowed presence on the Indian comics scene despite being out of print since it was first published, noncommercially, in 1994 by Kalpavriksh, a New Delhi–based, green NGO. This stunning graphic novel was the result of a grant awarded to Sen, a graphic designer who had been making comics since he was twelve years old. He won the grant for his proposal to combine words and images to record the bitter struggle of tribals and villagers, supported by activists and waged since 1989 against the building of the Sardar Sarovar dam across the Western Indian River Narmada.

Now operational since 2007, the dam remains one of India's most contentious development projects, with opinion split over its claimed benefits versus its environmental cost. *The River of Stories* tells of a tribal idyll destroyed in the name of progress by big money, bureaucrats, law enforcers, and politicians, and how the dispossessed joined protest groups such as the Narmada Bachao Andolan. *The River of Stories* was a cautionary—and sadly unheeded—tale for an India newly smitten with capitalism.

Sen clarifies that he never intended *The River of Stories* to present all sides of the issue. It was as a believer—not a journalist—aiming to ground his work in a real landscape and way of life that Sen visited the Narmada Valley and spent weeks sketching and talking to the people soon to be displaced. *The River of Stories'* simplistic politics and romanticization of pre-industrial economies arguably makes it propaganda literature. However, its picturesque realism, leavened with lyrical interludes tracing tribal creation myths, and within a sustained, unforced narrative albeit in conventional form, makes *The River of Stories* an impassioned plea for environmental sanity and the need to celebrate alternative ways of living. **HS**

Photo-realistic imagery helps to carry a powerful message. ➡

...Made a world full of pits and holes, projections and distortions...

Smooth in some places, rough in others, and held it in the palm of her hand, well pleased...

So she made trees, shrubs and grasses and planted them!

Beautiful looks my world. But what shall be the creatures to inhabit it?

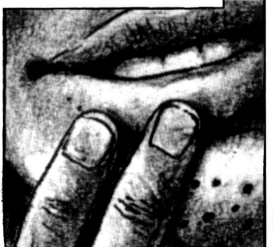

She took some clay and started shaping...shaped some lizards. Made some tigers and bears. Made snakes and birds..

We Are Reproducing 1994

✐✐ "Shungicu Uchida"

Title in original language *Watashitachi wa Hanshoku Shite Iru* **First published by** Bunkasha (Japan)
Creator Shigeko Uchida (Japanese, b.1959)
Genre Autobiography

Multifaceted Shungicu Uchida is a comics author and artist, novelist, actress, singer, and pop culture personality. Her idiosyncratic comic works defy easy classification. *We Are Reproducing* is a semiautobiographical series in which pregnancy, motherhood, and the attendant discomforts and pleasures are presented with charm and strong doses of sarcasm, honesty, and psychological realism.

One of Uchida's breezier and entertaining works, it has an unmistakable undertone of sexual politics. Begun in the early 1990s, it depicts feminism and motherhood as going hand in hand, the ideal of that decade's young Japanese career women. The protagonist—single, determined, and ambitious—wants to rear her child while climbing the corporate ladder. Just before giving birth and immediately after, she is seen diligently trying to meet a work project deadline. However, her drastically changed life situation has daunting dilemmas, including performance anxiety and self-doubt.

The subject matter is tackled with self-deprecating, ironic humor. The boyfriend (and child's father) is undeniably a one-dimensional character, but his behavior as a parent is so clichéd that he becomes a valuable asset to the story. Uchida's art is loose, sensual, and closely observed. Her cartoonlike figures have an uncanny realism and can be unabashedly erotic. *We Are Reproducing* has chronicled the pregnancies, births, and childhoods of Uchida's four children, named (in typically atypical Uchida fashion) Alpha, Beta, Gamma, and Delta. **TRL**

I Pity You: A Cartoonist's Diary 1994

✐✐ Philippe Dupuy and Charles Berbérian

Title in original language *Journal d'un album*
First published by L'Association (France)
Creators Berbérian (French, b.1959); Dupuy (French, b.1960) **Genre** Autobiography

By 1993 Philippe Dupuy and Charles Berbérian had been part of the French comics landscape for more than a decade. Their creative formula involved four hands—they shared the story line and drawing equally without either specifically claiming responsibility for one or the other. Their talent was recognized but they had not created the "big" book that would confirm them as major writers. *I Pity You* changed all that.

Initially, the project was simple: to record the progress of the album they were in the course of creating—the third volume of *Monsieur Jean*—closely following their daily work as creators. The whole point of the enterprise was to let it drift naturally toward related concerns, following the experiences of one and the other. This would be the piquancy of *I Pity You:* the mixing of genres and the continual overlapping of the creative project and "real life."

Dupuy and Berbérian hide nothing in their diary: the hesitations, anxieties, and hazards of their collaboration, as well as the parts played by those around them. Over the weeks, their moods change: sardonic and smiling when Berbérian is in control, darker and more introspective when Dupuy takes over. Affected by two deaths in his family, Dupuy does not seek to evade the difficulties he experiences at this moment, making his inner feelings one of the springs of his narrative. The result is a work of rare honesty, which made an impression with its subtle blend of lightness and gravity. Most importantly, *I Pity You* also highlighted the potential of autobiography as a comics genre. **NF**

From Inside 1994

🖉🖉 John Bergin

First published by Kitchen Sink Press (USA)
Creator American (Unknown)
Genre Science fiction
Adaptation Animated film (2008)

This strip has been compared with Cormac McCarthy's novel *The Road*—a vision of hell, complete with a sea of blood. In John Bergin's expressionistic, postapocalyptic graphic novel *From Inside*, a pregnant woman sees her husband die during a nuclear flash, before escaping on a train full of grotesque survivors through the ruins of a scorched Earth. The train passes one whistle-stop of devastation after another, a voyage of the damned bound for an unknown port.

The woman, who serves as the shocked narrator, is watched over by a mysterious man covered in bandages, and a dog with a skull for a head. All this is just a dream, she thinks again and again—but each time she awakens to find that most of the horrors are real. She is ambivalent about the impending birth of her child, unable to reconcile new life with the fast-approaching death of the world around her.

Bergin's dark vision of this journey, painted in red and brown tones, evokes blood, decay, and fire with the surreal clarity of a child's picture-book. *From Inside* is self-consciously a fable but definitely for adults. At times shocking, it is actually restrained, not exploitive in a way that one might expect from similar science fiction tales of doom. Written in a minimalist style, the narration may seem detached and the story unrelentingly claustrophobic, but there is always just enough hope to make readers want to turn the next page. Intense and graphic, an exploration of existential angst and the precarious nature of human life, it is deeply and tragically moving. **TRL**

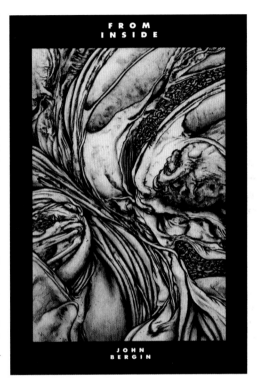

FROM INSIDE

JOHN BERGIN

"I reach for my baby …
But my hands are melting."

Similar reads
Blame! (*Buramu!*) Tsutomu Nihei
Bonesaw John Bergin
Dragon Head (***Doragon Heddo***) Minetaro Mochizuki
Panorama of Hell Hideshi Hino
The Crow James O'Barr

Hellboy: Seed of Destruction 1994

John Byrne Mike Mignola

First published by Dark Horse Comics (USA)
Creators Byrne (American, b.1950);
Mignola (American, b.1960)
Genre Horror, Adventure

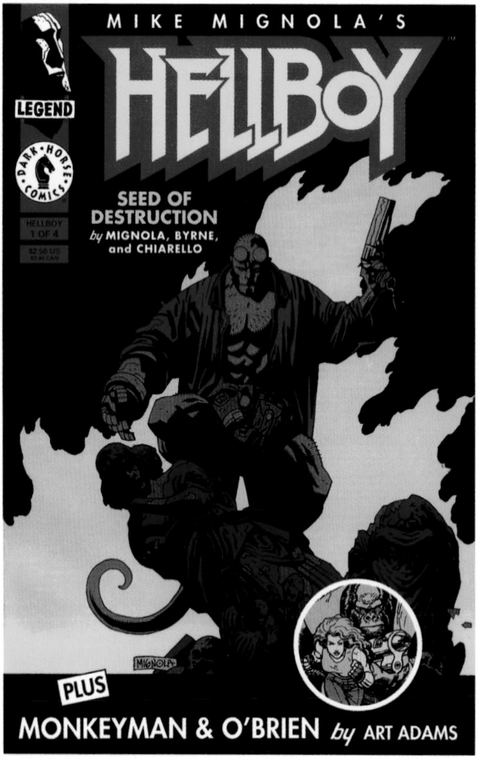
MIKE MIGNOLA'S
HELLBOY
LEGEND
DARK HORSE COMICS
SEED OF DESTRUCTION
by MIGNOLA, BYRNE, and CHIARELLO
HELLBOY 1 OF 4
PLUS
MONKEYMAN & O'BRIEN by ART ADAMS

Similar reads
B.P.R.D. Mike Mignola and Guy Davis
Death Note Tsugumi Ohba and Takeshi Obata
The Goon Eric Powell

Mike Mignola's obsession with myths and monsters may have started when, as a schoolboy, the richly detailed illustrations in a copy of John Bunyan's 1673 tract *Pilgrim's Progress* burned themselves into his impressionable brain. Still a novice writer in 1994, Mignola decided to keep Hellboy's origins secret until he was ready to tell them. All we learn is that on December, 23, 1944, in a massive fireball in an English church in East Bromwich, a bright red child first materializes on Earth. He had cloven hooves, sawn-off horns, forked tail, and a huge right hand made of stone.

He arrives at the site where Nazis are attempting to summon ancient monsters to their cause, a plot thwarted by a band of investigators who adopt the weird child and name him Hellboy. Raised on an army base in New Mexico and granted honorary human status by the United Nations in 1952, Hellboy eventually joins the Bureau for Paranormal Research and Defense.

"When I get angry, I sometimes do stupid things. Things like charging headlong into a pitch black room."

Mignola wanted to keep the concept simple: a big, cool-looking, demon guy battling monsters. He choreographs his colors and blacks to create an almost stained-glass effect. His learning curve as a writer took off from this first book, with some help from John Byrne, and he was soon rewriting his texts to make them less slick, more deliberately terse, even awkward. Sweeping the old tales he loved from world folklore into his plots, he was finding his voice. In subsequent stories, Mignola reveals more about Hellboy's past and adds sympathy by showing how he rejected his mission to wipe out humankind, his defiance symbolized by the horns that he himself severed. **PG**

The mystery of Hellboy's origins tantalizes both the character and readers.

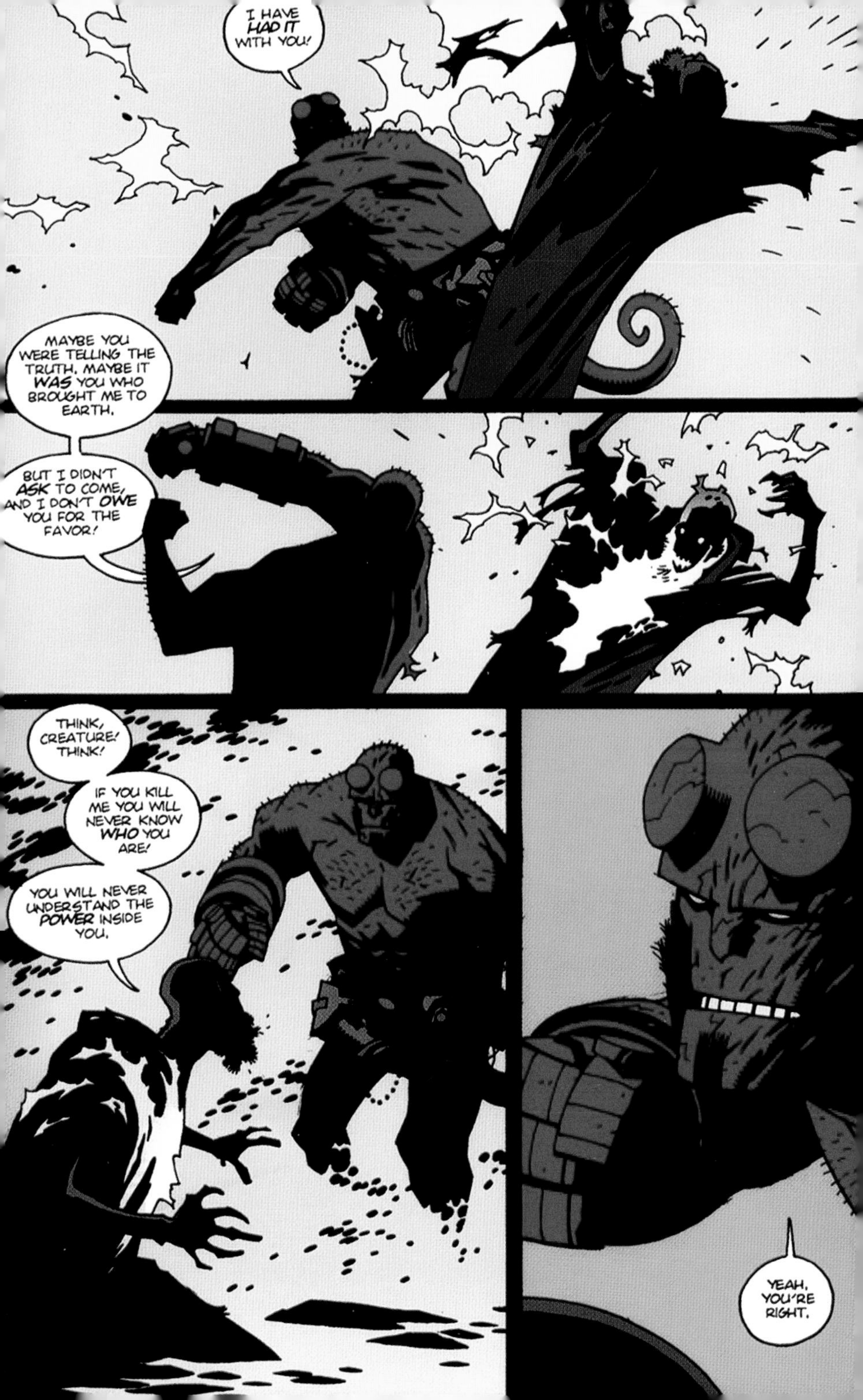
I HAVE HAD IT WITH YOU!
MAYBE YOU WERE TELLING THE TRUTH. MAYBE IT WAS YOU WHO BROUGHT ME TO EARTH.
BUT I DIDN'T ASK TO COME, AND I DON'T OWE YOU FOR THE FAVOR!
THINK, CREATURE! THINK!
IF YOU KILL ME YOU WILL NEVER KNOW WHO YOU ARE!
YOU WILL NEVER UNDERSTAND THE POWER INSIDE YOU.
YEAH, YOU'RE RIGHT.

The Invisibles 1994

Grant Morrison Various

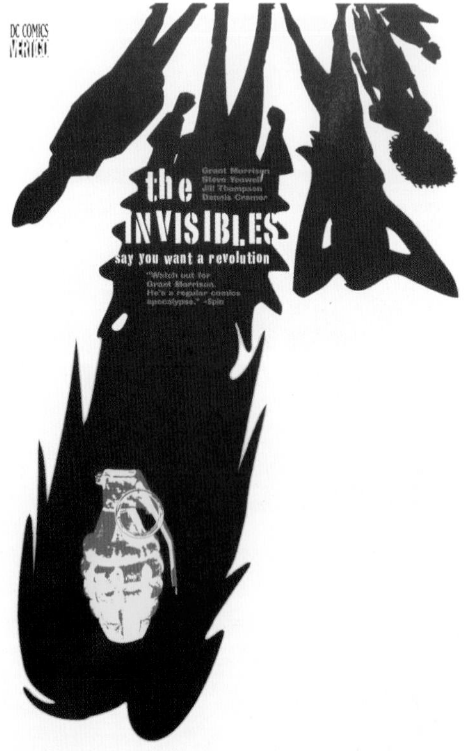
DC COMICS VERTIGO
the INVISIBLES
Grant Morrison
Steve Yeowell
Jill Thompson
Dennis Cramer
say you want a revolution
"Watch out for Grant Morrison. He's a regular comics apocalypse." -Spin

"Jump out of the world, jump to the place I showed you and you'll not fall."

Similar reads

Promethea Alan Moore, J. H. Williams III, and Mick Gray
Sebastian O Grant Morrison and Steve Yeowell
The Filth Grant Morrison, Chris Weston, and Gary Erskine
Zenith Grant Morrison and Steve Yeowell

First published by Vertigo/DC Comics (USA)
Creator British (b.1960)
Genre Science fiction
Adaptation Documentary: *Talking with Gods* (2010)

By the time Grant Morrison wrote *The Invisibles*, he was already famous for his astonishing, fourth-wall-puncturing reinvention of the minor DC Comics character Animal Man and his loopy reimagining of obscure superhero team Doom Patrol. *The Invisibles* gave him the opportunity to create an ongoing series of original characters and to fully indulge his interest in the esoteric and obscure for the first time.

It also marked the moment when he first began to experiment living as a chaos magician, and he launched his flagship series as an international spell that would change himself, comics, and, by extension, the world. The series started with a bang, breaking various taboos with strong language, a graphic portrayal of crime, and a fabulous cast of colorful counterculture characters, including tramps, terrorists, mad magicians, kids gone wrong, and a fabulous Brazilian transsexual called Lord Fanny.

Initially drawn by longtime Morrison collaborator Steve Yeowell, the series had a powerfully realistic feel. Later, more artists from the Vertigo stable, including Jill Thompson, Philip Bond, and Duncan Fegredo, joined Morrison in constructing his visceral collision of half-revealed stories and a magical system not so much described as suddenly and violently experienced. While later story lines occasionally foundered in self-indulgent rambling (once the series was brought back from the brink by a notorious fan campaign), Morrison's erratic genius kept those flashes of brilliance going right until the bitter end. **JD**

Mutts 1994

✐✐ Patrick McDonnell

First published by King Features Syndicate (USA)
Creator American (b.1956)
Genre Humor
Awards Five Harvey Awards for Best Comic Strip

Patrick McDonnell's *Mutts* is one of a small number of works that keeps the faltering heart of the U.S. comic strip beating. As strips become increasingly target-marketed and read as if they were assembled by a committee of bureaucrats, *Mutts* is an expression of pure whimsy in every morning's newspaper.

Launched in 1994, the strip is minimalist in all the best ways. The stars are Earl, a Jack Russell terrier who lives with Ozzie, and the neighboring cat, Mooch, who lives with Millie and Frank. Told from the point of view of the animals, *Mutts*, in contradistinction to Charles Schulz's Snoopy or Jim Davis's Garfield, presents animals that are not simply furry versions of humans. The jokes in *Mutts* are often rooted in simplicity but are presented with impeccable comic timing and a genuine fondness for the characters. McDonnell, who has published a book on the other beloved cat and dog (and mouse) strip, George Herriman's *Krazy Kat*, is one of the most knowledgeable and canny of contemporary cartoonists. He is a connoisseur of the visual image, and the title panels for his Sunday strips frequently use his characters to parody everything from punk rock graphics to the paintings of Johannes Vermeer.

As the years have passed, *Mutts* has moved beyond the confines of its original cast. Extended story lines are more common, and each summer Earl and Mooch visit their friends on the Jersey Shore. McDonnell has also used the strip as a platform to educate readers on animal welfare issues, always with an eye toward a celebration of the role that animals play in our lives. **BB**

Homo Metropolis 1994

✐✐ Nikoline Werdelin

First published by *Politiken* (Denmark)
Creator Danish (b.1960)
Genre Parody
Award Nominated for Eisner Award (2009)

Nikoline Werdelin has been steadily chronicling the life and times of her countrymen in a distinctive voice, blending quotidian realism and biting satire, since her debut as a strip cartoonist with *Café* in the daily *Politiken* in 1984. In addition to being a cartoonist, she is a celebrated playwright, and, taken as a whole, her work can be seen as an ongoing narrative portrait of Denmark through the medium of its people.

Café ended in 1988, but *Homo Metropolis*, launched in *Politiken* in 1994, was essentially its continuation under a different name. Drawing upon the tradition of Jules Feiffer, Gérard Lauzier, and Claire Brétecher, it is a big city strip with a sprawling cast of characters that has consistently captured and skewered the bourgeois zeitgeist of a privileged, parochial nation through what seemed, until recently, a more or less never-ending economic boom.

Werdelin is primarily distinguished by her sensitive ear for contemporary vernacular and for her sense of spoken rhythm broken down into a variable number of daily panels. Her drawing is arguably her main weakness, but, over the years, she has managed to refine its formulae and to harness her inelegant line into remarkably expressive, ugly portraits of her fellows. sometimes almost scabrous in their satire. Her coldness is tempered by an exacting sense of humor that brings a rare clarity to her vision. She is a diagnostician rather than a nihilist and a refined observer of people who has been writing and drawing the great Danish generation novel of her time. **MWi**

Palepoli 1994

Usamaru Furuya

First published by Ohta Shuppan (Japan)
Creator Japanese (b.1971)
Genre Underground
Collection *Secret Comics Japan* (2000)

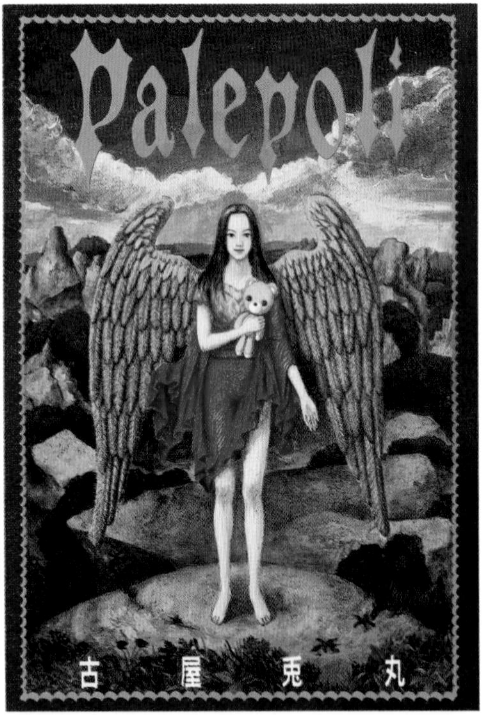
Palepoli
古屋兎丸

Also by Usamaru Furuya
Genkaku Picasso
Ningen Shikkaku
Short Cuts
The Lychee Light Club (*Norimizu Ameya*)

Yonkoma manga, which follow the four-panel style of newspaper strips, usually feature accessible, light comedic content. *Palepoli* adopts this deceptively simple format; however, its content exists at the opposite end to other popular four-panel mangas. The themes of *Palepoli* fly wildly between sadomasochistic fantasy, religion, childhood dreams, philosophy, and pop songs. These subjects are often punctuated with dark, enigmatic, and silly-yet-profound punch lines.

Readers will be spellbound by Usamaru Furuya's eclectic and striking graphic style in this, his debut comic series. His art shows exquisite craftsmanship, and he consciously references (revealing his fine art background) various master artists—Hieronymus Bosch, Sandro Botticelli, Escher—and art styles such as Victorian etchings and baroque painting, as well as mainstream anime. Furuya also pays homage to other manga artists, such as Fujiko Fujio, Fujio Akatsuka, and Yasuji Tanioka. Page by page, he skillfully embraces numerous art styles, tones, and techniques, which clash with one another yet make for a fascinating visual experience. Like most manga, *Palepoli* is predominantly printed in black and white, but the pages occasionally explode unexpectedly into small splashes, or sometimes whole pages, of color.

There are also brilliant experimental touches in the book. Time after time, a comical-looking ghost comes out from the page and peers down on Furuya as he finishes the page that is being read by the reader. These pages are always hilariously sabotaged by the impish ghost, showing traces of ink drips, doodles, and daamaging creases. *Palepoli* is an extraordinary manga book and it delivers so much more than just comedy. Its polished art and dark imaginings also combine to make for an absorbing, amusing, and memorable read. **AT-L**

The mischievous ghost strikes again in Usamaru Furuya's *Palepoli*. ➡

没のおばけ ③

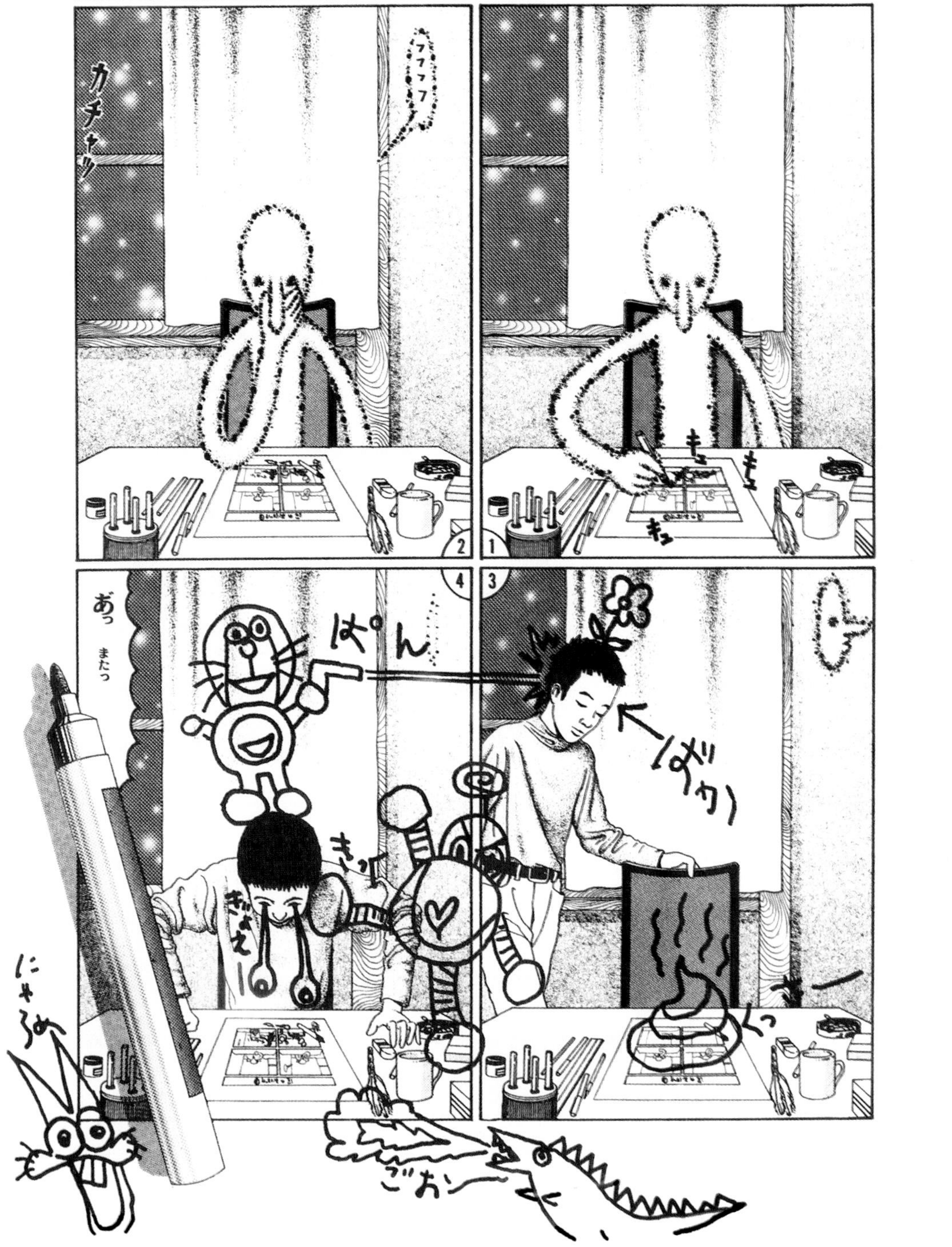

Tekkon Kinkreet
Black & White 1994

✐✐ Taiyo Matsumoto

Title in original language *Tekkon Kinkurlito*
First published by Shogakukan (Japan)
Creator Japanese (b.1967)
Genre Drama

Taiyo Matsumoto's edgy visual aesthetic and morally compromised characters bring a new level of sophistication and grittiness to manga in *Tekkon Kinkreet*. It is set in the fictitious Treasure Town, an urban mecca overflowing with high school thugs, yakuza mafia, emasculated cops, and homeless people. The heart of Treasure Town belongs to Black and White, two ten-year-old orphans who live in a derelict car and run the streets with steel rods and a penchant for violence. With a quiet rage and a desperate love, Black looks after his best friend, White, a slow-witted innocent with a clairvoyant streak. The yakuza plan is to clean up Treasure Town by building a theme park in the city's center, essentially giving the town an antiseptic gloss and luring families to enjoy the sights and sounds of a sterile playworld. The construction threatens to destroy the only home Black and White and other unfortunates have ever known, and it sends them into a tailspin of vengeance.

Matsumoto's style is heavily influenced by French *bande dessinée* creators Moebius and Enki Bilal, giving his work a Western feel. The paneling and action sequences, however, are purely Matsumoto. He implements some of the most progressive page layouts seen in manga. Certain stylistic elements in *Tekkon Kinkreet* even give a nod to The Beatles' *Yellow Submarine*. The three assassins recall the Blue Meanies, and one of White's outfits is similar to those of the *Sgt. Pepper* sleeve. Matsumoto creates a dark fantastical world that is both twisted and highly imaginative. **K-MC**

Blade of the
Immortal 1994

✐✐ Hiroaki Samura

Title in original language *Mugen no Junin*
First published by Kodansha (Japan)
Creator Japanese (b.1970)
Genre Adventure

Hiroaki Samura is the Quentin Tarantino of samurai manga—his torture scenes are horrific, even in the context of a comic book drenched in bloody battles and dismemberments. Or perhaps he is the Sam Peckinpah, for never has comic book violence looked so balletic or beautiful. With *Blade of the Immortal*, Samura modernized the genre, delivering a remarkable work that is also, paradoxically, subtle and humane.

Manji is a samurai cursed with immortality after killing his lord. Once known as "100-cop-killer" because of the lawmen he slew at his lord's behest, he wanders the land having vowed to kill 1,000 evil men to make up for his misdeeds. The trouble is that now that he recognizes his lord's betrayal, he is having increasing difficulty working out who the truly evil men are. Manji falls in with Rin, a teenage swordswoman, who is seeking the renegade fighters who wiped out her family.

Blade of the Immortal is about loyalty, revenge, and honor. Samura depicts the key event that sets Rin's quest in motion from numerous perspectives and creates moral conundrums for his characters as they discover that not all the men they seek are monsters. His language is quixotic and startlingly modern, jumping from formal sentences through street slang to insults traded in rhyming couplets. His range of art styles is also immense. He employs pencil and pastel as well as inks that range from the frenetic to the almost ethereal, and switches from depicting great detail to wild and audacious sketchiness in a heartbeat. An epic story and a visual tour de force. **FJ**

Astro City
Life in the Big City 1995

Kurt Busiek · Brent Anderson and Alex Ross

First published by WildStorm (USA)
Creators Busiek (American, b.1960); Anderson (American, b.1955); Ross (American, b.1970)
Genre Superhero

KURT BUSIEK'S
ASTRO CITY
WILDSTORM
LIFE IN THE BIG CITY
BUSIEK • ANDERSON • ROSS

Astro City is a pivotal superhero series, part of a trend that developed in the mid-1990s to move away from the grim, ultraviolent stories and heroes that had proliferated in the recent past. It was created to reinvent the superhero as an ethical and social being.

To achieve this, Kurt Busiek and Alex Ross created a whole new city and culture to support their heroes—Astro City—and depicted a society in which the actions of the heroes were embedded in the culture from which they emerged. *Astro City* dispenses with the social alienation that had become the hallmark of so many post-Rorshach, post-*Dark Knight* superheroes, and trains the spotlight on the ways in which a society can foster a culture of heroism and support the heroes that protect it. The characterization of the heroes almost marks a return to Stan Lee's Silver Age concept of a "hero with problems." But Busiek brings a contemporary awareness to the context of his heroes, which makes the experience of reading *Astro City* anything but retro.

Some stories are told from the point of view of the characters with no superpowers, which further emphasizes Busiek's theme of the superhero as part of the social and civic structure of the city. A number of memorable and quirky heroes appear in the series, including Samaritan, the egocentric Crackerjack, the eerie Hanged Man, and the clownlike Jack in the Box.

New issues of *Astro City* continue to be published. In 2010 the film rights for *Astro City* were acquired by Working Title Productions, and Busiek was reported to be working on a draft screenplay. **RR**

"The world's most prominent superhero and superheroine, and neither of us has been out on a date in so long . . . we've forgotten how it works."

Similar reads
Kingdom Come Mark Waid and Alex Ross
Marvels Kurt Busiek and Alex Ross

Johnny the Homicidal Maniac 1995

Jhonen Vasquez

First published by Slave Labor Graphics (USA)
Creator American (b.1974)
Genre Horror, Comedy
Award Nominated for Eisner Award (1998)

JOHNNY
#1
$2.95 US
$3.95
THE HOMICIDAL MANIAC

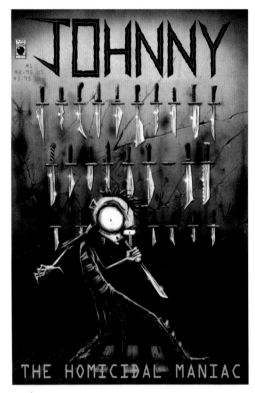

Similar reads
Lenore Roman Dirge
Red Meat Ted Rall
Squee Jhonen Vasquez

In a sense, *Johnny the Homicidal Maniac* is the ultimate "goth" comic, both as a founding publication and the perfect aesthetic example of the genre. Drawn in stark black and white, the art is often rough and full of angles, with text invading every inch of the page. The whole comic bursts with unchanneled energy—an aspect that is linked to Jhonen Vasquez's own way of doing things, mostly by improvising on the spot and producing the comic with constant urgency.

The filler strips included in the book have only a tenuous link with the main narrative: the always atrocious *Happy Noodle Boy* is Johnny's own minicomic, while the confidence issues of poor goth wannabee Anne Guish provide a welcome counterpoint (as well as

"I stuffed some dolls full of dead rats I put in the blender . . . maybe, there really is something wrong with me."

a dose of self-derision) to the rest of the book. Published by Slave Labor Graphics (another hint that *Johnny the Homicidal Maniac* should not be taken at face value), the title says it all: ultraviolent and laced with dark humor. The story starts out as a nihilistic, angst-ridden ride and progressively evolves into something more complex. While the first stories are limited to Johnny being his homicidal self (and traumatizing his young neighbor, Squee, in the process), the later episodes dive into the troubled psyche of the main character.

Sometimes overindulgent and bordering on caricature, *Johnny the Homicidal Maniac* is clearly a product of youth (Jhonen Vasquez was barely twenty-one years old when he created it), full of half-expressed ideas. With its flair for the dramatic and its genuinely funny moments, it remains an unequaled goth reference. **XG**

Stray Bullets 1995

David Lapham

A glimpse into a sleazy underworld where children wander aimlessly through parties full of drugs, booze, and sex, and adults end each others' lives at the drop of a baseball cap, *Stray Bullets* presents different ways of fighting back against our backgrounds—some more suitable than others. Straitlaced Orson is dragged into a world of low-level gangsters and less than subtle homicide when he witnesses an accident on the streets of Baltimore.

Little Ginny Applejack goes on the run after her attempt to strike back at bullies leaves her scarred, physically and psychologically. Joey avenges the only woman he has ever loved in a night that makes the Grand Guignol look tame. And then there is Amy Racecar, who has quite a lot in common with Ginny, but who she is when she is not robbing banks remains unclear.

"Christ, Ginny, do you know how many people vote in these things?"

Characters appear at different stages in their lives, some recognizable, some not. With eight tightly packed panels on most pages, each roughly the shape of a movie screen, reading *Stray Bullets* can feel like watching a lost Quentin Tarantino film. Action flies by in David Lapham's stark, brushy artwork, the story zigzagging wildly through time, with no crosshatching and no gradients along the way.

This mix of sex, violence, and gallows humor got attention right from the start. Lapham brought the series to a premature close in 2005, leaving readers one issue from the end. Hopefully those new to this messy gathering of criminals, romantics, and lost kids have time to catch up before the master of mayhem drags one last bloody rabbit out of his hat. **EL**

First published by El Capitan Books (USA)
Creator American (b.1970)
Genre Crime
Award Eisner Award Best Graphic Album Reprint (1997)

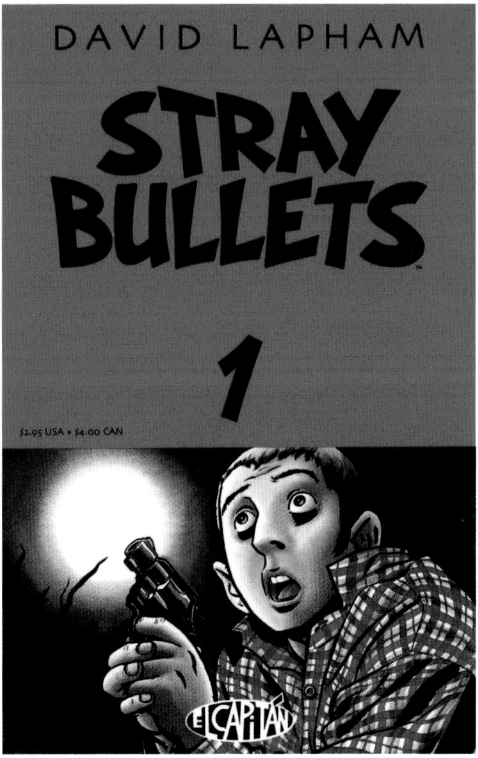
DAVID LAPHAM
STRAY BULLETS
1
$2.95 USA • $4.00 CAN
ELCAPITAN

Similar reads
Fishtown Kevin Colden
Silverfish David Lapham
Sin City Frank Miller

Misery Loves Comedy 1995

✐✐ Ivan Brunetti

First published by Fantagraphics Books (USA)
Creator American (b.1967)
Genre Humor
Award Ignatz Award (2007)

The driving factor behind this collected edition of Ivan Brunetti's nihilistic work is his basement-level self-esteem. He constantly questions his own self-worth. Brunetti's therapist provides an introduction to *Misery Loves Comedy,* relating the author's painful creation process, productive only when fear of his publisher's anger overwhelms his dread of criticism. No other cartoonist has unleashed their internal fear and rage to such a degree.

There are two primary strands to Brunetti's brilliant cartooning. The first could be likened to a glimpse inside the mind of a killer who wished the whole world had but one throat and his hands were around it. These pieces, including single or four-panel gags, are overwhelmed by violent obscenities as Brunetti purges himself. He points out that as appalling as his fantasies are, he could never act on them.

The other large body of work consists of introspective autobiographical strips in which Brunetti obsesses over human nature, his interaction with the wider world, his work, and the full spectrum of terrors that, on some days, confine him to bed unable to move for fear. His childhood tormentors affect him to this day; he delivers a philosophical discussion with Jesus Christ, and one strip is subtitled *1,784 Things That Make Me Vomit*. As bleak as this sounds, the cutting self-deprecation ensures the strips retain a modicum of jocularity even at their darkest moments. The cartooning is brilliant, immersing readers in *Misery Loves Comedy* and one of the world's funniest cartoonists. **FP**

Nudl Nude 1995

✐✐ Youngsoon Yang

First published by Seju (South Korea)
Creator South Korean (b.1970)
Genre Erotic, Humor
Adaptation Animated TV series (1999)

When *Nudl Nude* debuted, it redefined erotic humor in Korean *manhwa* (comics). Where most previous erotic comedies utilized sex as satirical elements to tackle a more adult sensibility, or plainly went abstract, this one tried an entirely different approach. It forces the reader to reimagine nonerotic situations as highly erotic ones through clever visual innuendos. By becoming an active participant, the reader is rewarded with great offbeat humor.

There are short stories about a superhero with a third leg that kicks his opponent when his female sidekick visually arouses him. In other stories, a "bridge" between two sides of a cliff only stands when a female traveler shows some skin. Sometimes the simple act of two biologists catching a butterfly can resemble the act of making love, without either of them realizing it. There are occasional stories that are surprisingly emotional, such as lovers who wait for each other so long that they turn into trees.

This new approach to erotic comics spawned a generation of copycats. It became all the more evident that *Nudl Nude* worked so well, not only because of the blatant eroticism, but because it was based on genuine visual imagination and backed up by Yang's skill in drawing human figures. *Nudl Nude* was made into two rather mediocre animated movies as well, which was proof that the reading experience of *Nudl Nude* clearly benefits from carefully selected moments for each panel and the brilliant layout of those panels. **NK**

Stuck Rubber Baby 1995

Howard Cruse

First published by Paradox Press/DC Comics (USA)
Creator American (b.1944)
Genre Reality drama
Award French Prix de la critique (2002)

Stuck Rubber Baby
A NOVEL
Howard Cruse
Introduction by Tony Kushner

Howard Cruse's *Stuck Rubber Baby* is a fictional coming-of-age story inspired by the artist's own teenage years in the American South of the 1960s. Toland Polk is a young white man in a small town who tries to hide his homosexuality by dating women. He falls in love with Ginger, who introduces Toland to the civil rights movement, and her friend Sammy, who in turn shows them the city's gay community.

The story is told by Toland's older self, who comments on events from the safe distance of a happy gay relationship, although he has chosen not to edit out his younger self's more embarrassing moments. The upheaval in U.S. society and contemporary homophobia and racism coincide with Toland's construction of his identity. At times the struggles of black people in the South are selfishly ignored and overshadowed by his personal misgivings about being gay. When Ginger becomes pregnant, Toland's biggest preoccupation is again himself. For all Toland's faults, he manages to tell this very moving story—the truly courageous act of the otherwise wonderfully confused and self-absorbed Toland Polk.

Cruse's drawing style is dense, with soft, rounded lines, crosshatched shadow effects, and close-ups that emphasize facial expressions. His imaginative page layouts stress the narrative's mood, and the dramatic events are recounted in a somber tone, but not without humor. *Stuck Rubber Baby* is brutally honest in its portrayal of the formative years of a man and his society—a painful and ultimately uplifting journey. **RPC**

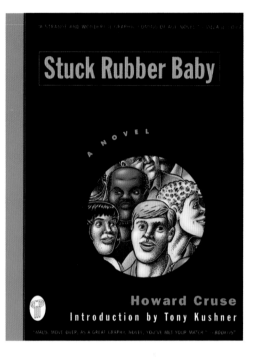

"I'm not absolutely sure that I'm really a homo. Things aren't always what they seem y'know."

Similar reads
American Born Chinese Gene Luen Yang
Bull's Balls Ralf König
Fun Home Alison Bechdel
King Ho Che Anderson
Wendel Howard Cruse

Ragmop 1995

Rob Walton

First published by Planet Lucy Press (USA)
Creator Canadian (b.1958)
Genre Humor
Awards Nominated for two Joe Shuster Awards (2007)

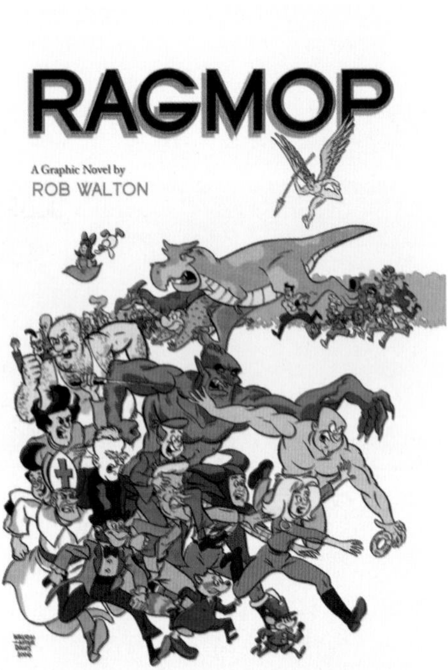
RAGMOP
A Graphic Novel by
ROB WALTON

Similar reads

Colville Stephen Gilbert
New X-Men Grant Morrison and various artists
Ronin Frank Miller
Truth Serum Jon Adams

Ragmop begins 248 million years ago and encompasses intelligent dinosaurs, a missing physicist, a Vatican assassin, Adolf Hitler, assorted U.S. covert agents—some of whom may have grassy-knoll credentials—a fighting misogynistic psychiatrist, the missing link, a giant rabbit with a gun, a controversial portrayal of God, and a device that can reset the known universe. And that's merely the half of it.

Gluing everything together is the adaptable Alice Hawkings, whose career as a second-rate criminal is not paying off. Political lectures are presented in superhero tropes, background information is delivered in the form of old-style Marvel comics pinup pages, and, irrespective of how chaotic this seems, creator Rob Walton never loses control. For sheer inventiveness alone, *Ragmop* is off the charts.

Walton's background in animation ensured accomplished cartooning was a hallmark when *Ragmop* was first serialized in thirteen largely self-published issues. However, when it failed to draw an audience that enabled a living income, Walton debunked to the world of animation. On returning to complete *Ragmop* several years later, Walton's approach was as novel as his story. Taking his cue from the music industry, he remixed the series. Original pages and plots were dropped or placed elsewhere in the continuity, and completely new plots were introduced. This resulted in a well-drawn, ambitious, and wildly creative comic. What raises *Ragmop* above a merely funny story is Walton's constant prodding about topics such as organized Christianity and U.S. beliefs about how the world should be run, among others. Walton has a lot to say and phrases it very well. "Unique" is an overused term in comics, commonly applied to superhero comics with a new wrinkle, but *Ragmop* is the genuine article. **FP**

Approximately 1995

"Lewis Trondheim"

One of the most remarkable autobiographical comics of the 1990s, Lewis Trondheim's *Approximately* eschews the simple chronicling of the quotidian aspects of its author's life, opting instead for a wide-ranging exploration of the psychology of the artist.

As far as autobiographical works go, *Approximately* is, in many ways, more closely aligned with the fantasy works that have defined Trondheim's most commercial successes. This is a daydreamer's comic. Throughout, Trondheim allows himself to be distracted, following seemingly random thoughts to the point where they reveal some truth about his personality. From his megalomaniacal aspirations for the Japanese version of his wordless comic *La Mouche* to his constant fantasies of inflicting harm on those who pester and annoy him, and the insecurities that he feels about leaving his close-knit community of friends in Paris for the southern French town of Montpellier, he has included it all for the reader to relish.

With the virtue of hindsight, one of the most appealing aspects of the work is its depiction of a generation of cartoonists who would transform French comics publishing in the 1990s. Frequent cameo appearances are made by individuals such as Philippe Dupuy and Charles Berberian, Jean-Christophe Menu, David B., Killoffer, and Émile Bravo, all of whom were eventually among the most influential and important cartoonists of their generation. *Approximately* opens up the lid on the early 1990s small-press comics scene in Paris; however, the real revelation comes in the way that Trondheim tugs at his own mask, revealing a complex and contradictory figure. *Approximately* is funny, trenchant, bittersweet, and disillusioned in almost equal measure. It is a comic book of many moods, from an artist of numerous interests and talents. **BB**

Title in original language *Approximativement*
First published by Cornélius (France)
Creator Laurent Chabosy (French, b.1964)
Genre Autobiography

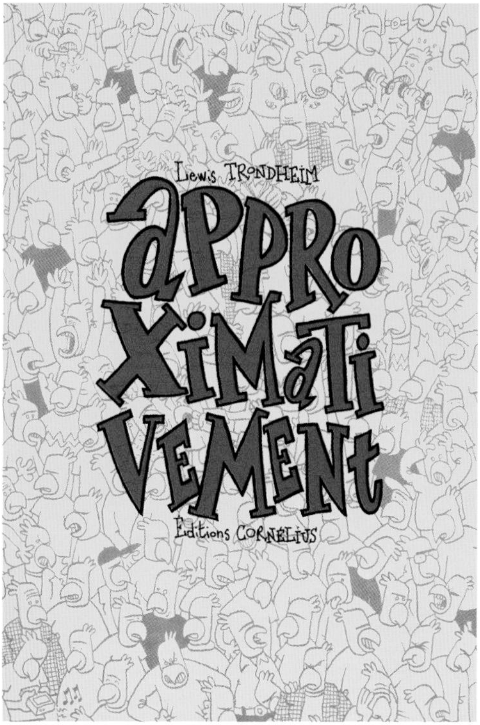
Lewis TRONDHEIM
approximativement
Éditions CORNÉLIUS

Also by Lewis Trondheim

Lapinot and Carrots in Patagonia (*Lapinot et les carottes de Patagonie*)

Little Nothings (*Les petits riens*)

The Fly (*La Mouche*)

Storeyville 1995

✐✐ Frank Santoro

First published by Sirk Productions (USA)
Creator American (b.1972)
Genre History, Autobiography
Influence on Multiforce

Frank Santoro's *Storeyville* may be the largest minicomic ever made. It was originally self-published in 1995 on inexpensive newsprint, the sort that had a preordained deterioration date. It immediately suggested itself as a comic with few parallel counterparts. The package matched the imagery, which combined elements almost as antiquated as newsprint: hobo melodrama, fixed-background animation, and a shipyard thriller.

The scope of the comic was interesting, merging its historical Depression-era scenario with a personal, world-weary aesthetic. It was an epic produced with gestural figurations and loose black-on-white drawings burnished with shades of brown. Credit for the coloring, such an important part of *Storeyville*'s telling, goes to Katie Glicksberg, Santoro's girlfriend at the time, and his co-conspirator in a spew of fragmented minicomics credited to their self-published *Sirk*.

Storeyville tells the story of an American who is down on his luck and trying to reconnect with a former mentor. The narrative moves north from Pittsburgh through city and country, civilization and squalor, and then it comes to an end on a two-page spread of intense beauty. A single panel, against a fading horizon, the yellow and brown of the dingy story has suddenly transformed into sun and sea, that single panel subdivided into the thirty rough-lined, hand-delineated panes, as if it were being seen through a factory window that just happens to be floating way up in the clouds. **MW**

Dragon Head 1995

✐✐ Minetaro Mochizuki

Title in original language *Doragon Heddo*
First published by Kodansha (Japan)
Creator Japanese (b.1964)
Genre Horror

Toward the end of the twentieth century, Japan was hit by a massive "apocalypse boom" along with the rest of the world, prompting the comics industry to launch a number of titles embracing the subject. One of the most successful of these was Minetaro Mochizuki's *Dragon Head*, which ran from 1995 to 1999 in Kodansha's *Young Magazine*.

This terrifying tale of postapocalyptic tragedy opens when a huge earthquake derails a bullet train, trapping it under the destroyed walls of a tunnel. The only survivors are three middle school students: Teru, Ako, and Nobuo, who had been on their way back from a school excursion. Hoping to be rescued, the students attempt to find means of survival. However, the longer they wait, the more desperate the situation becomes.

Nobuo, who had been bullied in school, loses his sanity, covers his face with horrifying makeup, and mutilates the dead body of his tormenter. He then hails the corpse of his teacher, claiming that they need an "adult's guidance." Teru and Ako eventually find a way out of the tunnel, only to realize that the situation outside is more horrifying than they had anticipated. Although the plot simulates the end of the world, this is a psychological thriller that drags readers into the harsh reality of the fragile human mind. There have been divided opinions on the author's graphic artwork and frank portrayal of the brutal survival war between humans, but the comic has won the hearts of enough readers to sell 6.5 million copies and be developed into a hit live-action film in 2003. **TS**

Preacher 1995

Garth Ennis Steve Dillon

First published by Vertigo/DC Comics (USA)
Creators Ennis (British, b.1960); Dillon (British, b.1962)
Genre Fantasy
Adaptation Film (in development)

DC COMICS VERTIGO
"MORE FUN THAN GOING TO THE MOVIES."
PREACHER
GONE TO TEXAS
GLENN FABRY 95
GARTH ENNIS STEVE DILLON
Foreword by Joe R. Lansdale

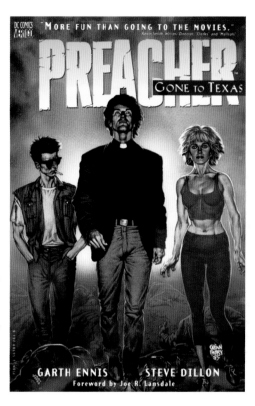

When the bastard child of an angel and a demon decides to live in the mind of preacher Jesse Custer, he finds himself speaking with the very persuasive word of God. Along with his sharp-shooting girlfriend, Tulip O'Hare, and the Irish alcoholic vampire Cassidy, Jesse sets out to find the God that has left Heaven and give Him a good talking to. Along the way their quest is constantly disturbed, and the narrative takes a number of detours to reveal the many characters' origin stories.

Among the threesome's adversaries are the Saint of Killers, sent by Heaven to stop the preacher, Herr Starr, and the secret society he represents, The Grail, who are looking to bring about Armageddon. Garth Ennis mixes up sexual deviancies, bodily fluids, cannibalism, profanities, and blood-gushing violence with sentimental soap opera–like scenes, gothic horror, and horrific stereotypes. Awash with Americana, *Preacher* uses the mythology of the United States to discuss subjects such as the Vietnam war, the consequences of exaggerated fame, gender roles, religion, and racism, while never once missing a beat as entertainment thanks to liberal doses of grotesque humor.

Steve Dillon's clear and crisp drawing style captures every sordid detail of this frenzied tale, supporting the dynamic forward motion of the stories with care and skill. Glenn Fabry's painted covers expose the ugly faces of humanity and divinity with a nauseating tactile quality. Gross humor aside, *Preacher* is essentially a moral fable about doing what is right in the face of power and loving truly until the end of the world. **RPC**

"The creation cannot make demands of its creator! / Then the creator shouldn't piss on his creation."

Similar reads

Hitman Garth Ennis and John McCrea
The Punisher Gerry Conway, John Romita, Sr., and Ross Andru

Bakune Young 1995

✎ Toyokazu Matsunaga

First published by Shogakukan (Japan)
Creator Japanese (b.1964)
Genre Adventure
Influenced by *Happy People*

Toyokazu Matsunaga debuted as a comics artist after his apprenticeship with Yuji Aoki, whose best known work, *Naniwa Kinyudo*, centers on a loan shark and illustrates the harsh realities of debt-stricken lives. In Matsunaga's *Bakune Young*, the artistic and thematic influences of his mentor are evident throughout.

First serialized in 1995, *Bakune Young* was launched during one of Japan's most tragic years. Only two months after 6,000 lives were lost in the Great Kobe earthquake in January, the notorious cult Aum Shinrikyo carried out a mass terrorist attack in Tokyo. With the country still trying to recover from economic depression after the bubble burst in 1992, it was a truly dark time.

Matsunaga captures the era in this controversial tale of crime, focusing on the violent acts of Shoichi Bakune, its brutal leading character. Set in Osaka, the story begins when Bakune beats up a yakuza member in a *Pachinko* parlor, inflicting fatal injuries. In an attempt to take revenge, ten members from the yakuza turn up at his door, not knowing that Bakune has set deadly traps. All ten are killed, and Bakune soon destroys the entire gang. The incident hits the news, and, outrageously, Bakune appears on television, provoking the nation with photographs of the massacre. The police and yakuza are desperate to capture him, but Bakune escapes, taking Japan's infamous yakuza boss hostage in Osaka Castle. Matsunaga has confessed that, before the release of the series, he was warned by his editor, "After this, you may never see a new title launch again." Fortunately this was not the case. **TS**

Black Hole 1995

✎ Charles Burns

First published by Kitchen Sink Press (USA)
Creator American (b.1955)
Genre Horror
Awards Seven Harvey Awards for Best Inker (Burns)

The horror of *Black Hole* is losing control over one's own body. Exaggerated from his own 1970s adolescence, Charles Burns combines raging hormones with "the bug," a sexually transmitted pandemic mutating U.S. high school students. One acquires a tail, another lionlike facial hair, another sheds skin like a snake— and all see themselves as freaks.

This is no simplistic cautionary AIDS tale or gruesome freak show, but a sensitive portrait of sympathetic misfits at the mercy of peer pressure and their sex drives who long to esape the sterility of home and school and emotionally connect with others.Burns restrains his shocks, working on the reader's imagination, making the revelatory moments all the more disturbing. In one chilling scene, while first making love to her boyfriend Rob, the uninfected Chris discovers something while kissing Rob's neck, a tiny second mouth. Now both infected, Chris and Rob feel ostracized and join other mutated kids hiding in a fragile, supportive community. Rob's orifice is one of several "black holes," vaginal symbols for burgeoning sexuality.

Burns also fills the wild outdoors with phallic symbols such as branches, snakes, and broken bones. He reveals the crossed paths of his tragic players, adding rippled edges to his panels to move in and out of nightmares, drug-induced trips, or dreams for the future, blurring boundaries between memory and fantasy. *Black Hole* exposes, in psychological and biological intimacy, the cost of the desperate desire humans have for acceptance. **PG**

There is no room for grays or tones, only black and white. ➡

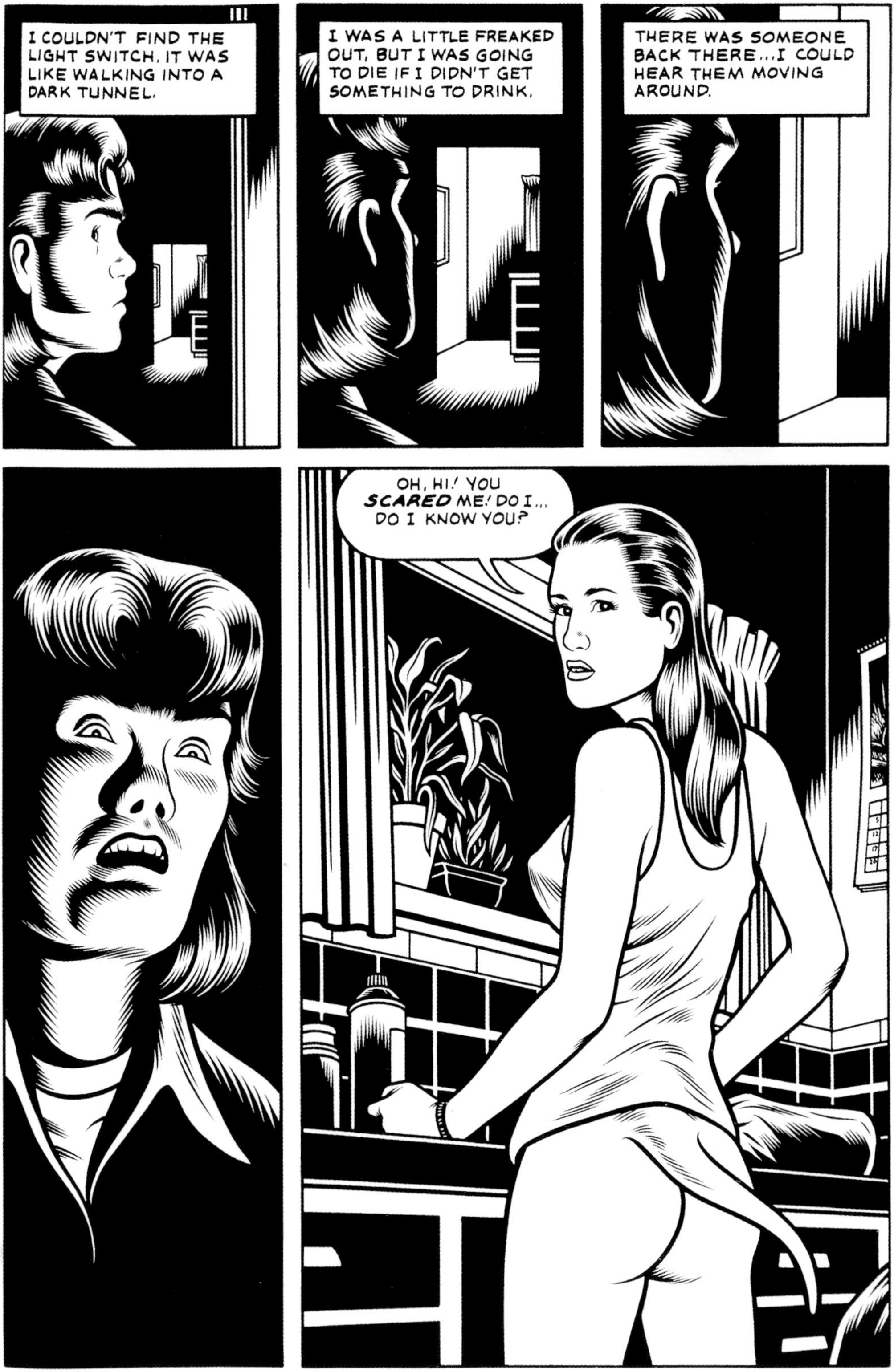
I COULDN'T FIND THE LIGHT SWITCH. IT WAS LIKE WALKING INTO A DARK TUNNEL.
I WAS A LITTLE FREAKED OUT, BUT I WAS GOING TO DIE IF I DIDN'T GET SOMETHING TO DRINK.
THERE WAS SOMEONE BACK THERE... I COULD HEAR THEM MOVING AROUND.
OH, HI! YOU SCARED ME! DO I... DO I KNOW YOU?

Beg the Question 1995

Bob Fingerman

First published by Fantagraphics Books (USA)
Creator American (b.1964)
Genre Humor, Drama
Awards Nominated for two Eisner Awards

BEG THE QUESTION
BOB FINGERMAN

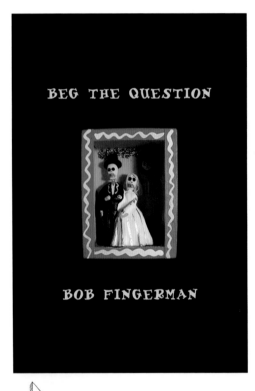

Also by Bob Fingerman
Connective Tissue
From the Ashes
Recess Pieces
You Deserved It

Beg the Question details the progression of the relationship between cartoonist Rob Hoffman and beauty parlor manager Syliva Fanucci. Rob is generally relaxed and easygoing, occasionally lapsing into insensitivity, while the bisexual Sylvia's outwardly rebellious confidence conceals the insecurities engendered by a large family and a strict Catholic upbringing. There is a quality sitcom sharpness to the narrative as Rob and Sylvia search for a new apartment, meet each other's families, and address the troublesome question of whether their relationship should be formalized. The supporting characters are equally well conceived, each of them distinct, while New York is as important a character as the cast, with the daily annoyances and experiences of life in the Big Apple informing and reflecting the two protagonists.

"I should be in the flower of my liberalism, but this lousy city sucks it right out of me."

In one way Bob Fingerman's career could hardly have had a more prestigious start, selling cartoons to the legendary Harvey Kurtzman. These were, however, for Kurtzman's poorly regarded and short-lived 1980s *Nuts!* project, and a decade of contributions ranging from *Screw* magazine to *MAD Magazine*'s most successful imitator, *Cracked*, followed.

This period of chasing assignments is very much reflected in Rob's experiences, and the sheer variety provided a solid background for *Minimum Wage* when Fingerman first introduced Rob and Sylvia. Fingerman's cartooning is excellent, particularly in characterizing his cast, who are far from the parade of perfection often common to comics. Fingerman has recently begun a parallel career as a novelist. **FP**

Hotel Africa 1995

Hee Jung Park

Hotel Africa is one of the most prominent Korean *shojo* comics from the mid to late 1990s, an era when the genre delved deeper into mature themes and new styles. It is a story about a place where many people flow in and out the doors—visiting for a while before moving on. Some meet and become friends; others become lovers, and some become enemies.

As time passes and many relationships develop so does a natural drama with emotion and depth. Hotel Africa is the name of a small roadside hotel in Utah. The protagonists are the hotel employees and the occasional guests who come and go—some return; others do not. Readers look through the eyes of a boy called Elvis, catching glimpses of the past and present

"People meet coincidentally and then become the most important beings in the world to each other."

of the many people who have built connections with each other at the hotel. Each person has his or her own dramatic story to tell. Mostly they have scars on their hearts, and eventually they come to reflect on their lives at Hotel Africa and find closure. It is a place where people tend to heal themselves.

Part *Bagdad Café* and part *Cinema Paradiso*, this work mixes in its own insights on life. Looking back, every tie with another human being is precious, no matter how fleeting or strong the bond. Loved ones can meet each other again or not, but the emotion is there to stay. What really counts is accepting life as it is. *Hotel Africa* carefully manages to explore these mature themes without becoming overwhelmingly preachy. The stylish artwork also contributes to the calm and otherworldly feeling of the hotel, which is needed to achieve that balance. **NK**

First published by Seoulmunhwasa (South Korea)
Creator South Korean (b.1970)
Genre Drama
Adaptation Radio (2000)

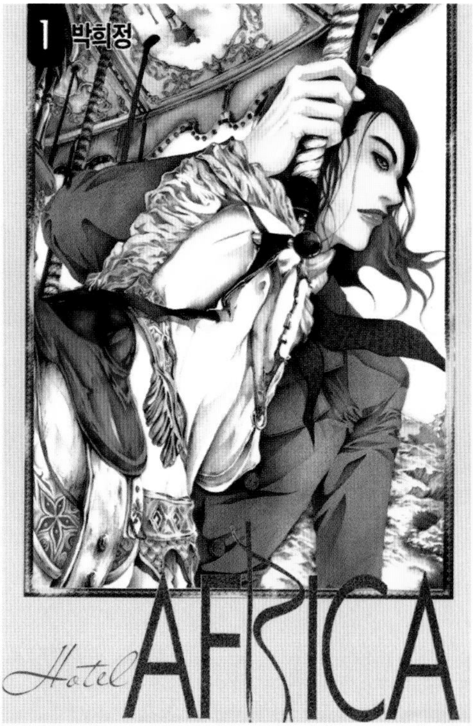
1 박희정
Hotel AFRICA

Similar reads

Fever Hee Jung Park
Martin and John Hee Jung Park
Ristorante Paradiso Natsume Ono
Secret Hee Jung Park

Neon Genesis Evangelion 1995

✏️ Yoshiyuki Sadamoto

Title in original language *Shin Seiki Evangelion*
First published by Kadokawa Shoten (Japan)
Creator Japanese (b.1962)
Genre Science fiction

In 1995 genius director Hideaki Anno took Japan—and subsequently the world—by storm with the launch of his revolutionary anime *Neon Genesis Evangelion*. Its plotline was full of mysteries within mysteries, and its production packed with the latest animation technology—everything was innovative, and it triggered a social phenomenon across Japan.

The comic version is an adaptation by Yoshiyuki Sadamoto, who also designed the characters for the anime. Critics have praised his exquisite signature illustrations. Particularly impressive is his ability to capture subtle changes of emotion for the famously expressionless character Rei Ayanami. The central character, Shinji, is a fourteen-year-old boy, raised by relatives from a young age. One day he is summoned by his father, Gendo, who works for a paramilitary organization called NERV. Following Gendo's orders, Shinji faces battles with invading enemies using gigantic robots known as Evangelion.

Unable to make sense of the situation, Shinji is full of questions, but, contrary to the audience's expectations, his questions are not about how he could save the world, or how he could make himself stronger. Shinji wants to know why he is forced to fight, why the enemies attack, and the meaning of his existence. It was the protagonist's pessimistic attitude that crucially distinguished the story from anything else that had been seen before. Shinji's character was emblematic of the negative youth of the time, and others were captivated by the plot. **TS**

The Boondocks 1996

✏️ Aaron McGruder

First published by *The Diamondback*, University of Maryland student newspaper (USA)
Creator American (b.1974)
Genre Humor

The bundoks are a mountainous region in the Philippines used to great advantage by Filipino freedom fighters in their struggle for independence during the Philippine-American War of 1899 to 1902. The word entered the U.S. lexicon soon after as "boondock," and refers to a sort of no-man's land, a wilderness, an unwelcoming, unfamiliar place.

This is an apt term for how the all-white, fictional suburb of Woodcrest, Maryland, now appears to African American brothers Huey (ten) and Riley (eight) Freeman, after they are taken out of their home in south Chicago by their grandfather, Robert Jebedia. Huey, named after the founder of the revolutionary Black Panthers Huey Newton, is angry and distrustful of authority, but also thoughtful and intelligent. Riley's hero is the Columbian drug lord Pablo Escobar. At school Huey makes friends with the rather more optimistic Micheal Caesar, and together the three direct their rhetoric not so much at overt racism but at the insidious, pervasive ignorance of it. Complacency and indifference are the bad guys here.

Drawn in a style inspired by Japanese anime, *The Boondocks* has never been far from controversy. When Huey wanted to find a boyfriend for the then–National Security Advisor Condoleezza Rice so she would not be so "hellbent" on destroying the world, *The Washington Post* killed the strips in question. It was also a tacit admission that *The Boondocks*, like the *Post*'s editorials, had the power to influence and shape public opinion. **BS**

Kingdom Come 1996

Mark Waid   Alex Ross

First published by DC Comics (USA)
Creators Waid (American, b.1962); Ross (American, b.1970)
Genre Superhero
Award Eisner Award (1997)

KINGDOM COME
Mark WAID Alex ROSS

Kingdom Come is a parable told in the form of a superhero story. Set during an unspecified time in the future, it describes the conflict between two generations of superheroes—Superman, Wonder Woman, Batman, and other heroes of the Justice League—and a new generation of superhumans, led by the violent Magog, who do not embrace the traditional role of the hero.

Mark Waid and Alex Ross offer a critique of the direction that the superhero genre had taken since the end of the Silver Age. The chivalrous heroism of the earlier heroes is set against the destructive violence of characters intended to personify the values of the so-called Iron Age—a phrase used to describe the style of superhero storytelling that developed in the 1980s. It was legitimized by the acclaim given to *Watchmen*, *The Dark Knight Returns*, *American Flagg*, and other downbeat superhero comics and graphic novels.

Alex Ross's artwork reinvents Superman, Wonder Woman, and a tormented Billy Batson (the original Captain Marvel) in a bright world of vertical light sources and backlit tableaux. Ross also emphasizes the intense and constant moral debate that engages almost every character in *Kingdom Come*. Mention should also be made of the theme restaurant populated by waiting staff dressed as superheroes and heroines. Into this environment, Waid and Ross introduce the out-of-costume Clark Kent, Diana Prince, and Bruce Wayne in an inspired moment of visual punning that celebrates all the absurd conventions that underpin the superhero genre. **RR**

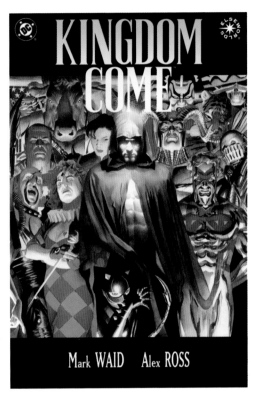

"Once, earth boasted other saviors who might have stemmed the tide of destruction."

Similar reads

Astro City Kurt Busiek, Brent Anderson, and Alex Ross
Justice Jim Krueger, Alex Ross, and Doug Braithwaite
Marvels Kurt Busiek, Alex Ross

It's a Good Life, If You Don't Weaken 1996

"Seth"

First published by Drawn & Quarterly (Canada)
Creator Gregory Gallant (Canadian, b.1962)
Genre Autobiography
Award Ignatz Award (1997)

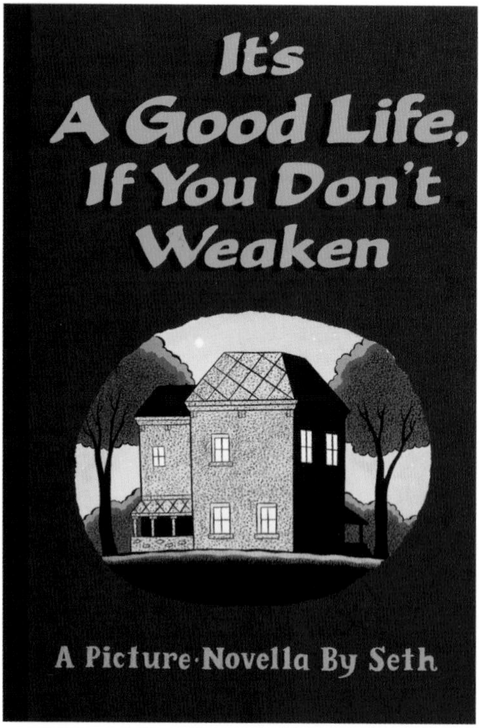
It's A Good Life, If You Don't Weaken
A Picture·Novella By Seth

Also by Seth
Clyde Fans
George Sprott
Palookaville
Wimbledon Green

A melancholy tale filled with longing and remembrance, Seth's fictional autobiography is the signature book by one of Canada's greatest comics talents. An intimate and revealing look at the aspirations of the cartoonist, *It's A Good Life, If You Don't Weaken* turns nostalgia into a thing of beauty.

Although the story depicts Seth and his close friend and fellow cartoonist Chester Brown as they really are, the bulk of the plot, including the specifics of the romance, is a work of fiction. The book follows Seth's growing interest in a fictional Canadian gag cartoonist, who works under the name "Kalo." When Seth learns that Jack Kalloway is, like himself, from a small town in Southern Ontario, he begins to identify strongly with the artist, who seems to have had only one significant success in his career: a single gag cartoon published by *The New Yorker*.

"With my old house as a starting point, I bet I could find any place in this town with my eyes closed."

Where *It's A Good Life, If You Don't Weaken* shines is in the calm, almost Zenlike moments of introspection. Seth's elegant drawings are a pitch-perfect reflection of his interests, harkening back as they do to an era long since past. The artist's use of fragile figures and carefully spotted patches of color recall a simpler time that seems all too sadly to have passed us by. In the end, Seth is taught a thing or two about life. He is reminded that a career is not a life, and that our lives are not defined so much by the work that we create as by the impression that we leave on those closest to us. Seth asks readers to consider what they want when they seek a "good life," and he finds his own answer very close to home. **BB**

Epileptic 1996

"David B."

A strong contender for the title of the greatest autobiographical comic of all time, David B.'s stunning memoir of growing up with a severely epileptic brother is more than a comic that makes great use of the form; it is a work that teaches its audience how to read comics anew.

Epileptic tells the story of Pierre-François Beauchard as he grows up from the age of five to become the cartoonist known as "David B." His life is shaped for better or worse by two forces: his astonishing imagination and his elder brother Jean-Christophe's illness, the latter of which forces the family to uproot itself constantly in efforts to seek a cure for his severe epilepsy. If Pierre-François eventually comes to conceptualize his brother's

"My brother is far away. I no longer believe in anything. I lock myself ever more tightly in my armor."

problems as an obstacle that is to be overcome, he triumphs by embracing the worlds of dreams and history, which he effortlessly combines in so much of his work.

What is most compelling about *Epileptic* is the personalized form of visual storytelling that David B. employs. More than any other cartoonist, he uses highly particularized visual metaphors that are built slowly through the work. As Pierre-François retreats into himself, he pulls his readers with him by making them complicit with his own fantastical imagery. This tendency is seen most clearly in the physicalization of Jean-Christophe's illness as a dragon that haunts the characters throughout the book. By literalizing the emotional and conceptual elements of his world, David B. creates the kind of story that could only ever be told in the comics form. **BB**

Title in original language *L'Ascension du Haut Mal*
First published by L'Association (France)
Creator Pierre-François Beauchard (French, b.1959)
Genre Autobiography

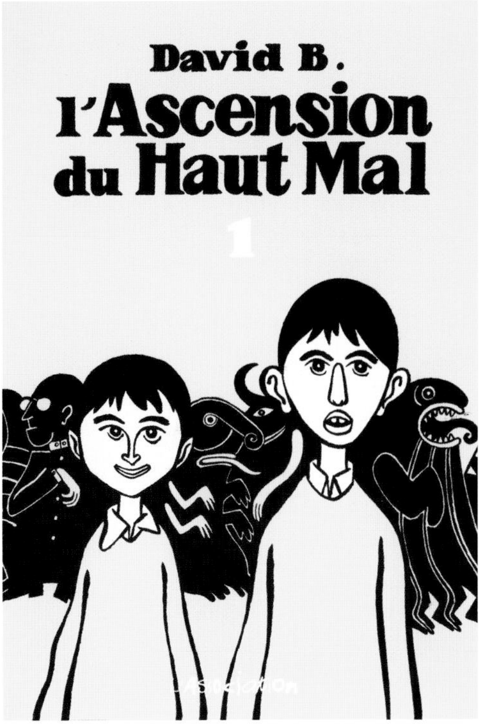
David B.
l'Ascension du Haut Mal
1
L'Association

Also by David B.

Black Paths (*Par les chemins noirs*)
Le cheval blême
Le tengû carré
Nocturnal Conspiracies (*Les complots nocturnes*)

The System 1996

✐✐ Peter Kuper

First published by Vertigo /DC Comics (USA)
Creator American (b.1958)
Genre Drama
Influenced by Lynd Ward

Peter Kuper described his wordless story *The System* as "a combination of my experiences and imagination." The starting point was Kuper always taking the same subway car and considering the lives of the changing cast of people in that carriage. From this relatively simple idea he developed an intricate story of class warfare set against a backdrop of women being murdered in New York City. It has a cast of dozens, and viewpoints shift, at first whenever one of them encounters another. A comic without words might suggest simplicity, but Kuper's story mechanism is complex. The transitions between scenes become increasingly subtle, indicated by artistic cues as well as by characters passing or interacting. And, although it is not immediately apparent, each character has a part to play in the bigger story, which affects all life in the city.

The System is a musing on the way people connect with one another. Being wordless, the comic can be understood globally. The work is not as overtly political as some of Kuper's other material, but it stresses that a capitalist society works well for the winners but ensures that there are also losers. This theme, however, is secondary to story considerations.

Kuper's richly colored artwork is unique in comic books. Starting with pages penciled in blunt outline, he produces stencils through which he sprays paint to create the finished page. While not a straightforward approach, it is a unique device that immediately distinguishes Kuper's work from that of any other artist working in comics. **FP**

Box Office Poison 1996

✐✐ Alex Robinson

First published by Antarctic Press (USA)
Creator American (b.1960)
Genre Drama
Award Angoulême Prize for First Comic Book (2005)

Sherman Davies is employed by a bookshop and hates his job and most of the customers. His friend, Ed Velasquez, wants a girlfriend and to be a comics artist, but currently assists irascible Irving Flavor, a man who has been working in comics for decades. At the start, Sherman moves in with laid-back couple Jane Pekar and Stephen Gaedel, and is about to meet Dorothy Lestrade. By virtue of her flaws, Dorothy is the most compelling character. An assistant editor at a trendy magazine, she is the infuriating girlfriend your best friend went out with for years: manipulative, messy, prone to alcoholic excess, and described by Alex Robinson, who based her on an ex-roommate, as "being constantly just one step ahead of catastrophe." Yet, like your best friend, Sherman sticks with her.

The stories are punctuated by pages in which Robinson has his cast answer questions, an endearing shorthand method of confirming their personalities, subtly foreshadowed early on. Revelations later in the story twist previous scenes completely, primarily with regard to a plot based on real-life events: a crusading magazine attempts to shame a major publisher into properly rewarding Flavor, who created their million-dollar assets under a work-for-hire contract.

Robinson sets out his stall with a sitcomlike precision and sophistication, providing naturalistic dialogue and expressive cartooning from the start. Memorable cameos abound, and, just like in real life, while there is a conclusion, it might not be all you want for people who have become your friends. **FP**

W the Whore 1996

Anke Feuchtenberger

Title in original language *Die Hure H*
First published by Jochen Enterprises (Germany)
Creator German (b.1963)
Genre Fantasy

W the Whore is undoubtedly one of the most fascinating and at the same time one of the most disturbing characters in the history of comics. Illustrator, artist, and visual storyteller Anke Feuchtenberger developed the character with writer Katrin de Vries in the 1990s and has since regularly published nightmarish tales with W the Whore as the main character.

The enigmatic drawings of *W the Whore* are distinguished by a sleepwalking character who is reflected in surreal motifs and texts. Even when the illustrations are arranged sequentially, they stand alone in their own right because of their atmospheric density and powerful graphic style. Keeping graphics and words separate, Feuchtenberger offers the reader several narrative levels at once, levels that only the reader can connect with and join together. This individual reading opens up the profound and ambivalent content of her comic narrative, which deals with real themes such as physicality, sexuality, and birth in dreamlike settings.

Having grown up in the former German Democratic Republic, Feuchtenberger is familiar with Eastern European styles of illustration and graphics. *W the Whore* is one of Feuchtenberger's early comics in which her drawings are still dominated by angular outlines. She draws her characters and subjects using hard strokes, reminiscent of wood engravings and linocuts. This trained commercial artist has successfully combined words and pictures to form a self-contained graphic texture while opening up new aesthetic and narrative perspectives in the comics medium. **MS**

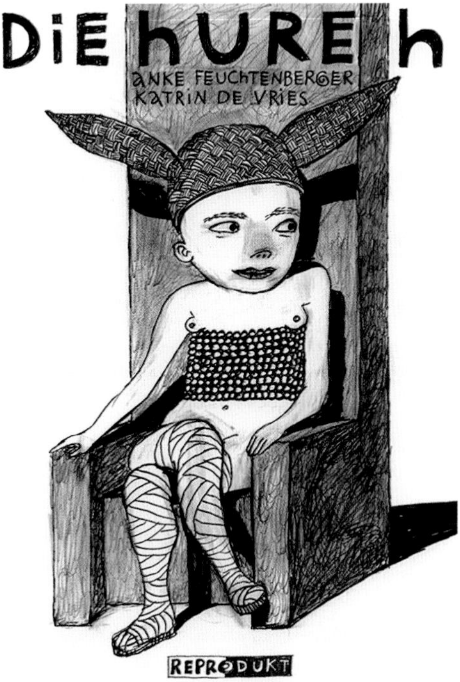
DiE hURE h
ANKE FEUCHTENBERGER
KATRIN DE VRIES
REPRODUKT

"Today she is the best-known comic artist in Germany. Her art is admired or hated."

Frankfurter Allgemeine Zeitung

Similar reads
Humus Vertebra Stefano Ricci
Love is Blind Line Hoven
Secret Volume Judith Mall
The House Anke Feuchtenberger

Finder 1996

Carla Speed McNeil

First published by Lightspeed Press (USA)
Creator American (b.1969)
Genre Science fiction
Award Lulu Kimberley Yale Award (1997)

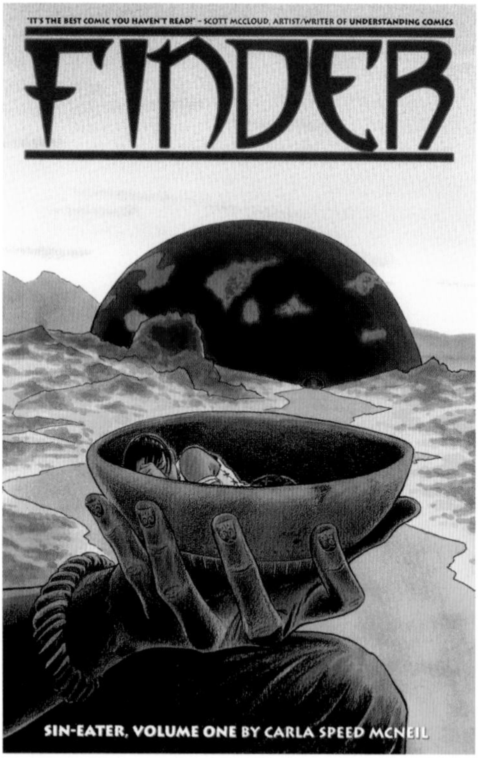
"IT'S THE BEST COMIC YOU HAVEN'T READ!" – SCOTT MCCLOUD, ARTIST/WRITER OF UNDERSTANDING COMICS
FINDER
SIN-EATER, VOLUME ONE BY CARLA SPEED MCNEIL

Similar reads
Finder: Dream Sequence Carla Speed McNeil
Finder: Mystery Date Carla Speed McNeil
Le Transperceneige Jacques Lob and Jean-Marc Rochette

In *Finder*, the ancient and the futuristic are part of everyday life. Races, faiths, and tribes maintain customs whose meanings may be lost, while technologies lurch ahead unchecked. Charismatic leading man Jaeger Ayers is a Finder, a supreme tracker, exuding animal physicality and a cocky confidence that masks his vulnerability (Carla Speed McNeil clearly loves drawing the male face and figure, capturing his shifting expressions and musculature). A loner and nomad, Jaeger is drawn back to the city of Anvard and the dysfunctional Grosvenor household, the nearest he has to a family.

In "Sin-Eater," Jaeger finds himself caught between the two Grosvenor parents, recruited by the abusive father desperate to be reunited with his family, while

"The strangeness of the world, the mere possiblities, they were so exciting to me."

being a secret lover of the mother and innately protective of her and her children. To this predicament, Jaeger brings a gift; as a young man, he chose to become a Sin-Eater, an almost Christlike scapegoat who takes on a guilty person's sins and punishments.

Jaeger hits the road again in "King of the Cats," guarding pilgrims to Munkytown, a supposed holy city. McNeil sends up the theme park excesses of religion while disclosing more about Jaeger's roots and ambivalence toward his people. In "Talisman," McNeil features the youngest Grosvenor, Marcie, bibliophile and aspiring author. McNeil contrasts Marcie's love of books with a near future where few read print when they can access multimedia via skull computers or jacks plugged straight into their brains. McNeil crafts some of the most sophisticated, satisfying "aboriginal science fiction" in modern comics. **PG**

Past, present, and future mingle in the world of *Finder*. ➡

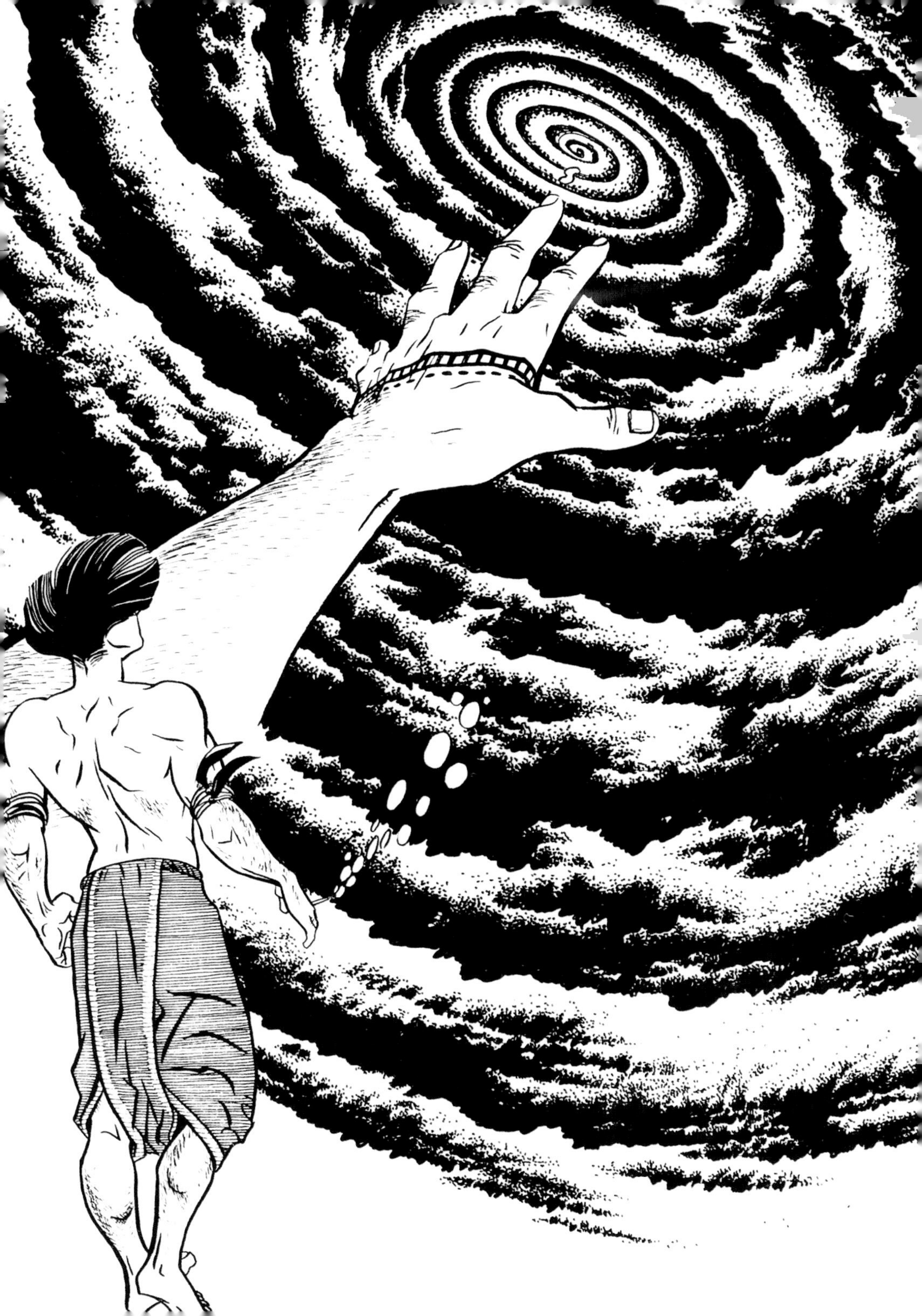

Journal 1996

✎✎ Fabrice Neaud

First published by Ego Comme X (France)
Creator French (b.1968)
Genre Autobiography
Award Angoulême Prize (1997)

One of the greatest achievments in autobiographical comics, the four-volume *Journal* is the gold standard of self-expression. Combining a deeply felt portrait of the artist's subjectivity with a masterful understanding of contemporary philosophical thought, it is one of the most thought-provoking comics ever published.

Fabrice Neaud is one of the rare cartoonists to have opted to work primarily in the autobiographical vein. Relying heavily on photographic notes, the artist has made himself the subject of his work nearly to the exclusion of other topics. His exploration of his personal artistic growth and his reflections on life as a gay man in a small French town are the hallmarks of his production. Yet it is the astounding reflective capacity of his comics that make them indispensable.

Neaud uses autobiography to meditate on broader social topics, ranging from gay rights to personal privacy. His masterpiece, *Journal (III)*, depicts his unrequited love for a classmate, a straight man named Dominique. Two set pieces in this volume are among the most powerful passages in comics: the Oubapo-inspired wordless conversation and Dominique's heartbreaking monologue in which he chastises Neaud for invading his privacy. In each, Neaud takes the representation of dialogue so central to our understanding of human communication and invents new ways to express it in the comics form. As the series progresses, Neaud's drawings become increasingly complex and referential. This is a bold and beautiful testament to what it meant to be alive in the late twentieth century. **BB**

Happy Mania 1996

✎✎ Moyocco Anno

First published by Shodensha (Japan)
Creator Japanese (b.1971)
Genre Romance, Humor
Adaptation TV series (1998)

We all want true love—but when it comes to actually finding it, some of us are more hopeless than others. Ms. Shigeta, Moyocco Anno's protagonist in the hilarious *Happy Mania*, is convinced that every man who agrees to a steamy night of lovemaking is "the one"—or soon will be. These love affairs offer plenty of distraction from the attentions of her nerdy coworker Takahashi, although—in true romantic comedy style—there is more to this quiet student than there seems. Certainly, Shigeta is clueless, but somehow her endless preening, schemes, and moments of utter desperation (not to mention her constant attempts to borrow money) make her all the more lovable.

Over the course of this eleven-book series, which appeared in Japan between 1996 and 2001, Shigeta's adventures become increasingly bizarre, as she meets—and falls in love with—slightly deranged men from all walks of life. Some readers will undoubtedly identify with Shigeta more than they would like to admit. After all, who has not gone to ridiculous lengths to try and get the attention of a man (or woman) and then failed?

A genre-challenging classic of *josei* manga—manga aimed at adult women—*Happy Mania* features explicit sex, but it is the moment when Shigeta begs a Shinto deity for a boyfriend that is most memorable. Anno's art—drawn in a springy, even pen line reminiscent of Taiyo Matsumoto—captures Shigeta's frenetic mood-swings with ease. If you think all manga is full of misty-eyed, cute characters, the adventures of *Happy Mania*'s exuberant antiheroine will make you think again. **EL**

Yongbi the Invincible 1996

Junghoo Moon

Title in original language *Yong Bi Bul Pae*
First published by Haksan (South Korea)
Creator South Korean (b.1967)
Genre Adventure

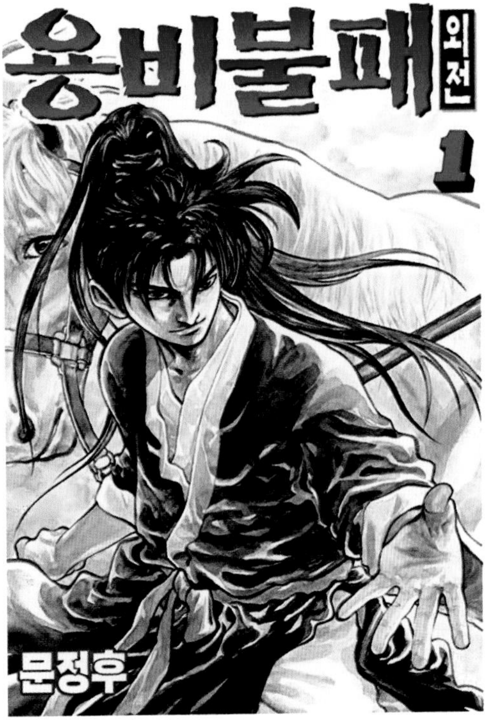

용비불패
외전
1
문정후

Popular in many East Asian cultures, the *wuxia* genre is essentially martial arts fantasy and superhero adventure rolled into one. It has different branches of fighting styles and training manuals to attain higher levels of *chi*. The protagonists train themselves to gain superhuman capabilities and fight against each other to gain power or to pursue greater justice. With a smart setting and story, *wuxia* can be a thrilling epic adventure with complex themes of vengeance, the vanity of power, and redemption. Add to that a healthy dose of comedy, and you get *Yongbi the Invincible*.

The protagonist Yongbi is a notoriously greedy bounty hunter in medieval China and is exceptionally skilled with the lance. When he rescues a little noble boy, he is hired by the boy to be his bodyguard in the quest to find the mysterious Golden Castle. Along the journey, different clans clash, swords and fist cross, old vengeances are pursued, and Yongbi has to face his troubled past.

The foremost strength of this work is its smooth integration of serious action sequences on all scales and flat-out hilarious comedy. Furthermore, the vast ensemble cast of characters and their interactions are compelling, with their rich back stories and morally ambiguous positions. Traditional gracefulness of the *wuxia* genre melds with contemporary character comedy. The pacing of the whole story is excellent, leaving no great character wasted in the middle and concluding with the immense climactic showdown at the Golden Castle. **NK**

"I don't know what kind of life you lived. But I too did not live a human life!"

Similar reads
Gehyupjun Junghoo Moon
Paladin Junghoo Moon
Spiral Junghoo Moon
The Legend of the Condor Heroes Jin Yong
The Return of the Condor Heroes Jin Yong

The Zabîme Sisters 1996

"Aristophane"

Title in original language *Les Soeurs Zabîme*
First published by Ego Comme X (France)
Creator Firmin Aristophane Boulon (French, 1967–2004)
Genre Drama

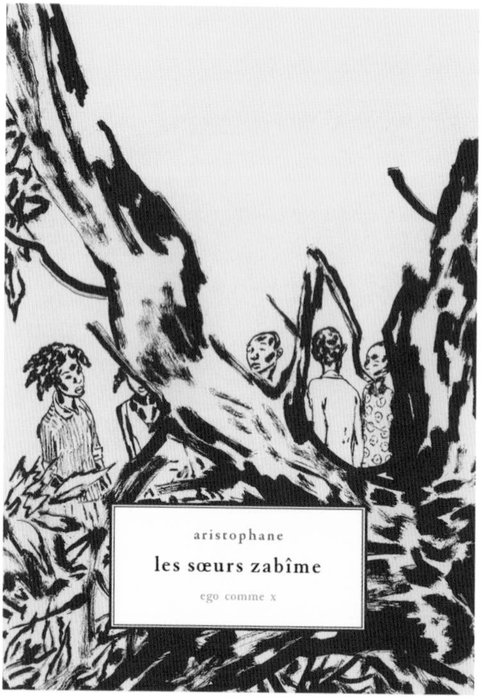
aristophane
les sœurs zabîme
ego comme x

"This modest work is dedicated to the divine, to the oneness whose domain is everything and which can be found in each one of us."

Aristophane

In Firmin Aristophane Boulon's tragically short career, there are three books that, at first glance, look very different from one another: *Faun* (*Faune*), *Demonic Tale* (*Conte démoniaque*), and *The Zabîme Sisters* (*Les Soeurs Zabîme*). However, two common themes span all of Aristophane's oeuvre: humankind's links both to the sacred and to evil.

Faune is about a mythological character who has such a drive to be evil that he poses the problem of which place is occupied by evil in the universe. Aristophane's answer is magnificent: "Why would the stars bother with states of mind?" *Demonic Tale* (a massive 300-page book) is set in Hell, but all the demons' cruelty, hubris, and will to power unequivocally remind readers of their own world.

In his last book, *The Zabîme Sisters*, Aristophane tells the story of three teenage sisters on the brink of adulthood. The story is an intoxicating mix of summertime exploits involving boys, arguments, thieving, and alcohol, set against the backdrop of the Caribbean island of Guadeloupe. In Aristophane's earlier works, readers might expect a demon and a faun to obey their own evil instincts. It is far more surprising to find the exact same reactions in children. The subtlety of their situations and the truthfulness of the characters' reactions are unmatched in comics.

Aristophane's drawing style is impressionistic, with small juxtaposed brush touches of black ink creating dramatic textures and shadows. He also uses the dry brush masterfully. In *The Zabîme Sisters*, these techniques help to convey the perfect feeling of a summer's day. Showing birds, bees, and lush vegetation, the artist wanted to convey the idea that life is all around us. Aristophane died prematurely in 2004. We can only imagine what great work he would have produced had he lived. **DI**

Aristophane subtly expresses the perplexities of the young. ➡

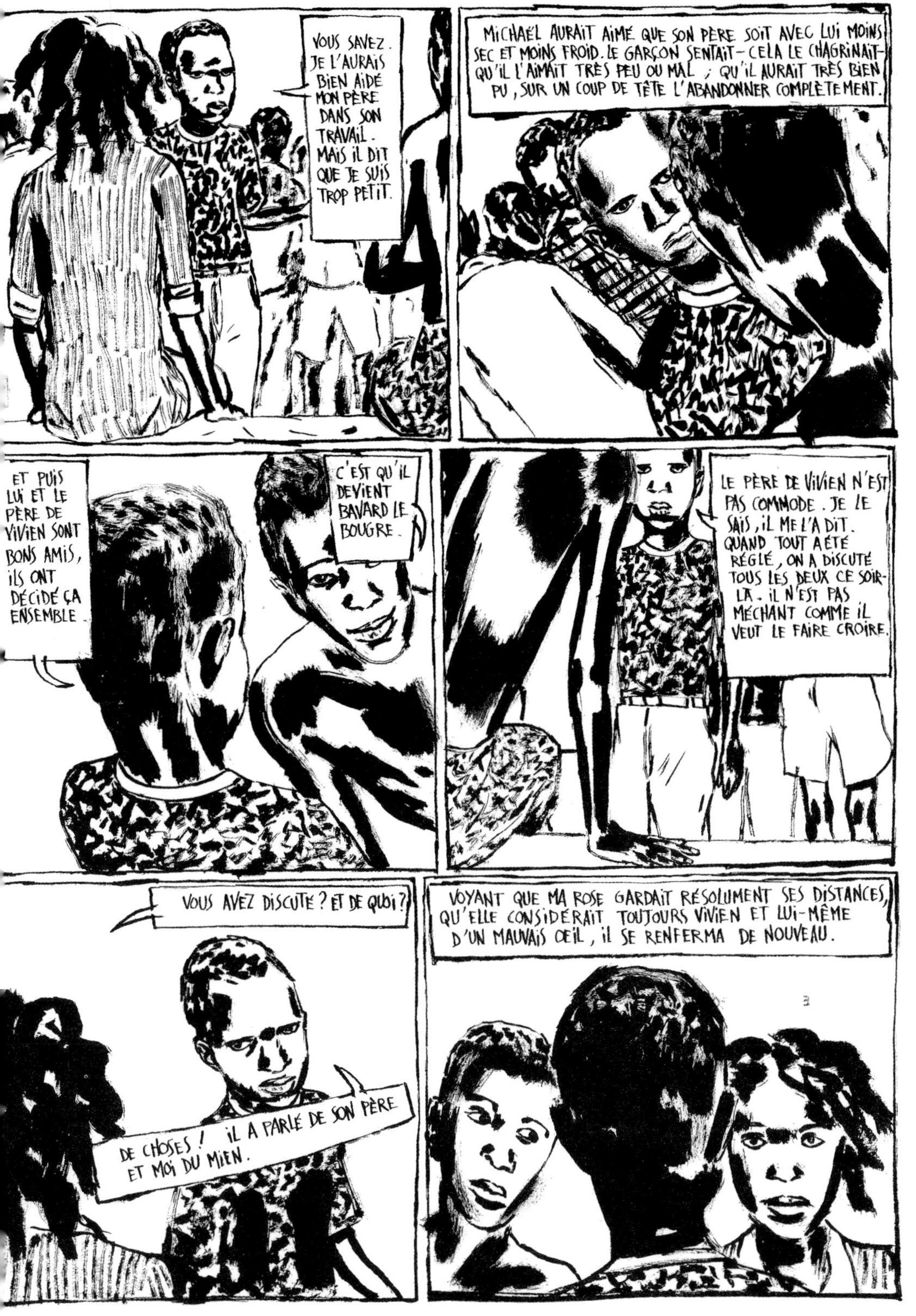
VOUS SAVEZ. JE L'AURAIS BIEN AIDÉ MON PÈRE DANS SON TRAVAIL. MAIS IL DIT QUE JE SUIS TROP PETIT.
MICHAËL AURAIT AIMÉ QUE SON PÈRE SOIT AVEC LUI MOINS SEC ET MOINS FROID. LE GARÇON SENTAIT – CELA LE CHAGRINAIT – QU'IL L'AIMAIT TRÈS PEU OU MAL ; QU'IL AURAIT TRÈS BIEN PU, SUR UN COUP DE TÊTE L'ABANDONNER COMPLÈTEMENT.
ET PUIS LUI ET LE PÈRE DE VIVIEN SONT BONS AMIS, ILS ONT DÉCIDÉ ÇA ENSEMBLE.
C'EST QU'IL DEVIENT BAVARD LE BOUGRE.
LE PÈRE DE VIVIEN N'EST PAS COMMODE. JE LE SAIS, IL ME L'A DIT. QUAND TOUT A ÉTÉ RÉGLÉ, ON A DISCUTÉ TOUS LES DEUX CE SOIR-LÀ. IL N'EST PAS MÉCHANT COMME IL VEUT LE FAIRE CROIRE.
VOUS AVEZ DISCUTÉ ? ET DE QUOI ?
DE CHOSES ! IL A PARLÉ DE SON PÈRE ET MOI DU MIEN.
VOYANT QUE MA ROSE GARDAIT RÉSOLUMENT SES DISTANCES, QU'ELLE CONSIDÉRAIT TOUJOURS VIVIEN ET LUI-MÊME D'UN MAUVAIS OEIL, IL SE RENFERMA DE NOUVEAU.

Yu Gi Oh! 1996

✎✎ Kazuki Takahashi

First published by Shueisha (Japan)
Creator Japanese (b.1961)
Genre Action, Fantasy
Adaptation TV anime (various series)

Yugi Moto is a diminutive, nerdy, underachieving high school student who lives with his grandfather in the fictional Domino City. His life changes forever when he is given the remains of an ancient Egyptian millennium puzzle, a puzzle that promises to grant a wish to whomever solves it. When Yugi assembles the puzzle in his bedroom, he wishes for a true and loyal friend who will always be with him. Enter the sadistic and malevolent Dark Yugi, the spirit of an ancient Egyptian pharaoh who manifests himself in Yugi's body whenever he perceives his powers are needed, dispensing "justice" in deadly shadow games that have grisly consequences for the loser. He takes an especially sadistic pleasure in the suffering of his victims, something that will come as a shock to fans of the television anime series, which features a much kinder Yugi. As Yugi learns more about his dark alter ego, he realizes that they must work together to discover the secrets of the pharaoh and fulfill their destinies.

The characters, which start off looking decidedly childlike, become more adult as this long series progresses. The battles are entertaining, although a little repetitive, and any lack of tension in the panels is caused by the inevitability of Yugi always emerging triumphant. Kazuki Takahashi came to manga in his thirties yet gave birth to a phenomenon that built a worldwide Yu Gi Oh industry. Manga adaptations include *Yu Gi Oh! R*, *Yu Gi Oh! GX*, and *Yu Gi Oh! 5D's*, and there have been several television anime series, movies, and the trading card game. **BS**

Blue 1996

✎✎ Kiriko Nananan

First serialized in *Comic Are!* magazine (Japan)
Creator Japanese (b.1972)
Genre Drama
Adaptation Live-action film (2001)

At the start of the school year in a provincial Japanese secondary school not far from the sea, two adolescent girls discover that they are irresistibly attracted to each other. Their friendship soon develops into love. Told through a series of subtle but very intense events, *Blue* is an almost daily chronicle of this decisive period in the lives of two girls reaching adulthood. It is a simple story that ends with an expected breakup in an atmosphere of tenderness and bitterness, marked by a profound feeling for the hopelessness of the situation.

In *Blue*, Kiriko Nananan produced a brilliant interpretation of a relatively conventional theme. Through this lucid, carnal story, she acknowledges her love of the intimate female chronicle—a liking that is confirmed by her subsequent publications. Freely using detailed drawings and with a remarkably sober narrative style, Nananan places her readers at the center of the relationship between the heroines, with close-ups of their faces, bodies, and the almost violent fervor of their emotions. With a tightly controlled structure, the book is impressive from a visual point of view: an outstanding graphic artist, the illustrator uses black and white (and without many of the crosshatching effects that are traditional in Japanese comics) to develop a very original way of working with empty spaces to suggest silences, the unsaid, and the quiet passion of eyes searching for each other. Sensual without affectation, and with an almost painful intensity, Nananan's is a remarkable female voice of which there have been relatively few in the comics world. **NF**

Castle Waiting 1996

Linda Medley

First published by Olio Press (USA)
Creator American (b.1964)
Genre Fantasy, Humor
Award Eisner Award (1998)

Castle Waiting represents a new take on fantasy. Instead of a preponderance of medieval English and endless swordplay, Linda Medley presents a community of cast-offs who find sanctuary and a sense of belonging in an old castle. A softer, feminine version of Robert Howard's *Conan*, *Castle Waiting* challenges long-held perceptions of beauty: there are no voluptuous Red Sonjas or soft-porn images here. Weighty matters include the washing of pots and dishes, the routine of everyday chores, and the maintenance of a proper household budget. The story may begin like a fairy tale, with a princess and a wicked witch, but these are quickly dispatched as the story focuses on what can happen to a once-beautiful castle now overgrown and abandoned by its princess (who rode off with her Prince Charming) and to those she left behind.

The three abandoned ladies-in-waiting decide to open their doors to strangers, and overnight the castle becomes a sort of medieval drop-in center, a refuge for a complex mix of anthropomorphic creatures, including a bearded nun, a knight with the head of a horse, a demented surgeon, and Lady Jain, who is pregnant and seeking refuge from her abusive husband.

In its quips and allusions, the book presupposes a certain familiarity with the fantasy genre. Although giants, fairies, and talking animals abound, there is no parody. Story lines are an intriguing mix of classic fairy tale, fantasy, and folklore, and the plot is complex, intricate, and rooted in the interpersonal relationships of multifaceted characters seeking acceptance. **BS**

$2.95 U.S./$4.05 CANADA
olio ISSN 1090-9494
L I N D A M E D L E Y
CASTLE WAITING
MEDLEY
NUMBER ONE

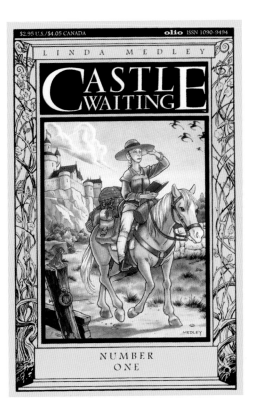

"If ifs and ands were pots and pans, there'd be no need for tinkers' hands!"

Similar reads
Emiko Superstar Mariko Tamaki
Fables Bill Willingham, Mark Buckingham, and others
Mouse Guard: Fall 1152 David Petersen
Polly and the Pirates Ted Naifeh

Old Boy 1996

✐ Garon Tsuchiya ✐ Nobuaki Minegishi

First published by Futabasha (Japan)
Creators Tsuchiya (Japanese, b.1947);
Minegishi (Japanese, b.1959)
Genre Crime

ACTION COMICS
FUTABASHA

オールド
ボーイ

【作】土屋ガロン　ルーズ戦記
【画】嶺岸信明

1

Similar reads
Crime and Punishment Osamu Tezuka
Freesia Jiro Matsumoto
Mike Hammer Mickey Spillane
Sin City Frank Miller

A man has been locked in a room for ten years. With no knowledge of the reason for his imprisonment or who is behind it, he spends his days, months, and years exercising and watching television. One day, he is freed without explanation, bundled into a suitcase, and deposited in a park. With his life ruined, there is just one thing on his mind: revenge.

Old Boy explores the psychology of the revenge thriller. The protagonist does not subject his enemies to a typical series of brutal punishments, but rather tries to make sense of his life and the person he has become. Nobuaki Minegishi's artwork presents a classic troubled hero: a silent, musclebound type with a face aged by hard years, who develops a

"Who the hell did this to me, and what for?"

relationship with a young waitress. In later volumes, more of his backstory is revealed, but to begin with, the enigmatic "Mister" is just a man sporting a mysterious scar and wandering through a bleak and sprawling Tokyo. The city is rendered in straight lines and concrete-colored tones, a cosmopolitan world with a faceless population and mysterious figures who monitor our hero's every move.

The moral territory between good and evil appears as gray as the nighttime alleys of the city. *Old Boy* is an unsentimental thriller, showing the mundane life of people working, eating, and living in a contemporary world but peeking below the surface to discover a terrifying criminal underworld. South Korean director Chan-wook Park made this dark manga into an equally pitch-black movie that does an admirable job of condensing Tsuchiya's saga; it won the Grand Jury Prize at the 2004 Cannes Film Festival. **SW**

"Mister" endures the purgatory of his unexplained imprisonment. ➡

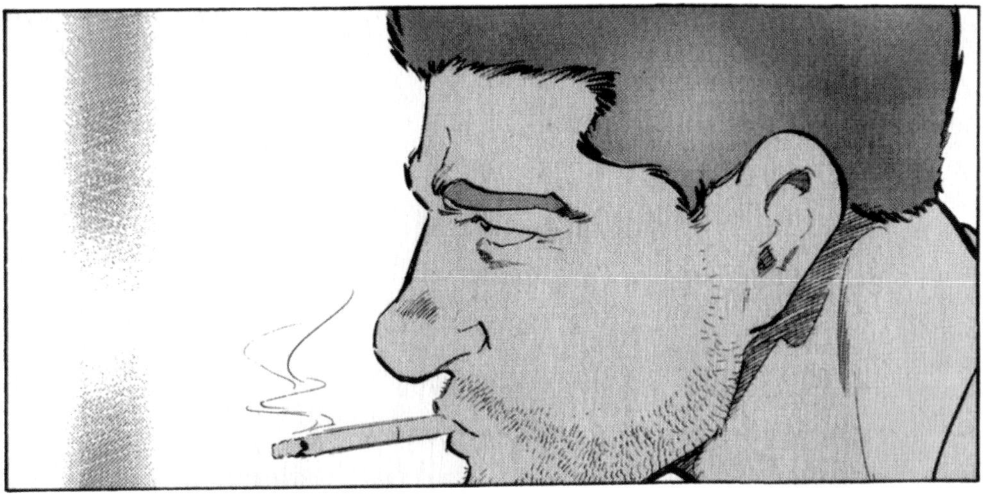
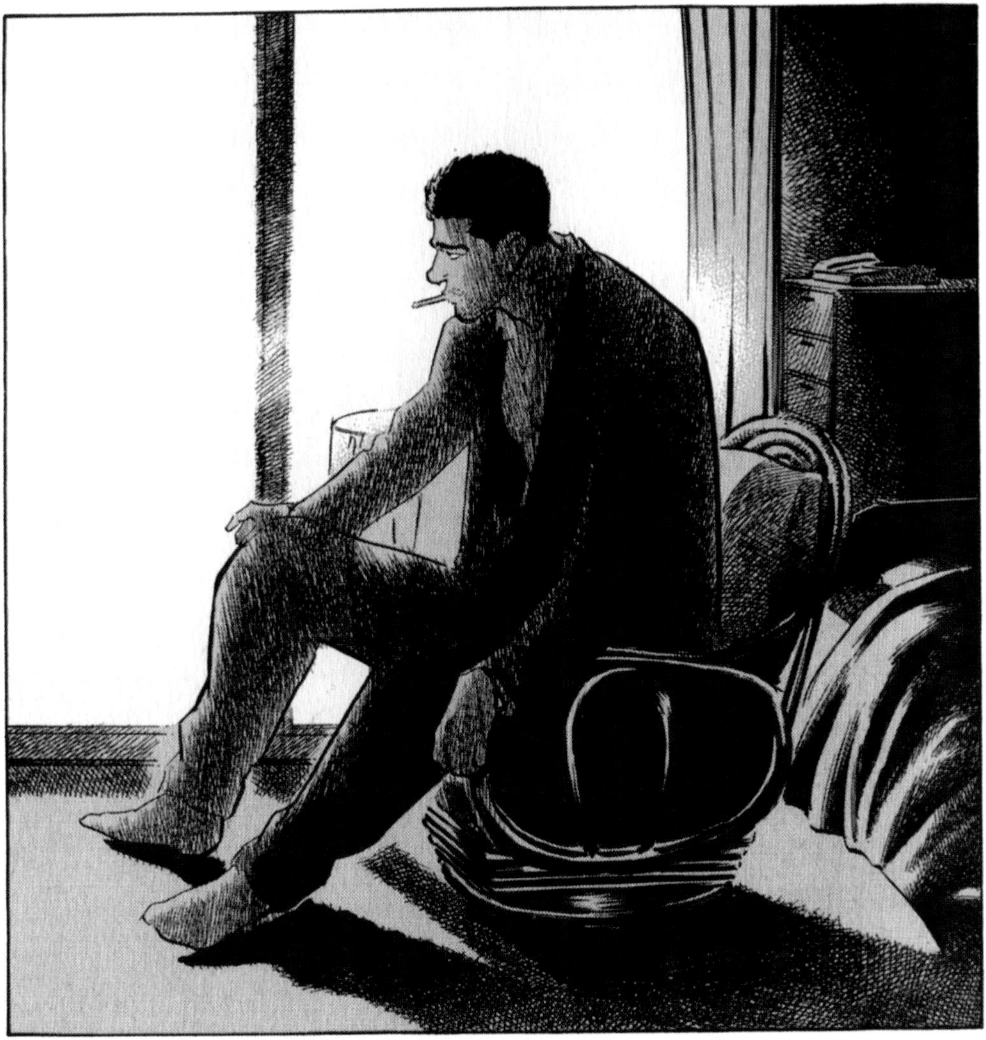

Seven Miles a Second 1996

David Wojnarowicz James Romberger, Marguerite Van Cook (Colorist)

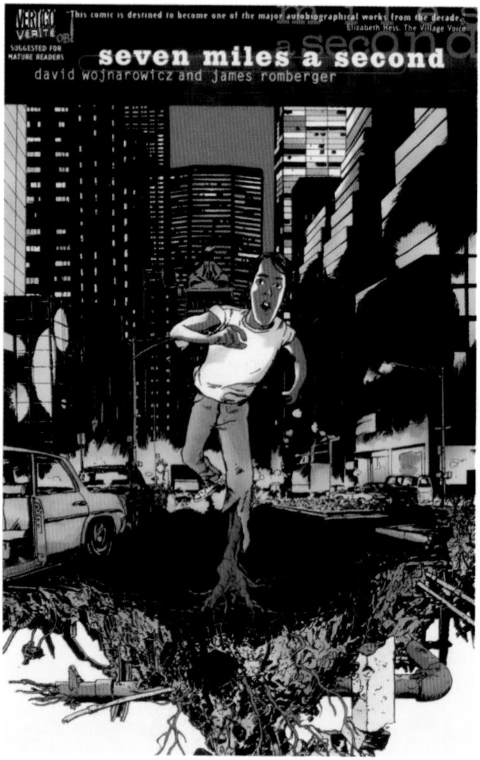
VERTIGO VERITÉ
This comic is destined to become one of the major autobiographical works from the decade.
Elizabeth Hess, The Village Voice
SUGGESTED FOR MATURE READERS
seven miles a second
david wojnarowicz and james romberger

First published by Vertigo/DC Comics (USA)
Creators Wojnarowicz (American, 1954–92); Romberger (American, b.1958)
Genre Biography

David Wojnarowicz found fame in the mid-1980s as a writer, painter, filmmaker, actor, and political activist. He died from AIDS at age thirty-seven, and in his final years was collaborating on this graphic novel with fellow artist and friend James Romberger. The project was completed by Romberger after David's death.

Wojnarowicz fled from home as a youth, and, like so many, struggled on the streets, inevitably turning to prostitution and petty crime to keep himself alive. Two-thirds of *Seven Miles a Second* deals with those days, a collection of his adolescent recollections, from abuse at the hands of middle-aged clients to his experiences with Willy, his friend and lover, as they both strive to make it through another day.

It would be very easy to candycoat a story such as this, but just as Wojnarowicz's words pull no punches, Romberger's raw, expressionistic drawings are alive with the poverty, vomit, and decay of the streets. Marguerite Van Cook's coloring favors impression over formality, adding much to the atmosphere and heightening the sense of reality.

The final part of *Seven Miles a Second* shows an adult David nearing the end of his life. The narrative veers largely into stream-of-consciousness polemic—very passionately—with some wonderfully evocative visuals to match. If anything positive emerges from a story that was bound to end tragically, it is in the enduring strength of belief expressed defiantly. *Seven Miles a Second* is a very challenging book, but an extremely intense and worthwhile one. **CH**

"The worst thing about the wait between customers was having to move every five minutes. . . ."

Also by James Romberger

2020 Visions with Jamie Delano
Aaron and Ahmed with Jay Cantor
Ares with Brian Azzarello and Marguerite Van Cook
The Bronx Kill with Peter Milligan

Daddy's Girl 1996

🖊 Debbie Drechsler

First published by Fantagraphics Books (USA)
Creator American (b.1953)
Genre Reality drama
Influenced by Lynda Barry

Daddy's Girl is, quite simply, one of the most harrowing comic books ever published. A collection of stories that first appeared in the *Seattle Stranger* and occasional *Drawn & Quarterly* anthologies, the overarching narrative of this book—a young girl subjected to regular sexual abuse and her subsequent teenaged attempts to enter the world of romantic relationships—will churn your stomach and break your heart.

Based on Debbie Drechsler's own experiences—although she refrains from calling it an "autobiographical comic"—*Daddy's Girl* forces readers to face up to a reality that is never discussed in society, except in the context of sensationalist news stories: incest. In this respect, *Daddy's Girl* feels like the apogee of the taboo-smashing in comics that began in the 1970s. However, what makes this graphic novel so completely affecting is Drechsler's ability to channel a child's voice as she tells the story of the young girls—named Lily in the earlier stories, and renamed Franny as she gets older.

The father is a terrifying presence, invading his daughter's sleep every night to ensure his sexual "needs" are met. Her coldhearted mother seems interested only in making sure that her daughters are dressed appropriately. It is almost as if she is keeping Lily, and then Franny, at a distance for fear one of them will say something about what is going on after dark. Secrets breed secrets as Franny grows up and finds out that her father is not the only sexual predator she needs to watch out for. Delve into *Daddy's Girl*, but be forewarned: this book might ruin that expression for you forever. **EL**

Great Teacher Onizuka 1997

🖊 Toru Fujisawa

First published by Kodansha (Japan)
Creator Japanese (b.1967)
Genre Drama
Adaptation TV anime series (1999–2000)

Around the time when *Great Teacher Onizuka* was first released, Japanese schools were faced with a dilemma known as *gakkyuu hokai*, or "collapse of the classroom." All over the country, teachers were troubled by a lack of student discipline in the classrooms. Amid such anarchy, *Great Teacher Onizuka* questioned the true meanings of the "ideal school" and the "ideal teacher."

Although the concept of reeducating delinquent youths is common in Japanese comics, the students featured in this plot are much harder to tame. Their rebellious natures are hidden under their seemingly innocent veils, and their cunningly intelligent minds know how to cover up whatever they do. Unlike traditional troubled youth, they do not break the school rules and are not openly violent—they are much shadier and more treacherous.

The central character, Eichi Onizuka, becomes a high school teacher for a rather illicit purpose: to date a schoolgirl. However, he soon comes face to face with the problems surrounding his new workplace: bullying, lack of love at home, inferiority complexes, and selfish teachers. Onizuka's unconventional teaching methods tackle these issues one by one, gradually winning the hearts of his students and colleagues. A factor that contributed to the comic's huge success was that its readers were men who grew up reading traditional school drama comics and could relate to Onizuka rather than to his students. *Great Teacher Onizuka* won the Boys' Comic Prize at the Kodansha Manga Award in 1998. **TS**

A History of Violence 1997

John Wagner   Vince Locke

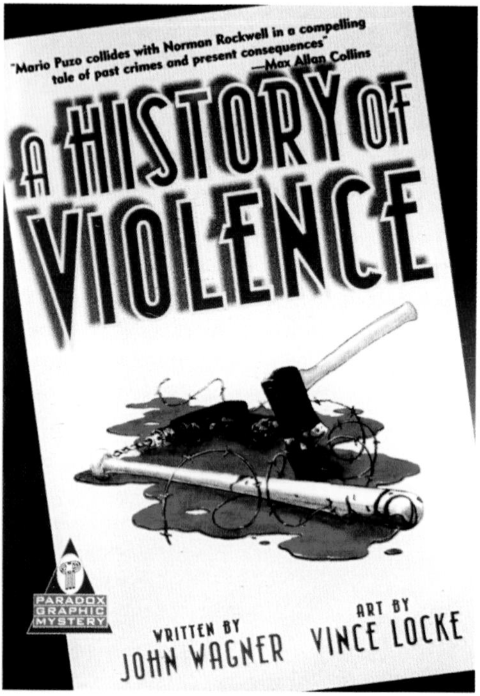
"Mario Puzo collides with Norman Rockwell in a compelling tale of past crimes and present consequences" —Max Allan Collins
A HISTORY OF VIOLENCE
PARADOX GRAPHIC MYSTERY
WRITTEN BY JOHN WAGNER
ART BY VINCE LOCKE

"My God—all these years and I don't even know you . . . Who are you Tom?"

Similar reads

Judge Dredd John Wagner and Carlos Ezquerra
Robo-Hunter John Wagner and Ian Gibson
Strontium Dog John Wagner and Carlos Ezquerra
The Last American John Wagner, Alan Grant, and Mike McMahon

First published by Paradox Press/DC Comics (USA)
Creators Wagner (British, b.1949); Locke (American, Unknown)
Genre Crime

As a mild-mannered soda shop owner in small-town Michigan, Tom McKenna becomes a reluctant hero after fighting off two armed robbers. His story reaches the national news, drawing unwanted fame and questions about how such a man could be capable of singlehandedly defeating two armed killers. Tom has hidden depths, and when the New York mafia arrive asking questions about him, his hidden past is forced to the surface.

A History of Violence was not widely read on first release, but experienced resurgence after David Cronenberg's movie adaptation hit the screens. The book and the movie are substantially different, however, branching off in other directions midway through, and with far more of Tom's past revealed in the book. His story is an audacious tale of murder, robbery, and revenge against the New York mob, the kind that mobsters would never forget, much less forgive.

John Wagner's mastery of amoral characterization, so brilliantly displayed in work such as *Button Man*, is turned on its head here as readers witness a man who finds his morals and bitterly regrets his past. Tom—or Joey to use his real name—is a likable character at odds with his youthful self. However, the mark of Cain is not easily removed, and he cannot outrun his past. Vince Locke uses a loose, scratchy style to give the book a fevered energy that, along with the gradual reveal of the narrative, sweeps the reader along. Illustrated in black and white, *A History of Violence* is a powerful mix of secrets, lies, revenge, and murder—and one of the most truly horrifying reveals ever seen in comics. **BD**

Eagle 1997

✎ Kaiji Kawaguchi

Title in original language *Iguru*
First published by Shogakukan (Japan)
Creator Japanese (b.1948)
Genre Drama

Long before the election of Barack Obama, manga artist Kaiji Kawaguchi imagined the idea of a visible minority running for president of the United States as a liberal senator. Kawaguchi's Kenneth Yamaoka is a wealthy man, a hero of the Vietnam war, a third-generation Japanese-American, and a man of many secrets. He also just might be the next leader of the free world.

Eagle: The Making of an Asian-American President tells the story of Senator Yamaoka's rise to power through the eyes of an outsider, a Japanese reporter who is sent to cover the campaign and slowly becomes drawn into the inner circle. As Takashi Jo digs into the background story of this powerful man, he reveals a disturbing, complex, and often contradictory figure, a man who is more than capable of doing the wrong thing if he believes that it is for the right reason.

Set in 2000, *Eagle* rewrites recent U.S. history in often thinly veiled terms. Yamaoka's rival for the Democratic nomination is Al Noah, vicepresident under Bill Clydon. The mixture of real and imagined figures provides a semblance of verisimilitude in the work. Kawaguchi couples this with striking melodrama. Primaries are won and lost on the strength of rousing speeches, and *Eagle* sometimes comes across as an enjoyable fantasy of electioneering worthy of a Frank Capra movie. Kawaguchi's outsider perspective on U.S. politics is a curious and compelling one. The mundanities of the electoral process become the stuff of fast-paced drama, with enough romance, intrigue, betrayal, and suspense to thrill even the most jaded political junkie. **BB**

One Piece 1997

✎ Eiichiro Oda

First published by Shueisha (Japan)
Creator Japanese (b.1975)
Genre Adventure, Humor
Adaptation TV anime series (1999–)

The plot of *One Piece* focuses on the adventures of Luffy, the central character, who is on a hunt for secret treasures hidden by a legendary pirate crew. While the general story line of the comic is simple, its attraction is in the dramatic events that occur along the way on Luffy's journey, often involving the coming and going of new friends and rescuing people from bizarre disasters that strike in Eiichiro Oda's exuberant world of fantasy adventure. The crew, which he calls *Mugiwara no ichimi*, or the Straw Hat Pirates, is made up of a unique mixture of characters, including the green-haired swordsman Zoro, the seventeen-year-old blue-nosed reindeer called Chopper, and Sanji, the well-dressed chef, as well as the beautiful navigator Nami, whose cleavage-enhancing tops make her the love interest of many adolescent boys.

In 1999, two years after its launch as a serial comic in *Weekly Shonen Jump*, *One Piece* was developed into an animation. This turned out to be a record-breaking hit, and in 2000, the first of many *One Piece* films was released. Although the fast pace of the series, which swiftly takes the reader from one episode to another, is a typical characteristic of *Weekly Shonen Jump*, what distinguishes the title from others is the fact that beneath the humor and action, there is indeed a tear-jerking drama that touches children and adults alike. Oda's romanticized vision of pirates is certainly captivating, and readers become hooked by the passion that drives Luffy and his crew to continue boarding that pirate ship week after week. **TS**

One Hundred Views of the Speicherstadt 1997

Martin tom Dieck

Title in original language *Hundert Ansichten der Speicherstadt*
First published by L'Arrache-Coeur (Switzerland)
Creator German (b.1963) **Genre** Fantasy

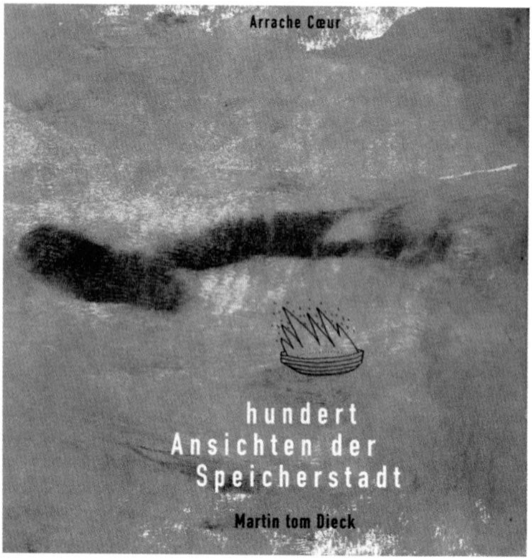
Arrache Cœur
hundert
Ansichten der
Speicherstadt
Martin tom Dieck

"I found out . . . that the water and a boat are very strong images. They're existential metaphors."

Martin tom Dieck

Also by Martin tom Dieck

Lingus, Wise Man of the Waters (*Lingus savant des eaux*)
Salut, Deleuze! with Jens Balzer
The Innocent Passenger (*Der unschuldige Passagier*)
The Silent Oud (*L'Oud Silencieux*)

This comic creator's working method includes the intuitive exploration and improvisation of visual recurrent motifs. He explores images in the same way that jazz musicians explore sounds or Dada and surrealist poets explore words. He also has affinities with Zen art, Cy Twombly, and, in comics, with Jean "Moebius" Giraud's *Le Garage hermétique de Jerry Cornelius*.

Martin tom Dieck prefers to leave his stories open to interpretation because he likes the idea that the story is not completed when he finishes it, permitting numerous versions to be imagined by its readers. He uses words sparsely because, as he put it, words specify too much, and only images know how to keep secrets.

Two leitmotifs punctuate Martin tom Dieck's oeuvre: water (with boats) and a city map that is also a heart. Both are present in the wordless *One Hundred Views of the Speicherstadt*. Water, in its multifarious manifestations, features throughout the work: heavy rain, air bubbles, foam, waves, vortices, tsunamis, cascades, and light reflections on and in the liquid element. Water behaves in a way that is very Deleuzian and Zen: it is always the same and yet it is always moving and it is always different; the appeal is in its difference and repetition. All these bodies of water and these reflections are masterfully executed in a caricatural but elegant style.

The Speicherstadt of the title (inventing a wordplay in German, "the city of memories") is a district in Hamburg, now disused, but still with impressive, old dockland facilities. With a little imagination, readers may very well see that, when viewed from above, the Speicherstadt has the form of a heart. Maybe that is where our most cherished memories come from, after all. According to Zen Buddhism, the artist and the thing being drawn must become one: one heart feeling the throb of life. **DI**

Martin tom Dieck's style conveys a forgotten, water-dominated Hamburg. ➡

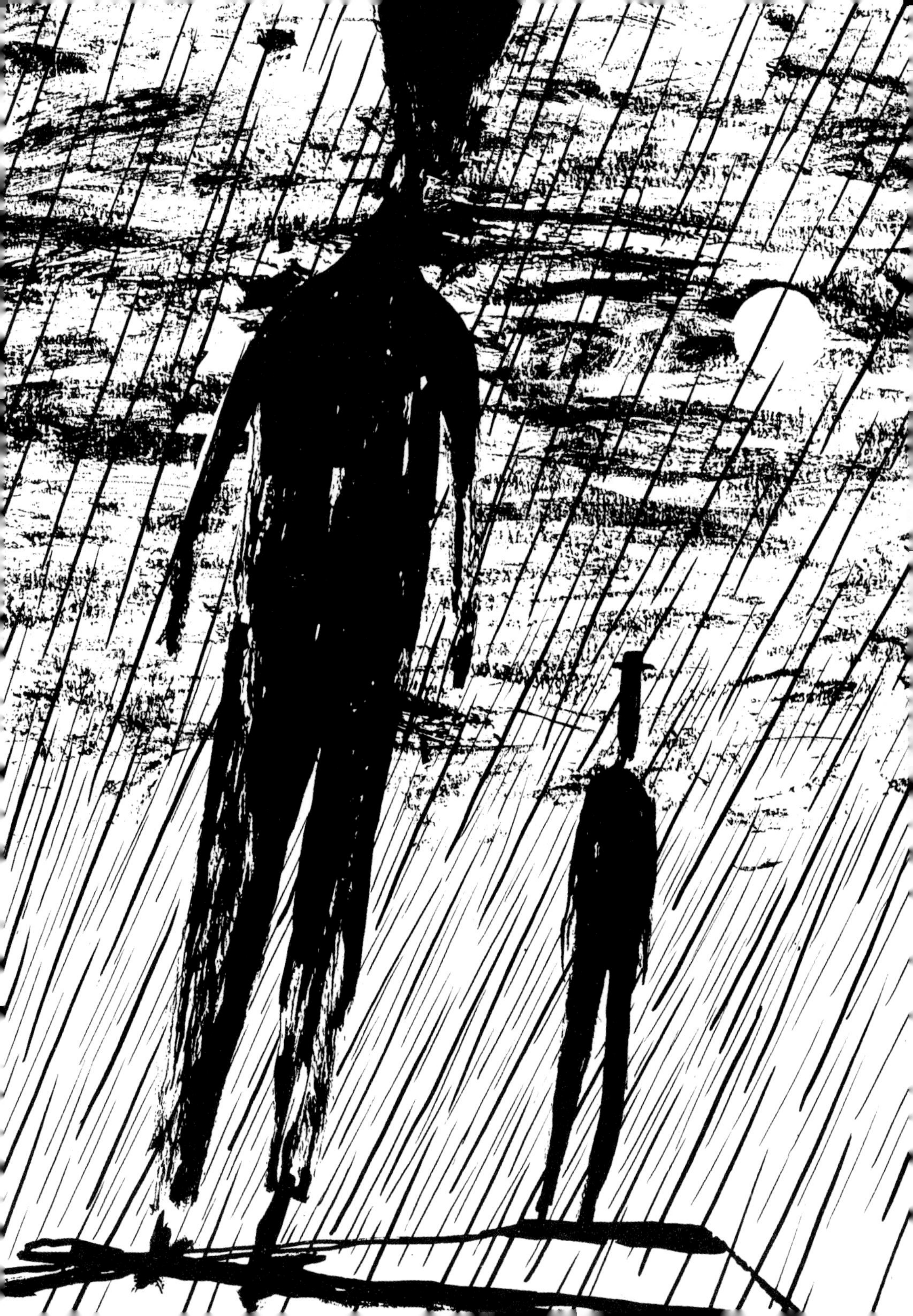

Swords of Rome 1997

✎ Jean Dufaux ✎ Phillipe Delaby

Title in original language *Murena*
First published by Dargaud (France)
Creators Dufaux (Belgian, b.1949); Delaby
(Belgian, b.1961) **Genre** History

Swords of Rome is set in the heart of the Roman Empire, picking up in 54 A.D. when Emperor Claudius is ruler. He is married to the scheming Agrippa, whose plan is that her malicious son Nero will inherit the empire. Claudius, though, favors his own son, Britannicus, as his successor. Claudius also has a mistress, and her son, Murena, is the fictitious pivot inserted to prod historical fact.

Swords of Rome is a dense political thriller. Page after page of talking heads delineate the machinations that move the plot forward in an undercurrent of terror, only to be abruptly punctuated by moments of shock and extreme violence. In the French tradition, *Swords of Rome* occupied an initial four volumes, and the recently completed second story arc courted controversy by involving early Christians. A third sequence is planned.

Jean Dufaux is a prolific writer whose backlist and ongoing series include a wide range of genres. He researches thoroughly, listing his sources at the end of each chapter, and *Swords of Rome* is commended by several historians. Delaby's contribution is detailed, well-researched art distinguishing a large cast and ensuring that a necessarily verbose script never becomes dull. Ancient Rome is portrayed in all its debauchery, but for all the brutality, there is nothing as savage as the censorship that spares the English language reader the sight of genitals or unfettered mammary glands. The full dose of bloody violence survived uncensored. As the potentially distressing content increases in later volumes, perhaps it is just as well that only the first two volumes were translated into English. **FP**

Vellevision 1997

✎✎ Maurice Vellekoop

First published by Drawn & Quarterly (Canada)
Creator Canadian (b.1964)
Genre Alternative, Humor
Influenced by Tom of Finland

What do Edward Gorey, Ziggy Stardust, soap operas, Barbie, and Puccini have in common? Nothing obvious, but Maurice Vellekoop puts them all together in this incredibly funny hodge-podge called *Vellevision*. It is a collection spanning ten years of the author's work as both an illustrator and cartoonist, and it comprises one-pagers and short stories alongside illustration series, fashion season reportages, and fake advertisements.

Most of the narrative works are about gay life: from the budding angst of adolescence to routine nightclubbing, from semiautobiographical confessions to comic book genre fantasies. Some elements are not about gay culture, but *Vellevision* is teeming with the customary references, concentrated and emphasized in the inspired four-page "8 Pillars of Gay Culture" piece. Clichés abound and are stretched to their limits throughout, with hilarious consequences. By mixing references from various sources, the author creates a celebration of diversity, sexual playfulness, and pleasures. In "The Adventures of Gloria Badcock," the protagonist is sent to outer space to experience the inner world of dreams and fantasies, beneath the sea, and even to a deluxe all-male bordello to find all kinds of orgasmic bliss ("I came, I saw, I came," she delightfully says).

Expect loads of glitz, glamour, and panache, with Vellekoop's fine lines and intensive watercolors providing the right ambience for his portrayal of such diverse worlds. *Vellevision* is filled with the sheer fun of sex, which comes in all colors and sizes. **PM**

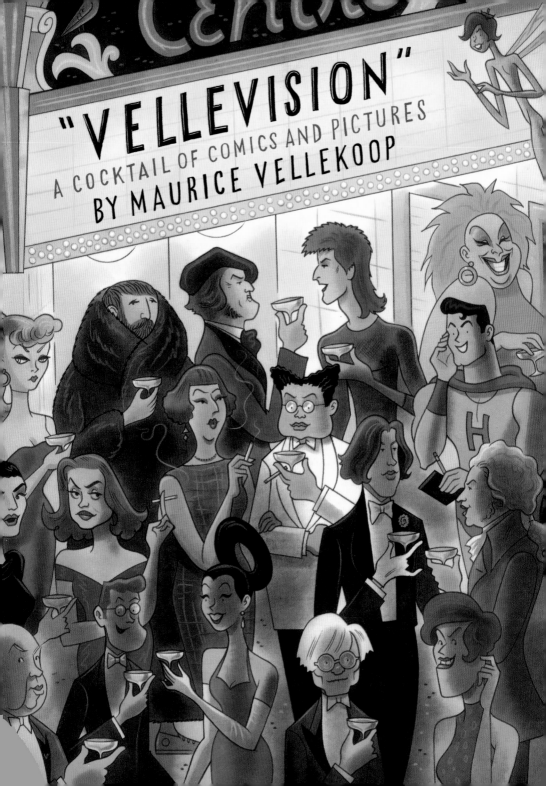

"VELLEVISION"
A COCKTAIL OF COMICS AND PICTURES
BY MAURICE VELLEKOOP

Bardin the Superrealist 1997

"Max"

Title in original language *Bardín el Superrealista*
First published by *El Víbora* (Spain)
Creator Francesc Capdevila (Spanish, b.1956)
Genre Fantasy

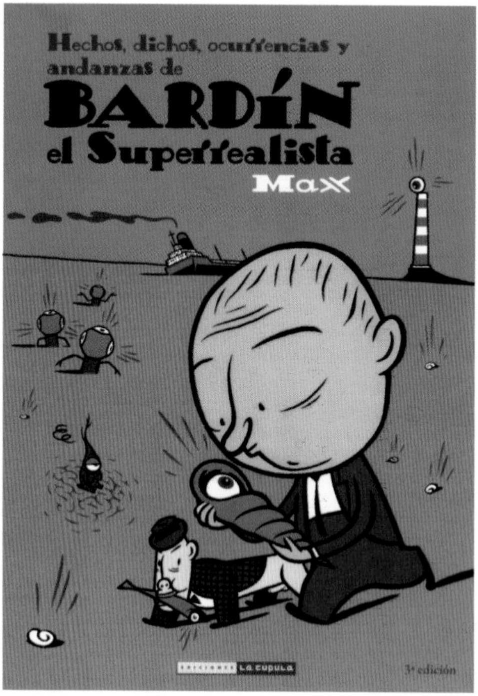
Hechos, dichos, ocurrencias y andanzas de
BARDÍN
el Superrealista
Max
3ª edición

Also by Max
El carnaval de los Ciervos
Gustavo
La biblioteca de Turpin
Peter Pank
The Extended Dream of Mr. D

The title hero of *Bardin the Superrealist* is a lonely, big-headed little man in a gray suit who stars in a series of short parables (usually one or two pages long), in which he oscillates between the real world and the superrealist worlds that are a figment—or not—of his imagination. (Max prefers the term "superrealism"—a more accurate transcription of the French word "surréalisme," meaning literally "above realism"—rather than "surrealism.") Max concentrates all of his main artistic influences into *Bardin*, which include Chris Ware's *Jimmy Corrigan*, but also Hergé's *ligne claire*, Robert Crumb, George Herrimann, and especially the classic Spanish comic weeklies such as *Pulgarcito* and *DDT*. There are also allusions to Luis Buñuel and

"Don't give yourself over to panic, Bardín!! You've been granted some extraordinary powers . . ."

Salvador Dalí (*Un chien andalou*), Pieter Bruegel the Elder (*The Triumph of Death*), and Henry Fuseli (*The Nightmare*). All this results in one of the author's most personal works, in which he explores such topics as existentialism, sex, and religion: one of *Bardin's* most visually notorious stories faces him with the Holy Trinity, represented in the shape of a well-known round-eared mouse.

A volume of all the *Bardin* material so far was issued by La Cúpula in 2006. It includes a specially produced, dialogueless story, "The Sound and the Fury," an allegory of violence in which the protagonist has to fight an archetypical dragon. This same volume has been published in English by Fantagraphics Books. *Bardin* has received many awards, including the Premio Nacional del Comic in 2007, granted by the Spanish Ministry of Culture. **AM**

The Sojourn 1997

Jean-Pierre Gibrat

In 1997 Jean-Pierre Gibrat was an accomplished artist with two decades of work behind him. Lauded for his depiction of alluring women, Gibrat was far more rounded than his reputation suggested, and, after years of illustrating the narratives of others, he made the leap into telling his own stories with *The Sojourn*.

Having escaped from the train sending him to work in Germany from occupied France in 1943, Julien returns to his rural village of Cambeyrac. He cannot risk capture by collaborators, so he hides in an empty house overlooking the village square and roams the streets at night. Forced into voyeurism, he observes what eludes others while becoming increasingly frustrated at being unable to make himself known to attractive waitress Cécile. Julien is eventually drawn out of hiding and into peril as he becomes involved with the Resistance. Despite the ever-present wartime dangers, this is a human drama. Gibrat recognizes that the heroics of ordinary people helped his country survive the occupation, and he creates a paean to the beauty of a way of life in the French countryside that has changed only superficially over decades.

"At the end of the day Cécile's smiles escaping from the café knotted my stomach."

One character returns in *The Raven's Flight*, which is set several months later in occupied Paris. Resistance fighter Jeanne has been captured and decides to take a chance to escape and flees across the rooftops with petty thief François. Both books are populated with an endearingly eccentric cast that never lapses into caricature. They are characterized by strong plotting, lushly drawn by an artist who never sacrifices storytelling for the sake of illustration. **FP**

Title in original language *Le sursis*
First published by Dupuis (France)
Creator French (b.1954)
Genre Drama

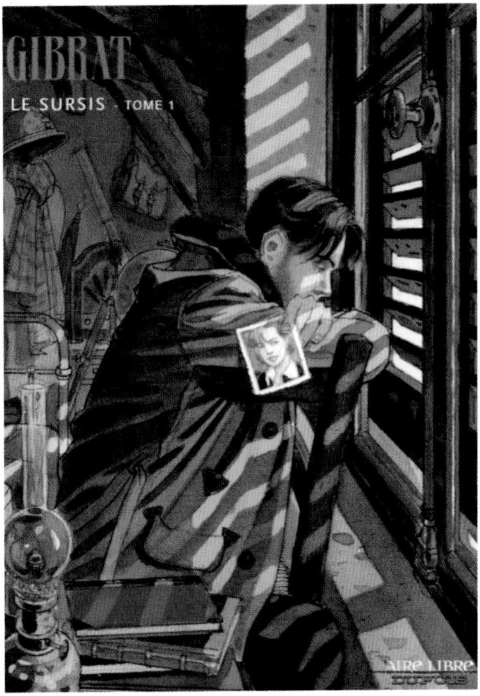

GIBRAT
LE SURSIS - TOME 1
AIRE LIBRE
DUPUIS

Similar reads
A Thorn in the Side Bill Knapp
Berlin: City of Stones Jason Lutes
Les Années Goudard Jean-Pierre Gibrat
Marée Basse Daniel Pecqueur and Jean-Pierre Gibrat
War Stories Garth Ennis and others

Transmetropolitan 1997

✎ Warren Ellis ✎ Darick Robertson

First published by Vertigo/DC Comics (USA)
Creators Ellis (British, b.1968); Robertson
(American, b.1968)
Genre Science fiction

Set in the future, *Transmetropolitan* is the account of journalist Spider Jerusalem's fight for telling the truth in a U.S. society that is becoming increasingly blasé and uninterested in politics. Jerusalem's Hunter S. Thompson–like demeanor is underlined by his bald head, colored glasses, enormous drug use, and gonzo take on journalism. His truth crusade is aided reluctantly by assistant Yelena Rossini and bodyguard Channon Yarrow, who are both in a complicated love/hate relationship with their chain-smoking boss. Jerusalem decides to take on the new president—"The Smiler"— by digging up dirt and exposing his wicked ways.

Transmetropolitan combines hilarious dialogue with futuristic elements, extreme violence, and a colorful cast in an effort to reveal the power structures that run through both the fictional and real worlds. The story is about one man's battle against lies, bigotry, and social injustice, armed with nothing but language, which, like the series itself, tends to include a wide variety of insults, profanities, and toilet humor at its most extreme.

Darick Robertson's illustrations match Warren Ellis's rambling writings by including a lot of close-ups of faces and crowded cityscapes in order to underline that this story is about the people and their city. By introducing guest artists and subtly changing his own style, Robertson makes sure that Spider Jerusalem and his "filthy assistants" are always in flux. Spider Jerusalem might have the foulest mouth in comics, but his quest is justified by the fact that he is pure at heart and will oppose unscrupulous people in power. **RPC**

Eiland 1997

✎✎ Stefan van Dinther and Tobias Tycho Schalken

First published by Self-published (Netherlands)
Creators Van Dinther (Dutch, b.1969);
Schalken (Dutch, b.1972)
Genre Alternative

The work of the cartoonists behind *Eiland* bears out the theory that one of the key elements of the comics form is the representation of time as space. Stefan van Dinther and Tobias Tycho Schalken, two Dutch artists who met in art school, have interrogated aggressively the limits of the comics form in their two-man anthology. They have raised formal experimentation to an art.

Eiland started off as a black-and-white fanzine but has grown over time to become a full-color art book. Each issue comprises a series of short, poetic works that reveal a tremendous formal ingenuity. The works are created in a wide variety of media and rendering styles, from the coldly analytic to the hauntingly human. Abstraction is one of *Eiland*'s key values, and individual pieces can be challenging for readers to follow. Nonetheless, the work is carefully crafted and always totally controlled. The duo have more in common with deliberate formalists such as Richard McGuire, Kevin Huizenga, and Chris Ware than with the anarchic experimentalists associated with the Fort Thunder collective based in Rhode Island.

The highlight of the earliest issues of *Eiland* was Van Dinther's *CHRZ*, a comic whose narrative is structured prismatically like the eye of a housefly. It is a wordless comic and its various stories interweave themes of loneliness, alienation, and love. Published as a stand-alone book, *CHRZ* is the most complex work to come out of the anthology. Schalken's "Folklore," in the fifth issue, is a similarly fascinating work, more emotionally laden but no less structurally inventive. **BB**

Puzzling events in *Eiland* #3 from the "masters of sequence." ➡

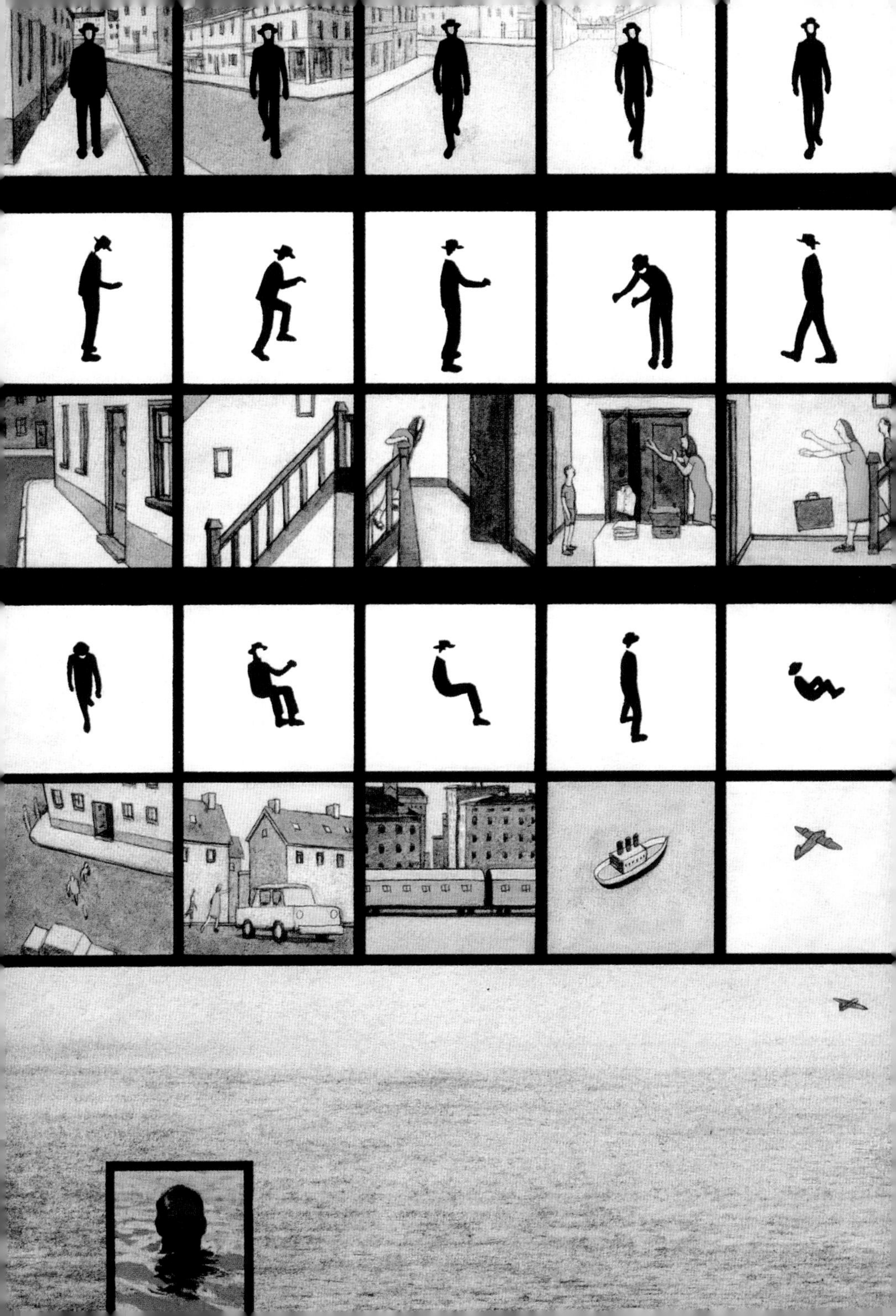

MPD Psycho 1997

Eiji Otsuka Sho-u Tajima

First published by Kadokawa Shoten (Japan)
Creators Otsuka (Japanese, b.1961); Tajima, (Japanese, b.1966)
Genre Horror

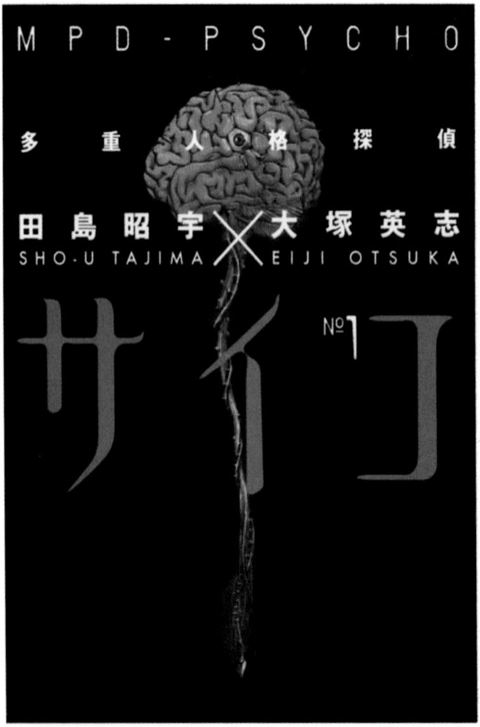

M P D - P S Y C H O
多重人格探偵
田島昭宇 大塚英志
SHO-U TAJIMA
EIJI OTSUKA
サイコ
№1

Similar reads
Battle Royale Koushun Takami
Death Note Tsugumi Ohba and Takeshi Obata
Madara Eiji Otsuka and Sho-u Tajima
The Kurosagi Corpse Delivery Service Eiji Otsuka

Mothers with mysterious barcodes tattooed on their eyeballs have their babies ripped from their wombs. Carefully numbered body parts are found in a field. A sadistic murderer buries his female victims in the ground up to their necks before turning their heads into flowerpots. There are dismemberments, disembowelments, and decapitations galore that take place not behind closed doors, but right before our eyes, and in abundance. *MPD Psycho* is, without doubt, the new yardstick in the "eighteen years of age and over" world of brutality, nudity, and manga.

When Yosuke Kobayashi's girlfriend is mutilated at the hands of a serial killer, he relentlessly hunts down her murderer. When he corners him, however, the confrontation triggers a multiple personality disorder (MPD) in Kobayashi's tortured mind, which sees Shinji Nishizono, a ruthless psychopath, split from deep within Kobayashi's subconscious to promptly murder his girlfriend's killer. A second, more dominant personality also emerges: Kazuhiko Amamiya. It is as the character of Amamiya that Kobayashi is imprisoned for murder, and he remains Amamiya for most of the remainder of the series. When released from prison, he joins a private detective agency as a criminal profiler and becomes involved in solving a series of increasingly gruesome serial killings that seem to be leading him toward a greater mystery.

MPD Psycho's predominantly black-and-white panels, often devoid of text, can seem almost sterile in the absence of anything even resembling gray shadings or shadows. Sho-u Tajima, however, saves his detail for the gore: muscles, veins, bone, brains, leaking fluid, and severed torsos, which, when combined with Eiji Otsuka's fresh, inventive plot twists, are guaranteed to keep even the most desensitized manga reader content until the very end. **BS**

The World Is Mine 1997

Hideki Arai

First serialized in *Weekly Young Sunday*, published by Shogakukan (Japan)
Creator Japanese (b.1963)
Genre Crime

Away from the civilized and polished streets of Tokyo, *The World Is Mine* embarks on an ultraviolent trip through the countryside, following the exploits of "natural-born killers" Toshi and Mon-chan. They are an unlikely pair—Toshi is a genius bomber with self-confidence issues; Mon-chan is a feral being, dominated by primal urges (eating, fornicating, killing) that he is happy to give in to—and soon have the Japanese public terrified. They also become the darlings of the media, until evidence emerges that a mysterious creature nicknamed "Higumadon" is on the loose. The monster is rampaging around northern Japan, leaving a bloody trail of slaughtered livestock and unlucky hunters. Higumadon continues to increase in size until it is big enough to destroy buildings and even small towns. Not willing to be outdone by this newcomer, Toshi and Mon-chan take their game to an entirely new level. As chaos engulfs Japan and unconventional politicians and tough cops take over, they decide that the only possible solution is to fight fire with fire.

This series is mainly about men trying to exert their power over the world. There are very few women who play a significant part, with the exception of the virginal Maria and the withered crone Hamaki Tashoko, both of whom are attracted to the animalistic nature of Mon-chan. Even as explosions and deaths abound, with Hideki Arai violence is never glamorous: it is about blood and tears and pain and destruction and despair. "When did Japan become like this?" wonders one elderly lady, shaking her head at the tragic headlines—maybe it always has been. With *The World Is Mine*, Arai peels off the polished surface of civilization to uncover the raw ugliness underneath. This is a modern tale of the apocalypse, a story about the end of time—a book on freedom and violence from which no one escapes unscathed. **XG**

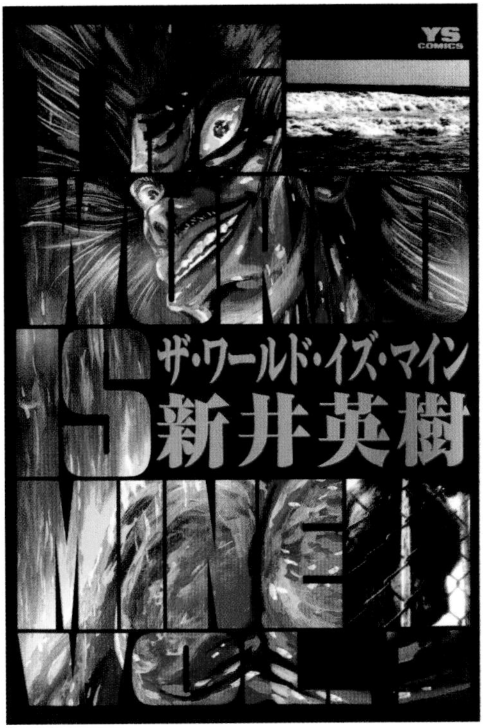
YS COMICS
ザ・ワールド・イズ・マイン
新井英樹

Similar reads

Bambi Atsushi Kaneko
Dragon Head Minetaro Mochizuki
Freesia Jirou Matsumoto
TOKYO TRIBE2 Santa Inoue

300 1998

Frank Miller and Lynn Varley

First published by Dark Horse Comics (USA)
Creators Miller (American, b.1957); Varley (American, Unknown)
Genre History

Almost everyone has at least heard of the Battle of Thermopylae (480 B.C.). This heroic deed of arms—a few hundred Greek soldiers fighting to the last man against a Persian army more than ten times their number—has become a legend over the centuries, ultimately symbolizing the spirit of resistance of every minority in the face of a numerically superior adversary.

Such a heroic situation could not fail to attract an author as naturally declamatory as Frank Miller. Temporarily abandoning uniformed righters of wrongs and hard-boiled heroes, Miller plunges his readers into the very heart of this warlike event, at the side of King Leonidas with his 300 hoplites and wave upon wave of enemy warriors in action. The historical plausibility of the story that Miller tells is of little interest to him. With Lynn Varley—then his colorist and his wife—Miller focuses on three days of frenzy, during which the future of a world is played out.

300 is published in a horizontal format, which is very unusual in the world of comics. Like the Frenchman Philippe Druillet, who twenty years earlier related the fall of Carthage in comics form—following the plot used by the great nineteenth-century writer Gustave Flaubert in his novel *Salammbô*—Miller manages to make his book a barbaric, thundering grand opera: as heady as a drug and as bewitching as a spell. Readers will not quickly forget the arresting portrait he paints of Xerxes, the god-king, a pagan idol incarnate, nor the spectacular end of the Greeks, engulfed by the multitude. **NF**

King Leonidas confers, from a dramatic perspective. ➡

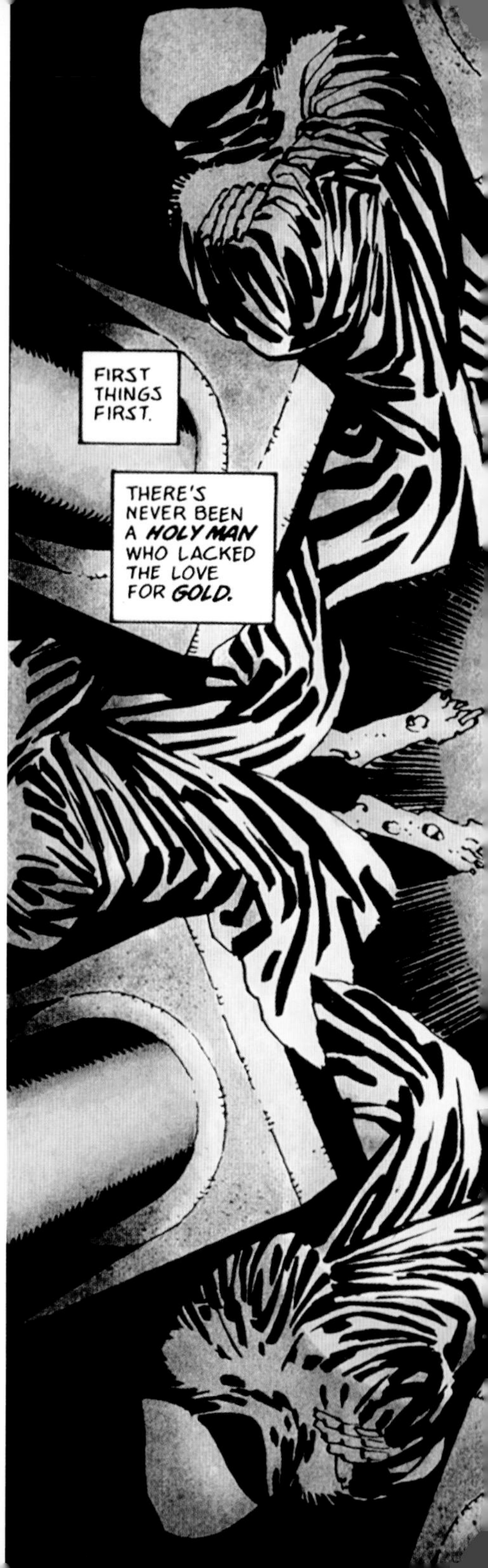
FIRST THINGS FIRST.
THERE'S NEVER BEEN A HOLY MAN WHO LACKED THE LOVE FOR GOLD.

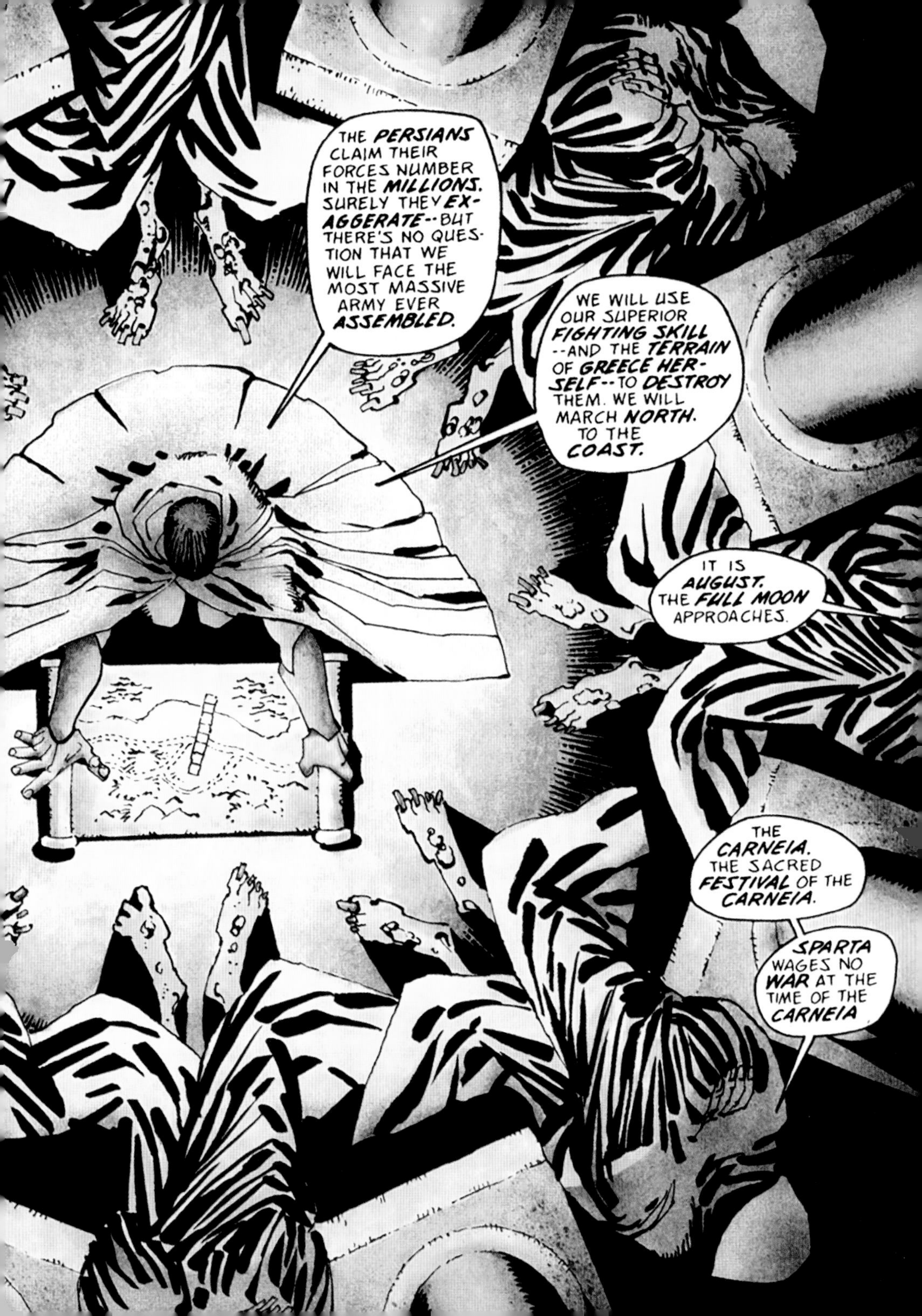
THE PERSIANS CLAIM THEIR FORCES NUMBER IN THE MILLIONS. SURELY THEY EXAGGERATE-- BUT THERE'S NO QUESTION THAT WE WILL FACE THE MOST MASSIVE ARMY EVER ASSEMBLED.
WE WILL USE OUR SUPERIOR FIGHTING SKILL --AND THE TERRAIN OF GREECE HERSELF-- TO DESTROY THEM. WE WILL MARCH NORTH. TO THE COAST.
IT IS AUGUST. THE FULL MOON APPROACHES.
THE CARNEIA. THE SACRED FESTIVAL OF THE CARNEIA.
SPARTA WAGES NO WAR AT THE TIME OF THE CARNEIA

The Killer 1998

"Matz" Luc Jacamon

Title in original language *Le tueur T. 1: Long feu*
First published by Casterman (Belgium)
Creators Alexis Nolent (French, b.1967); Jacamon (French, b.1967) **Genre** Crime

JACAMON & MATZ
LE TUEUR
Long feu
casterman

Also by Matz
Cyclops with Luc Jacamon
Headshot with Colin Wilson
Lost Effort with Jean-Christophe Chauzy
Savage Night with Miles Hyman
Shandy with Dominique Bertail

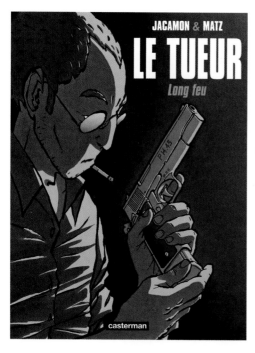

What are the thoughts of a killer who is about to pull the trigger to fulfill his contract? What convinces him to do the job of an assassin? Strongly inspired by crime fiction writing, Alexis Nolent, known as "Matz," puts the reader in the shoes of a killer whose identity is never made known. The setting focuses on close-ups but also provides plenty of room for recitatives by the killer. We learn the character's reflections on how the world is organized and run, and come to understand his valuation of his role and the way he justifies his actions. "Man's history is just an endless list of atrocities and we're not through with it," he asserts. "The first one who lectures me about life, liberty, and all that crap, I should just shoot him. That's what he'd deserve."

"The Killer is an independent character, conscientious . . . or rather with a conscience, which is not quite the same."

The protagonist is presented as a regular guy, who is doing a job to earn a living, and the way in which he approaches the assassinations is chillingly matter-of-fact. He often remains silent, which prompts readers to feel empathy toward him. The drawings of Luc Jacamon bring to life the intimate scenes as well as the action scenes, punctuated by incisive cut-outs such as broken glass. Jacamon's realist use of color is also exemplary because it does not fall into the clichés of the genre.

Lonely, the Killer eventually forges bonds of friendship and a lasting relationship with an Indian companion who has a child. Furthermore, in order to keep the story convincing, Matz moves the action between Venezuela, Mexico, the United States, and Cuba. This enables him to mix geostrategic ingredients related to the drug and oil industries with local political and economic ideologies. **CM**

Stigmata 1998

Claudio Piersanti Lorenzo Mattotti

A shambling hulk of a man, a loner at age forty-one, without any family, friends, or self-esteem, scraping a meager existence and drinking his life away, is the last person anyone would expect to receive the marks of being a saint. Yet one morning, an unnamed hero wakes from a strange dream to find the palms of his hands bleeding profusely from stigmata. These signs change his life, although not for the better.

Doctors dismiss his wounds as self-inflicted, but when they refuse to heal, he is forced to quit his job as a waiter, although not before beating up his boss and then accidentally burning down his own apartment. Homeless and hopeless, he finally finds work, love, and eventually marriage in a traveling carnival. When the stigmata reopen, the carnival folk persuade him to profit from them by becoming a sideshow attraction and pretending to heal the paying public. However, exploiting his "gift" backfires when his ex-boss catches up with him and rapes his wife, who is later swept away in a flood. Spiraling ever downward, he hits rock bottom and collapses in a cemetery, his tears and blood washing over a gravestone. At this point, the narrative voice shifts from his first-person monologue to the diary of Sister Anne in a hospital, observing his painful withdrawal and gradual recovery.

"Why me? Me, who doesn't believe in God, who's never believed in him."

This graphic novel grew out of an earlier comic, which first united novelist and screenwriter Claudio Piersanti with artist Lorenzo Mattotti. Drawing pure emotion, Mattotti makes readers feel the main character's pain in a raging fury of febrile linework along with the beauty of his redemptive reawakening. **PG**

Title in original language *Stigmates*
First published by Éditions du Seuil (France)
Creators Piersanti (Italian, b.1954); Mattotti (Italian, b.1954) **Genre** Drama

STIGMATES
MATTOTTI PIERSANTI
SEUIL

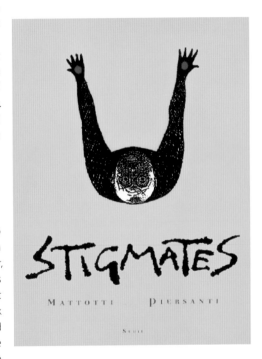

Similar reads
Fragile Line (Ligne fragile) Lorenzo Mattotti
The Man at the Window (L'homme à la fenêtre) Lilia Ambrosi and Lorenzo Mattoti
The Sound of the Frost (Le Bruit du givre) Jorge Zentner and Lorenzo Mattotti

Vagabond 1998

✐✐ Takehiko Inoue

First published by Kodansha (Japan)
Creator Japanese (b.1967)
Genre History, Adventure **Award** Japan Media
Arts Festival Grand Prize for Manga (2000)

Takehiko Inoue's *Vagabond* is an adaptation of an historical novel from the 1930s titled *Miyamoto Musashi* by Eiji Yoshikawa. Illustrating a fictional story of the life of the legendary swordsman Musashi, it follows his travels as he meets an array of masters. The comic may be based on a eighty-year-old novel about a man who lived in the seventeenth century, but Inoue's version is hardly old-fashioned. By carefully weaving in a string of modernity, *Vagabond* has attracted a young and diverse audience, both in and outside of Japan. Inoue's story line does not compromise the original plot, but the artist's own twist is evident in parts of the series. For example, Musashi's older sister has been deliberately left out, and the swordsman's rival, Kojiro Sasaki, has impaired hearing in Inoue's version. The author's powerful art brings Musashi's adventures to life, and his fierce brushwork is particularly effective in the hair-raising battle scenes.

Inoue, who made his debut in 1988, has produced a number of successful comics, including *Slam Dunk* and *Real*, which both focus on the theme of basketball. When the former was serialized in 1990, it caused a craze for the sport, and the comic has sold at least 100 million copies in Japan. The title came to be known as one of the "three pillars" that supported *Weekly Shonen Jump*, alongside Akira Toriyama's *Dragon Ball* and Yoshiiro Togashi's *Yu Yu Hakusho. Vagabond* has been turned into thirty-three successful volumes, and it has now been published in more than twenty countries, selling 22 million copies worldwide. **TS**

Ethel & Ernest 1998

✐✐ Raymond Briggs

First published by Jonathan Cape (UK)
Creator British (b.1934)
Genre Biography
Award British Book Awards Best Illustrated Book (1999)

Lovers of Raymond Briggs's earlier works will find much to remind them of his finest moments, although this biography is an unexpected departure from his tales of bogeymen, snowmen, and grumbling Father Christmases. The quiet narrative of his parents' lives together is played straight; the humor comes from the well-observed details of interplay between two very ordinary people and the changing times through which they live.

The understated tone takes readers from Briggs's parents' courtship in 1928 through to their deaths within months of each other in 1971. Each page or spread focuses on one or two anecdotes or snippets: moving into the house that they stay in for all those decades; building the Anderson bomb shelter in the back garden; receiving Raymond and his wife-to-be back at home. Subtle repetitions add depth, as readers see the shelter being dismantled and turned into a coal bunker, or the pear tree that Raymond grew from a seed closing the story on the final page.

Changes tick through the pages, faster and faster: new material goods, such as a television and telephone, are greeted with fresh eyes that convey the impact of these changes on everyday lives. Life events like Ethel's increasing illness are shown in the background. Despite the minimalist storytelling, there is much in the way of emotion. Briggs clearly loved his parents as well as being frustrated by them (there are some very funny moments when his mother's snobbery is played off against his father's leftist leanings), and the nearly wordless closing scenes will draw tears even on rereading. **JS**

Hicksville 1998

Dylan Horrocks

First published by Black Eye Books (Canada)
Creator New Zealander (b.1966)
Genre Drama
Influenced by Chester Brown

HICKSVILLE
A COMIC BOOK BY DYLAN HORROCKS

Readers are introduced to Hicksville through the eyes of Leonard Batts, a U.S. reporter conducting research on Dick Burger, a phenomenally successful comics creator and publisher who grew up there. The town is a veritable comics Shangri-La, where all the residents are immersed in comics, and rare first editions are readily available. Naturally, these inhabitants eschew the trashy superhero fare that Burger publishes, ensuring that Batts endures a frosty reception. However, he perseveres and eventually uncovers more than he expected about Burger, and, more importantly, discovers a rich history of comics that he never knew existed.

Dylan Horrocks invents a history containing the comics that serious readers dreamed of in the mid-1990s: the comics that would engender the cultural respectability that was so lacking in the age of Image Comics, when *Hicksville* appeared. As such, some criticized *Hicksville* for providing a cozy delusion, but that is unfair. *Hicksville* is a rousing call to claim those levels of respect and recognition for comics that Horrocks imagines, even if the history is made up. Additionally, *Hicksville* is simply a delight: funny and charming, appealingly drawn, and with a satisfying plot of corrupted ambition. It is also imaginatively structured, weaving maps, reproductions of fictional comics, and homages into the fabric of the story. Today, comics enjoy an unprecedented level of respectability in many countries. This does not mean that *Hicksville* is dated or irrelevant, rather that it can proudly take its place in the history of comics. **SB**

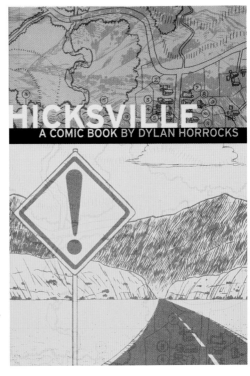

"Hicksville *is an unmistakenly modern, urbane, attractive, highly gratifying, and very, very smart tale.*"

The Comics Journal

Similar reads

Artichoke Tales Megan Kelso
Black Candy Matt Madden
Curses Kevin Huizenga
La Perdida Jessica Abel

Planetary 1998

Warren Ellis John Cassaday

First published by WildStorm Productions (USA)
Creators Ellis (British, b.1968);
Cassaday (American, b.1971)
Genre Superhero

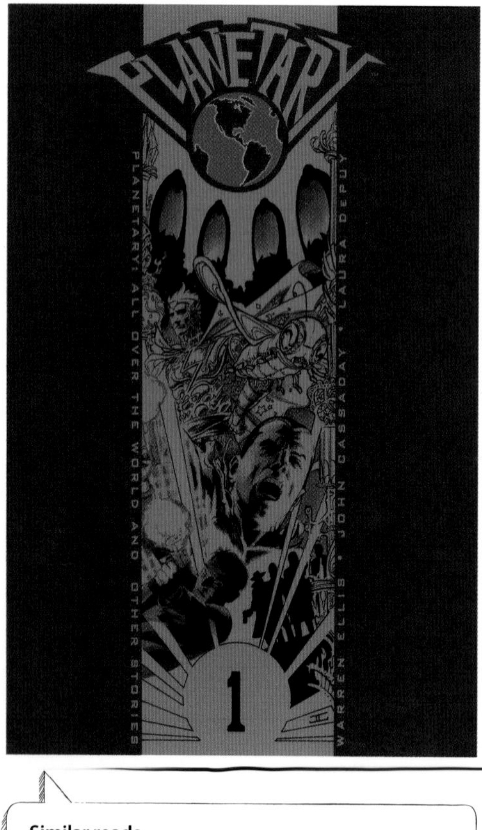
PLANETARY
PLANETARY: ALL OVER THE WORLD AND OTHER STORIES
WARREN ELLIS • JOHN CASSADAY • LAURA DEPUY
1

Similar reads
Miracleman Alan Moore and Neil Gaiman
Stormwatch Warren Ellis
X-Men Grant Morrison

In the late 1990s, Warren Ellis was busy exploring just how big he could make superheroes. This story started when he inherited the WildStorm title *Stormwatch* and began subjecting its colorful superhero team to a brutal reimagining. The characters that emerged, first into the later *Stormwatch* episodes, then as part of the new series *The Authority,* were on an altogether different scale: earth-shaking, game-changing, and a very long way from being human.

Planetary took this process to its final destination, with superheroes who are strange, unknowable animals that casually change the shape of the world they inhabit. The central characters are quite deliberately unlikable: a cold, angry old man, an easily bored superpowered heiress, and a fantastically irritating supercommunicator. They quip and carp their way through fantastic environments, all the more alien and astonishing for being buried in the cracks of a realistic, recognizable world, not that different to our own. They claim to be archaeologists of mysteries, of the fantastic rubble that clutters and colonizes every part of their world. In this world, superheroes have existed for generations, and many of our fictions are real. Each bizarre environment, each loving reimagining of a familiar genre or fictional space, is rendered in elaborate and careful detail by longtime Ellis collaborator John Cassaday, who lends realism and weight to every bizarre secret the antiheroes uncover.

The slow advancement of the plot, which sees the characters uncover gruesome conspiracies and secret societies piloting the world toward a terrible future, is fairly standard fare, but this is almost incidental. The real star is the world they inhabit, and the diverse and curious stories they excavate within it, in a series of unsettling and wonderful glimpses of a terrible hidden history. **JD**

Superman For All Seasons 1998

Jeph Loeb Tim Sale

Superman For All Seasons may be stripped of the more overt and traditional science fiction staples associated with the Man of Steel's beginnings, but, despite a lack of exploding alien planets and infant-bearing rocketships, it remains one of the most poignant of the many explorations of the Superman origin story in the character's decades-long history.

Split into four thematic chapters based on the seasonal calendar, Jeph Loeb's tale focuses on the formative moments in Clark Kent's maturation. It traces, in stages, his often lonely and self-doubting journey from childhood's end in Smallville to recognition of his ultimate destiny in the "adult world" of Metropolis. Each "season" is narrated by a key member of the supporting cast, rather than by Superman himself, with their differing perspectives underlining how his burgeoning heroism shapes and inspires those around him.

Tim Sale grounds his artistic interpretation of Superman firmly in the Golden Age, transposing the hero's iconic imagery to a modern sensibility in standout, double-page spreads that emphasize his majesty and grandeur. As dynamic as these scenes are, however, it is the artist's more subdued character pieces in Smallville, rendered in beautifully muted pastel shades by colorist Bjarne Hansen, that will stay with the reader the longest.

Although Loeb and Sale firmly root the Superman mythos in a cozily nostalgic atmosphere of Rockwellian Americana, they avoid the obvious trap of descending into mawkish sentimentality. Instead, an astonishing synchronicity of meaning and intent between the storytellers provides a rich celebration of the smalltown homeliness and values that Superman embodies. *Superman For All Seasons* is a definitive example of a superhero story that humanizes the superhuman without ever having to resort to the more cynical tricks of deconstructionism. **AO**

First published by DC Comics (USA)
Creators Loeb (American, b.1958); Sale (American, b.1956)
Genre Superhero

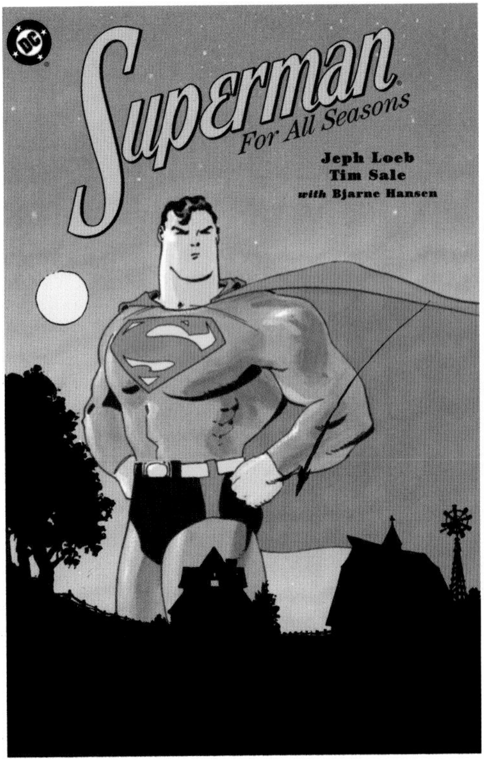
DC
Superman
For All Seasons
Jeph Loeb
Tim Sale
with Bjarne Hansen

Similar reads

Batman: The Long Halloween Jeph Loeb and Tim Sale
Kryptonite Nevermore! O'Neil, Swan, and Anderson
The Man of Steel John Byrne

Torso 1998

Brian Michael Bendis and Marc Andreyko

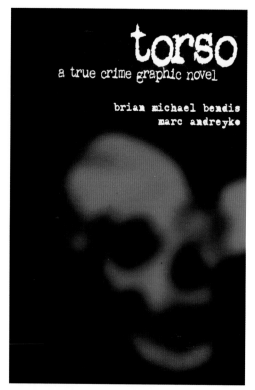

torso
a true crime graphic novel
brian michael bendis
marc andreyko

"The killer guy. They think it's him. He did it again."

Similar reads

Due Michele Petrucci
Filthy Rich Brian Azzarello and Victor Santos
Fortune and Glory Brian Michael Bendis
From Hell Alan Moore and Eddie Campbell
Road to Perdition Max Allan Collins and Richard Rayner

First published by Image Comics (USA)
Creators Bendis (American, b.1967); Andreyko (American, b.1970)
Genre Crime

Eliot Ness is well known as the whiter-than-white Federal agent who, as a member of The Untouchables, helped to bring Al Capone to justice. Less well known is what Ness did next. *Torso* follows the true story of the shocking murders that took place in Cleveland in 1935, while Ness was safety inspector for the city. More than a dozen people were beheaded and, in some cases, dismembered, sparking a media frenzy and leaving police struggling for answers. *Torso* is part mystery drama and part police procedural, and Bendis and Andreyko do not shy away from the intricacies of detective work. Nor do they soften the gruesome realities of the case, re-creating the victims in their macabre frankness and even including genuine coroner's photographs of bodies and scenes of crimes.

Depression-era Cleveland is likewise realized by samples from period newspaper pages and by using photographs of streets and buildings as backgrounds to the black-and-white artwork. While the juxtaposition of these captured moments and the hand-drawn images can be a little jarring, it helps to make *Torso* an historical document that serves as an education on this little-known dark chapter of twentieth-century America.

Bendis has cited David Mamet as an influence, and this is never more evident than in this series. The banter between characters zings along at a fast pace, filled with interjections, rhythmic repetitions, and characters who know all the angles. This is first and foremost a character piece and is as much a story about Ness as it is about his notorious and terrifying adversary. **SW**

Pure Trance 1998

✎✎ Junko Mizuno

Title in original language *Pyua Toransu*
First published by East Press (Japan)
Creator Japanese (b.1973)
Genre Science fiction

The publishing history of *Pure Trance* is rather unusual because it started off as a series of inserts for techno music CDs titled *Pure Trance*. The overall framework of the story has its origin in science fiction. After a major conflict has destroyed the surface of planet Earth, humanity has taken refuge underground. The concept of food no longer exists, having been replaced by nutritional capsules, called Pure Trance, the overconsumption of which—almost unavoidable in this claustrophobic, anxiety-provoking world—leads in the end to serious problems. The main plot of the story is centered on one of the hospitals dealing with cases of Pure Trance overdoses and their consequences. In this psychedelic atmosphere, populated by robots, lolitas, film stars, television personalities, and artificial animals, Nurse Kaori and her colleagues become involved in strange adventures, full of abnormalities, obsessions, ill-treatments, and addictions of every kind. Now and again, their incursions outside the hospital depict an equally bizarre world where frivolity fights with the existential anguish of these volunteer underground dwellers, an anguish that some of them try to combat by organizing expeditions to the surface.

Seductive and at the same time disconcerting, with its pop aesthetic crossed with bondage, violence, postfeminism, and hypersexuality, Mizuno's book is distinctive for its visual, almost hypnotic impact. Her subsequent work has been very consistent in continuing the exploration of this unique universe. **NF**

Best of Bitterkomix 1998

✎✎ Conrad Botes and Anton Kannemeyer ("Joe Dog")

First published by Bitterkomix Pulp (South Africa)
Creators Botes (South African, b.1969);
Kannemeyer (South African, b.1967)
Genre Underground

Conrad Botes and Anton Kannemeyer grew up in South Africa during apartheid. The architecture of discrimination hid the black communities from the view of white families, and white kids knew nothing about the black families and their conditions.

In their comics, Botes and Kannemeyer broke all the inhibitions and taboos, both political and personal. At school, they had been taught to pray and not to even think of sex and violence; consequently, their comics are full of sex and violence. They rip apart the power figure of the White Man with a rage that has been built up by their restrictive upbringing. The rebellion is indeed bitter, even more so than in the U.S. underground comix of the 1960s.

Bitterkomix was part of the South African counterculture, which mostly consisted of punk music and theater. The movement arose especially among the Afrikaner. The Afrikaner had held the political power while the English-speakers dominated the economy. For this reason Afrikaans has been labeled the language of guilt with regard to apartheid, and the underground culture rebelled against this view.

South Africa has hardly any tradition of comics. Botes and Kannemeyer soon started to gravitate toward gallery art alongside comics, and both are establishing an international reputation in the art world. Their work still carries the themes of their comics, but they are evolving stylistically, particularly Kannemeyer who tackles the worst fears of the South African white population with masterful black humor. **HR**

Dungeon 1998

Joann Sfar and "Lewis Trondheim"

Title in original language *Donjon*
First published by Delcourt (France)
Creators Sfar (French, b.1971); Laurent Chabosy (French, b.1964) **Genre** Fantasy, Humor

Joann SFAR & Lewis TRONDHEIM
Donjon
CŒUR de CANARD
DELCOURT

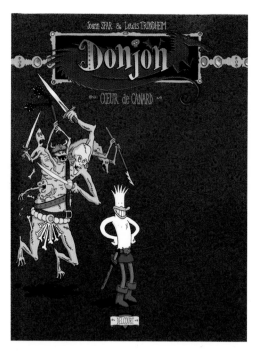

Also by Joann Sfar and Lewis Trondheim
Donjon Crépuscule
Donjon Monstres
Donjon Parade
Donjon Potron-Minet
Donjon Zenith

In parodying a genre that is defined by its own elaborately expansive fictional worlds, Joann Sfar and Lewis Trondheim have constructed one of the most ludicrously convoluted narratives in comics. *Dungeon* is fantasy comics publishing as performance art.

In 1998 Sfar and Trondheim launched the *Dungeon* series with *Duck's Heart*, a parody of sword-and-sorcery fantasy adventure comics starring a cowardly duck named Herbert and his mentor, a vegetarian dragon named Marvin. The book was cowritten by the duo but drawn by Trondheim. The next year, they added a second series, set in the future of their fictional universe, this time drawn by Sfar, and a third, set in the past, drawn by Christophe Blain. The numbering on the books indicated that each series would run one hundred volumes and tell a unified story when completed. The authors then proceeded to produce all three series at once, creating chapters out of chronological sequence. In 2001 they added another series, *Dungeon Monsters*, which featured the adventures of the supporting cast. These books were written by Sfar and Trondheim but drawn by various different guest artists.

One of the great sources of humor in the *Dungeon* comics stems from the fact that the series is almost impossible to follow. Reading the books in publication order means jumping seemingly randomly through narrative time. Reading them by series means missing out on the nested trilogies that the authors have hidden within the structure. Reading them at all means accepting the fact that there will never be 300 books in this series, and that the story will never be fully told. And yet, each individual book is clever enough, and funny enough, to merit readers' attention no matter what absences might deliberately exist in the logic of the plot. **BB**

Herbert and Marvin struggle to overcome their intense fears. ➡

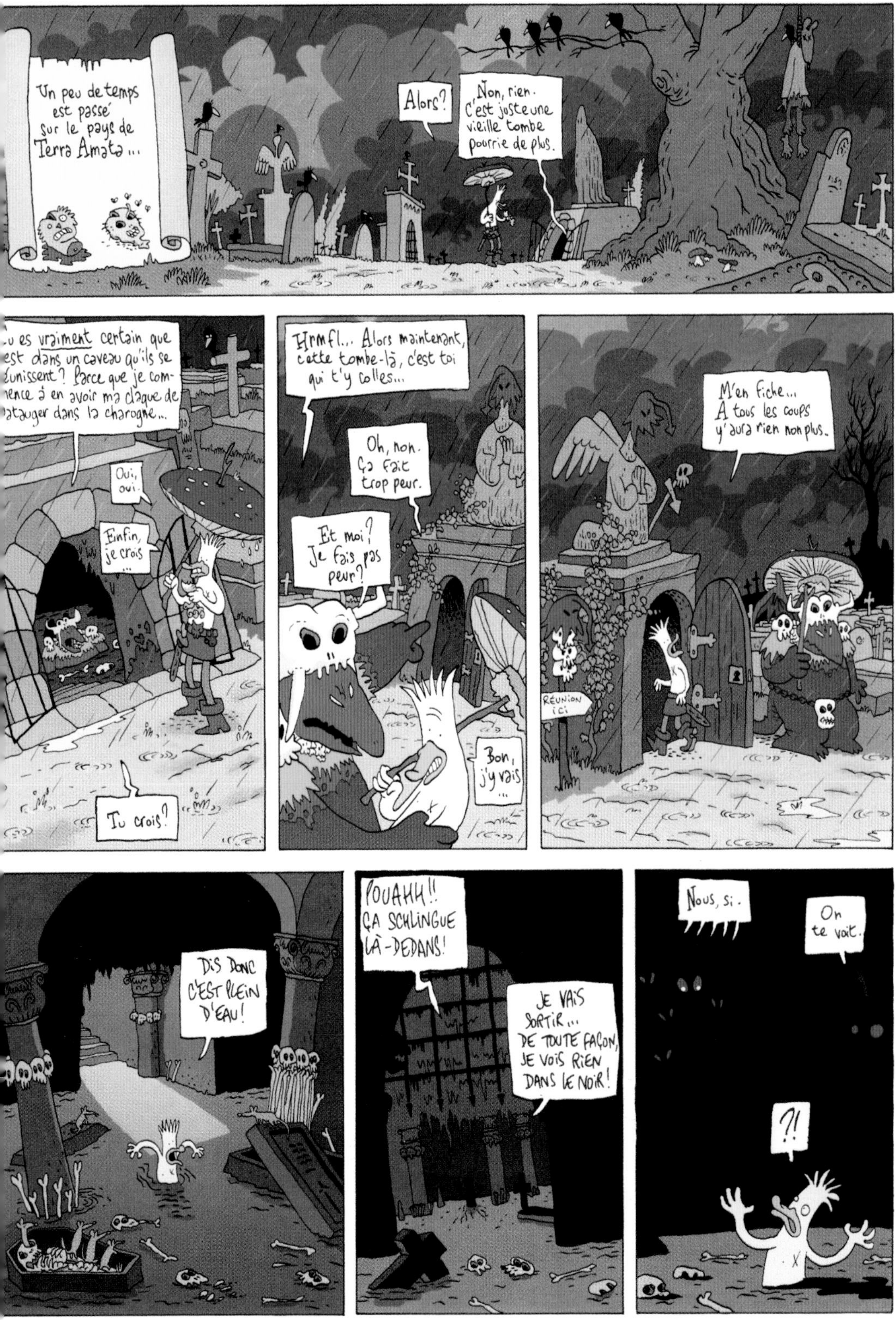
Un peu de temps est passé sur le pays de Terra Amata...
Alors?
Non, rien. C'est juste une vieille tombe pourrie de plus.
u es vraiment certain que est dans un caveau qu'ils se éunissent? Parce que je commence à en avoir ma claque de atauger dans la charogne...
Oui, oui.
Einfin, je crois...
Tu crois?
Hrmfl... Alors maintenant, cette tombe-là, c'est toi qui t'y colles...
Oh, non. Ça fait trop peur.
Et moi? Je fais pas peur?
Bon, j'y vais...
M'en fiche... A tous les coups y'aura rien non plus.
RÉUNION ICI
DIS DONC C'EST PLEIN D'EAU!
POUAHH!! ÇA SCHLINGUE LÀ-DEDANS!
JE VAIS SORTIR... DE TOUTE FAÇON, JE VOIS RIEN DANS LE NOIR!
Nous, si.
On te voit.
?!

A Child's Life and Other Stories 1998

Phoebe Gloeckner

PHOEBE GLOECKNER
a child's life
and other stories
introduction by
R. CRUMB

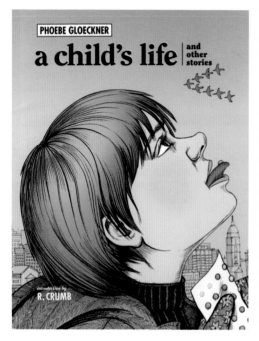

"My big brother got arrested and then my parents started fighting and my daddy hit me bad and he left and my mom got real sad."

Similar reads

Assume Nothing Leanne Franson
Daddy's Girl Debbie Drechsler
My Troubles With Women Robert Crumb
Peep Show Joe Matt
Real Girl Various

First published by Frog Books (USA)
Creator American (b.1960)
Genre Autobiography
Influenced by Aline Kominsky

Many of the strips collected in *A Child's Life* originally appeared in anthology comics from the early 1980s. Taken in isolation, they could be dismissed as solitary, albeit disturbing, childhood incidents that remain in the creator's memory. Collected together, they present a harrowing catalog of abuse that will have any right-minded person wishing they could reach back into the past to throttle some of the individuals involved.

This book, however, is a sugar-coated pill. Its pages are populated by appealing wide-eyed innocents, accentuating the allure and, by extension, rendering all readers complicit in vicarious fashion. The art is stylistically varied by choice, not just as a consequence of development.

Phoebe Gloeckner's childhood is personified by Millie, whose friends are routinely beaten by their parents. Her stepfather's behavior, though, is altogether more insidious. Overbearing, violent, prone to skin-crawlingly inappropriate suggestions and sexually abusing his teenage charge, he can be allocated a place among the greatest of comic villains. By inculcating insecurities and promiscuity in his stepdaughter, the predictable consequence is that she is shoved completely off the rails by her mid teens.

A Child's Life is a very uncomfortable read, but there are moments of humor and childhood innocence, albeit generally followed by shocking incidents. The other stories concern adult relationships that can perhaps be viewed as fiction rather than autobiography, although they are equally centered on issues of self-esteem. **FP**

The Jew of New York 1998

✒️ Ben Katchor

First published by Pantheon Books (USA)
Creator American (b.1951)
Genre Humor
Influenced by Edward Gorey

Ben Katchor is a cartoonist's cartoonist. Long heralded as one of the greatest practitioners of the form, he is best known for his serialized strip, *Julius Knipl, Real Estate Photographer*, a collection of loosely related episodic comics about the uncanny elements of contemporary urban life. When he turned his attention to New York in the 1820s, and to a novel-length work, some readers were puzzled. They need not have been. In *The Jew of New York* are all the hallmarks of Katchor's genius, sustained over a gripping, if highly unusual, narrative.

Katchor's approach to comics is shambling. His panels rarely align in neat fashion and often have parts that stick up or out. The gray washes that he applies to his figures can make them seem sinister and sometimes sloppy. The best way to describe his characters might be "rumpled." Yet his aesthetic outlook is a perfect match for characters that are often disoriented in the world, narrowly pursuing their own unique and esoteric interests. In *The Jew of New York*, a graphic novel based on the efforts of Mordecai Manuel Noah to found a Jewish homeland in upstate New York in the first part of the nineteenth century, these interests converge with tremendous force. Although the plot has bizarre trappings—characters include a man wandering around in an India rubber suit, a disgraced kosher butcher, a man mourning the impending extinction of the beaver, and another who enters into a Kabbalistic dreamworld at the sound of people eating—the central themes concerning the origins of a Jewish-American mythology could not be more clear. **BB**

The Trumpets They Play! 1998

✒️ Al Columbia

First published by Fantagraphics Books (USA)
Creator American (b.1970)
Genre Epic
Influence on Gerard Way

Al Columbia first shot to fame at the tender age of nineteen as Bill Sienkiewicz's assistant on the madly ambitious *Big Numbers*, written by Alan Moore. Several years later, he began developing his distinct, disturbing vaudeville of "body humor" of the queasiest kind.

Little Knishkebibble the Monkey-Boy and clown Seymour Sunshine may hark back to early black-and-white animation, but their escapades become increasingly nightmarish. In panels resembling soft-focused stills from vintage cinema, these bouncy, "bigfoot" characters scurry about among richly textured, photo-realist period buildings and backgrounds, bathed centerstage in glowing light but shrouded in the wings by threatening shadow. These terrors climax in the ten-page *The Trumpets They Play!*, which thrusts poor Knishkebibble and Seymour into St. John's Book of Revelations. After a newsflash announces the imminent end of the millennium, Columbia narrates without words, crafting some of his most detailed compositions, charged with dread. These are the end times, as debauchery and death pour from every window: Knish runs a bath that turns to blood; horrible locusts break down their door; and in the story's largest panel, the city is rent asunder and overrun by ghastly, grinning, sword-wielding monstrosities. And through all this, there is the slapstick of his cute duo desperate to flee destruction. Their trials end with a transcendent Seymour in color enjoying an idyllic afterlife. This cartoon apocalypse terrifies profoundly, like a Fleischer Brothers animated movie designed by Hieronymus Bosch. **PG**

Pastil 1998

✏️ Francesca Ghermandi

First published by Phoenix Enterprises (Italy)
Creator Italian (b.1964)
Genre Humor
Award Ignatz Award (2000)

Pastil is a hapless and cantankerous girl who lives in the slums of a world that is too large and too hard for her, and travels around meeting strange and dangerous people. The story begins when Pastil is the victim of a cruel joke inflicted on her by other children. The "joke" takes the small girl on an adventurous trip by bus, apparently heading for home, but not truly. It leaves her lost in the big city, where she bumps into an array of unknown men, bad women, and whimsical children. Taken home by the bus driver, she is soon forced—by his wife—to do all the housework, so she decides to run away. Moving through carnivals, circuses, and cramped apartments, Pastil not only experiences the diversity of humanity, but also a complete repertoire of childhood fears.

The work is entirely silent—no words or captions—and drawn with graphite pencil. Like many of Francesca Ghermandi's stories, *Pastil* is a "cartoon journey" through a threatening world; it offers no escapes except a sort of dreamlike dimension superimposed on reality. The artist's style is at its best here: cartoonish and "rubbery" characters and objects, panels filled with graphic elements, and a wildly imaginative and playful design. Ghermandi is a true heir to the Italian master of surrealist comics, Benito Jacovitti.

Much of Ghermandi's work has been translated and appears abroad published by magazines such as *L'Echo des savanes*, *Rubber Blankets*, and *El Vibora*. She is also active as an illustrator and designed the animated opening sequence for the Venice Film Festival in 2005. **MS**

Uzumaki 1998

✏️ Junji Ito

First published by Shogakukan (Japan)
Creator Japanese (b. 1971)
Genre Horror
Adaptation Live-action film (2000)

There are numerous spine-chilling incidences occurring in a fictional town, Kurozu-cho, where a high school student, Kirie, and her depressed boyfriend, Shuichi, live. As time passes, the town morphs into an unrealistic dark world. The creepy incidents are somehow connected to one strange aspect—an obsession with spirals.

Each episode of *Uzumaki* (which means "spiral") is a self-contained tale with the same location and regular characters, and the tales always turn into something incredibly creepy. Junji Ito executes each episode to perfection, even when the premise seems to verge on the insane. Readers may wonder how spirals can be a theme for a horror manga, but they will be left squirming in their seats. Ito's bizarre imagination is greatly supported by his distinctive style of art. As well as the very graphic scenes in which actual horror is unveiled, there are plenty of "normal" moments. Throughout, Ito's compelling, dense drawings—a pattern in the sky, a slit in a wall, the texture of skin and hair—convey a certain heaviness and eerie stillness that is reminiscent of U.S. author H. P. Lovecraft.

The superb book design celebrates the darkness of the contents by limiting colors to only white, red, and black. The cover art, which features a black glossy image on a black matt cover paper, is equally disturbing. The first four color pages of amazingly detailed illustrations, executed in a pale and eerie palette, serve to lure readers into the horrific adventure of the mysterious world of spirals. **AT-L**

Cages 1998

Dave McKean

First published by Tundra Publishing (USA)
Creator British (b.1963)
Genre Fantasy
Award Harvey Award (1992)

CAGES
a comic novel by
Dave McKean
"Mesmerizing"
Terry Gilliam

The 1990s saw a number of cartoonists driving the comics form in new and unexpected directions. It was a time of grand imaginings and books that shocked and inspired. Yet few works rose to the heights achieved by Dave McKean's *Cages*, one of the most audacious comics ever published and a landmark in visual expressivity.

Cages tells the story of Leo Sabarsky, a painter struggling to reclaim inspiration in his work. When he moves into a townhouse, he finds himself living under the same roof as Jonathan Rush, a writer whose novel, also called *Cages*, has touched such a nerve with the public that he lives anonymously, in fear of the rioters, who seek to send him to Hell, and of the protectors, who are slowly stripping bare his soul. The cast is rounded out by Leo's new girlfriend, Karen, a mystically powered jazz musician named Angel, and a black cat who moves freely among the apartments. McKean is an unabashed romantic in this work, mixing the quotidian aspects of his characters' lives with ruminations on the nature of God, history, mythology, and creation.

The greatness of *Cages* stems from its art. McKean is among a small handful of the most talented imagists, and he unleashes all of his talents here. He switches modes and media at will, ranging from inky drawings to photomontages and fully painted imagery, depending on the needs of the story. He excels in both wordless scenes, which take on a dreamlike quality, and wordy monologues, as in the chapter devoted to the landlady. *Cages* is the type of book that makes you think that there is nothing that comics cannot do. **BB**

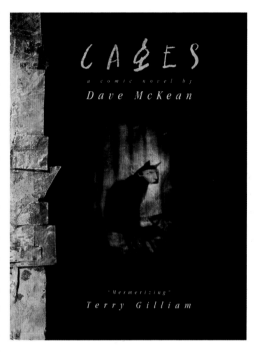

"Despite much evidence to the contrary, how could anyone not realize that this is just the best of all possible worlds?"

Also by Dave McKean
Arkham Asylum with Grant Morrison
Black Orchid with Neil Gaiman
Mr. Punch with Neil Gaiman
Signal to Noise with Neil Gaiman
Violent Cases with Neil Gaiman

White Death 1998

Robbie Morrison Charlie Adlard

First published by Les Cartoonistes Dangereux (France)
Creators Morrison (British, 1968);
Adlard (British, b.1966)
Genre War

morrison adlard
white death

The Trentino mountain range, fought over by Italy and Austria, is a largely forgotten battlefield of World War I. The fact that the Austro-Hungarian Empire contained ethnic Italians meant that if such a man were captured, he might find himself redrafted to fight against his former comrades. Such is the plight of Pietro Aquasanta in Robbie Morrison's graphic novel *White Death*.

Publicly declared untrustworthy by his commanding officer, Pietro is nevertheless a good soldier who proves his worth. He is a native of the mountain, and when on a reconnaissance mission he spots an Austrian advance using poison gas and purposefully triggers a huge avalanche that wipes out the entire advance. Pietro's superiors are highly impressed and order him to go on other missions to deliberately bring down avalanches on the enemy. A new form of warfare is born.

"An avalanche is like war. It starts small then escalates, consuming everything."

Heavily inspired by the work of Jacques Tardi and Pat Mills, and like many pieces about World War I, *White Death* focuses on the idiocy and futility of a war fought in unimaginable conditions, and the dehumanizing effect it has on all. Pietro describes himself as feeling "like a dead man," and, indeed, readers are told from the beginning of the book that this is exactly what he is. Furthermore, his Austrian enemies are frequently also his friends; the first man he kills knows him by name.

The unique circumstances in which Pietro finds himself, coupled with the relatively obscure setting, gives *White Death* a fresh and original feel. Charlie Adlard's art pushes the originality still further by almost entirely using charcoal blacks on gray paper, saving the whites only for the snow. **BD**

Similar reads
Alan's War Emmanuel Guibert
Charley's War Pat Mills and Joe Colhoun
Fucking War! Jacques Tardi and Jean-Pierre Verney
It Was the War of the Trenches Jacques Tardi
Onward Toward Our Noble Deaths Shigeru Mizuki

White Death is a powerful tribute to the fallen. ➡

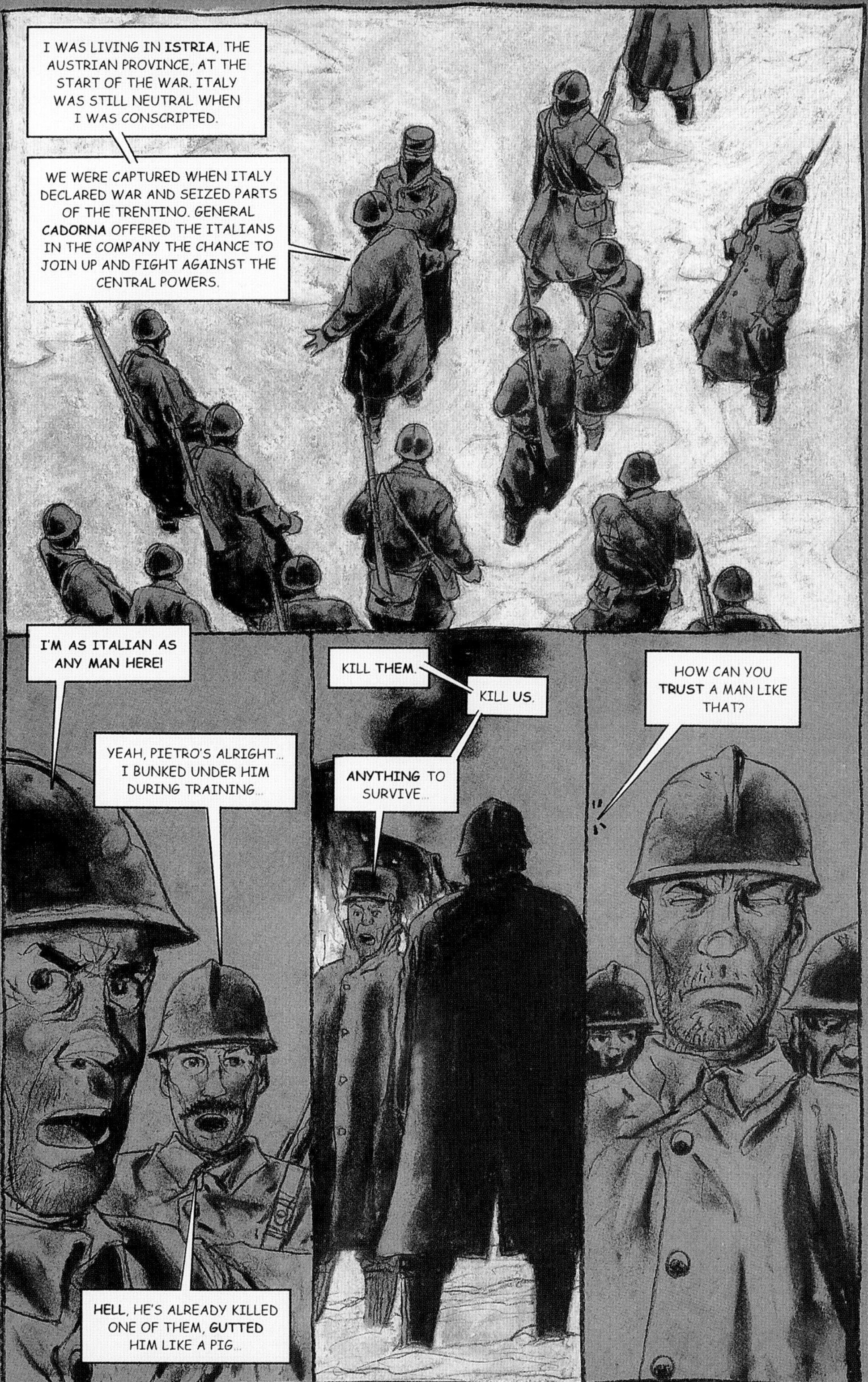
I WAS LIVING IN ISTRIA, THE AUSTRIAN PROVINCE, AT THE START OF THE WAR. ITALY WAS STILL NEUTRAL WHEN I WAS CONSCRIPTED.
WE WERE CAPTURED WHEN ITALY DECLARED WAR AND SEIZED PARTS OF THE TRENTINO. GENERAL CADORNA OFFERED THE ITALIANS IN THE COMPANY THE CHANCE TO JOIN UP AND FIGHT AGAINST THE CENTRAL POWERS.
I'M AS ITALIAN AS ANY MAN HERE!
YEAH, PIETRO'S ALRIGHT... I BUNKED UNDER HIM DURING TRAINING...
HELL, HE'S ALREADY KILLED ONE OF THEM, GUTTED HIM LIKE A PIG...
KILL THEM.
KILL US.
ANYTHING TO SURVIVE...
HOW CAN YOU TRUST A MAN LIKE THAT?

Age of Bronze 1998

Eric Shanower

First published by Image Comics (USA)
Creator American (b.1963)
Genre History, Drama
Collections *A Thousand Ships, Sacrifice, Betrayal*

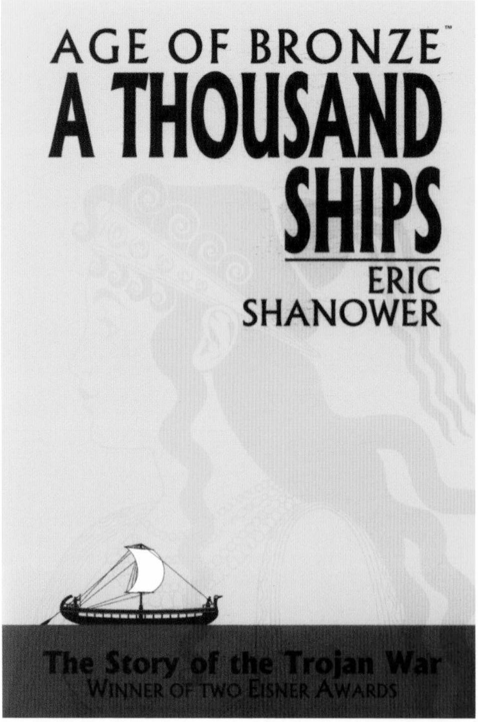
AGE OF BRONZE™
A THOUSAND SHIPS
ERIC SHANOWER
The Story of the Trojan War
WINNER OF TWO EISNER AWARDS

Similar reads
300 Frank Miller
Berlin: City of Stones Jason Lutes
Buddha Osamu Tezuka
Ikkyu Hisashi Sakaguchi

Eric Shanower's seven-volume *Age of Bronze*, an audaciously ambitious project, tells the story of the Trojan War by combining "the myriad versions of Greek myth with the archaeological record," presenting the tale in "authentic historical detail." With sources ranging from Homer to Hollywood, Shakespeare to Shelley, and Tennison to Troy, Shanower clearly has his work cut out.

The author made the somewhat controversial decision to toss the gods out of Olympus. There are no supernatural visitations or machinations by Zeus or the rest of the pantheon. The human characters that feature in the story believe in the gods and their actions, but these are left to interpretation. After the sacrifice of Iphigenia, the wind comes up and the

"Look hard at your own marriage, Achilles, before you question mine."

ships set sail and it may—or may not—be a god at work. However, dreams and visions have been retained.

The mortals, on the other hand, have never been more believable: Odysseus as a cunning statesman; Achilles as a glory-seeker; Paris and Helen as narcissists with overwhelming lust for each other. The characterizations make this story of power, sex, and human responsibility come alive—as does Shanower's draftsmanship and devotion to detail in vividly re-creating their world. The visuals may be unfamiliar because they are not the anachronistic stereotypes to which readers might be accustomed. Shanower's pen-and-ink style, somewhat stiff at times, is actually a plus in rendering images inspired by ancient pottery and murals. His storytelling and layouts are straightforward, never self-consciously flashy; his prose is elegantly understated—classic in every sense. *Age of Bronze*, Shanower's Herculean labor of love, is a true epic. **TL**

Road to Perdition 1998

✎ Max Allan Collins ✎ Richard Piers Rayner

Loosely based on the 1970s manga *Lone Wolf and Cub*, about a hunted samurai warrior on the run with his three-year-old child, *Road to Perdition* is the story of Michael O'Sullivan, Jr., whose father is a paid assassin for the Looneys, a Midwestern Irish gangster dynasty. When his mother and younger brother are murdered by the Looney's henchmen after he inadvertently witnesses one of his father's bloody executions, Michael and his father are forced into hiding.

They drive across the Midwest, stealing the Looney's laundered money from banks as they make their way to the town of Perdition, Kansas, where Michael Jr.'s uncle and aunt and a hoped-for sanctuary await. The story is told in a series of recollections written down years

"We're all sinners, son. That's the way we enter this world."

after the events by Michael Jr., his memories conveyed in the black-and-white images of illustrator Richard Piers Rayner, whose thick blacks create wonderfully atmospheric and moody panels that give the book a truly "pulp" look that resembles, in the words of Michael, "some people's dreams."

Unlike the 2002 film adaptation that saw Tom Hanks as a restrained, somber Michael Sr., the father here is a one-man wrecking crew, able to dispatch assassins en masse even while sliding down a banister. The focus is on the son, not the father, whose fate is already sealed, his soul lost. A harsh Irish Catholicism pervades these pages, but there is always the hope of salvation for the son should he refuse the temptation of succumbing to the evil around him by following in his father's footsteps. It is his fate more than his father's that engages readers and makes *Road to Perdition* such a powerful example of the triumph of good over evil. **BS**

First published by Paradox Press/DC Comics (USA)
Creators Collins (American, b.1948);
Rayner (British, b.1952)
Genre Crime

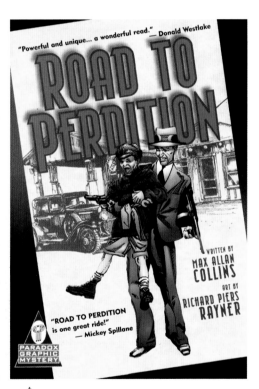

"Powerful and unique... a wonderful read." — Donald Westlake

ROAD TO PERDITION

WRITTEN BY
MAX ALLAN
COLLINS
ART BY
RICHARD PIERS
RAYNER

"ROAD TO PERDITION
is one great ride!"
— Mickey Spillane

PARADOX
GRAPHIC
MYSTERY

Similar reads
Dick Tracy Chester Gould
Ms Tree Max Allan Collins and Terry Beatty
Road to Perdition: On the Road Max Allan Collins
    and José Luis García-López

A Distant Neighborhood 1998

Jiro Taniguchi

Title in original language *Haruka na Machi e*
First published by Shogukukan (Japan)
Creator Japanese (b.1947)
Genre Drama

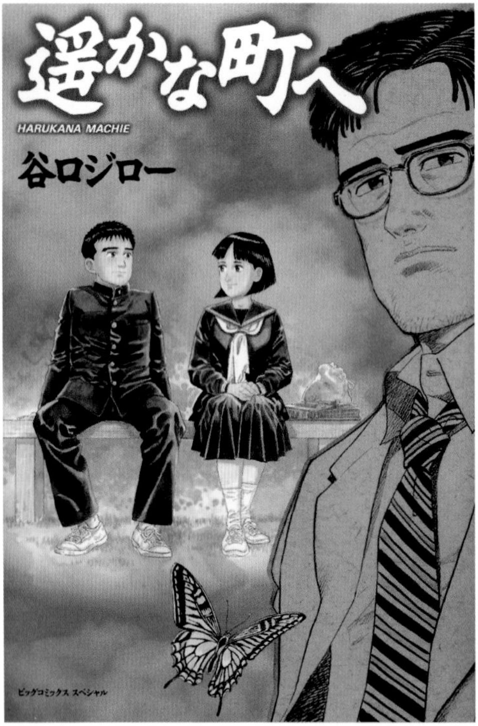
遥かな町へ
HARUKANA MACHIE
谷口ジロー
ビッグコミックス スペシャル

Also by Jiro Taniguchi
A Zoo in Winter
Icarus with Moebius
The Summit of the Gods with Yumemakura Baku
The Times of Botchan with Natsuo Sekikawa

It is not uncommon in Japan for the responsibilities of some husbands and fathers to become too much and force them to abandon everything. In Jiro Taniguchi's *A Distant Neighborhood*, a salaryman and father, Hiroshi, boards the wrong train one morning in 1998, only to find himself traveling to the town where he was born. He is forty-eight, the same age at which his mother died, and he decides to visit her grave. Praying in the tranquil cemetery, he loses track of time. When he comes to, he feels his heavy adult body has grown lighter and is astonished to find that he has become his fourteen-year-old self, with all his adult knowledge intact.

Hiroshi marvels at the chance to experience again the sensations of his teenage years, from cigarettes to young love, with all the benefits of hindsight. Now he can also ask his parents, grandmother, and friends all those unanswered questions—above all why one day, out of the blue, his father disappeared without explanation, forever. Hiroshi is determined to prevent this happening again, but the more answers he finds, the more uncertain he is that he can change the past.

"The . . . cemetery seemed slightly different. I sensed that even the smell in the air around me had changed."

In naturalistic and exquisitely detailed gray-toned artwork, with a dual soundtrack interweaving external dialogues and Hiroshi's internal monologue, Taniguchi crafts a subtle meditation on whether these two generations, father and son, are living the life they have chosen or the life chosen for them by others. With this tender story, crisp and clear in its illustration and narration, Taniguchi was the first Japanese creator to win one of France's highest awards for comics at the Angoulême International Festival in 2003. **PG**

Apocalypse Meow 1998

Motofumi Kobayashi

War is probably one of the most common themes when it comes to popular culture, and the Vietnam war is no exception. There are many songs referring to it, including The Beatles' "Revolution," the film *Apocalypse Now* (1979), and also a comic book series featuring cats and rabbits.

Apocalypse Meow is a story about a U.S. reconnaissance team called "Cat Shit One" and their missions during the Vietnam war. Motofumi Kobayashi pays great attention to war strategies and terminology. There are many side notes that explain words and facts; some of them even take a whole page. Weapons and vehicles are drawn realistically, so that every military maniac can recognize them, yet the characters are

"Pretz-L to Cat Shit One. I'm about two klicks north of you. There's somethin' moving down there... It's the gooks!"

anthropomorphic animals. Rabbits that are Americans and cats that are Vietnamese can be described in no other word but "cute." The contrast between the cruelty of war and the sweet little creatures, which sometimes look quite comical, helps to reiterate that the kind of battle mayhem that happened in Vietnam was in many cases pointless. At the same time, readers start to like the team of individuals: Packy, the optimistic leader; Rats, a sniper and interpreter from the Bronx; and Bota, a coward and racist radio operator. Each chapter follows one of their missions.

The last part of volume one is called "Dog Shit One." It features realistic human characters instead of animals, which reinforces the point that all the other chapters are actual war stories. There is also a sequel to the series, *Cat Shit One '80*, and a successful computer-generated animated series as well. **RB**

Title in original language *Cat Shit One*
First published by Softbank Publishing (Japan)
Creator Japanese (b.1951)
Genre War, Drama

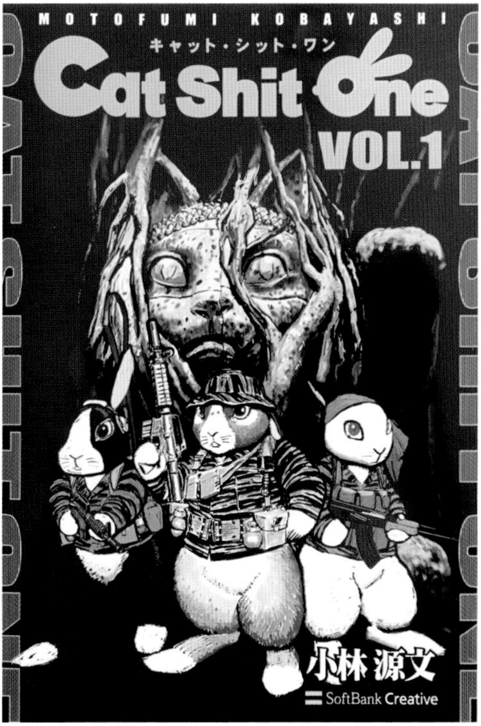
MOTOFUMI KOBAYASHI
キャット・シット・ワン
Cat Shit One
VOL.1
小林源文
SoftBank Creative

Similar reads

Cat Shit One '80 Motofumi Kobayashi
Maus Art Spiegelman
The 'Nam Various artists
War Stories Garth Ennis and others

Bosnian Fables 1998

"TBC"

Title in original language *Fables de Bosnie*
First published by Glénat (France)
Creator Tomaž Lavrič (Slovenian, b.1964)
Genre Drama

GRANDS CHAPITRES
Tomaž Lavrič TBC
fables de
BOSNIE
HARK
Glénat

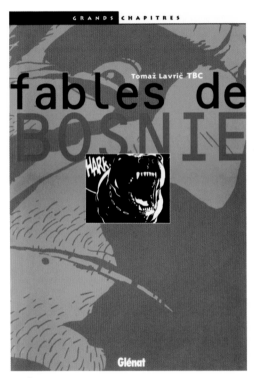

Similar reads
L'Echarde Frank Giroud and Marianne Duvivier
Le Décalogue Frank Giroud and others
Lomm Tomaž Lavrič
Sophaletta Erik Arnoux

Tomaž Lavrič has established himself as one of the all-time greatest comics artists from Slovenia. His works are characterized by his ability to draw in a variety of styles, whether in a grotesque or more realistic manner. He started with *Diarrhea*, political comic strips published continuously from 1988 in *Mladina* magazine, in which he summarized the frustrations of young Slovenians during the disintegration of Yugoslavia and beyond. He continued with his more realistically drawn *Red Alarm*, a political and social album about the punk music generation, which struggles with "hot beer and cold females." This is followed by *The Blind Sun*, allegorical and philosophical stories in condensed and simplified style, and later with realistic style works in the science fiction, crime noir, and historical genres. His work is well respected throughout the West and in his home country.

"A controversial and powerful comic album . . . perfectly told"

Marko Stojanović, artist

Bosnian Fables, drawn and written by Lavrič, is an award-winning graphic novel comprising several stories, intriguingly carrying the names of different animals (Pig, Dog, Mouse, Parrot). The stories are to an extent about the animals, but as in all classical fables, the narrative is actually about people: in this case during the tragic civil war in Bosnia at the end of the twentieth century. Lavrič uses strong, realistic, black-and-white pages to bring his message home. The stories are about ordinary people (and animals) who struggle under the brutality of war, and they are told with a genuine understanding and humanism, touched by the artist's personal distress. The narratives have great psychological depth, coming together as an outcry against this and any other war. **ZT**

Wake
Fire & Ash 1998

Jean-David Morvan Philippe Buchet

Title in original language *Sillage: A feu et à cendres*
First published by Delcourt (France)
Creators Morvan (French, b.1969); Buchet (French, b.1962) **Genre** Science fiction

The teenage Navee is the sole human occupant of a verdant planet with an abundance of animal life. Her tamed companion is a tigerlike creature, and she possesses the intelligence and adaptability to use tools and technology from the spacecraft that brought her to the planet as an infant.

Her carefree existence ends with the arrival of a probe dispatched from an inconceivably large convoy moving through space, aiming to locate inhabitable worlds for all constituent races. It is known as Wake, and Navee's discovery prompts a quandry about the morality of terraforming a planet in order to ensure the survival of a species if it means displacing even a single intelligent life-form. A further philosophical matter concerns the legitimacy of genetically engineering and utilizing even basically intelligent life-forms as slaves. Navee intrigues Wake's administration, which has never seen a human, nor encountered a being that cannot be telepathically accessed.

"Each album would subvert comic genres."
Jean-David Morvan

Philippe Buchet's art is remarkable. Solid storytelling, thoughtful characterization, and cinematic action are taken for granted, and he additionally creates a dozen new alien races for every volume. Unusually, he is equally confident with alien technology and the wonders of nature. Morvan and Buchet continue to surprise and delight with every volume. Time passes between each volume, and along the way Navee discovers aspects of her origins and corrupt dealings within the administration. Any volume serves as a good sample, drawing the reader in with an absorbing plot and stunning art. **FP**

MORVAN • BUCHET
SILLAGE
1. A FEU ET A CENDRES
DELCOURT

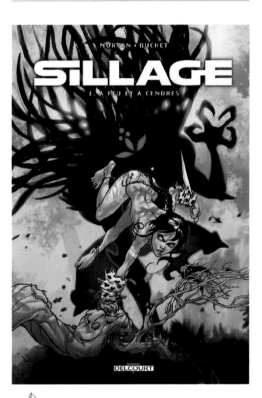

Similar reads
Nexus Mike Baron and Steve Rude
Orbital Serge Pellé and Sylvain Runberg
Planetes Makoto Yukimura
Wonton Soup James Stokoe

Tokyo Zombie 1999

✐✐ Yusaku Hanakuma

First published by Seirinkogeisha (Japan)
Creator Japanese (b.1967)
Genre Horror, Humor
Adaptation Live-action film (2005)

The *heta-uma* style (literally "clumsy skilled") is something of an acquired taste. Established in the early 1970s in the pages of *Garo* by the influential "King Terry" (the alias of Teruhiko Yumura), this genre embraced the sheer exuberance and enthusiasm of unpolished art over technical skill. One of the torchbearers of the style today, Yusaku Hanakuma has been putting his two iconic characters, Hage ("Baldie") and Afro in some of the most over-the-top situations, and this book is no exception.

In *Tokyo Zombie*, the Japanese capital is besieged by zombies who have started to spew out of a gigantic dump (nicknamed "the Dark Fuji") on the outskirts of town, where shady characters had been disposing of embarrassing corpses. Working at a nearby factory, Fujio (Afro) and Mitsuo (Hage) manage to escape the sudden uprising in a big truck. Hanakuma then decides to quickly move the story forward and introduces the new pastime of the rich and wealthy: "zombie fight," in which a human and a zombie battle to the death. Naturally, Fujio and Mitsuo are soon caught up in this new development.

As expected, the art is crude, there is gore aplenty, and the outlandish ideas keep on coming. Readers might detect an element of social commentary but it should not be taken too seriously. Laden with Hanakuma's trademark obsessions and quirks (a fascination for wrestling, combined with a hefty dose of homoerotic undertones), *Tokyo Zombie* is an unusual ride. It has also been adapted into a movie by Sakichi Sato. **XG**

Comix 2000 1999

✐✐ Various, edited by Jean-Christophe Menu

First published by L'Association (France)
Creator Menu (Editor, French, b.1964)
Genre Alternative
Award Eisner Award (2000)

Comix 2000 is the wordless work of 324 creators from twenty-four different countries. It is arranged dictionary-style and takes readers through alphabetically by author rather than using other possible arrangements (by theme, style, or geography). It is quite a task to read from cover to cover.

Readers who intend to use *Comix 2000* as a reference work containing unfeasible amounts of outrageous, impressive comics by many fantastic European, Japanese, and North American comics creators will not be disappointed. There are entries by Lewis Trondheim, Chris Ware, Julie Doucet, Alexandar Zograf, Megan Kelso, Dylan Horrocks, and many others. However, there are some odd omissions: no R. Crumb, for example, who would fit in perfectly stylistically.

The collection's theme is the twentieth century: this seems to be an invitation to produce cynical, nasty, violent comics about murders, rapes, war, destruction, and ugliness. Sadly, few of the stories take the opportunity to presents serious looks at pervasive social issues such as racism or sexism. However, readers experience a real sense of wonderment at the varied ways in which creators have resolved the wordlessness constraint. Many of the contributors use a straightforward approach: omit the speech bubbles and words, tell the story purely in images. The grand master of this method has to be Thomas Ott. The cleverer solutions, though, use nonsense squiggles, images within speech bubbles, or even company logos to tell their stories with panache and inventiveness. **JS**

Big Questions 1999

Anders Nilsen

First published by Self-published (Canada)
Creator American (b.1973)
Genre Drama
Influenced by Hergé and Chester Brown

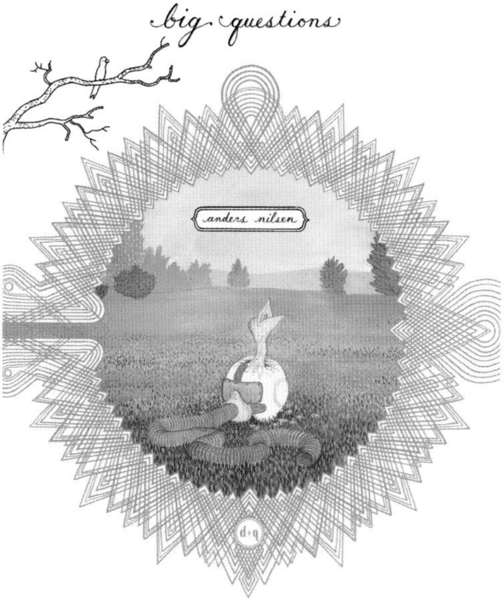
big questions
anders nilsen
d+q

The first thing that strikes readers when they pick up an issue of Anders Nilsen's *Big Questions* is its size. It is smaller and squarer than expected, and its paper is thicker. Inside, the drawings often lack borders. Nilsen occasionally crams up to ten panels on a page, and his sparse landscapes, with their empty white spaces and fine line work, give emphasis to a carefully crafted world of mild angst in which "less is more."

Told at a refreshingly leisurely pace, *Big Questions* is an existential tale set in a dreamlike world resembling the Russian steppes. The predominant characters are a community of identically drawn birds, finches mostly. In the third issue of the series, their world is turned upside-down when an air force plane crashes to Earth. They see the plane as a giant bird and the unexploded bomb it is carrying as its egg. The pilot survives, "hatches" from the cockpit, and tensions soon arise between birds that doggedly attempt to befriend him and birds that see him as a threat. Why birds? "Because they are easy to draw," says Nilsen, and because they possess the requisite humility and innocence the artist requires. A "depressive optimist," Nilsen feels an affinity with Existentialist writers Albert Camus and Friedrich Nietzsche, although at the series' end he offers no great moral answers to life's complexities.

Nilsen spent ten years creating the sprawling series' fifteen issues of minimalist purity. Readers should be grateful that this talented writer and illustrator dropped out of Chicago's Art Institute to concentrate on his dream of creating comic books of substance. **BS**

"So what do you think? Do you think it's a giant bird? / A giant bird? No, no, that's ridiculous."

Also by Anders Nilsen
Ballad of the Two Headed Boy
Dogs and Water
Don't Go Where I Can't Follow
Monologue for the Coming Plague
Sisyphus

The Authority 1999

✎ Warren Ellis ✎ Bryan Hitch

First published by WildStorm/DC Comics (USA)
Creators Ellis (British, b.1968); Hitch (British, b.1966)
Genre Superhero
Influenced by *Stormwatch*

Warren Ellis honed his vision of widescreen superheroics on *Stormwatch*, then ramped it up a gear for *The Authority*, posing the question, "What if a group of superheroes set themselves up as arbiters of the greater good?"

Under deep cover, a superhero covert action team locate a large alien vessel existing between dimensions, capable of providing instant access to any point on Earth. Then Stormwatch, their previous global peace-keeping squad, is disbanded, so they decide to become Earth's moral authority instead. "The Authority" first deals with a despot intent on carving his corporate logo on Earth, then an invasion from an alternate Earth where alien contact occurred in the sixteenth century. This is followed by the return of Earth's original owners and threats requiring individuals powerful enough to affect events on a planetary scale.

Ellis was matched with an artist entering his prime. Bryan Hitch had always been competent, but during his *Stormwatch* run he moved away from a style that had been strongly influenced by Alan Davis yet retained the first-rate storytelling skills learned from Davis. Here, his interpretative skills are captivating, and it is obvious that he does far more than slavishly follow the script.

The title's excessive violence and derisive attitudes offended readers expecting superheroes to radiate positivity and moral certainty. However, *The Authority* is high-octane excitement and kicks its superheroes into the twenty-first century. After Ellis and Hitch departed, their successors—Mark Millar and Frank Quitely—rose to the challenge, and *The Authority* remains essential. **FP**

The Goon 1999

✎✎ Eric Powell

First published by Avatar Press (USA)
Creator American (b.1975)
Genre Horror, Comedy
Award Eisner Award (2004)

Circus freaks, zombies, Lovecraftian cephalopods, and cigar-chomping arachnids—Eric Powell's exuberant pulp pastiche piles up the pop culture references. The vest-wearing, flat-capped, buck-toothed mob enforcer Goon is ably assisted by his glassy-eyed, fedora-wearing, vertically challenged sidekick Franky, and together they take on the ranks of the living dead and their master, the Zombie Priest. Raised in the circus by Aunt Kizzie, Goon started out working for the mysteriously absent gangster Labrazio. Later adventures reveal Labrazio and introduce giant rats, skunk apes, triads, aliens, mad scientists, and a tragic former sheriff, the Buzzard.

As much as the lurid pulp gothic atmosphere contributes to *The Goon*, this comic is about larger than life characters. Alongside the eponymous protagonist and his pint-sized sidekick comes a colorful cast of background creatures, including the Hobos, masters of the Hobo Jungle; Dr. Hieronymous Alloy's army of robots, all named "Bruno"; and assorted bog lurks, hags, vampires, and giant squids. Special mention goes to the angry, foul-mouthed Atomic Rage, a golden age superhero send-up; and Dwight T. Albatross, an intoxicated "friend" of Eric Powell given to venting his splenetic opinions in the newspaper letters page.

Powell's lively slapstick cartoon violence is a direct descendant of EC's notorious horror comics from the 1950s. The animated "so dumb it's smart" tone recalls giants of trash culture such as The Ramones, Ed Roth, and Russ Meyer, but the characters stay just the right side of caricature, strenuously avoiding sentiment. **TV**

Even the Undead Fear Him!
THE GOON™
IN
ROUGH STUFF
WRITTEN AND ILLUSTRATED BY
ERIC POWELL
Eric Powell

Ripple 1999

Dave Cooper

First published by Fantagraphics Books (USA)
Creator Canadian (b.1967)
Genre Drama
Influenced by Chester Brown and Joe Matt

ripple
a predilection for Tina
dave cooper
with an introduction by David Cronenberg

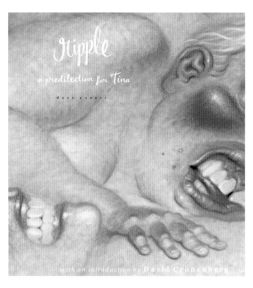

"I could hardly recognize her. I was quite taken aback by how young she looked and how . . . ugly."

Similar reads

Dan and Larry Dave Cooper
Mon bel amour Frédéric Poincelet
Pascin Joann Sfar
The Playboy: A Comic Book Chester Brown

In *Suckle* and *Crumple*, his first two published books, Dave Cooper had established a weirdly unsettling world in which sensuality seemed to be able to pervade everything and anything—a world that was peopled by strong, dominating women and weak, unassuming men. Moving away from this fantasy setting for modern-day Canada, *Ripple* is the first book in which Dave Cooper fully explores the dark recesses of desire and fascination, at which he had only hinted previously.

Ripple (subtitled "A Predilection for Tina") tells the uncomfortable story of Martin DeSerres, a struggling artist who receives a grant for "a gallery show of 'thought-provoking' and erotic fine art" and suddenly finds himself in urgent need of a model. This is how he encounters Tina, a young and ugly girl, who seems at first to be the complete opposite to what he would look for in a woman but turns out to be the perfect incarnation of his deepest, darkest fantasy. *Ripple* is the story of a long descent into the realms of desire and fascination, and follows the opposite trajectories of the two main characters. What started out as a casual, work-oriented encounter quickly evolves into something that is far more complex and troubling. Shy and submissive at first, Tina becomes more and more dominating as Martin progressively loses any kind of authority he might have had. Without a doubt, things do not end well.

As expected, Dave Cooper's realistic drawing style manages to flesh out his characters perfectly—rendering them both fascinating and repulsive at the same time, and expressing the strange dynamics that are at work between them. However, it is the authenticity of the writing that turns *Ripple* into a truly engaging (if often unsettling) graphic novel—and a dramatic masterpiece. **XG**

Rocky 1999

Martin Kellerman

Autobiography was big in the comics scene in the 1990s, with the Canadian trio of Joe Matt, Chester Brown, and Seth leading the way. A rather unorthodox way to use autobiographical material is to combine it with humor and tell stories in the traditional strip cartoon format. Undoubtedly one of the most successful practitioners of this is the Swedish cartoonist Martin Kellerman, and the way to success for him has been to filter his experiences through a funny animal style and publish the comics first in daily newspapers, then in comic books, and finally in collected volumes. Although Kellerman's *Rocky* cartoon strip was canceled by various newspapers when readers complained of its explicit sexual content, the *Rocky* comics are extremely popular in Sweden and have to date been collected in almost twenty volumes.

Kellerman tells the story of his life as a young man living in Stockholm, desperately looking for employment, a partner, and somewhere to live. The themes in *Rocky* are more mature than in traditional comic strips, and the stories are often told more via the dialogue than the pictures. As Kellerman has become increasingly successful, this has been mirrored in the strip, which nowadays is more about him quietly working in his house in the countryside or traveling around the world.

Besides the autobiographical element, which gives readers an opportunity to peek into Kellerman's life, the charm of *Rocky* lies partly in the fact that all the characters are rendered as anthropomorphic creatures—this gives a humorous distance to what is happening—and partly in Kellerman's dialogue, which is very well written and consistently credible. The character Rocky is not always very likable, but it is probably the blunt frankness of Kellerman's style that has made the comic so popular. **FS**

First published by *Galago* (Sweden)
Creator Swedish (b.1973)
Genre Humor, Autobiography
Collection *Rocky Vol. 2: Strictly Business* (2008)

ROCKY
VOL. 1: THE BIG PAYBACK
BY MARTIN KELLERMAN

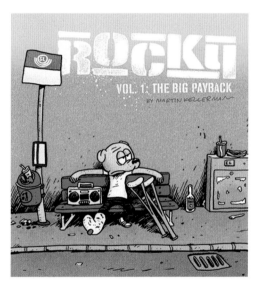

"It seems to work best when I'm at my lowest, whenever I feel good . . . people start complaining."

Martin Kellerman

Similar reads
Fritz the Cat Robert Crumb
Hate Peter Bagge
My New York Diary Julie Doucet
The Playboy: A Comic Book Chester Brown

Fruits Basket 1999

"Natsuki Takaya"

Title in original language *Furūtso Basuketto*
First published by Hakusensha (Japan)
Creator Naka Hatake (Japanese, b.1973)
Genre Fantasy

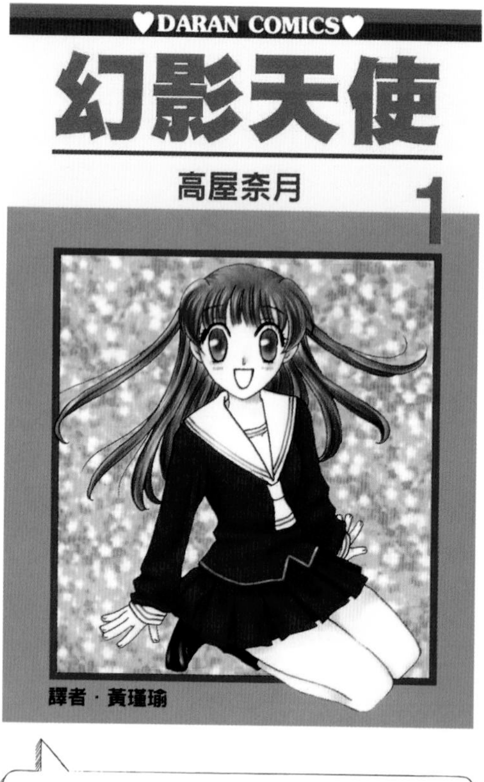
DARAN COMICS
幻影天使
高屋奈月
1
譯者・黃瑾瑜

Similar reads
Kekkaishi Yellow Tanabe
Maison Ikkoku Rumiko Takahashi
Ranma ½ Rumiko Takahashi
Tenchi Mujo Masaki Kajishima and Hiroki Hayashi

Natsuki Takaya's epic exploration of high school comedy and supernatural romance is a perfect example of the genre. It follows the adventures of disadvantaged, clumsy, and sweetly pitiable orphan Tohru Honda as she falls under the spell of a family of strange, beautiful people haunted by a dark past, cruel childhoods, and the confused spirits of the Chinese Zodiac. While common themes like cross-dressing and martial arts fights create a familiar manga environment, the story never strays too deeply into supernatural excesses or high school hijinks. Instead, the focus is on people; time and again, a comic aside or exaggerated character is suddenly given focus and finely drawn out as being different, individual, and important. This strong

"You may be a black belt fighter, but you're still a white belt in dealing with people."

characterization and careful attention to detail creates an exciting and engaging supporting cast each with their own issues, hopes, and ideas.

The leisurely pace of a full-length series allows Tohru and her friends to grow and change over time, while the flashbacks and memories afforded by the fractured timeline give great emotional depth to the briefest scene or aside. For all her expressive faces and delicate shading, Natsuki Takaya never flinches from the darker and cruel aspects of life; at her most ambitious, she is drawing an emotional map of the crises of adolescence, from dealing with crushes to understanding that parents are sometimes wrong. From this, a story emerges that is at once breathtaking, ambitious, and shockingly honest. At the heart lies a series of deceptively simple revelations; these are the tools that the child characters need to live better and finally grow up. **JD**

Nana 1999

Ai Yazawa

Meet Nana Komatsu (nicknamed Hachi), the constantly lovesick, archetypal girl of the modern day, and Nana Osaki, the vocalist of a hard-core punk band. The two Nanas become roommates after meeting on a train to Tokyo, and their friendship gradually deepens. Apart from their names and the fact that they are both twenty years old, the two are complete opposites. Hachi, who has lived a typically "ordinary" life, is naive and easily love-struck, whereas Nana has a darker past: her parents have left her forever, and she lost her foster grandmother when she was fifteen. Fearless and tough, Nana is the vocalist in a band that includes three male members. The story begins from Hachi's perspective as she recollects the days she spent with Nana.

"Nana, do you remember the first time we met? Because I believe it was fated for us to become good friends."

Comparable to Sid and Nancy, the core of the plot is the relationship between rock guitarist Ren and Nana. Beneath their punk facade is a captivating story of tragic romance, and their fragile sensibilities have moved readers worldwide. However, perhaps the key factor that led the comic to a staggering circulation of 40 million, as well as two successful film adaptations, is Hachi herself. Unlike the monogamous Nana, Hachi finds romance in order to avoid loneliness, and as a result gets tangled up in a chain of complex relationships. It may not be the ideal lovelife, but it is certainly one that many female readers can relate to. While the story line flows smoothly with no dramatic ups or downs, its juxtaposition of the two Nanas' contrasting lives and personalities makes up for it. Deeply engraving her exquisite drawings in her reader's memory, Ai Yazawa's artwork fully captures the characters' emotions. **TS**

First published by Shueisha (Japan)
Creator Japanese (b.1967)
Genre Drama
Award Shogakukan Manga Award (2003)

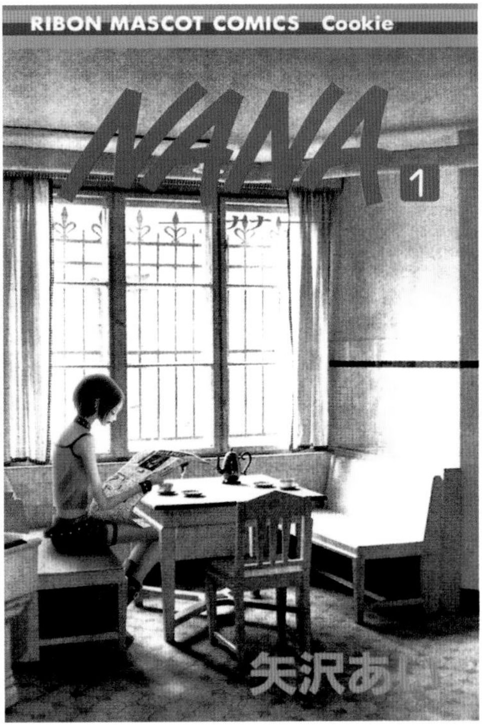
RIBON MASCOT COMICS Cookie
NANA
1
矢沢あ

Also by Ai Yazawa
Gokinjo Monogatari
Kagen no Tsuki
Marine Blue no Kaze ni Dakarete
Tenshi Nankaja Nai

Promethea 1999

Alan Moore J. H. Williams III

First published by America's Best Comics/DC Comics (USA) **Creators** Moore (British, b.1953); Williams III (American, b.1965)
Genre Fantasy, Superhero

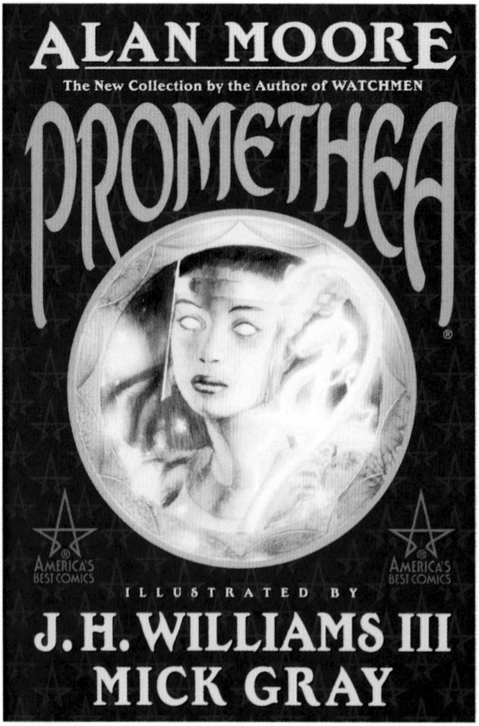
ALAN MOORE
The New Collection by the Author of WATCHMEN
PROMETHEA
AMERICA'S BEST COMICS
AMERICA'S BEST COMICS
ILLUSTRATED BY
J. H. WILLIAMS III
MICK GRAY

Similar reads
Angel Passage Alan Moore and Tim Perkins
Snakes and Ladders Alan Moore and Eddie Campbell
The Birth Caul Alan Moore and Eddie Campbell
The Sandman Neil Gaiman and others

Promethea is an attempt to explain the universe in a superhero comic. But it is not the universe exactly; it is us. When this series began in 1999, it appeared to be Alan Moore's version of Wonder Woman: a superheroine with mythological connections. It turned out to be something very different: his take on Kabbalistic philosophy in a psychedelic magical mystery tour. The series is a brash comics experiment: an exposition of philosophy behind the mask of superhero fiction.

The story begins in a futuristic, alternative New York City. College student Sophie Bangs is researching recurring sightings of Promethea—the female embodiment of imagination—when she brings the spirit of the goddess into herself through poetry. From there, she is led through a mystical journey that reveals the essence behind all symbolic structures: the tarot, sex magic, the "Tree of Life." She returns to her world just in time to usher in Armageddon before dinner.

"There are 1,000 comic books . . . that don't contain a philosophy lecture, and one that does."

Alan Moore

Moore's trippy epic is embellished in a plethora of palettes and homages to artists past and present by J. H. Williams III. Williams's role in this "experience" cannot be overstated; in portraying shifting states of consciousness and levels of reality, he exhibits astonishing craft. Moore creates a universe and guides it to destruction through imagination (Promethea) and beyond to renewal. More importantly, the systems he illuminates in telling the tale are metaphors for the full range of human nature and experience. There is ample room for works such as this, which help readers understand themselves a bit better. **TRL**

Priest 1999

Minwoo Hyung

When *Priest* was first serialized in Korea, it was recognized as having been influenced by North American comic books such as *Hellboy*. It soon became evident that it was so successful because it combined unusual angular artwork with a dark and grim story line that reinvented the Christian mythology of good and evil—with a devilish antihero as its protagonist.

The story unfolds in the Wild West, where a former priest who has risen from the dead is embarking on a one-man vengeance war against a world filled with ghouls. Young priest Ivan Isaacs lost his life and the life of his forbidden loved one as a result of a devilish ritual by the fallen archangel Temozalea. By giving half of his soul to the former witch hunter, Ivan comes back to life and vows to seek vengeance. With nothing but hatred and anger in his heart, Ivan goes on a killing spree against Temozalea, who is trying to complete his spell to bring hell on Earth.

"I like in my comic how I can be more philosophical and more detailed. It's not easy to do that in a movie."

Minwoo Hyung

Evil smiles, anger-filled empty eyes, bloody gloves, large knives, and machine guns on a man wearing a priest's outfit is indeed an awesome sight. On top of this, the recurring theme of religious existentialism is added, such as what good and evil really are and what God wants with his people on Earth. The fact that the gun action is stunningly choreographed also helps to make *Priest* a remarkable work. It found instant appeal with readers outside of Korea, making it one of the first real hit *manhwa* (Korean comic) in the North American market and even spawning a successful Hollywood action movie. **NK**

First published by Daiwon (South Korea)
Creator South Korean (b.1974)
Genre Horror, Western
Adaptation Film (2011)

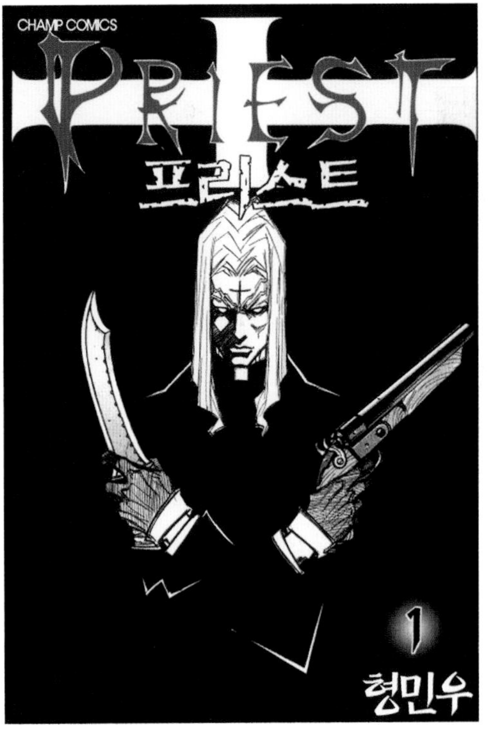
CHAMP COMICS
PRIEST
프리스트
1
형민우

Similar reads

Berserk Kentara Miura
Hellblazer Peter Milligan and Alan Moore
Hellboy Mike Mignola
Trigun Nasuhiro Nightow

Gemma Bovery 1999

"Posy" Simmonds

POSY SIMMONDS
Gemma Bovery

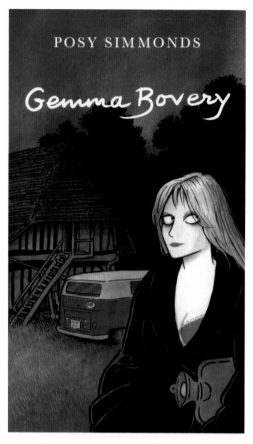

First published by Jonathan Cape (UK)
Creator Rosemary Elizabeth Simmonds (British, b.1945)
Genre Drama
Influenced by Gustave Flaubert

Since her first comic strip appeared in the *Guardian* newspaper in 1977, Posy Simmonds has held a unique place in the consciousness of British readers. However, with *Gemma Bovery*, her first graphic novel, Simmonds focuses on the British contemporary experience through a different kind of lens. Here she tells the story of an Englishwoman abroad by reinterpreting Flaubert's classic tale of infidelity, *Madame Bovary*.

One would think that times have changed. However, the temptations that spelled trouble for the first Mrs. B. are, for better or for worse, eternal. Gemma, an illustrator, is in a relationship with Charles Bovery, a furniture restorer with a demanding ex-wife and two sulky children. Gemma comes into some money and persuades Charles to give France a try—more old furniture for him to play with, fewer screaming matches with the ex. And, of course, they are both subject to the lure of France itself: open-air markets, cheap wine, and quiet country life. But all does not go to plan.

Bored by their new lifestyle, Gemma finds illicit fun with a law student, under the overly watchful eye of Joubert, the local baker, who obsesses endlessly over parallels between "l'anglaise" and her famous counterpart. We know from the start that this tale ends in tragedy, but the hows and whys make for exceptionally compelling reading. Simmonds's soft pencil strokes create a lush environment for human intransigence. However, it is her way with plotting and an unerring ear for dialogue that make *Gemma Bovery* such an affectingly modern tale. **EL**

Similar reads

Embroideries Marjane Satrapi
Faire Semblant, C'est Mentir Dominique Goblet
La Perdida Jessica Abel
Shortcomings Adrian Tomine
Tamara Drewe Posy Simmonds

The Adventures of Hergé 1999

✏ Bocquet and Fromental   ✏ Stanislas Barthélémy

First published by Éditions Reporter (France)
Creators José-Louis Bocquet (French, b.1962); Jean-Luc Fromental (French, b.1950); Barthélémy (French, b.1961)
Genre Biography

The most unusual comics biography ever published also happens to be one of the best. Sacrificing strict factual accuracy for creative license, the trio of José-Louis Bocquet, Jean-Luc Fromental, and Stanislas Barthélémy produced a biography that is a true celebration of its subject.

Hergé, the world-renowned creator of *The Adventures of Tintin*, had a much less glamorous and exciting life than did his beloved character, but you would never know it from reading his life as it is depicted here. Tracing his life in short scenes from his boyhood until his death in 1983, *The Adventures of Hergé* posits the author's rise to fame as a series of creative triumphs troubled by personal demons, anxieties, and bouts of depression. Into this mixture the artists have tossed a variety of counterfactual elements, suppositions, and playful homages to Tintin and his globe-trotting adventures.

The most enjoyable part of this biography is the clever way in which its creators have blended the story of creator and creation, attributing nearly every significant aspect of the *Tintin* books—from Castafiore's pushiness to the overlapping dialogue of Thomson and Thompson—to real people in Hergé's life, all the while respecting the general outlines of his life as he actually lived it. Stanislas's art choices, including a contemporary updating of the clear line style that Hergé pioneered, are consistently excellent, and the very style of the book serves as a loving tribute to one of the most influential cartoonists of all time. **BB**

My New York Diary 1999

✏✏ Julie Doucet

First published by Drawn & Quarterly (Canada)
Creator Canadian (b.1965)
Genre Autobiography
Award Firecracker Award (2000)

With her series *Dirty Plotte*, Montreal native Julie Doucet set a new standard of sexual frankness in comics. True to form, *My New York Diary* focuses on tales of emotional impulse and its aftermath, opening with two accounts of Doucet's formative sexual experiences. However, while these stories involve a range of disturbing behavior, from a suicide attempt to possible statutory rape, they are, literally, just the beginning. Doucet is simply warning readers to take crash positions as she relates an even more worrying decision: to move to New York and start over with a man she barely knows. Her friends and family seem concerned, but Doucet blithely swears that she has found her soulmate. She just left out a few details: her recently divorced beau lives in an isolated neighborhood where Doucet is afraid to leave the house alone after dark. Instead of going out, they get high or drunk and play boardgames. This lifestyle leads to complications for her health, her career, and, eventually, her sanity.

Doucet has a knack for imparting slightly alarming details in a laid-back, matter-of-fact tone that keeps readers engrossed even when they feel like they should look away. Her art sucks readers in, with every squalid detail given a loving flourish—dirty socks have never looked so good. Perhaps displaying a debt to Hergé, Doucet's panels tend to be from a fixed frontal perspective, with figures depicted head to toe. This creates the feeling of having a front-row ticket to a particularly disturbing domestic drama—one you would not want to miss. **EL**

Mushishi 1999

✎✎ Yuki Urushibara

First published by Kodansha (Japan)
Creator Japanese (b.1974)
Genre Supernatural
Adaptation TV anime (2005–06)

Mythical spirits, ghosts, and fairies: humans have long debated the relationship between inexplicable events and the existence of the supernatural. In the world of Yuki Urushibara's *Mushishi*, it seems that mysterious creatures called the "mushi" are the cause of such curious incidents.

While the mushi are invisible to most, there are a few exceptions, including Ginko, the main character of the series. Ginko is capable of attracting various types of the mushi, which can bring happiness as well as misfortune to people. He uses his gift to become a mushi master, or Mushishi, and travels around solving people's problems concerning the creatures.

Unlike other mushi masters who aim to banish the creatures, Ginko wants harmony. Appearing in various forms, from animals and plants to rainbows and fire, the mushi are described as something close to the core of life. At times they are harmful to humans, but only for their own survival. In reality, the concept is just everyday life—all living things and natural phenomena are capable of hurting humans, and the cause may not necessarily be a supernatural being. However, Urushibara's gripping storytelling and somewhat nostalgic illustrations raise fundamental questions of the human condition.

The comic ran in *Afternoon* magazine from 1999 to 2008 and has been developed into an animation series as well as a live-action film. It won the Excellence Prize at Japan Media Arts Festival and Kodansha's Comic Award in 2006. **TS**

Planetes 1999

✎✎ Makoto Yukimura

Title in original language *Puranetesu*
First published by Kodansha (Japan)
Creator Japanese (b.1976)
Genre Science fiction

Toward the end of the twenty-first century, humanity has finally started to spread beyond its original planet and settle on other planets in the solar system. As always, human expansion comes at a cost. In space, this cost is calculated, among other things, on the basis of the amount of debris left behind by space travelers: the remains of satellites, scraps of metal, devices, and bits of equipment of every kind. In order to make space travel safer, other men (they too are spacemen, but much less glorious) have been assigned to collect this debris. Garbage collectors, in other words.

It is these space garbage collectors, the proletariat of the space dream, whom Makato Yukimura invites readers to follow in their everyday lives in the suburbs of Earth, both in their far-from-gratifying job and in their private lives with their expectations and disappointments. His graphic style is a perfect match for this script: a moderate, precise realism without unnecessary special effects, more concerned with arousing empathy with "real life" than with telling the story of improbable adventures.

This is the fascination of this shrewd and sensitive series, in which a work of science fiction is created that is neither crude nor stentorian but full of subtle nuances. In contrast to most of the clichés of the genre (here there is no time travel, hyperspace, or extraterrestrials), Yukimura is more interested in the realism of his characters and their profound humanity—yet does not lose touch with what has always been the foundation of great science. **NF**

100 Bullets 1999

Brian Azzarello Eduardo Risso

First published by Vertigo/DC Comics (USA)
Creators Azzarello (American, Unknown); Risso (Argentinian, b.1959)
Genre Crime

VERTIGO
"A Criminal Masterpiece."
-Steranko
100
BULLETS
FIRST SHOT, LAST CALL
BRIAN AZZARELLO
EDUARDO RISSO

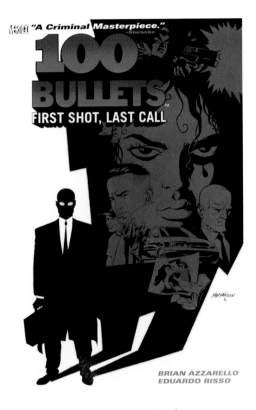

100 Bullets is a noir story in which a complicated conspiracy plot structures the underlining mechanics of the story arcs. It gets its title from the one hundred bullets in an attaché case passed on to a character by the mysterious Agent Graves, along with the irrefutable evidence against somebody who has wronged the recipient of the case. It becomes clear that Graves has a connection to The Trust, a powerful organization that has a team of protectors called the Minutemen. Two of the receivers of the case are contacted in order to enroll them in whatever master plan Agent Graves is plotting. This involves waking all the sleeping Minutemen agents and fighting off any adversaries in the process. It is sometimes hard to keep track of all the characters as their alliances shift regularly, but the dialogue flows freely and the many side stories—betrayal, tricks of fate, violent gun fights, and interesting characters—help *100 Bullets* in its quest for the truth.

Eduardo Risso's drawings are extremely expressive, with a heavy use of black for large areas as shadows and facial expressions are often distorted or parts of the action obscured by the choice of point of view. Eyes bulge, veins are visible, noses are broad and broken, and clothes are draped and folded in impressive ways in order to help shape the characters and their environment. The exaggerated depiction of bodies and slight disproportion of faces only make the people appear more believable, in such a way that readers can almost smell the blood, sweat, and tears gushing through the story. **RPC**

"Look li'l girl, understand a fact of life. If you're weak, you die. Don' be weak, baby."

Also by Brian Azzarello
El Diablo
Filthy Rich
Jonny Double
Loveless

Top 10 1999

Alan Moore   Gene Ha

First published by America's Best Comics/ DC Comics (USA) **Creators** Moore (British, b.1953); Ha (American, Unknown)
Genre Superhero

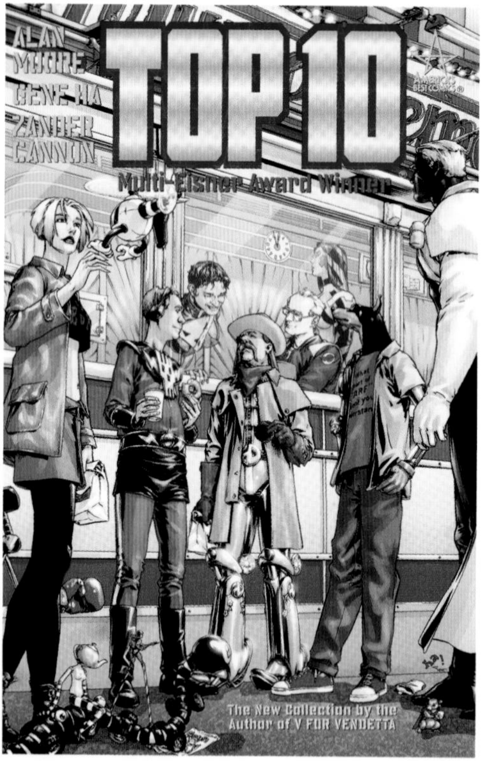
ALAN MOORE
GENE HA
ZANDER CANNON
TOP 10
Multi-Eisner Award Winner
The New Collection by the Author of V FOR VENDETTA

Also by Alan Moore
Promethea
Tom Strong
Supreme

When Alan Moore returned to superhero comics at the end of the 1990s, *Top 10* was the least remarked-upon of all his titles, yet it was also the most original and the most interesting. Set in Neopolis, a city in which everyone—cops, criminals, civilians—has superpowers and a secret identity, *Top 10* focuses on the exploits of a precinct full of eccentric police officers charged with the nearly impossible task of keeping the peace. Robyn "Toybox" Slinger is the new recruit, and Jeff Smax is her taciturn partner. *Top 10* moved through its initial run as if it were a procedural cop television series like *Homicide: Life on the Streets* (from which it shamelessly borrowed plots). The catch was the superpowers and Moore's deep and abiding interest in superhero storytelling.

"Huh? I heard they put a lot of Nazi villains and mad scientists and stuff to work designing it after the war."

More than any other superhero comic book, *Top 10* is awash with puns, allusions, and sight gags. From a street vendor roasting hotdogs with his heat vision to a boy band called Sidekix, Moore ladles on the ironies with reckless abandon. Entire plotlines are left to play out in the background of action-packed panels, and superheroes move through by the thousands. Not since *Watchmen* had Moore created a world that was so utterly dependent on the reader's ability to decode the various histories of superhero storytelling, and never before had he written with such unabashed joy for the genre.

After the original series ran its course, Moore and Gene Ha followed up with the mini-series *Smax* and the graphic novel *The Forty-Niners*, but both paled in comparison to *Top 10*, one of the smartest commentaries on superheroes ever published. **BB**

Naruto 1999

Masashi Kishimoto

One of the world's most popular comics of the late 1990s, Masashi Kishimoto's *Naruto* applies the traditional Japanese theme of ninja to the modern-day logic of boys' comics, illustrating the adventures of Naruto as he trains in ninja skills and faces various battles with rivals and enemies. A struggling student at Ninja Academy, Naruto is far from a gifted ninja; he is just an ordinary boy who hates studying and loves being a prankster. His so-called rival, Sasuke, is an attractive honors student who comes from an upper-class ninja clan. While Naruto insists that there is rivalry between the two, Sasuke pays no attention to him. However, as Naruto's intense training begins to pay off, Sasuke gradually acknowledges Naruto's courage and efforts,

"I'm a bum whose favorite thing to do is to watch the clouds . . . the last thing I'd want to be doing is giving out orders."

leading the unlikely pair to bond. Naruto and Sasuke share the same goal, which is to become the strongest ninja to ever exist. Yet their dreams are painfully different: Naruto wants to become the next Kokage (the leader of Konohagakure), whereas Sasuke plans to murder his entire clan, then hunt down and kill his missing brother.

Despite the characters' mutual goals, the pair's contrasting dreams lead them to a complicated future. However, Naruto, who still believes in their friendship and rivalry, does not give up on his companion. Perfectly embracing all three of *Shukan Shonen Jump*'s golden "key words"—friendship, effort, and triumph—*Naruto* has won the hearts of fans all over the world. Its U.S. adaptation was serialized by *Viz Media* in 2003, and the title has sold more than 100 million copies in Japan alone. **TS**

First published by Shueisha (Japan)
Creator Japanese (b.1974)
Genre Adventure, Fantasy
Adaptation TV anime (2002–07)

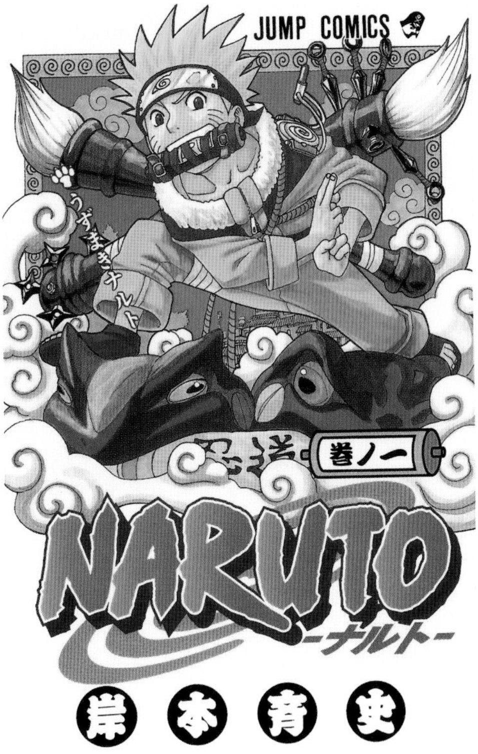
JUMP COMICS
巻ノ一
NARUTO
-ナルト-
岸本斉史

Similar reads

Bench Masashi Kishimoto
Karakuri Masashi Kishimoto
Ninku Kiriyama Koji

Louis Riel 1999

Chester Brown

First published by Drawn & Quarterly (Canada)
Creator Canadian (b.1960)
Genre Biography
Award Harvey Award (2004)

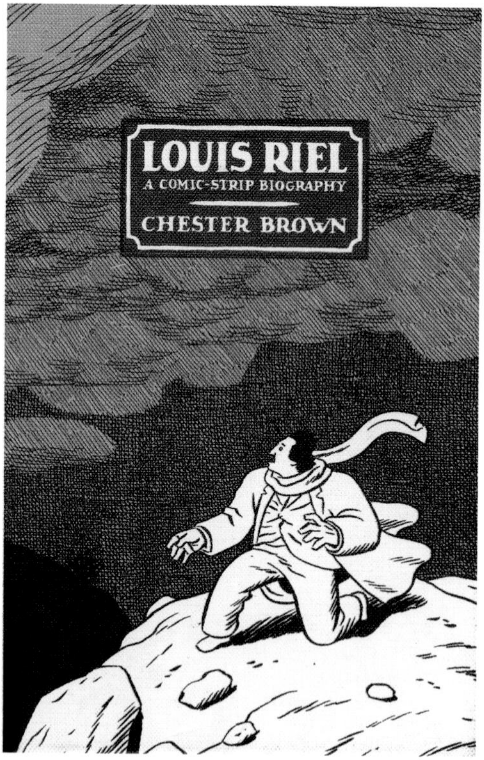
LOUIS RIEL
A COMIC-STRIP BIOGRAPHY
CHESTER BROWN

Also by Chester Brown
Ed the Happy Clown
I Never Liked You
Paying For It

In the last thirty years of the nineteenth century, the young Canadian nation, then part of the British Empire, began to expand its territories westward toward the Pacific. Canada bought Rupert's Land, an enormous territory that included a community of some 12,000 inhabitants, not far from the border with the U.S. state of Minnesota: the Red River settlement.

The people of Red River—mostly of French and Indian origin, Catholic, and French-speaking—did not accept that their future should be dictated by English speakers living thousands of miles away. Among them, one man stood up: Louis Riel. Charismatic, inspired, and a mystic, he became the thinking head of a rebellion against the far-distant city of Ottawa.

"I propose that we set up our own . . . government and that we take up arms to defend our right to do so!"

With amazing determination, inspired by political psychology and a good measure of military pressure, he persuaded the Canadian government to found a new state, Manitoba.

Although Louis Riel is today a symbol of resistance to imperialism and oppression, he is almost unknown outside of his own country. The detailed portrayal of Louis Riel in this comic by Chester Brown has helped to gain him greater recognition. But Brown has gone further by making the story of Manitoba's rebel a thrilling and poignant one in which he emerges as a champion of all minorities crushed by history. Louis Riel is shown to transcend all local references and cultures, and, because of the empathy aroused by his achievements and the new familiarity that has drawn attention to his situation as an outcast, he has finally achieved the status of universality. **NF**

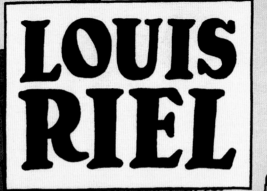

LOUIS RIEL

WRITTEN AND DRAWN BY **CHESTER BROWN** AND PUBLISHED BY DRAWN AND QUARTERLY.

THIS IS THE FIRST OF APPROXIMATELY TEN COMIC-BOOKS WHICH WILL TELL THE TRUE STORY OF THIS 19TH CENTURY INDIVIDUAL.

PLEASE PAY $ 2.95 IN THE UNITED STATES OF AMERICA, OR $ 4.25 IN CANADA.

The Double of Five 1999

Lourenço Mutarelli

Title in original language *O Dobro De Cinco*
First published by Devir (Brazil)
Creator Brazilian (b.1964)
Genre Crime, Drama

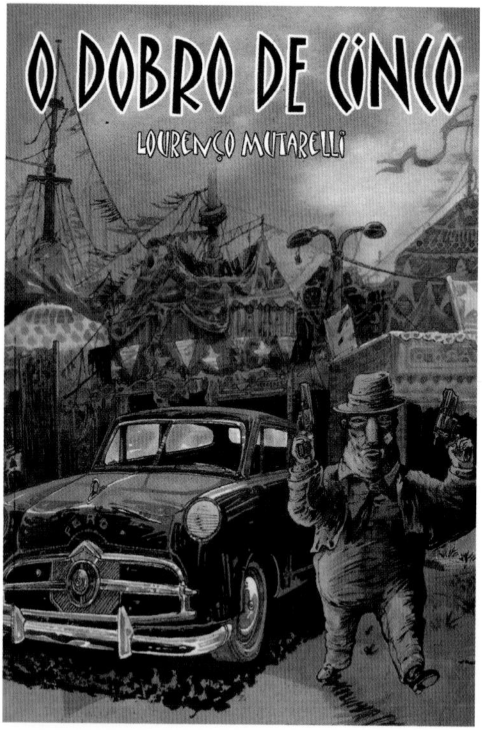
O DOBRO DE CINCO
LOURENÇO MUTARELLI

Also by Lourenço Mutarelli
The King of the Point (*O Rei Do Ponto*)
The "Pet" World (*Mundo Pet*)
The Sandbox (*A Caixa De Areia*)
The Sum of Everything (*A Soma De Tudo*)

With this ironic, acerbic graphic novel, Lourenço Mutarelli injected humor into his tragic worldview. His storytelling grew more agile, and it seems he had learned to laugh. His vision matured, and he consolidated his position as a cutting-edge author.

In *The Double of Five*, readers are introduced to Diomedes, a short, fat, lazy excuse for a private investigator, who nevertheless manages to laugh about the continuous troubles in which he finds himself. Trying to model himself on the Chandlerian prototype, Diomedes experiences a series of misadventures in which he achieves some understanding, if not victory. Of course, some of his conclusions are completely wrong, but they come accompanied by some correct ones,

"We are the illness! Us, the human race, the fungus, the rottenness, the scars . . . is what we are!!"

and Diomedes derives comfort from them. However, getting paid for his efforts proves more daunting than the investigation itself. The other main character in the book is his client, who also appears to be a sorry failure of a person. However, he may not be who he at first purports to be. Frail or not, he manages to establish a very original dialogue with Diomedes' gumshoe imagination. The occasional presence of Diomedes' lying wife helps the falsehoods to spread.

Rendered in very sharp contrast, with an expressionistic flavor, the artwork is on a par with the writing mood and is a welcome surprise at a time when even the most traditional comics had trouble finding readers. With this book, the commercial viability of a truly authorial vision was established in the small Brazilian market. Mutarelli has remained present in bookstores and now writes prose as well. **CB**

The Birth Caul: A Shamanism of Childhood 1999

Alan Moore Eddie Campbell

As the subtitle to *The Birth Caul* indicates, magic plays an important part in this comic. In fact, *The Birth Caul* began life as a one-off multimedia performance piece presented on November 18, 1995, before being adapted by Eddie Campbell. On his fortieth birthday Moore declared himself a magician, wanting to explore his complex ideas on the cultural significance of magic. This found an outlet in a series of site-specific performance art in collaboration with artists, musicians, and dancers.

A birth caul is the thin veil of the placenta that sometimes covers a newborn's head and is traditionally kept as a good luck charm. After the death of his mother, Moore found one in her effects. Using this experience as a starting point, he riffs on a reverse chronology

"We cut ourselves to suit the cloth. We cut ourselves to size when first we are delivered to the world's blunt engine."

of a fictional counterpart, charting a regression from adulthood to adolescence through infancy to a prenatal state of grace. The story recalls one of Moore's most famous *2000AD Time Twister* tales "The Reversible Man," which began with a man's death and ended with his birth.

The Birth Caul is as much Campbell's work as Moore's: the vivid, at times, disorienting layouts are every bit as daring and original as their previous collaboration. This results in a dazzling visual collage that incorporates Campbell's signature scribbled handwriting and images alongside fading photographs and direct pictorial quotations from Katsushika Hokusai and Hieronymus Bosch presenting a perfect analogue to Moore's regressive narrative. This enhances *The Birth Caul*'s sense of occult esotericism, dispensing with conventional comics breakdowns to provide a strong visual sense of visionary performance. **TV**

First published by Knockabout Comics (UK)
Creators Moore (British, b.1953); Campbell (British, b.1955)
Genre Fantasy

alan moore
& eddie campbell
theBirthCaul

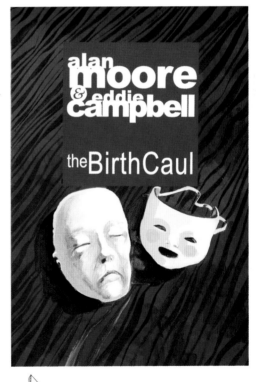

Similar reads

Alice in Sunderland Bryan Talbot
Promethea Alan Moore and J. H. Williams III
Snakes and Ladders Alan Moore and Eddie Campbell
The Spiral Cage Al Davison

The League of Extraordinary Gentlemen 1999

Alan Moore   Kevin O'Neill

First published by America's Best Comics/DC Comics (USA) **Creators** Moore (British, b.1953); O'Neill (British, b.1953)
Genre Alternative

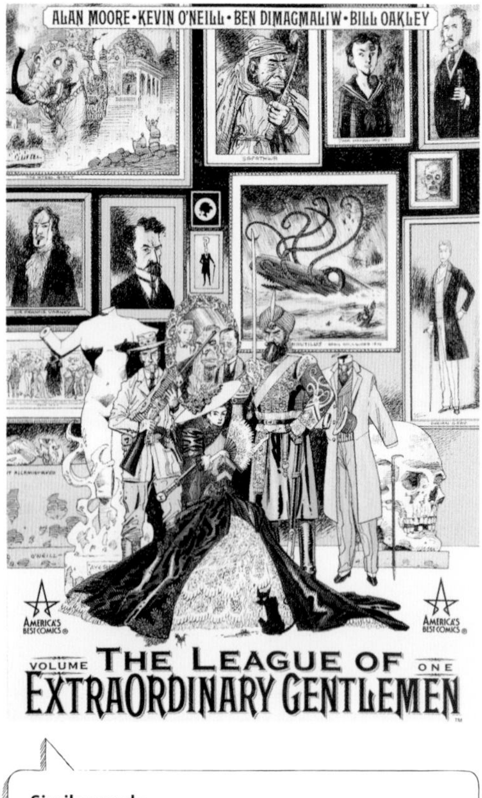
ALAN MOORE • KEVIN O'NEILL • BEN DIMAGMALIW • BILL OAKLEY
AMERICA'S BEST COMICS
AMERICA'S BEST COMICS
VOLUME THE LEAGUE OF ONE
EXTRAORDINARY GENTLEMEN

Similar reads
From Hell Alan Moore and Eddie Campbell
Marshal Law Pat Mills and Kevin O'Neill
Scarlet Traces Ian Edgington and Brooker Matt
Watchmen Alan Moore and Dave Gibbons

Alan Moore has always had fun subverting genre formula into interesting new shapes. In *The League of Extraordinary Gentlemen,* he takes the superhero team-up concept of DC's *Justice League* or Marvel's *The Avengers* and applies it to classic nineteenth-century literary characters and events, collapsing their worlds into one single continuum, creating a world that feels both fresh and familiar, rich with possibility.

In this first volume, the year is 1898 and the mysterious Miss Mina Murray is charged by the British Secret Service to form a league of secret agents to serve and protect the British Empire. Among her recruited "menagerie" are the adventurer Allan Quartermain, the submariner Captain Nemo, the dual character of Dr. Jekyll and Mr. Hyde, and the invisible Hawley Griffin. Together they are sent to Limehouse in London to foil plans to build an airship capable of aerial bombardment.

"The British Empire has always encountered difficulty in distinguishing between its heroes and monsters."

Campion Bond

If you know nothing about Victorian fiction, *The League of Extraordinary Gentlemen* is still an enormously entertaining adventure yarn. But even a passing familiarity with works such as *Dracula* or *Murders in the Rue Morgue* will bring added benefits, because the book is crammed full of nods to its myriad source material and produces extraordinary results as some of the most unique concepts in Victorian fiction collide. Kevin O'Neill's art is highly distinctive, using lithograph-style crosshatching and other elements commonly used in Victorian illustration; many panels carry literary in-jokes. Later volumes move to more recent times and a new set of characters but the fun never fails. **BD**

Hey, Wait... 1999

"Jason"

Title in original language *Vent litt*
First published by Jippi (Norway)
Creator John Arne Sæterøy (Norwegian, b.1965)
Genre Funny animal

This anthropomorphic tale, which starts with a childhood friendship, is a story of guilt, loss, and haunting memories. As in most of Jason's stories, there is a strong sense of melancholy, which places his work within a long Scandinavian tradition. The comics have a dark, black humor, often absurd, which is played out on the surface of life's innermost problems.

Hey, Wait... is Jason's first longer work that features characters with animal-shaped heads, a trait that has become something of a trademark of his today. This makes the characters more universal, and, strangely enough, easier to relate to. His finesse for details and a magnificent artistic virtuosity allow these animal faces to express every possible human feeling. The characters have the quality of an archetype, often with a clear reference to popular culture. While the artist's later works have been mainly executed with ink and pen for colorization, *Hey, Wait...* is rendered in brushwork in black and white. The rhythm between lines and shapes, dark and light, suits the tale in such a way that the reader is drawn into the story. Jason shows with *Hey, Wait...* that he is a trained storyteller who works in a minimalistic style where no word and no panel is redundant. His slow-paced style, with abrupt changes in time and space, sets the reader in an almost fragile state, and few have read *Hey, Wait...* without the story having made a strong impression on them. No wonder this novella established Jason as an international star and has been published all over the world. **TAH**

"Careful—think twice before you read this book. It is very, very beautiful, but it will utterly break your heart."

Dylan Horrocks

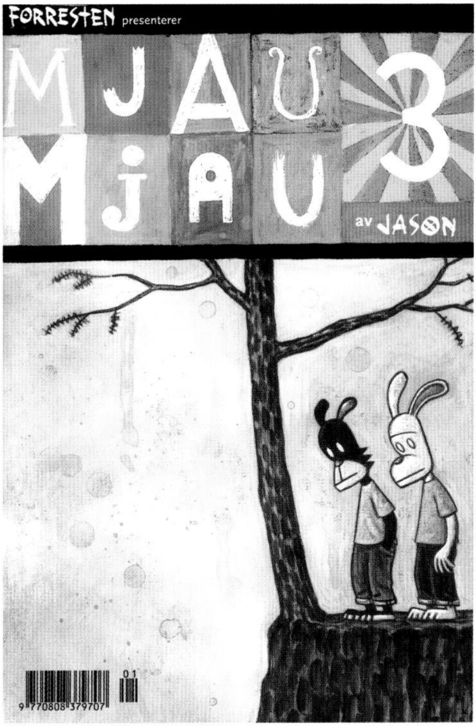
FORRESTEN presenterer
MJAU MJAU 3
av JASON

Also by Jason
I Killed Adolf Hitler
Low Moon
The Iron Wagon
The Left Bank Gang

6 2000–Present

Doing Time 2000

📖 Kazuichi Hanawa

Title in original language *Keimusyo no Naka*
First published by Seirinkogeisha (Japan)
Creator Japanese (b.1947)
Genre Reality drama, Autobiography

In 1994, the author Kazuichi Hanawa was arrested for violating the Japanese law on firearms. Sentenced to serve three years in jail, he decided to create a manga, entitled *Doing Time*, based on his experiences. The strip is a special treat for anyone who wants a peek into a different life—especially a life in jail.

With his beautiful pen drawing, Hanawa shows prison life as one of endless monotony hedged by restrictions on insignificant actions, such as rolling up one's sleeves or working on a word puzzle. Readers feel Hanawa's pain when he has to beg desperately for an officer's attention, shouting to ask permission to simply pick up an eraser from the floor.

From his amazingly precise depiction of the jail interior, readers might easily assume that Hanawa sketched every aspect from life. In fact, it was strictly forbidden to take notes and make sketches in the jail buildings, and all his drawings were produced from memory. Details such as the kinds of food he ate and the way he had to fold his clothes are vividly recalled.

Hanawa playfully adopts an illustrative style typical of children's encyclopedias for his precise depictions, with captions such as "An illustrated story for good children" referring to work that obviously is *not* for children. For anyone wanting to research life in a Japanese jail, they provide the perfect reference material. The book is unique in Hanawa's work, which otherwise tends to be set in medieval times, with stories about the grotesqueness of human nature illustrated in a sometimes gory manner. **AT-L**

Safe Area Goražde 2000

📖 Joe Sacco

First published by Fantagraphics Books (USA)
Creator Maltese-American (b.1960)
Genre War
Award Eisner Award (2001)

When journalist and comic book artist Joe Sacco produced the powerful Bosnian-war set *Safe Area Goražde* he was at the peak of his creative abilities: his characters were individualized and more true to life than in his earlier work. Sacco based his narrative on conversations he had with people trapped in Goražde.

Sacco is a better landscape artist than a portraitist. His views of the war-ravaged city of Goražde are magnificent. He uses all his formal resources—black gutters indicating flashbacks, flying short captions, and bleeding panels, pages, and spreads—effectively in the service of the storytelling. *Safe Area Goražde* is well structured. As the author explains: "to make it more powerful it's better to introduce the characters. Let them grow on the reader, as they grew on me, and as you get to know the characters through the atmospheric track, the historic track is building up. You go from history, to tension, to disintegration to the first shock, the first attack. Then the horrors just start to pile up."

And what horrors they are. Sacco does not spare his readers: war is hell. He portrays himself as a caricature that contrasts with all the other characters in the comic book because he believes that it is easier for his readers to identify with his cartoon self than with a realistic depiction. His caricature self wears eyeglasses, but there are no eyes shown behind them, which makes him look mousy and impenetrable. This approach by the author conveys the sense that Sacco himself is insignificant; it is the inhabitants of Goražde and their gruesome stories that are what matters. **DI**

Kraut 2000

"Peter Pontiac"

First published by Podium (Netherlands)
Creator Petrus J. G. Pollmann (Dutch, b.1951)
Genre Autobiography
Awards Stripschapprijs (1997), Marten Toonderprijs (2011)

In early 1978, fifty-five-year-old Dutch gossip journalist Joop Pollmann—divorced and his career drowned in booze—took a one-way ticket to the Dutch Antilles. The day after, lit pipe in hand, he walked into the water of a Curaçao bay; then, swimming on his back into the Caribbean Sea, looking up, slowly rocking, he blew out his last puffs of smoke and sank into oblivion.

But not for Peter, his first son, who had been told to leave home in 1969. His *Kraut*—an egodocument in the form of a long letter to a father he cannot love—zaps any theory of what a comic or a biography should or shouldn't be. Subtitled *biografiek* (biographics), its art and lettering were on photocopy paper in Bic ballpoint, with Staedtler marker for the heavy blacks and some Wite-Out. The 168-page tale soon turns into a maelstrom of visual and textual flashbacks, full of collage, half-joking comments, Church and Nazi paraphernalia, and doubts and theories about his family's Catholic background and his father's choice to join the Dutch fascists in World War II. While interspersed with beautifully drawn passages in strip form, it is hard to read at times because the lettered texts are often too long and set too wide.

Peter Pollmann went from 1960s anarchist through years of drug abuse to elderly punk to father of a family himself. In 1969 his first work was published unsigned: intense art for bootleg songbook covers. He soon began signing as "Dr. Faith" and "Holy Cat" and, after 1971, as "Peter Pontiac" or "Ponti." His works, often about himself, externalize his burning love. Emptiness or silence are not in his repertoire. **HvO**

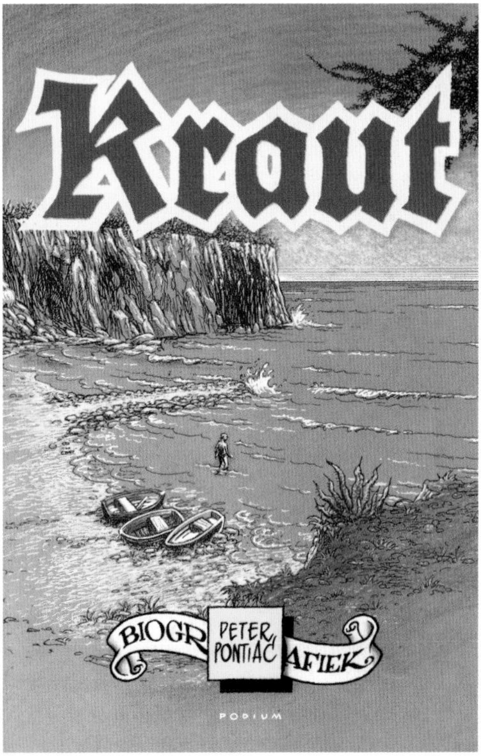
Kraut
BIOGR PETER PONTIAC AFIEK
PODIUM

"Were you in such a hurry to get to the water you simply forgot to get your stuff, or did you leave everything deliberately?"

Similar reads
Herinneringen Rudolf Kahl
Visual Addiction Robert Williams

Skibber Bee-Bye 2000

✎✎ Ron Regé, Jr.

First published by Highwater Books (USA)
Creator American (b.1969)
Genre Romance
Influenced by John Porcellino

Very few cartoonists aspire to be poets, and even fewer succeed in that goal. Ron Regé Jr., is one of the most notable. *Skibber Bee-Bye*, his most important book-length work, is a haunting tale that combines history, romance, and epic violence in a magical world where fairies exist and people's illnesses erupt on their bodies in the most unexpected ways.

Regé emerged from the Providence, Rhode Island art and minicomics scene that produced the likes of Brian Chippendale, Brian Ralph, and Matt Brinkman. His art is deliberately childlike, and filled with wonder. While some might imagine that his drawings are naive, closer inspection reveals his thin lines to be extremely controlled and deliberately executed. He fills his panels with seemingly extraneous lines that connote both movement and the pure power of emotional intensity. These are complex images, made all the more so by the unusual structure of the story.

Narratively, *Skibber Bee-Bye* is a difficult work. The story revolves round the interaction between a nattily dressed elephant, replete with fedora, and a brother and sister who work as bookbinders. Initially it seems to be about the budding romance between the elephant and the female bookbinder, which is delicately handled and beautifully rendered, until a lengthy flashback about the abandonment of the siblings by their father interrupts the flow. By the end, the story devolves into abstract violence in contrast with the earlier chapters. *Skibber Bee-Bye* is the expression of a mind fully engaged with the potential of the comics form. **BB**

Kramers Ergot 2000

✎✎ Edited by Sammy Harkham

First published by Avodah Books (USA)
Creator American (b.1980)
Genre Alternative
Influenced by Gary Panter

The defining art-comics anthology of the 2000s, *Kramers Ergot* began inauspiciously as a minicomic edited by Sammy Harkham in 2000 featuring work by him, Justin Howe, David Brook, and Luke Quigley. In 2003, with the fourth issue, Harkham moved the title to Gingko Press, where he radically expanded the size and scope of his anthology, creating a sensation in the comics scene by boldly foregrounding the expanded visual possibilities of the comics form. More than any comics project since *RAW*, *Kramers Ergot* pushed the limits of the form by drawing on the aesthetics of the contemporary art world.

The fourth, fifth, and sixth issues of *Kramers Ergot* were all thick, full-color anthologies combining the best of a new generation of comics, graphic artists, and photographers. Many of the contributors were young, relatively unknown, and had an aesthetic disposition that belied their art school backgrounds. The range of work included was extremely Catholic, running from assaulting graphic stylings of Leif Goldberg and Matt Brinkman, to the more introspective narratives of Kevin Huizenga and Tom Gauld. The seventh and final issue of *Kramers Ergot* is the most unusual. Inspired by the size of the strip reprint collections published by Sunday Press, Harkham invited contributors to submit pages to an enormous hardcover collection. The resulting anthology includes an international who's who of crossgenerational comics stars, and seems less like a comic book than a curated art show, capturing the explosive vitality of a generation of cartoonists. **BB**

Persepolis 2000

Marjane Satrapi

First published by L'Association (France)
Creator Iranian (b.1969)
Genre Autobiography
Award Coup de Coeur (2001)

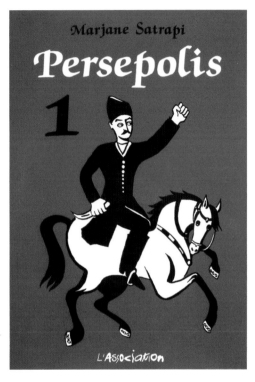

Marjane Satrapi's seminal autobiography has been well received all over the Western world, telling as it does the story of a fiery young girl growing up in both Iran and Austria. Satrapi is the daughter of liberal parents, and her favorite comic book is about Karl Marx. As a young girl she witnessed the downfall of the Shah and the subsequent Islamic revolution, and at ten years old was forced to wear the veil. As the Iran-Iraq War raged, the regime clamped down on any dissent, eventually forcing the willful and rebellious young Satrapi to flee to Austria.

Perhaps the most remarkable thing about *Persepolis* is how exceptionally intimate it is. Satrapi does not shy away from portraying her own mistakes, even when they are cruel, selfish, or horribly embarrassing—something that lends a stark truthfulness to her memoir. Her black-and-white illustrations also lend a strong sense of intimacy to the work, drawn as they are with a deceptively childlike simplicity.

Persepolis walks a fine line between opposites. It is at once the memoir of an innocent girl playing with friends and a stark insight into her learning of horrors, such as the deliberate burning of a "decadent" cinema with all its occupants locked inside. Satrapi's book fiercely criticizes her country and its politics, yet equally expresses a deep love for her homeland and its people. Her work is a powerful antidote to Western stereotyping of the Middle East and gives the reader a sense of seeing the real Iran through the eyes of someone who truly understands it. **BD**

Marjane Satrapi
Persepolis
1
L'Association

"We didn't really like to wear the veil, especially since we didn't understand why we had to."

Similar reads
Embroideries (Broderies) Marjane Satrapi
Epileptic (L'Ascension du Haut Mal) David B.
Forget Sorrow: An Ancestral Tale Belle Yang
Habibi Craig Thompson
Maus: A Survivor's Tale Art Spiegelman

Blacksad 2000

Juan Díaz Canales Juanjo Guarnido

Title in original language *Quelque Part Entre les Ombres*
First published by Dargaud (France)
Creators Canales (Spanish, b.1972);
Guarnido (Spanish, b.1967) **Genre** Crime

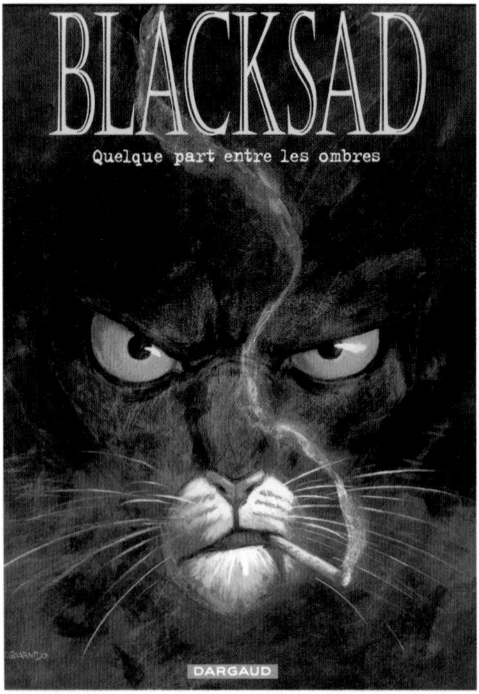
BLACKSAD
Quelque part entre les ombres
DARGAUD

Also by Juan Díaz Canales and Juanjo Guarnido
Arctic Nation (*Arctic-nation*)
L'histoire des Aquarelles, Tome 2
Red Soul (*Ame rouge*)
The Hell, The Silence (*L'enfer, le Silence*)
The Sketch Files (*L'histoire des Aquarelles, Tome 1*)

Like a bastard son of Walt Disney, John Blacksad is a feline private detective in a seedy world of talking animals. When the actress Natalia Wilford—Blacksad's former lover—is murdered, business becomes personal. His investigations quickly lead him to search for a mysterious "guy with bulging eyes" who does not want to be found and is willing to send hired muscle against Blacksad to stop him.

While the writing is excellent, the most striking thing about *Blacksad* is the stunning artwork. An ex-Disney animator and storyboard artist, Juanjo Guarnido has taken all he learned about visual style from Disney and applied it to the dark underworld of Dashiell Hammett, Raymond Chandler, and Mickey Spillane. Painted in beautifully warm and detailed watercolors, Guarnido brings the world of American noir and anthropomorphism together in a powerful head-on collision. The stories are well trodden but expertly told; and the simple act of placing them in the usually safe world of anthropomorphized animals gives them a fresh energy.

"When I walk into my office, I get the impression that I'm walking among the ruins of a lost civilization."

Later stories include *Arctic Nation* (*Arctic-nation*), in which the anthropomorphic theme is explored to its fullest with the rise of a white supremacist organization, led by an Arctic fox, which begins with the lynching of a vulture. *Red Soul* (*Ame rouge*), the third volume, explores Cold War paranoia and nuclear fears, as Blacksad becomes embroiled in the assassination of Communist intellectuals. All explore tough themes, but Juan Díaz Canales approaches them with the brazenness of his hero, making *Blacksad* one of the most important works to emerge in contemporary European comics. **BD**

Alan's War 2000

Emmanuel Guibert

Emmanuel Guibert was thirty years old when he met Alan Ingram Cope, a sixty-nine-year-old retired American World War II veteran living in l'Ile de Ré. The men became close friends, and the author used an old recorder to archive Cope's memories, beginning from childhood to his arrival as a G.I. in France in 1945. Guibert then translated Cope's memories into comics, literally "drawing Alan's memories" to give them a second life.

Prepublished in L'Association's anthology magazine *Lapin*, the three *Alan's War* books retell Cope's life from the beginning of the war to his old age and death. Guibert reveals his plans to revisit Cope's childhood in California in the future. Despite this description, Cope's memories do not linger in any sort of romanticized perspective on war, and even less so on a heroic stance. Most of the episodes are prosaic, but that is what makes this work such an emotionally moving and relevant title: it explores what constitutes a common humanity, with insights that are both humorous and poignant. It is also about the workings of memory and forgetting and the role they play in forming an individual.

"Uncle Sam told me he'd like me to put on a uniform and go off to fight a guy by the name of Adolf. So I did."

Guibert uses Indian ink mixed with water in a container he created himself, which allows him to draw quickly and calligraphically. His figures are solid, with thick outlines and complex textures. He plays with chiaroscuro and blinding whites, taking advantage of an apparently limited medium. *Alan's War* is a multilayered comic in a simple package that reveals an unusual side to wartime life. **PM**

Title in original language *La guerre d'Alan*
First published by L'Association (France)
Creator French (b.1964)
Genre War

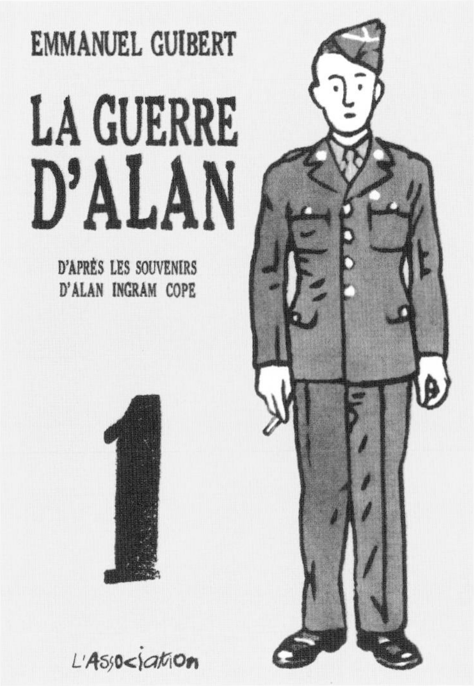
EMMANUEL GUIBERT
LA GUERRE D'ALAN
D'APRÈS LES SOUVENIRS D'ALAN INGRAM COPE
1
L'Association

Also by Emmanuel Guibert

Ariol
Sardine in Outer Space (*Sardine de l'espace*)
The Photographer: Into War-torn Afghanistan with Doctors Without Borders (*Le Photographe*)
The Professor's Daughter (*La fille du Professeur*)

Louis 2000

✎ John Chalmers ✎ Sandra Marrs

First published by Metaphrog (UK)
Creators Chalmers (British, b.1965);
Marrs (French, b.1974)
Genre Children's

Louis lives and works alone in the town of Hamlet, alone except for his companion and pet, F.C. (short for Formulaic Companion), a mechanical bird confined to a cage. The other inhabitants of Hamlet are content to eat their rations and occupy their spare time with entertainment centers, but Louis dreams about the mountains. Louis has been convinced by his not-so-friendly neighbors, Clean and Jerk Quidnunc, that he has an aunt, and he writes to her about his daily activities.

In "Red Letter Day," Louis has to rescue F.C. from his neighbors and attempts to reach the mountains. In "Lying to Clive," Louis is arrested and sent to a bee farm where he meets Clive, a bee trying to fly. "The Clown's Last Words" sees Louis back in Hamlet, facing weekly interrogations by the Cheeseman Information Agency, which wants to find out what he knows about the underground. Louis is diverted, however, by trying to design a new game for a competition associated with a mandatory fun day. In "Dreams Never Die," Louis decides to visit Aunt Alison, believing her to be ill, and in "Night Salad," Louis and F.C. succumb to the effects of a chemical spill and go looking for a cure.

Louis appears to be a naive everyman, strangely ignorant of his surroundings and role in life. The stories explore themes of friendship, control through surveillance, narcotics, and authoritarianism in surreal, fantastic ways. Ostensibly comics for children, these are multilayered adventures for all ages, proving themselves enigmatic and oddly disturbing. Although sometimes hard to fathom, they are ultimately charming. **NFI**

Sky Doll 2000

✎ Barbara Canepa ✎ Alessandro Barbucci

First published by Vittorio Pavesio (Italy), Soleil (France)
Creators Canepa (Italian, b.1969);
Barbucci (Italian, b.1973)
Genre Science fiction

In the late 1990s, European authors started to incorporate manga elements into their comics. Among them were Barbara Canepa and Alessandro Barbucci, whose pop series *Sky Doll* became a trendsetting model for a general shift to postmanga styles in the character design of Italian and French comics.

The main character of this dystopian science fiction saga, set on the planets Papathea and Aqua, is Noa. She is one of many android dolls created for the sexual purposes of their owners, for them to use without committing sin. Her personality is unusual for an android, and unlike an ordinary robot, she has a certain spirituality. Noa's universe is thrown into conflict by two female "popes": the spiritual and ethereal Agape, and the sensual and spectacular Lodovica. After Noa's owner is murdered, she meets two interstellar missionaries, Roy and Jahu, and joins them to help spread the heretic religion of Lodovica. During the series, elements of Noa's repressed memories arise, implying she has a connection to Agape.

Religion, media power, and sexuality are the main subjects of this acute and provocative sci-fi comedy. Prior to *Sky Doll*, Barbucci and Canepa cocreated the best-selling Disney preteen girl comic *W.I.T.C.H.*, and the horror comedy *Monster Allergy*. With *Sky Doll* the duo deliver a more adult mood, with complex themes and nudity. *Sky Doll* also offers a richer aesthetic, influenced by French comics, anime, Disney, and baroque and psychedelic art. Its distinctive, stunning style is also notable for its lavish and nuanced digital coloring. **MS**

Sky Doll tackles heavy issues, including religion and sexuality. ➡

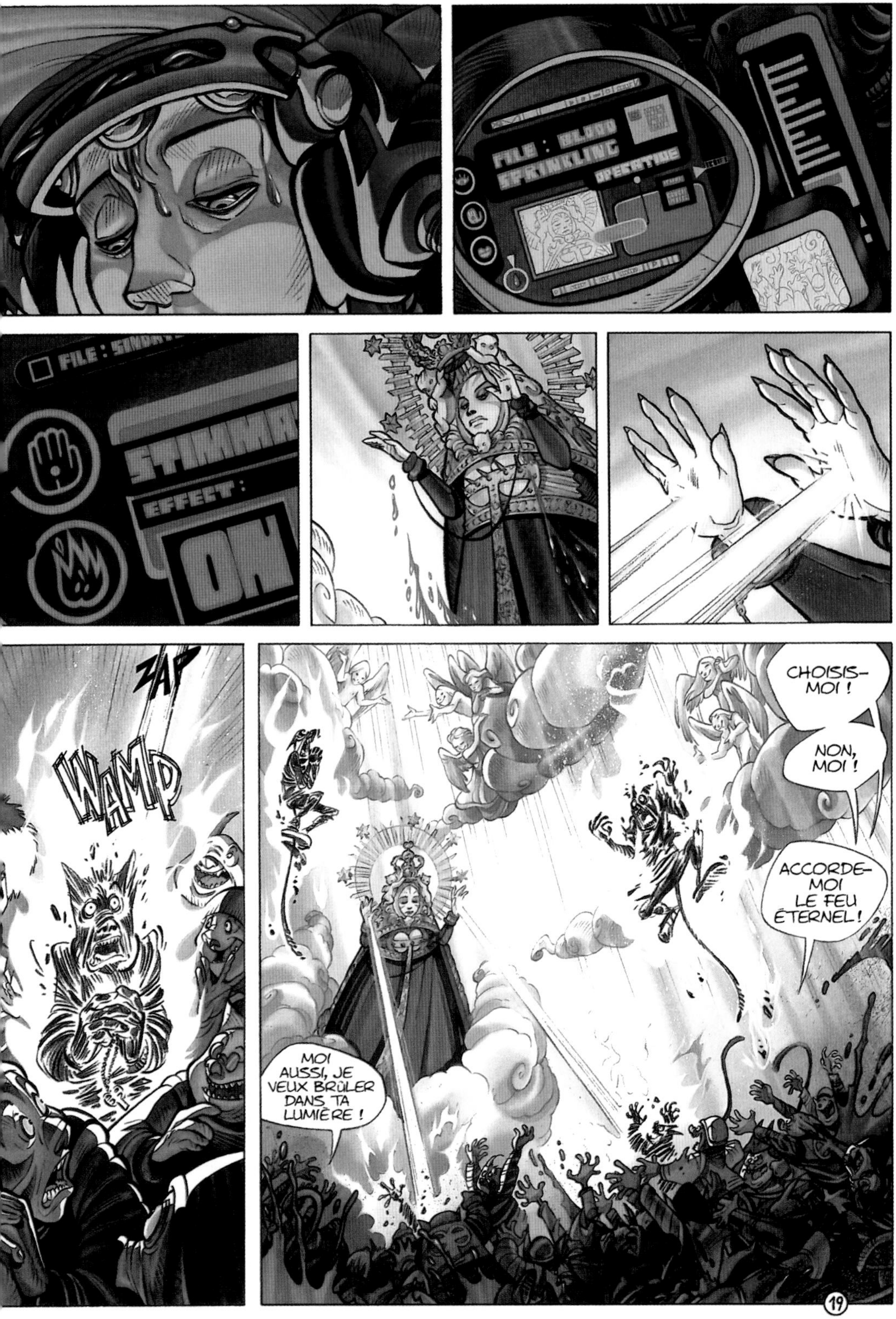
FILE : BLOOD
SPRINKLING
OPERATING
EFFECT :
ON
ZAP
WAMP
CHOISIS-MOI !
NON, MOI !
ACCORDE-MOI LE FEU ÉTERNEL !
MOI AUSSI, JE VEUX BRÛLER DANS TA LUMIÈRE !

Honey and Clover 2000

Chica Umino

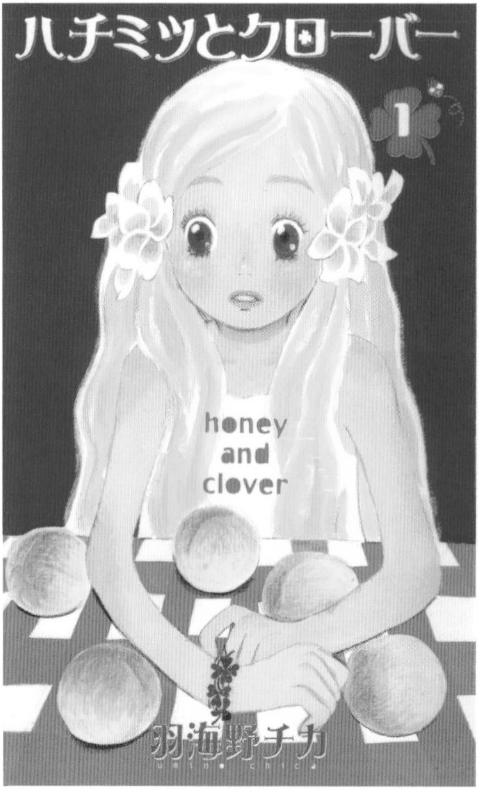
ハチミツとクローバー
1
honey
and
clover
羽海野チカ

"I realized why I'm lost. It is not because I don't have a map. What I do not have is . . . my destination."

Similar reads

Flower of Life (*Furawā obu Raifu*) Fumi Yoshinaga
March Comes in Like a Lion (*Sangatsu no Raionx*) Chica Umino

Title in original language *Hachimitsu to Kurōbā*
First published by Shueisha (Japan)
Creator Japanese (Unknown)
Genre Soap opera

Honey and Clover is wonderfully funny, sweet, and cute, but also contains some harsh realities. One of the central characters of this ensemble cast manga is Yuta Takemoto, an art student in Tokyo, who lives in the same apartment complex as his fellow students, Takumi Mayama and Shinobu Morita. One day Takemoto meets a shy girl, Hagumi Hanamoto, a promising artist, and falls in love with her. However, his senior colleague, the eccentric genius Shinobu, is also interested in her.

The characters are close friends and spend their life at art college together happily (most of the time), but sometimes they struggle as they wonder about their unknown futures and lose themselves in their relationships. The narrative tells of unrequited love, friendship, and how the characters find their way in the world after they leave college.

Chica Umino's drawing style is cute yet realistically detailed, paying special attention to the props and backgrounds and reflecting the complex tensions in her characters' lives. She designs her characters well and in minute detail, both inside and out, which is one of the reasons the story works. Some of them are perfectly average, and the way they dress, behave, think, feel, and talk make them appear familiar, as if the reader may know them in real life. Adolescent readers can identify with their problems, and older ones relive their youth and enjoy the bittersweet taste of nostalgia.

Umino's love and passion for her characters infuses them with spirit, making *Honey and Clover* a work for everyone, irrespective of age or gender. **CK**

20th Century Boys 2000

✐✐ Naoki Urasawa

Title in original language *Nijusseiki Shonen*
First published by Shogakukan (Japan)
Creator Japanese (b.1960)
Genre Science fiction

In Japan at the end of the 1960s, a group of children wrote a science fiction story. The book retraced the numerous disasters that have battered humanity and threatened its very existence, and starred the kids as saviors who intervened to preserve the Earth.

Almost three decades later, one of the children, Kenji Endo, remembers the childhood story after a member of the group commits suicide, accompanied by the enigmatic reappearance of the pictogram that the children used as a rallying sign and a symbol of their unbreakable friendship. Reluctantly, he follows in the steps of a millenarist sect run by a mysterious charismatic leader and discovers the elements of a plot, the consequences of which could turn out to be dire for humanity. But the most astonishing occurrence is that events copy the Book of Prophecy in which the children had related the story of the end of the world.

Like *Monster* (*Monsuta*), the other outstanding work of Naoki Urasawa, *20th Century Boys* is a series filled with multiple ramifications, populated by a large number of characters, but with a level of complexity added. The story interweaves several distinct timelines, an incomparable technique for maintaining the suspense while sustaining the plot. A great thriller and an impressive science fiction story, *20th Century Boys* throws light on contemporary concerns regarding propaganda, manipulation, and conspiracy theories, and these weighty issues are readily assimilated in the course of reading. It is also a parable with much to say on the creative power of the imagination. **NF**

Sexy Voice and Robo 2000

✐✐ Iou Kuroda

First published by Shogakukan (Japan)
Creator Japanese (b.1971)
Genre Crime
Award Manga Grand Prize (2002)

Nico Hayashi (Sexy Voice) is a perky fourteen-year-old girl posing as a phone-sex operator for anthropological amusement. With an uncanny ability to remember and mimic any voice she hears, she is hired by an aging gangster to investigate cases involving a kidnapped boy, a disillusioned businessman, a manipulative lover, and a *Memento*-like amnesiac assassin. She teams up with one of her clients, a nerdy man named Iichiro Sudo—nicknamed "Robo" for his love of robot action figures. Naive and dull-witted, the antithesis of the confident and savvy Hayashi, Sudo becomes Nico's comic sidekick.

Iou Kuroda writes clever, convincing dialogue to complement his serial mystery episodes. Each of the thirteen character-driven stories in *Sexy Voice and Robo* is complete, but the volume is a unified work, containing ongoing themes and subplots full of witty, ironic humor. Although some stories present extreme circumstances, they are full of understated, keenly observed moments with delicate attention to detail. Kuroda's quirky, engaging characters are placed within an accurate portrait of modern Tokyo with its love hotels, shops, subways, bookshops, and cafés.

Kuroda's drawing is extraordinarily dynamic. With command of brush, marker, or pen, he can capture naturalistic, personality-revealing gestures with a few casual lines, imbuing his characters with easy grace. He is not afraid to use broad, exuberant brushstrokes and scratchy pen lines, and his backgrounds are fluid and evocative. His storytelling makes use of both fragmented time and cinematic crosscutting. **TRL**

Jimmy Corrigan, The Smartest Kid on Earth 2000

Chris Ware

First published by Pantheon Books (USA)
Creator American (b.1967)
Genre Drama
Award Eisner Award (2000)

JIMMY
THE SMARTEST KID ON EARTH
OFFICIAL
PAPERBOUND
APOLOGUE

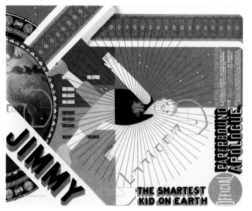

"Comics, at least in periodical form, exist almost entirely free of any pretense; the critical world of art hardly touches them, and they're 100 percent personal."

Chris Ware

Also by Chris Ware:
Acme Novelty Library
Building Stories
Quimby the Mouse
Rusty Brown
The Super-Man

The comic strips of *Jimmy Corrigan, The Smartest Kid on Earth* first appeared in 1992—as a series and without an overall plan—in a free weekly publication in Chicago. By the following year they had been partly republished in the *ACME Novelty Library*, a series of short books containing Chris Ware's work. At that time there was nothing to suggest that these weekly comic strips would add up to this brilliant, perfectly coherent album of 380 pages published by Pantheon Books in 2000.

The book caused a sensation in the strip cartoon world, similar to that caused in his day by Art Spiegelman with *Maus*. The homogenous quality of Ware's work is all the more surprising in that it is a saga that spans more than a century. The unparalleled tale has a story line of almost Proustian complexity, hinged on endless shuttling back and forth across three generations of characters of the same family, each of whom bears a resemblance to Jimmy and also shares the same name or nickname, as if they were all nursing the same atavism.

Ware describes his hero as "a lonely, emotionally impaired human castaway," clearly confirming the impression of overriding melancholy that permeates his work. In minute detail the reader follows the trials and tribulations of a lonely thirty-something who is seriously inhibited as far as action is concerned and devoid of all ambition, but who nevertheless dreams desperately about being Superman. In this context, where waiting is always predominant, Ware's genius comes into its own in his inventive representation and constantly renewed vision of someone bogged down by everyday life. *Jimmy Corrigan*'s almost slow-motion representation of life and its languor expresses the sensation of time, its architecture, density, modulation, and ductility providing the background for a discreet melody: the outpouring of a conscience. **JS**

I'll Be Back Shortly 2000

Frank Odoi

"Out of Africa always something new," said the Roman general Scipio Africanus a long time ago. And *I'll Be Back Shortly* is another shining confirmation of this truth.

Frank Odoi's *Golgoti* series was first published as consecutive strips in Tanzania, Uganda, Ghana, and Kenya. *Golgoti* is Odoi's native Ghana, which was known for its gold. The name is a corruption of Gold Coast, Ghana's colonial name. Part one of *Golgoti* has been published as the album *I'll Be Back Shortly*, and parts two, three, and four follow it up.

Although ostensibly about a white man who comes to Africa, the stories are told from an African man's perspective and written as a satire that is never cruel. Odoi makes fun of the constantly sweating colonialists who arrive for the gold, exploit the country, and break numerous taboos and traditions along the way.

The story begins when Gomez, a white man, lands in West Africa and trades his gun to Goma, a son of the soil, for some gold balls. Gomez returns for more gold, and nominates himself as father, eventually coming to stay. He explains to Goma: "I have been promoted, from today you will call me Master". At the independence negotiations Goma accepts that new strings must be attached. He becomes president and, just one week after inauguration, detains his first dissident. The stories also explore modern-day Africa, which Odoi portrays with subtle and poignant satire.

Odoi is an African comics artist whose stories always have a moral ingredient, just like the region's traditional oral stories. Born in Tarkwa, a mining town in western Ghana, he studied at Ghanatta Art College in Accra before joining the Medical School in Ghana as an assistant medical artist. He moved to Nairobi, Kenya, in 1979 and started drawing political cartoons for the *Daily Nation*. His production is immense, his themes reflective, and his pen is both quick and elegant. **LP**

First published by Oxford University Press (East Africa)
Creator Ghanaian (b.1948)
Genre Political fable
Award Ghana Cartoonist of the Year (2005)

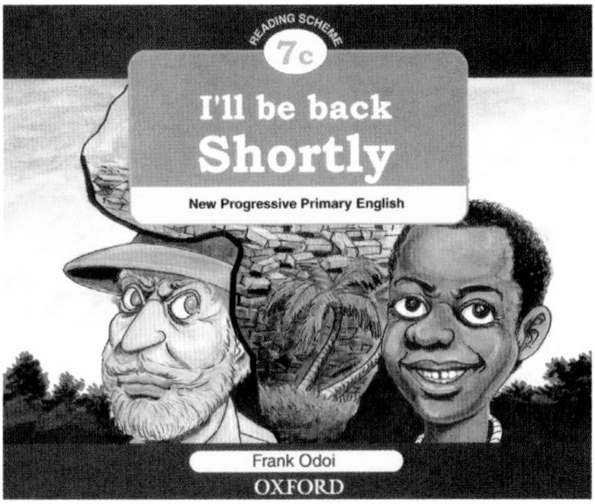
READING SCHEME
7c
I'll be back
Shortly
New Progressive Primary English
Frank Odoi
OXFORD

"I like watching Hollywood blockbuster, fantasy/horror/suspense movies. These and the follies of human nature inspire me. My role models were the artists . . . I hold in high esteem."

Frank Odoi

Also by Frank Odoi

Akokhan
Laban
The Mermaid of Motaba
The Wisdom of Africa : A Unique Collection of Listener's Proverbs

La Perdida 2000

Jessica Abel

First published by Fantagraphics Books (USA)
Creator American (b.1969)
Genre Reality drama
Award Harvey Award for Best New Series (2002)

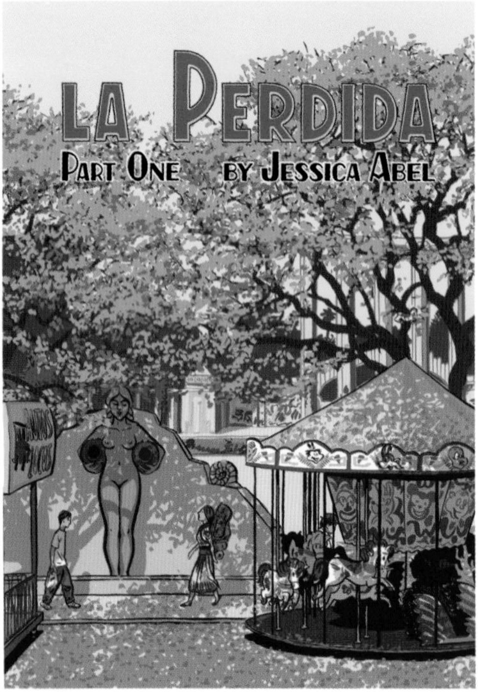
LA PERDIDA
PART ONE BY JESSICA ABEL

Similar reads
Artbabe Jessica Abel
Ghost World Daniel Clowes
Life Sucks Jessica Abel, Gabriel Soria, and Warren Pleece
Locas Jaime Hernández
Palomar Gilbert Hernández

The title translates as "the lost girl," although the story is more about finding oneself through sometimes bitter understanding. Carla is a twenty-something American girl estranged from an absent Mexican father and has an unhealthy fixation with Frida Kahlo She decides to reconnect with her roots south of the border by moving to Mexico City despite barely speaking Spanish.

Her experiences are narrated in three overlapping acts that move her from ignorance and innocence to hard-earned experience. At first she lives with a group of largely insular expatriates, including a truly obnoxious boyfriend. Then, craving more authenticity, Carla moves closer to a group of Mexican friends and lovers, losing her embarrassing ethnic accessories in the process. Finally, the story turns toward something darker that dramatically puts into context all the minor acts and decisions that have led Carla along thus far.

As the title character attempts to shed her American skin in this *bildungsroman*, the reader becomes aware that such a disavowal of her identity is problematic. Some of her Mexican friends are content to denounce American imperialism continually, while others would be only too happy to trade the day-to-day tribulations of Mexico City for opportunities across the border.

Initially, *La Perdida* was serialized by Fantagraphics from 2000 to 2005, before being revised and collected as a graphic novel by Pantheon in 2006. Despite some superficial resemblances with her protagonist—Abel moved for a brief period to Mexico City with her husband, comics artist Matt Madden—the story is not autobiographical. However, her sojourn helps create a strong sense of authenticity with its vivid depiction of physical environment and social milieu. Abel's black-and-white, ink-and-brush style expressively charts and complements Carla's transformation from an innocent abroad to an experienced young woman. **TV**

Betelgeuse 2000

"Léo"

Betelgeuse is the most successful of the narrative cycles that make up the epic that is the *Worlds of Aldebaran* (*Les Mondes d'Aldébaran*). It deals with the exploration of space and human expansion in the universe.

In the twenty-second century, encouraged to leave the solar system by the twin effects of the worsening conditions of life on Earth and the progress made in the technology of interstellar travel, humans have begun to colonize other worlds. Having settled successfully in the system of Aldebaran, the explorers have sent a mission to the sixth planet of Betelgeuse. But the expedition goes wrong. Isolated from their spacecraft, which has remained in orbit, and unable to make contact with the base they have left, the crew settles on the planet and founds two communities: one on the cliff side, the canyon group, and the other in the middle of a plain, the desert group. The two groups soon become enemies.

The heroine of the saga, Kim Keller, is sent by the Aldebaran colony to help the planet of Betelgeuse, and discovers a situation of conflict on her arrival. Tugged between the opposing survivors, she transfers her interest to the strange animals she discovers there, the "iums," the behavior of which suggests that they might be a more evolved species—a discovery that could put a stop to the process of colonization. She also finds on Betelgeuse traces of the "mantrisse," an extraterrestrial animal with mysterious powers that had been discovered on the planet of her birth.

While including various adventures typical of epic stories, *Betelgeuse* is, above all, a story about exploration. Léo is fascinated by the fauna and flora of the strange worlds he creates, portraying them with a profusion of details of rare luxuriance. The breath of a distant world can be felt throughout each episode of this rich saga, the evocative power of which has made it a classic in science fiction comics. **NF**

First published by Dargaud (France)
Creator Luiz Eduardo de Oliviera (Brazilian, b.1944)
Genre Science fiction
Award Nominated for Angoulême Series Award (2004)

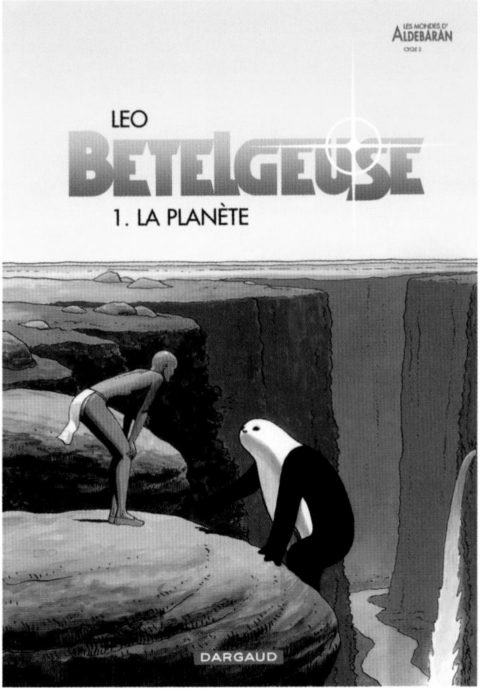
LES MONDES D' ALDEBARAN
LEO
BETELGEUSE
1. LA PLANÈTE
DARGAUD

Also by Léo

Dexter London with Sergio García
Gandhi, the Pilgrim of Peace (*Gandhi, le Pèlerin de la Paix*) with Benoît Marchon
Kenya with Rodolphe
Trent with Rodolphe and Scarlett Smulkowski

GoGo Monster 2000

Taiyo Matsumoto

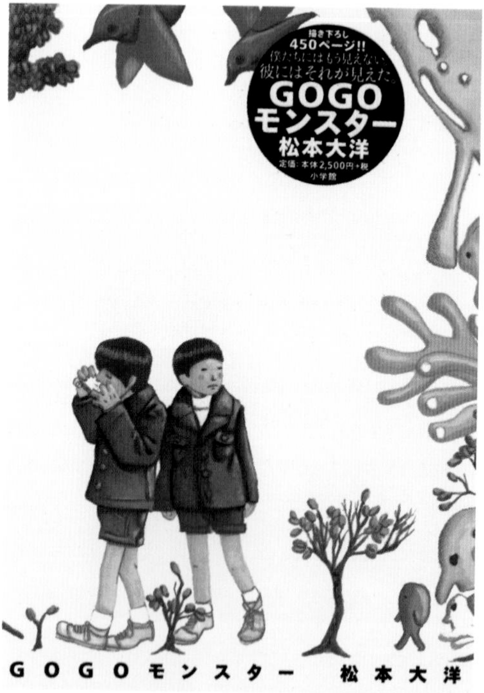

描き下ろし
450ページ!!
僕たちにはもう見えない。
彼にはそれが見えた。
GOGO
モンスター
松本大洋
定価：本体2,500円+税
小学館
GOGOモンスター 松本大洋

"I drew GoGo Monster *on commission for over three years, and it didn't go as smoothly as I thought it would."*

Also by Taiyo Matsumoto

Blue Spring (*Aoi Haru*)
Hana Otoko
Number Five
Ping Pong
Tekkonkinkreet **(*Tekkon Kinkurīto*)**

First published in Shogakukan (Japan)
Creator Japanese (b.1967)
Genre Fantasy
Award Excellence Award for Manga (2007)

Yuki Tachibana is an ordinary-looking student who readily conjures up "the others," imaginary creatures that are ubiquitous in his surroundings, but he is the only person who can see them. Since the rest of the school cannot understand the situation, his talent keeps him apart from his fellow students, who ignore him and treat him like a pariah.

Fortunately there are a few exceptions, such as old Gantsu, the school odd-job man, who shows tolerance and affection for the dreamlike sensitivity of the little boy, and in particular Makoto Suzuki, a student newly arrived at the school. This is the beginning of a friendship reinforced by Makoto's gradual awakening to the world of invisible spirits that Yuki inhabits. Throughout this sumptuous graphic novel, it is never revealed exactly what the perceptions of young Yuki are. An infectious illness? The inner visions of an autistic child? Or a dazzling glimpse of that secret world to which only children, empowered in their innocence, have the key?

Without resorting to sensationalism, Matsumoto makes a powerful impression with his fluency and boldness. This is the work of an author that can be read as a metaphor of the transition to adulthood, complete with all its bittersweetness. One can also interpret it as a ballet of elemental spirits, an ecological and contemporary extension of the old Japanese animism. Whatever it is, following many striking works such as *Number Five* and *Tekkonkinkreet*, *GoGo Monster* is an outstanding work that everyone can enjoy. **NF**

80°C 2000

✏️ Yao Fei La

Published by Big Kana (France)
Creator Chinese (b.1974)
Genre Reality drama
Influence on *Pink Diary*

80°C. The title reveals Yao Gei La's agenda from the start and he explains its significance in the subtitle to remind those of us who may have forgotten: "If love had a temperature, you would remember what it was. . . ." This is the background for a long series—*80°C* consists of eight volumes of short stories—all of which gravitate around the daily (and emotional) lives of Chinese youth.

There is nothing fundamentally revolutionary in these stories marked with the stamp of "real life": they exhibit the freshness of tone and acute observations that are typical of Yao Fei La's work. In one story is a young girl who blossoms on coming into contact with a stage director more than ten years older than herself; in another a video games enthusiast compares his virtual experience with the games of seduction he encounters in reality.

Making matters even more interesting are the slices of life that provide an account of a modern urban Chinese reality, which is little known to the rest of the world and are far removed from the usual clichés about China. Yao Fei La began producing manhua (comics) in 1995 when he was barely more than twenty, and since then he has not stopped observing the world in his unique way. The natural leader of a new generation of authors who have started to liberate the narrative and formal conventions of China, with *80°C* Yao Fei La has created a comics series that is inspired by the spirit of freedom. It only remains to hope that he will continue to be allowed to express himself. **NF**

Yukiko's Spinach 2000

✏️ Frédéric Boilet

Title in original languages *L'Epinard de Yukiko / Yukiko no Hôrensô* **First published by** Ego comme X (France); Ohta Shuppan (Japan)
Creator French (b.1960) **Genre** Romance

One April day in Japan, at the opening of an exhibition, the narrator of this story—a French comics author based in Tokyo who bears a striking resemblance to Frédéric Boilet—meets a beautiful, young Japanese woman, Yukiko, to whom he declares his love. Although tempted, Yukiko does not hide the fact that she is also attracted to another man, Boilet's friend Hashimoto.

After a dogged courtship, the narrator persuades Yukiko to venture into a romantic relationship with him, even if it is a short one without a future. The relationship, in which she becomes the artist's model also allows the author to explore the ambiguous relationship between an artist and his muse. Boilet opts for a deliberately frank style in portraying the intimacy of a relationship, including graphic sex scenes that manage to remain tender. Such frankness is accentuated by his photo-realist technique, which is based on graphically reworked photographs. Nonetheless, this graphic novel also provides an interesting account of everyday life in Tokyo.

After being prepublished in a Japanese magazine, the book was issued simultaneously in 2001 by French publisher Ego comme X, which has almost exclusively adopted autobiographical comics as its speciality. Such an unusual positioning only lends more weight to this singular, perfectly realized book. The initiative also reflects Boilet's unusual status as one of the few Western authors to have lived in Japan and become sufficiently immersed in the culture to act as a conduit between the worlds of Japanese and European comics. **NF**

Deogratias, a Tale of Rwanda 2000

Jean-Philippe Stassen

Title in original language *Déogratias*
First published by Dupuis (Belgium)
Creator Belgian (b.1966)
Genre Reality drama

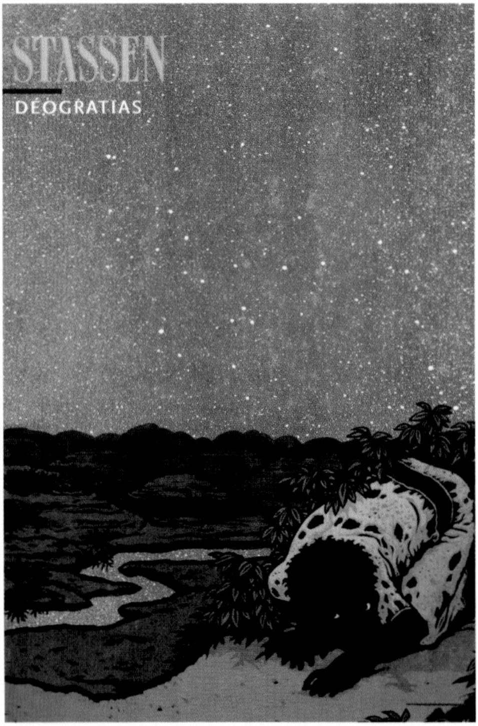
STASSEN
DÉOGRATIAS

Also by Jean-Philippe Stassen
Le bar du vieux Français with Denis Lapière
Les enfants
Louis le Portuguais
Pawa, chronique des monts de la lune

How can a comics artist portray unspeakable events? Jean-Philippe Stassen's subject in *Deogratias* is the 1994 genocide in Rwanda. His title means "Thanks be to God," and is also the name of his teenage protagonist. Its irony hangs heavily over the work. The graphic style, with distinctive thick black outlines and dense color, gives the comic book the look of a children's book, and so renders all the more disturbing the horror that takes an ordinary young man into the heart of darkness.

Deogratias is the witness upon whom the reader must rely, but the narration of his story is not straightforward because he displays the symptoms of trauma. The character is introduced in the aftermath of the massacre, crazed and intoxicated by alcohol.

"Deogratias . . . keeps the reader distant from the atrocities."

Publishers Weekly

The sudden flashbacks, which occur with no transition, evoke the involuntary memories that torment him. They also create suspense, as the reader becomes apprehensive about what must have happened to reduce the boy to this abject state.

The episodes recollected from before the atrocities depict Deogratias as a mischievous adolescent, a Hutu with a crush on a Tutsi girl. Any resemblance to the French photo-romances that he reads ends there. The buildup to the slaughter gathers momentum against a background of ethnic rivalries fomented by the former colonial occupiers. Deogratias's imagination is haunted by bigoted teachers, arrogant soldiers, hypocritical Catholic priests, and by his own actions. Stassen does not attempt to chronicle the historical process, preferring to draw the reader deep into the nightmare from which his protagonist can never wake. **AM**

Powers
Who Killed Retro Girl? 2000

Brian Michael Bendis   Michael Avon Oeming

A 1993 comic called *Cape City* showcased private investigators handling cases in a city populated by superpowered individuals. Entertainingly written but poorly drawn, it flopped. Several years later a very similar concept, far better handled, proved a gold mine for Brian Michael Bendis and Michael Avon Oeming.

In terms of comics, Oeming was an artistic prodigy, paid for his talents as young as fourteen. Five years later he was given the poisoned chalice of drawing original *Judge Dredd* stories for the U.S. market, and in the wake of the subsequent criticism his career foundered.

Who Killed Retro Girl? introduces police detectives Christian Walker and his new partner Deena Pilgrim, operating in a city overflowing with superpowers. Parity is only restored in customized cells and interview rooms where abilities are deactivated. Pilgrim is short, motor-mouthed, and aggressive, while Walker is large, reserved, and cautious. It's a classic setup of contrasts that plays to Bendis's facility for smart,yet never unrealistic dialogue, and Oeming adopts a style prioritizing light and shade. He initially wanted the comic black and white, but the thoughtfully applied color by Pat Garrahy creates a unique look.

The investigation into the murder of the nation's favorite superhero turns over several stones and offers insight into the detectives beyond their initial broad strokes. A witty page-turner, the volume more than adequately established *Powers*. Walker generates several surprises, one here, then in subsequent volumes, which stand as more than just reruns. There is a continuity, but it is not all-important, so each stands individually. **FP**

"I'm a storyteller; that means writing as well as art."

Michael Avon Oeming

First published by Image Comics (USA)
Creators Bendis (American, b.1967); Oeming (American, b.1975)
Genre Superhero

POWERS
Who Killed Retro Girl?
BRIAN MICHAEL BENDIS
MICHAEL AVON OEMING
PAT GARRAHY

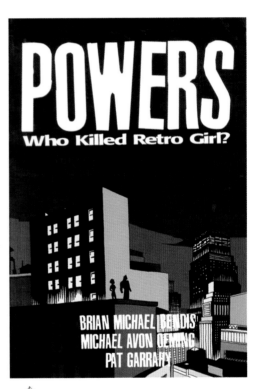

Also by Michael Avon Oeming
Powers with Brian Michael Bendis
Rapture with Taki Soma
The Foot Soldiers with Jim Krueger
The Mice Templar with Bryan J. L. Glass

Berlin: City of Stones 2001

✎ Jason Lutes

JASON LUTES
AUTHOR OF JAR OF FOOLS

Berlin

CITY OF STONES

BOOK ONE

"Have you ever seen such madness? Look at them all racing about in their machines. An affront...."

Similar reads

Exit Wounds Rutu Modan
Jar of Fools Jason Lutes
Locas Jaime Hernandez
Maus: A Survivor's Tale Art Speigelman
Palomar Gilbert Hernandez

First published by Black Eye Productions (Canada) and Drawn & Quarterly (Canada)
Creator American (b.1967)
Genre History, Drama

The first of a planned trilogy, *Berlin: City of Stones* is a hugely ambitious work, and one that displays a calm confidence. Part soap opera and part historical drama, it is the story of ordinary people living in Berlin during the tumultuous period of the Weimar Republic. Beginning with art student Marthe Müller's journey to Berlin by train, we are introduced to Müller and her future boyfriend, Kurt Severing.

Beside them in the railway car is a member of the Nazi Party, fast asleep; it is an apt metaphor for the time in which the story starts. As readers watch Müller go about her art course, make friends, and grow more attached to Severing, they also see many political factions fighting one another for dominance. A family is torn apart by politics as one half joins the Nazis and the other half the Communists, while police try to contain these warring sides. Acts of comradeship and acts of cruelty are seen through multiple viewpoints and from all sides, building up to the fateful May Day Parade of 1929.

Lutes's writing is meticulous and unsensational; he isn't interested in flashy images and snappy scenes. He confidently takes the time to develop his characters and explain the nuances of the city, neatly drawn in black and white, allowing the reader to feel fully immersed in Weimar-era Berlin. It's clear that Lutes has done his research. This feels very much like a living, breathing city—a window into a place that has, more than any other, been at the heart of the twentieth century and sliding toward its darkest hour. **BD**

Cola Madness 2001

✐🖊 Gary Panter

First published by Funny Garbage (USA)
Creator American (b.1950)
Genre Alternative, Science fiction
Awards Masters of American Comics (2006–7)

The great lost graphic novel by one of the form's towering talents, *Cola Madness* was originally created in 1983 but was not published for eighteen years. Having seen Panter's work in *RAW*, Shizuo Ishii enquired about publishing it in Japanese. Thinking that he had been asked to create an entirely new work, Panter produced this, his longest story to date. When no publisher was subsequently found to take on the project, the story languished for nearly two decades.

Like much of Panter's work, *Cola Madness* revolves around characters in a tribal, postapocalyptic future. The cast is more expansive here than in his better-known *Jimbo* books, but the characters are just as archetypal. The story focuses on a motley crew of misfits including Bob War, the crocodilelike Uncle Garcia, Salari Fuzz, and Kokomo, a tribal figure who introduces the story. Working with a Japanese audience in mind, Panter throws huge clumps of Americana into a blender and whips up a concoction that aims for universal significance. The result is sheer madness.

The significant difference between *Cola Madness* and Panter's other works resides in the framing. The vast bulk of the book is presented as two discrete panels per page. In the absence of the sprawling, anarchic page layouts that define his *Jimbo* work, the reader is left to contemplate his masterfully scratchy line work and the clear expression of a narrative dimension. In many ways *Cola Madness* is the most traditional of Panter's work. This change of pace allows an entirely different set of the artist's skills to take center stage. **BB**

Cromartie High School 2001

✐🖊 Eiji Nonaka

Title in original language *Sakigake!! Cromartie Koko*
First published by Kodansha (Japan)
Creator Japanese (b.1965)
Genre Humor

To fully appreciate the central theme of this comic, one should acknowledge the culture of the Japanese *Yanki* (derived from the word "Yankee," although there is no direct link between the two meanings). *Yanki* refers to a subculture of delinquent youths who vaguely stand somewhere between hooligans and gangs, and since first appearing in the 1980s have become a popular subject in the Japanese boys' comic scene. A subgenre dubbed *Yanki* comics has emerged as a result. While the *Yanki* in *Cromartie High School* maintain the stereotypical nature of this culture, Eiji Nonaka parodies the subgenre by replacing the typical themes with gags of utter nonsense.

The plot revolves around delinquent students of the notoriously low-ranking Cromartie High School who are feared for their *Yanki* reputation, although in reality they are just a group of surprisingly dull-witted boys. Insanely imaginative, Nonaka places the characters in crazy situations, like being hijacked during an excursion and getting lost in a mysterious underground empire.

The beauty of these stories is that there is nothing deep or coherent about its concept. The main characters that are supposedly teenagers look middle-aged, excluding one named β (Beta) Mechazawa, who looks like a robot. Takashi Kamiyama, the central character, is extremely low profile, and at one point he did not appear in the series for seven consecutive weeks. *Cromartie High School* was serialized in *Shukan Shonen Magazine* in 2000 and received the Kodansha Manga Award for Boys' Manga in 2002. **TS**

Chobits 2001

✎✎ "CLAMP"

First published by Kodansha (Japan)
Creators Japanese: Ageha Ohkawa (b.1967); Tsubaki Nekoi (b.1969); Mokona Apapa (b.1968); Satsuki Igarashi (b.1969)
Genre Science fiction, Romance

First released at the beginning of the twenty-first century, *Chobits* is a futuristic romance by comics collective CLAMP. The story focuses on a young man's life with Chi, the *bishōjo* android. CLAMP, a group of four Japanese female comic artists, is known for girls' comics and their animated series *Card Captor Sakura* and *Magic Knight Rayearth*. *Chobits* is an exception the rule, however, and targets a male audience. It was originally serialized in the boys' comic *Young Magazine*.

Set in a world where computers have developed into androids, the story questions the classic theme of romance between humans and robots. The central character, Hideki Motosuwa, moves from Hokkaido to Tokyo in order to attend a preparatory school after failing to pass the entrance exam to a university. A *ronin,* or "held-back" student (a high school graduate studying for another chance to enter the next level), is featured in various boys' comics, applying the golden rule that if a *bishōjo* is involved, the central male character should be less than perfect.

On the day of his arrival, Hideki finds a *bishojo* android computer and names it Chi after the only word she seems able to say. Hideki teaches the android words and manners, but struggles to keep his distance from Chi, who seems to be developing feelings for him. Hideki begins to question Chi's behavior, suspecting that she could be one of the Chobits, or androids with emotion. Many agree that the story line of this comic, though distinctly different from most CLAMP titles, best reflects the essence of the group's talent. **TS**

The Journal of K. 2001

✎ Raul Brandão ✎ Filipe Abranches

Title in original language *O Diário de K.*
First published by Edições Polvo (Portugal)
Creators Brandão (Portuguese, 1867–1930); Abranches (Portuguese, b.1965) **Genre** Drama

---

Filipe Abranches belongs to the *Lx Comics* generation. The "Lx" acronym doesn't stand for *lux* (light), although it could well have that additional meaning, but rather for Lisbon. *Lx Comics* was a magazine published from 1990 to 1991. Alternative comics were booming globally at the time, and Portugal was no exception. Sadly, *Lx Comics* ended after only four issues. A few years later, the Bedeteca de Lisboa (Lisbon's comics library) was founded, allowing the noncommercial art movement to survive. Also, for a brief period, the Portuguese central government gave grants to comic artists, allowing them to focus on their comics for a year. *The Journal of K.* was the first work aided by the grant and was released by boutique publisher Edições Polvo.

Raul Brandão was a Portuguese symbolist writer who published *The Clown's Death* (*A Morte do Palhaço*) in 1896. He was obsessed by social evil and human suffering. The grotesque, the pathetic, and the tragic are all part of his expressive palette. *The Journal of K.* is an adaptation of *The Clown's Death*. Filipe Abranches started his career influenced by *ligne claire* (clear line) drawing but, by 2001, he had switched to what is known as oily line. This is a very dark book, illustrated by Abranches's expressionist drawings. The clown's circus is a metaphor for life, where shattered illusions and evil hide behind the sparkle and glitter of lights and sequins. The story ends in derision, with someone shouting, *Fora o autor!* ("Boo to the author!"). But who exactly is this author? Raul Brandão, Filipe Abranches, or could it be an some unknown deity? **DI**

Oily lines and dark imagery evoke menace and mystery in *The Journal of K.* ➡

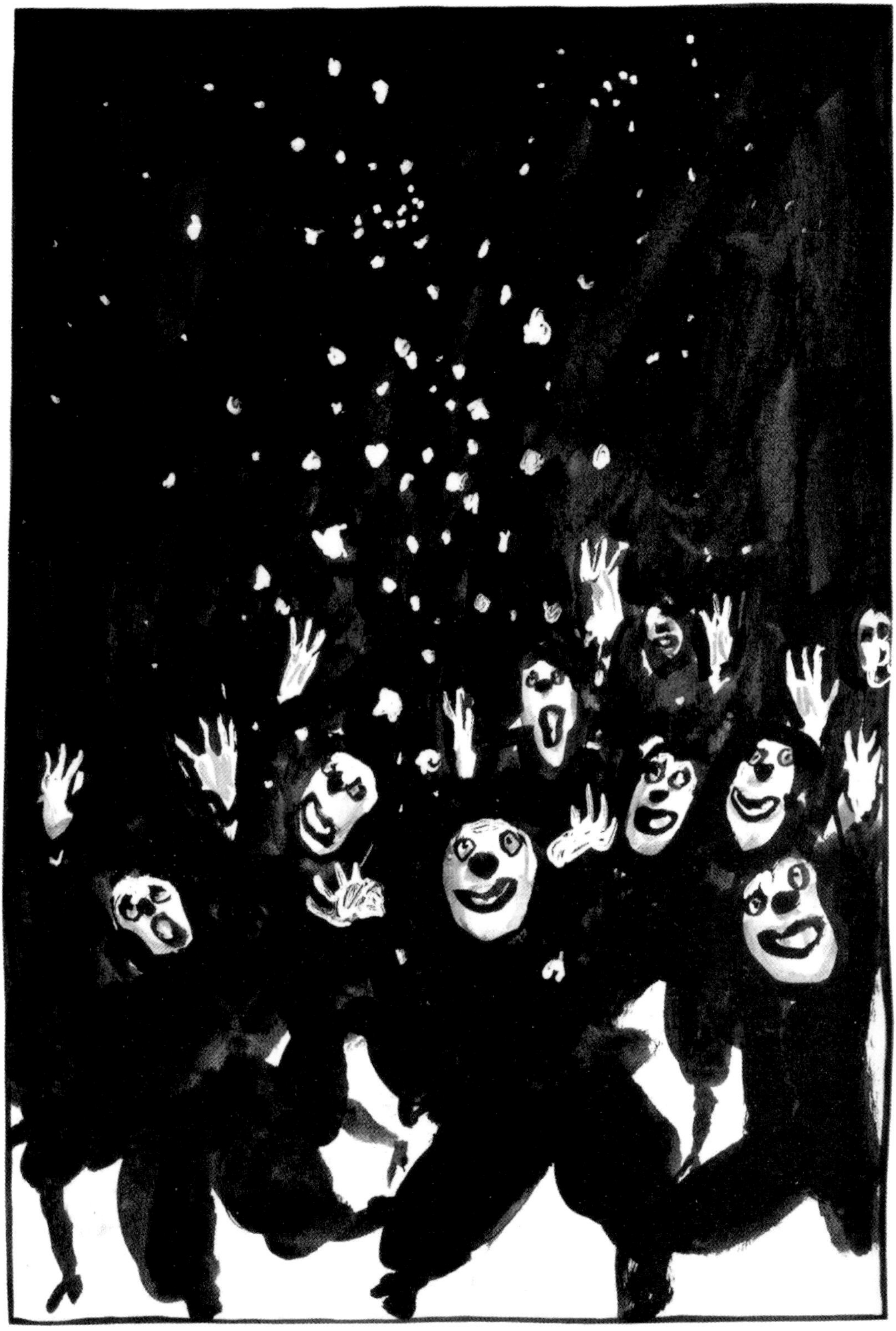

Mail Order Bride 2001

✎ Mark Kalesniko

First published by Fantagraphics Books (USA)
Creator Canadian (b.1958)
Genre Romance, Drama
Influenced by Eddie Campbell

Monty Wheeler is thirty-nine, single, a virgin, and a self-confessed geek who runs a comics, games, and toy business, living with his vast collection at the back of the store. Monty likes Asian girls, or at least the dreams promised in his porn mags, and through a classified ad orders Kyung Seo from Korea to be his "cute, exotic, loyal, hardworking, traditional Asian wife." But elegant, intelligent Kyung comes to the United States determined to leave her past behind. Growing disillusioned with Monty's jealousies and porn collection, she befriends a liberated Western-born Asian woman, a photographer, who introduces her to life-modeling, dance, and new friends, prompting Kyung to think of escaping.

Kalesniko crafts a perceptive portrayal of the false promises and thwarted aspirations on both sides of a mail-order marriage. Charting the disintegrating relationship, Kalesniko uses several powerful symbols. A lone female dancer, naked and masked, mirrors Kyung's shifting hopes; threatened by funereal cheerleaders, she breaks free, only to be engulfed later by the troupe's pom-poms. Monty's oppression is personified by his toys, in particular a threatening, grinning jack-in-the-box and a pair of dangling puppets, one a horned devil, the other a maiden with broken strings. Kalesniko also punctuates the pages with pouting girls from Monty's porn mags, juxtaposed, when Kyung tries to be more independent, with words from the ads promising a bride who will be "domestic" and "simple." Tensions escalate to an explosive confrontation that tests how independent either of them can ever be. **PG**

Perry Bible Fellowship 2001

✎ Nicholas Gurewitch

First published by *The Daily Orange*, Syracuse University (USA) **Creator** American (b.1982)
Genre Humor
Award Ignatz Award (2005–06)

Delve into the colorful, demented world of Nicholas Gurewitch's *Perry Bible Fellowship* and you might not come back the same person. This trickster of cartooning started the work for his college newspaper, getting an early start on honing his unique humor—and his skills with a pen—to a razor edge. Gurewitch defies summarization and it is hard to describe a strip where something different happens all the time and in a mind-boggling array of styles. In this, Gurewitch is like a good stand-up comedian—so endlessly surprising in his material that you want to recommend him to your friends by repeating his routines verbatim.

But the genius of Gurewitch's cartooning is that readers really do have to see the image to make the joke work. It helps that these cartoons are an unmissable visual treat, with source material coming from fairy tales to the space program, from Charles Atlas to bloodthirsty dinosaurs. Gurewitch is also a master of pastiche, seamlessly channeling the style of Edward Gorey, Quentin Blake, and the long-forgotten children's book illustrators of his childhood to create environments where associations with these artists set readers up to be flummoxed once again.

Despite having won every major award in the American comics world, Gurewitch has now stopped the stream of disturbing images issuing forth from the *Perry Bible Fellowship*. However, fans of the comic strip will never stop hoping that Gurewitch will return one day—bringing even more jokes, and even more astonishing drawings, to the world. **EL**

Miss Remarkable & Her Career 2001

Joanna Rubin Dranger

Title in original language *Fröken Märkvärdig & Karriären*
First published by Albert Bonniers (Sweden)
Creator Swedish (b.1970)
Genre Satire

Joanna Rubin Dranger
Albert Bonniers Förlag
fröken
Märkvärdig
&
Karriären

Sometimes a comic appears that changes readers' perceptions of what a comic can be. That was the case for many who read the graphic novel *Miss Remarkable & Her Career*. The Swedish artist Joanna Rubin Dranger, had a problem with conventional comics in that she felt there was just too much information on each page. She was exhausted by everything that she was supposed to take in. When she sat down to create a comic of her own, she decided to have only one large panel on a page and to make her characters highly iconic by drawing them in crisp black and white. All this reduced the amount of information on the page but did not dumb down the comic. In fact, it had the opposite effect.

Miss Remarkable & Her Career follows a young woman bent on success, simultaneously attending a prestigious art school and working as a freelance artist. She is always putting on a brave face but inwardly crumbling from the pressure. The story is told with imagery full of symbolism; for example, the pressure of expectations is depicted in the form of a big black monster slowly closing in on the main character.

The story is likely autobiographical to some extent, not the least implied by the resemblance of the artist to the main character. It is not autobiographical in a traditional sense, however, as Dranger has mixed her own experiences with elements of fiction in order to tell a story that is both personal and universal: a moral fable for the twenty-first century. *Miss Remarkable & Her Career* has also been made into a critically acclaimed animated film. **FS**

"Anyway, it doesn't matter what I do . . . As long as it's completely innovative and revolutionizing."

Similar reads
Cinderella's Sister and Other Moral Tales (Askungens Syster och Andra Sedelärande Berättelser) J. Rubin Dranger
Miss Terrified and Her Career (Fröken Livrädd och Karriären) J. Rubin Dranger
Passionella and Other Stories Jules Feiffer

Daredevil 2001

Brian Michael Bendis Alex Maleev

First published by Marvel Comics (USA)
Creators Bendis (American, b.1967); Maleev (Bulgarian, b.1971)
Genre Superhero

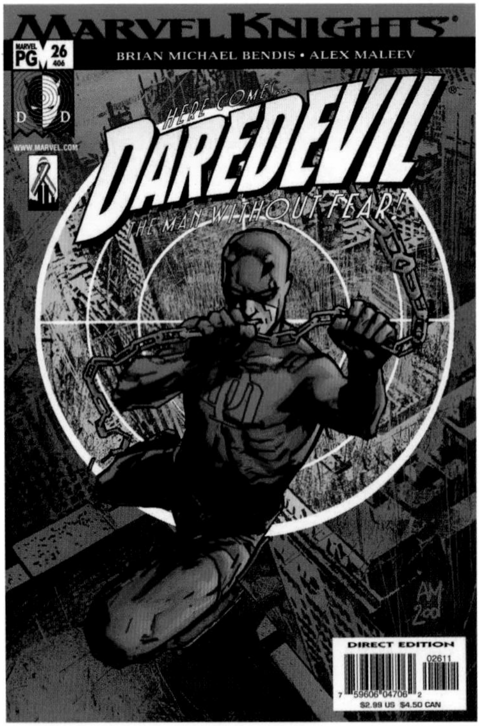
MARVEL KNIGHTS
BRIAN MICHAEL BENDIS • ALEX MALEEV
HERE COMES...
DAREDEVIL
THE MAN WITHOUT FEAR!
DIRECT EDITION
$2.99 US $4.50 CAN

Also by Brian Michael Bendis
Alias
Powers
Torso
Ultimate Spider-Man

A complicated character like Daredevil has had more downs than ups. In the 1980s, Frank Miller reinvented the somewhat unlikely hero in grim and gritty terms, spicing the title with ninjas and extreme violence. The title receded when Miller left, with new creators seemingly intimidated by his legacy. Not so Brian Michael Bendis and Alex Maleev. They faced the Miller legacy head on and took the character to heights previously unrealized.

Bendis and Maleev's four-year run on the *Daredevil* title was the heroic highlight of the 2000s. Introducing new characters such as Matt Murdock's wife, Milla Donovan, as well as new situations, the creators pushed Daredevil well past his breaking point and into territory rarely seen in mainstream superhero comics.

"I know before I wake up . . . I know my life is over."

The dramatic breakthrough stemmed from their desire to take the ramifications of Daredevil's actions seriously from a psychological point of view. The crucial turn was the revelation of his secret identity.

In story after story, Daredevil is a hunted man, with all of his old nemeses appearing out of the woodwork, hell-bent on retribution for the numerous times that the hero had thwarted their evil intentions. These *Daredevil* comics contain drama in a way that few superhero comics do because it is never clear that everything will work out for the best in the end.

Quite to the contrary, in fact. Bendis and Maleev drive Daredevil into a nightmarish, noirish universe, highlighting the alienation of this blind man whose abilities allow him to see what others turn away from. Maleev's gritty, photo-based artwork creates a New York that is entirely believable and genuinely intimidating in this superheroic tour de force. **BB**

The Birthday Riots 2001

Nabiel Kanan

The Birthday Riots explores issues about the gypsies, or "travelers" of Britain, and the crises of conscience they trigger in one man and his teenage daughter. Max Collins is a married, forty-something with two kids, and a house in the country. A former political science teacher, he has landed a well-paid job as an advisor to Thom Conran, the independent candidate for Mayor of London. Planning Conran's campaign, Max insists they ignore controversial government legislation that prohibits nomadic persons occupying private or public land, but his resolve is tested when a gypsy group turns up on the land behind his house.

Max calls the council to have them moved, but a week later they are still there. Meanwhile, his daughter Natalie, about to turn fifteen, befriends a new gypsy boy at her school who is the target of offensive graffiti and bullying. Their friendship only compounds her growing anger about the unjust land law and deepens the rift with her father. They argue over the breakfast table and it all comes to a head on her birthday when she runs away from home to London.

"I think people should keep the promises they make, don't you?"

The emotional journey to find her again, and learning that a hunger striker protesting the law is one of his former students, prompts Max to reevaluate how many promises he has broken: the little white lies, the marital infidelities, the treehouse he never finished for his daughter, and the bigger betrayal of his ideals. Author Nabiel Kanan continues his knack for capturing disaffected teenagers proven in his debut, *Exit*. He builds sympathy for Max as the discovery of how much he has given up by settling for comfort and compromise reawakens his political and moral conscience. **PG**

First published by NBM Publishing (USA)
Creator British (b.1971)
Genre Teen, Drama
Award Eisner Award nomination (2000)

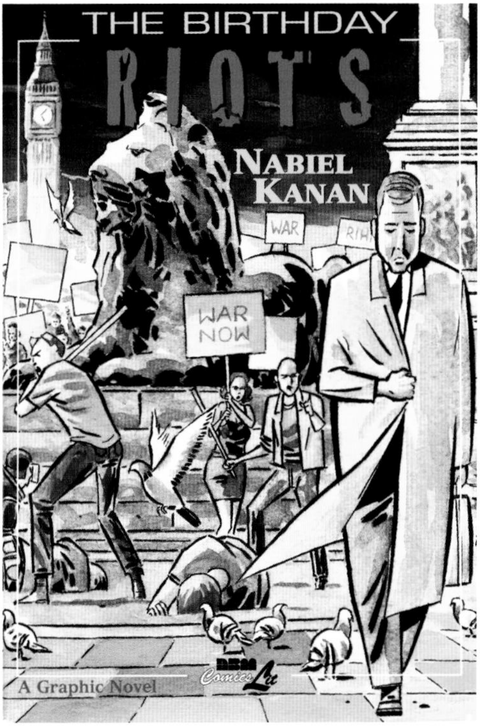

THE BIRTHDAY
RIOTS
NABIEL
KANAN
WAR
WAR
NOW
A Graphic Novel

Similar reads

A Small Killing Alan Moore and Oscar Zarate
Exit Nabiel Kanan
Lost Girl Nabiel Kanan
The Drowners Nabiel Kanan

Get Your War On 2001

✎✎ David Rees

First published by Soft Skull Press (USA)
Creator American (b.1972)
Genre Satire
Adaptation Theater (2007)

Back in the early days of the War on Terror, when New York City had just fallen victim to the September 11 attacks and television news reeled from anthrax poisonings to anti-Islamist hate crimes, David Rees's *Get Your War On* was one of the few things that seemed to make sense. His artistic courage was admirable. His creative, spleen-venting combination of clip art and crass wisecracks captured and held readers' attention.

Get Your War On felt like the interoffice memo to end them all—someone else was out there, pretending to crunch numbers while the stock market crashed and recession settled in, and he was just as confused and angry as we were. Rees's characters, ordinary office drones from the graphics pack that comes with word processing software, were so shocked by September 11, it barely fazed them when Voltron turned up in their office.

They spoke in curse words and lurid clichés but still managed to make more sense than supposed political leaders. Of course, as the geopolitical situation worsened and the Bush administration charged first into Afghanistan and then Iraq, Rees's vitriol only intensified. In the history of media there have been few who have spoken for the common person when the powers-that-be looked more invincible than ever. Comparing David Rees to Edward R. Murrow might be a little over the top, but it can be argued that he articulated the frustration of the ordinary (albeit somewhat liberal) American, watching their country's international reputation turn to ashes. **EL**

Fullmetal Alchemist 2001

✎✎ Hiromu Arakawa

Title in original language *Hagane no Renkinjutsushi*
First published by *Monthly Shonen Gangan* (Japan)
Creator Japanese (b.1973)
Genre Fantasy

From the *Monthly Shonen Gangan* magazine by Square Enix, the developer of *Final Fantasy* video games, comes *Fullmetal Alchemist*, another hugely popular franchise. Alphonse and Edward Elric are two brothers in a futuristic, steampunk-infused Japan. Alphonse is an armor-plated giant whose soul is contained within his hollow body. His brother Edward appears more human but has two steel prosthetic limbs and is the state's certified alchemist—someone able to manipulate metals and shape them to their will.

The fundamental rule of alchemy is "equivalent exchange," the idea that "to obtain something, something of equal value must be lost." This is linked to the themes that run throughout the series: consequence and fairness. One part adventure, another part social commentary, Arakawa devotes equal attention to discussing corrupt religion and unjust ruling classes as she does to creating sound effect-filled action sequences. *Fullmetal Alchemist* is a child's fantasy on paper.

It has much in common with a video game, complete with bosses and a thoroughly interactive environment. Magic and science meet in the Elrics's world and the methods Edward uses are similar to tapping the controls to deliver a video game character's special move. *Fullmetal Alchemist* has since become an industry, spawning an anime and video game series. It is a multilayered adventure where, beneath its metal-infused chest, lies the story of two brothers trying to reclaim their bodies and retain their humanity. **SW**

Edward's alchemical prowess gives him immense power. ➡

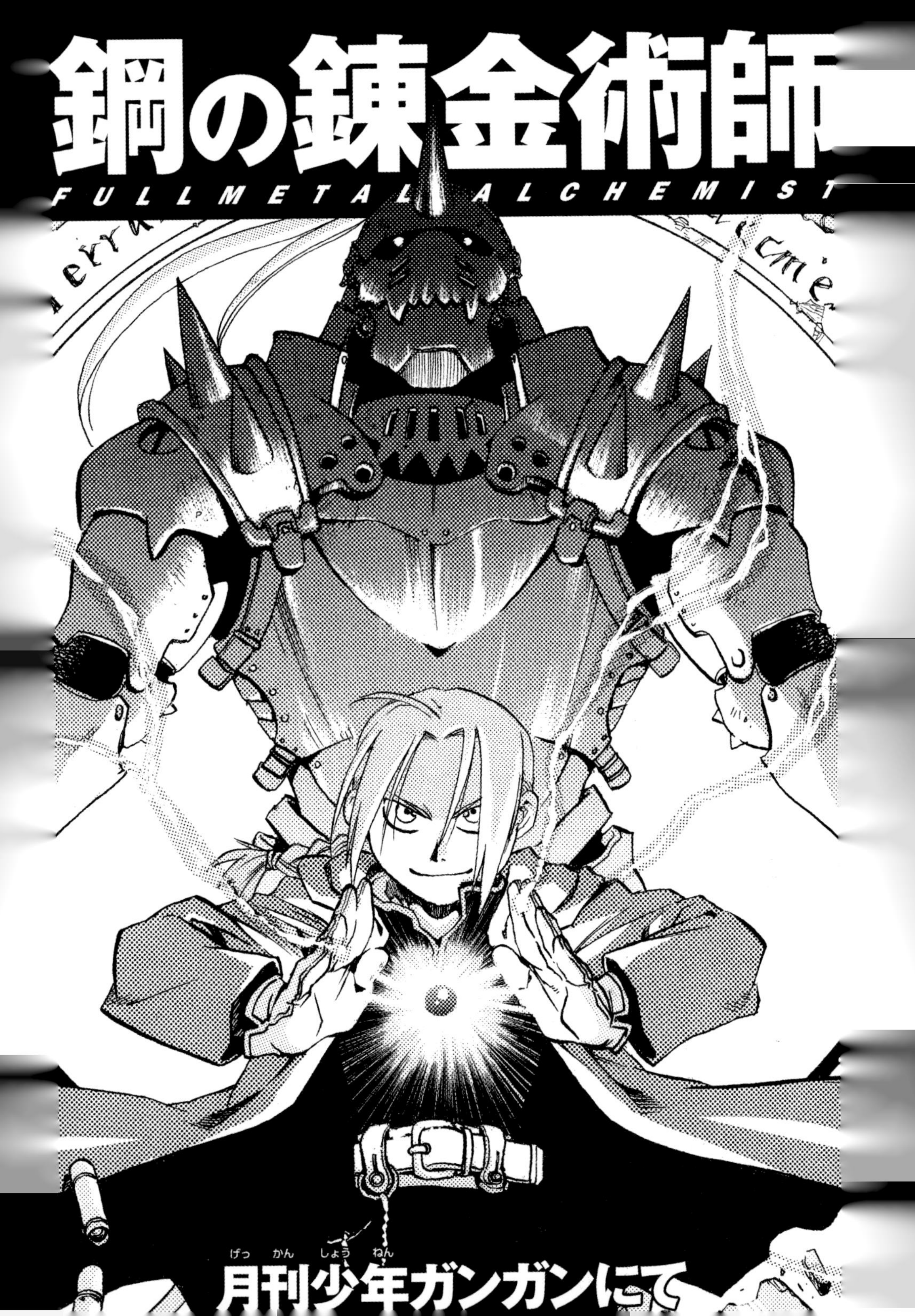
鋼の錬金術師
FULLMETAL ALCHEMIST
月刊少年ガンガンにて

Bleach 2001

✎🖊 "Tite Kubo"

First published by Shueisha (USA)
Creator Noriaki Kubo (Japanese, b.1977)
Genre Fantasy
Award Shogakukan Manga Award (2005)

Ichigo Kurosaki is a high school student who lives with his high-spirited father and younger twin sisters. Although he has the secret ability to see dead people, Ichigo lives an ordinary life until he meets a girl named Rukia Kuchiki, who claims to be a Soul Reaper.

Bleach is a series from Japanese manga magazine, *Weekly Shonen Jump*. The main themes of this popular title are friendship, effort, and victory. In a nutshell, it is the story about how a young boy grows up. The first few episodes are neat little pieces introducing Ichigo's struggles as a substitute Soul Reaper. He has to perform duties for Rukia and fight against "Hollows," the corrupt souls of the dead.

The story becomes increasingly gripping, especially after Ichigo goes to the Soul Society, the realm of the afterlife and a base for the Soul Reaper military. There, he becomes entangled in grand conspiracies and forced to overcome many ordeals. As this stage, the comic expands. The plentiful and captivating sub-characters are introduced, and their charms are clearly one of the most attractive aspects of *Bleach*.

The cool and stylish composition and drawing style are other appealing features. Thanks to its noncartoony, nonchildish style, this work attracts readers across all age groups. *Bleach* contains moments of genuine humor, varied and rich, and are deftly interspersed amid the dramatic and suspenseful elements. The deeply evocative coming-of-age story as a central theme works well alongside the artistic expertise and humor, delivering a true epic. **CK**

Ultra-Gash Inferno 2001

✎🖊 Suehiro Maruo

First published by Seirindô (Japan)
Creator Japanese (b.1956)
Genre Erotic, Horror
Influenced by German expressionist films

Ultra-Gash Inferno is a British collection of short story comics (and one graphic novella) that were originally published in Japan between 1981 and 1993. A frequent contributor to the underground manga magazine *Garo*, Suehiro Maruo's genre of extremely graphic sex and violent horror—dubbed "erotic grotesque"—draws on the tradition of gruesome *muzan-e* woodblock prints of the nineteenth century. Maruo also cites David Lynch as an inspiration, as well as German expressionist movies of the 1920s and 1930s. Several of the shorts in *Ultra-Gash Inferno* are experimental and designed to shock.

Others emphasize absurdity, surreal nightmare logic, and themes of alienation. In "Putrid Night" it is lust, not love, that conquers all—even pain and death. A couple—mutilated, tortured, and left to die—crawl together for one last tryst. "A Season in Hell" is a fever dream of lost memory and madness in which an adolescent boy, ridiculed by his parents, descends into hallucinogenic, murderous revenge.

"Non-Resistance City," the most sustained narrative in the collection, is set in postwar, occupied Tokyo, a ruined, insect-filled city in which American soldiers terrorize a disheartened populace. Amid the upheaval, a woman succumbs to the attentions of a dwarf whom she discovers later has butchered her son. All of this is rendered with Maruo's razor-sharp, sensuous pen and ink. The horrors have an intense (and disturbing) beauty, seducing the reader into becoming a reluctant, but fascinated, voyeur. There is no denying the visceral power of *Ultra-Gash Inferno*. **TL**

Blue Pills 2001

Frederik Peeters

Title in original language *Pilules Bleues*
First published by Atrabile (Switzerland)
Creator Swiss (b.1974)
Genre Autobiography

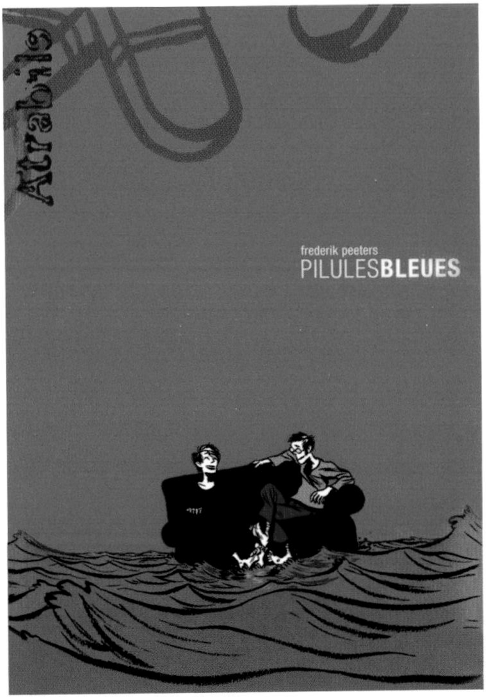

Atrabile
frederik peeters
PILULESBLEUES

On several occasions Frederik, a Geneva-born comics artist, meets the pretty Cati, a girl he knew at secondary school. The young pair, flustered and delighted, realize that they are strongly attracted to one another. But at the moment of giving herself to him, Cati hesitates and pulls away. She finally admits to Frederik that she is HIV-positive, as is her three-year-old son. It is their love story, marked by this initial revelation, which is related in *Blue Pills*. It is told in the first person from the point of view of the illustrator.

How to react to such news? How can one accept it? Frederik, who is slightly surprised at his own reaction, welcomes Cati into his life and sets up house with her and her son. Then he begins to record all the aspects of their everyday life in the form of a graphic novel. It includes all the details that help readers understand HIV, omitting none of the apparently insignificant details that convey depth and subtlety to this surprising autobiography: the meticulous inspection of bodies, looking for any little cuts or wounds that could prove dangerous; the ritual of visits to the doctor; the moments of intimacy and even sex, which remains in spite of everything a reassuring and affirmative reference point for both parties as their lives are turned upside down.

Before Frederik Peeters, no one had ever tried to describe daily life with HIV in such closely observed detail. This talented artist's narrative, supported by his confident graphic style, is expressed simply, without ever sinking into any theatricality. **NF**

"The woman that I love has HIV . . . and so does her little boy. That's not a bone of contention!"

Also by Frederik Peeters
Koma with Pierre Wazem
Lupus
Pachyderme
RG with Pierre Dragon
Sandcastle (*Château de sable*)

Isaac the Pirate 2001

✏️ Christophe Blain

Title in original language *Isaac le Pirate*
First published by Dargaud (France)
Creator French (b.1970)
Genre Adventure

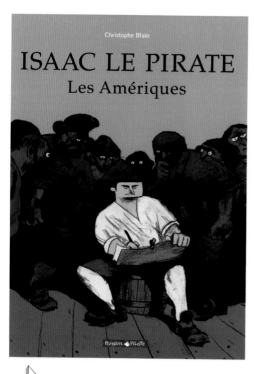

Christophe Blain

ISAAC LE PIRATE
Les Amériques

Poisson Pilote

Also by Christophe Blain
Socrates the Half-Dog (*Socrate le Demi-Chien*)
 with Joann Sfar
The Revolt of Hop Frog (*La Révolte d'Hop Frog*)
 with David B.
The Speed Abater (*Le Reducteur de Vitesse*)

A talented, young, ambitious painter, Isaac Sofer seems certain to find artistic glory one day. Alas, his life does not follow this course: a chronic lack of money is a recurring bone of contention between him and his girlfriend Alice. Isaac's chance encounter with John Demelin, a surgeon, causes his destiny to change in a completely unexpected way. Demelin asks Isaac to join him on a voyage with a famous captain who, like all men of taste during the eighteenth century when nautical painting was very fashionable, would employ an artist to document their sea voyages.

According to Demelin, Isaac's fortune will be made. It is an irrefutable argument that the young man goes along with: he goes on board, convinced that the

> ## "Isaac the Pirate . . . is based on my own experiences, my memories. . . ."
> **Christophe Blain**

voyage will be short and that he will quickly return to his love Alice. Once out at sea, however, he discovers that the shipowner, Jean Mainbasse, is actually a pirate who, tired of his life as an outlaw, plans to set sail for the South Pole. He dreams of finding glory as the explorer who discovers a new land. And he is counting on Isaac to immortalize this great adventure in pictures.

A talented author who became well-known in the mid-1990s, Christophe Blain gathers together the proven ingredients of a highly popular pirate story. Collisions, storms, pretty women, and unknown lands are all set against an exotic background. Where Blain excels most, however, is in the depiction of his characters, who are complex, passionate, nuanced, ambivalent, and profoundly human. Traditionally drawn with great skill, *Isaac the Pirate* reinvigorates the genre with great enthusiasm and spirit. **NF**

Saint Jean's Way 2001

Edmond Baudoin

Edmond Baudoin was already in his thirties when he decided to quit his job as an accountant to pursue his dream of being an artist and dedicating his life to drawing. In 1973 he started to create comics for a few magazines until, a few years later in 1981, he met avant-garde Futuropolis publisher Étienne Robial.

In Baudoin's own words: "It was a meeting of vital importance. It was one of those meetings that blows one up." At Futuropolis, Baudoin created a solid body of work. He was one of the first comics artists in France to produce autobiographical comics with works such as *Time Passes* (*Passe le Temps*) and *Like This* (*Couma Acò*). *Saint Jean's Way* is also an autobiographical book, but it is a peculiar one. Saint Jean's Way is a path on a mountain near Villars-sur-Var, the isolated village where Baudoin spent his childhood in postwar France. The author uses these places—as Marcel Proust used his famous madeleine—to spark his memories. He completed numerous, detailed sketches of small sections of the countryside and worked over them back at home in his studio. Elements of this lengthy process are still apparent in the final result, visible in the collages or enlargements.

Baudoin is a master of the brush: either dry, a technique that he uses to achieve texture and nuance, or wet, when he draws lines reminiscent of Chinese painting with its freedom and precision (landscape aritst Tao Chi was an important influence for Baudoin). Baudoin examines his life and his past, but he also raises questions about how difficult it is to draw experiences such as oppression, sex, and death. **DI**

"Baudoin does not write, he sings. His pen does not draw, it flies . . . "

Thierry Bellefroid, reviewer

Title in original language *Le Chemin de Saint-Jean*
First published by L'Association (France)
Creator French (b.1942)
Genre Autobiography

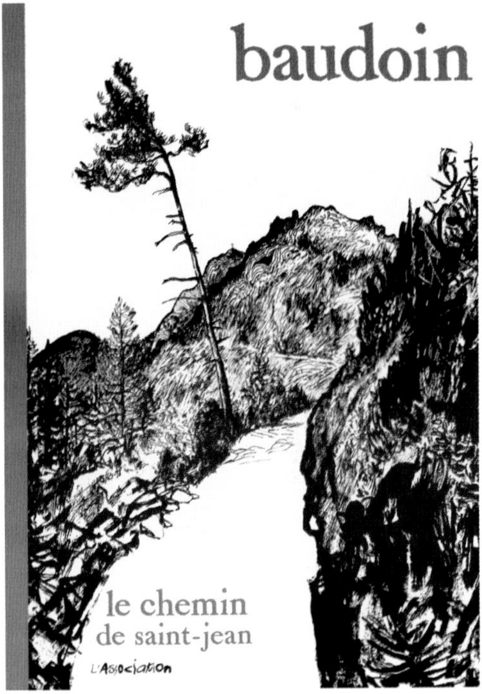
baudoin
le chemin
de saint-jean
L'Association

Similar reads

Approximately (Approximativement) Lewis Trondheim
In Praise of Dust (Éloge de la Poussière) Edmond Baudoin
Journal (III) Fabrice Neaud
The Portrait (Le Portrait) Edmond Baudoin
Wasteland (Terrains Vagues) Edmond Baudoin

Abe: Wrong for all the Right Reasons 2001

Glenn Dakin

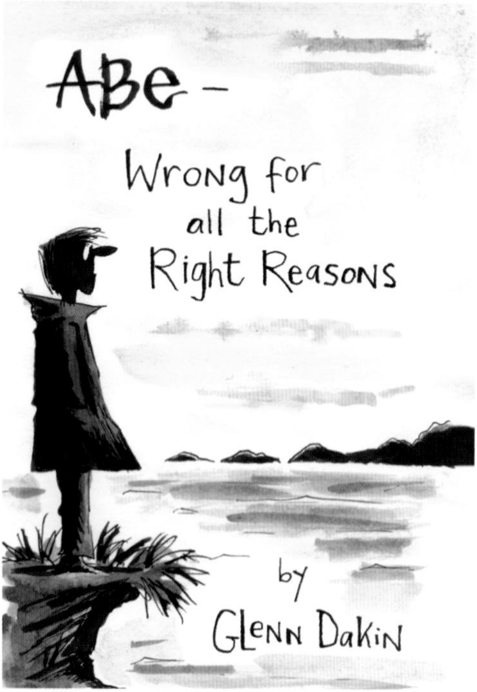
Abe -
Wrong for all the Right Reasons
by
Glenn Dakin

"I like to live intangibly, always between one thing and another…"

Similar reads

Alec: The Years Have Pants Eddie Campbell *Jerome Alphagraph (Jérôme d'Alphagraph)* Nylso
Le Pont du Havre Luc Giard
Mauretania Chris Reynolds
The Sands Tom Hart

First published by Top Shelf Productions (USA)
Creators British (b.1960)
Genre Superhero
Influenced by Eddie Campbell

Glenn Dakin was a teenager when he created his Abe Rat/Captain Oblivion characters. Abe stayed with him through thick and thin, outgrowing simple superheroics to become Dakin's stand-in for poetical musings, travelogues, and flights of fancy. This book is a collection of stories published from the mid-1980s to mid-1990s. The early stories take place in a future world of peace and advanced technology. In later stories Abe continues to fight such superpowered villains as the evil Milton Keenz, but the tales gain additional layers of meaning. In "Blinkers," for example, Keenz is pushing a new product, a headphonelike contraption that enables you "to stick ruthlessly to one narrow path in life." The people are ready to restrict their minds for the sake of getting things done. In the end Keenz is defeated with the help of the device's creator, Doctor Deepend.

Over the years, Dakin has abandoned his sci-fi surroundings to concentrate on everyday occurrences, such as changes in the weather, impressions of a trip to Sweden, or a visit to an old friend. The mood is quieter, more contemplative, and sometimes melancholic. The final story in the collection, "A Dream England," has Abe walking about "the beautiful England that is no longer seen and talked about," talking with Rupert Bear and having his ice cream stolen by King Arthur. Dakin muses on the paths people take in life, the loss of the enchantment of childhood, and the need to find it again in adult life in order to live with meaning and purpose. A straightforward description of his whimsical, thoughtful, poetic stories does not do them justice. **J-PJ**

Nodame Cantabile 2001

✎✎ Tomoko Ninomiya

First published by Kodansha (Japan)
Creators Japanese (b.1969)
Genre Romance, Humor
Adaptations TV (2006 and 2008)

In 2006, a classic music compilation CD unexpectedly hit the top ten sales ranking in Japan. This CD was the soundtrack of a hit television drama based on the manga *Nodame Cantabile*.

Shinichi Chiaki is an elite music student who hopes to become a world-famous conductor. However, his life is not going smoothly. Thanks to his flying phobia, he is unable to study abroad, and this is a big disadvantage to fulfilling his dreams. One day he drinks too much, passes out, and finds himself in an extremely untidy room. Wild but wondrous piano playing wakes him up, and he meets its source, Megumi Noda, or Nodame. Her playing is amazing and intuitive, and Chiaki notices her incomparable talent. She wants to enjoy the piano without competing with others, but Chiaki tries to persuade her to become a pianist. They then start influencing each other in many unexpected ways.

The overall tone of *Nodame Cantible* is comical, and even the romantic scenes often end in punch lines. The characters are faintly caricatured and the drawing style is simple. However, the funny and sweet humor is not the only beauty of this manga. There are key musical scenes that can give you goose bumps. The mood changes and the music "flows" into the reader as if they can hear Nodame playing her piano and Chiaki conducting the orchestra. This story will have you alternating between laughter and tears. And, when the reading is done and the tears wiped away, you can't help but feel the need to listen to a beautiful piece of classical music. **CK**

The Dark Knight Strikes Again 2001

✎ Frank Miller ✎ Frank Miller and Lynn Varley

First published by DC Comics (USA)
Creators American (b.1957)
Genre Superhero
Awards Six Eisner Awards (Miller)

Frank Miller's bizarre sequel to his 1986 masterwork, *The Dark Knight Returns*, was a polarizing work when published that has only gained in resonance over time. It was, in part, a disgusted reaction on the author's part to the dark "realist" paradigm of superhero storytelling that the original had helped inaugurate and which persists today. It was also a return to the genre in which he had made his mark, to distill as potently as possible his long-standing, conflicted ideas about heroism as an expression both of power and freedom.

The Dark Knight Strikes Again, or *DK2*, ostensibly picks up the story where its predecessor left off, but is really an independent work. It concerns Batman's underground struggle against an authoritarian U.S. government secretly controlled by the villains Lex Luthor and Brainiac, who have managed to pacify all his superhero colleagues. But Batman and his sidekick Catgirl end the plans for world domination by liberating Earth's superheroes and effectively starting a youth-led revolution. The tragedy of 9/11, which occurred as Miller was drawing the story, profoundly affects its tone, lending its manic four-color proceedings an apocalyptic edge. The cartooning is passionately expressive, the characterization recklessly idiosyncratic, the tone alternately irreverent and mournful, and the ideology contradictory. It adds up to an intoxicating read which is given a deliriously enzymatic boost by Lynn Varley's utterly confident, brutally beautiful coloring. With this comic Miller caught the raw energy and primeval fascination of heroism like lightning in a bottle. **MWi**

Buja's Diary 2001

Seyeong O.

Title in original language *Puja Ui Kurim Ilgi*
First published by Siat Publishing (South Korea)
Creator Korean (b.1955)
Genre Drama

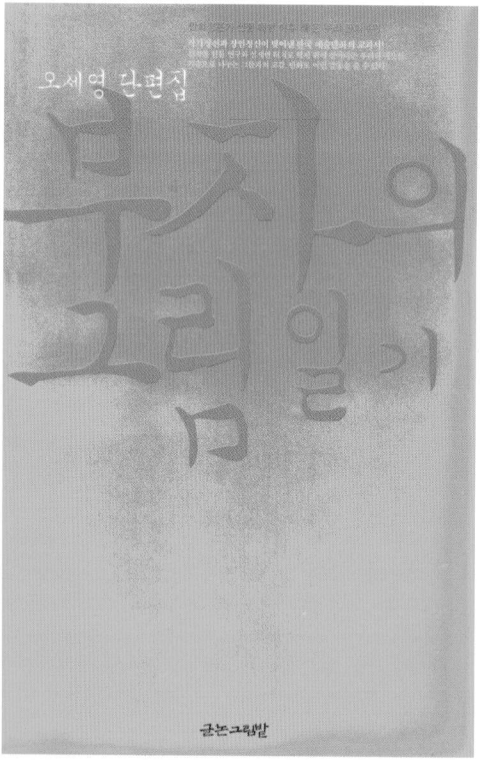
오세영 단편집
부자의 그림일기
글논그림밭

"After the war Korea was divided in two. Henceforth, our homeland was in North Korea behind an impenetrable frontier."

With subtle little touches—sometimes dramatic, funny, or bitter—the stories in *Buja's Diary* give the reader a composite picture of that very special moment in recent Korean history, which saw the country move, rather suddenly, from a military dictatorship to democracy. All these stories were published in various magazines between 1988 and 1993, spanning the years when South Korea entered a new era after hosting the Olympic Games in Seoul in 1988.

These stories do not all take place in that particular historical context, but through their themes they all reflect the breath of freedom and change that subsequently rippled throughout Korean society. In the background, they also tell the story of the political convulsions that have rocked the Korean peninsula—the Japanese occupation until the end of World War II, the partition of the country into two politically opposed entities after the Korean War, and the sporadic but violent student rebellion in favor of democracy that followed, as well as the social tensions and contradictions resulting from it.

Almost all these twelve stories deal with everyday life in Korea. With an extremely sharp sense of observation, a constant concern for authenticity, and always with confident strokes, Seyeong O. has appointed himself the chronicler of the world surrounding him. He portrays the rural exodus, the poverty, the often difficult relationships between generations, and the arrival of modernity in a country that had remained inward-looking for a long time.

There is also melancholy and sadness, as seen in the short, fifteen-page story that gives the collection its title, the tale of a very poor childhood in a single-parent family. Seyeong O. has painted a sensitive portrait of a country and its people in an elegant and realistic style. It is a deeply moving comic book experience. **NF**

Observant and deeply moving, *Buja's Diary* is a powerful read.

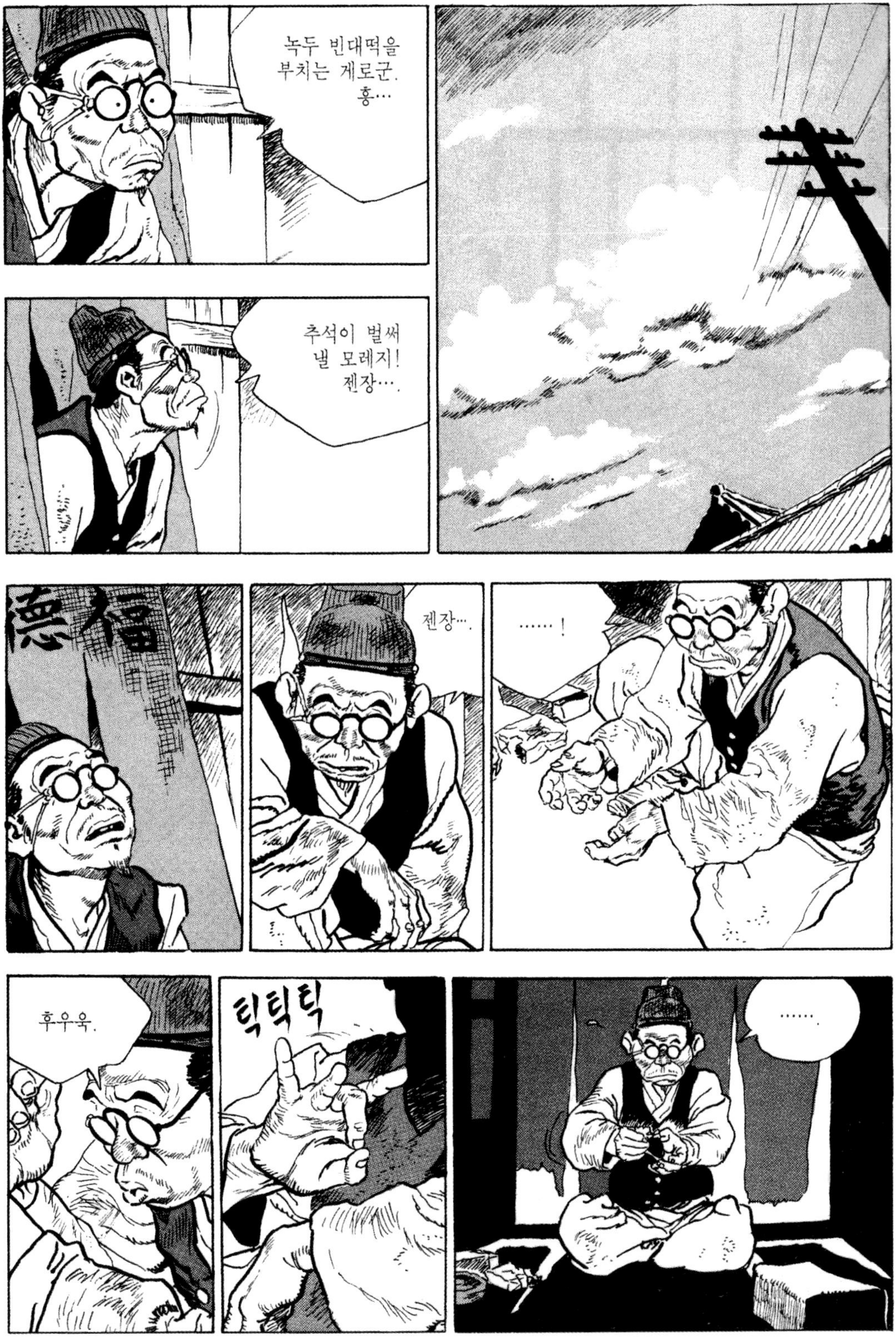
녹두 빈대떡을 부치는 게로군. 흥…
추석이 벌써 낼 모레지! 젠장….
젠장….
……!
후우욱.
틱틱틱
…….

Meanwhile 2001

Jason Shiga

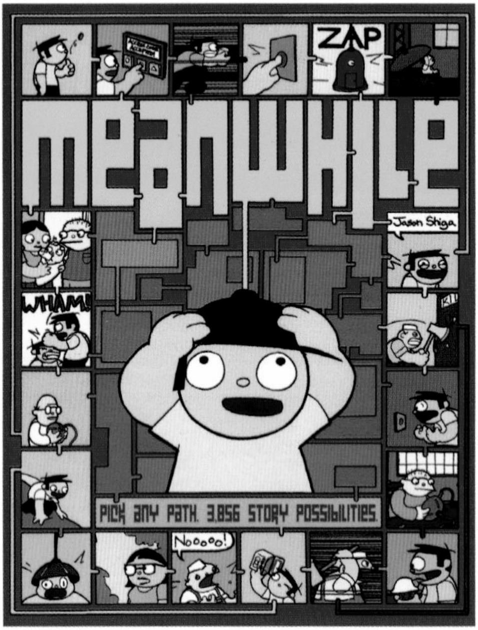
ZAP
MEANWHILE
Jason Shiga
WHAM!
PICK ANY PATH. 3,856 STORY POSSIBILITIES.
Noooo!

"I wanted to start the book off with the type of choice we make every day . . . I try and graduate to weirder choices like whether to kill every human on the planet . . ."

Similar reads

Bookhunter Jason Shiga
Double Happiness Jason Shiga
Fleep Jason Shiga
Lint Chris Ware
Little Nemo in Slumberland Winsor McCay

First published by Self-published (USA)
Creator American (b.1976)
Genre Science fiction, Fantasy
Award Eisner Award (2004)

Oakland, CA native Jason Shiga's *Meanwhile* first emerged as a self-published minicomic, too crazy for the world of comics, let alone mainstream publishing. But challenging comics such as *Meanwhile* are increasingly appreciated as the comic book matures as an art form. If you want to play a comic the way you might a video game, *Meanwhile* could be the book for you. In this choose-your-own-adventure world, where picking chocolate over vanilla ice cream can lead to the Apocalypse, readers follow an avatar—adventurous little Jimmy—through a panoply of possibilities.

The story begins innocently enough as Jimmy visits an ice cream parlor. Shiga's free-wheeling narrative quickly picks up (and occasionally loses) momentum depending on your decisions. Which of the mad scientist's inventions do you want to try out? How hard will you flip the coin? And just how deadly is the Killitron 3000? Altogether, as the cover to the book proclaims, there are 3,856 potential stories. A world of such vast options that Shiga—who studied pure mathematics in college—needed to write a series of computer algorithms to master it all.

The book is organized with a series of brightly colored tabs so that flipping backward and forward is easy. You'll read this extra-strength comic with your fingertips as much as your eyes as you trace the linear paths of Jimmy's destiny through tangles, page-to-page transitions, and the occasional backtrack to another conclusion. The author's drawings and character design are simple and utilitarian, but always charming. **EL**

The Great Catsby 2001

✎🖊 Kang Do-ha

Title in original language *Widaehan Kaetcheubi*
First published by Daum (South Korea)
Creator South Korean (b.1969)
Genre Humor

Catsby, twenty-six years old and jobless, is a man gently drifting and poorly equipped to deal with modern life. Fortunately two people help him through the trials and tribulations of everyday life. One is his friend Houndu, who temporarily earns a living as a teacher and with whom Catsby shares a studio in an old quarter of Seoul. The other is his girlfriend, Persu. Theirs is a relationship of true love, even though they do not yet feel ready to make plans for a future together.

Catsby's already precarious world suddenly collapses when Persu, whom he has been with for six years, tells him that she is going to marry an older widower. Catsby wants to give in to despair but under pressure from his father, who expects him to marry and give him heirs, he agrees to register at a marriage bureau. There he meets a delicate, young woman, Sun, who is clearly not indifferent to his charms.

Although the story is set in present-day Korea (and as a result *The Great Catsby* gives the reader interesting cultural insights into Korean life), Kang Do-ha's comedy of manners contains sufficiently familiar, timeless elements to have an immediate universal resonance. The animal-like features of the main characters paradoxically make them even more human.

From unexpected twists to sudden situation reversals, Do-ha delights in entangling the fates of his heroes to highlight what drives them. His approach has been influenced by the way this strip was initially published—on the internet. *The Great Catsby* has the same vivacity and rhythm as a serialized novel. **NF**

Amelia Rules! 2001

✎🖊 Jimmy Gownley

First published by Renaissance Press (USA)
Creator American (b.1972)
Genre Humor, Drama
Awards Four Eisner Award nominations

Amelia Rules! is that very rare thing, a comic for all ages to enjoy. Older than *Little Lulu*, yet younger than *Lou*, Amelia McBride is in the twilight days before puberty. Amelia's parents are divorced, and she moves to a new town with her mother as the series starts. She's outwardly confident and quickly makes new friends, but the situation has taken its toll.

Topics subsequently taking center stage are a friend with an incurable illness, and another concerned about her soldier father leaving for a two-year stint in Afghanistan. Gownley handles these subjects with subtlety and sympathy. He never provides easy answers, and shows that the hurt from all experiences fades with time. Importantly, he never forgets that without entertainment there is no point to any message. Artistically, Gownley has become an excellent expressive cartoonist, and, combined with computer wizardry and bold coloring, the result is a series that is instantly attractive to children. His storytelling portfolio encompasses repetition, use of fake publications, assorted methods of distinguishing the past, visual quirks, notable pastiches, and letting his cast age.

Gownley's foreshadowing is particularly impressive. The most innocuous or preposterous line or aside can have a purpose later. Amelia's world has grown to encompass around a dozen regular characters, with intriguing personalities. Why is cheerleader Britney so ambitious and cutting? Why does Pajamaman wear his pajamas outside school? The answers are likely to break your heart. **FP**

How Blue Was My Valley 2002

✐✐ Hok Tak Yeung

First published by Self-published (Hong Kong)
Creator Chinese (b.1970)
Genre Reality drama
Influenced by Richard Llewellyn

In the outlying districts of Hong Kong, where no tourist ever goes, life is shaped by the many little everyday things that form the fabric of human existence: the rowdiness of primary school children, visits to grandparents, chattering to neighbors on the stoops of tower blocks, unruly gangs of teenagers, the cheerful chaos of the market, and families that withdraw into the coolness of apartments on days when it is very hot.

Hok Tak Yeung invites readers to explore one of these neighborhoods—his own—over the summer of 1979. Bluefield (or in Chinese, *Lam Tim*, literally "jade blue field") is a fairly anonymous suburb on the south coast of the Kowloon peninsula, far away from the better known, more glittering areas of the city. In the course of Yeung's wanderings, punctuated by numerous memories of childhood and adolescence, readers learn to love his neighborhood, built by the British colonial government on unwelcoming land for the humblest social classes. The narrative sticks closely to the many details of local life, which are playfully repeated: typhoons, with which every Hong Kong resident has somehow learned to live, food marinated in vinegar, a soccer field built on a reservoir, and crowded apartment living.

Consisting of a series of genre scenes, the book is attractive to the eye with its bold use of color and large areas of very bright hues, as well as the unexpected way in which Hok Tak Yeung juggles with volume and form. *How Blue Was My Valley* is a comic book to savor, and it marks the appearance on the scene of an author to watch. **NF**

Paul Has a Summer Job 2002

✐✐ Michel Rabagliati

Title in original language *Paul a un travail d'été*
First published by La Pastèque (Canada)
Creator Canadian (b.1961)
Genre Autobiography

It is the summer of 1979. Paul is a young man working a series of dead-end jobs in Montreal. An old friend offers him the opportunity to spend the summer as a camp counselor on the shores of Lac Morin. Although he is initially put off by the experience of camping, Paul gradually adapts to his new job, and his life is transformed by his experiences with his coworkers and the children in his care.

When Michel Rabagliati published his first semiautobiographical graphic novel, *Paul in the Country* (*Paul à la campagne*), to tremendous acclaim in 1999, some wondered if he was a one-hit wonder. They need not have worried. His follow-up, *Paul Has a Summer Job*, with its abundance of slang and the trappings of youth, is a nearly pitch-perfect reminiscence of the Quebecois summer experience at the end of the "me" decade. Although he would continue to recount the adventures of Paul in a series of books that is still ongoing, this remains the single best expression of Rabagliati's charming mixture of youthful naïveté and fond nostalgia.

Much of the appeal of the *Paul* books can be found in Rabagliati's confident drawing style. Using a slightly abstract approach derived from animation, and filtered through the Franco-Belgian tradition, he mixes a cartoon style with slightly off-kilter realism. Remarkably, given his skill in the form, Rabagliati was nearly forty when he began to create comics, and his books are marked by a seriousness that comes from experience, even when his subject is the carefree exploits of the young. **BB**

Six Hundred and Seventy-Six Apparitions of Killoffer 2002

Patrice Killoffer

Title in original language *Six cent soixante-seize apparitions de Killoffer*
First published by L'Association (France)
Creator French (b.1966) **Genre** Autobiography

SIX CENT
SOIXANTE-SEIZE
APPARITIONS DE
KILLOFFER
L'ASSOCIATION

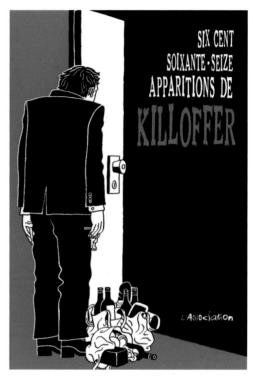

During a stay in Quebec, Parisian cartoonist Patrice Killoffer ruminates on his existence and scrutinizes his sexual encounters with the opposite sex in a foreign country. Away from his familiar turf, he digs deeper into himself and very honestly admits to his weaknesses and addictions. Part confession, part autobiography, part magical realism, this story speaks to the ugliness and uncomfortable truths within us all. Killoffer imagines the organic matter growing in his dirty dishes back home as being akin to the human condition and the way in which people interact with each other in the world: spreading like fungus, out of control. Killoffer imagines that there are numerous duplicate versions of himself, and his egocentric fantasy becomes increasingly violent and narcissistic. As the narrative progresses, he visualizes himself taking part in gang rape, murder, and extreme brutality.

As with many publications from French publisher L'Association, this comic eschews the traditional European album format. The larger pages allow Killoffer the space to play with more complicated page layouts without obscuring the clarity of his drawings or text. The narrative in black and white is equally funguslike, covering the pages, while his stylized *ligne claire* sits in stark contrast to the sprawling story, helping the less palatable details go down more easily. With multiple versions of himself on display, Killoffer leaves readers with the sense that he feels overcrowded by himself, along with the realization that to overcome existential terror is to come to terms with being fallible. **RPC**

"Who knows? Perhaps I discovered the formula for life in that compost of greasy casseroles."

Similar reads

Epileptic (*L'Ascension du haut-mal*) David B.
Little Nothings Lewis Trondheim
Self-Loathing Comics R. Crumb and Aline Kominsky-Crumb
Spent Joe Matt

Y: The Last Man 2002

Brian K. Vaughan Pia Guerra

First published by Vertigo/DC Comics (USA)
Creators Vaughan (American, b.1976); Guerra (American, b.1971)
Genre Science fiction

VERTIGO
ISSUE 1
SEPT 2002
BRIAN K. VAUGHAN
PIA GUERRA
JOSE MARZAN
SUGGESTED FOR MATURE READERS
Y
THE LAST MAN
DIRECT SALES
vertigocomics.com

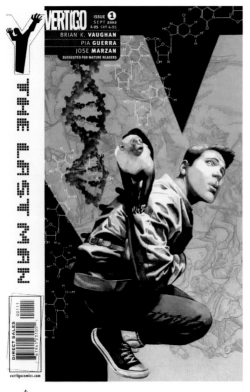

Also by Brian K. Vaughan
Ex Machina with Tony Harris
Pride of Baghdad with Niko Henrichon
Runaways with Adrian Alphona

When readers first meet Yorick, the hero of Brian K. Vaughan's "genderpocalypse" epic *Y: The Last Man*, he is on a long-distance call to his girlfriend, desperately trying to propose marriage while performing an upside-down escape from a straitjacket. Mere minutes after this idyllic scene a mysterious plague has killed off all the males of every species on Earth—with the exception of Yorick and his pet monkey, Ampersand. Yorick then hits the road intent on reaching his girlfriend in Australia—if only to find out her reaction to his proposal. But being the last man on Earth does not have the advantages one might imagine. With the world's infrastructure jammed up and governments depleted, a level of chaos that would make Mad Max feel anxious is the

"Saddle up, sisters! Somewhere out there, the last of our oppressors still lives!"

rule of the day. The Daughters of the Amazon, a radical pseudofeminist group, strives for power—and pounces upon any resistance with vicious fury. Meanwhile, the world's only fully gender-blind military organization, the Israeli Defense Force, has survived with its power structure—and political agenda—intact. Yorick, whom we discover is the son of a U.S. Congresswoman, receives protection from Agent 355, a member of the shadowy Culpeper Ring. But 355's mission—and her relationship with Yorick—is not what it seems.

Vaughan serves up the end of the world as it has never been seen before, taking readers through cunning and logic into a future where all expectations about the sexes are turned on their heads. It is gorgeously illustrated by Pia Guerra's compelling brand of comic book realism, which gives the feeling of a film where all the characters play themselves. **EL**

100% 2002

Paul Pope

In the New York of the future, three romances play out in and around the Catshack, a popular "Gastro" club. Strel is a single mother who manages the dancers. The father of her child is Hiatous, a boxer whom she threw out when they disagreed about his fighting career. John is a busboy. He gave up a career in education when he realized that he did not have a clue what he really wanted. Now at the club, he starts an affair with the dancer Daisy, who sees herself as a passerby, disconnected from everyone else.

Strel takes Daisy to meet Eloy, a struggling artist who is working on a project to create a symphony of one hundred boiling kettles. Kim, a barmaid at the club, starts a relationship with Eloy, but their relationship is threatened when Eloy considers compromising his vision in order to win a grant. Taking place over a couple of weeks, the stories of these couples are enriched by the elaborate, inventive setting that Paul Pope creates. The dancers are not merely strippers; Gastro dancers use magnetic resonance imaging to project three-dimensional images of their internal bodily functions to the audience. Light pollution indicators are used to reduce the effect of strobe lights, mood altering drugs are legal, and there are plans for a man versus robot soccer match.

"In the old days, a flash of ankle was enough. Then a calf, then a thigh . . . But it all got boring. All of it."

In black and white, with his heavily inked panels and fluid lines, Pope evokes a threatening yet vibrant noirish atmosphere. This serves as the backdrop to what are otherwise relatively straightforward tales of people struggling with decisions of how best to live life to the full in a futuristic world. **NFI**

First published by Vertigo/DC Comics (USA)
Creator American (b.1970)
Genre Science fiction
Influenced by Daniel Torres and Jack Kirby

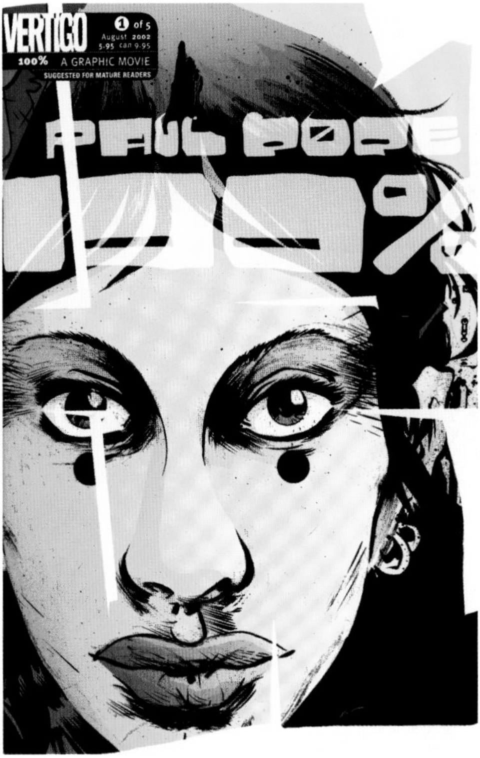
VERTIGO
1 of 5
August 2002
5.95 can 9.95
100% A GRAPHIC MOVIE
SUGGESTED FOR MATURE READERS
PAUL POPE
100%

Also by Paul Pope
Heavy Liquid
THB
The Ballad of Doctor Richardson

The Secret 2002

Andrzej Klimowski

First published by Faber & Faber (UK)
Creator Polish (b.1949)
Genre Drama
Influenced by Harold Pinter

ff
Andrzej Klimowski
THE SECRET

Similar reads
The Depository Andrzej Klimowski
Heights (Cimes) Vincent Fortemps
Horace Dorlan Andrzej Klimowski

The Secret starts relatively normally with a Christmas party scene set in suburbia. What happens next is kind of a Freudian or Poe-esque dream-within-a-dream experience. Freud saw such dreams as being "the most decided confirmation of the reality of the event—the strongest affirmation of it. [...] [It] is used with quite surprising frequency for representing its concealed subject matter." At a certain point in the wordless narrative, the main character dreams that he is shocked by the sight of perfectly normal people being transformed into monsters by a camera obscura (a darkened chamber that projects on one of its walls, through a hole in the opposite side, upside-down images of its surroundings).

The problem of voyeurism is introduced at the beginning. The novel starts with a disturbing voyeuristic eye looking at us, the readers, and ends with the same image. There is also a memorable pair of double-page spreads that is a kind of prologue, showing a woman's face with her eyes closed (spread one) followed by the same image of the woman with her eyes now open (spread two). The voyeur is viewed, and that is as disturbing as the razor knife cutting the (audience's) eye in *Un Chien Andalou*, the surrealist film directed by Salvador Dalí and Luis Buñuel in 1929.

Andrzej Klimowski's drawings are simple but effective. He is a master of crafting disturbing images in which a bright (often artificial) light and well-defined black shadows reveal strange proceedings. The secret is inside the camera obscura: it is how images are produced, how other people's eyes can look at us and see monsters. No one can really escape the camera obscura—and, sometimes, it is pretty bleak and dark in there. This appears to be the story of a husband losing his wife's affection, but it is also a dream that demands interpretation. **DI**

Invincible 2002

Robert Kirkman Cory Walker and Ryan Ottley

Mark Grayson is an average teenager: he hangs out with friends, has a part-time job in a fast food restaurant, and is preparing to go to college. What sets Mark apart is that his father is the most powerful man in the world. He goes by the name Omni-Man and protects humankind. Now that Mark is entering puberty, he has begun to gain his own powers and decides to become a superhero in his own right under the name Invincible. In *Invincible*, Robert Kirkman and his artists have paid homage to or subverted every superhero cliché in what the writer has labeled his "love letter" to superheroes. There are numerous in-jokes to entertain the avid comics reader, such as the *Invincible* version of *Watchmen*'s Rorschach and Dr. Manhattan, or the zombie night that Mark hosts, linking this comic to Kirkman's other title, *The Walking Dead*. A dark twist on the classic image of a hero ripping open his shirt to reveal his costume is transformed here into the shirt being opened and revealing a bomb strapped to a chest that is about to detonate.

The comic takes time to find its feet, and readers may wonder at first what it has to add to the well-trodden path of the superhero genre, playing as it does like a greatest hits of memorable superhero moments: the exhilaration of that first flight, putting on the costume, yearning after the unattainable girl. The first half of volume one is light and lacks anything to define it, until a major development changes the entire tone and the comic delves into decidedly bloodier and more mature territory.

Kirkman is a master of long-form storytelling, having the confidence and patience to craft an intricate world filled with many plot twists and original characters. With *Invincible* he has created both a brave new superhero and superhero comic that may in time earn its place among the great masked legends. **SW**

First published by Image Comics (USA)
Creators Kirkman (American, b.1978); Walker (American, b.1980); Ottley (American, Unknown)
Genre Superhero

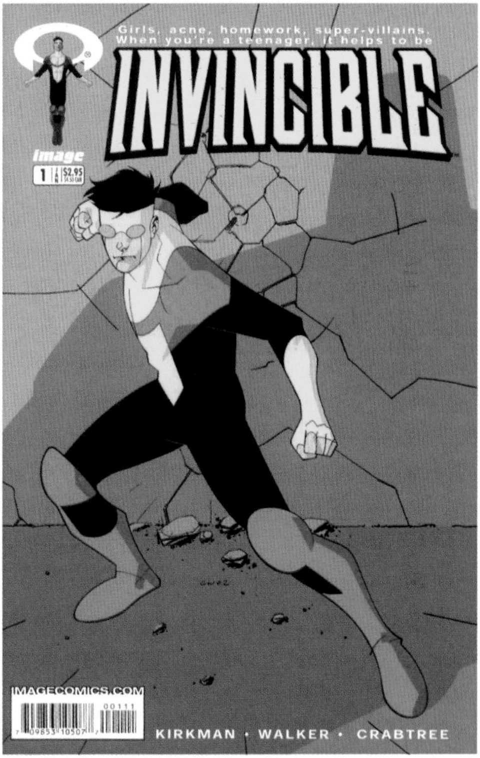
Girls, acne, homework, super-villains.
When you're a teenager, it helps to be
INVINCIBLE
image
1
$2.95
IMAGECOMICS.COM
KIRKMAN • WALKER • CRABTREE

Similar reads

Capes Robert Kirkman and Mark Englert
I Shall Destroy All the Civilized Planets Fletcher Hanks
Kick-Ass Mark Millar and John Romita Jr.

Good Bye 2002

✏✏ Yoshihiro Tatsumi

Title in original language *Daihakken*
First published by Seirinkogeisha (Japan)
Creator Japanese (b.1935)
Genre Drama

Good Bye, the story that gives the collection its title, is grim. Without indulgence and in only a few frames, it paints a picture of a young prostitute in the postwar period who, deciding to come to terms with what she is, shamelessly flaunts herself to her clients: the U.S. soldiers of the occupation forces. Arrogant, she even comes to abuse her own father, a poor devil to whom she regularly gives a little money as a handout. However, after the Americans have left she realizes that her life is at a dead end, and, after an impromptu drinking session, ends up giving herself to her father; it is her way of sealing a hopeless fate. The story ends with a close-up of the father, terrified of his own weakness, repeating incredulously, "We are beasts, we are beasts."

The three other stories in the collection are in a similar vein, as have been almost all the works created by Yoshihiro Tatsumi in the course of his prolific career. He tells of the other side of modern Japan—its dark side—the harshness of which he had experienced personally. A Japan of uprooted people, losers and outcasts, whom the postwar period of frantic reconstruction had ignored—or mercilessly crushed. Unlike the lighthearted, Manichean comic strip, brutal reality carries its full weight here. Spurning aestheticism, Tatsumi's stories are marked by shortage of money, disillusionment, commercialized sex, and impotence. The resigned sadness of his characters and the hopeless feelings that cling to their lives give them a poignant dimension. **NF**

Scarlet Traces 2002

✏ Ian Edginton   ✏ "D'Israeli"

First published by Cool Beans World (UK)
Creators Edginton (British, b.1963);
Matt Brooker (British, Unknown)
Genre Science fiction

A decade after H. G. Wells's failed Martian invasion, London is not quite the place it was. Martian technology has been reverse-engineered and now forms a part of everyday life: taxis walk on mechanical legs, homes are warmed by heat-ray, and London is the undisputed center of the world—but blood-drained bodies are turning up in the low-tide mudflats of the Thames.

When retired Major Robert Autumn and former sergeant turned manservant Archie Currie are informed that Currie's niece is missing after answering an ad for agency workers in southern England, Autumn and Currie decide to investigate. A trip to Scotland shows that the prosperity of the south stays in the south; northern Britain is under martial law. It soon becomes clear that a vast conspiracy is at work, in which the blood of young girls is being used to fuel the dark heart of a technologically dominant British Empire.

Scarlet Traces was commissioned to be a web comic with limited animation for the short-lived Cool Beans World website. It would be a daunting task for anyone to develop a sequel to such an iconic novel as *The War of the Worlds*, but Ian Edginton rises to it with surety, and the tale is ably illustrated by D'Israeli in a style that blends cartoon faces with dark shadows and bright, vivid colors. Echoing Wells's own feelings about the darker side of humanity and empire, *Scarlet Traces* makes for disturbing reading at times. Empires often run on the exploitation of the poor. In winning the war of the worlds and adapting alien technology, Britain's upper class effectively become the Martians. **BD**

Fables 2002

Bill Willingham Mark Buckingham

First published by Vertigo/DC Comics (USA)
Creators Willingham (American, b.1956); Buckingham (British, b.1966)
Genre Fantasy

Outside our mundane world lie the Homelands, the original residences of the displaced characters of myth, legend, and fantasy fiction. In recent times, a mysterious Adversary declared war on these "Fables," conquering their lands and forcing them to escape to New York. There, those who can pass as human live in an underground community called Fabletown, whereas their more fantastical counterparts are kept in seclusion at a more remote institution known as "The Farm."

Fables began its run with a murder-mystery story, and the strength of its premise is immediately apparent; by its very nature it is a comic that utilizes a vast company of characters to embrace virtually any genre of storytelling. In the opening arc, Fabletown's sheriff Bigby (the former Big Bad) Wolf investigates the death of Rose Red, with a number of very familiar faces, including Bluebeard, Snow White, and Prince Charming involved in the process. Bill Willingham playfully recasts *Fables'* main players in inventive extrapolations of their original roles, whether it be Prince Charming as an irredeemable womanizer or Bigby Wolf as a poacher turned gamekeeper.

Artist Mark Buckingham brings a storybook design sense to his page layouts, and a deceptively cartoony style that is a perfect counterpoint to the darker themes of the comic. Later story lines continue to expand upon the war in the Homelands and explore both the true identity of the Adversary and the fractious relationship between Fabletown and the Farm. There have even been a number of spin-off titles, such as *Jack of Fables* and the nonillustrated novel *Peter & Max*. **AO**

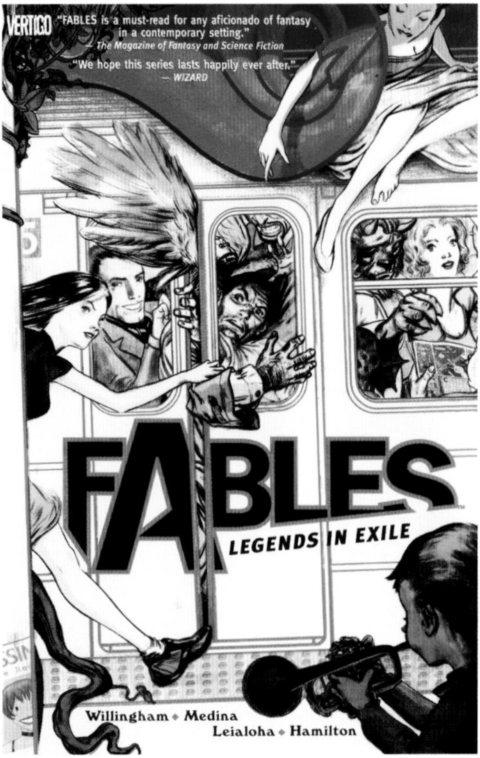
VERTIGO
"FABLES is a must-read for any aficionado of fantasy in a contemporary setting."
— The Magazine of Fantasy and Science Fiction
"We hope this series lasts happily ever after."
— WIZARD
FABLES
LEGENDS IN EXILE
Willingham • Medina
Leialoha • Hamilton

"No Fable shall, by action or inaction, cause our magical nature to become known to the mundane world."

Similar reads

Castle Waiting Linda Medley
Cinderella: From Fabletown with Love Chris Roberson
House of Mystery Matthew Sturges and Bill Willingham
Jack of Fables Matthew Sturges and Bill Willingham

American Elf 2002

James Kochalka

First published by americanelf.com
Creator American (b.1967)
Genre Fantasy
Award Ignatz Award (2002)

Many poet laureates have been named in the United States, at national and state levels. In 2011, an individual was named the country's first ever cartoonist laureate: James Kochalka, in his native Vermont.

The idea of Kochalka as laureate helped cement the reputation of his largest body of work, the ongoing _American Elf_ sketchbook series—a collection of square-format, generally four-panel windows—into Kochalka's daily life. The title confirms the sketches as a kind of comic, everyday poetry, in which pretty patterns turn out to be cat barf, the sensation of the universe's enormity leads to nothing more eventful than one's hair standing on end, and an adult refers to his lost umbrella as a magic wand.

The sketchbooks are loosely drawn: thick lines with limited detail, cartoons about real life in which real life is imbued with the wonderment of cartoons. There are elements of surrealism in the artist's portrayal of himself and his wife as elves. Kochalka started drawing his sketches in 1998, initially self-publishing them through his website and later collecting them into volumes for Top Shelf Productions and various other publishers.

The cartoon is published daily, and each strip documents an actual event Kochalka experiences that day; some are significant, others trivial. In one early strip, he attends a concert by U.S. singer-songwriter Daniel Johnston. In the narrative, Kochalka, a musician himself, describes Johnston's music as "excruciatingly, extraordinarily awkward . . . but beautiful," and the same applies to Kochalka's work. **MW**

30 Days of Night 2002

Steve Niles   _Ben Templesmith_

First published by IDW Publishing (USA)
Creators Niles (American, b.1965);
Templesmith (Australian, b.1978)
Genre Horror

Before _Twilight_ and _True Blood_ made bloodsuckers sexy again, _30 Days of Night_ took the vampire idea to its logical extreme with a suitably high concept: a very long night. The Alaskan town of Barrow is entering winter. It is at this time every year that the community is plunged into a month of darkness, literally thirty days of night. Miles from major cities and any hope of aid, Barrow is alone and completely vulnerable—the perfect hunting ground for the horde of bloodthirsty undead that descends on the town.

An unashamed genre piece, Steve Niles and Ben Templesmith move away from the idea of vampires as romantic, tragic antiheroes and return them to their terrifying roots as wild, monstrous, undead creatures. Templesmith's richly dark pen-and-ink artwork captures the gloomy atmosphere of the wintery locale, the blurry blues and chromatic grays punctuated by flashes of pallid, vampiric faces marked with blood-smeared fangs. The look of the comic perfectly captures the tone and feel of the situation—nothing less than a nightmare.

The horror in _30 Days of Night_ is explicit, and what the comic lacks in subtlety it makes up for in visceral action as Barrow's residents are hunted and ripped apart. This is a comic that takes its idea and runs with it, putting the reader in the middle of a horrific scenario. While not a psychological or layered exploration of terror, _30 Days of Night_ is a high-impact work that announced Niles and Templesmith as brave new talents possessed of a strong visual expression and uncompromising ideas. **SW**

Darkness falls on the ill-fated town of Barrow in _30 Days of Night_. ➡

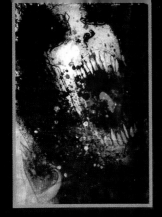

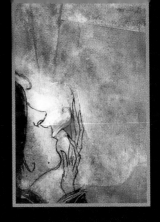

IT COULDN'T HAVE WORKED OUT BETTER.

THE HUMANS NEVER SAW THEM COMING, AND DIDN'T KNOW WHAT TO DO ONCE THEY ARRIVED.

IT WAS EVERYTHING MARLOW DREAMED.

EVERYTHING HE HAD PLANNED...

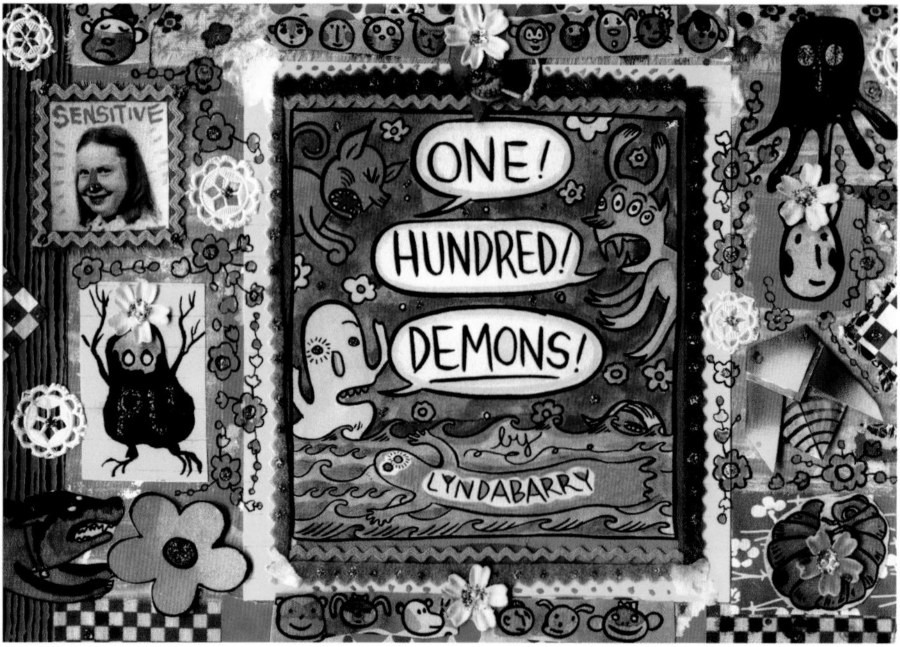
SENSITIVE
ONE!
HUNDRED!
DEMONS!
by
LYNDABARRY

One! Hundred! Demons! 2002

Lynda Barry

First published by Salon.com
Creator American (b.1956)
Genre Reality drama
Award Eisner Award (2003)

Lynda Barry was first published when Matt Groening secretly decided to run one of her cartoons in their college newspaper, and she has spent the ensuing decades making a name for herself with both influential strips (*Ernie Pook's Comeek* is the best known) and groundbreaking novels. With *One! Hundred! Demons!*, her most autobiographical work to date, Barry returns to one of her favorite themes: the pangs of growing up. Inspired by a Japanese monk's illustrated scroll cataloging the world's devils, these tales each take for their subject some of Barry's more mundane bugbears, such as head lice. Each of the seventeen short works in this collection—full of the sort of moments that seem ordinary at the time, but extraordinary in memory—give rise not just to greater clarity on Barry's part, but beautiful moments of meditation for readers. These anecdotes are also sometimes extremely amusing—no one draws the fierce indignation of an angry child like Barry, and no one writes better childish insults. The precision of her dialogue is crucial in bringing to life her mother and grandmother. However, Barry is equally as good with the casual put-downs of teenage boys or the paranoid ramblings of hippies. Barry believes in the power of writing by hand as a creative tool, and this book—hand-drawn and lettered with a Japanese ink and wash *sumi* brush, then effusively, colorfully collaged—channels such deep emotions that it is hard to argue with her. One is left hoping that Barry is secretly working on exorcizing more demons soon. **EL**

"A wild mixture of art history and mystery...His depiction of artists--Picasso, Braque, Stein, Satie, and Appollinaire... is strange, humorous, and thrilling." --Jonathan Ames, *Wake Up, Sir!*

THE SALON BY Nick Bertozzi

The Salon 2002

Nick Bertozzi

First published by Serializer.net
Creator American (b.1970)
Genre Fantasy
Award Ignatz Nomination (2003)

First appearing in 2002 as a web comic on the influential Serializer.net, *The Salon*'s tale begins when the young Georges Braque enters the bohemian coterie of Gertrude and Leo Stein, sibling art enthusiasts living in Paris in the early twentieth century. There he discovers a world in turmoil. The Steins should be joyously happy in their avant-garde paradise. After all, their salon includes such epochal talents as Henri Matisse, Erik Satie, Guillaume Apollinaire, and, in a memorable appearance, Pablo Picasso. Instead, they are terrified by a series of murders—with painters and their associates the victims—that they suspect have a root in the sad fate of Paul Gauguin and his Polynesian bride Annah.

With the help of their artist comrades, the Steins visit brothels, rival galleries, and back alleys in search of the killers. Along the way, they discover the secret of the blue absinthe that enables the brave (and slightly foolhardy) to enter paintings, exploring them as they would the streets of Montmartre. In this great feat of imagination and construction, Nick Bertozzi—the author of the Xeric grant-winning map comic *Boswash* and the short story collection *The Masochists*—is in fine form, enjoying his Parisian setting and relishing an opportunity to play with the phonetics of the French language (sound effects include "fronc," "dangue," and "monche"). With his juicy lines and coolly modulated colors that bring to mind the unconventional palette of the modernist painters, Bertozzi brings the Steins's salon—and its mystery—to convincing life. **EL**

Genshiken 2002

✐✐ Kio Shimoku

First published by Kodansha (Japan)
Creator Japanese (b.1974)
Genre Adult humor
Adaptation TV anime (2004)

This comic is aimed at the passionate fans of *otaku* (geek) culture, be it animation, comics, videogames, or cosplay. *Genshiken* explores the lives of young geeks in Japan, from where the term originated.

The story begins when Kanji Sasahara, the central character, enters college. He is a closet *otaku* but is determined to change, so he joins a club called the Genshiken, or The Society for the Study of Modern Visual Culture. There he is introduced to an array of eccentric characters: Makoto Kousaka, whose looks are unusually handsome for an *otaku*; Harunobe Madarame, the stereotypical *otaku*; the overweight Mitsunori Kugayama, who stutters when he speaks; the large-breasted cosplayer Kanako Ohno; and Saki Kasukabe, the *otaku*-hating girlfriend of Kousaka. Throughout the four years he spends with them, the "semi-*otaku*" Sasahara comes face to face with his true identity and gradually discovers the right path to his future. While embracing Japan's *otaku* culture, the comic also chronicles a tale of moral growth.

In modern-day Japan, *otaku* are often still a target for mockery. Yet Shimoku Kio's characters remain unaffected, collecting animations featuring *bishojo* (beautiful young girls), adult video games, and magazines on which the general public frowns. The students still care about what others think, but they have vowed to stay true to their hearts, and, as Sasahara says when entering college, they are prepared to stick to their passions in spite of criticism, providing a glimpse of what the world of *otaku* is all about. **TS**

Prosopopus 2002

✐✐ Nicolas de Crécy

First published by Dupuis (Belgium)
Creator French (b.1966)
Genre Crime, Fantasy
Influence on Sylvain Chomet

This wordless, genre mash-up of gritty crime thriller and cartoon craziness revolves around the forgery of an abstract painter's valuable masterpiece. To fabricate this fake, gangsters coerce the artist's boyfriend to steal her most unique mark—her thumbprint—with which she signs her works, first by sneaking a wax impression, then, horrifyingly, by cutting off her hand and disposing of her body in a faked car accident—all for cold cash.

Like the doomed figure in a classic noir, the lover-turned-killer tries to hit back by assassinating the mob boss, but this only triggers the apparition of Prosopopus, a giant cartoonlike bear. He is a smothering nightmarish creature with two protruding front teeth and swollen blubbery lips, as impossibly indestructible as any animated funny animal. But is he a savior or a monster? Prosopopus seems to adore the murderous protagonist and sets out to help him by retrieving incriminating evidence from the FBI's offices.

Some have interpreted this increasingly unhinged urban fairy tale as an allegory for Nicolas de Crécy's breakup with his creative partner, Sylvain Chomet, who directed the acclaimed 2003 animated movie *Belleville Rendez-vous* without him, and for de Crécy's sense of betrayal at this perceived theft of his identity and his mixed feelings about how and whether to seek retribution. All the book's piled-up vendettas, toppling domino-style, suggest that ultimately revenge is fruitless and will more than likely backfire. Whether it grew from cathartic autobiography or pure fancy, *Prosopopus* stands as a rich, bizarre chiller of rare quality. **PG**

A–Z 2002

Lars Arrhenius

First published by Peer (UK)
Creator Swedish (b.1966)
Genre Reality drama
Award Nominated for Carnegie Art Award (2002)

Commissioned by London gallery Peer to create a large wall display, Swedish artist Lars Arrhenius chose the classic *A to Z* map book of London over which to weave his multiple story paths. The result was also published as a stylized facsimile of an actual *A to Z*. London's popular street guide breaks down the capital into a grid of double-page spreads. On each page, arrows point to the four compass points, directing the reader to where the map on that page continues, sometimes on the next spread, sometimes several pages before or after. This format forms a perfect labyrinthine reading system for Arrhenius's overlapping streams of wry urban encounters. He draws his nameless characters in a detached *ligne claire* style, flatly colored, with their thoughts and speech communicated through symbols similar to those used on airline passenger safety cards. In eighteen varied scenarios that evolve through more than 250 circular textless illustrations, characters flow into the map book and navigate through the pages—often crossing paths with other characters—before flowing out to continue their narratives unobserved. Conventional reading order is confounded, so the reader has no choice but to investigate where each story leads.

The back pages compare *A–Z* to Hergé's "web of intertextuality" in the *Tintin* album *The Castafiore Emerald*, while Geoff Ryman's questionnaire serves to stimulate reader interpretation. Critics have long noted similarities between comics and maps in the way both enable users to navigate using signs and symbols. This book puts those theories into fascinating practice. **PG**

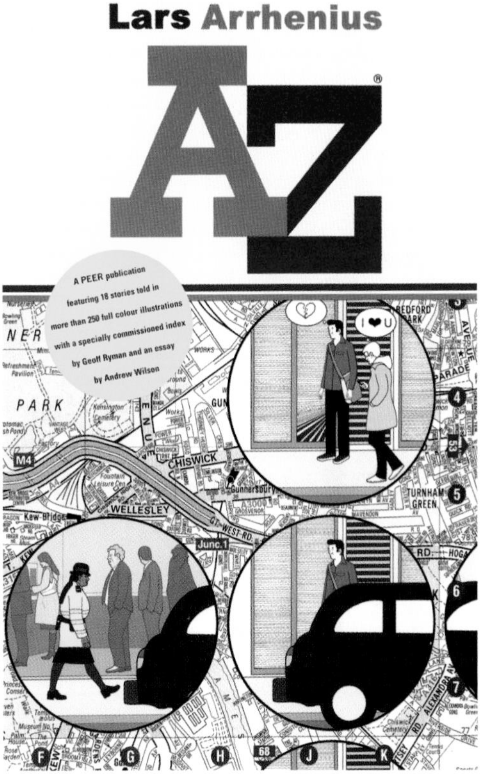

Lars Arrhenius
AZ
A PEER publication featuring 18 stories told in more than 250 full colour illustrations with a specially commissioned index by Geoff Ryman and an essay by Andrew Wilson
PARK
CHISWICK
WELLESLEY
TURNHAM GREEN

"Something interesting has just happened. What is it?"

Geoff Ryman's reader questionnaire

Similar reads
Acme Novelty Library 20 Chris Ware
Hieronymous Pop Daniel Merlin Goodbrey
The Man Without One Way Lars Arrhenius

The Filth 2002

Grant Morrison   Chris Weston and Gary Erskine

First published by Vertigo/DC Comics (USA)
Creators Morrison (British, b.1960); Weston (British, b.1969); Erskine (British, b.1968)
Genre Fantasy

The Filth
01. us vs them
A SERIES OF 13 BOOKS
AUGUST 2002
USA $2.95 CAN $4.95
SUGGESTED FOR MATURE READERS
vs
Grant Morrison
Chris Weston
Gary Erskine
Contains
23 Pages
DIRECT SALES
dccomics.com

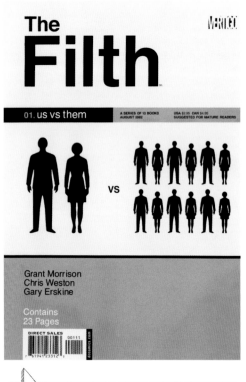

Similar reads

Fluorescent Black M. F. Wilson and Nathan Fox
The Invisibles Grant Morrison and various
We3 Grant Morrison and Frank Quitely
X'ed Out Charles Burns

Veering between the populism of Warren Ellis and the mystical, shamanic qualities of Alan Moore, Grant Morrison—author of *The Invisibles*, *Arkham Asylum*, *Doom Patrol*, and more—is known as an artistic explorer among comic book writers. With *The Filth*, the writer goes further into our subconscious than ever before.

Readers first meet Greg Feely, a seemingly ordinary man, when he is relaxing at home after shopping for hard-core pornography and cat food. Enter Agent Miami, a psychedelic Pam Greer lookalike and willing tool of the Hand, a shadowy organization operating on the fringes of public consciousness. She drags Greg back to his "real" life as Agent Ned Slade. Their mission as Hand operatives is to stop society from tearing itself apart.

"Luteinizing hormone, progesterone, estrogen . . . talk dirty to me, Slade."

Ned is back on duty—but how much longer will he play the Hand's game? And why has a seemingly identical Greg Feely moved into Greg's old apartment, albeit one with considerably less concern for Greg's cat's welfare? Meanwhile, a variety of nefarious plots have hatched in the underworld of the porn industry. Will the Hand triumph in its battle against chaos? Will Ned ever be truly free? In this postmodern, postsuperhero world, Morrison invents a panoply of great characters, including Dmitri-9, a chimpanzee assassin whose aphorisms on the fall of the Soviet Empire must be read to be believed.

While titillating readers' minds with images from an alternate reality drenched in madness, Morrison cunningly spins a mind-bendingly metafictive tale that defies traditional narrative conventions, and with the painfully colorful art by Chris Weston and Gary Erskine, *The Filth* is less a story than an experience. **EL**

Clumsy 2002

Jeffrey Brown

A brutally honest portrait of young love, Jeffrey Brown's first graphic novel, *Clumsy*, established him as one of the most important cartoonists to emerge in the 2000s. *Clumsy* tells the true story of his relationship with Theresa, from their first meeting to their eventual breakup. Brown presents the work in roughly chronological order, although the short chapters frequently appear out of order. This complex narrative structure recalls the way that memory works—selectively and somewhat arbitrarily—contributing to the sense that the feelings and emotions that define the work are completely genuine. More than almost any other autobiographical comic, *Clumsy* creates an impression that the artist is laying himself bare to the reader.

"I'm not ready to read about you being in love with someone else."

Readers are divided on the subject of Brown's drawings. The entire book is rendered in an extremely spare visual style that strikes some readers as unaccomplished. A more fitting description would be direct, or unmediated. Brown's work carries with it the force of brutal honesty, and, in reading *Clumsy*, one cannot help but be struck with the idea that one is peeking into a very personal diary. Much of *Clumsy* deals with sex, and because those acts are presented in a way that is intimate and almost completely devoid of prurient eroticism, the book has a deeply personal quality that would most likely be mitigated by a more traditionally polished visual tone.

Jeffrey Brown continued to explore his relationships with women in subsequent graphic novels, but *Clumsy* established the template for what would follow and it remains the most powerful and direct expression of his relationship preoccupations. **BB**

First published by Top Shelf Productions (USA)
Creator American (b.1975)
Genre Reality drama
Influenced by Chris Ware and Julie Doucet

CLUMSY
A NOVEL
BY JEFFREY BROWN
$10.00
PARENTAL ADVISORY EXPLICIT CONTENT

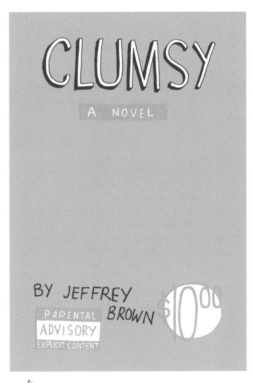

Similar reads
Blankets Craig Thompson
Journal Fabrice Neaud
King-Cat John Porcellino
Spent Joe Matt

The Boulevard of Broken Dreams 2002

Kim Deitch

First published by Pantheon Books (USA)
Creator American (b.1944)
Genre Political fable
Influenced by Gene Deitch

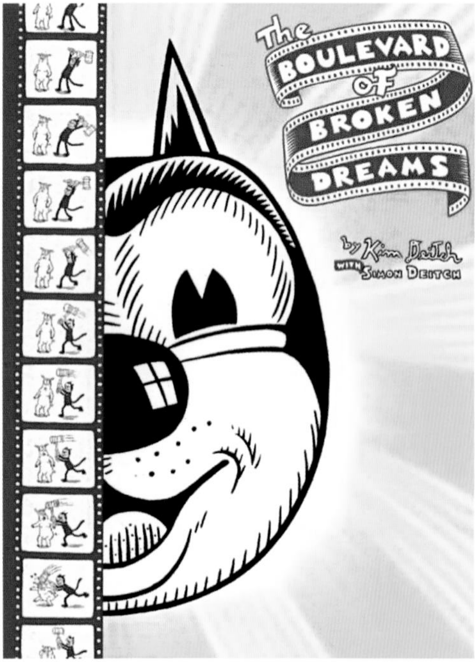

The Boulevard of Broken Dreams
by Kim Deitch
with Simon Deitch

Also by Kim Deitch
A Shroud for Waldo
All Waldo Comics
Beyond the Pale
Shadowland
The Stuff of Dreams

An animation studio called Fontaine Talking Fables has as its star a character named "Waldo," who used to be animator Ted Mishkin's imaginary friend. That is what his brother Al thinks. It seems Ted still sees and talks to Waldo.

Ted's studio is facing financial ruin unless it can find a way to compete with Disney. Jack Schick, who has just quit Disney, is brought in to soften up Waldo's image, making him bright-eyed and ruddy-cheeked. As Ted is an alcoholic and not very stable mentally, these sudden changes precipitate a decline that his assistant, Lillian, cannot conceal from his bosses. Following a nervous breakdown, Ted begins working with animation pioneer Winsor Newton, creator of Milton the Mastodon, in an attempt to win the war between art and commercialism.

Waldo's "history" and those of Ted, Al, and Lillian, from 1927 until 1993, are shown against the backdrop of the history of American cinema, drawing on the changes brought about by Disney's success, the hearings of the House Un-American Activities Committee, the birth of the amusement park, and the rise of product merchandising.

Kim Deitch's depiction of alcoholism and delusion makes for unsettling, sometimes almost hallucinatory, reading. This is a remarkable twisted "history" of U.S. animation. Waldo is largely a secondary character, but his malevolent presence always adds a dark humor to the proceedings, particularly when he is reacting to his new, cuter depiction on screen. Deitch's sharply inked black-and-white line work is perfectly suited to the emotional drama, capable of capturing complex detail. Working here with his brother Simon, Kim is the son of animator and Oscar-winning director Gene, and grew up with an interest in animation and vaudeville. He first introduced Waldo in strips for the paper *The East Village Other,* where he started work in 1967. **NFI**

Modern Speed 2002

"Blutch"

As she leaves her dance class, a young Parisian woman named Lola is approached in the street by a person whom she does not know. This person, Renée, insistently asks her to agree to be the subject of her next book. She will have to agree to being followed by Renée everywhere, day and night, to the heart of her most private intimate experiences. Lola accepts the proposal spontaneously, without really knowing why—perhaps in order to be temporarily relieved of Rudy, an obese cellist and her stubborn suitor, who has also come to wait for her to emerge from her dance class.

So begins an apparently random journey through an often incongruous Paris that leads the two young women into improbable situations (the city is suddenly emptied of all its inhabitants subject to a complete power cut, and then a giant flood) in unknown places, all set to the rhythm of classic French songs. Readers learn little of the backgrounds or the motives of the key characters, or even what drives this strange story. However, by the end of the book they will have met an interesting cast of people whose impulses, deviations, and obsessions reflect—to varying degrees—the poetry that is often nestled deep within the fabric of everyday life.

Modern Speed is a UFO in the landscape of comics. Perhaps it is the closest graphic equivalent to what the European surrealists tried to practice in literature with the invention of automatic writing. Blutch is regarded by many to be one of the most talented writers of his generation in Franco-Belgian comics, and he does nothing to dispel the enigmatic dimension of his book or to restore the constantly distorted internal consistency. The only things that really matter to him as an artist are the raw primal beauty of line and the flight of the creative imagination in a state of complete freedom. **NF**

Title in original language *Vitesse moderne*
First published by Dupuis (Belgium)
Creator Christian Hincker (French, b.1967)
Genre Alternative

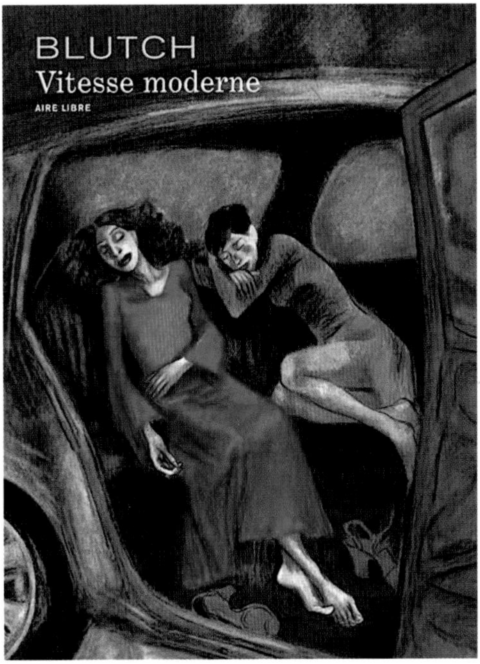
BLUTCH
Vitesse moderne
AIRE LIBRE

Also by Blutch
C'était le bonheur
Donjon Monster with Lewis Trondheim and Joann Sfar
Mitchum
Péplum
Rancho Bravo with Jean-Louis Capron

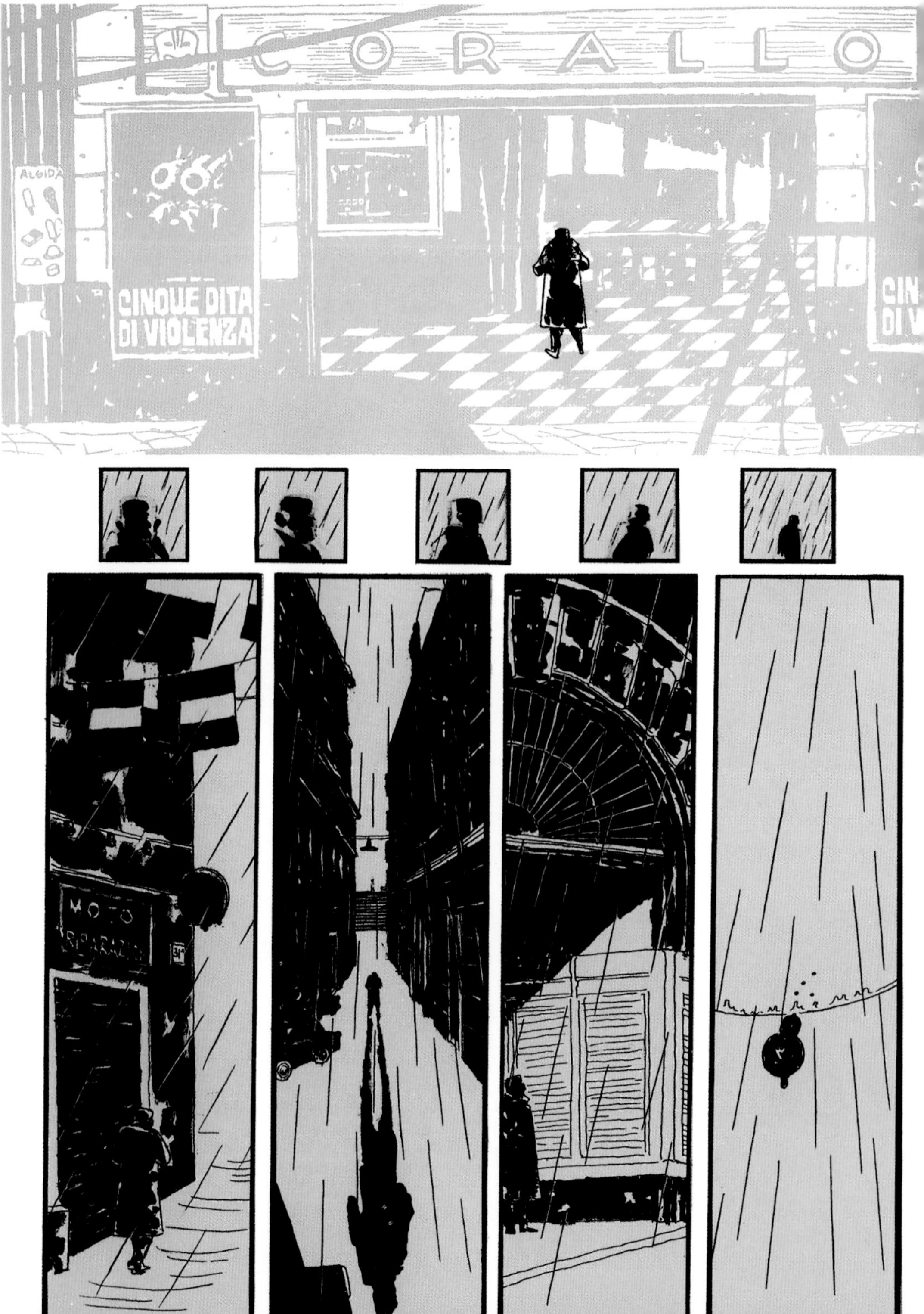
CORALLO
ALGIDA
CINQUE DITA DI VIOLENZA
MOTO

5 Is the Perfect Number 2002

✐✐ "Igort"

Title in original language *5 è il numero perfetto*
First published by Coconino Press (Italy)
Creator Igor Tuveri (Italian, b.1958)
Genre Drama

Peppino Lo Cicero—whom everyone calls only by his nickname, Peppi—is a delicate, sensitive, old man. The bulk of his life is now devoted to looking after his son Nino, and to recollecting the good times of days gone by, an era in which he was a virtuoso killer feared by all . . .

One evening, Nino, who has become Peppi's successor, has to go to Naples on business. "Don't come back too late," his father tells him on the doorstep. "That way, we can go fishing together tomorrow." But Nino will not return: the contract on which he has been sent is a fatal setup, and Peppi is the next target. The rest of the narrative has the old man using his lifetime of experience to seek revenge, insensitive to the prospect of his own death, which he has been expecting.

Presented in the format of a graphic novel and employing a subtle bluish two-tone technique that makes the contrasts stand out, *5 Is the Perfect Number* appeals in the manner of a cinematographic creation, like a dark choreography that has been secretly filmed. Peppi's vendetta is depicted as dry and meticulously planned; each gesture is measured, every word hits the target, each decorative element has a meaning. Skilled in constructing a pure visual language and full of symbolism, Igort composes even the smallest of his frames with extreme care, the empty spaces and silences all working to convey the dramatic narrative.

The story of *5 Is a Perfect Number* has an uncommon intensity that propels the reader through the narrative, in what is Igort's best work to date. **NF**

The Color of Earth 2003

✐✐ Kim Dong Hwa

Title in original language *Hwangtobit Iyagi*
First published by Happy Comics Works (Korea)
Creator South Korean (b.1950)
Genre Drama

It has always been rare in the world of comics for stories about women to attract the attention of male authors, and even rarer that the latter succeed in achieving a genuine empathy with their subject. This ambitious comic tells the story of two women, a mother and her daughter, living in the rural world of deepest Korea in a period that is not exactly specified by the author, Kim Dong Hwa, but that is roughly before World War II, in the 1930s.

The story is a personal one: it not only tells of the relationship between mother and daughter, but also describes their individual adventures in love. In this respect, their profile is atypical. The mother is a widow and is bringing up her daughter on her own while at the same time running the little country restaurant that provides them with an income. However, living without a man in the home is not always easy, not to mention the problems caused in the eyes of the community by their choice of an independent life. Hwa paints a portrait of two liberated women that is both unexpected and engaging. Their sensual freedom and closeness lead to a strong bond that will resist all the blows dealt by fate.

Hwa has created a genuine historical document by bringing to life a Korea that no longer exists. However, it is the deep humanity of his moving story that really makes an impression: punctuated by moments of grace, the relationship between mother and daughter acquires a universal resonance—a characteristic that is always the mark of a masterpiece. **NF**

◀ The silences add greatly to the noirish atmosphere in *5 Is the Perfect Number*.

Death Note 2003

Tsugumi Ohba   Takeshi Obata

First published by Shueisha (Japan)
Creators Ohba (Japanese, b.1969); Obata (Japanese, b.1969)
Genre Horror

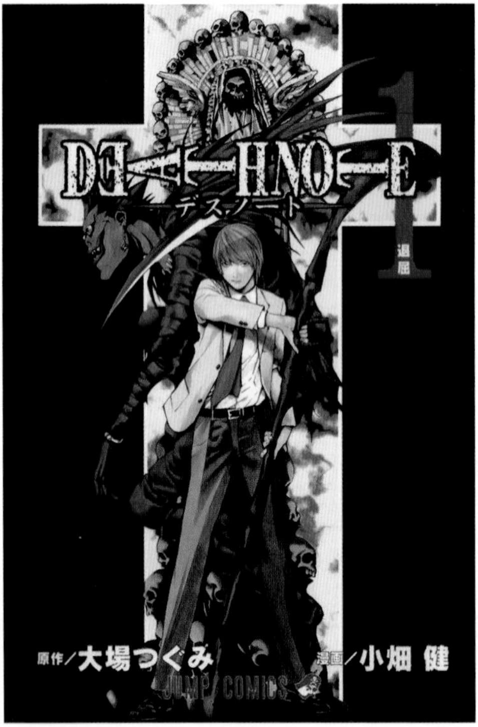
デスノート
1
原作/大場つぐみ
漫画/小畑 健
JUMP COMICS

Similar reads

Bakuman Tsugumi Ohba and Takeshi Obata
Darker Than Black Tensai Okamura, Bones, and Nokiya
Devilman Go Nagai
MPD Psycho Eiji Otsuka

Ryuuk is a supernatural Shinigami (death god), one of a race of beings who inhabit a realm beyond Earth where, despite their immense powers and the circumstances of their existence, not a lot happens. In a bid to overcome his boredom, Ryuuk decides to randomly leave a "Death Note" book on Earth. The notebook enables the human in possession of it to kill anyone by inscribing their name on it while imagining their face. If a cause of death is written within forty seconds of writing a name, that person will die as specified. Ryuuk thought it would be entertaining to see how whomever picked it up decided to respond to it.

Seventeen-year-old Light Yagami, a student similarly bored with life, is the one who finds Ryuuk's experiment. Picking the notebook up off the sidewalk outside his school, he takes it home and reads it. He decides it is a powerful tool for good and begins to use it to rid the world of the evil he sees everywhere. When criminals and evildoers start dropping like flies the famous detective L. is given the task of finding their killer, and a battle of wits ensues between L. and the increasingly psychotic and self-righteous Yagami, who is seeking to create an earthly utopia.

"What's going to happen to me . . . ? Are you going to take my soul?"

Writer Tsugumi Ohba wanted to produce concise dialogue for *Death Note* because he felt reading too many words would be counterproductive to the visual suspense he was attempting to create. Obata's art elegantly blends Yagami's earthly and Ryuuk's interdimensional worlds. There is also an intriguing cast of intelligent characters fueled by a refreshingly original plot with twists aplenty, together with a good serving of manga-style bloodshed. **BS**

Derek the Sheep 2003

Gary Northfield

It is a harder life than one might think, being a sheep. Whether it is being bothered by bulls, wolves, or fire-breathing trolls, there is always something to spoil your day. Such is the lot of Derek, an impulsive, charming, and rather silly sheep living with his woolly brethren on a farm in the English countryside. Derek is a magnet for trouble; whatever he tries to do, it always goes wrong.

Individual *Derek* stories run between four and eight pages long, each one a short, concentrated burst of insanity. Derek finds himself stealing Farmer Jack's tractor in a low-speed getaway, discovers a pot of gold at the end of a rainbow (along with a very annoyed leprechaun), is kidnapped by a wolf with a surprisingly nice house, goes sledding with some

"Hey, cow-pat breath. Fancy a tango with the best-looking sheep in Britain?"

of the other animals, and enters the "Farmyard Best Haircut" competition. Yet he faces more down-to-earth problems too, such as getting rid of annoying flies from his behind or coping with bad weather. Accompanied (and sometimes led on) by his sheep friends Lenny, Daisy, and Daphne, as well as Cecil the Bee and Nobby the Hedgehog, life never seems to be quiet.

Gary Northfield is the first cartoonist to have a creator-owned strip appear in *The Beano*; his stories are loosely plotted and very charming in their simplicity. One gets the impression that he begins a story without necessarily knowing where it might end, giving his tales a sense of free-flowing delirium where practically anything could happen. The stories are brightly colored and drawn with a roughness that, in Northfield's hands, has a charming style similar to the work of Quentin Blake and harks back to subversive creators such as Leo Baxendale, but with a voice that is fresh and new. **BD**

First published by D. C. Thomson (UK)
Creator British (b.1969)
Genre Humor, Children's
Influenced by Peter Bagge and Jim Woodring

Derek the Sheep
Gary Northfield
As featured in The Beano

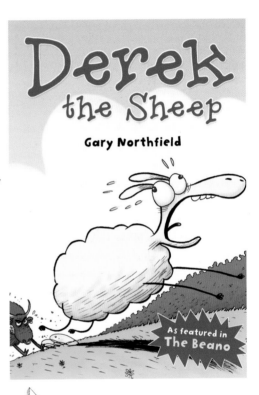

Similar reads

Bad Dog Gary Northfield
Good Dog Bad Dog Dave Shelton
Little Cutie Gary Northfield
Vern and Lettuce Sarah McIntyre

Pluto 2003

🖉 Naoki Urasawa, Takashi Nagasaki 🖉 Naoki Urasawa

Title in original language *PLUTO: Urasawa x Tezuka*
First published by Shogakukan (Japan)
Creators Urasawa (Japanese, b.1960); Nagasaki
(Japanese, b.1956) **Genre** Science fiction

Astro Boy is one of the most recognizable series created by Osamu Tezuka. The problem is that while many people have heard of *Astro Boy*, not as many have actually read it. Today, Astro Boy is more widely renowned as a pop-culture figure than for the quality of the original manga in which he first appeared. Although *Pluto* features characters from *Astro Boy*, it is far from a spin-off or a remake of Tezuka's *Astro Boy* story "The Greatest Robot on Earth."

Firstly, it is aimed at a more mature audience. The story is about a robot killer, but, unlike the original story line, it does not focus on robot fight scenes. It is a darker, almost noirish, detective story. Like *Astro Boy*, there is an element of a modern Pinocchio tale about *Pluto* as robots pose the question of how they are different from humans. Such questions force readers to consider what it means to actually be human.

Secondly, *Pluto* does not put Astro Boy at the center of the story. Instead, background characters from that series are brought to the fore and provided with more developed identities. A further distinction is that the drawing style of both stories is completely different because Macoto Tezuka (the son of *Astro Boy* creator Osamu Tezuka) asked Naoki Urasawa not to copy Osamu Tezuka's style but draw in his own manner, a request that Urasawa honored. With all the awards and critical acclaim that *Pluto* has garnered over the years, it would seem that readers agree that it is a significant standalone work and not merely another *Astro Boy* spin-off. **RB**

Fluffy 2003

🖉🖉 Simone Lia

First published by Cabanon Press (UK)
Creator British (b.1974)
Genre Humor, Funny animal
Award Deutsche Bank Pyramid Award for Design (2004)

A British-born Maltese with parallel careers in children's books and illustration, Simone Lia developed her first graphic novel, *Fluffy*, as a series of four booklets when she joined Tom Gauld in the self-publishing partnership Cabanon Press. Step aside Bugs Bunny, Thumper, and McConey, there's an even more aggravating yet adorable cartoon rabbit in the shape of Fluffy.

Fluffy is a long-eared, white-furred chatterbox who goes to nursery school in English suburbia and is being raised by harried and unmarried Michael Pulcino. The long-suffering Michael keeps trying to tell Fluffy, "I'm not your real daddy" and "I'm a man and you're a bunny," but nothing seems to diminish Fluffy's love for this unlikely father figure. Their peculiar, touching relationship develops on a trip to Sicily. Michael wants to escape various stresses, including the persistent attention of Fluffy's schoolmistress Miss Owers, who wants to be his girlfriend so badly that she flies out to the island to "surprise" him.

In *Fluffy*, Lia has created an unpredictable, slightly surreal, and reflective human drama without losing her childlike playfulness. She inserts diagrams of the thoughts cramming a character's head and wacky asides from guest narrators—a cheery dust particle or a grouchy piece of dandruff. Lia can animate the most minimal figures into characters with vibrant human personalities. The secret behind her simple-looking comics is how they wittily question preconceived ideas and pose philosophical puzzles. *Fluffy* is a unique parable about the needful, loving bunny inside us all. **PG**

Blankets 2003

Craig Thompson

First published by Top Shelf Productions (USA)
Creator American (b.1975)
Genre Reality drama
Awards Harvey (2004); Eisner (2004); Ignatz (2004)

This poignant, beautifully drawn memoir vividly re-creates the tribulations of growing up as a talented and sensitive artist in small-town America. Intricately structured, and as multilayered as a good novel, the 600 pages of this intimate epic fly by, so subtle and finely rendered are its characters.

In Craig Thompson's childhood struggles with his brother, their imaginative play becomes a refuge from their harsh fundamentalist Christian parents and abusive babysitters. Thompson's nascent career as an artist meets with criticism from his family and deeply Christian community, who only want him to fit in with their ideology. He goes off to church camp with a heavy heart, yet, to his amazement, he falls in love with the complex and popular Raina. Their story is one of the most boldly romantic yet realistic love stories you will ever read.

The artwork is truly gorgeous, amplifying the inner lives of its characters while gently and affectionately mocking them. Thompson's growth as a character is augmented by his storytelling in this visually arresting, graceful celebration of the subtleties of comic art. Thompson has commented: "I just kind of fell in love with [comics], suddenly. It filled all my needs—I was able to draw cartoons, to tell a story; but I also had total control, and I wasn't just a cog in some machine somewhere." The challenge of being an individual in a world of conformity, and of finding something new to say about love in all its forms—from friendship to erotic love—is at the core of this big-hearted book. **AK**

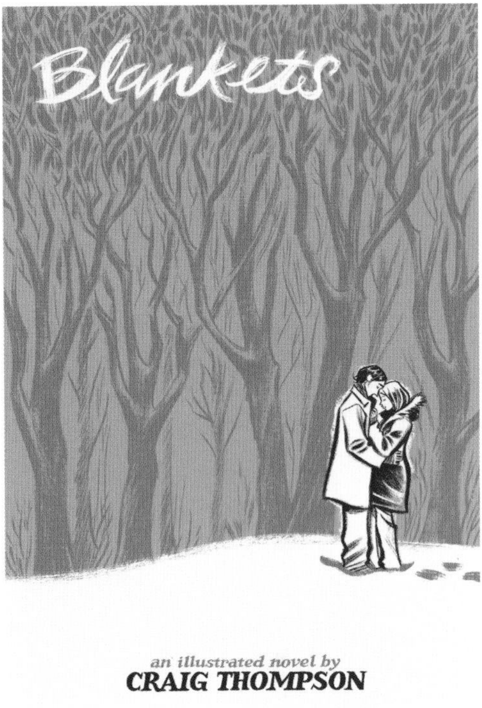

Blankets
an illustrated novel by
CRAIG THOMPSON

"Pressed against her I can hear ETERNITY—hollow lonely spaces and currents that churn ceaselessly. . . ."

Similar reads

Binky Brown Meets the Holy Virgin Mary Justin Green
Black Hole Charles Burns
Fun Home Alison Bechdel
Good-bye, Chunky Rice Craig Thompson
My New York Diary Julie Doucet

Lou! 2003

Julien Neel

First published by Glénat (France)
Creator French (b.1976)
Genre Teen
Award Angoulême Youth Award (2005)

Julien Neel
T1.
Lou!
JOURNAL INTIME
Glénat

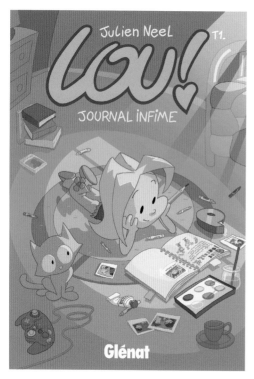

"The story of Lou is a kind of restructuring of my own life."

Julien Neel

"Lou, the story you are not going to be able to resist!" was the slogan on the cover of issue #61 of *Tchô*, which came out in September 2003. Conceived by Zep and the publisher Jean-Claude Camano, the "mégazine" had already launched a considerable number of young talents. *Lou!* chronicles the life of a young girl from preadolescence to late teens. When it appeared, Julien Neel was twenty-seven years old, and it was not long before a first collection was published. From the very start, Neel intended the miniseries to end with volume eight, when the heroine turned eighteen.

The narrative structure meant that there were particular events to be told in each album, carefully selected slices of life that were all rendered sensitively because the author included numerous personal elements. With its autobiographical touch, *Lou!* was not as humorous as most of the other cartoons in the magazine that published it, but being sincere, sensitive, and generous, it has attracted an increasingly wide readership.

Its charm lies in the detailed, realistic description of the temperament of this independent young girl. Her story starts when she is twelve years old, surrounded by good friends including Mina, her best friend, and Tristan, her boyfriend. Lou has never met her father and lives in the city with her mother, who is a writer. She persuades Lou to make the acquaintance of Richard, who lives on the same floor in the apartment block. The narrative follows Lou year by year: one summer she stays on vacation with her grandmother, meets new friends, has her first adolescent crisis, and experiences her first romance. Significantly, Julien Neel's delicate drawing style, with colored outlining strokes (a technique derived from his experience in animated cartoons), enables him to be gentle in his approach to some of the more serious themes. **CM**

Pyongyang 2003

Guy Delisle

Without wanting to overstate its importance, *Pyongyang* is one of the few reliable documents available in the West to give some kind of insight into daily life in North Korea in the twenty-first century. The story, as told by Quebecois animator and cartoonist Guy Delisle, is pretty much autobiographical.

A supervisor at a French-language animation company, Delisle is dispatched to the North Korean capital, Pyongyang, for a few months in order to coordinate the work of a local animation subcontractor. A standard practice of modern animation production, where it is often only the initial design work that is still done directly in Europe or the United States, the bulk of the work in hand-drawn animation is usually outsourced to countries with lower labor costs. And few countries can match North Korea for its cheapness.

What awaits Delisle when he arrives in Pyongyang is far removed from what he is accustomed to. At his side, readers witness the numerous absurd constraints of a strange and culturally sealed country that was cooped up for half a century in totalitarian paranoia. Over the days, the reader becomes familiar with all aspects of Delisle's regimented life as a foreigner, as he settles in at the special hotel where all the other foreigners live on the fifteenth floor (apparently the only one with electricity). Readers are privy to the countless restrictions on food and energy that pervade North Korean society and the ubiquitous propaganda—the invisible iron fist—that weighs down on every citizen. The incongruities of Korean life are funny and awful at the same time.

Part diary, part travel narrative, and part fiction, Delisle mobilizes all his skills as an animator to craft a tale that is far more polished than a mere improvisation. But it is still a vivid demonstration of the ability of the individual to chronicle an absurd reality. **NF**

First published by L'Association (France)
Creator Canadian (b.1966)
Genre Reality drama
Influenced by *Shenzhen*

GUY DELISLE
PYONGYANG
L'Association

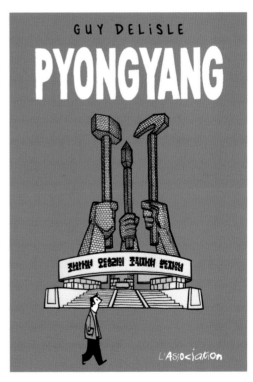

"If anyone did talk to me they'd probably be viewed as suspect, so looking the other way is probably the safest thing to do."

xxxHolic 2003

🖉🖉 "CLAMP"

Title in original language *Horikku*
First published by Kodansha (Japan) **Creators** Japanese
Ageha Ohkawa (b.1967); Tsubaki Nekoi (b.1969); Mokona
Apapa (b.1968); Satsuki Igarashi (b.1969) **Genre** Fantasy

The astonishing *xxxHolic* started life as a side story from the massive *Tsubasa* series, but there is little to link it stylistically to the all-female CLAMP collective's flagship title. Its subtle, delicate story lines and weird, ambiguous characters belong to a stranger world. Owing more to the traditional ghost stories of Japanese horror titles than to *Tsubasa*'s frenetic world, *xxxHolic* focuses on Kimihiro Watanuki, a young man haunted by spirits. He accidentally becomes the employee of a secretive witch who runs a mysterious shop that can only be visited by people who have wishes they want granted. Wishing, as any lover of ghost stories knows, is a risky business, and these tales are dark, frequently disturbing, and possessed of a cruel and quirky morality.

Ghost fans will find a new and attractive take on familiar stories here, alongside tales that are original. Although much of the action is suitably glamorous, there is enough humor and farce to keep the story lively and sharp. The charm of the cast of tragic women, cat spirits, cute monsters, and hyperactive children with rude names is balanced by interesting and engaging central characters, each boasting their own obsessions, particularly relating to food. The art style is elegant, decorative, flowing, and decadently preoccupied with elaborate costumes and ornamentation. Any crossover moments are handled well; there is no need to read other books to understand what is going on. *xxxHolic* is a strange flower that has grown from *Tusbasa*'s roots and should appeal to any lover of pretty clothes, high drama, and delicious food. **JD**

Yotsuba &! 2003

🖉🖉 Kiyohiko Azuma

First published by Media Works (Japan)
Creator Japanese (b.1968)
Genre Humor, Children's
Award Excellence Award for Manga (2006)

Many comics depict kids in terms of what they can symbolize instead of observing them just as they are. Such portrayals often show children as caricatures of the adult world, or representations of naive but bold adventurers. However, sometimes simply observing the behavior of a realistic child in detail can be great fun. Even without all the fictional magic, everyday is something new, an adventure.

Yotsuba &! is the lighthearted story of a single father raising his five-year-old daughter. As is the case with most modern suburban life, the daily grind seldom provides life-threatening adventures, just ordinary events in an ordinary town with regular next-door neighbors. If you are curious and fun-seeking enough, you do not need to imagine a stuffed tiger as your close partner in intergalactic quests to enjoy your day. Accompanying dad to the grocery store for the first time is an adventure. Going to the public pool and meeting new people is exciting. The school fair at the local high school is a place filled with wonders. Every little detail of life has an element of joy, and all the characters help make the world a better place for a little girl to make some new discoveries.

As one might expect from such a life-affirming tale, *Yotsuba &!* incorporates both a *kawaii* (cute) drawing style and Kiyohiko Azuma's keen eye for subtle details in the background, which means there is plenty for the reader to appreciate in this immersive work of cartoony fun. Yotsuba's seemingly endless curiosity and childish boldness are a joy to experience. **NK**

The Photographer 2003

Emmanuel Guibert, Didier Lefèvre, and Frédéric Lemercier

Title in original language *Le Photographe*
First published by Dupuis (Belgium)
Creators Guibert (French, b.1964); Lefèvre (French, 1957–2007); Lemercier (b.1962) **Genre** History

Photojournalist Didier Lefèvre took many more shots than he ever had published. He showed Emmanuel Guibert boxes of photographs recounting his grueling mission with Doctors Without Borders in 1986, traveling in and out of Afghanistan to bring medical care to those in remote regions on both sides during the Soviet occupation. Guibert was determined that Lefèvre's story should reach the public and found a way, with designer and colorist Frédéric Lemercier, to integrate these black-and-white photographs into comic book panels, by leaving them uncropped and text free. Guibert had to visualize any incidents that were unphotographed, including portrayals of Lefèvre who took few shots of himself. The surfeit of information within the photographs, recorded in shades of gray, contrasts with the muted, flat colors of the concise drawings.

Lefèvre's first-person narration describes Afghan customs and the bonds he forms with the doctors. His photographs capture the human suffering of operations carried out with the minimum of medical supplies. On one house call to a young girl, the room is too dark to take pictures, so Guibert draws the scene in silhouettes lit by the doctor's flashlight. He spots a tiny hole in her back, made by a piece of shrapnel. She will never walk again. Lefèvre breaks down, unable to take any more photographs, but is jolted out of this by the mission's leader, Jamila, who has just filmed a child's death. She tells him, "The mother said to me, 'Film it, Jamila. People have to know.'" Now more people can learn about this tragic war through this deeply humane chronicle. **PG**

GUIBERT • LEFÈVRE • LEMERCIER
LE PHOTOGRAPHE - TOME 1
AIRE LIBRE
DUPUIS

"Helicopter! The shout makes its way down the caravan, just ahead of the engine hum everyone fears."

Similar reads

Alan's War (*La Guerre d'Alan*) Emmanuel Guibert
Chimo David Collier
Palestine Joe Sacco
To Afghanistan and Back Ted Rall
War Is Boring David Axe and Matt Bors

The Walking Dead 2003

Robert Kirkman   Tony Moore and Charlie Adlard

First published by Image Comics (USA)
Creators Kirkman (American, b.1978); Moore (American, b.1978); Adlard (British, b.1966)
Genre Horror

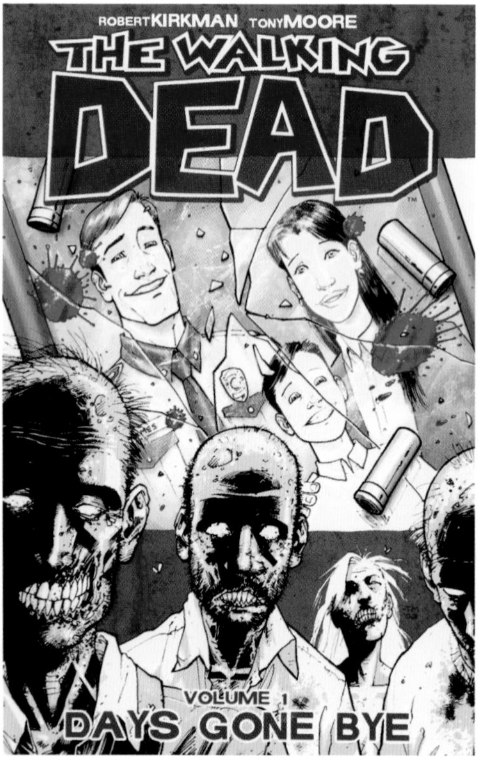
ROBERT KIRKMAN TONY MOORE
THE WALKING DEAD
VOLUME 1
DAYS GONE BYE

Similar reads
Deadworld Gary Reed and Vince Locke
Marvel Zombies Robert Kirkman and Sean Phillips
Zombo! Al Ewing and Henry Flint

While zombies have never really gone away, there have been numerous attempts to reinvent them in film and novels. In his bleak and brutal zombie saga, creator Robert Kirkman has sought not to revolutionize the zombie mythos but instead to craft a moving human drama that just happens to feature hordes of ravenous undead consuming all in their path.

Rick Grimes is a police officer who wakes up in hospital to find the city overrun by zombies. His wife and son are missing, and the life he knew is gone. After equipping himself with guns, ammunition, and a hatchet, Rick sets out across a devastated United States in order to find his family. He encounters several fellow survivors, and together they attempt to forge a new existence, despite jealousies and burning resentments. The emotional turmoil and dramatic beats are punctuated by moments of graphic violence, which embrace the gory, explicit tradition of zombie horror, but ground that horror by showing the actual cost of such bloodshed.In both its theme (ordinary people in extraordinary circumstances) and look (stark black and white), *The Walking Dead* harks back to George A. Romero's classic 1968 horror movie *Night of the Living Dead*.

Kirkman's writing is constantly surprising, and while the dialogue is not as naturalistic as in later volumes, this first arc sets up the concept and emotional investment in his key characters that make later events all the more shattering. The initial volume is drawn by Tony Moore, with art chores on later issues handled by Charlie Adlard. Moore's energetic style relishes in the detail of postapocalyptic cities and is akin to an action movie, a contrast to Adlard's more atmospheric work.

With more than eighty issues to date, and with Kirkman claiming he would like to write at least another 200, like its titular antagonists, *The Walking Dead* shows no signs of lying down anytime soon. **SW**

Yossel: April 19, 1943 2003

Joe Kubert

First published by I Books (USA)
Creator American (b.1926)
Genre Autobiography
Award Will Eisner Hall of Fame Inductee (1998)

Joe Kubert takes us back to November 1926, when he was only two months old, and he, his parents, and elder sister managed to escape Poland for a new life in the New World, where he became one of the twentieth century's most versatile and acclaimed comic book storytellers. Earlier that year, the Kubert family had been refused a visa to the United States because Joe's mother was still pregnant with him. How very different his life might have been if they had been forced to remain behind and he had grown up in Nazi-occupied Poland as a Jew named Yossel.

Kubert rewrites the course of his life from this pivotal point into an alternative but utterly believable autobiography, one that ends on that fateful day in 1943 during the Warsaw Ghetto Uprising. Gifted at drawing, Yossel's talents become his solace and inspiration. They win him favors from the Germans but cannot save his parents and sister from being deported to the death camps. Rather than meet the same fate, he and the others left in the ghetto choose to die fighting against their Nazi persecutors.

Kubert draws the whole graphic novel, including Yossel's own artwork, in raw, uninked pencils, giving readers the impression that they have stumbled across the original, unfinished sketches. The drawings allow readers to get to know young Yossel, a teenager and barely a man, caught up in the harrowing immediacy of the Holocaust, speaking through history to readers' hearts. For Kubert, creating this book was "very personal, a little scary, and sort of cleansing," and in the introduction he writes, "There's no question in my mind that what you are about to read could have happened." At the age of seventy-seven, he has given at least some of his life over to his other self and allowed *Yossel* to give readers a lasting testimony of a life that very nearly could have been. **PG**

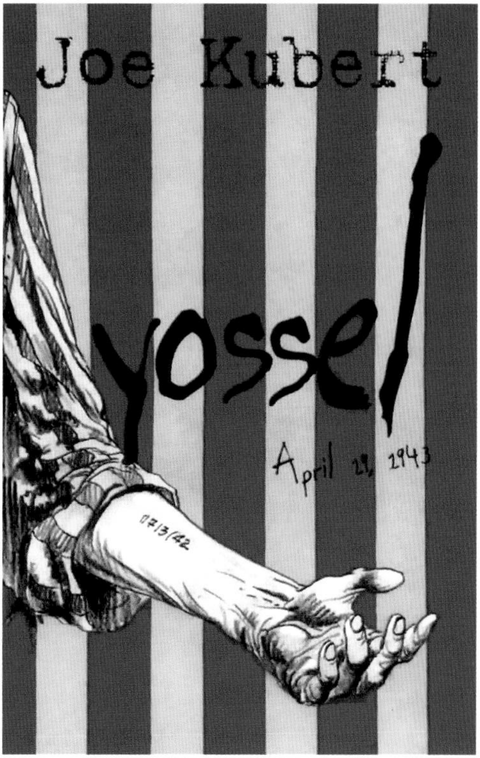
Joe Kubert
Yossel
April 19, 1943
07/13/42

Also by Joe Kubert
Dong Xaoi, Vietnam 1965
Fax from Sarajevo
Sgt. Rock: The Prophecy

Town of Evening Calm, Country of Cherry Blossom 2003

Fumiyo Kouno

Title in original language *Yunagi no machi sakura no kuni*
First published by Futubasha (Japan
Creator Japanese (b.1968)
Genre Drama

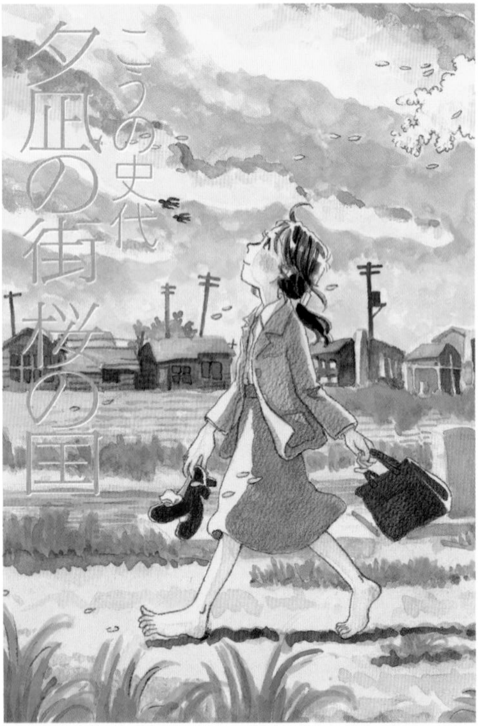
こうの史代
夕凪の街桜の国

Similar reads
A Drifting Life Yoshihiro Tatsumi
Barefoot Gen **(*Hadashi no Gen*)** Keiji Nagazawa
Kono Sekai no Katasumi ni Fumiyo Kouno
Maus: A Survivor's Tale Art Spiegelman

In the afterword to the two short stories contained in this highly acclaimed anthology, Fumiyo Kouno writes that it was her publisher who suggested that she should produce a book about Hiroshima and the atomic bomb, adding that at the time she had to try extremely hard to overcome her reluctance at undertaking such a project. A native of Hiroshima, she is very familiar with the problem of the *hibakusha*—literally, the "victims of the bombs." Survivors of the atomic bombing in 1945, who were often ostracized by the rest of the Japanese population, frequently felt burdened by the fact of their survival, although this was not the case with Kouno and her family.

This is the sensitive subject of this manga, which stands out as atypical in the world of comics: how to live with the memory of what happened in Hiroshima and how to understand the quite incomprehensible suffering caused by surviving such a terrible catastrophe. Kouno's talent lies in her down-to-earth approach to the subject. In just a few dozen pages, the first story in the book, "The Town of Yunagi," tells the poignant tale of a young woman, who in her private life is still feeling the aftereffects of the bomb, in spite of her efforts to return to a "normal" life. The next story is longer, but is told in the same personal, unpretentious tone. Containing numerous flashbacks from the narrator's childhood, "Country of Cherry Blossom" tells the story of a family from Hiroshima, the relationships between its various members, and the way in which memories, darkened by the ghost of the bomb, are passed down through the generations.

Kouno's approach is discreet, sensitive, and enormously human; combined with a subtle graphic style, it is never shocking. In 2005, *Town of Evening Calm, Country of Cherry Blossom* was justly awarded the Tezuka Prize of Culture in Japan. **NF**

The Building Opposite 2003

"Vanyda"

The first collection by French-Laotian artist Vanyda, *The Building Opposite* follows the everyday lives of three sets of neighbors, each occupying one floor of a split-level building. After beginning life as a series of comics in the French fanzine *Porophore* between 1999 and 2002, the story was collected and published in album format, with two further volumes appearing later.

An example of the recent French comics trend of *la nouvelle manga* (the new manga), Vanyda's first album belies a Japanese influence not in its artistic style, but in both its narrative structure and its *mise-en-page*. The story is divided into twenty-six short chapters with strips and frames of varying size and page placement. Each brief episode builds up a picture of both the separate and communal lives of the building's six inhabitants (plus one rather large dog). They mix inconsequential daily occurrences—young couple Claire and Louis's discovery that they have run out of toothpaste or their middle-aged, married neighbors' discussions about the dog—with more serious aspects of the characters' lives, such as single mother Béatrice's waters breaking in the building's stairwell, or the refusal of her children's father to involve himself in their lives.

The apparently incongruous intermingling of these short narratives is held together masterfully by Vanyda's innovative manipulation of structure. Some chapters adhere to a classically linear progression of frames while others follow the actions of the three sets of characters simultaneously, using a page layout that reflects the structure of the building itself. This fluctuating page composition—coupled with the flawlessly realistic dialogue and a stark, expressive artistic style—produces an impressive first offering from a young artist whose bold manipulation of the comics medium adds life to the everyday and indicates enormous artistic potential for the future. **CMac**

Title in original language *L'immeuble d'en face*
First published by La Boîte à bulles (France)
Creator Savatier Vanyda (French, b.1979)
Genre Teen

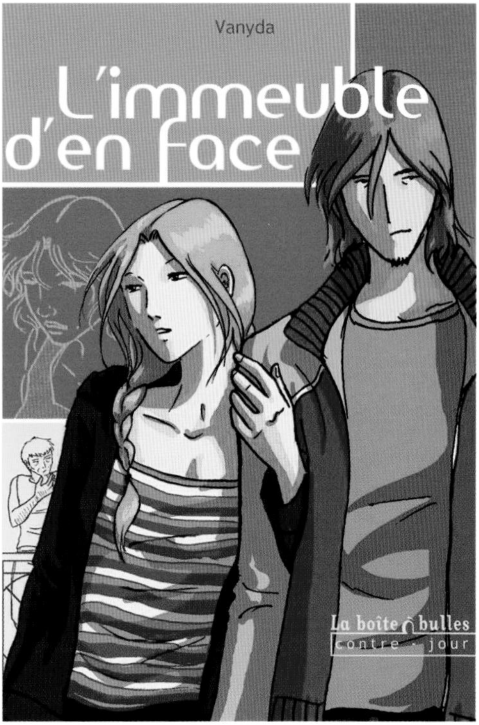
Vanyda
L'immeuble d'en face
La boîte à bulles
contre · jour

Similar reads
Blue Kiriko Nanana
Emile Fabrice Neaud
The Walking Man Jiro Taniguchi
Tokyo est mon jardin Frédéric Boilet and Benoît Peeters

Same Difference 2003

✐✐ Derek Kirk Kim

First published by Top Shelf Productions (USA)
Creator American (b.1974)
Genre Teen
Awards Eisner and Harvey Awards (2004)

Nancy and Simon are two twentysomethings who live in the San Francisco Bay Area of California. They are very close and have been friends for a long time. Both are originally of Korean descent, but have perfectly integrated into their host country. The story follows the aimless activities of the pair until they plan a strange outing to Pacifica, a very ordinary Bay Area suburb.

There they set off on the trail of a stranger who, just for fun, they have decided to track down. In the course of this escapade Nancy and Simon enjoy a brief moment of true intimacy without having really planned it. While helping each other do some serious and honest soul-searching for the first time, they simultaneously pass through a rite of passage to adulthood, driven by their amorous friendship and a quest for identity.

This engaging, naturalistic, and droll story is told with delicacy and sensitivity. Kim, also a Korean-American, initially self-published his debut collection of stories about Korean-American life on his website. His drawing style has been influenced by European comics, particularly the Franco-Belgian *ligne claire* (clean line) school. His narrative approach, on the other hand, was inspired by the independent U.S. comics tradition led by authors such as Daniel Clowes and Adrian Tomine.

Less tormented and less caustic than his Korean elders, Kim conveys a rather tender, lightweight self-mockery that gives his works a very individual feel. Equally, *Same Difference* provides an enlightening insight into the existence of young adults who live in anonymous and interchangeable U.S. suburbs. **NF**

The Rabbi's Cat 2003

✐✐ Joann Sfar

Title in original language *Le Chat du Rabbin*
First published by Dargaud (France)
Creator French (b.1971)
Genre Humor

This is one of the wisest and most hilarious comics from an extraordinary artistic talent. In his native France, where he is venerated, Joann Sfar has published over one hundred books aimed at both children and adults.

Sfar's family was forced to flee Algeria in the 1920s. In the first collected volume of *The Rabbi's Cat*, he pays homage to the stories he grew up with, creating a sharply observed and richly detailed portrait of the arrival of modernity in one Algerian household. This comprises a rabbinic father, his beautiful daughter Zlabya, and a cat. When the cat swallows the family parrot, it acquires the ability to talk. The cat's barbed wit defeats both the rabbi and the rabbi's rabbi, as it embarks on a quest to become bar mitzvahed and learn Kabbalah. Sfar uses the cat's perspective both to gently deflate the hypocrisies and pomposities of the traditional Moroccan Jewish community, and to highlight the cat's delightful self-absorption.

Both rabbi and cat are thrown into crisis by the arrival of a very modern Parisian rabbi, a prospective husband for Zlabya. The cat (and the artist's line) are very much in love with Zlabya, who forms the elusive and passionate center of the book. Their collective journey to Paris pits rationalism against superstition, and explores the nature of prejudice, the possibility of belief in the twentieth century, and what a cat might say if it had swallowed a library of classical Jewish sources. Sfar's line is fluid and playful, recreating a forgotten world with an intimacy, humor, and pathos that offer rare insights into our own predicament today. **AK**

Cat and rabbi interact in Sfar's thoughtful critique of modernity. ➡

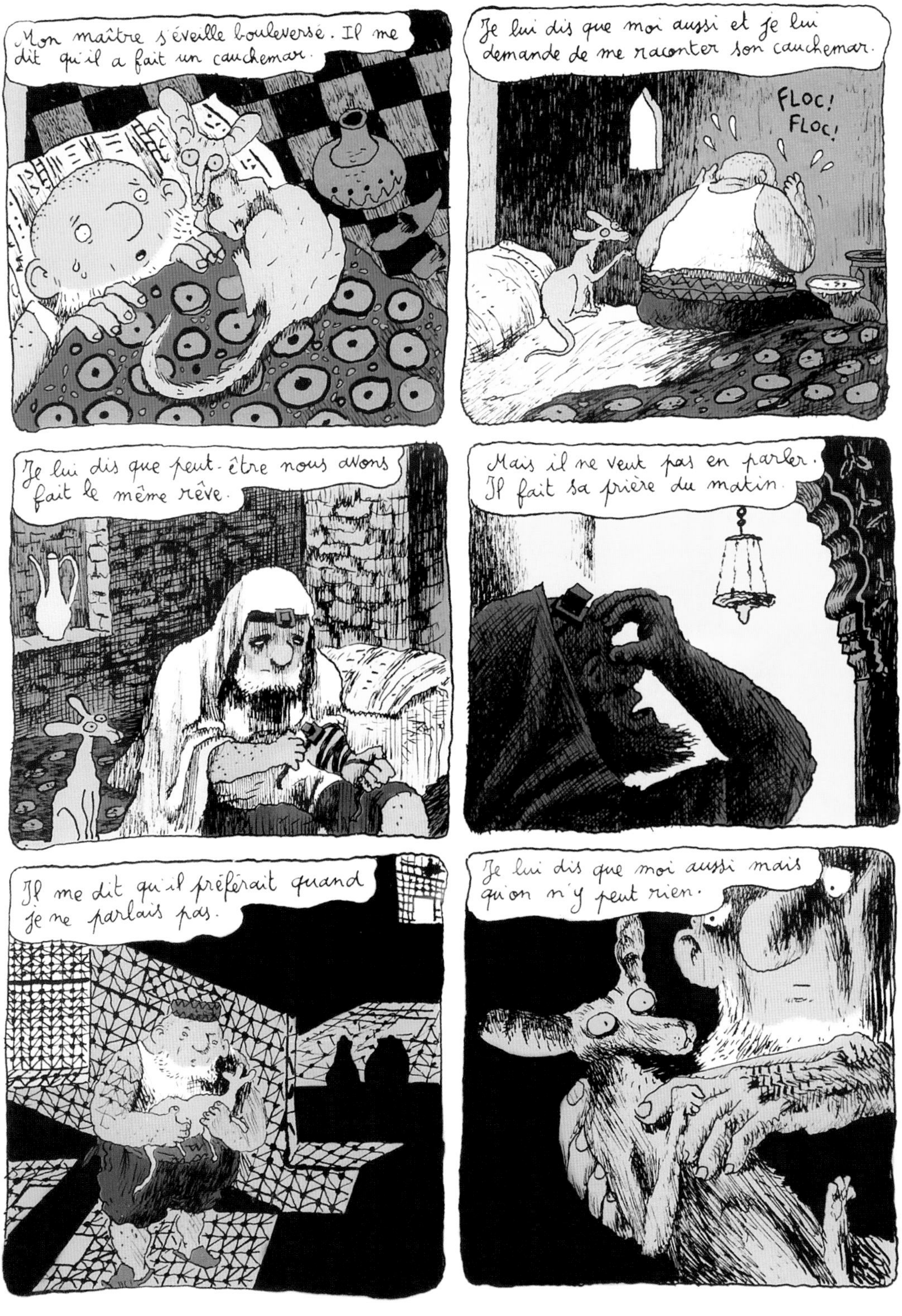
Mon maître s'éveille bouleversé. Il me dit qu'il a fait un cauchemar.
Je lui dis que moi aussi et je lui demande de me raconter son cauchemar.
FLOC! FLOC!
Je lui dis que peut-être nous avons fait le même rêve.
Mais il ne veut pas en parler. Il fait sa prière du matin.
Il me dit qu'il préférait quand je ne parlais pas.
Je lui dis que moi aussi mais qu'on n'y peut rien.

The Bellybuttons 2004

"Dubuc and Delaf" "Delaf"

Title in original language *Les Nombrils*
First published by Les Artistocrates (Canada)
Creators Maryse Dubuc (Canadian, b.1977); Marc Delafontaine (Canadian, b.1973) **Genre** Humor, Teen

1 Delaf - Dubuc
les Nombrils
Pour qui tu te prends ?
DUPUIS

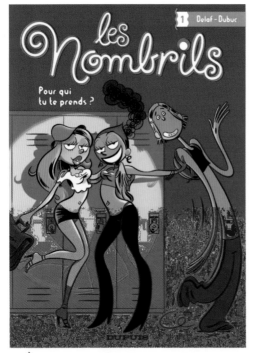

Similar reads
Amelia Rules! Jimmy Gownley
Get a Life Dupuy and Berberian
Les Filles Christopher
Maybe Later Dupuy and Berberian
Where's it at Sugar Kat? Ian Carney and Woodrow Phoenix

After publishing six pages of *The Bellybuttons* in the Quebec humorous monthly magazine *Safarir* in 2004, Maryse Dubuc and her companion, Marc Delafontaine, also known as Delaf, realized that they would have to look outside their native Canada to publish their series as a hardcover album. To their great surprise, the Belgian publisher Dupuis immediately accepted the series, running it in the weekly magazine *Spirou* starting in May 2005. Success came quickly. A few months later *The Bellybuttons* was the most popular comic in *Spirou*; a first album was published in February 2006. In another surprise for the authors, the publisher fully accepted the caustic tone of their imagined adolescent world and made no comments about their merciless descriptions—on the contrary, they loved them.

Who are the Bellybuttons? The title has a double meaning; it refers to the heroines' way of dressing in short T-shirts that reveal their bellybuttons, but it also alludes to the navel-gazing aspect of their behavior. The Bellybuttons are three girls attending secondary school. Jenny (a redhead) and Vicky (a brunette) are forever attracting the attention of boys and manipulating them. The pair also have an ideal and consenting victim in Karine, a tall, gangly girl who is constantly humiliated by her two "friends."

The characteristic feature of the series is its humor based on jokes and gags, but it follows the example of the *shonen* manga in that there is an internal progression in its talk about adolescence. The psychology of the characters evolves, and their school lives and social milieu are described in order to create backgroound and context to the story. The fluctuations of their loves and friendships are detailed. Every word and scenario are carefully chosen to achieve the consistent atmosphere of timelessness and universality that has made this comic such a publishing success. **CM**

Cul de Sac 2004

Richard Thompson

The world of *Cul de Sac* is a suburban community in an unnamed part of the United States. The strip chronicles the daily lives of four-year-old Alice Otterloop, her eight-year-old brother Petey, and their parents. Alice is a bossy little girl who attends the Blisshaven Academy preschool along with a number of friends. These include Beni, whose favorite toy is a hammer; Marcus, whose every action is recorded by his mother as a memento for her scrapbooks; and Dill, a naive and imaginative boy whose unseen older brothers are always busy fashioning bizarre objects, such as a trebuchet, in their family's front garden.

Alice's brother Petey is her near opposite, a peculiar boy who tries to be as unobstrusive as he can, prides himself in being one of the world's pickiest eaters, and whose favorite comic, *Little Neuro*, stars a character so self-conscious that he never does anything. Petey has his own "supporting cast," including big Andre and Ernesto Lacuna, a "James Bond villain in the making" whom Petey suspects is imaginary.

Among other notable strange characters in the strip is Alice and Petey's grandmother, who throws deviled eggs at passing cars and lives with an enormous dog called Big Shirley. Alice's class at school has a hamster, Mr. Danders, with delusions of grandeur. And there is the dreaded uh-oh baby, whose appearance is considered by Alice and Dill to be a portent of doom.

Cartoonist Richard Thompson developed *Cul de Sac* in 2004 as a weekly Sunday color page in the *Washington Post Magazine*, and the strip became syndicated in 2007. It is difficult to explain quite what makes it so very charming, but it has a subtle mixture of the everyday (Thompson has a frighteningly accurate grasp of the thinking processes of four year olds) and the surreal. **J-PJ**

First published by *The Washington Post Magazine* (USA)
Creator American (b.1957)
Genre Humor
Adaptation Online animated movies

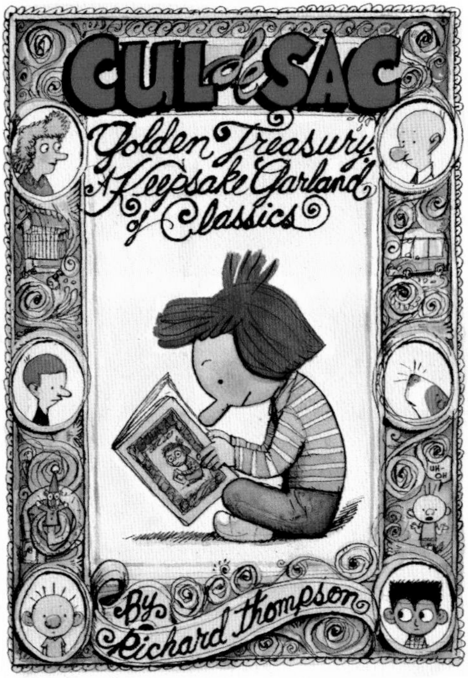
CUL de SAC
Golden Treasury
A Keepsake Garland of Classics
By Richard Thompson

Similar reads

Calvin and Hobbes Bill Watterson
Hansel and Gretel (*Hans en Gritje*) Fred Julsing
Little Lulu John Stanley
Peanuts Charles Schulz
The Perishers Maurice Dodd and Dennis Collins

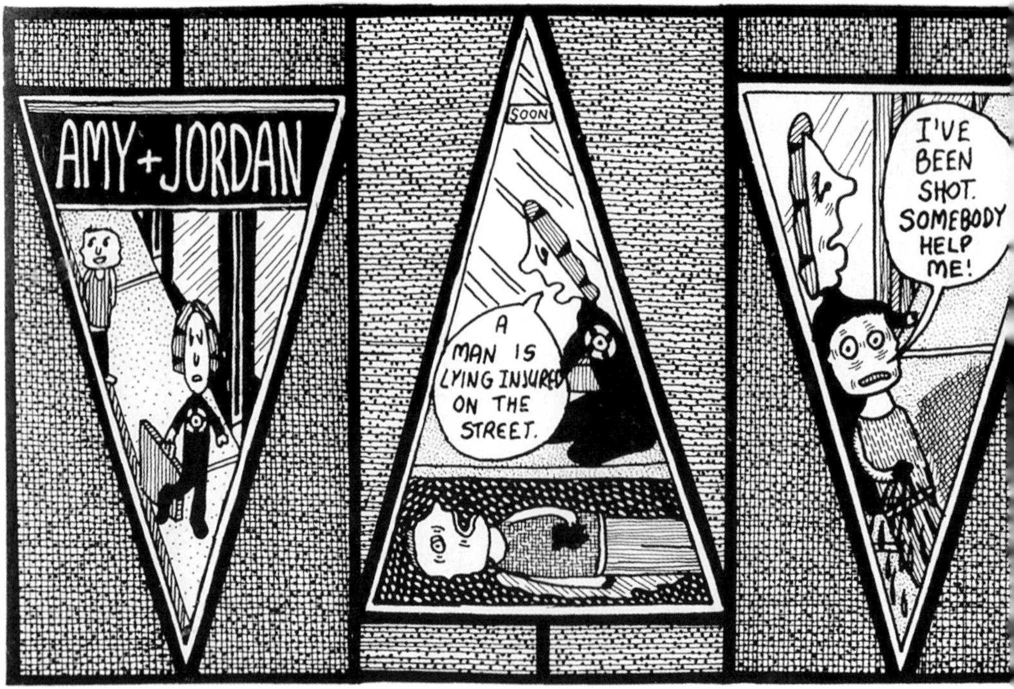
AMY+JORDAN
SOON
A MAN IS LYING INJURED ON THE STREET.
I'VE BEEN SHOT. SOMEBODY HELP ME!

Amy and Jordan 2004

Mark Beyer

First published by Pantheon Books (USA)
Creator American (b.1950)
Genre Humor
Award *TIME* magazine's Best Comix of 2004

With the exception of editor Art Spiegelman, Mark Beyer was the only artist featured in every issue of the cutting-edge magazine *RAW*. The two-page short story "Dead Things" introduced Beyer's signature couple in the first issue in 1979, and he has been detailing their bleak lives ever since. The result has been a relentlessly downbeat vision of contemporary life and relationships told through geometric abstraction.

The most striking thing about *Amy and Jordan* is not its tone of disaffected isolation but the unusual visual choices that Beyer consistently makes. Both Amy and Jordan are drawn with flattened heads, primarily in profile. They exist in a world of almost pure abstraction and in spaces that range from dank inner-city high-rises to the wide-open vistas of the American southwest. Beyer's construction of panels defies easy description. He commonly adopts oddly angular shapes and complements them with extraneous drawings that serve no narrative function. The work creates a genuine sense of anxiety in the reader.

There is little or no narrative cohesion in *Amy and Jordan*, and the strips carry no consequences. When Jordan rips off his arms in one strip, they are miraculously returned to him in the next. In some ways, Amy and Jordan are like Samuel Beckett's Vladimir and Estragon: they are waiting forever for something—anything—to happen in their lives. In other ways, the work reads like the vividly nightmarish imaginings of a child, a sense that is strengthened by Beyer's powerfully direct faux-naive rendering style. **BB**

Amy and Jordan's scenarios play on the insecurities of the modern reader. ↑

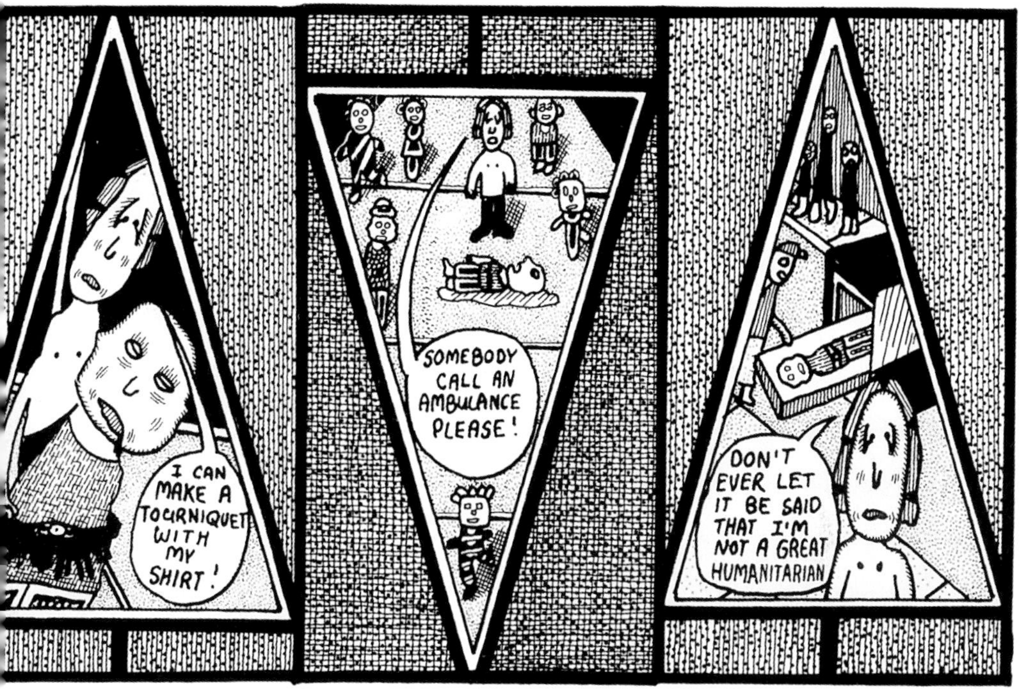
I CAN MAKE A TOURNIQUET WITH MY SHIRT!
SOMEBODY CALL AN AMBULANCE PLEASE!
DON'T EVER LET IT BE SAID THAT I'M NOT A GREAT HUMANITARIAN

Kekkonen 2004

Matti Hagelberg

First published by Otava (Finland)
Creator Finnish (b.1964)
Genre Satire
Award Puupää hat Award (1997)

As president of Finland from 1956 to 1982, Urho Kekkonen controlled Finnish relations with the Soviet Union during the Cold War. In the 1980s Matti Hagelberg's irreverent use of him as the hero of a comic book would have caused quite a stir, but by 2004 the long-prevailing unity of Finnish society, culture, and values was almost as long gone as Kekkonen's era, and Hagelberg's book was universally well received.

Hagelberg's *Kekkonen* is not a biography. The book portrays the president's adventures with other mythical figures—both real and fictional—such as Elvis Presley, Pinocchio, and Jesus, and he travels in the belly of a whale as Jonah did in the Bible. Hagelberg's Kekkonen is easily recognizable, fishing and skiing as eagerly as his real-life counterpart. Halfway through the book, Kekkonen dies, but that barely slows him down.

Kekkonen was produced on scratchboard in Hagelberg's signature style. The technique is extremely time-consuming, and Hagelberg needed four years to complete more than 200 pages. The visually stunning drawings have a sharp, semiotic quality that helps make the comic easy to read. The book has been published in French, Swedish, and partially in English.

Hagelberg's oeuvre includes three major books. After *Holmenkollen* (2000), *Kekkonen* marked a change of pace to more explicit political commentary and satire. *Kekkonen* is a very funny book, but since then Hagelberg's views have become increasingly acerbic. In his third book, *Silvia Regina* (2010), he turns toward more contemporary social issues. **HR**

Bosnian Flat Dog 2004

Max Andersson Lars Sjunnesson

First published by *Galago* magazine (Sweden)
Creators Andersson (Swedish, b.1962); Sjunnesson (Swedish, b.1962)
Genre Satire

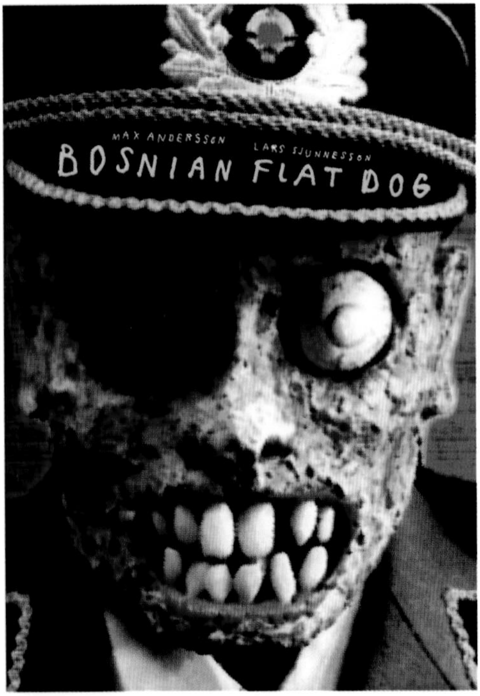
MAX ANDERSSON
LARS SJUNNESSON
BOSNIAN FLAT DOG

Similar reads
Black Hole Charles Burns
Death & Candy Max Andersson and Lars Sjunnesson
Ed the Happy Clown Chester Brown
Pixy Max Andersson
Socker-Conny Joakim Pirinen

Max Andersson and Lars Sjunnesson are among the most expressive and idiosyncratic of Swedish comic artists. Both come from the so-called Galago Generation, which uses the Swedish anthology *Galago* as its preferred residence, and both men are numbered among the most successful Swedish cartoonists abroad.

Max Andersson was one of the first modern Swedish artists to have a graphic novel (*Pixy*) published in the United States. Andersson's comics showcase a dark, Kafkaesque future where everything is turned upside down and dead objects come alive. His visions are disturbing yet compelling. Sjunnesson has, since the 1980s, consistently told strange, poetic, and political stories featuring Åke Jävel and Tjocke-Bo, his anarchic male characters. Both artists have worked in Berlin since the 1990s. With *Bosnian Flat Dog*, they did something entirely new—a graphic novel written and drawn by both of them in such a symbiotic artistic relationship that they themselves do not know who did what.

"Listen! I want you to draw me as a naked princess with a ray gun, killing all the fuckers."

The drawings are black and white, with absurdist, sharply caricatured characters. The story concerns a psychedelic trip taken by the two artists through the bombed-out Balkans; they visit a comics festival, among other things. Realism is soon mixed with surrealism at multiple levels, and eventually the reader realizes that this is not a journey in a physical sense, but rather a journey into the creators' psyches, a processing of the trauma that the wars in the former Yugoslavia have left behind. The result is a strange, harrowing, hilarious, and overwhelming read that is probably unlike anything you will have come across before. **FS**

Apartment 2004

"Kang Full"

Apartments have a special position in modern urban South Korea. The capital city of Seoul has a ridiculously high population density, and the dominant form of housing consists of endless blocks of similar looking high-rise apartment buildings. People are very close to their neighbors but never actually get to know them. Each closely situated home has its own story yet is isolated from the homes around it. This is the near-perfect setting for a complex horror-drama.

Apartment is a horror story that starts off like Hitchcock's movie *Rear Window*, jumps into occult horror, and eventually ends with a strong human drama about how people's lives are ultimately connected. It asks, how would you respond if all the lights in your apartment block went out at the same time, and in the building opposite your window you saw the same dead woman, over and over again? Your next-door neighbors, the delivery man, and the other residents all seem to be something other than they appear. And the other protagonists suspect the same of everyone else. Dead souls, past grudges, family conflicts, and human redemption cross paths in this compelling comic book, and a surprise ending is guaranteed.

"We can make them understand. They were humans like you and me once, before they died."

Korean author Kang Full has been recognized as a masterful storyteller since the 2000s. All his longer stories have been serialized online as vertical scrolling pages. Although critics have passed comment on his loose artwork, he compensates with superb story lines and a large ensemble cast, and is not afraid to convey profound human emotions. *Apartment* is a great read that demonstrates Kang Full's many strengths. **NK**

First published by Munhaksegyesa (Korea)
Creator Kang Do-young (South Korean, b.1974)
Genre Horror, Drama
Adaptation Film: *APT* (2006)

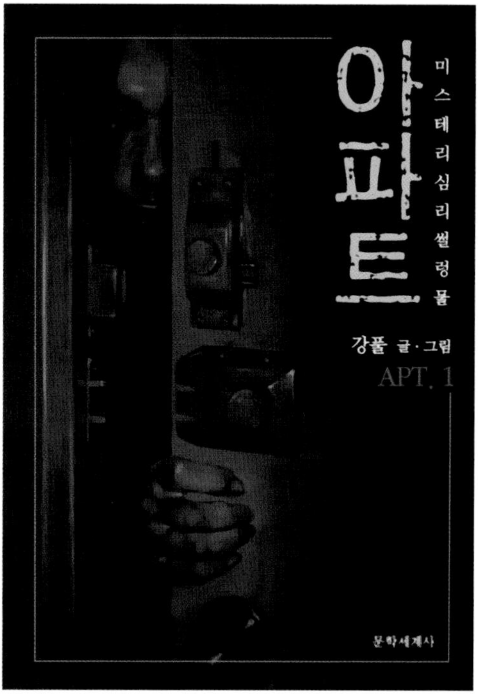
아파트
미스테리심리썰렁물
강풀 글·그림
APT. 1
문학세계사

Similar reads

26 Years Kang Full
Normal City Kang Kyung-ok
Romance Comics Kang Full
Someone Behind You Kang Kyung-ok
Timing Kang Full

Achtung Zelig! 2004

🖋 Krystian Rosenberg   ✒ Krzysztof Gawronkiewicz

First published by Zin Zin Press (Poland)
Creators Rosenberg (Polish, Unknown);
Gawronkiewicz (Polish, b.1969)
Genre Political fable

Through a menacing forest stumble two males—a father and son. They are Jews, and this is Nazi-occupied Poland during World War II. On the surface, the story seems straightforward: the protagonists meet a German patrol and are arrested, only to be rescued eventually by a group of partisans.

Yet the reader does not need to scratch the surface of *Achtung Zelig!* to realize that this is nothing like a routine heroic war story. The father looks like Ridley Scott's Alien, his son resembles a giant frog, and the arresting German officer wears a magician's costume and a pointy hat. With the story itself drawing upon the improbable—the Germans are transporting a truckload of prisoner kittens, the partisans are helped out by wild animals, and the rescue operation is made to look like instructions for a board game—it is obvious that this is not the domain of reality, in spite of the emotional effects of the album's beautifully rendered and realistic black-and-white art.

Is it a dream, then? Could this surreal, nightmarish vision serve as some kind of catharsis for the already traumatized Polish national psyche? Or perhaps *Achtung Zelig!* is a story of war seen through a child's eyes, the passage of time having replaced the cruelty of conflict with bizarre imagery, not denial so much as repressed memory. In this sense, Gawronkiewicz and Rosenberg follow the lead of Art Spiegelman's *Maus: A Survivor's Tale* in trying to understand the largest massacre in human history, but accomplish it in their own unique and strangely beautiful way. **MB**

Playback 2004

🖋 Raymond Chandler   ✒ Ted Benoit, François Ayroles

First published by Editions Denoël (France)
Creators Chandler (American, 1888–1959);
Benoit (French, b.1947); Ayroles (French, b.1969)
Genre Crime

Elizabeth Kinsolving, found guilty by a compromised jury of the murder of her husband, is freed by the judge but runs away to Vancouver when her father-in-law swears revenge. Under the name of Betty Mayfield, Kinsolving checks into a hotel and meets brash ladies' man Larry Mitchell and rich playboy Clark Brandon, both of whom try to win her affection. When Kinsolving wakes to find Mitchell's body lying on her balcony in the pouring rain, she knows she's in serious trouble.

Based on Raymond Chandler's last screenplay, presumed lost until the mid-1980s, this graphic novel adaptation is not to be confused with Chandler's Philip Marlowe novel *Playback*, which was loosely adapted from the same screenplay but carries a significantly different plot. It is easy to imagine what the film might have been, thanks to Ayroles's stark black-and-white illustrations of burly men in trenchcoats and fedoras, and icy but glamorous women. But Kinsolving is not a typical femme fatale; she is a vulnerable woman stuck between a rock and a hard place, just barely hanging on. The plot is dialogue- and character-driven, with everyone potentially playing an angle. In Chandler's world nobody is truly innocent; it's simply a matter of degree, and love is something that happens against your better judgment. *Playback* feels very much a part of the golden era of film noir, sitting well with such works as *The Maltese Falcon* or *The Third Man*.

Playback may not be Chandler's best, but it has everything that made him such a master storyteller. And this adaptation stands tall against any rival. **BD**

We3 2004

Grant Morrison "Frank Quitely"

First published by Vertigo/DC Comics (USA)
Creators Morrison (British, b.1960);
Vincent Deighan (British, b.1968)
Genre Science fiction

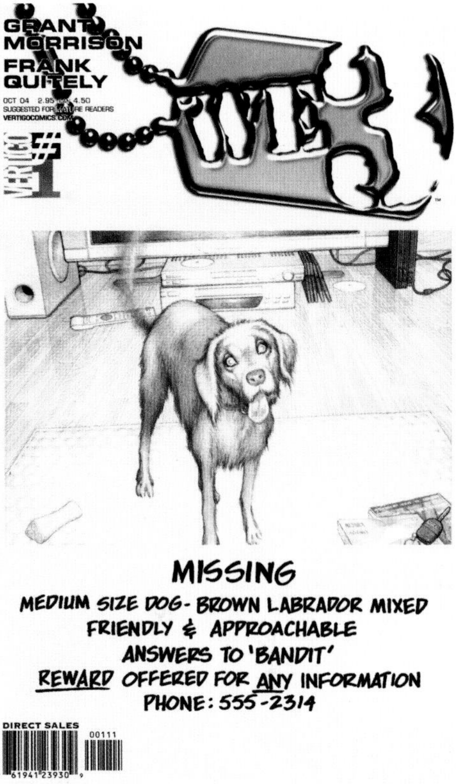

GRANT MORRISON
FRANK QUITELY
VERTIGO
WE3
MISSING
MEDIUM SIZE DOG - BROWN LABRADOR MIXED
FRIENDLY & APPROACHABLE
ANSWERS TO 'BANDIT'
REWARD OFFERED FOR ANY INFORMATION
PHONE: 555-2314
DIRECT SALES

The United States Air Force has been working on modifying animals with technology and has turned a dog, a cat, and a rabbit into killer machines. For political reasons it is decided that they should be terminated, but their trainer, Dr. Roseanne Berry, helps them escape. As lethal weapons, the three can defend themselves fiercely, but they are also vulnerable in their robot shells because they need special medication. We3—the three animals—run away in search of something called "home," and the miniseries follows them in their collective effort to stay alive despite being heavily pursued by the military.

Frank Quitely's extremely fluid drawing style captures every gory detail and makes frequent use of inserted tiny panels to zoom in on simultaneous actions and underline a very fast-paced narrative. He also manages to give the animals facial expressions that maintain the reader's sympathy in even the most horrifying scenes. The soft style of the covers effectively spells out the tragedy of the protagonist animals.

The story is primarily driven by the visual content, but Grant Morrison's economic use of text achieves a heartbreaking effect by having the mechanically altered animals interact in broken spoken sentences. The reader never doubts that these are living, feeling creatures. Even if their language skills leave something to be desired, communication and teamwork is their only chance of survival. The story of *We3* shows us the meaning of compassion, loyalty, and affection in a world dominated by deceit and horrible violence. **RPC**

Also by Grant Morrison
All Star Superman with Frank Quitely
Animal Man with Charles Truog
Batman and Robin with Frank Quitely
Flex Mentallo with Frank Quitely
The Invisibles with others

Astonishing X-Men 2004

Joss Whedon John Cassaday

First published by Marvel Comics (USA)
Creators Whedon (American, b.1964); Cassaday (American, b.1971)
Genre Superhero

MARVEL
ASTONISHING
X-MEN
WHEDON • CASSADAY
GIFTED

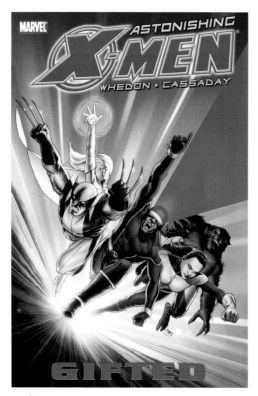

Similar reads
Buffy the Vampire Slayer Joss Whedon
Runaways Brian K. Vaughan
Serenity: Those Left Behind Brett Matthews

Astonishing X-Men was geek god Joss Whedon's first project with Marvel Comics. Having experienced the heroics and difficulties of teamwork with *Buffy the Vampire Slayer* and *Firefly*, Whedon emerged as the perfect fit for the ensemble cast of the X-Men.

At the beginning of the story, Xavier's School for Gifted Youngsters is welcoming new students, but Professor X himself is absent. Indeed, so are Storm, Jean Grey, and other staple X-Men. Events in the larger X-Men universe mean that the new X-Men team comprises Cyclops, Wolverine, Emma Frost, Beast, and Kitty Pryde. With the world as much in need of their help as ever before, Cyclops and Emma have decided to astonish the world with their new team.

Concurrently comes the announcement of a way to eliminate mutant genes in humans. X-Men comics are most potent when working as an allegory, when a so-called "mutant disease" can be applied to any marginalized sector of society, such as homosexuals or those who deal with mental health issues. Such themes are difficult to contend with, and amid the action scenes, there are thoughtful moments when the Beast contends with his emotional and existential stress. With de facto leaders such as Cyclops and Wolverine relegated to secondary roles, it is left to the Beast and Kitty Pryde—two underappreciated characters—to carry most of the emotional baggage. Kitty is a classic Whedon heroine: beautiful, possessing great power, and on the cusp of discovering herself.

The artwork is glossy and filmic and filled with great detail (Kitty's ability to pass through solid objects is shown, while the Beast's ears perk up when he drinks coffee). Whedon's writing hits the action beats while also filled with his trademark witticisms—Wolverine's self-aware response upon hearing the pitch for the new team is: "Is this gonna be about tights?" **SW**

Astonishing X-Men's intense action is rendered with truly cinematic art. ➡

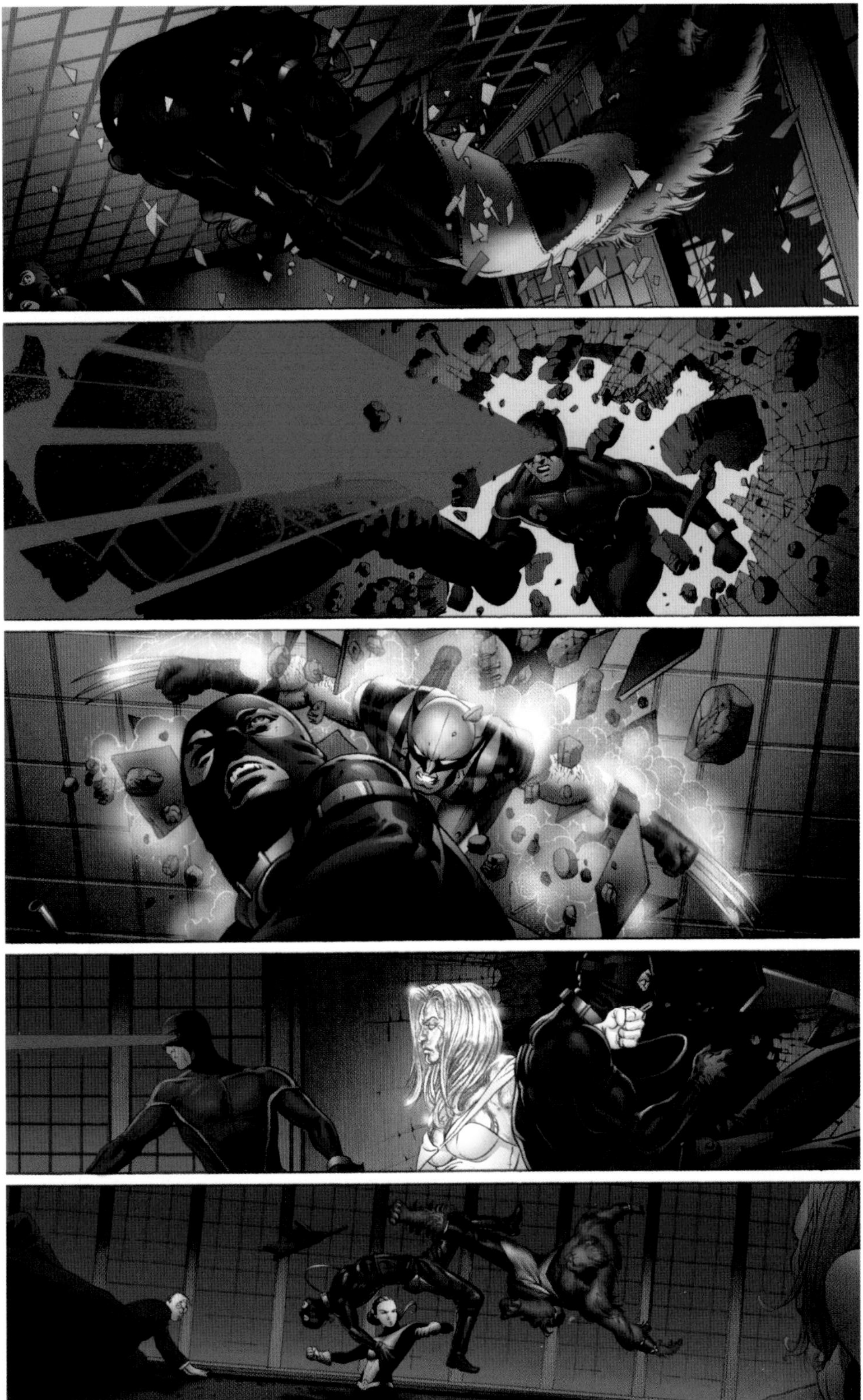

The Ultimates 2004

Mark Millar   Bryan Hitch

First published by Marvel Comics (USA)
Creators Millar (British, b.1969); Hitch (British, b.1966)
Genre Superhero **Adaptations** Films: *Ultimate Avengers* (2006), *Ultimate Avengers 2* (2006)

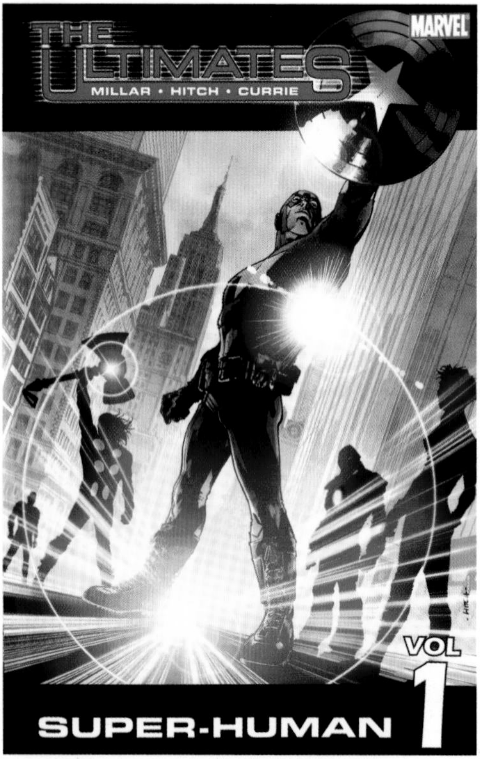
MARVEL
THE ULTIMATES
MILLAR • HITCH • CURRIE
VOL 1
SUPER-HUMAN

Similar reads
Supreme Power J. Michael Straczynski and Gary Frank
The Dark Knight Returns Frank Miller
Watchmen Alan Moore and Dave Gibbons

The Ultimates helped launch Marvel's Ultimate Universe, a new imprint dedicated to the reimagining of their main trademark characters with a more contemporary, sometimes adult-oriented and cinematic approach.

As a creative reengineering of the classic Avengers, *The Ultimates* are a team put together by the U.S. government-funded agency S.H.I.E.L.D. under the auspices of Nick Fury (a "cool and tough" Samuel L. Jackson lookalike in this universe). In the team are Steve Rogers/Captain America, the newly resuscitated and nationalistic supersoldier; Tony Stark/Iron Man, a cocktail-swilling and supermodel-dating billionaire; Hank Pym/Giant Man and Janet Pym/Wasp, married scientists-cum-superheroes; Bruce Banner/the Hulk, the crazed and jealous lab nerd; and Thor, ecologist and headcase/god of thunder, among others.

The major plot revolves around the presence on Earth of shape-shifting aliens known as the Chitauri, who helped the Nazi regime back in World War II and are once again attempting to conquer the world. While the premise fights shy of originality, it is the treatment that makes this a light yet thrilling read. Hitch's art is crisp, clear, realistic, and yet as dynamic as it can get, while Millar's words bring a healthy degree of cynicism and darkness to the otherwise facetious interaction between the main characters.

As entertainment, *The Ultimates* works best for readers who have some familiarity with classic Marvel superhero stories, this being a revision that pulls out all the stops and cranks up the volume. A visual feast packed with action and razor-sharp one-liners, Millar and Hitch's *The Ultimates* is also sprinkled with themes such as domestic violence, drunkenness, secret ops, U.S. external policies, broken trust, and unrequited love, treated in a way that is sometimes serious and often funny. **PM**

Ex Machina 2004

Brian K. Vaughan Tony Harris

Blending *The West Wing* with superhero standbys hardly seems a winning idea, and even less so when slapped onto a Latin title referencing ancient Greek tragedy. Applying more thought, however, there is unlikely to be a more appropriate title for summing up a superhero intervention than deus ex machina, or "God from a machine," which refers to the theatrical constructions from which actors playing Greek gods were lowered to the stage from the skies.

The series cleverly plays as two simultaneous strands set several years apart. In 1999 civil engineer Mitchell Hundred examines a glowing device that endows him with the ability to hear machinery and speak to it. Lights dim at his command, guns jam, and telephones cease ringing. A subsequent stuttering superhero career involves a critical intervention in the events of 9/11, and Hundred parlays his acclaim into a successful campaign to be elected mayor of New York. Flashbacks to his previous career are run alongside the issues besetting him as mayor, enabling the narrative structure to unpeel Hundred and his cohorts in increments.

Citing Norman Rockwell as an influence, Tony Harris's highly detailed approach to the art involved casting the entire series, photographing the actors for every single panel, then working in the detail. The results are occasionally static, but more often offer an emotional range rare to comics dependent on talking heads. Additionally, the technique ensured a consistent look from start to completion.

As with Brian K. Vaughan's other important work, *Y: The Last Man*, *Ex Machina* was conceived as a finite series. Although the concept demands political debate, the story is never a forum for shoving opinions down throats. Narrative is paramount as Hundred gradually discovers where his powers come from and realizes that political status has inbuilt limitations. **FP**

First published by WildStorm/DC Comics (USA)
Creators Vaughan (American, b.1976); Harris (American, b.1969)
Genre Drama, Superhero

EX MACHINA
THE FIRST HUNDRED DAYS
BRIAN K. VAUGHAN TONY HARRIS TOM FEISTER

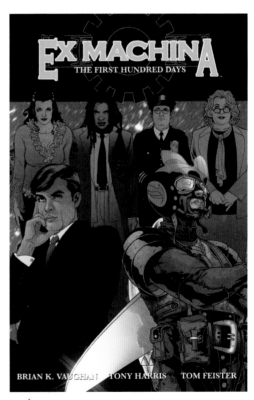

Similar reads

Pride of Bagdhad Niko Henrichon
Runaways Brian K. Vaughan, Adrian Alphona, and others
The Hood Kyle Hotz

Macanudo 2004

Ricardo Siri Liniers

First published by Ediciones de La Flor (Argentina)
Creator Argentinian (b.1973)
Genre Humor
Influenced by Francisco Solano López

Nº1
MACANUDO
POR LINIERS
EDICIONES DE LA FLOR

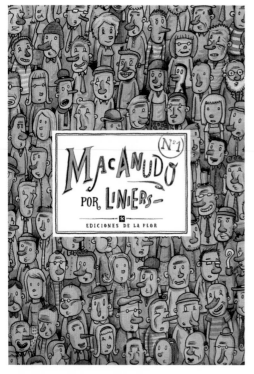

"I focus on the smallest things. I get the arbitrary feeling that small is good and big is bad."

Ricardo Siri Liniers

By 2002, the Argentinian weekly strip *Bonjour!* had already revealed Ricardo Siri Liniers as a devil in disguise. What the disguise was hiding was his innovative, deadpan, and devilish use—alchemy, you could say—of pop-culture sources, absurdity, and Argentinian idiosyncrasies. He was an atomic bomb, an Elvis who would come and rock modern Argentinian comics with his new daily strip, *Macanudo*. But Liniers was a beautiful A-bomb, strangely positive and good. His heartfelt yet savage take is simultaneously an extremely sincere and unprecedented blast of light tenderness. Although a few of his characters recur, Liniers never compromises his "anything can happen" formula for the daily comic strip. It was a formula that successfully mutated the prejudices of readers unaccustomed to comics.

A cat named Fellini, an emotional robot, autobiographical stories, a troglodyte ball, tongue-in-cheek comments on Argentinian everyday expressions, goblins, anthropomorphic penguins: all *Macanudo* inhabitants and references are arbitrary and heart-to-heart. Although Liniers's style is defined by his watercolor vignettes and surreal yet simple use of line, the reader has a sense of Liniers as someone who creates as if building a ship in a bottle, with feelings of love and nostalgia. But Liniers has no punch line. Sometimes he even disregards the funny factor, relying on a natural—yet warmly radioactive—trust in the medium, the readers, and his work.

Ranting against the modern world (or the stupid one at least), *Macanudo* functions as a shelter—cute but wild, melancholic but happy, personal but universal. It is a masterpiece that feels like something a gifted and beloved five year old—but one with an absolute comprehension of the comics medium—has created solely for us to treasure. It is perhaps the one thing to save when the real atomic bomb comes. **JMD**

Chicken with Plums 2004

Marjane Satrapi

Tehran, 1958: Nasser Ali, a professional musician and player of the tar (a kind of Iranian lute with a long neck), cannot get over the loss of his unique instrument, broken by his wife during a violent fight. After briefly trying to make do with a replacement, the desperate musician takes to his bed to await the release of death. Eight days later, he is buried next to his mother in a cemetery to the north of the Iranian capital.

This simple plot, inspired by the real story of Marjane Satrapi's great-uncle, is only the framework of *Chicken with Plums*. The real story of the book is about the eight days in which Nasser Ali waits for Azraël, the angel of death. Eight days of brooding, flashbacks, memories, fantasies, legendary stories, and unexpected digressions that Satrapi takes enormous pleasure in narrating.

Far from being a sinister book as this summary might suggest, *Chicken with Plums* is a rather amusing, playful chronicle of everyday life in Iran in the 1950s. Through a few journeys back and forth in time, Satrapi is able to evoke her own bond with the hero of her book. The story also briefly mentions a few of the political events in Iran at the time but, as in her work *Persepolis*, its main theme is the family. It is the family that lies at the center of the author's imagination and forms the fundamental thread of the story.

It is obvious that the illustrator takes great delight—and she excels at this—in exploring the complex meanderings and ramifications of the life of a family, one that we guess must be representative of all Iranian families. At the same time she infuses the story with the discreet irony that is one of her distinctive characteristics. After the international success of *Persepolis*, Satrapi was determined to prove that she could write about something other than the formative experiences of her childhood in Iran, followed by her exile in Europe. This is a mission well accomplished. **NF**

Title in original language *Poulet aux prunes*
First published by L'Association (France)
Creator Iranian (b.1969) **Genre** Drama
Adaptation Live-action movie (2011)

Marjane Satrapi
poulet
aux prunes
L'Association

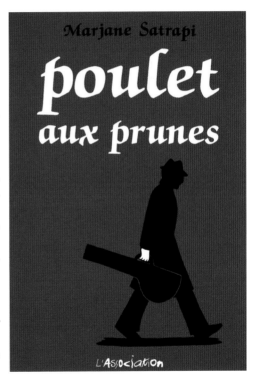

"Satrapi's deceptively simple, remarkably powerful drawings match the precise but flexible prose."

***The New Yorker* magazine**

Dokebi Bride 2004

✎ Marley

First published by Seju (Korea)
Creator South Korean (b.1972)
Genre Fantasy, Romance
Influenced by *xxxHolic*

In comics the occult genre involves protagonists who can mostly be categorized as exorcists or shamans. While exorcists ward off ghosts and demons, shamans communicate with them. Fictions about the latter tend to be less exciting in terms of action but have better potential as mature stories of coexistence.

Marley's *Dokebi Bride* is the coming-of-age story of high-school girl Sunbi, who has inherited the strong shamanic powers of her family's female side. More cursed than gifted, she has grown up alienated from her classmates and targeted by spirits who want to possess her. When Sunbi's grandmother dies, she has to move from her rural fishing village to her father's home in the big city. Over time she learns the truth of her late mother and the true value of her own abilities and enlists local demons to cooperate in helping the living and the dead, humans and demons. Sunbi seeks to take a different path from her grandmother, who devoted her life fully to the spirits, and her mother, who refused to accept that calling and lost her sanity.

Dokebi Bride seamlessly mashes up the spiritual world of traditional Korean folklore with modern city life. The artwork blends elements from mainstream comics and traditional folk paintings to create a unique style. The author explains that otherworldly beings are neither good nor evil, just acting on their own unique logic. While the mainstream *shojo* genre was retreating to lighter romantic comedy by the mid-2000s, *Dokebi Bride* was a reminder that emotional depth and a feminine touch are what make the romantic genre great. **NK**

Flower 2004

✎ Park Kun-woong

First published by Sai Comics (Korea)
Creator South Korean (b.1972)
Genre Reality drama
Influence on *Massacre at No Gun Ri Bridge*

In the darkness of a prison cell, broken by ill-treatment, an elderly prisoner lives with his memories. His recollections are painful because even his oldest childhood memories are marked by suffering—the suffering of the entire Korean people, who for decades were forced to experience the daily humiliation of the Japanese occupation.

The 1,000-odd pages of *Flower* echo the first sequences of the work, a long flashback during which the prisoner, Jaeng-tcho, summons the numerous ghosts inhabiting his long memory to recount his, and Korea's, biography. Thus we travel through imagery of striking beauty to discover the cruel, violent Japanese occupation, with its attempt to eradicate the Korean language, followed by the fresh tragedy of civil war.

Jaeng-tcho, having miraculously returned alive from a labor camp in Manchuria, is once again the victim of violence, this time at the hands of new American conquerors and their Korean allies, defenders of the "free world." He must learn to fight and kill his own brothers in a paroxysm of absurd violence.

The *Flower* trilogy—the first volume is entirely without words—reads as a striking testimony to the Korean psyche today, marked by so many horrors and tragedies. The title was chosen by Park Kun-woong to question what can remain of the flowers of love and friendship when they are swept away by the devastating hurricane of history. Deeply moving from beginning to end, this monumental work is also a magnificent graphic achievement. **NF**

Flowers represent human fragility in Park Kun-woong's historic tale. ➡

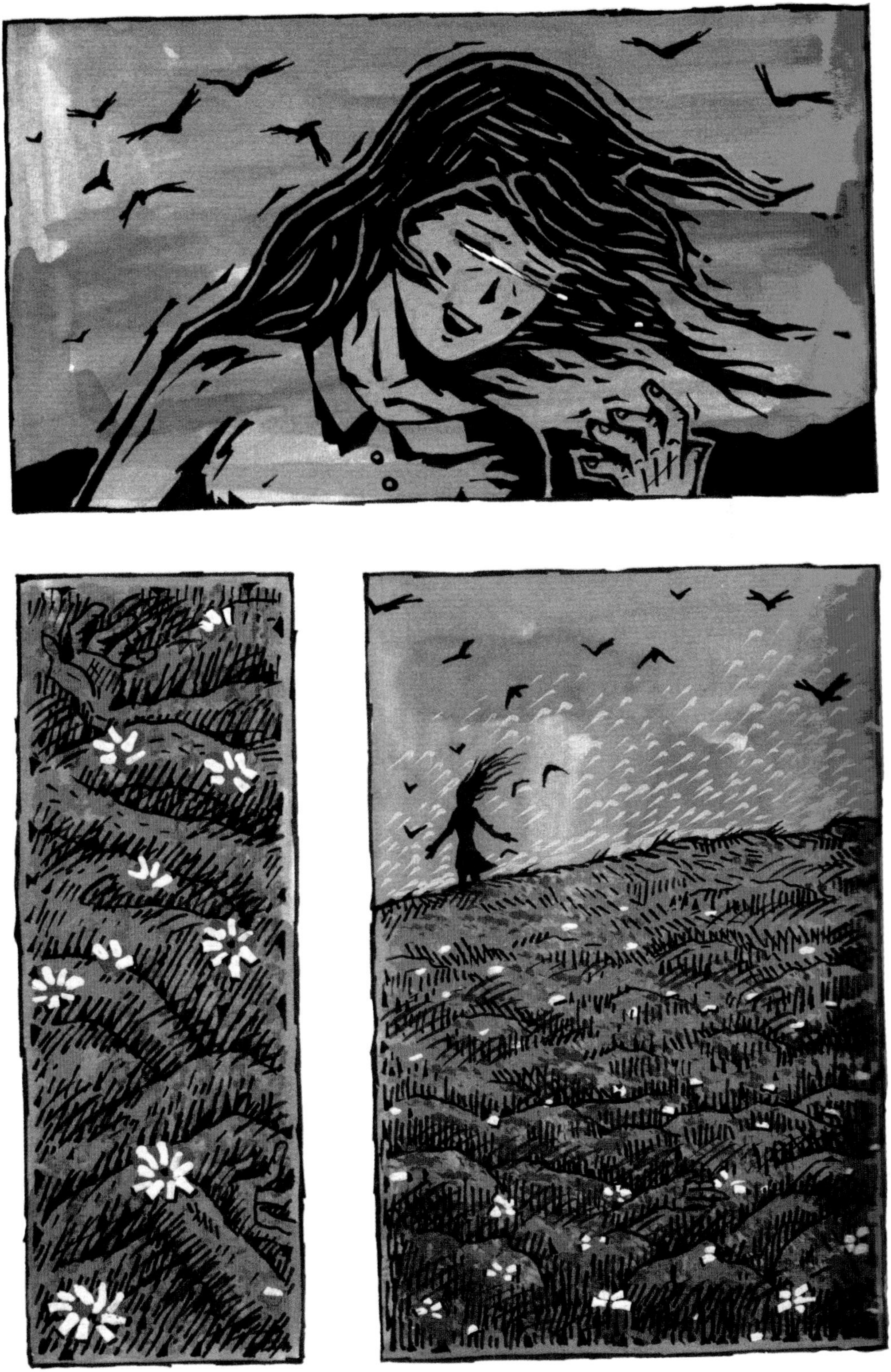

Different Ugliness, Different Madness 2004

Marc Malès

Title in original language *L'autre laideur, l'autre folie*
First published by Les Humanoïdes Associés (France)
Creator French (b.1954)
Genre Reality drama

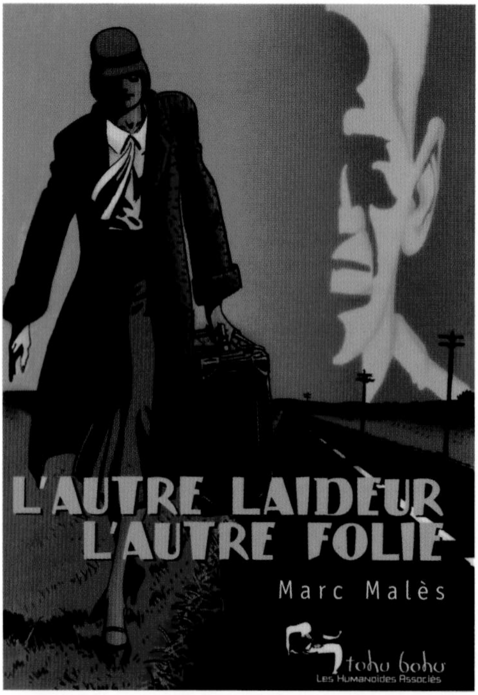
L'AUTRE LAIDEUR
L'AUTRE FOLIE
Marc Malès
tohu bohu
Les Humanoïdes Associés

Also illustrated by Marc Malès
A Thousand Faces Philippe Thirault
Katharine Cornwell Marc Malès
Of Silence and Blood François Corteggiani
The Mutineers (*Les Révoltés*) Jean Dufaux
Under His Gaze (*Sous son regard*) Marc Malès

Emotional despondency is the theme of Marc Malès's award-nominated story. In the Depression-era United States, radio presenter Lloyd Goodman has the nation at his feet as the purveyor of hope, providing brief interludes from hardship. His smooth baritone seduces millions over the airwaves, while publicity posters revealing his handsome looks render him even more alluring. Except that it's all a lie. Goodman has the voice, certainly, but he is in reality an ugly man whose promotional material and public appearances make use of a more acceptable-looking model.

Helen possesses the good looks Goodman pretends to have, but is mentally scarred by the recent death of her twin sister, with whom she converses via mirrors and other reflective surfaces. Trying to forget the tragedy by boarding random trains and hitchhiking, she arrives at the remote house to which Goodman has retreated to escape the false existence he created but can no longer live with. The taciturn Goodman offers her a room without strings, and the two splintered individuals bolster each other's self-esteem in order to repair themselves. The story includes scenes set fifty years later, which indicate that while determined resolutions can be made, some emotional scars never heal and have consequences for future generations.

After twenty years of drawing the material of others, often set in the United States, this bleak depiction of fractured emotional health was a major break from the mainstream for Malès, and his first solo project. The break and the isolated setting were accentuated by stepping away from color pages into a stark black-and-white world. Malès doesn't offer a comfortable read, nor a market-dictated upbeat conclusion. What he does provide is an exceptionally moving drama that reaffirms the humanity that underlies attributes that will inevitably set some people above others. **FP**

Notes for a War Story 2004

"Gipi"

Somewhere in contemporary western Europe, three boys barely out of adolescence—Christian, the narrator, Julian, and Stephen (nicknamed Small Caliber)—are sticking together to try and survive a war. None has been prepared for war, but each will soon learn. In the dangerous and uncertain world they now inhabit, it is hard to know who is a soldier, a mercenary, or a mafioso. Dangers of every kind lurk around every corner, and a series of exhilarating and traumatic episodes soon train the boys into a new mentality of complete amorality. In just a few months all traces of their childhood innocence will be gone as they turn into true dogs of war.

We will never know exactly which modern conflict inspired *Notes for a War Story*, but that is not the point. What affects readers most in Gipi's gripping story is the portrayal of the process by which, in situations of crisis and permanent tension, moral taboos are abandoned, especially by naive young men tempted by the power gained by the exercise of brute force.

Gipi's report is blunt and crude but not bitter, even though it offers no basis for hope or optimism. The illustrator approaches his story from the right distance to describe with cold logic the psychological metamorphosis of his characters and their violent apprenticeship to their new adult status. Yet here and there are touches of unconcealed admiration for the way young men form staunch friendships, and a certain regret for their lost innocence.

Graphically, Gipi the illustrator shows himself to be remarkably inventive. He uses a wide palette of techniques, adapting his strokes to variations in the story: a deep-wash drawing style for panoramas or interior scenes, almost childlike representations of the dream scenes, and so on. Gipi has a masterful comics style. **NF**

Title in original language *Apunti per una storia di guerra*
First published by Coconino Press (Italy)
Creator Gianni Pacinotti (Italian, b.1963)
Genre Reality drama, War

GIPI
APPUNTI PER UNA STORIA DI GUERRA
COCONINO PRESS

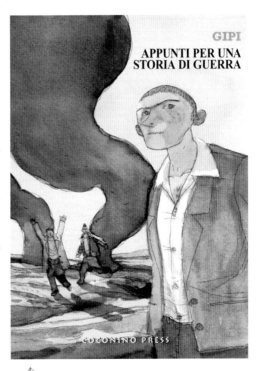

Similar reads
Garage Band Gipi
Lost & Found Shaun Tan
My Life Badly Drawn Gipi
Tales from Outer Suburbia Shaun Tan
The Innocents Gipi

Headshot 2004

"Matz" Colin Wilson

Title in original language *Du Plomb dans la tête*
First published by Casterman (Belgium)
Creators Alexis Nolent (French, b.1967); Wilson (New Zealander, b.1949) **Genre** Crime

WILSON & MATZ
DU PLOMB DANS LA TÊTE
LES PETITS POISSONS
casterman Ligne Rouge

Similar reads
Cyclops Matz and Luc Jacamon
Savage Night Matz and Miles Hyman (adaptation of the 1953 novel by Jim Thompson)
Shandy Matz and Dominique Bertail
The Killer Matz and Luc Jacamon

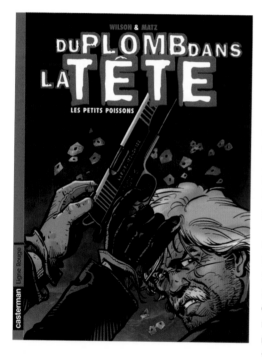

Dispatched to New York City to carry out a contract killing, two loudmouth professional killers, Louis and Jimmy, soon find themselves caught up in the unexpected consequences of their mission. The man they have killed, after surprising him while he is with an underage prostitute, is a well-known senator. Hunted by two determined policemen, trailed by the press, and abandoned by those who ordered the killing, the assassins are now themselves the prime targets.

A string of violent deaths ends with the murder of Louis. Jimmy is then obliged to join forces with Carlisle, one of the policemen who pursued him. But Carlisle is himself in the FBI's line of sight and the object of death threats. The ramifications of the senator's murder seem to be interfering with the interests of some very powerful people. Taking the initiative, this curious team of killer and policeman—by the end we no longer really know who represents good and who evil—decide to get rid of those around them and strike at the very top.

Using all the classic motifs and tricks of the modern thriller, *Headshot* is a brilliant stylistic creation, mainly due to the depth and flavor of its main characters. Readers will enjoy the psychoanalysed killer's sense of propriety in that he does not hesitate to blow $2,000 on "pimp shoes" while admitting that he first had sex rather late in life; also enjoyable is the unexpectedly refined psychological profile of Jimmy, the killer who is fascinated by actress Kim Basinger.

The diffuse humor of the trilogy, as well as the rhythm and action, owe much to the talent of the cheeky, truculent dialogue writer Matz. With their strong contrasts, the realistic and uncommonly vigorous drawings of Colin Wilson provide a perfect counterbalance. Black humor, displaced events, and energy add up to a compelling story that does not let go of the reader until the last trenchant retort. **NF**

Olaf G. 2004

Lars Fiske and Steffen Kverneland

Olaf G. is a graphic novel both by and about artists Lars Fiske and Steffen Kverneland as they travel to Bavaria to study the infamous Norwegian illustrator and cartoonist Olaf Gulbransson (1873–1958), the hero of the title. The comic also serves as a retrospective biography and brief art history of an artist who never distanced himself from the Nazi regime, something that was never forgotten or forgiven in postwar Norway, and which accounts for the artist's move to Bavaria.

The book is an odd collaboration of two highly talented artists possessing very different and distinct styles. Fiske has an elegant cubist style, whereas Kverneland has developed a superb cartoonish style derived from photo-realism. They blend their varying artistic approaches with photographs of Olaf G., with examples of both his art and that of other artists. The result is a fantastic visual mix that is rarely seen anywhere else.

Olaf G. starts with the two artists visiting an exhibition of Olaf G.'s work for the German satirical weekly magazine *Simplicissimus*. They are displeased with the exhibition and decide to travel to Germany to see the body of Olaf G.'s work for themselves. The idea of a coffee-table book is born, and the story takes off. Fiske and Kverneland, often intoxicated by the products of local breweries, tell anecdotes about their stay in Gulbransson's Bavarian landscape and the life of the artist himself, all the while reflecting and analysing with seriousness and self-irony. The complex whole could easily be likened to a strong cocktail.

Olaf G. may be the best graphic novel ever published in Norway. It was listed among the country's best books published in 2004. Without question it is an insightful, hilarious, and accessible combination of artist portrait, gonzo journalism, and travelogue, just as colorful and larger than life as Olaf G. himself. **TAH**

First published by No Comprendo Press (Norway)
Creators Fiske (Norwegian, b.1966); Kverneland (Norwegian, b.1963)
Genre Biography

OLAF G.
LARS FISKE
STEFFEN KVERNELAND

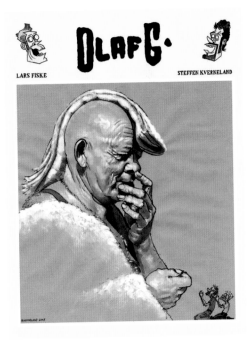

Also by Steffen Kverneland

Canon (*Kanon*) with Lars Fishing
Canon II (*Kanon II*) *Epic Amputations* (*Episke amputasjoner*) with Lars Fishing
Rascal (*Slyngel*)
Storytellers with Jan Erik Vold

It's a Bird 2004

Steven T. Seagle   Teddy Kristiansen

First published by Vertigo/DC Comics (USA)
Creators Seagle (American, b.1965); Kristiansen (Danish, b.1964)
Genre Autobiography, Superhero

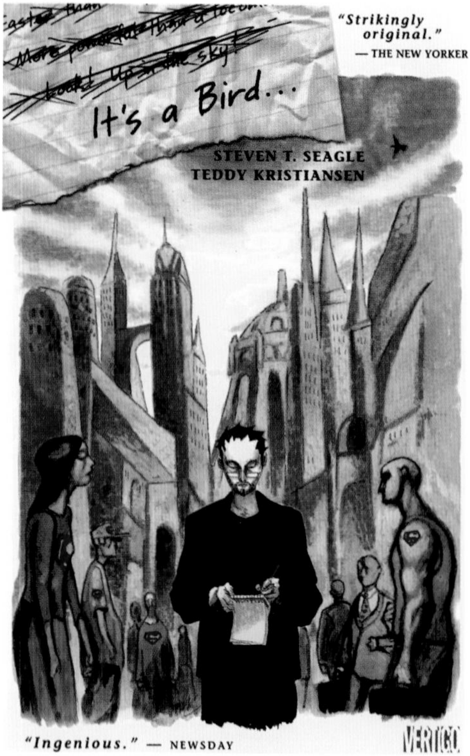
"Strikingly original." — THE NEW YORKER
It's a Bird...
STEVEN T. SEAGLE
TEDDY KRISTIANSEN
"Ingenious." — NEWSDAY
VERTIGO

Similar reads
Blue Pills Frederik Peeters
Our Cancer Year Harvey Pekar and Joyce Brabner
Stitches David Small

It's a Bird is an inspired, semiautobiographical account of writer Steven T. Seagle's own family history. Seagle has an alter ego, Steve Superman, associated with the death of his grandmother from Huntington's disease when he was very young. When his editor commissions him to write a Superman story, it brings up repressed anxiety about a family secret that everyone thinks about but no one addresses: "For me to write Superman, I have to believe he could live in our world, but he *can't*," the author tried to explain. Huntington's disease is hereditary, so all of his family potentially face a premature decline in their mental and physical abilities.

By debating the improbable myth of Superman, Steve tries to come to terms with his angst. Both the Steve and Superman characters benefit from the discussion as Steve challenges the iconic DC Comics figure, discovers his more human side, and comes closer to the frailty of ordinary people. Artist Teddy Kristiansen, who won an Eisner Award in 2005 for his work on the book, switches his drawing style from scene to scene, from Steve's own life to the many fragmentary Superman episodes. His delicate lines and pale coloring express the reality of the distressed writer as he worries about passing the disease on to future children. Primary colors are used for a discussion of the symbolism of Superman's costume, while earthen tones accompany his experiences in Smallville.

> *"For me to write Superman, I have to believe he could live in our world, but he can't."*

It's a Bird explores the cultural significance of a comic book icon. Beautifully crafted and expertly told, its combination of superhero and fatal disease might seem odd, but it works wonders in many ways. **RPC**

Me & The Devil Blues 2004

Akira Hiramoto

In this comic, Akira Hiramoto takes the story of virtuoso blues guitarist Robert Johnson selling his soul to the devil and weaves a disturbing speculative meander around the few known facts of the musician's life.

The book opens with harrowing colored images from the black-and-white story, concluding with Johnson (referred to throughout as R.J.) standing at the crossroads where his satanic pact was allegedly made, before backtracking to the months before it occurred. Comics have barely tried to convey the thrill of music, yet when R.J. and others play in the local bar, Hiramoto's art is a stunning cinematic mélange of scratchy movement, pulling the reader into the performance via large images and small details. In more than a thousand pages there is no poor artwork, but these atmospheric early scenes in particular drip with mood.

"What we bluesmen do is take the blues everyone has inside their heart and pull it out."

Once R.J. has acquired his talent, Hiramoto moves to a wider exploration of rural America in the 1930s. For long periods R.J. is absent from the narrative, which switches to a young Clyde Barrow, the outlaw behind the legend of Bonnie and Clyde. In different circumstances, both end up in a town that strictly upholds prohibition yet revels in lynching—and that's what they've got planned for R.J.

Hiramoto pointedly contrasts the hell supposedly awaiting R.J. for having sold his soul with the everyday trials of black Americans during that era. He also contrasts Barrow, a man whose criminal future we know, with people who would at that time have been considered upstanding citizens. These are unsavory realizations in an altogether unsettling read. **FP**

First published by Kodansha (Japan)
Creators Japanese (Unknown)
Genre Biography, Drama
Award Glyph Comic Award (2009)

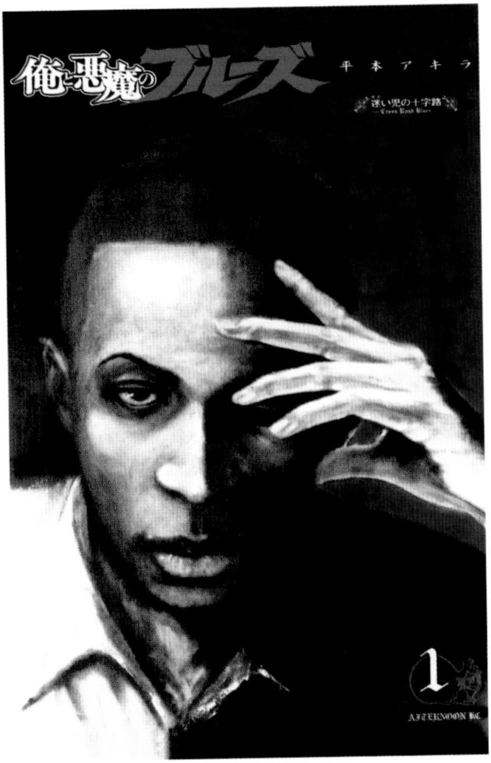
俺と悪魔のブルーズ
平本アキラ
1

Similar reads
Bluesman Rob Vollmar and Pablo G. Callejo
Kings in Disguise James Vance and Dan Burr
R. Crumb Sings the Blues Robert Crumb

Ordinary Victories 2004

Manu Larcenet

Title in original language *Le combat ordinaire*
First published by Dargaud (France)
Creator French (b.1969)
Genre Reality drama

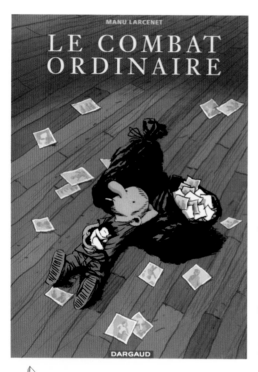

MANU LARCENET

LE COMBAT ORDINAIRE

DARGAUD

Similar reads

Artist of the Family (L'artiste de la famiille) Manu Larcenet
Blast Vol. 1: Fat Carcass (Grasse carcasse) Manu Larcenet
Dallas Cowboy Manu Larcenet
Highway of the Sun (L'autoroute du soleil) Baru
Nearly (Presque) Manu Larcenet

As its title implies, Manu Larcenet's subject is the battleground of everyday life as experienced by his protagonist Marco, former war photographer and son of a shipyard worker. Over four volumes, Marco grapples with the decline and death of a father whose intimate self remained elusive to him, as well as with his own difficulties in accepting commitments and taking up the paternal role.

The character's restless days and nights are depicted in a cartoon style that dissolves into lines and blobs when anxiety tightens its grip. Emotional highs and lows are expressed through color, with a striking use of different background shades to suggest changes in mood. Occasional monochrome pages, made up of more realistic images that appear to represent photographs, are accompanied by a first-person narrative voiceover, offering Marco's thoughts on fear, loss, and the purpose of art.

The strength of *Ordinary Victories* lies in the contextualization of a credible and engaging personal story within a larger political framework. The incomprehension that marks the relationship between Marco and his father cannot be divorced from the latter's past involvement—as a conscript—in the shameful events of the Algerian war. Marco's proposed project of photographing his father's former workmates provokes sharp disagreement with his mother: should the memory of a now-dying tradition of industrial labor be preserved, or would that just be a sentimental celebration of a miserable history of exploitation? The macho posturing of celebrity war photographers who show casual disdain for Marco's work is hilarious, but it also raises questions about the aestheticization of suffering, and the link, if any, between beauty and ethics. Will Larcenet come down on the side of life, cats, Harvey Keitel, and poetry? Read and find out. **AM**

Siberia 2004

Nikolai Maslov

There is no longstanding tradition of comics in Russia. Decades of Soviet government sidelined the art form, denouncing it as beneath the attention of serious artists, and years later that legacy remains. This alone renders *Siberia* noteworthy, but the story of the publication is as astonishing as the work itself.

Nikolai Maslov, then working as a night watchman in Moscow, turned up at the bookstore owned by the French-born publisher of *Asterix*. Presenting the first three pages of *Siberia*, he requested an advance to complete a full graphic novel. The quality and intensity of those pages earned Maslov the opportunity to quit his job, and he spent the next three years working on the story of his youth.

A talented artist since childhood, Maslov was raised in Siberia, and his recollections of it are as forbidding and bleak as the landscape itself. He details his military service in Mongolia, his mind-numbing employment, and his psychiatric breakdown, existing as an everyman in a society where people are supposedly equal, but some are more equal than others. Bullying and intimidation, often in the form of petty bureaucracy, are daily experiences. Moments of beauty are brief, and often defiled, yet they nourish a spirit doused in alcohol and brutality. The clash of culture and establishment, prevalent throughout, is exemplified by Maslov's employment in a Moscow art gallery. At first envisioning a productive artistic environment, he spends his days packaging state-sanctioned portraits of Lenin for distribution.

Maslov's pages are entirely in gray pencil wash, a further anomaly in a world accustomed to inked artwork. That choice of medium is not explained, but it surely reflects an enclosed and isolated world where variations on the shades of gray are defining. *Siberia* may be a brief read, but it is a compelling story. **FP**

Title in original language *Une jeunesse soviétique*
First published by Editions Denoël (France)
Creator Russian (b.1954)
Genre Autobiography

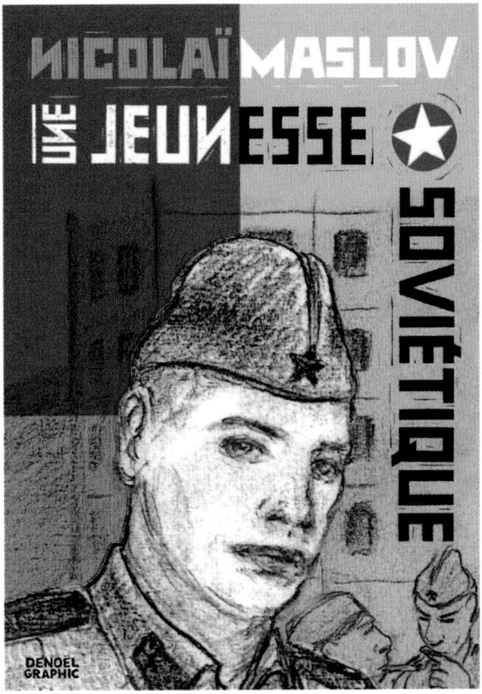
NICOLAÏ MASLOV
UNE JEUNESSE SOVIÉTIQUE
DENOËL GRAPHIC

Similar reads
A Drifting Life Yoshihiro Tatsumi
Burma Chronicles Guy Delisle
Psychiatric Tales Darryl Cunningham
The Alcoholic Jonathan Ames and Dean Haspiel
Tribeca Sunset Henrik Rehr

Scott Pilgrim's Precious Little Life 2004

Bryan Lee O'Malley

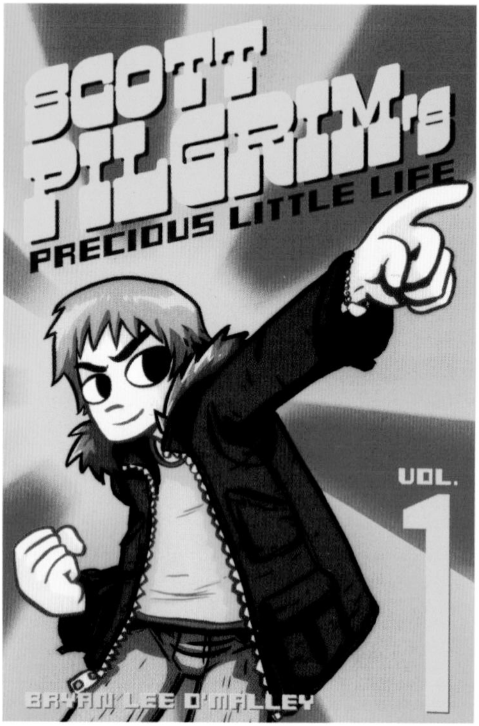
SCOTT PILGRIM'S
PRECIOUS LITTLE LIFE
VOL. 1
BRYAN LEE O'MALLEY

"Dear Mr. Pilgrim. It has come to my attention that we will be fighting soon. My name is Matthew Patel . . . "

Other *Scott Pilgrim* stories

Scott Pilgrim and the Infinite Sadness
Scott Pilgrim's Finest Hour
Scott Pilgrim Gets It Together
Scott Pilgrim vs. the Universe
Scott Pilgrim vs. the World

First published by Oni Press (USA)
Creator Canadian (b.1979)
Genre Romance, Humor
Adaptation Film: *Scott Pilgrim vs. the World* (2010)

The signature comic book of the 2000s is this improbable fusion of young love, Nintendo games, and Canadian winters. A revolutionary hybrid of manga-style storytelling and slacker characterizations, the six volumes of the *Scott Pilgrim* series were to define nerd cool for a generation.

Scott Pilgrim is an unemployed slacker living with his gay friend Wallace in a basement apartment in Toronto. His "precious little life," as the subtitle suggests, is interrupted by Ramona Flowers trespassing in his dreams. As Scott's bandmates and friends watch in disbelief, Scott is compelled to battle and defeat seven evil guys from Ramona's past in order to win her love. Scott's struggle involves a series of increasingly dangerous showdowns with Ramona's childhood crushes and notorious former flames. Complicating matters is the fact that Scott has more than a little romantic baggage himself.

Creator Bryan Lee O'Malley's ability to mix romantic melodrama with playful irony and copious references to contemporary popular culture made *Scott Pilgrim* a generation-defining sensation. O'Malley's writing shows a consistently mature voice throughout. With the art improving with each volume, the work itself seems to grow and develop alongside its own lead character.

The final volume, released in conjunction with the movie of the same name, was met with frenzied celebration. Despite the hype, neither Scott nor O'Malley ever lost touch with their roots. *Scott Pilgrim* is the most bittersweet of all comic book romances. **BB**

DC: The New Frontier 2004

✏️ Darwyn Cooke

First published by DC Comics (USA)
Creator Canadian (b.1962)
Genre Superhero
Adaptation Film: *Justice League: The New Frontier* (2008)

The New Frontier is a reinvention of DC's Silver Age, melded together with the world of 1950s and 1960s test pilots and astronauts—very much as envisioned by Tom Wolfe in *The Right Stuff*, or in Phil Kaufman's classic movie adaptation of Wolfe's book. The term "New Frontier" itself was coined by John F. Kennedy during his acceptance speech after his success in the 1960 U.S. presidential election.

The Old Frontier was the fabled Wild West. Kennedy's New Frontier did not specifically refer to the contemporary challenge of the Space Race; rather, it was a call to move on from the supposed torpor of the Eisenhower years and to meet the economic, scientific, and military challenges of the 1960s.

Darwyn Cooke brilliantly translates Kennedy's rallying cry into a metaphor for the heroism of the DC Silver Age superheroes, as well as real-life heroes—the test pilots and astronauts of the same period. By depicting fictional characters such as Carol Ferris and Hal (Green Lantern) Jordan in the same narrative space as historical figures such as Pancho Barnes and Chuck Yeager, Cooke delivers an unexpected insight into the ways in which the Silver Age heroes embodied the dynamic aspirations of their era.

Cooke's lightness of touch, his humor, his bright colors and bold, cartoonlike art banish at first glance the grim-and-gritty superheroes so prevalent today. Cooke's world of playful forms and witty details captures the Silver Age, but he does so with a knowing smile and a sense of irony so that it all feels fresh. **RR**

Moyasimon: Tales of Agriculture 2004

✏️ Masayuki Ishikawa

First published by Kodansha (Japan)
Creator Japanese (b.1974)
Genre Humor
Award Osamu Tezuka Cultural Prize (2008)

Set in an agricultural university and centered around a superhuman student whose qualities include the ability to see and communicate with bacteria and viruses, this comic is seemingly a cliché in Japan's overdone genre of sci-fi-cum-college-drama. But it turns out to be a pleasant surprise, introducing readers to a peculiar and unexplored marriage of drama and bacteria. *Moyasimon* is full of agricultural information, from the effects of bacteria in alcoholic drinks and how they can change flavors to international analyses of various food cultures. The comic is particularly informative on fermented produce, such as Korean *hongeohoe* (fermented skate), Greenland's *kiviak* (birds fermented inside disemboweled seals), and Swedish *surströmming* (fermented herring).

Equally impressive is the plot, which portrays a typical Japanese agricultural university with delightful realism. When the leading character, Tadayasu Souemon Sawaki, enters agricultural university in Tokyo, he is determined to enjoy the usual student package of dating, partying, and freedom. He soon discovers, however, that campus life involves looking after pigs, growing gigantic vegetables, and sweeping up animal feces. Into this plot Ishikawa plants a theme of maturity, drawing attention to the realization that unlike high school, where students are told what to learn, university allows students the opportunity to learn about their passions—in Sawaki's case, bacteria. The comic has won awards, including the Soy Sauce Culture Prize for its accurate information about soy sauce. **TS**

Disappearance Diary 2005

Hideo Azuma

Title in original language *Shisso Nikki*
First published by East Press (Japan)
Creator Japanese (b.1950)
Genre Autobiography, Drama

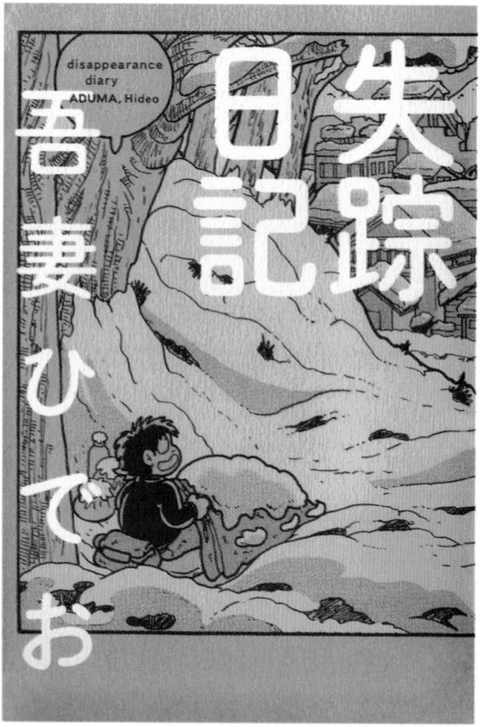
disappearance
diary
ADUMA, Hideo
失踪
日記
吾妻ひでお

Hideo Azuma's résumé is certainly unique. After the success of his softly erotic gag comic *Futari to 5-nin*, serialized in the weekly *Shonen Champion*, his illustrations of *bishojo* (beautiful young girls) became popular among the *Otaku*, prompting him to launch a pornographic comic series. This was *Fujori nikki*, published in erotic comics magazine *Kiso tengai*. With the series, the artist developed a clever concept that combined mysterious reality with fantasy, and this style came to be known as the *Fujori* genre.

Yet later the artist dropped the comic without warning, and suddenly disappeared. During this time he lived a vagrant life with the homeless, sleeping in parks; he once woke to find that it had snowed overnight, nearly freezing him to death. After picking up food from the street he suffered acute diarrhea. These are the kind of episodes that later made up the story of 2005's *Disappearance Diary*.

"Since they're totally frozen, I can't tell from the smell if they're rotten or not."

Azuma decided to take up sewer work, and although he took pleasure in repairing pipes he eventually put an end to his "disappearance" and returned home. Having lost the trust of the comics industry he remained unemployed, but he completed his autobiographical *Disappearance Diary*. Azuma's warm, mellow illustrations and characters, as well as his genuine efforts to entertain his audience, paid off in a delightful piece of work, despite its basis in tragic real-life events.

After its release, the comic won several prestigious awards, including the Grand Prize at the Japan Media Arts Festival. *Disappearance Diary* has joined the other masterpieces in Azuma's diverse portfolio. **TS**

Similar reads

Nanako SOS Hideo Azuma
Pollon of Olympus (*Olympus no Pollon*) Hideo Azuma
The Story of Little Goddess Roly-Poly Pollon (*Ochamegami Monogatari Korokoro Poron*) Hideo Azuma

Ikigami: The Ultimate Limit 2005

Motoro Mase

What would you do if you had just twenty-four hours to live? In the alternative world of *Ikigami*, one in every thousand Japanese must answer that question. In primary school every child is injected with a special vaccine, not to prevent any disease, but to improve economic growth, reduce crime, and make everyone value their lives. Once in every thousand injections, on a random basis, a child is given a nano-capsule containing a bomb that will kill him or her at some time between the ages of eighteen and twenty-four. Awareness of this supposedly makes people better behaved, more productive, and appreciative of life. All those destined to die are sent a twenty-four-hour advanced notice called an *Ikigami*, delivered by a special government official, to give them time to part with loved ones, sort out unfinished business, or just enjoy themselves. They are considered heroes who die for their country; their families get a pension in return. But some turn to violence or other reckless acts, undeterred by the knowledge that their family will face a trial and become outcasts in society. The Japanese support the law because disagreeing with the system is a crime.

"You have been randomly selected by the government . . . to die in 24 hours!"

Motoro Mase, by means of subplots showing how different *Ikigami* receivers spend the last day of their lives, and the main plot involving Kengo Fujimoto, an *Ikigami* deliverer, reveals not only an antiutopian society under totalitarian rule, but also individual tragedies and joys. He is a craftsman able to present every emotion, and his skillful layouts include full-page portraits that effectively heighten the drama. *Ikigami* is a best seller that has received various awards and was made into live-action movie. **RB**

First published by Shogakukan (Japan)
Creator Japanese (b.1969)
Genre Political fable
Adaptation Film (2008)

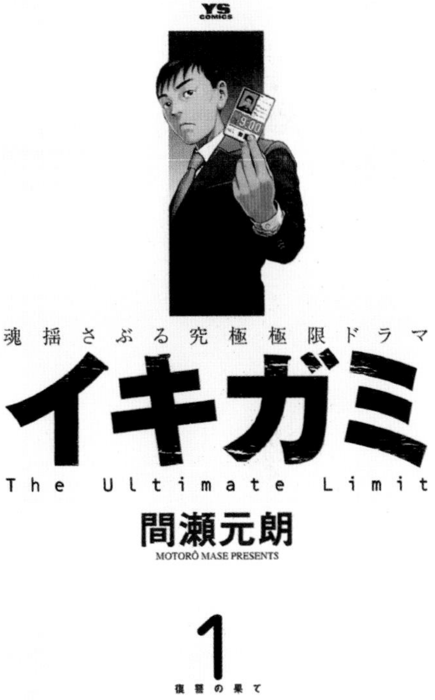
YS COMICS
魂揺さぶる究極極限ドラマ
イキガミ
The Ultimate Limit
間瀬元朗
MOTORŌ MASE PRESENTS
1

Similar reads

A.D. Police Tony Takezaki
HEADS Motoro Mase and Higashino Keigo
The Hunting Party Pierre Christin and Enki Bilal
V for Vendetta Alan Moore and David Lloyd

Aya from Yopougon 2005

Marguerite Abouet Clément Oubrerie

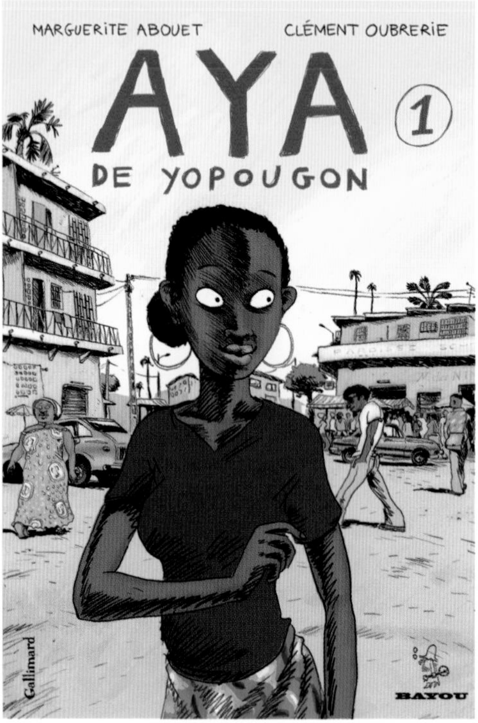
MARGUERITE ABOUET
CLÉMENT OUBRERIE
AYA 1
DE YOPOUGON
Gallimard
BAYOU

"Life isn't complicated. You're the one complicating it, Adjoua."

Similar reads

Bhimayana Srividya Natarajan and S. Anand
Deogratias J. P. Stassen
Eva K. Frank Giroud and Bally Baruti,
***Le Chat du Rabbin* (*The Rabbi's Cat*)** Joann Sfar
Zazie dans le metro Clément Oubrerie

Title in original language *Aya de Yopougon*
First published by Gallimard (France)
Creators (Ivory Coastean-French, b.1971); Oubrerie (French, b.1966) **Genre** Reality drama

Drawing inspiration from her own childhood growing up in the Ivory Coast of the late 1970s, Margurite Abouet tells the story of teenager Aya, who lives with her family in the former capital of Abidjan (now Yamoussoukro). The lives of the inhabitants seem far removed from the images of mass hunger and civil war that the Western reader has come to identify with the whole continent of Africa. Indeed, the issue topping the agenda of most Ivorians in this comic seems to be how to have a good time.

Aya is the odd one out when she concentrates on her homework, helps her friends, and dreams about becoming a doctor. In fact, it is much more interesting to follow the life of her family and friends, who never miss out on an opportunity to get new clothes or stage a party, a funeral, or a beauty contest in their good-natured efforts to better their living conditions, perhaps by attempting to marry someone from a higher social class or take on a second wife. The stories are told with real warmth and humor and the wives definitely wear the pants, even if they let their men think otherwise.

In a straightforward, simple drawing style, Clément Oubrerie makes the everyday Ivory Coast come alive with warm colors and a diverse cast of quirky characters. Oubrerie keeps the seething city's action in check with a tight, squared-panel layout. Whether the stories appear in full-flowering polychrome underneath a high noon sun or in shadowy venues in the middle of the night, *Aya from Yopougon* is a story of Africa that can appeal to readers of any nationality. **RPC**

King of the Flies 2005

✎ "Pirus" ✎ "Mezzo"

Title in original language *Le Roi des mouches*
First published by Albin Michel (France)
Creators Michel Pirus (French, b.1962);
Pascal Mesemberg (French, b.1960) **Genre** Drama

In a small town, possibly in eastern France, a dozen characters of various ages are mingling the emptiness of their lives with family neuroses, hopeless jobs, poorly kept secrets, joyless enjoyments, and addictions of every kind. The suburban setting, like the wanderings of the characters, is terrifying in its banality: Shopping centers, residential areas, sanitized cafeterias, medical offices, interiors so anonymous that they have become inhuman. In this psychotic world, plagued by communication failure, how could meetings be anything other than violent or sexual?

King of the Flies—the nickname of a character—works in the manner of a choral narrative. Chapters are each told from the unique perspective of a different narrator, gradually building into a vast history with many ramifications in which all the characters eventually intersect. The subjectivity of each chapter—often a pure monologue—enables some significant details to be highlighted and others to be hidden.

Remarkably delicate in tone, *King of the Flies* is a striking achievement by the writer. The toxic intensity of the characters and the stifling nature of their suburban universe, so evocative of the American suburbs, recalls David Lynch's *Twin Peaks* and the artificially distanced stories of Brett Easton Ellis. Mezzo's incredible artwork is the perfect counterpoint to the malaise with which all Pirus's characters are burdened. This panorama of everyday terror has a haunted tone, dark and at the same time icy and thrilling; "possessed" would probably be the best word. **NF**

Ice Haven 2005

✎✎ Daniel Clowes

First published by Pantheon Books (USA)
Creator American (b.1961)
Genre Fantasy, Reality drama
Award Harvey Award Best Writer (2005)

Ice Haven first appeared in an issue of *Eightball*, but the expanded graphic novel version is preferable because its landscape format affects the pacing and the way it is read. *Ice Haven* is very much about the experience of taking in information. At first it seems to be a random series of jottings about the town of Ice Haven's inhabitants and visitors—largely embittered losers, strange children, and frustrated teens—told from the viewpoints of a series of unreliable narrators. Most of the plot actually happens off-panel, in the cracks between the differing narrators' accounts of the events.

Daniel Clowes uses the disappearance of an unlovely and uncommunicative local boy to loosely gather together the various narrative strands. He creates a "comic within a comic" to tell the story of the famous "intellectual" murderers Leopold and Loeb, and hints at a similar motivation in the boy's abduction. He also inserts various short strips such as "Rocky," a riff on *The Flintstones* set in prehistoric Ice Haven, and "Blue Bunny," the hard-boiled adventures of a character's stuffed toy. Ultimately the missing boy returns. No one knows what has happened to him, but there is an outburst of optimism among Ice Haven's routinely isolated residents.

Clowes switches styles and color palettes to provoke echoes of many familiar strips. The regularity of his grids highlights how much is going on that readers are not seeing. The tone of *Ice Haven* harks back to his early masterpiece, *Like A Velvet Glove Cast In Iron*, while his art is almost clinically controlled, with perfectly weighted lines and very simplified characters. **FJ**

Interiorae 2005

Gabriella Giandelli

First published by Coconino Press (Italy)
Creator Italian (b.1963)
Genre Drama
Award Ignatz Award Nominee (2009)

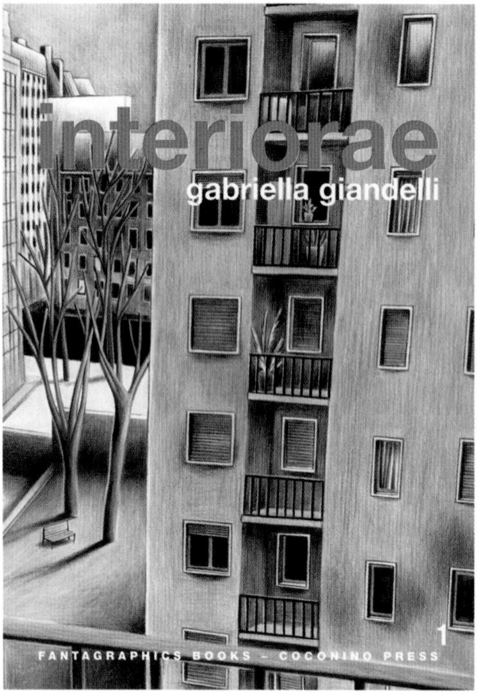
interiorae
gabriella giandelli
1
FANTAGRAPHICS BOOKS - COCONINO PRESS

Similar reads
Abstractions Shintaro Kago
Cages Dave McKean
Fever in Urbicand Peeters and Schuiten
Sandman: World's End Neil Gaiman
The Building Will Eisner

In the same vein as Will Eisner's *The Building*, this story is an exploration of a city building and the people who inhabit it. But *Interiorae* is a more mental and dreamy journey, loosely related to the real appearance of things. The strange building is a sort of living creature, and we look at people's lives are seen as organs in its body. Aided by a white rabbit, an observer serving an entity of the building called the Great Darkness (whose favorite dish is people's dreams), we dig into the desires and frustrations of some typical urban individuals.

There is an old lady whose immigrant caregiver falls asleep after dinner, always dreaming of things he saw as a child; two young friends who fantasize about boys and pop idols; a mother whose phone calls mourn her wrong choice of husband; a young drug dealer; two lovers who kiss and imagine some future that may never exist; and the ghosts of a happy family, already dead, reliving their best moments together.

"... [in] my favorite apartment, all is peaceful and where it should be."

Gabriella Giandelli's building is a metaphor of the vastness of inner spaces, and her book is one of the most intense psychological contemporary graphic novels: severe, elegant, and enigmatic. The narrative derives from her thoughts—a mix of neurosis and distant quietness—about the aura of things and the secrets embedded in everyday lives. Giandelli's atmosphere recalls David Lynch's explorations of the human mind, or Roman Polanski's movie *The Tenant*. But most striking is her graphic technique: an incredibly fine and heavily textured art, made of precise pencil lines. In her mastery of the control and emotional design of color (famously appreciated by Lorenzo Mattotti), she oscillates between stiffness and sensitivity. **MS**

Toys in the Basement 2005

Stéphane Blanquet

A self-publisher from the age of sixteen, Stéphane Blanquet creates deliciously creepy narratives laced with pitch-black humor to confront doomed desires and physical dysfunction, deformation, and decay. His comics often hark back to the moralizing tradition of cautionary tales, such as the German Heinrich Hoffman's *Struwwelpeter* (1845), which were designed to frighten youngsters into behaving properly.

In this vein, *Toys in the Basement*, his first solo graphic novel in color, was conceived for children but can chill and charm every age. It follows a spoiled boy who is sulking at having to wear a pink rabbit outfit to a Halloween party. Descending into the basement in search of refreshments, he and a girl follow a tunnel into a hidden society of damaged, abandoned, and angry toys. These mistake the children in their furry costumes for newly arrived stuffed toys. The boy and girl play along at first, but a mistake exposes them as humans, capable of crimes of cruelty against their playthings. As punishment the children are fed to Amelia, a grotesque giantess built from broken toys.

"When you least expect it he'll snap you in two. . . ."

Blanquet makes readers question who are the true monsters of the story, building sympathy for the rejects with their ripped seams and wrenched-off hands and arms. The theme relates to Blanquet's condition: for years he has been confined to a wheelchair by muscular dystrophy. His deteriorating condition has made him an intense, prolific artist, whose output goes beyond comics. His work embraces gallery installations and animated films using jointed shadow-play, cut-outs and his own stuffed dolls and toys, forming an urgent personal self-mythology. **PG**

Title in original language *Chocottes au sous-sol!*
First published by Éditions La Joie de Lire (France)
Creator French (b.1973)
Genre Fantasy, Children's

Blanquet
Chocottes
au sous-sol!
LA JOIE DE LIRE

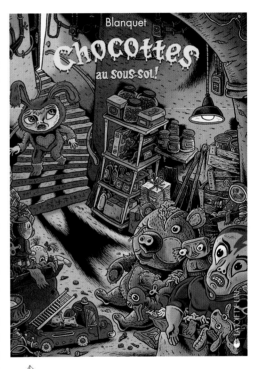

Similar reads

Dungeon Monsters Book 2: The Dark Lord Lewis Trondheim and Joann Sfar
Kingdom of the Wicked Ian Edgington and D'Israeli
Monographie Lacrymale Stéphane Blanquet
Silent Stories in Zero Zero Stéphane Blanquet

Bad People 2005

🖉🖉 Étienne Davodeau

Title in original language *Les mauvaises gens*
First published by Delcourt (France)
Creator French (b.1965)
Genre Reality drama

What is more unusual than a comic strip that portrays the lives of working-class people? Answer: one in which they refuse to stay in their allotted place. *Bad People* is a biography of Étienne Davodeau's parents, both factory workers, brought up in a conservative Catholic milieu in the years following World War II, in a tradition of docile obedience to their employers. Under the influence of a worker priest, they set up union branches and campaign for the Socialist Party.

Davodeau uses a delicate black-and-white drawing style, washed in shades of gray, to document his parents' stories. He is concerned above all to be faithful to their experience as he re-creates now-demolished sites, conditions of work, and political struggles. These may be rendered literally (repeated images convey the monotony of gluing leather onto shoe heels) or metaphorically (the shadow of the factory looms over his mother, who is forced to leave school at fourteen).

The interplay of points of view and time frames is complex. Davodeau not only records scenes from the past, but also the process, in the present, of producing his album. The artist is shown sketching, with his parents commenting on his drafts. Panels in which these modest people look back on their younger selves as they achieve the confidence to speak out against authoritarian bosses are moving and inspirational. History provided no happy end for the socialist dream, but in a brilliant final panel Davodeau suspends time, literally, through a freeze frame, defying the cynicism that hindsight makes inevitable. **AM**

Jacaranda 2005

🖉🖉 Kotobuki Shiriagari

First published by Seirinkôgeisha (Japan)
Creator Japanese (b.1957)
Genre Fantasy, Humor
Influenced by *Ereki na Haru*

In his afterword to the Japanese edition of *Jacaranda*, Kotobuki Shiriagari apologizes twice. First for turning what should have been the idea for a single strip—namely, what if a giant tree destroyed Tokyo overnight?—into a 300-page book. Second, he apologizes to the jacaranda, a large South African tree with purple-blue flowers, for giving it a bad name.

By many accounts, Shiriagari is a funny man. But while he has produced nonsensical stories, such as *Hige no OL Yabuuchi Sasako*, where a young woman's mustache becomes a matter of national importance, other works (in particular, *Hinshi no Essayist* and *AOsu*) have revealed a darker side, dealing with more serious topics such as death and solitude.

This darker trait is present in *Jacaranda*, and echoes *Hako-bune*, Shiriagari's take on the story of Noah's Ark. Where *Hako-bune* described the slow and quiet disappearance of civilization underwater, *Jacaranda* is full of explosions and spectacular destruction, in a strange mix of dark humor and social commentary. The early pages present acerbic criticism of contemporary Japanese society and its fascination with media and appearances—and then all hell breaks loose. From here onward the book is rooted in parody, playing on the usual tropes of disaster movies (worried families, separated couples) but inevitably leading them to a violent and deadly conclusion. Shiriagari might go a little overboard with the pyrotechnic finale, but for all the cynicism he displays in this book, he cannot help but finish on a positive note. There is always hope. **XG**

Solanin 2005

Inio Asano

First published by Shogakukan (Japan)
Creator Japanese (b.1980)
Genre Reality drama
Award Harvey Award (2009)

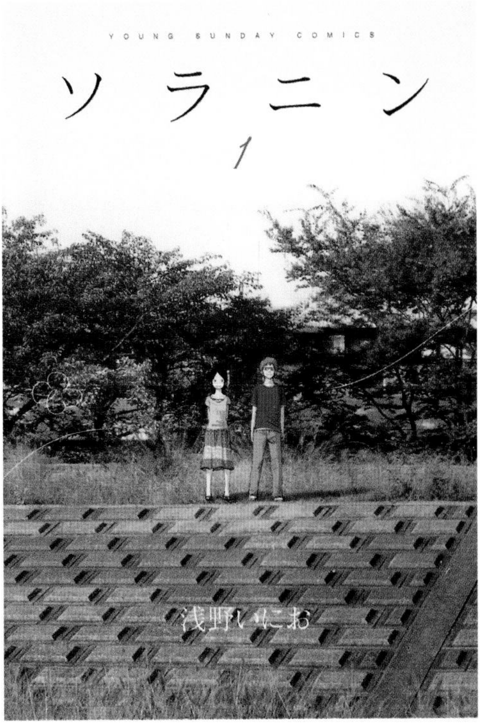

YOUNG SUNDAY COMICS
ソラニン
1
浅野いにお

In Japan, Inio Asano is considered a voice of the younger generation, but the problems addressed in his works are far more universal than that suggests. *Solanin* is concerned with how some things will never change no matter where you live. Gaining entrance to the adult world is not easy, and the characters of this story know that from their own experience.

Meiko has quit being an "office lady" and is living with her boyfriend Naruo, who only does odd jobs and dreams about becoming a rock star. Their relationship becomes more and more complicated, not because they don't love each other, but because they feel lost and are unable to find their place in the world. However, they know they can depend on their friends: Jirÿ, a drummer who works at his father's pharmacy; Ken'ichi, a bass player who started to study at the university but so far has failed to graduate; and Ai, Ken'ichi's girlfriend, who works in a shoe shop. In Japan you are expected to become part of society after graduation, to get a full-time job and start a family, but the characters of *Solanin* seem unable to do so, or maybe really do not want to.

The story of *Solanin* may sound dispiriting, but the dialogue and the drawings transform it with comedy, making it a very pleasant read. The images are detailed, with numerous jokes hidden in the backgrounds. Sometimes photographs are used instead of drawings, but in a way that does not disturb the narrative.

The universality of *Solanin* has been fully appreciated. It has been nominated for various awards, and was the basis for a live-action movie. **RB**

"There's probably a dimensional warp in the Machida area."

Similar reads
A Distant Neighborhood Jiro Taniguchi
BECK Harold Sakuishi
Pumpkin with Mayonnaise Kiriko Nananan
The Band Mawil
What a Wonderful World! Inio Asano

Little Star 2005

Andi Watson

First published by Oni Press (USA)
Creator British (b.1969)
Genre Reality drama
Influenced by *Blankets*

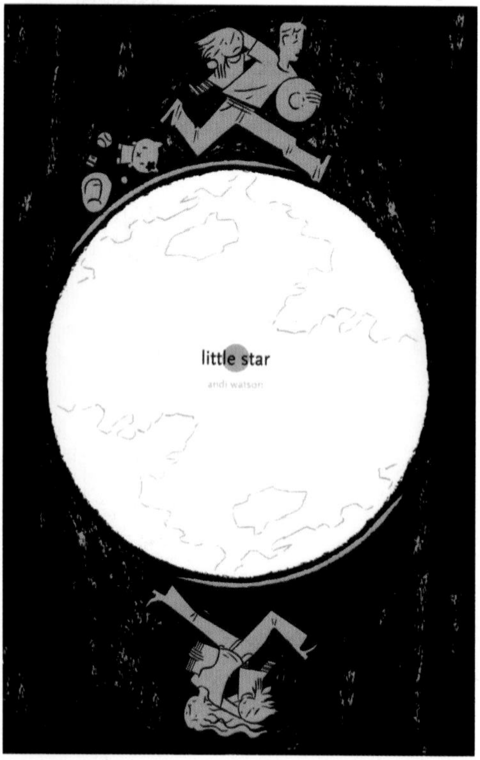
little star
andi watson

Also by Andi Watson
Breakfast After Noon
Skeleton Key
Slow News Day

When he was a child, *Little Star*'s Simon Adams longed to be an astronaut. His evenings were spent gazing into the night sky, considering its constellations of distant suns and the blackness that separated them, and imagining an infinite void of possibilities, a vast canvas of new worlds and as yet unrealized dreams. Now an adult with a mortgage, a family, and a part-time job that barely pays the bills, Simon still spends his nights stargazing, although the universe no longer beckons as it did before.

Married to wife Meg and with an ungrateful daughter named Cassie, who barely acknowledges his existence, the stars now seem more benign, representing little more than a diversion from the

"When did my daughter become a feminist extremist?"

pressures of everyday life. Beset with financial concerns and losing touch with Cassie, who loves her mother but increasingly sees him as an irrelevance, he finds the complexity of the universe transformed into a metaphor for his own confusion and angst.

Struggling as he may be, he is not some overwhelmed, deadbeat father. He has changed diapers and suffered the sleepless nights, although his awareness of masses of black space provides a powerful emotional contrast.

Little Star is about staying the course, about not giving in or giving up. By its nature it may appeal more readily to parents than nonparents, but there are lessons here for anyone who sees time passing too quickly. Its creator, Andi Watson, became a father in 2002, so it's tempting to suggest this may be in part an autobiographical work. Watson denies this, but is happy to add that "babies are very hard work." **BS**

DMZ 2005

Brian Wood Riccardo Burchielli

In the near future, the United States is embroiled in a second civil war, this time with the "Free States". An uneasy stalemate has emerged between the two sides, with Manhattan lying directly in between. The island has become a demilitarized zone, or DMZ, with both sides vying for power and influence. Into this world comes Matty Roth, a Liberty News intern who finds himself stranded in the DMZ when his news helicopter is attacked. Matty turns crisis into opportunity, establishing himself as the only journalist in the DMZ and reporting on the suffering of residents as various factions fight for power and influence.

DMZ is essentially a protracted criticism of how the United States wages war today. The DMZ itself includes

"Everyone knows everyone. Stay close. If you're with me, you should be cool."

a little of everything; there are shades of Kosovo, Korea, and Somalia here, but mostly Brian Wood is commenting on Iraq and Afghanistan. Matty explores terrorist cells, unearths a civilian massacre, interviews Free States commanders, and sees for himself the atrocities being committed by private security contractors. Matty's story gradually becomes entwined with that of the DMZ itself, his investigative reports able to sway public opinion and change the very nature of the war.

Riccardo Burchielli's art is detailed and organic, bringing an Italian visual sensibility and an outsider's view to a very American series, but it is Wood's political views that are being explored here. By bringing the war to Manhattan, Wood is able to show that things associated with far-off regions of the world could happen in the United States. He humanizes the conflicts normally only seen on television, exposing their barbarism by staging them on home soil. **BD**

First published by Vertigo/DC Comics (USA)
Creators Wood (American, b.1972); Burchielli (Italian, b.1975)
Genre Political fable

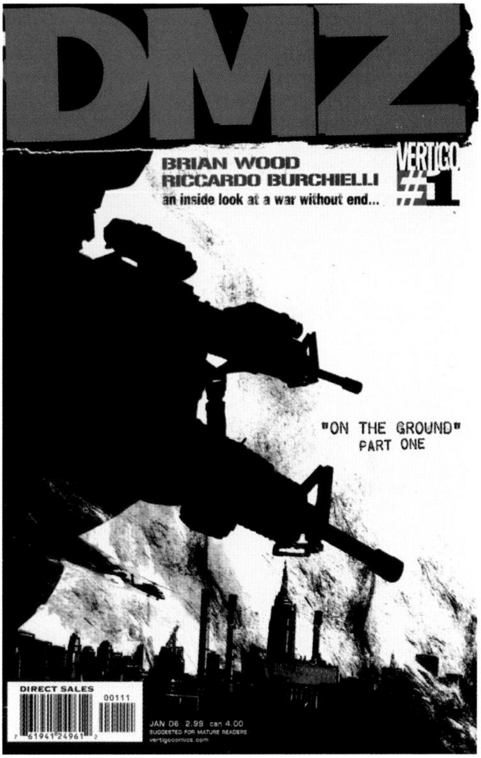
DMZ
BRIAN WOOD
RICCARDO BURCHIELLI
an inside look at a war without end...
VERTIGO
#1
"ON THE GROUND" PART ONE
DIRECT SALES

Similar reads

Channel Zero Brian Wood
Local Brian Wood and Ryan Kelly
Northlanders Brian Wood and others

Cinema Panopticum 2005

Thomas Ott

First published by Edition Moderne (Switzerland)
Creator Swiss (b.1966)
Genre Fantasy
Award Ignatz Award Nominee (2005)

THOMAS OTT
CINEMA
PANOPTICUM

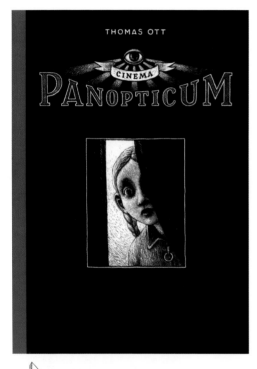

Similar reads
Black Hole Charles Burns
Greetings from Hellville Thomas Ott
In Vitro Marc Caro
Perdita Durango Barry Gifford and Scott Gillis
Tales of Error Thomas Ott

The Swiss comic draftsman, or rather comic scraper, Thomas Ott is a master of somber stories. Gradually becoming aware that his drawings consisted mainly of black lines, and inspired by the French comic strip artist Marc Caro, Ott decided that he would work with scraperboard exclusively. Over the years Ott has perfected this time-consuming technique, in which white lines and areas are scraped or scratched out of black-coated card with a scalpel or needle. The scraperboard technique not only gives his pictures a surprising plasticity, but also confers an almost three-dimensional quality, which is fascinating in its weight and depth.

With Ott's stories one is taken directly into the deepest abysses of destiny and the human soul. Even when fortune suddenly seems to smile on his heroes or heroines, the moment of happiness is always brief, followed by even greater misery and unhappiness. In *Cinema Panopticum*, Ott has assembled a collection of short stories within an overarching plot. Disappointed that she does not have enough money to go on the roundabout or enjoy herself in other ways at the annual fair, a little girl finally discovers a Nickelodeon movie theater where she can just about afford to watch short films. These include "The Champion," in which a wrestler fights the Grim Reaper and in the end manages to defeat him. But when the apparent winner arrives home, he realizes that Death has only diverted his attention because he has taken away his greatest treasure—his daughter.

Ott's heroine is fascinated by the Nickelodeon, but as she watches the last film, "The Girl," it is evident just from her wide eyes and her panic-stricken flight that she must have seen something terrifying. In the same way, the reader of Ott's story may also suddenly feel the need to put the comic down. **MS**

Ott's scraperboard technique gives a sinister air to even the simplest scenes. ➡

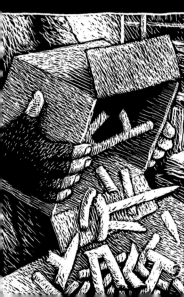

erman 2005

Morrison 🖊 "Frank Quitely"

shed by DC Comics (USA)

Morrison (British, b.1969); Vincent Deighan
986)

erhero

urse of writing *All Star Superman*, Grant
ecalled interviewing a costumed "Superman"
s convention. "My entire approach . . . had
n the way that guy had been sitting . . . as
able to all physical harm, he could . . . be
us and warm." Morrison's twelve-part "love
uperman" distills his essence from comics,
and movies into an elegant, nostalgic, yet
sion. Morrison's take is gentler, more idealistic,
d freer than other imaginings, but retains
dgy science fiction quirks. The result can be
ked, affecting, or absurd, often all at once.
from an overdose of solar radiation inflicted
hemesis Lex Luthor, Superman must compress
worth of feats into mere days and prepare
to live without him. This framework allows
play with ideas that include the Underverse,
so strong time stops; the anti-Bizarro Zibarro,
tive in an insane world; all of human history
in twenty-four hours on an alternate world;
ttle city of Kandor reborn on Mars. Morrison's
cast is perfect, but his overarching theme is
ering faith his hero has in humanity.

Frank Quitely creates a palpably real world
fantastic and wondrous. Combining a quirky,
lity with idiosyncratic figurework and faces,
when called for, or masterfully subtle in
d detail. Morrison and Quitely have created

Exercises in Style

🖊🖊 Matt Madden

First published by Chamberlain Brothers (USA)
Creator American (b.1968)
Genre Alternative
Influenced by *Exercises in Style* Raymond Quen

A man gets up from his computer, walks into h
speaks to his wife and opens his refrigerato
discover that he can't recall what he was lo
In the simplest terms, that is all that happen
Madden's book. Of course, nothing about this
be described in simple terms.

Each of the ninety-nine pages tells the ex
story, but each introduces a new way of
Inspired by the French writer Raymond Quen
once wrote the same mundane anecdote nin
different ways, Madden tests the limits of th
form by introducing innovative ways of pr
the same information to the reader. With this
he links himself to the experimental comics
developed by the French OuBaPo group; he p
slight story well past the point of narrative ex
and delivers, in the process, some profound
into the way comics work.

The challenge presented by the project
simply the identification of possible styles,
the execution of them. Madden subjects his c
story to transformations of all kinds: changin
points-of-view, and drawing styles. He substit
text, new images, and entirely new logical pat

When he is not working as a cartoonist,
is employed as a teacher of comics. He has,
wife Jessica Abel, authored a textbook that
interested readers how to make comics,

Detroit Metal City 2005

Kiminori Wakasugi

First published by Hakusensha (Japan)
Creator Japanese (b.1971)
Genre Humor
Adaptation Original video animation (2008)

With eccentric costumes, devilish makeup, and the word "murder" inscribed on his forehead, Johannes Krauser II is the guitarist of death metal band Detroit Metal City (DMC). He is excessively provocative onstage, and his insane crowd of hardcore fans rock to the band's outrageous lyrics and psychotic performances. But offstage his real name is Soichi Negishi, and back at the office of his boss, the sadistic woman who owns his record company, he's utterly powerless.

In fact, he is only in the band because he has to be. His actual dream is a career in pop, playing the acoustic guitar and singing tunes of love and hope. Hopelessly unstylish, his real bobbed-hair self is a cheerful but shy street singer. However, despite loathing the role of his alter ego, Negishi is naturally gifted at death metal, and once he's dressed for the part he suddenly transforms into a destructive, sinister, and sadistic guitarist.

Detroit Metal City humorously presents Negishi's struggles to juggle his two personalities without his loved ones noticing and the hilarious gap between his peaceful self and the world of death metal he is forced to inhabit. Other characters in the comic are every bit as good, creating a rare work of laugh-out-loud comedy that has gained plenty of admirers. Passionate fans have even written music for the DMC lyrics featured in the story. When the comic was developed into an Original Video Animation (OVA) in 2009, DMC's songs traveled beyond fiction and were released on CD. The following year it was adapted as a film featuring Kenichi Matsuyama, star of *Norwegian Wood* (2010). **TS**

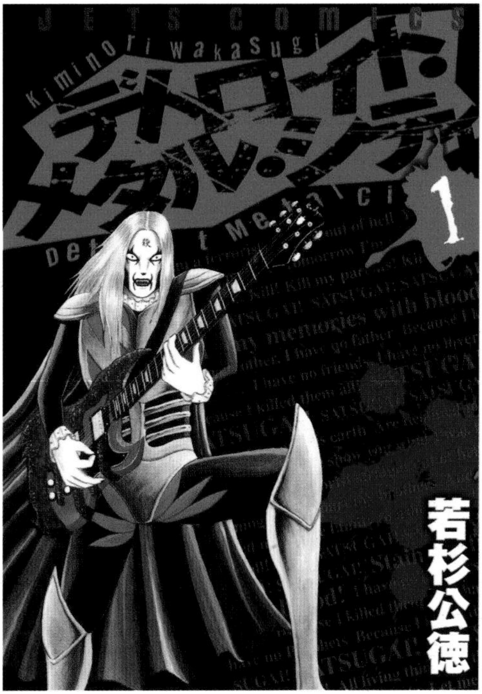
Kiminori Wakasugi
1
若杉公徳

"Carve my name into your souls! Extol me as the true demonic emperor! I am the real Krauser and we are the real Detroit Metal City!"

Similar reads
Amaresu Ken-chan Kiminori Wakasugi
BECK Harold Sakuishi
Fire! Hideko Mizuno
Minna! Esper Dayo! Kiminori Wakasugi
Woodstock Yukai Asada

Ooku: The Inner Chamber 2005

Fumi Yoshinaga

Title in original language *Ooku*
First published by Hakusensha (Japan)
Creator Japanese (b.1971)
Genre Political fable, Romance

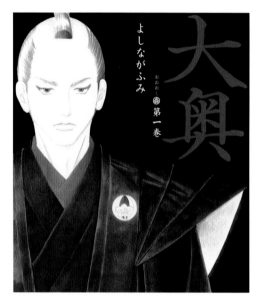

"Forgive me. I shall call you Onobu tonight, just for this one night."

Also by Fumi Yoshinaga
All My Darling Daughters
Antique Bakery
Flower of Life
Kodomo no Taion
What Did You Eat Yesterday?

During the Edo period of seventeenth- to nineteenth-century Japan, a section known as the Ooku existed in the shogun's castle at Edo (Tokyo). Forbidden to males and sometimes referred to as a harem, it was the home of the shogun's female attendants whose responsibilities included producing candidates for the throne. Fumi Yoshinaga's comic, however, tells the story a little differently. She illustrates a theoretical interpretation of Ooku where the roles of males and females are reversed.

In Yoshinaga's version, young men fall victim to a mysterious plague, reducing the male population to only a quarter of the female. Men are therefore protected, leaving labor to women, and even the shogunate is taken over by a female successor. The Ooku becomes a place for beautiful young males to entertain the female shogun. Famous male figures in history such as Yoshimune Tokugawa are depicted as women, although their names remain unchanged.

The focal point of the plot is Mizuno, a handsome attendant of the Ooku. He may be surrounded by women, but in the reversed world of Ooku, Mizuno's masculine looks draw the attention of his fellow flamboyant men. The strong-minded swordsman is unconcerned. His progress catches the eye of his highest-ranked boss, Fujinami, and he is promoted.

The appeal of this comic is its structure, which mixes carefully researched historical facts with imaginative fiction. The story of Mizuno and Yoshimune early in the series paints the relationship between a female shogun and manservant; the theme of love and hatred between men and women in this scenario is intriguing. When the focus shifts to Iemitsu Tokugawa, the unraveling of the mystery behind this reversed world and the vivid portrayal of the Ooku system once again enthralls the reader. **TS**

Tamara Drewe 2005

✍ Posy Simmonds

Welcome to Ewedown, a dull, class-ridden, "event-proofed" English village, with "no shop, no bus, no school, no post office," three-quarters of its residents "stinking rich incomers," the rest poor and stuck on benefits. Bequeathed the family home by her late mother, Tamara Drewe returns to her birthplace. Thanks to plastic surgery on her nose, Tamara is now transformed into a seductive beauty.

In no time four men succumb to her charms: her former teenage sweetheart, handyman Adam Cobb; a cool new romance with drummer Ben Sergeant; a famous local crime writer named Nicholas Hardiman; and U.S. academic Glen Larson, who is visiting Hardiman's writers' retreat. Tamara's provocative presence ignites chain reactions in Hardiman's long-suffering wife, Beth, who is weary of her manipulative husband's philandering, and in thrill-seeking teenager Jody Long, who is determined to lose her "V plates" (or virginity) to Tamara's rockstar lover Ben. The final spark is Jody's prank email, supposedly from Tamara, offering three of her admirers "the biggest shagging of your life."

Thomas Hardy's *Far From The Madding Crowd* provided Posy Simmonds with the dynamics of desire, while her "Literary Life" satires supplied the milieu of writers' egos and rivalries. Simmonds substantially revised and expanded the 110 installments serialized in *The Guardian* newspaper for the 124-page graphic novel, reining in Beth's ruminations and enhancing Glen's role as outsider-commentator. She intersperses ample passages of typeset text among her more conventional comic strip layouts, giving each character's voice its own font, or heighten tension by drawing whole pages without words. Always an astute observer of the British middle classes, Simmonds also makes readers empathize with the celebrity-obsessed desperation of abandoned, working-class youth. **PG**

First published by Jonathan Cape (UK)
Creator British (b.1945)
Genre Satire
Award Prix de la critique (2009)

Posy Simmonds
TAMARA DREWE

"The real secret of being a writer is learning to be a convincing liar."

Similar reads
Gemma Bovery Posy Simmonds
La Marie en plastique Pascal Rabaté and
    David Prudhomme
Literary Lives Posy Simmonds
Summer of Love Debbie Drechsler

The Boys 2006

Garth Ennis Darick Robertson

First published by WildStorm/DC Comics (USA)
Creators Ennis (Irish, b.1970);
Robertson (American, b.1968)
Genre Adult, Superhero

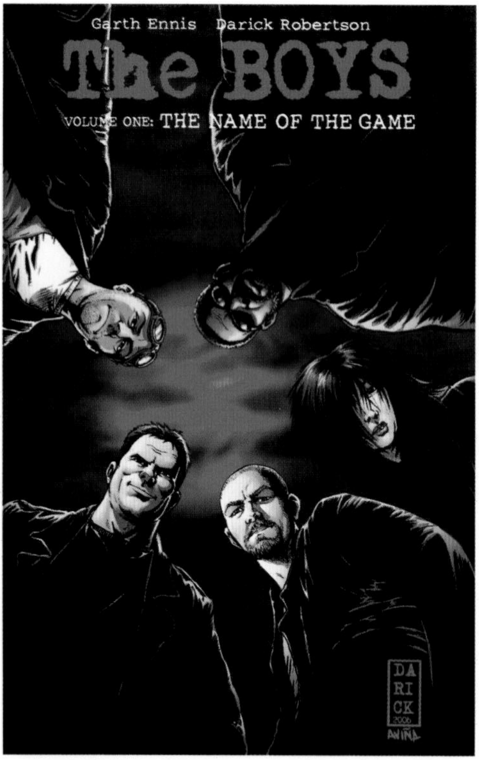
Garth Ennis Darick Robertson
The BOYS
VOLUME ONE: THE NAME OF THE GAME
DA RI CK 2006

Similar reads
Irredeemable Mark Waid and Peter Krause
Powers Brian Michael Bendis
Top Ten Alan Moore

Superheroes are far from perfect, as Garth Ennis's brutal and uncompromising *The Boys* is keen to remind us. The Boys are the opposite of costumed heroes. They have bad hair and grim faces, talk in thick colloquial accents, and operate in trenchcoats and T-shirts. Butcher, the rough but highly capable Englishman, is the leader; the Frenchman is part romantic, part psychopath; Mother's Milk is a responsible, versatile giant of a man; and the final member, the Female, is a mute sociopath with a gentle streak. The first volume (*The Name of the Game*) in this ongoing series concerns the introduction of the newest member of the team: Wee Hughie, a timid, Simon Pegg lookalike whose girlfriend has just been killed in a collision with a speeding superhero.

"It's the superheroes, right? The supes. We were the ones who kept an eye on 'em."

In typically explicit Ennis fashion, the Boys' efforts to intimidate and punish reckless "supes" is expressed in wall-to-wall sex, violence, and strong language. They are out to punish superheroes, and the team members all have personal motivations that are explored in later issues. It is a dirty, bitter, and angry series, offering an alternative to the masked heroes that dominate the market.

In a cynical, corrupt world, the superheroes are portrayed as arrogant celebrities, whereas the real heroes are the ones who refuse to let their world be ruled by The Seven (a thinly veiled parody of the Justice League of America) and are prepared to use blackmail and intimidation where they see fit. *The Boys* is a bone-crunching, cult masterwork, featuring a new breed of heroes who look out for their own, are not afraid to get their hands dirty, and whom the creators dare you to hero-worship. **SW**

Ultimate Spider-Man Clone Saga 2006

Brian Michael Bendis   Mark Bagley

First published by Marvel Comics (USA)
Creators Bendis (American, b.1967); Bagley (American, b.1957)
Genre Superhero

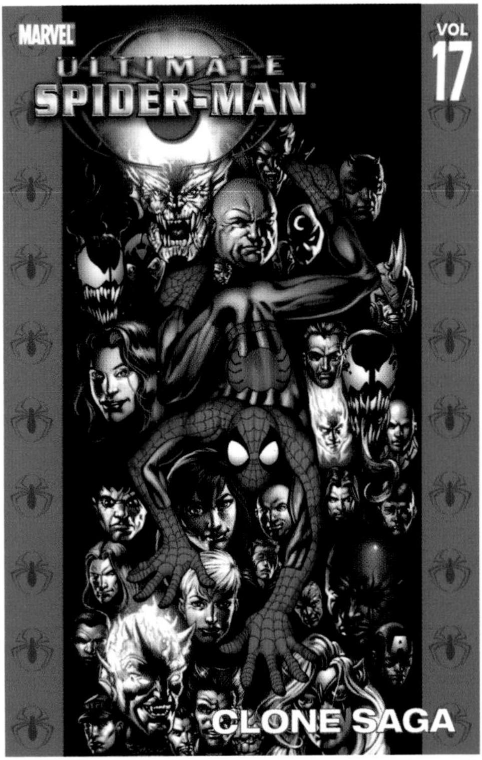
MARVEL
VOL 17
ULTIMATE
SPIDER-MAN
CLONE SAGA

Throughout his career, Brian Michael Bendis had honed a collection of narrative tics on which he relied heavily. *Ultimate Spider-Man* dragged away much of this safety blanket by requiring all-ages content—reworking Spider-Man's recognized history and cast for a fusion of familiarity and freshness. Bendis excelled and surprised many by making an astounding success from an initially scorned idea.

Five years into what became the longest run of consecutive monthly issues by the same creative team, he tackled the most derided of all *Spider-Man* stories, the *Clone Saga*: a dismal sprawling mess by third-rate creators overseen by even less competent editors and occupying all *Spider-Man* titles for a year.

"This is my life!! This is Peter's life!! And you can't have it!! So you just go on back to where you came from!!"

Bendis focused on the plot as the primary strength. This Spider-Man is fifteen years old, uncertain and inexperienced, when disturbing variations of his own DNA manifest to complicate his life. The morally ambivalent pragmatism of the real world is reflected by one of Spider-Man's malevolent foes, who is believed to be incarcerated, yet turns up employed by a government agency. There is also a much-anticipated conversation with Peter Parker's adoptive mother, Aunt May.

Artist Mark Bagley is notable for winning a talent competition run by Marvel in 1983. He became a favorite artist of editors, able to turn out twenty-five pages of competent superhero action month after month without ever relying on pinup pages or skimping on detail. Almost the entire run of *Ultimate Spider-Man* provides an entertaining read, but the *Clone Saga* is a surprise-packed, page-turning peak. **FP**

Similar reads
Hawkworld Tim Truman
Ultimate X-Men: The Tomorrow People Mark Millar, Adam Kubert, and Andy Kubert

Travel 2006

✐✐ Yuichi Yokoyama

Title in original language *Toraberu*
First published by East Press (Japan)
Creator Japanese (b.1967)
Genre Humor

Yuichi Yokoyama's books are a curious mix of classical storytelling and formal experimentation, where everything is abstracted in the visual field of composition. His *Travel* is a spectacular clash between graphic design and comics.

The plot is rather simple and linear, reminding readers of modern comic's obsession with travel and fast-paced movement (Rodolphe Töpffer and Rafael Bordalo Pinheiro, for example) or, more contemporarily, the highly dynamic and movement-obsessed manga series *Gon* by Masashi Tanaka. In *Travel*, the so-called narrative follows three characters who get on a train that travels through many landscapes, and who get off at a waterfront at the journey's end. While on the train, they perambulate, look at the other passengers, and light up cigarettes: nothing particularly exciting in itself. However, each of these apparently simple actions is blown out of proportion with the author's various visual tricks—pure pattern, and stunning perspectives and angles, for example—transforming every occurrence into a fantastic, epic gesture. As readers, we are traveling not only with these characters but also in and out of all the possible points of view around and within the train in a frenzied attempt to control as much information as possible. Even the lighting of a cigarette and the act of smoking it turns into a titanic event.

The lack of dialogue and real interaction shows that Yokoyama is less interested in the creation of characters than of agents, functions of action, and mere excuses for this frantic kinetic spree. **PM**

Criminal 2006

✐ Ed Brubaker   ✐ Sean Phillips

First published by Icon/Marvel Comics (USA)
Creators Brubaker (American, b.1966);
Phillips (British, b.1965)
Genre Crime

Before superheroes came to dominate U.S. comic books from the 1960s onward, crime stories flourished. The best-selling *Crime Does Not Pay* concentrated on the battle between cops and gangsters, and *Crime SuspenStories* and *Shock SuspenStories* drew more directly on pulp fiction and film noir sources.

Criminal, by writer Ed Brubaker and artist Sean Phillips, succeeds in bringing back that same noirish intensity to the comic page. The title houses a number of four- or five-issue story arcs that are essentially self-contained, although certain locations, events, and minor characters are common throughout. Focusing on the small-time crooks and low-life losers who feed and fight at the bottom of the underworld, *Criminal* is in many ways a very traditional crime comic. Here passions are always murderous, cops invariably corrupt, and femmes guaranteed to be fatale. But it is also more than fifty years since the peak of film noir, and in that time both comics and crime fiction have changed considerably.

Criminal is more sexually explicit, more profane, more brutally violent, and more morally ambiguous than its comic book predecessors. The dialogue has the same slangy zing as the crime fiction of writers such as Elmore Leonard and George V. Higgins, and the whole series is imbued with a certain ironic self-awareness that inevitably invites comparisons with Quentin Tarantino. The fourth and best *Criminal* story, "Bad Night," even features a cartoonist (who draws the Dick Tracy–ish strip *Frank Kafka PI*) as the main protagonist. **AL**

American Born Chinese 2006

Gene Luen Yang

First published by First Second Books (USA)
Creator American (b.1973)
Genre Teen, Humor
Award Michael L. Printz Award (2007)

American Born Chinese deals with identity, acceptance, and high school insecurity via three seemingly unrelated strands. An adaptation of *The Monkey King* legends and the lessons to be learned from them is the opening sequence. The strand most rooted in realism spotlights Chinese-American Jin's experiences growing up, and his difficulties in adapting to a largely white neighborhood and school. In 1950s sitcom-style sequences, apparently white student Danny is embarrassed continually by the antics of his visiting Chinese cousin, Chin Kee, whose name reflects his portrayal in the exaggerated racist manner of 1940s comics.

The three different strands of the tale address the question of how much of their background and culture a person should discard in order to assimilate into a different society. It is a weighty topic that a lack of subtlety could render unsympathetic, but with Gene Luen Yang's deft handling, *American Born Chinese* is compassionate, sensitive, and, in places, very funny. The artwork is drawn in vivid cartoon style, yet it never distracts the adult reader, and the simplicity of the narrative resonates positively with teenagers whose experiences resemble the situations depicted.

American Born Chinese has drawn considerable attention outside the comics community. In 2006 it was selected as one of the five nominees for the National Book Award in the Young People's Literature category. It was the first comic ever honored by the judges, providing the best possible indication of its widespread accessibility. **FP**

AMERICAN BORN CHINESE
Gene Luen Yang

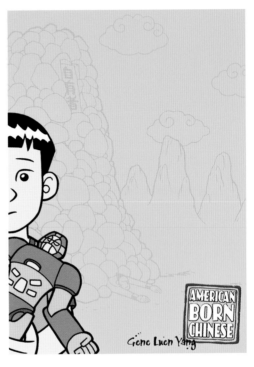

"It's easy to become anything you wish . . . so long as you are willing to forfeit your soul."

Similar reads

Animal Crackers Gene Luen Yang
Astronauts of the Future (Les cosmonautes du futur) Lewis Trondheim and Manu Larcenet
Leçon de chose Grégory Mardon
Stuck Rubber Baby Howard Cruse

The Arrival 2006

✐✐ Shaun Tan

First published by Lothian Children's Books (Australia)
Creator Australian (b.1974) **Genre** Fantasy, Biography
Award Children's Book Council of Australia:
Picture Book of the Year (2007)

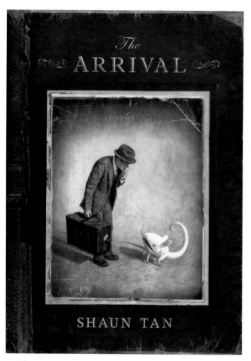

Similar reads
A Week of Kindness (Un Semaine de Bonte) Max Ernst
Flood! A Novel in Pictures Eric Drooker
Passionate Journey Frans Masereel
Tales from Outer Suburbia Shaun Tan
The Invention of Hugo Cabret Brian Selznick

Shaun Tan's *The Arrival* has a rare quality: it conjures up the breathless excitement and wonder of a first cinematic experience. The book feels crafted rather than drawn, as it tells the story of a migrant through a series of wordless images.

Tan's trademark fusion of the suburban and the surreal imbues the narrative with wonder, joy, and a delicious hint of danger. The lack of words is deliberately unsettling and highlights the way the migrant is feeling as he flees a nameless, but nonetheless terrifying, force. Tan's dreamlike imagery taps directly into our deepest fears and aspirations, giving the book the quality of a shared dream. The size and shape of the panels vary with a musical rhythm, expanding or contracting depending

"I'd like to keep it quite personal, challenging and unexpected . . ."

Shaun Tan

on the kind of experience they depict. Moving close-ups that follow the gaze of the characters alternate with extraordinarily detailed double-page spreads that recall the art of Salvador Dalí. Tan draws on a range of eclectic influences, from silent film to science, plumbing, and anthropology, all to powerfully original effect.

In keeping with the theme of the book, Tan never allows readers any comfort or certainty; as soon as an image can be interpreted, it becomes something else in the next panel. Handled with such assurance, this never becomes confusing—readers are drawn in repeatedly, discovering new connections and associations in a fully realized world. Yet this is also a book that can be shared with younger people, empowering them to add their own voices and meanings. *The Arrival* takes its audience on a journey, touched by wonder, poetry, and a tragic sense of the absurd. A true masterpiece. **AK**

Tan's pencil drawings have a sepia tone that recalls old photograph albums. ➡

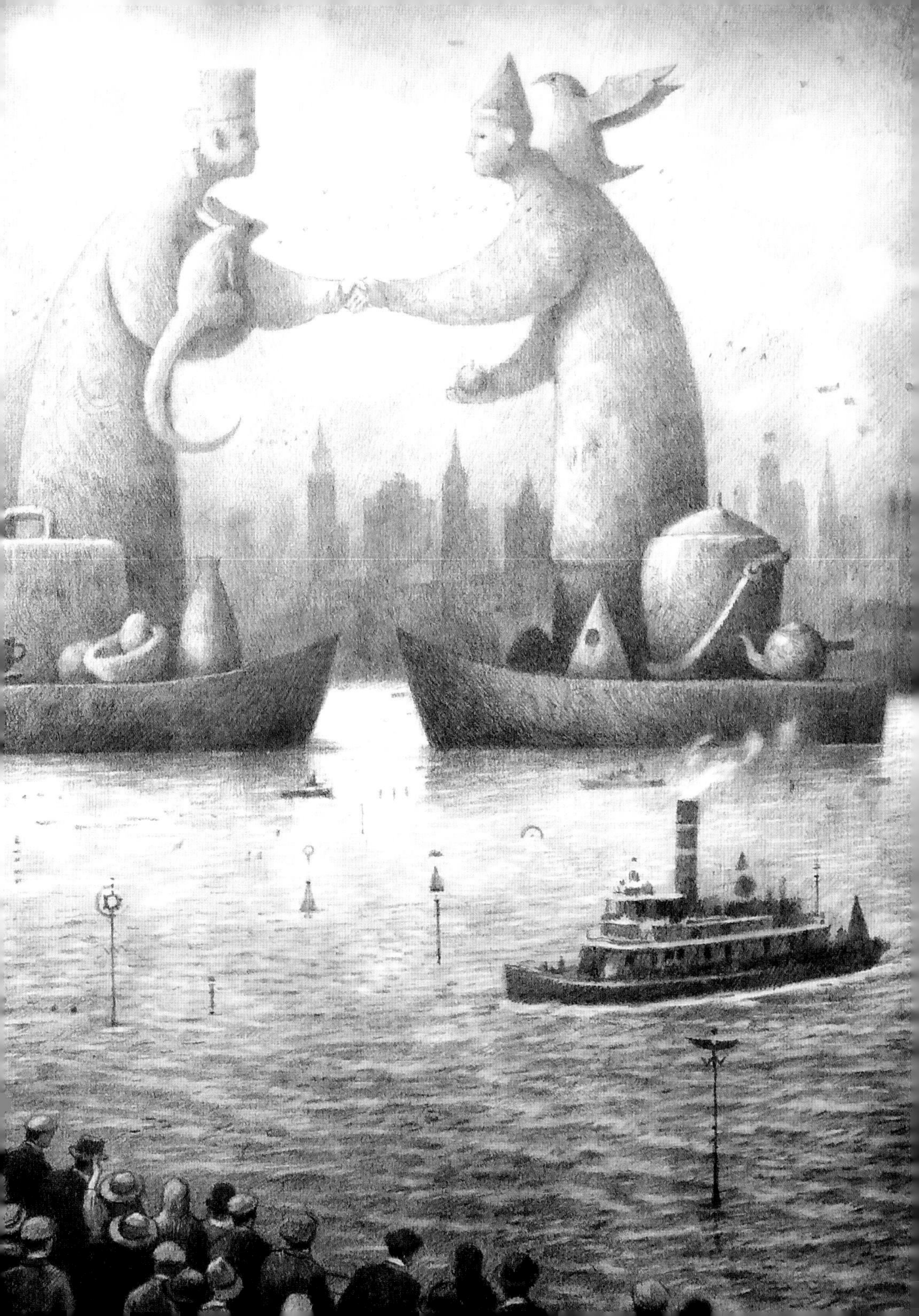

The Museum Vaults 2006

Marc-Antoine Mathieu

Title in original language *Les Sous-sols du Révolu*
First published by Louvre Editions/Futuropolis (France)
Creator French (b.1959)
Genre Humor

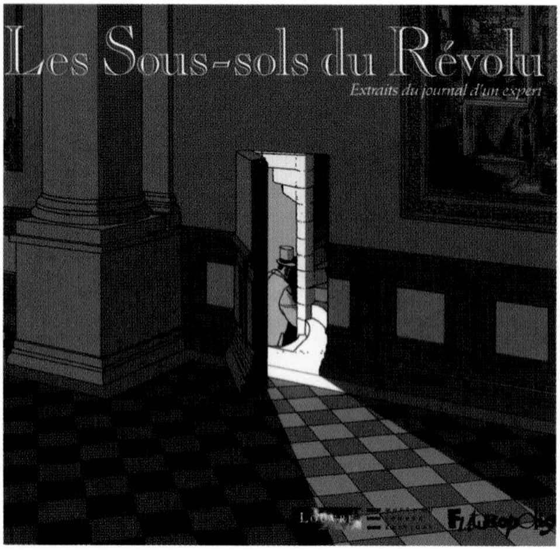
Les Sous-sols du Révolu
Extraits du journal d'un expert

"One can imagine a series of pictures in chronological order . . . forming a story. In other words, a sequential pictorial narrative."

Also by Marc-Antoine Mathieu
Dead Memory (Mémoire morte)
Dieu en personne
La Qu . . .
Le Dessin
Le Processus

This album is the fruit of the second collaboration between Futuropolis and the Musée du Louvre, the letters of which recur as a series of anagrams, beginning with the title and the name of the main character: Eudes le Volumeur, an art assessor, who is charged in 1840 with surveying the content of the museum's innumerable underground rooms. The realist style is tempered by the chiseled faces of the characters, and the palette of black, white and grays, intensifies the Kafkaesque atmosphere of the labyrinthine building.

Author and illustrator Marc-Antoine Mathieu stresses the paradoxes inherent in the art museum's function: colors are best preserved by darkness, some copies of artworks may attain the coveted status of fakes and be exhibited, and changing fashions demand that restoration should appear deliberately inauthentic. The meditation on art and its conservation is compelling, but still more appealing is a series of brilliant allusions to the medium of comic art, arguably always the real subject of Mathieu's work. The architecture of the comics page is constantly evoked, from the lattice of paving stones in the opening splash panel to the scaffolding and ladders negotiated by Volumeur across the gridlike surface of the archives room, or in front of the vast reconstructed sculpture of an eye. The latter not only provides a metaphor for human sensitivity to art but also—as a fragment believed to belong to a much greater whole—suggests the process by which comic art operates, through details that conjure up a larger scene.

With typically deadpan humor, Mathieu finally stakes an explicit claim for the artistic prestige of his own medium. Down in the museum's frame depot, a worker neatly arranges empty rectangles on a wall and imagines a new art form based on framed images in a narrative sequence. **AM**

We Are on Our Own 2006

Miriam Katin

A glamorous mother, a hometown rich in history and culture—Miriam Katin's life should have been so different. However, instead of enjoying a comfortable childhood, she and her mother were chased out of their Budapest home by the arrival of the Nazis, leaving behind their friends, family, and belongings.

We Are on Our Own tells the story of the choices Katin's mother makes as she strives to save herself and her daughter from the German troops and to reunite with her husband, who is fighting in the Hungarian army. It is also the moving tale of the spiritual disappointment of an entire people told through the experience of a young girl. "Where is God?" wonders tiny Miriam as she struggles to comprehend how God could tolerate the atrocities of war. The answer varies, but He is never there to protect her. Only her mother, despite suffering terrible indignities, manages to do that. The story also follows Katin as an adult and raising a family of her own and dealing with the metaphysical and personal repercussions of the traumatic time that she and her mother spent in hiding.

Katin's pencil artwork, always stylishly delicate, rises to the demanding occasion of a personal memoir spanning two continents. It starts off with her usual polish, as her mother and a friend discuss the impending Nazi requisition of Jewish citizens' dogs. However, as their lives start to fall apart, the pencil lines turn angular, and the lettering becomes more hurried and jagged. The full-color pages that narrate the story of Katin as an adult are an oasis of calm as black-and-white chaos reigns in Europe and the panels struggle to contain a whirlwind of frenetic energy. A written epilogue fills in what happened next, but readers are left with the same worry as Katin's mother—how much of the experience has scarred young Miriam forever? **EL**

First published by Drawn & Quarterly (Canada)
Creator Hungarian-American (b.1942)
Genre Autobiography, History
Influenced by *To the Heart of the Storm*

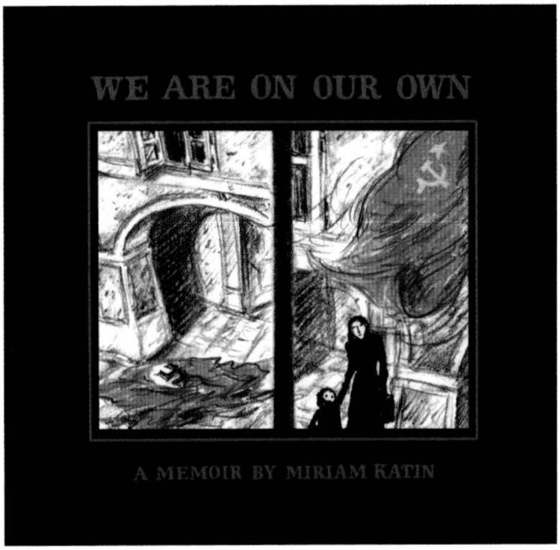
WE ARE ON OUR OWN
A MEMOIR BY MIRIAM KATIN

"I wonder if any more postcards arrived from the front. If we will ever return to our lives. For now, a servant with a bastard child. But safe. SAFE."

Similar reads

A Contract with God Will Eisner
Exit Wounds Rutu Modan
Maus II: A Survivor's Tale Art Spiegelman
Persepolis Marjane Satrapi
The Rabbi's Cat (Le Chat du Rabbin) Joann Sfar

Lucky 2006

✐✐ Gabrielle Bell

First published by Drawn & Quarterly (Canada)
Creator American (b.1976)
Genre Autobiography
Award Igntaz Award (2003)

"I am interested in reality and in storytelling, and those two things sometimes stay on the same path and sometimes diverge," explains Gabrielle Bell about her comics. She was born in England and moved to the United States when she was two years old; she now lives in New York, where these comics are based. *Lucky* invites readers into the imaginative reality of Bell's semiautobiography and tells of an itinerant and unsettled twentysomething artist looking for apartments and studios while working at (mostly) unenjoyable jobs. Bell's comics allow her to travel outside of the uncertainty of minimum wage jobs and the bone-numbing boredom of life with humor: "When I woke up I wished I was still in the dream. At least then I would have a job".

Beautifully drawn, with often just a single, simple, black outline on a white page and tempered by the occasional rich black background, Bell displays not only skill but also a subtle weaving of form and content. The artist acknowledges her influences are Robert Crumb and Julie Doucet because both have "the homemade feeling . . . that invites you to try it for yourself." Both Crumb and Doucet, like Bell, are fascinated by the art of the everyday, which, aligned with their often eye-watering intimacy, contributes to this sense of the approachable familiarity of the "homemade."

Lucky is the collection of three earlier self-published works: *Lucky 1*, *Lucky 2*, and *Lucky 3*. Bell writes: "In *Lucky 3* my work became more introspective and revealing. I realized it was too embarrassing to publish." **SL**

My Boy 2006

✐✐ Olivier Schrauwen

First published by Bries (Belgium)
Creator Belgian (b.1977)
Genre Fantasy
Influenced by *Little Nemo in Slumberland*

Flemish animator Olivier Schrauwen devises a unique response to the potential for distance, distrust, and dysfunction between fathers and sons, prevalent themes in comics such as *Maus* and *Jimmy Corrigan*. He begins with the birth of "beamish boy," who is overdue and finally born in the coffin of his dead mother. No wonder his bereaved father's hair turns white.

This strange, timid son—dot-eyed and red-haired like Tintin—is nameless, barely audible, and apparently stunted. He remains so tiny that his broad-shouldered father can hold him in his hand or carry him around in his jacket pocket. The father seems outwardly proud of the boy while trying to raise him on his own, but an atmosphere of shame, unease, and menace creeps into these five vignettes. Readers start to worry about the safety of this miniature firstborn, privately a disappointment to his manly father, not to mention the likely cause of his mother's demise. At any moment, the mundane can evaporate into the bizarre, whether at home or on their trips to a golf course, a gallery of medieval art in Bruges, or the zoo. Here, for example, the boy is swallowed whole by a crocodile, but escapes thanks to a tribe of pygmies residing inside the beast's stomach, whose acrobatics and arrows proceed to liberate all the caged animals.

My Boy is much more than a cool pastiche; it questions and subverts prevailing beliefs in the security of childhood and the expectations of masculinity. Schrauwen's faded colors and lack of white borders make it resemble a lost relic from U.S. newspapers. **PG**

Miss Don't Touch Me 2006

"Hubert" "Kerascoët" and Sébastien Cosset

Title in original language *Miss Pas Touche*
First published by Dargaud (France) **Creators** Hubert Boulard (French, b.1971); Marie Pommepuy (French, b.1978); Cosset (French, b.1975) **Genre** Adventure

Miss Don't Touch Me is set in Paris in the 1930s. Blanche and Agathe, two sisters employed as servants by an older woman, are making their first forays into adult life. They live in an attic room and take advantage of what little freedom they have to go out and have fun, in spite of the threat of a serial killer known as the Butcher who leaves the dismembered bodies of women all over the capital and its surroundings. By great coincidence, the two girls discover that the killer lives nearby, but they have no time to make use of this information. Agathe is killed, and the police take no notice of Blanche's fearful explanation. Devastated and alone, Blanche becomes obsessed by one thought: to unmask the Butcher and avenge her sister.

Her search for the killer leads her into the world of prostitution. She joins a brothel, where one of the victims used to work. To keep her credibility, Blanche must become integrated in the life of the brothel, but she refuses to lose her virginity. Against all expectations, she finds a niche in the brothel by becoming the "iron virgin," a resident much appreciated by the masochistic patrons of the establishment.

Very light-spirited and whimsical in spite of the potentially slippery subject, *Miss Don't Touch Me* sparkles like a glass of champagne. This does not mean there is no subtlety or sharpness. The portrait of a luxury brothel in 1930s Paris feels authentic, with its share of politicians, police officers, and other notables. Hubert achieves a fine balance between crudeness and freshness, and the picturesque settings and dramatic tension. **NF**

Hubert & Kerascoët
MISS PAS TOUCHE
1. La Vierge du bordel
Poisson Pilote

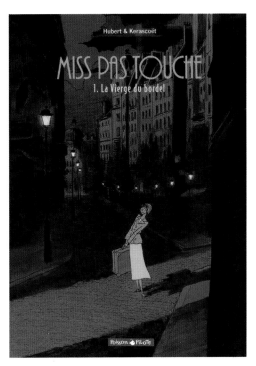

"You will see your dear Annette rolling around in the mud. You'll like that won't you . . . Maybe you'll even discover what an orgasm is."

Also by Hubert
Critters (*Bestioles*)
Flesh of the Spider (*La Chair de l'araignée*)
Green Eyes (*Les Yeux verts*)
The Alchemist's Legs (*Le Legs de l'alchimiste*)
The Fire Siren (*La Sirène des pompiers*)

Why I Killed Peter 2006

✒ Olivier Ka ✏ "Alfred"

Title in original language *Pourquoi j'ai tué Pierre*
First published by Delcourt (France)
Creators Ka (Lebanese, b.1967); Lionel Papagelli
(French, b.1976) **Genre** Autobiography

Writer Olivier Ka describes this book as "a painful autobiographical comic which returns to a number of anecdotes from my life, from the age of seven to thirty-five, all with a link to the story's central event: the manipulation, which I was a victim of when I was twelve, by a family friend, a priest, and summer camp director." Olivier is a boy of nine on a family vacation when he first meets the cheery, guitar-playing priest Peter. The following year, Olivier goes away alone for the first time to a summer camp that Peter has set up, where a simple friendship blossoms. But when Olivier is twelve, Peter abuses their bond, talking him into a single sexual encounter and insisting it must remain their secret. This secret gnaws at Olivier's self-esteem as he grows up and Peter becomes a judgmental presence in the adolescent's mind, spoiling his first romantic flings, making him fearful and resentful.

A spoiler alert cannot defuse the closing chapter's impact. Olivier, now thirty-five and married with a daughter aged twelve, is sleeping poorly, haunted by his conflicted feelings. He decides to write the story down and then asks illustrator Alfred to convert it into a graphic novel. With sixty pages completed they revisit the summer camp for reference photographs, and who should Olivier spot but Peter himself. Unable to speak, Olivier hands him the comic in its current state, the pages we have already read. Peter's confrontation with their secret creates a profoundly moving and redemptive denouement. In *Why I Killed Peter* Ka takes us on a journey of exceptional candor and catharsis. **PG**

Mouse Guard Fall 1152 2006

✒✏ David Petersen

First published by Archaia Entertainment (USA)
Creator American (b.1977)
Genre Fantasy, Adventure, Children's
Award Eisner Award (2008)

Mouse Guard: Fall 1152 collects the first story line in David Petersen's ongoing *Mouse Guard* series, a swashbuckling adventure with a medieval setting in which all of the characters are mice. It works thanks to Petersen's brilliant use of scale. When every obstacle is overwhelmingly big compared to the protagonists, all the stories become epics: A leaf is large enough to be used as a boat; a crab looks like a monster; and a snake seems like a dragon as it towers over a solitary mouse.

Surrounded by so many huge and dangerous foes, the mice of Petersen's world prefer to remain in their hidden towns and cities. When they must travel, they are escorted by the Mouse Guard, an organization that is dedicated to ensuring that the mice cities remain untroubled. The tale of *Mouse Guard: Fall 1152* follows three members of the Guard—Lieam, Kenzie, and Saxon—as they investigate the possibility of a traitor within their ranks.

The narrative moves along rapidly, and Petersen keeps dialogue to a minimum to focus on the artwork. The panel layouts are beautifully clear, and color is used to great effect, with a palette of fall colors—oranges, browns, reds, and yellows—setting the scene. Backgrounds are detailed but uncluttered, keeping readers' attention centered on the characters, which are both cute and ferocious. Their broad foreheads, wide black eyes, and tiny paws give them a lovable appearance, even as they rush into battle against insurmountable odds wielding swords and axes. How could readers, both young and old, not fall for their charms? **HB**

The mice guard tackle a snake, which they believe devoured a missing mouse. ➡

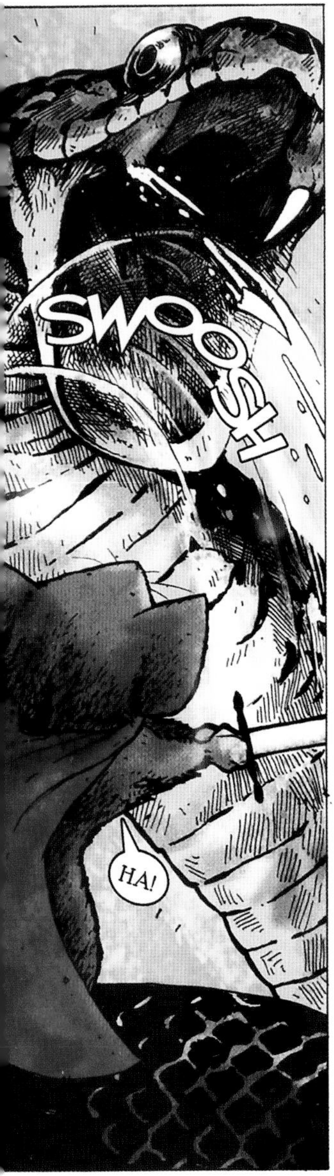
SWOOSH
HA!
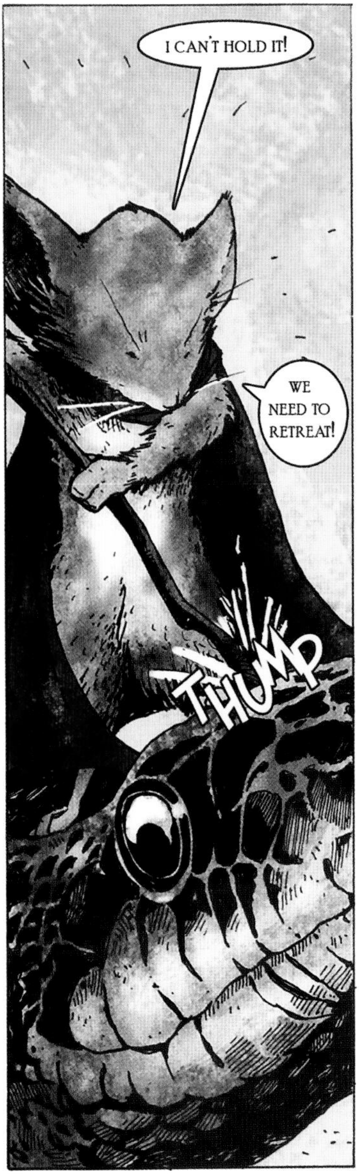
I CAN'T HOLD IT!
WE NEED TO RETREAT!
THUMP
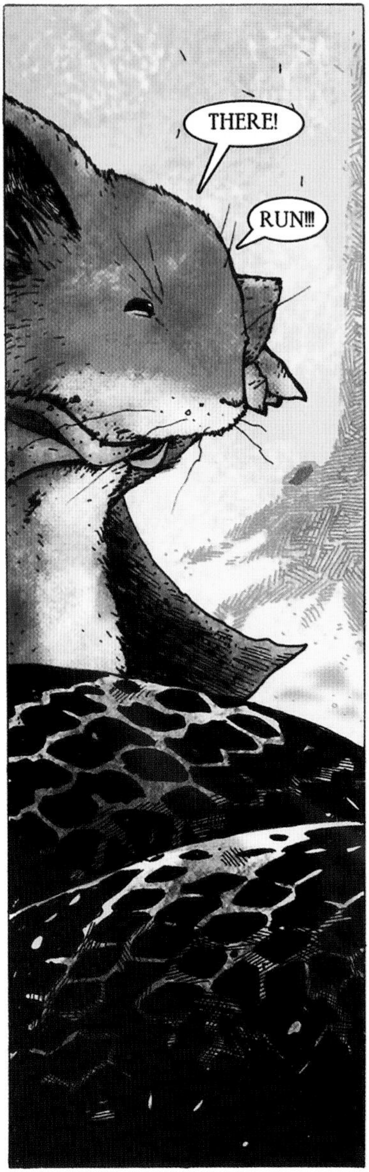
THERE!
RUN!!!

The Lost Colony
The Snodgrass Conspiracy 2006

Grady Klein

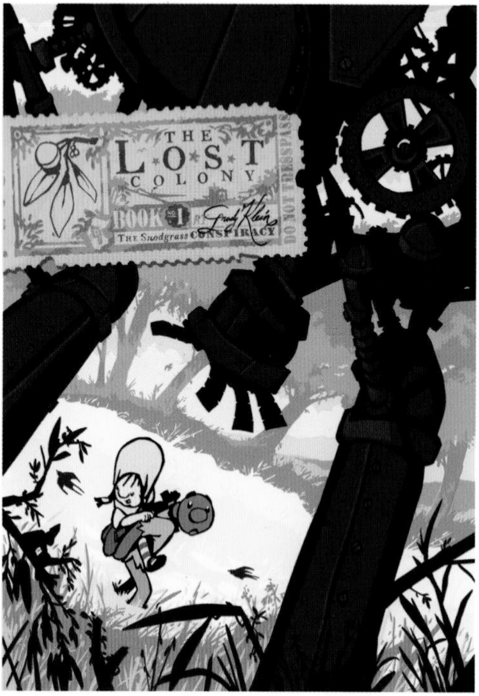
THE
LOST
COLONY
BOOK No. 1
The Snodgrass CONSPIRACY
DO NOT TRESSPASS

"For so long I have yearned to be free of my slaves! So I've invented a machine that will rid me of them."

Similar reads

Asterix and the Great Crossing René Goscinny
Birth of a Nation Aaron McGruder and Reginald Hudlin
Journey into Mohawk Country George O'Connor
Marvel 1602 Neil Gaiman
Trickster: Native American Tales Matt Dembicki (editor)

First published by First Second Books (USA)
Creator American (b.1974)
Genre Drama, History
Influenced by Ralph Steadman

Set on a mysterious island in the nineteenth century, *The Lost Colony* explores antebellum problems and paranoia that still reverberate through contemporary America: racial tensions, federal conspiracies, and the dichotomy between Puritanism and free market economics.

Stumbling upon the hidden island by accident, slave trader Mr. Stoops causes a fuss among the inhabitants, some of whom fear he will expose their home to hordes of mainlanders, while others are intrigued by his plans for a slave auction. The spoiled and rambunctious Birdy Snodgrass, young daughter of the island's banker and governor, fancies buying a slave to do her household chores and so follows Stoops back to the mainland, purchasing slave Louis John at the auction.

Louis befriends the young girl, however, convincing her to free him. They return to the island together, where Governor Snodgrass is engaged in nefarious plans to control the local currency and works with inventor Rex Carter to build a robot so that they can free themselves from the burden of looking after slaves.

Klein's digital art and bright coloring contrasts with the book's setting, a juxtaposition he works into his writing, too, weaving De Tocqueville with pop culture as he deconstructs the U.S. shift from agrarian plantocracy to industrialized capitalism. Further volumes in the series tackle the McCarthyist Cold War (book two: *The Red Menace*) and look at the exploitative power of frontier religion (book three: *Last Rites*). Teenage and more mature readers alike will enjoy the dripping gothic menace and satirical colonial history. **DN**

Sardine in Outer Space 2006

✏ Emmanuel Guibert ✏ Joann Sfar

Title in original language *Sardine de l'espace*
First published by Bayard (France)
Creators Guibert (French, b.1964); Sfar (French, b.1971)
Genre Children's

Sardine in Outer Space is deliriously inventive with its unpredictable and imaginative plots. Intergalactic explorer Sardine accompanies her uncle, the notorious space pirate Captain Yellow Shoulder, as he raids the orphanages of villain Supermuscleman and frees the children within to stop them from being brainwashed into "proper behavior." Yellow Shoulder sets his own rules though; luckily for him, Sardine and her pal Little Louie ignore them enough to rescue him when required.

Emmanuel Guibert and Joann Sfar created the sort of wildly imaginative story that children themselves might have come up with, and Sfar's art is deliberately naive, as if a child had drawn it. Sardine is a memorable visual creation, with her red hair topped by a witch's hat, on which her cat is permanently perched. Supermuscleman is a steroid nightmare in a Shazam shirt with a silent movie villain's mustache, whereas Yellow Shoulder looks to have picked up the Hulk's tattered pants at a thrift store.

Split into a dozen chapters, *Sardine in Outer Space* is ideal for bedtime reading. The monsters are not threatening enough to prompt nightmares, the coarse jokes are pitched just right, and a complete story told in twelve pages is just the right length. There is also a wealth of content to wash over younger heads, including visual asides, literary gags, and planets that resemble disco glitterballs. Guibert and Sfar are both writers and cartoonists, and their collaboration on *La Fille du Professeur*—about an Egyptian mummy that comes back to life—reverses their contributions here. **FP**

Ristorante Paradiso 2006

✏✏ Natsume Ono

First published by Ohta Books (Japan)
Creator Japanese (b.1977)
Genre Reality drama
Adaptation TV anime (2009)

Good-looking, charming, with great manners, a bit older, and must wear glasses—that is the type of man who works in Ristorante Paradiso, a typical Italian restaurant in Rome with some not so typical personnel. One day Nicoletta, the adult daughter of the owner's fiancée Olga, suddenly appears at the restaurant. The problem is that Olga has never told her future husband that she has a child. Nicoletta was raised by her grandparents and does not get along well with her mother; nevertheless she decides to stay in Rome. The mother-daughter relations are not the only complicated ones; other characters also have their own stories and problems.

This heartwarming tale about love, friendship, family, and cuisine puts its readers in a good mood. *Ristorante Paradiso* is not packed with surprises, but the atmosphere of the little restaurant is something not to be missed. It should be savored slowly like an elegant feast, with delicate and tasteful dishes that everyone can enjoy.

Natsume Ono's artwork is magnificent and has more of an Italian than Japanese feel. It resembles the drawings of Italian comic illustrators such as Igort and Gipi. Ono's use of black captures the reader's attention as the eye is drawn from one black area to another: the eyes of the main heroine, sharp suits, coffee, or other minor details. The composition is not packed tightly, as seen in *shojo* manga (Japanese comics for girls), and there is much space between the irregular but geometric panels. There is also a three-volume anime TV series of *Ristorante Paradiso*. **RB**

Lucille 2006

✐✐ Ludovic Debeurme

First published by Futuropolis (France)
Creators French (b.1971)
Genre Drama
Award Essentials of Angoulême (2007)

The remarkable story of the damage people do to one another, and to themselves, *Lucille* was the breakout graphic novel from the talented Ludovic Debeurme. He had long been tagged as an important new voice in French comics, but it was only with this epic undertaking that he began to reach his true potential.

Lucille is a sixteen-year-old anorexic girl living in a small French town by the sea. Driven to death's door by her disease, her life is saved by a romantic relationship with a young man calling himself Vladimir, the son of an alcoholic father who has committed suicide. This unlikely duo flee their homes for Paris and, eventually, Tuscany. When Lucille is pursued relentlessly by the son of a wealthy landowner, Vladimir kills him, then attempts to take his own life in prison. The story concludes in a complexly narrated sequel, *Renée* (2010), which introduces new characters, including the damaged young woman of the title.

Seemingly unique among cartoonists, Debeurme's comics are informed by theoretical issues and concerns. *Lucille* focuses on personal psychology, particularly Debeurme's readings of Jacques Lacan. At the same time the work is influenced by surrealism, and his characters often veer off into fantasies, flashbacks, and uncued dreamscapes. Debeurme's floating, panel-less images highlight the uncertainty that surrounds his characters, who live their lives in a world that seems both subjective and undetermined. Debeurme's art style suits characters who, though well developed, lead lives that are anything but finished. **BB**

Reflections 2006

✐✐ Marco Corona

Title in original language *Riflessi*
First published by Coconino Press (Italy)
Creator Italian (b.1967)
Genre Drama

The story follows the life of a woman named Miranda who is visiting her sick twin brother Riccardo and her wise old grandmother. Riccardo is obsessed with pirates and lives in a fantasy world in which he imagines himself to be the captain of a ship. When Miranda meets her twin and grandmother at the seaside hospital, she flashes back to her days as a child and teenager, dreaming about relationships with her brother and the harsh reality of living with unfeeling parents. The central scene of the book takes place as a dream sequence in which Miranda walks through a large house decorated with a crystal chandelier. She is led in front of a mirror by her mother, and asked what she sees—perhaps her destiny?

The narrative shifts between the past, present, and a dream world as readers are confronted by a haunting story, narrated by Miranda, that contrasts adolescent memories with visions of beauty. The result is an intense reading experience in which readers are drawn to the characters through their thoughts, dreams, and emotions.

Corona's impressive drawing talent was first seen in 1998 in his biography of the artist Frida Kahlo. His style emerged from the "art brut" element of the Italian underground comics movement and is close to Pakito Bolino or Stéphane Blanquet in mood. He is one of the most imaginative storytellers writing in Italian comics today. His artistic sense is visionary and elegant—rich in detail yet somewhat disheveled—clearly influenced by Carlos Nine, Robert Crumb, and Enrique Breccia. **MS**

The drawing style of *Reflections* is sketchy with dense crosshatching. ➡

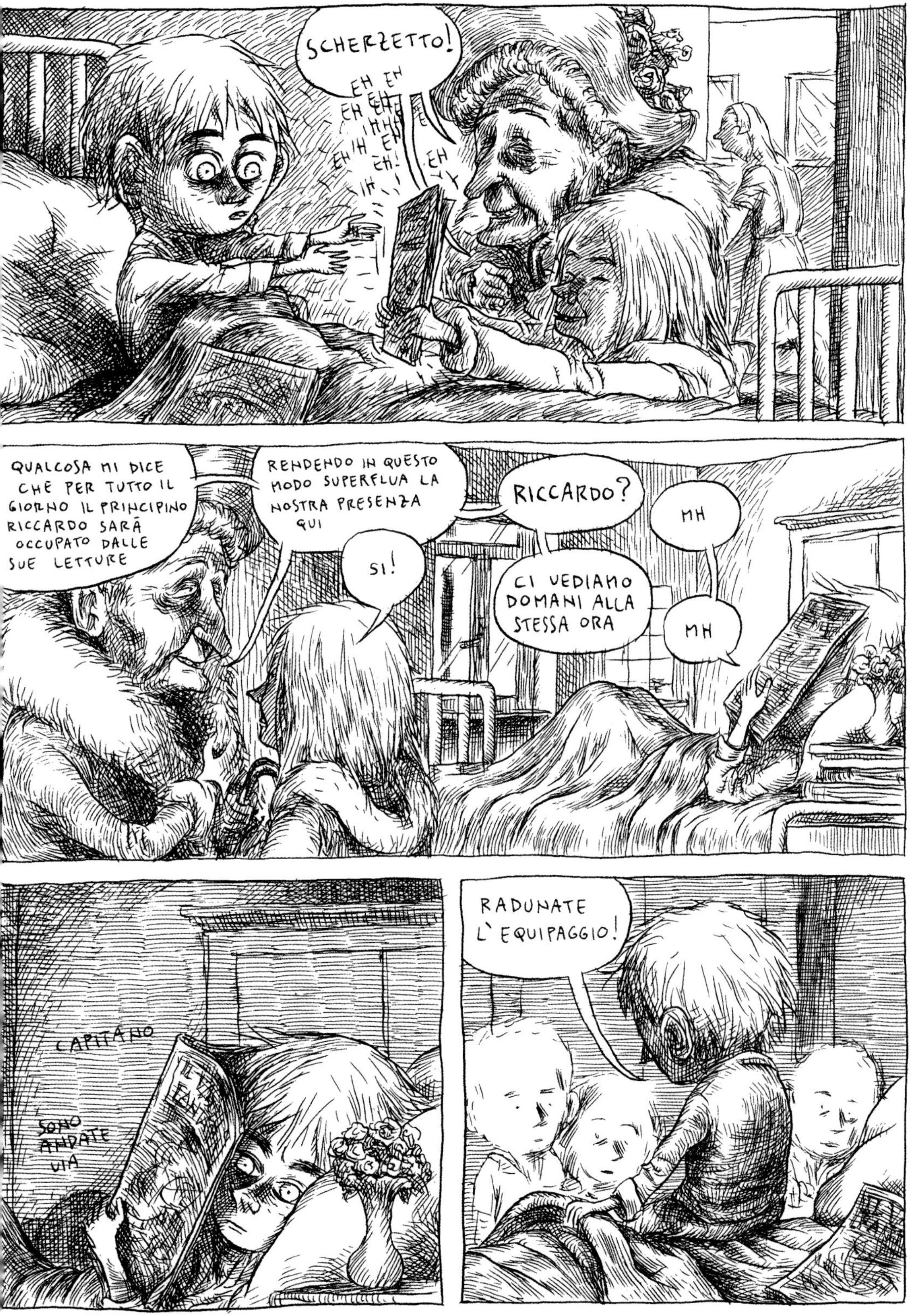
SCHERZETTO!
EH EH
QUALCOSA MI DICE CHE PER TUTTO IL GIORNO IL PRINCIPINO RICCARDO SARÀ OCCUPATO DALLE SUE LETTURE
RENDENDO IN QUESTO MODO SUPERFLUA LA NOSTRA PRESENZA QUI
SÌ!
RICCARDO?
CI VEDIAMO DOMANI ALLA STESSA ORA
MH
MH
CAPITANO
SONO ANDATE VIA
RADUNATE L'EQUIPAGGIO!

Orange 2006

🖋 "Benjamin"

First published by Xiao Pan (France)
Creator Zhang Bin (Chinese, b.1974)
Genre Teen
Influenced by Fashion illustration

Orange has all the trappings of both Western comics and manga: a glossy finish, a beautiful—if not conflicted—female protagonist, stylish clothing, and accessories. However, what sets this narrative apart from the rest is its location. Coming from Communist China, *Orange* is something of a mixed bag. The story is a bizarre combination of angst and extremes: the titular character, Orange, is an average adolescent girl with a penchant for makeup and boys, but she also feels lonely, angry, and dissatisfied with her life. Like many teenagers, she is looking for something with meaning to give her life resonance. She finds it in a mysterious and attractive stranger, Dashu. He saves her from committing suicide, only to kill himself later.

At the time of its U.S. publication, *Orange* was not well-received by critics or readers. The distinctive graphic characteristics of Benjamin's work are his dynamic and forceful use of flashy color and his sweeping, broad strokes that wash over specifics and detail. Rather than reading the narrative of *Orange* as a story simply about teenage angst, it can also be interpreted as a fantasy about upper-middle-class anxiety and freedom, especially within its Communist China context. Alongside the cargo pants, Nike shoes, and Fossil watches—brands and styles that litter Benjamin's comic—is a bonafide sense of ennui and privilege, a sense of decadence and fatigue that is as affected as it is accurate. *Orange* may not be the best comic, but it is the best reflection of the Mainland to come out of China. **K–MC**

Curses 2006

🖋 Kevin Huizenga

First published by Drawn & Quarterly (Canada)
Creator American (b.1977)
Genre Reality drama
Awards *Time* Magazine Top Ten Comics (2005 and 2006)

Kevin Huizenga's *Curses* is a collection of nine stories about everyday life in Midwestern America featuring his recurring character Glenn Ganges. The artwork is simplistic—dots are eyes and mouths are single lines—as imagination and tangents take center stage in the narrative. For example, when late one night Glenn and his wife Wendy are woken by starlings, Huizenga ignores their plight and instead tells readers how the bird was introduced to North America.

The most poignant story, "28th St.," is loosely based on *The Feathered Ogre*, itself an adaptation of a folktale by Italy's Italo Calvino. It chronicles Glenn and Wendy's desperate attempts to conceive a child. "You have the most half-ass sperms I have ever seen," the doctor tells Glenn. He learns that he and Wendy are cursed, and so begins a search for a feathered ogre who will lift the curse and pave the way for parenthood. Other stories range from the poetic to the scientific, but addressing big issues such as faith and the origin of life do not interest Huizenga, who enjoys providing dense visual information within complex drawings only as a tool for the telling of a good story. His concern is with the character's response to any questions posed, rather than the questions themselves.

Ganges is a nebulous character, deliberately kept vague so Huizenga can use him as a starting point regardless of the message he intends to convey. "It's nice to have a landmark . . . variations all come from the same starting place." After all, he likes to remind us, "Drawing comics is really hard." **BS**

Cash: I See a Darkness 2006

Reinhard Kleist

First published by Carlsen Comics (Germany)
Creator German (b.1970)
Genre Biography
Award Max and Moritz Award (2008)

Reinhard Kleist
CASH
I see a darkness
CARLSEN

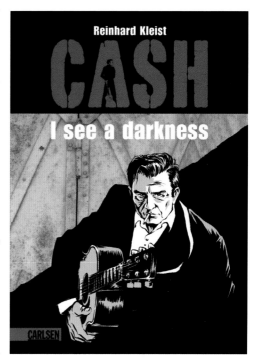

Reinhard Kleist's comic book biography of Johnny Cash was already completed when James Mangold's movie *Walk the Line* (2005) was released. For weeks, the Berlin comic book artist was plagued by anxiety, fearing that the film might be "more authentic and personal," and he considered revising his comic book. Fortunately, Kleist retained his independent approach and remained true to his version. While the Hollywood film concentrated on the love story between June Carter and Johnny Cash, Kleist was keen to explore the darker side of the famous country singer.

Kleist uses Cash's legendary performance in a high security prison as the narrative background for his biography. Music helps Cash's social standing, but above all, it provides him with an audience to whom he can express his anger about the injustices of U.S. society. Kleist puts the "angry man" on the stage across a sophisticated page layout and in picturesque comic drawings that show Cash holding his guitar so high that it looks like a gun clamped under his arm.

Using expressive and cinematically dynamic images, Kleist portrays the highs and lows of the "Man in Black," his successes and his debacles fueled by excessive drugs and alcohol. However, it was this very complexity that was at the heart of Cash's personality, because it gave him the energy to rebel against the politics prevalent in the United States and to hold his own against everyone during the eras of McCarthy, Vietnam, and the Ku Klux Klan, and to fight for the rights of outlaws. **MS**

"Kleist's version of the Man in Black [is] a dynamic pattern of black lines, a 220-page portfolio of inky expressionism."

Michel Faber, novelist

Similar reads

Bigbeatland Andreas Michalke
Castro Reinhard Kleist
Hank Williams—Lost Highway Sören G. Mosdal
Love and Rockets Los Bros Hernández
The Secrets of Coney Island Reinhard Kleist

Exit Wounds 2007

Rutu Modan

First published by Drawn & Quarterly (Canada)
Creator Israeli (b.1966)
Genre Drama
Award Eisner Award Best Graphic Novel (2008)

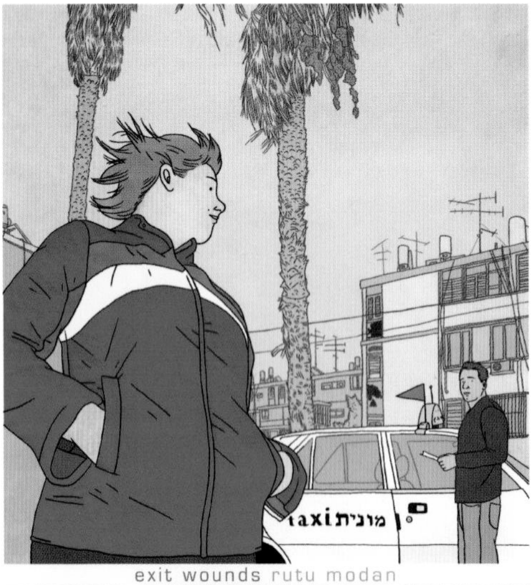
taxi מונית
exit wounds rutu modan

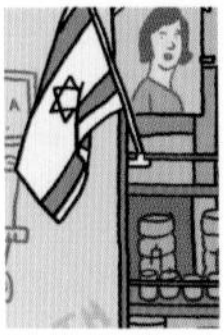

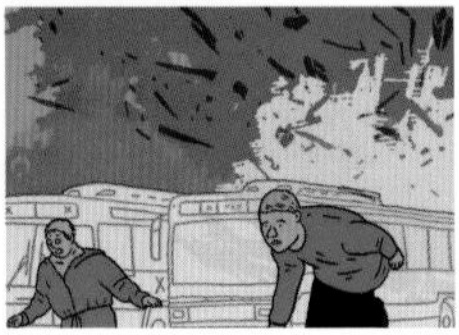

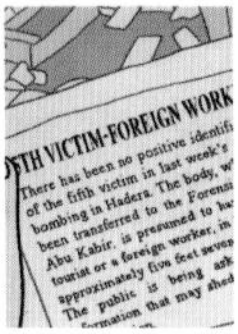

Similar reads

Cargo Rutu Modan, Pinkus, and others
Farm 54 Galit and Gilad Seliktar
Jamilti Rutu Modan
Pizzeria Kamikaze Etgar Keret and Asaf Hanuka
The Placebo Man Tomer Hanuka

A romantic comedy set against a background of class divides, *Exit Wounds* features suicide bombers, missing bodies, absent parents, and family dysfunction through a uniquely Israeli sensibility while touching on universal themes. It is both beautifully drawn and powerfully written; Rutu Modan's ear for dialogue is reminiscent of U.S. novelist Don DeLillo.

Exit Wounds is the story of a young man's search for his father's corpse after a bus is blown up by a suicide bomber. Koby's journey becomes a fascinating road trip that takes him across the social and religious divides of Israeli society, accompanied by his father's young lover, Numi. On his quest, Koby discovers commonalities of loss and longing, but maintains

"One of the bodies was so badly burned that they still don't know who it was."

hope amid many disappointments. Modan got the idea for the book after seeing David Ofek's 2003 *Documentary No. 17* about the unclaimed body of a suicide bombing victim. "For me," Modan commented in an interview, "the drama is always behind the words. No one mentions the word 'love' in the novel, even though it is a central focus for all of them."

The book is colored beautifully: each chapter has its own palette that emphasizes its themes and gives the visuals a musical feel. Despite the seriousness of her subject, Modan's text is witty, playful, and often laugh-out-loud funny. There are surprises at the turn of every page, because nothing and no one are quite what they seem. Modan's tender, haunting evocation of these characters' trials and tribulations will involve readers deeply in their fate, and through them, toward a deeper understanding of Israeli society. **AK**

Yorahop 2007

"Ancco"

Coming of age is less fun if you inhabit the real world rather than an adolescent comic. You are about to get kicked out into the adult life and realize you have not really done much so far. You are not smart, rich, or self-confident. Worst of all, you are not even witty enough to live through life with a dose of cynicism. *Yorahop* (literally "19") is a fictional, semiautobiographical anthology of short stories focusing on this stage of life. Showing influences from autobiographical U.S. indie comics, Ancco weaves through life's episodes.

The stories deal either with her life or the lives she saw as she grew up. As a teenager, she was neither a well-behaved kid nor a delinquent one. In the titular short story *Yorahop*, she gets beaten up by her dad because she comes back from school drunk and draws crude pornographic comics starring her teacher. The dialogue is without any hint of wit or poetic metaphor, just short, empty expressions of genuine angst. In other stories, the author observes other peoples' lives that are marginalized as well. These include a grandmother who is gradually losing her place in society as she gets older, mentally disabled people, and a young HIV-positive man among others. The characters are not filled with hopes for a brighter future, and society does not expect them to be. Their stories explore the realities of their situations without decorating them with overtly emotional drama. Real life is mediocre for most of us, and we will come to accept it. It is ironic, though, that the author's stories about life's mediocrity and marginalization showed off her talent to the world and earned her international acclaim. **NK**

"Do you think I'm pathetic? / Not really pathetic . . . I mean, I'm just the same as you."

First published by Sai Comics (Korea)
Creator Choi Gyeong-jin (South Korean, b.1983)
Genre Reality drama
Influenced by *I Never Liked You*

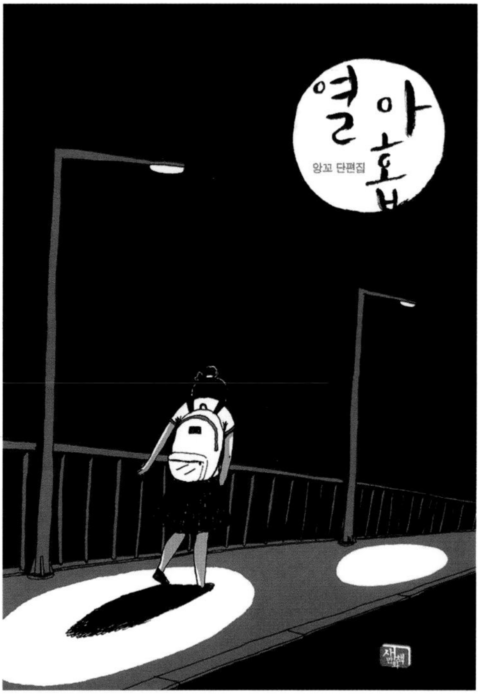
열아홉
앙꼬 단편집

Similar reads

Analog Man Jeff Pfaller and Joseph Arnold
Ancco-ui Grimilgi Ancco
Ghost World Daniel Clowes
I Never Liked You Chester Brown
My Love Yang Young Soon

How to Be Everywhere 2007

✎✎ Warren Craghead III

First published by Self-published (USA)
Creator American (b.1970)
Genre Alternative
Award Nominated for Pushcart Prize (2006)

On the one hand, *How to be Everywhere* is a collection of drawings based on Guillaume Apollinaire's modernist poetry, mainly works from *Alcools* and *Calligrammes*. In this sense it is a fusion of comics and poetry. However, *How to be Everywhere* could perhaps also be described as a "translation," "transformation," or "dialogue."

Artist Warren Craghead III delved into the realm of comic books in an attempt to expand their possibilities. He states, "My work explores the absurd idea of how to be everywhere; it insists that art can be accessible, cryptic, and beautiful all at the same time." Influenced by Martin Vaughn-James, Richard McGuire, and Andrei Molotiu, Craghead is inspired by everyday experiences. He creates spontaneous nonlinear narratives that often originate from notes or sketches he made on a particular day: bicycle and gun parts, lamps and flowers, stockings in bodiless legs, soldiers and trenches, burned forests, and a face whose eye is not drawn but written instead.

Apollinaire reinvented poetry as a vehicle for the uncanniness of the twentieth century through typography and calligraphy. Craghead uses his own art style to combine images with words and pictures with poetry and prose. The author's figures or spaces are never fully complete, as if the blanks between the panels were brought into the panels themselves. Verses are scattered across a page, with each letter written spaciously. "Merveille de la guerre" reads, "I bequeath to the future the story of Guillaume Apollinaire / who was lucky in the war and knew how to be everywhere." **PM**

I Shall Destroy all the Civilized Planets! 2007

✎✎ Fletcher Hanks and Paul Karasik

First published by Fox Publications (USA)
Creators Hanks (American, 1887–1976);
Karasik (American, b.1956)
Genre Superhero, Biography

The strange, disturbing comic strips of Fletcher Hanks raise a number of intriguing questions. Was he an idiosyncratic "outsider artist," expressing a dark but deeply personal vision as he toiled away unnoticed in the world of pulp comics? Or was he a cynical hack who, hiding behind pseudonyms such as "Barclay Flagg" and "Hank Christy," showed a flagrant disregard for the niceties of anatomical realism and coherent narrative?

Hanks's major characters, Stardust, the Super Wizard, "the most remarkable man who ever lived," and Fantomah, "the most remarkable woman in the universe," are minimally characterized superheroes who remorselessly punish the guilty. Their intense, surreally detailed story lines bristle with barely repressed fantasies of dominance and control. The abiding atmosphere throughout is rigidly humorless and authoritarian, and the bodies and faces drawn by Hanks are invariably distended, grotesque, and weirdly sexualized. In their naivety and crudity, however, these strips are very much of their time, and sometimes seem to anticipate the individuality of many later underground strips.

I Shall Destroy all the Civilized Planets! concludes with a strip written and drawn by its editor, Paul Karasik, in which he expresses the belief that Hanks, "one of the greatest cartoonists of the twentieth century," has created "a new heroic mythology." While researching Hanks's work, Karasik learned that the artist was an abusive alcoholic who abandoned his family and was later found frozen to death on a park bench, a macabre detail that somehow unifies his life and art. **AL**

The Umbrella Academy 2007

Gerard Way Gabriel Bá

First published by Dark Horse Comics (USA)
Creators Way (American, b.1977); Bá (Brazilian, b.1976)
Genre Adventure **Collection** *The Umbrella Academy: The Apocalypse Suite* (2008)

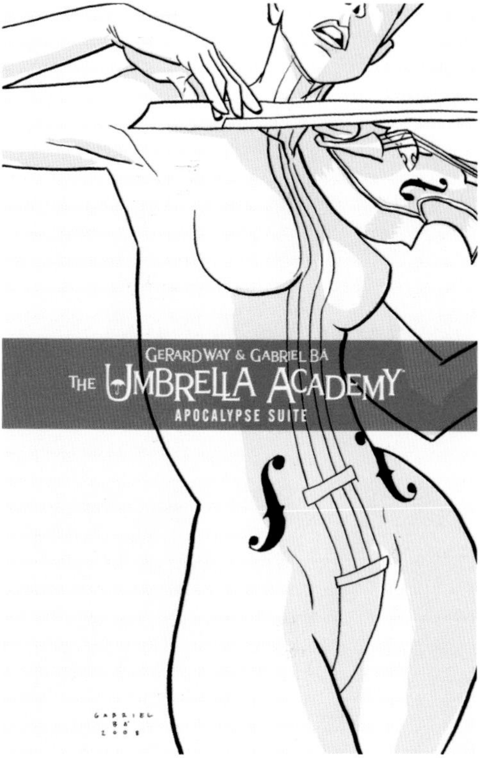
GERARD WAY & GABRIEL BÁ
THE UMBRELLA ACADEMY
APOCALYPSE SUITE

The products of an incident in which forty-three children are suddenly born to women who do not know they are pregnant, the members of the Umbrella Academy are raised as a family by the mysterious Sir Reginald Hargreeves. The children grow up in an utterly cold atmosphere in which they are known only by a number. As they grow older they discover that they have superpowers—all except one child, tiny violin-playing Number 07.

The plot of the first series of *Umbrella Academy* centers around the older 07—now known as Vanya. In a flashback, the academy is seen in action against the Eiffel Tower, which is being manipulated by a cyborg—with 07 held back, seemingly useless. In the present day—now estranged from her family, and the author of a damning memoir of her childhood—Vanya joins an apocalyptic plot by the sinister Verdammten Orchestra. Meanwhile, her adopted brother 05, who escaped using his special power of time travel, is about to return from the future to tell of the devastation to come. He becomes the focus of *Umbrella Academy*'s second series, in which 05 has to prevent his older, lunatic self from assassinating President Kennedy.

Full of wild imagination and love for the superhero genre, Gerard Way's script is packed with hilariously sad touches, such as when the young superheroes are given ice cream for saving the world. Gabriel Bá's artwork captures all the frenetic action in inky and sculptural chiaroscuro. Readers who like the idea of a modern, dysfunctional *Fantastic Four* will love it. **EL**

"I wake up in the morning with the finest impulses known to man—and thanks to you I slaughter them."

Similar reads
100% Paul Pope
20th Century Boys Naoki Urasawa
Ex Machina Brian K. Vaughan and Tony Harris
FreakAngels Warren Ellis and Paul Duffield

Essex County Trilogy 2007

Jeff Lemire

First published by Top Shelf Productions (USA)
Creator Canadian (b.1976)
Genre Drama
Award Joe Shuster Award (2008)

JEFF LEMIRE
COLLECTED
ESSEX COUNTY
9

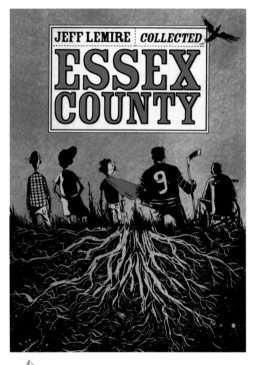

Similar reads
Blankets Craig Thompson
Ghost World Daniel Clowes
Swallow Me Whole Nate Powell
Sweet Tooth Jeff Lemire
The Nobody Jeff Lemire

In *Essex County Trilogy,* blackbirds fly from house to hut and home, connecting the lives of a recently orphaned boy, an elderly former ice hockey player, and a meddling country nurse. They all live in the same Canadian county, and their lives are intertwined in ways the reader will only fully appreciate when sensing their shared feeling of loneliness and isolation.

Jeff Lemire weaves the stories together through time and space by allowing the sport of ice hockey to act as common ground. It unites the lonely and provides the language for all the things that are left unsaid yet continually keep people apart. Interpreting very basic and recognizable emotions, the three main characters have more in common than initially meets

"The game is like family . . . it won't let you go, no matter how long you've been away."

the eye, and it is both a heartbreaking and beautiful experience to follow them as their stories unravel.

With his sketchy black-and-white drawings, Lemire scratches with equal eloquence the fine lines of a hockey player's gnarled old face, the wide open eyes of a boy in mourning, and the chirpy, good-natured smile of a nurse. Forests, cities, and vast open plains come to life through a very deliberate use of empty white paper and heavy black ink. The past is always heavily present, distinguished from current events by lighter washes of gray that characterize memories out of focus but never completely out of sight.

One leaves Essex County feeling sad and perhaps tearful, but harboring a deep sense of having been enriched by the people and their surrounding places. Like the blackbirds, readers will probably have trouble staying away and will return to visit again. **RPC**

Three Shadows 2007

Cyril Pedrosa

The singular terror provoked by the threat of losing a child and the extraordinary lengths a parent will go in attempting to stave off such a threat are at the core of Cyril Pedrosa's heartbreaking but ultimately beautiful fable. *Three Shadows* lays open both the paralysis and the monstrous violence of a parent's grief, and how that unimaginable torment might be survived.

Louis and Lise lead a quiet life of rustic subsistence with their young son Joachim. One night, three dark riders appear on the horizon, stalking them from a distance. Louis investigates the terrorizing shadows, but they disappear in the mist like apparitions.Against Louis's will, Lise travels to the city to seek out an old friend, Mistress Pike, who is a soothsayer. She tells Lise

"Back then life was simple and sweet. Everything was simple and sweet . . . Then everything changed."

that the three shadows have come for Joachim and there is nothing anyone can do. Refusing to accept his son's fate, Louis flees with the boy, hoping to travel to his father's homeland far away across a vast and capricious river. Along the way they meet a colorful cast of characters, from conjurers and slave traders to necromancers, and Louis's fear of the pursuing shadows eventually drives him to madness.

A former Disney animator, Pedrosa has illustrated and created comics in France for more than a decade, and *Three Shadows* is his first work that has been translated into English. His loose monochromatic art suggests that he has shaken off the shackles of his former employer, although the fluidity and control of gesture in his work betray his roots in animation. The dark vision, bleakness tempered by love, has more in common, at least in scope if not aesthetic, with Hayao Miyazaki. **DN**

Title in original language *Trois ombres*
First published by Delcourt (France)
Creator French (b.1972)
Genre Drama

Trois Ombres
Cyril Pedrosa
shampooing

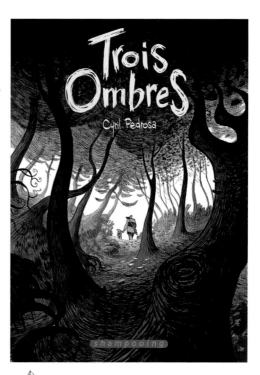

Similar reads

A Small Killing Alan Moore
Black Hole Charles Burns
Blankets Craig Thompson
Fun Home Alison Bechdel
Epileptic (*L'Ascension du haut-mal*) David B.

Regards from Serbia 2007

✏️✏️ "Aleksandar Zograf"

First published by Top Shelf Productions (USA)
Creator Saša Rakevic (Serbian, b.1963)
Genre Reality drama, Fantasy
Award Hector Oesterheld Award (1999)

Aleksandar Zograf is an alternative and innovative Serbian cartoonist renowned for his striking black-and-white drawings. His narrative themes were originally about his own dreams, visions, or interpretations of the real world. However, having been exposed to the brutal situation in Serbia during the civil wars in Yugoslavia, he has become a storyteller of real-life incidents, all interpreted in his deeply intimate, sociological, dreamlike, and sometimes skeptical manner. This sensitive and autobiographical approach reminds readers of other great "dreamers," such as Czech novelist Franz Kafka, whose writing combined inner anxieties with real life, and Russian painter Mark Chagall, who incorporated memories and dreams into his paintings. It is no surprise that Zograf is referred to by critics as a "comic painter" or "painter storyteller."

Regards from Serbia is Zograf's visual diary about his life in the small Serbian town of Pančevo, during the bombardments by NATO forces in the late 1990s. The terrible circumstances associated with the bitter conflict made real life seem surreal, and Zograf conveys this to his readers not only with the precision of a witness, but also with a distance, to protect his own sanity. He combines grimly realistic situations with serious thoughts about human existence. Everything is drawn from his actual life and own inner thoughts in a striking and distinguished, semigrotesque style. However, he presents it as if it were happening to somebody else who is not present and who exists in his own dreamlike reality. **ZT**

The Chimpanzee Complex 2007

✏️ Richard Marazano ✏️ Jean-Michel Ponzio

Title in original language *Le Complexe du Chimpanzé*
First published by Dargaud (France)
Creators Marazano (French, b.1971); Ponzio (French, b.1967) **Genre** Science fiction

A space module falls from orbit in 2035, and inside are Neil Armstrong and Buzz Aldrin, the first men to walk on the Moon in 1969. Contemporary astronaut Helen Freeman is assigned to liaise with them, having just learned that the Mars mission she was to command has been postponed for a decade. She is now unlikely to be the first human to set foot on Mars. However, evidence emerges that while NASA was concentrating on the Moon in the 1960s and 1970s, Soviet astronauts had a more distant target. Covert agency forces co-opt Helen and offer her a mission to Mars; ultimately her scientific curiosity and ambition take priority over her pre-teen daughter Sofia.

The Chimpanzee Complex is an epic science fiction tale splashed across a hard science canvas, but it is created from a succession of little moments not widescreen battles. As intriguing as the mystery on Mars and the action it prompts become, the heart of this story is whether Helen has sacrificed her daughter for objectives that have moved beyond her control. Despite the art being heavily photo referenced, Jean-Michel Ponzio overcomes the shortfalls of the technique and successfully depicts movement and emotion. His characters come alive, and his locations display their accumulated grime.

The title refers to the experiences of chimpanzees sent into space. They have the intelligence to realize they cannot control their environment, leading to a breakdown. For Helen, the conclusion echoes the outset, and fittingly ends a very satisfying read. **FP**

Richard Marazano allows the art to tell the story when required. ➡️

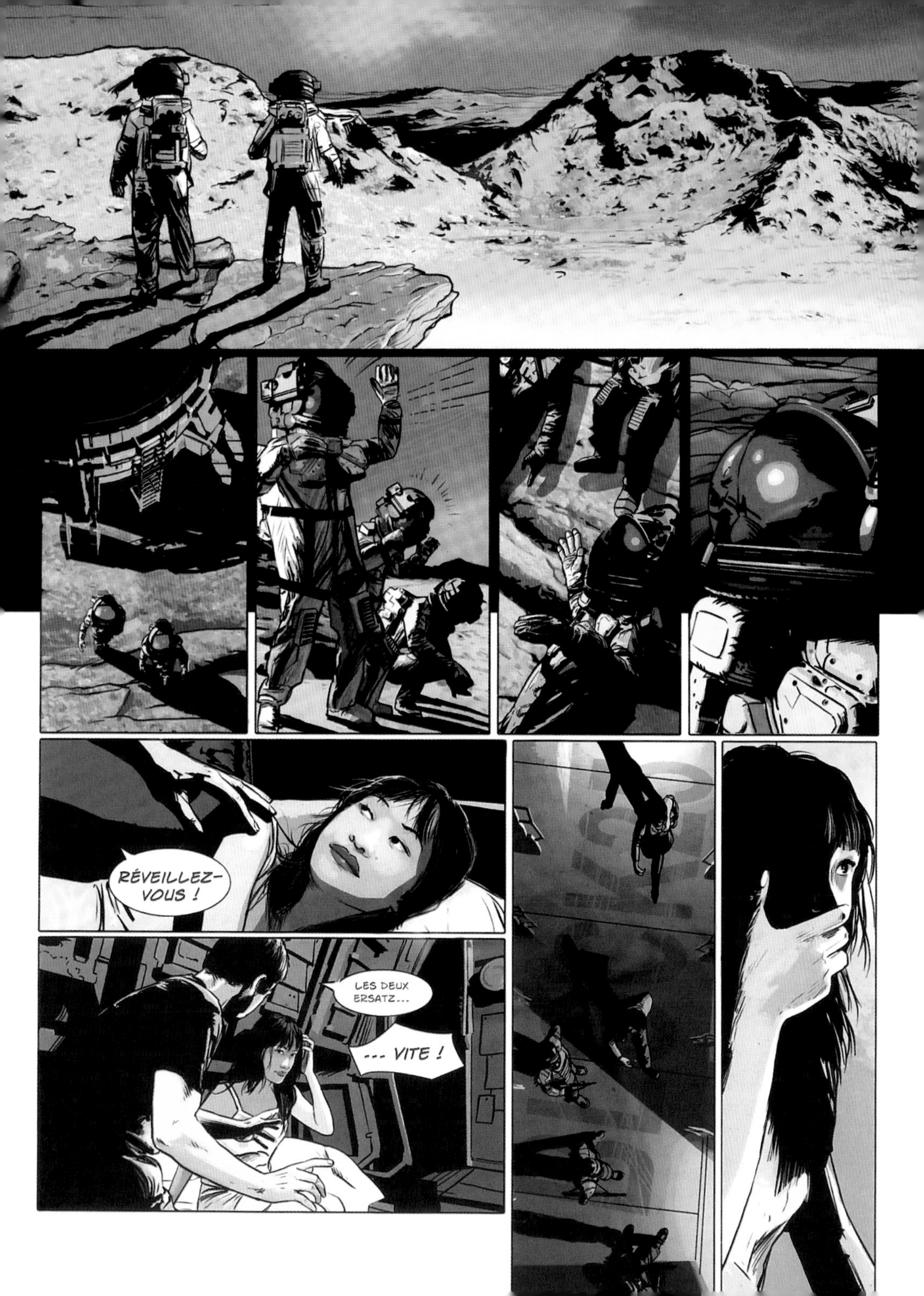
RÉVEILLEZ-VOUS !
LES DEUX ERSATZ...
... VITE !

Years of the Elephant 2007

✐✐ Willy Linthout

Title in original language *Het Jaar van de Olifant*
First published by Bries (Belgium)
Creator Belgian (b.1953)
Genre Autobiography

Many years may pass, but an elephant never forgets. And how could any parent forget when their child takes their own life? There is no escaping the constant reminders and unanswered questions, but Willy Linthout attempts to express his feelings in this surreal yet poignant comic book memoir based on his reactions to the 2004 suicide of his own son, Sam, who was twenty-one.

Linthout implements his skills as a best-selling Flemish illustrator to convey a roller-coaster ride of bewilderment, grief, anger, despair, paranoia, and ultimately enduring love felt by his alter ego Charles for his son Jack. Linthout omits all captions to give the reader no grounding in place or time, reality or fantasy, and to instil the same disorientation felt by Charles as he flounders through home, work, and everyday life. Similarly, Linthout almost never portrays Charles's wife in order to make readers share in his feelings of extreme isolation.

Linthout's masterstroke is to personify the son by bringing back to life the chalk outline on the ground where his body fell. He also deliberately leaves his drawings in their uninked pencil stage, as if to emphasize the human hand and heart behind them. As he explains, "My son Sam's life didn't get the chance to go all the way, it stayed unfinished, so the same goes for my pencils." By finishing this cathartic graphic novel, Linthout has given himself, and perhaps others, a way to remember and possibly come to terms with a young life lost. **PG**

Faire semblant c'est mentir 2007

✐✐ Dominique Goblet

First published by L'Association (France)
Creator Belgian (b.1967)
Genre Autobiography
Award École Européenne Supérieure de l'Image (2010)

One of the most beautiful comics of the decade is also one of the most harrowing and the most haunting. The initial attraction of Dominique Goblet's stunning autobiographical masterpiece is the overwhelming power of the art. The purple ink drawings that create the playfully cute opening give way to a series of penciled images that are truly evocative of the power of memory. Goblet recounts her relationship with her hard-drinking father with a mixture of honest appraisal and strong sentiment. In later chapters the small panels that characterize the book's opening are replaced by large, darkly disturbing images of caged dogs and the industrial parts of Belgium. A tone of menace quickly enters this compelling and disturbing work.

Faire semblant c'est mentir takes a turn into darkness when Goblet reveals a truly terrifying memory of her father's abuse. Cutting between television coverage of the death of Roger Williamson in a Formula One race and her own imprisonment in the attic of the family house where she is literally tied to the rafters, Goblet lays her past bare in a manner that is both unsettling and inherently trusting of her readers.

The horror of the latter part of the story is not its defining characteristic, however. Goblet's book is about much more than her past. Most notably, it is about her own role as a mother and her struggle to negotiate her personal history so that she might provide the best future for her little girl. The final pages, which feature an astoundingly beautiful array of dissolving images, are among the most optimistic in comics. **BB**

Omega the Unknown 2007

Jonathan Lethem · Farel Dalrymple

First published by Marvel Comics (USA)
Creators Lethem (American, b.1964); Dalrymple (American, b.1972)
Genre Superhero

MARVEL
LIMITED SERIES
1 of 10
JONATHAN LETHEM
FAREL DALRYMPLE
OMEGA
THE UNKNOWN

Loosely based on the short-lived Marvel creation of Steve Gerber and Mary Skrenes, *Omega the Unknown* begins with a bang: the car crash in which teen whiz Titus Alexander Island's parents are both killed. However, as Alex and the reader discover, their death is not all it seems. The crash exposes that they were not, in fact humans, but sophisticated robots. But who built them? And where have Alex's strange powers—and the glowing, burning omega symbols on his hands—suddenly come from?

These events send Alex, whose awkward speech and actions reflect his childhood in the company of automatons, on a search to discover his identity. However, he must also foil a nanotechnological plot while hindered by the Mink, a superstar superhero who has used his media millions to construct an underground labyrinth with both physical and metaphysical horrors lurking within. The prison is not the only labyrinth in town, and the plot of *Omega the Unknown* unrolls in a dense medley of druidic chant, cryptic comics created by an incarnation of *Omega* (and guest drawn by Gary Panter), and unintelligible gibberish spouted by victims of the nanorobots.

Fans of Jonathan Lethem's inventive novels will find a lot to absorb in this endlessly creative narrative. As drawn by indie superstar Farel Dalrymple, readers see the fantastical events of *Omega the Unknown*—a giant necklace absorbed into its owner, a life-saving salt shaker, and a seething crowd of fast-food zombies—effortlessly inhabit a rough and tumble Upper Manhattan. **EL**

"Some ticked-off superhero's busting up the joint."

Similar reads
Fortress of Solitude Jonathan Lethem
Pop Gun War Farel Dalrymple
Project: Superior Various artists
Watchmen Alan Moore and Dave Gibbons

Shortcomings 2007

Adrian Tomine

First published by Drawn & Quarterly (Canada)
Creator American (b.1974)
Genre Reality drama
Collection *Summer Blonde* (*Optic Nerve* series, 2002)

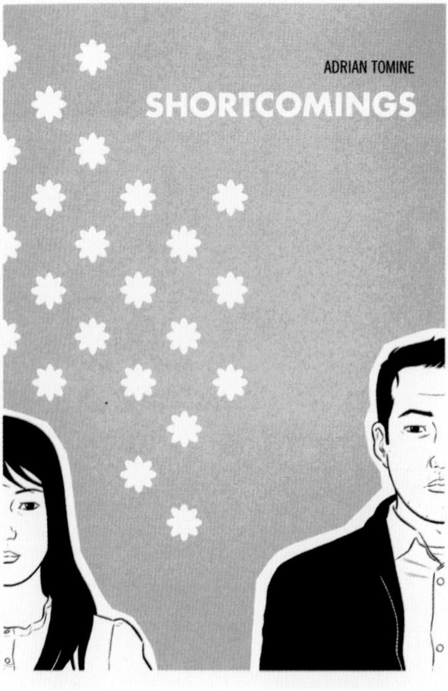
ADRIAN TOMINE
SHORTCOMINGS

Similar reads
American Born Chinese Gene Luen Yang
Box Office Poison Alex Robinson
Sleepwalk and Other Stories Adrian Tomine
Summer Blonde Adrian Tomine
Why I Hate Saturn Kyle Baker

Adrian Tomine's first full-length work is a contemplative and, at times, pleasingly frustrating meditation on race, relationships, and identity. Semiautobiographical in tone and content, the protagonist is Ben Tanaka—a young Japanese-American college dropout who works as a movie theater manager in California—whose fading relationship with his more politically active girlfriend Miko is charted via a series of everyday micromoments. As Miko leaves to find herself in New York, Tanaka becomes increasingly drawn to Caucasian women. He is a self-centered character, singularly uninterested in what he sees as clichéd statements about ethnicity, in contrast to Miko's increasing engagement with her Asian heritage. While the focus is on Tanaka, the story carefully balances his pessimistic and, at times, immature outlook against Miko's more positive point of view. Tanaka's friend Alice, a lesbian Korean-American whose ease with relationships Tanaka envies, offers another perspective.

Tomine, a fourth-generation Japanese-American, established himself in the early 1990s with the self-published minicomic *Optic Nerve*, subsequently published by Drawn & Quarterly. His clean, crisp visual style owes a debt to Daniel Clowes (who has been vocal in supporting Tomine's work), and also to Jaime Hernández. Like Hernández, Tomine makes use of an anonymous California setting in which racial identities are generally normalized. The clear black-and-white lines and regular grids add a sense of rhythmic unity to the unfolding story, further emphasized by panels that focus on quiet moments, such as the wordless pause after a telephone argument. Like its antiheroic main character, *Shortcomings* studiously avoids making a big statement on race, but in doing so manages to make a profound one on the ambiguous nature of identity. **TV**

Laika 2007

Nick Abadzis

In *Laika*, Nick Abadzis examines the political machinations behind the race between Russia and the United States to get the first man into space, and he uses the story of the first animal successfully launched in *Sputnik II* as the lynchpin around which to build his tale. Or maybe he is just writing a sad story about a dog. Laika was the first dog to be successfully launched into space, but she never came back. She died slowly and alone, unable to understand why the scientists who had rescued and befriended her had suddenly disappeared. If you are an animal lover, get a box of tissues ready.

Written for young adults but also tackling some complex themes, *Laika* is drawn in an extremely expressive but simple style, with soft, thick lines. Abadzis is a wonderful creator of characters, and he perfectly captures the peculiar circumstances in which space program members found themselves, pressured to succeed at all costs and rubbing up against each other day in and day out. Sergei Pavlovich, a brilliant scientist, was at the forefront of the Russian Space Race. Readers first encounter him half-dead, walking away from one of Stalin's gulags. The steely drive that enables him to survive then informs his later research, and he remains one of the most fascinating characters at the heart of the story.

Abadzis balances the inevitable sadness of the ending with an understanding of the noble vision that prompted the Space Race, and the questioning and occasional confusion of the scientists and dog handler, Yelena Dubrovsky, who prepared Laika for her mission. Laika is never anthropomorphized—her responses are interpreted through her body language in the same way that humans interact with any animal—and it is a mark of Abadzis's skill as an illustrator how much readers can come to care about a two-dimensional drawing that does not speak. **FJ**

First published by First Second Books (USA)
Creator British (b.1965)
Genre Teen
Award Eisner Best Publication for Teens (2008)

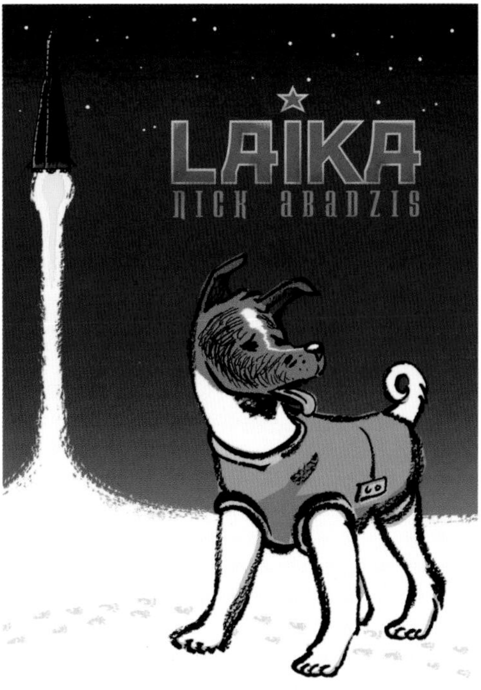
LAIKA
NICK ABADZIS

Similar reads

Hugo Tate: O'America Nick Abadzis
The Ballad of Halo Jones Alan Moore and Ian Gibson
The Hunting Party Christin and Bilal
Tintin Hergé
When the Wind Blows Raymond Briggs

Kiki de Montparnasse 2007

✎ José-Louis Bocquet ✎ "Catel"

First published by Casterman (Belgium)
Creators Bocquet (French, b.1962);
Catherine Muller (French, b.1964)
Genre Biography

The twentieth century had just begun when little Alice Prin came into the world in 1901 in a small town near Paris. Her childhood was poor and frugal, and once she reached adolescence, Alice quickly learned that the world does not cater for people in her situation: like everyone else, she must win her happiness, often at the cost of bitter lessons or superhuman efforts.

Happily, the young girl has a fierce determination, uninhibited nature, and an appetite for life. Having had several domestic jobs that she lost as a result of her impulsive nature, it is in the company of artists that Alice finds a way out. She begins to pose for painters and sculptors—and also shares their beds—gradually winning economic freedom and an independence of spirit.

In France, after World War I, "Kiki"—as Alice is now known—meets many of the avant-garde artists of Paris: Soutine, Modigliani, Kisling, Fujita, Man Ray, Picasso, Cocteau, Tristan Tzara. Kiki knows them all and can ask them for anything. For years, in the parts of Paris where they live, work, and socialize, she will be their famous muse—Kiki de Montparnasse.

Catel and Bocquet's handsome book is devoted to an astonishing character and is the comic book equivalent of a movie biopic: the evocation of a life reconstructed through its key episodes. The authors rightly chose to focus on their heroine's most flamboyant period—the 1920s and 1930s—without dwelling on her final, sadder years. Erudite without ever being ponderous, this portrait full of life is also an endearing chronicle of a legendary era in Paris. **NF**

Body World 2007

✎✎ Dash Shaw

First published by Self-published (USA)
Creator American (b.1983)
Genre Science fiction
Award Nominated for Eisner Award (2009)

When Dash Shaw first started to self-publish *BodyWorld* online in 2007, its rich colors and harshly determined grid suggested something beyond print. The story flowed like a futurist drug trip along the lines of the writing of William S. Burroughs or J. G. Ballard, told with a sensuality that seemed to ooze off the screen. The story took place in the future, and the telling of it seemed to as well. However, three years later it was handsomely collected by the publisher Pantheon and lost none of its vibrancy in the translation from computer screen to page.

Grids define Shaw's story: there is the page, its panels laid out like skyscraper windows, there is the locale—a city whose precise geography suggests some time spent in Dungeons & Dragons, and there is the love quadrangle at the heart of the story. A man comes to town to investigate the properties of a rare plant that has druggy side effects. He flirts with a teacher and seduces a student, whose ex-boyfriend in turn falls in love with the teacher.

Shaw's drawing style varies as the story explores its own metaphysical nether regions. At times it is downright diagrammatic in charting the interactions of its characters, the dialogue a deliciously deadpan pulp noir. However, once the grid is set, Shaw does not so much play out the narrative within it as splash paint and imagery around it. As it becomes clear that the effect of the drug is to blur the personalities of the individuals taking it in unison, the comic becomes a series of pages spanning op art abandon. **MW**

Shaw uses computer software to color and layer his drawings. ➡

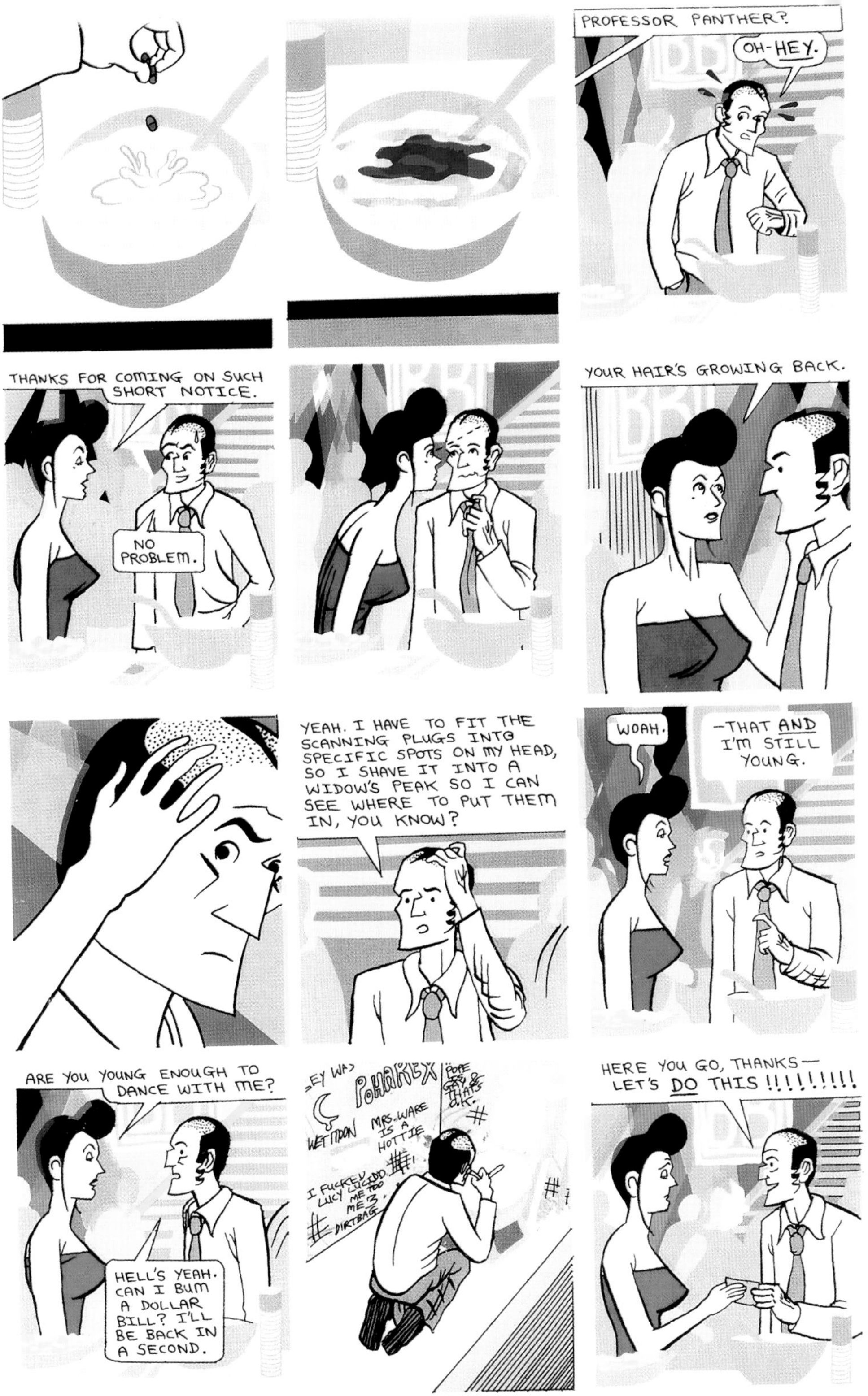
PROFESSOR PANTHER?
OH-HEY.
THANKS FOR COMING ON SUCH SHORT NOTICE.
NO PROBLEM.
YOUR HAIR'S GROWING BACK.
YEAH. I HAVE TO FIT THE SCANNING PLUGS INTO SPECIFIC SPOTS ON MY HEAD, SO I SHAVE IT INTO A WIDOW'S PEAK SO I CAN SEE WHERE TO PUT THEM IN, YOU KNOW?
WOAH.
—THAT AND I'M STILL YOUNG.
ARE YOU YOUNG ENOUGH TO DANCE WITH ME?
HELL'S YEAH. CAN I BUM A DOLLAR BILL? I'LL BE BACK IN A SECOND.
WET MOON
MRS. WARE IS A HOTTIE
POPE IS GAY & THAT'S O.K.
I FUCKED LUCY
ME TOO
ME 3
DIRTBAG
HERE YOU GO, THANKS— LET'S DO THIS !!!!!!!!!

A.D.–New Orleans After the Deluge 2007

Josh Neufeld

First published by *Smith Magazine* (USA)
Creator American (b.1967)
Genre Autobiography, History
Award Xeric Award (2004)

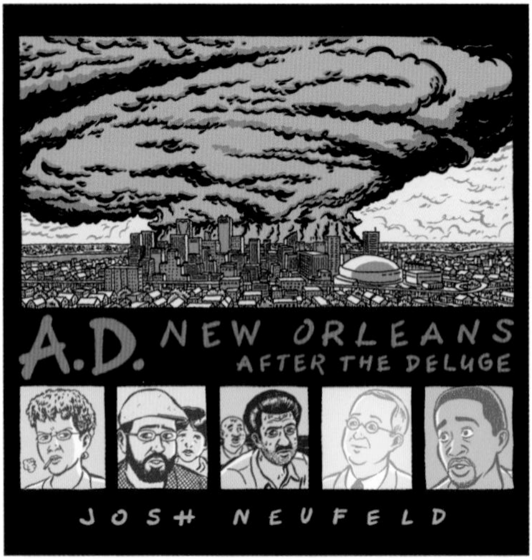
A.D. NEW ORLEANS
AFTER THE DELUGE
JOSH NEUFELD

"But, Mansell, why stick around? The store's totally flooded. For goodness' sake, there are rats runnin' around in trees!"

Similar reads
A Few Perfect Hours Josh Neufeld
Burma Chronicles Guy Delisle
Dark Rain Mat Johnson and Simon Gane
The Photographer: Into War-Torn Afghanistan With Doctors Without Borders Emmanuel Guibert

Based on Josh Neufeld's experiences as a Red Cross volunteer in the immediate aftermath of Hurricane Katrina in 2005, *A.D.–New Orleans After the Deluge* will exhilarate and devastate readers in equal measure. Neufeld worked with a crew of storm survivors to create this record of the hurricane, and readers can experience their stories taking shape in real time as Hurricane Katrina approaches.

The narrative reveals to the reader what is most important to each survivor. Denise, a sixth generation New Orleanian, treasures her city and her family but also values her independence very highly. Abbas, whose family is far away and safe, decides to stay behind with a friend, Darnell, to help protect his convenience store. And a doctor who is out of immediate danger on the higher ground of the French Quarter, wants to believe that the city of New Orleans will continue to be what it has always been—a great place for a party. Through the eyes of these real people—and those of other New Orleanians that enter the narrative as the rain starts to fall —readers experience feelings of hope and confidence, both of which are soon shattered.

As the storm situation worsens, readers revisit scenes that had been flashed on the television news—but now the story is told from the inside, reporting conversations and visiting places that the news did not have time for. Neufeld's comic book includes the protestations of folks turned back at the county border and the shock of starving, dehydrated citizens witnessing troops rolling by, their guns trained on the innocent victims of a natural disaster. But *A.D.–New Orleans After the Deluge* also captures something that is difficult to convey in a news report or editorial: the terror of having every thing you have ever known washed away, and knowing that even if it all comes back, *you* will never be the same again. **EL**

Cecil's Quest 2007

František Skála

Title in original language *Skutečný příběh Cílka a Lídy*
First published by Arbor vitae (Czech Republic)
Creator Czech (b.1956)
Genre Fantasy, Adventure

František Skála is an extraordinarily versatile artist: he studied animation, is a respected author on contemporary Czech art, performs comedy sketches, is a member of several musical groups, and occasionally makes comics, too.

Cecil's Quest was created by a very unique method: he photographed the entire book on a traditional cine-film camera in a woodland location. Skála made puppets of all the characters, as well as their homes, tools, and vehicles from natural materials, supplemented with discarded items such as plastic bottles, plastic bags, and remnants of an old television. He created a world that is visually original and full of postmodern, playful, and slightly ironic romanticism. This approach echoes the aesthetics of artwork that he exhibits in galleries.

Work on the project was very similar to making an animated film, except that Skála alone replaced an entire film crew, and taking the photographs took almost a year. The final comic book consists of 322 photographs that are accompanied by handwritten speech balloons.

The main hero of the story is a manikin, Cecil, who lives in a small house under an old cherry tree. One day he goes to visit his friend Lida, only to discover that she has been kidnapped with her magic mirror. Cecil decides he must try to find her and meets a number of strange forest creatures in the process. It is gradually revealed that Lida's kidnapper is Murdock, the ruler of evil spirits, so Cecil and his friend Homer go by wooden car to Murdock's tower to rescue Lida. Like every spectacular thriller, the plot culminates in a grandiose explosion followed by a happy ending. The humor of the story lies somewhere between J. R. R. Tolkien's *The Hobbit* and the absurdity of *Monty Python's Flying Circus*. **TP**

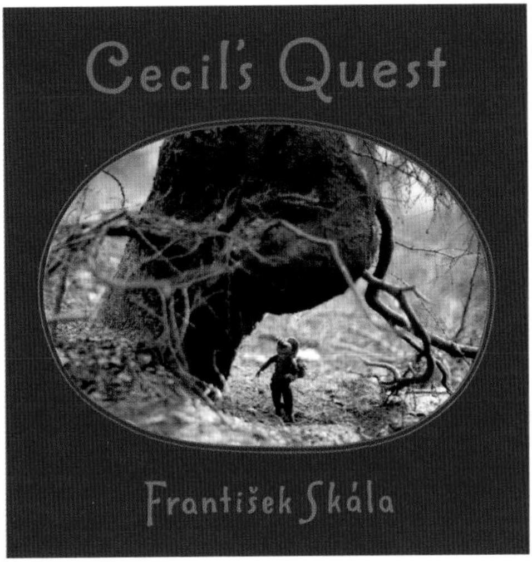

Cecil's Quest
František Skála

"Benedict Bone lives under a stone and sleeps there all day long. But at dead of night when the moon is bright he joins the ghostly throng."

Similar reads
Anča a Pepík Lucie Lomová
Dědečkové Pavel Čech
Péťa Medánek Alžběta Skálová
Tajemství ostrova za prkennou ohradou Pavel Čech
Velké putování Vlase a Brady František Skála

Dance by the Light of the Moon 2007

Judith Vanistendael

Title in original language *De maagd en de neger*
First published by Oog & Blik (Netherlands)
Creator Belgian (b.1974)
Genre Drama, Autobiography

In Brussels, in 1994–95, a black man, a political refugee from Togo, lived in an asylum and in the parental home of a white Flemish girl, who fell in love with him. His favorite read was Hergé's classic *Tintin in the Congo* (1930–31), a comic the British once considered unsuitable for publication in translation. The black man and his friends enjoyed the album endlessly, taking no offense at its content, just as Hergé intended.

The French-speaking refugee and the Dutch-speaking student, Judith Vanistendael, eventually married and lived in the bilingual (Dutch, French) Belgian capital. She lovingly called him her *petit nègre*, "little negro"—a term that was not considered offensive there. They split up in 1999 because he could not cope with freedom. Later, Judith was shocked to learn that, without her consent, her journalist father had written a short story about her and her black lover.

Years later, having studied the art of comic making at Sint-Lukas University College of Art and Design in Brussels, she paid her father back by retelling the story in her own 136-page graphic novel *De maagd en de neger* ("The Virgin and the Negro"), or *Dance by the Light of the Moon* in the English edition. Published in two parts in 2007 and 2009, it contained the viewpoints of both parent and child. The story was an instant classic.

Vanistendael rarely reads comics. She loves language, color, experimentation, human emotion, and silence. Sadly, the rawness of the original Flemish words, and also the larger size of the original Dutch edition, are lost in translation. **HvO**

Fun Home 2007

Alison Bechdel

First published by Houghton Mifflin (USA)
Creator American (b.1960)
Genre Autobiography
Award Eisner Award for Best Reality-Based Work (2007)

Alison Bechdel has kept a journal since she was ten. In *Fun Home* she crafts a graphic memoir about herself and her late father. Bruce Bechdel is a literature-loving teacher, a funeral parlor director, an obsessive restorer of the family's Victorian home, and a difficult, dominating husband and father, remote from both his wife and children. Father and daughter share a love of books, as well as an unspoken bond of homosexuality, which they must hide in small town 1960s America.

Not long after Alison came out as a lesbian to her parents in 1980, her father was hit by a truck and killed. She believes it was not an accident but a suicide, and her coming out may have triggered it. A year after his death, she discovered a vacation snapshot by her father of a young man reclining on a bed in only his briefs. She recognizes it as Roy, her babysitter and one of her father's students—and likely an underage lover. The year printed on the photo, 1969, is half hidden under blue magic-marker pen. Bechdel chooses the same hue to watercolor the pages of her "family tragicomic," which discloses her father's secrets, as well as her own.

Unlike her father, Bechdel has chosen to live proudly as the United States's foremost lesbian cartoonist, but she needed twenty years' hindsight after his death before she could confront his double life. She has come to understand how his refined, repressed personality helped to shape her own identity. This work of brave honesty, counterpointing two generations' attitudes toward homosexual self-acceptance, was chosen by *Time* as its Fiction Book of the Year. **J-PJ**

Alice in Sunderland 2007

Bryan Talbot

First published by Jonathan Cape (UK)
Creator British (b.1952)
Genre Fantasy
Award Eisner Award Best Graphic Album (1996)

This stylistic tour de force reveals the surprisingly interwoven histories of Lewis Carroll, his young muse Alice Liddell, and the city of Sunderland. Shrewdly, Bryan Talbot avoids turning this minefield of information into a dry "educational" tract by converting it into a theatrical entertainment on paper, set in the city's Empire Theatre, complete with an intermission, a visit backstage, two finales, and "numerous diversions and digressions."

Talbot uses digital software to merge images, objects, maps, and photographs into multilayered fantasias. These serve as backdrops and sets for Talbot's three alter egos: the performer, the plebeian, and himself. Aware that his narrator's sometimes dense monologues risk seeming like lessons, he undercuts them with outbursts by the grouchy plebeian, or the ghost of the late *Carry On* comedian Sid James, who died here onstage and is said to haunt the theater still, or at one point by the "real" Talbot, waking from a nightmare and plagued by doubt. Talbot taps into the heritage of comics: a Tintin-style Moroccan interlude; the battle speech from Shakespeare's *Henry V* spoofed in *MAD Magazine*; a meticulously engraved retelling of "Jabberwocky;" the Battle of Hastings given a Marvel Comics makeover; and even a page scripted by *Beano* legend Leo Baxendale. These coalesce to celebrate the alchemy of words and pictures, from the Bayeux Tapestry and Hogarth's prints to the *Alice* books themselves.

In the second of two endings, as Bryan Talbot stirs Alice-like, as if from a dream, the same climax awakens the reader to the connectedness of all our lives. **PG**

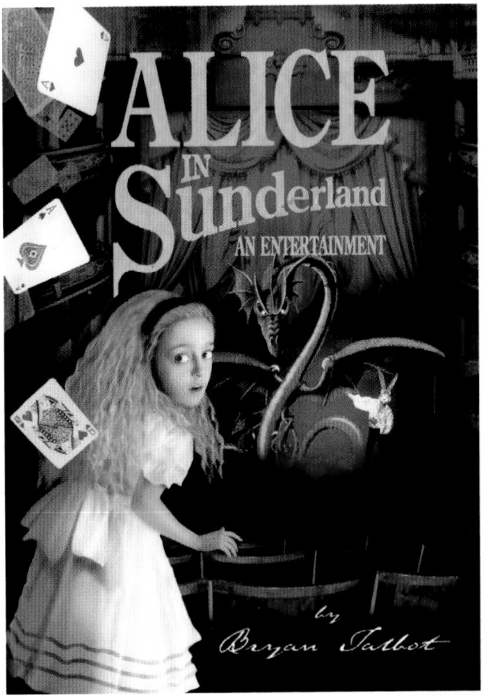
ALICE
IN
Sunderland
AN ENTERTAINMENT
by
Bryan Talbot

"Before she sails, she autographs a copy of Alice for the future Queen Elizabeth II 'From the original Alice.'"

Also by Bryan Talbot
Cherubs! with Mark Stafford
Grandville
Heart of Empire
The Adventures of Luther Arkwright
The Tale of One Bad Rat

Scalped 2007

Jason Aaron R. M. Guéra

First published by Vertigo/DC Comics (USA)
Creators Aaron (American, b.1973);
Guéra (Yugoslavian, b.1959)
Genre Crime

SCALPED
JASON
AARON
R.M.
GUÉRA
INDIAN
COUNTRY
Introduction by
BRIAN K.
VAUGHAN
CASINO
VERTIGO

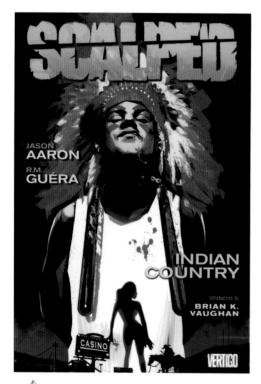

Similar reads
100 Bullets Brian Azzarello and Eduardo Risso
Criminal Ed Brubaker and Sean Phillips
The Goon Eric Powell
The Other Side Jason Aaron and Cameron Stewart

Scalped is a series that defies easy definition. A fusion of genres: part crime noir, part contemporary Western—with an occasional sprinkle of morbid humor, it provides a brutal examination of the slow and painful decline of a vanishing American Indian culture, a once proud way of life now plagued by the social problems of poverty, addiction, vice, and crime. The initial story arc follows the return of drifter Dashiell Bad Horse to the Prairie Rose Indian Reservation after many years away. Estranged from his activist mother Gina, he falls into the uneasy employ of tribal leader and local crime boss Lincoln Red Crow. As the impending opening of Red Crow's controversial casino promises to change life on "the Rez" forever, long-buried secrets are unearthed, opposing criminal interests vie for control, and the shocking truth behind Dash's homecoming is revealed.

As all good noir should, *Scalped* invites its audience to immerse itself in the plight of doomed individuals who are spiraling downward toward inevitable self-destruction through the inescapable consequences of their own life choices and the circumstances that dictate them. Jason Aaron relentlessly plays on readers' presumptions about his cast with multilayered characterization and unexpected revelations that provoke a constant need to reevaluate the motivations of the main players. Matching Aaron's raw storytelling, R. M. Guéra's grimy atmospheric art is a perfect reflection of the despair that often permeates life on the reservation. The oppressive claustrophobia of his layouts is eerily exacerbated by the murky, muddy coloring.

Scalped commands attention not only because it is an intricate, tightly plotted crime drama, but also because it sets itself against a cultural backdrop that the comic book medium has, traditionally, often failed to represent in anything but the most superficial and stereotypical of ways. **AO**

Children of the Sea 2007

✎ Daisuke Igarashi

Daisuke Igarashi's meditation on the ocean incorporates magic, folklore, and luminescence into a narrative that is part natural mystery, part fairy tale, and part coming-of-age story. Tough, adolescent, and conflicted, elite athlete Ruka is kicked off her high school sports team after a bloody bout with a teammate. Her frustration and sense of loss are soon replaced with wonder when she forms a bond with two strange visitors, Umi and Sora, who have come ashore from their natural habitat of the ocean. Their visit coincides with a series of bizarre phenomena: deep-water fish coming to the surface, large whales getting beached, and fish disappearing from aquariums across Japan. As the two visitors search for reasons behind these incidents, Ruka's involvement begins adding to the riddle.

Children of the Sea is a slow yarn that unfolds at a measured, careful pace, following the rhythm of a calm ocean. There is an element of secrecy and the unknown, but without any real sense of foreboding. Even the most unsettling sequences are portrayed as dreamlike, haunting the characters without drawing upon cheap, visceral reaction from the reader. Igarashi's love for worlds natural and supernatural anchors the characters and setting in familiar territory while stretching the narrative to places far away and imaginary. His aesthetic sensibility is one of feeling and texture, and his illustrations capture the details of water and light, crevices in skin, and sea foam on sand.

Drawings of marine wildlife are portrayed accurately and distinctly, with careful attention paid to gills, whiskers, and scales. However, Igarashi's affinity lies with contradictions and ironic possibilities: the fish that surface when we turn away, the phosphorescence that illuminates after we have passed. The result is a quietly playful world of wildlife and mystery that is as intimate as it is startling. **K-MC**

Title in original language *Kaiju no Kodomo*
First published by Shogakukan (Japan)
Creator Japanese (b.1969)
Genre Drama

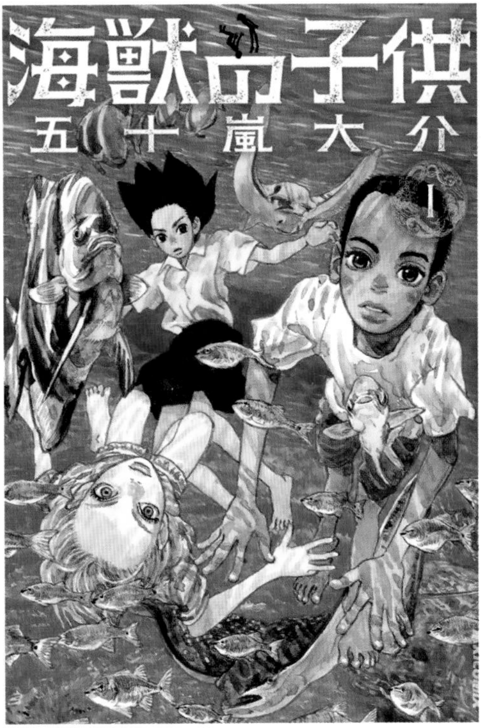
海獣の子供
五十嵐大介
1

Also by Daisuke Igarashi

Hanashippanashi
Little Forest
Saru
Witches

Nothing Broth 2007

✏️ Andrea Bruno

Title in original language *Brodo di niente*
First published by *Canicola* (Italy)
Creator Italian (b.1972)
Genre Drama

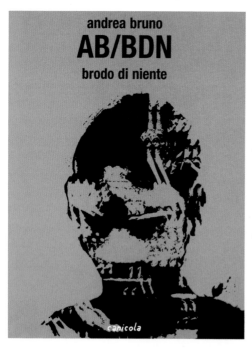

andrea bruno
AB/BDN
brodo di niente

canicola

Similar reads
A.D.–New Orleans After the Deluge Josh Neufeld
Alack Sinner José Antonio Muñoz
Rifles Andrea Bruno
Mort Cinder Alberto Breccia
The Walking Dead Robert Kirkman

Nothing Broth is set in the darker echelons of the Italian suburbs. Far from the vitalism of comic book creators such as Gipi and Baru, Andrea Bruno writes about small and suburban provinces from a desperate perspective.

In Bruno's first novel-length comic book, readers follow a young deserter named Red who is escaping toward an unrecognizable Italian city. Outside the town there is a strange war taking place between military forces and a group of priests. Red decides to stay in the violent town, taking part in robberies and visiting brothels, all the time hoping for a return to normality.

The title refers to the absence of food and comfort that faces Red in his extreme living conditions. However, the comic does not focus so much on its characters as

"I heard that somebody who was living down there found a piece of a priest in his soup!"

on the de-industrialized suburban environment, where "the city smells of incense and roast meat. It smells of many other things, because the trash collection services don't work."

Nothing Broth envisions a society paralyzed by its own destruction. Bruno's impressive, innovative black ink drawings recall the best works of José Muñoz or Alberto Breccia. The dense ink looks as if it has been mixed with lime and thrown onto the page. Like pieces of despair, his dark spots drip on the dazzling white paper. The first parts of the story were published in *Canicola*, a magazine that celebrated the tradition of avant-garde European publications such as *Frigobox*. In the 2000s, *Canicola* has been a leading light in the Italian art comics scene by showcasing the talents of Davide Catania, Giacomo Nanni, Giacomo Monti, Alessandro Tota, and Amanda Vähämäki. **MS**

Bruno's artwork is influenced by expressionism and informal painting. ➡️

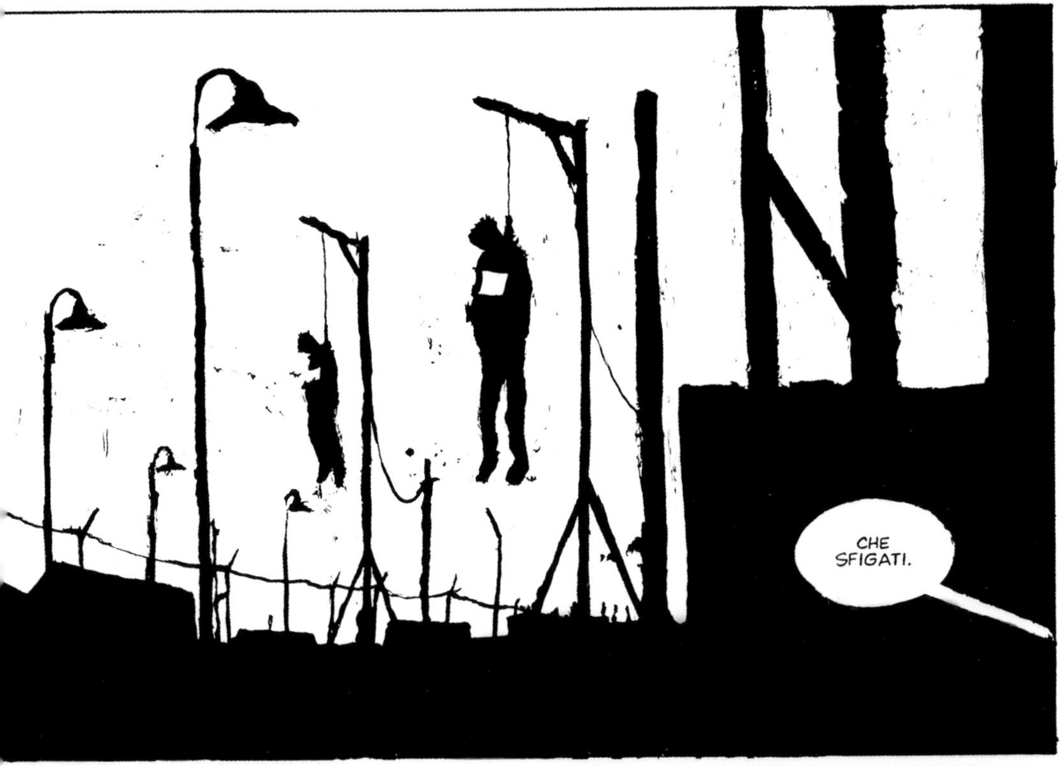
CHE SFIGATI.

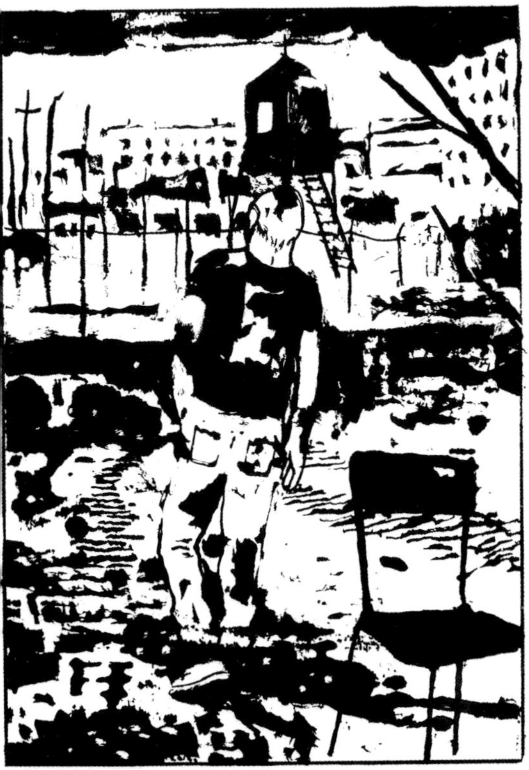

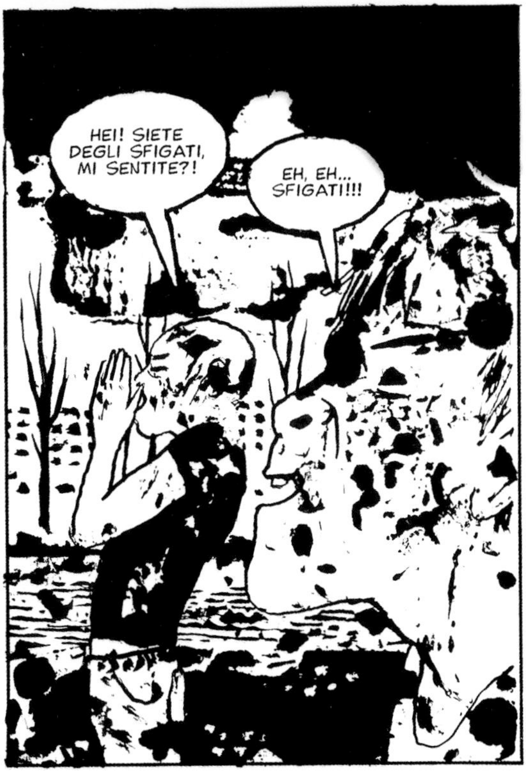
HEI! SIETE DEGLI SFIGATI, MI SENTITE?!
EH, EH... SFIGATI!!!

Sleepyheads 2007

✏️✏️ "Randall C."

Title in original language *Slaapkoppen*
First published by Oogachtend (Belgium)
Creator Randall Caesar (Belgian, b.1967)
Genre Drama

Cartoonists such as Julie Doucet or David B. had already brought their dreams to the comic page, but no other author had ever transposed dream logic to a long book the way Randall C. did with *Sleepyheads*. This, his first graphic novel, contains a clearly structured and easy to follow story, but the portrayed events are so surreal that an aesthetic and emotional reading is as rewarding as discovering the unusual story itself.

Sleepyheads features an ensemble cast. A boy and girl are traveling in a fantastic landscape. They walk through the sea, meet a brontosaurus, sit on an elephant, and get eaten alive but manage to escape. Two Russians on a small island seem to be the only remaining survivors of a submarine searching for a sunken treasure ship. They spend the day talking and playing games. A wolf tells stories about American Indians and about his own past. Slowly, all these story lines come together as one collective dream.

Sleepyheads deals with big topics such as love, colonization, and the power of imagination, but the book never feels heavy. Randall C. achieves lightness by switching from the serious to the comical. His drawing style reinforces the dreamlike quality of the book as he sketches cute creatures and changing landscapes without sticking to realistic proportions. The line work is spontaneous, reminiscent of Christophe Blain, and the colors in *Sleepyheads* are the decisive finishing touch. Randall C. uses just a few colors in many different shades because these suffice to evoke his intended dreamy feel. **GM**

Maggots 2007

✏️✏️ Brian Chippendale

First published by PictureBox (USA)
Creator American (b.1973)
Genre Experimental
Influenced by Matt Brinkman

Brian Chippendale's *Maggots* is one of the few graphic novels that come with complex reading instructions. Rather than reading from left to right and top to bottom (or from right to left as in the Japanese manga tradition), the narrative of *Maggots* proceeds in alternating tiers from left to right and then back again, with odd numbered pages reading from bottom to top and even numbered pages from top to bottom. Except where it doesn't. "Stay alert!" warns the book jacket, and this is good advice.

Created between 1996 and 1997 when Chippendale was a student at the Rhode Island School of Design, *Maggots* is a several-hundred-page story drawn into a Japanese art book. On nearly every page Japanese characters peek through the art, which is scratched across the pages as if it were the product of a fever dream. *Maggots* feels at times more like a compulsive act than a fully thought-out comic book story. To immerse oneself in it is to enter into an alien space, and to give oneself over to a creation that is as unsettling as it is compelling.

Maggots is not a story-centered comic. Although there is a discernible action narrative involving strange flying creatures and a living pyramid, the appeal of the work resides in its explosive visual energy. At times Chippendale's imagination is seemingly at war with the comic book form because he is seeking to express himself in a medium that is reliant on the printed page, which may be too limiting for an artist who once described himself as "drowning in ideas." **BB**

Kiichi!! 2007

Hideki Arai

First published by Shogakukan (Japan)
Creator Japanese (b.1963)
Genre Drama
Award Shogakukan Manga Award (1993)

In Japanese comic books, one of the most common qualities of a leading character is überintelligence. Traditionally, in order for genius characters to connect with their audience they are required to show some kind of vulnerability. Yet most of Hideki Arai's main characters, such as Mon-chan from *The World Is Mine* and the titular role in *Kiichi!!*, are not so traditional. Kiichi accomplishes the impossible with utter ease and calmness. Although the unorthodox genius is seen as an outsider by most people, he gains a charismatic status among his admirers.

It is Kiichi's tragic past that earns the sympathy of readers. When he is just four years old his parents are brutally murdered by a street slasher. Standing over their dead bodies, Kiichi does not shed a tear, but instead spends three insomniac days, followed by three days of sleep, and finally another three days of steady weeping. He then decides to run away from his grandparents' home and is adopted by a homeless woman called Momo. This marks the beginning of his turbulent life.

Young Kiichi goes on to tackle the dark sides of modern society, such as homelessness, the *yakuza* (mafia), and child prostitution. Ignoring political correctness and convention, he confronts whatever issue he is faced with, captivating readers with a wisdom that prevails over orthodoxy. Arai's core-shaking dialogue, fiercely intense illustrations, and innovative characters depict a story with overwhelming fervor. After being published for nine volumes in *Big Comics Superior*, its sequel, *Kiichi VS*, was launched in 2007. **TS**

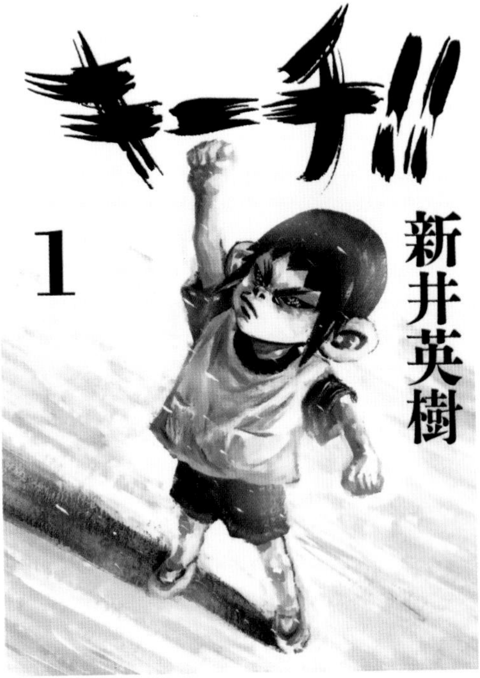
キーチ!!
1
新井英樹

"I guess he doesn't perceive the world like we do . . . It's only normal for him to have bad days!"

Also by Hideki Arai
I Love Irene
Kiichi VS
Rin
Sugar
The World Is Mine

Spent 2007

Joe Matt

First published by Drawn & Quarterly (Canada)
Creator American (b.1963)
Genre Autobiography
Awards Nominated for four Harvey Awards

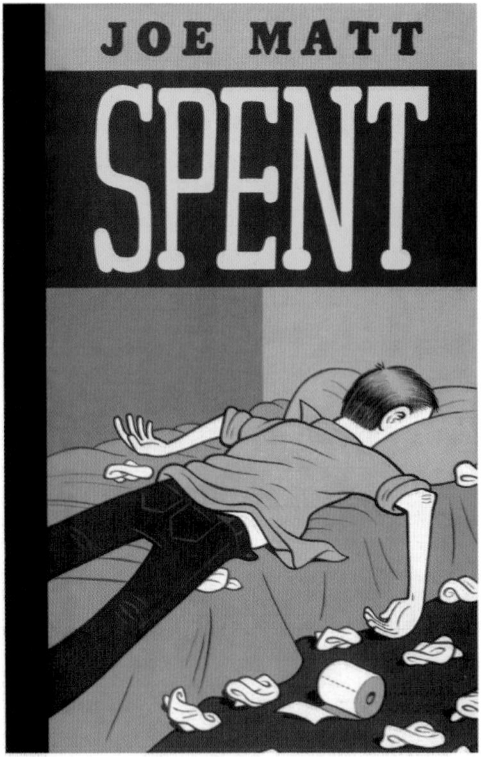
JOE MATT
SPENT

Similar reads
It's A Good Life, If You Don't Weaken Seth Brown
Paying for It Chester Brown
The Playboy Chester Brown

One of the most unusual of all autobiographical comics, Joe Matt's *Spent* is a love letter from the author to himself. Although all autobiographical works might be charged with a certain degree of narcissism, few cartoonists revel in personal humiliation to the extent that Matt does here. If autobiographical comics were a race toward the revelation of the most disturbing levels of personal embarrassment, *Spent* would win hands down.

Spent takes place during four single days over a nine-year period in which, apparently, very little happens in the life of Joe Matt. He spends time with his friends, cartoonists Seth and Chester Brown, hanging out in Toronto, but when he is alone he passes his time in his room obsessively masturbating. *Spent* describes, with astonishing levels of detail, Matt's enormous pornography collection, which he has painstakingly edited to fulfill his own particular sexual needs. The rest of his life is shown to revolve around a deeply felt sense of childhood trauma and loss, with Joe desperately seeking out the old comics and toys that he cherished when he was young. Throughout, Matt presents himself in the least flattering light imaginable, as if his sole desire is to make the world pity and detest him.

"Do you think that maybe . . . we could have an intelligent discussion about something other than masturbation?"

One of the reasons that the book works so well, aside from the spectacle of watching Joe's train-wreck life, is that the illustrations are superlative. The images, produced in an unvarying eight-panel grid, display all the mastery of a superb craftsman untroubled by deadline. *Spent* is an astonishing, hilarious, and deeply touching portrait of self-obsession. **BB**

Gus 2007

Christophe Blain

Gus Flynn is possibly the least likely hero of a Western comic, which is fine, because *Gus* is also the least likely of all Western comics. Part Western, part romance, part fantasy, part sex farce, Christophe Blain thumbs his nose at every piece of pulpy Americana that has structured the myth of westward expansion for more than a century-and-a-half. The result is a beautifully irreverent take on the American Wild West that has more in common with Tex Avery than it does with Tex Ritter.

Having established his name with his widely acclaimed work in the fantasy (*Donjon*) and sea-faring (*Isaac the Pirate*) genres, Blain returned in 2007 to a familiar genre. *The Revolt of Hop-Frog*, written by David B., had positioned Blain among the most impressive visual stylists to emerge from the so-called *nouvelle bande dessinée* movement of the 1990s. *Gus* demonstrates just how deserving that reputation is. Working in a stripped-down, sparer style, Blain's images seem to flow straight from his pen. His lines are nimble and playful, with the coloring (by Walter) setting a pitch-perfect tone.

"A letter! From a girl. From Natalie. I knew her five years ago, in Cincinnati. . . . I chose her out of the audience."

The stories in the *Gus* series are chaotically slapstick, filled with improbable sight gags (none funnier than Gus's ridiculously long nose), and the fast-paced adventure of Saturday morning cartoons. Gus and his compadres are ladies' men first and bank robbers second, constantly scheming and plotting to find romance in the arms of a schoolmarm or bank teller. In Blain's America it is sex, not violence, that tamed the West, and it is the fantasy of love that keeps the cowboy awake at night. **BB**

First published by Dargaud (France)
Creator French (b.1970)
Genre Western
Award Angoulême Festival Best Album (2002)

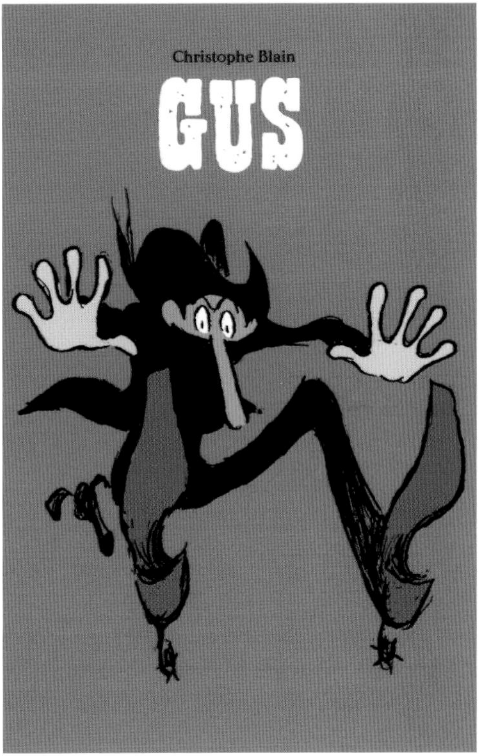
Christophe Blain
GUS

Also by Christophe Blain
Isaac the Pirate
The Revolt of Hop-Frog (*La Révolte d'Hop-Frog*) with David B.

The Train 2007

✏️ Chi Hoi

First published by Black Eye Culture (China)
Creator Hong Kong Chinese (b.1977)
Genre Alternative
Collection *Hijacking: Hong Kong Comic Literature* (2007)

Seemingly trapped within a loop, two men travel on a train. At every stop, passengers are exchanged, and the train itself never seems to end its metamorphosis, with cars being added and removed—dining and sleeping cars, but also a library, cinema, karaoke, sauna, and supermarkets. One of the protagonists finds a woman in the bar and introduces himself as "Cheng Yik, friend of Tze Wah," but she seems not to know him. He tries again later, but this time he says he is "Tsang Lik, friend of Lok Shan." A mistake? Duplicity? A parallel reality? A distraction by the author? In this endless voyage, everything is in flux yet remains the same.

Based on a story by writer Hung Hung, *The Train* is not a simple adaptation but rather a transformation of its setting and surreal contours. Although Chihoi employs a conventional structure, using characters, dialogue, and a psychological approach, he plays with the minds of his readers in this disturbing tale. His pencil drawings are comparable to those of Amanda Vähämäki and Blaise Larmee, but his art is sharper and more focused where figuration and page structure are concerned. With a few exceptions the book follows a strict, simple grid of two panels per page, thereby conveying a controlled rhythm. Yet this seeming fidelity to naturalistic and narrative conventions only serves better to pull the rug from under the readers' feet.

This absurdist tale starts and ends without explanations, and its main subject remains elusive. Like a dream, it seems to speak to readers about the most important things in life. **PM**

Powr Mastrs 2007

✏️ "C.F."

First published by PictureBox (USA)
Creator Christopher Forgues (American, b.1980)
Genre Science fiction, Fantasy
Influenced by Chester Brown

One of the most unusual fantasy comics ever published, C.F.'s *Powr Mastrs* takes the tropes of science fiction and Dungeons & Dragons–style adventure and completely inverts them to create what is almost an entirely new genre. Blending hilariously deadpan dialogue with the outrageous narrative conventions of fantasy, C.F. has produced a work that seems oriented toward a reality that is only tangentially related to our own.

Powr Mastrs charts the lives of a series of mystical warriors in Known New China. Subra Ptareo is the reader's initial guide to this strange world, but C.F. introduces new characters with little apparent rhyme or reason. Eschewing traditional exposition, *Powr Mastrs* is a fictional world in which the reader can, at times, feel entirely lost. As an example of world creation, the work is groundbreaking for the way in which it suggests that fantasy should not be a simple thing.

The great appeal of *Powr Mastrs* stems from its unusual visual aesthetic. At first glance some images appear crude and plainly drawn, with unimaginative framing and points of view. A closer look refutes this impression. What is clear is that these panels are carefully considered, and that gesture and expression are maximized for emotional and narrative impact. The delicate lines create compositions that are inherently fragile and that are perfectly suited to a make-believe world in which physical and psychological change is the rule rather than the exception. Moreover, the brilliantly designed settings and costumes show a level of deep investment on the part of the artist. **BB**

My Mommy is in America and She Met Buffalo Bill 2007

Jean Regnaud Emile Bravo

Title in original language *Ma maman est en Amérique elle a rencontré Buffalo Bill* **First published by** Éditions Gallimard (France) **Creators** Regnaud (French, b.1968); Bravo (French, b.1964) **Genre** Autobiography

Few autobiographical comics have dealt with childhood as movingly as this one by Jean Regnaud and Emile Bravo. Regnaud's mother passed away when he was a young boy, but his father opted not to let him and his brother know this fact. It tells the extremely unusual story of a young man growing up with a mother whom he believes has gone to the United States to live among Native American Indians.

The writing throughout is remarkably charming. At times the work seems like a more serious version of *Calvin and Hobbes*, exploring as it does, the imaginative life of a young boy. However, the book is filled with vital humor, particularly in a series of comic interludes that appears between the chapters. Unlike many comics that feature young children as stand-ins for adults, Regnaud writes a truly believable young man struggling to deal with a distant father, a school psychiatrist, aging grandparents, and concerns about what Santa Claus might bring him for Christmas.

Bravo's art has been justifiably acclaimed. Working in a classically Franco-Belgian visual style with astonishing supple coloring, Bravo mixes sketchy realism with an understated cartoony vibe. Many of the best pages are those in which he drops out backgrounds altogether, placing his focus on sharply realized characters on flat backgrounds. This comic is noteworthy not only for its remarkable honesty, but also for the truly memorable way in which it crafts characters and events through the eyes of a young man determined to deal with the world on his own terms. **BB**

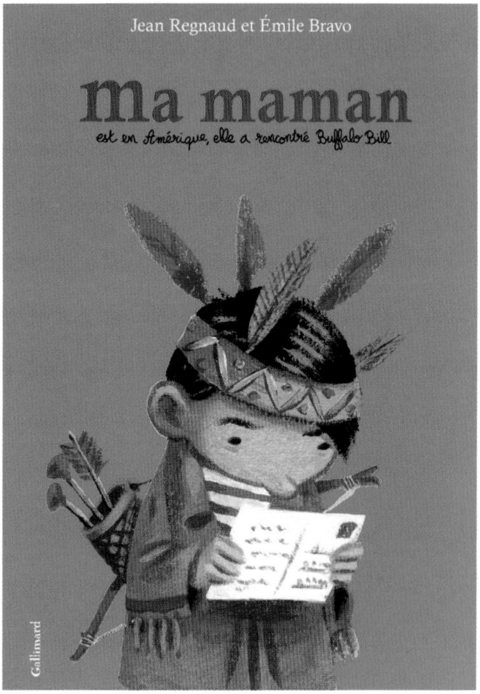
Jean Regnaud et Émile Bravo
Ma maman
est en Amérique, elle a rencontré Buffalo Bill
Gallimard

"At nursery school last year, Miss got us to make Mother's Day gifts. I made a necklace out of little bits of pasta which I painted different colors."

Also by Emile Bravo

Ivoire: Les Tribulations de Joost Vanlabecke with Jean Regnaud
Les Véritables aventures d'Aleksis Strogonov with Jean Regnaud
Spirou: Le journal d'un ingénu

Metro 2008

Magdy El Shafee

First published by Malaamih Publishing House (Egypt)
Creator Egyptian (b.1972)
Genre Political fable
Influenced by *Palestine*

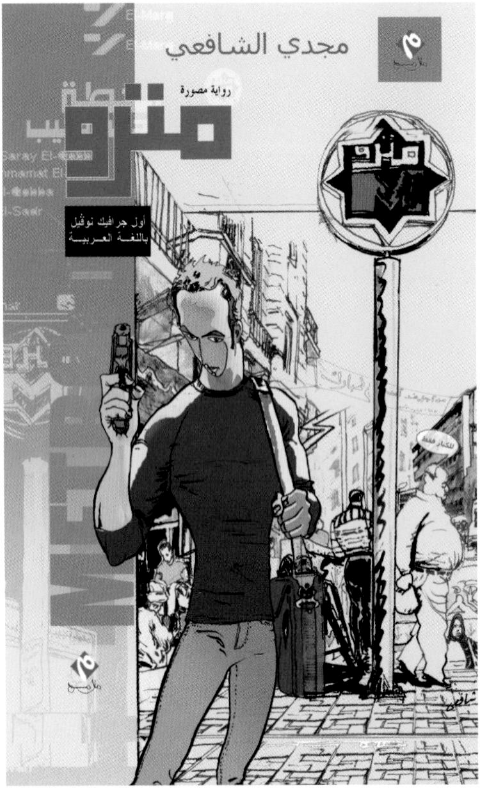

مجدي الشافعي
رواية مصورة
أول جرافيك نوفيل
باللغة العربية

Similar reads

L'Association en Egypte Baudoin, David B., Golo, and Menu
Mes Mille et une nuits au Caire Golo

Metro was the first adult graphic novel published in Egypt, and it could have been the last. Not long after publication, all copies of the comic book were looted in a raid without a warrant on the publisher's offices and removed from bookstores. In November 2009, a Cairo court fined both its publisher and creator and banned the book for being "offensive to public morals." While *Metro* contains one mild sex scene and some edgy language—in colloquial Egyptian instead of formal Arabic—what probably offended the authorities far more was its accessible critique of the country's corrupt regime and its advocacy of protest and democracy. Its publisher Mohammed Sharqawy, an acitivist, had been arrested and tortured before.

Author Magdy El Shafee creates a provocative antihero in Shihab, whose small software company is about to go under because it lacks the right connections to secure a bank loan. Disillusioned with the system, Shihab decides to get the money for himself by staging an armed bank robbery and dismisses his assistant's anxieties about the police, stating "They're all busy with the peace and security of one single person," a reference to the unseen, unnamed but ever-present President Mubarak. Several of Mubarak's cohorts do appear, thinly disguised but instantly recognizable to Egyptian readers; one "piece of garbage" is shown being thrown onto the street and assaulted by a furious public.

El Shafee combines a heist thriller based around Cairo's subway with a portrait of his people, so caught in the "trap" of day-to-day survival that most cannot contemplate challenging state repression. *Metro* was part of a call for change that culminated in the successful ousting of Mubarak and his regime in 2011. It also paves the way for other Egyptian graphic novels to be published in post-Mubarak Egypt. **PG**

Fueye 2008

✎ Jorge González

Taking its title from the Argentinian concertina often used for tango music, this graphic novel focuses on Argentina's immigrant past and the social, political, and cultural development of the country. An immigrant himself, Jorge González left Argentina to live in Spain, and writes here of an Argentina he never knew, the Argentina of the 1920s with its romance and tango music.

Fueye is a tale of two halves; the first half is dedicated to the story of immigrant musician Horacio as he explores Argentina's tango-laced musical scene. The second half is more confessional, a nonfictional account of the author's brief return to Argentina to visit friends and family, a trip that enables him to reflect on his Argentinian roots, his love of tango, his doubts, and his creative identity. The book is also a sketch of a vanished age filled with side-notes, loose strokes, and watercolors. It is an argument for uncertainty that, although based on reality, is always aware of its own artifice. Its constant sepia tones, at least in the historical sections, seem to perpetuate the scent of a lonely, old family photograph album.

González's characters feel the nostalgia too, not for the Argentinian history through which they are living, but for the lives they have left behind. There is a double-edged nature to this nostalgia: the excitement of escaping a war-ravaged Europe versus the hurt of being uprooted from home and family.

Frequently employing low-angled or caricaturelike panels, it is as if González wants readers to view his world through the eyes of a child seeing Buenos Aires's vibrant streets and nightlife for the first time. Distance is something felt by those of us who live in lands we were not born in and who are both rejecting and taking pride in different aspects of our own roots. And being an immigrant is certainly something González knows all about. **JMD**

First published by Sins Entido (Spain)
Creator Argentinian (b.1970)
Genre Reality drama
Award Novela Gráfica Fnac-Sins Entido Award (2008)

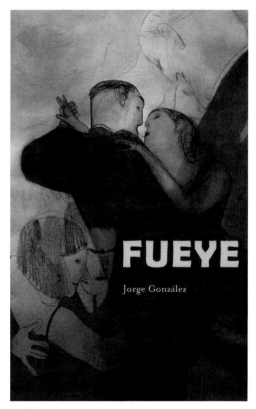

Similar reads
Persepolis Marjane Satrapi
The Four Immigrants Manga Henry Kiyama

Giraffes in My Hair 2008

✒ Bruce Paley ✒ Carol Swain

Title in original language *Rock 'n' Roll Life*
First published by Ça et La (France)
Creators Paley (American, b.1949); Swain (British, b.1962)
Genre Reality drama

Bruce Paley was eighteen in 1967 when his father threw him out and he embarked on a road trip across America. With added hindsight, his recollections of sex, drugs, and rock 'n' roll have now been visualized by his British partner Carol Swain in *Rock 'n' Roll Life*. In a series of short chronological episodes of assorted scrapes and schemes, Paley is our guide on a summer odyssey spanning the heady promise of the 1960s through to the disillusionment of the 1970s. Paley sets out as a wide-eyed, Kerouac-loving hippy with his seventeen-year-old girlfriend, encountering dope fiends, cops, rednecks, Disneyland, Black Panthers, and rock stars. He winds up as a punk on cocaine, single and jobless, screwing a five-dollar hooker for his thirtieth birthday.

Swain's charcoal drawings are the perfect accompaniment to Paley's tales, infused as they are with the atmosphere of Edward Hopper's paintings and American urban and landscape photography. She contrasts textures and shadows, especially in nature and skies, with harder outlines for figures and the man-made world. Her characters' expressions are understated, emotions largely internalized, mouths rarely smiling or even open. Her viewpoint is almost always shifting, one moment sweeping into the air, the next plunging to Earth, this circling and hovering suggesting the restlessness of the protagonists as well as the reader's voyeurism. People say that if you can remember the 1960s, you probably weren't there. Unlike some of the people he meets, Paley survived his walks on the wild side to pen this frank, unsweetened memoir. **PG**

Britten and Brülightly 2008

✒✒ Hannah Berry

First published by Jonathan Cape (UK)
Creator British (b.1982))
Genre Crime
Influenced by Raymond Briggs

Known as "The Heartbreaker," Fernández Britten is a private detective specializing in extramarital affairs. A career of destroying marriages has driven his self-esteem into the ground, so when the beautiful young Charlotte Maughan asks Britten to investigate the suspicious suicide of her fiancé Bernie Kudos, it seems like a break from his normal work. Unfortunately, nothing in this rain-soaked world is quite that simple, and along with his bizarre partner Brülightly, Britten descends into a world of lies, deceit, treachery, blackmail, and murder, as well as the full consequences of his own profession.

Britten and Brülightly is an exceptionally confident debut from a young author. Berry's world of secrets and lies is never clear-cut and forces the reader to question the morality of telling the whole truth. Berry keeps many key details from the reader; Britten's partner is a teabag whose voice only he can hear, yet it's never specified whether or not Britten is actually mad. Equally, the time and location where the story takes place are never specified; it is clearly Britain, but when and where is difficult to tell. Narratively complex, darkly humorous, and with well-drawn characters, this is a book that rewards attentive readers. Apparently insignificant details turn out to be crucial as the story twists and turns toward an understated yet devastating climax.

Beautifully painted in acrylics, Berry's art has a distinctive noir style. Her hand-lettering gives the book a personal feel, eschewing the standard computer fonts for her own imperfect handwriting and the charming expressiveness and authenticity that it brings. **BD**

Britten & Brülightly

Hannah Berry

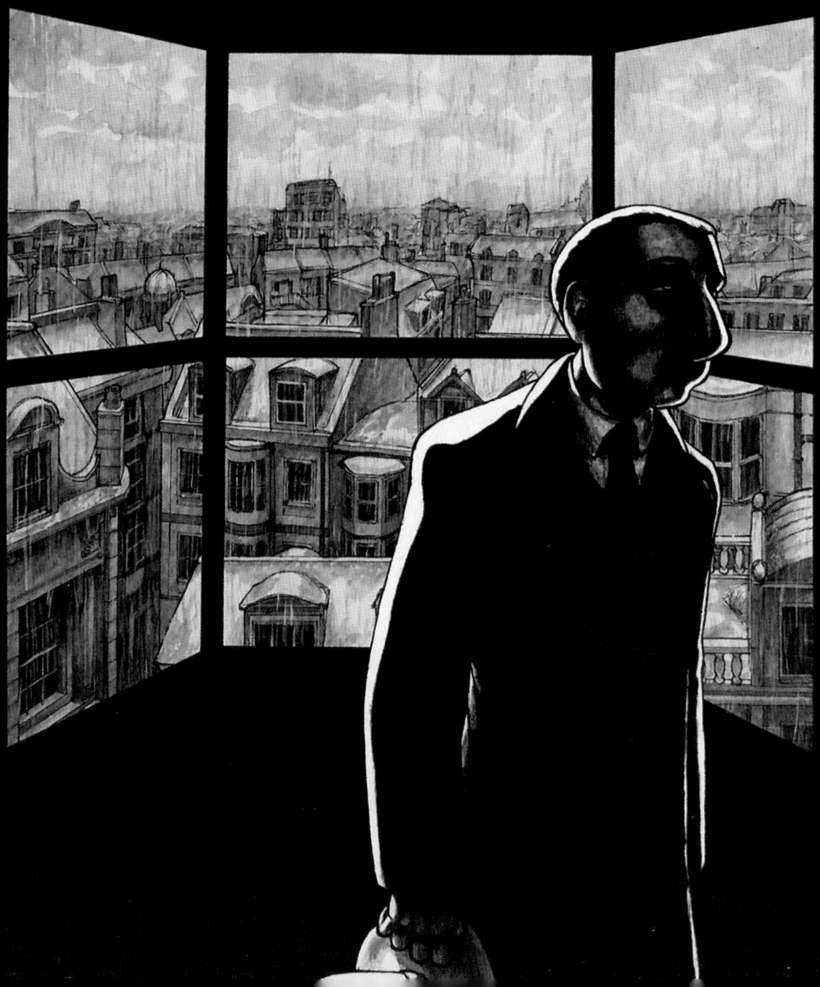

The Sacrifice 2008

✑✑ Bruce Mutard

First published by Allen & Unwin (Australia)
Creator Australian (b.1963)
Genre War
Influenced by Albert Tucker

When Bruce Mutard began to commit *The Sacrifice* to paper, the words came first because he wanted to leave the illustrating until the story and its intended message had been worked out and properly told. For Mutard, the words determine the images. In fact, it took a year of writing before he even drew his first panel, and then the rest took two more years to craft. For the dedicated writer/illustrator, creating a graphic novel can be a time-consuming task.

The first book in a trilogy that will keep Mutard busy through to 2016 at his current pace, *The Sacrifice* is set in 1939 Australia in the Melbourne bayside suburb of St. Kilda in 1939, during the final weeks of peace prior to the outbreak of World War II. The city is as much an intrinsic part of the story as any of the characters. It is fabulously rendered, though in tantalizing glimpses, in Mutard's pen-and-ink, black-and-white compositions as he takes it from its "provincial and complacent" starting point to its time as a frenetic wartime hub overflowing with soldiers, bureaucrats, and administrators. The city is also the home of Robert Wells, a respectable member of the middle class who finds himself struggling with the moral dilemma the war poses to his deeply held socialist and pacifist principles. After his brother Artie enlists and is killed in Crete, Robert feels compelled to follow his example and joins up.

Meticulously researched, *The Sacrifice* represents another big step forward in what is something of a resurgence of the graphic novel in Australia, showing much promise of great things to come. **BS**

Kajaani 2008

✑✑ Ville Ranta

First published by Asema Publishing (Finland)
Creator Finnish (b.1978)
Genre Reality drama
Award Nominee at Angoulême (2011)

Ville Ranta's *Kajaani* (named after a Finnish town) is a portrait of a man trying to balance his personal morals with an illicit relationship. It matters little that the protagonist lives in rural Finland in the 1830s: this story of conflicted morals and forbidden passion is universal. However, for Finns the story also carries historical weight in that the person is Elias Lönnrot, the compiler of *The Kalevala*, an epic poem of profound significance to Finland's sense of national identity made up of smaller folk poems collected and edited by Lönnrot. Fortunately, knowing *The Kalevala* or the history of Finland is by no means necessary for enjoying *Kajaani*.

Ranta uses the real-life Lönnrot as an actor in his period piece, an actor who also bears some resemblance to Ranta himself. The book's snowbound landscapes may be even more enchanting for non-Finns than they are to those who live there all year round.

The black-and-white images allow us to feel the enjoyment Ranta takes from the very act of drawing. The beautiful brush lines seem spontaneous and capture the scenery both boldly and poetically. His images are not restricted to traditional panels but float more freely on the page, and he has been known to draw some pages as many as sixteen times before they felt "right." Hence the book retains the feel of improvisation despite its careful composition.

Ultimately, the Lönnrot portrayed in *Kajaani* is more human than just a name in a history book, and Ranta succeeds in bringing him to life more vividly than any biography ever could. **HR**

What It Is 2008

Lynda Barry

First published by Drawn & Quarterly (Canada)
Creator American (b.1956)
Genre Reality drama
Award Eisner Award for Best Reality-Based Work (2009)

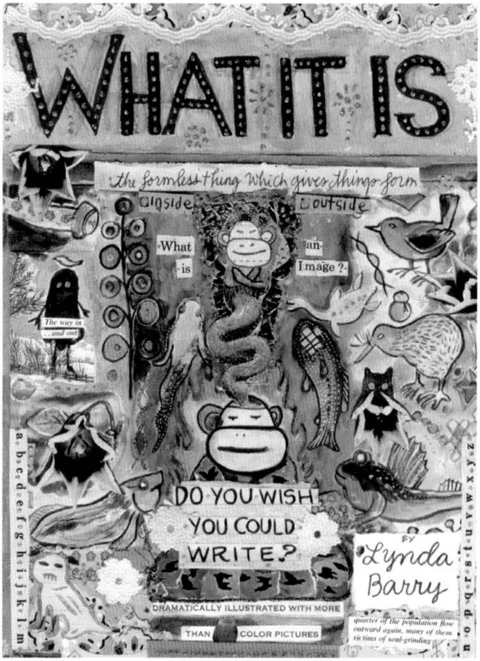
WHAT IT IS
the formless thing which gives things form
inside
outside
What is an Image?
DO YOU WISH YOU COULD WRITE?
BY Lynda Barry
DRAMATICALLY ILLUSTRATED WITH MORE THAN COLOR PICTURES

What longtime cartoonist and novelist Lynda Barry offers here is a unique book that is part memoir and part how-to guide, on the subject of creativity. Much of *What It Is* is spent exploring Barry's own relationship to creativity. Through her own example she shows how art helps us deal with the real world but can also easily get stifled by self-doubt and the demands of society that something "make sense."

Barry explores the nature of creativity through essays in collage form that mix her own words and pictures with found material, a great deal of which was originally collected by a retired primary school teacher during her long career. How do narratives from inside us become "real" stories? How do we give them form? Or not? Such questions alternate with autobiographical passages that recount Barry's own relationship to creativity—how images sprang up when she was a child, how "making art" later became a social embarrassment, something you had to be good at to have the right to make, so that she'd do it at night or when others weren't looking, and still later how she rediscovered the pleasure of telling stories under the guidance of a college art teacher.

Barry also describes methods and exercises one can use to enhance creativity and express the stories one has always had inside but never managed to get out, finishing with a series of entries from her own notes. Lynda Barry is at her best here in this exploration of the creative process that is both a continuation and a reflection upon her own comics. **J-PJ**

"I wanted it to make people just itch to make something. To me, writing or painting or collage are not different at all."

Lynda Barry

Similar reads

Making Comics Scott McCloud
One! Hundred! Demons! Lynda Barry
Picture This Lynda Barry
The Greatest of Marlys Lynda Barry

Kari 2008

Amruta Patil

First published by HarperCollins (India)
Creator Indian (b.1979)
Genre Teen
Influenced by Dave McKean

Amruta Patil caused a stir in India's literary circles with *Kari*, not only the first Indian graphic novel by a woman but the first to deal forthrightly with lesbianism. Patil chose to avoid the stylistic norms of comics, preferring to work on instinct instead. She draws in strong black lines, shading in charcoal grays, occasionally in colors or loose scrawls, and incorporating photos and collage. Seeing herself more as a writer than a graphic novelist, Patil indulges in rich, barbed first-person prose to reveal her titular character's turbulent inner life in "smog city" Mumbai. Patil's fictional antiheroine broods behind dark, burning eyes and knotted brows, a tousled boyish girl turning twenty-one, an advertising copywriter, introverted, gender-fluid, describing herself not as a "proper lesbian" but an "armchair straight, armchair gay, active loner." Kari's story opens and closes with her standing on the edge of her apartment block roof, ready to jump. When her intense romance with her lover Ruth ends, both decide to take their lives. Ruth jumps first from the block opposite, but is rescued by the building's safety net; Kari jumps and lands in the sewer. Both survive, but Ruth departs India, leaving Kari to struggle on. As alone and as alienated as she feels, Kari's wry monologues reveal a web of supportive relationships: shallow female roommates; conservative parents; an awkward male admirer; and Angel, a client with terminal breast cancer, with whom Kari forms a life-changing attachment. Patil captures all the self-mythologizing bravado and fragility of a woman living every moment as another postponed suicide. **PG**

Äitienpäivä 2008

Amanda Vähämäki

First published by Drawn & Quarterly (Canada)
Creator Finnish (b.1981)
Genre Drama
Influenced by Michelangelo Setola

Amanda Vähämäki's *Äitienpäivä* (*Mother's Day*) was included, without an English title, in *Drawn & Quarterly Showcase: Book Five*. Her second major work, it was later published in Finland as a stand-alone pamphlet by Huuda Huuda.

Vähämäki builds strong atmospheres without too much explanation or background. *Äitienpäivä* is a story of two boys embarking on time travel using a television remote control. Vähämäki doesn't explain the technical side of time travel here—this is not science fiction. The boys live on islands with an abundance of spare time, but not much to do with it. For them, time travel is merely a distraction. It could be their fantasy if the times they travel to were not so mundane.

In the past, the boys come across shepherds transporting sheep by a boat. They swim in the sea and use rocks to construct a Troy Town turf maze. Then it is time to return to the present and a meal with mother. The boys are able to travel in time but not in space so they cannot escape the familiar surroundings. For Vähämäki, time travel is a way to highlight the boys' sense of boredom and frustration. The innocence of childhood is coming to an end, but their youthful rebellion has not fully begun.

Vähämäki studied art in Bologna, Italy, where she joined the *Canicola* collective and started creating comics. Her early dreamlike, atmospheric work was crafted in simple pencils. While *Äitienpäivä* is in full color, it is far from naturalistic, and the use of color reflects the boys' state of mind more than the setting. **HR**

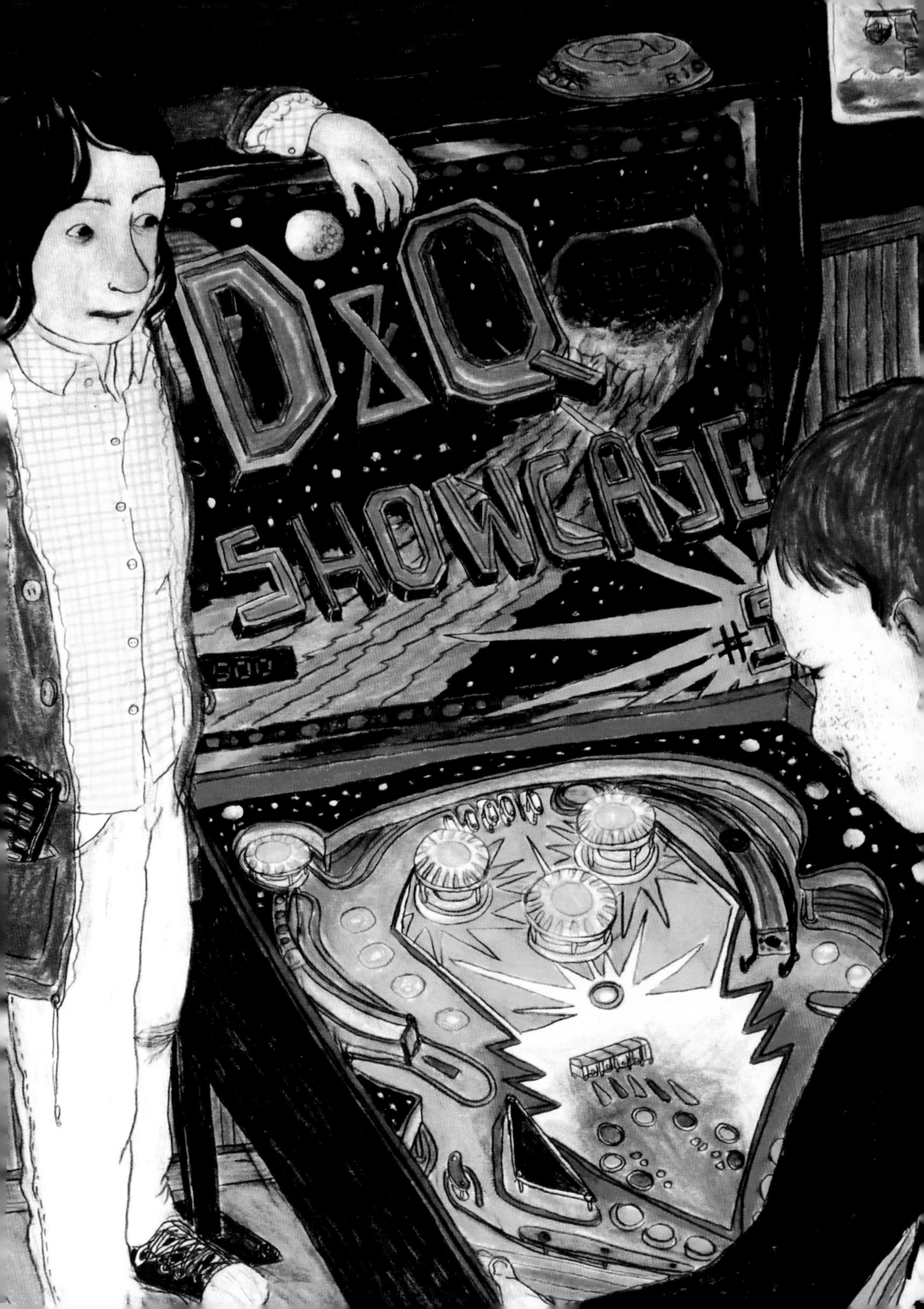
D&Q
SHOWCASE
#5

Frances 2008

✏️✏️ Joanna Hellgren

First published by Édition Cambourakis (France)
Creator Swedish (b.1981)
Genre Soap opera
Award Urhunden Award (2009)

Joanna Hellgren made her comics debut in 2008, arriving seemingly out of nowhere, but from the start proving herself to be a surprisingly deft storyteller. Her first graphic novel, *Mon frère nocturne* (*My Night Brother*), was immediately nominated as one of the best French-language graphic novels, and her next book, *Frances,* was praised unanimously by the critics. The latter even garnered her the prestigious Urhunden Award for best graphic novel in Sweden in 2009. Hellgren is Swedish but releases her books first in France—proof, if any is needed, that the world is becoming smaller and more international.

Frances is a quiet, somber drama about relationships and growing up. Readers follow a little girl named Frances who is taken from the orphanage where her father has left her and sent to live with her aunt in the city. The aunt lives with her old, senile father, and the trio form a dysfunctional family as the aunt starts a love affair with a woman living next door. As this plot line suggests, *Frances* is not an average comic story, but a dense and rewarding read. Hellgren does not resort to pedestrian characters and predictable plot lines, but tells a story that feels both fresh and convincing.

She employs a lush, free-flowing graphic style in which her art is drawn in pencil and left uninked. The effect opens her art up and gives a more natural feel to the characters. Hellgren predicts that *Frances* will encompass three volumes when completed. It promises to be a wonderful voyage of discovery when it can be read as a whole. **FS**

Kick-Ass 2008

✏️ Mark Millar ✏️ John Romita, Jr.

First published by Marvel Comics (USA)
Creators Millar (British, b.1969);
Romita, Jr. (American b.1956)
Genre Superhero

Superhero comics are often cited as the ultimate solution to adolescent wish-fulfillment fantasies, and, in *Kick-Ass*, Millar extrapolates this to its logical, self-referential conclusion. Dave Lizewski is an average U.S. teenager who pays homage to his comic book heroes by creating a real-world superhero identity. After being beaten nearly to death while on patrol, his incompetent but fearless Kick-Ass alter ego becomes an overnight sensation when footage of him tackling a group of thugs is posted on YouTube. But fame leads to notoriety, and Kick-Ass is soon out of his depth and caught in the middle of a brutal conflict between organized crime and the murderous vigilantes Big Daddy and Hit-Girl.

Millar underlines the comic's reality-based setting with an uncompromising depiction of Tarantinoesque violence surrounding the hapless Kick-Ass and cast. Ten-year-old assassin Hit-Girl is a particularly provocative example of this. Romita Jr., a veteran superhero artist who has drawn most Marvel characters at some point in his career, provides some uncharacteristically gory art and proves to be more than a match for the casual, over-the-top carnage Millar's scripts throw his way.

Kick-Ass may appear to sit somewhere between parody and satire, but at its geeky heart, it is actually an affectionate celebration of the superhero genre. It also champions the underdogs and outsiders who traditionally reside both within and outside its four-color pages. In perhaps his greatest character, Dave Lizewski, Millar has caught the zeitgeist and given us a true Peter Parker for the social networking age. **AO**

Logicomix: An Epic Search for Truth 2008

Apostolos Doxiadis and Christos Papadimitriou Alecos Papadatos

First published by Ikaros (Greece)
Creators Doxiadis (Greek, 1953); Papadimitriou (Greek, 1959); Papadatos (Greek, 1959)
Genre History

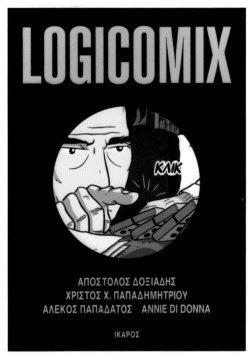

ΑΠΟΣΤΟΛΟΣ ΔΟΞΙΑΔΗΣ
ΧΡΙΣΤΟΣ Χ. ΠΑΠΑΔΗΜΗΤΡΙΟΥ
ΑΛΕΚΟΣ ΠΑΠΑΔΑΤΟΣ   ANNIE DI DONNA

ΙΚΑΡΟΣ

This is a graphic novel that few would have predicted in advance: a serious work about philosophy, philosophers, and logicians in the form of an extended look at Bertrand Russell's quest for logical certainty. Part-biography, part-disquisition, this is an engaging and lively work that stands with Douglas Hofstadter's *Gödel, Escher, Bach* as an introduction to the problems of logic, and Scott McCloud's *Understanding Comics* as a self-referential illustration of its own subject.

Written and drawn by a predominantly Greek team (colorist Annie di Donna is the only non-Greek), *Logicomix* has been a massive publishing success not only in its home country, where its first three printings sold out in a few months, but also around the world. It has been a hit with logicians and philosophers as well as the general public.

It's a great piece of work. It is concerned with truth and rationality—the really difficult questions in philosophy—but it manages to be clear, exciting, engaging, and up front about the liberties it has taken with the facts to make the story work. The ideas take center-stage, but so too do the personalities: Bertrand Russell the womanizer, obsessed with rationality and terrified of the ultimate irrationality of madness, and Ludwig Wittgenstein, prepared to deny the reality of empirical fact, even down to seeming absurdity. The art and the writing work in harmony to tell the whole story, whether they are showing the creative team self-referentially discussing how best to explain the issues, or showing logicians in action. **JS**

"Only by being 'stupid' can you break the barrier of the seemingly obvious … With time and persistence, the 'stupidification' began to pay off."

Similar reads
Cartoon History of the Universe Larry Gonick
Psychiatric Tales Darryl Cunningham
The Thrilling Adventures of Lovelace & Babbage Sydney Padua
Understanding Comics Scott McCloud

Monster Men Bureiko Lullaby 2008

✐✐ Takashi Nemoto

Title in original language *Kaijin bureiko lullaby*
First published by Seirinkogeisha (Japan)
Creator Japanese (b.1958)
Genre Adult humor

Monster Men Bureiko Lullaby is a collection of Takashi Nemoto's seminal early manga work. Not for the squeamish, and definitely not safe for the workplace, the book begins with a short manga introduction by Tomofusa Kure, which features Nemoto as a character showing his work to a saleswoman totally unprepared for its graphic nature. It seems Tomofusa, and perhaps Nemoto himself, is resigned to the fact that the comic book's Grand Guignol antics have a select readership with few women part of it. You will either love Nemoto's work or find it repellent.

Nemoto is not seeking to be controversial or subversive simply for the sake of it as he remarks in his essays "Life is just full of nonsense and silly mishaps." Cynicism would probably be the best word to describe his view of the world.

The last piece in the book, "The World according to Takeo" is worth reading in one sitting. Takeo is a giant irradiated sperm with a human head. Readers are likely to feel utterly exhausted as they, like Takeo, endure a sequence of terrible misfortunes. The tale plays with similar themes to *The Phantom of the Opera* and *Frankenstein,* but with a massive twist.

His satirical work has earned him the moniker "the Japanese Robert Crumb," but it is also reminiscent of William Burroughs and Charles Bukowski. While Nemoto's work will not appeal to everybody—and it is certainly not for the faint of heart—it is a real shame not to at least experience its strangeness and finish reading it once you have started. **AT-L**

Stalin's Spy in Tokyo 2008

✐✐ Isabel Kreitz

Title in original language *Die Sache mit Sorge*
First published by Carlsen Comics (Germany)
Creator German (b.1967)
Genre Reality drama, Political fable

Isabel Kreitz's voluminous 258-page political graphic novel *Stalin's Spy in Tokyo* was conceived after some lengthy in-depth research into the Russian Dr. Richard Sorge, a journalist with a legendary reputation who, during the Nazi period, worked at the German Embassy in Tokyo while also working as an agent for Stalin. Kreitz carried out painstaking research into the historical settings for her comic, and with her realistic drawing style she creates striking scenes dense with detail and brimming with atmosphere.

There are many stories and legends surrounding the man-about-town Sorge. As an agent of the Soviet secret service, Sorge started spying on the German ambassador Eugen Ott in 1933 as well as on prominent Nazis then living in Tokyo. After his arrest by the Japanese secret service, Sorge was executed in 1944. As a Communist dissident he was considered a hero in the former German Democratic Republic; conversely he was hardly mentioned in West Germany. Since German reunification, he has virtually disappeared from the history books. Long after his death, the controversial Dr. Sorge remains a political enigma.

Stalin's Spy in Tokyo is the most ambitious project undertaken to date by Kreitz, who is one of Germany's most political comics creators. She uses extreme, dramatically changing perspectives with enormous skill to echo the varied political viewpoints of her protagonists and adds a breathtakingly dynamic dimension to the story of a little known and intriguing historical figure. **MS**

Freak Angels 2008

Warren Ellis   Paul Duffield

First published by Avatar Press (USA)
Creators Ellis (British, b.1968); Duffield (British, b.1984)
Genre Science fiction
Award Eagle Award for Best Webcomic (2010)

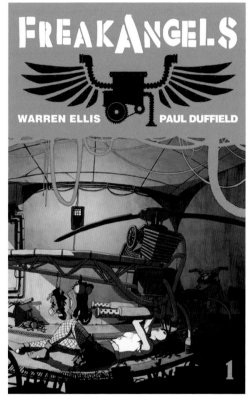

FreakAngels is an ongoing free web comic subsequently collected and published in book form. The FreakAngels of the title are a group with psychically enhanced powers, such as telepathy and telekinesis, who live in London in a postapocalyptic near future. Eleven of the protagonists live in Whitechapel, now an island due to flooding, while the last is an apparent outcast for some vaguely described transgression, and it is strongly hinted that the FreakAngels themselves had a hand in causing the unspecified apocalypse. Whitechapel is now their mini-utopia, its small group of survivors watched over by the FreakAngels, who communally organize resources and a medical clinic as they come to terms with external attacks and internal dissent.

Warren Ellis is a writer who has often gravitated to science fiction, while Paul Duffield is heavily influenced by the techno-landscapes of manga and European sci-fi comics. Ellis grapples with issues of refugees, petty crime, and overcrowding in front of lovingly constructed images of a flooded, decayed London.

FreakAngels taps into the literary tradition of using London as a postapocalypic setting and owes a clear debt to sci-fi writer John Wyndham, particularly *The Midwich Cuckoos*. Like Wyndham's work, *FreakAngels* at times resembles what Brian Aldiss called "the cozy catastrophe" where civilization collapses except for a group of plucky survivors. Despite this, the series manages to keep the reader hooked by cannily withholding the full extent of the protagonists' culpability while focusing on their efforts at redemption. **TV**

FREAKANGELS
WARREN ELLIS
PAUL DUFFIELD
1

"23 years ago, twelve strange children were born in England at exactly the same moment. 6 years ago, the world ended."

Also by Warren Ellis
Fell with Ben Templesmith
Red with Cully Hammer

Pinocchio 2008

"Winshluss"

First published by Les Requins Marteaux (France)
Creator Vincent Paronnaud (French, b.1970)
Genre Adult humor
Award Best Album Award, Angoulême (2009)

WINSHLUSS
Pinocchio
REQUINS MARTEAUX

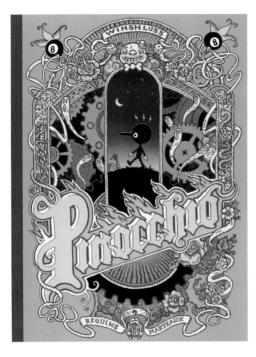

Similar reads

Fritz the Cat R. Crumb
Fun with Milk and Cheese Evan Dorkin
Is Nothing Sacred? Gahan Wilson
The Tinpot Foreign General and the Old Iron Woman Raymond Briggs

Winshluss has always been attracted by the imagery and stereotypes of the popular literature on which he has often based his work (for instance, he has cheerfully parodied the Walt Disney *Silly Symphonies* cartoons). He has also applied his caustic humor and impressive graphic skills to a loose adaptation of Carlo Collodi's famous tale *Pinocchio*.

Everyone knows the story of the wooden puppet carved by the carpenter Geppetto and his adventures that end in his transformation into a real boy. But things do not go so smoothly in Winshluss's reworking of the tale. Built from scraps of iron by a greedy engineer who intends to sell his little robot to the army as a potential killing machine, Pinocchio starts life with a torrid and deadly sex scene (he is not really equipped for this but, as everyone knows, he has a nose that can grow) before setting off to travel the great wide world, ready for the worst life can throw at him.

Obviously the worst is exactly what he encounters. Indeed, as in the Disney cartoon version, this metal Pinocchio has a conscience within him, but here Jiminy Cricket is a brutal and amoral character only interested in satisfying his base instincts, which are usually conveyed graphically. Under his influence, Pinocchio experiences a series of horrors of every kind: children's forced labor, murders, rapes, massacres, and various other traumas—lovingly illustrated in all their gory details. Fortunately, there is a happy (or almost-happy) ending. In one of the last sequences, the avaricious Geppetto, locked up in prison, is forced at knifepoint to submit to the lecherous lascivious urges of the seven dwarfs in a section simply entitled "All You Need is Love!"

Admittedly, Winshluss's *Pincocchio* does not paint a pretty picture of humanity. However, it does serve to remind readers of humanity's many brutal faults and failings. **NF**

No Comment 2008

✒️ Ivan Brun

Ivan Brun's *No Comment* offers readers a few brief glimpses into some suffocating worlds where madness, oppression, and death may suddenly loom at a moment's notice. These worlds—that are seemingly very similar to ours—are inhabited by cruel creatures looking as if they are operated by remote control, moved only by the most primitive urges.

With one- or two-word titles, the short stories contained in *No Comment* are chilling. "Eyes," for instance, in only four pages tells the story of the unstoppable decline of a fired worker who is driven to despair and the point of no return under the omnipresent eye of video-surveillance cameras. "Balls" concentrates on chauvinist hysteria in the workplace, and "Burned Hearts" satirizes the everyday pornography of our lives. With sinister humor, "Wasteland" evokes the unpunished massacres of Mexican women workers close to the factories near the U.S. border. And so on. There is never a hint of complacency in these stories of the horrors of everyday life. There is no let-out, not the slightest light at the end of the tunnel to give readers even a little hope.

Known to cult enthusiasts since the 1990s, but only discovered by the general public when it was published in the French magazine *L'Écho des savanes* in 2005, Ivan Brun chooses to express himself in perhaps the earliest form of comics: the wordless story. In *No Comment* Brun portrays the communication between his characters by means of thought bubbles containing small images, sometimes very close to pictograms—thereby emphasizing the feeling of deep dehumanization in his stories. Graphically, the illustrations do not belong to any particular genre or school, but they do seem to take some inspiration from the extreme humor of Philippe Vuillemin, and that is no small compliment. **NF**

First published by L'Écho des Savanes (France)
Creator French (b.1958)
Genre Horror
Influenced by Katsuhiro Otomo

Ivan Brun   **NO COMMENT**

DRUGSTORE

Also by Ivan Brun
Lieux Communs
Low Life
Otaku with Lionel Tran
Panoramique
War Songs

Pushwagners Soft City 2008

✏️ "Hariton Pushwagner" 🖋️ Alex Jensen

First published by No Comprendo Press (Norway)
Creators Terje Brofoss (Norwegian, b.1940);
Jensen (Norwegian, 1932–2003);
Genre Political fable

Almost forty years in the making, *Pushwagners Soft City* is probably Norway's most iconic graphic novel. The creators started it in 1969; it was finished in 1976, but the original art and manuscript were misplaced in the early 1980s and not found for over twenty years.

Set in a futuristic landscape, the titular Soft City is a metropolis where consumption and entertainment are key, people are production units and class distinctions are enormous. The social criticism is not subtle and is expressed through society's alienation of the individual. *Pushwagners Soft City* fronts a liberal criticism of society, a typical zeitgeist concern of the 1970s. Another layer is a child named Bingo, and his perception of Soft City. As a reader, we are passive viewers to the naive presentation of the automated people of the metropolis not too far from Bingo's own perspective.

Both creators were influenced by the theories of Wilhelm Reich, and crowd psychology is an important element in the book. So is the brutal authority of Mr. Soft, the city's undisputed ruler. Mr. Soft represents everything the creators hated and feared in their society. "Pick me up before the party, Helmut," Mr. Soft tells his chauffeur, in a dystopian moment. Soft City is doomed and Mr. Soft plans to escape in a rocket. "Who controls the controller?" is another essential sentence in the book, an echo of Juvenal's "Who Watches the Watchmen?"

Pushwagners Soft City is the story of how the engineers, the pharmaceutical industry, and the exercise of power have corrupted the world. It is as revelevant today as the decade in which it was written. **TAH**

Rumble Strip 2008

✏️🖋️ Woodrow Phoenix

First published by Myriad Editions (UK)
Creator British (b.1961)
Genre Reality drama
Influenced by Kate Charlesworth and Lynda Barry

How could Londoner Woodrow Phoenix ever forget the death of his younger sister in a car accident when she was eleven? Instead of turning this tragedy into a heartfelt autobiographical comic, Phoenix chooses to enquire into the invasive impact automobiles are having on our lives. Naming his graphic novel *Rumble Strip*, his intention is to create a similar effect to those road safety ads that attempt to shake people awake to the dangers of driving. Phoenix is no pedestrian lobbyist; he is a driver himself, and it is precisely because he loves his Audi A3 and the pleasures of being behind the wheel that he can deliver such a cool yet heartfelt polemic about the absurdities of road deaths, which claim over 1.2 million lives worldwide each year. He wants readers to question how they have come to accept the risks of living with cars and why killer-drivers are often allowed to get away with little more than a fine, a reprimand, or perhaps a temporary ban on driving.

Phoenix adopts an unsettling approach by avoiding dialogue, using only captions for his acerbic commentary. He portrays no characters, only the stick-figure people from road signs, and no other cars except for the one from which the readers view the action through subjective windows. Detached, we watch hypnotic highways speed by, eerily devoid of all traffic, abstracted into their painted markings, in the kind of "autopia" found in seductive car commercials.

Despite not showing a single human being, this is a very human book, and one that makes us examine how we interact with automobiles. **PG**

Swallow Me Whole 2008

Nate Powell

First published by Top Shelf Productions (USA)
Creator American (b.1978)
Genre Drama
Award Eisner Award for Best New Graphic Novel (2009)

Twins Ruth and Perry both suffer from schizophrenia. The two lead an overlapping life, heavily intertwined for adolescent siblings. They go to the same school, have friends in the same social circles, visit each other during and between classes, and walk home together. But their closeness is a result of their medical condition. Ruth is consumed by hallucinations of swarms of insects that threaten to swallow her whole. Perry, meanwhile, is plagued by a tiny wizard who commands him to draw. It becomes obvious that Ruth and Perry treat schizophrenia as a dirty, shameful secret, kept not just from their classmates but from their parents as well. Powell's sincere and ruthless portrayal of living with a mental disorder is sickeningly honest. There is sadness and irony in the fate of these two siblings. While Ruth's schizophrenia leaves her almost unable to function without her meds, Perry's schizophrenia manifests itself as artistic talent, his sketchbook filled with drawings dictated by his little wizard. Just as Ruth appears to find her way in life, securing an internship at the local natural history museum, she is consumed by her illness. While Perry is diagnosed as the "healthy one," he is still left to manage his condition alone.

Powell's borderless artwork conveys a truly organic feel. These are not heavily directed illustrations, but ones that push, suggest, and linger. His sharp, black inks eat up the page, leaving the reader with a sense of tension and a looming fear of being sucked into a dark place. This is a terrifying and sad story that will leave readers feeling as unsteady as the characters who "lived" it. **K-MC**

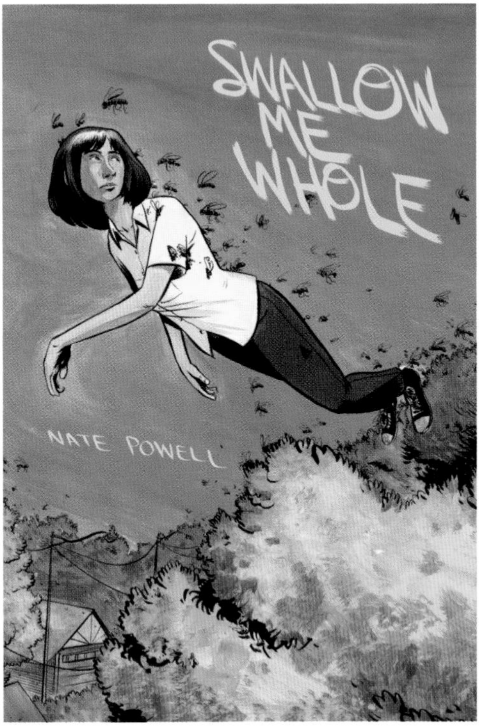
SWALLOW ME WHOLE
NATE POWELL

"At times arranging and reordering was all I could do to handle the day."

Also by Nate Powell
Any Empire
It Disappears
Please Release
Tiny Giants
Wonderful Broken Thing

Skim 2008

Mariko Tamaki Jillian Tamaki

First published by Groundwood Books (Canada)
Creators Mariko (Canadian, Unknown); Jillian (Canadian, Unknown) **Genre** Teen
Award Ignatz Award for Outstanding Graphic Novel (2008)

SKIM
WORDS BY Mariko Tamaki
DRAWINGS BY Jillian Tamaki

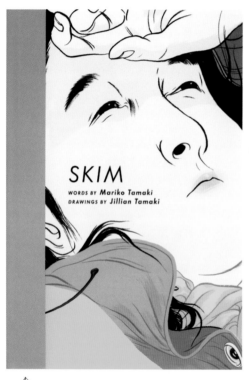

Similar reads
Ghost World Daniel Clowes
Girls and Boys Lynda Barry
Lost Girl Kiriko Nananan
X-Day Setona Mizushiro

On the cover of *Skim*, a young woman shields her eyes from the sun; her oval, moon-white face, petite mouth, and high eyebrows almost classically Japanese. But *Skim* is not about some geisha from eighteenth-century prints. Skim is the nickname of a modern, "not-slim" teenager, Kimberley Keiko Cameron, a half-Japanese, goth loner and wannabe witch at a Canadian Catholic girls' school in 1993. Skim's adolescent anxieties are understood and sympathetically conveyed by Japanese-Canadian cousins Mariko and Jillian Tamaki, who craft this graphic novel as Skim's self-absorbed diary, its spine warning; "Skim's Journal, Private Property!" The intimate truths readers glean within are not always what its diarist intends. Skim's written entries are sometimes crossed

"Being sixteen is officially the worst thing I've ever been."

out and her thought-track captions counterpoint or contradict what is shown of her conduct and comments to others. Vulnerable beneath her veneer of cynicism, she copes with a broken arm, her separated parents, disillusionment, and her awakening sense of self. When one girl's boyfriend, a jock rumored to be gay, commits suicide, Skim's teachers overcompensate with fervent student grief counseling. All except Skim's favorite, the drama and English tutor Ms. Archer, who becomes the first person to whom Skim opens up over shared cigarettes. This sparks Skim's first love; their discreet, illicit kiss in the woods is set within one silent double-page spread. Jillian draws in brush, soft pencil and gray tones in the manner of the *ukiyo-e* (floating world) Japanese woodblock tradition. The two Tamakis stunningly bring the acute dialogue and visual riches together to illuminate an ephemeral "floating world" of tentative, conflicted romance. **PG**

A Taste of Chlorine 2008

Bastien Vivès

Forced to go swimming regularly to treat his back pain, a young man notices an unknown girl about his age at the local swimming pool. This is the starting point for an unlikely game of seduction played almost silently, with only rudimentary gestures and unspoken terms. Readers get to know almost nothing about the identity of the characters or their backgrounds, but evidently this is not important. As in the films of Eric Rohmer, it is not the "why" that matters, but the "how."

In the anonymous, quiet, and somewhat strange environment of the swimming pool, which depersonalizes all its users, turning them into mere bodies, the dominant images are the eyes. These eyes seek out an object of desire and attempt to avoid

"Have you ever asked yourself what you're ready to die for?"

the gaze of others; they watch skin as length after monotonous, rhythmic length of the pool is swum.

Appearing on the scene in 2007, the graphically gifted Vivès, who has a background in animation, has quickly established himself as a name to be reckoned with. The new French generation of comic books owes much to this young author. Most of his stories revolve around the exploration of emotions, and *A Taste of Chlorine*, his third book published, is no exception to this trend.

Demonstrating nuance and modesty combined with remarkable control and fluidity, Vivès presents a sophisticated, intimate approach to comics that seeks above all to allow the images to express themselves and convey the narrative. With their simplicity, lightness, and silence, the wordless pages of *A Taste of Chlorine*, and its balletlike movement of bodies underwater will not quickly be forgotten. **NF**

Title in original language *Le goût du chlore*
First published by Casterman (Belgium)
Creator French (b.1984)
Genre Romance

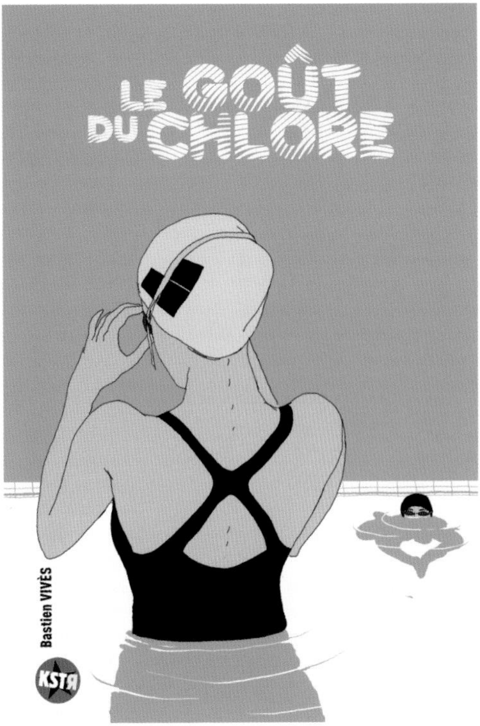
LE GOÛT DU CHLORE
Bastien VIVÈS
KSTR

Similar reads

Clumsy Jeffrey Brown
Likewise Ariel Schrag
Rumble Strip Woodrow Phoenix
Scott Pilgrim Brian Lee O'Malley

Van Helsing's Night Off 2008

Nicolas Mahler

Title in original language *Van Helsing macht blau*
First published by Reprodukt (Germany)
Creator Austrian (b.1969)
Genre Humor

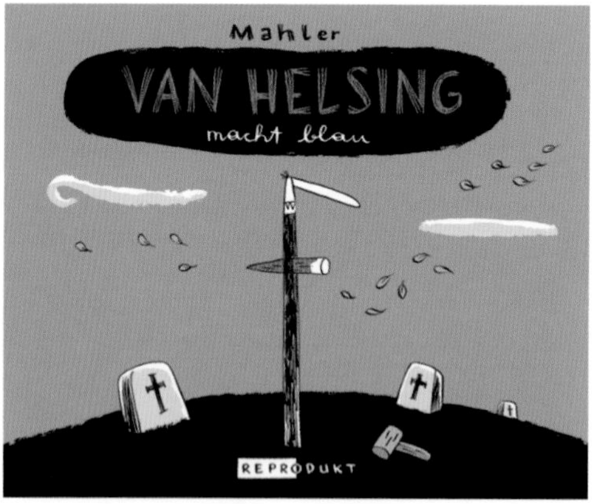
Mahler
VAN HELSING
macht blau
REPRODUKT

"I always wanted to get ideas fast, and have a style of drawing that would get that idea onto paper in a direct and also quick way."

Nicolas Mahler

Similar reads

Amy and Jordan Mark Beyer
Flaschko Nicolas Mahler
Kratochvil Nicolas Mahler
Krazy Kat George Herriman
Zippy The Pinhead Bill Griffith

Nicolas Mahler is a master of all kinds of bizarre worlds, many of which he uses as the setting for his humorous and surreal stories. He distorts the appearance of his characters as if they are seen through a fairground mirror. Large, slender figures are as tall as telephone poles, while the plump short characters are almost square, their noses disproportionately long and their feet abnormally short. With his mute dry humor expressed through horror-movie characters, Mahler could be compared to the Finnish director Aki Kaurismäki in creating engaging wordless narratives in black and white.

In *Van Helsing's Night Off*, Mahler portrays fictional figures such as Dracula, Frankenstein, werewolves, and the Invisible Man as lovable scatterbrains. They are not monsters in Mahler's world but normal people who happen to have some very strange physical peculiarities that leave them vulnerable to a variety of everyday pitfalls. For instance, the Invisible Man is, unsurprisingly, overlooked by the barkeeper as he desperately tries to order a beer. The mummy, on the other hand, is on a romantic date with his beloved, but when things get frisky he is forced to fight her off as she attempts to remove his bandages. And Dracula has serious problems finding his grave again after having one too many beers in a bar.

Mahler's humor is always a brilliantly acute combination of words and pictures. Whether he was inspired by the silent films of Buster Keaton and his stoical, fatalistic attitude to life's vicissitudes is not known. In any event he draws his characters with the same stone-faced expression, and his characters behave in similar fashions as well. *Van Helsing's Night Off* is the work of an exceptionally gifted humorist whose whimsical spin on the archetypes of horror pushes its "monsters" to the extremes of absurdity in their banal scenarios. **MS**

You'll Never Know: A Good and Decent Man 2009

Carol Tyler

Carol Tyler's father Charles kept much of what he saw in World War II beneath tons of what she calls "mental concrete." Not a secretive man by nature, like the millions of other American servicemen of that generation he kept silent about the war for over six decades, a time that gave rise to a distance between father and daughter that is bridged here by fragmentary memories, assorted memorabilia, and the outpourings of a burdened heart.

The title alludes to how someone can seemingly construct a new life from the fragments of a difficult past. More a meditation than a memoir, this is a disarming account of a daughter's struggle to understand her father and how his silence impacted upon her ability to relate to those around her.

The book's foundations were laid in 2002 after an unexpected phone call. "Hey Dad, what's up?" "Rivers of blood," came the reply. Presented in the form of a scrapbook, *You'll Never Know* employs a variety of illustrative techniques used with great emotional effect. Tyler's recollections blend a mix of vividly colored splash pages of Midwestern landscapes, hand-drawn renditions of sepia photographs, and subtle watercolors that wash over the book's pages. The art style fluctuates from symbolism to realism to fantasy, occasionally even within the same panel. Tyler's father is the good man of the title, depicted alternately as a fox, a tree, a child, and a soldier.

The author lays the chaos and dysfunction in her family bare and cleverly depicts it in overlapping ribbons of conversation. But there are no sour grapes here, no finger pointing, just vignettes and memories told using fifty-three, custom-mixed inks. *You'll Never Know* is only the first installment of an uncompromising and revealing family saga that will, once finished, span three must-read volumes. **BS**

First published by Fantagraphics Books (USA)
Creator American (b.1951)
Genre Reality drama, Autobiography
Award Best Writer/Artist Eisner Award nominee (2010)

YOU'LL NEVER KNOW
A Graphic Memoir
by C. Tyler
BOOK ONE:
A GOOD AND
DECENT MAN

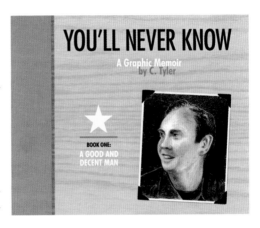

"I gotta get at this. I gotta somehow figure out a way to talk about this, ALL of it, the history, the drama. . . ."

Similar reads

Alan's War Alan Cope
Ethel and Ernest Raymond Briggs
Late Bloomer Carol Tyler
Maus: A Survivor's Tale Art Spiegelman
Persepolis Marjane Satrapi

Alec: The Years Have Pants 2009

✐✐ Eddie Campbell

First published by Top Shelf Productions (USA)
Creator British-Australian (b.1955)
Genre Autobiography
Award Ignatz Award for Outstanding Artist (2010)

Alec is artist Eddie Campbell's pen-and-ink persona in his series of autobiographical comics begun in the early 1980s and still continuing, although Campbell has since done away with the Alec guise to play his own part in his comic himself. The *Alec* strips were originally issued as short stories in various small-press publications, then as book collections by Escape, Acme, Eddie Campbell Comics (his own imprint), then Top Shelf. *The Years Have Pants* is the combining of several books previously issued as individual volumes chronicling different periods, with new added material.

Early on, in what was to become *The King Canute Crowd* and *Graffiti Kitchen* collections, Alec is a young man with artistic aspirations working in a menial job and enjoying a life of reveling and long bar conversations with his coworker Danny Grey, who becomes a mentor and hero-figure. These segue into *How to Be an Artist*, *Little Italy*, and *The Dead Muse*, which focus on the hero's artistic career, first in small press, then as an aspiring professional, including his move to his wife's native Australia and his struggle to find work there. *The Dance of Lifey Death*, *After the Snooter*, and *The Years Have Pants* collect vignettes and short stories centering around Campbell's daily life and his family, as well as the three completed chapters of an unfinished, abandoned project called *The History of Humor*.

Campbell's stories recount everyday occurrences in a lyrical and whimsical voice, with the underlying theme that life is there to be enjoyed and that human beings are strange and wonderful creatures. **J-PJ**

My Dear Saturday 2009

✐✐ Marcello Quintanilha

Title in original language *Sábado dos meus amores*
First published by Conrad (Brazil)
Creator Brazilian (b.1971)
Genre Political fable

A tremendous and remarkable collection of short stories, this volume is the product of many years work, and in putting the strips it contains together Quintanilha expended a great deal of time and effort to look at the people and places he was depicting. Written, penciled, inked, colored, and lettered by the artist alone, the tales in this collection all take place in authentic Brazilian environments, are recorded with painstaking care, and bear witness to how carefully the author looks at people. The shortest piece is just one page but captures its moment perfectly.

These strips are not about pretty images; they're made to convey an emotion. They neatly tie in with the Brazilian literary tradition of the "chronicle," a short text in which mood is usually more important than any plot. Even in the case of the longest story, which seems to have been made specifically for the book and takes twenty pages, what matters most is the mood. As most of the stories in this sixty-two-page book are shorter, this longer piece really stands out, and while each of its pages are as elaborate and rich in detail as the shorter stories, it possesses a different rhythm.

Dealing with one man's sense of shame, with another's love of soccer, with a girl's first love, these stories are not just about their protagonists. They also act as windows through which Quintanilha's powers of observation and memory mingle with his technical expertise to bring readers unforgettable glimpses of a traditional Brazil. These vignettes were slowly crafted and, like a fine wine, they age well. **CB**

Quintanilha's art seeks to capture the essence of rural life in Brazil. ➡

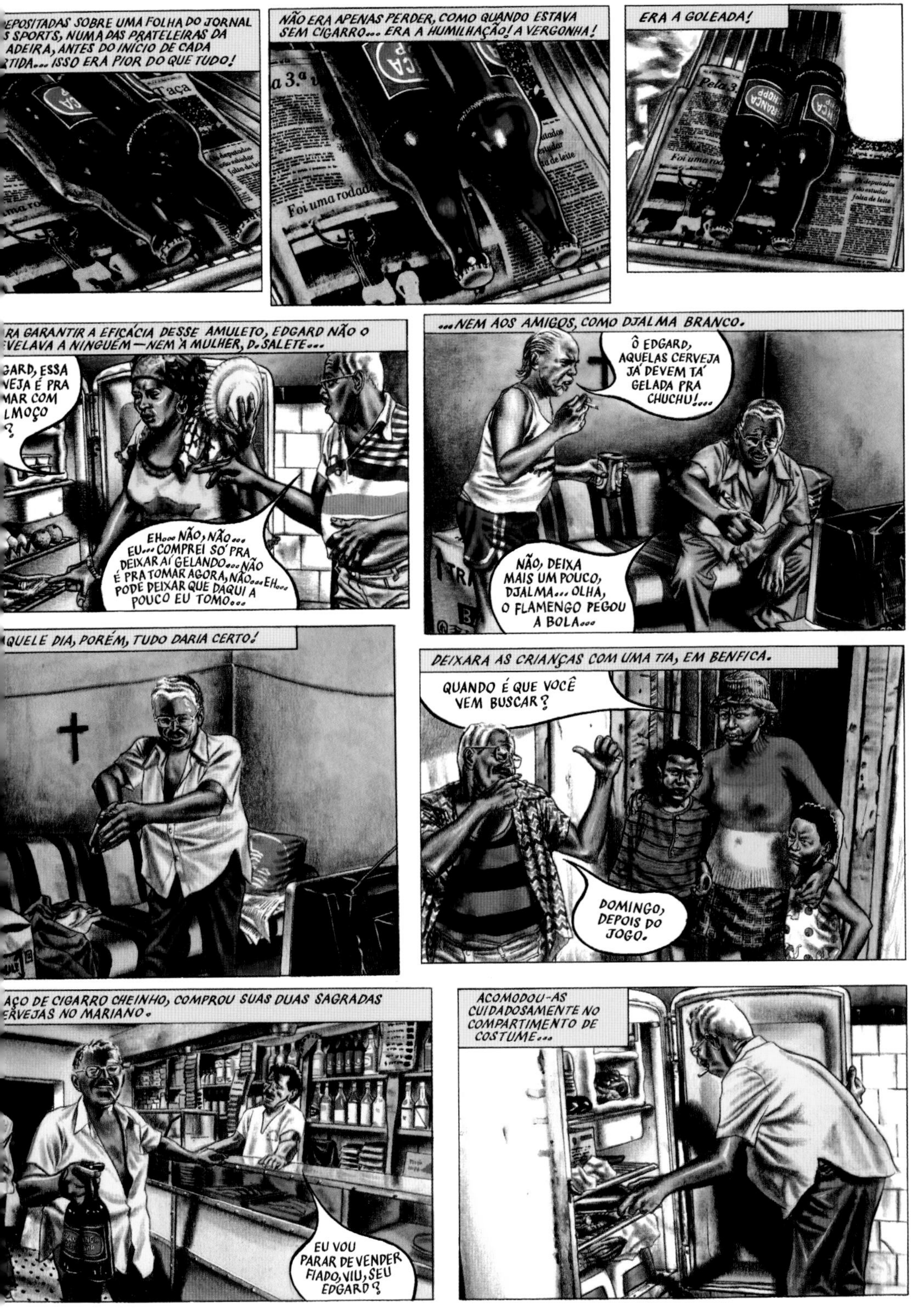
EPOSITADAS SOBRE UMA FOLHA DO JORNAL
S SPORTS, NUMA DAS PRATELEIRAS DA
ADEIRA, ANTES DO INÍCIO DE CADA
RTIDA... ISSO ERA PIOR DO QUE TUDO!
NÃO ERA APENAS PERDER, COMO QUANDO ESTAVA SEM CIGARRO... ERA A HUMILHAÇÃO! A VERGONHA!
ERA A GOLEADA!
RA GARANTIR A EFICÁCIA DESSE AMULETO, EDGARD NÃO O
EVELAVA A NINGUÉM — NEM À MULHER, D. SALETE...
GARD, ESSA
VEJA É PRA
MAR COM
LMOÇO
?
EH... NÃO, NÃO... EU... COMPREI SÓ PRA DEIXAR AÍ GELANDO... NÃO É PRA TOMAR AGORA, NÃO... EH... PODE DEIXAR QUE DAQUI A POUCO EU TOMO...
...NEM AOS AMIGOS, COMO DJALMA BRANCO.
Ô EDGARD, AQUELAS CERVEJA JÁ DEVEM TÁ GELADA PRA CHUCHU!...
NÃO, DEIXA MAIS UM POUCO, DJALMA... OLHA, O FLAMENGO PEGOU A BOLA...
QUELE DIA, PORÉM, TUDO DARIA CERTO!
DEIXARA AS CRIANÇAS COM UMA TIA, EM BENFICA.
QUANDO É QUE VOCÊ VEM BUSCAR?
DOMINGO, DEPOIS DO JOGO.
AÇO DE CIGARRO CHEINHO, COMPROU SUAS DUAS SAGRADAS
ERVEJAS NO MARIANO.
EU VOU PARAR DE VENDER FIADO, VIU, SEU EDGARD?
ACOMODOU-AS CUIDADOSAMENTE NO COMPARTIMENTO DE COSTUME...

Masterpiece Comics 2009

Robert Sikoryak

First published by Drawn & Quarterly (Canada)
Creator American (b.1964)
Genre Parody
Award Ignatz Award for Outstanding Anthology (2010)

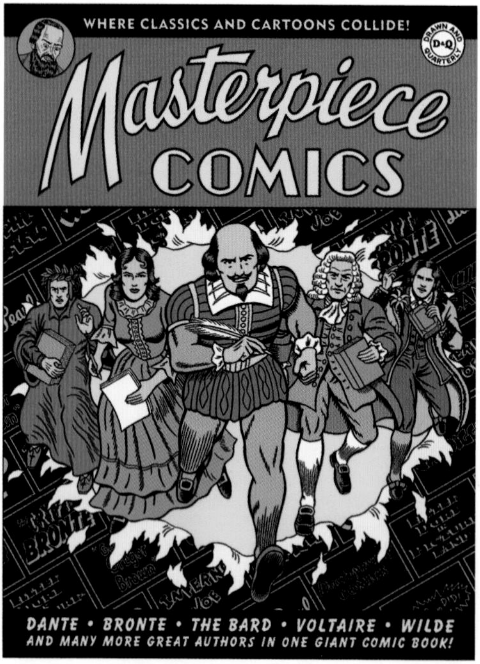
WHERE CLASSICS AND CARTOONS COLLIDE!
DRAWN AND QUARTERLY D+Q
Masterpiece COMICS
DANTE • BRONTE • THE BARD • VOLTAIRE • WILDE
AND MANY MORE GREAT AUTHORS IN ONE GIANT COMIC BOOK!

Similar reads

Casanova's Last Stand Hunt Emerson
Classics Illustrated Albert Kanter and others
The League of Extraordinary Gentlemen Alan Moore and Kevin O'Neill
The War of The Worlds Ian Edginton and D'Israeli

Attempts at adapting classic works of literature into comic books, as seen in the *Classics Illustrated* comics series, have always been plagued by the problem of not having the space to do the stories justice. Crucial scenes were often, out of necessity, omitted, and minor though pivotal characters sometimes all but ignored. Artwork was frequently workmanlike, with little in the way of background art. There were even instances of altered story lines. It must have seemed that comics and the classics were destined to never find common ground, and then along came Robert Sikoryak.

Sikoryak specializes in taking classic literary works and instead of attempting to tell the story in a condensed form, he opts for parody, concentrating

"I went to bed feeling okay, but now... What an awful life I have!!"

only on those essential elements that he feels best translate to the comic book medium. In his *Tales from the Crypt*–like adaptation of Emily Brontë's *Wuthering Heights*, "The Crypt of Brontë," Sikoryak cleverly elevates the housekeeper Elly Dean to the status of narrator and uses her to tell carefully selected, lurid extracts from Brontë's novel. In "Good ol' Gregor Brown," he uses the characters in *Peanuts* to highlight Franz Kafka's *The Metamorphosis*, the story of salesman Gregor Samsa, who wakes to find himself inexplicably changed into a giant insect. "Happiness is a pest-free home", says Snoopy, looking down at a dead cockroach.

Sikoryak uses jokes and sight gags to give emphasis to his chosen themes and combines his narrative with a chameleonlike ability to mimic whatever artistic style the story's history and setting require. It might be tongue-in-cheek, but it is still unquestionably a significant achievement. **BS**

Asterios Polyp 2009

David Mazzucchelli

Meet Asterios Polyp, a prickly, stiff, self-important "paper architect," lauded for his designs, although none have actually been constructed. His comfortable world is turned upside down when a lightning bolt decimates his apartment block and belongings. What should he rescue? Readers gradually learn why he saved a cigarette lighter, a watch, and a Swiss army knife as he reevaluates his unfulfilled career and his broken relationship with Hana Sonnenschein, the woman he loved, and relocates to small-town America to get by as a car mechanic. Our fantastical narrator here is Asterios's identical twin brother Ignazio, whose death in childbirth has haunted Asterios ever since with the fear that he could have been his twin's murderer in the womb.

"There's this palpable tension between order and chaos."

Dazzlingly innovative, Mazzucchelli taps fresh formal possibilities in the medium by giving each main character their own appropriate drawing style, speech balloon shape, and dialogue font. While Asterios holds forth in emphatic capitals inside rectangular blocks, Hana's softer voice is evoked through a cursive upper- and lowercase script in curvaceous bubbles. When the couple first meet at a party, they are drawn in different styles; Asterios made up of blue outlined Aristotelean forms, Hana resembling a pink carved statuette in textured volume. As the two of them fall in love, they take on each other's visual register, literally harmonizing. Palettes also shift to suit settings or moods: magenta for a nipple, the color of Asterios's desires, or ochre for philosophical interludes where he communes with Ignazio. Yet, for all these techniques, Mazzucchelli has a purpose: to reflect on how one man grapples with what in his life is truly worth his attention. **PG**

First published by Pantheon Books (USA)
Creators American (b.1960)
Genre Romance
Award Los Angeles Times Book Prize (2009)

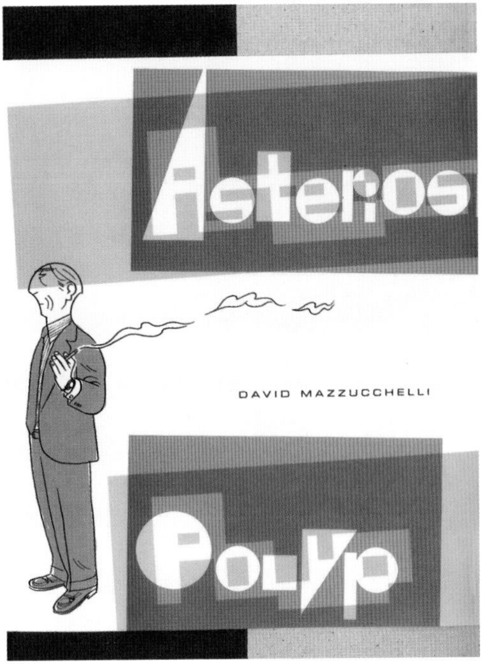

Asterios
DAVID MAZZUCCHELLI
Polyp

Similar reads

Big Man David Mazzucchelli
City of Glass Paul Auster, Paul Karasik, and David Mazzucchelli
George Sprott Seth
Rubber Blanket David Mazzucchelli

Attack of the Titans 2009

Hajime Isayama

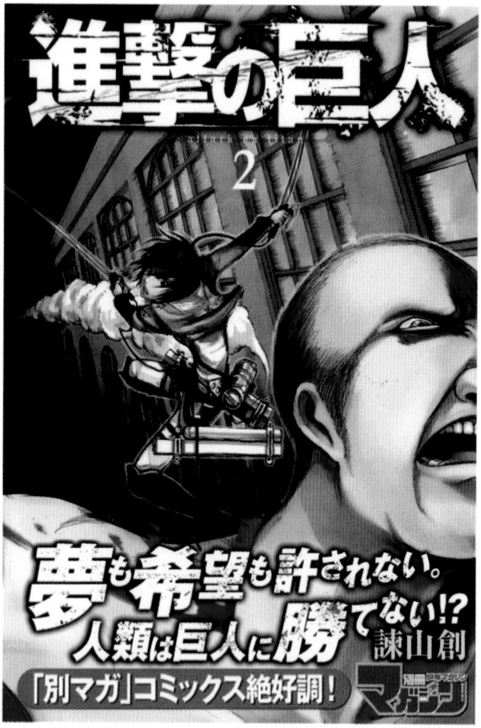
進撃の巨人
2
夢も希望も許されない。
人類は巨人に勝てない!?
諫山創
「別マガ」コミックス絶好調!

"On that day, humanity remembered the terror of being ruled, the frustration of living inside a cage."

Title in original language *Shingeki no Kyojin*
First published by Kodansha (Japan)
Creator Japanese (b.1988)
Genre Science fiction, Fantasy, Horror

As a young, aspiring *mangaka* (cartoonist), Hajime Isayama submitted his work to the editors of the best-selling comic magazine in Japan. They turned him down. Fortunately, a far less famous magazine, *Bessatsu Shonen,* was willing to publish his work. Both readers and critics quickly hailed him as the hottest newcomer, and his work soon topped the sales charts and picked up a number of major awards.

Deemed too dark and intense, and with unpolished art that was seen as lacking in mainstream appeal, his story nonetheless seems to have been exactly what the Japanese manga scene had been craving. It is a tale of desperate survival, drawn in a dramatic style with some of the most powerful small-guy-against-a-huge-enemy action scenes in manga history.

In some distant future, humans have been hunted down and eaten—almost to the point of extinction—by a race of huge, unintelligent giants that came out of nowhere. A group of humans have managed to survive the onslaught by building high castle walls around their territory, a tactic that has kept them safe for one hundred years. When the story begins, their sanctuary is breached by the sudden appearance of an even bigger giant, enabling other giants to get into the city. Amid the war for survival three teenage friends, Elen, Mikasa, and Armin, join the army to avenge the death of their families and fight for the survival of humanity. Isayama's compelling manga is filled with a sense of overwhelming threat, desperation, and fear toward an implacable, unknowable foe. **NK**

Similar reads

Berserk Kentaro Miura
Linebarrels of Iron Eiichi Shimizu and Tomohiro Shimoguchi
Neon Genesis Evangelion Yoshiyuki Sadamoto

The Wrong Place 2009

Brecht Evens

Title in original language *Ergens waar je niet wil zijn*
First published by Oogachtend (Belgium)
Creator Belgian (b.1986)
Genre Reality drama

Who is hot and who is not? That is what it is all about in *The Wrong Place*, Brecht Evens's fourth book and the first to be translated into English. The focus on popularity and late-night partying may not come as a surprise. After all, when Evens started painting this book he was still a student. Partying was very much a part of his life, and as he says himself: "I draw what I see."

Evens has a keen eye for human conversation and behavior. This is clear from the first scene in which he throws a dull party in Francis's home where everybody seems to have come because of the popular Robbie. This Robbie is elsewhere, however, at his regular disco haunt where his sex appeal and crowd-pleasing capabilities attract men and women alike. The contrast between shy Francis and extrovert Robbie is extreme, but they still turn out to become very good friends. A lot of attention is paid to the rendition of small talk, mostly about members of the opposite sex, clothing, and appearance.

Evens hardly ever uses panel borders. The dialogue is written directly on the page, with a different text color for each speaker, which makes speech balloons superfluous and allows for a colorful interplay between text and drawing. The art is spread on the page as well and varies in size. Costumes are carnivalesque, and detailed backgrounds turn a disco into an Alicelike wonderland. The exuberant use of watercolor in warm reds, blues, and greens creates a cheerful hymn to the freedom of carefree partying. Evens's book is a feast for the eye, a holiday for the mind, and a joy to read. **GM**

Bayou 2009

Jeremy Love

First published by Zuda/DC Comics (USA)
Creator American (b.1980)
Genre Fantasy
Award Glyph Award for Best Comic Story (2009)

Bayou is set in 1933 in the dreamy, Lewis Carroll–like parallel world of "Dixie," somewhere on the Mississippi Delta, a place that grew out of the spilt blood of America's Civil War. Nine-year-old Lee Wagstaff is our "Alice," a black girl and the daughter of a poor sharecropper who grows up with a fear of the bayou after being forced to retrieve the dead body of a lynched black boy from its depths.

Lee befriends a white girl named Lily, only to see her swallowed by a giant swamp creature called Bog. Lee's father is accused of Lily's disappearance, and Lee is again forced to enter this mysterious world to rescue her friend and redeem her father. On her journey she meets Bayou, a benevolent Blues-singing swamp monster tormented by memories whose meaning Lee cannot fathom. Together, they search for Lily.

Bayou had its origins in DC's web-based Zuda imprint. Its lush colors, the work of the strip's colorist Patrick Morgan, imbue it with great aesthetic appeal. You simply cannot look away. But eye candy on this scale is a double-edged sword. The art, both sumptuous and menacing, draws the eye in, only to confront readers with the disturbing realities of Lee's segregated 1930s world. Words such as "piccaninny" and "nigra" occur with enough frequency to knock readers out of their complacency. Visually the pace may seem slow and the dialogue sparse, but the art speaks volumes. *Bayou*'s panels say plenty, raising the readers' awareness of just what a comic book is capable of conveying. **BS**

The Impostor's Daughter 2009

✎ Laurie Sandell

First published by Little, Brown and Company (USA)
Creators Sandell (American, Unknown)
Genre Reality drama
Award Eisner Award nomination (2010)

The daughter of a college professor, Laurie Sandell grew up secure in the belief that her father was the smartest, handsomest, bravest dad in the world. After all, he'd been imprisoned for his political beliefs back in Argentina, survived a grenade attack, and enjoyed a brilliant teaching career at Stanford. Or had he? As she grows up, Sandell starts to wonder why her father receives mail addressed to a series of unrecognizable names, and why, when fired from his teaching job, he starts hanging around the house in his underwear—and photocopying her diary.

It's perhaps a testament to the strength of the love between Sandell and her father that not even this betrayal shakes her belief in him for long. But when she realizes he may have ruined her credit forever, she starts asking questions that expose a lot more than she bargained for. She also starts asking herself what effect have her father's inventions and half-truths had on her own relationships, especially with the opposite sex.

With *The Impostor's Daughter*, Sandell takes the skill she originally used to impress her father—funny drawings of him that she'd leave on the family credenza—and turns it into a tool for plumbing the depths of her family's identity. Each emotion is easily readable on the Sandell family's faces. The pages sing with gorgeous color and texture, supplied by supporting artist Paige Pooler. Over 245 pages, Laurie Sandell makes a compelling case that no matter what our parents tell us about themselves, it's what they don't tell us that shapes our lives. **EL**

Alpha... directions 2009

✎ Jens Harder

First published by Actes Sud/L'An 2 (France)
Creator German (b.1970)
Genre History
Award The "Audacity" Award at Angoulême (2010)

Few comic strips have such ambitious objectives as *Alpha . . .directions*, Jens Harder's literally demiurgic attempt to retell in a single book fourteen billion years of history, from the Big Bang up to the appearance of the human species in the Quaternary period. The sheer volume of research that Harder has conducted is evident. He has tried to remain as close as possible to the latest scientific knowledge in the field—although he explicitly states his subjectivity in the choices he made as to what to cut out.

Readers follow a chronological guide to the adventures of the universe, passing through each of the ages of matter, first on the scale of the cosmos and then, once the Earth forms, on that of the planet through geological time. There is an immense brew of data here, and on a vertiginous timescale, but what really captures the reader's attention is the art.

Very skilfully, in an effective two-tone color scheme that enables each period covered to be readily identified, Harder combines scientific drawings detailing aspects of paleontology, biology, chemistry, physics, and astronomy, with images of the great myths of humanity, borrowing from all iconographic traditions. Syncretic to the end, here and there he allows himself to glance at paintings, sculptures, architecture, and even the odd cartoon strip.

It is this ability to stimulate the imagination about a subject so immense that makes this impressive work so appealing. In all the 350 pages of this meta-history, humans occupy just one. **NF**

Alpha . . . directions conveys the history of the universe through multiple images. ➡

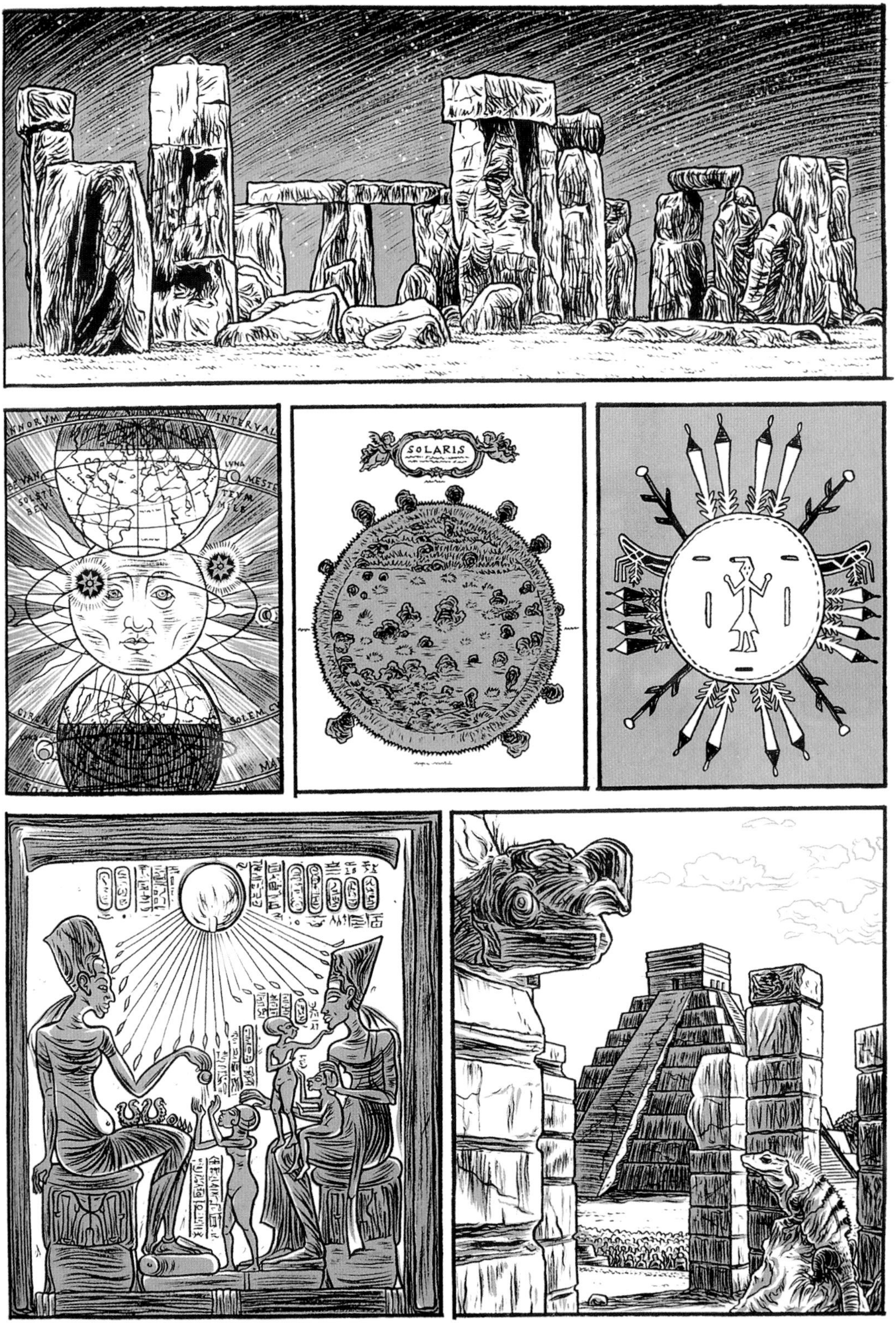
SOLARIS
INNORVM
INTERVAL
LVNA
SOLEM

Eden 2009

"Kioskerman"

First published by Editorial Sudamericana (Argentina)
Creator Pablo Holmberg (Argentinian, b.1979)
Genre Fantasy
Influenced by Tove Jansson

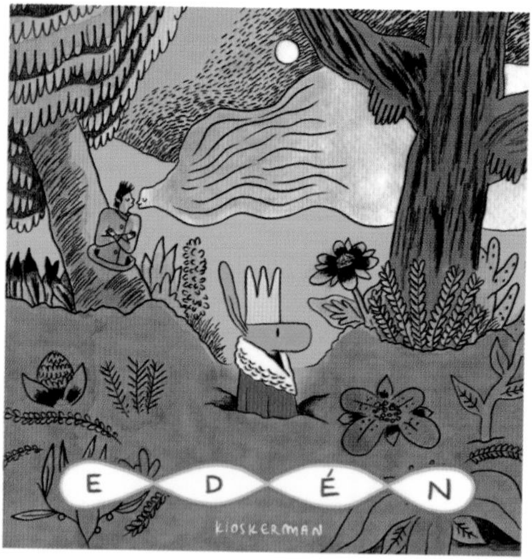
E D É N
KIOSKERMAN

"I think that when you work on a day-to-day basis, the barrier that stops us from knowing our true self starts to give up."

Pablo Holmberg

Similar reads
Curses Kevin Huizenga
Macanudo Liniers
Map of My Heart John Porcellino

What we think of as Eden is an illusion. *Eden* is, of course, also an Argentinian web comic subsequently turned into Drawn & Quarterly's first print-published book by a Latin American author, but at heart it is an illusion. What the *Eden* comic hides inside its formal classicism of one-page strips, each four panels in length, is an experimental approach to expressing what it means to be human—the doubts, the fear, the love, all the inexplicable things. It is as if J. R. R. Tolkien, with his world-creating romanticism and capacity for giving life and feelings to nature, were somehow merged with the Frank King of *Gasoline Alley*, with his subtle, yet discernible autobiographical surrealism. The result is the most basic, powerfully human comic.

Readers follow Kioskerman's diminutive character, the Forest King, as he talks to the moon and wanders his kingdom. Kioskerman compresses a lot into this epic little volume on both being alive and comic books themselves, and he does so in a quiet, subtle, poetic way. At first glance the art appears to be drawn in a simple, imperfect style, but Kioskerman's use of space and silence is a mark of his precision-engineered cartooning. In fact, hundreds of small references to various aspects of comic book history pepper each and every one of his vignettes. Far from being simple, this is clearly a work of great knowledge and passion.

The *Eden* tales may seem familiar but that perception is also an illusion, although the roots of the narratives can be traced to the wild imaginings of primal folklore. The Forest King cannot be blamed for his land filled with anthrophomorphic entities; that emotional wilderness is just Kioskerman jumping into the void while expressing his feelings.

Eden may be set in a tiny and dreamlike paradise but the painful realities of our day-to-day existence are always felt and never forgotten. **JMD**

Walking the Dog 2009

David Hughes

David Hughes is an acclaimed illustrator's illustrator, but his health is suffering due to his sedentary occupation, drinking, and high blood pressure. The best medicine, prescribed by his doctor and bought by his wife, is a "whft"—a wire-haired fox terrier named Dexter. For this maverick 304-page, semiautobiographical rumination, Hughes draws himself as a Jacques Tati-like grouch, bag of poop held daintily between his fingers, whose dog-walking forces him to socialize with complete strangers.

Hughes's self-representations keep slipping too, as walking lets his mind meander back to his memories, some of which are by turns disturbing and funny. On Dexter's first excursion to Brighton, Hughes spots himself as a boy named William (his second name) lost on the pier. He then spots his anxious father asking "Have you seen my little Willie?", in the manner of a saucy seaside postcard by Donald McGill.

The darker flashbacks soon accumulate as well: a classmate strangled by his own mother with a school tie; a gay molestation at summer camp; the local landlord's suicide; a brutal assault on a Polish immigrant; a chilling Ouija seance. Death is never more than a dog walk away, it seems.

There is little comfort in Hughes's idealized alter ego John Crawford, a deranged hit man whose next contract may be Hughes's wife. Yet despite this grim undertow, Hughes takes a dogged pleasure in both the absurd and in toilet humor, from barrages of farts to Hughes's own stool samples, produced for his doctor. Whether in neat manuscript or inky typewriting, photo-collages, dense comics, or whole-page pictures, Hughes modulates his precise pencilings; hard to fragile, sharp to smudgy, evidence of the hand and mind behind them, which, like Paul Klee, are making "a line go for a walk." **PG**

First published by Jonathan Cape (UK)
Creator British (b.1947)
Genre Fantasy, Autobiography
Influenced by Arthur Sarnoff

WALKING
THE
DOG
AUTHOR: DAVID HUGHES:

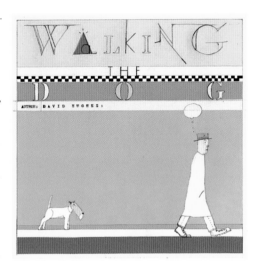

"He turns around with a quizzical, slightly bemused look and I brandish the Colt .45 Magnum Python Revolver."

Similar reads
Drawings? David Hughes
Duncan the Wonder Dog Adam Hines
Othello by William Shakespeare David Hughes

Footnotes in Gaza 2009

✏️ Joe Sacco

First published by Metropolitan Books (USA)
Creator Maltese-American (b.1960)
Genre Reality drama
Award The Ridenhour Book Prize (2010)

The foremost practitioner of graphic journalism, a growing genre of comics as reportage, *Footnotes in Gaza* is perhaps Joe Sacco's most ambitious work. The book was inspired by a reference made by Noam Chomsky to the killing of Palestinian civilians by the Israeli Defense Forces (IDF) in the town of Khan Younis in 1956. Sacco's research unearths details of another incident in the neighboring town of Rafah in which 111 Palestinians were killed by the IDF. Such incidents, buried deep in a UN report, form footnotes to "a forgotten war," a reference to the postimperial fiasco that was the Suez conflict. *Footnotes in Gaza* is divided between accounts from Khan Younis and those from Rafah, the latter forming the longer section in the book.

Sacco embeds himself within the story; we follow him as he conducts his research, collecting oral testimony and visiting sites, and it is this investigative process that forms the narrative. He remains ever-present even as he foregrounds eyewitness accounts, eyes hidden behind his signature glasses, his own features ironically caricatured as a counterpoint to the more realistic depictions of the speakers who often gaze directly at the reader, breaking the fourth wall.

Sacco's style is well established, drawing on the influence of underground comix and New Journalism, taking the shock value of the former and the reflexive narration of the latter, to create a hybrid of Robert Crumb and Michael Herr. Yet Sacco adds more—copious footnotes that reinforce the graphic novel's title and underline the research that went into it. **TV**

Map of My Heart 2009

✏️ John Porcellino

First published by Drawn & Quarterly (Canada)
Creator American (b.1968)
Genre Reality drama
Influenced by *Mark Trail*

John Porcellino has been self-publishing his photocopied *King-Cat Comics and Stories* since 1989. Unlike many artists for whom fanzines were just a stepping stone to bigger things, Porcellino has doggedly persisted producing *King-Cat,* and although collections of his work have been published, he still considers his fanzine the "real" work, of which collections can only be incomplete reflections.

Map of My Heart is the closest readers can come to actually experiencing *King-Cat* in a collected form as it is a compilation of issues #51 to #61. Since some of the material from those fanzines had already been collected into a book, some issues are incomplete, but all have their covers, editorial pages, and readers' pages, and there are still plenty of comic strips.

Most of Porcellino's comics are either recollections of childhood and teenage memories or vignettes from his adult life. There are also the "Zen stories," anecdotes from the life of a Zen monk, which reflect Porcellino's personal interest in Buddhism. *Map of My Heart* covers some important periods in his life, starting with Porcellino living in Denver with his wife, then moving back to his native Illinois after his divorce. All through these years he was battling with depression and a number of other health problems.

Porcellino tells of very simple events in a clear and straightforward fashion. His style has the childlike simplicity and clarity of a diagram, and its sparseness gives his comics a Zenlike quality that is totally appropriate to his subjects. **J-PJ**

The Art of Flying 2009

Antonio Altarriba "Kim"

Title in original language *El Arte de Volar*
First published by Edicions de Ponent (Spain)
Creators Altarriba (Spanish, b.1952); Joaquim Aubert (Spanish, b.1942) **Genre** Biography

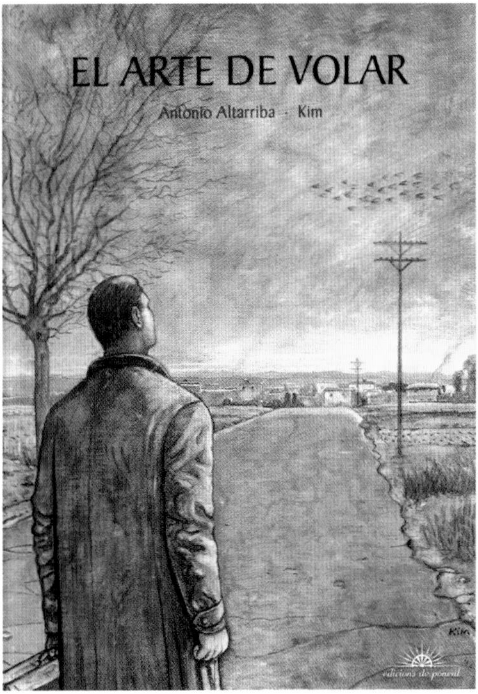
EL ARTE DE VOLAR
Antonio Altarriba · Kim
Kim
edicions de ponent

Published as a 208-page graphic novel, this story tells the real-life tale of Antonio Altarriba Sr., the father of the writer, and is divided into four parts that cover: the protagonist's youth during the 1920s in poverty-stricken rural Spain; his participation in the Spanish Civil War, where he fought for the Republican side, and his later exile to France after Franco's triumph; his return to Francoist Spain in the late 1940s, and his eventual marriage, birth of his son, and his final years after Franco's death and Spain's return to democracy in an old people's home. In spite of all the hardships suffered throughout his life, Altarriba Sr. never gave up hope, always trying to learn to "fly" with the wings of illusion up to the very last moment of his life. His story could be the chronicle of many Spaniards who lived through those years, with all of their dreams and frustrations. The younger Altarriba's poignant script is enhanced by Kim's half-realistic, half-cartoony artwork, done in black-and-white wash, which took him four years to complete, and whose richness of details—none of them superfluous—allows the reader to dive into the action. The authors succeed in creating a narrative that, despite its density, remains accessible to readers, while also being a valuable piece of documentation of twentieth-century Spain.

Regarded as an instant classic, and one of Spain's major contributions to the graphic novel field, *The Art of Flying* has won several awards, including the Premio Nacional de Comic in 2009, granted by the Spanish Ministry of Culture. **AMo**

"We are beside a masterwork which recovers the story of the Spanish people and which will make history."

Antonio Martín Martínez, comics historian

Similar reads

Arrugas (*Wrinkles*) Paco Roca
El invierno del dibujante (*Winter Cartoonist*) Paco Roca
Miguel: 15 años en la calle (*Miguel: 15 years on the Street*) Miguel Fuster

Walking with Samuel 2009

✐✐ Tommi Musturi

Title in original language *Samuelin matkassa*
First published by Huuda Huuda (Finland)
Creator Finnish (b.1975)
Genre Fantasy

It is said that we live in a visual world, yet reading wordless comics often reveals how visually illiterate we are. It can take considerably more effort to decipher narratives constructed only of pictures than those accompanied and explained by text. The fact that the wordless comic book *Walking with Samuel* (*Samuelin matkassa*) is easy to follow demonstrates a great deal about the skill of its creator, Tommi Musturi.

The stories center on a white, expressionless humanoid called Samuel, and take place in a psychedelically colorful dreamworld, a garden paradise. Samuel leaves for the gray, dull, and sinful city, taking his colorful rainbows with him. Musturi's narrative resembles a stream of consciousness and his surreal stories are drawn in bright colors. Sometimes events slightly contradict those related in an earlier tale, but the lack of internal narrative cohesion heightens the dreamlike quality of the work.

Artistic creation is a central theme of the book. Samuel himself appears to be a dispenser of color on several occasions. He crafts his own image, then burns it to ashes. At one point, the finger of God—or the artist—even pounds Samuel's round figure into a cubist form. With these events Musturi is taking an ironic, even mocking view of making art. He acknowledges the harshness of the world, in which art is often swept aside, but opposes it in the book's abundantly visual style. The artist's true strength, however, lies in not being obvious—he leaves plenty of space for interpretation by the reader. **HR**

Stitches 2009

✐✐ David Small

First published by W. W. Norton & Co. (USA)
Creator American (b.1945)
Genre Reality drama
Influenced by Anton Chekov

Curses and prayers abound in this angry, unforgettable memoir, the first graphic novel by children's book illustrator David Small. The pages, drawn in ink wash and black and white, evoke the cinematic conventions—camera angles, sweeps, and transitions—of Ingmar Bergman or Roman Polanski.

The first words, "Mama had her little cough," are chilling. Her nonverbal language typifies the silence and denial in a home with many closeted skeletons. At fourteen, Small undergoes a routine operation that reduces his voice to a whisper. This and subsequent shocking revelations comprise the rest of the narrative.

Small's mastery of the form is assured. Dreams pass into reality seamlessly, and his childhood retreat into his art is shown literally and beautifully. In a striking series of transition pages, the stitches in his neck morph into a staircase his mother ascends to write a letter—a letter he later finds by chance. He learns that he has had cancer and was expected to die. Furthermore, treatments he had received from his radiologist father were the cause of the illness.

Later, in therapy, his psychiatrist is portrayed as the White Rabbit, referencing Small's early love of *Alice in Wonderland*, the world of imagination that was the only sanctuary from his family's dysfunction. It is to Small's credit that he does not reduce his parents to monsters, but shows great understanding of their own struggles. *Stitches* is the story of a child who loses his voice, and finds it again in his ability to draw. And as Small clearly knows, drawing well is the best revenge. **TRL**

David Small's use of a nine-panel grid gives a steady pace to the action it displays. ➡

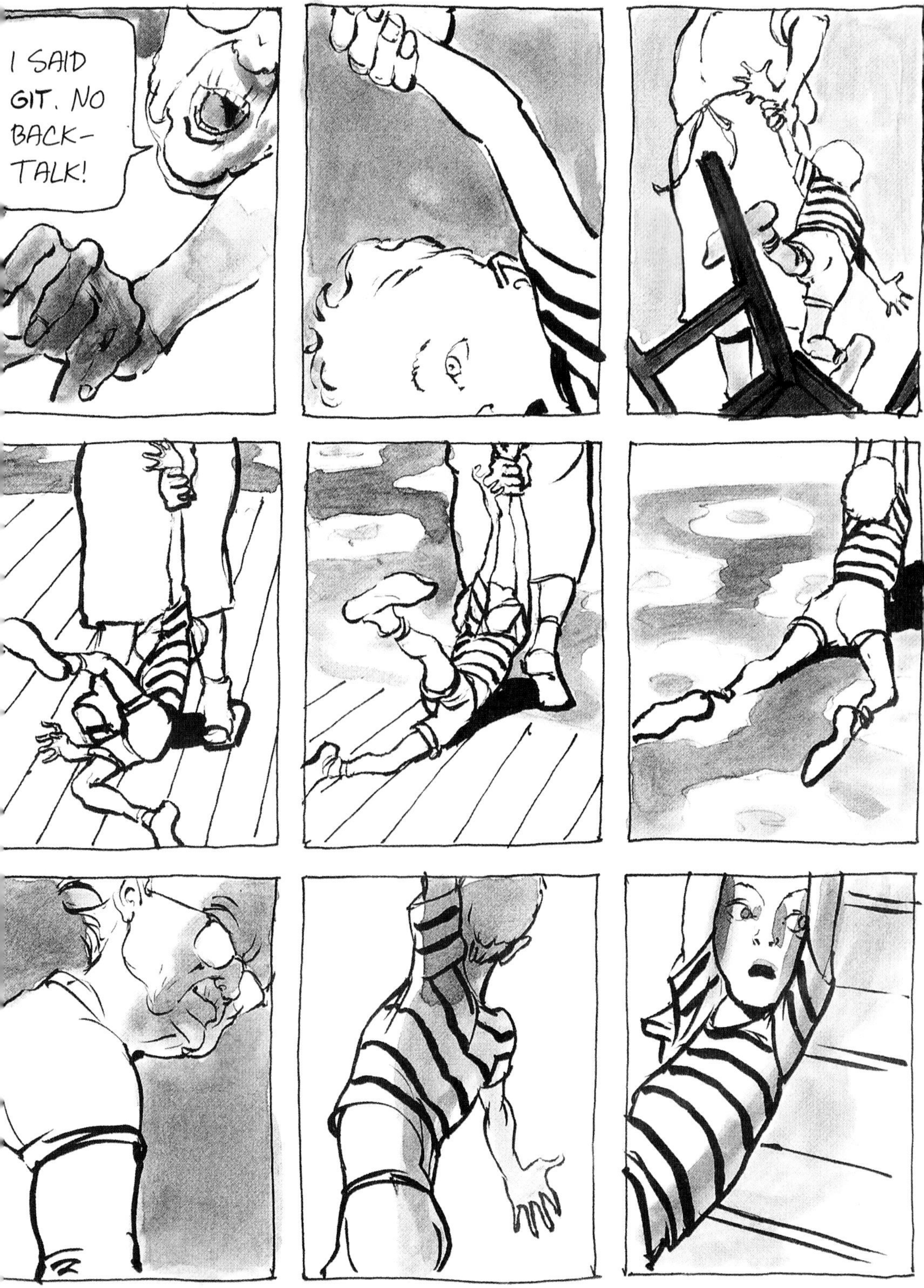
I SAID GIT. NO BACK-TALK!

Temperance 2009

Cathy Malkasian

First published by Fantagraphics Books (USA)
Creator American (b.1959)
Genre Fantasy
Influenced by Mort Drucker and Don Martin

TEMPERANCE
CATHY MALKASIAN

Similar reads
Castle Waiting Linda Medley
Cerebus: High Society Dave Sim
Dungeon Joann Sfar and Lewis Trondheim
Percy Gloom Cathy Malkasian
The Lost Colony Grady Klein

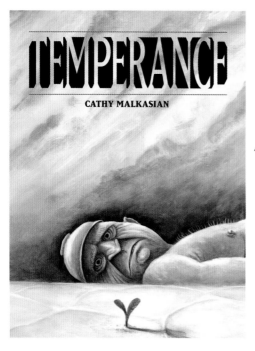

Temperance weaves a quirky, turbulent fantasy about two daughters who are victims of their father's cruelties and fear-mongering. Radiant, ethereal Peggy insists that their "Pa" is nobody's father and has "torn us all apart," whereas drowsy Minerva is too afraid to disbelieve his tales of a terrible looming enemy. The paternal ax first cuts down a trembling tree and then chops off the lower leg of Lester, a young man, who rescues Peggy from some unwanted paternal attentions. In the fight, Lester also loses his memory, so Pa permits Minerva to keep him and "fix" him as her husband. Tree and man, felled together, bond further as Lester's peg leg is carved from the trunk and becomes our narrator. Can his new leg's rings help him remember?

"It must have been my knot . . . a swirl in my grain that looked like sympathy."

From a wooden doll that springs to life in a medieval-like castle, Cathy Malkasian revitalizes familiar storybook tropes, blending them with Cold War–style paranoia and siege mentality. Minerva becomes her people's leader, sealing them off from a nonexistent enemy within the city of Blessedbowl, a vast ship built of stone. Daily she fabricates reports from her vanished father to brainwash the citizens into unquestioning loyalty, and fills her husband Lester's head with tales of his glorious past as a war hero.

Malkasian draws in tremulous pencil tinted in shades of gray, with sepia tones denoting the truth invading Lester's dreams. An acclaimed animator, Malkasian repeats characters within a single frame to suggest motion or time passing. *Temperance* confounds fairy-tale expectations with a disturbing parable about the power of propaganda, memories, and lies. **PG**

Likewise 2009

Ariel Schrag

"My memories of my teen years are definitely all intermingled with images from the comic . . . I've ended up with a very warped, fictionalized version of my life," acknowledges Ariel Schrag, creator of acclaimed chronicles of her time at Berkeley High School in California. As befits the last and most mature book of the series, *Likewise* is stylistically the most sophisticated, self-consciously aware of its own production, a work of art about living and a life becoming art. It reflects on the construction of memory and thus the process of creating an autobiography. Schrag was reading James Joyce's *Ulysses* as she wrote *Likewise*, and she combines this highbrow reference within a comic homage that is conceptually and experientially challenging for both

> ## "Well, so like, if you HAD to say why you're gay, what would your answer be?"

artist and reader. She introduces the use of stream of consciousness and fluctuating visual styles to distinguish differing timescales.

Schrag later references her machinery of memory: the tape recorder, camera, notebook, and computer she used at the time. This will-to-recall almost paralyzes her, as she confesses: "The methods in which I recorded the present became more relevant than reality."

When you've read Schrag's work, you feel that you know her intimately: you've seen her on the toilet, pine painfully over an ex, and research the scientific reasons for lesbianism. But even she grew exhausted of living within her own reality comic. Of the final panels in *Likewise,* Schrag says: "Senior year is over and Ariel finally doesn't have to keep recording her life for everyone to read. For the first time, in a long time, she experiences a private moment." **SL**

First published by Slave Labor Graphics (USA)
Creator American (b.1979)
Genre Autobiography
Award LAMBDA Literary Award nominee (2010)

"A scathing and meticulously documented autobiographical triumph." —Alison Bechdel, author of *Fun Home*

LIKEWISE

The High School Comic Chronicles of

ARIEL SCHRAG

Author of **Potential**

Similar reads

Awkward Ariel Schrag
Dykes to Watch Out For Alison Bechdel
Potential Ariel Schrag
Stuck in the Middle: 17 Comics from an Unpleasant Age edited by Ariel Schrag

Special Exits 2010

✎✎ Joyce Farmer

First published by Fantagraphics Books (USA)
Creator American (b.1938)
Genre Reality drama
Award National Cartoonists' Award nominee (2010)

A work of heartbreaking honesty from one of the pioneers of underground cartooning, Joyce Farmer's *Special Exits* tells the story of Lars and Rachel, two older people struggling to maintain their independence in the face of worsening illness. Based on Farmer's own experiences of caring for her parents, *Special Exits* tells a story that is both personally and socially relevant.

Readers meet Lars, a former engineer, who is caring for Rachel, his wife of many years. Rachel has gone blind because of glaucoma. Laura, Lars's daughter, acts as their advocate in the wider world and generally tries to lend a hand. Together they navigate a world of Meals on Wheels, waiting lists, doctor's appointments, and even the occasional riot. We hear Lars and Rachel's stories of childhood, of meeting each other, and of disagreements that still rankle decades on. We watch as life becomes more difficult for them—and while we're cheering them on, we know that their time is drawing to a close. Thirteen years in the making, this book's ink drawings vibrate with detail, convincingly conjuring the claustrophobic but loving world of an elderly couple in worsening circumstances. *Special Exits* can be emotionally wrenching at times, but Farmer has clearly decided that her readers deserve the truth.

One of a generation of women cartoonists who explored topics such as sex and abortion unflinchingly, Farmer has a long history of making an impact with words and pictures. *Special Exits* is a frank depiction of the aging process, as well as a gentle reminder to never take the people we love for granted. **EL**

Psychiatric Tales 2010

✎✎ Darryl Cunningham

First published by Blank Slate Books (UK)
Creator British (b.1960)
Genre Autobiography
Influenced by Paul Grist

A former health care assistant in an acute psychiatric ward, Yorkshireman Darryl Cunningham began recording his experiences of working with sufferers of depression, dementia, self-harm, schizophrenia, and other mental illnesses online. His demanding job took its toll, not just physically, but also from coping with its impact on his sensitive spirit.

Carers care, and can rarely avoid being affected, and that is certainly true for Cunningham and his feelings of guilt that he failed to prevent the two suicides he witnessed at work. In stark graphics, he wants to destigmatize the unsettling, sometimes harrowing nature of mental disorders by having readers view them through his eyes. The circular lenses of his glasses reappear as a motif threaded through these short stories, their shape echoed in bicycle wheels, handcuffs, and finally in a high-contrast photo of the bespectacled author himself. Looking out at us he affirms, "I redeemed myself in my own eyes."

Psychiatric Tales comes with a touching epiphany in the closing chapter, "How I Lived Again." Using himself as his last case study, Cunningham discloses that the four-year break from creating these stories was due to his own severe depression after having to drop a demanding nurse training course with only one year to go. In his case, "with glacial slowness," he found crafting these internet comics and the encouragement they generated brought him a measure of self-worth. Cunningham's survival through his art suggests that one's means to recovery may be creativity itself. **PG**

Today Is the Last Day of the Rest of Your Life 2010

Ulli Lust

Title in original language *Heute ist der letzte tag vom rest deines lebens*
First published by Avant (Germany)
Creator Austrian (b.1967) **Genre** Autobiography

Today Is the Last Day of the Rest of Your Life starts with a dream, a dream that inspired seventeen-year-old Ulli Lust and her female friend to leave Austria for Italy to spend the winter in the milder Mediterranean climate. But their dream turned into a nightmare.

Originally an autobiographical web comic, Lust's graphic narrative is the arena in which she describes, quite openly and with relentless candor, her adventurous travels in 1984. The two young punks hitchhiked to Sicily without passports, with just a little money and a sleeping bag as luggage. Although they hit rock-bottom more than once, they held on to the freedom of their Italian dream far from the parental or social restrictions they would have suffered back home. However, the reality Lust and her friend experienced was far from rosy. Although the two girls were taken under the wing of other punks and homeless people when they stopped in Rome, their naivety was taken advantage of, and they were deceived, lied to, and robbed. In addition, they also had to deal with the bigoted, macho society of Italy at every turn.

While her friend was able to enjoy her sexuality freely, Lust was sadly raped. She compares the experience to running a gauntlet, especially when she tried to avoid the looks of the men around her. With time, though, her fear turned into strength. Lust grew more self-confident and learned to assert herself, whether confronting drug dealers and mafiosi or in crafting a 450-page autobiographical comic. **MS**

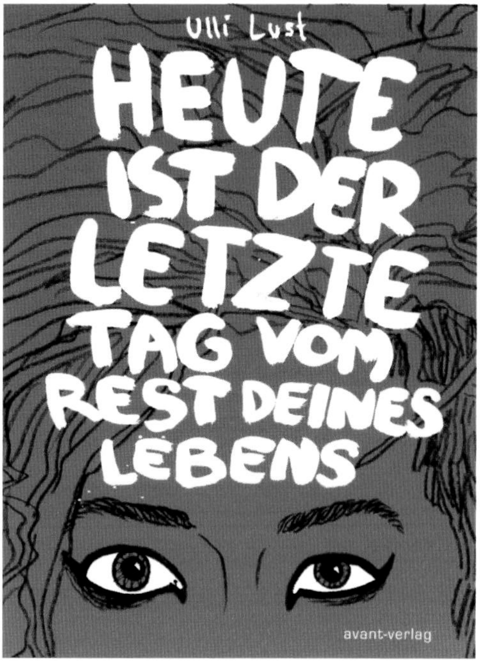
Ulli Lust
HEUTE IST DER LETZTE TAG VOM REST DEINES LEBENS
avant-verlag

"This comic is a sensation. Not because it has so many pages, but because Ulli Lust tells a story which is second to none."

Andreas Platthaus, *Frankfurter Allgemeine Zeitung*

Similar reads

Alltagsspionage Monogatari
Cargo Jens Harder
Fashionvictims Ulli Lust
L'Autoroute du Soleil Baru

Hair Shirt 2010

🖊🖊 Patrick McEown

First published by Éditions Gallimard (France)
Creator Canadian (b.1968)
Genre Romance
Influenced by Matt Wagner

John is an introspective soul, fractured by the death years before of Chris, a friend from whom he'd drifted away. He buries his problems rather than confronting them, and is plagued by disturbing dreams of a sinister dog. A chance meeting reunites John and Naomi, Chris's sister, who had moved away with her family after her brother's death, but is now studying at a nearby university. Prior to Chris's death the pair had grown closer, but had never actually embarked on a relationship. Both grasp their second chance, but despite their happy memories of childhood, they are both equally tormented by their shared past. All goes well to begin with, but each has their secrets, and incidents from their past accrue additional meaning when viewed from an adult's perspective.

The career path to *Hair Shirt* is an eccentric one for Patrick McEown, starting with his own guilty secret: ghastly fantasy comics produced when he was eighteen. He progressed to work on an award-winning comics series, after which he turned his hand to illustration work for both children's and adult magazines, animation storyboarding for superhero cartoons, and far more personal strips contributed to anthology titles.

The art of this disturbing story draws on the lumpy style of Dave Cooper. During the more surreal sequences, characters appear a mere panel away from becoming Edvard Munch's *The Scream*. *Hair Shirt* is not a pleasant read at times, and with such material created so convincingly, it's hard to resist asking how much of it is autobiographical. **FP**

Market Day 2010

🖊🖊 James Sturm

First published by Drawn & Quarterly (Canada)
Creator American (b.1965)
Genre Political fable
Award Ignatz Award for Outstanding Graphic Novel (2010)

As the title suggests, *Market Day* narrates a single day in the life of a rug-maker named Mendleman. One morning he goes to the market, where he tries to sell his goods, returning the next day a changed man.

Reminiscent of early twentieth century *Mitteleuropa* (central European) literature, and once again exploring Ashkenazic Jewishness, Sturm is not preoccupied here with ethnical-political contrasts or historical examination, but more with human nature. If there is a contrast, it is at an economic level, juxtaposing waning craftsmanship with the emergence of commodity capitalism and all the upheaval that brings to the fabric of society.

Mendleman is a man who attentively observes the world around him, from the soothing dawning sun on the still-dark horizon to the bustling narrow streets of the city center. All is translatable by his hands into rug patterns. Superficially he may be an artisan, but at heart he is an artist. One day before his first child is born, Mendleman finds he can no longer sell his rugs. "What is to be done?" seems to be the hovering question that sends him into a maelstrom of painful reflections and recollections, inner conflicts, and even fantasies of escapism, turning Mendleman into an emotional Sisyphus. But will he emerge a better man?

Sturm plunders the spectrum of tools that comics have to offer perfectly, using them effectively and knowingly without unnecessary fanfare. Many of these serene pages are almost interludes, conveying some of the most soothing and meditative moments in comic book history. **PM**

The way Sturm bleeds the landscape across the panels gives a sense of the passage of time. ➡

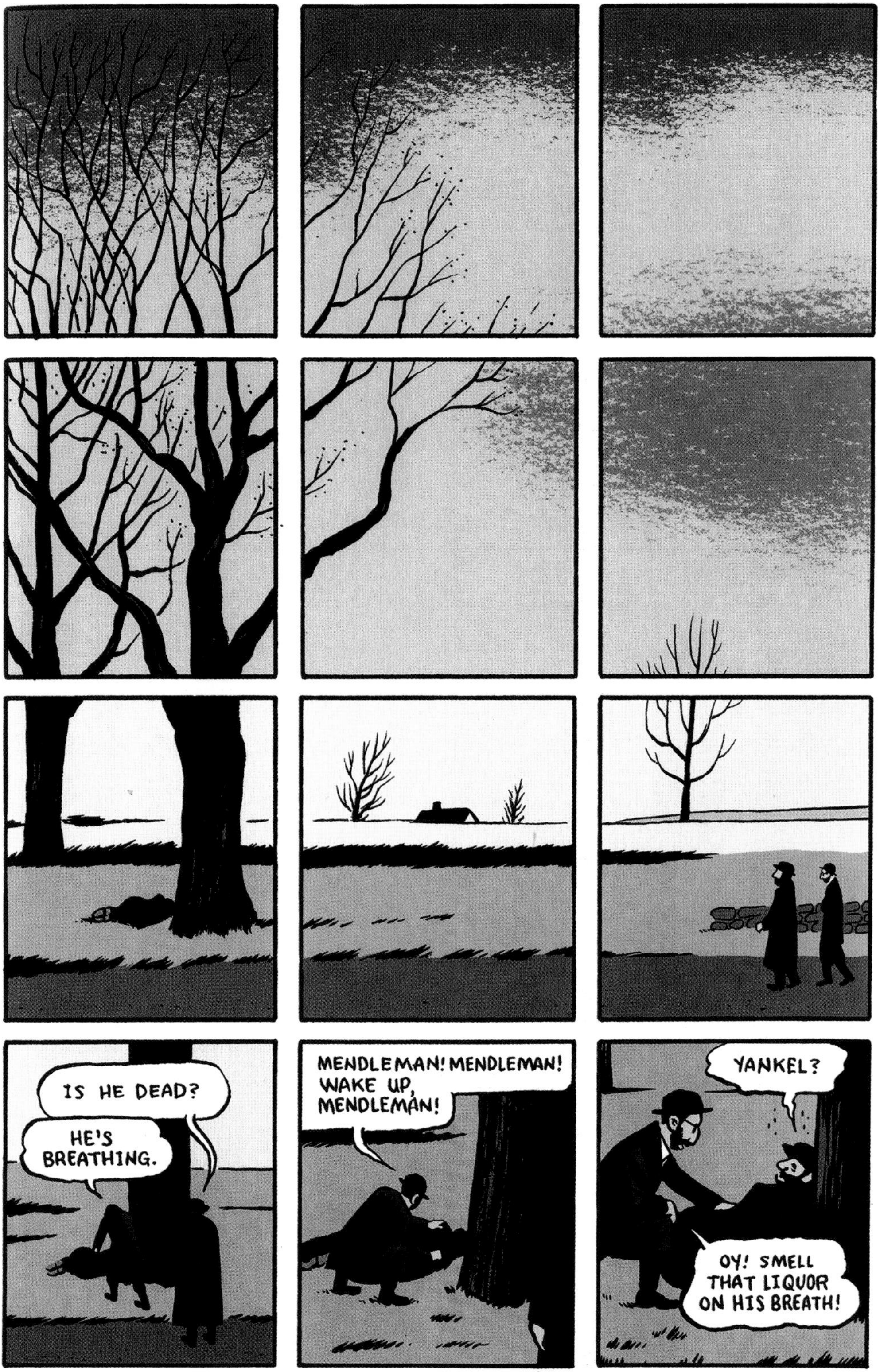
IS HE DEAD?
HE'S BREATHING.
MENDLEMAN! MENDLEMAN! WAKE UP, MENDLEMAN!
YANKEL?
OY! SMELL THAT LIQUOR ON HIS BREATH!

Baby's in Black 2010

Arne Bellstorf

First published by Reprodukt (Germany)
Creator German (b.1979)
Genre Reality drama
Award ICOM Independent Comic Prize (2006)

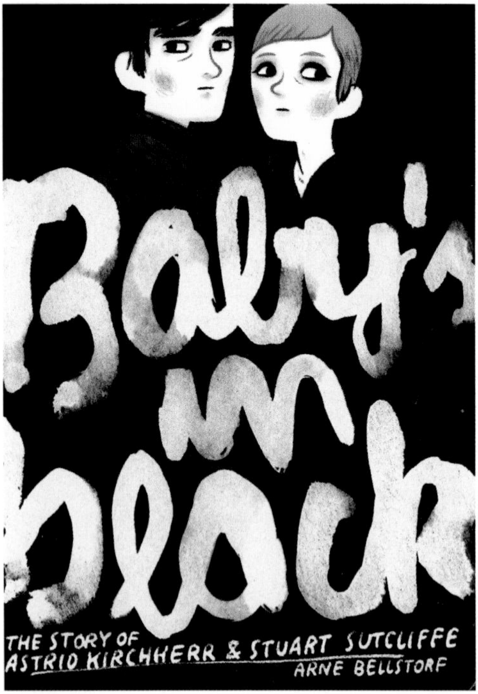
Baby's in black
THE STORY OF ASTRID KIRCHHERR & STUART SUTCLIFFE
ARNE BELLSTORF

Similar reads

Acht, neun, zehn Arne Bellstorf
Insekt Sascha Hommer
Liebe schaut weg Line Hoven
Orang Comic-Anthologie
Wandering Ghost Moki

Arne Bellstorf's comic book *Baby's in Black* is set in the 1960s and centers on the relationship between German photographer Astrid Kirchherr and Stuart Sutcliffe, the British painter and first bass player of The Beatles. Their love flourished during the Liverpool group's early performances in Hamburg before they became the world-famous band everyone knows today.

Sutcliffe was the fifth Beatle. At that time The Beatles were a typical rock 'n' roll band, performing every evening in Hamburg's St. Pauli district. Bellstorff searches for clues to discover how the group emerged out of various youth subcultures of the period. Extensive interviews with Astrid Kirchherr were the starting point for this sensitive and perceptive comic. Kirchherr had photographed The Beatles when they were still in their early period, which is reflected in their hairstyles and clothing. This was shortly before they adopted their famous haircut and started their rise to legendary fame and commercial success.

"He's got something . . . something different to the others . . . I just wish he'd take off those sunglasses."

Together with her former boyfriend Klaus Voormann, who years later designed the celebrated *Revolver* album cover, Kirchherr had stumbled upon the band in the sweaty clubs of Hamburg in 1960 and found themselves on the brink of a completely new musical world. As style icons The Beatles would have a considerable influence on a whole generation. Bellstorf knows every detail of the history of the Fab Four, but he is also a professional and carried out exhaustive research before starting work on *Baby's in Black*. Using stylized black-and-white drawings he tells the brief and tragic love story of Kirchherr and Sutcliffe. **MS**

Duncan the Wonder Dog 2010

Adam Hines

Hugh Lofting's *Doctor Dollittle* asked us to imagine "If we could talk to the animals," but what would we honestly say to each other, and how would we react when they start answering back? In his ambitious 400-page debut, Adam Hines explores the complex connections and questions raised by interspecies relations, whether as pets, food, performers, partners, or fellow citizens.

A cattle farmer en route to the slaughterhouse berates an injured cow who "breaks the rules" and starts quizzing him about the building where he saw "our prints . . . going in . . . But I didn't see any . . . going out." In turn, the farmer's trip to the abattoir disturbs his dog Clementine, who asks where beef comes from. Later, left to mind their baby daughter, Clementine apparently sits on the child's face to stop her crying. Readers are privy to further extraordinary conversations: a circus tiger and a monkey's philosophical discussion; a fight between apes and a "perv" filmmaker wanting to record their mating; a cat scolding her owner for not looking after an ailing dog. Adept at subtle, slow, unfolding tales, Hines avoids explicit depictions of humans' oppression of animals. He knows readers will quickly grasp their nonstatus in our society and how this polarizes reactions: from human politician Aaron Vollmann's maneuvers to impose controls on animals, through Voltaire, an enlightened mandrill in a relationship with a woman seeking mediation, to Pompeii, a psychotic macaque monkey whose militant group masterminds bombings and kidnappings. But, hang on, where is Duncan the Wonder Dog? Hines promises eight more volumes to answer that question. **PG**

"The poorest, most pathetic humans live like gods compared to any animal!"

First published by AdHouse Books (USA)
Creator American (b.1984)
Genre Political fable
Award Los Angeles Times Book Prize (2010)

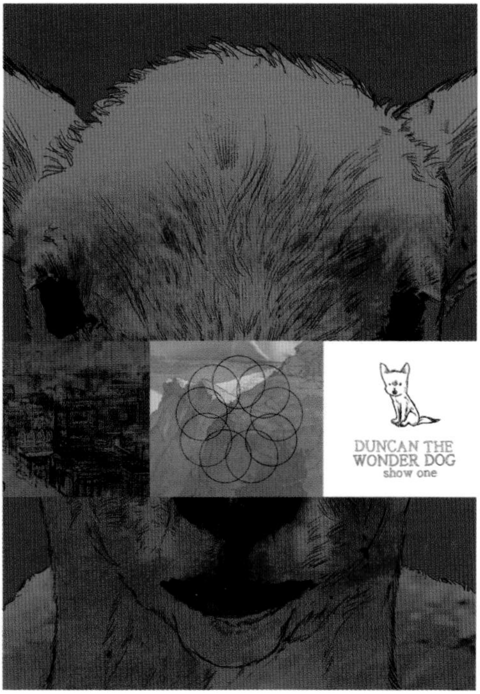
DUNCAN THE
WONDER DOG
show one

Similar reads

Children of the Sea Daisuke Igarashi
Pride of Baghdad Brian K. Vaughan and Niko Henrichon
Puma Blues Michael Zulli
True Swamp Jon Lewis
We3 Grant Morrison and Frank Quitely

Magic Mirror 2010

✐✐ Ed Pinsent

First published by Eibonvale Press (UK)
Creator British (b.1960)
Genre Fantasy
Influenced by Thomas Hardy and M. R. James

Ed Pinsent emerged on the British small-press scene in the early 1980s, and this book collects works going back as far as the mid-1990s, when he left comics to pursue an interest in electronic music, producing the magazine *The Sound Projector*. Pinsent's comics have a mythic quality involving elementary forces to which Pinsent gives fanciful humanlike appearance.

Around half of the book is made up of short stories or rather, as described in the contents page, "Tales, poems and fables," some written by Denny Derbyshire. They are in turn wistful, as with "The Last Eskimo," larger than life, as in the "Astorial Anecdotes," which takes place in a hotel that seems to contain the whole world, or verge on the sinister, as with "Ioren and Marja," a tale about a curse striking a couple through their child.

The rest of the book contains stories featuring Pinsent's recurring character Windy Wilberforce, including his long narrative "The Saga of the Scroll." Windy is a blusterous character, a linguist who goes around the world helping people. His stories evolve from whimsical adventures into more mythical sagas, where religion and philosophy seem to be the main subjects, although shrouded in the artist's strange and poetic storytelling. Pinsent tantalizes the reader with glimpses of faraway lands that appear to exist beyond space and time. "The Saga of the Scroll" itself is a symbolic tale that takes hero Windy and friend Harry Excess to different times and lands where they are faced with four enemies who represent the evils of the world. **J-PJ**

La Faille 2010

✐ Carlos Sampayo ✐ Oscar Zárate

First published by Futuropolis (France)
Creators Sampayo (Argentinian, b.1943);
Zárate (Argentinian, b.1942)
Genre Drama, Satire

In the slightly distorted funhouse mirror of *La Faille*, today's London is cracking up, physically and mentally. Everywhere cracks are spreading across buildings, even within the Houses of Parliament themselves. Could these widening faultlines be caused by renewed terrorist attacks? Or by the delayed effects from the Blitz? Or are they symptoms of a fundamental fear of the city finally collapsing? Posters reassure citizens that "We are watching you (for your happiness)," and yet, despite London having the most surveillance cameras in the world, their efficiency proves debatable against threats by everyone from the Afghans to "the Sioux, the Welsh, the fishermen, or perhaps the Norwegian Mafia." Cracks are also appearing in our protagonists' gradually intertwined lives. Bomb specialist Peter Greene must trace the supplier of Titadine explosives from a fresh attack. Reality TV star Helen Rosen must save her show *Your Problem Is Our Problem* from falling ratings. When Jeremy McPhee applies to Rosen's show to raise £15,000 for plastic surgery to give him the face God denied him, he becomes an overnight celebrity. Money pours in, but cynical television executives postpone paying him to maximize their viewing figures. Growing desperate, Jeremy then orders a suspicious package.

For this satire of twenty-first century absurdity, Zárate brings a caustic sting to his watercolor caricatures, and an outsider's insight into what makes London tick. He has found his ideal cocreator in fellow Argentinian exile Carlos Sampayo, two friends hitting their prime and falling in love again with making comics. **PG**

Forget Sorrow: An Ancestral Tale 2010

Belle Yang

First published by W. W. Norton & Co. (USA)
Creator Taiwanese-American (b.1960)
Genre Reality drama
Influenced by Marjane Satrapi

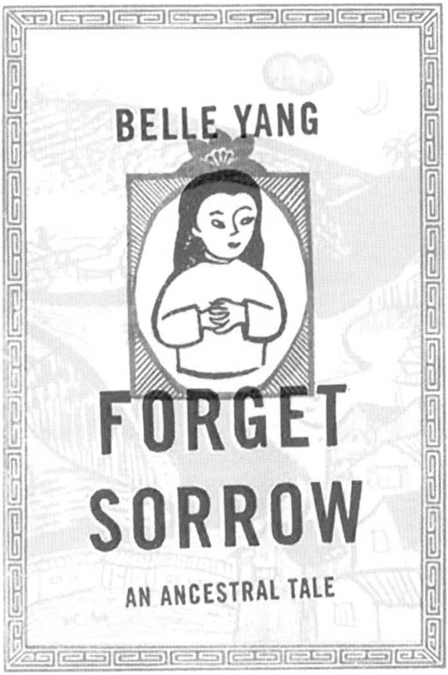
BELLE YANG
FORGET SORROW
AN ANCESTRAL TALE

The generational gap is more of a generational chasm between Belle Yang, born in Taiwan but raised in the United States, and her mainland Chinese parents. When her boyfriend turns into an abusive stalker, Yang is forced to take refuge in the family home. She is used to being a free-spirited, independent Westernized woman, but with nowhere else to go, she cautiously reconnects to her Old World Chinese father, Baba, who wants her to understand more about his own grandfather's ancestry in Manchuria.

Forget Sorrow illuminates the tides of early twentieth-century Chinese history, which swept over the House of Yang, from warlord battles and the Japanese occupation to the Soviet invasion and civil war. In successive generations, parallel tensions emerge between parents and their children over duties and desires, as bonds are stretched sometimes to breaking point.

Coming fresh to graphic novels from making illustrated books for adults and children, Yang evokes the Chinese soul, capturing its phraseologies and philosophies. She varies her brushstrokes, from bold to dry, and taps into a long tradition of "simplicity" in Chinese art and notably the observations of everyday life by master Chinese cartoonist Feng Zikai. Yang admires Zikai's "loose-limbed yet robust brush work." By the redemptive conclusion of Yang's graphic memoir, her newfound perspective on her family's heritage allows her to fulfil the promise of her Chinese name, Xuan, which means "Forget Sorrow." **PG**

"I spent the Chinese New Year with my grandparents. Their heads were frosted white with layers of memories. Grandmother was senile."

Similar reads
A Chinese Life (Une vie Chinoise) P. Ôtié and Li Kunwu
How to Understand Israel in 60 Days or Less Sarah Glidden
Persepolis Marjane Satrapi
Vietnamerica G. B. Tran
Wild Animals Song Yang

MeZolith 2010

Ben Haggarty Adam Brockbank

First published by David Fickling Books (UK)
Creators Haggarty (British, b.1958); Brockbank (British, b.1963)
Genre Fantasy, Horror

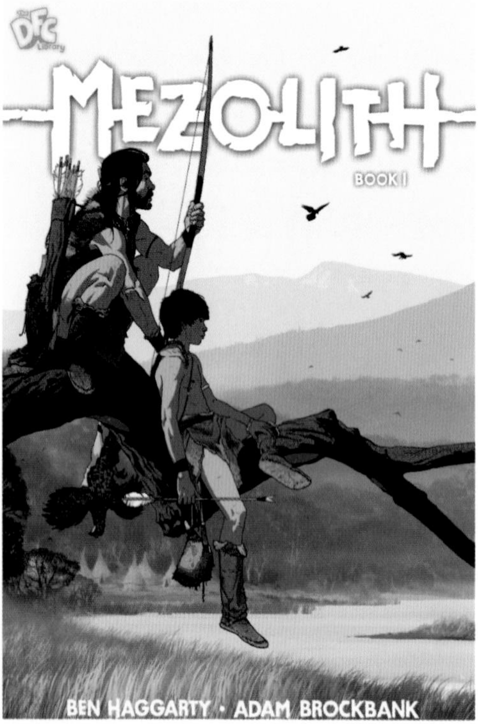
MEZOLITH
BOOK I
BEN HAGGARTY · ADAM BROCKBANK

Similar reads
Heros the Spartan Tom Tully and Frank Bellamy
Prince Valiant Hal Foster
Thorgal Jean Van Hamme and Grzegorz Rosiński
Wulf the Briton Ron Embleton

Random House's charismatic children's publisher, David Fickling, revived the British tradition of a weekly comic in 2008 with *The DFC*. While the credit crunch led to the comic's closure a year later, a number of future classics have come out of Fickling's stable—*MeZolith* being one of the finest.

The DFC reached out to embrace many talents not featured elsewhere on the comics map; *MeZolith* is no exception, written as it is by Ben Haggarty, a professional storyteller, and drawn by Adam Brockbank, a Hollywood concept artist. It may be this freshness of talent that made the story and art strike with readers so strongly because it is free of the usual tropes of comics, whether aimed at younger or older readers.

"The bee is fast . . . but Poika, greatest-hunter-of-all, is gaining on him. . . . "

This is billed as "stone-age horror," which is not exactly a well-trodden path. And horrific it is, with stunning set pieces, such as a giantess whose filthy hair must be combed before she will help a child, who is a cross between a raven and a corpse, and the cruel torture of a member of a neighboring tribe.

The story describes the central character's journey from child to adult: Poika becomes a man at the end of the many stories within the overall tale. Inside this classic "coming of age" structure readers encounter both the familiar (William Tell–style archery) and the shocking (a giant baby devouring all it finds). It is hard to tell what is real and what is not: appropriately so for a narrative dealing in myth and legend. Nevertheless, at its core this is a grounded work that avoids too many magical excesses. Even the fantastical mirror stone brought back from another world is ultimately revealed as a real archaeological find. **JS**

A Single Match 2010

Oji Suzuki

Gekiga is generally translated as "dramatic pictures" and is a term often applied to the work of Japanese manga artist Oji Suzuki. The association is appropriate but misleading, although unintentionally so. Confusion arises because much of the *gekiga* reprinted outside Japan, especially in English, has typically been autobiographical or realist, or both, whereas Suzuki's work is far more surrealist.

The *art brut* (outsider art) stories that Suzuki draws may be no more or less true than the godfather of *gekiga* Yoshihiro Tatsumi's, but they're often true in the way that recounted dreams are true. Each of the stories in this collection walks a surreal line where sensations blur, memories surface ferociously, and metaphors become tangible. A severed head floats in the air, but without the humor of Garry Trudeau's famously imprecise head caricatures. A conductor appears as an oversized bird cawing directions. A man and boy meet on the road and have a conversation worthy of Samuel Beckett.

"Again and again and again and again the stars came falling down."

The stories share an inconsolable sense of sadness. An old woman recounts her ritual ostracization, a child witnesses his father's humiliation, and a boy catches such a cold that readers fear for his sanity. This last story appears first in the collection, and the sequencing seems intentional: each subsequent story, rendered in a mix of rough lines and beautiful imagery (distant mountains, firefly lamps, decaying buildings), arrives like another, deeper dream as the boy veers toward coma. The interconnectedness is abetted by themes of wronged women, transportation, and an uneasy peace between built and natural environments. **MW**

First published by Drawn & Quarterly (Canada)
Creator Japanese (b.1949)
Genre Fantasy
Influenced by Zhuangzi

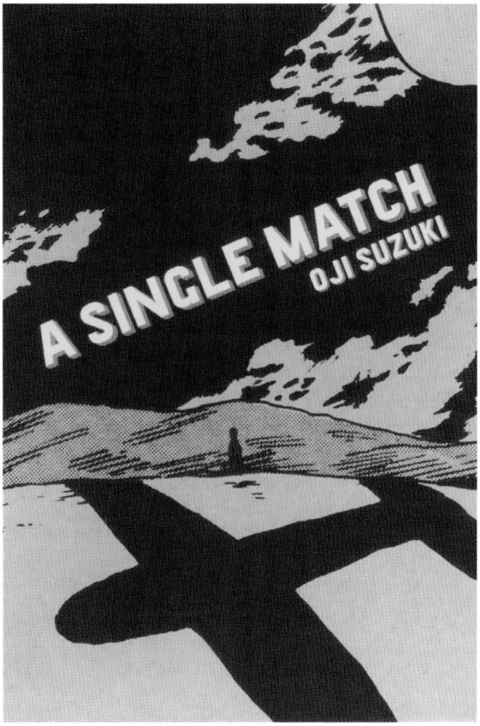
A SINGLE MATCH
OJI SUZUKI

Similar reads

MW Osamu Tezuka
Red Snow Susumu Katsumata
The Push Man and Other Stories Yoshihiro Tatsumi
The Walking Man Jiro Taniguchi

Daytripper 2010

✏ Fábio Moon ✏ Gabriel Bá

First published by Vertigo/DC Comics (USA)
Creators Moon (Brazilian, b.1976); Bá (Brazilian, b.1976)
Genre Fantasy, Romance
Influenced by Laerte Coutinho and Will Eisner

Best known for their Eisner Award-winning art on Gerard Way's *Umbrella Academy* and Joss Whedon's *Sugarshock*, Brazilian twins Moon and Bá came to prominence as writers with *Daytripper*. Abandoning the supernatural bent of their earlier work, *Daytripper* tells the life story of Brás de Oliva Domingo, an obituary writer for a São Paulo newspaper who aspires to be a novelist, but lives in the shadow of his father, a great Brazilian writer. Each issue deals with a single day in Brás's life, flitting back and forth from his youth to his old age and his midlife crises inbetween.

Fusing magical realism with quantum mechanics, *Daytripper* builds on the idea that on any given day, despite our best plans and intentions, the unexpected can radically change or even end our lives. When readers first meet Brás on his thirty-second birthday, he reminisces with his best friend Jorge (a fixture at his side throughout his life) about the traveling they did as young men. Readers wonder how that carefree and vivacious youth could grow into a man who writes about death all day. *Daytripper* feels just like that—a man's life seen from a journey through his memories, each one sparking a new recollection.

By exploring the different days and deaths of Brás, Moon and Bá paint a larger picture where every day of Brás's life shares in some mediated connection with every other day. If he accepts that the unexpected can touch his life with happiness or tragedy on any day, what he has left is the power of choice to experience everything that day has to offer him. **DN**

100 Months 2010

✏✏ John Hicklenton

First published by Cutting Edge Press (UK)
Creator British (1967–2010)
Genre Horror
Influenced by Pat Mills and Bryan Talbot

"We have less than 100 months to alter our behavior before we risk catastrophe," said Prince Charles in Rio in 2009, delivering his dire warning on climate change. "I am 100 months … You may call me the end of all things," says Mara, Earth goddess, daughter of Satan, and the Antichrist protagonist of John Hicklenton's final work. Hicklenton cut his creative teeth as an artist at *2000 A.D.*, where he illustrated Neil Gaiman's first published story and he cultivated a reputation for shocking, visceral art, particularly in his work with Pat Mills (the demented and hellish *The Tenth Circle* was disturbing even by *Judge Dredd* standards). In this regard, *100 Months* is Hicklenton's magnum opus.

Released into a world ravaged by its own decadence, Mara resolves to kill the swine god Longpig and bring forth Armageddon upon its worshippers, the "shaven apes tearing up the image of god." The violent mayhem that follows is breathtaking in both its savagery and its beauty. Relentlessly brutal, the bleak and ambiguous narrative is an augur of the end of the world. There are no panels; each page is filled with a single monstrous image accompanied by handwritten captions.

Hicklenton suffered with multiple sclerosis for over a decade, and *100 Months* was only completed shortly before his assisted suicide in Switzerland. Shorn of any of the commercial considerations or the editorial requests to "tone it down" that had blighted his career, it is undoubtedly the purest distillation of Hicklenton's vision and, given the context of its completion, it is difficult to read it as anything other than a valediction. **DN**

Angry, visceral images are a hallmark of Hicklenton's work. ➡

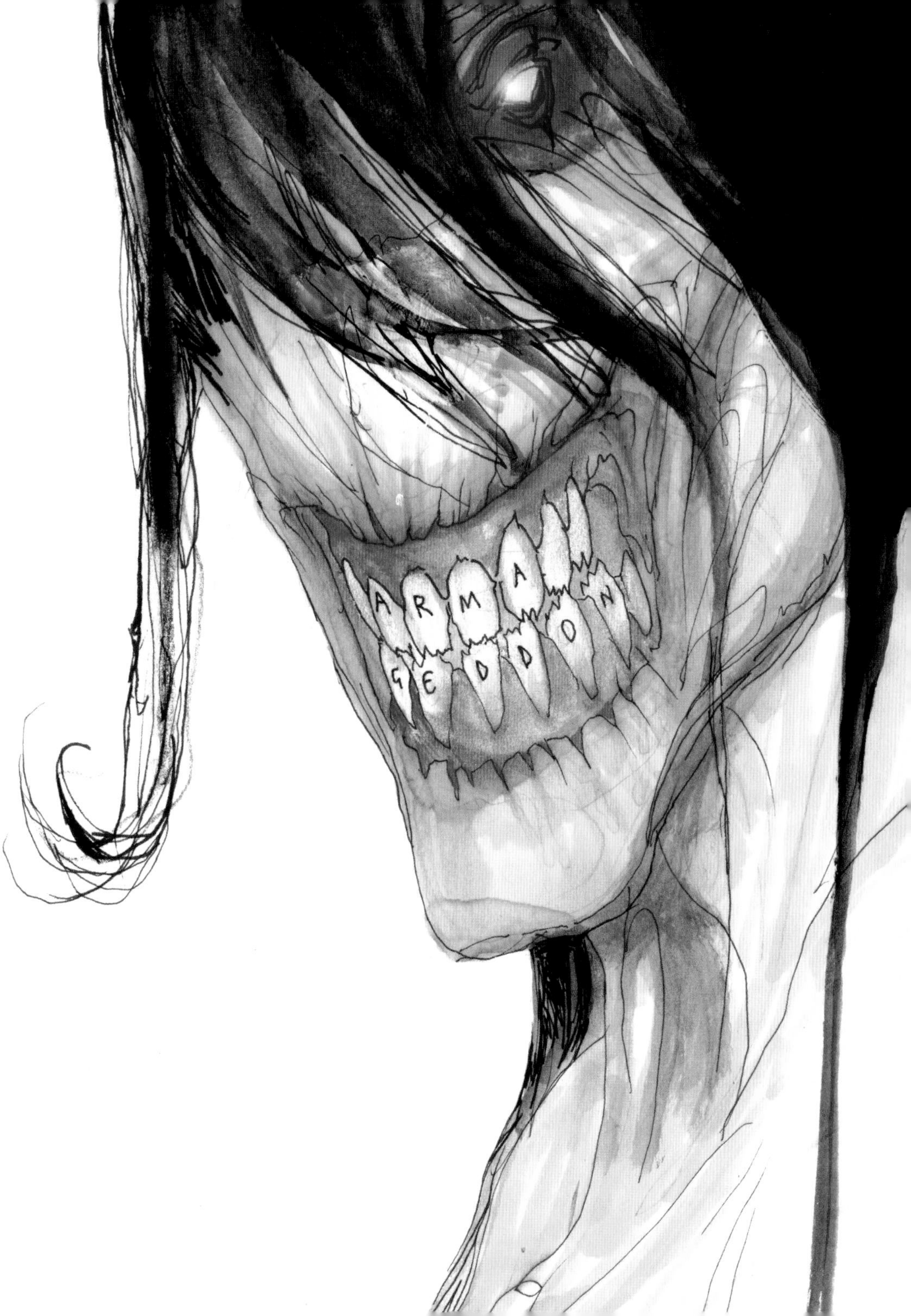
ARMAGEDDON

The Great Unwashed 2011

✐ Gary Pleece ✐ Warren Pleece

First published by Velocity Comics (UK)
Creators Gary Pleece (British, b.1966);
Warren Pleece (British, b.1965)
Genre Drama, Humor

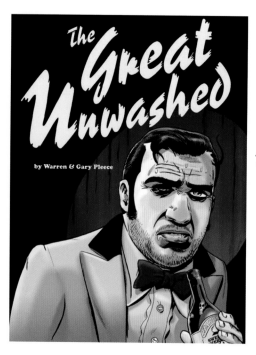

by Warren & Gary Pleece

Also by Warren Pleece
Incognegro with Mat Johnson
Life Sucks with Jessica Abel and Gabriel Soria
Mobfire with Gary Ushaw
Sandman Mystery Theater with Matt Wagner
True Faith with Garth Ennis

If there's a unifying theme to this collection from the Pleece brothers it is the question "Is anyone truly happy?" Their stories are splashed across eras, yet almost all feature someone dissatisfied with their lot, be it a pirate trapped in the clichés of his trade, a drug dealer in a society merely a step away from our own, or an old man sitting on a train regretting the turning point of his life.

The strips are often very funny, sometimes in the darkest fashion, with the humor accentuated by Warren's art playing it straight for the most part. This additionally lends pathos to characters such as Reg Chivers, a former music hall comedian whose career ended in scandal. The characters ooze sweat and grime in starkly contrasting, cinematic black and white.

"Any more relish stains on your reports and I'll bust yer ass."

Started in 1991, the title strip is the longest and is concluded here for the first time. Such a prolonged pause might have rendered the work redundant, but if anything it is more relevant. George and Buster predate slackers, yet in addition to being idiots, they devote their time to daytime television soaps, playing at preposterous careers, and sleeping with the same woman, Michelle. She is the only one who has any belief in their talents and intends to see they receive their due no matter what it takes.

Out-and-out comedy material in *The Great Unwashed* features such memorable characters as mercenary former football player-turned-pundit Len Shackleswick, and Dave Crotcherelli, a cop who distills the preposterous essence of 1970s American police shows. The sheer variety of topics and characters is a prescription for experiencing life beyond the computer and drawing board. **FP**

The Harappa Files 2011

Sarnath Banerjee

With 2004's *Corridor*, India's first commercial graphic novel, Sarnath Banerjee single-handedly started a modest graphic novel revolution in India. By his second, 2007's *The Barn Owl's Wondrous Capers*, Banerjee had tamed a form associated with the exotic and the strange in the Indian mind, and yoked it to the everyday Indian reality, helped by his distinct, rigorous, ancient Kalighat style-inspired artwork.

In *The Harappa Files*, Banerjee combines his skills as an astute observer and social commentator with his flair for what he calls a "graphic essay." These vignettes can take the form of character studies or short, wry, insightful digressions on arcane subjects, such as buying hilsa fish in Calcutta, to fulfill his ambition to

"Jagat Bahadur smelled of Lifebuoy soap . . . the smell of the working class."

come up with a form and a graphic language that relies on few received notions outside the broad desire to communicate effectively using a combination of words and images.

Heeding a hired marketing agency's counsel, a group of Indian mandarins and intellectuals calling themselves the Harappa Committee hire a graphic artist, Banerjee himself, to present the findings of a "grand survey" of "current ethnography and urban mythologies" they have undertaken. A series of sardonic vignettes follows dealing out anonymous, personal histories and sketches bound together only with the finest lines of logic. A fusion of pop art and satire builds an iconography of middle-class India in the 1980s. *The Harappa Files* is a commentary on life and ethnicity that reads like an oblique, alternative, everyman's history of urban India throughout its most transformative period in modern times. **HS**

First published by HarperCollins (India)
Creator Indian (b.1972)
Genre Parody, Humor
Influenced by Hergé

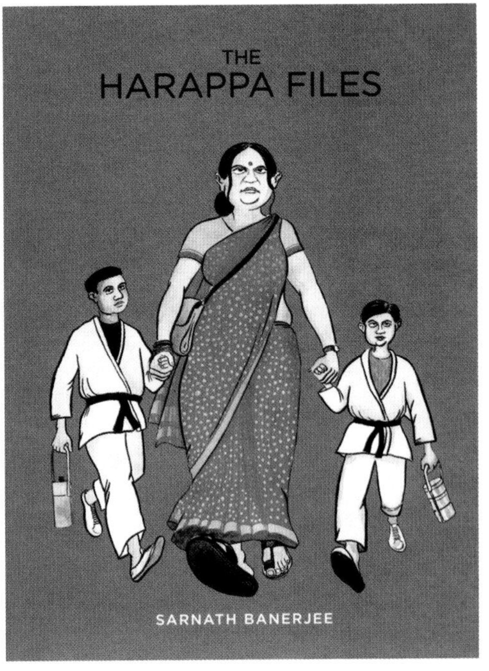
THE HARAPPA FILES
SARNATH BANERJEE

Similar reads
Boulevard of Broken Dreams Kim Deitch
Corridor Sarnath Banerjee
Lie Gautam Bhatia
The Barn Owl's Wondrous Capers Sarnath Banerjee
Three Fingers Rich Koslowski

Bhimayana 2011

Srividya Natarajan and S. Anand   Durgabai Vyam and Subhash Vyam

First published by Navayana Publishing (India) **Creators** Natarajan (Indian, b.1967); Anand (Indian, b.1973), Durgabai Vyam, (Indian, b.1974); Subhash Vyam (Indian, b.1970) **Genre** Biography

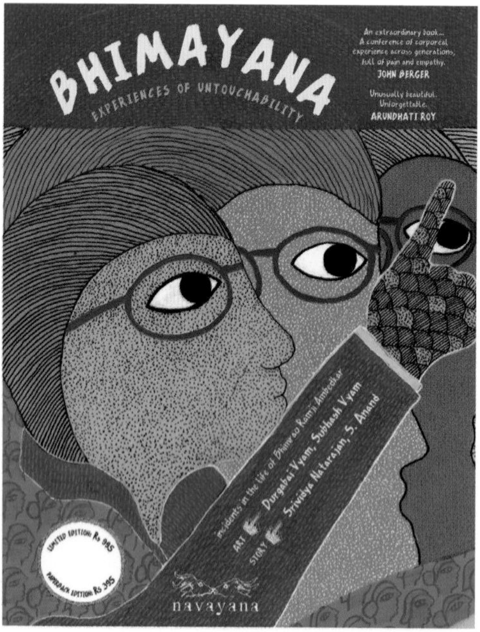
BHIMAYANA
EXPERIENCES OF UNTOUCHABILITY
An extraordinary book... A conference of corporeal experience across generations, full of pain and empathy.
JOHN BERGER
Unusually beautiful. Unforgettable.
ARUNDHATI ROY
incidents in the life of Bhimrao Ramji Ambedkar
ART Durgabai Vyam, Subhash Vyam
STORY Srividya Natarajan, S. Anand
LIMITED EDITION: Rs 995
PAPERBACK EDITION: Rs 395
navayana

One sixth of the world's population lives in India, and one sixth of Indians are classified as *dalits* (untouchables). The caste system continues to deny most of India's 170 million *dalits* the basic dignities of life; in 2008 a crime was committed against a *dalit* every eighteen minutes. Today Dr. Bhimrao Ambedkar is remembered mainly for drafting India's national constitution, which came into effect upon its independence from Britain in 1947, but his significance as an untouchable himself who rose to prominence and as a lifelong activist against discrimination, has been largely neglected. His plea for justice is reaffirmed in this graphic biography.

Framed by a passionate present-day debate at a bus stop between a young man who believes "Caste isn't real any longer. It's a non-issue" and a woman who brings to the young man's attention recent harrowing outrages reported in the media is an account of Dr. Ambedkar's historical experiences of prejudice, starting in school at the age of ten.

Dr. Ambedkar's story flows through three chapters based on his reminiscences about the injustices concerning basic rights to water, shelter, and travel, while the fourth explains how the husband-and-wife art team adapted their tribal drawings into comics. Such art does not represent, it signifies, so here a train becomes a snake, a fortress is a lion, and happiness is a peacock. Refusing to "force our characters into boxes [because] it stifles them," the Vyams make their panels sinuous and organic, outlined by *dignas* (decorative borders normally applied to buildings with colored earth). The art's intense patterning, its faces shown mainly in profile with large single eyes, and its word balloons—birdlike for gentleness, with a scorpion's sting for venomous dialogue or the mind's eye for thought—show how traditional artists can startlingly reinvent and reinvigorate the medium. **PG**

Similar reads

Jotirao Phule: Slavery Gulamgiri Srividya Natarajan and Aparajita Ninan
Lie Gautam Bhatia, Shankar and Birju Lal Bhopa, and Ghanshyam
Sita's Ramayana Samhita Arni and Moyna Chitrakar

Paying For It 2011

Chester Brown

Subtitled "a comic-strip memoir about being a john," Chester Brown's latest work documents his experiences paying prostitutes for sex over several years. After breaking up with his girlfriend (and continuing to live with her and her new boyfriend, because he is THAT liberal), Brown suddenly realizes that, at least for him, romantic relationships don't work. He much prefers the intimacy of friendship with his former partners than getting between the sheets with them.

As he thinks more about what motivates him to fall in love he realizes that paying for sex is actually a sensible and viable option. He gets better quality sex and greater variety than he can in a relationship. Brown is the kind of cartoonist who can mock his own insecurities with great subtlety, and who isn't afraid to examine the nuances of his behavior, while at the same time keeping up a documentary account of his numerous sexual encounters, from the dull and brief through to his eventual monogamous relationship with one of the girls he meets. The art is simple but not simplistic, using an eight-panel-per-page grid to tell the story in small movements and changes of expression.

Levelheaded is perhaps the best adjective to describe *Paying For It*. In countless discussions with his friends Brown analyses his motivations and their reactions to his frank attitude to being "a whoremonger." The art holds nothing back either. The only things he doesn't share are clues that might allow anyone to identify the various prostitutes who entertained him—a far more immoral act, in Brown's mind, than paying for sex. The only thing that slightly spoils *Paying For It* is the lengthy expository text sections at the back on why prostitution is not immoral and the various issues surrounding its legal position. The comic covers these areas better on its own terms and is strong enough to stand on its own merits. **FJ**

First published by Drawn & Quarterly (Canada)
Creator Canadian (b.1960)
Genre Reality drama
Influence on Joe Matt

I'd like a room.
PAYING FOR IT
This is your boyfriend?
a comic-strip memoir about being a john
Yeah.
CHESTER BROWN
Right.
thought you were my boyfriend.
Uh, the usual.
Oh, you know what? I forgot to bring condoms.
introduction by ROBERT CRUMB

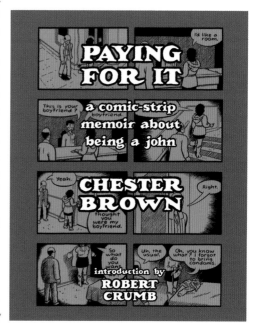

Also by Chester Brown
Ed the Happy Clown
I Never Liked You
Louis Riel: A Comic Book Biography
The Playboy
Underwater

Habibi 2011

✏✏ Craig Thompson

First published by Pantheon Books (USA) and Faber (UK)
Creator American (b.1966)
Genre Political fable
Influenced by *Arabian Nights*

Can comics be a means of cultural dialogue and transformation? Building on the strengths of his outstanding autobiographical comic *Blankets*, Craig Thompson steeps himself in the Arab world and emerges with an intimate epic, a startlingly vivid portrait of two unforgettable characters, Dodola and Habibi, set in the imagined kingdom of Wanatolia. This kingdom has both skyscrapers and a sultan, and vibrates urgently between the past and the present, between pollution and despair, redemption and rebirth.

When we first meet them, Dodola is a former child bride, who, with a young black slave she names Habibi, has escaped from the slavers who would also have sold her. Their relationship changes as they grow, and becomes a love story blazing with erotic yearning and intelligence.

Dodola becomes a passionate, articulate, and witty woman who struggles against the patriarchal world in which she finds herself. As he becomes an adolescent, Habibi discovers a terrible secret that threatens to destroy both how he sees Dodola, as well as his own identity. The choice he makes defines their lives for years to come. Now separated, Dodola and Habibi make arduous journeys in search of one another. As we follow them from the desert to the city, from slum to sultan's harem, the narrative moves seamlessly between gritty realism, fairy tale, and religious imagery.

Like Scheherazade, Dodola and Habibi use stories to think with, to shape their identities, and to save themselves and others. They draw on key passages from the Bible and the Koran, bringing them to urgent, contemporary life. Theirs is a world full of pollution, corruption, and dangers. Stories are not an escape, but a challenge to remake ourselves and the world. There are often competing versions of the same stories due to different religious and cultural traditions, but their differences are unified visually in the comic to create a richer, more nuanced whole. Thompson presents his comic as myth, a way of revising and reconciling the opposed visual and storytelling traditions of East and West, and of giving voice to the marginalized.

At nearly 700 pages, this is a labor of love. Thompson has steeped himself in Arabic and Arab culture, and the fluid line of Arabic script becomes a unifying motif in the story. Each character becomes associated with a different strand of the arabesque, a symbol of unity in Islamic thought. There are different dimensions of arabesque here, each of which resonates through the novel. One is the parallel between human and divine creativity; the geometric shapes that link his chapters point beyond themselves to the organizing hand of the world's artist, and the possibility of finding meaning, in both life and narrative.

Calligraphy is a further layer of the arabesque that Thompson uses to extraordinary effect, as words become characters, the shapes of particular letters reflecting the shape of their lives, and of our reading experience. Thompson brilliantly combines each of these strands to create unity through diversity, a key Islamic concept and a central theme in the novel. *Habibi* is a transformative journey for both its characters and the reader, a uniquely immersive visual and literary encounter with a cultural other that has original things to say. It is a compelling experience that builds vital bridges between past and present, art and nature, love and faith. It'll change the way you think about comics, too. **AK**

habibi

CRAIG THOMPSON

author of BLANKETS

Index by Author/Illustrator

Contributors

Gerry Alanguilan (GA) is a comic book writer and artist. He has worked as an inker for Marvel and DC comics, most notably on *Superman: Birthright*, *X-Men*, and *Batman*. His own stories include *Wasted*, *Humanis Rex!*, and the Eisner-nominated *Elmer*.

Rachid Alik (RA) has run public relations for the Algiers International Comics Festival (FIBDA) since 2009. Prior to this he worked as a journalist on the Algerian daily newspapers *Le Matin* and *Liberté*, and in French-speaking radio at Alger Chaine 3.

Helena Baser (HB) has nursed a passion for comics since first reading Neil Gaiman's *Sandman* over a decade ago. She volunteered for several years at the UK Web and Mini Comix Thing, an annual small press expo. In order to fund her comic-buying she works for a London-based publishing company.

Bart Beaty (BB) is professor of English at the University of Calgary, Canada. He is the author of several books, including *Fredric Wertham and the Critique of Mass Culture* and *Comics Versus Art*. He writes on European comics for ComicsReporter.com.

Stephen Betts (SB) is a lifelong comics reader, with a particular interest in European comics. Frustrated by his

paltry language skills, he developed and runs Comix Influx, the community Web site for comics translation.

Michał Błażejczyk is the founder, editor, and publisher of *Zeszyty Komiksowe* (www.zeszytykomiksowe.org), the only Polish journal for the critique and study of comics.

Radosław Bolałek (RB) is a freelance comics scholar. Since 2005 he has run Hanami, a company that focuses on Polish-Japanese cultural and economic exchange, and publishes award-winning Japanese graphic novels in Polish and Czech.

Cha, Kai-ming (K-MC) is a writer for *Publishers Weekly*.

Les Coleman (LC) is a London-based artist and writer with an extensive collection of underground and alternative comics. In 2003, he organized the Foo, Zap, Yow & Now exhibition with Paul Gravett at the ICA.

Hikmat Darmawan (HD) writes on Indonesian and international comics. He is a fellow of the Asian Public Intellectuals Program, concerning the globalization of manga subculture and visual identity.

Jeremy Day (JD) is a member of the UK small press comics community, and a founding member of the Caption comics convention. He believes everyone can make comics and that everyone should, at least once.

Ben Dickson (BD) is the author of graphic novels *Falling Sky*, *Slumdroid*, and *Kestrels*. He is also an accomplished painter and community artist, working with children and vulnerable adults.

Juan Manuel Domínguez (JMD) wanted to be a superhero. Now, the Batman-Gorey lover drowns his dreams of saving the universe with comics and film criticism.

Carlos Eugênio Baptista (CB) is a Brazilian comics writer and researcher, who loves horror, monsters, and sci-fi. His books include the award-winning graphic novels *Sangue Bom* and *A Guerra dos Dinossauros*.

Nicolas Finet (NF) is an author, editor, journalist, curator, and inveterate traveler. He has worked in comics for more than twenty-five years. An expert in Asian comics, he notably headed up *DicoManga*, the definitive manga dictionary, in 2007. He lives near Paris.

Nigel Fletcher (NFl) is a business consultant and the publisher of fanzine *The Panelhouse*. He also contributed to *The Slings and Arrows Comics Guide* and *500 Essential Graphic Novels: The Ultimate Guide*.

Melanie Gibson (MG) is based at Northumbria University, where her research and publications in childhood studies focus on comics and their audiences. She is also a consultant on traditional and visual literacies (http://www.dr-mel-comics.co.uk).

Paul Gravett (PG) has been described by *The Times* as "the greatest historian of the comics and graphic novel form in this country." After working on UK magazine *pssst!,* he went on to publish *Escape* magazine. He became director of The Cartoon Art Trust in 1992 and has directed Comica, the London International Comics Festival since 2003. He is the author of several books, including *Graphic Novels: Stories to Change Your Life* (2005).

Maggie Gray (MG) completed a history of art PhD at University College London in 2010, with a thesis about Alan Moore. Her work has been published in *Studies in Comics* and the *Journal of Graphic Novels and Comics*, as well as a forthcoming anthology on Alan Moore and the gothic tradition.

Xavier Guilbert (XG) is the acting editor-in-chief of *du9—l'autre bande dessinée* (http://du9.org), a French-language Web site for indepth criticism of alternative comics. He has also written articles in *Neuvième Art* and *Le Monde Diplomatique,* among others.

Chrissie Harper (CH) is a journalist, cartoonist, and designer. She has self-published a number of fanzines and comics, and is currently working on a series entitled *Club Comicana* (www.chezchrissie.co.uk).

Tor Arne Hegna (TAH) writes about comics in newspapers, magazines, and Web sites in Norway. He has also published comics and books about

comics, and received the Raptus Festival prize of honor in 2004.

Domingos Isabelinho (DI) is a Portuguese comics critic. He has written for *The Comics Journal, The International Journal of Comic Art* (USA), and magazines in Portugal such as *Splash!* and *Quadrado.* His main interest is in international alternative comics.

Jean-Paul Jennequin (J-PJ) is a comics translator, critic, and author. Among his translations in French are works by Alan Moore, Eddie Campbell, Howard Cruse, Dave McKean, Will Eisner, Charles Burns, Harvey Pekar, and Daniel Clowes. He has also written a biography of Osamu Tezuka.

Fiona Jerome (FJ) began her journalism career working on the comics magazine *Speakeasy.* She launched *Bizarre* magazine and has contributed to several comics guides. She is now the creative director of a small publishing company.

Ariel Kahn (AK) is a senior lecturer at Roehampton University, London, where he teaches the UK's first undergraduate course in scriptwriting for comics. He regularly reviews comics in the print media and online.

Chie Kutsuwada (CK) is a Japan-born manga enthusiast. A graduate of the Royal College of Art, she lives in London, working as a manga artist and running manga workshops. Her work includes *King of a Miniature Garden.*

Guy Lawley (GL) is a Londoner who became hooked on the Marvel universe at the age of seven. He likes to remind people that the comics medium evolved in the American Sunday newspapers, circa 1895 to 1902. Hail Opper, Dirks, and Outcault!

Timothy R. Lehmann (TRL) is an award-winning journalist, artist, and designer. He is the author of *Manga: Masters of the Art,* a book of interviews and studio visits with Japanese manga creators. He is currently working on a book about European comics.

Sarah Lightman (SL) is an artist and curator, who is researching a PhD on autobiography in comics at the University of Glasgow. She codirects Laydeez Do Comics and chairs the annual Women in Comics conferences (www.sarahlightman.com).

Ellen Lindner (EL) trained as an art historian while harboring ambitions of a career in comics. Today she's a London-based cartoonist and illustrator, and the author of *Undertow,* a graphic novel about Brooklyn in the 1960s.

Andrew Littlefield (AL) is a freelance author and editor who writes about comics and popular culture.

Catriona MacLeod (CM) specializes in the representation of women in French-language comics, and is completing a PhD on the subject. Her articles for journals include "Contemporary French Civilisation" and "L'Esprit Créateur."

Christian Marmonnier (CM) has worked on several comics dictionaries and is the author of works on René Goscinny, the magazine *Métal Hurlant*, the relationship between music and art, and on various popular subjects, including a history of sex toys.

Gert Meesters (GM) has a PhD in Dutch linguistics from the University of Leuven and teaches at the University of Liege, Belgium. He also works as a comics critic and journalist, and is currently writing about comics for the Flemish news weekly *Knack*.

Ann Miller (AM) has published widely on French-language comics, including *Reading Bande Dessinée: Critical Approaches to French-language Comic Strip* (Intellect, 2007). She is joint editor of *European Comic Art*, published biannually by Liverpool University Press.

Alfons Moliné (AMo) is an animator, translator, and writer on the subjects of comics, animation, and manga. He is the author of a number of books, including *El Gran Libro de los Manga* (Glénat, 2002) and biographies of Osamu Tezuka, Carl Barks, and Rumiko Takahashi.

Pedro Moura (PM) is a Portuguese PhD student researching trauma and comics. He writes mainly for his own blog (lerbd.blogspot.com) but has published several articles and worked as a teacher, curator, translator, and conference director in comics.

Nakho Kim (NK) is a Korean comics researcher who has worked as editor-in-chief for the comics critic webzine Dugoboza, organized an exhibition on Korean comics at the Angoulême Festival 2003, and is the author of a *History of Modern Korean Comics 1945–2009*.

Dom Tarquin Nolan (DN) enjoys reading comics, writing about comics, and reading about people writing about comics.

Andy Oliver (AO) is the managing editor of the comics site www.brokenfrontier.com, home of digital magazine *The Frontiersman*. He contributes there as an interviewer, feature writer, and reviewer.

Huib van Opstal (HvO) is a Dutch designer, picture researcher, and author of *Essay RG. Het fenomeen Hergé* (1994), an analysis of the life and work of the Belgian comic strip author.

Leif Packalen (LP) is chairman of World Comics Finland (www.worldcomics.fi). He has extensive experience of promoting comics as a development communication tool in Africa and Asia.

Rikke Platz Cortsen (RPC) is a PhD scholar at the University of Copenhagen, working on a thesis concerning time in comics. She has written articles on various Scandinavian comics artists and on time and space in the work of Alan Moore.

Frank Plowright (FP), as a teen, reasoned that should comics graduate from "dem funnybooks" to "graphic novels," courses might be taught at those universities visionary enough to discard science and classics. At that point, he realized, he would then be able to make a living writing about comics.

Edwin Pouncey (EP), aka Savage Pencil, is an artist and writer whose work has appeared in publications and galleries in the UK, Europe, and the United States. He is currently working —with writer David Quantick—on a graphic novel about Edwardian cat artist Louis Wain.

Ernesto Priego (EPr) is a Mexican comics scholar who works as an editor, journalist, translator, poet, and curator. He lives in London and is a founding member and coeditor of The Comics Grid, a collaborative, peer-edited, and authored blog dedicated to comics.

Ian Rakoff (IR) is a screenwriter, film editor, comic book collector, and the author of *Inside The Prisoner: Radical Television and Film in the 1960s*. Two of his collections of comics are held at the National Art Library and the Victoria & Albert Museum.

Richard Reynolds (RR) is an author, publisher, and lecturer at Central Saint Martins College of Art and Design, London. He is the author of *Superheroes: A Modern Mythology*.

David A. Roach (DAR) is an artist, writer, and comic book historian. As an artist he has worked on numerous comics including *Judge Dredd*, *Batman*, and *Dr. Who*. Among his publications are *The Warren Companion* and *The Superhero Book*. He lives in Cardiff with his family and mountains of comics.

Harri Römpötti (HR) is a freelance journalist who writes about comics, cinema, music, and literature. He is the coauthor of *Päin näköä!* (2011), a book about contemporary Finnish comics.

Roger Sabin (RS) is the author of several books including *Adult Comics: An Introduction* and *Comics, Comix and Graphic Novels*. He lectures at Central Saint Martins College of Art and Design, London.

Jacques Samson (JS) lives in Montreal, Canada. His passion for comics is kept alive with articles in various journals, including *Neuvième Art*. Along with Benoît Peeters, he recently published *Chris Ware. La bande dessinée réinventée* ("Chris Ware. Comics reinvented").

Hemant Sareen (HS) lives and works in New Delhi, India. He is an associate editor at *ArtAsiapacific* magazine, devoted to contemporary visual art.

Matthias Schneider (MS), cultural scientist and music agent, is based in Berlin. As artistic director he has organized two Berlin comic festivals. He publishes books and articles and regularly curates exhibitions on illustration and comics, including exhibitions for the Goethe-Institut. www.schneiderplus.com

Jenni Scott (JS) co-organizes the UK's longest-running comics convention, Caption, held in Oxford each year since 1992. She has written about comics since the late 1980s.

Tatsuya Seto (TS) is a Japanese manga critic and the CEO of publisher G.B. Company. The founding editor-in-chief of manga magazine *comnavi*, his numerous books include *The Ten Men Behind Great Comics*, *The Giant Robots Reader*, and *Gakuen Manga Reader*.

Matteo Stefanelli (MS) is a scholar, curator, and media consultant based in Italy. He has developed comics-related projects for television, and organized exhibitions and conferences. His books include *Il Secolo del Corriere dei Piccoli* and *Antonio Rubino*.

Barry Stone (BS) is an internationally published history author and freelance travel writer, with 2,000-plus comics shrink-wrapped and squirrelled away in his garage in Sydney, Australia.

Fredrik Strömberg (FS) is president of the Swedish Comics Association, editor of the magazine *Bild & Bubbla*, and a professor at Malmö's Comic Art School. His books include *Swedish Comics History* and *Comic Art Propaganda*.

Ai Takita-Lucas (AT-L) was born and grew up with manga comics in Japan. She studied at London's Central Saint Martins College of Art and Design, works as a manga artist, and published charity comics anthology *Spirit of Hope*.

Živojin Tamburić (ZT) is a reader, collector, critic, and historian of comics from Belgrade. His book, *Comics We Loved* is a selection of twentieth-century comics and creators from the region of former Yugoslavia.

Tony Venezia (TV) is a teaching fellow at Birkbeck College, who is completing a PhD on Alan Moore and the question of history. He has written on comics for the *International Journal of Comic Art* and *Radical Philosophy* and is also a founding member and editor of the scholarly blog, comicsgrid.com.

Simon Ward (SW) is a writer and editor working in London. He has won awards for his short story work and has written widely on cinema and comics.

Marc Weidenbaum (MW) has edited comics that appear in books by Jessica Abel, Justin Green, Carol Swain, Adrian Tomine, and others. A former editor-in-chief of manga magazines *Shonen Jump* and *Shojo Beat*, he founded electronic music site Disquiet.com in 1996.

Matthias Wivel (MWi) is an art historian based at the State Museum of Art in Copenhagen. He is a cofounder and board member of the Danish Comics Council, a critic for *The Comics Journal*, and recently edited the Nordic comics anthology *Kolor Klimax*.

Picture Credits

Every effort has been made to credit the copyright holders of the images used in this book. We apologize for any unintentional omissions or errors and will insert the appropriate acknowledgment to any companies or individuals in subsequent editions of the work.

2 Photo by Morris Engel/Getty Images **22-23** Palto / Shutterstock Images **31** Rudolph Dirks **37** Feininger Lyonel **38** DC Comics **39** Antonio Rubino **40** Cliff Sterrett **41** George McManus / Emil Zekley **44-45** Rube Goldberg **48** © Trina Robbins **51** Dover Publications Inc. / Frans Masereel **52** Billy DeBeck **53** Mirrorpix / Daily Mirror **54** Oscar Jacobsson **55** Mary Tourtel / Alfred Bestall **57** John Millar Watt **58** Jimmy Bancks **61** Otto Messmer **63** Frank Willard **64-65** Percy Crosby **66** Harold Gray **67** Otto Nückel **69** Philip Nowlan / Dick Calkins **70** Lynd Ward **72-73** Palto / Shutterstock Images **75** © Hergé/ Moulinsart 2011. Supplied by Huib Van Opstal. **76** Doubleday / Milt Gross **78** Ham Fisher **79** Otto Soglow **80** Hal Foster / Burne Hogarth **81** Chester Gould **83** V. T. Hamlin **84** Mirrorpix / Daily Mirror **87** CASTERMAN **88** Milton Caniff **90** e. o. plauen **91** e. o. plauen **92** King Features Syndicate / Lee Falk and Phil Davis **93** King Features Syndicate / Dahsiell Hammett and Alex Raymond **94** © Gajo Sakamoto / Tankuro Publication **95** © Gajo Sakamoto / Tankuro Publication **96-97** King Features Syndicate / Alex Raymond and Don Moore **99** © St Ogan / Greg - Hyphen Comics **100** Jesús Blasco **103** King Features Syndicate / Lee Falk and Ray Moore **105** King Features Syndicate / Hal Foster **106** Andrija Maurović **109** United Media / Fred Harman **110** DC Comics **111** DC Comics **112** Gladys Parker **113** Dick Briefer **115** Tarpé **116** DC Comics **117** DC Comics **118** Captain America and all other Marvel characters: TM & © Marvel Entertainment, LLC and its subsidiaries. All Rights Reserved. **120** DC Comics **122** George Carlson **123** Basil Wolverton **125** © Hergé / Moulinsart 2011 **127** Victor Dancette / Edmond-François Calvo **128** Joaquim Buigas / Marino Benejam **129** CASTERMAN **130** DC Comics **131** Willy Vandersteen **133** John Stanley / Irving Tripp / Dark Horse Comics **134** Alex Raymond **135** John Willie **136** Miné Okubo **138** DC Comics **139** Marc Sleen **140** Gaylord Dubois / Jesse Mace Marsh / Dark Horse Comics **141** Les aventures de Buck Danny © DUPUIS 1947 by Jean-Michel Charlier and Victor Hubinon www.dupuis.com All rights reserved **142** CASTERMAN **143** Gordon Rogers **144** Simon & Schuster / Walt Kelly **147** Douglas Mount / Trog **148** DC Comics **150-151** Palto / Shutterstock Images **153** Jack Kirby / Joe Simon **154** DC Comics **155** DC Comics **156** Frank Hampson **158** Manfred Schmidt **159** United Media / Charles M. Schulz **160** Edgar P. Jacobs **161** King Features Syndicate / Mort Walker **162** King Features Syndicate / Hank Ketcham **164** © Tezuka Production / Shogakukan Inc. **167** Francisco V. Coching **168** © Disney **169** © Disney **170** José G. Cruz / José Trinidad Romero **172** DC Comics **173** DC Comics **174** Rolf Kauka **176** © Osamu Tezuka / Kodansha Ltd. **178** Jerry Spring © DUPUIS 1954 by Jijé www.dupuis.com All rights reserved **179** Tove Jansson **181** Les voleurs du Marsupilami © DUPUIS 1954 by André Franquin www.dupuis.com All rights reserved **182** Alan Moore / Garry Leach **185** Palle Nielsen **186-187** Reg Taylor / James Edgar / Tony Weare **188** Yoshihiro Tatsumi **189** © Mitsuharu Yokoyama, Kobunsha, monthly magazine "Shonen" **190** Edgar P. Jacobs **192** Michael Butterworth / Ronald Embleton **194** DC Comics **195** © Disney **196** © Shigeru Sugiura , Kobunsha , monthly magazine "Shonen" **197** DC Comics **198** Bob Bolling **199** H. G. Oesterheld / Francisco Solano Lopez **200-201** Leonard Starr **202** Gaston Lagaffe © DUPUIS 1957 by André Franquin www.dupuis.com All rights reserved **203** Gaston Lagaffe © DUPUIS 1957 by André Franquin www.dupuis.com All rights reserved **204** Zvonimir Furtinger / Julio Radilović **206** La flûte à six schtroumpfs © DUPUIS 1958 by Peyo www.dupuis.com All rights reserved **207** Gil Jourdan: La voiture immergée © DUPUIS 1958 by Maurice Tillieux www.dupuis.com All rights reserved **208** Ediciones B / Francisco Ibañez **211** D C Thompson / Walter Fearne / Ken Reid **212-213** Mirrorpix / Daily Mirror **214** Harvey Kurtzman **215** Kim Sanho **216** © Shigeru Mizuki / Kodansha Ltd. **218** Edgar P. Jacobs **219** Guillermo Mendizábal / Rubén Lara y Romero **220** George Beardmore / Frank Bellamy **221** George Beardmore / Frank Bellamy **222** The Fantastic Four and all other Marvel characters: TM & © Marvel Entertainment, LLC and its subsidiaries. All Rights Reserved. **223** The Fantastic Four and all other Marvel characters: TM & © Marvel Entertainment, LLC and its subsidiaries. All Rights Reserved. **225** Z comme Zorglub © DUPUIS **1961** by André Franquin www.dupuis.com All rights reserved **226** Frank Dickens **227** DC Comics **228** Santiago Armada **229** Santiago Armada **231** Ediciones Colihue / H. G. Oesterheld / Alberto Breccia **232** © 2011 LES EDITIONS ALBERT RENE / GOSCINNY-UDERZO **234** Kenneth Bulmer / Jesús Blasco **235** Angela Giussani / Luciana Giussani **236** The Incredible Hulk and all other Marvel characters: TM & © Marvel Entertainment, LLC and its subsidiaries. All Rights Reserved. **237** Thor and all other Marvel characters: TM & © Marvel Entertainment, LLC and its subsidiaries. All Rights Reserved. **239** Jean-Claude Forest **240** Spider-Man and all other Marvel characters: TM & © Marvel Entertainment, LLC and its subsidiaries. All Rights Reserved. **241** The Avengers and all other Marvel characters: TM & © Marvel Entertainment, LLC and its subsidiaries. All Rights Reserved. **242** Dr. Strange and all other Marvel characters: TM & © Marvel Entertainment, LLC and its subsidiaries. All Rights Reserved. **244** Modesty Blaise © Associated Newspapers/Solo Syndication. Cover art reproduced by kind permission of Titan Publishing Group Ltd. **246** Joe Brainard **247** Joe Brainard **249** Richard E. Hughes / Ogden Whitney **250** KAMUIDEN © 1967 Sanpei SHIRATO / Shogakukan Inc. **253** Jean-Claude Forest / Paul Gillon **255** © Ishinomori Shotaro / Kodansha Ltd. **257** © 2011 LES EDITIONS ALBERT RENE / GOSCINNY-UDERZO **259** Jean-Jacques Sempé **260** Michael O'Donoghue / Frank Springer **261** Sonoyama Shunji **263** Guido Crepax **264** Le Concombre Masqué © DARGAUD 2004 by Mandryka www.dargaud.com All rights reserved **265** R. Crumb **266** DC Comics **267** Rafael Cutberto Navarro / Roberto Vásquez **268** Archie Goodwin **270** Nick Fury and all other Marvel characters: TM & © Marvel Entertainment, LLC and its subsidiaries. All Rights Reserved. **271** Jiro Kuwata **272** Albin Michel / Philippe Druillet **273** Albin Michel / Philippe Druillet **274** Archie Goodwin / Steve Ditko **275** Archie Goodwin / Steve Ditko **276** Vaughn Bodé **278** DC Comics **279** Asao Takamori / Tetsuya Chiba **280** R. Crumb **281** CASTERMAN **283** Osamu Tezuka **285** Gilbert Shelton **286** © 2011 LES EDITIONS ALBERT RENE / GOSCINNY-UDERZO **287** DC Comics **289** R. Crumb **290** Rubrique-à-Brac © Dargaud by Gotlib www.dargaud.com All rights reserved **291** Tom of Finland **292** Yoshiharu Tsuge **293** Yoshiharu Tsuge **294** The Silver Surfer and all other Marvel characters: TM & © Marvel Entertainment, LLC and its subsidiaries. All Rights Reserved. **296** Philémon et le naufragé du "A" ©DARGAUD 1972 by Fred www.dargaud.com All rights reserved **297** Roger Lécureux / André Chéret **298** Gian Luigi Bonelli / Aurelio Galleppini **299** Max Bunker / Magnus **300** DORAEMON © 1974 Fujiko-Pro / Shogakukan Inc. **302** Tom Tully / Francisco Solano Lopez **303** Rory Hayes **304** Dino Buzzati **306** The X-Men and all other Marvel characters: TM & © Marvel Entertainment, LLC and its subsidiaries. All Rights Reserved. **307** The X-Men and all other Marvel characters: TM & © Marvel Entertainment, LLC and its subsidiaries. All Rights Reserved. **308-309** Palto / Shutterstock Images **310** Maurício De Sousa **311** George Akiyama **313** © Tezuka Production / Shogakukan Inc. **314** Lucky Luke: Tortillas pour les Dalton © DUPUIS 1970 by René Goscinny and Morris www.dupuis.com All rights reserved **315** Jean-Marc Reiser **316** DC Comics **318** Gianluigi Gonano / Gianni De Luca **320** DC Comics **321** Seiichi Hayashi **323** S. Clay Wilson **325** Dan O'Neill / Bobby London / Gary Hallgren / Ted Richards **326** Sio **327** Tom Veitch / Greg Irons **329** La jeunesse de Blueberry: La Mine de l'Allemand perdu © DARGAUD 1972 by Charlier & Giraud www.dargaud.com All rights reserved **330** The Man-Thing and all other Marvel characters: TM & © Marvel Entertainment, LLC and its subsidiaries. All Rights Reserved. **331** Victor De la Fuente **332** Justin Green **334** DC Comics **335** The Tomb of Dracula and all other Marvel characters: TM & © Marvel Entertainment, LLC and its subsidiaries. All Rights Reserved. **337** Edward Gorey **338** Jacques Lob / Philippe Druillet **339** Kazuo Kamimura **341** Kazuo Koike / Kazuo Kamimura **343** Rick Griffin **345** Mordillo **347** Roy Thomas / Barry Windsor-Smith **348** Spider-Man and all other Marvel characters: TM & © Marvel Entertainment, LLC and its subsidiaries. All Rights Reserved. **349** Spider-Man and all other Marvel characters: TM & © Marvel Entertainment, LLC and its subsidiaries. All Rights Reserved. **350** © 2011 LES EDITIONS ALBERT RENE / GOSCINNY-UDERZO **353** Howard the Duck and all other Marvel characters: TM & © Marvel Entertainment, LLC and its subsidiaries. All Rights Reserved. **355** Bruce Jones / Bernie Wrightson / Dark Horse Comics **356** THOMA NO SHINZO © 1975 Moto HAGIO / Shogakukan Inc. **359** Philippe Picaret / Jacques Tardi **360** Carlos Sampayo / José Muñoz **363** Moebius **364** Martin Vaughn-James

366 Claus Deleuran **368** © KEIKO TAKEMIYA / Shogakukan Inc. **370** © Tezuka Production / Shogakukan Inc. **371** Aabid Surti / Jagit Uppai / Govind Brahmania **372** Harvey Pekar **375** © Miuchi Suzue / Hakusensha **377** Art Spiegelman **378** Job / Derib **379** Georges Pichard **380** Richard Corben **381** CASTERMAN **382** The X-Men and all other Marvel characters: TM & © Marvel Entertainment, LLC and its subsidiaries. All Rights Reserved. **383** DC Comics **384** David E. Boswell **387** Stefano Tamburini / Tanino Liberatore **389** CASTERMAN **390** Bryan Talbot **392** DC Comics **393** Larry Gonick **395** Dave Stevens / Dark Horse Comics **396-397** Universal Press Syndicate / Jim Davis **399** W.W. Norton & Company / Will Eisner **400** Kate Worley / Reed Waller **402** Martin Veyron **403** Martin Veyron **405** CASTERMAN **406** CASTERMAN **408** Jeremiah © DUPUIS **1979** by Hermann www.dupuis.com All rights reserved **409** Pierre Christin / Enki Bilal **410** Binet Christian **412** Universal Press Syndicate / Lynn Johnston **413** © Posy Simmonds by permission of United Agents Ltd. (www.unitedagents.co.uk) on behalf of the author. **414** Iron Man and all other Marvel characters: TM & © Marvel Entertainment, LLC and its subsidiaries. All Rights Reserved. **417** Alejandro Jodorowsky / Moebius **419** Les passagers du Vent / François Bourgeon (ed. 12bis). **420** © Yamagishi Ryoko **421** MAISON IKKOKU © 1982 Rumiko TAKAHASHI / Shogakukan Inc. **422** CASTERMAN **424** Jean Van Hamme / Grzegorz Rosiński **425** Jean Van Hamme / Grzegorz Rosiński **426** Mattioli **429** Pierre Christin / Enki Bilal **430** Slim **431** Andrea Pazienza **432** Mirka Martini / Magnus **435** Kamagurka / Herr Seele **436** © Katsuhiro Otomo / Kodansha Ltd. **437** © Katsuhiro Otomo / Kodansha Ltd. **438** Mick Kidd / Chris Garratt **439** Raoul Cauvin / Lambil **440** CASTERMAN **441** CASTERMAN **442** Sergio Aragonés / Mark Evanier **443** Enrique Sánchez Abulí / Jordi Bernet **444** Judge Dredd: The Apocalypse War by John Wagner, Alan Grant & Carlos Ezquerra © 1982, 2011 Rebellion A/S **445** Judge Dredd: The Apocalypse War by John Wagner, Alan Grant & Carlos Ezquerra © 1982, 2011 Rebellion A/S **446** Gilbert Hernández **448** DC Comics **450** Raymond Briggs **453** ©Hergé/Moulinsart 2011 **454** The Shit Generation **455** © Jaime Hernandez **457** La Quête de l'Oiseau du Temps 1/La Conque de Ramor © DARGAUD, Paris, 1998, by Letendre and Loisel www.dargaud.com All rights reserved. **458** CASTERMAN **460** CASTERMAN **462** Howard Chaykin **463** Pascal Doury **465** CASTERMAN **467** DC Comics **468** CASTERMAN **469** CASTERMAN **470** Hermann **471** CASTERMAN **472** Scott McCloud **474** The Ballad of Halo Jones by Alan Moore & Ian Gibson © 1984, 2011 Rebellion A/S **475** Chantal Montellier **476** XIII: Le jour du soleil noir © DUPUIS 1984 by Jean Van Hamme and William Vance www.dupuis.com All rights reserved **478** Tadeusz Baranowski **479** Joakim Pirinen **480** Patrick Cothias / Philippe Adamov **482** DC Comics **483** Balac / Yslaire **485** Albin Michel / Paul Gillon **487** Universal Press Syndicate / Bill Watterson **489** Magnus **490** DC Comics **491** © MIKIO IGARASHI / TAKE SHOBO **492** Elektra and all other Marvel characters: TM & © Marvel Entertainment, LLC and its subsidiaries. All Rights Reserved. **493** CASTERMAN **495** CASTERMAN **496** CASTERMAN **497** © Guy Delcourt Productions – 1990 **498** Yves Chaland / Yann Chaland **499** DC Comics **500** DC Comics **501** Daredevil and all other Marvel characters: TM & © Marvel Entertainment, LLC and its subsidiaries. All Rights Reserved. **502** Dave Sim **505** © Hirohiko Araki / Shueisha **506** Zenith by Grant Morrison & Steve Yeowell © 1987, 2011 Rebellion A/S **507** Daniel Goossens **508-509** René Windig / Eddie de Jong **510** CASTERMAN **511** Miguelanxo Prado **513** DC Comics **514** Rick Geary **516** © Guy Delcourt Productions – 1988 **517** Le Voyage en Italie © DUPUIS 1988 by Cosey www.dupuis.com All rights reserved **518** Al Davison **520** Tank Girl © Deadline Magazine. Art reproduced by kind permission of Titan Publishing Group Ltd. **521** Tank Girl © Alan Martin and Jamie Hewlett. Art reproduced by kind permission of Titan Publishing Group Ltd. **523** Doubleday / Kyle Baker **525** DC Comics **526-527** Ben Katchor **528** DC Comics **529** DC Comics **530** Alan Moore and Eddie Campbell **531** © Masamune Shirow / Kodansha Ltd. **532** CASTERMAN **533** DC Comics **535** Sláine: the Horned God by Pat Mills and Simon Bisley Copyright © 1989, 2011 Rebellion A/S **536** © Daniel Clowes **537** DC Comics **538** Charles Berbérian / Philippe Dupuy **540-541** Palto / Shutterstock Images **543** Frank Miller / Dave Gibbons / Dark Horse Comics **545** Alan Moore / Bill Sienkiewicz **546** Régis Loisel **547** Albin Michel / Baru / Jean-Marc Thévenet **548** Judge Dredd: America by John Wagner & Colin MacNeil © 1990, 2011 Rebellion A/S **550** Django / Igor Kordej **551** DC Comics **552** © Hitoshi Iwaaki / Kodansha Ltd. **553** L'héritier et Le Groupe W © DUPUIS 1990 by Jean Van Hamme and Philippe Francq www.dupuis.com All rights reserved **554** DC Comics **555** Peter Milligan / Brendan McCarthy **556** Chris Reynolds **557** © Jim Woodring, Published by Fantagraphics Books **558** Danijel Žeželj **560** © Aline Kominsky-Crumb **561** © Chris Ware, Published by Fantagraphics Books **562** © Kishiro Yukito / Shueisha **564** Jeff Smith **565** © Masahi Tanaka / Kodansha Ltd. **566** Alan Moore and Melinda Gebbie **567** Chester Brown **569** DC Comics **570** Wolverine and all other Marvel characters: TM & © Marvel Entertainment, LLC and its subsidiaries. All Rights Reserved. **571** Wolverine and all other Marvel characters: TM & © Marvel Entertainment, LLC and its subsidiaries. All Rights Reserved. **572** Ted McKeever **575** Archer Prewitt **576** Button Man by John Wagner & Arthur Ranson © 1992, 2011 John Wagner and Arthur Ranson **577** Miguelanxo Prado **579** Eric Drooker / Dark Horse Comics **580** © Ho Che Anderson **582** Savage Pencil **583** Zep **584** © Joe Sacco, Published by Fantagraphics Books **585** © Joe Sacco, Published by Fantagraphics Books **586** Peter Blegvad **587** Carol Lay **588** Barron Storey **589** Paul Grist **590** CASTERMAN **591** CASTERMAN **592** Design and art by David Hine **593** Hunt Emerson **596** DC Comics **595** © Daniel Clowes, Published by Fantagraphics Books **597** Frank Miller / Dark Horse Comics **598** Scott McCloud **599** Scott McCloud **600** © Hisashi Sakaguchi / Kodansha Ltd. **601** © Tatsuya EGAWA / Shogakukan Inc. **602** © Okano Reiko / Hakusensha **603** Sam Keith / William Messner-Loebs **604** Henrik Dorgathen **605** DC Comics **607** Harvey Pekar / Joyce Brabner / Frank Stack **608** Jorge Zentner / Rubén Pellejero **609** Circo Editorial / Laerte Coutinho **610** Paul Auster / Paul Karasik / David Mazzucchelli **611** Paul Auster / Paul Karasik / David Mazzucchelli **612** © Baru / Kodansha Ltd. **613** Christophe Arleston / Didier Tarquin **614** Marvels and all other Marvel characters: TM & © Marvel Entertainment, LLC and its subsidiaries. All Rights Reserved. **615** Yvan Alagbé **616** Bryan Talbot / Dark Horse Comics **617** DC Comics **618** © Peter Bagge **620** Neil Gaiman / Dave McKean **621** Neil Gaiman / Dave McKean **622** © Disney **623** DC Comics **624** Orijit Sen **625** Orijit Sen **627** John Bergin **628** Mike Mignola / John Bryne / Dark Horse Comics **629** Mike Mignola / John Bryne / Dark Horse Comics **630** DC Comics **632** © Usamaru Furuya / Ohta Publishing Company **633** © Usamaru Furuya / Ohta Publishing Company **635** Kurt Busiek / Brent Anderson / Alex Ross **636** © 2011 Jhonen Vasquez. Used with permission. **637** David Lapham **639** Howard Cruse **640** Rob Walton **641** Lewis Trondheim **643** DC Comics **645** © Charles Burns **646** © Bob Fingerman **647** Hee Jung Park **649** DC Comics **650** Seth **651** L'Association / David B. **653** Feuchtenberger, Anke **654** Carla Speed McNeil / Dark Horse Comics **655** Carla Speed McNeil / Dark Horse Comics **657** Junghoo Moon **658** Aristophane **659** Aristophane **661** © Linda Medley, Published by Fantagraphics Books **662** © 1996 Tsuchiya Gallon, Minegishi Nobuaki / Futabasha **663** © 1996 Tsuchiya Gallon, Minegishi Nobuaki / Futabasha **664** DC Comics **666** DC Comics **668** Edition Moderne / Martin tom Dieck **669** Edition Moderne / Martin tom Dieck **671** Maurice Vellekoop **672** Max **673** Le sursis © DUPUIS **1997** by Jean-Pierre Gibrat www.dupuis.com All rights reserved **675** Bries / Stefan van Dinther / Tobias Tycho Schalken **676** © OTSUKA Eiji Jimusyo, Sho-u TAJIMA / KADOKAWA SHOTEN 2011 **677** THE WORLD IS MINE © **1997** Hideki ARAI / Shogakukan Inc. **678-679** Frank Miller / Lynne Varley / Dark Horse Comics **680** CASTERMAN **681** Claudio Piersanti / Lorenzo Mattotti **683** Dylan Horrocks **684** DC Comics **685** DC Comics **686** Brian Michael Bendis / Marc Andreyko **688** © Guy Delcourt Productions – 1998 **689** © Guy Delcourt Productions – 1998 **690** Phoebe Gloeckner **693** Dave McKean **694** Robbie Morrison / Charlie Adlard **695** Robbie Morrison / Charlie Adlard **696** Eric Shanower **697** DC Comics **698** HARUKANAMACHI-E © 1998 Jiro TANIGUCHI / Shogakukan Inc. **699** © MOTOFUMI KOBAYASHI © SOFTBANK Creative Corp. **700** Tomaž Lavrič **701** © Guy Delcourt Productions – 2006 **703** Anders Nilsen **705** Eric Powell / Dark Horse Comics **706** © Dave Cooper **707** Martin Kellerman **708** © Takaya Natsuki / Hakusensha **709** © Yazawa Manga Seisakusho / Shueisha **710** DC Comics **711** Minwoo Hyung **712** from Gemma Bovery by Posy Simmonds, published by Jonathan Cape. Reprinted by permission of The Random House Group Ltd. **715** DC Comics **716** DC Comics **717** © MASASHI KISHIMOTO SCOT / SHUEISHA **718** Chester Brown **719** Chester Brown **720** Lourenço Mutarelli **721** Eddie Campbell Comics / Alan Moore **722** DC Comics **723** Jason **724-725** Palto / Shutterstock Images **727** Peter Pontiac **729** L'Association / Marjane Satrapi **730** Blacksad © DARGAUD 2000 by Diaz Canales & Guarnido www.dargaud.com All rights reserved **731** L'Association / Emmanuel Guibert **733** Barbara Canepa / Alessandro Barbucci **734** © Umino Chica / Shueisha **736** © Chris Ware, Published by Pantheon Books **737** Frank Odoi **738** © Jessica Abel **739** Beltégense l'Intégrale © DARGAUD 2006 by Leo www.dargaud.com All rights reserved **740** GO GO MONSTER © 2000 Taiyou MATSUMOTO / Shogakukan Inc. **742** Déogratias © DUPUIS 2000 by Jean-Philippe Stassen www.dupuis.com All rights reserved **743** Brian Michael Bendis / Michael Avon Oeming **744** Jason Lutes **747** Raul Brandão / Filipe Abranches **749** Joanna Rubin Dranger **750** Daredevil and all other Marvel characters: TM & © Marvel Entertainment, LLC and its subsidiaries. All Rights Reserved. **751** Nabiel Kanan

753 © Hiromu Arakawa / SQUARE ENIX **755** Frederik Peeters **756** Issac le Pirate 1/les Amériques © DARGAUD, Paris, 2001 by Blain www.dargaud.com All rights reserved **757** L'Association / Edmond Baudoin **758** Glenn Dakin **760** Seyeong O. **761** Seyeong O. **762** Jason Shiga **765** L'Association / Patrice Killoffer **766** DC Comics **767** DC Comics **768** Andrzej Klimowski **769** Robert Kirkman / Cory Walker / Ryan Ottley **771** DC Comics **773** Steve Niles / Ben Templesmith **774** Lynda Barry **775** Nick Bertozzi **777** Lars Arrhenius **778** DC Comics **779** Jeffrey Brown **780** © Kim Deitch **781** Vitesse moderne © DUPUIS 2002 by Blutch www.dupuis.com All rights reserved **782** Coconino Press / Igort **784** © TSUGUMI OHBA, TAKESHI OBATA / SHUEISHA **785** D C Thompson / Gary Northfield **787** Craig Thompson **788** Julien Neel **789** L'Association / Guy Delisle **791** Le photographe © DUPUIS 2003 by Emmanuel Guibert, Didier Lefèvre and Frédéric Lemercier www.dupuis.com All rights reserved **792** Robert Kirkman / Tony Moore / Charlie Adlard **793** Joe Kubert **794** © Fumiyo Kouno 2003 / Futabasha **795** Vanyda **797** Le Chat du Rabbin T1 – LA BAR MITSVA © DARGAUD 2002 by Joann Sfar www.dargaud.com All rights reserved. This comic is the author's homage to the painters of Algiers in the 20th century. It makes a particular point of quoting the work of Marion Vidal-Bué, Algiers and its Painters: 1830-1960, published by Editions Paris Méditerranée. **798** Les nombrils © DUPUIS 2004 by Dubuc and Delaf www.dupuis.com All rights reserved **799** Richard Thompson **800-801** Mark Beyer **802** Max Andersson / Lars Sjunnesson **803** Kang Full **805** DC Comics **806** The X-Men and all other Marvel characters: TM & © Marvel Entertainment, LLC and its subsidiaries. All Rights Reserved. **807** The X-Men and all other Marvel characters: TM & © Marvel Entertainment, LLC and its subsidiaries. All Rights Reserved. **808** The Ultimates and all other Marvel characters: TM & © Marvel Entertainment, LLC and its subsidiaries. All Rights Reserved. **809** DC Comics **810** Ediciones de la Flor / Ricardo Siri Liniers **811** L'Association / Marjane Satrapi **813** Park Kun-woong **814** Marc Malès **815** Gipi **816** CASTERMAN **817** Lars Fiske / Steffen Kverneland **818** DC Comics **819** © Akira Hiramoto / Kodansha Ltd. **820** T1 – Le Combat ordinaire © DARGAUD 2003 by Larcenet www.dargaud.com All rights reserved **821** Nikolai Maslov **822** Bryan Lee O'Malley **824** Hideo Azuma **825** IKIGAMI © 2005 Motoro MASE / Shogakukan Inc. **826** Marguerite Abouet / Clément Oubrérie **828** © Gabriella Giandelli **829** Stéphane Blanquet **831** SOLANIN © 2006 Inio ASANO / Shogakukan Inc. **832** Andi Watson **833** DC Comics **834** Thomas Ott **835** Thomas Ott **837** © Wakasugi Kiminori / Hakusensha **838** © Yoshinaga Fumi / Hakusensha **839** from Tamara Drewe by Posy Simmonds, published by Jonathan Cape. Reprinted by permission of The Random House Group Ltd. **840** DC Comics **841** Spider-Man and all other Marvel characters: TM & © Marvel Entertainment, LLC and its subsidiaries. All Rights Reserved. **843** Gene Luen Yang **844** Shaun Tan **845** Shaun Tan **846** Marc-Antoine Mathieu **847** Miriam Katin **849** Miss Pas Touche T1 – La Vierge du Bordel © Dargaud 2006 by Hubert & Kerascoët www.dargaud.com All rights reserved **851** David Petersen **852** Grady Klein **855** Coconino Press / Marco Corona **857** © by Carlsen Verlag GmbH, Hamburg, Germany **858** Rutu Modan **859** Ancco **861** Gerard Way / Gabriel Bá / Dark Horse Comics **862** Jeff Lemire **863** © Guy Delcourt Productions – 2007 **865** Le Complexe du Chimpanzé T. 1 Paradoxe © Dargaud 2007 by Marazano & Ponzio www.dargaud.com All rights reserved **867** Omega the Unknown and all other Marvel characters: TM & © Marvel Entertainment, LLC and its subsidiaries. All Rights Reserved. **868** Adrian Tomine **869** Nick Abadzis **871** Dash Shaw **872** Josh Neufeld **873** Skála František **875** from Alice in Sunderland by Bryan Talbot, published by Jonathan Cape. Reprinted by permission of The Random House Group Ltd. **876** DC Comics **877** KAIJU NO KODOMO © 2007 Daisuke IGARASHI / Shogakukan Inc. **878** Andrea Bruno **879** Andrea Bruno **881** KIICHI!! © 2002 Hideki ARAI / Shogakukan Inc. **882** Joe Matt **883** Gus © Dargaud by Blain www.dargaud.com All rights reserved **885** Jean Regnaud / Emile Bravo **886** Magdy El Shafee **887** Jorge González **889** from Britten and Brülightly by Hannah Berry, published by Jonathan Cape. Reprinted by permission of The Random House Group Ltd. **891** Lynda Barry **893** Amanda Vähämäki **895** Apostolos Doxiadis / Chirstos Papadimitrou / Alecos Papadatos **897** Warren Ellis / Paul Duffield **898** Winshluss **899** Ivan Brun **901** Nate Powell **902** Mariko Tamaki / Jilian Tamai **903** CASTERMAN **904** Nicolas Mahler **905** © C. Tyler **907** Conrad Editora / Marcello Quintanilha **908** Robert Sikoryak **909** David Mazzucchelli **910** © Hajime Isayama / Kodansha Ltd. **913** Jens Harder **914** Kloskerman **915** from Walking the Dog by David Hughesy, published by Jonathan Cape. Reprinted by permission of The Random House Group Ltd. **917** Ediciones de Ponent / Antonio Altarriba / Kim **919** W.W. Norton & Company / David Small **920** © Cathy Malkasian **921** Ariel Schrag **923** Ulli Lust **925** James Sturm **926** Arne Bellstorf **927** Adam Hines **929** W.W. Norton & Company / Belle Yang **930** Ben Haggarty / Adam Brockbank **931** Oji Suzuki **933** John Hicklenton **934** Gary Pleece / Warren Pleece **935** Sarnath Banerjee **936** Srividya Natarajan / S. Anand / Durgabai Vyam / Subhash Vyam **937** Chester Brown **939** Craig Thompson

Acknowledgements

Paul Gravett and Quintessence would like to thank the following individuals and organizations for their assistance in the creation of this book:

Helena Baser at Quintessence; Thierry Bombillon, Anders Hjorth-Jørgensen, Peter van Hooydonck, Yves Kerremans, Cyril Koopmeiners, and Marcel Wilmet for the loan of books; John Dunning; Curtis Hoffmann for supplying images; Jeremy Sutton-Hibbert and Yuko Hirono for help with copyright clearances; Carol King for editorial work; Guy Lawley for scanning; Aubrey Lawrence and Danielle Lawrence-de Froidmont at Rosetta Translations SARL, France; Delphine Maubert at Moulinsart; Aki Omori for picture research; Dominic Nolan for picture research; Randall W. Scott at Michigan State University Libraries; Tamaki Seto for her translations; Jon Wainwright for design work; Olivia Young at Quintessence.

Photography for this book was carried out by Simon Pask and Jeremy Sutton-Hibbert.

Paul Gravett dedicates this book to Maurice Horn, editor of *The World Encyclopedia of Comics* (1976), for truly opening up the world of comics to him.

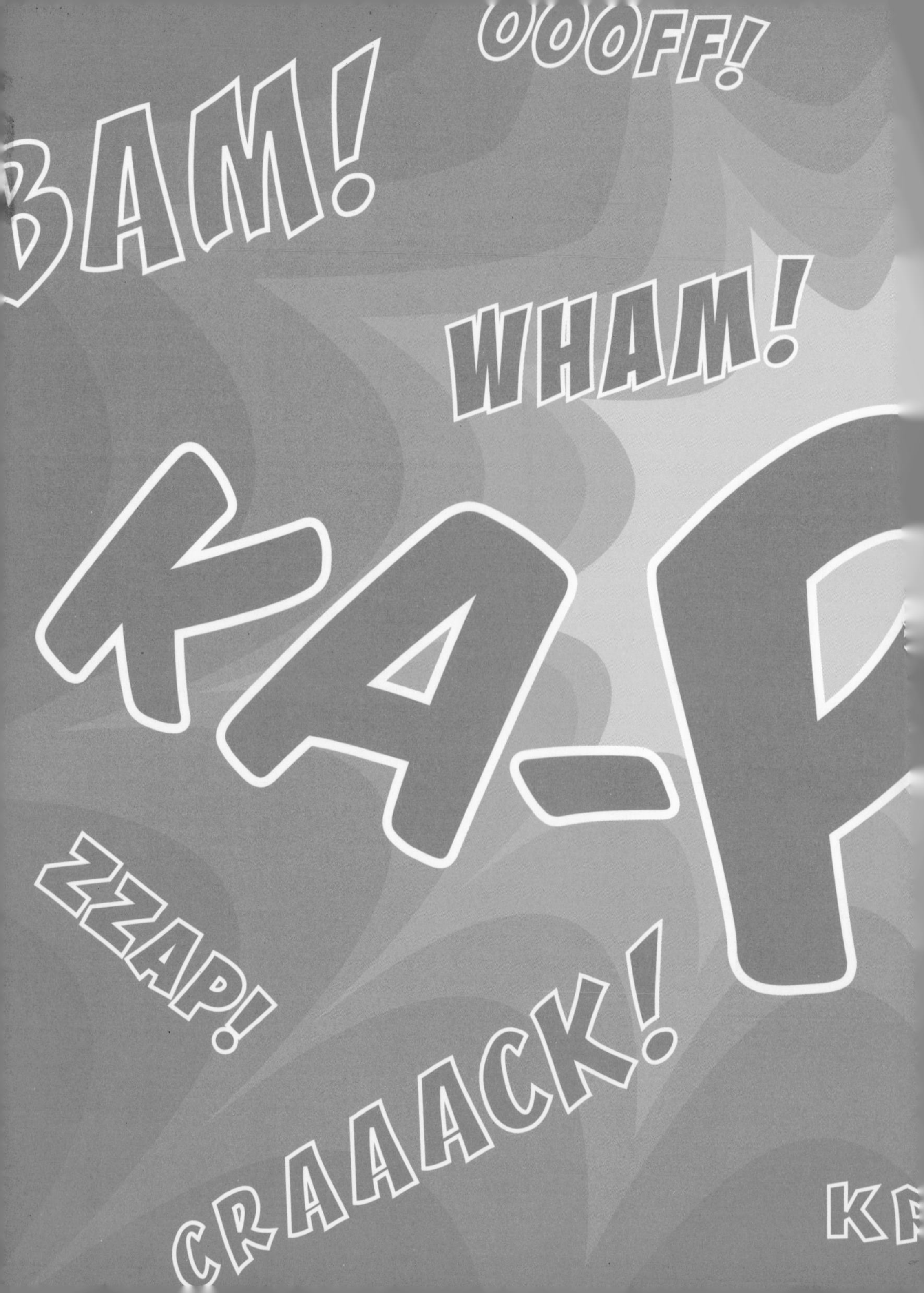
OOOFF!
BAM!
WHAM!
KA-P
ZZAP!
CRAAACK!